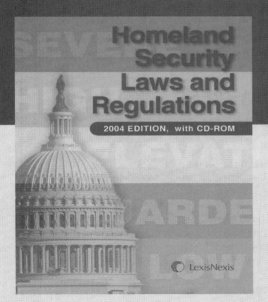

HOMELAND SECURITY LAWS AND REGULATIONS

*This guide presents all the relevant **Homeland Security Laws and Regulations** in one convenient softbound book. The accompanying CD-ROM includes the entire contents of the book, plus the full text of relevant court opinions.*

Contents include:

- United States Code Service
  - Title 6: Domestic Security
  - Title 8: Aliens and Nationality
  - Title 18: Crimes and Criminal Procedure
  - Title 31: Money and Finance
  - Title 42: The Public Health and Welfare
    (Bioterrorism Preparedness)
  - Title 49: Transportation
  - Title 50: War and National Defense
- United States Code Service – Federal Rules
  - Alien Terrorist Removal Court of the United States, Rules 1-14
- Code of Federal Regulations
  - Title 6: Homeland Security
- Full text of relevant cases
  - Hamdi v. Rumsfeld
  - Doe v. Ashcroft
- State Homeland Security Contacts
- Legislative Summaries

And More!

 LexisNexis®

ESSENTIAL GUIDES

OFFICER'S ARREST HANDBOOK, WITH CD-ROM

John A. Stephen

Officer's Arrest Handbook is an easy to read, concise manual that will sharpen an officer's knowledge of arrest and seizure law. Topics include:

- Reasonable suspicion and probable cause
- Arrests without a warrant
- Distinguishing encounters, seizures, and arrests
- Statements obtained during encounters
- Informant information as basis for arrest
- Analysis of *Miranda* and "in custody" factors
- Specific issues concerning automobiles
- Racial profiling in law enforcement

$30 Softbound with CD-ROM, © 2001
item #37596-10, ISBN 0-327-01773-2

OFFICER'S SEARCH AND SEIZURE, WITH CD-ROM

John A. Stephen

A short, nuts-and-bolts guide on the application of the Fourth Amendment to everyday police work, **Search and Seizure Handbook** will prove invaluable to veteran officers as well as officers new to the force. Topics include:

- Basic search and seizure principles
- Practical advice on preparing and executing search warrants
- Search warrant exceptions for persons, effects, etc.
- Warrantless searches of automobiles
- "Stop and frisk" and other investigative searches

$30 Softbound with CD-ROM, Supplemented Annually, ©2004
item #37590, ISBN 0-8205-8623-4

ORDER TODAY!

Call toll-free at **800-833-9844**
Fax your order toll-free at **800-828-8341**
Order online at *www.lexisnexis.com/bookstore*
Bulk purchase discounts available.

FOR POLICE OFFICERS

OFFICER'S DUI HANDBOOK,
WITH CD-ROM
Kwasnoski, Partridge, and Stephen

Now with state-to-state case summaries, updated annually

Officer's DUI Handbook contains practical advice for police officers on how to handle the arrest, investigation, and trial of an individual found guilty of driving under the influence of alcohol. Tips and checklists include:

- Checklists to aid in DUI investigations
- Arrest and custody issues
- Landmines to avoid during investigations
- Tips to increase conviction rates
- Drug recognition evaluation

$30 Softbound with CD-ROM, ©2003
item #37553-14, ISBN 0-8205-9212-9

COURTROOM SURVIVAL:
MAKING THE TRAFFIC OFFICER A POWERFUL WITNESS
Kwasnoski, Partridge, and Stephen

This handbook provides the principles and skills needed to be an effective and persuasive courtroom witness. Topics include:

- Preparing the traffic officer
- Preparing the prosecutor
- Stages of witness preparation
- Structure of the direct examination
- The three goals of a witness during cross-examination
- How to tell winners from losers
- How to investigate the defense attorney
- The four realities of cross-examination
- How the defense attorney controls you
- Profile of a competent police witness

$25 Softbound, ©1999
item #37580-10, ISBN 0-327-04950-2

ORDER TODAY!

Call toll-free at **800-833-9844**
Fax your order toll-free at **800-828-8341**
Order online at *www.lexis.com/bookstore*
Bulk purchase discounts available.

M74

DRUGS and the LAW
Detection, Recognition & Investigation

(Third Edition)

by
Gary J. Miller

QUESTIONS ABOUT THIS PUBLICATION?

For Customer Service matters concerning shipments, billing, reprint permission, or other matters, please call the Customer Service Department at 800-833-9844, e-mail customer.support@lexisnexis.com, or visit our customer service website at http://www.lexisnexis.com/custserv/default.asp.

For Editorial content questions concerning this publication, please call 800-446-3410 ext. 7447, or e-mail LLP.CLP@lexisnexis.com.

For information on other LEXISNEXIS MATTHEW BENDER publications, please call 800-223-1940, or visit our online bookstore at: http://bookstore.lexis.com/bookstore/catalog.

ISBN: 1-4224-0296-7

Matthew Bender & Company, Inc.
Editorial Offices
P.O. Box 7587
Charlottesville, VA 22906-7587
800-446-3410
www.lexisnexis.com

Product Number 2919511

(Pub. 29195)

PREFACE

One of the most serious problems in the world today is the use and abuse of a wide variety of chemical substances. Most Americans consider illicit drugs and alcohol in particular among the major problems facing our nation. The concern is not only the high financial cost of enforcement, education, and treatment, but the high social cost of American lives and the drug-related street crime that has made our cities increasingly unsafe.

America has been involved in a global war on drugs. Arrests have increased, the prison jail population has increased, drug seizures have gone up, and millions of dollars in financial assets have been seized. Yet the problem is still there, and drug cartels continue to flourish. While drug abuse has stabilized somewhat, the problems of drug-related crime and unsafe streets continue to increase.

For the past 40 years, the U.S. strategy in combating the problem of illegal drug use and trafficking has been to reduce the demand for drugs through education, treatment, and rehabilitation and to reduce the supply of drugs through crop eradication, arrests, interdiction and seizures, asset forfeitures, etc. Current efforts involve a comprehensive program to control each phase from the grower to the user. Intensified investigations into money laundering are being conducted. Pressure is being applied at all points in the chain, resulting in increased seizures of drugs and financial assets, and increased arrests and prosecution of traffickers. More effective education, prevention, treatment, and rehabilitation programs are needed to reduce the demand for drugs.

Drugs and the Law—Detection, Recognition & Investigation is an attempt to reach law enforcement officers, narcotics enforcement officers, students, counselors, educators, parents, and all the other dedicated people who are concerned with the drug problem. To be effective, it is important to have an accurate understanding of the law and procedures, the identification of drugs, the various ways drugs are packaged, the identification of people under the influence, the recognition of the characteristics of addiction, and all the related topics covered herein.

Officers must recognize and be able to handle many situations, including encounters with motorists under the influence of a drug, or citizens under the influence of a drug on the street, in a residence, or in a public place. An officer must realize when he or she is witnessing the buying or selling of controlled substances. The officer must know the elements of the crime and how to safely handle the situation. Knowledge about drugs is important, because the officer can only enforce the law if violations of the law are recognized. It is also important because many drugs alter behavior as well as mood, perception, and physiology. Some people become violent, combative, and assaultive when under the influence. Early recognition of drug influence could save lives.

In our society, people use drugs to modify how they perceive and feel about themselves and the world about them. Drugs are used to relieve pain, reduce anxiety, counter depression, heighten pleasure, aid in healing, and for a variety of other reasons. Hopefully, the knowledge you gain in studying this text will help you to become an effective force in reducing the drug problem and consequently decreasing those criminal offenses which are related to drug abuse.

There are numerous references to sections of the United States Code (USC) in the text. Unless otherwise noted, other sections of law cited in the text are from the California statutes, e.g., the Penal Code (Pen. Code), the Vehicle Code (Veh. Code), the Health and Safety Code (H&S), the Business and Professions Code (B&P), etc. You should refer to your own state's statutes for sections of law concerning drug laws in your state. At the end of this volume is a complete and comprehensive index.

Comments from users of this publication and ways to improve it to facilitate its use would be appreciated by the publisher.

ABOUT THE AUTHOR

Gary Miller first became interested in law enforcement while serving in the United States Navy. After an honorable discharge, Mr. Miller attended Santa Rosa Junior College, receiving an A.A. degree in Police Science. He continued his education at Sacramento State University, earning a B.A. degree. He furthered his educational goals at Washington State University where he received an M.A. degree in Police Science.

Mr. Miller has worked in a variety of jobs in the criminal justice system. He served as a correctional officer with the California Department of Corrections and as a probation officer with the Sonoma County Probation Department. His interest in drug abuse and addiction began while he was employed by the California Department of Justice, Bureau of Narcotics Enforcement, as a narcotics agent. From 1979-1991, he served as the Director of the Central Coast Counties Police Academy. He was involved in police education and training as an assistant professor in the Administration of Justice Department at San Jose State University, as a program specialist at Modesto Junior College Police Academy, and as an instructor and program coordinator at San Jose City College. Additionally, he is a former instructor in the Police Academy, the Administration of Justice Degree Program, and the in-service training program for police officers at Gavilan Community College. Mr. Miller is now retired.

DEDICATION

This book is dedicated to all those who have devoted their lives to making this world a safer place to live.

A special dedication to those who have lost their lives to protect us.

A personal dedication to a friend and partner in fighting the drug war who tragically lost his life. To all that knew him, Lauren Platt, Special Agent with the California Bureau of Narcotic Enforcement, we miss you.

TABLE OF CONTENTS

TABLE OF CONTENTS
(Continued)

TABLE OF CONTENTS
(Continued)

TABLE OF CONTENTS
(Continued)

TABLE OF CONTENTS
(Continued)

TABLE OF CONTENTS
(Continued)

TABLE OF CONTENTS
(Continued)

CHAPTER 1

CURRENT PATTERNS OF DRUG USE

§ 1.1 INTRODUCTION

For the last 30 years, the available indicators on drug use, abuse, and addiction have reported conflicting and confusing results. On the one hand, surveys of the general population show a sharp decline in drug use in the late 1980s and essentially no change in the 1990s. On the other hand, more direct measures of drug use, such as the number of drug-related deaths and emergency room admissions, have increased steadily and are much higher than they were in 1980.

However, according to the survey, illicit drug usage declined significantly from 1985 to 1995. The total number of individuals from the survey reporting current illicit drug use declined from 23.2 million users in 1985 to 12.8 million users in 1995. A decline in marijuana use that began after 1979 accounts for most of this success. The total number of current marijuana users declined from 23.7 million users in 1979 to 9.8 million users in 1995. During that same period, current cocaine use declined from 4.7 million to 1.4 million users. Although this long-term trend is encouraging, the results from the 1995 Household Survey suggest that the general decline may have ended. Illicit drug use reported in 1995 was 12.8 million compared to 12.5 million for 1994 and 12.2 million in 1993. Current drug use appears to have stabilized in the general population with the exception of illicit drug use by adolescents, which is on the increase.

§ 1.2 THE BIG PICTURE: DRUG USE IN THE LAST 30 YEARS

Drug use can be categorized in several ways: initiation or first-time use, continued use (which can be either frequent or occasional), and abuse (which causes both the user and society significant problems). The trends for each category vary.

§ 1.2.1   First-time use

Initiation into the use of illicit drugs rose through the late 1970s and perhaps into the early 1980s, then began a sharp decline around 1983. First-time drug use started to rise again in 1992, but by 1997 it was still well below the peaks of the early 1980s.

§ 1.2.2   Continued use

Although the number of people who continued using drugs may have risen steadily into the mid-1980s, the numbers were almost certainly in decline after 1987. Since 1990, the percentage of the population using drugs has remained essentially flat.

§ 1.2.3   Drug abuse

Drug abuse continued to rise through the 1980s, even as the rates of first-time and continued use declined, because it usually takes several years to move from first-time use to the beginning of dependent use. The number of drug abusers probably flattened out at the end of the 1980s, but it has declined only modestly since then.

The fraction of today's population using illicit drugs is well below the peak of the early 1980s. However, the severity of drug-related problems has not declined much, probably because drug abusers have such difficulty quitting and because the problems they cause themselves and society change, but do not abate, as their drug-using careers lengthen and their health deteriorates.

Since 1980, a higher fraction of all users have been problematic users—a phenomenon that increases the association between drug abuse and crime—and the population of drug abusers has aged. Drug use is declining across all demographic groups.

§ 1.2.4   Drugs and the Young
Drug use among high school seniors peaked in 1979, and declined until 1992, when it increased again.

§ 1.2.5   Arrestees' Drug Use
While drug abuse among young people was decreasing in the 1980s, it was increasing significantly among persons arrested for crimes. For example, ADAM's trend data show that cocaine-using criminals are getting older. This suggests that cocaine use is increasingly a problem of a group of long-term users who developed their addiction in the early stages of the cocaine epidemic. Other drug indicators such as hospital and coroner data also show this aging of cocaine addicts and a strong relationship between drug use and crime. The data also supports the idea that efforts to decrease recidivism are most effective when they focus on decreasing drug use among criminals at all stages of the criminal justice process (pretrial, trial, jail/prison, probation/parole).

§ 1.2.6   Hospital and Coroner Studies
The most direct measure of serious drug problems comes from reports of deaths and emergency room treatment related to drug abuse (DAWN). As with data from other drug indicators, DAWN reports show the changing population of cocaine and heroin addicts—they are getting older. Almost half of reported deaths related to cocaine and heroin were people 30 years old or older in 1982; by 1996, two-thirds were 35 or older.

The data also shows that a greater proportion of the cocaine-using population is addicted—a finding that is consistent with the observation that cocaine users develop their addiction over time and are now experiencing the problems that stem from long-term use.

§ 1.2.7   What it all Means
It should be apparent that the various indicators need careful reconciliation and interpretation mixed with solid understanding of drug-use patterns.

But these apparent inconsistencies do not necessarily point to conflict or inaccuracy. Rather, they point to a need to recognize cocaine and heroin use as a career rather than as an event. During the late 1970s and early 1980s, many individuals (mostly young adults) experimented with cocaine. Some became regular, but occasional users; a smaller group went on to become regular and frequent users. By the mid-1980s, the percentage of first-time users had slowed substantially and remained low through the mid-1990s. But the total number of cocaine users did not begin to decline because one-third of the users continued to use and most likely became addicted.

As the dangers—medical rather than legal—of cocaine use became more apparent and widely known, regular users who were not addicts and generally using only occasionally were increasingly likely to quit. But as cocaine became cheaper and more addictive in the form of crack, users who had not quit were more likely to become addicted. They were also more likely to be among the urban poor, whose use has serious consequences, both for themselves and for society. As a result, there is now a stronger association between cocaine use and health problems (as reflected in DAWN's rise) and a strong association with crime.

Each indicator provides useful information. Monitoring the Future provided the early indications of the cocaine epidemic, while ADAM did a good job in tracking its later stages. DAWN has shown that drug problems can increase even as the rate of drug use in the population stabilizes, and has provided compelling evidence that drug problems are disproportionately borne by poor and urban minority populations. The National Household Survey on Drug Abuse has provided an essential measure of the decline of drug use in the general population through the 1980s.

§ 1.3 EMERGING DRUG TRENDS: CEWG
The landscape of drug abuse is never static. Fluctuations in drug availability, generational shifts, and variations in cultural influences fuel the ongoing emergence of new drug abuse trends.

How do we identify new drugs of abuse? How do policymakers at all levels of government and addiction professionals receive the most up-to-date data and information about rapidly changing drug abuse situations? How do we monitor and assess emerging patterns of drug abuse? The answer is the Community Epidemiology Work Group (CEWG), which is the epidemiological compass of the National Institute on Drug Abuse (NIDA).

Established in 1976 by NIDA, the CEWG consists of researchers from 20 major cities across the United States (from West to East Coast) and the state of Texas. CEWG has been around for 28 of NIDA's 30-year history.

CEWG is based on the notion that drug abuse trends are uniquely specific to the communities in which they occur. A drug abuse pattern in one community may look quite different in another area or be entirely absent. For example, in 2004, while Minneapolis-St. Paul area reported the rising abuse of methamphetamine, particularly among girls attracted by the promise of heightened energy and rapid weight loss, eastern cities have not experienced this trend.

The CEWG has been the first to identify every major drug abuse trend in the U.S. It was the first to identify the rapidly rising abuse of the smokable form of cocaine known as "crack" in the 1980s. Though initially known by different names in different cities, such as "gravel," "rock," "freebase," or "bozuco," by 1986, everyone knew it by the name of crack. The epidemic of crack use peaked in most U.S. cities by the late 1980s.

In the early 1990s, the CEWG identified rising heroin abuse among middle class, young suburbanites who smoked it. CEWG in Philadelphia first reported the use of "blunts"—hollowed our cigars that are refilled with marijuana. In 1992, CEWG in Florida was the first to detect the emerging abuse of Rohypnol, also known as "roofies." Rohypnol, the acting benzodiazepine that induces memory loss, soon became widely known as the date-rape drug.

Later in the 1990s, CEWG reported the increasing use of MDMA (Ecstasy), ketamine, and GHB by young adults and teenagers at party settings ("raves"). And along with abuse came the "word on the street" that these drugs were essentially low risk and harmless. In response, in 1999 NIDA began a comprehensive public information campaign about the actual dangers of these "club drugs": heart attack, stroke, hyperthermia, and respiratory arrest.

The CEWG meeting held June 2004 in Washington, D.C., found arising nonmedical use of prescription drugs across all cities, the expanding ravages of methamphetamine abuse, especially in the western and central states, and a resurgence of cocaine abuse in some cities.

§ 1.4 IMPLICATIONS FOR THE FUTURE

While the general population surveys have shown very stable use figures throughout the 1990s, aggregate stability masks a great deal of change in patterns of drug use.

The rapid rise in marijuana use among adolescents since 1992, for example, has been accompanied by an unexplained decline in marijuana use among adults, so that the prevalence of marijuana in the total population remains unchanged. This rise in adolescent marijuana use has led to a general call to arms that has been reinforced by the diffusion of methamphetamine from its established base in the Southwest and by claims that heroin use is growing among young adults as heroin prices have plummeted and purity has risen. However, marijuana use among youth is a weak predictor of future cocaine use, methamphetamine is still primarily a regional drug, and indicators of heroin use are very inconsistent. ADAM data, for example, show minimal increases in heroin use among young arrestees.

Measuring the extent of a nation's drug problems requires more than estimating the number of persons using illicit drugs. Drug use differs in the damage it does to individuals and in the damage those individuals do to the rest of society. The task for local decision makers and their social science partners is how to use the expanded federal data systems to better understand changes in local drug problems.

§ 1.5 WHAT ABOUT CHRONIC DRUG USERS?

The Office of National Drug Control Policy estimates the size of the chronic drug user population with a statistical estimation technique that uses data drawn from several sources. The results indicated by this method suggest that the number of chronic users of cocaine and heroin has remained almost unchanged since 1988; the total number was 2.7 million in 1993 with about 2.1 million people using primarily cocaine and 600,000 using primarily heroin. Chronic drug users continue to be responsible for the bulk of illicit drug consumption in America today.

Chronic drug users are only one-fifth of the drug-using population, but consume two-thirds of the total amount of cocaine in the United States. The large amount of cocaine consumed by a minority of users makes one thing clear: the goal of reducing the overall rate of illicit drug use in this country cannot be achieved without targeting chronic drug users (Office of National Drug Control Policy 1995).

§ 1.6 CURRENT DRUG FACTS

In 2002, an estimated 35.1 million people aged 12 and older reported using an illicit drug with the past year; an estimated 3.2 million people were dependent on or abusers of illicit drugs. To counter the overall threat, federal, state, and local agencies nationwide commit significant portions of their resources annually to antidrug law enforcement initiatives, education, and treatment (National Drug Intelligence Center 2004).

The National Drug Control Strategy report of March 2004 lays out in detail the President's drug control budget for fiscal year 2005. Forty-five percent of the drug control budget is to be spent on drug treatment and education and prevention; the remaining fifty-five percent, among law enforcement budgets, international programs, drug-related intelligence spending, and interdiction activities.

Americans spend approximately $66 billion on the use of illegal drugs each year (Office of National Drug Control Policy 2000). Law enforcement and public health agency reporting reveals regional variations in the drug threat; however, data from the National Drug Intelligence Center National Drug Threat Survey 2003 indicate that, nationally, 37.0% of state and local law enforcement agencies identified cocaine (either powder or crack) as their greatest drug threat, followed by methamphetamine (36.2%), marijuana (13.1%), heroin (8.2%), and MDMA, or Ecstasy, (0.9%). National Drug Threat Survey 2003 data further show that more agencies identified cocaine (either powder or crack) as the drug that most contributes to violent crime (50.1%) and property crime (42.0%) than methamphetamine (31.6% and 29.8%), marijuana (4.6% and 11.8%), heroin (4.6% and 10.9%), or MDMA (0.2% and 0.1%).

§ 1.6.1 Cocaine

Cocaine trafficking and abuse represent a significant drug threat to the United States. Both powder and crack cocaine are readily available throughout the country, and overall availability appears to be stable. All Drug Enforcement Administration Field Divisions and High Intensity Drug Trafficking Areas report that powder and crack cocaine are readily available in their areas. Law enforcement reporting indicates that the number of cocaine-related federal investigations and arrests remained relatively stable over the past year. Federal seizures of cocaine have decreased; however, cocaine remains second only to marijuana as the drug most seized by federal agencies. National Drug Threat Survey data for 2003 indicate that 37.0 percent of state and local law enforcement agencies nationwide identify cocaine (both powder and crack) as their greatest drug threat, which is higher than any other drug type.

The demand for cocaine is high, and adults appear to be the largest users of both powder and crack cocaine. Across the United States, powder cocaine ranges in purity from 30 to 95 percent. The price ranges from $25 to $150 per gram, with an average of $100 per gram.

Crack cocaine purity ranges from 30 to 85 percent with most purity levels around 55 percent. The most common unit of crack sold is one rock approximately 0.1-0.2 grams for $2 to $40 each, with the standard rock price of $10 (ONDCP 2004).

Worldwide cocaine production decreased significantly in 2002, largely because of intensified coca eradication in Colombia. Cocaine continues to be smuggled into the United States primarily overland from Mexico in private and commercial vehicles. Cocaine is transported within the United States primarily via commercial and private vehicles but also by trains, buses, mail services, and couriers on commercial flights. The distribution of powder cocaine and crack occurs throughout the country, and the market for the drug appears to be stable overall. All Drug Enforcement Administration Field Divisions and High Intensity Drug Trafficking Areas report that powder cocaine is distributed in their areas. Most report that crack cocaine is distributed particularly in inner cities, and some report that crack distribution is increasing in smaller towns and communities. The primary market areas for cocaine are Atlanta, Chicago, Houston, Los Angeles, Miami, and New York.

§ 1.6.2 Methamphetamine

The threat posed to the United States by the trafficking and abuse of methamphetamine is high. Methamphetamine availability is very high in the Pacific, Southwest, and West Central regions. In the Great Lakes and Southeast regions, methamphetamine availability has increased to such a level that most state and local law enforcement agencies now report that availability of the drug is either high or moderate in their areas (National Drug Intelligence Center 2003).

Current Patterns of Drug Use

Methamphetamine use appears to be highest among young adults, and the consequences of such use are trending upward. However, domestic methamphetamine production appears to be increasing. The number of methamphetamine laboratory seizures increased overall from 2002 to 2003, while the number of seizures of high-capacity superlabs appears to have remained stable.

The DEA reports that methamphetamine production in Mexico (which is the primary foreign source area for the drug) appears to have increased.

Methamphetamine availability in the Northeast/Mid-Atlantic region is low but increasing. Despite wide-ranging reports of increasing availability, the number of methamphetamine-related Organized Crime Drug Enforcement Task Force investigations and Drug Enforcement Administration arrests, as well as the amount of methamphetamine seized by federal agencies, all decreased from 2001 to 2002. Methamphetamine is transported primarily by Mexican criminal groups as well as gangs (including outlaw motorcycle gangs) and independent methamphetamine producers primarily via private vehicles and, to a much lesser extent, by mail services to drug markets throughout the country. Southeast Asia methamphetamine available in the United States typically is transported to the country via commercial air carriers primarily for distribution in Asian communities in western states. Mexican criminal groups control most methamphetamine distribution in the Pacific, Southwest, and West Central regions and supply much of the wholesale methamphetamine to eastern states where Caucasian independent dealers and outlaw motorcycle gangs control mid-level and retail distribution of the drug. The primary market areas for methamphetamine are Los Angeles, Phoenix, San Diego, San Francisco, and the Central States (Arkansas, Illinois, Indiana, Iowa and Missouri).

Locally produced methamphetamine has become easier to purchase overall. Mexican amphetamine is also readily available in most areas. The ease of purchasing "ice," highly pure, smokable methamphetamine, has increased across the United States (ONDCP 2004).

Purity of methamphetamine ranges from 8 to 95 percent with an average across the United States around 30 to 40 percent. Methamphetamine sells for an average of $100/gram (*Ibid*).

§ 1.6.3 Marijuana

Both law enforcement and public health agencies consistently identify marijuana as the most commonly used illicit drug in the country. The overall demand for marijuana is at high levels. Drug markets across the country are supplied with significant quantities of marijuana produced in foreign source areas (chiefly Mexico, but also Canada, Colombia, and Jamaica) as well as domestic sources. Marijuana transportation and subsequent distribution by a wide range of criminal groups, gangs, and independent dealers are commonplace throughout the country, result in an overall domestic market for marijuana that is strong and stable. Primary market areas for marijuana, based on national-level distribution only, include Chicago, Dallas/Houston, Los Angeles/San Diego, Miami, New York, Phoenix/Tucson, and Seattle (NDIC 2004).

Marijuana is the most easily purchased drug across the United States. Mexican commercial grade marijuana is the most common variety and can be purchased with little or no difficulty. Local commercial grade marijuana is the next most common variety. Depending on where you live, Sinsemilla, hydroponically grown marijuana, and British Columbian marijuana (BC Bud) can be purchased with little difficulty (ONDCP 2004).

Reported THC levels range from 1 to 10 percent for commercial grade marijuana to as much as 30 percent for BC Bud. Most ounce prices for commercial grade marijuana are about $100 (ONDCP 2004).

In an article appearing in the May 5, 2003 issue of the Journal of the American Medical Association (JAMA), addiction researchers at the National Institutes of Health compared marijuana use in the United States adult population in 1991-92 and 2001-02. They found that the number of people reporting use of the drug remained substantially the same in both time periods, but the prevalence of marijuana abuse or dependence increased markedly. This new study also showed that increases in the prevalence of abuse or dependence were most notable among young African-American men and women and young Hispanic men. The increase in potency of marijuana over the last decade may be partly responsible for the drug's increased abuse and dependence, particularly since marijuana use patterns have not changed over this period. However, no single factor can account entirely for the increases seen in minority populations, the authors report. Numerous cultural, psychosocial, economic, and lifestyle factors likely play roles.

§ 1.6.4   Heroin

Heroin trafficking and abuse pose a significant drug threat to the country. Law enforcement reporting indicates that heroin remains readily available throughout most major metropolitan areas, and availability is increasing in many suburban and rural areas, particularly in the northeastern United States. Heroin from South America and Mexico is most prevalent in the United States, although lesser quantities of Southeast and Southwest Asian heroin are available.

However, the overall demand for heroin in the United States appears to be lower overall than for other major drugs of abuse such as cocaine, methamphetamine, marijuana, and MDMA, and the rates of heroin use appear to be trending downward for most age groups. Estimates of worldwide heroin production increased considerably between 2001 and 2002 primarily because of increases in Afghanistan—a primary source of heroin destined for Europe. Heroin production estimates for Colombia and Mexico also decreased.

Heroin typically is smuggled into the country, either carried by couriers on commercial flights from source and transit countries or hidden in private and commercial vehicles driven across the U.S.-Mexico and, to a lesser extent, U.S.-Canada borders. Heroin is smuggled into the country via maritime conveyances and mail services as well.

Heroin is distributed by a wide range of criminal groups, gangs, and independent dealers. The primary market areas for heroin are Chicago, Los Angeles, New York, and on a smaller scale, Boston. Other significant heroin markets also include Baltimore, Detroit, Miami, Newark, Philadelphia, San Francisco, Seattle, and Washington, D.C. (National Drug Intelligence Center 2004).

At the retail level, the purity of heroin in the U.S. market increased from an average of 11% in 1981 to an average of 32% in 2003. Starting 1993, there was seen a growing trend to inhale rather than to inject heroin. As long as heroin purity remains high, many heroin users will continue to inhale heroin rather than inject it ("Price and Purity" 62).

High-purity, snortable white South American (Colombia) heroin still predominates the Eastern United States, while lower-purity Mexican black tar heroin predominates throughout the Western United States. Southeast Asian heroin is not as available. South American heroin ranges in purity from 40 to 95 percent. Mexican black tar heroin ranges from 5 to 64 percent pure. One dose of 0.1 gram of heroin sells for $4 to $30. Heroin prices have been declining (ONDCP 2004).

§ 1.6.5 MDMA (Ecstasy)

MDMA trafficking and abuse represent a moderate threat to the United States. Law enforcement reporting indicates that MDMA (Ecstasy) is readily available in all regions of the country, particularly in metropolitan areas, and that availability is stable overall. National-level drug prevalence studies also indicate that MDMA use is trending downward, particularly among adolescents.

Most of the MDMA available in the United States is produced in clandestine laboratories located in the Netherlands and Belgium. To a much lesser extent, MDMA is produced in other foreign countries, such as Canada and Mexico. Domestic MDMA production remains limited as evidenced by very few MDMA laboratory seizures.

MDMA typically is smuggled directly from Europe to the United States primarily by couriers on commercial flights and via mail services; however, lesser amounts of MDMA are transported to the United States from Europe via Canada and Mexico. Israeli and Russian criminal groups and, to a lesser extent, Asian, Colombian, Dominican, Middle Eastern, and traditional organized crime groups control most wholesale MDMA distribution in the United States. These groups, along with African-American gangs and Mexican criminal groups, also control most mid-level MDMA distribution in the country. Retail MDMA distribution typically occurs in venues such as rave parties, dance clubs, and bars. The primary market areas for MDMA are Los Angeles, Miami, and New York (NDIC 2004).

One tablet of Ecstasy is the most common unit sold and prices range from $7.50 to $40, depending on the area of the United States.

§ 1.6.6 Pharmaceuticals

The diversion and abuse of pharmaceuticals, which include narcotics, depressants, and stimulants, pose an increasing threat to the country. Most pharmaceutical controlled substances abused in the United States are diverted by forged prescriptions, doctor shopping, and theft; however, law enforcement agencies report that pharmaceuticals are increasingly being obtained from Mexico and through Internet pharmacies whose sources of supply often are in Mexico, and in other foreign countries.

Pharmaceutical narcotics such as hydrocodone (Vicodin), oxycodone (OxyContin), hydromorphone (Dilaudid), and codeine are available and abused throughout the country. The demand, availability, and abuse of these drugs are high and appear to be increasing, but the abuse of hydrocodone and oxycodone drugs in particular pose the greatest threat (NDIC 2004).

OxyContin, in many areas of the country, has become more difficult to obtain because of increased awareness of the problem by law enforcement, the manufacturer, the medical community, and pharmacists. Many pharmacies no longer carry it, and they post notices to that effect. In some areas the cost of the drug has increased, causing demand to decline, which causes supply to decline. In other cases doctors and pharmacists have become more stringent with prescriptions, so less is available on the street and the price has increased. Law enforcement arrests of large diversion cases have made a difference in supply. Also following major law enforcement activity, availability has declined around methadone clinics, where it used to be sold.

Because many areas of the country are experiencing a decline in availability of OxyContin, addicts are using heroin or diverted methadone, Percocet or clonazepam. Other abused substances include cold medications containing dextromethorphan, often found in Coricidin products, commonly referred to as "triple C" (ONDCP 2004). Diverted OxyContin is typically sold by the 20 or 40 milligram tablet at $1.00 per milligram.

Depressants (including barbiturates and benzodiazepines), Alprazolam (Xanax) and diazepam (Valium) are among the most widely abused pharmaceutical depressants, particularly in the Southeast region.

Stimulants, particularly dextroamphetamine (Adderall) and methylphenidate (Ritalin), are widely available in most areas. Ritalin abuse is most noted in school settings where students with legitimate prescriptions often share the drug with friends. In addition to adolescents, many young adults abuse these drugs; however, overall abuse appears to be stable (NDIC 2004).

§ 1.6.7   Other Dangerous Drugs

The production, distribution, and abuse of other dangerous drugs, including the club drugs GHB, ketamine, and Rohypnol as well as the hallucinogens LSD, PCP, and psilocybin, pose only a moderate threat to the country overall. The availability and use of these drugs are moderate and relatively stable.

However, PCP is emerging as a problem in many cities in the United States. It is sometimes sold as a liquid in vials. Often cigarettes or marijuana blunts are dipped in PCP, then sold. PCP arrests have increased (ONDCP 2004).

Particularly popular among adolescents and young adults, other dangerous drugs are most prevalent in metropolitan areas. Some club drugs, particularly GHB and Rohypnol, are used in drug-facilitated sexual assaults because of their sedative properties. Although law enforcement reporting indicates increased availability of hallucinogens within college and rave communities, the most recent drug prevalence data indicate that overall use of these drugs is relatively stable (NDIC 2004).

Khat is an emerging drug among Minneapolis/St. Paul's Somalian community, which is the largest in the country. This natural stimulant, which loses potency in 48 hours, has leaves that contain psychoactive ingredients structurally and chemically similar to d-amphetamine. It is overnight-mailed or shipped in luggage on airplanes from Kenya. The drug has also increasingly appeared on the St. Louis drug market, with three seizures by law enforcement during fall 2002.

There is a continuing interest among drug users in hallucinogens such as LSD, peyote, and psilocybin. However, there are some different hallucinogens appearing on the street.

Jimson weed is a plant that produces the toxin belladonna. Users either chew its seeds, make a tea from the roots, or smoke the leaves. It was mentioned in books on psychedelics in the 1960s. During 1994, in Trenton/Newark, New Jersey, 27 youths were taken to local emergency rooms for treatment of jimson weed poisoning. In the San Antonio/El Paso area, two adolescent males died from drinking tea made from jimson weed, and there was additional use reported in the summer of 1994. While these are probably isolated events, it is important to note the interest they represent in experimenting with naturally occurring hallucinogens.

The Washington, D.C., police reported in 1994 the appearance of a hallucinogen that is extracted from fluid excreted by a certain variety of toad. The fluid is collected, dried, and then smoked. Like jimson weed, the toad extract phenomenon is a reincarnation of events reported in the 1960s.

§ 1.6.8 Inhalants

The abuse of inhalants is a relatively low threat to the country; however, inhalant abuse, particularly among adolescents, is a concern among law enforcement and public health agencies. Common household products, including solvents, aerosols, gases, and nitrites, are legally available and are commonly misused as inhalants. Individuals of all ages use inhalants, but teens and young adults account for a large portion of the inhalant abuse in the United States.

1.6.9 Drugs on a College Campus

Any drug that can be found in the community will be available on a college campus. Alcohol is the primary drug used. Past-month alcohol use was reported by 65 percent of full-time college students in 2003. Binge and heavy alcohol drinking was reported by 44 percent of the students (SAMHSA 2003). Marijuana is the next most common drug on a college campus. To a much lesser extent, hallucinogens like LSD are used. Of course, other drugs like amphetamines, cocaine, and MDMA (Ecstasy) are used by college students as well.

§ 1.7 MONEY LAUNDERING

Traffickers of illicit drugs, primarily Colombian and Mexican criminal groups, launder their drug sale proceeds to minimize the risk of detection or seizure when using the funds. A principal method used to launder drug proceeds is the physical transportation of bulk currency and monetary instruments, such as money orders and checks, to destinations outside the United States. Drug proceeds also are laundered through money service businesses, including money remittance, money exchange, and check cashing firms. In addition, traffickers introduce their illicit proceeds into the United States' financial system by structuring currency transactions in amounts that fall under threshold reporting requirements established by the Bank Secrecy Act, by co-opting cash-intensive businesses to commingle drug proceeds with legitimate funds, and by purchasing real estate, vehicles, and businesses. Another technique is for traffickers to consign their proceeds to money brokers who launder the funds for a fee or a commission. This technique frees drug trafficking organizations or criminal groups of responsibility for the security and transportation of bulk proceeds, and it separates the traffickers from the laundering process (NDIC 2004).

§ 1.8 IMPACT OF CALIFORNIA PROPOSITION 36

Since its implementation in July 2001, California's Substance Abuse and Crime Prevention Act, known as Proposition 36, has diverted more than 37,000 people, usually those arrested for petty crimes or drug possession, into treatment. Respondents view this initiative as having a major impact on treatment programs in several cities: A Sacramento treatment respondent states that these new clients include many older drug users with mental health problems (especially schizophrenia) who are new to treatment. The Sacramento methadone treatment reports general increases in treatment caseloads and court referrals due to Proposition 36.

In Sacramento, males have increased as a proportion of treatment admissions. Before Proposition 36, females dominated because they were referred to treatment through child welfare cases.

In Los Angeles, younger users, more females, and more users new to treatment are referred for drug treatment, especially heroin addiction. Also in Los Angeles, more methamphetamine users are referred to treatment due to the changes in funding established by Proposition 36.

Overall, it appears that Proposition 36 has been successful (ONDCP 2004).

§ 1.9 DRUG ABUSE TREATMENT

According to Pulse Check treatment sources, most heroin addicts in methadone programs are individually referred. In other treatment programs, 50 percent of the heroin addicts are individual referrals and 50 percent are court/criminal justice referrals.

Crack cocaine and methamphetamine addicts are more likely to be court/criminal justice referrals to treatment programs. Powder cocaine addicts are more likely to be individually referred to treatment.

Marijuana addicts are predominately court and criminal justice referrals to treatment. Some referrals involve marijuana possession only and others include referrals for both possession and sales. Challenges involved in treating marijuana addicts over the past 10 years have increased and include earlier initiation of marijuana use, increased marijuana potency and a decline in users' perception of harm. Court referrals to treatment for marijuana abuse have had a positive effect of getting users into treatment earlier. Several sources in the Northeast (in Baltimore, New York, and Philadelphia) report increased criminal justice referrals for all drugs. For marijuana in particular, drug court referrals have increased in San Francisco, and referrals from mental health centers (mostly for generalized anxiety) have increased in Chicago (ONDCP 2004).

§ 1.10 ALL SEGMENTS OF SOCIETY AFFECTED

No population group is immune to substance abuse and its effects. Men and women and people of all ages, racial and ethnic groups, and levels of education smoke, drink alcohol, and use illicit drugs. There are, however, significant differences in substance use among groups.

Young adults are the group most likely to use alcohol, illicit drugs, and tobacco. Men are more likely than women to use most substances. Men are particularly more likely to be heavy users of alcohol and to be problem drinkers.

Whites are more likely than blacks or Hispanics to drink, but they are no more likely to drink heavily. Native Americans are more apt to have problems with alcohol. Illicit drug use disproportionately affects minority groups at an additional risk for a range of adverse consequences, because they are more likely to use these drugs intravenously.

Level of education is increasingly recognized as an important correlate of substance use, with heavier use among those who are less educated. People with higher education levels are more likely to drink, but those with less education are more likely to drink heavily. Among less educated people, smoking is more common and smoking cessation less likely.

The impact of substance abuse is felt from earliest infancy through old age. Some infants are born already compromised through exposure to chemical substances by their mothers during pregnancy. For example, nationwide, one in ten children born has been exposed to cocaine in the womb, affecting 350,000 babies a year. Throughout childhood, children are affected in many ways by their parents' substance use, from neglect and abuse, to psychological, physical, and mental problems.

Adolescence is a period of experimentation with substance use, and teenagers are particularly at risk for being involved in alcohol- and drug-related vehicle injuries and death. Because drug use is higher among young adults, men and women in this age group are more likely to experience problems. For example, workplace problems and family disruption can develop during this time. But it is later in life that the long-term health effects from alcohol and tobacco use are most apparent. A lifetime of drinking, smoking, and use of illicit drugs exacts a heavy toll in chronic health problems and premature death (Clark).

A study released by the National Institute on Drug Abuse (NIDA) and the National Institute on Alcohol Abuse and Alcoholism (NIAAA), National Institutes of Health (NIH), estimates that the economic cost of alcohol and drug abuse was $246 billion in 1998, the most recent year for which sufficient data were available. This estimate represents $965 for every man, woman, and child living in the United States in 1998. The study reports that alcohol abuse and alcoholism generated about 60 percent of the estimated costs ($148 billion), while drug abuse and dependence accounted for the remaining 40 percent ($98 billion).

The international illicit drug business generates $400 billion in trade annually. According to the United Nations International Drug Control program, that figure amounts to 8% of all international trade. In 1999, the National Drug Control Policy reported that federal expenditures in control of illegal drugs was $17 billion and, when combined with expenditures by federal, state, and local governments, exceeded $30 billion. This is a protracted cost. The U.S. has spent roughly this amount throughout the 1990s. In 1992, the economic costs of alcohol abuse was $148 billion; by 1998, this cost had increased to $185 billion—a 25% increase or 3.8% per year on average.

The distribution of alcohol and drug costs differed significantly. Two-thirds of the costs of alcohol abuse related to lost productivity, either due to alcohol-related illness (45.7 percent) or premature death (21.2 percent). Most of the remaining costs of alcohol abuse were in the form of health care expenditures to treat alcohol use disorders and the medical consequences of alcohol consumption (12.7 percent), property and administrative costs of alcohol-related motor vehicle crashes (9.2 percent), and various additional costs of alcohol-related crime (8.6 percent).

It costs approximately $8.6 billion a year to keep drug law violators behind bars (BJS 1996, 1997).[1]

According to the United Nations, illegal drugs create enormous profits. In 2001, a kilogram (2.2 lbs.) of heroin in Pakistan sold for an average of $610. The UN reports that in the U.S. in 2001, heroin cost an average of $25,000 per kilogram (UNODC 2003).

According to the United Nations, profits in illegal drugs are so inflated that three-quarters of all drug shipments would have to be intercepted to seriously reduce the profitability of the business. Current efforts only intercept 30% of cocaine shipments and 10%-15% of heroin shipments (Associated Press).

The Federal Government's Drug Control budget request for fiscal year 2006 proposes to spend 38.7% of the budget on drug treatment and prevention, while 61.3% will be shared among law enforcement budgets, international programs, drug-related intelligence spending, and interdiction activities (ONDCP 2005).

New estimates of the amount of money Americans spend on illegal drugs reveal something remarkable about the extent to which the concentration of drug users in our cities hurt those cities economically. In five cities (Atlanta, Chicago, New York, Los Angeles, and San Diego), estimated annual expenditures by drug users total $1 billion or more— and this is money that is drained out of the legitimate economy. Not surprisingly, three of the same cities have to spend $1 billion or more in costs directly attributable to their residents' drug use, with health care cost the single biggest expense. Such costs represent an unacceptable drain on the economics of American's cities (ONDCP 2005).

The enormous social consequences of drug use would be far worse were the price and availability of illegal drugs not so successfully circumscribed by the activities of interdiction and law enforcement. The drug trade is a market phenomenon. As we interrupt the supply of drugs, we make them scarcer and more expensive, diminishing drug use and leading some to seek treatment. We also know that an even greater impact than price of drugs on behavior is the overall legal status of substances. Sixteen million Americans are dependent on alcohol compared to 5 million who are dependent on an illegal drug.

§ 1.11   PATTERNS OF USE/PERCEPTION OF RISK

Americans increasingly recognize that the use of alcohol, illicit drugs, and tobacco involves substantial health risks. Not all substances are perceived as equally risky. Illicit drug use is viewed by people of all ages

---

[1] The Criminal Justice Institute estimates cost of a day of jail to be $55.41/day or $20,237/year, and the cost of prison to be about $64.49/day or $23,554/year.

as much riskier than smoking or drinking, and regular or heavier use of drugs or alcohol is seen as riskier than occasional or experimental use. There are also differences in perception of risk by age. In general, older people are more likely than young people to think that substance use is risky. Over half of the youth do not think that smoking tobacco is risky.

§ 1.11.1 Implications of Early Use

Age is one of the most important factors defining the likelihood of using alcohol, illicit drugs, and tobacco. Young adults, ages 18 to 25, are the group most likely to use alcohol or illicit drugs or engage in heavy alcohol use. Those between the ages of 18 and 34 are the ones likeliest to smoke tobacco.

Many young people begin to experiment with alcohol, illicit drugs, and tobacco at very early ages, although not all who try drugs once or twice continue to use them.

Because cigarettes and alcohol usually are tried before illicit drugs such as marijuana, hallucinogens, or cocaine, they are often referred to as "gateway drugs." However, many youth who use alcohol or cigarettes never try illegal drugs. The age when young people first start using alcohol and illicit drugs is a predictor of later alcohol and drug problems, especially if use begins around 13 years of age. People who begin using alcohol or smoking when they are very young are more likely to be heavy users of these substances later on. Serious problems related to alcohol and drug dependence typically begin to appear in men by age 20. For women, problems with alcohol and drugs frequently occur later, when they are in their thirties (Christe et al).

§ 1.11.2 Consequences of Use

Cigarette smoking accounts for over 400,000 deaths a year or 20 percent of all United States deaths. Cigarette smoking has long been known to cause cancer, and nearly 90 percent of lung cancer deaths result from smoking. While lung cancer rates are a good marker for long-term use of tobacco, lung cancer accounts for only one-quarter of all deaths attributed to smoking. Smoking also is a major contributor in deaths from coronary heart disease, chronic bronchitis and emphysema, and cancers of the pancreas, trachea, and larynx. Smoking during pregnancy is associated with fetal and infant deaths. In fact, smoking is probably the most important modifiable cause of poor pregnancy outcome, according to the U.S. Surgeon General (CDC 2004).

Alcohol is a major cause of premature death in the United States. Excessive alcohol consumption is the third leading preventable cause of death in the U.S., and is associated with multiple adverse health consequences, including liver cirrhosis, various cancers, unintentional injuries, and violence. Vehicular accidents remain the single greatest cause of death among youth and young adults. During 2003, alcohol-related motor vehicle accidents accounted for nearly 40% of all traffic fatalities in the U.S. Evidence links drinking and deaths from falls, fires and burns, and drowning. Various studies estimate that between 17 and 53 percent of falls are alcohol-related and between 48 and 64 percent of people dying in fires had blood alcohol levels indicating intoxication. One common cause of fire among intoxicated people is falling asleep or passing out with a lit cigarette (CDC 1990,1992).

It is difficult to determine the extent of deaths caused by illicit drugs. Reported deaths directly related to drugs are gross underestimates of the mortality toll from illicit drugs since they exclude deaths from associated diseases, such as hepatitis or TB, and all other causes where illicit drugs contribute to death, such as homicides, falls, and motor vehicle crashes. Medical examiner data from 1990 indicate that about one-third of all drug deaths involve illicit drugs as a contributing factor, but not the direct cause of death. Deaths from drug causes often involve a lethal combination of two or more illicit drugs or drugs combined with alcohol. Heroin or cocaine is involved in two-thirds of drug deaths.

Nearly 40 percent of illicit drug deaths are among adults between 30 and 39 years old, an age group that has high rates of many chronic problems due to drug abuse. Overall rates are higher for men than for women, and for blacks than for whites. Injection drug use is a risk factor for AIDS in that he drug users become infected with AIDS through sharing injection drug equipment with HIV infected persons. However, since 1995, AIDS incidence among injection drug use has declined (CDC 2003).

Substance abuse places tremendous psychological and financial burdens on families. Problem drinking can affect a family in many ways, such as violence, divorce, child abuse and neglect, and spousal abuse. The children of alcoholic families show emotional and adjustment problems like aggressive behavior, difficulties with peers, behavior problems, hyperactivity, and poor school adjustment. Another impact of substance abuse on families is the financial cost. The costs of smoking, drinking, and using illicit drugs are high (Bijur et al).

Significant amounts of substance abuse takes place among the American work force, and some of this use occurs at work. Smoking is a costly expenditure for employers. In addition to health care costs for the smokers, smoking poses health hazards to nonsmokers at work and increases the risk of workplace fires and product contamination, as well as the cost of facility cleaning and ventilation.

Seventy percent of illicit drug users age 18-49 are employed full time; 6.3 million of full-time workers are illicit drug users. Two-thirds of drug users work full or part-time. Some 27 percent of the full-time employed illicit drug users report that in the past 30 days they had missed work due to illness or injury, and 18 percent just did not go to work. Many have reported that they go to work high or a little drunk (NIDA 1991). Illicit drug and alcohol use are also costly to employers. Health insurance costs for employees with alcohol problems are about twice those of other employees. There are costs related to workplace injuries, higher employee turnover, and lost productivity.

§ 1.12 CONCLUSION

All the indicators of drug use and abuse point to an important strategy of preventing drug use by young people. The various documents affirm that no single approach will work. Drug prevention, education, treatment, and research must be complemented by supply-reduction and a strong law enforcement approach.

We know that drug use is preventable; that the negative social consequences of drug-related crime and violence show the extent drug abuse impacts individuals; that drug addiction is a chronic and relapsing problem; that the United States is obligated to protect its citizens from the threats passed by illegal drugs; and that the rule of law, human rights, and democratic institutions are threatened by drug trafficking and use.

The metaphor of a "war on drugs" is misleading. Although wars are expected to end, drug prevention and education is a continuous process.

For More Information

Arrestee Drug Abuse Monitoring (ADAM) Program: www.adam-nij.net

Arrestee Drug Abuse Monitoring (ADAM), sponsored by the National Institute of Justice, has been conducted quarterly since 1987.

Bureau of Justice Statistics: www.ojp.usdoj.gov/bjs/

Community Epidemiology Work Group: www.drugabuse.gov/about/organization/cewg

The Community Epidemiology Work Group (CEWG) is a group of experts from 21 metropolitan areas who report on various local indicators every 6 months and assess developing drug use trends in their local communities. CEWG is sponsored by NIDA.

Drug Abuse Warning Network: dawninfo.samhsa.gov

Drug Abuse Warning Network (DAWN), sponsored by SAMHSA, has been collecting data since 1975.

Monitoring the Future: www.drugabuse.gov/DrugPages/MTF.html

Monitoring the Future sponsored by National Institute on Drug Abuse (NIDA) has been conducted annually since 1975.

National Drug Intelligence Center: www.usdoj.gov/ndic

National Drug Threat Assessment, sponsored by the National Drug Intelligence Center, annually reports results. Started in 2001, synthesizes all federal, state, and local reporting into a single source.

National Household Survey on Drug Abuse: www.oas.samhsa.gov/nhsda.htm

National Household Survey on Drug Abuse (NHSDA), sponsored by the U.S. Department of Health and Human Services' Substance Abuse and Mental Health Services Administration (SAMHSA), has been conducted periodically from 1971 to 1990 and annually since then.

National Institute on Drug Abuse: www.nida.nih.gov

Current Patterns of Drug Use

The National Institute on Drug Abuse (NIDA) is a component of the National Institutes of Health, U.S. Department of Health and Human Services. NIDA supports more than 85 percent of the world's research on the health aspects of drug abuse and addiction. The Institute carries out a large variety of programs to ensure the rapid dissemination of research information and its implementation in policy and practice. Fact sheets on the health effects of drugs of abuse and information on NIDA research and other activities can be found on the NIDA home page at www.drugabuse.gov.

National Institute of Justice: www.ojp.usdoj.gov/nij

Office of National Drug Control Policy: www.whitehousedrugpolicy.gov

Pulse Check was developed by the Office of National Drug Control Policy (ONDCP) in 1992. It collects quarterly interview data from 20 metropolitan areas in the United States.

Substance Abuse and Mental Health Services Administration: www.samhsa.gov

References

"Alcohol: Attributable Deaths and Years of Potential Life Lost." JAMA 292 (2004): 2831-32.

Bijur, Kerzon, Overpeck, and Scheidt. "Parental Alcohol Use, Problem Drinking, and Children's Injuries." Journal of the American Medical Association 267. 23 (1992): 3166-3171.

Bureau of Justice Statistics. Profile of Jail Inmates 1996. Washington, D.C.: U.S. Government Printing Office, 1996.

----------. Prisoners in 1996. Washington, D.C.: U.S. Government Printing Office, 1997.

Centers for Disease Control & Prevention. HIV Diagnosis Among Injection Drug Users in States with HIV Surveillance: 25 States, 1994-2004. Atlanta: CDC, 2003.

---------- "Factors Potentially Associated with Reductions in Alcohol-Related Traffic Fatalities, United States, 1990-1991." Morbidity and Mortality Weekly Report. Atlanta: CDC, 1990 and 1992.

---------- Morbidity and Mortality Weekly Report. Atlanta: CDC, 2003.

---------- Tobacco Information and Prevention Source (TIPS). Atlanta: CDC, 2003.

Christe, Burke, Regier, et al. "Epidemiologic Evidence For Early Onset of Mental Disorders and Higher Risk of Drug Abuse In Young Adults." American Journal of Psychiatry 145 (1988): 971-975.

Criminal Justice Institute, Inc. The Corrections Yearbook 1997. South Salem: Criminal Justice Institute, Inc., 1997.

Clark, W.D., and Hilton, M.E. Alcohol in America: Drinking Practices and Problems. Albany: State University of New York Press, 1991.

National Drug Intelligence Center. "National Drug Threat Survey 2003." Washington, D.C.:U.S. Department of Justice, 2003.

----------. National Drug Threat Survey 2004. Washington, D.C.: U.S. Department of Justice, 2004.

National Institute on Drug Abuse. "National Household Survey on Drug Abuse." Rockville, MD: Department of Health and Human Services, 1991.

National Institute on Drug Abuse and National Institute on Alcohol Abuse and Alcoholism. "The Economic Costs of Alcohol and Drug Abuse in the United States, 1992." Washington, D.C.: U.S. Department of Health and Human Services, 1998.

Chapter 1

National Research Council/National Academy of Sciences. "Reforming America's Policy on Illegal Drugs: What We Don't Know Keeps Hurting Us." Washington, D.C.: National Academy Press, 2005.

Office of National Drug Control Policy. "National Drug Control Strategy." Washington, D.C.: Executive Office of the President, 1995.

----------. "Pulse Check." National Trends in Drug Abuse. Washington, D.C.: Executive Office of the President, December, 1994.

----------. "Pulse Check." National Trends in Drug Abuse. Washington, D.C: Executive Office of the President, 2004

----------. "National Drug Control Strategy Update 2005." The President's National Drug Control Strategy. Executive Office of the President, February 2005.

----------. "The Price and Purity of Illicit Drugs: 1981 Through Second Quarter 2003." Washington, D.C.: Executive Office of the President, 2004.

----------. "What America's Users Spend on Illegal Drugs." The President's National Drug Control Strategy. Washington, D.C.: Executive Office of the President, Washington, D.C., 2000.

Substance Abuse and Mental Health Services Administration. "National Household Survey on Drug Abuse: Main Findings 1994." Rockville, MD: Department of Health and Human Services,1994.

---------- "Overview of Finding from the 2003 National Survey on Drug Use & Health." Rockville, MD: Department of Health and Human Services, 2004.

----------. "Worker Drug Use & Workplace Policies and Programs: Results from 1994-1999." Rockville, MD: Department of Health and Human Services, 1999.

Surgeon General's Report. The Health Consequences of Smoking on the Human Body. 2004.

"U.N. Estimates Drug Business Equal to 8 Percent of World Trade." Associated Press, 26 June 1997.

United Nations Office for Drug Control and Crime Prevention. Economic and Social Consequences of Drug Abuse and Illicit Trafficking. New York: UNODC, 1998.

United Nations Office on Drugs and Crime. Global Illicit Drug Trends: 2003. New York: UNODC, 2003.

CHAPTER 2

DRUGS, CRIME AND VIOLENCE

§ 2.1 INTRODUCTION

Nowhere are the consequences of illicit drug use, addiction, and trafficking more visible than in the extent and patterns of drug crime and drug-related violence.

Drugs are related to crime in multiple ways. Most directly, it is a crime to use, possess, manufacture, or distribute drugs classified as having a potential for abuse (such as cocaine, heroin, marijuana, and amphetamines). Drugs are also related to crime through the effects they have on the user's behavior and by generating violence and other illegal activity in connection with drug trafficking.

The three most important causal links between drugs and crime are the behavioral effects of drug use, the urgent need of addicts for money to feed their habits, and the side-effects of illicit markets. We will examine each in turn.

§ 2.2 THE FIRST LINK

Intoxication and addiction, in certain circumstances, appear to encourage careless and combative behavior. The key empirical observation here is that more crimes—and, in particular, more violent crimes—are committed under the influence of alcohol than under the influence of all illegal drugs combined.

The Bureau of Justice Statistics (B.S.) report *Substance Abuse and Treatment, State and Federal Prisoners*, 1997, reports on the strong association between alcohol and crime. Most political attention is focused on illicit drugs. Drug surveys concentrate on illicit drugs. Alcohol, the licit drug, is really the forgotten drug when it comes to our national efforts. The fact is that alcohol plays a significant role and link to crime and violence.

In the B.S. report itself, illicit-drug involvement by offenders is categorized in terms of lifetime use and monthly use, while past use of alcohol is defined in terms of "abuse" measures, such as binge drinking and alcohol dependence. So whereas past use of illicit drugs is used to infer a relationship with crime, no such inference is drawn for past use of alcohol. This may be in line with government policy (which states that all illicit drug use is abuse), but for comparing the relative relationship between alcohol and other drugs to crime, it's strictly apples and oranges.

There is, however, one category where the relationship between alcohol and illicit drugs is clearly considered on equal grounds by the

B.S. report: use at the time the prisoner committed the offense for which he or she was incarcerated. Here, a comparison reveals that alcohol and other drugs have roughly equal roles in crime. The B.S. report also shows that alcohol plays a greater role in assault, murder, and sexual assault than illicit drugs.

Not surprisingly, prisoners who were under the influence of illicit drugs when they committed their crime were more likely to have been convicted of drug offenses than those who were under the influence of alcohol. Also, one in six offenders reported that they committed their crime to get money to buy illicit drugs. In the 1997 Survey of Inmates in State and Federal Correctional Facilities, over 570,000 of the nation's prisoners (51%) reported the use of alcohol or drugs while committing their offense. Also in 1997, 83% of state prisoners reported past drug use as compared to 73% of federal prisoners. Sixty-three percent of federal prisoners were incarcerated for drug offenses in 1997. Marijuana use was the most commonly used illicit drug by state prisoners (77%) in 1997, and there is not much change today.

When 33% of state prisoners and 22% of federal prisoners landed in prison committing their crime under the influence of illicit drugs, 30% reported intoxication with alcohol alone and at least 17% used alcohol and illicit drugs. That alcohol, a legal and inexpensive drug, is implicated in so much crime suggests that substance abuse itself, and not just economic motivation or the perverse effects of illicit markets, can play a significant role in crime.

According to the National Crime Victimization Survey (NCVS), in 2002, there were 5.3 million violent victimizations of residents age 12 or older. Victims of violence were asked to describe whether they perceived the offender to have been drinking or using drugs. About 29% of the victims of violence reported that the offender was using drugs, alone or in combination with alcohol. Based on victim perceptions, about 1.0 million violent crimes occurred each year in which victims were certain that the offender had been drinking. For about one in five of these violent victimizations involving alcohol use by the offender, victims believed the offender was also using drugs at the time of the offense.

This connection is hardly surprising. Anything that weakens self-control and reduces foresight is likely to increase lawbreaking activities. Most crime doesn't pay, and being high is one good way to forget that fact. (Drunk driving, for example, rarely stands up to cost-benefit analysis from the drunk driver's viewpoint, yet many otherwise sensible people engage in it.) Some forms of intoxication also make certain crimes seem more rewarding, as well as making punishments seem less threatening. And most of us know people who become aggressive when drunk or high.

So alcohol, aside from affecting an individual's reasoning and judgment, elicits aggression and violent behavior. Alcohol is the most widespread and frequently abused drug associated with violence. Forty percent (40%) of criminal offenders reported using alcohol at the time of their offense, as did 36% of convicted violent offenders (Greenfeld). Even the mere presence of alcohol can increase violent crimes. Researchers have found that the number of alcohol outlets in a given area is related to the rate of violent crime. Each liquor outlet contributes an average of 3.4 violent crimes a year for each city (Respers).

Alcohol-influenced driving is considered the nation's worst frequently committed violent crime (MADD 1996). Every weekday night from 10 p.m. to 1 a.m., one in thirteen drivers is drunk, and between 1 a.m. and 6 a.m., on weekend mornings, one in seven drivers are drunk (Miller). In 1998, drunk drivers caused 38.4% of all traffic fatalities (NHTSA 1998).

Alcohol is the only psychoactive drug that in many individuals tends to increase aggressive behavior temporarily while it is taking effect. However, the setting or where people are drinking (home, bar), the mind-set while the person is drinking, and the local drinking customs influence the strength of this relationship.

Alcohol has a particularly strong relationship with domestic violence. Alcohol is present in more than one-half of all incidents of domestic violence (Collins). Two-thirds of partner abuse victims reported that alcohol was a factor, and for spouse abuse victims, the offender was drinking in three out of four cases (Greenfeld). Husbands who binge drink are also three times more likely to abuse their wives than husbands who abstain (Kaufman). A recent study examines the connection between intimate partner abuse and alcohol and drug use. Researchers have found that increased substance use results in more severe violence, male perpetrators were more often problem drinkers (Sharps). Similarly, alcohol is largely related to sexual aggression and violence. Increased drinking frequency and intensity are both associated with sexually aggressive behavior by white male college students, and researchers estimate that alcohol is implicated in one- to two-thirds of sexual assault and acquaintance or "date rape" cases among teens and college students (OIG 1992). According to surveys of probationers and local, state, and federal prisoners, 27% to 36% of offenders convicted of rape and/or sexual assault were drinking at the time of the offense (Greenfeld). Furthermore, as the consumption of alcohol by either the victim or perpetrator increases, the rate of serious injuries associated with dating violence also increases (Makepeace).

Other drugs like marijuana and opiates inhibit violent behavior. Withdrawal from opiate addiction tends to increase aggressive behavior that may lead to violence.

There is no evidence to support the claim that central nervous system (CNS) stimulants directly stimulate violent behavior. However, the paranoid psychosis created by heavy use and abuse of CNS stimulants can make this person very dangerous to handle in arrest situations. Law enforcement officers must take great caution when dealing with people under the influence of CNS stimulants because of the strong unpredictable psycho-activity of the drugs. There is no doubt that users with histories of psychosis and/or antisocial behavior can become very violent with the chronic use of these drugs.

Early childhood aggression is a predictor of later heavy drinking, and the combination is associated with an above average risk of adult violent behavior, especially among those who also abuse other psychoactive drugs.

Preexisting psychosis appears to account for violent outbursts by people who are under the influence of amphetamines, cocaine, and especially PCP. While these drugs are known to cause disorganized, bizarre behavior, they trigger violence in few people who are not psychotic (of course the drugs trigger psychosis). In studies of laboratory mice and monkeys, bizarre behavior of the animals under the influence of PCP commonly provokes violent attacks by others in the group. Newspaper reports and police reports identify similar attacks on humans using alcohol, cocaine, HCL, crack cocaine, and PCP, but this relationship has not been systematically studied in humans (NIJ 1994).

Remember, the immediate effects of intoxication are not the only, or necessarily the most significant, connection between drug-taking and crime. Chronic intoxication impairs school and job performance, makes its victims less able to delay gratification, and damages relationships with friends and family. All of these tend to increase criminality.

§ 2.3 THE SECOND LINK
The second important link between drugs and crime involves drug users' need for large amounts of quick cash due to the high costs of maintaining an illegal drug habit. The average heavy heroin or cocaine user consumes about $10,000 to $15,000 worth of drugs per year, a sum that most of them cannot generate legally.

Twenty-five percent of jail inmates convicted of property and drug crimes had committed their crimes to get money for drugs (BJS 1998). In 1997, 19% of state prisoners and 16% of federal prisoners committed their current offense to obtain money for drugs (BJS 1997).

Nonetheless, the economic links between drug use and income-generating crime go both ways. Drug users commit crimes to obtain drug money—in part because their drug use reduces opportunities for legitimate work—but there is also the "paycheck effect." Just as some heavy drinkers splurge at the local bar on payday, drug-involved offenders may buy drugs because crime gives them the money to do so. This income-generating crime may lead to drug use, as well as the other way around.

§2.4 THE THIRD LINK
The drug trade provides the third connection between drugs and crime. Because selling drugs is illegal, business arrangements among dealers cannot be enforced by law. Consequently, territorial disputes among dealers, employer-employee disagreements, and arguments over the price, quantity, and quality of drugs are all subject to settlement by

force. Since dealers have an incentive to be at least as well-armed as their competitors, violent encounters among dealers, or between a dealer and a customer, often prove deadly.

Moreover, perpetrators of inter-dealer or dealer-customer violence are unlikely to be apprehended: Enforcement drives transactions into locations that are hidden from the police, and victims—themselves involved in illegal behavior—are unlikely to complain to the authorities. An increasingly common form of drug-market violence is simple robbery-murder by gangs that are in the drug trade only in the sense that hijackers of truckloads of microchips are in the electronics business.

The Uniform Crime Reporting Program (UCR) of the Federal Bureau of Investigation (FBI) reported that in 2003, 4.6% of the 14,408 homicides in which circumstances were known were narcotics-related. Murders that occurred specifically during a narcotics felony, such as drug trafficking or manufacturing, are considered drug-related.

§ 2.4.1 Drug-Related Homicides

Year	Number of homicides	% Drug-related
1993	23,180	5.5
1994	22,084	5.6
1995	20,232	5.1
1996	16,967	5.0
1997	15,837	5.1
1998	14,276	4.8
1999	13,011	4.5
2000	13,230	4.5
2001	14,061	4.1
2002	14,263	4.7
2003	14,408	4.6

Note: The percentages are based on data from the Supplementary Homicide Reports (SHR) while the totals are from the Uniform Crime Reports (UCR). Not all homicides in the UCR result in reports in the SHR. Table constructed by ONDCP Drug Policy Information Clearinghouse staff from FBI, Uniform Crime Reports, Crime in the United States, annually.

Still, it is not clear how much of the violence among drug dealers is attributable to the drug trade itself, as opposed to the personal propensities of the individuals employed in it, or to the economic, social, and cultural conditions of drug-plagued communities. Violent drug dealers tend to live and work in poor, inner-city neighborhoods, where violence is common independent of the drug business. On an individual level, a willingness to engage in violence is part of the implicit job description of a drug dealer in many markets. And the Darwinian logic of criminal enterprise suggests that surviving dealers are those who are best able to use violence, intimidation, and corruption to protect their positions.

Even the degree to which the drug trade provides the immediate pretext for violence among drug dealers is hard to pin down. Many violent incidents that are commonly described as drug-related—because they occur between dealers, between members of drug-dealing gangs, or at a known dealing location—turn out on close inspection to have personal rather than commercial motives, involving gang territory, an insult, sexual competition, or just a confrontation between two, edgy, armed youngsters.

Finally, the drug trade also contributes to crime by diverting inner-city youths away from school and legitimate employment. Not only does drug dealing introduce them to criminal enterprise, it also increases their risk of substance abuse and weakens their prospects for legitimate work (a recorded conviction and prison time are two obvious reasons), all of which make it more likely that they will engage in criminal activity, both in and out of the drug business.

Connections between drugs and crime vary across drugs—of the three most popular illicit drugs, marijuana, cocaine, and heroin, marijuana is the least implicated in violent crime. In a 2003 ADAM report, marijuana was the leading drug used among juveniles. Cocaine came in a distant second and methamphetamine use was low (NIJ 2003).

Marijuana users do not typically become violent, and marijuana habits are less expensive to support than cocaine or heroin habits. And marijuana is bought and sold in markets that, while not free of violence, are less violent than cocaine and heroin markets. This is in part because marijuana users make fewer purchases than do heroin or cocaine users, and in part because much marijuana is sold in residential settings by dealers who do not themselves have expensive habits.

Cocaine, on the other hand, is an expensive drug whose use and distribution are often accompanied by violent behavior. Heroin is less often tied to violence than cocaine, but because of the persistence of heroin addiction and the more regular use of the drug, it is possible that heroin addicts typically commit more income-producing crimes over time than cocaine addicts.

This analysis suggests that a reduction in heroin or cocaine use is likely to mean a bigger decrease in crime than a comparable reduction in cannabis use. As for other illegal substances, methamphetamine would tend to resemble heroin and cocaine in this regard, while MDMA ("ecstasy") and diverted pharmaceuticals, including painkillers such as OxyContin and Vicodin and the benzodiazepine tranquilizers such as Valium and Xanax, would look more like cannabis.

§ 2.5 DRUG TRAFFICKERS

In 2000, drug offenders accounted for a third (1/3) of all persons convicted of a felony in state courts. Drug traffickers accounted for 22% of all convicted felons and drug possession accounted for 13% of all convicted felons (BJS "Felony" 2003).

In 1996, those jail inmates convicted of drug trafficking (60%), drug possession (57%), fraud (45%), or robbery (44%) were most likely to have reported to be using drugs at the time of the offense (BJS 1998).

§ 2.5.1   Federal Courts

Drug trafficking has a 92% conviction rate. Drug offense defendants served an average of 97 months in federal prison, compared to 44 months for property offenders (BJS "Money" 2003).

§ 2.6 SPECIAL POPULATION GROUPS AND CRIME

Overall, 41% of violent crimes committed against college students and 38% of non-students were committed by an offender perceived to be using drugs between the years 1995 and 2000. About 2 in 5 of all rape/sexual assaults and about a quarter of all robberies against a college student were committed by an offender perceived to be using drugs (BJS "violent" 2003)..

Almost half of college students who were victims of campus crime said they were drinking or using other drugs when they were victimized (Bausell).

The drug Rohypnol has gained widespread publicity due to its involvement in several incidences of rape and sexual assault. Victims are unwittingly given the drug by their attacker and its tranquilizer-like effects make them susceptible to assault. However, alcohol is most often cited as increasing a victim's vulnerability to sexual assault, especially in college settings.

College binge drinkers, or individuals drinking five or more drinks at one time, are more than twice as likely as nonbinge drinkers to have experienced forced sexual touching and almost three times as likely to endure unwanted sexual intercourse (Presley). Eight percent (8%) of female college students said they have had sexual intercourse when they didn't want to because a man gave them alcohol or drugs (Koss 1987). Eighteen percent (18%) of high school females and 39% of males said it was acceptable for a boy to force sex if the girl is drunk or stoned (OIG 1992). Interviews with college fraternity members indicated a tendency to give alcohol to women on the theory that women who are drinking are less resistant to sexual advances (Martin).

§ 2.6.1   Victims of Workplace Violence

Of workplace victims of violence—

35% believed the offender was drinking or using drugs at the time of the incident;

36% did not know if the offender had been drinking or using drugs;

27% of all workplace offenders had not been drinking or using drugs;

Victims of workplace violence varied in their perception of whether the offender used alcohol or drugs by occupation—

47% of those in law enforcement perceived the offender to be using alcohol or drugs;

35% of those in the medical field perceived the offender to be using alcohol or drugs;

31% of those in retail sales perceived the offender to be using alcohol or drugs;

§ 2.7 DRUG CRIME AT THE LOCAL LEVEL

Federal, state, and local agencies share responsibility for enforcing the nation's drug laws, although most arrests are made by state and local authorities. In 2003 the Federal Bureau of Investigation's Uniform Crime Reports (UCR) estimated that there were 1,678,192 state and local arrests for drug abuse violations in the United States. (Source: FBI, Uniform Crime Reports, Crime in the United States).

According to the UCR, drug abuse violations are defined as state and/or local offenses relating to the unlawful possession, sale, use, growing, and manufacturing of narcotic drugs, including opium or cocaine and their derivatives, marijuana, synthetic narcotics, and non-narcotic drugs.

In 2003, according to the UCR, law enforcement agencies nationwide arrested 1.7 million people for drug abuse crimes. From 1987 to 1995, more drug arrests involved heroin or cocaine than other types of drugs. Since 1996, the number of arrests involving marijuana exceeded that for other types of drugs.

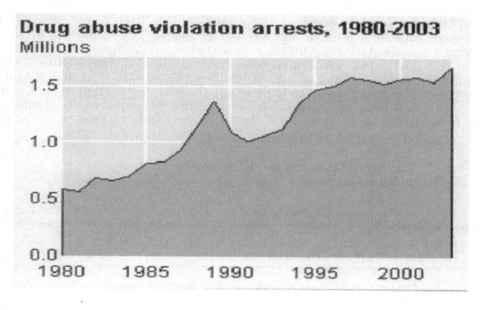

Drugs, Crime and Violence

More than four-fifths of drug law violation arrests are for possession. (Source: FBI, Uniform Crime Reports, Crime in the United States, annually).

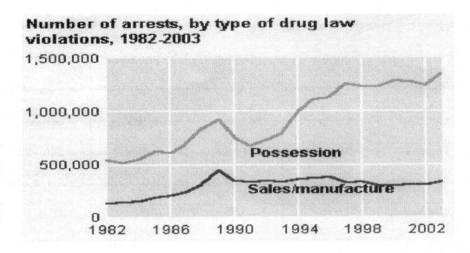

Number of arrests, by type of drug law violations, 1982-2003

While the number of drug arrests for juveniles has remained fairly steady, the number of adults arrested has continued to increase. (Source: FBI, Uniform Crime Reports, Crime in the United States, annually. Juveniles are defined as persons under age 18. Adults are defined as persons age 18 or older).

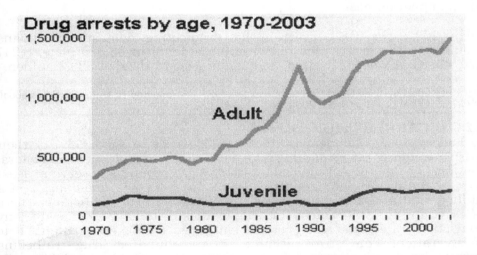

Drug arrests by age, 1970-2003

Source: FBI, Uniform Crime Reports, <u>Crime in the United States</u>. Juveniles are defined as persons under age 18.

§ 2.8 DRUG SEIZURES

Many federal agencies are involved in the removal of illicit drugs from the market. The Federal-Wide Drug Seizure System (FDSS) contains information about drug seizures made within the jurisdiction of the United States by the FBI, Drug Enforcement Administration (DEA), U.S. Customs Service (USCS), and U.S. Border Patrol, as well as maritime seizures made by the U.S. Coast Guard.

§ 2.8.1   Seizures in Pounds

	2000	2001	2002	2003
Total	2,919,608	2,894,200	2,571,355	2,644,580
Cocaine	2,733	6,640	4,392	6,900
Heroin	284,631	248,827	239,957	225,122
Marijuana	2,282,313	2,614,746	2,674,826	2,412,365
Hashish	1,678	23,987	433	193

Table constructed by staff of the DEA, FDSS, Sourcebook of Criminal Justice Statistics, 2002, NCJ 203301, July 2004.

According to the DEA—

The federal government seized 16,270 illegal drug laboratories between fiscal years 1975 and 2002

In 2002, of the 570 labs seized, 544 (95%) manufactured methamphetamines

In 2002, the DEA program for eradicating domestic marijuana resulted in the destruction of 3.3 million plants in 33,329 plots, 8,247 arrests, 3,511 weapons seized, and assets seized valued at $28.3 million.

Data provided by U.S. Department of Justice, DEA as reported in the BJS, Sourcebook of Criminal Justice Statistics, 2002, NCJ 203301, July 2004.

§ 2.9 INCARCERATION TREND

Federal drug offenders in 1986 could expect to serve 58% of their prison sentence, the remaining time served on parole. Under the Federal Sentencing Reform Act, defendants today are required to serve at least 87% of the prison sentence (BJS 1999). In 2000 over one-quarter of a million adults were arrested at the state level for drug trafficking. There is a trend in the state courts for drug traffickers to have increased felony conviction rates and an increase in drug traffickers sentenced to incarceration. Thirty-two out of every one hundred drug trafficking arrests result in a state prison sentence (BJS 2003). In 2000, drug offenders comprised a third of all persons convicted of a felony in state courts. Drug traffickers accounted for 22% of all convicted felons; drug possession accounted for 13% of all convicted felons.

§ 2.10 A CHANGE IN PERSPECTIVE

Now in the 21st century, the United States continues to grapple with the twin scourges of addiction and crime. The search for viable solutions is as urgent today as it was 35 years ago when Weissman and DuPont looked at the problem. The expenditures now being made in both criminal justice and the prevention and treatment of addiction are staggeringly large compared to the expenditures in the late 1960s. They exceed even the most aggressive plans of that era. Despite these efforts, the problems of drugs and crime remain huge, although most people would now describe them as "endemic" rather than "epidemic" since they have become chronic and apparently intractable (Du Pont et al).

The study of drugs, crime, and violence is confusing and contradicting at times. A 1998 study by the National Center on Addiction and Substance Abuse at Columbia University found that 3% of violent criminals in state prisons were under the influence of cocaine at the time their crime was committed and 1% were under the influence of heroin. In jails, none (0%) of the violent criminals was under the influence of heroin at the time their crime was committed. However, 21% of state inmates incarcerated for violent crime were under the influence of alcohol alone at the time they committed their crime (CASA 1998).

The linkage of drug use and crime remains fraught with controversy as many people believe that the connection is no more than coincidental. While historically the Drug Use Forecasting Data (DUF) has given us the best evidence of the high correlation of illegal drug use and crime, others can point to an equally high correlation of crime and cigarette smoking, pointing to the fact that a larger percentage of incarcerated felons smoke cigarettes than the general population.

We know the offensive in the war on drugs has included more money to fight the war, new resources for the police, and new laws to incarcerate people for longer sentences. We know, also, that the war on drugs has created violence and crime where once there was only addiction. Today the cost of drug-related crime and violence actually exceeds the cost of the drug itself.

We have seen that the trafficking in illicit drugs tends to be associated with the commission of violent crimes. The reasons for the relationship include competition for drug markets and customers, disputes and rip-offs, and a tendency toward violence of individuals involved in drug trafficking. In addition, locations in which street drug markets proliferate tend to be disadvantaged economically and socially; legal and social controls against violence in such areas tend to be ineffective. The proliferation of lethal weapons in recent years has also made drug violence more deadly.

Does drug use cause violence? Yes and no. Many experts believe that drug-related violence is actually a by-product of a black market and the types of people who engage in drug trafficking. According to members of the Panel on the Understanding and Control of Violent Behavior for the National Academy of Sciences, most of the violence associated with cocaine and narcotic drugs results from the business of supplying, dealing, and acquiring these substances, not from the direct neurobiological actions of these drugs (Miczek et al).

The drug/crime relationship should be interpreted cautiously. The relationship is difficult to quantify because most crimes result from a variety of factors that are personal, situational, cultural, and economic. Even when drugs are a cause, they are likely to be only one factor among many. Also, what is meant by "drug related" varies from study to study; some studies interpret the mere presence of drugs as having a causal relevance, whereas other studies interpret the relationship more narrowly. The reports by offenders about their drug use may exaggerate or minimize their involvement in drugs. Drug use measures, such as urinalysis, identify only very recent drug use.

The evidence indicates that drug users are more likely than nonusers to commit crimes that arrestees frequently were under the influence of a drug at the time they committed their offense, and that drugs generate violence. Assessing the nature and extent of the influence of drugs on crime requires that reliable information about the offense and the offender is available and that definitions be consistent. In the face of problematic evidence, it is impossible to say quantitatively how much drugs influence the occurrence of crime.

If we are going to have any effect on reducing the incidence of drug violence, criminal justice agencies must disrupt illegal drug markets. We must know who is using drugs by monitoring drug use of arrestees. We must establish drug abuse treatment for convicted criminals and create effective drug abuse prevention programs. Eventually, efforts to prevent drug-related violence may be assisted by pharmacological therapies to reduce the aggression-promoting effects of alcohol and the craving for other psychoactive drugs. And finally, we need to deal effectively with violence in the American family.

Drugs, Crime and Violence

References

Bausell, C.R. The Links Among Drugs, Alcohol, and Campus Crime. Towson State University Center for Study and Prevention of Campus Violence, 1990.

Bureau of Justice Statistics. DWI Offenders Under Correctional Supervision. Washington, D.C.: National Center for Justice, 1999.

----------. Felony Sentences in State Courts, 2000. Washington, D.C.: National Center for Justice, 2003.

----------. Profile of Jail Inmates, 1996. Washington, D.C.: National Center for Justice, 1998.

----------. Money Laundering Offenders. Washington, D.C.: National Center for Justice, 2003.

----------. Substance Abuse and Treatment, State and Federal Prisoners. Washington, D.C.: National Center for Justice, 1997.

----------. Substance Abuse and Treatment, State and Federal Prisoners. Washington, D.C.: National Center for Justice, 1999.

----------. Time Served in Prison by Federal Offenders, 1986-1997. Washington, D.C.: National Center for Justice, 1999.

----------. Violence in the Workplace, 1993-1999. Washington, D.C.: National Center for Justice, 2001.

----------. Violent Victimization of College Students, 1995-2000. Washington, D.C.: National Center for Justice, 2003.

Collins, J., and Messerschmidt, P. "Epidemiology of Alcohol-Related Violence." Alcohol Health and Research World 17.2 (1993).

DuPont, R.L., and MacKenzie, D.L. "Narcotics and drug abuse: An Unforeseen Tidal Wave." The 1967 President's Crime Commission Report: Its Impact 25 Years Later. Cincinnati: Academy of Criminal Justice Sciences & Anderson Publishing Co., 1994.

Greenfeld, L.A. Alcohol and Crime: An Analysis of National Data on the Prevalence of Alcohol Involvement in Crime. Washington, D.C.: U.S. Department of Justice, Office of Justice Programs, 1998.

Kaufman Kantor, G., and M. Straus. "The 'Drunken Bum' Theory of Wife Beating." Social Problems 34.3 (1987).

Koss, M., and Gaines, J. "The prediction of sexual aggression by alcohol use, athletic participation, and fraternity affiliation." Journal of Interpersonal Violence 8.1 (1993).

Koss, M., Gidyez, and Wisniewski, N. "The Scope of Rape: Incidence and Prevalence of Sexual Aggression and Victimization in a National Sample of High Education Students." Journal of Consulting and Clinical Psychology 55.22 (1997).

Makepeace, J.M. "The severity of courtship and the effectiveness of individual precautions." Family Abuse and Its Consequences: New Directions in Research. Thousand Oaks: SAGE Publications, 1988.

Martin, P., and Hummer, R. "Fraternities and Rape on Campus." Gender & Society 3.4 (1998).

Miczek, Klaus A., Joseph F. DeBold, et al. "Alcohol, Drugs of Abuse, Aggression and Violence." Understanding and Preventing Violence: Social Influences, Vol. 3. Ed. Albert Reiss. Washington, D.C.: National Academy Press, 1994.

Miller, T.R., Spicer, R.S., Levy, D.T. How Drunk Are the Drivers? (Working Paper). Washington, D.C.: National Public Service Institute, 1996.

National Center on Addiction and Substance Abuse (CASA). Behind Bars: Substance Abuse and America's Prison Population. New York: Columbia University, 1998.

National Highway Traffic Safety Administration. Fatal Accident Reporting System. 1998.

Chapter 2

National Institute of Justice. <u>Psychoactive Substances and Violence</u>. Washington, D.C., U.S. Department of Justice, 1994.

----------. <u>2000 Annual Report on Drug Use Among Adult and Juvenile Arrestees, Arrestees Drug Abuse Monitoring Program (ADAM)</u>. Washington, D.C., U.S. Department of Justice, 2003.

Office of Inspector General. <u>Youth and Alcohol: Dangerous and Deadly Consequences</u>. Washington, D.C.: U.S. Department of Health and Human Services, 1992.

Presley, C.A., Meilman, P.D., Cashin, J.R., and Leichliter, J.S. <u>Alcohol and Drugs on American College Campuses: Issues of Violence and Harassment: A Report to College Presidents</u>. Carbondale: The Core Institute, Southern Illinois University, 1997.

Respers, L. "USC Study Links Crime Rate and Number of Liquor Outlets." <u>Los Angeles Times</u> 1 May 1995.

Sharps, Campbell, Gary & Webster. <u>Risky Mix: Drug Use and Homicide</u>. NIJ Journal, 250 (2001).

Weissman, J.C., and DuPont, R.L. <u>Criminal Justice and Drugs: The Unresolved Connection</u>. Port Washington, N.Y.: Kennikat Press, 1982.

CHAPTER 3

DRUG PHARMACOLOGY, CLASSIFICATION, AND TESTING

§ 3.1 PHARMACOLOGY

The branch of science that deals with the interaction of chemical agents and living organisms is known as pharmacology. Traditionally, the major concern of pharmacology has been the study of drugs intended for medicinal use, i.e., drugs used to diagnose, prevent, treat, or cure disease. Even when such chemicals were misused and abused, and used for recreational purposes rather than for treating disease, the standard description of a drug was considered adequate. However, with the introduction of oral contraceptives in the mid-1950s, pharmacologists had to revise their definition of a drug. The "pill" was not used in the diagnosis, prevention, treatment, or cure of disease—unless pregnancy was to be considered a disease.

Consequently, pharmacologists have revised their definition of drugs to include "all chemicals that affect living processes." This newer definition seems more appropriate, especially with the increased use of "street drugs," many of which never had any intended medical use.

The science of pharmacology has given rise to three major subdivisions now recognized as special areas of study and practice:

1. Psychopharmacology—the study of where and how drugs act in the body, how drugs are changed by the body, and how drug action affects behavior.

2. Therapeutics—the use of drugs in treating disease. When drugs are used specifically to destroy or weaken invading organisms, the treatment is referred to as chemotherapy.

3. Toxicology—the study of poisons and the treatment of drug poisoning, including intoxication, resulting from the presence of harmful chemicals in the body.

§ 3.2 THE NERVOUS SYSTEM

In order to understand the impact of various drugs on the human body, one must first understand the uniqueness and processes of the nervous system. People take drugs recreationally to feel good and to alter their consciousness. Consciousness takes place through the nervous system.

All drugs are capable of producing more than a single response. Psychoactive drugs or substances have their primary effect on the human nervous system.

The nervous system is separated into three major divisions. It is important to realize however, that these divisions are not independent of each other. They interact; they are subsystems of the total system of our body. The three major divisions include the central nervous system, the autonomic nervous system, and the peripheral nervous system.

§ 3.2.1   THE CENTRAL NERVOUS SYSTEM (CNS)
The central nervous system (CNS) is composed of the brain and spinal cord. The central nervous system is encased in bone; the brain is covered by the skull, and the spinal cord resides within the vertebral column. The spinal cord serves as the conduit of information bringing signals to the brain from organs (including sensory organs) and muscles. In turn, the brain sends messages to motor fiber, which effect change in the activity of glands and muscles.

§ 3.2.2   THE AUTONOMIC NERVOUS SYSTEM (ANS)
The autonomic nervous system (ANS) is a regulatory system for smooth muscles, which form much of the viscera and internal organs. Smooth muscles are specialized for slow, sustained functions, such as digestive movement. The autonomic nervous system is regulated by hypothalamic activity and is divided into the parasympathetic and sympathetic systems. These two systems act in opposite ways. The parasympathetic nervous system is primarily concerned with maintaining organ function; the sympathetic nervous system takes over under conditions of excitation, stress, or threat.

Many drugs affect the autonomic nervous system. Furthermore, many drugs do not act on the central nervous system; rather, their effects are observed in the autonomic nervous system. Drugs that are similar to or act like adrenaline activate the sympathetic nervous system. Since these drugs mimic the effects of adrenaline and therefore stimulate the sympathetic nervous system, they are called sympatho-mimietic agents. The activation of the sympathetic nervous system produces the fight or flight response, which includes the following signs: increased respiration, increased cardiovascular output, dilation of the pupils, constriction of blood flow in the digestive system, and other stimulating effects.

§ 3.2.3   THE PERIPHERAL NERVOUS SYSTEM (PNS)
The ANS is actually a specialized portion of the peripheral nervous system (PNS). The nerves of the body that connect the brain and spinal cord to the sense organs and muscles make up the peripheral (motor-somatic) nervous system. When a receptor nerve is stimulated, it carries this excitation from the receptor to the central nervous system. When the brain has deciphered the message and acted on the information, it in turn activates motor nerves that carry excitation from the CNS to the glands and muscles. These nerves are known as effectors; they "effect" or stimulate the action required by the central nervous system in the peripheral nervous system.

Interestingly, many drugs (such as certain muscle relaxants) have what are called "peripheral effect," since their action is on the peripheral nervous system. A drug may have peripheral effects alone, or peripheral effects and central effects, or only central effects.

§ 3.2.4 SUMMARY

Human consciousness includes some very pleasurable states, which may be sought for their own sake. Drugs are sometimes used for the purpose of altering a state of consciousness, because such states take place through the action of the nervous system (a vastly complicated entity that is subject to the impact of various substances). The study of three subsystems—the central, autonomic, and peripheral nervous systems—can help in understanding some pharmacological concepts. The actual activity of the nervous system involves communication between nerve cells called neurons. This communication is carried out by electrical impulses within the cells and by neurotransmitters between cells. Drugs can affect both cells and neurotransmitters, sometimes causing profound behavioral and/or physical effects. The higher-order brain functions—those which make us most human—are the most susceptible to destruction by drugs.

§ 3.3 NEUROTRANSMITTERS: MEDIATORS OF THE NERVOUS SYSTEM

A neurotransmitter is a naturally occurring chemical in the nervous system which carries electrical impulses between neurons (brain cells).

The brain and peripheral nervous system is comprised of neurons separated by small gaps called "synapses." Neurotransmitters act within the synapses to determine the quantity and quality of electrical impulses that will be transmitted.

Although there are over one hundred chemicals in the brain, no more than about two dozen are probably true neurotransmitters. Research to date indicates that some of these are very important in the development and continuation of drug dependence.

Some transmitters implicated in drug dependence are: dopamine, acetylcholine, serotonin, norepinephrine, and gamma amino butyric acid (GABA).

§ 3.4 NEUROHORMONES: THE REGULATORS OF THE BODY

A neurohormone is a chemical that is made in a gland, leaves it, and acts on nervous tissue and/or other glands to maintain equilibrium in the body. Many neurohormones are made in the pituitary gland which is located at the base of the brain. The pituitary gland makes hormones which regulate most of the body's other glands. These include: thymus, thyroid, pancreas, ovary, testicle, adrenal, and breast glands. The pituitary gland also makes the neurohormones that are greatly responsible for pain relief, stress relief, and mental stability.

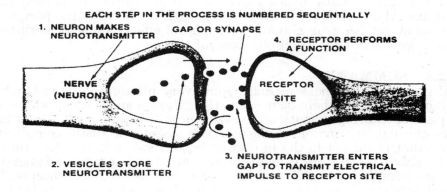

Diagram of How a Neurotransmitter Works

§ 3.5 RECEPTOR SITES

In 1974, the opioid receptor site was discovered. Opioids are opium derivatives which include heroin, morphine, codeine, Talwin, Darvon, Dilaudid, Demerol, methadone, Percodan, and fentanyl. When one of these drugs is taken, it goes to the brain and attaches to the opioid receptor site.

The opioid receptor site is known to help the brain perform the following functions:

—Relieve Pain
—Control Stress
—Promote Mental Stability
—Prevent Depression
—Regulate Food Intake
—Control Breathing Rate
—Produce Euphoria

Receptor sites have also been discovered for benzodiazepines.

During natural brain activity, neurotransmitters and neurohormones attach to specific brain receptor sites to carry out different functions. Drugs of abuse mimic the brain's natural neurotransmitters and neurohormones in that they have similar chemical effects on the nervous system.

§ 3.6 HOW DRUGS ENTER THE BODY

In order for a drug to have any more than a superficial effect, such as antacids in the stomach or antidandruff shampoos on the scalp, the chemical agent must enter the blood-vascular system. It must be absorbed or transported from the site of administration into the bloodstream, and then distributed by the blood throughout the body to various tissues and fluids. The manner in which the drug is introduced (the route of administration) is an important factor in determining how fast the drug acts, how long its effects will be sustained, the intensity of the drug's action, and the degree of localization of the drug's action.

Although drugs can be administered in several ways, they are usually given orally, rectally, parenterally, and by inhalation. Most often, drugs are taken into the body by way of the mouth. From the mouth, the liquid or solid drug passes into the stomach, and eventually into the intestine where most of the chemicals are absorbed (transferred) into the bloodstream. Oral administration is convenient, permits self-medication, and avoids the physical and psychological discomforts of injection. However, this route of administration is not ideal for all drugs. Absorption is sometimes slowed by the presence of food in the stomach and the excessive movement of the gastrointestinal tract.

Less commonly, drugs can be given rectally, i.e., through the rectum, which is the terminal end of the digestive tract. This method is particularly advantageous if the person is unconscious, has difficulty in swallowing, or is vomiting. However, drugs administered rectally in the form of a suppository or even an enema may be incompletely and irregularly absorbed.

The term parenteral describes the administration of drugs, such as antibiotics, insulin, and anticlotting medicine, into the bloodstream directly or indirectly by injection, without having to be absorbed through the digestive tract. This can be accomplished by intravenous injection (known as an IV or "mainlining," by which a drug in inserted directly into a vein); intramuscular injection or IM (directly into muscle tissue); or by subcutaneous injection or "skin-popping" (just beneath the skin's surface). While each of these routes of administration has its distinct advantages and disadvantages, some features are commonly shared, as noted below.

Administration of drugs by injection:

1   Produces a more rapid response than can be obtained by oral or rectal administration.

2. Achieves more accurate dosage, since drug destruction in the digestive tract is avoided.

3. Bypasses the unpredictable absorption processes occurring in the stomach and intestine.

4. Provides insufficient time, in comparison with orally administered drugs, to counteract unexpected drug reactions or accidental overdose. Once given, an injection cannot be recalled.

5. Requires sterile conditions in order to avoid infectious disease caused by bacteria and viruses that can damage the liver, heart, and other body organs.

6. Presents a potentially painful situation for the drug taker.

Certain drugs can be administered by *inhalation* in which chemicals are absorbed into the blood stream by passing through the lungs. Volatile anesthetic gases, paint thinner and gasoline vapors, and non-volatile aerosols, as well as tobacco, marijuana smoke and crack cocaine can pass through the thin membranes of the lung's air sacs and readily enter the bloodstream. In certain instances, inhalation of drugs produces an effect nearly as fast as or faster than intravenous injection. Consequently, control of dose is a major advantage of inhaling or breathing in drug vapors and drug smoke.

A variation of inhalation is known as snorting, which is the intranasal administration of drugs. In this route of entry, a water-soluble drug such as cocaine is snorted or sniffed, which is being absorbed through the moist mucous membranes that line the nasal passages. The drug enters the blood vessels near the surface lining.

While most psychoactive drugs are administered by mouth, rectum, injection, or inhaling, the future of drug use could be changed dramatically by a relatively new form of administration. The U.S. Food and Drug Administration authorized use of the first rate-controlled, transdermal drug system in which a drug is absorbed through the skin. Worn on the skin's surface as a disk or patch, the drug is absorbed directly into the bloodstream at programmed rates.

§ 3.7 DRUG DISTRIBUTION AND ELIMINATION IN THE BODY

After a drug has been absorbed into the bloodstream, it is widely distributed throughout the body. Such dispersal, however, reflects the physical and chemical nature of the drug and its ability to pass through various membranes—cell walls, capillaries, the brain, and the placenta.

Four basic patterns of drug distribution have been identified:

1. Some drugs, including blood-plasma substitutes, remain largely within the bloodstream.

2. Other compounds, such as ethyl alcohol and certain sulfa drugs, become almost uniformly distributed throughout each and every body cell.

3. Most drugs are unevenly distributed in the body in accordance with their ability to penetrate different membranes of the body.

4. Very few drugs actually concentrate in one or more body tissues or organs that may not even be the sites of drug action.

It should be noted that although psychoactive drugs affect mood and behavior—functions controlled by the nervous system—most of these chemicals will be found outside the brain at any given time, even during states of drug intoxication and poisoning.

Drug Pharmacology, Classification, and Testing

As drugs are circulated throughout the body, they undergo processes of metabolism and excretion, both of which are responsible for the elimination of the drugs and the termination of drug action.

The complex chemical changes that alter drugs and convert them to substances that can be eliminated from the body are known collectively as metabolism. A special system of enzymes in the liver cells carries out these metabolic reactions. Thus, the liver is an important body organ that functions in detoxification, the natural process of making substances nonpoisonous.

When the recently detoxified substances are carried by the blood to the kidneys, the metabolized drug by-products are excreted, i.e., eliminated from the body in the urine. Consequently, the kidneys with their filtering action are the major route of eliminating toxic substances from the human body. This action of the kidneys helps maintain the body's chemical homeostasis, that internal state of constancy or equilibrium necessary for normal functioning.

Although most drugs are excreted by the kidneys, small amounts will also be eliminated via several minor pathways of excretion. These routes include sweat, saliva, gastric secretions, bile, feces, breast milk, and the lungs. Though several psychoactive substances are absorbed through the lungs, including nicotine and marijuana, only the highly volatile drugs, such as anesthetic gases and alcohol, are excreted through the lungs.

§ 3.8 DRUG ACTIONS AND DRUG EFFECTS

Although there are technical differences between drug actions and drug effects, these terms will be used interchangeably throughout this section.

Drug actions are the result of a chemical interaction with some part of the human organism. In general, drugs change cell function by one or more of the following actions:

1. <u>Stimulation</u>—an increase in the rate of functional activity. Cocaine and amphetamines speed up central nervous system function.

2. <u>Depression</u>—a reduction in the rate of functional activity. Ethyl alcohol and barbiturates slow down or depress the function of the central nervous system.

3. <u>Blocking</u>—an obstruction that effectively prevents a particular action or response. This action is probably the consequence of depression. Antihistamine drugs block typical allergic reactions.

4. <u>Replacement</u>—the provision of a substitute or equivalent substance to restore an optimal condition. The administration of insulin to diabetics is an example of replacement therapy.

5. <u>Killing or inactivating organisms</u>—the destruction or prevention of the growth of disease-causing organisms. Antibiotics kill bacteria by interfering with the manufacture of bacterial cell walls.

6. <u>Irritation</u>—the abnormal excitation of some body part or function. This action may be an exaggerated form of stimulation. Laxatives irritate the large intestine to initiate defecation.

§ 3.9 FACTORS INFLUENCING DRUG ACTIONS

In addition to the route of administration, drug distribution throughout the body, and the processes of drug metabolism and elimination, the following factors should also be noted as influencing drug responses.

§ 3.9.1   Dose

The quantity or amount of drug that is taken at any particular time is called the dose or dosage. The greater the dose, the greater the drug effect will be. Threshold dose or minimal dose refers to the smallest amount of a given drug capable of producing a detectable response. By contrast, the median effective dose describes the dose required to produce a specific response in one-half or 50 percent of test subjects. If the response to a dosage is death, it is described as the lethal dose. Drugs are also said to have a maximum effect, the greatest response produced by a specific drug, regardless of the dose administered.

§ 3.9.2   Age

In comparison with so-called average 18- to 65-year-old adults, both infants and the elderly generally display more sensitivity to the effects of drugs. Infants tend to have underdeveloped abilities to metabolize and excrete drugs. As a consequence, drug actions within their bodies tend to be prolonged. The elderly, too, are likely to have impaired ability to metabolize and eliminate drugs from their bodies, part of the phenomenon of aging. Poor absorption in some older people is also a factor in reducing the effects of certain drugs. In another instance, one drug has a special reputation for reacting differently in children than in adults. Ritalin, a powerful stimulant for adults, acts as a depressant in children.

§ 3.9.3   Body Weight

Placing the same amount of a drug in a 90-pound person and a 200-pound person is likely to produce significantly different results because of the greater concentration of the drug in the blood of the lighter-weight individual. Lightweight people usually experience a greater drug effect than heavier people, when all other factors, including dosage, are similar. By contrast, the heavier individual with more blood and body fluids to dilute an absorbed drug has a reduced concentration of the dissolved drug—the amount of the drug contained per unit volume of body fluid.

§ 3.9.4 Sex

Contrary to popular belief, the sex of a drug taker has very little influence on the effect of a drug. Males and females tend to respond equivalently to drugs. However, women should be extremely cautious about taking any drugs during pregnancy, because many drugs, including beverage alcohol, cross the placenta and can damage the embryo and fetus.

§ 3.9.5 Time

The length of time between the taking of a drug and the observation of the anticipated effect is referred to as the "onset of action." Some drugs act shortly after entering the body; others may require several hours or even days before their effects become apparent. After the onset of action, drugs will vary in terms of the time required to achieve their maximum effects, as well as the duration of time during which drugs continue to have an effect.

§ 3.9.6 Disease

The presence or absence of a disease condition will often alter a person's response to a drug. For instance, aspirin reduces fever, but has no effect in lowering normal temperature. People with impaired liver and kidney function often have difficulty in metabolizing and excreting drugs, and thus experience prolonged drug effects. Such people are unable to eliminate drugs from their bodies in a normal period of time. On the other hand, when a condition of diarrhea exists, some drugs are transported through the gastrointestinal tract so rapidly that drug absorption is significantly reduced.

§ 3.9.7 Mind-set

Often referred to as the mind-set, one's emotional state or climate is now recognized as having a potentially significant impact on drug responses. Temperament marked by anger, fear, sadness, joy, or any other emotion can bring about changes in various body processes, namely, secretion of gastric juices and hormones, and alteration of blood pressure, heart rate, pulse, and respiration. These bodily processes, in turn, influence drug absorption, distribution, metabolism, and excretion—all of which can modify the response to a drug.

Taking a drug, especially a psychoactive one, in anticipation of "getting high," feeling more powerful or secure, or experiencing a new, altered state of consciousness, can also result in an exaggerated behavioral effect. Similarly, the use of a fake or inert substance that produces a drug response (the placebo effect) is also based upon a mind-set of trust, belief in a physician's judgment, and expectation of relief.

§ 3.9.8 Environmental Setting

Closely related to mind-set in changing a drug response are the various factors of the environmental setting. The environment includes not only the physical place in which a drug is taken, but also the psychosocial circumstances surrounding the drug use.

The impact of the environment on drug action can be very significant with mood- and behavior-modifying chemicals. For example, using a psychedelic drug in a controlled laboratory situation, or among caring, protective friends, will likely result in fewer "bad trips" than would be experienced in "street use" of the same drug.

§ 3.10 DRUG DEPENDENCE

Described as a state of psychological or physical need, or both, drug dependence can occur in an individual who uses a drug periodically or on a continual basis. Even though drug dependence is not exclusively associated with psychoactive drugs, the term is often used in reference to chemical modifiers which affect mood and behavior.

For many years, the word *addiction* was used to define compulsive use of drug substances, especially narcotics and alcohol. During the recent past, considerable difficulty arose in distinguishing among the various interpretations of addiction and habituation, especially as differences in the newer drugs and recreational ones became apparent. Eventually, the World Health Organization proposed substituting the more neutral term *drug dependence* for addiction. More recent variations in drug-abuse terminology include chemical dependence, substance abuse, more inclusive perhaps than the older terms.

Although not everyone who uses psychoactive agents develops a drug dependency, such a condition is a distinct possibility. The most extreme forma of drug dependence arecharacterized by (1) psychological dependence, (2) the development of tolerance, and (3) physical dependence. Fortunately, not all of these phenomena occur in each instance of drug dependency. Some drugs carry the potential for psychological dependence only, whereas others involve the aspect of physical dependence, too.

§ 3.10.1 Psychological Dependence

This sort of dependence occurs when a person takes a drug primarily for its effects. An individual who develops psychological dependence on a particular drug has a strong desire to repeat the use of that drug either occasionally or continuously. Although the body may not require the drug in a physical sense, the person has an intense craving for it to maintain drug-induced pleasure, a feeling of well-being, to achieve a maximum level of functioning, to reduce tensions, or to alter reality. When drug seeking becomes a compulsive and regular behavioral pattern, psychological dependence has reached its peak intensity. Deprived of the drug, the user will usually experience a period of readjustment, accompanied by some degree of anxiety, irritability, and restlessness.

§ 3.10.2 Tolerance

With the repeated use of certain drugs, a condition known as tolerance develops. Tolerance is defined as taking more and more of the drug to obtain the same effect. Put another way, it is the development of body or tissue resistance to the effects of a drug so that larger doses are required to reproduce the original effect.

The onset of tolerance may be rapid or gradual, depending upon the drug used. However, this condition is not an all-or-none phenomenon, since a person may develop a tolerance to one aspect of a particular drug's action, but not to another. It should also be noted that tolerance can accompany psychological dependence upon a drug without the occurrence of physical dependence.

Theories that explain the mechanisms of physiological or tissue tolerance may appear both contradictory or complementary. One major theory holds that tolerance is the result of alterations in how a drug is processed in the body after repeated doses are taken. Changes occur in the normal processes of drug absorption, distribution, metabolism, or elimination. For instance, the liver begins to destroy the drug substance more quickly. As a result less of the drug reaches the site of its action. Another contrasting theory is based on the reduced sensitivity of nerve-cell receptor sites that takes place over a long period of drug taking. This represents a form of cellular or tissue adaptation in which reaction to the drug is diminished.

One additional concern with tolerance is the development of cross-tolerance, a condition in which the reduced pharmacological response to one drug results in a lessened response to another drug. Cross-tolerance, however, typically occurs among drugs belonging to the same class of chemical agents. For example, persons tolerant to morphine are also tolerant to heroin, methadone, and other narcotic agents, but not to alcohol or barbarities, which belong to another class of drugs, the sedatives. On the other hand, persons tolerant to alcohol have a degree of tolerance to barbiturates and vice versa, but have no tolerance to narcotics.

Tolerance to some drugs develops very rapidly after the first dose, but occurs more slowly with other drugs.

Rate of Tolerance Development

Fast Tolerance Development	Intermediate Development	Slow Development
Cocaine	PCP	Nicotine
Opioids (Heroin, etc.)	Amphetamines	Benzodiazepines (Valium, etc.)
	Marijuana	Caffeine

§ 3.10.3 Physical Dependence

Simply stated, physical dependence is the presence of a withdrawal syndrome. One can also define physical dependence as the dependence of the body tissues on the continued presence of a drug revealed by withdrawal symptoms that develop when the drug is discontinued.

Thus, physical dependence is a state of functional adaptation to a drug in which the presence of a foreign chemical becomes "normal" and necessary. The absence of a drug would constitute an abnormality. The presence of a drug is required for normal function.

The condition of physical dependence is revealed only when drug use is discontinued. If the drug is removed abruptly, "normal" cell function is disturbed, resulting in hyper-excitability or over-activity of the nervous system. These drastic alterations in physical functions and behavior, observed or experienced after drug use is terminated, are known collectively as withdrawal or the abstinence syndrome.

DRUG DEPENDENCIES WHICH HAVE RECOGNIZED WITHDRAWAL TREATMENTS

Standard Medical Withdrawal Treatments	Recognized Withdrawal Treatments
Alcohol	Benzodiazepines
Heroin	Methadone, clonidine
Nicotine	Nicotine gum

Drug dependencies which have no standard medical withdrawal treatments are caffeine, cocaine, marijuana, phencyclindine (PCP) and amphetamines.

§ 3.10.4 Antagonists for Drug Dependence

Antagonists are drugs which can neutralize a drug and prevent relapse. In contrast to medical agents who help a drug dependent person stop using the drug, antagonists actually prevent the re-use of a drug once someone has completely stopped use.

There are two antagonists now available for use in preventing relapse to drug dependence.

Drug Dependence	Antagonist
Alcohol	Disulfiram (Antabuse)
Heroin	Naltrexone (Trexan)

There are also experimental antagonists for nicotine and benzodiazepines.

§ 3.10.5 Why Know about Drug Dependencies?

Why should you learn about drug dependencies? Understanding drug characteristics will help you to understand what will happen to a user of a particular drug. For example, a user of a drug with strong pleasurable effects, tolerance and physical dependence will no doubt continue to use the drug for the pleasurable effects, will increase the dosage to obtain the pleasurable effects (tolerance), and will at some point in time experience withdrawals when the drug is discontinued.

§ 3.11   WHAT IS PLASMA LIFE?

Plasma life is the length of time that a drug will remain in the plasma, which is the clear part of the blood.

Knowing the plasma life of a drug is critical for the following reasons:

1. This is the approximate length of time that a drug produces maximal activity or influence; for example, pupil constriction with heroin, or pupil dilation with cocaine.

2. This is the approximate length of time that a drug will saturate the target areas or receptor sites in the brain.

3. An addict person will take a drug at about the end of the plasma life. For example, the average heroin addict will use every 4 to 6 hours, and the average nicotine addict about every 20 to 40 minutes.

PLASMA LIFE OF SOME COMMON DRUGS OF ABUSE

Drugs	Approximate Maximal Plasma Life
Heroin (Morphine)	4 to 6 hours
Cocaine	3 to 5 hours
Amphetamine	4 to 6 hours
Phencyclidine	15 to 24 hours

§ 3.12   WHAT ARE METABOLITES OR SECONDARY DRUGS?

A metabolite is a new drug(s) that is formed when the drug originally taken comes into contact with enzymes and/or other reactors in the blood.

Drugs and/or their fat-soluble metabolites stay in the plasma for long periods of time.

SOME IMPORTANT METABOLIC CONVERSIONS WITH DRUGS OF ABUSE

Primary Drug	Metabolite(s)	Importance of Conversion
Heroin	Morphine	Changes to morphine in blood after 2 or 3 minutes and found in urine as morphine.
Cocaine	Benzoyle-cognine	Changes to benzoyle-cognine in blood and found in urine in this form.
Marijuana (Tetrahydro-cannabinol-THC)	A. 11-Hydroxy THC B. Carboxy THC	THC is active for only about two hours and produces euphoria. The metabolites are fat-soluble, non-euphoric, and stay in plasma 5 to 8 days. They are found in urine for 30 or more days.
Nicotine	Cotinine	Nicotine is active for 20 to 40 minutes. Cotinine lasts about 18 hours, which explains why a nicotine addict can sleep all night and not need a cigarette.

§ 3.13   HOW AND WHY TO DIAGNOSE ADDICTION

In dealing with drug abusers, the first consideration must be determining whether or not the individual is addicted.

You can usually make a diagnosis of addiction simply by knowing how often a person uses the drug. If addicted, the individual will reuse the drug within an interval which will approximate the plasma life of the drug the addict is dependent upon.

Once a diagnosis of addiction is made, stopping drug use is best accomplished by gradually reducing the daily intake of the drug over a 4 to 8 week period. If stopping is to be done in a shorter time-period, medical assistance to suppress withdrawal symptoms will almost always be necessary or the individual will relapse.

Unfortunately, a medical agent to assist withdrawal by suppressing symptoms is not available for all drugs which produce addiction.

§ 3.14   POST-DRUG IMPAIRMENT SYNDROME (PDIS)

One of the most exciting findings regarding addiction was found by Dr. Forest Tennant; he refers to it as the Post-Drug Impairment Syndrome (PDIS). It is a combination of signs and symptoms found in persons who have taken certain drugs and developed a permanent chemical imbalance of the brain. It is thought that drug abuse may damage specific receptor sites, neurotransmitters, and metabolism in the brain. If a receptor site is damaged, one of the brain's natural neurotransmitters cannot attach to it and perform its natural function. When the metabolism of a neurotransmitter is altered, the brain will either have too much or too little brain chemical or neurotransmitter. Thus, PDIS is basically a permanent imbalance of the chemical equilibrium of the brain.

The drugs that commonly produce PDIS are phencyclidine (PCP), marijuana, amphetamines, cocaine, and hallucinogens (MDMA, mescaline, LSD, psilocybin).

When one knows the signs and symptoms of PDIS, it is relatively easy to recognize. Today, many parents, relatives, employers, and friends realize that there is something wrong with an individual who has previously used drugs, but they do not quite know how to characterize it or understand what has happened.

A primary symptom of PDIS is the inability of the individual to maintain patterns of consistency; e.g., hold a job, engage in marital relationships, save money, complete school, or take care of personal belongings (such as a car) for very long. This inability is partially related to the fact that the PDIS-impaired individual cannot withstand much stress. This inability is often manifested in sudden outbursts of temper, depression, or bizarre behavior that may include delusions. Further, this inability is sometimes manifested by these individuals moving from town to town, or house to house, never living in one place very long. Oftentimes, they will stay with their parents for a few weeks, suddenly disappear for a few weeks, and then show up without warning—completely oblivious to the fact that they left, and they cannot understand their parents' concern. These individuals frequently join communes, residential groups, or religious cults because there they experience less stress and less responsibility.

Another typical symptom is the inability to concentrate or maintain attention. This results in the PDIS person constantly changing his or her mind or not completing tasks.

Although these individuals state that they have "lots of friends," close observation reveals the contrary; they have only one or two persons of either sex that they stay in close contact with for very long. In other words, they are very much "loners," but do not perceive themselves as such. In general, the PDIS individual does not perceive the world as most people do.

There are many situations in which PDIS individuals exhibit faulty perception. They generally feel that there is absolutely nothing wrong with them or any behavior they exhibit. These individuals do not respond well to any type of authority or advice and may not understand what is told to them by an employer, teacher, or parent. The reason for these symptoms is obvious. The ability of the PDIS individual to comprehend is impaired due to a chemical imbalance of the nervous system. It is important to emphasize that PDIS may vary in intensity from person to person.

§ 3.15   DRUG PHENOMENON

Drugs of abuse produce dependence and promote relapse. They also produce a phenomenon of taking a chemical substance (that mimics a naturally produced substance) into the body which causes the body to stop producing the natural substance.

WELL-KNOWN EXAMPLES

Thyroid	Stops thyroid production
Estrogen	Stops ovary production
Testosterone	Stops testicle production
Cortisone	Stops adrenal production

A dramatic example is cortisone. This natural drug, and particularly its potent analogs like prednisone, may suppress and atrophy the adrenal gland so much that the adrenal gland may stop producing cortisone after just 10 to 20 days of continuous treatment. This may result in some individuals taking cortisone for the rest of their lives.

§ 3.16   GENETIC THEORY

Alcoholism is known to run in some families. There is also preliminary scientific evidence that this may occur in families who are dependent upon other drugs.

The working genetic theory (which is not a proven fact), and which is recommended by most authorities on drug dependence suggests that some persons may be born with excesses or deficiencies of either neurotransmitters, neurohormones, or receptor sites.

It is hypothesized that some genetic defects may be at least partially responsible for the following:

—Low resistance to peer pressure.

—Willingness to try drugs at a young age.

—Susceptibility to drug phenomenon.

—Childhood hyperactivity, deviancy, poor response to adult authority, inability to develop interpersonal relationships.

—Other poor health habits almost always observed in drug abusers: for example, failure to brush teeth, maintain diet, drive safely, etc.

§ 3.17 PHARMACOLOGICAL DRUG CLASSIFICATION

There are many different drug classifications, including a legal classification. In the California Controlled Substances Act, a legal classification can be found. For example, narcotic drugs (section 11019 H&S) include such substances as opium, opiates, coca leaves and cocaine. Drugs are also classified in the Controlled Substances Act under certain schedules as to their medical usage, potential for abuse, and dependencies.

For our purposes, a pharmacological drug classification is more useful because it groups drugs together for their effects. Pharmacology is the study of a drug, the action the drug has on the body, how the cells of the body are changed because of the drug, and how the modifications affect the body overall. By grouping drugs as to their effects (a pharmacological classification), it is easier to remember that, for the most part, drugs listed under a certain classification will have similar effects on the body (the differences might only be in intensity and duration of action).

Therefore, there are many reasons to pharmacologically classify drugs. First, if one drug of a class is physically addicting, it is very likely that other drugs of that class will also share this property. Second, if one drug of a group is likely to be associated with severe psychotic symptoms (e.g., cocaine), similar symptoms are likely to be observed with abuse of other drugs of the same group (e.g., amphetamines). Third, if an individual develops tolerance to one drug of a group, when the first drug is stopped and a second substance of that same category is taken within a relatively short period of time, cross-tolerance for the second drug is likely to be observed (e.g., tolerance developed to alcohol can result in cross-tolerance to diazepam or Valium). Finally, if two drugs of the same class are taken at the same time, they are likely to boost or potentiate the effects of each other with a potentially lethal overdose as a consequence (e.g., the concomitant mixing of alcohol and diazepam).

Drug Pharmacology, Classification, and Testing

§ 3.17.1 Narcotics (Opiates)

At the usual doses, these drugs have as their most prominent actions a dampening of pain with comparatively weak, general CNS depression (sedation). Substances that fall into this category include opium and all of its derivatives (e.g., morphine, heroin, codeine, etc.) and almost all non-anti-inflammatory prescription analgesics (e.g., meperidine or Demerol, propoxyphene or Darvon, etc.). Each of these drugs can be dangerous in overdose; all are physically addicting. These substances share cross-tolerance and can potentiate the other's actions, but the opiates are unlikely to precipitate psychoses, major depressions, or major anxiety syndromes. A narcotic is defined as a substance that relieves pain and produces sleep.

§ 3. 17.2 Hallucinogens (Psychedelics)

At relatively low doses, these substances share the ability to induce intense emotional feeling states characterized by a magnification of sensory perceptions and to induce possible visual hallucinations. They include drugs such as LSD, psilocybin, mescaline or peyote, MDA, MDMA or ecstasy, and STP. Hallucinogens do not produce prominent tolerance, have no clinically relevant physical withdrawal syndromes and are not likely to (but can) induce death in overdose. The symptoms of overdose are likely to resemble a CNS stimulant overdose. Hallucinogens do produce emotional instability and flashbacks (an unwanted recurrence of drug effects), which is a hyperstimulated state that includes panic and can produce states of confusion at doses close to those that induce a toxic reaction. Psychedelic is defined as mind-expanding or mind-altering.

§ 3.17.3 Phencyclidine

This drug cannot logically be placed in any of the other groups. An analog of this agent was first developed as a dissociative anesthetic, but the human form, ketamine, is now rarely used because a substantial number of people developed a state of extreme agitation and confusion when emerging from surgery. A similar drug, Sernyl, is still used as a veterinary anesthetic. Based on its clinical use, one would have predicted PCP would be a CNS depressant, but it is abused on the streets primarily as a hallucinogen or stimulant, or as a substitute for other drugs that are more expensive or more difficult to manufacture (e.g., THC). The clinical effects observed at a relatively low dose include changes in sensory perceptions and visual hallucinations similar to those described for the hallucinogens. At slightly higher doses, patients exhibit a syndrome, however, of mixed cholinergic and adrenergic disturbances marked by intense agitation and confusion. Thus, the most prominent clinical syndrome associated with this drug is a severe organic brain syndrome (OBS) that (as is true with all confused states) can be associated with hallucinations and/or delusions. Contrary to the general rules that acute drug-induced psychiatric syndromes are likely to disappear within several days to several weeks, the PCP-induced OBS can last several months or more.

§ 3.17.4 Cannabis

All drugs deriving from cannabis have one active ingredient: delta-9 tetrahydrocannabinol (THC). All cannabis derivatives originate in the marijuana plant. At usual doses, the most prominent effects of these drugs are a change in the sense of time, an increase in appetite, and a floating sensation, similar to sedation or mild euphoria. At clinical doses, cannabis derivatives do not produce hallucination, although this psychedelic effect may occur at very high levels of intake.

§ 3.17.5 Central Nervous System (CNS) Stimulants

The CNS stimulants are a group of drugs for which the most prominent effects at the usual doses center on enhancement or stimulation of nervous tissue activity. These agents include all forms of cocaine (including cocaine hydrochloride, "freebase" cocaine, and rock), all forms of amphetamines (e.g., methedrine and benzedrine), prescription weight-reducing products, amphetamine-like drugs such as methylphenidate (Ritalin), and even some over-the-counter weight-reducing drugs (e.g., Dexatrim), if taken in very high doses. The more potent agents have been listed first (i.e., the ones most likely to induce states of severe psychopathology and medical problems) while the less potent (e.g., weight-reducing products) require very high doses in the average individual to cause the same pattern of problems. These difficulties include possible lethal overdoses, physical addiction, dramatic psychoses, severe depressions, and all anxiety syndromes including panic attacks and obsessions. Although caffeine and nicotine are included here because they can induce and exacerbate anxiety, they are not capable of producing intense psychiatric syndromes, such as psychoses and major depressions.

§ 3.17.6 Central Nervous System (CNS) Depressants

These drugs dampen CNS activity, while carrying relatively weak analgesic effects. Included among the CNS depressants are ethanol (beverage alcohol), barbiturates, barbiturate-like hypnotics (e.g., methaqualone or Quaalude), meprobamate (Miltown or Equanil), and all benzodiazepines (e.g., alprazolam or Xanax; diazepam or Valium, etc.). In other words, the CNS depressants include all prescription hypnotics and all prescription antianxiety drugs except for buspirone (Buspar). All drugs in this class share the properties of lethality in overdose, physical addiction, cross-tolerance, potentiation, the ability to induce severe depressions, prominent anxiety during withdrawal, and so on.

§ 3.17.7 Solvents

All drugs in this category are capable of dissolving stains and oils and some are used as fuels or industrial solvents. The most prominent psychological actions of these drugs at the usual doses are feelings of excitement and confusion. Substances in this class include gasoline, toluene, paints and paint thinners, some glues, the solvent used in typing correction fluid, and so on. The problems associated with these agents include the potential for severe cardiac arrhythmias, liver damage and kidney failure, but psychiatrically, the most frequent clinical outcome is confusion.

§ 3.17.8 Miscellaneous Substances

It is unlikely that any simple categorization will fit all substances likely to be abused. Other drugs with relatively distinct side effect profiles include nitrous oxide (with effects and problems somewhat similar to mild CNS depressants), amyl nitrite (inducing mood swings and confusion), and anticholinergic type prescription anti-parkinsonian drugs (e.g., procyclidine or Kemadrin, trihexphenidyl or Artane, benztropine or Cogentin), producing states of mild euphoria and confusion. Also not discussed in the abbreviated overview are over-the-counter (OTC) drugs on which people can at least demonstrate psychological dependence, including laxatives and antihistamines, the latter being the major component of OTC sleeping pills, and sedatives.

§ 3.18 PSYCHIATRIC PROBLEMS AND SUBSTANCE ABUSERS

All substances of abuse affect the brain and produce changes in a person's normal level of functioning. Therefore, it is not surprising that such drugs are likely to show alterations in mood, ability to reason, and content of cognition.

When drugs are placed into categories based on the effects of the substances, the substances within each classification are likely to share the same problems. The two categories of substances most intimately tied to states of psychiatric symptoms are the brain depressants (e.g., alcohol, the benzodiazepines, and the barbiturates), and the brain stimulants (e.g., cocaine, all forms of amphetamine, methylphenidate or Ritalin, and all prescription as well as most over-the-counter weight-reducing products).

When a person shows no obvious signs of confusion, with stable vital signs, but who has hallucinations (e.g., hearing things that are not there and believing they are real) or delusions (e.g., believing people are plotting against him and trying to harm him), such auditory hallucinations and/or paranoid delusions without confusion are likely to be seen with abuse of brain stimulants or brain depressants. The stimulants (especially the more potent ones such as cocaine and amphetamines) are likely to produce a severe psychosis in anyone after hours to days of escalating doses. Although this level of severe psychiatric impairment can mimic schizophrenia, the psychosis developed in the context of abuse of drugs is likely to disappear within several days to several weeks of abstinence, even if antipsychotic medications (e.g., haloperidol or Haldol) are not used. Identical symptoms may develop in the context of abuse of brain depressants such as alcohol, although this is much less common among alcoholics than among stimulant abusers.

Severe depression involving suicidal tendencies most often occurs among abusers of brain depressants during active intoxication and withdrawal. This level of depression is also likely to be a symptom of stimulant withdrawal.

On the other hand, a state of anxiety (panic attacks, paranoia, obsessive thinking, etc.) most often occurs during intoxication with brain stimulants (e.g., cocaine and amphetamines). Signs of general anxiety, panic, and phobia are also likely to occur during the acute withdrawal from brain depressants such as alcohol.

PHARMACOLOGICAL CLASSIFICATION OF DRUGS

Narcotics (Opiates)

Natural	Synthetic
Opium	Demerol
Morphine	Percodan (oxycodone)
Heroin (diacetylmorphine)	Methadone (dolophine)
Codeine (methylmorphine)	Dilaudid (hydromorphone)

Hallucinogens (Psychedelics)

Peyote (mescaline)
Psilocybin
Bufotenine
LSD (d-lysergic acid diethylamide)
Nexus (4-bromo-2,5 dimethoxyphenethylamine)
DMT
SRP
DET
MDA
MDMA
MDEA
MMDA (Ecstasy)

Cannabis

Marijuana
Hashish
Hash Oil
THC
Sinsemilla (buds)

Central Nervous System Depressants

Barbiturates	Secobarbital (Seconal) Amobarbital (Amylal) Phenobarbital
Non-barbiturate Sedative	Doridan
Benzodiazepines	Librium (clordiazepoxide) Valium (diazepam) Miltown or Equanil (meprobamate) Rohypnol
Methaqualone	Quaalude
Chloral Hydrate	
Alcohol	

Central Nervous System Stimulants

Amphetamines (Benzadrine)
Dextroamphetamine (Dexadrine)
Methamphetamine (desoxyn, methadrine)
Ritalin
Preludin
Parnate
Cocaine hydrochloride
Crack Cocaine
Caffeine
Nicotine

Phencyclidine

PCP
Ketamine
Sernyl

Solvents

Gasoline
Toluene
Paints
Glue
Paint Thinners

Misc. Substances

Amyl Nitrite
Ether
Nitrous Oxide
Morning Glory Seeds (Lysergic Acid Amide)
OTC Drugs

§ 3.19   IDENTIFYING THE DRUG ABUSER

There has not been much attention given to the use of urine testing to identify the drug abuser who has been arrested or under supervision of the criminal justice system, despite the high prevalence of drug abuse and associated health problems in criminals. There are many stated reasons why the drug abuse criminal should be identified.

To target active criminals. Researchers have found that drug-abusing offenders are among the most active criminals. Addicts commit more crimes during periods when they are frequently using drugs than during periods of lesser drug use. The association between high rates of criminality and drug abuse has been found predominantly in persons who use expensive dependence-producing drugs like cocaine and heroin. Less is known about the criminal activities of people who abuse PCP or other illicit drugs. In youths, however, heavy marijuana use is also associated with problem behavior and is often accompanied by the use of other illicit drugs.

To protect the public from crimes by persons released to the community. Judges are often faulted when persons they have released pending trial or on probation are found to have committed another crime, especially a violent crime. If those persons who are released to the community before trial, or who are under probation or parole supervision were tested for illicit drug use, it might be possible to initiate treatment or urine monitoring for those who test positive. Due to the association between drug use andcrime, effective programs for controlling or monitoring drug use may be a means of reducing crimes of released arrestees and offenders.

To reduce jail or prison crowding. Jail and prison populations in large cities contain substantial numbers of drug-dependent persons. By identifying drug-dependent persons and placing them in residential treatment programs or urine monitoring programs, we may be able to reduce jail and prison populations, and to lessen future drug abuse and crime. One jurisdiction in Indiana is adopting a program in which arrestees charged with minor offenses can be released without bail if they agree to participate in a urine monitoring program. The cost of testing is charged to the defendant but is less than the amount for bail and should result in the early release of more defendants. Judges in Washington, D.C. report that because of their pretrial testing program, they are more likely to release suspected drug users because they know that their drug problems are being addressed.

To reduce drug abuse and crime. There is growing evidence that criminal justice referral of offenders to drug abuse treatment programs, often accompanied by urine monitoring, can lead to a longer treatment period and therefore reductions in both drug abuse and crime. Since younger offenders are less likely than older offenders to inject hard drugs and to use heroin, identification of youthful offenders who are abusing drugs such as marijuana, PCP, or cocaine, may hold promise for preventing more extensive drug use.

To address public health problems. Abusers of hard drugs, especially persons who inject drugs, are at high risk for health problems. Intravenous drug users are most at risk for contracting AIDS by sharing dirty needles that contain blood from other infected addicts. Prostitutes are also likely to have serious drug abuse and associated health problems. In a three-year study, the Bureau of Justice Statistics (BJS) revealed in 1986 that 53 percent of probationers had a drug abuse problem. In 1992, BJS reported that more than twice as many women as men in jail reported using a major drug daily. The criminal justice system may have an unusual opportunity to identify persons with health problems.

To monitor community drug use trends. As illicit drugs become more available in a community, the more deviant persons can be expected to be among the first to use them. Thus, an ongoing urine testing program may provide warning of drug epidemics, and information on changing patterns of drug availability. The results from the DUF urine testing program have been useful for tracking the use of drugs in the United States (BJS, "Identifying the Drug Abuser").

§ 3.20 DRUG TESTING

In the current atmosphere of heightened concern about drug abuse in America, there is growing interest in the use of chemical tests, especially urine tests for identifying drug users. Public debate, which is often heated, has focused on the advisability and legality of using urine tests to identify drug use in athletes, celebrities, and employees performing sensitive jobs.

In 1995, the Supreme Court made a groundbreaking decision in the case of *Vernonina School District v. Acton* (115 S.Ct. 2386 (1995)), a case that asked whether of not the drug testing of student athletes at a school in Oregon was reasonable under the Fourth Amendment. The Supreme Court upheld the school's policy, and noted that the state's interest in preventing drug addiction among students was compelling given the alarming increase in the use of drugs at the school in question. Student athletes have a decreased expectation of privacy, often are student leaders, and are at risk for physical harm if practicing sports while intoxicated.

In the case *Earls v. Board of Educ. of Tecumseh Public School Dist.* (now entitled *Bd. of Education of Independent School District No. 92 of Pottawatomie County v. Earls*, No. 01-332) high school students in the Tecumseh Public School District in Oklahoma challenged the constitutionality of their high school's mandatory drug testing policy which required that all high school students participating in non-athletic extracurricular activities—whether academic, artistic, vocational, or otherwise—submit to drug tests. The drug testing wasmandated even though there wasno suspicion that any of the students tested had ever used an illegal drug, or absent any evidence that the school had a widespread drug problem. In June 2002, the U.S. Supreme Court upheld the Oklahoma school's policy, opening the doors for suspicionless drug testing of students who wish to participate in extracurricular activities around the country. The Court's decision broadens the 1995 ruling that allowed urinalysis of student athletes by expanding testing for activities that can be key to students' high school years. After the 1995 ruling, only about 5% of the nation's schools began drug-testing programs for athletes, mainly because of the cost of such programs. School districts can now force the nation's 23 million middle and high school students to take drug tests before they join the band, choir, chess club, or any other extracurricular activities where they compete with other schools.

Employers are warning employees that they will not tolerate drug use in or out of the workplace. Professional sports officials are also cracking down. The military already requires mandatory urinalysis.

In 1989, two U.S. Supreme Court decisions upheld drug testing programs that were set up by the railroads and by the U.S. Customs Service. These programs allow employers to test employees for drugs without any belief that the employees in question have ever used drugs. Contrary to a long line of legal precedents, these programs were found to be constitutionally valid. The Supreme Court supported this constitutionality on two grounds: first, that present drug use is a major menace to our society which must be addressed, and second, that the mandatory testing programs were only minimal intrusions on an employee's privacy. The two cases were *Skinner v. Railroad Labor Executive Association*, 489 U.S. 602, 109 S.Ct. 1402, 1411 (1989), and *National Treasury Employees Union v. Von Raab,* 489 U.S. 656, 109 S.Ct. 1384 (1989).

Since the Supreme Court decisions, courts across the country have been grappling with numerous challenges to drug testing programs in government workplaces. Although the case law is still evolving, some trends have emerged.

In general, federal courts are upholding random drug testing programs for the following kinds of jobs:

1. Those implicating public safety: e.g., motor vehicle operators, locomotive engineers, aircraft pilots and boat operators working for the Department of the Navy (*AFGE v. Cheney*, ___F.Supp. ___ (N.D.Ca., 1990)); but not pathology technicians, diagnostic radiology technicians and dental hygienists (*AFGE v. Cheney*).

2. Those requiring the carrying of firearms: E.g., prison guards (*Taylor v. O'Grady*, 888 F.2d 1189 (7th Cir., 1989)); police officers (*Brown v. City of Detroit*, 715 F.Supp. 832 (E.D. Mich., 1989)).

3. Those with access to highly classified information: E.g., Department of Justice lawyers who hold top secret national security clearances (*Harmon v. Thornburgh*, 878 F.2d 484 (D.C. Cir., 1989), cert. den., 110 S.Ct. 865 (1990)).

The courts are, in general, not permitting the blanket testing of entire workforces.

Few courts have afforded private sector employees protection against random drug testing. To date, there have only been a handful of cases won by private sector employees who either refused to take the test on privacy grounds and were fired, or whose test results were inaccurate. In most states, courts have ruled that the employment-at-will doctrine outweighs employees' privacy rights. Only in California has the highest state court held otherwise. In that state, private sector employees (but not job applicants) have been found to be protected by the right to privacy contained in the state constitution.

The International Association of Chiefs of Police (IACP), which developed a model drug testing policy for local police departments to consider in identifying and dealing with the use of illegal drugs by police officers. The policy calls for:

1. Testing applicants and recruits for drug or narcotics use as part of their pre-employment medical exams;

2. Testing a current employee when documentation indicates that the employee is impaired or incapable of performing assigned duties, or experiences reduced productivity, excessive vehicle accidents, high absenteeism, or other behavior inconsistent with previous performance;

3. Testing a current employee when an allegation involves the use, possession, or sale of drugs or narcotics, or the use of force, or when there is serious on-duty injury to the employee or another person;

4. Requiring current sworn employees assigned to drug, narcotics, or vice enforcement units to submit to periodic drug tests.

§ 3.21   CRITICISMS OF DRUG TESTING

Fourth Amendment rights against illegal search and seizure. Does the government have the right to impose mandatory testing on a person in the absence of individualized suspicion? It is argued that the invasion of privacy, the costs, and the intrusiveness of urine testing are too great to justify the testing of persons at random, when there is no clear suspicion that the person is using drugs. In some instances, mandatory urine testing has been sustained by the courts when unique institutional requirements existed. For example, such tests have been upheld for jockeys, in the context of regulation and reduction of criminal influence in the racetrack industry, as well as for prison inmates and in the military, to promote security.

Critics of mandatory urine testing argue that the need to watch the person providing the specimen is an unacceptable infringement of privacy. When an employee offender who has received advance notice is tested, special precautions must be made to ensure that the person does not substitute someone else's urine.

Fourteenth Amendment due process rights. Considerable litigation has occurred over the accuracy of urine tests and whether punitive actions taken against a person on the basis of a single unconfirmed urine test violate the 14th Amendment's guarantees of due process. Because of the extensive use of the EMIT test most of this discussion has concerned the accuracy of that particular test.[2]

When persons are tested repeatedly, other issues become relevant. For example, a contempt of court ruling for a person who was on pretrial release in Washington, D.C., who also tested positive for PCP on 16 tests over a 60-day period, was denied when expert witnesses could not specify the length of time that PCP could be detected in urine. Unlike cocaine and opiates, which are eliminated from the body within days after

---

[2] EMIT is Enzyme Multiplied Immunoassay Technique. EMIT is a popular test because it is relatively inexpensive and it has a reputation for accuracy. However, gas chromatography/mass spectrometry are even more accurate and are considered necessary to ensure that the initial EMIT results are correct.

ingestion, PCP and marijuana may be stored and released weeks after use.

Another important issue is the confidentiality of test result information. For example, is information about drug use at arrest to be made available at the time of sentencing or parole? A person labeled a drug user after a positive test result is obtained can suffer prolonged adverse consequences from that label.

Perhaps the greatest danger posed by urine testing programs is the belief that use of the tests will somehow solve the drug abuse problem. Testing will uncover the magnitude of the drug problem in a jurisdiction and identify some of the affected persons. However, in the absence of pre-developed plans on how to assess a person's level of drug involvement and how to plan effective responses, the testing program may fail to achieve its goal of reducing drug abuse.

§ 3.22 DRUG TESTING THROUGH URINALYSIS OR HAIR ANALYSIS

As public concern over drug use has increased and employers and travelers recognize the impact that substance abuse can have on public safety, there is an increasing interest in the mandatory drug testing of employees, pilots, and others employed in sensitive positions. In addition, treatment programs have turned to drug monitoring in an attempt to measure the outcome on their patients and clients, thus gathering evidence of the efficacy of their particular program.

Urine samples for drug screens have many inherent assets. They are relatively easy to collect, not exorbitantly expensive, and are relatively accurate. At the same time, however, they are not perfect. Drug testing or monitoring through urinalysis is a way of determining whether drugs have been used, but it is of little benefit if one wants to measure the amount of drug that was present in the body—that is, it is a qualitative rather than a quantitative test. In addition, there are difficulties that can lead to falsely negative results, including the possibility that a subject might give a sample that is not his own urine, and the possibility that, for drugs which stay in the body for very short periods of time, a urine sample might be falsely negative even when the drug has been ingested the same day. Additional problems relate to the inability to determine whether a positive sample indicates only one instance of drug use, or whether the subject has engaged in repeated drug intake over a matter of many days or weeks. This approach also has inherent dangers of false positive results due to contaminants such as poppy seeds. Finally, the careful supervision of gathering urine samples is embarrassing and may lead to a reluctance on the part of many programs to actually supervise the urine collection procedure.

While these difficulties are not insurmountable, they do underscore the reason why clinicians and other people interested in public health issues continue to search for additional approaches to drug monitoring. In this regard, the use of hair to determine drug intake patterns has many potential advantages. The samples are easy to gather under close supervision, thus decreasing the possibility of false negative results. Since hair grows steadily at approximately 1.3 cm per month, the procedure offers the opportunity to observe sequential drug-taking patterns week by week. Because drugs finding their way into the hair follicles are there permanently until the hair is cut, this approach also minimizes the chance that the drug use will be missed because the substance is present in the blood or urine for a relatively short time.

The approach to hair analysis is based on the hypothesis and subsequent documentation that drugs circulating in the blood are incorporated into hair roots and follicles. Work with animals as well as some studies with humans indicates that the period of time when the drug was taken can be isolated in a specific area of the hair strand which grows out from the scalp at approximately 1.3 cm per month. Work with animals exposed to drugs indicates that the amount of drug ingested is likely to impact the amount of the substance found in the hair strand, although there are even less impressive data regarding this quantitative association in humans.

The hair to be selected for analysis is ideally from the rear portion of the top of the head. It is usually suggested that a spot approximately 1 to 2 inches back from an imaginary line that could be drawn across the top of the head from ear to ear would be the ideal place for sampling between 10 and 20 hairs comprising a weight of approximately 10 milligrams. This point, also called the posterior vertex, is said to have hair growth that is least influenced by sex and age, as well as a more constant proportion of hair (perhaps 85 percent) that is in a growth phase. The samples are subsequently taken and carefully washed. There are data to indicate that if this procedure is followed, it is not likely that hair dyes, shampoos, or any form of damage to the hair follicle will interfere markedly with the determination of the presence or absence of a drug. It is possible, however, that some of these factors might make a difference to the amount of drug present within the hair. After the hair is washed, the strands can then be cut into segments that relate to a specific time period. This is made possible by cutting strands as close to the scalp as possible. Next, the hair is dissolved through a series of steps. This procedure allows for the release of proteins related to the drugs used, proteins that can be identified by specific antibodies. The samples can then be scanned for the presence (and perhaps amount) of heroin, methadone, phencyclidine (PCP), cocaine, marijuana, nicotine, and benzodiazapines (like diazepam or Valium).

Research on hair analysis for detecting drugs began in 1954, according to pharmacologists Martha R. Harkey and Gary L. Henderson of the University of California at Davis. However, according to the consensus report of a conference on hair analysis held May 31, 1990, in Washington, D.C., by the Society of Forensic Toxicologists, Inc., and the National Institute on Drug Abuse, "there are no generally accepted procedures for hair analysis for drugs of abuse and there is no information on the accuracy, precision, sensitivity, specificity, or appropriate cutoffs that define potentially false positive or false negative results for either screening or confirmation procedures." The report notes that studies conducted so far are essentially anecdotal.[3]

One organization that does not consider hair analysis controversial is the Federal Bureau of Investigation. The FBI's chemical toxicology unit uses both gas chromatography/mass spectrometry (GC/MC) and a more advanced technology that analyzes hair with a tandem mass spectrometer. The status of hair test findings as legally admissible evidence is still uncertain, although they have been accepted in some jurisdictions. In Massachusetts, Ohio, and New Jersey, hair testing has been used in correctional settings (Gropper).

There are many potential benefits to using samples of hair to determine drug-taking patterns. These would be of little use, however, unless there were data to demonstrate the relevance of this approach to real life situations.

§ 3.23   THE ACCURACY OF HAIR ANALYSIS

While few laboratories have developed data, there are indications that an impressive level of accuracy may exist. One group of investigators asserts that their analytic techniques will identify as little as 100 milligrams of cocaine per week (one "line" of "snorted" cocaine contains somewhere between 25 and 50 milligrams). Analysis of hair samples can also identify the use of as few as 3.5 "bags" of heroin per month and less than 2 "joints" of marijuana in a 30-day period. The authors state that even lower levels of drug use can be identified if larger samples of hair are obtained (Baumgartner).

There are also indications that the approach may be relatively reliable. One study gathered hair from 20 PCP users and 18 control persons, and reported that hair evaluations correctly identified all 38 people (Sramek). Another study compared the efficacy of urinalysis and hair evaluations on 60 patients with histories of prior drug use. Through hair analysis, positive results were obtained from all subjects; but with urine samples only 30 percent of the individuals tested positive. The latter result probably reflects the limited number of hours after drug intake when the substance still appears in the urine. Other data utilizing individual case reports have related remarkable correlations between the history of monthly drug use and specific hair segment evaluations which reflect that period of use.

In a research project conducted in Pinellas County, Florida, drug use among arrestees at the county jail was evaluated by comparing results of hair testing, urinalysis, and self-reports. Both hair testing and urinalysis produced a larger number of positive results than did self-reports; more significantly, there was a greater proportion of positive hair assays than positive urine samples. The most important result was that 88 of the 256 specimens analyzed for opiates and cocaine were identified as drug positive by the radioimmunoassay of hair (RIAH) but negative by both urine testing techniques used. Confirmatory testing by GC/MC was

---

[3] See also *Lucky v. Southern Pacific Transportation Co.,* 267 (Cal Ct. App. 1990), petition to review denied, S014832 (Cal. Sup. Ct. May 31, 1990).

completed on 9 of the 88 specimens and cocaine was detected in all 9. This indicates RIAH's potential to identify drug users who have not taken drugs within a day or two of a urine test (Mieczkowski).

Of course, as was true of urinalysis, hair evaluations are far from perfect. First, not many laboratories have this evaluation available, and it is likely to be quite expensive. Second, while the evaluations can tell us about drug intake on a weekly or monthly basis, they are of little use with regards to day-by-day or current use patterns. Hair has complicated structures which can be damaged by sun and chemicals, yielding varying results. There are also racial differences in the amount of a drug that is incorporated into hair, with one study finding that black hair is more absorbent of drugs than brown hair, and that certain drugs wash out of brown hair more easily than black hair. Some of the research is anecdotal, and much research has not yet been published.

The following questions need to be investigated before the results of hair analysis can be reliably interpreted:

—How are drugs incorporated into hair?
—What is the relationship between the amount of the drug used and the concentration of the drug or its metabolites in hair?
—What is the minimum dose required to produce a positive result?
—How is drug incorporation and retention in hair biased by race, age, sex, or other individual differences?
—To what extent is an externally applied drug (whether by sweat, glandular secretion, or environmental exposure) retained in the hair?
—What is the effect of various washing or hair treatment procedures in removing externally applied drugs and internally incorporated/bound drugs?

In summary, hair testing appears to have a number of advantages, including its less invasive method of collection, the extended time window of results, the stability of the medium, and the difficulty of tampering with the medium to evade positive test results (INEOA 1990). However, standards have not yet been established for hair analysis that would place it on a par with urinalysis for widespread application by the criminal justice system—either in decision making or as evidence.

Chapter 3

References

"Advantages of Hair Analysis Over Urinalysis." The Narc Officer. International Narcotic Enforcement Officers Association, 1990.

Baumgartner, W.A., et al. "Hair analysis for drugs of abuse." Journal of Forensic Sciences 34 (1989): 1433-1453.

Bureau of Justice Statistics. "Federal Criminal Case Processing, 1980-1989 with Preliminary Data for 1990." Washington: D.C.: U.S. Department of Justice, 1991.

----------. Women in Jail, A BJS Special Report. Washington: D.C.: U.S. Department of Justice, 1992.

Gropper, Bernard, and Judy Reardon."Developing Drug Testing by Hair Analysis." National Institute of Justice, Research in Brief. Washington: D.C.: U.S. Department of Justice,1993.

Mieczkowski, Tom, et al. "Testing Hair for Illicit Drug Use." National Institute of Justice, Research in Brief. Washington: D.C.: U.S. Department of Justice, 1993.

National Institute of Justice. "Identifying the Drug Abuser: Drug Testing." Crime File Study Guide. Washington, D.C. U.S. Department of Justice, 1993.

Sramek, J.J., et al. "Hair analysis for detection of PCP in newly admitted psychiatric patients." American Journal of Psychiatry 142 (1985): 950-953.

CHAPTER 4

DRUG ADDICTION AND BEHAVIOR

§ 4.1 DRUG ADDICTION: CRIME OR DISEASE?

In the past, efforts to eliminate drug addiction have been aimed mainly at isolated aspects of the problem. The common focus upon the individual user as "the problem" has helped create the image of the user as an outcast and has frequently resulted in his being regarded as a criminal. Recently, addiction has been redefined as a disease.

In order to obtain some clarity about whether or not the addict is a criminal or suffering from a disease or both, it is necessary to explore each of the concepts.

§ 4.2 DRUG ADDICTION AS A CRIME

The use of narcotic substances in the United States evolved from the pain-killer phase in the mid-1800s, through the recognition of opiate addiction by 1910, to its definition as a criminal activity in 1914 by the passage of the Harrison Act—which is still this country's basic narcotics law. The Harrison Act is a tax law, part of the Internal Revenue Act, and is administered by the Drug Enforcement Administration. The law was designed to make narcotics distribution a matter of record. The act does not make drug use illegal, nor does it allow or forbid a doctor to give drugs to a user regularly. Nevertheless, its vague terminology that states that drugs must be dispensed in "professional practice only" has never been legislatively defined, and the act has become the basis for over fifty years of legal problems for the user, the doctor, and the community. The prosecution of many doctors that followed the introduction of the Harrison Act had the effect of depriving the user of medically supervised treatment with opiates; it became legally impossible for a doctor to prescribe narcotics except for withdrawal. The user was forced to turn to illegal channels to obtain drugs, and thus his dependence on the criminal world became established. Before the prosecution of physicians for medical treatment of users and the prosecution of users themselves for possession of narcotics, users were generally not involved in criminal behavior.

Some attempt was made between 1919 and 1923 to deal with drug abuse as a medical problem. Forty-four public outpatient narcotics clinics were opened throughout the country. By 1923, the last clinic was closed. The clinics were started as an emergency measure and were generally unsuccessful. On the basis of an alleged rise in narcotics arrests, it was claimed that the clinics spread drug use by making drugs easily available. In fact, the arrest rate climbed substantially after the clinics were closed.

When we think of drug addiction, someone like the heroin addict comes to mind. The image of the addict is someone who is motivated to crime by the effects of heroin and that he will do anything to get his "fix." Heroin addicts are defined as criminal in the sense that possession and use/influence of heroin is a criminal offense.

§4.3 DRUG ADDICTION AS A DISEASE

The treatment of chemical dependency has undergone dramatic changes during the past several years. One of the factors which has stimulated this change is the increasing acceptance of addiction as a disease. Since Jellinek first proposed this concept in 1960 with specific reference to alcohol, it has been broadened to include all psychoactive drugs. It is thought that addictive disease is primarily a biochemical/genetic disorder which is activated by the environment.

The genetic predisposition to alcoholism has been well established. While other psychoactive drugs have been less well studied, there does appear to be higher incidence of psychoactive drug addiction in the families of addicts than in the population at large.

§ 4.4 DRUG DEFINITION

One of two definitions of the word "drug" in the dictionary is: "a substance intended for the cure, treatment, or prevention of disease." The second one is "a habit-forming substance, especially a narcotic." And if we look up "narcotic," we read that it is "a substance that blunts the senses, produces euphoria, stupor, or coma, and can cause addiction; used in medicine to relieve pain, cause sedation, and induce sleep."

However, these definitions are based on society's concept of the use of drugs and its beliefs about drugs. A scientific definition must be, first, objective and, second, descriptive. It must make no assumptions about proper or improper use, social factors, or value judgment. A basic pharmacological definition is: *A drug is a substance which by its chemical nature affects the structure and function of the living organism* (DEA 1990). This definition is a workable one because it includes prescription drugs, over-the-counter drugs, illicit drugs, recreational drugs—drugs which in our wisdom or folly we prefer to call beverages, like alcohol and caffeine food additives, industrial chemicals, agricultural chemicals, pollutants, and food.

The second reason this is a workable definition is that it will remind us always that a drug is a drug, no matter what we call it. They all operate according to the same basic pharmacological principles. It doesn't make any difference whether it's a wonder drug, whether it's heroin, or whether it's food. There are basic principles according to which all of these substances act.

Therefore, we're all drug users, not only of alcohol and caffeine but cigarettes—nicotine, which is a drug—and over-the-counter drugs, drugs to relieve anything that ails us. The largest single group of prescribed drugs is for modifying mood and feeling, the minor tranquilizers and the related drugs. Some people use these wisely. Some use them unwisely. So, from one point of view, we are all drug users, and an increasing number of us are drug abusers.

§ 4.5 WHY USE DRUGS?

The most popular drugs used today are caffeine, nicotine, and alcohol. This is true on every significant measure: number of people who have ever used, number of regular users, number of daily users, number of man-hours spent under the influence of the drugs, and money spent for the drug. The amount of harm done to the human body by nicotine and alcohol, moreover, vastly exceeds the physical harm done by all of the other psychoactive drugs put together. Also, the amount of damage done to the human mind by alcohol alone, as measured by mental hospital data, vastly exceeds the mental harm done by all of the other psychoactive drugs put together.

These facts are commonly masked by the categorization of caffeine, nicotine, and alcohol as nondrugs. Many people think that drug abuse is new. However, history tells us that drug use has been around since the beginning of recorded time. There are numerous descriptions in ancient literature of the use of mushrooms, marijuana, opium, alcohol, etc.

Some drug use led to attempts to regulate it legally. For instance, problem drinking is addressed in the Code of Hammurabi (2240 B.C.) and is described as a problem of men with too much leisure time and lazy dispositions. Nearly every culture has as part of its historical record laws controlling the use of a wide range of drugs, including tobacco.

Human beings have always experimented with natural drugs. Why does this experimentation occur? Many users claim to be bored, in pain, frustrated, unable to enjoy life, or alienated. They turn to drugs in the hope of finding oblivion, peace, togetherness, or euphoria. The fact that few drugs actually cause the effects for which they are taken—or if they do, they do so for only a brief time—seems to be no deterrent. People continue to take drugs for other than medical reasons because:

1. Drugs make them feel good.

2. Drugs may relieve stress or tension, or provide a temporary escape.

3. Peer pressure is strong, especially for young people. The use of drugs has become a "rite of passage" in some parts of our society. Sometimes it is part of the thrill of risk-taking.

4. From an early age we are "programmed;" the media tell us that drugs are part of the technology that can help make life a little bit better. They urge us to seek "better living through chemistry." One national commission studying the drug-abuse problem estimated that by the age of 18 the average American has seen 180,000 television commercials, many of which give the impression that pleasure and relief are to be found in sources outside oneself.

5. In some cases the drugs may enhance religious or mystical experiences. A few cultures teach their children how to use specific drugs for this purpose.

There is a distinction between the use and abuse of drugs. Almost everyone uses a psychoactive substance, even if it is a socially acceptable substance such as alcohol, coffee, tobacco, or over-the-counter drugs. Not everyone misuses or abuses drugs.

Misusing a drug means using it in a way that can have detrimental effects. Getting drunk may be a misuse of alcohol, but it does not necessarily mean the drunk person is an alcoholic or that he or she has sustained bodily damage from the episode. There are many definitions of abuse of a drug. The National Institute on Drug Abuse (NIDA) defines drug abuse as *drug use that results in the physical, mental, emotional, or social impairment of the user.* There are other definitions linked more to social relationships—that is, use becomes abuse if the drug has a negative effect not just on the user, but on others with whom the person is in contact. The reasons for abusing a drug vary widely, but most drug abusers have at least one thing in common: *they use drugs to feel good.* Feeling good involves individual interpretation. For some, feeling good means feeling good about yourself; for others, feeling good involves association with a peer group, relieving boredom, etc.

Drugs might be used as a substitute for the achievement of a goal, such as the satisfaction of the need for affection and a sense of belonging or for a feeling of self-confidence. If the drug satisfies the need to some extent, the user may not learn how to give and receive affection or develop a sense of self-worth and confidence. Such a person would be stunted in his or her personality development and may continue to turn to drugs as a way to satisfy his or her needs.

Another consideration of drug use is that American society has produced an atmosphere leading to the naturalness of using drugs—no matter what the underlying complaint or need.

It seems simplistic but people use drugs because they want to and people will only stop drug use when they want to. To understand this, there are principles that can be applied to understanding drug use practices.

Principle I.—People take drugs because they want to.

Principle II.—People use drugs to "feel better" or to "get high." Individuals experiment with drugs out of curiosity, or out of the hope that using drugs can make them feel better.

Principle III.—People have been taught by cultural example and the media that drugs are an effective way to make them feel better.

Principle IV.—"Feeling better" encompasses a huge range of shifts in mood or consciousness, including such aspects as oblivion or sleep, emotional shifts, energy modification, visions of the Divine, etc.

Principle V.—With many mind- or mood-altering drugs, which are taken principally for that purpose, individuals may temporarily feel better. However, drugs have substantial short- and long-term disadvantages related to the motive for their use. These include possible physiological, psychological, or cognitive deterioration. The psychoactive effects of drugs also tend to be temporary, relatively devoid of adequate translation to the ordinary non-drug state of consciousness, and siphon off energy necessary for long-term constructive growth.

Principle VI.—Individuals do not stop using drugs until they discover "something better."

Principle VII.—The keys to meeting the problems of drug abuse are to focus on the "something better" and to maximize opportunities for experiencing satisfying non-chemical experimentation or, more likely, to keep experimentation from progressing to dependency.

§ 4.6 CHARACTERISTICS OF DRUG ABUSERS

According to Richard Blum,[1] the majority of drug abusers have the following characteristics in common:

—Their drug use usually follows clear-cut developmental steps and sequences. Use of one of the legal drugs, such as alcohol, almost always precedes use of illegal drugs.

—The dysfunctional attributes of drug use usually appear to precede rather than to derive from drug use. In other words, the "amotivational syndrome" often attributed to a person's heavy marijuana use was probably part of that person's personality before he or she started the drug.

—Immaturity and maladjustment usually precede the use of marijuana and of other illicit drugs.

—Those who will try illicit drugs usually have a history of poor school performance.

—Delinquent and deviant activities usually precede involvement with illicit drugs.

—A constellation of attitudes and values that facilitate the development of deviant behavior exists before the person tries illicit drugs.

---

[1] Richard Blum served as the Director of the Joint Program in Drugs, Crime and Community Studies at the Institute of Public Policy Analysis. He is a consulting Professor of Psychology at Stanford University.

Chapter 4

—There is a process of anticipatory socialization during which youngsters who will later try drugs first develop attitudes favorable to the use of legal and illegal drugs. A social setting favorable to drug use usually reinforces and increases individual predisposition to use.

—Drug behavior and drug-related attitudes of peers are usually among the most potent predictors of subsequent drug involvement.

—Parents' behaviors, attitudes, and closeness to their children usually have varying influence at different stages of their children's involvement in drugs.

—Highly deviant children start using drugs at a younger age than less deviant children.

—When drug use begins at a later age, the user is less likely to become intensely involved and more likely to eventually cease drug use. The period of greatest risk of initiation into illicit drug use is usually over by the mid-20s.

—A certain amount of rebelliousness is not unusual in youngsters as they try to assert themselves and gain self-identity. Some experiment with drugs to annoy and upset their parents.

Illegal drug use offers the individual both benefits and disadvantages. The benefit is usually a short-term gain, such as increased positive feelings or a decrease in discomfort. The disadvantages are multiple but usually remote. For example, there is a decrease in the chance of reaching permanent solutions to underlying problems. There is also, in our society, a probable decrease in the rewards an individual can obtain if he or she persists in drug use.

Possibly 70 percent of the U.S. adult population are able to use alcohol—a potent psychoactive agent—in moderation, even to the point of strong psychological dependence, with minimal personal injury and social consequence. Many persons use other powerful psychoactive drugs under the supervision of a physician without becoming drug dependent. The study of the use of these powerful psychoactive drugs is fascinating and surprising. Morphine, for example, produces no significant pain relief in as much as 25 percent of persons given it; in fact, it may produce unfavorable reactions. Some people can take small amounts of heroin for years without becoming dependent on it, whereas a few become physically addicted after a few intravenous doses. Perhaps 10 percent to 15 percent of the population would be or could be classified as susceptible to these powerful psychoactive agents; drugs dominate these people's lives. Stimulated by their need for drugs, some of these people become directed toward one goal only—obtaining the money to buy their drug. After talking to many such people, one has the feeling that they could have been successful in almost any legitimate endeavor if they had applied to it only half of their drive to obtain drugs.

§ 4.7 THE ADDICTED

Addiction is found in all races, religions, and social strata. The only difference is that some social classes have greater percentages of addiction to particular types of drugs.

Alcohol addiction is the drug dependency that affects the greatest number of professionals (and laypersons). A study by the American Medical Association estimated that 400 doctors are lost from the medical profession each year because of alcoholism. That does not sound like a significant number until you realize that it is the equivalent of the graduating classes from four large medical schools each year. This figure does not include those doctors lost because of their use of narcotics or other drugs. Of the professionals addicted to drugs other than alcohol, physicians have one of the highest addiction rates. This is partly due to their access to narcotics and other potent drugs and partly due to the stress of the medical profession. The nursing profession has also had similar problems with certain kinds of addiction, particularly tranquilizers, narcotics (to a lesser extent than physicians), and stimulants. Nurses have the opportunity to divert drugs prescribed for patients, and this diversion appears to provide the major drug supply. Furthermore, nurses often receive little professional respect and may be pressured by physicians, which, combined with irregular working schedules, leads to considerable job-related stress.

The Catholic Church has for years had special rehabilitation centers for priests with alcohol problems. The usual causes of alcoholism are reported to be the use of alcohol for socialization and for the psychological stresses and pressures of handling the problems of the congregation. The legal profession has also developed programs to help lawyers who are having difficulty performing well because of heavy use of alcohol and other drugs. Furthermore, the armed forces have admitted, in the last decade, that there are many service personnel with serious drug problems. Part of the drive to develop treatment programs in the armed forces began with the realization that many of the service personnel in Vietnam were using narcotics. Subsequently, a great deal of money was funneled into the Veterans' Administration (VA) hospitals to help treat addicts.

Substance abuse in the workplace has recently become an issue of widespread public interest and pandemic media attention. It is commonly believed that drug abuse in the workplace is increasing in prevalence, but this is difficult to substantiate. Although drug abuse in industry—particularly the abuse of alcohol—has been recognized as a cause of industry-worker dysfunction since the beginning of the industrial revolution, why is drug abuse surfacing *now* as a major issue?

One important factor to consider is *who* is using drugs in the workplace. Those who grew up in the late 1960s, and who have accepting attitudes towards drugs, have assumed positions of technical, professional, and executive responsibility. As the complexity of industrial and managerial tasks continues to increase, so do the economic and safety risks to both employers and employees. The serious consequences resulting from errors of judgment are making drug-induced impairment unacceptable at all levels of employment.

For many industries and corporations (as well as the U.S. military) technological improvements in urinalysis have led to large-scale drug testing. However, the promise of urinalysis to provide an objective appraisal of an individual's drug use has proved elusive. Drug testing has also raised some civil rights, legal, and technological challenges. One challenge was recently brought about by the U.S. Army, which has questioned the efficacy of urinalysis due to "improper processing, handling, or recordkeeping" of samples.

Unsurprisingly, industry has been the most visible nexus of the increasingly litigious climate of the last 15 years. Drug abuse by employees significantly increases an industry's vulnerability to suits from employees disciplined for drug use, liability suits from employees injured by other employees under the influence of drugs, and worker's compensation disputes.

Fortunately, employee assistance programs (EAPs), which provide an alternative to disciplining employees with alcohol or other drug problems, have resulted in numerous individuals seeking treatment. In some industries, EAPs have increased the visibility of drug-impaired employees. The net result of all these factors has been significant. Most notably, there has been an increasing sensitivity on the part of management, EAPs, medical and legal departments, industrial security officers, and unions toward employees who come to work impaired by the use of drugs.

The alcohol or drug addiction problem among women was ignored for many years. According to various estimates, anywhere from 24 to 50 percent of problem drinkers are women. When you consider that the National Institute on Alcohol Abuse and Alcoholism (NIAAA) estimates that 15 percent of the total population has a drinking problem, then you are talking about a large number of people in the United States. The use of prescription sedatives combined with alcohol is also likely to be more common among women than men. Sixty percent of psychoactive drugs and 71 percent of antidepressant drugs are prescribed for women in response to symptoms of anxiety. Apparently, physicians are more likely to prescribe psychoactive drugs (Valium is number one) for women than for men. Due to the widespread availability of these drugs (and the availability of alcohol) many women develop poly-drug addictions that affect the home and the workplace.

Another population affected by addiction is that of the elderly. As many as 90 percent of those over age 65 have suffered side effects from drugs. About 20 percent have been hospitalized for these effects. Frequently, exposure to or use of drugs results in addiction. At one time, people believed that there were no elderly narcotics addicts. We now know that there are drug abusers and addicts throughout all levels of the population—young, old, blue-collar workers, professionals, male, and female.

§ 4.8 THE HARDCORE ADDICT

Even if incarcerating drug addicts on a long-term basis was economically feasible for society, it would not address the addict's drug addiction and its destructive consequences. What is most appropriate for the addict and for society is treatment and rehabilitation for the addict. Many studies reinforce the fact that when addicts receive drug treatment, they decrease their drug use, decrease their criminal activity, increase their employment, improve their social and interpersonal functioning, and improve their physical health.

Treatment of chronic, hardcore addicts is a cost-effective solution. The most compelling demonstration of the cost effectiveness of treatment is from a California study assessing alcohol and drug treatment effectiveness. The study found that in 1992 the cost of treating 150,000 drug users in California was $209 million. Approximately $1.5 billion was saved while these individuals were in treatment and during the first year after their treatment. Most of these savings were in the form of reductions in drug-related crime because there was a two-thirds decline in crime during pretreatment to posttreatment.

The most recent Arrestee Drug Abuse Monitoring (ADAM) program data indicate that the criminal justice system offers an opportunity to identify addicts and to match their specific needs to appropriate drug treatment programs. On any given day, more than 4 million people are under the custody of a correctional agency, either on probation, on parole, in jail, or in federal or state prisons.

Managed care has shown that treatment capacity can be allocated more efficiently. For example, Massachusetts and Minnesota have demonstrated that the more efficient the use of drug treatment resources, the greater the number of individuals that can be served at a low cost.

The United States lacks adequate programs to help all individuals who need drug treatment. There are long waiting lists to get into public drug treatment programs. The U.S. Department of Health and Human Services estimates that more than 1 million hardcore addicts currently are caught up in the "gap" of available treatment services. Furthermore, many drug treatment programs do not address many of the addicts' problems, such as health and unemployment. We need to take a close look at what we are doing to alleviate this social problem, strengthen existing programs, and duplicate them across the nation so they are available to all addicts. Then we can truly offer them a choice of treatment or prison.

§4.9 FACTS ABOUT DRUG DEPENDENCE

People take drugs because drugs feel good. Each time the person takes a drug, the experience is rewarding and the behavior is positively reinforced. In the case of depressants that may cause physical dependence following repeated use, a second type of behavior, secondary psychological dependence, results. Secondary psychological dependence is a negative experience, or avoidance, as it is sometimes called. It is also called aversive reinforcement because the feeling of withdrawal from the depressant is unpleasant, and the depressant drug is taken to prevent the occurrence of withdrawal symptoms. For example, once an alcoholic starts to experience the symptoms of withdrawal, the alcoholic is motivated to drink to avert the symptoms. The use of depressants is especially difficult to stop because of tolerance. As tolerance increases the dosage needed must be increased, and the reward of taking the drug becomes less important. Then the need to prevent the occurrence of withdrawal, or secondary psychological dependence, becomes the most important factor that will encourage use of the drug.

Drugs have multiple effects that vary with the amount of the drug used and the personality of the user, as well as the user's expectations of the drug's effects. Whether or not a person decides to use drugs depends on his or her background, present environment, and the availability of the drugs. People look for rapid solutions to problems, and drugs are one of the options our society makes available.

§ 4.10   ADDICTIONOLOGY

Addictionology is a subspecialty in the field of medicine in the study and treatment of addictive disease. It is based on the disease concept of addiction. By this concept, addictive disease is defined as: the abuse of drugs which interferes with health, economic, or social functioning, characterized by compulsion, loss of control, and continued use in spite of adverse consequences. In the past most definitions of addiction concerned themselves with the action of the drugs, so addiction was viewed as the result of physical withdrawal that compelled "hooked" users to continue using the drug. Drugs that were physically dependent were addictive—others were not. This created a false picture of addiction. For example, cocaine was thought to be a "benign" drug compared to heroin. However, cocaine is a highly potent reinforcing central nervous system stimulant that can lead to compulsion and, therefore, very addicting. The disease concept of addiction turns the focus from the drug to the person using the drug.

The question is not whether the drug is addictive but whether the user has an addictive disease. A drug user has an addictive disease when there is present a compulsion, loss of control, and continued use in spite of adverse consequences. You can tell if a person is addicted to a drug or drugs by his behavior. You look for a compulsive individual—a person who has a drive to get the drug, to use it, to get it, etc.; you look for a person who has lost control over his drug use—a person who cannot say no. It is manifest in the thought process of the addict. In the beginning they think of ways to control their drug use. For example, don't drink before noon, only drink beer, etc. Eventually, the loss of control is evident in that the addict recognizes how powerless he is over the drug. In a sense the addict surrenders to the power. The last behavior you look for in the addicted person is his continued use of the drug in spite of adverse consequences such as deteriorating health, loss of job, family, incarceration, etc (Inaba et al).

Researchers agree that addiction—whether to cocaine, heroin, amphetamines, or some other chemical substance—is a single disease. According to much of the latest evidence, addicts will switch drugs when their choice is not available (Inaba). An addict will compulsively attempt to repeat and even to intensify the feeling produced by drugs—no matter what the consequences. The key to the diagnosis of addictive disease is in the observation that the addict persists in using drugs in spite of the adverse consequences. Simply taking away drugs, even if it could be done, would not solve the problem of drug addiction. At treatment centers across the country, it has been learned that if the addict's cocaine is taken away, he will become addicted to alcohol; if his alcohol is taken away, he will be addicted to Valium; if his Valium is taken away, you will find him somewhere down the line, taking heroin; and if his heroin is taken away, he will find morphine, Demerol, codeine, Talwin, Percodan, Dilaudid...the list is endless. Many individuals with addictive disease are in a state of denial about the severity of their addiction. Family, friends, and employers should intervene to break through this denial system to get the person into treatment.

Addiction cannot be cured. But it can be brought under remission. Remission is known as recovery. It is brought about by learning to live a comfortable, rewarding, and satisfying life that does not include drugs. Methods used to bring about recovery are: long-term counseling, AA and other support groups, long-term residential care, and individual and family treatment programs. Recovery does not mean "cured." Cured would mean addicts could go back to using drugs. The primary treatment is no drugs—a chemical-free philosophy.

Addicts are taught that the particular drugs they have been using are not the essential problem; once they have developed addictive disease, they are equally vulnerable to all mood-altering drugs. The recovering cocaine addict cannot go out and become a social drinker. The recovering heroin addict cannot smoke an occasional joint. Even going to the hospital for surgery can be risky, because a shot of morphine that would not affect most people adversely could trigger the cycle of addictive behavior.

Therefore, the only treatment for addictive disease is to give up all mood-altering chemicals. It used to be thought that taking drugs or drinking to excess was a symptom of some other disorder, but it is not. It is an illness in its own right—the cause, not the effect.

§ 4.11 SCIENCE OF ADDICTION

Until a few years ago, the concept of addictive disease did not exist. No one had suggested that all addictions were the same. In "Cocaine: A Special Report" (*Playboy*, September, 1984), Contributing Editor Lawrence Gonzales wrote:

> Cocaine somehow gets access to the areas of the brain (the amygdalae and lateral hypothalamus) in which those chemical changes occur and allows you to make those changes at will. In addition, cocaine takes control of the use and manufacture within the body of essential chemical message transmitters, such as dopamine, which transmits sexual and

feeding signals, and norepinephrine, which transmits signals to flee in the face of danger. When you take cocaine, it feels as if it is the most important function in life, because cocaine causes your body and brain to send those essential life-protecting and life-producing signals: the need for sex, food, water, flight. So, of course, you take more.

Artificially stimulating those areas of the brain has serious psychological consequences which are symptomatic of addictive disease. For one thing, after being over-stimulated, the pleasure circuits do not work anymore. Pleasure cannot be experienced. Pain is all that is left— pain and craving. The result is often the classic clinical picture of addictive behavior: continued compulsive use of the drug despite the adverse consequences.

When the pleasure circuits in the brain no longer produce pleasure, the result is depression, anxiety, and panic. The brain says, "You are dying of thirst. Get cocaine or you will die." Later, when the chemicals are gone from his brain, the addict cannot believe he did it. He cannot remember why he did it, because the memory states do not match. Remorse and anxiety set in. And not even getting high will make everything all right again. That is why addicts talk about needing to take drugs just to feel normal.

One of the most difficult jobs in treating addicts is to convince them that they cannot recover unless they avoid all mood-altering chemicals forever. Cocaine addicts will want to be treated only for cocaine addiction: "Hey, I have never had a problem with drinking a few beers." Therapists hear it all the time: "How did this happen to me? "I cannot understand it. I never drank before." Or even worse for the addict, "Hey, what is the problem if I smoke a joint after work? Grass isn't even addictive." But it's not the drug, it's the person; and any mood-altering drug can reignite the inferno. Indeed, animal tests bear out the fact. No laboratory monkey, when offered a particular drug, says, "No, thanks. I use only Peruvian flake." An animal addicted to cocaine will substitute alcohol if it is deprived of cocaine. If heroin is substituted, it will become a junkie. Give it the choice of any drug and it will choose cocaine. Cocaine appears to be most dangerous because it is most efficient in triggering the reward circuitry of the brain.

In fact, mood-altering drugs interfere with the addict's ability to remember why he cannot use drugs. That sets him up for relapse. In fact, even while abstaining, most addicts have to be reminded daily why they cannot use drugs, because their worst experiences happened while they were high. Because the memory is dependent upon the state of mind, those memories are not readily accessible to the sober brain.

Once you are an addict, you are always at risk for relapse. What that means to a scientist is that relapse is a biological imperative. This is more or less a new principle of drug addiction: There is an active drive to relapse.

We can now understand a few of the mysteries of addictive disease. For example, why is the first drug experience free? It is free because it is free of anxiety. To inebriate means to exhilarate and then to stupefy. That is why the first high is free, because the first one is the exhilarating one. Then comes the stupefaction. The first experience gives direct access to the controls in the brain that operate the most fundamental circuitry of pleasure and happiness. The first time out, the addict is God, with his hand on the throttle of ecstasy.

Why, then, doesn't everyone repeat this ecstatic process over and over again? No one knows. As Dr. David E. Smith, founder of the Haight-Ashbury Clinic in San Francisco and one of the pioneers of addiction research, said, the potential addict "responds differently the very first time he uses" a drug. Most addicts interviewed said the same thing: "I was hooked the first time I got high. I was no longer lonely, no longer self-conscious; I could be with people; I was not afraid." Normal people do not react to chemicals that way when they first take them. That is why normal people can take them or leave them.

What, then, are the new scientific secrets of treatment? If, say, cocaine depletes dopamine, a chemical messenger to the brain, then is there some nonaddictive, benign drug that we can use to replace dopamine? An approved treatment for low-dopamine diseases called bromocriptine is used in cocaine withdrawal and it works. It is given during the first ten days of abstinence. Similarly, the drug clonidine is used for heroin addiction.

§ 4.12   SCIENCE OF THE BRAIN—NEW RESEARCH

Why is it that addicts crave drugs long after they stop using? Why do addicts continue to relapse? Why do addicts clean up and then start using again? The answer lies in the brain. With the use of MRI and PET scans, neuroscientists are finding answers to these questions. Scientists are finding out what happens to the brain during highs and lows, why withdrawal is unbearable, and how changes caused by addictive drugs persist long after the addict stops using. Drugs of abuse change the brain, hijack its motivational systems, and even change how its genes function.

An addicted brain is different, both physically and chemically, from a normal brain. A lot of neurobiological changes accompany the transition from voluntary to compulsive drug use. Drugs like cocaine, heroin, nicotine, CNS stimulants, and depressants (alcohol), etc., alter the brain's pleasure circuits. Activating this circuit, called the reward circuit, produces a feel-good sensation. The pleasure circuit communicates in the chemical language of dopamine; this neurotransmitter goes from neuron to neuron, affecting the firing of other neurons, and producing feelings from mild happiness to euphoria.

What happens to the circuit when you inject, inhale, or swallow an addictive drug? These drugs increase the amount of dopamine in the brain's reward circuit. Each drug affects this good feeling in a different way. But what they all have in common is that they make more dopamine available in the brain, meaning more firing of neurons in the pleasure circuit. Chronic use produces enduring changes, and it reduces the number of dopamine receptors. With fewer dopamine receptors, a level of use that once produced pleasure, doesn't. This is the molecular basis for tolerance. To get the original high, the addict has to increase the dose. In addition, the decrease in dopamine receptors means that experiences that used to bring pleasure no longer do. Therefore, the only escape from chronic dysphoria is to take more of the drug. Initial drug use is about feeling good. Addiction is about trying to stay normal.

Withdrawal is also a direct result of the drug resetting the brain's dopamine system—withdrawal and abstinence deprive the brain of the only source of dopamine that produces any sense of joy. Without it, life does not seem worth living.

§ 4.13   TREATMENT

If it is a characteristic of the disease to deny its existence, how, then, can an addict be persuaded to seek treatment? Denial is one reason that drug-treatment centers use what is known as the Minnesota Model of therapy. The Minnesota Model is the method of treatment developed by the Hazelden Foundation.

An essential part of Minnesota Model treatment is direct intervention in the addict's life. Since denial is a central characteristic in addiction, the Minnesota Model supports getting the practicing addict into treatment through constructive coercion, if necessary, by using either involuntary commitment or "voluntary" admission resulting from an arranged crisis confrontation. The addict is a motivated person, motivated to feel better, and drug-taking is used as a means of trying to feel better. Once the denial system is dismantled, the motivation to feel better can be used constructively in the rehabilitation process.

The most important fact about intervention is that it works. People who seek treatment voluntarily do no better than people coerced into it.

A typical intervention involves getting the addict's relatives, friends, employer—anyone who has influence over him—to have, as it were, a surprise party for him, coordinated by a professional counselor. Each person has a prepared list of what the addict has done lately to make life miserable. (A daughter might be enlisted, for example, to say, "Mom, I brought my new boyfriend over and you came out of the bathroom naked." Or "Dad, you missed my graduation because you couldn't get out of bed.") Each person also has an ultimatum. (A boss might be brought in to say, "Jim, if you do not get into this treatment program, you are going to be fired.") This is organized coercion. The addict's family may have called Customs to arrange an involuntary commitment. They will call the local police and say, "I will turn in my loved one if you promise me that you will give him the choice of treatment or prosecution." Once the addict's relationship to the drug is stronger than any other relationships, then there is a need for some organized intervention. Timing may be of the essence. There may be just an instant when the person is truly receptive to getting help.

Once the addict is in treatment, especially treatment before he has hit bottom, it appears that the person is never more than 51 percent in favor of getting better. "There really are these two forces within him: the drug speaking and trying to preserve itself—the parasite trying to remain in some equilibrium with the host—and the other side of the person that is getting all this support from work, from friends, from loved ones, to try to bolster itself, to make it assert itself so that treatment becomes possible," claims the National Institute on Drug Abuse.

The essential aim of Hazelden's treatment plan—the Minnesota Model—is to get the addict fully involved in AA or one of its sister organizations, so when he leaves treatment, he will continue going to meetings. The same is true of Gateway, Fair Oaks, the Betty Ford Center, Comprehensive Care Units, and every responsible treatment facility. In fact, one measure of a treatment program's effectiveness is how far it will go to get the addict to join AA after his insurance money is gone. At some hospitals, a staff member will hand the phone to the addict when his 28 days are up and say, "Call AA Here is the number. Good luck." Others have AA meetings in the hospital throughout the treatment program and insist upon follow-up meetings on hospital grounds. Some private programs will not accept anyone who cannot commit himself to at least a year of treatment. Another key to good treatment is when the family is included. The addict cannot go it alone. Addiction is a disease that affects the entire family. Being married to an addict, being the child or a parent of an addict makes one ill. Family members must be treated, or the patient will relapse (Nelson). And even with AA, there is a 50 percent chance of relapse within 24 months.

§ 4.14 RELAPSE

The small percentage of the people in any society who suffer from addictive disease suffer greatly. Part of the reason is relapse. The American Medical Association includes in its definition of alcoholism the fact that it is a disease "characterized by a tendency to relapse." (The same is true of addiction to any other drug.) Of those who are treated, half to two-thirds relapse within two years, whatever their method of treatment. Yet few treatment facilities address that issue, either before or during treatment; and few programs provide the long-term therapy necessary to give the patient the best chance against relapse. The reason for that is simple: Treatment costs money; and most insurance policies cover only 28 easy treatments in the hospital and extremely limited follow-up and outpatient treatment.

When relapse occurs, it seems to come out of the blue, blanking out all reason, all experience, all logic. But there are warning signs. It may begin as anger or depression. It may begin as a sense of well-being, confidence, a warm glow of pride at how well everything is going. As one AA member said, "In my 30 years, no one ever called me to ask to be prevented from taking a drink. I myself never called for help at the threshold of relapse, probably because I did not want to be stopped." From "Alcoholics Anonymous," here is a description of relapse after a promising period of sobriety:

Chapter 4

"I felt hungry, so I stopped at a roadside place where they have a bar. I had no intention of drinking. I just thought I would get a sandwich...I had eaten there many times during the months I was sober. I sat down at a table and ordered a sandwich and a glass of milk, still with no thought of drinking. I ordered another sandwich and decided to have another glass of milk. Suddenly the thought crossed my mind that if I were to put an ounce of whiskey in my milk, it could not hurt me on a full stomach. I ordered a whiskey and poured it into the milk. I vaguely sensed I was not being any too smart but felt reassured as I was taking the whiskey on a full stomach. The experiment went so well that I ordered another whiskey and poured it into more milk. That did not seem to bother me, so I tried another."

The scientists would call what happened to him selective memory or euphoric recall, in which the addict suddenly remembers the good times he had while high. It is a cunning and baffling and cruel trick of neurochemistry. The tendency to relapse should receive as much attention as does initial recovery. In other words, any program that slights the importance of a deep and lifelong involvement in AA (or Cocaine Anonymous or Narcotics Anonymous) is not for the addict who is serious about protecting his recovery.

The AA tradition of telling stories is not for the benefit of the person to whom they are told. It is for the benefit of the person telling them. The sober alcoholic told his own story out of the conviction that such honesty was required only by and necessary only to his own sobriety. This example was evidence of the AA understanding that honesty was necessary to get sobriety. The happy byproduct of self-therapy for the one who has already attained sobriety is that the would-be AA member identifies with the stories he hears. He says, "Hey, this guy was almost as pan-fried as I was. And look at him now. How did he get sober?" Once that moment of identification—of constructive envy—is achieved, the addict is on his way to recovery.

Becoming addicted is like being in a near-fatal car accident and having both legs cut off. In relative terms, it does not happen to many people, and it should not discourage everyone else from driving. But for those unfortunate enough to be victims, there is no quick fix, only a lifetime of coping; and any advertisement that suggests otherwise is misleading people.

There is only one proven way to maintain abstinence: one day at a time for a lifetime. Drug treatment has become big business, but no one stays in business providing lifelong treatment. No one could afford it, and no insurance company would cover it. Not even the nonprofit places offer unlimited treatment. And that is why, no matter where an addict goes for his initial treatment or detoxification, he will find the same thing: All roads lead to AA (or C.A. or N.A.). The reason is simple. It is free and it works.

§ 4.15 DRUGS AND BEHAVIOR

We have already discussed why people take drugs. We have seen that drug use is as old as recorded history and has occurred in all civilizations. The most important point of this discussion is that drug use is an established part of human behavior, and as such it follows the same rules and principles of any other behavioral pattern. One basic behavioral principle is that behavior persists when it either increases the individual's pleasure or reduces his or her discomfort (psychic or physical). People do not take just any drug—they take only those substances that affect them pleasurably or that make a situation less intolerable. Furthermore, of those drugs that do increase pleasure or decrease discomfort, the ones chosen must be acceptable within the user's cultural setting.

Thus, there is no single cause of drug abuse. Studies with laboratory animals show that susceptibility to narcotics addiction is at least partially determined by genetics. Strains of laboratory animals have been bred that are either susceptible or resistant to induced addiction. Similarly, strains of laboratory animals have been developed that prefer alcoholic solutions over drinking water, whereas most animals will select tap water if given the choice. This finding suggests that alcoholism in humans may be partially based on hereditary predisposition.

Drug use, whether influenced by genetic factors or not, is also the result of a complex interaction of past experiences and present environments. This principle is true of any behavior. It is possible to group some persons together by a common history and environment, thus to predict whether or not they will have a predisposition to drug use, and to predict whether or not they will have a predisposition to a particular type of drug. This fact does not mean that potential users can be readily identified; rather, it means that some groups of individuals can be identified according to the *probability* of their becoming drug users. Various types of drug users may also be classified according to differences in personality and background. For example, narcotics addicts usually start drinking alcoholic beverages in their early teens, before their age and social-class peers do. After experimenting with alcohol, narcotics addicts often try marijuana or inhalants, such as those found in model airplane glue. The average age of first narcotics use is the late teens. As one drug becomes more acceptable in society—for example, marijuana—the next drug selected is usually less socially acceptable than the previous one.

§ 4.16 ADOLESCENT DRUG USE

Public concern about drugs intensified during the campus turmoil of the 1960s, and since then Congressional hearings on drug use have been frequent. At the grass-roots level, local organizations of parents who were worried about adolescent drug use sprang up in a few places in the mid-1970s, and soon mushroomed into a national movement. That concern is based on the growing numbers of adolescents who take drugs.

Adolescent drug use is troubling mainly because of the risks involved in taking psychoactive substances. The principal risks are toxic effects, impairment of function, the potential for physical or psychic dependence, and the long-term effects of an addictive disease.

There are several grounds for special concern about drug use by children and adolescents. First, all psychoactive drugs have acute effects on mood, concentration, and cognitive functioning, including memory, and hence use may interfere with learning and impair school performance.

Second, if a young person will eventually use drugs, it is at least advisable to put off starting as long as possible. Many toxic substances require prolonged exposure to produce an effect, or a long incubation period for the effect to become manifest. Thus, postponing the onset of use reduces the likelihood of adverse effects, and may reduce the chance of becoming a chronic user.

Third, a conservative course of action is especially appropriate when dealing with children and adolescents. In medicine it is generally accepted that a drug should not be administered when it is not known to be safe. When safety is in doubt—for example, during pregnancy or immaturity—special restrictions often are imposed to avoid harm. In the case of illicit drugs, none has been sufficiently studied to warrant a claim of safety.

§ 4.17   INFLUENCE OF PARENTS AND PEERS

Parents are concerned with the use of drugs among children and youth. Many parents believe that their authority is being undermined by various social elements such as the media, the government, and the peer group. Although many parents may see the media and the government as the ultimate sources of this erosion of control, it is with the more proximate and accessible peer group that most parent groups are primarily concerned. They feel that more can be accomplished by actively attempting to regain control on a local, more manageable level while continuing to exert pressure on the more nationally oriented media and government.

This concern with conflict between parents and peers is, of course, not new. It is one of the most predictable and, in Western society, probably least avoidable of developmental conflicts. What is new, however, is the sharp and specific focus upon the relative influence of parents and peers on youthful drug use. This focus upon drug use is not surprising since this behavior has increased substantially over the past several years and attitudes toward drug use provide what is one of the most distinctive and emotional conflicts between the generations.

There have been many studies that have researched adolescent drug use and abuse. There is extensive and growing literature concerning the role of the family in drug use and abuse. For example parental drinking patterns are the single most important tool for predicting adolescent drinking patterns. Thus parental drinking behavior is a strong factor in influencing adolescent initiation into alcohol use. However, parental influence on adolescent marijuana use is quite small. What parental influence was found appeared to be based on parental attitudes and closeness of relationship with their children, i.e., parents whose relationships strongly discourage marijuana use and still hold the relationship together were more successful in minimizing initiation than those parents whose attitudes and behavior suggested a more permissive stance.

Adolescent initiation into the use of illicit drugs other than marijuana appears to be strongly related to parental influences. The quality of the parent-child relationship appears to be particularly important. The adolescent's feelings of closeness to the family predicted low likelihood of initiation into other illicit drugs, while strict controls and parental disagreement about discipline predicted higher likelihood of initiation. Additionally, parental drug use was, again, an important predictor.

The influence of the family differs in each stage of adolescent drug use. Parents appear to be influential concerning adolescents' initiation into hard liquor use and, in particular, their initiation into use of illicit drugs other than marijuana. Parental influence appears to be somewhat diminished, however, with regard to initiation into marijuana use.

Peer influences on adolescent drug use have received less research attention than the role of the family in this behavior. The role of peers has not been ignored as much as it has been considered as one of many factors influencing adolescent drug use; the role of the family, on the other hand, has often been singled out for study.

Peer influence has, nevertheless, been examined by a significant number of researchers. Adolescents' and their friends' perceptions of how many of their friends are using hard liquor, actual use of hard liquor by friends, best friends' attitudes about the harmfulness of hard liquor, and the degree of adolescent involvement in peer activities (e.g., attending parties, driving around) were the most important peer factors found to predict adolescent initiation into hard liquor use. The modeling effect based on friends' actual use, however, may be the most important factor in initiation to hard liquor use.

Friends' actual and perceived use, friends' actual and perceived espousal of values and attitudes conducive to use, and availability of the drug are peer factors that strongly predict adolescent initiation to marijuana use. Marijuana, as opposed to alcohol, is a substance associated with youth, and that the range and importance of peer factors in predicting use are considerably greater for marijuana than for alcohol. As such, exposure to peers who use marijuana and/or have favorable attitudes toward it has in fact become a source of adolescent socialization.

The strength of peer influence, direct and indirect, on marijuana use has considerable support in the literature (NIDA 1985). It seems as attachment to parents diminishes, peer orientation grows and so does initiation to marijuana use.

In summary, parental alcohol use seems to be the strongest interpersonal predictor of adolescent alcohol use, peer marijuana use appears to be the strongest interpersonal predictor of marijuana use, and family and best friends' use of other illicit drugs appears to be among the better interpersonal predictors of adolescent use of these substances.

§ 4.18 DRUG ADDICTION—A FAMILY PROBLEM

I don't know how many times people have asked me how to deal with an alcoholic or drug addict in the family. Questions like: How can I get him to stop drinking? How can I get him help? Into treatment? In the *Hazelden Voice*, Winter 2003, page 5, there is an article by Dr. Robert Meyers worth mentioning. He has developed a family approach to addiction called CRAFT, which stands for Community Reinforcement and Family Training. It is a family intervention approach for engaging unmotivated addicts into treatment. It is a model to give family members an optimal strategy for getting their loved one into treatment. For more information on the CRAFT program, contact Dr. Meyers at bmeyers@unm.edu.

§ 4.19 LINKING CRIMINAL JUSTICE AND TREATMENT

We know the number of drug arrests made each year is staggering. Drug abuse continues to burden the prison system because the majority of prisoners are drug offenders as well as criminals. The courts and the correctional system must use their power to convince addicts to "clean up their act." Studies have demonstrated that when drug addicts within the criminal justice system receive effective treatment, they commit fewer crimes. The Violent Crime Control and Law Enforcement Act of 1994 formalizes the linkage between criminal justice and treatment systems and empowers judges to use a valuable range of treatment and punishment options.

The Violent Crime Control and Law Enforcement Act of 1994 authorizes $1 billion over 6 years for drug courts. These drug courts should free up jail and prison space for violent, predatory criminals. To be effective, drug courts and offender management programs must provide integrated services and sanctions that include continuing close supervision; mandatory drug testing, and aftercare services; and a system of escalating sanctions for those who fail to meet program requirements. This reasonable and fair but tough treatment for drug addicts can help ensure that addicts do not revert to the same criminal activity and continue to pass through the criminal justice system.

§ 4.20 THE CHANGING WAR ON ADDICTION: DRUG COURTS

While policy revolutions like legalizing drugs or eradicating the supply of drugs are pipe dreams, change is coming to the world of addiction and drug policy. Several states are far ahead of politicians in approving ballot initiatives that include treatment programs. For example, drug courts that allow judges to impose treatment in place of jail sentences have increased fifty-fold since the mid-1990s, part of a new understanding that even with frequent relapses, treatment is much less expensive for society than prison.

Drug Addiction and Behavior

Part of the reason for the change is the growing prison population. The prison population has more than tripled over the past 20 years to nearly 2 million, with 60% to 70% testing positive for drug abuse on arrest (BJS 2000). These inmates are parents to 2.4 million children, all of whom are disproportionately likely to follow their parents to prison. If the prison population were to continue to grow at the current rate, by 2053 the United States would have more people in prison than out. So in an attempt to break the cycle, drug addiction is increasingly being viewed more as a disease than a crime.

In 2000 California approved Proposition 36, which offers treatment options in place of jail for nonviolent offenders.

Of course, old habits die hard. Washington still directs two-thirds of the federal drug budget, including 1.1 billion in military aid to Colombia, to law enforcement. So-called "harm-reduction" strategies, like needle exchange programs, have a tough time getting approval, despite many studies proving they save lives.

Even so, at the local level where the real money is spent, we see flexible law enforcement with mandatory treatment. Most prosecutors like the drug court system. It is know as coercive abstinence by using the threat of jail to motivate drug addicts into treatment. The real issue is motivation. The research shows that those forced into treatment do at least as well as addicts who enter voluntarily and sometimes better because they must stay in treatment longer or go to jail. The best indication of treatment success is the length of treatment. While relapse is common, those who remain in treatment for a year or more are twice as likely to stay clean.

Drug treatment experts are finally realizing that law enforcement and treatment programs must work together because the nature of addiction is that the addict is resistant to treatment. Therefore, the arrest by law enforcement can have a tremendous impact on the addict providing that there is intensive drug treatment in jail where addicts are a captive audience and after release, with after-jail treatment. As in all treatment, the vast majority drop out before completing the program, but those who stay the year or more, approximately three-fourths who graduate from a twelve-month program are employed, drug-free and not in jail five years later. The results of in-prison programs and outpatient therapy are worse than long-term residential treatment; the key variable is length of treatment.

Therefore, any program that can increase an addict's stay in treatment will have a more successful outcome for the addict. Drug courts divert addicts out of incarceration to community treatment. Drug courts seek to reduce drug use and criminal behavior by keeping drug addicts in treatment. Addicts who complete the program either have their charges dismissed (in a diversion or presentence model) or probation sentence reduced (in a postsentence model).

Chapter 4

Title V of the Violent Crime Control and Law Enforcement Act of 1994 has had a large impact on the establishment of state drug courts. The act authorizes the Attorney General to make grants to state and local governments to establish drug courts. As of October 2000, there were 593 drug courts nationwide with 456 more in the planning stages, up from 12 in 1994. For more information about drug courts, go to www.drugcourt.org.

Drug courts are an important component in the criminal justice system by forcing addicts into treatment. By 2001 over 57,000 addicts have successfully completed drug court programs. A review of 24 drug courts found that twice (as many stay in treatment as compared to noncourt programs) with reduced drug use and criminal behavior. See Blanko, S., "Research on Drug Courts: A Critical Review," <u>National Drug Court Institute Review</u>, 1.1 (1998).

References

Blum, Richard H. <u>Society and Drugs</u>. San Francisco: Jassey-Bass Press, 1969.

Bureau of Justice Statistics. <u>Prisoners in 1999</u>. Washington, D.C., National Center for Justice, 2000.

Byrne, M.M., and J.H. Holes. "The Co-Alcoholic Syndrome." <u>Labor-Management Alcoholism Journal</u>, 9.2 (1979).

Drug Enforcement Administration. <u>Controlled Substances: Use, Abuse and Effect</u>. Washington: D.C.: U.S. Department of Justice, 1990.

Inaba and Cohen. <u>Uppers, Downers, All Arounders. The Haight-Ashbury Detox Clinic</u>. San Francisco, CA, 1989.

Jellinek, E.M. <u>The Disease Concept of Alcoholism</u>. New Haven, CT: College and University Press, 1960.

"National Commission on Drug Free Schools and Toward a Drug Free Generation: A Nation's Responsibility, Final Report." Washington, D.C.: U.S. Government Printing Office, September, 1990.

National Institute on Drug Abuse. "Drug Abuse Treatment." 1988.

----------. "Preventing Adolescent Drug Abuse." <u>Research Monograph Series</u> 47 (1985).

Nelson, Charles. <u>Styles of Enabling in Codependents of Cocaine Abusers</u>. San Diego: United States International University, 1984.

Smith, David E., and Wesson, Arnold R. <u>Treating the Cocaine Abuser</u>. Center City, MN: Hazelden Foundation, 1985.

Teshner, Alan. "Addiction as a Brain Disease." <u>Issues in Science and Technology</u> (2001).

CHAPTER 5

AN EXAMINATION OF ONE STATE'S DRUG POLICY ENFORCEMENT

§ 5.1 INTRODUCTION TO DRUG TRAFFICKING

Due to California's diverse culture and unique geography, there are many issues that affect the drug situation in California. Drugs such as cocaine, heroin, methamphetamine, and marijuana are smuggled into the state from Mexico; however, methamphetamine and marijuana are produced or cultivated in large quantities within the state.

5.1.1 Drug Trafficking

San Diego and Imperial Counties remain a principal transshipment zone for a variety of drugs—cocaine, heroin, marijuana, and methamphetamine—smuggled from Mexico. Most drug traffickers/organizations that are encountered by law enforcement continue to be poly-drug traffickers rather than specializing in one type of drug. Since September 11, 2001, greater emphasis has been placed on carefully screening people and vehicles at all California ports of entry into the United States from Mexico. This has forced traffickers to attempt other means to smuggle their contraband into the United States, including the use of tunnels that run underneath the border and more sophisticated hidden compartments in vehicles.

Los Angeles is a distribution center for all types of illicit drugs destined for other major metropolitan areas throughout the United States as well as locally. Increased security measures at Los Angeles International Airport continue to deter drug traffickers from traveling through the airport. Although the more rural areas in the northern half of California are awash in methamphetamine, heroin remains the number one drug of abuse in San Francisco, heroin and crack cocaine continue to impact Oakland, and methamphetamine use continues in and around Sacramento.

5.1.1(a) Frequently Trafficked Drugs

Cocaine: Mexican trafficking organizations, working closely with Colombian suppliers, dominate the wholesale cocaine trade. However, the Mexican traffickers continue to specialize in cross-border cocaine transportation by air, land, and sea.

Heroin: California-based law enforcement agencies primarily seize Mexican black tar heroin throughout the state and, to a lesser extent, Mexican brown tar heroin. Reports that high-purity Colombian heroin is now available in the counties surrounding Los Angeles is supported by the recent seizure of 200 grams of Colombian heroin by law enforcement in Ventura County. A 40,000-poppy-plant grow was discovered by hikers in the Sierra National Forest in June 2003. That was the only poppy grow located in California in recent history.

Methamphetamine (Meth): Methamphetamine is the primary drug threat in California. Mexican organizations continue to dominate the production and distribution of high-quality meth, while a secondary trafficking group, composed primarily of Caucasians, operates small, unsophisticated laboratories.

Club Drugs: Although MDMA, or Ecstasy, was considered the most popular "club drug" in the state among teens and young adults, there are indicators that its use may be decreasing across the board, yet it is consistently available in geographical pockets. Compton street gangs continue to control both production and distribution of PCP. Though not as widely popular as most rave drugs, LSD remains readily available throughout the Los Angeles area. The ample supply of LSD is due to the number of LSD laboratories operating in remote areas of Northern California, which has been the center of LSD production since the 1960s. Internet sales of GHB and GBL persist.

Prescription Drugs: Due to the discrepancy in national laws between the United States and Mexico, the prolific "border pharmacies" within walking distance across the border in Tijuana and other Mexican border towns remain the primary source of controlled substances in the San Diego metropolitan area. Doctor shopping and prescription forgery are the primary methods of prescription drug abuse in the Los Angeles and San Francisco metropolitan areas. In Northern California, OxyContin, Vicodin, benzodiazepines, and carisoprodol are most commonly abused. In the Los Angeles area, Demerol, Dilaudid, Diazepam, Hydrocodone, and steroids remain the principal drugs abused. The San Diego area prescription drugs of choice are Vicodin, Vicodin ES, Lortab, and Vicoprofen. Rohypnol remains readily available throughout the Los Angeles area, due primarily to the city's proximity to Mexico.

Marijuana: Marijuana remains the most widely available and abused illicit substance in California. Large quantities of low-grade marijuana are smuggled into the state from Mexico. Highly potent Canadian marijuana, commonly referred to as "BC bud," is also smuggled into the state. Potent domestic marijuana is also cultivated in sophisticated indoor, hydroponic gardens throughout the state.

Crack: Los Angeles-based gangs dominate the street-level distribution of crack cocaine throughout the Los Angeles and San Diego metropolitan areas. Cocaine bought by the gangs is "rocked" or converted into crack cocaine in the Los Angeles area (including Santa Ana and Riverside) and then sold locally or distributed to other cities in California and nationally. These organizations frequently use intimidation and violence to facilitate their narcotics trafficking activities. Gang members involved in the street distribution of crack are often armed and have a propensity towards violence against other gang members whom they feel are invading their areas of control.

California Drug Policy Enforcement

State Facts	2004 Federal Drug Seizures
Population: 34, 501,130	Cocaine: 3,186.6 kg
Law Enforcement Officers: 85,736	Heroin 121.4 kg
State Prison Population: 239,900	Methamphetamine: 786.5 kg (Methamphetamine Labs 730)
Probation Population: 350,768	Marijuana: 131,871.5 kg
Violent Crime Rate Nat. Ranking: 10	Ecstasy: 329,973 tablets

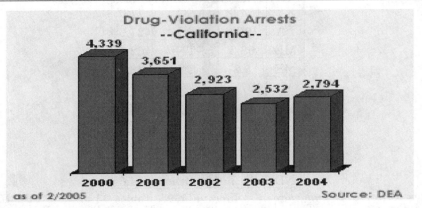

5.1.2 Cracking Down: Arrests and Imprisonments

As stated, due to California's diverse culture and unique geography, there are many issues that affect the drug situation in the state. California shares, more or less, the same problems and drug issues present in the other states. An examination of California's drug policy enforcement might help in understanding this thing we call the "War on Drugs." We might begin to focus on a more effective approach if we can understand where we have been and what direction we are headed.

During the past two decades, California experienced a 25-fold increase in the number of drug offenders sentenced to state prison. As a result of this increase, California led the nation in drug offender incarceration with a rate of 115 per 100,000 of the population—**2.5 times the national average** of 45 per 100,000 population for 36 reporting states in 1996 (Table 1). By 1999, California's drug imprisonment rate rose to 132 per 100,000.

Table 1. Arrest rate for drug offenses per 100,000, 1998:

	1980	1998	Change
California	553.6	811.1	+46.5
U.S.	256.0	596.2	+132.9

Chapter 5

Table 2. Drug imprisonment rate per 100,000, 1996:

AL	48.5	NE	25.9
AR	28.3	NH	9.7
CA	114.6	NJ	85.3
CO	32.8	NY	80.8
FL	34.7	NV	59.1
GA	64.5	OH	55.8
HI	10.6	OK	44.4
IA	20.6	OR	53.3
IL	73.3	PA	23.3
KY	54.3	SC	71.0
LA	106.6	SD	27.6
MD	68.3	TN	62.4
ME	5.2	TX	48.7
MI	27.2	UT	35.4
MN	10.6	VA	52.7
MO	54.5	WA	37.5
MS	68.3	WI	26.1
NC	76.7	WV	7.6
ND	14.7	Other	44.6

Sources: *Crime & Delinquency in California*, 1998, Tables 33 and 36; FBI, *Uniform Crime Reports*, 1998, Table 38; Data Analysis Unit, California Department of Corrections, 1999; Justice Policy Institute (2000). *Peer Prescription: The Cost of Imprisoning Drug Offenders in the United States*, http://www.cjcj.org/drug.

This unprecedented imprisonment increase is partly attributable to escalating drug arrests. These escalating drug arrests result from harsher sentencing statutes that have expanded the pool of prison-eligible offenders and promoted incarceration as a primary response to illicit drug use (Maxwell, 1999; Tonry, 1999).

California's uniquely harsher approach to drug crime is founded on deterrence and incapacitation theory. Deterrence and incapacitation theory promotes increased arrests, prosecutions, and prison sentences as the primary means to dissuade drug use and reduce street crime, by removing the drug-involved offender from the community. The theory also holds that stricter sanctions targeting low-level and first-time drug offenders further reduces drug-related crime by increasing the personal costs of drug use among incipient users (Maxwell, 1999; Tonry, 1999; Henham, 1999). The theory subscribes to the belief that failure to strictly enforce drug laws promotes other forms of crimes as undeterred drug users seek money to supply their drug needs (Lurigio & Swartz, 1999).

Supporters of deterrence and incapacitation theory associate the recent declines in California crime rates as a testament to these policies (Jones, 1999). Opponents argue that this theory is misguided and ineffective because simple punishment does not address the underlying causes of drug use and addiction (Sentencing Project, 1998). In addition, national statistics show that crime rates are declining across the nation regardless of individual state enforcement policies (Tonry, 1999). California presents an unusual opportunity to examine the impact of arrest and incarceration drug control policies. As California drug arrests doubled from 131,000 in 1980 to 265,000 in 1998, major variations developed. In the 1980s, two-thirds of the state's drug arrest increases were high-level felonies such as illegal drug manufacture, sale, or possession in large quantity. However, in the 1990s, nearly all drug arrest increases were for low-level possession offenses.

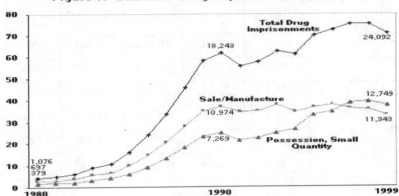

Figure 1: California Drug Imprisonments, 1980-99

These variations in arrest patterns are reflected in imprisonment rates (Figure 1). In 1980, only 379 Californians were sent to prison for drug possession offenses compared to 12,749 in 1999, a population-adjusted rate increase of over 20-fold (2,244%). The per capita imprisonment growth rate for all drug offenses was 1,473%, while the per capita growth rate in prison commitments for sale/manufacture drug offenders was 1,048%. By the late 1990s, in a radical departure from the past, more than half of Californians imprisoned for drugs were locked up for possession (Table 3)

Table 3. CA New drug imprisonments and rates per 100,000, 1980-99

YEAR	% Nationally.	% Sale/ Manuf*	% Possess*	Total #	# Sale/ Manuf	# Possess	Per 100,000
1980	4.5	2.9	1.6	1,076	697	379	35.2%
81	5.1	3.2	1.9	1,224	777	447	36.5%
82	6.1	4.1	2.0	1,498	1,005	493	32.9%
83	9.0	5.9	3.0	2,250	1,488	762	33.9%
84	10.8	6.8	4.0	2,767	1,747	1,020	36.9%

85	16.1	10.1	6.0	4,210	2,634	1,576	37.4%
86	24.2	14.9	9.2	6,460	3,988	2,472	38.3%
87	33.8	20.5	13.3	9,255	5,603	3,652	39.5%
88	46.1	28.2	18.0	12,945	7,903	5,042	38.9%
89	58.2	35.1	23.1	16,750	10,101	6,649	39.7%
1990	61.7	37.1	24.6	18,243	10,974	7,269	39.8%
91	55.8	34.7	21.2	17,113	10,627	6,486	37.9%
92	57.7	35.1	22.6	18,063	10,983	7,080	39.2%
93	62.7	38.0	24.7	19,902	12,075	7,827	39.3%
94	61.3	34.8	26.5	19,692	11,185	8,507	43.2%
95	70.1	36.9	33.2	22,472	11,816	10,656	47.4%
96	72.6	38.1	34.5	23,510	12,354	11,156	47.5%
97	75.1	36.4	38.7	24,748	11,984	12,764	51.6%
98	75.1	35.7	39.4	25,152	11,949	13,203	52.5%
99	70.8	33.3	37.5	24,092	11,343	12,749	52.9%

Table 4. Five-year averages

YEAR	% Nationally.	% Sale/Manuf*	% Possess*	Per 100,000
80-84	7.2	4.6	2.5	34.7%
85-89	36.2	22.1	14.1	39.0%
90-94	59.9	35.9	23.9	39.9%
95-99	72.7	36.0	36.7	50.5%

*"Sale/manuf" refers to high-level drug offenses (drug sale, manufacture, or possession in quantity large enough to presume intent to sell). "Possess" refers to low-level possession of drugs in small quantity for personal use.
Source: Data Analysis Unit, California Department of Corrections (imprisonments); Demographic Research Unit, California Department of Finance (populations used to calculate rates).

This dramatic rise in drug offender imprisonment throughout California is not uniform, as jurisdictions show wide variations in policy and practice. While many counties adopted strict doctrinaire enforcement policies that targeted serious and low-level offenders, others opted to target more serious and chronic offenders.

To determine the impact of different enforcement policies, a look at California's 12 largest counties—which account for 25 million people, or 3/4 of the state's population, and 4/5 of the state's drug arrests—is in order. It is necessary to analyze the impact of strict drug enforcement on violent crime, property crime, and drug abuse rates. According to deterrence and incapacitation theory, the counties that adopted strict enforcement approaches should show the greatest declines in drug-related crime and drug abuse (see figure 2).

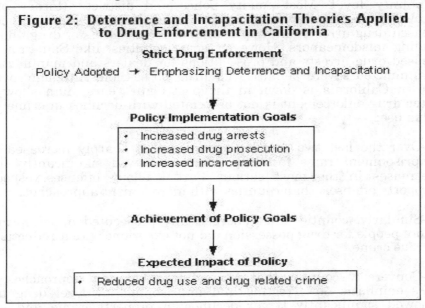

Figure 2: Deterrence and Incapacitation Theories Applied to Drug Enforcement in California

Strict Drug Enforcement

Policy Adopted → Emphasizing Deterrence and Incapacitation

Policy Implementation Goals
- Increased drug arrests
- Increased drug prosecution
- Increased incarceration

Achievement of Policy Goals

Expected Impact of Policy
- Reduced drug use and drug related crime

An examination of the 1990s drug law arrest and imprisonment patterns shows a distinct pattern shift from the 1980s and prior decades. During the 1990s, California drug enforcement targeted an ever-increasing pool of marginal drug users, with possession accounting for virtually all the increase in drug-related imprisonments. From 1989 to 1999, imprisonment for drug possession nearly doubled while felony drug imprisonment for manufacturing and trafficking remained steady. In a radical departure from past drug enforcement, more Californians were imprisoned in the last three years for simple drug possession (38,716) than for sale or manufacturing drug offenses (35,276). Even more surprising, while a drug dealer or manufacturer was much more likely to be imprisoned than a drug possession offender in the 1980s and before, today an offender arrested for low-level drug possession is considerably more likely to be imprisoned than one arrested for felony drug manufacture or sale. Further, 6,191 Californians were imprisoned in 1999 for possession of a small amount of drugs with no prior offense for violent or serious offenses and no other current offenses. These drug users comprise the state's fastest-growing inmate population and constitute 11% of those sent to prison for all offenses in 1999.

In summary, the imprisonment increases for California drug law violators during the past two decades are the result of harsher sentencing of lower-level drug users. This pattern suggests that incarceration has become the primary intervention tool for state drug prevention policy.

Although California laws are established by the state legislature, arrest, prosecution, and sentencing decisions are county functions. Because California counties pursued drug policy enforcement in sharply different ways, wide variations exist on how laws are implemented at the county level. Most county police and district attorney offices vigorously pursued new harsh enforcement statutes and significantly increased drug arrests and imprisonment for all forms of drug offenses, including misdemeanors. However, some counties, like San Francisco, increased drug arrests and prosecutions for dealers and manufacturers but minimized severe penalties for drug possession. Although, overall, crime in California is down in the past eight years, data show that stricter drug enforcement is not associated with declines in crime rates or drug use:

—Over the last two decades, counties that sharply increased their imprisonment rates for drug offenses showed significantly slower decreases in the most serious Part I felony offenses, especially property offenses, than counties with more lenient approaches.

—Similarly, counties that energetically prosecuted and imprisoned more people for drug possession did not experience great reductions in serous crime.

—Conversely, counties that adopted more balanced approaches, with less emphasis on arresting and imprisoning low-level drug users, showed significantly larger declines in property crime and larger (though not statistically significant) declines in violent crime as well.

These patterns remain consistent when a variety of crime measures and time periods are compared. The absence of differential effects between counties with strict drug enforcement policies and counties with more lenient drug enforcement policies does not support the deterrence and incapacitation arguments of drug enforcement advocates.

§ 5.2 CALIFORNIA DRUG POLICY: A DISCUSSION

As in other areas of crime control, during the past 20 years California implemented an unprecedented social experiment in its attempt to suppress illicit drug use. By emphasizing law enforcement strategies based on deterrence and incapacitation theories, the state's drug-offender prison population rose from 1,778 in 1980 to 45,455 in 1999. However, these policies were not adopted uniformly across the state, because of county-by-county variations.

Since 1990, many counties placed increased emphasis on the prosecution and imprisonment of low-level drug offenders, especially for drug possession offenses. For example, in 1980 only seven people from San Diego County were sentenced to prison for low-level drug possession, while in 1999 the county sent 1,002 drug possession offenders to state prison. Los Angeles sentenced only 145 drug possession offenders to prison in 1980, yet sentenced 5,109 in 1999.

The six counties that increased their imprisonment rates the most for low-level drug possession actually experienced greater increases in violent crime rates from 1980 to 1999 (up 11%, on average) than the six most lenient counties (up 1%). Further, no major differences emerged in violent or property crime rates between strict-enforcing counties and more lenient or balanced counties. Increased drug arrests and imprisonment are not correlated with decreases in violent and property crime (in fact, they are more likely to be associated with increases), and high levels of drug arrests and imprisonment are not associated with lower rates of crime (the results are entirely random).

A conclusion that fits all the facts, then, suggests that some counties chose to combat their drug abuse and crime problems by making more felony and misdemeanor drug arrests, while other counties made fewer drug arrests and/or concentrated only on the worst (felony) drug offenses (manufacturing and trafficking). The latter group of counties had considerably more success in reducing crime regardless of the dimension of their drug abuse and crime problems. Finally, counties that imposed high rates of imprisonment for drug violations generally experienced SLOWER declines in index felony offenses than low-imprisonment counties, though the results were not statistically significant.

A major reason for these outcome differences appears to be that simple possession drug offenses are not associated with high rates of crime or drug abuse—with correlations close to zero. Therefore, increasing arrests for low-level drug possession does nothing to control crime and may drain resources away from more productive strategies.

A second reason for the outcome differences is that felony drug offenses appear to reflect, rather than control, higher rates of drug abuse and crime. Counties that stepped up felony drug arrest rates did not show the most impressive improvements in violent and property crime rates (although the San Francisco exception indicates that areas with extremely high rates of drug abuse may benefit from policing of the worst drug offenses). For most jurisdictions, however, increasing felony drug arrests is a very limited strategy to control rising drug abuse and crime.

Finally, counties that reduced misdemeanor drug arrests and switched to judicious enforcement of felony drug laws enjoyed the healthiest reductions in violent and property crime. Taken together, these findings strongly suggest that (a) strong enforcement of drug possession laws is ineffective in reducing crime, and (b) felony drug arrest is a strategy that should be used sparingly and carefully targeted.

§ 5.2.1   Conclusion

After a decade and a half of skyrocketing drug arrests and imprisonment rates at a cost of billions of dollars, California (and the United States) now suffer the highest rates of drug abuse deaths in our history and no discernible impact on California crime is observed. Justice Department research reported that drug treatment is effective even with the most hardened addicts, and that concerted efforts towards treatment

Chapter 5

can reduce drug use and drug-related crime by over 40 percent (Harrell, Cavanaugh, & Roman, 2000).

Given the continued emphasis in California on law enforcement strategies despite the dearth of evidence showing effectiveness, future drug policy research should examine the political basis of current approaches. Questions to examine are whether current policies are better designed to accommodate vested interest groups and political agendas than to serve as a reasonable solution to the legitimate social issue of drug abuse.

§ 5.3 THE BASIC ELEMENT OF A NEW POLICY ON CRIME: HARM REDUCTION

Any discussion of crime policy in the United States necessarily confronts the issue of drugs, but the way that the drug issue interacts with other issues is neither simple nor obvious. Crime policy analysts generally agree that imprisonment for drug use, or even drug sale, is an ineffective strategy, but the public seems to demand increasingly severe sanctions for these behaviors. There are, however, ways of modifying rather than reversing the War on Drugs approach that may be politically feasible. A drug policy that retains existing prohibitions but focuses more directly on harm reduction would be substantially more effective than the existing approach.

There is a wide range of attitudes about drug use. For present purposes, three major views can be identified: first, that drug use is private conduct; second, that drug use is undesirable, even deviant, behavior that the state may prohibit (*mala prohibitum*); and third, that drug use is morally repugnant and the state is obligated to criminalize it as intrinsically bad (*mala in se*). The first National Drug Control Strategy report was published in 1989. The document set the tone and direction for the War on Drugs. The original strategy, as formulated by William Bennett, opted strongly for the *mala in se* approach; in it, the use of any drug, in whatever quantity, was attributable to the deficient moral character of individuals, a weakness of will. Adopting the "War on Drugs" as its overriding metaphor, the 1989 strategy fulfilled the metaphor's promise by advocating a vast expansion of the apparatus of social control, particularly of law enforcement and prisons.

Legalization has often been proposed as an alternative to the vast expansion of the criminal justice system, i.e., courts, law enforcement, and corrections. There are many complexities involving the legalization of drugs, but they are not necessarily insoluble. Any legalization program, however, would confront a further, and almost certainly fatal, difficulty—the pragmatic problem that legalization is politically unacceptable to the American people. Government officials may have dreamed up the notion of a War on Drugs, but they did not invent the underlying selection of the punitive or *mala in se* approach to drug use. Americans overwhelmingly regard drug use as reprehensible and demand severe punishment for those who sell drugs, possess them, or even simply use them. No politician in a democratic regime can safely ignore such a widespread sentiment.

The ineffectiveness of the War on Drugs approach and the political unacceptability of the legalization approach present a familiar divergence between expert and popular opinion. One is presented with two unappealing options: either frame recommendations that rest on valid research but stand no chance of real-world adoption or abandon the effort to frame rational responses and accept popular opinion as an absolute determinant of public policy.

The principle of harm reduction provides a possible solution. In essence, the idea is that the public's real fear is violent crime. Drugs are condemned primarily because of their connection to violent crime, and nonviolent drug use is condemned by association. The fact that drugs are used by all segments of the population indicate that drug use would not be regarded as serious enough to justify the current draconian approaches without being connected in the public's mind with violence. One possibility for drug policy, therefore, is to identify more effective ways of combating drug-related violent crime—in other words, ways of reducing harm—that would provide alternatives to current policy.

There are a variety of prevention programs operating at the early childhood or teenage levels that can produce significant reductions in the crime rate and thereby reduce the amount of crime, particularly violent crime. These programs would naturally reduce the level of drug use that has proved to be so criminogenic in inner-city populations, although the programs themselves are not specifically directed toward drugs.

Prevention programs are linked to a policy of minimizing harm for two separate reasons. First, if we can prevent some crime more cheaply than we can punish the perpetrators once the crime has occurred, we will avoid more victimization at any given level of expenditure. The second link between prevention and harm reduction is even more direct. Prevention means that the potential perpetrators will not victimize anyone, while punishment only means that the actual perpetrators will be incapacitated for some period of time after they have already created a certain number of victims. The "Three-Strikes" law provides for permanent incapacitation, but by definition those subject to this sanction have already victimized at least three people and possibly as many as 30 or more. Thus, prevention programs will prevent further victimization and achieve even greater cost-effectiveness for harm reduction.

§ 5.3.1 Results
There are a number of programs that have promising results.

Prenatal and Early Childhood Interventions with High-Risk Families: Inappropriate or inadequate parenting are among the strongest predictors of later delinquency. The following three factors are most consistently associated with such risks: poverty, being single and/or without the aid of a co-parent, and youthfulness. Additional risk factors include substance abuse, mental health problems, or criminality on the part of either parent; birth complications; or residence in a criminogenic neighborhood. During the past two decades, a number of experimental programs have demonstrated the value of home visits and early childhood education in reducing a range of problem behaviors.

Interventions for Acting-Out and At-Risk Youth: Programs that target acting-out adolescents and their families and train parents how to monitor their child's behavior and respond with appropriate rewards and punishments have been shown to reduce stealing and antisocial behavior over short periods of time. One approach to parenting intervention that focuses on modification of dysfunctional family communication processes—training family members to negotiate effectively and to set clear rules about privileges and responsibilities—has been shown to reduce recidivism. School-based programs that train middle and high school students in drug resistance skills and drug education also have been shown to reduce or delay initiation into drug use for a limited period following the training.

Early Interventions for Delinquent Youth: Most criminal careers begin in the juvenile years, and most chronic adult offenders have had multiple contacts with the juvenile justice system. Since the disposition of juvenile offenders is still supposed to be tailored to the individual needs and circumstances of each case, a wide variety of programs have been developed to meet these needs. Many states provide a continuum of increasingly restrictive settings ranging from isolated wilderness camps and ranches to very secure fenced and locked facilities, with individual placement decisions made on the basis of community safety, treatment needs, and amenability to treatment.

Although a number of programs appear to have reduced recidivism rates significantly, no particular intervention strategy was found to be consistently more effective than any other. Unfortunately, many of the youngest delinquents do not appear to be exposed to whatever benefits juvenile corrections programs have to offer until they are well on their way to developing a pattern of serious criminal behavior. In most jurisdictions the juvenile system has little in the way of programs to offer 11- or 12-year-old delinquent youth because they are not yet seen as dangerous, but such youth represent the greatest eventual risk to society of their entire group.

In addition, there are a variety of other prevention strategies that focus more directly on drug use and show considerable promise in minimizing harm. Perhaps the best known are needle exchange and methadone maintenance.

Programs to increase access to sterile intravenous equipment ("needle exchange") are not directed at violent crime, but they are intended to reduce the obvious harm of HIV (human immunodeficiency virus) infection. Transmission to adolescents and adults occurs either directly from contaminated drug paraphernalia or through sexual contact with an infected partner. Infants may become infected transplacentally or perinatally from mothers who themselves are intravenous drug users or who become infected by sex partners who are IV drug users. In an ideal world, treatment and prevention programs would seek to reduce drug use, not HIV infection alone. In the real world, drug users may not enter or remain in treatment, or abstain from injecting drugs while in treatment.

A similar argument can be made regarding methadone maintenance, a program that is more directly linked to crime prevention. When it is administered to previously intractable heroin addicts in an adequate, daily oral dose, methadone blocks acute narcotic effects and ceases the recurrent craving usually associated with long-term abstinence from heroin and other opiate drugs. Methadone does not cure narcotics addition. Instead, it controls withdrawal symptoms and normalizes the functioning of heroin addicts while the medication is being taken.

Another way of implementing a harm reduction policy with respect to drug use is to explore alternative sanctions for those arrested for or convicted of drug offenses. Alternative punishments are still punishment, but they reduce the severity of punishment in a manner that raises political difficulties of its own. The rationale for doing so, once again, is harm reduction. First, alternative sanctions, because they frequently incorporate treatment, offer a better chance of altering the drug-user's behavior, thus preventing further criminal activity once that person is released from the direct control of the criminal justice system. Second, these sanctions are often less expensive; when used for nonviolent offenders, they do not significantly increase the risk of harm for the citizenry in general, and they release resources for the apprehension and punishment of violent offenders. Two such sanctions that are now being used are drug courts, authorized by Title V of the Violent Crime Control and Enforcement Act of 1994, and supervised probation.

§ 5.4 THE GET-TOUGH APPROACH

The "get tough" approach is based on a theory of deterrence that is superficially persuasive. If we raise the cost of selling and using drugs by increasing penalties, it is assumed, we will drive out dealers and sellers. In the abstract, the theory seems to make sense. In practice, when we delve more deeply into its operation, we can understand how and why it doesn't work and may even worsen the drug problem.

One reason why the War on Drugs is inefficient is that there are specific impediments to law enforcement that do not seem soluble, no matter what level of resources is devoted to the effort. If we believe, as most observers of the drug trade believe, that authorities interdict around 10% to, at most, 15% of the shipments of drugs, record seizures suggest the enormity of the drug supply and the relatively efficient organization of the suppliers.

Data reported in the National Drug Control Strategy, February 2002, Trends in Heroin Supply 1996-2000, indicates the amount of heroin available for consumption in the United States has remained at a fairly constant level as well as heroin availability outside the United States.

While the current policy of interdiction does not appear to be particularly effective, it also seems unlikely that any other War on Drugs or crime control strategy would represent much of an improvement. In economic terms, much of the demand for drugs appears to be relatively inelastic. Addicts have a physical or powerful psychological need for the drug to which they are addicted, and their level of use tends to be driven by their needs rather than the price. Other users may have psychological needs that also make them relatively insensitive to price, as people are with respect to medical care and funeral services.

Not only has the War on Drugs been ineffective, but it has caused positive harm by corrupting the nation's character. Unfortunately, we are all too familiar with the legendary narcotics scandals that have plagued police departments in various cities. In addition, the desire of law enforcement officials to show results in the War on Drugs, specifically by obtaining large fines or large numbers of convictions, has led to a more subtle form of corruption. It has been shown that low-level drug offenders (possession of drugs) are most representative of our prison drug population. For example, for the total estimated drug arrests for the year 2000, approximately 41% were arrested for marijuana possession as contrasted to 5-6% for marijuana sales/cultivation (USDOJ 2001). Upper-level drug traffickers either do not get arrested or have money or information to trade, so they have a better chance of a plea bargain with district attorneys. It's no secret that law enforcement has grown dependent on asset seizures to offset drug investigation expenditures.

A second problem that the War on Drugs poses for the national character is that prison has begun to lose any sense of terror for many urban youth. As penalties for drug use and sale have escalated, increasing numbers of sellers and users have been incarcerated. As of March 7, 1996, the second anniversary of the passage of California's "Three-Strikes" law (See "California's Three Strikes Law," this chapter), data released by the California Department of Corrections and analyzed by San Francisco's Center on Juvenile and Criminal Justice showed that more persons have been imprisoned under the "Three-Strikes" law for possession (not sale) of drugs than for all violent offenses combined. Indeed, the data show that twice as many defendants have been imprisoned for marijuana possession under "Three-Strikes" than for murder, rape, and kidnaping combined. Prison ceases to be a dreaded punishment and becomes instead an integral part of the dominant culture for urban minorities. Moreover, it often reinforces troublesome behavior. Already consigned to the margins of society, prisoners join gangs, use drugs, and make useful connections for buying and selling drugs.

§ 5.5 POLICY IMPLICATIONS

An interesting question to ask is why crime control and victim advocate groups are not demanding expansion of parent training and interventions for young delinquents rather than mandatory sentences. One answer must be our society's current faith in the value of "toughness" as opposed to treatment or prevention-oriented approaches. We have seen this clearly illustrated in the War on Drugs, where enforcement has received much greater funding than treatment in spite of clear evidence that the latter is seven times more cost-effective than the former. It is apparently much easier and more satisfying to spend money forcibly restraining misbehavior than to spend it on programs designed to bring about voluntary changes in behavior, even though the latter are more efficient.

Another reason much be the basic mistrust in government to run complicated programs. A majority of citizens seem to believe that the government is not very good at anything, from delivering mail to running schools. However, this skepticism does not appear to extend to state-run prison systems, which have become the fastest-growing segment of government.

How to go about convincing policymakers and voters of the crime-control benefits to be derived from investing in early prevention programs appears to be a real problem. It would help considerably to have several pilot programs under way, which include rigorous impact evaluations. In order to detect a 10% reduction in recidivism, it is necessary to compare the outcomes for 200 or more participants randomly assigned to the experimental program against a similar size group randomly assigned to the current pattern of dispositions and/or treatment, which is usually no treatment or supervision at all. The cost for such an evaluation is likely to be well in excess of $2 million—much more than is currently available from governmental or foundation sources for program development and testing purposes.

This brings us to the final Catch-22 of crime prevention efforts. One of the reasons the public may have more faith in imprisonment than early prevention efforts is that the crime reduction benefits of prevention are more difficult and expensive to document. Yet most criminologists would argue that there will not be any substantial reduction in crime rates without significant prevention efforts that seriously address the root causes and risk factors that clearly contribute to the development of criminal behavior.

§ 5.6 COST-EFFECTIVENESS

Early intervention programs offer an alternative means of reducing serous crime. The parent training and early intervention programs for young juvenile offenders are 4-5 times more cost-effective than "Three-Strike" mandatory sentences in preventing serious and violent crimes. Even if the impacts of these programs are only half what we estimated from the literature, they will still be twice as effective as "Three-Strikes." Furthermore, not only are they less costly ways of achieving the reductions in serious crime, but their impacts are felt fairly soon after their imposition, with only three or four years' delay in the case of early intervention for delinquents and 7-10 years for parent training.

The cost-effectiveness of early childhood and broad school-based interventions, in comparison to mandatory sentences, in not nearly as clear-cut. These two interventions require very large expenditures to affect large numbers of youth and only begin to produce cost-effective crime reduction benefits 15-20 years after they are implemented. Of course, both of these interventions may have large collateral benefits in terms of improved school performance, lower healthcare costs, and gains in worker productivity. Justification of either of these large-scale programs on cost-effective grounds is likely to provide an alternative policy option for dealing with violent offenders by diverting them from turning violent and thereby preventing the harm that they would otherwise cause. The other half of the equation consists of the nonviolent offenders currently in prison, who are occupying California's incapacitation facilities and absorbing the relatively high annual expenditures that such incapacitation demands, The question is whether a more cost-effective means can be found for dealing with this large and rapidly growing population.

Again, the question must be asked in terms of political realities. Clearly, there is a strong public demand that criminals—even nonviolent criminals—be punished for their antisocial actions. The inclusion of burglars and drug sellers in California's "Three-Strikes" law received strong support from the public in general and from victims' rights groups in particular. But this does not conclude the issue. Prison is only one way of punishing criminals. It possesses the great virtue of incapacitating the criminal from committing other offenses, and for violent criminals, the principle of harm reduction supports the use of this approach. But when there is no reason to believe that the offender is violent, other means of punishment may be more cost-effective and still sufficiently punitive to be politically acceptable. Such alternatives can contribute to harm reduction by freeing prison beds and budgets for violent offenders. In addition, it may offer more effective strategies for deterring criminals who, even if imprisoned, will be back on the streets within a relatively short period of time. Such deterrence is important, because the decision of these people to obey the law or turn toward more serious violations will also affect how many citizens are victimized by crime.

§ 5.7 THE NATURE OF INTERMEDIATE SANCTIONS

Proponents of prison diversion often fail to answer the question: If not prison, then what? Many prisoners who might be diverted cannot simply be released outright with no supervision, and it is often not appropriate to sentence them to routine probation supervision. In large urban California counties, "routine" supervision often equates with minimal contacts between offenders and their probation officers, infrequent drug tests, and few referrals to substance abuse or employment programs. Such a sentence seems too lenient for felons and has been shown to be ineffective in forestalling recidivism in California and elsewhere.

Many states have addressed this problem by developing "intermediate sanctions" that are tougher than traditional probation but less stringent and expensive than prison. And perhaps most importantly, they are designed to provide "partial incapacitation" benefits either by reducing the time available to commit crime or reducing the contacts with tempting targets and/or victims. During the past decade nearly every state has implemented a variety of intermediate sanctions. California has experimented less with intermediate sanctions than have other states, especially since the passage in 1978 of Proposition 13, which restricted local revenues.

The most important finding from the intermediate sanctions literature is that programs must deliver high "doses" of *both* treatment and surveillance to assure public safety and reduce recidivism. "Treatment" alone is not enough, nor is "surveillance" by itself adequate. Implementing "surveillance-only" programs, in which offenders are simply watched more closely without being given treatment or work, simply identifies failures faster and ends up costing *more* because of the reprocessing and reincarceration costs attributable to the failures. This important finding has been seen in evaluations of different types of intermediate sanctions, including intensive supervision, boot camps, electronic monitoring, and house arrest. But programs that can increase offender-to-officer contacts *and* provide treatment (for substance abuse, individual, family, and employment problems) have reduced recidivism. Offenders who received drug counseling, held jobs, paid restitution and did community service were arrested at rates 10-20% lower than others. The researchers suggested that the overall results might have been better if a greater proportion of the sample had participated in treatment, particularly drug treatment.

One of the more successful treatment programs in Southern California is the Social Recovery System. A Social Model Recovery System is a multifaceted human service organization providing mental health and alcohol and other drug services at various locations throughout California.

What has helped direct criminal defendants into treatment is the California Substance Abuse and Crime Prevention Act of 2000 (known as Proposition 36). It amended existing drug sentencing laws to require that criminal defendants convicted of certain nonviolent drug offenses be placed in drug treatment as a condition of probation instead of incarceration.

None of this should be understood as a panacea or even a second-best solution. Ultimately, the best way to minimize the harm caused by drugs lies in education and social reform, not in crime policy. There is some indication that this approach is returning to the political mainstream after its long banishment. The 2002 Drug Control Strategy reveals a shift in priorities and a recognition that primary reliance on law enforcement is not as effective as previous administrations thought it to be.

§ 5.8 CALIFORNIA'S THREE STRIKES LAW

In 1994, the atmosphere in California was politically charged on the issue of violent crime, with the public outraged over several highly publicized murders. In June 1992, 18-year-old Kimberly Reynolds was shot and killed by two repeat felons with long arrest records. Kimberly's father, Mike Reynolds, started a ballot initiative called "Three-Strikes and You're Out," to subject repeat felons to long mandatory sentences. Then, in October 1993, 12-year-old Polly Klaas was kidnaped at her

Petaluma home and found murdered months later. Eventually, Richard Allen Davis, a repeat violent offender, was convicted for her murder. Polly's father, Marc Klaas, and the powerful California Prison Guards Union added their considerable support to the "Three-Strikes" initiative and propelled the measure to victory on the November 1994 ballot as Proposition 184.

Proposition 184 substantially lengthened prison sentences for persons who had previously been convicted of a violent or serious crime. Specifically, a person who committed one prior violent or serious offense and who committed any new felony could receive twice the normal prison sentence for the new felony (the "second strike"). A person who committed two or more prior violent or serious offenses and then committed any new felony would automatically receive 25 years to life in prison (the "third strike"). An identical legislative version of Proposition 184, AB 971, was introduced in the Assembly in March 1994 by Assembly member Bill Jones. The law quickly passed the legislature, and Governor Pete Wilson signed it into law on March 8, 1994. When Proposition 184 passed in November 1994, with an approval rate of 72% of the vote, its status as a voter-approved measure gave it special protection from legislative revision. Although challenged in the courts, Proposition 184's constitutionality was affirmed in two March 2003 U.S. Supreme Court decisions, *Lockyer v. Andrade* and *Ewing v. California*. The two cases involved repeat offenders who were sentenced to prison terms of 25 years and longer after stealing golf clubs and videotapes.

Criticism of Proposition 184 has centered on its cost. Large increases in the prison population and prison expenditures followed the law's implementation. By September 1999 almost 50,000 inmates were imprisoned as second- and third-strikers. From 1983 to 2004, the prison system budget increased from $1 billion to nearly $6 billion, a fact that many consider at least partially attributable to Proposition 184. Critics of the law also note that the majority of persons imprisoned under the law are second-strikers who have committed non-violent felonies such as property crime and drug offenses, and that the system has led to excessive incarceration rates. Some claim that the law was written to give the impression that its focus was violent offenders and didn't fairly convey its impact on all felons.

Assessments of Proposition 184's impact on the crime rate vary. Some conclude that major crime in California has decreased by 50% or more since the law's implementation, making it an obvious success. They say the law is effective against repeat criminal activity because it keeps dangerous habitual criminals behind bars. They say further that by reducing repeat criminal activity, the law reduces public expenditures on law enforcement and criminal justice. Opponents claim that crime rates decreased nationally for reasons other than the "Three-Strikes" law, such as a stronger economy in the 1990s and increased incarceration under other laws. They also say that the law unfairly sentences minor felons and costs California billions of dollars every year that could be better spent in other areas.

California Drug Policy Enforcement

It all came to a head in an initiative on the California November 2004 ballot, called Proposition 66. It made it to the ballot in a climate of concern over problems inside the California prison system and alarm over state budget deficits. It was spearheaded by Citizens Against Violent Crime, a California political action committee whose chairman, Joe Klaas, is the grandfather of Polly Klaas, whose murder helped ignite the support for Proposition 184 in 1994. Proposition 66 was also backed by Sacramento businessman Jerry Keenan whose son Richard is serving time for manslaughter after crashing his car while driving drunk and killing two passengers. Proposition 66 would limit felonies that trigger the second and third strike to violent or serious crimes. It would eliminate residential burglary from the list of serious felonies that qualify as strikes, except when prosecutors prove someone was in the home at the time of the burglary. It would also direct prosecutors to count only one strike per prosecution instead of one strike per conviction, as current law requires, and it would increase penalties for child molesters. Proponents contend that Proposition 66 restores the "Three-Strikes" law's original intent to keep serious and violent criminals in prison.

Opponents of Proposition 66 include Governor Arnold Schwarzenegger, Attorney General Bill Lockyer, and several crime victims advocates groups. They contend that Proposition 66 could allow as many as 26,000 inmates back on the streets. They also accuse the main financial backer of Proposition 66, Jerry Keenan, of trying to change the law to get his son out of prison early.

Public opinion on "Three-Strikes" legislation may be undergoing a significant shift. Proposition 184 passed with 72 percent of the vote. A July 1996 *Los Angeles Times* poll found that 75% of the respondents viewed the "Three-Strikes" law as a "good thing." However, a June 2004 Field Poll found 76% of the respondents in support of Proposition 66. A *Los Angeles Times* poll on October 19 found 62% of the respondents in support of Proposition 66. In July, opponents of Proposition 66 filed suit against the sponsors of the initiative, over language which claims that Proposition 66 would "restore the original intent" of the Three-Strikes law passed in 1994. Proponents announced that they would countersue over the language in their opponents' arguments. On August 10, a Sacramento Superior Court Judge ordered both sides in the Proposition 66 debate to make changes in the language they use in their arguments. Judge Raymond Cadei required opponents to cite a different illustration of a criminal whose sentence might be shorter if the initiative passes, targeting the use of violent offenders as examples. However, he did allow opponents to quote from a California District Attorney's estimate that as many as 26,000 felons could be released from prison if the law is enacted. He also required proponents to clarify that approving the changes would not release criminals currently serving sentences for violent offenses though they could have been previously convicted of those crimes. By October 2004, there was a noticeable declining of support for Proposition 66, and in the final analysis, statewide ballot returns from the California Secretary of State reported 47.3% supported Proposition 66 and 52.7% opposed it. Efforts to reform the "Three Strikes law" in California will likely be on the ballot again.

Chapter 5

For More Information

DiCamillo, Mark. Overwhelming support for "Three-Strikes and You're Out" initiative. San Francisco: Field Institute, 1994.

Jones, Bill. "Crime is down 38% after five years of Three-Strikes." Sacramento, CA: California Secretary of State, 1999.

Males, Mike A. Striking Out : the Failure of California's "Three-Strikes and You're Out. San Francisco, CA: Justice Policy Institute, 2000

Schmertmann, Carl P. "Three-Strikes and You're Out: A demography analysis of mandatory prison sentencing," Demography 35.4 (1998).

Skolnick, Jerome H. "Wild Pitch:'Three-Strikes, You're Out' and Other Bad Calls on Crime." The American Prospect 1 (Spring 1994).

Three-Strikes and You're Out" Law's Impact on State Prisons: an Update. Sacramento, CA: Legislative Analyst's Office, 1999.

Zimring, Franklin E. Crime and punishment in California : the Impact of Three-Strikes and You're Out. Berkeley: Institute of Government Studies Press, University of California, 1999.

References

Beatty, Phillip, Barry Holman and Vincent Schiraldi. Poor Prescription: The Costs of Imprisoning Drug Offenders in the United States. Washington, D.C.: The Justice Policy Institute, 2000.

Drug Enforcement Administration. Factsheet California, Drugs and Drug Abuse. DEA Regional Offices, 2005.

Drug Use and Justice: An Examination of California Drug Policy Enforcement. San Francisco: Center on Juvenile and Criminal Justice, 2000.

Federal Bureau of Investigation. Crime in the United States. Washington, D.C.: U.S. De partment of Justice, 2001.

Harrell, A., S. Cavanaugh, J. Roman. Evaluation of the D.C. Superior Court Intervention Programs. Washington, D.C.: United States Department of Justice, 2000.

Henham, Ralph. "Theory, Rights and Sentencing Policy." International Journal of the Sociology of Law 27 (1999).

Jones, Bill. "Why the Three Strikes Law Is Working in California." Stanford Law & Policy Review. 11.1 (1999).

Lurigio, Arthur and James A. Swartz. "The Nexus Between Drugs and Crime: Theory, Research, and Practice." Federal Probation 82 (1999).

Maxwell, Sheila R. "Conservative Sanctioning and Correctional Innovations in the United States: An Examination of Recent Trends." International Journal of the Sociology of Law 27 (1999).

Sentencing Project. Drug Policy and the Criminal Justice System. Washington, D.C: U.S. Department of Justice, 1998.

The White House. National Drug Control Strategy. Washington, D.C.: Supervisor of Documents, U.S. Government Printing Office, 2002.

Tonry, Michael. "Why Are U.S. Incarceration Rates So High?" Crime and Delinquency 45 (1999).

CHAPTER 6

CENTRAL NERVOUS SYSTEM DEPRESSANTS

§ 6.1 INTRODUCTION

Drugs that slow down mental and physical functions of the body are known generally as central nervous system (CNS) depressants. Since these chemical agents tend to produce a calming effect, relax muscles, and relieve feelings of tension, anxiety, and irritability, they are also described as having a sedative or sedating effect. Such drugs are referred to as sedatives.

At higher dose levels, sedatives also produce drowsiness and eventually a state resembling natural sleep. Drugs that have such a sleep-inducing effect are called hypnotics. This hypnotic effect has nothing to do whatsoever with the artificially induced state of suggestibility often associated with the word "hypnosis." Nevertheless, the combination term of "sedative/hypnotic" appropriately identifies the major pharmacological effects of these drugs.[1]

This term encompasses two overlapping classes of central nervous system depressant drugs, sedatives and hypnotics, which are similar in effect and are often used interchangeably. Although benzodiazepines and barbiturates may be included, the term may also be used when referring to a group of non-barbiturate drugs with properties similar to, but chemically distinct from, barbiturates and from each other.

§ 6.2 HISTORY OF DEPRESSANTS

Depressant drugs have been used throughout history. Herbs and alcohol were used to produce stupor and sleep. During the early 1900s, ether, chloroform, and nitrous oxide were used to produce a "high."

Rauwolfia serpentina, the Indian snakeroot shrub common to India and Southeast Asia, had been used for centuries to treat many diseases, including high blood pressure and mental disorders. It was not until the 1950s that Rauwolfia's active ingredient, reserpine, was used clinically as an antipsychotic agent. Reserpine ushered in the age of the so-called "major tranquilizers" that revolutionized treatment of the mentally ill. Because of reserpine's adverse side effects, the derivative of the Indian snakeroot was soon replaced by the chlorpromazine family of antipsychotic agents.

---

[1] Specific drugs include acetylcarbromal, Aquachloral, chloral hydrate, chlormethiazole, dexmedetomidine, Doriden, ethchlorvynol, ethinamate, Equanil, Felsules, glutethimide, Kessodrate, meprobamate, Mequin, methaqualone, methyprylon, Miltown, Noctec, Noludar, paraldehyde, Paxarel, Placidyl, Precedex, Quaalude, Salacen, Somnos, Sopor, thalidomide, Thalomid, tybamate, Tybatran, and Valmid.

Chapter 6

The very first drug introduced as a sedative/hypnotic was bromide. In the 1860s, potassium bromide entered the practice of medicine as a treatment for epileptic convulsions. Due to its irritating effects on the gastrointestinal tract and its tendency to accumulate in the body, leading to chronic bromide intoxication (bromism), bromide was replaced by barbiturates upon their introduction in the early 1900s.

Supposedly synthesized by Adolph von Baeyer on December 4, 1862 (St. Barbara's Day), the name "barbiturates" was derived from the popular local saint's name. In 1903, barbital, a derivative of barbituric acid, was introduced. Its sleep-inducing and anxiolytic effects made it very desirable in clinical medicine. It soon became popular as a treatment for anxiety and as the first "sleeping pill." In 1912, phenobarbital was introduced. Phenobarbital, in addition to sedative/hypnotic properties, has anticonvulsant properties and has become one of the most important pharmacological treatments for epilepsy. The success of barbital and phenobarbital spawned the synthesis of over 2,500 barbiturates. Of these many barbiturate analogues, only about 20 are still on the market. The effects of these various barbiturates are generally similar, only differing primarily in potency and duration of action.

The partial separation of sedative-hypnotic-anesthetic properties from anticonvulsant properties found in phenobarbital led researchers to search for agents with more selective effects on the functions of the CNS. In the late 1930s, relatively nonsedative anticonvulsants were developed (e.g., phenytoin and trimethadione). In 1957 the first benzodiazepine, chlordia-zepoxide (Librium) was synthesized. Benzodiazepines have demonstrated the ability to relieve symptoms of anxiety with relatively little interference with cognitive function or wakefulness. Benzodiazepines and barbiturates share very similar properties, but the benzodiazepines have been demonstrated to have a much safer pharmacological profile. Benzodiazepines have, therefore, replaced barbiturates for most uses, particularly for treatment of anxiety and sleep disturbances.

Sedative/hypnotic drugs depress behavior, moderate excitement, and induce calmness. These drugs depress the central nervous system; however, they usually produce therapeutic benefits at far lower doses than those causing substantial generalized depression of behavior.

§ 6.3 BARBITURATES
Barbiturates have a wider and more powerful effect on the central nervous system than the other sedatives. The barbiturates can produce varying degrees of depression of the CNS, ranging from mild sedation to general anesthesia. In low doses barbiturates have a calming effect, and some of the barbiturates (e.g., phenobarbital) have demonstrated selective anticonvulsant properties. In moderate doses they produce a drunken euphoric state, similar to alcohol. Sedation and sleep result from increased doses, and even higher doses produce surgical anesthesia. Because of their ability to produce sedation and decrease sleep latency, barbiturates were popular in the treatment of insomnia prior to the

advent of benzodiazepines. However, because of the high incidence of tolerance and physical dependence following chronic use and the relatively high danger of overdose, these drugs are rarely used today for the treatment of anxiety.

Today, about a dozen are in medical use. Barbiturates produce a wide spectrum of central nervous system depression, from mild sedation to coma, and have been used as sedatives, hypnotics, anesthetics, and anticonvulsants. The primary differences among many of these products are how fast they produce an effect and how long those effects last. Barbiturates are classified as ultrashort, short, intermediate, and long-acting.

The ultrashort-acting barbiturates produce anesthesia within about one minute after intravenous administration. Those in current medical use are the Schedule IV drug methohexital (Brevital), and the Schedule III drugs thiamyl (Surital) and thiopental (Pentothal). Barbiturate abusers prefer the Schedule II short-acting and intermediate-acting barbiturates that include amobarbital (Amytal), pentobarbital (Nembutal), secobarbital (Seconal), and Tuinal (an amobarbital/secobarbital combination product). Other short- and intermediate-acting barbiturates are in Schedule III and include butalbital (Fiorinal), butabarbital (Butisol), talbutal (Lotusate), and aprobarbital (Alurate). After oral administration, the onset of action is from 15 to 40 minutes, and the effects last up to six hours. These drugs are primarily used for insomnia and preoperative sedation. Veterinarians use pentobarbital for anesthesia and euthanasia.

Long-acting barbiturates include phenobarbital (Luminal) and mephobarbital (Mebaral), both of which are in Schedule IV. Effects of these drugs are realized in about one hour and last for about 12 hours and are used primarily for daytime sedation and the treatment of seizure disorders.

The two barbiturates that are still abused today in the United States are Mebaral (mephobarbital) and Nembutal (pentobarbital). These drugs have been replaced in therapeutic practice by benzodiazepines such as Valium (diazepam).

§ 6.4 BENZODIAZEPINES

Barbiturates and benzodiazepines act similarly to produce depression of central nervous system function and behavior. Both classes of drugs enhance the ability of the inhibitory neurotransmitter, gamma-aminobutyric acid (GABA), to activate a type of receptors known as GABA-A receptors. These drugs increase the effectiveness of GABA by altering the receptor so that GABA can bind more easily, an effect known as "allosteric regulation." Activation of the GABA-A receptor opens an ion channel, allowing negatively charged chloride ions to enter the cell, producing an inhibition of neuronal activity.

§ 6.4.1 Benzodiazepines & Allosteric Regulation

Therefore, benzodiazepines are drugs that reduce anxiety, enhance sleep, and reduce seizures. Examples of this drug class are Valium, Librium, Xanax, and Tranxene. These drugs are thought to work by enhancing or mimicking the effects of gamma-aminobutyric acid (GABA), an inhibitory neurotransmitter, in certain parts of the limbic system. The limbic system is the part of the brain where emotions and "mood" are thought to arise.

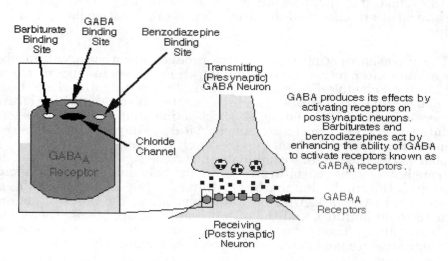

In addition to barbiturates and benzodiazepines, ethanol (alcohol) appears to produce depression of central nervous system function, in part by enhancing the ability of GABA to bind to the GABA-A receptor. This may explain why these three classes of drugs potentiate each others' effects and why tolerance to one results in cross-tolerance to another.

Benzodiazepines are effective in reducing anxiety (anxiolytics) and in promoting sleep (hypnotics). Anxiolytic benzodiazepines include alprazolam (Xanax), chlordiazepoxide (Librium), and diazepam (Valium). Hypnotic benzodiazepines include flurazepam (Dalmane), triazolam (Halcion), and temazepam (Restoril).

Benzodiazepines share the sedative-hypnotic properties, but produce fewer side effects than barbiturates. Like barbiturates, benzodiazepines have also been reported to produce anticonvulsant effects. In addition, these drug are used clinically as muscle relaxants, antiepileptic agents, and to produce sedation before operative procedures. The antianxiety effects of benzodiazepines are more selective than those of other sedative/hypnotics—they relieve anxiety at lower doses and thus produce minimal sedation and motor impairment. The benzodiazepines are currently the most important class of drugs for treatment of anxiety and sleep disorders.

Central Nervous System Depressants

In general, benzodiazepines act as hypnotics in high doses, anxiolytics in moderate doses, and sedatives in low doses. Of the drugs marketed in the United States that affect central nervous system function, benzodiazepines are among the most widely prescribed medications. Fifteen members of this group are presently marketed in the United States, and about 20 additional benzodiazepines are marketed in other countries. Benzodiazepines are controlled in Schedule IV of the U.S. Controlled Substances Act (CSA).

Short-acting benzodiazepines are generally used for patients with sleep-onset insomnia (difficulty falling asleep) without daytime anxiety. Shorter-acting benzodiazepines used to manage insomnia include estazolam (ProSom), flurazepam (Dalmane), temazepam (Restoril), and triazolam (Halcion). Midazolam (Versed), a short-acting benzodiazepine, is utilized for sedation, anxiety, and amnesia in critical care settings and prior to anesthesia. It is available in the United States as an injectable preparation and as a syrup (primarily for pediatric patients).

Benzodiazepines with a longer duration of action are utilized to treat insomnia in patients with daytime anxiety. These benzodiazepines include alprazolam (Xanax), chlordiazepoxide (Librium), clorazepate (Tranxene), diazepam (Valium), halazepam (Paxipam), lorazepam (Ativan), oxazepam (Serax), prazepam (Centrax), and quazepam (Doral). Clonazepam (Klonopin), diazepam, and clorazepate are also used as anticonvulsants.

Benzodiazepines are classified in the CSA as depressants. Repeated use of large doses or, in some cases, daily use of therapeutic doses of benzodiazepines is associated with amnesia, hostility, irritability, and vivid or disturbing dreams, as well as tolerance and physical dependence. The withdrawal syndrome is similar to that of alcohol and may require hospitalization. Abrupt cessation of benzodiazepines is not recommended and tapering down the dose eliminates many of the unpleasant symptoms.

Given the millions of prescriptions written for benzodiazepines (about 100 million in 1999), relatively few individuals increase their dose on their own initiative or engage in drug-seeking behavior. Those individuals who do abuse benzodiazepines often maintain their drug supply by getting prescriptions from several doctors, forging prescriptions, or buying diverted pharmaceutical products on the illicit market. Abuse is frequently associated with adolescents and young adults who take benzodiazepines to obtain a "high." This intoxicated state results in reduced inhibition and impaired judgment. Concurrent use of alcohol or other depressants with benzodiazepines can be life-threatening. Abuse of benzodiazepines is particularly high among heroin and cocaine abusers. A large percentage of people entering treatment for narcotic or cocaine addiction also report abusing benzodiazepines. Alprazolam and diazepam are the two most frequently encountered benzodiazepines on the illicit market.

Zolpidem (Ambien) and zaleplon (Sonata) are two relatively new, benzodiazepine-like CNS depressants that have been approved for the short-term treatment of insomnia. Both of these drugs share many of the same properties as the benzodiazepines and are in Schedule IV of the CSA.

§ 6.4.2 Xanax (Alprazolam)

Xanax is a benzodiazepine. It is medically used for anxiety disorders and short-term relief of symptoms of anxiety. Xanax is available in tablets of 0.25, 0.5, and 1 mg. Long-term use of Xanax creates drug tolerance and physical dependence and eventually addiction. Abrupt discontinuance or a rapid decrease in dosage can cause withdrawal seizures. Other barbiturate-like reactions, ranging from mild dysphoria and insomnia to a major syndrome characterized by abdominal and muscle cramps, vomiting, sweating, tremors, and convulsions, have resulted from abrupt withdrawal from benzodiazepine drugs.

§ 6.4.3 Valium (Diazepam)

Valium is a benzodiazepine, a minor tranquilizer used to relieve mild to moderate anxiety and nervous tension. It is also used for sleep and for muscle spasm. Valium is illegally used most often by polydrug users. Although the number of diazepam users has declined, it is still a widely used and misused benzodiazepine. Illicit use of diazepam-opioid(heroin) combination is very common among heroin addicts. Addicts may self-medicate to reduce the unpleasant effects of the withdrawal syndrome associated with a decrease in their supply of the drug.

§ 6.4.4 Dalmane (Flurazepam)

Dalmane is a benzodiazepine. Its primary medical use is for the treatment of insomnia. It is used exclusively as a minor tranquilizer at bedtime to induce sleep. Extensive use will create psychological dependency and physical dependency. A moderate overdose will induce drowsiness, drunkenness, and impairment of coordination. A larger overdose will create a stupor, deep sleep, and coma.

§ 6.5 CHLORAL HYDRATE

The oldest of the hypnotic (sleep-inducing) depressants, chloral hydrate was first synthesized in 1832. Marketed as syrups or soft gelatin capsules, chloral hydrate takes effect in a relatively short time (30 minutes) and will induce sleep in about an hour. A solution of chloral hydrate and alcohol constituted the infamous "knockout drops" or "Mickey Finn." At therapeutic doses, chloral hydrate has little effect on respiration and blood pressure; however, a toxic dose produces severe respiratory depression and very low blood pressure. Chronic use is associated with liver damage and a severe withdrawal syndrome. Although some physicians consider chloral hydrate to be the drug of choice for sedation of children before diagnostic, dental, or medical procedures, it's general use as a hypnotic has declined. Chloral hydrate (Noctec and other) and compounds, preparations, or mixtures containing chloral hydrate are in Schedule IV of the CSA.

§ 6.6 PARALDEHYDE

Paraldehyde (Paral) is a Schedule IV depressant used most frequently in hospital settings to treat delirium tremens ("the d.t.'s") associated with alcohol withdrawal. Many individuals who become addicted to paraldehyde have been initially exposed during treatment for alcoholism and, despite the disagreeable odor and taste, come to prefer it to alcohol. This drug is not used by injection because of tissue damage and, taken orally, it can be irritating to the throat and stomach. One of the signs of paraldehyde use is a strong, unpleasant breath odor that smells like a combination of acetic acid (vinegar) and sulfuric acid.

§ 6.7 GLUTETHIMIDE & METHAQUALONE

Glutethimide (Doriden) was introduced in 1954 and methaqualone ("Quaalude" Sopor) in 1965 as safe barbiturate substitutes. Experience demonstrated, however, that their addiction liability and the severity of withdrawal symptoms were similar to those of barbiturates. By 1972, "luding out," taking methaqualone with wine, was a popular college pastime. Excessive use leads to tolerance, dependence, and withdrawal symptoms similar to those of barbiturates. In the United States, the marketing of methaqualone pharmaceutical products stopped in 1984, and methaqualone was transferred to Schedule I of the CSA. In 1991, glutethimide was transferred into Schedule II in response to an upsurge in the prevalence of diversion, abuse, and overdose deaths. Today, there is little medical use of glutethimide in the United States.

§ 6.8 MEPROBAMATE

Whatever happened to meprobamate? It was introduced as an anti-anxiety drug in 1955, and was distributed under the brand names Miltown and Equanil. The drug is still being produced today but has been pretty much replaced by benzodiazepines. Meprobamate is characterized by its low potency (many milligrams needed to produce an effect), its hangover, and its addiction potential. One drug similar to meprobamate that still gives us trouble is Soma (carisoprodol), used to produce skeletal-muscle relaxation. Unfortunately, some individuals are abusing Soma because of its sedative qualities. Carisoprodol is metabolized to meprobamate. This conversion may account for some of the properties associated with carisoprodol and likely contributes to its abuse.

§ 6.9 PLACIDYL (ETHCHLORVYNOL)

Placidyl (trade name for ethchlorvynol) is a nonbarbiturate sedative/hypnotic. Users report that Placidyl seems to have the most euphoriant effects of the CNS depressants. Placidyl is available in 100-, 200-, 500-, and 750-mg capsules and is rapidly absorbed from the gastrointestinal tract. It has extremely rapid onset of action and short duration of action (about 3 to 5 hours). Peak plasma concentrations are observed within 1 to 1 hours after ingestion. It is metabolized by the liver, and inactive metabolites are excreted in urine.

Placidyl has anticonvulsant and muscle-relaxant properties. It only slightly affects REM sleep, and discontinuation produces less REM rebound than with many other sedative/hypnotics. It produces a mintlike

Chapter 6

aftertaste and hangover is frequently reported. Continued use results in concentrations of active metabolites stored in fatty tissue. If using it as a sedative (although they probably should not be), people should be urged not to drive or operate heavy equipment because coordination can be impaired. As for the euphoriant properties of Placidyl, rapid absorption results in giddiness. Paradoxical excitement can occur, with delirium and incoordination. Recreational users describe Placidyl's effects as very pleasant, calm, and happy with initial mild stimulation. Placidyl, when available, is usually the preferred sedative/hypnotic for the more experienced CNS depressant user-abuser. However, if someone who is psychologically depressed takes Placidyl, his or her depression may increase.

Tolerance can quickly develop to the sedative/hypnotic and mood effects of Placidyl. It is a drug that produces physical dependence quite readily. Physical dependence can occur with daily administration of one gram or more for four weeks. Note that one gram is only twice the hypnotic dose; as you can see, the safety margin of Placidyl is quite small. Once physical dependence develops, continued administration is necessary if withdrawal symptoms are to be avoided. Chronic abusers may take up to 4 grams daily. The chronic dependent abuser shows intoxication symptoms similar to those of an alcoholic. Symptoms include incoordination, tremors, slurred speech, and confusion. Abrupt discontinuation results in withdrawal symptoms remarkably similar to delirium tremens (the d.t.'s) or the major abstinence syndrome seen in alcohol withdrawal.

§ 6.10   PROZAC (FLUOXETINE HYDROCHLORIDE)
Prozac is found in either a light green oval pill with "Prozac 10 mg" imprinted on it or a green/white capsule with "Lilly 90 mg" printed on the side. It is an antidepressant for oral administration. It inhibits or blocks the uptake of serotonin (a brain chemical). The primary medical use of Prozac is for the treatment of depression. It is metabolized in the liver. The half-life of Prozac is 2 to 3 days, which means an accumulation of the chemical in the body with chronic use. Even when the drug is discontinued, the active drug substance will persist in the body for weeks. Prozac has not been systematically studied in animals or humans for its potential for abuse, tolerance, or physical dependency (PDR 1993).

There have been several deaths attributed to the overdose of Prozac. These involved the use of 1,800 mg to 3,000 mg of the drug. Nausea and vomiting are the prominent signs of a Prozac overdose. The other signs are agitation, restlessness, and central nervous system excitation. Most overdose cases recover.

§ 6.11   PREDATORY DRUGS
There are drugs that are used to facilitate sexual assault and to prey on other people. Some have been known as the "date rape" drug. People may unknowingly be given the drug which, when mixed with alcohol, can incapacitate a person and prevent him or her from resisting sexual assault. The drugs are odorless when dissolved in water. They are somewhat salty tasting but not detected when dissolved in alcohol, soda,

juice, or beer. Due to memory problems caused by the drug, the victim may not realize the attack until 8 to 12 hours after it occurred. The drugs are also metabolized quickly, so there may be little physical evidence that the drugs were used to facilitate an assault. Current predatory drugs are Rohypnol, GHB and its analogues GBL and 1, 4 BD, and Ketamine.

§ 6.11.1 Rohypnol (Flunitrazepam)

Flunitrazepam (Rohypnol) is a benzodiazepine that is not manufactured or legally marketed in the United States, but is smuggled in by traffickers. In the mid-1990s, flunitrazepam was extensively trafficked in Florida and Texas. Street names include R-2, Mexican Valium, rophies, roach, and roofies (ONDCP 1999).

Flunitrazepam gained popularity among younger individuals as a "party" drug. It has also been utilized as a "date rape" drug. In this context, flunitrazepam is placed in the alcoholic drink of an unsuspecting victim to incapacitate them and prevent resistance from sexual assault. The victim is frequently unaware of what has happened to them and often does not report the incident to authorities. A number of actions by the manufacturer of this drug and by government agencies have resulted in reducing the availability and abuse of flunitrazepam in the United States.

Rohypnol is manufactured in pill form. The licit market for the drug is currently supplied with a 1-milligram dose in an olive-green oblong tablet, imprinted with the number 542. The new tablet includes a dye that, according to Hoffman-La Roche (the makers of Rohypnol), will be visible if it slipped into a drink. Rohypnol is usually taken orally in pill form, but can also be crushed and snorted (NIDA 1999).

In Latin America and Europe, Rohypnol is prescribed to patients as a short-term treatment for insomnia and as a preanesthetic medication. Rohypnol continues to be abused among teenagers and young adults, usually at raves and nightclubs.[2]

Rohypnol is not approved for use in the United States and its importation is banned. Rohypnol is usually smuggled into the United States by way of mail or delivery services. The drug remains readily

---

[2] A rave (similar to a dance party) is a large get-together comprised mostly of young people. At raves, disc jockeys and synchronized light shows are featured, and drug use is condoned. Drugs used at raves include the so-called "club drugs"—MDMA (ecstasy), LSD, methamphetamine, Rohypnol ("roofies"), Ketamine ("special K," "vitamin K"), and GHB ("liquid ecstasy"). These are either used alone or in combination with alcohol. Most raves are well attended (generally 100 to 500 people), and are advertised on the Internet, in music stores (posters), and by word of mouth. While illegal drugs are bought and used at raves, authorities are usually outnumbered at such places, so the number of arrests is relatively small. Club drugs are presumably taken to enhance people's experiences during dance parties and raves. In spite of common belief, all of these drugs are dangerous and can trigger addiction. These drugs affect neurotransmitters in the brain, and most are lethal with mixed with alcohol.

available, mainly through pharmaceutical operators located in Mexico, especially Tijuana. Reports indicate that Rohypnol is often sold for between $2 and $5 per dosage unit, although it may sell for as much as $10 to $30 per dosage unit (DEA 2001).

One of the significant effects of the drug is anterograde amnesia, a factor that strongly contributed to its inclusion in the Drug-Induced Rape Prevention Act of 1996. Anterograde amnesia is a condition in which events that occurred while under the influence of the drug are forgotten. In addition to the chemically induced amnesia, Rohypnol often causes decreased blood pressure, drowsiness, visual disturbances, dizziness, confusion, gastrointestinal disturbances, urinary retention, and the development of physical and psychological dependence.

Another very similar drug is now being sold as "roofies" in Miami, Minnesota, and Texas. This is clonazepam, marketed in the United States as Klonopin and in Mexico as Rivotril. It sometimes is abused to enhance the effects of heroin and other opiates. Based on emergency room admission information, Boston, San Francisco, Phoenix, and Seattle appear to have the highest use rates of clonazepam.

§ 6.11.2 GHB

Since about 1990, GHB (gamma-hydroxybutyrate) has been abused in the United States for euphoric, sedative, and anabolic (body building) effects. As with Rohypnol and clonazepam, GHB has been associated with sexual assault in cities throughout the country. Gamma-hydroxybutyric acid (GHB) is a Schedule I depressant. GHB, as well as its analogs GBL (gamma-butyrolactone) and BD (1, 4-butanediol), is available in every region of the country. They are used as recreational drugs for their euphoric and sedative effects. GHB abuse became popular among teens and young adults at dance clubs and raves in the 1990s and also gained notoriety as a date rape drug.

GHB analogs often are abused in place of GHB. Both GBL and BD metabolize to GHB upon ingestion. However, only GBL is converted to GHB by a chemical reaction. the ingestion of these analogs produces physiological effects similar to GHB. GBL and BD are sold under the guise of cleaning products and nail polish remover.

On July 17, 2002, the U.S. Food and Drug Administration (FDA) approved a GHB-containing product, Xyrem (sodium oxybate, GHB) with Orphan Drug Status. Xyrem oral solution is approved as a treatment to reduce the incidences of cataplexy (sudden attacks of muscle weakness) in patients with narcolepsy. (The FDA's orphan drug program encourages research, development, and approval of products for diseases affecting fewer than 200,000 patients in the United States.)

§ 6.11.2(a)   Chemistry and Pharmacology:

Traffickers produce GHB using a simple chemical reaction between GBL and either sodium or potassium hydroxide. GHB itself is a solid substance but is generally dissolved in liquid. Confiscated samples have been found in a variety of plastic bottles.

GHB occurs naturally in the central nervous system in very small amounts. Scientific data suggest that GHB can function as a neurotransmitter or neuromodulator in the brain. It produces dose-dependent depressant effects similar to those of the barbiturates and methaqualone. Low doses of GHB produce drowsiness, nausea, and visual distortion. High doses of GHB can result in unconsciousness, seizures, slowed heart rate, severe respiratory depression, hypothermia, vomiting, coma, or death. 57% and 56% of GHB-related emergency room visits in 2001 and 2002, respectively, were due to an overdose and 29% and 33% of the visits, respectively, were for unexpected reactions. Chronic abuse of GHB can produce a withdrawal syndrome characterized by insomnia, anxiety, tremors, marked autonomic activation (i.e., increased heart rate and blood pressure), and occasional psychotic thoughts. Currently, there is no antidote available for GHB intoxication.

§ 6.11.2(b)   Illicit Uses:
GHB is abused for its euphoric and sedative effects and its alleged role as a growth-hormone-releasing agent to stimulate muscle growth. Because of its anesthetic properties, GHB also has been used by sexual predators to incapacitate their victims. GHB is mainly self-ingested orally in a liquid mixture. GHB is a solid that is easily dissolved in a liquid and packaged in vials or small bottles. In liquid form GHB is clear and colorless and slightly salty in taste. The presence of GHB in the liquid can be detected by shaking the liquid. If it becomes cloudy, GHB may be present. The average oral dose range is from 1 to 5 grams. The onset of action after oral ingestion occurs within 15 to 30 minutes, with duration of effects lasting 3 to 6 hours. The recreational dose is very close to the dose that can induce coma in humans.

§ 6.11.2(c)   Control Status:
On March 13, 2000, GHB, including its salts, isomers, and salts of isomers, were placed in Schedule I of the Controlled Substances Act. At the recommendation of the World Health Organization, on March 20, 2001, the Commission on Narcotic Drugs added GHB to Schedule IV of the 1971 Convention on Psychotropic Substances. GBL became a List I chemical, subject to the criminal, civil, and administrative sanctions of the CSA, on February 18, 2000, under the provisions of the "Hillary Farias and Samantha Reid Date-Rape Prohibition Act." Xyrem is a Schedule III controlled substance. Abuse of Xyrem will be subject to Schedule I sanctions per the "Hillary Farias and Samantha Reid Date-Rape Prohibition Act." Thus, any person who sells, distributes, or gives Xyrem to someone else, or who uses Xyrem for purposes other than what it is prescribed for, may be punished under federal and state laws.

§ 6.11.3 Ketamine
Ketamine is covered in Chapter XIII, Hallucinogenic/Psychedelic Drugs.

§6.12   SHORT-ACTING DEPRESSANTS & THEIR EFFECTS
–Onset of effect: 10-20 minutes
–Duration of effect: 4-5 hours
–Length of physical withdrawal symptoms: 1-4 days

Generic	Brand Name	Street Name
Pentobarbital	Nembutal	Yellows, Yellow Jackets
Secobarbital	Seconal	Reds, Red Devils
Ethchlorvynol	Placidyl	Dillies
Ethinamate	ValmidAmytal	
Paraldehyde	ParalAmytal	
Chloral Hydrate	Noctec, Kessodrate	Mickey Finns, Knock-out drops

§ 6.13 INTERMEDIATE-ACTING DEPRESSANTS & THEIR EFFECTS

—Onset of effect: 20-40 minutes
—Duration of effect: 6-8 hours
—Length of physical withdrawal symptoms: 7-8 days

Generic	Brand Name	Street Name
Amobarbital	Amytal	Blues, Blue Heavens
Amosecobarbital*	Tuinal	Rainbows, Tuies, Christmas trees
Butabarbital	Buticaps, Butisol	
Meprobamate	Miltown, Equanil	
Methaqualone	Quaalude, Sopor, Parest, Mequin	Quaalude, Sopor's
Methyprylon	Noludar	
Glutethimide	Doriden	

*Short onset of action, 10-20 minutes—Intermediate duration of effect.

§ 6.14 LONG-ACTING DEPRESSANTS & THEIR EFFECTS

—Onset of effect: 1 hour
—Duration of effect: 8-14 hours
—Length of physical withdrawal symptoms: 10-14 days

Generic	Brand Name	Street Name
Phenobarbital	Luminal	Pink Ladies

§ 6.15 EFFECTS OF SEDATIVE/HYPNOTIC ABUSE

In view of the widespread use of sedative/hypnotics drugs, it is not surprising that they are frequently overused or abused, either accidentally or intentionally. Many such cases are seen in hospital emergency rooms. The instances of serious intoxication and death caused solely by benzodiazepine overdose are unusual. However, it is common for emergency rooms to experience cases of overdose involving a combination of alcohol and other sedative/hypnotic substances, such as benzodiazepines. Benzodiazepines are relatively safe substances when medically used. Their major side effect is sedation. As with any type of sedative drug, the addition of other sedating substances, such as alcohol, leads to increased sedation. While a combination of alcohol in small quantities (one or two drinks with a normal dose of benzodiazepine, 20 to 30 mg/dose of diazepine) does not produce much of a problem, the overuse of either or both will produce serious consequences.

When abused, tranquilizers cause all of the objective symptoms displayed by a drunk, except that there is generally no odor of alcohol. The degree of intoxication can produce symptoms which may vary from a euphoric "high," to sloppy drunkenness, to unconsciousness. The abuser will be drowsy, confused, and unable to think clearly. His or her coordination may be impaired when standing or walking. The abuser will be dangerous to himself or herself and to others when driving a car. The individual's speech will be thick and slurred. He or she will tremble. The abuser's eyes will "bounce" involuntarily upon movement to either side (called "nystagmus") and he or she will not be able to hold a fixed position for very long. The individual may be irritable and hostile. With large doses, he or she may fall into a deep sleep and a delirious state is not uncommon. When taken with *alcohol,* tranquilizers *are* particularly deadly, because they increase the effects of both; this effect is called *synergism.* A person who is under the influence of alcohol may take a few pills and not survive. Tranquilizers can also be fatal when taken in combination with anesthetics and narcotics.

§ 6.15.1 Objective Symptoms of Sedative/Hypnotic Drug Influence
The following is a list of the objective symptoms of a person under the influence of a depressant drug:

—Drowsiness
—Staggered gait
—Impaired coordination
—Flushed face
—Thick and slurred speech
—Nystagmus (involuntary bouncing of the eyes)
—Confusion

When these symptoms are observed and investigation rules out alcohol as the lone intoxicant, the person is under the influence of a depressant drug.

§ 6.15.2 Effects of Sedative/Hypnotic Withdrawal
Sedative/hypnotics are highly addictive drugs. The abuser develops a tolerance to the drug so that he or she requires increasingly higher doses to achieve the same effects. The body develops a physical dependence on the drug, as well as the psychological dependence, which is part of every drug-abuse pattern. Continued use of the drug is required to prevent the characteristic symptoms which follow abrupt withdrawal.

Withdrawal symptoms can last 7 to 20 days for short-acting and up to 28 days for long-acting enzodiazepines. Called "protracted withdrawal," the symptoms of benzodiazepine withdrawal may persist for several months. Withdrawal from sedative/hypnotics is more dangerous than withdrawal from heroin. Under withdrawal, the abuser will be nervous, anxious, and delirious. He or she will tremble, be nauseated, and may have a headache. The abuser is quite likely to have convulsions. He or she may become unconscious and may die. *If you are handling a person who seems to be experiencing severe withdrawal symptoms, transport him or her to a hospital immediately!*

§ 6.15.3 Objective Symptoms of Sedative/Hypnotic Withdrawal
The following is a list of the objective symptoms of a person who is experiencing withdrawal from sedatives/hypnotics:

—Confusion   —Abdominal cramps
—Anxiety   —Delirium
—Hallucinations   —Convulsions
—Tremors   —Unconsciousness
—Insomnia   —Possible Death
—Nausea and Vomiting

§ 6.16   ALCOHOL COMBINED WITH DEPRESSANTS
When more than one drug enters the body, a chemical interaction of some type may occur. One compound may offset the effects of another, which is known as *antagonism*. When two drugs that act in a similar fashion enter the body, this would increase the total effect and is known as an *additive effect*. If two drugs act together to give an effect that is greater than addition, it is known as *synergism* (sometimes referred to as potentiation). Coroners have found in a number of cases that the drug and alcohol levels in the blood were insufficient to cause death; however, the combined effect caused death. This effect is greatest when the short-acting depressants are combined with alcohol. Since the short-acting depressants are very similar in effect to alcohol, and because of the multiplying effect when the two drugs are combined, the result is a very potent depressant to the central nervous system.

The easiest way to describe synergism is to use two mathematical formulas. If you equate a dosage of depressant to an ounce of alcohol, the two drugs added together would equal two ounces of alcohol or two dosages of depressants by way of physical effect on the user. This is an additive effect. Synergism, on the other hand, can be described as taking one dosage of a depressant and equating it to two dosages of a depressant when added to two dosages of alcohol, equaling four units in physical effect on the user.

§ 6.17   SEDATIVE/HYPNOTIC USE IN COMBINATION
In 2002, over 100,000 people were taken to emergency rooms (ER) involving benzodiazepines. Nearly half of the ER visits were the result of suicide attempts. From 1995 to 2002, drug abuse-related ER visits involving benzodiazepines increased by 41%. The majority of the ER incidents were the result of sedative/hypnotic drugs in combination with alcohol and other drugs (DAWN 2004). The best way to avoid the potential hazards is to avoid mixing alcohol with any prescription drug.

§ 6.17.1 Glutethimide and Codeine

Codeine is widely available as a minor narcotic analgesic and cough suppressant. Glutethimide is a tranquilizer and sleeping aid. These two drugs produce a high or euphoria when used together. Users refer to this combination of drugs as "loads" or "fours and dors" and use two to three times the therapeutic dosage.[3] The two drugs interact in a synergistic way to intensify the sedative/hypnotic effect. Glutethimide is especially dangerous since it is not readily metabolized and can be reabsorbed. The abusers who use "loads" six or seven times a day, which is common, run the risk of overdose and death.

§ 6.18 DEPRESSANT ABUSE BY INJECTION

The most common and easiest method of administering depressants is orally. The fast-acting depressants, which are the most commonly abused, begin taking effect within a very short period of time (10 to 20 minutes) when ingested orally. Because of this fact, the intravenous injection is less common. Intravenous use of sedatives is usually used only by those deeply involved in the drug culture. The use of the intravenous injection of sedatives is limited because the desired effect can be achieved almost as rapidly through oral administration; however, there is no orgasmic-type "flash" or "rush" when taken orally, as there is when injected.

§ 6.19 DEPRESSANT DETECTION AND IDENTIFICATION IN THE BODY

Drug detection in the body by law enforcement is usually accomplished by urinalysis. Another efficient and accurate method is through blood analysis, particularly for sedatives. When obtaining blood or urine samples, the following procedures should be followed:

1. Blood samples should only be drawn by qualified medical personnel.

2. The blood should be collected in Vacutainers that contain a blood preservative.

3. Two full Vacutainers of blood should be submitted to the laboratory for a complete analysis.

4. If amphetamines or opiates are suspected, a urine sample of at least three ounces should be submitted to the laboratory.

5. If the identity of the drug is unknown, submit both urine and blood samples for analysis.

6. Any tablets, capsules, medications, or prescription vials taken from a suspect or from his or her vehicle should be submitted to the laboratory with the blood and/or urine samples.

---

[3] Dors means Doriden. Doriden is the trade name for glutethimide.

7. Specifically instruct the laboratory to check the blood-alcohol level as well as drug levels. This is particularly important with respect to depressant drugs since the physical symptoms of intoxication are similar to alcohol.

When a person is suspected of driving under the influence of a sedative and the suspect refuses to give either a blood or urine sample, performing a breath-alcohol examination would be an additional factor for law enforcement personnel to consider. This may show the absence of alcohol or may show that the suspect's behavior is inconsistent with the alcohol level. By doing this, the officer could correctly assume and support drug intoxication.

§ 6.19.1   Nystagmus Test

"Nystagmus," according to *Webster's Dictionary,* is an involuntary rapid movement of the eyeball, usually from side to side on the lateral/horizontal plane.

The nystagmus test has been widely used to identify the presence of PCP. More recently, law enforcement officers have come to realize the value of nystagmus testing for DUI arrests. Alcohol, as well as many other sedative/hypnotics, will produce nystagmus. It can serve as a gauge to the user's level of intoxication.

When testing for horizontal gaze nystagmus, the angle of onset (where the eye begins to bounce) is the most critical point for diagnosing the person's internal level of alcohol at the time of the test.

The following factors assist administration of the test:

1. A reasonably well-lighted area

2. A safe area

3. A standing surface which is level and free of obstacles

4. A standardized test. If possible, always give your tests in the same order. Always ask your subject the location and time and note the answers in your report.

Gaze nystagmus is simply a preliminary investigative technique in which the officer looks for an involuntary jerking of the eyes. In court, the officer should not get too technical and should avoid the use of medical terms unless they are thoroughly understood. The officer must be prepared to testify to his or her training and experience and keep a log to record the actual number of gaze nystagmus exams conducted.

When performing the test, have the subject, if wearing glasses, remove them. Contact lenses do not need to be removed. Make sure that the subject can see you. Remember, there must be enough light for you to see the reaction.

Central Nervous System Depressants

Follow these steps when administering a nystagmus test:

1. Direct the subject to hold his or her head still.

2. Hold your finger or pen approximately 12 inches directly in front of the tip of the subject's nose; then direct the subject to follow the testing object (your finger or pen), moving only their eyes.

3. Move the testing object rapidly from the front of the nose toward the side of the head, keeping the testing object 12 inches from the subject's head at all times.

4. Observe the right eye when moving the testing object to the subject's right. Observe the left eye when moving the testing object to the subject's left.

In this test, called "rough pursuit," you are looking for the failure of the eye to follow the testing object smoothly. This is one of the objective indicators of intoxication or impairment if not performed well.

Now repeat the test again, but move the testing object much slower. Watch for the point at which the eyes start to bounce or vibrate sideways. Stop and see if the bounce continues. If not, continue to move your finger or pen to the side of the head until you have a confirmed bounce which continues after your finger or pen has stopped.

For alcohol intoxication, the degree or angle of the eyes at this point is critical to determine the person's actual level of intoxication. The degree is determined by measuring from directly in front of the suspect to the side of the head, and any movement to the left or right would be an increase in the number of degrees. There are two devices available to determine the degrees involved in the test. They are the DARTS Chart and the FOG Tool (folding onset gauge), two nystagmus tests from Santa Clara. The FOG Tool has also been called the Grillimeter for its inventor.

You can approximate the degree by considering that moving the iris of the eye (the iris is the colored part of the eye) from directly in front of the nose to where it starts to touch the outside corner of the eye is movement from 0 to 45 degrees. Nystagmus onset will occur between 0 and 45 degrees.

Assume you have a subject who produces a nystagmus onset at 35 degrees. Subtract 35 degrees from the number 50. The difference of 15 degrees is equivalent to .15 BAC (blood-alcohol content). (50 - 35° = .15 BAC)

To determine end-point nystagmus, move the eyes to the right or left as far as you can and you are at the end point. End-point nystagmus occurs between 45° and 50° or where the iris touches the outermost corner of the eye. About 50 percent of the general population will have end-point nystagmus without any alcohol in their body.

For alcohol intoxication, the nystagmus test can be used as one tool which, coupled with other signs of impairment, may prove that the suspect is under the influence. Do not base your arrest on the nystagmus test alone.

Some people will show nystagmus and not be under the influence of anything. About 4 percent of the population will have early-onset nystagmus, which can be mistaken for intoxication.

Check for eye injuries. Ask whether the subject has an artificial eye.

If the angle of the onset of nystagmus is not the same for each eye, check to see if the pupil sizes are different. The nystagmus may be the result of a head injury. Get the subject immediate medical treatment.

Some people who are intoxicated will not show any apparent sign of nystagmus.

When using nystagmus in DUI situations, it is not a pure science that can be used as the sole basis for determining whether a subject is under the influence. You must have other signs of alcohol intoxication.

Nystagmus tests are useful for determining the presence of drugs in the body. Sedative/hypnotics such as barbiturates, methaqualone, alcohol, and chloral hydrate cause horizontal nystagmus. PCP and toluene (glue) cause horizontal and vertical nystagmus. Tranquilizers such as Valium, in large doses, may cause nystagmus. Narcotics (heroin, methadone, Talwin, etc.) and central nervous system stimulants (amphetamine, cocaine) do not cause nystagmus.

§ 6.20　SUMMARY

Benzodiazepines, which are among the safest, most effective, and widely prescribed psychotropic compounds, have largely replaced barbiturates as anxiolytics, sedatives, and hypnotics over the last two decades. The nonmedical use (i.e., abuse) of barbiturates and benzodiazepines has tended to decrease in recent years. Clinical observation suggests that, in the illicit drug culture, these drugs are most frequently used by polydrug abusers. Benzodiazepines tend to be abused in combination with other drugs; diazepam-opioid combinations seem to be a particular problem in this regard. Studies in laboratory animals and humans have shown that abrupt termination of high chronic doses of barbiturates and benzodiazepines can produce a severe withdrawal syndrome, sometimes including delirium and grand mal convulsions. Some limited animal and human data suggest that high doses of barbiturates may produce a more severe withdrawal syndrome than high doses of benzodiazepines. It is now clear that benzodiazepines can produce a withdrawal syndrome after prolonged treatment with normal therapeutic doses. Although additional research will be required to adequately address the risk/benefit ratio of long-term benzodiazepine use, there is an increasing clinical consensus that chronic maintenance of patients on anxiolytics is not desirable and that such patients should be regularly evaluated for termination of medication.

§ 6.21   SLANG TERMINOLOGY
This is a partial list of drug jargon in use in California:

Bag............................ quantity of drugs packaged in various containers such as paper, balloons, Baggies, etc.
Barbs .... barbiturates
Barrel .... 100,000 pills
Bottle.......................... 100 pills
Cap.............................. capsule
Cap up .... transfer drug in bulk form into capsules
Downer .... drug with depressant effect, usually means secobarbital
Dropped .... taking drugs orally
Eat.............................. to swallow drugs
Factory....................... location where illicit drugs are manufactured
Forget Pill .... Rohypnol
Jar.............................. 1,000 pills
Jug .... 1,000 pills
Keg............................. 50,000 pills
Knockout drops........ chloral hydrate
Ludes.......................... methaqualone
Mequin .... methaqualone
Pill freak.................... user of any type of pills
Pillow .... 25,000 tablets, packaged in a black plastic bag
Pink Lady .... phenobarbital capsule
Q's.............................. methaqualone
Rack............................ 2 to 5 capsules wrapped in tinfoil
Sopors .... methaqualone
Tabs .... tablets

§ 6.22   EXAMPLES OF SEDATIVE/HYPNOTIC DRUGS

Drug Class	Chemical Name	Trade Name
Barbiturates (Ultra-Short Effect)	Thiopental	Pentothal
Barbiturates (Ultra-Short Effect)	Methohexital	Brevital
Barbiturates (Intermediate Effect)	Pentobarbital	Nembutal
Barbiturates (Intermediate Effect)	Secobarbital	Seconal
Barbiturates (Intermediate Effect)	Amobarbital	Amytal
Barbiturates (Intermediate Effect)	Butabarbital	Butisol
Barbiturates (Long Effect)	Phenobarbital	Luminal
Piperidinediones	Glutethimide	Doriden
Piperidinediones	Methprylon	Noludar
Quinazolinones	Methaqualone	Quaaludes
Tertiary Carbinol	Ethchlorynol	Placidyl
Benzodiazepines	Lorazepam	Activan
Benzodiazepines	Clorazepate	Tranxene
Benzodiazepines	Chlordiazepoxide	Librium
Benzodiazepines	Oxazepam	Serax
Benzodiazepines	Diazepam	Valium

Drug Class	Chemical Name	Trade Name
Benzodiazepines	Alprazolam	Xanax
Benzodiazepines	Clonazepam	Klonopin
Benzodiazepines	Flurazepam	Dalmane
Benzodiazepines	Nitrazepam	Mogodan
Benzodiazepines	Prazepam	Verstran (Centrax)
Benzodiazepines	Temazepam	Restoril
Benzodiazepines	Trialozam	Halcion
Benzodiazepines	Zopidem	Ambien
Carbamates	Meprobamate	Miltown, Equanil
Carbamates	Tybamate	Salacen, Tybatran
Halogenated hydrocarbons	Chloral hydrate	Noctec
Halogenated hydrocarbons	Paraldehyde	

Other sedative/hypnotic drugs, which are available in other countries but which are not legally available in the United States, are Zopiclone (Zimovane) known as "Zim Zims" and flunitrazepam (Rohypnol). Rohypnol will usually induce sleep at levels of 1 to 2 mg. The much older "Mickey Finn" is a mixture of Chloral Hydrate dissolved in alcohol.

References

"The APA Task Force Report on Benzodiazepine Dependence, Toxicity and Abuse." American Journal of Psychiatry 148 (1991): 151-152.

Barker, M.J. et al. "Cognitive Effects of Long-Term Benzodiazepine Use: A Meta-Analysis." CNS Drugs 18.1 (1995): 37-48.

Drug Enforcement Administration. Club Drugs: An Update. Washington, D.C.: U.S. Department of Justice, September 2001.

File, S.E. "The Pharmacology of Benzdiazepine Tolerance and Withdrawal." Clinical NeuroPharmacology 15 (1992): 100A-101A.

Mantooth, Robin. "Toxicity, Benzodiazepine." Emedicine Articles. 5 April 2005.

National Institute on Drug Abuse, Community Drug Alert Bulletin: Club Drugs. Rockville, M.D.: Department of Health and Human Services, 1999.

Office of National Drug Control Policy. Street Terms: Drugs and the Drug Trade. Washington, D.C.: Executive Office of the President, 1999.

Physician's Desk Reference. Thomson PDR,1993.

Substance Abuse and Mental Health Services Administration "Demographic Characteristics of Benzodiazepine Involved ER Visits." The DAWN Report. Rockville, M.D.: U.S. Department of Health, July 2004.

CHAPTER 7

ALCOHOL

§ 7.1 INTRODUCTION

Americans live in a culture in which the use of alcoholic beverages is widely, though not universally, accepted. At the same time, the misuse of alcohol represents a public health problem of major significance. The effects of excessive drinking on one individual, tragic as they may be, indicate only one aspect of the problem. The problem is further compounded by the effects of the individual's behavior on family, friends, fellow-workers, and neighbors.

§ 7.2 HISTORY

The use and misuse of alcoholic beverages is a major subject of controversy in America. It has nearly always been so.

Efforts to control drinking have ranged from sermons from the pulpit, to advice from physicians, and to judgments by the courts. The very political climate of the nation has been shaped by attitudes about drinking—attitudes as disparate as those which brought about the Whiskey Rebellion of 1794 and the Volstead Act of 1919.

America has tried nationwide prohibition by federal law and rejected it. Today, it is generally accepted that those adults who wish to drink have a right to do so, limited by local customs defined by either written or unwritten laws. But legal rights, written or unwritten, are not the only factors involved. Social rights and social pressures are also concerned, and these may vary widely in different groups and different regions.

Under these circumstances, there is no one national attitude toward moderate or social drinking that is acceptable to everyone. Perhaps there will never be such agreement. But there is developing a common attitude concerning the excessive drinker, the problem drinker, and the alcoholic. This is based in part on the growing awareness that the problem of excessive drinking in this country is of serious proportions. It is based also on the growing recognition that alcoholism and excessive drinking represent not simply moral issues but medical problems with complicated and interrelated chemical, physiological, psychological, and sociological aspects.

This new look at drinking is not a renewal of hostilities between "wets" and "drys." Instead, there seems to be an appreciation among many thoughtful people—including scientists, physicians, educators, jurists, and religious leaders—that the solution of drinking-related problems requires an understanding of drinking in its many complex facets. It is essential to consider not pure alcohol itself (which is almost unknown outside the laboratory), but the chemistry and the physiological effects of the alcoholic beverages consumed in real life by real people, as well as the psychological and sociological implications to a society in which abstinence, moderate drinking, excessive drinking, and alcoholism all occur as normal or abnormal behavioral patterns. It is likewise essential to consider the nature of the problems and their scope, to assess their true impact on American society, and to arrive—through study and research—at new knowledge that can help prevent and control excessive drinking and simultaneously improve the treatment and rehabilitation of the alcoholic.

Even though widespread public awareness of drinking problems is new, the existence of alcohol is exceedingly old. As with such natural phenomena as fire and water, the discovery of alcoholic beverages cannot be assigned a date or a patent number, nor credited to any man or place. Only a few basic ingredients—sugar, water, yeast, and a mild degree of warmth—are required for alcohol production. Where these occur together, it is virtually impossible for alcohol not to be produced. According to paleontologists, all four were present on earth in Paleozoic times, at least 200 million years ago.

It seems obvious, therefore, that alcohol preceded man and that he began to use it long before the beginnings of written history. Since the earliest civilizations, alcoholic beverages have been viewed as nutritious foods, valuable medicines, and sacred liquids for religious ceremonies.

§ 7.3 WHY PEOPLE DRINK

It is generally accepted today that alcohol, by strict definitions, is a food, since it is a source of calories. Like some other nutrients, it is not a perfect food; it contains no vitamins and is harmful when used to excess. Alcoholic beverages have a long record of medical use and were at one time among the most widely prescribed drugs. It is still accepted that alcohol may serve as a useful, although not a curative, medical agent. While some of the health values once attributed to beer, wine, and distilled spirits have been disproved, others have been confirmed by modern scientific study. For example, certain alcoholic beverages are used by some physicians as aids in the treatment of arthritis, digestive diseases, high blood pressure, and coronary disease and as tranquilizers or sedatives for convalescent and geriatric patients.

In one form or another, alcohol was probably the first tranquilizer known to human beings and remains today the most widely used. The drinking of alcoholic beverages also has long been established as a part of many religious rites and continues in that role.

In the majority of instances, however, drinking stems from the desire for an antidote to unpleasant reality, the need for an ego booster, as an aid to sociability, or for simple pleasure. Quite apart from any physiological effects, the custom of drinking has often been felt to be rewarding because of the social interrelationships, the status, and the behaviors and attitudes that accompany it.

§ 7.4 EXCESSIVE DRINKING

Throughout the history of alcoholic beverages, drunkenness has been considered a problem.

Alcoholic beverages were probably known in the New World long before Columbus. They were certainly brought to America in 1607 with the settling of the Virginia Colony. Twelve years later, their excessive use was such that a law decreed that any person found drunk for the first time was to be reproved privately by the minister; the second time, publicly; the third time, to "lye tin halter" for twelve hours and pay a fine. Yet in the same year, the Virginia Assembly passed other legislation encouraging the production of wines and distilled spirits in the colony. It was not the custom of drinking that was unacceptable in early Virginia, but drinking to excess (Goode).

In the Massachusetts Bay Colony, brewing came to rank next in importance to milling and baking. There, as in Virginia, occasional drunkenness was punished by whipping, fines, and confinement in the stocks. But, as Norbert Kelly writes, "The Puritans neither disdained nor prohibited the use of beverage alcohol. They were emphatic, however, in urging moderation in drinking" (Kelly).

The temperance movement—which sprang in considerable measure from the alcoholic excesses of the Industrial Revolution in England—was not long in coming to America. It began with the goal of temperance in its literal sense: moderation. At the peak of this early campaign, in the 1830s, temperance leaders—many of whom themselves drank beer and wine—maintained that the remedy for intemperance was abstinence from distilled spirits only.

But the subsequent decades brought a significant change. The meaning of temperance was gradually altered from moderation to total abstinence. All alcoholic beverages were attacked as unnecessary, harmful to health, and inherently poisonous. The demand arose for total prohibition.

This demand culminated in the United States in the passage of the 18th Amendment, which prohibited the manufacture and sale of all alcoholic beverages. Beginning in 1920, national prohibition lasted until 1933. Even now, Prohibition remains a controversial subject. Its defenders claim that it brought substantial reduction in drinking, a decrease in drunkenness, and marked economic improvement to the country. Those who oppose the concept say that the experiment curbed only the moderate drinker and brought new and dangerous glamour to drinking and intoxication. They claim that it destroyed public respect for law enforcement officers and bred the crime, violence, and general corruption that marked the bootlegging of illicit liquor. Whatever the validity of these views, one fact seemed fairly well established by the end of the Prohibition era: many Americans liked to drink and would insist with considerable vehemence on their right to drink. There are no signs that their views have changed to any extent today.

Chapter 7

But while it has become clear that many and perhaps most Americans would continue to insist on their right to drink, it has also become evident that many Americans are drinking to excess and endangering the lives and the welfare of themselves, their families, and all those around them. The problem of alcoholism, in fact, is now recognized as a serious public health problem that urgently demands intelligent, practical action based on better knowledge of its causes and potential cures.

§ 7.5 VARIETIES OF ALCOHOL

Among the many varieties of alcohol, *methyl alcohol* (commonly called "wood alcohol") is the variety used in commercial products such as antifreezes and fuels. A second type of alcohol—also poisonous—is *isopropyl alcohol*. While isopropyl alcohol is usually called "rubbing alcohol," it is also used as a disinfectant and a solvent.

The only kind of alcohol that can be consumed safely in alcoholic drinks is *ethyl alcohol,* or "grain alcohol." "Denatured" alcohol is ethyl alcohol to which poisonous chemicals have been added. The removal of these poisons requires complex laboratory procedures, so there is no household way to make denatured alcohol safe for drinking.

Ethyl alcohol is initially obtained through the fermentation of sugars and starches. However, to produce intoxicating beverages with a higher alcoholic content than that of beer or wine—say, for example, rum, whiskey, or gin—a process of distillation must also be undertaken.

In distillation, a liquid mixture is vaporized and the components of the vapor are collected by differential cooling during condensation. In distilling a previously fermented solution containing a low concentration of alcohol in order to produce a beverage with a greater alcoholic content, heat must be applied to the solution until the alcohol, which has a lower boiling point than water, is changed to a vapor. This vapor is then collected and condensed into a liquid form resulting in a new beverage having a higher alcoholic *proof* (one-half of the proof equals the percent of actual alcohol content—in other words, 86 proof means that the alcohol is 43 percent of the total liquid content).

Alcoholic beverages have no food value. Only insignificant amounts of vitamins, minerals, and proteins are provided. Calories, however, are abundant, and therefore alcohol is classified as an incomplete food (Doweiko 17). The caloric value of pure alcohol is 7 calories per gram. Thus alcohol is nearly as high in calories as pure fat or oil, which contains 9 calories per gram.

§ 7.6 IMMEDIATE EFFECTS OF INCREASING ALCOHOL CONCENTRATIONS ON THE CENTRAL NERVOUS SYSTEM

The immediate actions of alcohol as a drug are exerted mainly upon the central nervous system (CNS). As with other general depressant drugs, the effects of alcohol follow a pattern in which the highest intellectual functions of the CNS are the first to be interfered with and those vital functions that are under the control of brain stem regulatory centers are the last to go. The pattern of alcoholic depression of the CNS is characterized by a particularly long excitement, or delirium, stage. This prolonged hyperactivity is actually the result of the depression of the inhibitory areas of the brain which normally keep the more primitive parts of the CNS under control. Later, as the released areas are themselves depressed, the drinker falls into a stupor and may become comatose.

Thus, contrary to the belief that still persists among many people, alcohol is not a stimulant. It was, in fact, once employed in preparing patients for surgery. However, although it can help to put a person to sleep, raise his pain threshold, and finally produce unconsciousness, alcohol is not used as a general anesthetic in modern clinical practice.

The effects of alcohol on the functioning of the CNS are related largely to the level of alcohol in the blood and brain. Individuals, of course, differ to some degree in their reactions to the same concentration of alcohol in the CNS. However, it is certainly true that the lower the level of alcohol in a person's blood, the less the extent of nervous function impairment; and the higher its concentration in the blood and brain, the more profound and widespread the degree of CNS depression. As is true with other drugs, the concentration of alcohol in the brain at any given moment after ingestion depends upon its rates of absorption, distribution, and elimination—that is, to use the term broadly, upon its metabolism.

§ 7.7 METABOLISM

The average metabolism rate of alcohol is approximately 1 ounce of 100 percent alcohol per hour or about 1 ounce of whiskey per hour, or approximately one 12-ounce can of beer per hour. Metabolism rate is important in two respects: (1) determining the probable length of time of a hangover, and (2) determining the amount of time required to safely operate an automobile or other machinery. A hangover lasts approximately the same number of hours as the number of drinks ingested. Bear in mind that this is only a rule of thumb.

Because it takes approximately 1 hour for the body to metabolize the equivalent of 1 shot of whiskey or a 12 ounce can of beer, it is apparent how a person can fall "under the influence" of alcohol: by drinking more alcohol per unit of time than the body can metabolize. The greater the consumption per unit of time, the greater the increase in blood-alcohol concentration. The greater the concentration, the more noticeable the effects. There is, however, wide variation among people as to the effects of alcohol at any given blood level. People who have learned to "hold" their liquor (heavy drinkers) have learned how to behaviorally compensate (behavioral tolerance) for the effects of alcohol so that other people cannot see how much they have drunk. Behavioral tolerance is when a heavy drinker or alcoholic learns to act somewhat normal, even with a high blood alcohol content—there is a point of no return though. Interestingly, the same person may behave differently at different times on the same blood level. This variation is a function of mood, setting, or expectations.

Chapter 7

Absorption. Alcohol is a rapidly absorbed substance, because it requires no digestion and diffuses readily through the body. About 20 percent of the ingested alcohol is absorbed from the stomach, but the bulk of any drink makes its way into the blood stream only after it enters the small intestine. The CNS effects of a concentrated alcoholic drink can often be felt very quickly when it is taken on an empty stomach, because absorption begins immediately and reaches a peak in as little as twenty minutes. The period required for absorption may, however, be considerably delayed when the stomach contains a moderate amount of food. The presence of food tends to dilute the alcohol in the stomach and interfere with its absorption from that site. In addition, milk or other fat-containing foods tend to slow the rate at which the stomach empties into the first foot of the small intestine, from which most of the alcohol is ordinarily absorbed. Since more of the alcohol can be detoxified during such delayed absorption, its concentration in the blood and brain remains relatively low, and its effects on the CNS are less marked. Similarly, sipping a drink over a period of time results in lower blood-alcohol concentrations and fewer CNS effects than are likely to occur when the same amount of alcohol is downed all in one gulp.

Distribution. Once the alcohol enters the capillaries, it diffuses from the blood into all the body's tissues where it mixes with their water content. The better a tissue's blood supply, the more rapidly does its concentration of alcohol build up. Thus, the level of alcohol in the brain quickly comes into balance with that of the blood. Later, tissues that receive proportionally less blood or contain less water, finally take up their full share of the alcohol. Redistribution to secondary storage sites tends to draw some of the alcohol away from the brain and thus aids in the sobering-up process, provided that no further drinking is done.

Metabolic Breakdown. By far the most important factor in the reduction of brain levels of alcohol is the body's ability to burn up, or oxidize, the alcohol in the tissues. Between 90 and 95 percent of all the alcohol that is absorbed is broken down to carbon dioxide and water in a series of three enzymatically catalyzed steps. Most of the remaining alcohol leaves the body unchanged by way of the breath and urine.

The first steps in the metabolic breakdown of alcohol take place largely in the liver. Two enzymes catalyze the conversion of alcohol, first to acetaldehyde and then to acetate. Ordinarily, the second step immediately follows the first, so that there is little or no accumulation of acetaldehyde. However, sometimes—e.g., after the prior administration of certain drugs that suppress the activity of the oxidative enzymes— acetaldehyde may build up to toxic levels.

The final step in the metabolism of alcohol takes place in all the cells of the body. Here, the acetate derived from alcohol is fed into the cellular system for obtaining energy from foodstuffs. This is the Krebs tricarboxylic acid cycle, the main chemical pathway used by the body's cells to burn the acetate fragments from foods, producing energy and giving off water and carbon dioxide as waste products (Girdano et al).

§ 7.8 RELATIONSHIP OF BLOOD-ALCOHOL LEVELS TO BEHAVIOR

When a person drinks more of an alcoholic beverage than his body can burn, the excess alcohol accumulates in his blood and brain. The increasing levels of alcohol bring about behavioral changes that—within limits—can be correlated with the concentration of blood-alcohol. The most important application of this principle has been in determining a person's fitness to drive a motor vehicle. Chemists have devised many tests for estimating the amount of alcohol in a person's brain by analyzing his blood, urine, or breath. Analysis of a person's breath is the basis for the Intoxilyzer test that drivers are required to take. Such tests have nothing to do with the odor of a person's breath, which is caused not by alcohol itself but by other substances contained in alcoholic beverages. The breath serves instead as an index of the amount of alcohol in the person's blood, because the alcohol in the arteries is in balance with that of the air in the alveoli of the lungs.

Individuals vary in their ability to tolerate or withstand similar levels of alcohol in their brains; however, blood-alcohol levels correlate well with the expected impairment in the driving ability of the vast majority of people. For such purposes, blood-alcohol levels expressed in milligrams of alcohol per 100 milliliters of blood are related to probable fitness to drive on the basis of several broad categories, or zones.

BLOOD-ALCOHOL LEVELS RELATED TO FITNESS TO DRIVE

	2 DRINKS			4 DRINKS			6 DRINKS			8 DRINKS		
	120lb	150lb	180lb	120	150	180	120	150	180	120	150	180
1 Hour	.05	.04	.03	.11	.09	.07	.16	.13	.11	.21	.17	.14
2 Hours	.02	.01	—	.08	.05	.04	.14	.10	.08	.20	.15	.12
3 Hours				.06	.04	.02	.12	.08	.06	.18	.13	.10
4 Hours				.05	.02	.01	.11	.07	.04	.17	.12	.09

Note: The number of drinks is based on one ounce of 86 proof alcohol or one 12-ounce bottle of beer. This is the typical strength of a bar or restaurant drink; home drinks tend to be about twice as strong.

How To Use This Chart:
You can estimate figures that are not on this chart. For example, suppose you have been drinking for two hours, have had five drinks, and weigh 150 pounds. You would read down the left hand column to 2 hours, then read across. Four drinks would give you a blood-alcohol content of .05, and six drinks would give you a blood-alcohol content of .10. You could figure that your blood-alcohol content would be between these two figures, about .07 or .08. Since this indicates a loss of driving skill, and the possibility that you could be charged with driving under the influence of alcohol, you would want to wait for a while without drinking, about two hours at least (DMV).

BLOOD-ALCOHOL LEVEL AND BEHAVIORAL EFFECTS

.02 After approximately one drink, light or moderate drinkers experience some pleasant feelings, e.g., a sense of warmth and well-being.

.04 Most people feel relaxed, energetic, and happy. Time seems to pass quickly. Skin may flush and motor skills may be slightly impaired.

.05 More observable effects begin to occur. Individual may experience lightheadedness, giddiness, lowered inhibitions, and impaired judgment. Coordination may be slightly altered.

.06 Further impairment of judgment; individual's ability to make rational decisions concerning personal capabilities is affected, e.g., driving a car. Individual may be subject to mood swings.

.08 Muscle coordination definitely impaired and reaction time affected; driving ability is suspect. Heavy pulse and slow breathing. Sensory feelings of numbness in the cheeks, lips, and extremities may occur. Legally drunk, in most states.

.10 Clear deterioration of coordination and reaction time. Individual may stagger and speech may become slurred. Judgment and memory further affected.

.15 All individuals experience impairment of balance and movement. Severe impairment of reaction time.

.20 Marked depression in motor and sensory capability; slurred speech, double vision, difficulty standing and walking may all be present. Decidedly intoxicated.

.30 Individual is confused or stuporous; unable to comprehend what is seen or heard. May lose consciousness or pass out.

.40 Usually unconscious. Alcohol has become deep anesthetic. Skin may be sweaty and clammy.

.45 Circulatory and respiratory functions are depressed and may stop altogether.

.50 Near death.

§ 7.9 PHARMACOLOGICAL EFFECTS

What are the effects of alcohol on other parts of the body? Alcohol dilates the blood vessels close to the surface of the skin. This effect causes what people report as a warm feeling. However, this effect also increases heat loss. Therefore, alcohol consumption would not be advisable if you were in a cold climate and trying to keep warm. If you drank alcoholic beverages, you would freeze to death much sooner than someone who did not have alcohol in the bloodstream. Another mitigation against excess, alcohol can suppress the body's temperature regulatory mechanism, resulting in a sharp drop in body temperature.

Alcohol also dilates the coronary arteries, thereby increasing blood flow. This effect, along with certain changes in blood lipoproteins, may explain the recent finding that moderate drinkers have fewer myocardial infarctions (heart attacks) than do either abstainers or heavy drinkers.

Alcohol also appears to have some anticoagulant properties. This effect is problematic for automobile accident victims, because it increases the blood loss rate, adding to the risk of shock and/or of bleeding to death.

Alcohol also acts as a diuretic. Diuretics are agents that increase the volume of urine. This effect is one reason why someone who has drunk to excess may be quite thirsty the next morning. The diuretic action of alcohol may disturb the electrolyte balance necessary for normal body functions.

Alcohol, like many other CNS depressants, raises seizure threshold. This effect is thought to be why seizures occur in some heavy drinkers who suddenly stop drinking. Individuals with seizure disorders should, of course, be urged to use alcohol with extreme caution.

A further effect of alcohol is the suppression of REM (Rapid Eye Movement) sleep. Very often people who have difficulty falling asleep have a "few drinks" in order to sleep. The greater the number of drinks, the more REM suppression. Of course, the first night the individual does not have this nightly "dose," he or she will experience a very fitful sleep with perhaps very disturbing dreams from which he or she awakes feeling quite unrefreshed.

§ 7.9.1   Tolerance, Dependence, Withdrawal

Tolerance for many effects of alcohol is easily developed and is acquired by three mechanisms. First, alcohol is metabolized by the liver. It increases the formation and activity of the liver enzymes responsible for its metabolism. Therefore, chronic use results in higher "doses" if the user wants to continue certain effects. At the cellular level, chronic use results in the cells attempting to adapt to the effects of alcohol. Therefore, in a sense the cells become dependent, because cellular accommodation continues whether or not alcohol is present. In the absence of alcohol, these cells are still "accommodating" by cell excitation to a drug that is not present. This is probably the mechanism by which abstinence symptoms occur. The heavy drinker who wants to avoid the "shakes," produced by cellular accommodation to a drug that is not present, drinks more. It's a vicious cycle.

Behavioral tolerance to alcohol is also acquired. You are perhaps familiar with people who really can "hold their liquor." They may drink far more alcohol than you might drink, and yet do not appear drunk. This is an example of behavioral tolerance.

Tolerance, of course, can lead to both psychological and physical dependence. The chronic heavy drinker often feels that life cannot be lived without drinking. An important point is that psychological and physical dependence are not mutually exclusive. The chronic heavy drinker is at least psychologically dependent, but very possibly he or she is also physically dependent on alcohol.

Physical dependence is demonstrated by the appearance of abstinence symptoms when the alcoholic stops drinking. The severity of withdrawal symptoms is a function of the degree of physical dependence.

§ 7.9.2   Acute Withdrawal Syndromes

Many of the difficulties that occur after drinking are now recognized to be the result of its withdrawal. Symptoms may range in severity and depend mainly upon how much and how long someone has been drinking.

People with a relatively mild withdrawal syndrome may suffer only from what they call "the shakes," a state of tremulousness and relatively slight agitation. This is commonly managed by the parenteral administration of chlordiazepoxide (Librium), which reduces the person's psychomotor hyperactivity and tremors. The continued use of this minor tranquilizer during long-term convalescence, however, may be undesirable in alcoholic patients, because such people are prone to abuse depressant drugs in general. In the past, some alcoholics have become addicted to the barbiturates, paraldehyde, chloral hydrate, and other sedative/hypnotics with which they were being treated. Today, addiction to meprobamate, glutethimide, and other modern tranquilizers and sedatives is common among former alcoholics (Schuckit).

The development of the delirium tremens (the DTs) after several weeks of heavy drinking seems to be precipitated when the person can no longer keep his blood-alcohol up to the accustomed level. This falling off of blood-alcohol may occur as a result of persistent vomiting or other conditions that keep the person from continuing to drink. Users who are hospitalized for acute alcoholic intoxication, or alcoholics who are hospitalized for treatment of pneumonia or other conditions, may develop delirium tremens after a day or two of treatment, during which they have had no alcohol.

The Hangover. Some experts contend that hangover is actually an abstinence syndrome. The symptoms support this explanation because they are consistent with the symptoms of a minor abstinence syndrome (discussed earlier). The most commonly reported symptoms include nausea, vomiting, shaking, profound thirst, fatigue, dizziness, perhaps anxiety and/or depression, skin pallor, and sweating. The severity of the symptoms are a direct function of how much was consumed and how quickly. The more consumed per unit of time, the worse the hangover.

Two contributing factors that seem to be responsible for the hangover are acetaldehyde and cogeners. Acetaldehyde is a byproduct of the metabolism of alcohol in the liver and is very toxic, even in small quantities. It is thought to play a role in the severity of the hangover headache. Cogeners are naturally occurring by-products of the fermentation process that exists in alcoholic beverages and appear to contribute to the stomach upset, nausea, and headache. The more cogeners, the greater the severity of these effects. Beer has the fewest cogeners, while bourbon and whiskey have the most. Usually the lighter the color of the hard liquor, the fewer the cogeners. Of course, nausea and vomiting could also be a function of the gastric irritation caused by large amounts of alcohol itself.

Unfortunately, there is no cure for a hangover other than time. An analgesic such as buffered aspirin may ease the headache, and drinking water may help replace any lost fluids. However, most home remedies that you may have heard of do little if anything to moderate the symptoms of hangover.

§ 7.9.3 How Alcohol and Drugs Interact

To exert its desired effect, a drug generally must travel through the bloodstream to its site of action, where it produces some change in an organ or tissue. The drug's effects then diminish as it is processed (metabolized) by enzymes and eliminated from the body. Alcohol behaves similarly, traveling through the bloodstream, acting upon the brain to cause intoxication, and finally being metabolized and eliminated, principally by the liver. The extent to which an administered dose of a drug reaches its site of action may be termed its *availability*. Alcohol can influence the effectiveness of a drug by altering its availability.

Typical alcohol-drug interactions include the following. First, an acute dose of alcohol (a single drink or several drinks over several hours) may inhibit a drug's metabolism by competing with the drug for the same set of metabolizing enzymes. This interaction prolongs and enhances the drug's availability, potentially increasing the patient's risk of experiencing harmful side effects from the drug. Second, in contrast, *chronic* (long-term) alcohol ingestion may activate drug-metabolizing enzymes, thus decreasing the drug's availability and diminishing its effects. After these enzymes have been activated, they remain so even in the absence of alcohol, affecting the metabolism of certain drugs for several weeks after cessation of drinking (Guram). Thus, a recently abstinent chronic drinker may need higher doses of medications than those required by nondrinkers to achieve therapeutic levels of certain drugs. Third, enzymes activated by chronic alcohol consumption transform some drugs into toxic chemicals that can damage the liver or other organs. Fourth, alcohol can magnify the inhibitory effects of sedative and narcotic drugs at their sites of action in the brain. To add to the complexity of these interactions, some drugs affect the metabolism of alcohol, thus altering its potential for intoxication and the adverse effects associated with alcohol consumption (Lieber).

For example, the combination of opiates and alcohol enhances the sedative effect of both substances, increasing the risk of death from overdose (Kissin).

Also, acute alcohol consumption increases the availability of barbiturates, prolonging their sedative effect. Chronic alcohol consumption decreases barbiturate availability through enzyme activation (Sands et al). In addition, acute or chronic alcohol consumption enhances the sedative effect of barbiturates at their site of action in the brain, sometimes leading to coma or fatal respiratory depression (Forney).

§ 7.9.4 Possible Complications

Coma: Initially the victim is drowsy, very sad, and sick. He may be aggressive when disturbed. Later he may develop some definite physical signs, such as skin pallor. He may complain of ringing in his ears, numbness "all over," and seeing double. Later he may go into increasing stupor, from which it is difficult to arouse him, and he may die of two things:

Shock: Signs of shock are paleness, sweating, clammy skin, fainting, and weak pulse. Total anesthesia of the brain could also occur within two or three hours of first seeing the victim.

Convulsions: These are a potentially frightening and dangerous development of the hangover stage. The immediate dangers of convulsions are that the victim may fall and injure himself or herself, or that the victim's airway may also become blocked—often called "swallowing the tongue." The greatest danger is that convulsions may indicate a very serious medical condition. After administering first aid, a physician should be called; the person should then be watched until medical advice is obtained.

Alcoholic Hallucinations: This lasts from minutes to days. The victim sees and hears things that are not really there. He or she is convinced that they are real, and they may be vivid, frightening, and terrifying. Sometimes he may be paranoid (feeling perhaps someone is after his life). Apart from these abnormalities, however, he is rational, can talk, and knows who you are and what time of day it is. He doesn't usually have a fast pulse, fever, or tremor, and is not sweating, pale, or flushed. In fact, he looks all right, but "sees things."

Delirium Tremens: This is a serious possible complication of the hangover stage. The person suffering from delirium tremens is out of contact with his surroundings and does not know what is going on, though there may be clear periods. You may wear a uniform, but he will not necessarily recognize this or realize what it means. He may not know where he is, what time of day or what month it is, or even what nationality he is. He doesn't "know" anything! He often has some fever, is flushed, has a rapid pulse and intense tremor. In addition, he has the typical disturbing hallucinations and suffers from insomnia and great exhaustion. Usually the condition lasts from two to seven days. Fortunately, it is rare, but it is very serious and requires urgent medical attention.

In any of the above circumstances, after first aid is administered, if indicated, the person should be taken to the nearest medical facility.

Another possible complication resulting from alcohol abuse is that inebriated persons are often more inclined to injure themselves. As previously indicated, the suicide rate among alcoholics is extremely high. Thus, an officer should be aware of how to deal with a person who is threatening suicide. The following suggestion might be useful to remember when coming into contact with such a person.

1. Take all threats to commit suicide seriously.

2. Do not threaten someone who is threatening suicide.

3. Try to stimulate the "will to live" in the individual.

4. Do not make any sudden moves toward the person until you are close enough to grab a secure hold of him or her.

5. Send someone to get professional assistance (clergyman, doctor) while you are speaking to the suicidal person.

§ 7.9.5   Summary

The major pharmacological effects of alcohol are similar to those of the other CNS depressants. Alcohol is almost identical to the barbiturates in dependence and tolerance potential, toxic effects, and overdose risks. The absorption of alcohol takes place throughout the entire gastrointestinal tract and is affected by stomach contents and alcohol concentration and/or carbonation in the beverage. Alcohol crosses the blood-brain barrier quickly and is distributed through all body fluids, tissues, and organs. Its effects are clearly dose-related. The greater the consumption of alcohol per unit of time, the greater the blood-alcohol concentration. The table on pages 143 and 144 shows the behavioral effects of alcohol at various blood levels. Individual differences such as weight and tolerance affect blood serum levels. The greater the body mass, the less alcohol found in the blood and the fewer psychoactive effects. However, set and setting may cause a person to react differently at different times at the same blood level. (The set is the mindset: what is taking place in the brain. The setting is the environment where drinking takes place, e.g., a bar, party, home, etc.)

Large amounts of alcohol can lead to acute and chronic tolerance, in which higher and higher "doses" are needed to produce the desired effects. Tolerance can lead to both psychological and physical dependence, as demonstrated by abstinence symptoms ranging in severity from mild to life-threatening. Cellular accommodation to alcohol, blackouts, irreversible brain syndrome, digestive problems, gastritis, and liver problems, including cirrhosis and hepatitis, can result from chronic use. It also increases the risk of cancer. Some recent findings indicate that genetics may be a contributing factor in alcoholism. A physiological predisposition, particularly in males, is implicated.

§ 7.10   SOCIAL DRINKERS/ALCOHOLICS

The transition from being an abstainer to suddenly becoming an alcoholic is not the usual course. What is much more frequent is that someone who had been drinking moderately for years will shift the pattern of imbibing to one of problem drinking or alcoholism.

Chapter 7

Many students of the phenomenon separate alcoholism from problem drinking. *Alcoholism* is considered to be a physical addiction to alcohol: the build-up of tolerance over time, and an alcohol withdrawal syndrome varying from shakiness to DTs on sudden reduction or discontinuance of alcohol. A strong desire to continue to drink heavily is an associated effect. *Problem drinking* consists of difficulties in living directly related to excessive drinking. Marital, job, social, or health problems are some of the areas affected. Addiction may or may not coexist. In this publication, alcoholism refers to both problem drinking and alcohol addiction.

It is highly unlikely that an alcoholic person will make a deliberate decision to become an alcoholic. Rather, he or she slips imperceptibly, without conscious intent, into excessive drinking styles that culminate in alcoholism. This transformation period is important to identify by the individual and by the clinician.

Drinkers in a pre-alcoholic phase may be able to correct their drinking behavior more readily if they become aware of their progression toward a destructive mode of use. But exactly how can an early warning system be developed to alert the drinker of his or her approach to hazardous levels of consumption?

The transition to problem drinking is not a simple one; it consists of more than a quantitative change in consumption patterns. Some people can become impaired by consuming daily amounts of alcohol that would produce no impairments in others. Also, it is possible that a fatty liver or alcoholic hepatitis may develop in a person whose patterns of consumption are consistent with other relatively healthy drinkers. Many occupational and social groups consume alcohol rather heavily and consistently. Some of their members will get into difficulties early. Others may go indefinitely without encountering alcohol-related adverse effects.

Usually, an escalation of drinking practices occurs during periods of increased stress. A few extra drinks are taken to unwind, to forget, or to sleep. When the stressful period has passed, the newly established drinking routine continues. Under conditions of further stressful episodes, alcohol consumption increases again. Eventually, a point is reached when attempts to cut down or stop fail because of early withdrawal symptoms like the shakes or insomnia; these require alcohol for relief.

The pleasures of drinking can have an entrapping quality. The mild euphoria and social relaxation provided by a few drinks produce feelings of amiable fellowship and good cheer. This is an attractive state, very attractive to some, but some people make the error of assuming that the additional ingestion of beverages will serve to increase the fun. The memory of the immediate pleasure is of greater importance than the memory of distant bad effects.

With additional amounts, the mild and pleasant stimulation changes to an increasing depression and then to substantial loss of control over behavior. This up-then-down effect of ethanol on the central nervous system also is well known when alcohol is used as an antianxiety agent. Initially, alcohol reduces tension and anxiety. As heavy drinking becomes chronic, anxiety levels are elevated. It may be that this increase in anxiety perpetuates drinking in a vain search for relief. Using alcohol to evade an unpleasant reality, to forget one's worries, or to achieve mastery over life's stresses usually turns out to be a poor effort at self-treatment. This is compounded by the period of intoxication, the post-intoxication ineffectiveness and debility, and the pre-intoxication drive to escape from the consequences.

The dilemma is that the socially drinking individual has few guidelines to indicate that he or she may be at risk when his drinking pattern gradually changes. If one stays below two drinks a day and does not save up the drinks to go on a binge, impairment over the years will not occur. But many people in this culture drink more than that and appear to do well. At what point do we approach our personal danger zone? The answer is not entirely in the amount of ethanol ingested over time, but in how and why one drinks and what the effects are.

We must also remember that even two drinks a day are too much for some people. There are those who are hypersensitive to very small amounts of ethanol, reacting with a flush, hypotension, tachycardia, and chest constriction. Then there are the pathologic drinkers who become violent under the influence of one or two glasses. In addition, a long list of drugs interact adversely when combined with alcohol. These range from antibiotics, antihypertensives, and anticonvulsants to anticoagulants, diuretics, sleeping pills, and many other groups. Of course, people with peptic ulcer, pancreatitis, or liver ailments may increase the severity of their disorder by exposing themselves to alcohol. Diabetics and epileptics would be unwise to use alcohol, if only because of the risk of smelling like a drunk during a period of unconsciousness because a diabetic coma looks similar to an alcoholic coma (passed out), let alone the deleterious effects of alcohol in such conditions.

As a rule, the shift to dysfunctional drinking is a gradual one. In large doses, alcohol is a protoplasmic poison (able to change cell metabolism), but the danger level varies for each individual. People metabolize alcohol at different rates (even though there is an average). One becomes tolerant to alcohol effects because of change in cell metabolism. The higher the tolerance, the closer to overdose. Furthermore, to tell a person who has been regularly taking four drinks a day, and who has crept up to eight a day, that he is at risk will predictably accomplish little. In fact, anger at being unjustly accused or a complete denial that a problem exists are the usual responses. The advice is interpreted as nagging and may itself lead to additional drinking. It would seem more desirable for each person who drinks to regularly examine his own drinking practices and be willing to change them if the suspicion of dysfunctional drinking is uncovered.

Self-examination should be a part of the drinking person's routine and every effort should be made to be as candid with oneself as possible.

Examples of questions that could be indicative of a pre-alcoholic or an early alcoholic situation include:

1. Do I get drunk when I intend to stay sober?

This question speaks to early loss of control over one's drinking. The inability to stop once drinking has commenced is an ominous sign. Even an occasional loss of control may be a warning signal. Some confirmed alcoholics are unable to stop drinking after a single drink has been consumed.

2. When things get rough, do I need a drink or two to quiet my nerves?

Using alcohol as a tranquilizer can be precarious, because the dose is difficult to adjust and no other person is supervising the medication.

3. Do other people say I am drinking too much?

If the negative effects of drinking are evident to more than one person or to a single person on a number of occasions, this means that one's behavior is exceeding the social limits. It is advisable to listen to such comments, remembering that most people are reluctant to talk about the drinking troubles of their friends and relatives.

4. Have I gotten into trouble with the law, my family, or my business associates as a result of drinking?

Being arrested for drunk driving or drunk and disorderly conduct are not reliable early signs of excessive drinking. Only a minority of these acts are apprehended, so it is unlikely that this was the first such offense. Being confronted with difficulties at home or at work also tend to be the cumulative effect of a long series of objectionable behaviors.

5. Is it impossible for me to stop drinking for a week or more?

Resolving to stop and not being able to carry it off would indicate a definite psychological or physical dependence and points to potential problems in the future. Being able to stop is encouraging, but does not eliminate the possibility of a binge or other types of destructive drinking. Many alcoholics remain dry for long intervals. Therefore, being able to stop is not indicative of a danger-free situation.

6. Do I sometimes not remember what happened during a drinking episode?

Blackouts due to alcohol consist of variable periods of amnesia. They are to be differentiated from passing out into unconsciousness, which is the end state of intoxication. Blackouts, which are complete and cover periods of hours or more, are definite evidence of alcoholism. Passing out is an unfavorable indication of excessive drinking.

7. Has a doctor ever said that my drinking was impairing my health?

Although it is now possible to pick up early signs of harmful drinking, by the time a medical examination reveals abnormalities attributable to alcohol, it is clear that continuing current drinking patterns will further damage one's health. Abnormalities of amino acid ratios, plasma lipoproteins, or hepatic enzymes are signs that the liver cannot adequately metabolize the amount of ethanol being ingested.

8. Do I take a few drinks before going to a social gathering, just in case there won't be much to drink?

Assuring oneself of a sufficient supply of alcohol, "just in case," is evidence of an unhealthy preoccupation with such beverages and speaks for a need to feel "loaded" on social occasions.

9.   Am I impatient while waiting for my drink to be served?

The urgency to obtain a drink reflects a craving. Gulping drinks is another sign of over-involvement with alcohol.

10.   Have I tried to cut down but failed?

As with the inability to stop drinking for periods of time, the inability to cut down is a warning that dependence is present or impending. Cutting down successfully, but eventually slipping back up, is another sign of possible future trouble.

11.   Do I have to have a drink in the morning because I feel queasy or have the shakes?

The relief obtained from a drink after arising is often a relief of early, mild withdrawal symptoms. Therefore, drinking when one wakes up is a clear sign of increasing physical dependence.

12.   Can I hold my liquor better than other people?

Being able to hold one's liquor is not necessarily evidence of freedom from the complications of drinking. Holding one's liquor may indicate the development of tolerance due to the persistent consumption of large quantities. Although social disabilities may be avoided by holding one's liquor, physical impairment due to the amount consumed is inevitable.

13.   Have many members of my family been alcoholics?

There is some medical evidence of a genetic component to some instances of alcoholism. People whose parents or siblings had serious problems with alcohol have reason to be extra careful of their drinking habits. Not only may there be an inherited vulnerability, but the early life experience of an alcoholic parent may predispose the child to seek out consciousness-changing drugs or alcohol in later life.

The 13 indicators mentioned above are early or somewhat advanced signs of alcoholism. They should be assessed seriously by the individual concerned or by the health professional who is evaluating him. The recognition that a threat to one's future exists is a first step. The second step is taking realistic action on the basis of the threat. The third step is sustaining the new behavior. These steps are the critical blocks in altering the course of destructive drinking: refusal to accept the information, refusal to do anything about it, and refusal to maintain a corrective course of action once it is initiated.

§ 7.11   THE USE OF ALCOHOL AND THE CRIMINAL JUSTICE SYSTEM

Alcohol use has almost always been an issue of major importance for local, state, and federal criminal justice agencies in the United States. The primary concerns of these agencies center around the following issues regarding alcohol consumption:

1.   Regulation—Law

2.   Law enforcement

3.   Driving under the influence of alcohol.

§ 7.11.1 Regulation

In China, as early as 1100 B.C., laws were being imposed in connection with the sale and consumption of alcoholic beverages. Attempts in Europe to limit alcohol use spanned from the fourteenth to the early part of the twentieth century. In England we find typical examples of legal restrictions of alcohol use. In the sixth, fourteenth, and nineteenth centuries, religious edicts and civil laws were enacted in an effort to temper the use of alcohol. What is surprising, by contemporary standards, is that despite the emotional outcries of the day against alcohol's evil influences, many of the laws designed to temper alcohol abuse were relatively mild. In 1839, for example, the primary sections of the public drunkenness act initiated the policy of weekend closing times for establishments selling alcohol beverages and established a legal drinking age—one had to be at least sixteen years of age.

Once the colonies gained their independence they became free to enact new federal and state laws to regulate alcoholic beverages on their own. And that they did. In 1791, a federal excise tax was placed on whiskey; in 1834, a congressional law was passed prohibiting the sale of alcoholic beverages to Indians; and, in 1851, Maine enacted the first prohibition law.

Prohibition periods on local, state, and federal levels have been part of the American tradition. Beginning with Maine's law, a series of regulations would be passed and repealed until December 5, 1933, when the Twenty-first Amendment was ratified by thirty-six states, thus ending the "Great Prohibition."

Clearly, then, there was never any firm or lasting stand taken against the use of alcohol. This possibly stems not only from the fact that alcoholic beverages had accepted uses in religious ceremonies and unwritten medical prescriptions, but also because its social use—and the clubs and saloons that grew up around it—had become part of the American way of life.

Today, wine, beer, and liquor regulation enforcement by criminal justice agencies involves violations arising from sale of alcoholic beverages to minors, diluting alcohol by bars and restaurants, alcoholic beverage smuggling and other related tax evasion activities, and enforcement of "blue laws" and closing times of alcoholic beverage outlets (stores, bars, and so forth).

However, enforcement agencies today are primarily concerned with the problem of handling intoxicated persons, particularly those cited for driving under the influence of alcohol. The Federal Bureau of Investigation reports that one out of every three arrests involves alcohol abuse; approximately two million arrests for the offense of public drunkenness are made by police agencies annually in the United States; practically one-half of all fatal accidents today involve alcohol; over 90 percent of short-term prisoners are confined because of their contact with alcohol; and the suicide rate for alcoholics compared to nonalcoholics is 58 to 1.

§ 7.11.2 Handling the Intoxicated Person or the Alcoholic

Even in those few areas of the country where there are no specific laws dealing with drunkenness, inebriates are still often locked up under other charges such as vagrancy, loitering, and disorderly conduct. Maximum penalties for drunkenness range from five days to six months; for habitual drunkenness, some states even have statutes under which a person can be imprisoned for up to two years.

Until the laws are changed, the peace officer will continue to be responsible for handling inebriates. Therefore, to enable police, sheriffs, and correction officers to deal with drunken individuals as optimally as possible, information must be available to help them undertake this task. In response to this need, the Smithers Foundation published a handbook on the subject: *Alcohol and Alcoholism: A Police Handbook.* The following is an excerpt from the section titled "Handling the Intoxicated Person or Alcoholic."

"In handling the "drunk" or alcoholic in your course of duty as a police officer, you will encounter many different problems. Knowing how to handle these could, in some cases, mean the difference between life and death. Your very first problem will be to determine the extent of drunkenness. You must decide whether the person is in such a state as to be capable of hurting himself or others. If he does seem potentially dangerous, then he must be taken into custody, or at least protected.

With the sleepy, depressed type, you must be especially careful. He may appear quite capable of sleeping off his current state of intoxication. But he may have downed a pint or more of whiskey, or some such drink, just before you arrested him—in which case, he will get more and more intoxicated in the following hour or two. If left alone in a cell and not watched, he could die from absorption of extra alcohol during that time. So your second problem involves your ability to recognize some of the common danger signs and complications of severe intoxication."

§ 7.12   DRIVING UNDER THE INFLUENCE

Drunk driving is one of the most serious public health and safety problems facing the American people and their policy makers. In a 2-year period, 50,000 Americans die as a result of drunk driving—almost as many American lives as were lost in the entire 10 years of the Vietnam War. Conservative estimates place the annual economic loss from drunk driving accidents at $21 billion to $24 billion for property damage alone.

The first identification of alcohol as a highway safety problem came through anecdotal evidence of alcohol involvement in crashes. This evidence combined with the general societal knowledge of the effects of alcohol on human behavior led many to suspect an alcohol-crash problem.

This led to experimental studies of the effects of alcohol on driving skills. These experimental studies confirmed that alcohol as commonly used could impair driving performance. Chemical tests were developed to measure the amount of alcohol in the body. These allowed the correlation of specific amounts of alcohol in the body with effects on driving behavior.

The experimental studies were complemented by epidemiological studies that determined the incidence of alcohol in drivers who had been involved in crashes and in the general driving population. These studies revealed that alcohol was more frequently used by drivers involved in crashes and was used in greater amounts than by drivers who were not involved in crashes. The data obtained in the epidemiologic studies allowed a much more precise statement to be made about the relative risk of alcohol as a highway safety problem (i.e., the difference in probability of being involved in an accident when not drinking and the probability of being involved after having had a certain amount to drink).

As evidence emerged that alcohol was a highway safety problem, countermeasures were developed and implemented. Laws were passed prohibiting alcohol-impaired driving. As chemical tests to measure alcohol levels in the body became more widely available and, more importantly, as information correlating the effects of alcohol with its levels in the body was scientifically established, test results were gradually accepted in criminal trials as evidence of impairment.

At first, the alcohol level was used to establish the presumption of impairment. More recently, some state statutes have been passed that make it illegal per se to operate a motor vehicle with a level of alcohol in the body above a certain amount. Education and information efforts were undertaken to inform the public about alcohol and highway safety. This was done to deter people from driving unsafely and to create public support for actions against those who drove while impaired. Sanctions against those convicted of alcohol-impaired driving included the traditional sanctions of fine and imprisonment, driver license suspension and revocation, and referral to health and education programs. The last approach has been sometimes called the health/legal approach.

The National Highway Traffic Safety Administration estimates that approximately half of all fatal traffic accidents involve the use of alcohol and/or drugs; 50 percent of drivers killed have a blood-alcohol level of .10 percent or above; and 60 percent to 75 percent of drivers in single-vehicle collisions have a blood-alcohol level of .10 percent or above. The California Supreme Court has also recognized the gravity of the problem.

While California has 10 percent of the nation's licensed drivers, we account for 30 percent of the nation's total arrests for driving under the influence.

§ 7.13 DRIVING UNDER THE INFLUENCE DEFINED

For a person to be "under the influence," within the meaning of the Vehicle Code, the liquor or combination of liquor and drugs must have so far affected the nervous system, the brain, or muscles as to impair to an appreciable degree the ability to operate a vehicle in a manner like that of an ordinarily prudent and cautious person in full possession of his faculties using reasonable care and under like conditions. It is not necessary to prove any specific degree of intoxication. A person is impaired to an "appreciable degree" if intoxication causes him to operate his vehicle in a manner different from that in which it would be operated by an ordinarily cautious and prudent person. "Under the influence" does not require being affected to the extent commonly associated with terms like "intoxicated" or "drunk." A person's driving ability may be impaired even though others who see him may not readily see and know that he is intoxicated.

For example, pronounced weaving (2-foot drift) over a sustained period (3/4 mile) provides a basis to detain, for an officer sufficiently qualified (experienced) with DUI's, even though the vehicle stays within the lane and no actual traffic violation is observed. (*Perez* (1985) 175 Cal.App.3d Supp. 8, 11; *Bracken* (2000) 83 Cal.App.4th Supp.1.)

§ 7.13.1 Alcohol and Drugs

Under subdivision (a) of Section 23152, driving under the influence can include the combination of alcohol and any drug, or any drug alone. This includes any drug which is which is prescribed and is not illegal, e.g., insulin (*People v. Keith*, 184 Cal. App. 2d Supp. 884, 7 Cal. Rptr. 613 (Cal Super. 1960)). Addictive drugs are covered by subdivision (c).

§ 7.13.2 Vehicle Defined

A "vehicle" is any device which permits persons or property to be propelled, drawn, or moved upon a highway, except a device moved exclusively by human power or used exclusively upon stationary rails or tracks (Veh. Code § 670). It includes a bulldozer, forklift, go-cart, mobile crane, moped, tractor, snowmobile, horse-drawn vehicles, and the like (Veh. Code § 670). Although bicycles are not vehicles under the definition, there is a separate section applying driving under the influence laws to them (Veh. Code § 21200(a) and Veh. Code § 21200.5).

§ 7.13.3 Driver/Driving Defined

A "driver" is a person who drives or is in actual physical control of a vehicle (Veh. Code § 305). The person steering or controlling a vehicle is a "driver" even if the car is pushed or towed by others. To constitute "driving," only slight movement of the vehicle is necessary; it may be just a few feet or even inches (*People v. Jordan*, 75 Cal. App. 3d Supp. 1, 142 Cal. Rptr. 401 (Cal. App. 1977). For a motorized vehicle, it includes any movement with the motor off, such as coasting down a hill or pedaling a moped.

For example, defendant was "driving" and therefore properly convicted of violating Vehicle Code Section 23153, subdivision (a) where he was behind the wheel as his stalled vehicle came to a complete stop in the traffic lane, even though he had turned off the motor and gotten out before his car was hit by another vehicle. (*Hernandez* (1990) 219 Cal.App.3d 1177.)

§ 7.14 DUI: TWO SEPARATE CASES

In order to convict a person of DUI, the prosecutor must prove beyond a reasonable doubt that the accused drove a vehicle while under the influence of drugs, alcohol, or both; or, that the accused drove a vehicle with .08 or more, by weight, of alcohol in the blood. (The basic DUI law can be found in California Vehicle Code, Sections 23152 and 23153.)

A DUI case may be charged as a felony (meaning the punishment can be a term in state prison for a minimum of 16 months) where someone is injured or where the accused has three or more prior DUI convictions.

When someone is arrested for DUI, there are really two separate cases being prosecuted against the accused:

1. The DMV case. If you have been arrested for drunk driving, you must request a DMV hearing within 10 days of your arrest. If you do not request a DMV hearing within 10 days of your arrest, your license will be automatically suspended or revoked 30 days after your arrest.

2. The criminal case. This can result in jail, fines, an ignition interlock device being installed in the car, alcohol education classes, community service, impounding the defendant's vehicle, or a combination of these things, depending upon the facts of the case.

There are two ways to be convicted of DUI:

1. Failing to operate a vehicle with the same caution characteristic of a sober person under the same or similar conditions (being a sloppy driver as the result of drinking or taking drugs).

2. Driving a vehicle while having .08 or more, by weight, or alcohol in the blood.

DUI arrests of persons under age 21 also have separate rules and consequences. Because of California's "*zero tolerance*" for minors consuming alcohol and driving, anyone under 21 who drives with .01% or higher alcohol level can be subject to a one-year suspension of their driving privileges separate and apart from any action taken in court.

§ 7.15 PROSECUTION OF A DUI

The United States Supreme Court has upheld the practice of videotaping (with audio) the routine booking of DUI suspects. The tape, reflecting the suspect's slurred speech, his attempts to perform nonverbal sobriety tests, and any remarks he may blurt out, is not considered "testimonial" and therefore may be admitted into evidence, even though no *Miranda* warnings have been given. However, any incriminating *verbal* responses which you have solicited (such as asking him "the date of his sixth birthday," or asking him to count or recite the alphabet) will not be admissible because of the right against self-incrimination, unless *Miranda* warnings have first been given. (*Pennsylvania v. Muñiz*, 496 US 530, 110 L.Ed.2d 480 110 S.Ct. 2638 (1990)).

The primary elements of the misdemeanor labeled "Driving Under the Influence" are as follows (California Vehicle Code, § 23152):

1. Elements:

(a) It is unlawful for any person who is under the influence of any alcoholic beverage or drug, or under the combined influence of any alcoholic beverage and drug, to drive a vehicle.

(b) It is unlawful for any person who has 0.08 percent or more, by weight, of alcohol in his or her blood to drive a vehicle.

Note: The constitutionality of this subdivision was upheld by the California Supreme Court in *Burg v. Mun. Ct. for Santa Clara Jud. Dist.*, 35 Cal. 3d 257, 198 Cal. Rptr. 145, 673 P.2d 732 (Cal. 1983).

(c) It is unlawful for any person who is addicted to the use of any drug to drive a vehicle, except for a person who is participating in an approved narcotic treatment program.

(d) It is unlawful for any person who has 0.04 percent or more, by weight, of alcohol in his or her blood to drive a commercial motor vehicle.

It is unlawful for a person under the age of 21 years of age who has 0.05 percent or more, by weight, of alcohol in his or her blood to drive a vehicle (Veh. Code § 23140).

Section 23136 of the Vehicle Code requires an immediate one-year suspension of the driver's license of anyone under the age of 21 driving with a 0.01 percent alcohol concentration (BAC) or higher. An officer can use a preliminary alcohol screening test or a chemical test to determine if the person under 21 has a BAC of 0.01 or greater (Veh. Code § 23137).

2. Where Applicable:

Section 23152 applies to highways "and elsewhere" throughout the state (Veh. Code § 23100). It is no longer limited to only "public highways," but rather applied anywhere and everywhere a vehicle can be driven.

For example, defendant was guilty of violating Section 23152 when he drove a vehicle on a privately owned and paved area that was part of a locked storage facility. The facility was not open to the public, but lessees and others with business on the property could enter. (*Malvitz* (1992) 11 Cal.App.4th Supp. 9, 11.)

§ 7.15.1 "Parental" Responsibility (Business and Professional Code, § 25658.2)

It is a misdemeanor for a parent or guardian to permit a child living in the home or a minor in the company of a child in the home to consume an alcoholic beverage or use a controlled substance in the home if (1) the minor's blood-alcohol level is 0.05 percent or the minor is under the influence of the controlled substance, *and* (2) the parent allows the minor to drive a vehicle away from the home, *and* (3) the minor causes a traffic collision while driving the vehicle.

§ 7.15.2 Persons Under 21 Driving with Blood-Alcohol of .01 or More (Veh. Code, §§ 23136, 13388, 13390)—The "Zero Tolerance" law.

It is *unlawful* (but not an infraction, misdemeanor, or other public offense) for any person under the age of 21 to drive a vehicle while having a BAC of .01 or more as shown by a PAS (preliminary alcohol screening) device or other chemical test. (Veh. Code, § 23136.)

This law, which took effect in 1994, amounts to a *total* prohibition against drinking and driving for persons under 21. However, it does not bar prosecution under Section 23152 or 23153 or any other statute. (Veh. Code, § 23136.)

If you have lawfully detained a driver under the age of 21 and have "reasonable cause," i.e., probable cause, to suspect that the driver has been drinking, you "shall" request the driver to take a PAS test, if a PAS device is immediately available. If a PAS device is *not* immediately available, you may request the person to submit to a chemical test of his blood, breath or urine, as provided in Vehicle Code Section 23612. (Veh. Code, § 13388.)

You must also advise the driver that his or her failure to take or complete a PAS test or other chemical test as requested will result in a one- to three-year suspension or revocation of his or her driver's license. (Veh. Code, § 23136 (a) (3).)

If the test shows .01 or more, or if the driver refuses to take or to complete the PAS test or other chemical test, the usual "admin. per se" provisions apply. Accordingly, you should physically confiscate the driver's license, immediately issue a notice of the order of suspension endorsed as a temporary license, and forward the appropriate documents to DMV within five business days, as set out in Section 13388 (b).

A violation of Section 23136 is expressly stated to be neither an infraction nor a "public offense" (i.e., misdemeanor or felony). Rather, "A violation of Section 23136 is only subject to civil penalties." (Veh. Code, § 13390.)

§ 7.16   OFFENSES IN OFFICER'S PRESENCE

In the past, the "in your presence" requirement of Pen. Code Section 836 caused considerable difficulty for misdemeanor DUI arrests in situations where the officer did not actually see the vehicle move. (*Johanson* (1995) 36 Cal.App.4th 1209, 1216.) Indeed, arrests under such circumstances were ruled illegal even though, for example, the suspect and only occupant was found passed out behind the steering wheel, with seat belt fastened, the lights on, the engine running, etc. (*Mercer* (1991) 53 Cal.3d 753.)

Courts struggled to get around this problem by holding that, even without observing actual physical movement of the car, an officer could make or have made a lawful arrest for *attempted* drunk driving or for a violation of Pen. Code Section 647, subd. (f) (unable to exercise care for his or her own safety or the safety of others). (*Mercer* (1991) 53 Cal.3d 753, 769; *Wolterman* (1992) 11 Cal.App.4th Supp. 15.)

Now, however, this entire problem is apparently history, for beginning in 1997, three new exceptions to the "in your presence" requirement were added to the two which already existed under Vehicle Code Section 40300.5. According to that section, you are now permitted to make a DUI arrest whenever you have probable cause to believe that the person has been driving while under the influence, and the person:

- was involved in a traffic accident; or

- is in or about a vehicle which is obstructing a roadway; or

- will not be apprehended unless immediately arrested; or

- may cause injury to himself or herself or damage property unless immediately arrested; or

- may destroy or conceal evidence of the crime unless immediately arrested.

Since anyone under the influence is "destroying evidence" simply by letting time go by (since their blood-alcohol content is diminishing), it would appear that DUI arrests are now legal even where you do not actually see the vehicle being driven.

In addition, you should remember that when the facts establishing a misdemeanor DUI offense did not occur in your presence, you may make an arrest if a citizen observer places the defendant under citizen's arrest. (Pen. Code, §§ 837, 839; *Padilla* (1986) 184 Cal.App.3d 1022; *Lofthouse* (1981) 124 Cal.App.3d 730.) The private person's arrest may be express and formal or implied under the circumstances. (Johanson (1995) 36 Cal.App.4th 1209, 1216.)

And finally, there is another exception, under Vehicle Code Section 40600, which permits an officer who has been properly trained in accident investigation to issue a "written notice to appear" to the driver of a vehicle that was involved in a traffic accident anytime he or she has probable cause to believe that the driver violated any Vehicle Code provision or local ordinance, other than a felony, and that the violation was a factor in the occurrence of the accident.

§ 7.16.1 Circumstantial Evidence of Driver's Identity

The identity of the driver may sometimes be shown circumstantially. (*Moreno* (1987) 188 Cal.App.3d 1179.)

A highway patrolman attempted to stop an automobile he saw weaving erratically on a highway. The vehicle appeared to contain only its male driver. After the officer had turned on his red light, flashed his high beams, and blown his horn, the car pulled into the driveway of a house and drove behind its detached garage. The officer found the car parked there with the lights on, the driver's door open, and the driver gone. However, about 90 seconds later, the officer saw the defendant come through the side door of the garage. He appeared to be under the influence, and there was no one else in the vicinity. The court found sufficient circumstantial evidence to establish the defendant as the driver. (*Noia* (1973) 34 Cal.App.3d 691.)

Remember, however, that it was only the *identity* of the driver which was established by circumstantial evidence. The actual act of driving itself must occur in your presence, unless the situation comes under any of the exceptions. Normally, this will mean that you must actually *see* the car move — although, in theory, "driving" can be determined through any one of your senses.

§ 7.16.2 Drug Addicts

Subdivision (c) of Section 23152 is not a "driving under the influence" offense. Because a drug addict is subject to the physical infirmities caused by withdrawal, he is always a potential danger on the highway and it is proper to forbid him to drive. It is not necessary to show that his driving was impaired at the time of driving. Nor is it necessary to show that he was in a state of withdrawal. "Addicts," covered by Section 23152, subdivision (c), do not include drug users who do not use a drug producing a physical dependence so as to suffer withdrawal symptoms if deprived of their dosage.

§ 7.17 THE OFFENSE OF DRIVING UNDER THE INFLUENCE– CAUSING DEATH OR INJURY

Driving under the influence causing death or injury is found in Section 23153 of the Vehicle Code and is a felony offense. The elements of the crime are as follows:

(1) It is unlawful for any person, while under the influence of any alcoholic beverage or drug, or under the combined influence of any alcoholic beverage and drug, to drive a vehicle and, when so driving, do any act forbidden by law or neglect any duty imposed by law in the driving of the vehicle, which act or neglect proximately causes bodily injury to any person other than the driver.

(2) It is unlawful for any person, while having 0.08 percent or more, by weight, of alcohol in his or her blood, to drive a vehicle and, when so driving, do any act forbidden by law or neglect any duty imposed by law in the driving of the vehicle, which act or neglect proximately causes bodily injury to any person other than the driver.

(3) It is unlawful for any person, while having 0.04 percent or more, by weight of alcohol in his or her blood to drive a *commercial motor* vehicle and when so driving, do any act forbidden by law or neglect any duty imposed by law in driving the vehicle, which act or neglect proximately causes bodily injury to any person other than the driver.

A peace officer may make a felony arrest (1) when the person arrested has committed a felony, even though not in the officer's presence, or (2) when the officer has reasonable cause to believe the person has committed a felony, whether or not a felony has in fact been committed (Pen. Code §836; *Schmerber v. California*, 384 U.S. 757, 86 S.Ct. 1826, 16 L.Ed. 2d 908 (1966)). This distinguishes felony arrests from misdemeanor driving under the influence arrests.

§ 7.18 DRUGS AND DRIVING

Alcohol is a drug, but a unique one. Alcohol is a single substance with a simple chemical structure. Its absorption, distribution, and action within the body are comparatively simple and well understood. Its use is almost entirely nonmedical. Although a drug of abuse, it is a legal drug whose social use is generally approved by society.

In contrast, other drugs may include many substances. Most are very complex—often products of modern chemistry. In general their absorption, distribution, and actions are much more complex than those of alcohol. Some drugs are transformed by the body into new substances that also have effects on behavior.

Some drugs remain in the body for long periods of time. In some cases, a drug's effects may continue long after it can no longer be detected in the blood. In other cases, drug presence may be detected after the drug's action has effectively ceased.

From a highway safety perspective, several aspects of the differences are important. First, legitimate drug use can create a highway safety problem. Drugs taken as directed can still impair driving behavior. Conversely, drugs used for the treatment of some conditions may reasonably be expected to improve driving behavior. Second, the complex nature of many drugs may not allow the development and implementation of a drug measurement technique similar to that used for alcohol (i.e., breath analysis). Even when drugs are detected, the full meaning of the findings may be unclear because of the lack of knowledge of the drugs' effect on driving behavior and the lack of an epidemiological basis relating use of a particular drug in driving and crashes.

Chapter 7

The experience with alcohol has served as a starting point for examination of the drug and driving problem. However, the differences between alcohol and other drugs must be kept in mind. Not all aspects of experience with alcohol may be applicable.

§ 7.18.1 Secobarbital (Seconal)

Secobarbital is a widely-prescribed "short-acting" barbiturate typically used as a sleeping pill at 100 mg or preoperatively at 200 or 300 mg. Laboratory studies of skills associated with driving or flying have reported evidence of impairment after barbiturate use. The degree of behavioral impairment was found to be roughly proportional to the treatment dose level. The data as a whole showed impairment for extended time periods, clearly to 6 hours and intermittently beyond that time, especially in a divided-attention situation (e.g., multi-tasking).

§ 7.18.2 Diazepam (Valium)

Diazepam is the most frequently prescribed psychotropic drug in the world. Epidemiological studies found diazepam present in approximately 10 percent of samples of fatally injured drivers.

Laboratory studies of the effects of diazepam and of alcohol combined with diazepam clearly demonstrate that diazepam impairs psychomotor skills and that alcohol compounds the impairment. Studies have shown diazepam decreases the velocity and accuracy of eye movements, increases simulator accidents, and impairs tracking in a divided-attention situation (e.g., talking on the phone while driving).

§ 7.18.3 Marijuana

Laboratory studies have shown marijuana to impair perceptual and perceptual-motor functions important to driving. An example of an impaired perceptual function is the difficulty to accurately judge distances and speed, whereas a perceptual-motor function may be the belief that your driving motor skills (e.g., reaction time) is improved with alcohol when in reality they are slower and impaired.

Since marijuana is used extensively, both alone and in combination with alcohol, the effects of marijuana were examined under both of these conditions. Three epidemiological studies (484 fatally injured drivers in Toronto, Canada; 267 drivers responsible for fatal vehicular accidents in Boston; and 600 operators killed in single-vehicle accidents in North Carolina) suggest that marijuana-alcohol interactions are of greater concern for traffic safety than marijuana alone. In all three studies, 70 percent or more of the fatally injured drivers found with marijuana in their blood also had alcohol in their blood (NIDA 1985).

The effects of one marijuana cigarette are powerful enough to impair driving for up to eight hours or longer, according to a study published in *Psychopharmacology* by Cocchetto *et al.* The National Institute on Drug Abuse (NIDA) contracted and funded the research. The study marks the first time a link between tetrahydrocannabinol (THC) and impairment was established, according to Gene Barnett, a program officer at NIDA and coauthor of the study. The results indicated a one-to-one correlation between the level of THC and impairment, said Dr. Travis Thompson, who led the psychological aspect of the research. (THC is a metabolite formed when marijuana is broken down by the body). "What that boils down to forensically is that if you know somebody's level [of THC], then you know the amount of impairment," he said. Marijuana continues to impair driving even after the feeling of being intoxicated has worn off, said Dr. Thompson, professor of psychology at the University of Minnesota. People say they feel "high" up to two hours after smoking a marijuana cigarette, he said. But even when they no longer feel under the influence of the drug, their driving ability was impaired up to eight hours after smoking, he said.

§ 7.18.4 Drug-Alcohol Interactions
In both marijuana-alcohol and the diazepam-alcohol studies, the addition of alcohol to the drug resulted in greater impairment than was present when the drug was used alone.

§ 7.18.5 Conclusions
Secobarbital, diazepam, marijuana, and alcohol were all found to impair performance of a variety of simulated driving tasks. Drug levels tested for secobarbital and diazepam were therapeutic doses; the marijuana doses were considered moderate to strong by the subject population used; the alcohol effects were reported for levels up to and slightly above the legal limit. No clear-cut differences in the pattern of effects were found among the drugs tested. All drugs impaired perceptual-motor skills (e.g., tracking, speed, and headway control), perceptual tasks (those involving the visual and motor skills necessary to operate a motor vehicle) where response time and detection ability were measured, and decision-making tasks.

§ 7.19 ALCOHOLICS AND DRIVING
The National Safety Council has stated that, while alcoholics usually account for alcohol-related deaths on the highway, many accidents are still caused by non-alcoholics who drive under the influence of alcohol. Many drivers in this condition refuse to believe that as few as two drinks can cause impaired judgment, distorted vision, and slower reaction time. They somehow feel that they are immune to the effects of alcohol—"others" may be influenced, but not *them*. However, when such drivers are stopped by the police and asked to take the drunk-driving test, they might be subject to harsh penalties if found to be inebriated.

§ 7.20 DETECTING THE DRUNK DRIVER
Detection of the driver who is possibly "driving under the influence" is usually initiated in one of four ways:

—direct observation of the individual while driving;

—a report from some other person of the individual's driving;

—as a result of a call to the scene of an accident; or

Chapter 7

—as a result of stopping the individual for a traffic violation.

The police officer must mentally record, with accuracy, not only the normal actions which should be expected, but also the individual's abnormal or unusual actions. The use of video cameras greatly assist in this regard.

While parked, officers can easily keep moving traffic under surveillance to spot hazardous or unusual operation of a vehicle. The signs the officers are looking for, that would warrant stopping a motorist, are fairly straightforward, for they are similar to the signs manifested by a driver under the influence of drugs or by one who is an habitual reckless driver.

Once an officer has decided to stop a vehicle, he or she should signal the operator to pull over and then watch for a number of possible reactions in addition to the normal one in which the driver pulls over correctly. These include failure to stop soon after being signaled; attempted escape; an abrupt stop in the middle of the road; and/or a swerving, dangerous stop. How the person reacts after being signaled to stop can provide the first clue that the person may be intoxicated. By the time the motorist has pulled off the road, the officer has already had time to gather information about the driver—based on the manner in which the driver was acting prior to being signaled to pull over and the way in which the driver responded once requested to stop.

The next set of clues can be observed just prior to the driver's exiting from the vehicle. First, the driver may attempt to change seats with the person in the passenger seat. The driver may also try to quickly conceal alcoholic beverages in the glove compartment, under the seat, or by throwing them out of the window. Sometimes the motorist exits from the car immediately in an attempt to prove that everything is under control. Occasionally the driver may attempt to escape.

Once the officer comes into contact with the motorist, there are a number of physical signs that he or she should look for—again, these are usually quite evident and fairly easy to detect.

1. Flushed, pale, or bruised face

2. Bloodshot or crossed eyes

3. Alcohol on the breath

4. Belching, hiccuping, vomiting, or shallow and heavy breathing

5. Uncoordinated gait, stumbling, walking into objects

6. Profuse sweating

7. Unkempt appearance

8. Incontinence

9. Uncontrollable waving of the arms and hands

Some of the common psychological signs of intoxication are:

1. Inappropriate laughing, crying, or talking

2. General hostility for no apparent reason

3. Incoherent speech or mumbling

4. General disorientation; the suspect may not know where he or she is or even the time of day

5. Inappropriate behavior in response to the officer's requests

You must mentally record, with accuracy, not only the normal actions which should be expected, but also the individual's abnormal or unusual actions.

Apprehension

Stop any driver immediately who is operating a vehicle in any manner which would raise a doubt as to his sobriety or other abnormal condition and ascertain the cause of the erratic driving.

§ 7.20.1 Detecting Drunk Drivers at Night

To detect drunk drivers at night, a study was conducted in which cues observed in 4,600 patrol stops were correlated with driver blood-alcohol concentration (BAC). The 20 cues are the best ones for discriminating nighttime drunk drivers from nighttime sober drivers and account for more than 90 percent of all DUI detections (USDOT 1982). The cues are listed in descending order of probability that the person observed is driving while intoxicated. Also, the number given after each cue is the probability that a driver exhibiting that cue has a BAC equal to or greater than .10. For example, the 65 for the first cue, turning with wide radius, means that chances are 65 out of 100 that the driver will have a BAC of .10.

		Probability (percent)
1.	Turning with wide radius	65
2.	Straddling center of lane marker	65
3.	Appearing to be drunk	60
4.	Almost striking object or vehicle	60
5.	Weaving	60
6.	Driving on other than designated roadway	55
7.	Swerving	55
8.	Speed more than 10 mph below limit	50
9.	Stopping without cause in traffic lane	50
10.	Following too closely	50

11.	Drifting	50
12.	Tires on center or lane marker	45
13.	Braking erratically	45
14.	Driving into opposing or crossing traffic	45
15.	Signaling inconsistent with driving actions	40
16.	Slow response to traffic signals	40
17.	Stopping inappropriately (other than in lane)	35
18.	Turning abruptly or illegally	35
19.	Accelerating or decelerating rapidly	30
20.	Headlights off	30

If these signs are present, they will be observable when the motorist gets out of the vehicle and responds to a request to show a driver's license and registration. (Naturally, officers should visually survey the inside of the vehicle and its other occupants when approaching the vehicle and during the initial contact with the motorist.) If the driver does not appear to be intoxicated (but possibly just sleepy from traveling for a long time), and if motor vehicle documents are in order and the driver hasn't broken any traffic laws, the driver would, naturally, be permitted to proceed—with a warning if it is deemed necessary.

If, on the other hand, the driver appears to be intoxicated, then the officer should immediately advise the driver of legal rights and ask the driver to move to an area away from the vehicle and moving traffic so that dexterity-physical coordination tests can be administered immediately.

After these tests, if the officer feels that intoxication is not evident, and if the driver appears sober enough to drive, but has violated a moving traffic law, a citation should be issued and the driver should be allowed to proceed. If enough evidence of intoxication is present, the violator should be handcuffed and placed under arrest; searched for alcohol, drugs, and weapons; placed in the patrol car; and advised of legal rights under the so-called implied consent law. Following this procedure, any other occupants of the car should be interviewed, the suspect's car should be searched, and any evidence should be collected and receipted according to standard procedures.

Following the arrest, the violator's car should be secured until it can be moved to safety. Arrangements must also be made for transportation of the other occupants of the car. The suspect should then be taken either to a hospital—in the event that there is a severe alcohol-related problem requiring immediate medical attention, such as alcohol hallucinosis or convulsions—or to a detention facility for chemical tests, temporary incarceration, if necessary, and the booking process.

§ 7.20.2 Accident Investigations

During an accident investigation, police officers must also consider the possibility that one or more of the drivers involved might be under the influence of alcohol. In addition to the presence of open bottles in the vehicle, other signs which may indicate possible alcohol use on the part of a driver include failure to have lights on, reports by witnesses indicating that the driver was swerving or driving on the wrong side of the road, or an actual failure on the part of the motorist to comprehend how the accident occurred or that it even occurred at all (however, this sign may be a symptom of shock as well).

If officers are sensitive to the signs that a person is or has been drinking while driving, much can be done to prevent alcohol-related accidents. Of course, most states do have an efficient, well-organized training program for their officers in the area of detection, investigation, and arrest of intoxicated drivers. The job is mammoth, however, and the work of removing the intoxicated driver from the road is vitally important to driving safety. Therefore, the methods and techniques presented in this chapter are, at the very least, meant to reinforce this important police operation.

§ 7.20.3 Implied Consent Law
The other major decision affecting determination of inebriation is the implied consent law. This law contains two important provisions.

1. Upon receiving a license to drive, the motorist agrees as well to submit to a chemical test, if so requested by an officer.

2. If the driver refuses to be tested for being under the influence of alcohol, his or her license may be revoked.

§7.21   THE STANDARDIZED FIELD SOBRIETY TESTS
The National Highway Traffic Safety Administration (NHTSA) and the International Association of Chiefs of Police have approved and recommend that the Standardized Field Sobriety Test (SFST) be used to determine alcohol and/or drug impairment at roadside.

The SFST, which is also known as the NHTSA-e, consists of three tests: Horizontal Gaze Nystagmus (HGN), Walk and Turn (WAT), and the One-Leg Stand (OLS). The Walk and Turn and the One-Leg Stand tests are divided attention tasks. Specific, so-called validated, clues have been established for these two tests. In addition to these three tests, Drug Recognition Experts incorporate the Romberg Balance test and the Finger-to-Nose test into the battery.

When the three tests (HGN, WAT, and OLS) are administered, they should always be given in the order HGN, WAT, and OLS. When the additional tests are administered, the order should be HGN, Romberg, WAT, OLS, and Finger to Nose.

The WAT test requires the individual to maintain a heel to toe position while the remainder of the instructions are given. The individual is then instructed to take nine steps down a real or imaginary line, turn , and take nine steps back.

The OLS test requires the individual to raise either foot approximately six inches off the ground, and while looking at his foot, keep the arms at the sides. The individual then counts out loud "one thousand one, one thousand two," etc., for approximately thirty seconds. Drug Recognition Experts always have the individual attempt to perform this test on each foot.

The Romberg balance test requires the individual to stand erect, arms at the side, head tilted back, and eyes closed. The individual is instructed to estimate a thirty-second time lapse to his or herself. The individual's estimate is compared with the actual elapsed time.

The Finger-to-Nose test requires the individual to first stand erect, and to extend each hand's index finger. The individual then closes his or her eyes, tilts the head back, and keeps the arms at the side until told to touch the tip of the nose with either index finger. The individual is also instructed to immediately return the arm to the side after touching the tip of the nose.

§ 7.21.1 Horizontal Gaze Nystagmus Instructions
I am going to check your eyes. Please remove your glasses. Are you wearing contacts? Please look at the top of the stimulus. Keep your head still, and follow the top of the stimulus when I move it. Only move your eyes, not your head. Do you understand? (Check horizontal first, then vertical, holding the stimulus approximately 12 to 15 inches (30 to 38 centimeters) away.)

§ 7.21.1(a)   HGN Clues (six clues total, three in each eye):
—Lack of smooth pursuit

—Distinct nystagmus at maximum deviation

—Angle of onset prior to 45 degrees

§ 7.21.2 Romberg Balance Instructions
Please stand with your heels and toes together, and your arms at your sides. Do not begin until I tell you to. When I tell you to, tilt your head back like this and close your eyes. **Demonstrate, keeping your eyes open for officer safety reasons.** When I say "begin," estimate a 30-second time period to yourself. When you think that 30 seconds have passed, open your eyes, tilt your head forward, and tell me "stop." Do you understand? Tilt your head back, close your eyes, and begin.

§ 7.21.3 Walk and Turn Instructions
Please stand with your heels and toes together, and your arms at your sides. **Demonstrate**. Don't do anything until I tell you to. When I tell you to, raise your right foot approximately six inches (or 15 centimeters) off the ground, with your toes pointed out. Keep your left leg straight. Hold that position while you count out loud for 30 seconds in the following manner: "1001, 1002, 1003," and so on until I tell you to stop. If you put your foot down, immediately lift it back up and continue counting. Watch your raised foot while you are counting, and keep your arms at your sides. **Demonstrate**. Do you understand? Begin. (**Time**

the suspect for 30 seconds. If the suspect counts too slowly, stop the test at 30 seconds. If the suspect counts too fast, direct the suspect to keep the foot up and continue counting until 30 seconds have elapsed.) Repeat the test with the suspect standing on the right foot.

Additional: An acronym for the eight clues of the Walk-and-Turn test is "BS SO WHAT."
B - **Balance**
S - **S**tarts too soon
S - **S**tops walking
O - Steps **O**ff line
W - **W**rong number of steps
H - Misses **H**eel-to-toe
A - Uses **A**rms to balance
T - Improper **T**urn

§ 7.21.3(a)   Walk & Turn Clues:

1. Instruction phase

   —Cannot keep balance

   —Starts too soon

2. Walking phase

   —Stops while walking

   —Misses heel-to-toe

   —Steps off the line

   —Uses arms to balance

   —Improper turn

   —Wrong number of steps

§ 7.21.4 One-Leg-Stand Instructions

Please stand with your heels and toes together, and your arms at your sides. Make a fist, and extend your index fingers. Place your arms at your sides with your palms facing forward. **Demonstrate**. Do not begin until I tell you to. When I tell you to, touch the tip of your nose with the tip of your index finger. **Demonstrate**. I will tell you which hand to use. Return your hand to your side after touching your nose. Your eyes will be closed, and your head will be tilted back. **Demonstrate, but do not close eyes for officer safety reasons.** Do you understand? Tilt your head back and close your eyes. (Sequence: L,R,L,R,R,L)

An acronym for the four clues of the One-Leg Stand is "DASH."
D - Puts foot **D**own
A - Uses **A**rms to balance
S - **S**waying
H – **H**opping

Chapter 7

§ 7.21.4(a)   OLS clues:
—Swaying

—Uses arms to balance

—Hopping

—Puts foot down

—Finger to Nose

§ 7.21.5 Preliminary Alcohol Screening Test
One of the Field Sobriety Tests is the Preliminary Alcohol Screening test, also called the PAS test. This is a portable breath test to determine the presence of alcohol. The officer is supposed to advise the suspect that the test is voluntary. These PAS tests do not comply with Title 17 of the California Code of Regulations and the results should therefore not be allowed into court.

§ 7.22   SIGNS OF DRUGS (SYMPTOMS)
When conducting field sobriety tests (FST's) on a suspected impaired driver, you will find, more often than not, that your drug user will be mixing drugs and alcohol. The eyes are one of the best indicators of being under the influence of drugs. Eye tests are also utilized for alcohol use; for now we will concentrate on drug use.

1.   Cocaine—pupils will be dilated and will stay dilated in a well-lit area.

2.   Heroin and Opiates—pupils will constrict and remain constricted in a dark area.

3.   Marijuana—blood vessels of the eye will be dilated, producing a reddening effect. Also check for an increase in heart rate and the noticeable smell of marijuana.

4.   PCP—produces vertical nystagmus. The eye will appear to bounce up and down on a vertical plane. Vertical nystagmus will occur whether the subject has ingested small or large amounts of PCP. To test for vertical nystagmus, just direct the subject to look at your finger, which should be held approximately 12 inches directly in front of their nose. Then lift your finger upward while they keep their head steady, and the subject should follow your finger with just their eyes. Look for the eyes to bounce up and down. If the bounce is there, your subject has vertical nystagmus. You have to use other testing procedures to determine whether this vertical nystagmus is a product of PCP or high levels of alcohol and barbiturates.

Note: A high blood-alcohol level or a high concentration of barbiturates in the blood will also produce this vertical bounce or nystagmus. This effect has been determined from both field experience and laboratory testing.

§ 7.23   CHEMICAL TESTS

Chemical tests are incidental to arrest and are administered at the direction of a peace officer who has reasonable cause to believe the person was driving a motor vehicle in violation of Section 23140, 23152 or 23153 (Veh. Code §13353 (a) (1)). As long as you have probable cause to believe one of these offenses was committed, such as receiving a report from another officer, you may direct that a test be taken (*Mueller v. DMV*, 163 Cal. App. 3d 681, 210 Cal. Rptr. 14 (Cal. App. 1 Dist. 1985)).

§ 7.23.1 Blood Test

A blood sample must be drawn by one of the medically qualified persons specified in Vehicle Code §23158(a), which includes physicians, registered nurses, licensed vocational nurses, licensed clinical technologists or bioanalysts, or certified paramedics authorized by their employer.

§ 7.23.2 Breath Test

Ordinarily, the operator should be certified by a forensic alcohol supervisor, analyst, or trainee and employed by a licensed forensic alcohol laboratory whose breath testing instrument is being used (Cal. Admin. Code, title 17, §1221.4). A valid breath test requires two breath samples which are within 0.02 of each other. The purpose of the two-sample requirement is to insure that two samples of deep-lung air have been obtained, since samples of air higher in the lungs are being diluted and give a lower reading.

§ 7.23.3 Urine Test

The Vehicle Code provides that a urine sample shall be collected giving the subject such privacy as will ensure accuracy of the specimen while maintaining the dignity of the person involved (Veh. Code § 23158(e)). To avoid dilution of the sample with water, an officer or other person may remain and observe from several feet away. Women should be observed by a female officer or employee while the sample is being taken, rather than having the complete privacy of a stall. The only "privacy" necessary is that which is common to toilets found in a public restroom, school, military establishment, or similar places. The sample should be collected at a place where there are both toilet and handwashing facilities.

The subject is required to urinate twice. (*Kessler* (1992) 9 Cal.App.4th 1134, 1137.) First, the subject must void his or her bladder to remove previously accumulated urine which obviously would not accurately reflect the subject's present blood-alcohol level. However, there must be an actual "initial" urination; the inability to urinate, accompanied by a claim that the bladder is already empty, will not suffice and will require the subject to choose one of the other two tests. (*Kessler* (1992) 9 Cal.App.4th 1134, 1137-1139.) There is no legal requirement to retain this initial sample. (*Miles* (1981) 118 Cal.App.3d 555.)

The second and crucial urine specimen is then collected no sooner than 20 minutes after the first voiding of the bladder. (Cal. Code of Regs., Title 17, § 1219.2, sub. (a).) Failure to produce this sample after the 20 minutes have passed is also considered a refusal. (*Smith* (1972) 25 Cal.App.3d 300.) Although the regulations do not designate an outside time limit, you only need to wait a short but reasonable time beyond the 20 minutes for the driver to produce a sample. Failure to produce this sample within several minutes beyond the 20 minute period has been upheld as a refusal, requiring the subject to choose one of the other tests. (*McConville* (1979) 97 Cal.App.3d 593.)

§ 7.23.4 Elimination

Approximately 90 percent of the alcohol consumed is eliminated from the body by an oxidation metabolism occurring largely in the liver. The remaining alcohol is excreted through the breath, urine, and perspiration—the passive, predictable elimination of small amounts of alcohol concentration.

In the case of urine, water and metabolic wastes are removed from the blood in the kidneys. The small amount of water removed will carry with it the same concentration of alcohol as the blood. This is because alcohol and water are infinitely soluble. It has been well established that the concentration of alcohol found in the urine will reflect the concentration of alcohol in the blood by a ratio that has been determined to be 1.3 to 1. Because urine is constantly being produced by the kidneys, it is necessary to have a subject void his bladder before giving a urine sample for analysis. The void eliminates urine that would reflect the average blood-alcohol level from the time since the previous urination (which could have been several hours prior). The sample collected at least 20 minutes after the void reflects the blood-alcohol level over those 20 minutes.

In the case of breath, circulating blood travels throughout the lung tissues. The blood is exchanging gases with the lung air. At body temperature (37° C), a small amount of alcohol will become a gas. This amount has been determined as one part of alcohol as gas for every 2,100 parts of alcohol that stays in the blood as liquid. This equilibrium between blood and breath is established almost instantly in millions of tiny "pockets" in leading to the alveoli (throat, trachea, bronchial tubes, etc.) contains various mixtures of room air and deeper lung air. Consequently, this "top lung" air does not reflect the true blood-breath equilibrium. It is a varying amount less in alcohol concentration than deep-lung breath. For this reason, the first part of an exhale has the lowest concentration of alcohol in the breath. The highest concentration is reached from the last part of an exhale and contains the breath that reflects the true blood-alcohol concentration.

The total rate of elimination of alcohol (metabolism, breath, excretion) varies from person to person, but is reasonably constant for any one individual. This rate is about 0.02 percent of blood-alcohol concentration per hour, or about 1 oz. of 100 proof alcohol by a 150-pound man.

§ 7.23.5 Legal Basis to Chemically Test for Drugs

Breath test instruments are designed only to detect alcohol and will not detect or measure any drugs. If you have reasonable (i.e. probable) cause to believe that the driver is under the influence of drugs, or a combination of alcohol and drugs, and you have a clear indication that a blood or urine test would reveal that fact, then you may require a person who has already given a breath test to also submit to an additional blood or urine test. (Veh. Code, § 23612, subd. (a)(2)(C).) The subject has a choice of these other tests, and completion requirements are the same as with any other implied consent tests. (Veh. Code, § 23612, subd. (a)(2)(C).)

The statute requires that you set out in your report the facts giving rise to your belief that the driver is under the influence of drugs, or the combined influence of drugs and alcohol, as well as those facts giving you a clear indication that a blood or urine test will so reveal. (Veh. Code § 23612, subd. (a)(2)(C).) It is initially difficult to tell whether an intoxicated driver has ingested alcohol, drugs, or a combination. (See *Rice* (1981) 118 Cal.App.3d 30.) "Track marks," coupled with impaired condition, obviously suggest drugs. (See *Roach* (1980) 108 Cal.App.3d 891.) Impaired condition, physical symptoms of intoxication, but an absence of alcohol odor, also suggest drug usage. (See *Howell* (1973) 30 Cal.App.3d 228.) When the subject is obviously intoxicated with an odor of alcohol, but a breath test results in a reading lower than would be expected of a person exhibiting those symptoms of intoxication, then a combination is likely and further testing is in order. (See *Roach* (1980) 108 Cal.App.3d 891.)

Where you have a reasonable basis for requiring a test of blood or urine to determine the existence of intoxicating drugs, a refusal to provide that sample is a refusal warranting license suspension, even though the driver has already given a breath sample for the purpose of indicating alcohol intoxication. (Veh. Code, § 23612, subd. (a) (1) (D); *Roach* (1980) 108 Cal.App.3d 891.)

§ 7.23.6 Test by Physical Compulsion

Although the implied consent law was intended to avoid, or at least minimize, physical confrontations with intoxicated persons in connection with obtaining samples of blood, breath, or urine, it did not eliminate the possibility of having to "forcibly" remove a sample in situations where the officer wishes to obtain this type of evidence but the suspect refused to consent. Generally, a person lawfully arrested for driving under the influence may have a bodily fluid or breath sample forcibly removed without his consent, incident to the lawful arrest, provided it is done in a reasonable, medically approved manner. (*Mercer* (1991) 53 Cal.3d 753, 760; *Hawkins* (1972) 6 Cal.3d 757; *Sugarman* (2002) 96 Cal.App.4th 210, 214.) Furthermore, doing so does not violate the suspect's "due process" rights. (*Belgrade* (9th Cir. 1997) 123 F.3d 1210, 1214.)

A warrant to obtain the sample is not required. (*Schmerber* (1966) 384 U.S. 757; *Hawkins* (1972) 6 Cal.3d 757; *Carleton* (1985) 170 Cal.App.3d 1182; *Sugarman* (2002) 96 Cal.App.4th 210, 214.) According to two California Court of Appeal cases, a formal arrest is also *not* required, as long as probably cause to arrest exists. (*Trotman* (1989) 214 Cal.App.3d 430, 435; *Deltoro* (1989) 214 Cal.App.3d 1417, 1425.) The federal Ninth

Circuit Court of Appeals, after first holding otherwise, now also agrees. (*Chapel* (9th Cir. 1995) 55 F.3d 1416.)

"Forcible" removal means only that the sample is physically taken from the driver without his consent. It is thus a "forcible" removal of blood for constitutional purposes where the subject sits passively and his only "resistance" is his refusal to consent. (Compare *Cole* (1983) 139 Cal.App.3d 870; *Barrie* (1984) 151 Cal.App.3d 1157.) The physical compulsion or force used to accomplish sample collection must be reasonable under the circumstances. (*Kraft* (1970) 3 Cal.App.3d 890.) It definitely cannot be brutal or shocking to the conscience. (See *Kraft* (1970) 3 Cal. App.3d 890; *Fite* (1968) 267 Cal.App.2d 685.) Where the force is excessive, it is unreasonable. (*Hammer* (9th Cir. 1991) 932 F.2d 842; *Kraft* (1970) 3 Cal. App.3d 890.) Use of excessive force in obtaining a sample will make it inadmissible. (See *McDonnell* (1975) 45 Cal.App.3d 653; *Kraft* (1970) 3 Cal.App.3d 890.)

There can be no magic formula for "reasonableness"; each case must turn upon its own facts. (See *Vasquez* (1962) 199 Cal.App.2d 61.) The courts recognize that because a driver who is under the influence is typically recalcitrant, obstreperous, and frequently belligerent, restraints are often necessary and appropriate. (*Kraft* (1970) 3 Cal.App.3d 890.) The use of physical force is permissible. However, no more force or restraint can be used than is necessary to accomplish the purpose; it cannot be disproportionate to need. (*Hammer* (9th Cir. 1991) 932 F.2d 842; *Kraft* (1970) 3 Cal.App.3d 890; *Bass* (1963) 214 Cal.App.2d 742.) The most common "involuntary" sample taken is blood.

In felony arrests for driving under the influence, where there has been a death or such serious injury that the victim is likely to be permanently disabled or badly disfigured, a sample should be "forcibly" collected if there is any question of intoxication or its degree. The force used should be that reasonably necessary to accomplish collection of the sample without injury to the technician or physician, the attending officers, and as little injury as possible to the driver himself. Normally this requires restraints and multiple officers. If there is no felony, only a misdemeanor, the same rule applies. (*Ford* (1992) 4 Cal.App.4th 32, 38.) That is, it is legal to "forcibly" extract a blood sample without a warrant — even in a misdemeanor case — as long as (1) there are exigent circumstances (i.e., it is necessary to test promptly because, for example, the blood-alcohol level (important evidence) is dissipating); (2) you have a basis for believing the suspect is under the influence; (3) the sample is taken in a medically approved manner, i.e., without excessive force; and (4) it is taken incident to a lawful arrest. (*Mercer* (1991) 53 Cal.3d 753, 760; *Ford* (1992) 4 Cal.App.4th 32; *Sugarman* (2002) 96 Cal.App.4th 210, 214.)

In connection with forcible extractions, however, there are at least two related problem areas that you should be aware of.

First, if the suspect agrees to provide one type of sample (such as urine), and actually provides it, then you are not entitled to extract a different sample (such as blood) by force, i.e., against the suspect's will, no matter how nicely it is done. (*Nelson* (9th Cir. 1998) 143 F.3d 1196, 1200-1204.) You only get one sample, and you don't get to choose which type. (*Fiscalini* (1991) 228 Cal.App.3d 1639.)

Second, if the suspect at first refuses to give any sample, but then changes his mind and agrees to cooperate and give breath or urine just as you are about to forcibly extract the blood, you probably have a problem. (*Hammer* (1991) 932 F.2d 842.)

On the one hand, under the implied consent law, the suspect has already "refused"; he is not entitled to change his mind, so going ahead with the forcible blood withdrawal will not affect the administrative taking of his license for refusing. On the other hand, the forcible taking of blood under such circumstances has been ruled "unreasonable" under the fourth Amendment, so that going forward could subject you and your department to civil damages. (*Nelson* (9th Cir. 1998) 143 F.3d 1196, 1200-1204; see also Hammer (1991) 932 F.2d 842, 846-852.) To avoid this possibility, it would therefore be advisable to let the suspect have his way and provide the "other" type of sample, although there has to be some limit on how far the suspect must be allowed to take this technique.

Nonconsensual sample collection may also be necessary from persons not covered by the implied consent law, i.e., persons who are not driving a "motor vehicle," but who are nevertheless subject to the DUI laws or other laws forbidding intoxication, such as drivers of horse-drawn vehicles, horsemen, or bicyclists. It is also possible to invoke the implied consent law or justify a "forcible" sample collection where the initial arrest was for some offense other than driving under the influence.

Officers arrived at the scene of a fight and one of the assailants was placed under citizen's arrest for battery. Upon accepting custody, the officers noted classic signs of intoxication and gave the arrestee field sobriety tests, which he failed. They were also told by witnesses that the arrestee had been driving his car immediately before the assault. HELD: the battery arrest was sufficient to permit taking a sample, and there was no need to "arrest" the arrestee a second time for the driving under the influence offense. (*Bianco* (1975) 55 Cal.App.3d Supp. 8.)

Always remember, however, that even though obtaining samples against a suspect's will in a medically approved manner is legal under the circumstances outlined above, force should only be used as a last resort. The implied consent law was enacted to avoid violent confrontations, and you should always try, repeatedly if necessary, to obtain actual consent before resorting to force.

§ 7.23.7 Arrest Requirement
The implied consent law has always required, and still does, that there be a "lawful arrest" for a violation of Section 23140, 23152, or 23153. (Veh. Code, §§ 23612, 23612 (a)(1); *Mercer* (1991) 53 Cal.3d 753.)

Chapter 7

In 1972, the California Supreme Court decided that a "lawful arrest" was required not only under the implied consent law, but also under the *Fourth Amendment*. That is, the court held that the results of a blood, breath, or urine test, obtained without a warrant, were admissible in a criminal trial only if the sample was taken incident to a lawful arrest. (*Hawkins* (1972) 6 Cal.3d 757, 761.)

At least two subsequent appellate court cases have held that *no* formal arrest, felony *or* misdemeanor, is necessary anymore before blood may legally be withdrawn from a possibly intoxicated suspect. These cases say that as long as you have probably cause to arrest on suspicion of driving under the influence, it is legal to withdraw blood even though no formal arrest has yet been made, and the results of the sample will be admitted into evidence at the criminal trial. (*Trotman* (1989) 214 Cal.App.3d 430, 435; *Deltoro* (1989) 214 Cal.App.3d 1417, 1425.) The Ninth Circuit Court of Appeals has also made it clear that a formal arrest is not a prerequisite to lawfully withdrawing blood from a suspect.

Chapel was severely injured in a single vehicle motorcycle accident in a remote part of a national park. Rangers and a park medic came to assist Chapel, administered first aid, and prepared an IV In doing all this, the rangers noticed telltale signs of drinking. After Chapel refused to take a Breathalyzer test, and knowing the blood-alcohol content was dissipating, the rangers instructed the medic to obtain a blood sample for later testing, which he did. The BAC turned out to be .21, and Chapel was convicted of DUI. HELD: A sample may be legally withdrawn without a warrant where (1) exigent circumstances exist, (2) the officers have probable cause to believe the suspect has been driving while under the influence, and (3) the sample is taken by trained medical personnel in accordance with accepted practice. If these three requirements are met, "an arrest is not essential to support the intrusion in the absence of a warrant..." (*Chapel* (1995) 55 F.3d 1416, 1419.)

Accordingly, the "safest" course of action would be placing the suspect under arrest as contemporaneously as possible with the non-consensual extraction of the sample, i.e., shortly before or shortly after. (See *Nieto* (1990) 219 Cal.App.3d 1275, 1278.)

§ 7.23.8 Injured or Unconscious Driver
There is no specific legislation which provides for the testing of a person who is dead, unconscious, or in a condition where consent or refusal to provide a sample is not possible. A police officer may request that a doctor or the coroner take samples of both blood and urine.

§ 7.23.9 The Best Test Rule for Drugs
Drugs for which blood is the preferred sample are basically the sedative/hypnotic substances such as barbiturates (Seconal, Amytal, Tuinal, etc.), benzodiazepines (Valium, Librium), carbonates (Equanil, Valmid), nonbarbiturates (Dilantin, Doriden, methaqualone), and Darvon. Remember to obtain 10 ml or more (two Vacutainer tubes) of blood with preservative and anticoagulant.

Drugs for which urine is the preferred sample are a mixture of drugs. Basically, if the preferred sample is not blood, then collect urine. Drugs in this category would include amphetamines, cocaine, PCP, methadone, heroin, morphine, and codeine. If you suspect marijuana intoxication, then obtain a blood sample. The lab will be able to detect the presence of THC in the blood. Some labs can also detect THC in the urine.

§ 7.24   IMPLIED CONSENT LAW

A sample of the driver's blood, breath, or urine, taken soon after the act of driving, is the best scientific evidence of intoxication and supplements fallible human observations. The sample needs to be taken soon after the arrest because the amount of alcohol or drugs in the blood begins to diminish soon after drinking or ingestion stops, as the body eliminates it from the system. (*Schmerber* (1966) 384 U.S. 757; *Skinner* (1976) 58 Cal.App.3d 591, 598.)

Accordingly, the Legislature long ago enacted the "implied consent law" (now Veh. Code § 23612) under which drivers are deemed to have given their permission to undergo a test of their blood, breath, or urine to determine the presence of alcohol and/or drugs. As of 1999, however, this law was changed to distinguish between situations where the officer suspects only *alcohol* from situations where the officer suspects *drugs*, or a *combination* of alcohol and drugs. Under this revised law, in cases involving only the suspicion of *alcohol*, the driver now has a choice of only *two* tests: breath or blood — although a urine test is still permissible under certain limited circumstances.

In cases where *drug* use is suspected, or a *combination* of drugs and alcohol, the 1999 law did not change anything: The driver still can choose either blood, breath and urine, although, if he chooses breath, the officer can require an additional test of either blood or urine.

What follows is a more detailed discussion of this law and related statutes and topics, including the forcible taking of blood in the event a driver either refuses or is unable to take or complete the test(s).

§ 7.24.1 Chemical Blood, Breath, or Urine Tests (Veh. Code §23157)

The following California statute contains most of the language and provisions contained in the Vehicle Codes of other states:

Section 23612
Any person who drives a motor vehicle shall be deemed to have given his or her consent to chemical testing of his or her blood, breath, or urine for the purpose of determining the alcoholic content of his or her blood, and to have given his or her consent to chemical testing of his or her blood or urine for the purpose of determining the drug content of his or her blood, if lawfully arrested for any offense allegedly committed in violation of Section 23140, 23152 or 23153. The testing shall be incidental to a lawful arrest.

§ 7.24.2 Chemical Test Admonition (DS–367)

The person shall be told that his or her failure to submit to or complete the required chemical testing will result in a fine, mandatory imprisonment if the person is convicted of a violation of Section 23152 or

23153, *AND* a one-year suspension, or a two- or three-year revocation of the person's driving privilege, depending on his or her prior driving record.

A refusal to take or failure to complete a test may be used as evidence against him in court and will result in a fine and imprisonment if this arrest results in a conviction, he has no right to counsel in connection with the test, and if he is unable to complete one test, he must submit to one of the remaining tests.

Note: If taken to a medical facility for treatment, he must submit to whatever tests are available.

§ 7.24.3 Mandatory License Suspension
In giving the "chemical test admonition," you must make clear to the motorist that unless he submits to and completes one of the three tests, his privilege to operate a motor vehicle will be suspended.

§ 7.24.4 No *Miranda* Warning Needed Until Arrest
Field investigation prior to arrest need not be preceded by a Miranda warning. You may ask the suspect questions, such as how much he has had to drink, and require performance of field sobriety tests without a Miranda admonition (*Berkemer v. McCarty*, 468 U.S. 420, 104 S.Ct. 3138, 82 L.Ed. 2d 317 (1984); *People v. Carter*, 108 Cal. App. 3d 127, 166 Cal. Rptr. 304 (Cal. App. 2 Dist. 1980).

§ 7.24.5 No Right to Counsel at Test
You must place the driver under arrest before any chemical test may be given. (*Hawkins* (1972) 6 Cal.3d 757; *Engleman* (1981) 116 Cal.App.3d Supp. 14.) Because actual arrest amounts to "custody," the suspect will have a right to counsel under *Miranda* in the event he is subsequently "interrogated." On the other hand, under Vehicle Code Section 23612, you must advise the driver that the right to counsel does *not* apply to the chemical tests, and that he has no right to have an attorney present before stating whether he will submit to a test, deciding which test to take, or during administration of the test. If confusion arises because of this conflict, you must indicate that the *Miranda* right to counsel is not applicable to the chemical test. (*Rust* (1968) 267 Cal.App.2d 545; *McDonnell* (1975) 45 Cal.App.3d 653; *Smith* (1969) 1 Cal.App.3d 499.) If you wish, you can further explain that *Miranda* applies only to interrogation subsequent to arrest. (See *Maxsted* (1971) 14 Cal.App.3d 982.)

§ 7.24.6 No Right to Remain Silent when Asked to Select Test
The *Miranda* right to remain silent does not include the responses to the questions of whether to take a test and of which test the driver will take.

However, this qualification need not be added to the admonition unless it appears that the driver is confused about it (See *Lampman* (1972) 28 Cal.App.3d 922.)

§ 7.24.7 Failure to Admonish

Failure to give, or a defect in, the statutory admonition only precludes license suspension or revocation and does not affect a criminal prosecution for driving under the influence. Section 23158, subdivision (b), gives the driver the right to have a person of his own choice give him an additional chemical test, at the driver's own expense. However, there is no need to advise him of this right. (*Kesler* (1969) 1 Cal.3d 74.)

§ 7.24.8 "Retention Admonition" for Breath Tests (Veh. Code §26614)

In addition to the "chemical test admonition" requirements of Section 03612, a driver who chooses a breath test must also be informed that:

—breath test equipment does not retain a breath sample for later analysis by him or anyone else;

—if he wants a sample retained, he may provide a blood or urine sample which will be retained at no cost to him; and

—if he does so, the blood or urine sample may be tested for alcohol or drug content by either party in any criminal prosecution.

This additional advisement may be given either before or after the breath test has been administered (*In re Cheryl S.*, 189 Cal. App. 3d 1240, 235 Cal. Rptr. 42 (Cal. App. 1 Dist. 1987)). However, after the test is the preferred method.

§ 7.24.9 Drug Admonition (DS–367)

If the driver has already taken a breath test, and you have reasonable cause to believe he is under the influence of drugs, you must give him yet another advisement—namely, the "drug admonition."

This admonition advises the driver that:

—the breath test he took was only to detect alcohol;

—because you believe he is under the influence of drugs or the combined influence of drugs and alcohol, he must now submit to a blood or urine test; refusal to submit to or failure to complete a blood or urine test will result in suspension or revocation of his driving privilege;

—a refusal to take or failure to complete either test may be used as evidence against him in court, and will result in a fine and imprisonment if this arrest results in a conviction;

—he has no right to counsel in connection with the test; and

—if unable to complete one of these tests, he must take and complete the other (Veh. Code §23157).

Remember, give this admonition only after the driver has chosen and completed the breath test for alcohol, and only in situations where you have reason to believe he is under the influence of drugs or the combined influence of drugs and alcohol.

§ 7.25.10   Driver's Confusion

The purpose of the implied consent or "chemical test" admonition is to make the arrestee aware of his duty to submit to and complete a chemical test at that time and the consequences of his refusal to do so. As a general rule, you need only advise the driver in the statutory language. But this is subject to one important qualification: if the driver manifests confusion or a lack of understanding, which is or should be readily apparent to you, and this confusion or lack of understanding has been induced by the language you used in giving the various admonitions, then you have an affirmative duty to clarify the situation. Failure to take or complete a chemical test attributable to officer-induced confusion creates a legitimate basis for the refusal, so that the driver's license may not be suspended (*Joyce v. DMV*, (1979) 90 Cal. App. 3d 539, 153 Cal. Rptr. 404 (Cal. App. 2 Dist. 1979)).

§ 7.24.11   What Is a Refusal?

If, after being lawfully arrested and given a standard admonition, a driver refuses to submit to and promptly complete a chemical test, his driver's license will be suspended. You have no obligation to make a second offer, or to accommodate the driver if he subsequently changes his mind (*Dunlap v. DMV*, 156 Cal. App. 3d 279, 202 Cal. Rptr. 729 (Cal. App. 5 Dist. 1984)). But what is a "refusal"? A refusal is any statement, act, or conduct by the driver which expresses a determination not to comply.

The simple refusal ("No") is obviously the easiest. In all other instances, refusal is implied by the driver's acts and conduct or the qualifications he imposes before cooperating, provided that it is indeed a fair implication. When the driver remains silent after being asked whether he will submit to a test, it constitutes a refusal. If the driver is assaultive, shouting, etc., you are not obligated to complete the admonishment and the conduct is considered a refusal.

§ 7.24.12   Time Is of the Essence

In obtaining any sample of blood, breath, or urine, time is of the essence because bodily chemistry continually removes alcohol from the system. Unless the sample is promptly taken, its alcoholic content will be reduced and will be lower than the true blood-alcohol level at the time of driving. The statute specifies that the test shall be "administered at the direction" of the peace officer, which means that it is you who determines when the test will be given (Veh. Code § 23157(a)(1)). The driver must give the sample when directed and failure to do so is a refusal, even if the driver later changes his mind and offers to provide one.

§ 7.24.13   Refusal at Time Facilities Available

The driver must agree to submit to a test when the facilities for its administration are available. If he declines when the opportunity is offered, he does not get it again, and upon failure of a different test, officers have no obligation to offer him another chance. In *Noli* (1981) 125 Cal.App.3d 446, a combative driver who selected a urine test was told that blood and breath tests could only be done at the medical center and that if it was necessary to remove him to jail to collect the urine sample because of his behavior, blood and breath tests would no longer be available. This limitation was upheld even though he was unable to provide a urine sample. "[S]ection 13353 [now § 23612] did not require the officers to offer [him] another opportunity to choose one of the two tests he had categorically refused, when it would mean transporting him back ... The officers had more important things to do than play games with [him] in his condition." (*Noli* (1981) 125 Cal.App.3d 446.)

§ 7.25   DUI LEGAL DECISIONS

At present, determining whether a person is too inebriated to drive is based on a 1935 decision by the Arizona Supreme Court, which has been endorsed by the American Medical Association and the National Safety Council.

The expression "under the influence of intoxicating liquor" covers not only all the well-known and easily recognizable conditions and degrees of intoxication, but also any abnormal mental or physical condition that is the result of indulging to any degree in intoxicating liquors and which tends to deprive the individual of that clearness of intellect and control of himself which he would otherwise possess. If the ability of the driver of an automobile has been lessened in the slightest degree by the use of intoxicating liquors, then the driver is deemed to be under the influence of intoxicating liquor. The mere fact that a driver has taken a drink does not place him under the ban of the statute unless such drink has some influence upon him, lessening in some degree his ability to handle an automobile.

California has interpreted this decision in the following manner: The presumptive level of being under the influence of an alcoholic beverage under the California Vehicle Code is 0.08 (January 1, 1990). (Remember, this is a Vehicle Code standard, and is intended for Vehicle Code situations.)

Section 23610 Vehicle Code: Driving While Intoxicated (Presumption)
1. 0.05 percent or less = The person is NOT under the influence of alcohol.
2. 0.05 percent or more, but less than 0.03 percent = This level "shall not give rise to any presumption."
   (a) The law doesn't say whether the suspect is under the influence or not.
   (b) A person could be prosecuted for driving under the influence, and a number have been convicted.
   (c) Prosecution would really depend on the lack of driving skill, poor performance during field sobriety tests (FST's), and other signs of impairment for a District Attorney to decide.
3. 0.08 percent or more = "It shall be presumed that the person was under the influence of an alcoholic beverage."

Percent of weight of alcohol in the blood shall be based upon grams of alcohol per 100 milliliters of blood.

§ 7.26 DRUNK DRIVING LAWS

Drunk driving, driving under the influence, or driving while intoxicated (DUI/DWI) laws are defined by each state. For the most part, they follow similar guidelines or rules concerning drunk driving. No matter how strict or lenient the DUI laws are, the consequences of driving drunk can be severe and life-changing.

DUI laws may include specific details such as blood-alcohol content level, which varies with each state but generally must not exceed .08 percent. License suspension or revocation traditionally follows conviction for drunk driving. Forty-five states permit convicted drunk driving offenders to drive only if their vehicles have been equipped with ignition interlocks. Expungement of a DUI criminal conviction varies by state, the type of DUI conviction and sentence, age of DUI, offender, etc.

The California Supreme court has also recognized the gravity of the problem, (1) by upholding the blood-alcohol level provision of Vehicle Code Section 23152 (*Burg* (1983) 35 Cal.3d 257), and (2) by approving the use of "sobriety checkpoints" if certain safeguards are followed. (*Ingersoll* (1987) 43 Cal.3d 1321; *Banks* (1993) 6 Cal.4th 926.) Checkpoints have also been upheld by the United States Supreme Court. (*Sitz* (1990) 110 S.Ct. 2481.) Once you have detained a driver, your reasonable suspicion may develop into probable cause to arrest as a result of questioning, closer observation of the suspect, and administration of field sobriety tests and/or the horizontal gaze nystagmus (HGN) test.

For several years, a legal controversy swirled around the admissibility of in-court testimony from officers concerning HGN test results and their meaning. In 1994, the California Supreme Court finally ruled that HGN was indeed a "new scientific technique" that had to meet the Kelly/Frye standard of having gained general acceptance in the relevant scientific community (namely, behavioral psychologists, highway safety experts, criminalists, and medical doctors concerned with the recognition of alcohol intoxication). (Leahy (1994) 8 Cal.4th 587.) Following Leahy, however, a California appellate court (the Fourth District, in San Diego) ruled that the HGN test had in fact been shown to meet the Kelly/Frye standard. (Joehnk (1995) 35 Cal.App.4th 1488.) Therefore, it should now be settled that an officer, without any scientific qualification, can properly use HGN test results in the field to help form an opinion about whether a suspect is under the influence and in court may testify about how the HGN test was administered and what the results were — but without translating them into a specific BAC level.

§ 7.27 RELATED VEHICLE CODE SECTIONS

The following are related vehicle code sections.

1. Drinking While Driving (Veh. Code § 23220)—Infraction

No person shall drink any alcoholic beverage while driving a motor vehicle upon any highway or public lands.

Alcohol

2. Drinking in Motor Vehicle (Veh. Code § 23221)—Infraction

No person shall drink any alcoholic beverage while in a motor vehicle upon a highway.

3. Possession of Open Container While Driving (Veh. Code § 23222) —Infraction

No person shall have in his or her possession on his or her person, while driving a motor vehicle upon a highway, any bottle, can, or other receptacle, containing any alcoholic beverage which has been opened, or a seal broken, or the contents of which have been partially removed.

This section does *not* apply to a car which is parked (not moving) in a public parking lot. (*Lopez* (1987) 197 Cal.App.3d 93.)

4. Possession of Open Container in Motor Vehicle (Veh. Code § 23223) —Infraction

No person shall have in his or her possession on his or her person, while in a motor vehicle upon a highway, any bottle, can, or other receptacle, containing any alcoholic beverage which has been opened, or a seal broken, or the contents of which have been partially removed.

This section does not apply to a car which is parked (not traveling) in a public parking lot (*People v. Lopez*, 197 Cal. App. 3d 93, 242 Cal. Rptr. 668 (Cal. App. 4 Dist. 1987)).

5. Possession of Alcohol in Vehicle (Veh. Code § 23224)—Infraction

No person under the age of 21 years shall knowingly drive any motor vehicle carrying any alcoholic beverage, unless the person is accompanied by a parent, responsible adult relative, any other adult designated by the parent, or legal guardian for the purpose of transportation of an alcoholic beverage, or is employed by a licensee under the Alcoholic Beverage Control Act and is driving the motor vehicle during regular hours and in the course of the person's employment.

These same requirements also apply to passengers.

6. Storage of Open Container (Veh. Code § 23225)—Infraction

It is unlawful for the registered owner (RO) of any motor vehicle, or the driver if the RO is not then present, to keep any open container of alcohol in the vehicle, including inside the glove compartment, when the vehicle is upon any highway or designated public lands, unless the container is kept in the trunk or, if there is no trunk, some other area of the vehicle not normally occupied by the driver or passengers, meaning some place beyond their easy arm's reach. (*Souza* (1993) 15 Cal.App.4th 1646.)

If the vehicle is an off-highway motor vehicle, as defined, *and* has no trunk, the open container must be kept in a secure, fully enclosed container that is actually *locked*.

Also, this statute, by its own terms, does not apply to the living quarters of a housecar or camper.

7.   Storage of Open Container in Passenger Compartment (Veh. Code § 23226)—Infraction

It is unlawful for any person to keep in the passenger compartment of a motor vehicle, when the vehicle is upon any highway, any bottle, can, or other receptacle containing any alcoholic beverage which has been opened, or a seal broken, or the contents of which have been partially removed.

This section shall not apply to the living quarters of a housecar or camper.

8.   Possession of Alcoholic Beverage; Exceptions (Veh. Code § 23229)

Except as provided in Section 23229.1, Sections 23221 and 23223 do not apply to passengers in any bus, taxicab, or limousine for hire licensed to transport passengers pursuant to the Public Utilities Code or proper local authority, or the living quarters of a housecar or camper.

Except as provided in Section 23229.1, Section 23225 does not apply to the driver or owner of a bus, taxicab, or limousine for hire licensed to transport passengers pursuant to the Public Utilities Code or proper local authority.

9.   Possession of Alcoholic Beverage; Charter-Party Carriers (Veh. Code § 23229.1)

Subject to subdivision (b), Sections 23223 and 23225 do not apply to any charter-party carrier of passengers, as defined in Section 5360 of the Public Utilities Code, operating a limousine for hire when the driver of the vehicle transports any passenger under the age of 21.

For purposes of subdivision (a), it is not a violation of Section 23225 for any charter-party carrier of passengers operating a limousine for hire which is licensed pursuant to the Public Utilities Code to keep any bottle, can, or other receptacle containing any alcoholic beverage in a locked utility compartment within the area occupied by the driver and passengers.

§ 7.28   DO TOUGH DRUNK DRIVER LAWS WORK?

A 2002 study shows that states with tougher alcohol laws have significantly fewer fatal car crashes. So, as the strictness of a variety of alcohol regulations increase, the rate of alcohol-related traffic fatalities tends to decrease.

Alcohol

Using data from the National Highway and traffic Safety Administration, Cohen and her colleagues analyzed traffic-related fatalities from 97 cities in 38 U.S. states from 1995 through 1997. The researchers found that more than 44 percent of all urban car crashes during that time period involved alcohol. In cities with stricter regulations on access to alcohol and tougher penalties for violations, the alcohol-related fatality rates were lower than cities with looser laws. The researchers looked at 20 possible alcohol regulations, such as limiting the number of liquor licenses in a community, implementing harsher penalties for driving under the influence, publishing the names of drunk drivers in the local newspaper, and conducting sobriety checkpoints. Cohen's team found that cities that implemented fewer than nine of the regulations had a 46 percent higher rate of alcohol-related traffic accidents than cities with 15 or more of these regulations in place.

However, it is also reported that the rate of injuries and deaths in the U.S. highways is at its lowest in 38 years. Officials credit the drop to a decrease in drunken driving and increase in seatbelt use. According to the report from the National Highway Traffic Safety Administration (NHTSA), 42,643 people died in traffic crashes in 2003, a decline of 362 from 2002. The death rate was 1.48 per 100 million miles driven, the lowest level since record keeping began in 1966.For the fifth straight year, California experienced an increase in alcohol-related traffic deaths. On the positive side, however, alcohol-related injuries and fatalities declined in 2003 in areas of the state that conducted sobriety checkpoints.

So it is difficult to say which tough drunk driving law is effective. As more research is conducted, we will begin to see a clearer picture. For now, it looks like a combination of factors are responsible.

§ 7.29 BOATING UNDER THE INFLUENCE

In Chapter 5 of the California Harbors and Navigation Code, commencing with Section 650, address problems of operating a boat while intoxicated. Studies in fatal motorboat accidents show that in approximately 60 percent of the cases where blood-alcohol could be documented, alcohol was a factor in the accident. Although it is legal to operate a vessel with an open container aboard, and even to consume alcohol while operating the vessel, it is not legal to drink to the level of intoxication.

The law provides:

(1) a statutory presumption of intoxication at .08 percent (CHN Code § 655);

(2) "zero tolerance" (.01 BAC or more) for persons under the age of 21 (CHN Code § 655.6);

(3) the authority to arrest without a warrant in specified cases (CHN Code § 663.1);

(4) provisions for chemical testing which parallel those for DUI cases (CHN Code § 655.1);

(5) enhanced penalties upon conviction for refusal to submit to such tests (CHN Code § 655.5);

(6) classifications for manslaughter during operation of a vessel (including water skis, aquaplanes, etc.). This offense is specifically classified as a type of vehicular manslaughter and is governed by parallel provisions. (Pen. Code §§191.5(b), 192.5).

A comprehensive peace officer's guide on enforcement of intoxicated boater laws is available at no charge from the Department of Boating and Waterways, 2000 Evergreen Street, Suite 100, Sacramento, CA, 95815, or by calling (916) 263-8183.

§7.30 FLYING UNDER THE INFLUENCE

It is unlawful for any person who is under the influence of an alcoholic beverage or any drug or an alcohol/drug combination to operate an aircraft in the air or on the ground or water or to engage in parachuting for sport (Pub. Util. Code §21407.1(a)).

No person shall operate an aircraft who has 0.04 BAC or higher.

The Implied Consent Law applies (Pub. Util. Code §2 1407.2).

§ 7.31 SHOULD ALCOHOL BE PROHIBITED?

Alcohol addiction is second only to nicotine addiction in incidence and prevalence in the United States today. A conservative estimate is that ten million Americans are alcoholics, but figures as high as fifteen million alcoholics and "problem drinkers" are also cited. Alcoholics are unable to refrain from their drug even though they decide to, want to, and try to quit drinking alcohol; those who succeed for a time remain in imminent danger of relapse. To the millions of alcoholics must be added millions of "spree drinkers," who are not addicted but get roaring drunk from time to time.

Alcohol addiction is destructive to the human mind. In many states, alcoholic disorders lead all other diseases in mental hospital admissions. Alcohol abuse is also destructive to the human body. High concentrations of alcohol are directly irritating to the mucosal lining of the stomach, causing acute and chronic gastritis. Acute and chronic liver disease is common in people who have been drinking large amounts of alcohol for a long time. There is a progressive disturbance in neurological function that occurs as a result of an episode of acute alcohol intoxication. Withdrawal from alcohol may set off a variety of nervous system disturbances including delirium and convulsions.

In some of these disorders, the damage is due mainly to malnutrition rather than to the direct effects of alcohol. Such nutritional disorders include Wernicke's encephalopathy, Korsakoff's psychosis, and alcoholic polyneuropathy.

Alcohol

Wernicke-Korsakoff Syndrome. This syndrome is a brain disorder involving loss of specific brain function caused by thiamine deficiency. Alternative names are Korsakoff Psychosis, Alcoholic Encephalopathy, Encephalopathy - alcoholic, Wernicke's Disease. The syndrome is actually a spectrum, including two separate sets of symptoms, one of which tends to start when the other subsides. Wernicke's Encephalopathy involves damage to multiple nerves in both the central nervous system (brain and spinal cord) and the peripheral nervous system (the rest of the body). It may also include symptoms caused by alcohol withdrawal. The cause is generally attributed to malnutrition, especially lack of vitamin B1 (thiamine), which commonly accompanies habit alcohol use or alcoholism.

Heavy alcohol use interferes with the metabolism of thiamine, so even in the unusual cases where alcoholics are eating a balanced diet while drinking heavily, the metabolic problem persists because most of the thiamine is not absorbed.

Korsakoff Syndrome, or Korsakoff Psychosis, tends to develop as Wernicke's symptoms diminish. It involves impairment of memory out of proportion to problems with other cognitive functions. Patients often attempt to hide their poor memory by confabulating. The patient will create detailed, believable stories about experiences or situations to cover gaps in memory. This is not usually a deliberate attempt to deceive because the patient often believes what he or she is saying to be true. It can occur whether or not the thiamine deficiency was related to alcoholism and with other types of brain damage. Korsakoff Psychosis involves damage to areas of the brain involved with memory.

Symptoms of Wernicke-Korsakoff Syndrome include vision changes (double vision, eye movement abnormalities, eyelid drooping), loss of muscle coordination (unsteady, uncoordinated walking), loss of memory (can be profound), inability to form new memories, confabulation (making up stories to explain behavior that have little relation to reality), and hallucinations. Note that symptoms indicating alcohol withdrawal may also be present or may develop.

Alcoholic Polyneuropathy. Many patients show signs of damage to the motor and sensory fibers of peripheral nerves. Most complain of muscle weakness of the legs and arms or numbness and tingling of the skin. A few suffer from burning pain in the feet or hands or deep aching of the legs.

Whether alcohol is solely responsible for this damage to mind and body or whether defective nutrition also plays a role has long been debated. Alcohol contains calories; indeed, a heavy drinker may consume half or more of his caloric needs in the form of alcohol. The result is to reduce quite drastically his consumption of proteins, vitamins, and other essential nutrients. The informed consensus is that the two effects march hand in hand; irreversible brain and liver damage, for example, is less severe in the alcoholic who maintains adequate nutrition—but it can occur all the same. Making alcohol unavailable would thus contribute enormously to physical as well as mental health.

Alcohol is also, by a wide margin, the biggest law enforcement problem in the United States today. Forty percent of all arrests are for public drunkenness or for drunk driving. Many homicides are alcohol-related. Alcohol is a significant factor in domestic violence and child abuse. The relationship between alcohol and suicide is very close.

One of the most powerful arguments in favor of alcohol prohibition is rarely advanced—that it is useless to prohibit other drugs, so long as alcohol remains freely available.

This discussion hardly exhausts the arguments for alcohol prohibition, but perhaps it is sufficient to demonstrate the inherent logic of such a proposal. From the humanitarian as well as the societal point of view, for the benefit of drinkers and potential drinkers as well as teetotalers, for the benefit of ex-heroin addicts and users of other drugs, and especially for the benefit of young people, alcohol should be promptly prohibited—except for one consideration. In contrast to the many logical arguments in favor of alcohol prohibition, the one decisive argument *against* such a measure is purely pragmatic: prohibition doesn't work. It should work, but it doesn't. The evidence, of course, was accumulated during the thirteen-year period from 1920 to 1933. The arguments in favor of prohibition before 1920 were overwhelming. The Eighteenth Amendment (Prohibition) passed both houses of Congress by the required two-thirds majority in December 1917 and was ratified by the required three-fourths of the forty-eight state legislatures a bare thirteen months later. After experiencing alcohol prohibition for thirteen years, however, the nation rebelled. The Twenty-First Amendment (Prohibition Repeal) passed both houses of Congress by the required two-thirds majority in February 1933—and this time it took less than ten months to secure ratification by three-fourths of the forty-eight state legislatures.

Alcohol prohibition *was not* repealed because people decided that alcohol was a harmless drug. On the contrary, the United States learned during Prohibition, even more than in prior decades, the true horrors of the drug. What brought about repeal was the slowly dawning awareness that alcohol prohibition wasn't working.

Alcohol remained available during Prohibition. People still got drunk, still became alcoholics, still suffered delirium tremens. Drunk drivers remained a frequent menace on the highways. Drunks continued to commit suicide, to kill others, and to be killed by others. They continued to beat their own family, sometimes fatally. The courts, jails, hospitals, and mental hospitals were still filled with drunks. In some respects and in some parts of the country, perhaps, the situation was a little better during Prohibition—but in other respects it was unquestionably worse. Instead of consuming alcoholic beverages manufactured under the safeguards of state and federal standards, for example, people now drank "rotgut," some of it adulterated, some of it contaminated. The use of methyl alcohol, a poison, because ethyl alcohol was unavailable or too costly, led to blindness and death; "ginger jake," an adulterant found in bootleg beverages, produced paralysis and death. The disreputable saloon was replaced by the even less savory speakeasy. There was a shift from relatively mild light wines and beers to hard liquors—less bulky and therefore less hazardous to manufacture, transport, and sell on the black market. Young people—especially respectable young women, who rarely got drunk in public before 1920—now staggered out of speakeasies and reeled down the streets. There were legal closing hours for saloons; the speakeasies stayed open night and day. Organized crime syndicates took control of alcohol distribution, establishing power bases that (it is alleged) still survive. Marijuana, a drug previously little used in the United States, was first popularized during the period of Prohibition, and ether was also imbibed. The use of other drugs increased, also; coffee consumption, for example, soared from 9 pounds per capita in 1919 to 12.9 pounds in 1920. The list is long and could be lengthened—but we need not belabor the obvious.

During the early years of Prohibition, it was argued that all that was wrong was lack of effective law enforcement. So enforcement budgets were increased, more Prohibition agents were hired, arrests were facilitated by giving agents more power, and penalties were escalated. Prohibition still didn't work. The United States thus learned its lesson with respect to alcohol. More remarkably, the mere memory of Prohibition, years after Repeal, is still so repellent that no proposal to revive it would be taken seriously.

The Twenty-First Amendment left power in the states to retain statewide alcohol prohibition—and made it a federal offense to ship alcoholic beverages into a dry state. Statewide alcohol prohibition failed, however, like national prohibition. State after state repealed its statewide alcohol prohibition laws; Mississippi's, in 1966, was the last to go.

In summary, far more would be gained by making alcohol unavailable than by making any other drug unavailable. Yet the United States, after a thirteen-year trial, resolutely turned its face against alcohol prohibition. Society recognized that prohibition does not in fact prohibit and that it brings in its wake additional adverse effects.

Chapter 7

References

Coccheto, D.M., S.M. Owens, M. Perez-Reyes, et al. "Relationship Between Plasma Delta-9-THC Concentration and Pharmacological Effects in Man." Psychopharmacology 75 (1981): 158-164.

Cohen, Deborah. "Traffic Fatalities." Preventive Medicine (February 2002).

Doweiko, Harold. Concepts of Chemical Dependency. Pacific Grove: Cole Publishing Co., 1990.

Forney, R.B., & Hughes, F.W. "Meprobamate, ethanol or meprobamate-ethanol combinations on performance of human subjects under delayed autofeedback (DAF)." Journal of Psychology 57 (1964): 431-436.

Girdano and Dusek. Drug Education: Content and Methods. New York: Random House, 1988.

Goode, Erick. Drugs in American Society. New York: Alfred N. Knopf, Inc., 1989.

Guram, M.S.; Howden, C.W.; and Holt, S. "Alcohol and drug interactions." Practical Gastroenterology 16.8 (1992) 50-54.

International Association of Chiefs of Police and the Correctional Association of New York. Alcohol and Alcoholism: A Police Handbook. New York: Christopher D. Smithers Foundations, Inc., 1978.

"Intoxication." Drug Abuse and Alcoholism Newsletter. 15.7 (1986).

Kelly, Norbert L. "Social & Legal Programs of Control in the United States." Alcohol Education for Classroom and Community. Ed. McCarthy. New York: McGraw-Hill, 1964.

Kissin, B. "Interactions of ethyl alcohol and other drugs." The Biology of Alcoholism: Volume 3. New York: Plenum Press, 1974.

Lieber, C.S. "Interaction of ethanol with other drugs." Medical and Nutritional Complications of Alcoholism: Mechanisms and Management. New York: Plenum Press, 1992.

National Institute on Drug Abuse. "Drug Concentrations and Driving Impairment: Consensus Development Panel." Journal of American Medical Association 254 (1985) 2018-2021.

Oakley, Ray. S. Drugs, Society and Human Behavior. St. Louis, MO: C.V. Mosby Co., 1972.

Sands, B.F.; Knapp, C.M.; & Ciraulo, D.A. "Medical consequences of alcohol-drug interactions." Alcohol Health & Research World 17.4 (1993): 316-320.

Schuckit, Marc. "Is there a Protracted Abstinence Syndrome with Drugs?" Drug Abuse and Alcoholism Newsletter. Vol. 20.4 (1991).

U.S. Dept. of Transportation. "Guide for Detecting Drunk Drivers at Night." DOT HS 805-711, 2nd ed., January, 1982.

CHAPTER 8

NARCOTIC DRUGS OF ABUSE

§ 8.1 INTRODUCTION

The term "narcotic," which is derived from the Greek word for stupor, originally referred to a variety of substances that dulled the senses and relieved pain. Today, the term is used in a number of ways. Some individuals define narcotics as those substances that bind at opiate receptors (cellular membrane proteins activated by substances like heroin or morphine) while others refer to any illicit substance as a narcotic. The "narcotic drugs" (which originally referred to a variety of substances which relieve pain and produce sleep) in current usage refers to: (1) opium and its derivatives (heroin, morphine, and codeine), or (2) synthetic narcotics (such as methadone, Demerol, Talwin) which have properties similar to the opium derivatives.

Narcotic drugs are the most effective pain relievers known. They are among the most valuable drugs available to physicians, and are widely used to relieve short-term acute pain, reduce suffering during terminal illnesses, and promote rest so the body can restore itself. Because of the physical and/or psychological addiction which results from their abuse, the use of these substances is controlled. Heroin is illegal for anyone to use.

There are several substances legally listed with the narcotics which are not covered in this chapter. Because their effects on the body are different, they are covered in other chapters. These are cocaine (a stimulant), peyote, and psilocybin (psychedelic).

There are three sources of narcotics: natural, semi-synthetic, and synthetic.

§ 8.2 NARCOTICS OF NATURAL ORIGIN

Narcotics cultivation and trafficking has a long tradition in some parts of the world.

The poppy *Papaver somniferum* is the source for nonsynthetic narcotics. It was grown in the Mediterranean region as early as 5000 B.C., and has since been cultivated in a number of countries throughout the world.

Foreign sources of opium are responsible for the entire supply of heroin consumed in the United States. Efforts to reduce domestic heroin availability face significant problems. Unlike cocaine, which is concentrated in South America, opium production occurs in three source regions — Southeast Asia, Southwest Asia, and Latin America — creating a worldwide problem. While an undetermined amount of the opium is consumed in the producing regions, a significant amount of the drug is converted to heroin and sent to Europe and North America. The routes, volume, and methods for the transshipment of heroin vary between the producing regions. Heroin from all three regions reaches the United States using all forms of air, maritime, and overland conveyances. Rising purity levels and lower prices have helped contribute to heroin's popularity.

Historically, most of the world's illicit opium for heroin has been grown in the Golden Triangle of Southeast Asia. The Golden Triangle, an immense natural fortress of heavily forested highlands in Northern Thailand, Burma, and Laos, produces tons of opium that are converted to morphine and heroin for distribution in the United States and Europe.

While the United States does not receive large quantities of illegal drugs from Asia, historically the Golden Crescent of Pakistan and Afghanistan have provided the raw materials for much of the world heroin. The narcotic trade has a long and infamous tradition in the Middle East. Poppy fields have been cultivated for centuries. The drug trade is deeply entrenched throughout the Middle East, with Lebanon being the most widely known area for such activity. The other hot spot of drug activity in the region has been in the central Asian region. In 2000, the United States received about 5% of its heroin from Afghanistan (ONDCP 2004). By 2002, Afghanistan was reported to be the world's leading opium producer (BBC 2003). Opium cultivation could drop in 2005. Afghan President Hamid Karzai's call for a "holy war" on drugs and campaigns to eradicate opium poppy crops appear to have persuaded many farmers to plant legal crops.

Another area of opium production is Mexico. Much of the heroin consumed in the United States comes from Mexico. To explain this we need to go back a few years. The North American heroin traffic is a phenomenon of the heroin epidemic of the sixties. Then there was a demand for white heroin, which everybody knew was refined in Marseilles, France, from a morphine base of Turkish origin. In 1972 the Turkish government banned poppy production, creating a shortage of opium/heroin for the illicit market. From this point on Mexico became a major supplier of "brown" and "tar" heroin to the United States.

However, Latin America has emerged, in recent years, as the primary supplier of heroin to the United States. Colombian and Mexican heroin comprises 60 and 24 percent, respectively, of the heroin seized today in the United States. Low-level opium poppy cultivation in Venezuela and even more limited growing in Peru currently produce only marginal amounts of heroin but could become the foundation for an expanding opium and heroin industry beyond Colombia. Opium poppy cultivation in Venezuela is limited to the mountains opposite Colombia's growing area and appears to be a spillover from cultivation of the Colombian side of the border. Reports indicate that opium poppy cultivation in Peru over the last several years is nearly negligible.

Narcotic Drugs of Abuse

There were no legal restrictions on the importation or use of opium until the early 1900s. In those days patent medicines often contained opium without any warning label. Today there are state, federal, and international laws governing the production and distribution of narcotic substances. With long-established trafficking and distribution networks and exclusive markets for black tar and brown powder heroin, Mexico's hold on the United States heroin market in the West seems secure. Mexico grows only about two percent of the world's illicit opium, but virtually the entire crop is converted into heroin for the United States market. Opium cultivation and production in Mexico have been relatively stable through most of the 1990s.

After several years of intense focus on Mexico, United States drug officials are turning their attention to Central America and South America, where traffickers have developed new transit points for smuggling Columbian white heroin into the United States.

Heroin consumption and overdoses are rising in the United States, partly as a consequence of the diversified smuggling routes. With purity levels as high as 90 percent, Colombian white heroin is highly addictive and increasingly seen as chic. Sold as a bitter-tasting white powder, it is widely available in forms that can be smoked or snorted, taking away the stigma of injecting heroin with needles.

Traditionally, Colombian white heroin moved through Miami, New York, and Puerto Rico, but smugglers began moving it via Mexico in the late 1990s, often following the same routes as cocaine across the porous border into the United States. Central American countries such as Panama and Nicaragua are popular staging points for delivering the highly refined Colombian heroin to Mexico or directly into the United States via passengers on cruise ships or airliners, or as packets hidden in cargo shipments.

Another area of minor concern is the domestic cultivation of the opium poppy. How much this will be a problem in the future remains to be seen.

A two-acre field of 40,000 lavender opium poppies were discovered growing in the Sierra National Forest 35 miles northeast of Fresno, California. The 40,000 plants could have produced 40 pounds of raw opium or 4 pounds of heroin. A pound of heroin sells wholesale for between $16,000 to $18,000. Retail heroin sells for $50 to $100 a gram. In 1999, opium sold for $15,000 a pound. It has been illegal to grow opium poppies in the United States since 1932 (DEA 2003).

At least 25 alkaloids can be extracted from opium. These fall into two general categories. The first, known as the phenanthrene alkaloids, represented by morphine and codeine, are medically used as analgesics and cough suppressants. Heroin, an illicit narcotic, is also in this category. The second category is the isoquinoline alkaloids, represented by papaverine (an intestinal relaxant) and noscapine (a cough suppressant). Although a small amount of opium is medically used to make antidiarrheal preparations, such as paregoric, virtually all the opium imported in to the United States for medical use is broken down into its alkaloid constituents, principally morphine and codeine.

§ 8.2.1   Origin and History of Opium Poppy

The source of opium is the opium poppy, *Papaver somniferum*, one of the few species of Papaver that produces opium. Through centuries of cultivation and breeding the poppy for its opium, a species of the plant evolved that is now known as somniferum. The genus, Papaver, is the Greek word for "poppy." The species, somniferum, is Latin for "sleep-inducing."

The psychological effects of opium may have been known to the ancient Sumerians (circa 4000 B.C.) whose symbol for the poppy was hul (joy) and gil (plant). The plant was known in Europe at least 4,000 years ago, as evidenced by fossil remains of poppy seed cake and poppy pods found in the Swiss lake dwellings of the Neolithic Age. Opium was probably consumed by the ancient Egyptians and was known to the Greeks as well. References to the poppy are found in Homer's works, The Iliad and The Odyssey. Hippocrates (460-357 B.C.), the Father of Medicine, recommended drinking the juice of the white poppy mixed with the seed of nettle.

The opium poppy probably reached China about the 7th century A.D. through the efforts of Arab traders who advocated its use for medicinal purposes. In Chinese literature, however, there are earlier references to its use. The noted Chinese surgeon, Hua To of the Three Kingdoms (220-264 A.D.), used opium preparations and Cannabis indica for his patients to swallow before undergoing major surgery.

The beginning of widespread opium use in China has been associated by some historians with the introduction of tobacco into that country by the Dutch, from Java in the 17th century. The Chinese were reported to mix opium with tobacco. The practice was adopted throughout the area and eventually resulted in increased opium smoking with and without tobacco.

In 1803, the German pharmacist F. W. Serturner isolated and described the principal alkaloid in opium, which he named morphium after Morpheus, the Greek god of dreams. The invention of the syringe and the discovery of other alkaloids of opium soon followed: codeine in 1832 and papaverine in 1848. By the 1850s, the medicinal use of pure alkaloids, rather than crude opium preparations, was common in Europe.

In the United States, opium preparations became widely available in the 19th century, and morphine was used extensively as a painkiller for wounded soldiers during the Civil War. The inevitable result was opium addiction, contemporarily called "the army disease" or "soldier's disease." These opium and morphine abuse problems prompted scientific search for potent but nonaddictive painkillers. In the 1870s, chemists developed an opium-based and supposedly nonaddictive substitute for morphine.

The Bayer Pharmaceutical Company of Germany was the first to produce the new drug in large quantities under the brand name Heroin.

§ 8.2.1(a)   The Opium Poppy Plant

The opium poppy, Papaver somniferum, is an annual plant, i.e., the plant matures one time, and does not regenerate itself. New seed must be planted each season. From a small seed, it grows, flowers, and bears fruit (a pod) only once. The entire growth cycle for most varieties of this plant takes about 120 days. The tiny seeds (like the seeds on a poppy seed roll) germinate quickly in warm air and sufficient soil moisture. In less than 6 weeks, the young plants emerge from the soil, grow a set of four leaves, and resemble a small cabbage in appearance. The lobed, dentate (jagged-edged) leaves are glaucous green with a dull gray or blue tint.

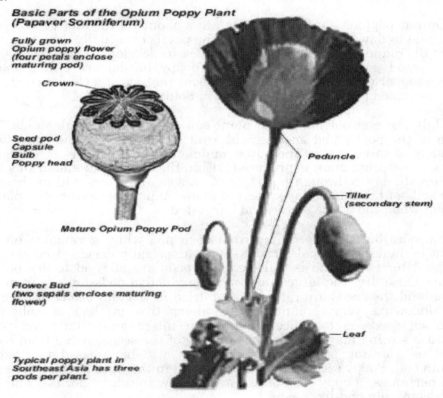

Basic Parts of the Opium Poppy Plant (Papaver Somniferum)

Fully grown Opium poppy flower (four petals enclose maturing pod)

Crown

Seed pod Capsule Bulb Poppy head

Peduncle

Mature Opium Poppy Pod

Tiller (secondary stem)

Flower Bud (two sepals enclose maturing flower)

Leaf

Typical poppy plant in Southeast Asia has three pods per plant.

Within 2 months, the plant will grow from 1 to 2 feet in height, with one primary, long, smooth stem. The upper portion of this stem is without leaves and is called the "peduncle." One or more secondary stems, called "tillers," may grow from the main step of the plant. Single poppy plants in Southeast Asia often have more than one tiller.

The main stem of a fully matured Papaver somniferum ranges between 2 and 5 feet in height. The green leaves are oblong, toothed, and lobed and vary between 4 to 15 inches in length at maturity. The

Chapter 8

matured leaves have no commercial value except for use as animal fodder.

As the plant grows tall, the main stem and each tiller terminate in a flower bud. During the development of the bud, the peduncle portion of the stem elongates and forms a distinctive "hook" that causes the bud to be turned upside down. As the flower develops, the peduncle straightens and the buds point upward. A day or two after the buds first point upward, the two outer segments of the bud, called "sepals," fall away, exposing the flower petals. At first, the exposed flower blossom is crushed and crinkled, but the petals soon expand and become smooth in the sun. Poppy flowers have four petals. The petals may be single or double and are either white, pink, reddish purple, crimson red, or variegated.

Opium poppies generally flower after about 90 days of growth and continue to flower for 2 to 3 weeks. The petals eventually drop to reveal a small, round, green pod that continues to develop. These pods (also called seed pods, capsules, bulbs, or poppy heads) are either oblate, elongated, or globular and mature to about the size of a chicken egg. The oblate-shaped pods are more common in Southeast Asia.

Only the pod portion of the plant can produce opium alkaloids. The skin of the poppy pod encloses the wall of the ovary. The ovary wall consists of three layers: the outer, middle and inner layers. The plant's latex (raw opium gum) is produced within the ovary wall and drains into the middle layer through a system of vessels and tubes within the pod. The cells of the middle layer secrete more than 95 percent of the plant's opium when the pod is scored and harvested.

Farmers harvest the opium from each pod while it remains on the plant by making vertical incisions with a specially designed homemade knife. After the opium is collected, the pods are allowed to dry on the stem. Once dry, the largest and most productive pods are cut from the stem, and the seeds are removed and dried in the sun before storing for the following year's planting. An alternative method of collecting planting seeds is to collect them from intentionally unscored pods, because scoring may diminish the quality of the seeds. Aside from being used as planting seed, poppy seed may also be pressed to produce cooking oil. Poppy seed oil may also be used in the manufacture of paints and perfumes. Poppy seed oil is straw yellow in color, odorless, and has a pleasant, almond-like taste.

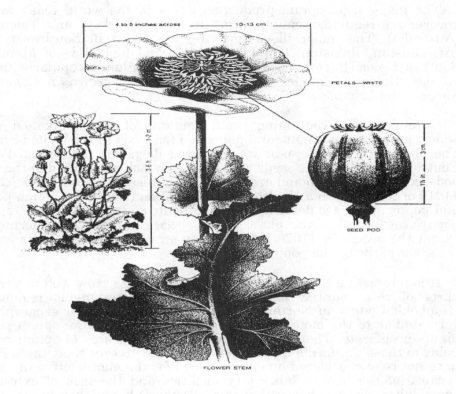

The Opium Poppy—*Papaver Somniferum*. (Source: Smith, Kline and French Laboratories.)

§ 8.2.1(b)   Opium Poppy Growing Areas

The opium poppy thrives in temperate, warm climates with low humidity and requires only a moderate amount of water before and during the early stages of growth.

The opium poppy plant can be grown in a variety of soils — clay, sandy loam, sandy, and sandy clay — but grows best in a sandy loam soil. This type of soil has good moisture-retentive and nutrient-retentive properties, is easily cultivated, and has a favorable structure for root development. Clay soil types are hard and difficult to pulverize into a good soil texture. The roots of a young poppy plant cannot readily penetrate clay soils, and growth is inhibited. Sand soil, by contrast, does not retain sufficient water or nutrients for proper growth of the plant.

Excessive moisture or extremely arid conditions will affect the poppy plant's growth adversely thus reducing the alkaloid content. Poppy plants can become waterlogged and die after a heavy rainfall in poorly drained soil. Heavy rainfall in the second and third months of growth can leach alkaloids from the plant and spoil the harvest. Dull, rainy or cloudy weather during this growth stage may reduce both the quantity and the quality of the alkaloid content.

Chapter 8

The major legal opium production areas in the world today are in government-regulated opium farms in India, Turkey, and Tasmania (Australia). The major illegal growing areas are in Southwest Asia (Afghanistan, Pakistan, and Iran) and in the highlands of Mainland Southeast Asia (Burma, Laos, Vietnam, and Thailand), popularly known as the "Golden Triangle." Opium poppy is also grown in Colombia, Mexico, and Lebanon.

Opium poppies containing small amounts of opium alkaloid were widely grown as an ornamental plant and for seeds in the United States. The possession of this plant was declared illegal by the Opium Poppy Control Act of 1942. The seeds of the poppy, which are located in the seed pods, contain no opium and are therefore not illegal. According to Section 11019 of the California Health and Safety Code (H&S), the opium poppy and poppy straw are defined as a narcotic drug. In 11021 H&S, "opium poppy" means all of the plant of the species papaver somniferium L. except the seeds. In 11025 H&S, "poppy straw" means all parts except the seeds of the opium poppy after mowing.

It is interesting to note that opium poppy plants grow well in various parts of this country, particularly in the mountainous regions of Humboldt County in Northern California. This particular geography is very similar to the mountainous regions of Mexico where opium poppy plants proliferate. There have been numerous seizures of opium poppy fields in these California mountains. But at the present time, these fields have not been considered an opium source for the manufacture of heroin because of the lack of laboratory facilities and the lack of extremely cheap labor. Because harvesting opium requires hand labor and is a very tedious, low-yielding process, it is feasible only in areas where hand labor is available and extremely cheap. It takes approximately three acres of poppies to produce 10 kilograms (22 pounds) of opium. Many of the opium fields in Northern California are believed to be "volunteer" crops which have reproduced naturally each year as a result of the original raw opium planted by Chinese immigrants in the 1800s and early 1900s.

§ 8.2.1(c)   Cooking Opium

Before opium is smoked, it is usually cooked. Uncooked opium contains moisture, vegetable matter, and other impurities that detract from a smooth-smoking product. The raw opium that is collected from the pod is placed in an open pot of boiling water where the sticky glob of opium alkaloids quickly dissolves. The soil, twigs, and plant scrapings remain undissolved. The solution is strained through cheesecloth to remove these impurities. The clear brown liquid, sometimes called "liquid opium," is actually opium in solution. This liquid then is reheated over a low flame until the water turns to steam. When the water has evaporated, a thick paste remains. This paste is called "prepared opium," "cooked opium," or "smoking opium" and is dried in the sun until it has a putty-like consistency. The net weight of the cooked opium is generally about 20 percent less than the original raw opium.

Cooked opium is suitable for smoking or eating by opium users. Traditionally, there is only one group of opium poppy farmers, the Hmong, who often do not cook their opium before smoking. Most other ethnic groups, including Chinese opium addicts, prefer smoking cooked opium.

Opium, either raw or cooked, will not degrade or otherwise spoil for an indefinite period of time, as long as it remains relatively dry and cool. These are the normal conditions in the highlands of mainland Southeast Asia. There are cases of opium being stored on a shelf for 10 years without deterioration.

§ 8.2.1(d)   Smoking Opium

Smoking opium is very popular in many parts of the world but not as popular in the United States. It was first introduced in the United States in the 1800s with the immigration of the Oriental community into San Francisco. Opium smoking dens were quite popular in the San Francisco area but enforcement efforts have practically phased them out. There may be an occasional opium den or facsimile encountered today, but their popularity has not been shown to be a significant problem. These opium dens were premises where opium users would meet and participate in the rituals of opium smoking. There was generally a leader or practitioner who would tend to the user by providing him with smoking paraphernalia and keeping the opium lighted. The word "opium" comes from the Greek term "opos," which means juice. Users often lay on the floor and form a circle by placing one's head on another's hip and so on. Another method was to lay their heads on special pillows. These pillows are still found on occasion, which suggests the probability that some opium smoking still exists. While lying upon the floor, the smoker lies on his side and smokes through the opium pipe while his head is elevated and on its side. The opium does not actually burn, but rather smolders and the user inhales the fumes through a specially constructed pipe.

Opiate Drugs: Their Origin and Potency

DRUG	ORIGIN	POTENCY
Laudanum	Alcoholic solution of 10% opium	0.10 x opium
Paregoric	4% tincture of opium	0.04 x opium
Morphine	Natural alkaloid	10 x opium
Codeine	Natural alkaloid	0.50 x opium
Heroin	Semisynthetic	3 x morphine
Dilaudid	Semisynthetic	3-4 x morphine
Meperidine	Semisynthetic	0.10 x morphine
Methadone	Synthetic	equals morphine

To smoke opium, you need an opium pipe about 24 inches long. The pipe has a bowl. There is a small square piece of cloth between the bowl and the stem of the pipe that forms a gasket. You need a peanut oil lamp and a metal pointed needle (resembling a knitting needle) to form the opium into small balls to light over the lamp and insert into the pipe bowl. The lamp is used to light the opium and to heat the bowl of the pipe. The opium releases a smoke or vapor that is inhaled into the lungs.

The alkaloid of opium is morphine. Opium usually contains 10 percent morphine, 0.5 percent codeine, 1.2 percent thebaine, and 1 percent papaverine. There are also approximately 20 other alkaloids in opium.

§ 8.2.2   Morphine

Morphine is the principal alkaloid of opium, the chemical formula of which is $C_{17}H_{19}NO_3$. Morphine was named after the Greek God of Dreams, Morpheus, by the German Serturner who first isolated the drug from opium in 1805.

Illicit morphine is produced from opium through a fairly simple process and at a ratio of 10 pounds of opium to produce one pound of morphine, one kilo of morphine will produce (one kilo of heroin). The chemist heats water in an oil drum over a wood fire until the proper temperature is reached. He will then dump raw opium into the oil drum and stir it with a heavy stick until it dissolves. At this time, ordinary lime fertilizer is added to the steaming solution, precipitating out organic waste and leaving the morphine suspended in chalky white water near the surface. The chemist then pours the solution into another oil drum through cheesecloth or a piece of flannel cloth, removing any waste matter. The solution is again heated and stirred at which time concentrated ammonia is added, causing the morphine to solidify and drop to the bottom. The solution is then filtered through cheesecloth or flannel, leaving chunky white kernels of morphine on the cloth. The morphine, called free morphine base, is dried and packaged for shipment to make into heroin.

Medical morphine, despite developments of various synthetic narcotics, is still the most widely used drug for relief of severe pain. It is desirable for these reasons: (1) it raises the patient's pain perception threshold; (2) it relieves the anxiety and fear that are natural emotional reactions to painful stimuli and are largely responsible for the unpleasantness of the pain experience; and (3) it can produce sleep even in the presence of severe pain.

There are a number of preparations that contain morphine, such as morphine sulphate, morphine hydrochloride, morphine acetate, and morphine tartrate. Of the morphine preparations, morphine sulphate is the most common. It appears as a white, crystalline powder. It is odorless, has a bitter taste, and darkens upon long exposure to light. It acts as a depressant on the central nervous system and when injected for the relief of pain, acts almost immediately.

Since 1990, there has been about a 3-fold increase in morphine products in the United States.

Morphine is marketed under generic and brand name products including "MS-Contin, Oramorph SR, MSIR, Roxanol, Kadian, and RMS. Morphine is used parenterally (by injection) for preoperative sedation, as a supplement to anesthesia, and for analgesia. It is the drug of choice for relieving pain of myocardial infarction and for its cardiovascular effects in the treatment of acute pulmonary edema. Traditionally, morphine was almost exclusively used by injection. Today morphine is marketed in a variety of forms, including oral solutions, immediate and sustained-release tablets and capsules, suppositories, and injectable preparations.

§ 8.2.3   Codeine (Methylmorphine)

Codeine is the most widely used, naturally occurring narcotic in medical treatment in the world. This alkaloid is found in opium in concentrations ranging from 0.7 to 2.5 percent. However, most codeine used in the United States is produced from morphine. Codeine is also the starting material for the production of two other narcotics, dihydrocodeine and hydrocodone.

Codeine is medically prescribed for the relief of moderate pain and cough suppression. Compared to morphine, codeine produces less analgesia, sedation, and respiratory depression, and is usually taken orally. It is made into tablets either alone (Schedule II) or in combination with aspirin or acetaminophen (i.e., Tylenol with Codeine, Schedule III). As a cough suppressant, codeine is found in a number of liquid preparations (these products are in Schedule V). Codeine is also used to a lesser extent as an injectable solution for the treatment of pain. Codeine products are diverted from legitimate sources and are encountered on the illicit market. Codeine is addicting and if taken in large amounts, produces an overdose. Cardiorespiratory depression accompanied by cyanosis occurs, followed by a fall in body temperature, circulatory collapse, coma, and death.

§ 8.2.4   Thebaine

Thebaine, a minor constituent of opium, is controlled in Schedule II of the CSA as well as under international law. Although chemically similar to both morphine and codeine, thebaine produces stimulatory rather than depressant effects. Thebaine is not used therapeutically, but is converted into a variety of substances including oxycodone, oxymorphone, nalbuphine, naloxone, naltrexone, and buprenorphine. The United States ranks first in the world in thebaine utilization.

§ 8.3 SEMI-SYNTHETIC NARCOTICS

Semi-synthetic narcotics come from the opium poppy but are chemically modified. The drugs included in this area are heroin, hydromorphone, hydro-codone, buprenorphine, and oxycodon.

§ 8.3.1   Heroin — Diacetylmorphine

A milestone in the history of opiate use was the chemical modification of morphine to diacetylmorphine. Heroin was first produced in 1874 by an English researcher, D.P. Wright. Wright experimented with heroin on dogs as an ideal non-addicting substitute for morphine, but later discontinued any further research. In 1898 the Bayer Chemical Company of Germany manufactured diacetylmorphine under the brand name of Heroin for its mass-marketing campaign. One of the original typical advertising slogans was "Heroin — A Sedative for Coughs."

Heroin soon became one of the most popular patent medicines on the market. In the United States, the St. Louis Pharmaceutical Company offered a sample box of heroin tablets free to physicians. Then in 1906 the American Medical Association approved heroin for general use and advised that it be used in place of morphine for various painful infections. Due to the unrestricted distribution by physicians and pharmacists in 1920, the enormous heroin addiction problem. In 1924 the importation and manufacture of heroin was prohibited in the United States. However, the first comprehensive control of heroin in the United States was established with the Harrison Act of 1914.

§ 8.3.1(a) The Manufacturing Process for Heroin

The manufacturing process for heroin is more complicated than that of prepared opium or morphine. The centers for heroin laboratories are Iran, Hong Kong, Mexico, Southeast Asia, and the Philippines. The goal of the five-stage process is to chemically bond morphine molecules with acetic acid and then process the compound into a fluffy white powder than can be injected by the use of a syringe and hypodermic needle. The process is as follows:

1. To produce ten kilos of pure heroin (the normal daily output of some labs) the chemist heats ten kilos of morphine and ten kilos of acetic anhydride in an enamel bin or glass flask. This mixture is heated for six hours at exactly 185 degrees. The morphine and acid become chemically bonded, creating an impure form of diacetylmorphine, or heroin.

2. To remove the impurities from the compound, the solution is treated with water and chloroform until the impurities precipitate out, leaving a higher grade of diacetylmorphine.

3. The solution is then drained into another container and sodium carbonate is added until the crude heroin particles begin to solidify and drop to the bottom.

4. After the heroin particles are filtered out of the sodium carbonate solution under pressure from a small suction pump, they are purified in a solution of alcohol and activated charcoal. The mixture is then heated until the alcohol begins to evaporate, leaving relatively pure granules of heroin at the bottom of the flask.

5. The final stage produces the fine white powder known as heroin. The heroin is placed in a large flask and dissolved with alcohol. As ether and hydrochloric acid are added to the solution, tiny white flakes begin to form. After the flakes are filtered out under pressure and dried through a special process, the end result is a white powder, 80 to 100 percent pure, known as Heroin No. 4. Under the hands of a careless chemist, the volatile ether may ignite and produce a violent explosion.

Narcotic Drugs of Abuse

The heroin produced from the labs in Hong Kong and France is usually white and pure. In the crude clandestine laboratories in Mexico, Mexican heroin is brown in color because the manufacturing process leaves impurities in the heroin. Raw opium is converted to heroin in a continuous three- day process. In contrast to the classical French procedures, morphine hydrochloride is produced instead of morphine base, simply by adding water, lime, salt, and probably hydrochloric acid. The morphine product is then filtered by squeezing it in a cloth. On the third day it is acetylated to produce heroin hydrochloride.

THE CONVERSION PROCESS REQUIRES A SERIES OF SUCCESSIVE STEPS. SHOWN ABOVE IS SOME OF THE EQUIPMENT USED.

§ 8.3.1(b)   Types of Heroin

Opium derivatives are traditionally numbered according to the four steps in the heroin production process. Heroin No. 1, a tan-to-brown-colored powder, is actually crude morphine base extracted from raw opium. It is the starting material for the various heroin products. Heroin No. 2, a white-to-gray powder, is a transitional product in the conversion of morphine base to heroin. Two marketable products are derived from it: smoking heroin and injectable heroin—both manufactured for illicit markets. Heroin No. 3, smoking heroin, is also known as "White Dragon Pearl." It is tan-to-gray in color, commonly seen in several shades of gray, blue, and light brown, and has a granular or lumpy composition. Heroin No. 4 is a mixture of heroin hydrochloride, 50 to 60 percent, caffeine, 30 to 50 percent, and often strychnine hydrochloride, 0.5 to 10 percent. It also has other impurities such as 3 or 6 monocetylmorphine, codeine, and thebaine. Heroin No. 3 is more available than Heroin No. 4. It is also easier to make than No. 4 in that it is manufactured without the final step. The final stage is not only dangerous but also doubles the time required to make the heroin.

Heroin No. 4, indictable heroin hydrochloride, is usually marketed as a fluffy white powder (the famous "China White" of the United States), and may vary in color from a bright white to creamy yellow. It is less dense than European-produced heroin since it is sold by volume rather than by weight.

§ 8.3.1(b)(1)   Mexican Brown

Beyond the basic numbered types, there are the varieties commonly sold in the United States. "Mexican Brown" heroin, a phenomenon of the western U.S., is usually pink-brown in color, a rather fine powder with dark brown flecks and/or white particles. The color may vary from a rather light brown to almost chocolate. The product's name does not necessarily mean that it originates in Mexico; originally, heroin from Mexico was a characteristic brown due to a particular method of manufacture, hence the name "Mexican Brown." Apparently, the name and the color both make the product more marketable, as this type of street heroin is one of the most avidly sought by consumers—it is "good." One ex-dealer/user reported that he used instant coffee to make "Mexican Brown from China White . . . I couldn't deal China White. It had to be brown." The active ingredients in this preparation are usually procaine, 55 percent, and heroin, 30 percent; diluents may be talc, flour, cornstarch, lactose and/or mannitol.

Though Mexico is the major source of brown heroin, Asian heroin is also entering the United States. Asian heroin may first be smuggled into Europe (Paris, Amsterdam and/or Brussels) and then be brought directly into the United States or it may enter via Canada, South America, or Mexico.

§ 8.3.1(b)(2)   Persian Heroin

Certain California law enforcement agencies have encountered a type of heroin called "Persian Heroin," "Lemon Heroin," "Persian Morphine," and "Salt n' Pepper." The heroin, as analyzed by the Drug Enforcement

Administration laboratory in San Francisco displayed the following characteristics: it is a "base" substance, not a hydrochloride. This means that it is not soluble in water. It is commonly light tan to near pink to reddish in color. Instead of adding water to the powder prior to "cooking," lemon juice (containing citric acid) or vinegar (containing acetic acid) is used to dissolve the heroin. The traditional spoon, solution, and heating procedure for cooking is used. Seizures have revealed consistently high percentages of heroin. Seizures of even small amounts have been as high as 98 percent pure.

It is possible that Persian heroin is a crude morphine base. In Iran, there is a common practice of "chasing the dragon"—that is, smoking this morphine base. There are many Iranians in California. It has been stated by "Persian heroin" dealers in San Francisco that they receive their supply from Iranians who brought the habit of smoking with them to California. They have connections in the homeland and receive the drug many different ways. The percentage of the morphine in the drug must be high in order to get a high from smoking. In the last several years "Persian heroin" has been cut to decrease potency and increase profits. Users have started injecting the drug to get more of an effect.

§ 8.3.1(b)(3) Brown Sugar Heroin

A common name for heroin (any source) which has the appearance of light brown, granulated sugar produced in Southwest Asia (Afghanistan, Pakistan, and Iran). Used in contrast with the white, fluffy crystal form of heroin, such as Southeast Asian "China White" heroin. Like white heroin, brown sugar heroin may be injected, snorted, or smoked.

§ 8.3.1(b)(4) Black Tar Heroin

Black tar heroin has been increasing in use in California. It began to appear in wholesale quantities in the United States in about 1979, two years after the Drug Enforcement Administration stopped eradication efforts in Mexico.

The Drug Enforcement Administration has encountered black tar heroin exhibits in all 50 states. It is believed that the material originates in the Mexican states of Durango, Sinaloa, Sonora, and Guerrero. The growing acceptance of this form of heroin over traditional forms is believed to be due primarily to its high purity at the "street" level. The purity has been found to be as high as 93 percent. Although purities as low as 2 percent have been encountered, the purities most frequently seen range between 40 and 80 percent pure. The smaller exhibits of black tar heroin are normally packaged in plastic bags, balloons and aluminum foil and usually conform to the shape of the packaging.

Even "brown" or "Mexican Brown" heroin is now almost always tar that has been cut and blended.

There are several street names for tar, including: gum, goma, chiva, raw heroin, and Mexican mud.

High purity and low volume account for the demand for tar. Most uncut tar ranges from 50 to 70 percent purity and is commonly injected at full strength in some areas of California and Oregon and Washington. A match-head size piece usually sells for about $25 and will give an experienced user one to five doses, depending on purity. A dealer can easily sell to fifty or sixty customers from five to six grams hidden in a sock, as a gram is about the size of a pea. If the same dealer wanted to conceal a comparable supply of white heroin, he would have to carry 25 to 30 grams. Street dealers have been known to carry a couple of grams of tar in a balloon in their mouths. If approached by law enforcement, they simply swallow the balloon and recover it later. Along with the high purity has come a rash of overdoses and overdose deaths. It is not unusual for an area to experience double or triple the amount of these incidents; but normally this happens only during the initial influx of tar. A consistently high incidence of overdoses usually occur where tar is sold both cut and uncut and purity fluctuates significantly.

The processes used to manufacture tar heroin are easier than those used for the white crystalline variety and take about one-third of the time. Also, there are no controls on any of the chemicals needed. Impurities such as hydrochloride, opium alkaloids, acetylated opium, acetylated codeine, and insoluble plant products are not removed. They are responsible for the final tar-like form and for some of the inflammation, infection, and scarring of the skin and veins of the user. The steps below result in a product that is about 60 to 70 percent heroin and 10 to 20 percent morphine:

1. Score poppies and gather opium.

2. Dissolve the opium in water and one of the following base solutions:

   a) Butanol and ammonia.

   b) Hydroxide

   c) Lye

   d) Lime and/or ammonia.

This will cause the active alkaloids (morphine, caffeine, etc.) to separate from the organic debris.

3. Cook with one of the following chemicals to convert the morphine to heroin:

   a) Acetic anhydride

   b) Acetyl chloride

4. Add baking soda

5. To clean the heroin, heat with acetone or alcohol and activated charcoal.

6. Add hydrochloric acid and ether to change the heroin base to heroin hydrochloride, a water-soluble salt suitable for injection.

In summary, raw opium is treated with acetic anhydride or acetyl chloride. The mixture is neutralized with baking soda, resulting in tar cut into 25-gram pieces; the tar heroin is then cut or diluted with lactose, cornstarch, cocoa, brown sugar, or procaine and divided into 0.5- to 1-gram pieces. The cutting or diluting method involves the tar heroin being rolled and blended with burnt cornstarch or molasses, placed in a 200-degree oven, and the diluent folded into the mixture with a putty knife; or the tar heroin is softened with acetone or ethyl acetate (fingernail polish) and the diluent or cut is stirred in.

Characteristics of Tar

A street level "bag" or "paper" of tar heroin is most often described as looking "like a rat turd." It is usually a very dark brown, nearly black color, and could be mistaken for a piece of hash. When cut excessively, it may become lighter in color or even translucent, like a chip off a beer bottle. The tar-like, sticky form is very common and is often pressed flat. Opinions differ on the significance of the degree of hardness. It may be hard when old or dry or when high in purity. Hardened tar can resemble a piece of obsidian, hardened roofing tar, or charcoal. Tar heroin smells strongly of vinegar but this does not begin until two or three hours after the manufacturing process is completed. During that time, it is possible for a smuggler to walk a small amount across the border without alerting drug-detecting dogs.

To cut tar, the dealer may use any of the common cutting agents such as lactose, inositol, or brown sugar; however, chocolate milk powder, instant coffee, raisins, molasses, and powdered Vitamins A, B3, and C have been reported. Blenders and coffee grinders are used to combine the heroin with the cutter. Freezing or drying the tar first to harden it will facilitate the process. Sometimes the heroin is spread on tin foil, then a cutting agent is sprinkled on top and melted in. Using a cutting agent usually alters the original gooey form, which may be undesirable in some areas. One ingenious dealer burns cornstarch in a cast-iron skillet until it is black, then rolls the ball of heroin in it until the desired amount of cutter has been absorbed. It still looks the same; but if the user cooks his heroin instead of dissolving it in cold water, the cornstarch will gel. (Lemon or lime juice are also often used to dissolve tar heroin prior to injecting.) Cut tar heroin is most often packaged in balloons, while uncut tar is wrapped in cellophane, tin foil, or both.

Black Tar Analyzed

The Idaho State Crime Laboratory, Pocatello, Idaho, has analyzed "black tar" heroin in exhibits submitted over a period of approximately two years. The purity has ranged from 4 percent to 100 percent heroin. Most frequently the purity is between 70 percent and 90 percent. Sample weights have ranged from 50 milligrams to 2 ounces. To date, the smaller samples are usually soft and gummy, while the larger samples have been received as hard blocks. There have been two documented cases of overdose deaths associated with this type of heroin. The Los Angeles County Sheriff's Criminolistics Laboratory recently tested an exhibit of 12 balloons containing a brown pliable substance similar to "tar heroin," with a grayish color coating on it. The analysis of this material showed it to contain a mixture of cocaine and heroin. The weight of the individual samples was approximately 0.24 grams.

§8.3.1(b)(5)   Paper Heroin

A form of heroin called "paper dope" is appearing on the streets of California. A 1 x 2-inch square of heavy grade artist's paper is soaked in heroin, which the user dissolves and injects. Each dose is equivalent to three-fourths of a gram of heroin at about 3 percent purity. The paper squares sometimes have a name on them and have a brown stain when held up to the light.

§ 8.3.1(b)(6)   China White

Southeast Asian Heroin No.4 in a white powder form has been called "China White." The term China White also has been used in recent years as an alternate name for fentanyl, a synthetic narcotic analgesic similar to morphine and meperidine (Demerol) that has caused a number of overdoses throughout the state. A more complete description of fentanyl is covered in Chapter X, Designer Drugs, under Narcotics Analog.

§ 8.3.1(b)(7)   Red Rock

Red Rock is No. 3 heroin manufactured in the Philippines and combined with barbital, strychnine, and caffeine. This form of heroin looks like small red rocks and is consumed by smoking.

Once the heroin has been manufactured, it is packaged and smuggled to various parts of the world with a large portion going to the United States. Heroin is smuggled into California usually in hermetically sealed plastic bags or rubber condoms; however, there are a variety of methods employed in smuggling. The wholesaler will dilute the heroin with some powdered agent to give the drug more quantity and lessen the quality. A wholesaler might sell large quantities of heroin in its original, smuggled form or dilute it once or twice, bringing the percentage of heroin down 50 to 25 percent. From the wholesaler who deals in pounds and kilos of heroin down to the ounce dealer through the gram dealer to the addict, the heroin is often "cut," diluted, or "stepped on" a number of times, leaving the street quality of the drug at .5 to 5 percent. That means that 0.5 to 5 percent of the total powder is actually heroin.

§ 8.3.1(b)(8)   South American Heroin

South American (Colombia, etc.) in heroin hydrochloride, a white powder. Samples seized in the United States show a purity level above 90% at the wholesale (kilo) level.

Narcotic Drugs of Abuse

For 2002, 80% of the heroin analyzed by the Drug Enforcement Administration was from South America — signature analysis is the only scientifically based source of information currently used to determine the origin of heroin entering the United States drug market.

Varieties of heroin analyzed by the Special Testing and Research Laboratory

Colombian opium poppies

HEROIN SIGNATURE PROGRAM DATA: 1977-2002
Geographic Source Area Distribution (in percent*)
Based on Net Weight of Heroin Seized and Analyzed

	MEXICO	S.E. ASIA	S.W. ASIA	S. AMERICA
1977	89	9	2	**
1978	82	15	3	**
1979	48	13	39	**
1980	38	11	51	**
1981	36	10	54	**
1982	34	14	52	**
1983	33	19	48	**
1984	32	17	51	**
1985	39	14	47	**
1986	42	22	36	**
1987	42	25	33	**
1988	29	46	25	**
1989	27	56	17	**
1990	21	56	23	**
1991	21	58	21	**
1992	10	58	32	**
1993	8	68	9	15***
1994	5	57	6	32
1995	5	17	16	62
1996	20	8	20	52
1997	14	5	6	75
1998	17	14	4	65
1999	24	10	6	60
2000	17	8	16	59
2001	30	7	7	56
2002	9	1	10	80

- The percentages are based on samples for which a signature was identified. In 2002, approximately 90 percent of the samples were classified.
- ** Not Applicable (The signature for heroin from South America was not developed until 1993.)
- *** The signature for heroin from South America was not developed until July 1993; therefore, this figure represents only partial-year data. Bold numbers indicate the dominant source area.

Prepared by the Domestic Strategic Unit, Office of Strategic Intelligence, Intelligence Division, DEA Headquarters, January 2004.

§ 8.3.1(c)   Cutting or Stepping on Heroin

The basic paraphernalia for adulteration of heroin consists of the cut (lactose, etc.), scales, measuring spoons, flat nonporous surface, razor blade or playing card, sifter or nylon stocking, funnel, and packing containers (toy balloons, paper bindles, plastic bags, etc.).

A common diluting agent is lactose or dextrose, a white, powdered milk sugar that is used as a baby food supplement and can be purchased in any drug store. Lactose is also used by druggists as a filler for capsules. Often heroin addicts have what they call a "milk sugar habit," causing them to crave sweets, soda pops, etc. It is not uncommon for a heroin addict to add three or four spoons of sugar to his/her coffee.

Besides lactose, any soluble powder that is not disruptive to the body can be used as a cutting agent. Dealers of Mexican Brown heroin will often use brown-colored diluting agents such as chocolate cake mix, cocoa, and instant coffee instead of white milk sugar. This maintains the brown color of their product and gives the visual impression of better quality. Other cutting agents include powdered quinine (used to treat leg cramps and malaria and having a bitter taste similar to heroin, making it an ideal cutting agent), procaine, baking soda, powdered sugar, powdered milk, menita, mannitol, starch, and Darvon.

The dealer will be able to approximate the percentage of heroin that he has purchased by injecting either himself or a second party. Some dealers use chemical testing kits that are now available on the street or in many paraphernalia shops. In an elaborate operation, a chemist ascertains the percentage of the heroin by chemical analysis.

Once a dealer has a general idea of the purity of the heroin, he will mix a small quantity of the heroin and cutting agent in the desired proportions and retest the heroin as a final check. When the dealer is sure of the ratio he wishes to use, he proceeds to dilute the remaining heroin. When a dealer cuts the heroin, he may use one of any number of dilution formulas. Two basic formulas are as follows:

Formula 1

1 ounce of lactose added to 1 ounce of 100 percent heroin = 2 ounces of 50 percent heroin.
2 ounces of lactose added to 2 ounces of 50 percent heroin = 4 ounces of 25 percent heroin.
4 ounces of lactose added to 4 ounces of 25 percent heroin = 8 ounces of 12 percent heroin.
8 ounces of lactose added to 8 ounces of 12 percent heroin = 16 ounces of 6 percent heroin.
16 ounces of lactose added to 16 ounces of 6 percent heroin = 32 ounces of 3 percent heroin.
32 ounces of lactose added to 32 ounces of 3 percent heroin = 65 ounces of approximately 1 percent heroin.

Formula 2

Cutting Agent added to 100 percent heroin = Heroin

Cutting Agent	100% Heroin	Heroin
1 oz.	1 oz.	2 oz. of 50 percent heroin
2 oz.	1 oz.	3 oz. of 33 percent heroin
3 oz.	1 oz.	4 oz. of 25 percent heroin
4 oz.	1 oz.	5 oz. of 20 percent heroin
5 oz.	1 oz.	6 oz. of 17 percent heroin
6 oz.	1 oz.	7 oz. of 14 percent heroin
7 oz.	1 oz.	8 oz. of 12 percent heroin
8 oz.	1 oz.	9 oz. of 11 percent heroin
9 oz.	1 oz.	10 oz. of 10 percent heroin
10 oz.	1 oz.	11 oz. of 9 percent heroin
11 oz.	1 oz.	12 oz. of 8 percent heroin
12 oz.	1 oz.	13 oz. of 7 percent heroin
13 oz.	1 oz.	14 oz. of 7 percent heroin
14 oz.	1 oz.	15 oz. of 6 percent heroin
15 oz.	1 oz.	16 oz. of 6 percent heroin

Cutting Agent	100% Heroin	Heroin
16 oz.	1 oz.	17 oz. of 5 percent heroin
17 oz.	1 oz.	18 oz. of 5 percent heroin
18 oz.	1 oz.	19 oz. of 5 percent heroin
19 oz.	1 oz.	20 oz. of 5 percent heroin
20 oz.	1 oz.	21 oz. of 4 percent heroin

This dilution formula could be continued until 64 oz. were created, which would result in 1 percent heroin.

The dealer will measure out the desired amount of heroin, for instance five level teaspoons, and place it in a pile on flat nonporous surface such as a mirror or glass plate. He will then measure out the desired amount of lactose and place it in a separate pile on the same surface. Then, using a playing card, razor blade, knife, or any sharp-edged instrument, the dealer chops the heroin to take out all the lumps so the heroin is fairly fine powder. The heroin is then sifted through a sifter or nylon stocking, producing a fine fluffed powder and removing foreign material from the substance. Once through the sifter, the heroin usually has a little more volume since it has been fluffed. The heroin is sifted into a pile and the same process is repeated with the diluting agent. The dealer will then mix the pile of heroin into the pile of diluting agent. Once this has been accomplished, he sifts the diluted heroin through a sifter, trying to get the mixture as equal as possible. The dealer may resift the diluted heroin to assure an equally distributed mixture. The sifted heroin is placed in a single pile. At this time, the dealer is ready to place the heroin into packages for sale.

In larger quantities, heroin is packed in plastic bags or rubber condoms, which generally hold from 1 oz to 3 oz. On the West Coast, smaller amounts are packaged in penny balloons and paper bindles. On the East Coast of the United States, heroin is packaged in 2 x 2 glassine envelopes and No. 5 gelatin capsules. The dealer will weigh the desired quantity of heroin on a scale or use a measuring spoon. When packaging in balloons, the balloons will be placed at the end of the funnel; the desired amount of heroin is then put in the balloon through the funnel. In the dope business, the amount received is usually less than the amount represented. For example, a "spoon" of heroin represents a level teaspoon of approximately 2 grams. However, most "spoons" have been found to contain from 0.7 to 1.5 grams. If the dealer is packaging ounces (referred to as "piece"), he will measure an ounce on a scale and measure an ounce in teaspoons. One ounce is 14 teaspoons. The dealer will commonly measure out 11 to 14 level teaspoons to the "piece." The usual weight of a "piece" is 22 to 25 grams. Paper bindles are also used for packaging small amounts of heroin. The paper bindle is a square piece of paper; the size will depend upon how much heroin will be placed in the paper. The heroin is placed inside the paper bindle in the middle. The paper is folded to make a triangle. The base of the triangle is folded, usually once or twice, then the outer wings of the paper are folded inside and the unfolded top of the triangle is folded and tucked into the wings. Paper bindles can be commercially purchased with directions on how to fold them. They have names such as Snow Seals, which are usually purchased to package cocaine.

When using a penny balloon, the heroin is placed at the bottom of the balloon. The balloon is knotted and rolled up to the end, which is then folded back over, forming a ball. Many times the dealer won't knot the balloon, but will twist it and roll it up as previously described. The rubber condoms are sometimes folded over to give extra, added protection. Once the heroin has been packaged in its container, it is ready for sale. The penny balloon is probably the most common form of packaging for street heroin due to the fact that the heroin is well protected and that the addict can carry the balloon in his mouth. If the dealer is approached by a police officer, he can swallow the balloon and later retrieve it.

In many geographical areas of California, the larger dealers, which we will refer to as distributors, will have several small-time user/dealers working for them. The distributor will "front" (furnish with understanding that payment will be made at a later time) several "bags" (terminology for balloons) to each of their user/dealers who will sell the heroin to other users and return the money to the distributor to pay for the fronted dope. This user/dealer's payment will be some free heroin from the distributor. As an example, a distributor will "front" the user/dealer 30 balloons of street-level quality, ready-to-use heroin. The user/dealer will sell 20 of the balloons and keep 10 for his own personal use and payment. He will take the proceeds from the 20 balloons back to the distributor and get 30 more balloons. This cycle continues and when a trust is developed by the distributor, he will front the user/dealer several packages of 30 each time. Another common size package is 12 balloons. The user/dealer sells ten of the balloons and keeps two for himself. These packages, whatever amount they may contain, are many times referred to as "paquettes," a Spanish term translated as packages. Throughout California, one will discover a variety of trends which may be unique to certain geographical areas. These paquettes, for example, will vary in size from one community to the next, but the principle remains the same.

§ 8.3.2 Hydromorphone

Hydromorphone (Dilaudid) is marketed in tablets (2, 4, and 8 mg), rectal suppositories, oral solutions, and injectable formulations. All products are in Schedule II of the CSA. Its analgesic potency is from two to eight times that of morphine, but it is shorter acting and produces more sedation than morphine. Much sought after by narcotic addicts, hydromorphone is usually obtained by the abuser through fraudulent prescriptions or theft. The tablets are often dissolved and injected as a substitute for heroin.

§ 8.3.3 Buprenorphine

This drug is a semi-synthetic narcotic derived from thebaine and is currently being investigated for the treatment of narcotic addiction. Like methadone and LAAM, buprenorphine is potent (30 to 50 times the analgesic potency of morphine), has a long duration of action, and does not need to be injected. The buprenorphine products under development are sublingual tablets (placed under the tongue). Unlike the other treatment drugs, buprenorphine produces far less respiratory depression and is thought to be safer in overdose. Buprenorphine is currently available in the United States as an injectable Schedule V narcotic analgesic (Buprenex) for human and veterinary use.

§ 8.3.4 Hydrocodone
Hydrocodone is an orally active analgesic and antitussive (cough suppressant) Schedule II narcotic that is marketed in multi-ingredient Schedule III products. Hydrocodone has an analgesic potency similar to or greater than that of oral morphine. Sales and production of this drug have increased significantly in recent years (a four-fold increase between 1990 and 2000), as have diversion and illicit use. Trade names include Anexsia, Hycodan, Hycomine, Lorcet, Lortab, Tussionex, Tylox, Vicodin, and Vicoprofen. These are available as tablets, capsules, and/or syrups. Generally, this drug is abused by oral rather than intravenous administration. Currently, about 20 tons of hydrocodone products are used annually in the United States.

§ 8.3.5 Oxycodone/OxyContin
OxyContin is a trade name for the narcotic oxycodone hydrochloride (HCl), an opiate agonist. Oxycodone, a semi-synthetic opioid derived from the opioid alkaloid thebaine, is similar to codeine, methadone, and morphine in producing opiate-like effects. Oxycodone is a Schedule II drug under the Controlled Substances Act because of its high propensity to cause dependence and abuse.

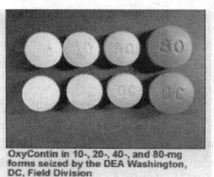

OxyContin in 10-, 20-, 40-, and 80-mg forms seized by the DEA Washington, DC, Field Division

Oxycodone is the active ingredient in a number of other commonly prescribed pain relief medications such as Percocet, Percodan, and Tylox. These medications contain oxycodone in smaller doses and are combined with other active ingredients like aspirin or acetaminophen. OxyContin contains oxycodone in various dosage strengths as the only active ingredient. These formulations are designed for a controlled release of the drug, to minimize the total number of tablets a patient must take for around-the-clock pain relief. OxyContin's intended application is the relief of moderate to severe pain of long duration, such as pain caused by rheumatoid arthritis and cancer.

OxyContin, marketed in 1996 by Purdue Pharma L.P., was the first product capable of giving 12 hours of pain relief, making it the longest lasting oxycodone product on the market. OxyContin was initially available in 10-, 20-, and 40-milligram (mg) strengths. In 1997, an 80-mg tablet was introduced and later followed by a 160-mg tablet in 2000. Purdue Pharma L.P. also produces OxyFast, an immediate-release liquid formulation containing 20-mg of oxycodone. Other pain medications such as Percocet, Percodan, and Percodan-Demi, which contain 5, 4.5, and 2.25 mg of oxycodone respectively, only provide short periods of pain relief (4 to 6 hours) and have to be taken at repeated intervals.

Beginning in 1996, the first full year it was marketed, the number of OxyContin prescriptions rose to approximately 5.8 million prescriptions in 2000. This makes OxyContin the number one prescribed Schedule II narcotic in the United States. Prescriptions dispensed for all other common opiod analgesics such as codeine, hydrocodone, morphine and hydromorphone have risen 23% during this same period (DEA 2002).

§ 8.3.5(a)   Abuse

Since 1996, Drug Abuse Warning Network (DAWN) data indicate an increasing number of emergency department mentions and deaths associated with oxycodone. This growing abuse of OxyContin, commonly known as Oxy's, OC's, Killers, Poor Man's Heroin, and Hillbilly Heroin, is leading to an increase in burglaries, thefts, and robberies of residences and pharmacies.

§ 8.3.5(b)   Illicit Use

OxyContin is designed to be administered orally in tablet form; however, many abusers chew the tablets or crush them and snort the powder to defeat the intended time-release action. However, most deaths appear to be the result of oral ingestion of the intact tablet. Injection also is possible, but it requires a preparation regimen similar to that of heroin. Such a regimen requires the removal of the tablet coating by either sucking on it or scraping it with the teeth or a razor blade, followed by melting the remainder on a spoon, adding water, and then injecting the solution. Snorting or injecting hastens the body's absorption of OxyContin.

Individuals abuse oxycodone to gain a euphoric high and to avoid the withdrawal symptoms associated with heroin. Because OxyContin contains large doses of oxycodone and produces opiate-like effects, it acts as a reasonable substitute for heroin; however, individuals do not necessarily need to be heroin addicts to become oxycodone abusers.

§ 8.3.5(c)   Effects

OxyContin is prescribed for the management of moderate to severe pain. Normal side effects include nausea, drowsiness, constipation, and to a lesser extent, dizziness, headache, vomiting, and sweating. An acute overdose of oxycodone may cause drowsiness, skeletal muscle flaccidity, cold and clammy skin, constricted pupils, bradycardia (slow heartbeat), hypotension, respiratory depression, coma, and death.

§ 8.4 SYNTHETIC NARCOTICS

In contrast to chemical substances derived directly or indirectly from the opium poppy, synthetic narcotics are produced entirely within the laboratory. A continuing search for a product that will retain the analgesic properties of morphine without the problems associated with addiction, tolerance, physical dependency has yet to produce a drug that is not susceptible to abuse. There are many synthetic narcotic substances. We will only cover a few of the most commonly used and abused.

§ 8.4.1   Darvon (Propoxyphene)

In the 1960s, Darvon was claimed to be a non-addicting, non-narcotic analgesic equal to codeine in pain-relieving potency for the relief of mild to moderate degrees of pain. Darvon is chemically related to methadone. Darvon is sold under trade names such as Darvon Compound, Darvocet-N, and under its scientific name, propoxyphene. It is a frequently prescribed drug in the United States. Propoxyphene is generally not dangerous when taken as directed but it is a dangerous drug in a number of ways. It is second to barbiturates as the prescription drug most often associated with suicides. It is an addictive drug and often abused. For all these reasons—suicides, accidental deaths, addictions—it is a drug that has raised serious concerns.

There are many Darvon-related deaths reported to the Drug Enforcement Administration's Drug Abuse Warning Network (DAWN). The exact cause is still uncertain, leaving many unresolved questions about Darvon. Overall, the best evidence thus far is that propoxyphene is no more effective and may be less effective than aspirin, codeine, and other pain relievers. It is a drug that is occasionally given to heroin addicts in county jails to ease the pains of withdrawals. But this usage only contributes to addiction.

Today, Darvon is considered a narcotic drug. It is known to be addictive and there are some very serious problems associated with the use of it. More than 100 tons of dextropropoxyphene are produced in the United States annually, and more than 30 million prescriptions are written for the products. This narcotic is associated with a number of toxic side effects and is among the top 10 drugs reported by medical examiners in drug abuse deaths.

§ 8.4.2   Demerol (Meperidine)

The first synthetic narcotic, meperidine is chemically dissimilar to morphine but resembles it in its analgesic potency. It is the most widely used medical drug for the relief of moderate to severe pain. It is a white crystalline substance, soluble in water and slightly bitter to the taste. Demerol produces less constipation and cough suppression than morphine. Sixty to eighty milligrams of Demerol is equivalent to ten milligrams of morphine for pain relief. Demerol also tends to dilate the pupils of the eyes. Demerol is the drug of choice of medical addicts: that is, doctors and nurses and others in the medical profession who become narcotic addicts.

§ 8.4.3   Talwin (Pentazocine)

The effort to find an effective analgesic with less dependence-producing consequences led to the development of pentazocine (Talwin). Introduced as an analgesic in 1967, it was frequently encountered in the illicit trade, usually in combination with tripelennamine and placed into Schedule IV of the CSA in 1979. An attempt at reducing the abuse of this drug was made with the introduction of Talwin Nx. This product contains a quantity of antagonist (naloxone) sufficient to counteract the morphine-like effects of pentazocine if the tablets are dissolved and injected.

§ 8.4.4   Fentanyl

First synthesized in Belgium in the late 1950s, fentanyl, with an analgesic potency of about 80 times that of morphine, was introduced into medical practice in the 1960s as an intravenous anesthetic under the trade name of Sublimaze. Thereafter, two other fentanyl analogues were introduced: alfentanil (Alffenta), an ultra-short-acting (5-10 minutes) analgesic, and sufentanil (Sufenta), an exceptionally potent analgesic (5 to 10 times more potent than fentanyl) for use in heart surgery.   Today, fentanyls are extensively used for anesthesia and analgesia. Duragesic, for example, is a fentanyl transdermal patch used in chronic pain management, and Actiq is a solid formulation of fentanyl citrate on a stick that dissolves slowly in the mouth for transmucosal absorption. Actiq is intended for opiate-tolerant individuals and is effective in treating breakthrough pain in cancer patients. Carfentanil (Wildnil) is an analogue of fentanyl with an analgesic potency 10,000 times that of morphine and is used in veterinary practice to immobilize certain large animals. Illicit use of pharmaceutical fentanyls first appeared in the mid-1970s in the medical community and continues to be a problem in the United States. To date, over 12 different analogues of fentanyl have been produced clandestinely and identified in the United States drug traffic. The biological effects of the fentanyls are indistinguishable from those of heroin, with the exception that the fentanyls may be hundreds of times more potent. Fentanyls are most commonly used by intravenous administration, but like heroin, they may also be smoked or snorted.

§ 8.4.4   Laam

Closely related to methadone, the synthetic compound levo alphacetyl-methadol, or LAAM (ORLMM), has an even longer duration of action (from 48 to 72 hours) than methadone, permitting a reduction in frequency of use. In 1994, it was approved as a Schedule II treatment drug for narcotic addiction. Both methadone and LAAM have high abuse potential. Their acceptability as narcotic treatment drugs is predicated upon their ability to substitute for heroin, the long duration of action, and their mode of oral administration.

§ 8.4.6   Methadone

German scientists synthesized methadone during World War II because of a shortage of morphine. Although chemically unlike morphine or heroin, methadone produces many of the same effects.

Introduced into the United States in 1947 as an analgesic (Dolophine), it is primarily used today for the treatment of narcotic addiction.

Methadone is a synthetic narcotic. There are a large number of synthetic compounds that have been tested in an effort to improve on the properties of the natural alkaloids of opium. Methadone is distinct from morphine in its longer duration of action (24 hours). The withdrawal state following prolonged use of methadone is more prolonged but of lesser intensity than heroin. Methadone has a cross-dependence with morphine and heroin and can therefore forestall the morphine or heroin abstinence syndrome (withdrawals). During the 1960s, it came into widespread use for heroin detoxification. Transfer from heroin to equivalent doses of methadone, followed by gradual reduction of the daily methadone dose, is the drug of choice for heroin detoxification. The 1973 FDA regulations define methadone detoxification as the administering of methadone in decreasing doses to reach a drug-free state in a period not to exceed 21 days; administering methadone for more than 21 days is deemed maintenance treatment.

§ 8.4.6(a)   Why Methadone Maintenance?

In an ideal world, there would be no need for drug treatment programs because no one would become addicted to heroin or other drugs in the first place. Even in the world as it is, there would be no need for maintenance treatment if there existed drug-free treatment programs capable of attracting all kinds of heroin addicts and of graduating them as responsible, effective, self-respecting, law-abiding ex-addicts able to live without opiates thereafter.

Drug-free treatment programs do not work for everybody. In fact, rehabilitated addicts who emerge from treatment programs each year to live drug-free are only a small proportion of the addict population.

Something must be done for addicts who refuse to enter a drug-free program, or who are refused admission to drug-free programs, or who fail in the drug-free programs. This is the target population for methadone maintenance.

There are reasons why methadone is superior to either morphine or heroin as a maintenance drug.

First, methadone is highly effective when taken by mouth rather than by injection. This means that the hazards of infection, AIDS, and the many other drawbacks associated with the intravenous injection of drugs several times each day are avoided.

Second, methadone is a long-acting drug. An adequate oral dose of methadone keeps the user from experiencing withdrawal for up to 24 hours. In contrast, addicts on morphine or heroin must "shoot up," or inject the drug, 3 to 4 times a day.

Third, methadone has a slower and more gradual onset of effect, especially when taken by mouth. Hence patients receiving oral methadone do not experience the "rush" or "bang" often experienced shortly after heroin is injected into a vein.

Fourth, some addicts have a tendency to escalate their doses of heroin. Once stabilized on an adequate daily dose of methadone, patients are content to remain on that dose year after year.

Methadone's fifth advantage is that it blocks the heroin effect. A patient stabilized on an adequate daily dose of methadone who uses heroin at the same time discovers that there is no effect. The higher the dose of methadone, the larger a dose of heroin is blocked. There is nothing mysterious about this blocking effect; it is a case of cross-tolerance. Any opiate or synthetic narcotic is blocked when one dose is substantially higher than the other.

Sixth advantage is the "rush" or "bang" is gone with methadone maintenance. Intravenous heroin is a tricky drug to administer even under skilled medical auspices. A patient on heroin tends to "bounce" from one physiological state to another throughout the day. Immediately after injection he may experience a "rush" or "bang." A period of somnolence or lethargy may follow. Then, after a relatively brief period of feeling more or less "normal," an addict on heroin begins to experience withdrawal anxiety and after that withdrawal distress—the abstinence syndrome. He may go through this cycle, or portions of it, two or three times in 24 hours.

It should be pointed out that the euphoria of a drug rush many times depends upon how a drug is used. For example, oral methadone does not produce a "rush" or "euphoria" but using the same drug by injection in the vein will produce a heroin-like euphoria.

Finally, methadone relieves the acute effects of withdrawal from heroin. On methadone, the addict no longer has to think where his next "fix" or shot of heroin is coming from. He no longer has to engage in crime to support his heroin habit. He no longer has to engage in compulsive drug-seeking behavior.

The key characteristic which makes methadone useful as a maintenance drug, however, is one which it shares with morphine and heroin. Patients on uniform daily doses of methadone perceive fewer and fewer of the initial effects of the drug; they develop tolerance and the effects which remain are experienced to a lessened degree.

After tolerance has developed—that is, after a patient has been stabilized on a uniform daily dose—patients on methadone cannot be distinguished from drug-free men and women. They look and act "normal," and they report that they feel "normal." However, methadone can cause some side effects, as reported by methadone addicts. Drs. William Bloom and Brian Butcher of Tulane University said possible side effects include:

Drowsiness—tended to disappear in all patients as they achieved a stable dose level.

Decreased sexual interest—reported in both men and women. In some patients, however, sexual interest increased.

Nausea—eventually grew less in long-term maintenance patients.

Alcohol abuse—older addicts and those on high methadone doses tended to drink more.

Difficulty in urination—younger patients and those taking higher doses had more trouble with this.

In addition, addicts have reported constipation, swelling of feet and ankles, blurring of vision, numbness of hands and feet, and weight gain.

There have been many complaints about methadone addicts continuing to commit crimes while on the methadone maintenance program. Methadone addicts are people who have, for the most part, lived a life of crime to support their heroin addiction. Thus, many of the addicts do not change their lifestyle, and continue their criminal ways while on methadone maintenance. One would think that the criminal justice system would treat the criminal methadone maintenance addict more harshly that the heroin addict. At least the methadone addict cannot claim that the crimes were committed to support a drug habit.

Today methadone maintenance is the most commonly used treatment for heroin addiction. It has been used to treat hundreds of thousands of heroin addicts over the past 25 years in a wide variety of social, economic, and geographical settings. This type of treatment is suppose to combine counseling and other rehabilitative services with methadone.

Current federal regulations encourage methadone programs to move users to total abstinence, although some methadone addicts have remained on the program for 10 or more years.

After a review of methadone treatment effectiveness research, the Office of Technology Assessment concluded in 1990 that methadone treatment's safety and effectiveness have been established in numerous studies and that, for a substantial majority of opiate users who enter methadone maintenance, drug use and criminality decrease and health improves (Office of Technology Assessment 1990).

Because most heroin users inject the drug, methadone maintenance is considered to be a key treatment to help prevent the spread of HIV. Some methadone supporters believe that injection heroin users placed on waiting lists for methadone maintenance should be provided methadone on an interim basis (even with limited or no counseling) until they can be admitted to a treatment program that provides methadone and full counseling services.

Methadone maintenance is a controversial type of drug treatment. Opponents believe it is not a valid treatment because it substitutes one addictive drug for another. Also, they point out that many methadone patients continue using heroin to varying degrees and some commit other crimes, including selling their take-home doses of methadone. In addition, although the methadone maintenance approach only treats heroin addiction, many heroin addicts also use other drugs. A Government Accounting Office (GAO) report in 1990 stated that the use of cocaine or methamphetamine and alcohol by many methadone patients was common (US General Accounting Office 1990).

No medication comparable to methadone has been shown to stabilize cocaine addicts. However, the use of antidepressant drugs to treat cocaine addiction is currently being studied.

§ 8.5 NARCOTIC ANTAGONISTS

The deliberate effort to find an effective analgesic that is not dependence-producing has led in recent years to the development of a class of compounds known as narcotic antagonists. These drugs, as the name implies, tend to block and reverse the effects of narcotics. These drugs have been shown to interact with opiate receptors in the brain, thus antagonizing the actions of not only the so-called narcotics but also other substances with an affinity for opiate receptors. The term "opioid antagonists" may be more appropriate.

Antagonists have a strong affinity for opiate receptors in the brain. If the narcotic antagonist is taken before the narcotic (heroin), the heroin effect is blocked because the narcotic receptor sites are already occupied.

There are several narcotic antagonists, such as nalorphine (Nalline), naloxone (Narcan), naltrexone, pentazocine (Talwin), and cyclazocine.

§ 8.5.1 Naloxone (Narcan)

Narcan is the drug of choice to treat narcotic overdoses (severe respiratory depression). Narcan quickly increases the respiratory rate and volume. Like other narcotic antagonists, Narcan precipitates withdrawal symptoms in people who are using narcotics such as heroin. The onset of the withdrawal is rapid and is usually observed within 2 minutes of IV injection of Narcan.

§ 8.5.2 Naltrexone

Naltrexone is a medication that blocks the effects of drugs known as opioids (a class that includes morphine, heroin, or codeine). It competes with these drugs for opioid receptors in the brain. It was originally used to treat dependence on opioid drugs but has recently been approved by the FDA as treatment for alcoholism. In clinical trials evaluating the effectiveness of Naltrexone, patients who received Naltrexone were twice as successful in remaining abstinent and in avoiding relapse as patients who received placebo—an inactive pill.

While the precise mechanism of action for Naltrexone's effect is unknown, reports from successfully treated patients suggest three kinds of effects. First, naltrexone can reduce craving, which is the urge or desire to drink. Second, Naltrexone helps patients remain abstinent. Third, naltrexone can interfere with the tendency to want to drink more if a recovering patient slips and has a drink.

Naltrexone's effects on blocking opioids occur shortly after taking the first dose. Findings to date suggest that the effects of Naltrexone in helping patients remain abstinent and avoid relapse to alcohol use also occur early (Rounsaville et al).

Essentially, Naltrexone is a long-lasting adaption of the classic "narcotic antagonist" drug Naloxone, which has been in use since the 1960s. Produced by Dupont under the brand name Narcan, Naloxone is used in hospital emergency wards everywhere to bring patients out of overdoses on heroin or other opiate drugs. Naloxone has saved untold thousands of lives in this way. "The patient will appear to be dead when brought into the emergency room," a veteran physician relates, "his lips

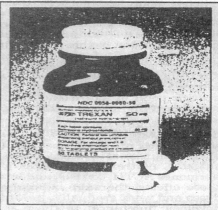

WARNING

"Drug abusers share medication," it is noted in NIDA's latest monograph on naltrexone. In fact, there have been several cases since 1973 of naltrexone clients slipping a dose of the drug to friends who were on methadone or street heroin. The results have been pretty spectacular: Instant withdrawals so drastic they required intensive hospital treatment.

Each white Trexan tablet will counteract a dose of 25 milligrams of heroin for 24 hours, the Dupont company warns; two Trexan tabs will last 48 hours, three tabs 72 hours, and so on. Opiate addicts who take Trexan will be in withdrawals for as long as the dose lasts.

"Symptoms of withdrawal have usually appeared within five minutes of ingestion of Trexan," cautions the Dupont product information in very small print, "and have lasted up to 48 hours. Mental status changes including confusion, somnolence and visual hallucinations have occurred." Such drastic mental changes are not typical at all of ordinary opiate withdrawals, and suggest that naltrexone's main active metabolic—6-Beta naltrexol—has special psychotrophic effects in people who are actively addicted.

Naltrexone-induced withdrawals need to be managed carefully by physicians, titrating into the patient just enough hydromorphone Dilaudid to overcome the naltrexone blockade, but not enough to overdose the patient dead. The same delicate and complicated routine must be undertaken when naltrexone clients accidentally injure themselves so badly that they require opiates for pain relief.

bright blue, no motion, no respiration, no detectable pulse. One shot of Narcan, and instantly the guy comes back to life with a 'bang,' sitting straight up on the gurney, coughing and spitting, quite often taking a swing at the ER intern who just brought him back from the dead." With Naloxone, these precipitated withdrawals are irreversible, even though they last for only 20 minutes.

Opiate dependence is a medical condition that has limited success rate with treatments. Ultra-Rapid Detox (URD) relapse rates are high. Naltrexone helps improve the success rate. However, administering it orally is often ineffective because patients either refuse to take their medicine or forget to take it. In order to improve these results, some programs are using a Naltrexone implant; it is placed under the skin, and the formula is slowly released over a 6-10 week period.

§ 8.5.3   Cyclazocine

Cyclazocine is a opiate antagonist. Treatment with cyclazocine involves first the withdrawal from heroin. Then cyclazocine is administered in increasing doses until tolerance develops, at about 4 mg a day. This level will block the subjective effects of 20 to 25 mg of heroin for a period of twenty to twenty-six hours. The user is usually tranquil and free of anxiety, without any appearance of sedation or mental disturbance. Most important is the absence of the drive to find heroin, which allows for social rehabilitation and increased productivity.

§ 8.6 SUMMARY AND CONCLUSIONS

Heroin and other opiates are narcotic sedatives and pain relievers that exert their effects by depressing the central nervous system and attaching to the pain receptor sites in the body. This depressant action works to relieve pain and to induce sleep. Overdose causes death because of the narcotic's selective depressant action on the respiratory center in the medulla.

Heroin has a rapid onset of action and proceeds with its analgesic effect. The results are a flush of euphoria, elevation of mood, and feeling of peace, contentment, and safety as the drug offers relief from the environment, both internal and external. This is one of the most significant reasons that heroin has the highest addiction potential of all the illicit drugs.

Common effects of narcotics (opiates) are respiratory depression, constipation, pupillary constriction, libido suppression, and the release of histamine, which causes the itching that may accompany heroin use. Nausea and vomiting also accompany heroin use, usually in the new user.

Contrary to popular belief, high-dose users of opiates can function quite adequately, and aside from the danger of unsterile needles and other catastrophes inherent in the lifestyle of the heroin user, the addict does not suffer any direct physical deterioration resulting from the drug.

In contrast to the pharmaceutical product derived form opium, synthetic narcotics are produced entirely within the laboratory. The continuing search for products that retain the analgesic properties of morphine without the consequent dangers of tolerance and dependence has yet to yield a product that is not susceptible to abuse. A number of clandestinely produced drugs, as well as drugs that have accepted medical uses, fall within this category.

Chapter 8

References

BBC News World Edition. March 3, 2003.

Drug Enforcement Administration. <u>Heroin Signature Program: 2002, Drug Intelligence Brief.</u> Washington, D.C.: U.S. Department of Justice, 2004.

----------. "Microgram Bulletin." <u>Forensic Drug Abuse Advisor</u> 15.7 (2003).

Drug Enforcement Administration. <u>Oxycontin: Drug Intelligence Brief.</u> Washington, D.C.: U.S. Department of Justice, 20024.

Office of National Drug Central Policy (ONDCP). <u>Breaking Heroin Sources of Supply</u>. Washington, D.C.: Executive Office of the President, 2004.

Office of Technology Assessment. <u>The Effectiveness of Drug Abuse Treatment: Implications for Controlling Aids/HIV Infection</u>. Washington, D.C.: U.S. Department of Justice, 1990.

Rounsaville, Bruce J., Stephanie O'Malley, and Patrick O'Connor. <u>Guidelines for the Use of Naltrexone in the Treatment of Alcoholism</u>. New Haven: The APT Foundation.

U.S. General Accounting Office. "Methadone Maintenance Report." GAO/T-HRD-90-19, March 23, 1990.

CHAPTER 9

HEROIN INFLUENCE

§ 9.1 THE CRIME

Being under the influence of heroin is a crime in all states of the United States. In California, the law is found in Section 11550 of the Health and Safety Code. Under subdivision (a) it reads:

(a) No person shall use, or be under the influence of any controlled substance which is (1) specified in subdivision (b) [opiates], (c) [opium derivatives], or (e) [depressants], or paragraph (1) of subdivision (f) [cocaine base stimulants] of Section 11054, specified in paragraph (14) [mescaline], (15) [peyote], (21) [phencyclidine], (22) [PHP-PCP analog], or (23) [TPCP, TCP-PCP analog] of subdivision (d) [hallucinogenics] of Section 11054, specified in subdivision (b) [raw opium, morphine, opium, codeine, cocaine] or (c) [methadone, fentanyl, etc.] of Section 11055, or specified in paragraph (1) [amphetamine] or (2) [methamphetamine] of subdivision (d) or in paragraph (3) [PCP] of subdivision (e) of Section 11055; or (2) a narcotic drug classified in Schedule III, IV, or V, except when administered by or under the direction of a person licensed by the state to dispense, prescribe, or administer controlled substances. It shall be the burden of the defense to show that it comes within the exception. Any person convicted of violating this subdivision is guilty of a misdemeanor and shall be sentenced to serve a term of not less than 90 days or more than one year in the county jail. The court may place a person convicted under this subdivision on probation for a period not to exceed five years and, except as provided in subdivision (c) [opium derivatives], shall in all cases in which probation is granted require, as a condition thereof, that the person be confined in a county jail for at least 90 days. Other than as provided by subdivision (c), in no event shall the court have the power to absolve a person who violates this subdivision from the obligation of spending at least 90 days in confinement in the county jail.

Although the above quoted material is the law against narcotic influence, this section is not to be used for arresting a narcotic addict for addiction. In a 1962 U.S. Supreme Court decision, *Robinson v. California*, 370 U.S. 660, 8 L.Ed.2d 758, 82 S.Ct. 1417 (1962), the court held that it was unconstitutional, cruel and unusual punishment, and against the 8th Amendment of the U.S. Constitution, to arrest a narcotic addict for addiction. Therefore, officers are said to be arresting narcotic users not for addiction but for being under the influence of a narcotic.

Legally, what is the difference between arresting a person for using heroin and arresting a person for being under the influence of heroin? According to jury instructions (Cal JIC 16.060), if a controlled substance is appreciably affecting the nervous system, brain, muscles and

other parts of a person's body, or is creating in him or her any perceptible abnormal mental or physical condition, such a person is considered
under the influence of a controlled substance. Generally, a person is
considered under the influence of heroin when you can identify the
physiological symptoms of heroin use: constricted pupils, scratching,
dry mouth, dull and indifferent, unsteady, needle marks, clammy skin,
etc. You must also prove venue; in other words, the crime must have
occurred within the county that brings the case to trial. When you observe the suspect under the influence, a crime is being committed in
your presence. The prosecutor will establish jurisdiction by asking you
where you observed the defendant under the influence. Almost all Section 11550 Health and Safety Code arrests are for influence.

It is confusing whether heroin withdrawals constitute heroin use or
influence. Below is a diagram of the physiological effects of heroin.

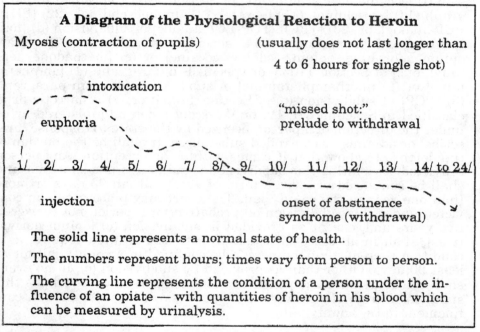

A Diagram of the Physiological Reaction to Heroin

Myosis (contraction of pupils)   (usually does not last longer than
4 to 6 hours for single shot)

intoxication

euphoria   "missed shot:"
prelude to withdrawal

1/ 2/ 3/ 4/ 5/ 6/ 7/ 8/ 9/ 10/ 11/ 12/ 13/ 14/ to 24/

injection   onset of abstinence
syndrome (withdrawal)

The solid line represents a normal state of health.

The numbers represent hours; times vary from person to person.

The curving line represents the condition of a person under the influence of an opiate — with quantities of heroin in his blood which
can be measured by urinalysis.

When does the law recognize that a person uses a controlled substance such as heroin? When a person is observed with fresh needle
marks, scar tissue, and admission of use, it is reasonable to conclude
that the person committed the crime of heroin use. When a person is
charged with use of heroin, venue must be established. There must be
evidence of where the suspect used heroin. To establish this, ask the
suspect, "Where did you have your last fix?" If the suspect refuses to
talk, then venue must be proven by a preponderance of the evidence.
For example, the apartment manager can state that the suspect lived
in the apartment for one year and has seen the suspect daily for two
weeks.

We know that heroin influence begins at the point of injection and
continues for up to 4 to 6 hours afterwards, or until the user begins to

experience the onset of an abstinence syndrome. Is the state of heroin withdrawal considered to be heroin use or influence? It could be successfully prosecuted that withdrawal symptoms fall within the scope of heroin influence. Medically, however, the question could be phrased as follows: is a person under the influence of an opiate while experiencing withdrawal symptoms? Withdrawal is actually the addict feeling the absence of an opiate. If the addict had not become addicted to heroin, then the withdrawal symptoms would not be present. Therefore, the use of heroin is creating a perceptible mental and physical condition, i.e., runny nose, dilated pupils, vomiting, cramps, fever, etc.

However, in *People v. Gutierrez*, 72 Cal. App. 3d 397, 140 Cal. Rptr. 122 (Cal. App. 2 Dist. 1977), Gutierrez was arrested for heroin use while being observed in a state of withdrawal. The court stated that to arrest for use, the crime must be committed in the officer's presence. Since Gutierrez did not inject the opiate in the officer's presence, the arrest was illegal. Another problem in arresting an addict during the withdrawal stage for heroin use is the officer's initial observations of the withdrawal syndrome. Withdrawal from opiates starts out similar to the symptoms of a common cold and progresses (if the tolerance is high enough) to the symptoms of a severe case of influenza or the flu. The point is this: a police officer cannot arrest a citizen for having a cold or the flu.

It has been established that heroin use in Section 11550 of the Health and Safety Code means withdrawals. Most prosecutors will not prosecute a use case only.

However, when a person is arrested for heroin influence, it is suggested that both influence and use be charged. Heroin influence relates to symptoms of heroin use from the moment of injection up to 4 to 6 hours later (constricted pupils, recent needle puncture wounds, etc.). If the prosecutor charges only influence, then it is possible that only the most recent needle marks can be admitted into evidence, which may be the one fresh needle mark you could find. However, if use is also charged, then all the marks are evidence that the addict had been using heroin on the other days prior to the time the defendant was observed to be under the influence.

It sounds confusing and juries also get confused with the terms "use of" and "under the influence." If the evidence shows that the defendant is a user of heroin (within several days prior to arrest) and the defendant was under the influence at the time of the arrest, then the defendant should be charged with two counts of Section 11550 H&S:

Count I: Did willfully and unlawfully use heroin.

Count II: Was willfully and unlawfully under the influence of heroin.

§ 9.2 SECTION 11550 H&S AND FIREARMS

According to Section 11550 (c) H&S, any person who is unlawfully under the influence of cocaine, cocaine base, heroin, methamphetamine, or phencyclidine while in the immediate personal possession of a loaded, operable firearm is guilty of a public offense punishable by imprisonment in county jail, not exceeding one year, or in state prison. As used in this subdivision, "immediate personal possession" includes, but is not limited to, the interior passenger compartment of a motor vehicle. Every person who violates subdivision (c) is punishable upon the second and each subsequent conviction by imprisonment in the state prison for two, three, or four years.

§ 9.2.1   Possession and Firearms (Section 11370.1 H&S)

Section 11370.1 H&S states that every person who unlawfully possesses one-half gram or less of a substance containing cocaine base, one gram or less of a substance containing cocaine, one gram or less of a substance containing heroin, one gram or less of a substance containing methamphetamine, one-eighth gram or less of a crystalline substance containing phencyclidine, and other specified weights of phencyclidine while in the immediate personal possession of a loaded, operable firearm is guilty of a felony punishable by imprisonment in the state prison for two, three, or four years.

§ 9.2.2   Summary Of § 11550 Prosecution

There are some important cases to remember when investigating a Section 11550 H&S case. In *People v. Gutierrez*, supra, the court made a distinction between an arrest for influence and use. The term "use" refers to the act of injecting or ingesting a drug. Therefore, you cannot arrest for use unless you see the addict inject the drug in your presence. The term "under the influence" refers to the presence of physical symptoms of the drug. If you can identify the physical symptoms of drug influence in your presence then you can arrest for influence. The withdrawal from the use of narcotics is not a crime.

In *People v. Snider*, 76 Cal.App.3d 560, 142 Cal. Rptr. 900 (Cal. App. 3 Dist. 1978), the court set out the factors that justify a detention in a Section 11550 H&S case.

a.   Pinned eyes;

b.   Defendant's coming from an area frequented by drug users; and,

c.   Prior knowledge of the defendant and his reputation.

Snider also approved the use of a flashlight to detect pupillary reaction.

In *People v. Rich*, 72 Cal. App. 3d 115, 139 Cal. Rptr. 819 (Cal. App. 2 Dist. 1977), the court held that a full search may be made of a person arrested for being under the influence.

In *People v. Carter*, 75 Cal. App. 3d 865, 142 Cal. Rptr. 517 (Cal. App. 2 Dist. 1977), the court held that a full search of a vehicle may be conducted when a suspect in the vehicle is arrested for Section 11550 H&S.

Heroin Influence

When you look at the elements of the crime of Section 11550 H&S remember that, in order to have a prosecutable case, certain elements must exist. The pupils must be constricted less than 3.0 mm. There should also be marks or injection sites of varying age. There should be old, recent, and fresh needle marks. There are some cases where no fresh marks are found. This presents a difficult problem of proof in that a necessary foundation to the officer's expert opinion is his observation of fresh needle marks. This information is then correlated with the amount of pupillary constriction. Of course, if the drug was inhaled or snorted, that would account for the lack of marks. Remember, if you testify to the age of an injection site, make sure you can differentiate between a fresh, recent, and old track mark.

There should also be some evidence of the addict's behavior at the time of the arrest. There should be some evidence of narcotic influence in the addict's behavior. There should be either a positive urine test showing an opiate present or a valid refusal.

§ 9.3 ARRESTS FOR VIOLATION OF SECTION 11550 OF THE HEALTH AND SAFETY CODE

To secure an arrest for violation of Section 11550 H&S, an officer should be able to articulate the facts that justify the contact or detention of an individual; investigate the readily observable symptoms that are possible narcotic indicators by:

—establishing reasons for the person's condition that confirm or eliminate the possible use of heroin;

—detaining the person for a pupilometer test; if person refuses, conduct the test at the police station.

The officer can form the conclusion that the person is under the influence of heroin (or a narcotic or controlled substance) when his investigation shows that no physical or mental illnesses or other intoxicants are involved. This conclusion is probable cause for an arrest. Once the officer reaches this conclusion, the subject should be admonished before questioning continues.

Viewing areas of the body (e.g., the arms) which are in plain sight does not constitute a search. The officer is permitted to obtain the subject's voluntary consent to view unexposed parts of the body. If the subject refuses consent, the officer may only demand such exposure as incident to an arrest, i.e., as a search for further evidence of the crime. Provided that the officer has first formed the intention to arrest, the officer may make this demand before informing the person that he or she is under arrest.

§ 9.3.1 Probable Cause

An officer's reasons for contacting, or stopping and investigating a subject, must always be stated clearly in the crime report. This contact may be the result of a vehicle stop, nonvehicle contact, or residential investigations.

§ 9.3.2   Vehicle Stop

Reasons for a vehicle stop include: moving violations, equipment violation, occupant resembles wanted suspect, near scene of recently reported crime, and/or stolen vehicle.

§ 9.3.3   Nonvehicle Stop

Reason for a nonvehicle stop include: received prior information of suspicious person in area, person appears lost or ill, person appears under the influence of something, person resembles wanted suspect, and/or pedestrian vehicle code violation.

§ 9.3.4   Residential Investigations

If you receive information on suspicious circumstances at a residence, (Section 415 Pen. Code[1], etc.), then knock on the door and allow the occupant to open it. You cannot enter the residence without consent unless you see a crime being committed or enter to check on the safety of a victim (if your call was Section 242 Pen. Code in progress, shot fired, etc.). If you have probable cause to arrest, then make an entry into the residence after knocking, identifying yourself, and stating your purpose.

Contact with a private citizen need not necessarily be based on a suspicion of criminal activity. It may be initiated due to a need for service or aid, such as traffic advice, directions, etc. For example, an officer has encountered a situation which calls for an investigation when he observes a person whose conduct or demeanor gives a reasonable indication that the person is:

−sick
−in need of help
−under the influence of an intoxicant (whether alcohol or a narcotic).

It is proper for the officer to contact a person falling into one of these categories.

If the officer develops a reasonable suspicion during the contact that the person has committed, is committing, or is about to commit a crime, the officer has the authority to detain (stop) the person long enough to complete his or her investigation. An officer may exercise this authority anywhere the officer has a right to be. Possible violation of Section 11550 H&S is a valid basis for a stop.

When the contact or stop begins under other circumstances (e.g., the issuance of a citation for a motor vehicle violation), if the officer observes narcotic indicators, he or she has probable cause for a self-initiated investigation of the subject's condition.

An officer will also have probable cause to begin an investigation on the basis of information supplied by personal knowledge of the area, knowledge of the suspect, police sources, or informers.

---

[1] Section 415 Pen. Code in California means disturbing the peace, domestic disturbance, party, etc. Section 242 Pen. Code in California means assault and battery.

Heroin Influence

Note that to violate the statute a person must be "under the influence" of a controlled substance or "narcotic drug" on the date (at the time) he or she is charged with the violation.

Remember, Section 11550 H&S does not have to be in a public place like Section 647f Pen. Code.

§ 9.4 PRELIMINARY § 11550 H&S INDICATORS

There are many preliminary narcotic indicators. A part of the Oakland Police Department Narcotics Influence Report lists some of these narcotic indicators

—eyes constricted
—balance impaired (new users)
—coordination impaired (new users)
—skin cold, clammy to touch
—mental state (euphoria)

The indicators under these headings are not, in and by themselves, conclusive. A combination of several from different categories is necessary before one has a probable indication of the influence of narcotics. A combination is necessary because prolonged addiction produces a tolerance which can cause some indicators to become less visible, such as the disruption of coordination. (A short sample form follows and a longer sample Narcotics Influence Report form is included at end of this chapter.)

PART I: PHYSICAL OBSERVATIONS (check as applicable)

EYES (PUPILS)	BALANCE COORDINATION	MENTAL STATE
___ Constricted	___ Normal	___ Cooperative
___ Dilated	___ Sways	___ Depressed
___ Watery	___ Staggers	___ Confused
___ Sensitive to Light	___ Unable to Stand	___ Passive
___ Reaction Test	___ Other: _____	___ Argumentative
___ mm. to ___ mm		___ Nervous
Comparision: ___	SKIN	___ Other: _____
___ No Reaction Observed	___ Scabs	
___ Eyelids Droop	___ Cold-Clammy	
___ Squints	___ Sweating	SPEECH
___ Glassy Appearance	___ Other: _____	___ Normal
___ Other: _____		___ Slurred
	OTHER	___ Incoherent
	___ Nose — runny, sniffling	___ Excited
	___ Yawning	___ Other: _____
	___ Scratching	
	___ Dry Mouth	
LIGHTING CONDITIONS	___ Drowsy ("On the Nod")	MECHANICAL AIDS USED
___ Daylight	___ Drooling	___ Flashlight
___ Nighttime	___ Nauseated	___ Pupilometer
___ Artifical Light	___ No Odor Alcoholic Beverage	___ Photos taken by ___
___ Other: _____	___ Other: _____	___ Other: _____

Chapter 9

§ 9.4.1 Eyes (Pupils)

Pupil size is extremely important in determining the status of a narcotic user. In the case of a heroin addict, a constricted pupil indicates recent use (within about 4 to 6 hours), while a dilated pupil usually means the addict is entering or is already in active physical withdrawal.

In a normal pupil an increase in light causes the pupil to constrict, and a decrease in light causes the pupil to dilate.

Below is a graph showing pupil size of a normal human under very bright and very dark experimental conditions. It can be seen in this graph that the pupil does not go beyond a normal range of 2.9 mm and 6.5 mm, despite a high range of illumination.

Most narcotic drugs constrict the pupil below the normal range (below 2.9 mm) for a short period of time.

Range of Pupil Size Under Different Light Exposure

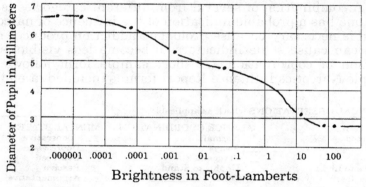

Although each narcotic has a predictable, consistent effect on pupil size as indicated in the "Pupil Size with Use of Some Common Opioids" chart, there are some drug interactions that may alter the expected result (Tennant).

No matter how long an individual has used an opiate, its influence will always cause the pupils of his eyes to constrict, except in the case of Demerol, which causes the pupils to dilate.

The size of normal pupils changes according to lighting conditions. In a very bright light, the pupils constrict (i.e., they become smaller); when the light diminishes, the pupils dilate (i.e., they become larger). The size of a normal pupil varies with each person, but the normal range of variation is between 2 and 5 mm in diameter.

Opiates can cause difficulties with vision. The pupils of a person "under the influence" grow so small that they are frequently described as being "pinpointed," although this particular word is medically and legally imprecise.

Heroin Influence

In their constricted state, the user's pupils do not respond normally to changes in light. They do not visibly constrict when a light is focused on them suddenly. (In fact, medical instruments could record changes in pupils, but the changes are so slight as to be almost undetectable to an unaided observer.)

When subjected to the same changes in light, the pupils of the eyes of a person not under the influence of an opiate will show obvious visible changes in size.

In conjunction with any combination of the narcotic indicators discussed previously, constricted pupils furnish reasonable grounds for an arrest of violation of Section 11550 H&S. When the condition of the pupils has been verified by comparison with those of another officer, the subject may be placed under arrest and admonished (see Admonition of Rights below). The officer with whom the subject's eyes have been compared must be identified in the crime report.

PART IV: ADMONITION OF RIGHTS

1. YOU HAVE THE RIGHT TO REMAIN SILENT 2. ANYTHING YOU SAY CAN AND WILL BE USED AGAINST YOU IN A COURT OF LAW	3. YOU HAVE THE RIGHT TO TALK TO A LAWYER AND HAVE HIM PRESENT WITH YOU WHILE YOU ARE BEING QUESTIONED	4. IF YOU CANNOT AFFORD TO HIRE A LAWYER ONE WILL BE APPOINTED TO REPRESENT YOU BEFORE QUESTIONING, IF YOU WISH ONE
THE ABOVE STATEMENT WAS READ TO THE ARRESTEE BY Smith, A.	SERIAL NO. 1001 P	TIME 1930
DO YOUR UNDERSTAND EACH OF THESE RIGHTS I HAVE EXPLAINED TO YOU? Yea, I know them.	HAVING THESE RIGHTS IN MIND, DO YOU WISH TO TALK TO US NOW? (WAIVER STATEMENT) Sure. You got me now.	

§ 9.4.1(a)   Pupil Size with the Use of Some Common Opioids

Opioid	Approx. Minimal Dose Required to Produce Constriction Below 3 mm dia.	Approx. Length of Time Between Dose and Constriction	Approx. Length of Time Constriction Lasts
Heroin	4-6 mg	15 minutes	4-6 hours
Morphine	10-20 mg	15 minutes	4-6 hours
Codeine	200-300 mg	30-60 minutes	3-4 hours
Propoxyphene	400-600 mg	1-2 hours	4-6 hours
Methadone	10-20 mg	1-2 hours	Variable
Meperidine	May produce no change or even dilation	n/a	n/a

§ 9.4.1 (b)   Causes of Non-Narcotic Pupillary Constriction

CAUSE	WAY TO IDENTIFY CAUSE
Medication for glaucoma	Individual will have doctor's prescription and obtainable medical records.
Tertiary (neuro-) syphilis	Condition is usually permanent and affects only one eye, while narcotics always affect both. Iris around pupil gives "eroded" or "degenerated" appearance. Have subject wait 4 hours to see if dilation occurs. This dilation will occur when heroin influence wears off.
Injury to eye or nerves	Will have past history of injury or disease, usually on one side. Will not dilate even in the darkness. Have subject wait for 4 hours as with syphilis.
Congenital	Condition is permanent and subject will know this. Usually on one side. Will not dilate even in darkness. Have subject wait for 4 hours as with syphilis.
Phencyclidine (PCP)	Will produce constriction in some individuals. Determine PCP presence by urine test.
Age under 18 years or over 65 years	Young and older persons have naturally constricted pupils under 2.9 mm in diameter.
Excessively high doses of barbiturates and benzodiazepines	These individuals are usually in a coma or so intoxicated they cannot walk.
Hippus	Hippus is an abnormally exaggerated rhythmic contraction and dilation of the pupil. It is occasionally seen when the pupil dilates in narcotic withdrawal. Since Hippus is not a consistent and predictable finding, it does not have many medico-legal implications.

§ 9.4.1(c)   Measurement of Pupil Size

Although pupil size can be photographed, it can be measured quite accurately with a simple card called a pupilometer. With the card, simply measure the pupil size to determine whether or not it is outside the normal range (2.9 to 6.5 mm). A pupil size smaller than 2.9 mm in diameter most likely indicates recent narcotic use.

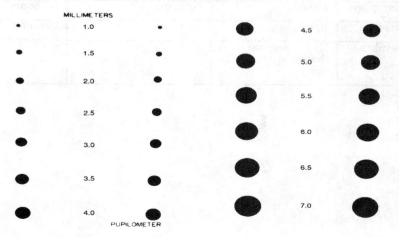

MILLIMETERS

1.0 1.5 2.0 2.5 3.0 3.5 4.0

PUPILOMETER

4.5 5.0 5.5 6.0 6.5 7.0

§ 9.4.1(d)   Pupil Test Procedures

1. During the day, test the subject away from bright sun. At night test the subject in light. Plain room lighting is best.

2. Measure pupil size by holding a flashlight at a 45-degree angle from the subject's lateral side. Never shine the light directly into the eye from the front, or the pupil will constrict and destroy the measurement.

3. Compare subject's pupil size to a pupilometer. Note sizes in millimeters.

4. Keep flashlight about 1 foot away.

5. Note the reaction or absence of reaction in subject's pupils by "flicking" the light beam on and off the pupil.

6. Repeat above procedures on at least one non-drug-using person in the same light and note results for comparison.

7. Remember that those few persons with a very dark iris surrounding the pupil cannot be adequately measured.

If you use the pupilometer, courtroom testimony might go something like this:

"Defendant and I (officer) then entered a small interview room. I dimmed the lights. After waiting a few minutes I performed a light reflex test on the defendant's eyes by directing a flashlight above the left eye and then above the right eye. I observed the response of his pupils. The pupils of the defendant's eyes remained at approximately 1.5 millimeters in size despite the change in the amount of light to which his eyes were exposed."

§ 9.4.1(e)   Photographic Documentation of Pupil Size and Reaction

There are some legal and clinical occasions when photographic evidence of pupil size and/or reaction may be advantageous. Consult the following key points when using this procedure:

1. A standard camera with a flash is sufficient, since it reacts faster than the pupil can.

2. Take photograph with pupilometer next to the eye for comparison.

3. Make sure room light is satisfactory. Avoid bright light or darkness.

4. To demonstrate nonreactivity by photograph, take a picture in room light. Then place the subject in a very dark room for 5 minutes and repeat the same photograph. A nonreactive pupil

will not dilate in darkness. It is advisable to take photographs of a control subject at the same time and in the same light to demonstrate the difference.

§ 9.4.1(f)   Summary

The normal pupil diameter of the adult (age 18-65 years) is considered to be 2.9 to 6.5 mm. Basis for this is a review of pertinent scientific literature dating back to 1941.

—Teenagers and persons over age 65 years may naturally have very small pupils under 2.9 mm in diameter.

—Pupil size under 2.9 mm in diameter is one of the most reliable indicators of acute heroin influence.

—If a pupil is constricted under 2.9 mm in diameter, its reactions to light will usually be imperceptible to the common observer.

—Even if a pupil is not constricted under 2.9 mm in diameter with heroin, the pupil may still be nonreactive. In addition, nonreactivity of the pupil generally last slightly longer than constriction.

—The pupil usually constricts within 10 to 15 minutes after intravenous heroin use, and it usually remains constricted for 4 to 6 hours. It may remain constricted 8 to 10 hours if a very high heroin dose is used.

—For unknown reasons, little tolerance develops to the pupillary effects of heroin. Therefore, pupillary constriction and nonreactivity may be present in a user who shows no other influence signs, such as droopy eyelids, slow speech, or itching.

§ 9.4.2   Needle Marks

Needle marks over veins are narcotic indicators usually present on the arms. They are corroborative physical evidence. These marks, scar tissue, "tracks," or "tattooing" can usually be found over the veins.

When checking for needle marks, examine the veins of the arms carefully. Feel the scar tissue. Make a close inspection of the scabbed areas. Press raised areas gently and ask about pain or tenderness. During the investigation, ask the addict if he fixes himself and how he feels. Is he going to get sick (withdrawals)? Make the addict feel comfortable when interviewing him.

Heroin Influence

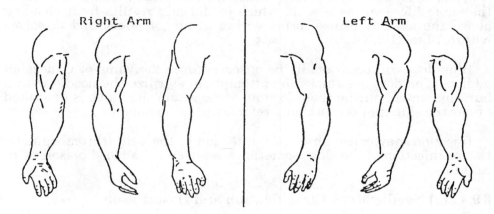

Scar tissue (the "tracks") will form over a vein after a period of repeated injections in the same spot. Some sources estimate that it takes approximately 50 injections to form one inch of permanent scar tissue. Repeated injections into the scar tissue will cause the skin to abscess. The same injections cause hardening (sclerosis) and collapse of the vein.

Old needle marks, scabs, tattooing, bruises, and tracks may be signs of addiction, but they do not prove present use. Only indications of a recent injection confirm that the person is "under the influence."

The heroin addict usually injects heroin directly into his veins in order to produce euphoria (called a "rush") as rapidly as possible.

Most addicts inject heroin into the inner folds of the arm and the back of the hand. Veins in places other than the arm are very thin and can seldom be used.

Addicts rarely, if ever, use proper medical procedures to administer drugs intravenously. Most heroin addicts have scabs (crusts of hardened blood and serum), inflammatory tissue, and scar tissue over their veins from constant injections, many of which are unsterile.

Immediately after an addict "fixes," a small pink swelling will occur at the point of injection. This forms a scab, which is a distinctive light pinkish-orange in color. The swelling may appear as a tiny hole, and sometimes it will have clotted blood around it. The injection site may bleed, leaving a stain on the user's shirt sleeve. If the site is pressed after a recent injection, it may ooze. A scab can normally form within 24 hours after injection. The approximate age of a scab can be estimated by its color and by the condition of the tissue around it. After three or four days, it becomes predominantly orange. As it grows older, the color darkens. A scab may last as long as 21 days.

If the tissue around a scab swells, the swelling will be pronounced for the first two days after the injection. Subsequently, it will subside.

Chapter 9

A bruise is essentially bleeding under the skin, and a bruise has about the same life span as a scab, which essentially results from bleeding above the skin. A bruise forms within about 24 hours and dissolves within 14 to 21 days.

Blue dots will occasionally be observed over the veins of Caucasian addicts. The dots are caused by attempts to sterilize the needle with a burning match; during the injection, carbon from the flame is deposited under the skin and is commonly referred to as "tattooing."

Injection may cause abscesses, infection of the vein (thrombophlebitis), or infection of the skin, sometimes referred to as blood poisoning or cellulitis.

§ 9.4.2(a) Needle Mark Classification and Description

Classification	Approx. Time after Injection	Major Appearance Characteristic	Major Texture of Site
Fresh	0-24 hours	Red dot	Oozing
Early	24-96 hours	Light scab Light bruise Reddened Border	Mild elevation
Late	5-14 days Dark Bruise	Dark scab ("tracks")	Elevated ridges
Healing	14 days and older	Scar/fiber formation ("Silver streaks")	Indentation

§ 9.4.3 Withdrawals (not an indicator for heroin influence)

While questioning the addict, watch for obvious withdrawal symptoms: yawning, sniffling and/or excreting through the nasal passages, perspiration, gooseflesh, chills, restlessness, clearing of the throat and the desire to expectorate. These signs will give the officer an idea of what to expect in the way of marks and an estimate of the daily amount of narcotics being used. Quantity used will vary with the quality currently being sold. These observations will assist in overcoming declarations of weekend use of "only chipping." Recently, the term "chipping" has been loosely used by hypes (heroin addicts) concurrent with the admission of using only one or two caps a day. The original definition, of sporadic use with varying intervals between injections, cannot always be construed.

Withdrawal symptoms or the abstinence syndrome, a term more often used by the medical profession, varies in intensity depending on the amount of narcotic used.

Doctors Himmelsbach and Small conducted extensive research into opiate addiction and withdrawal symptoms at the United States Government Hospital, Lexington, Kentucky. They describe the symptoms and severity in the following terms.

MILD (+)	MODERATE (++)	MARKED (+++)	SEVERE (++++)
When only those signs	When these signs are added	When these signs are added	When these signs are added
Yawning	Loss of appetite	Deep breathing	Vomiting
Watery eyes	Dilated pupils	Fever	Diarrhea
Runny nose	Tremors	Insomnia	Weight loss
Sneezing	Gooseflesh	Restlessness	
Perspiration		Rise in BP	

These studies made by Drs. Himmelsbach and Small were controlled conditions with specific doses at regular periods, circumstances a narcotics officer will not encounter.

Users prefer heroin, but will use anything that will forestall withdrawal pains. A capsule of heroin may in reality contain only 3 percent heroin to 48 percent heroin. Through interviewing and the withdrawal symptoms exhibited, the officer can speculate as to the quality currently being sold.

Experience and observation will be the only method the officer has to evaluate the admissions made to him. For example, a user will say he uses a cap a day, but shows mild (+) through severe (++++) symptoms; also his arms are decidedly marked. It is then obvious he is lying. Another user may say he is using a gram a day and exhibits mild (+) symptoms or none at all. The dealer he is buying from is apparently adulterating the heroin to the point where the user has what is known as a "mild sugar habit." These are extreme examples, but nonetheless true. The officer may not always observe all the symptoms, but only see part of any of the four categories. From these symptoms he can make an estimate of the user's habit.

Even though you are not basing your arrest for heroin influence on the fact that withdrawals are present because withdrawals indicate use, not influence, it is very important that you understand the degrees of withdrawal, and be observant of any symptoms during the interview process.

§ 9.4.4   Problems of Recognition

A person under the influence of opiates shows a distinctly different combination of symptoms than a person in some other condition. Some problems of recognizing opiate influence may involve the following:

—long-time addicts

—the symptoms of other drugs

—non-drug-abuse situations

§ 9.4.4(a) Prolonged addiction

The primary difficulty in recognizing a chronic addict lies in the fact that, because the addict has developed an abnormal tolerance for the drug, he or she may not display many of the visible indicators of opiate abuse as clearly as someone who has less tolerance. This principle parallels alcohol tolerance, wherein an alcoholic may show fewer outward signs of intoxication when compared to an equally intoxicated nonalcoholic.

As a consequence, a chronic addict may or may not exhibit the following symptoms:

—reduced coordination

—impaired comprehension

—drowsiness

In such cases, the officer must rely on the other narcotic indicators, such as the subject's familiarity with the argot, or specialized slang, of the drug abusers, the wearing of warmer clothing than necessary for the weather, prior arrests, and so forth. It should be emphasized, though, that the difficulty is limited to the preliminary indicators. Every user of opiates, no matter how tolerant of the drugs, will have constriction of the pupils of the eyes.

§ 9.4.5 Summary of Heroin Influence

To validly state that a person is under the influence of heroin, an officer must have physical evidence of heroin activity (such as constricted pupils, nonreactive pupils, or muscle relaxation) and laboratory evidence of heroin activity (evidence of heroin or a heroin derivative such as morphine in the blood or urine).

More than one item of evidence must be found in order to make the diagnosis of heroin influence.

If an officer observes a constricted pupil below 2.9 mm, he or she has probable cause to arrest the suspect for violation of Section 11550 of the Health and Safety Code of California. If, after a blood or urine analysis, a heroin derivative (morphine) is detected, the individual is definitely under the influence of heroin.

In another situation, the pupil may be under 4.0 mm. and be nonreactive. In this case, the pupils should be photographed in lighted and darkened conditions; a control subject should be photographed under the same conditions with the same camera. If fresh needle marks are present or heroin is present in the nasal passage and heroin or a derivative is found in the urine, the person is under the influence of heroin.

In a third situation, you may find a suspect who exhibits muscle relaxation including one or more of the following symptoms: droopy eyelids, slurred or slow speech, abnormal gait, nodding. If you find fresh needle marks and the person is negative on alcohol breath, blood, or urine, and a heroin derivative is found in the urine, the person is under the influence of heroin.

§ 9.4.6 Summary of Narcotic Indicators

Narcotic indicators are signs and symptoms of opiate use that you can observe with your eyes. Remember, no narcotic indicator alone is conclusive; a combination of indicators is required for probable cause to arrest. Below is a list of narcotic indicators that might be observed by an officer while performing law enforcement duties:

1. Poor coordination.

    a. A user under the influence may exhibit poor physical co-ordination and poor balance (stumbling).

    b. Chronic users become tolerant to this effect unless they use enough of the drug to exceed their tolerance level.

2. An appearance of drowsiness or sleepiness ("on the nod").

    a. A tendency to sit looking off into space (known to addicts as "goofing") may indicate the use of heroin, barbiturates, or both. Head may bob back and forth.

    b. Slow, shallow breathing, a dry mouth, slow reflexes, and a general retardation of physical activity.

3. Appearance and clothing.

    a. Excessively warm clothing on a warm day (to counter hypothermia, the lowered temperature of the skin caused by opiates). On a hot day may be carrying a jacket. Unkempt appearance, not interested in a neat, clean appearance.

4. An undernourished appearance.

    a. More interested in feeding the heroin habit than in feeding the body's necessary nutrients.

    b. Thin, frail, or run-down bodily appearance.

5. Pupils of the eyes.

    a. Sunglasses to conceal myosis (constricted pupils) of the eyes (encountered less frequently now than in years past).

    b. Droopy eyelids from sedation of drug.

6. Flushed complexion (caused by dilation of the facial blood vessels after an injection).

    a.   A tendency to scratch facial areas, particularly the nose, may indicate a slight overdose or an allergic response to the drug.

    b.   A tendency to scratch other areas of the body. Injection sites frequently itch

    c.   Sweating due to relaxation of the blood vessels.

7. Excessive desire for sugar in coffee, sweets, and other foods.

    a.   The mild sugar diluent in heroin causes hyperglycemia (excess sugar in the blood stream), and an addict becomes habituated to this condition; hence, the "milk sugar habit."

8. Inhibited comprehension due to drug influence.

    a.   The subject's mind may function rationally but very slowly, and may easily be confused by conversation carried on at a normal speed.

    b.   Some addicts become very talkative when under the influence.

    c.   Inhibited speech that is slow and deliberate but understandable.

9. Use of the characteristic vocabulary of heroin addicts.

10. Needle marks and tracks on the arms, hands, and other areas where veins can be reached by a person who injects himself.

    a.   Long-sleeve shirts (to hide needle marks).

    b.   Bloodstains on clothing near or at the site of an injection.

11. A statement by the subject that he is an addict or that he is under the influence of a drug.

12. Possession of prescription drugs without adequate medical explanation.

13. Possession of paraphernalia associated with the sale or use of drugs.

    a.   An "outfit" including a spoon, a hypodermic syringe (pharmaceutical or homemade), a needle, a tourniquet, matches, and other miscellaneous items.

b.　　The spoon will have a characteristically bent handle, and may be blackened from being held over lighted matches.

c.　　A belt used as a "tie rag" (tourniquet) will have teeth marks at one end. Other tie rags include rubber tubing, neckties, and ripped T-shirts.

14. Withdrawal symptoms (see text). No known deaths have been recorded due to withdrawal symptoms.

15. Overdose symptoms (see text).

§ 9.5 WHAT IS HEROIN?

Heroin is a diactylmorphine and it is made by the chemical conversion of morphine, which is synthesized from opium.

Heroin is classified as an "opioid." This term is now preferred over "narcotic" since it is more descriptive, in that "narcosis" refers to sleep and sedation which is produced by many drugs rather than specifically relating to the unique characteristics of an opioid.

An opioid is any drug that:

1.　　Will relieve pain.

2.　　Will produce withdrawal symptoms when the drug is withheld after chronic administration.

3.　　Will suppress withdrawal symptoms which occur as a result of withholding chronic opioid administration.

Opioids come from three sources:

1.　　Opium poppy plant, e.g., heroin

2.　　Synthetic manufacturer, e.g., propoxyphene

3.　　Nervous tissue in human body, e.g., endorphin

§ 9.5.1　How is Heroin Used?

Proper identification of heroin use can only be made by understanding its various use patterns.

Heroin is usually used intravenously, but it can be smoked, sniffed, taken orally, or by rectal suppository.

Most single doses of street heroin contain about 4 to 8 mg of heroin. For example, a 2 percent street sample that weighs 250 mg or gm contains 5 mg of heroin, as does a 1 percent sample which weighs 500 mg or gm.

Most persons dependent upon heroin begin to use it in their late teenage years after they have experiences with nicotine, alcohol, caffeine, marijuana, and one or more other illicit drugs such as PCP, cocaine, and/or amphetamines.

A few heroin users may begin to use in late adolescence or in adulthood and may not have extensive experience with other abusable drugs.

Once addicted to intravenous heroin, approximately 70 to 80 percent of addicts continue intermittent use for many years or for life.

Addiction periods or "runs" usually last 4 to 6 months, and the cessation of a "run" is often brought about by arrest or entry into treatment. Periods of abstinence usually last no more than a few weeks or months, and relapse is usually precipitated by physical or mental stress.

§ 9.5.2   How Does Heroin Work?

Heroin is converted to morphine within about 2 to 3 minutes after it is injected into the bloodstream.

Before total conversion to morphine, heroin enters the brain and helps produce a brief yet intense euphoria called a "rush."

Heroin and morphine attach to small areas in the brain known as receptor sites. Upon drug use, these sites are triggered to help produce the following signs and symptoms, defined as "being under the influence":

—Constricted pupils (less than 2.9 mm diameter)

—Muscle relaxation (e.g., droopy eyelids, slurred speech, slow gait, sleepy appearance, etc.)

—Decrease in pulse, reflexes, blood pressure, and respiration rate.

—Nonreactive pupils

In addition to the "under-the-influence" signs listed above, the user may experience pain relief, euphoria, and psychic stimulation.

§ 9.5.2(a)   Heroin Metabolism

Modern research has identified how the human body accepts, deactivates, and eliminates drugs. This process is usually called "metabolism" or "pharmacokinetics."

§ 9.5.2(b)   Schematic Diagram of Heroin Metabolism

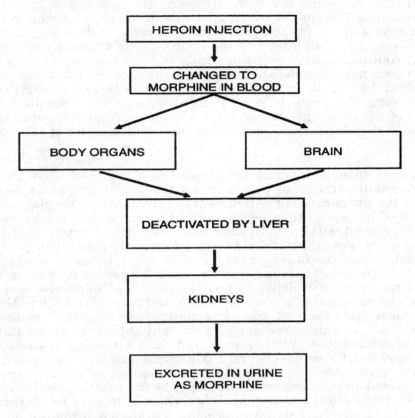

Heroin is very soluble and can be taken by injection, oral, nasal, smoking, and suppository routes.

After heroin reaches the bloodstream, most of it is transformed to morphine within 2 to 3 minutes. After 4 to 6 hours the liver deactivates most of the heroin-morphine and it is then primarily eliminated through the bile and urine.

It takes approximately 1 to 2 hours for heroin-morphine to reach the urine after heroin is injected.

Although a small amount of codeine will often be found in urine specimens from heroin addicts, it is due to codeine being in mixtures of heroin sold on the streets and not due to metabolism.

After a single injection of heroin, morphine can be found in the urine for 48 to 72 hours.

§ 9.5.3   Tolerance, Physical Dependence & Withdrawal
The chronic administration of a therapeutic dose of heroin over a period of a few weeks will reduce the respiratory depressant, analgesic, sedative, and euphorigenic effects initially introduced by the drug. At

this point larger doses will become necessary to produce the same effects elicited by earlier use of the drug and the user is said to have become tolerant. The rate at which tolerance develops is a function of the size of dose and the frequency of administration. It does not, however, develop equally to all effects of the drug—highly tolerant persons will usually continue to have pinpoint pupils and constipation. Development of tolerance may considerably elevate the dosage that is lethal to the individual, but death by respiratory depression can occur even in the chronic user. Tolerance to heroin will disappear after complete withdrawal of the drug; this can be fatal when a previously dependent opiate user takes his "usual" dose after weeks or months of total abstinence.

Physical dependence may be defined as a condition that requires regular administration of heroin at higher than therapeutic doses to prevent the appearance of withdrawal syndrome. Even regular administration of heroin at therapeutic doses for one or two weeks usually precipitate mild withdrawal symptoms when it is discontinued. If the usual dose of heroin is withheld from a physically dependent person, a predictable sequence of responses will usually occur, many of which are opposite to the effects produced by the drug. The severity of these withdrawal responses will depend upon the degree of tolerance, length of time of chronic administration and the usual dose of the drug. About 8 to 12 hours after the last dose, lacrimation (eyes tearing), rhinorrhea (runny nose), yawning, and perspiration will appear; at about 12 to 14 hours afterward, the individual may fall into a tossing, restless sleep which may last for several hours. Upon awakening, she/he is more restless and "miserable." As the syndrome progresses, additional signs appear: dilated pupils, anorexia (no appetite for food), gooseflesh, restlessness, irritability, and tremor. When these responses reach their intensity, the individual shows increasing irritability, insomnia, marked anorexia, violent yawning, severe sneezing, lacrimation, and stuffy nose. Nausea and vomiting are common, as well as intestinal spasm and diarrhea. Heart rate and blood pressure are elevated; the person feels cold, alternating with periods of flushing and excessive sweating. Abdominal cramps usually occur, as well as pains in the bones and muscles of the back and extremities, muscle spasms, and kicking movements.

Without treatment or drug use, the symptoms usually subside in 7 to 10 days. Restoring physiological equilibrium takes considerably longer. There appears to be more subtle behavioral manifestations upon a protracted period of abstinence which include failure to tolerate stress, overconcern of discomfort, and a poor self-image. It is probable that these factors contribute to the tendency of the compulsive user to relapse following withdrawal.

From a medico-legal viewpoint, it is generally not correct to describe an individual as being "under the influence" because withdrawal doesn't occur until there is essentially no narcotic left in the bloodstream. Remember that all narcotics develop physical dependency (withdrawals) at the same rate (see table below).

§ 9.5.3(a) Minimal Time and Dosage Requirements for Dependence Upon Some Opioids

Drug	Usual Dose	Approximate Daily Dose Required to Produce Dependency	Minimal Length of Time Required to Produce Dependency
HEROIN	4-8 mg	20-25 mg	1-2 Weeks
MORPHINE	8-20 mg	50-100 mg	1-2 Weeks
CODEINE	30-60 mg	1200-1800 mg	1-3 Weeks
PROPOXYPHENE	65-130 mg	800-1000 mg	2-3 Weeks
MEPERIDINE	50-1000 mg	Over 1000 mg	2-3 Weeks
METHADONE	5-10 mg	20-40 mg	1-2 Weeks

Note: Lower dosages given over a longer period of time may also produce dependence. Intravenous administration will produce tolerance and dependence faster than will oral administration.

§ 9.5.3(b) Withdrawal Symptoms and Signs from Heroin Addiction

Symptoms: Feelings experienced by the addict 4 to 6 hours after last use:

—Insomnia
—Chills
—Aching muscles (myalgia)
—Aching joints (arthralgia)
—Nausea'

Things an observer can feel or see, which begin about 8-12 hours after last heroin use.

—Sweating (diaphoresis)–Usually first sign to appear
—Gooseflesh (piloerection)–Usually second sign to appear
—Hyperactive reflexes–Usually third sign to appear
—Yawning–Only occurs with marked withdrawal
—Tearing (lacrimation)–Only occurs with marked withdrawal
—Runny nose (rhinorrhea)–Only occurs with marked withdrawal
—Vomiting–Only occurs with marked withdrawal
—Diarrhea–Only occurs with marked withdrawal
—Pupil dilates above 6.5 mm–Only occurs after prolonged withdrawal

§ 9.5.4 Other Physiological Symptoms

Often after the addict has injected the opiate, there is a tendency to scratch the skin, particularly around the face area. The addict's mouth will be dry, his face will be flushed, and his skin temperature lowered. The opiates have a direct effect on the gastrointestinal tract, causing constipation. This is one reason why opiates are very common for the relief of diarrhea. In addition to a flushing of skin, opiates often cause sweating due primarily to the relaxation of the blood vessels. Since the continual use of opiates causes a general dehydration of fluids, the skin of the addicted person will often become dry and the fingernails pale and brittle. Opiates tend to diminish sexual desire.

Due to the fact that the opiates generally act as a depressant upon the central nervous system, the addict's movements, pulse, breathing, and heartbeat will be slower than normal.

§ 9.5.5 The Difference Between the New User and Chronic User

Not all addicts are the same. There are differences in the observable and unobservable effects of the intravenous use of heroin.

§ 9.5.5(a) Observable Effects of Intravenous Heroin on New Users and Chronic Users

New User	Approx. Time after Last Injection	Chronic User	Approx. Time after Last Injection
Sedation "nodding"	.25-4 hours	Little or no sedation	.25-4 hours
Poor motor	.25-4 hours	Little or no motor loss (slurred speech)	.25-4 hours
Pupillary Constriction	.5-6 hours	Pupillary Constriction	.5-6 hours
Depressed Reflexes	.5-4 hours	Depressed Reflexes	.5-4 hours
Scratching	.25-6 hours	Scratching	.25-6 hours
Vomiting	.25-2 hours		
Relaxation	.25-12 hours	Relaxation	.25-6 hours
Decreased Respiratory Rate	5-4 hours	Decreased Respiratory Rate	.5-4
No Withdrawal Signs	.5-4 hours	Withdrawal Signs: runny nose, gooseflesh, dilated pupil	8-72 hours
"Rush"	30 seconds -	"Rush"	(Depending on amount used over tolerance)
Euphoria & Psychic Stimulation	.25-6 hours	Little Euphoria & Psychic Stimulation	.25-6 hours
Pain Relief	.25-6 hours	Little Pain Relief	.25-6 hours
Constipation	—	Constipation	Constant
Suppressed Cough	.25-6 hours	Suppressed Cough	.25-6 hours
Morphine in Blood	.25-12 hours	Morphine in Blood	.25-12 hours
Morphine in Urine	2-4 hours	Morphine in Urine	2-24 hours

§ 9.5.6 How Much Heroin Does An Addict Use?

An addict will use several balloons or bindles a day to support his habit. A balloon of heroin contains about a gram, enough heroin for one or two injections, depending upon the extent of the user's habit. A gram equals 500 mg of total weight. If there is 1 percent heroin in the gram, then there is actually 5 mg of heroin in the gram or spoon.

If an addict has enough resources to maintain a regular supply of heroin, how much will an addict use? Contrary to popular belief, heroin addicts do not seek to escalate their heroin dosage indefinitely. Both humans and laboratory monkeys with unlimited access to heroin/morphine tend to slowly increase their use until they self-administer a stable and subjective optimal amount of the drug.

§ 9.5.7 Heroin Paraphernalia

Heroin can be taken orally (although it is not very effective), snorted in the nose, or injected. The most common method of using heroin is injecting it into the veins. Paraphernalia for injecting heroin is variously called an "outfit," "kit," "rig," or the "works," and includes a spoon or bottle cap, syringe, needle, needle sheath, cotton, tourniquet, and matches.

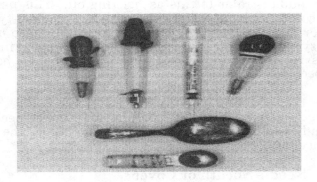

§ 9.5.7(a)   A Spoon

The heroin addict will take a teaspoon, tablespoon, measuring spoon, or the metal top of a bottle and use any one of these items to hold the heroin solution. The spoon will typically be burnt on the bottom from heating the solution and crimped up in the center to make the spoon more stable, thereby decreasing the chances of spilling the heroin. Sometimes the spoon handle will be bent back in a U-shape, leaving the bowl off the surface so the solution can be heated without the addict holding it. Depending on the cleanliness of the addict, some heroin residue or a dirty piece of cotton may remain inside the spoon.

§ 9.5.7(b)   Hypodermic Syringe

The medical-type syringes were at one time unpopular, especially if the addict injects himself, because depressing and releasing the plunger with one hand is often cumbersome. Addicts would take a professional syringe, take out the plunger and cut the syringe smaller. For an air source, the addict would use a plastic grape or a baby pacifier and this "homemade" outfit enabled the addict to "work" or "play" with the bulb while injecting heroin .In 1976, the law requiring syringes to be obtained through a doctor's prescription was changed, enabling a person to purchase the insulin-type disposable syringes across the pharmacy counter.

Addicts no longer had to use the same precious but dirty, misused and abused needle and syringe that they had shared with other addicts. They could now use a new, sharp, and sterile needle and syringe each time they injected if they chose to do so. Clean and sterile needles would decrease the incidents of infection, diseases such as hepatitis, AIDS, and a host of other problems. The injection sites would heal more quickly, thereby reducing the chances of having the telltale marks of heroin use.

Addicts enjoy not only the effects from the heroin after it is injected, but also the foreplay which precedes the actual injection. They derive much pleasure from watching the needle penetrate the vein while holding the bulb of the syringe between the thumb and fingers. When the needle "registers" (the blood enters the syringe indicating that the needle has entered the vein) the addict can manipulate the bulb with one available hand. The addict will often manipulate or play with the bulb, squeezing and then backing off, to allow his blood and the heroin to intermix. Many addicts refer to this as "jacking off." This particular part of the ritual could not be accomplished with the medical-type (plunger) syringe. Other addicts, however, have opted to purchase or obtain the insulin-type syringes and will use them. Generally speaking, the addict will use the syringe over and over again until the needle bends or until the syringe becomes inoperative.

§ 9.5.7(c)   Hypodermic Needle
The needle is usually a #25 or #26 pharmaceutical needle, the preferred size and opening for injecting heroin. The higher the number, the smaller the needle.

§ 9.5.7(d)   Needle Sheath or Cover
The needle sheath is a plastic covering used to protect the needle. If a needle sheath is not available, the addict will often use the back part of a matchbook cover by rolling it up, tying it with a rubber band, and placing the needle directly inside. Sometimes the plastic needle sheath is used to stir the heroin while it is being dissolved in water.

§ 9.5.7(e)   Cotton
Common cotton is formed into a ball and used as a filter between the needle and the heroin solution when the heroin solution is drawn into the syringe. The cotton balls are often saved so that when the addict is desperate, he can dissolve them in water and remove any residual heroin they contain.

§ 9.5.7(f)   Tourniquet
The tourniquet or "tie rag" may be a piece of rubber tubing, a necktie, a belt, a piece of cloth, a nylon stocking, or any strong, soft, elongated material. The tourniquet stops the flow of blood and forces the vein to the surface, making it easier for the addict to locate the vein for injection.

§ 9.5.7(g)   A Book of Matches
The addict uses any kind of heating device, usually matches, to heat the heroin in water.

Miscellaneous items are sometimes found with injection paraphernalia, such as a small container for water, tissue paper or cloth to wipe up blood, and a special container for the outfit.

§ 9.5.8   Injecting Heroin

Once the addict is in possession of the injection paraphernalia and the heroin (which is most commonly packaged in toy balloons), he is ready to "fix" himself (inject the heroin into his veins).

The heroin will be taken out of the balloon and put the proper amount in the empty spoon. The amount will depend on the addict's habit, purity of the drug, and how much heroin the addict could get. The addict will put water in the syringe and then put the water from the syringe into the spoon containing the heroin. The mixture is then heated with matches (four or five matches) until the first bubble rises to the surface of the solution and the powder dissolves. Below is an illustration of cooking up heroin.

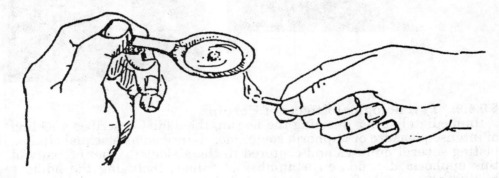

A small amount of cotton is placed in the bowl of the spoon to prevent clogging of the needle. A syringe or eyedropper with a hypodermic needle attached is then stuck in the cotton, and the solution is drawn into the syringe or tube of the eyedropper through the cotton. Later, if the addict cannot get more heroin or morphine, the cotton may be "cooked" to obtain whatever drug residue is left in it.

Most addicts inject the heroin into the inner elbow area. The injection is made easier by tying a rag, belt, or rope around the arm above the elbow, which causes the veins to swell and stand out. The needle is then placed on top of a vein and the puncture is made. When blood appears in the eyedropper or syringe, the addict knows that the needle is inside the vein.

Some addicts will "clean" their "works" by running water back and forth through the syringe a number of times. Other addicts will just put the outfit away dirty.

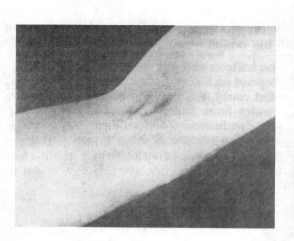
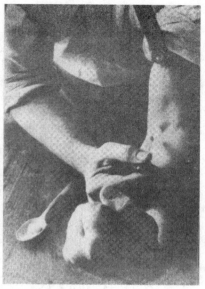

§ 9.5.9   Psychological Effects of Heroin

Immediately after injecting the heroin, the addict describes a feeling of intense pleasure or euphoria sometimes described as a sexual climax, lasting several minutes and centered in the abdomen. The intensity of this euphoria depends on a number of things, including the addict's habit, the amount of tolerance developed, the normal amount and purity of the heroin injected, and the user's psychological state of mind. An addict who is heavily addicted and beginning withdrawal symptoms may only experience a slight euphoric effect after injection. In this case, the injection only negates the sickness, allowing the addict to feel normal. He will normally feel relief from pain and a mental sluggishness or drowsiness (a dream-like state) often called "on the nod." Psychologically, he may feel relief from problems and responsibilities. The feeling of ease and a floating sensation are common. Some heroin addicts become very talkative after fixing. Generally, both male and female addicts have a reduced sexual desire after using opiates.

The central nervous system and analgesic effects of heroin (diacetylmorphine) depend upon the conversion of heroin to morphine in the body. This conversion occurs rapidly in a two-step process: the first stage produces 6-monoacetylmorphine; the second produces morphine. A study of the metabolism of intravenously-administered heroin showed that significant quantities of morphine were excreted in the urine within two hours of administration (Yeh et al). Thus, when considering the pharmacological activities of injected heroin, it is actually morphine which is studied. Morphine is the point of reference for all narcotic analgesics, including heroin; extensive use and study of morphine over many years has made it a standard of comparison.

Heroin Influence

Intramuscular administration of the therapeutic dose (10 to 20 mg) of morphine (equivalent to 5 to 10 mg of heroin) in a "normal" adult (weight approximately 150 lbs.) will cause a range of effects from drowsiness and euphoria to anxiety and nausea. One of the most significant effects produced by heroin and morphine is depression of the respiratory center. The degree of depression is usually dose-dependent, particularly in the nontolerant (nondependent) individual, although in hypersensitive individuals, a drastic depression may result, regardless of dosage.

Another effect which appears after administration of morphine or heroin is constricted pupils. Chronic uses do not develop tolerance to the pupillary constrictor action of the drug. The opiates also have a marked constipating effect. While morphine tends to increase the tone of intestinal smooth muscle, it decreases propulsive movement and thereby delays gastric emptying. Morphine also affects the smooth muscle of the urinary tract and tends to contract the ureter and the detrusor muscle of the bladder. Urinary retention depresses the response to the stimulus of a full bladder.

§ 9.5.9(a)   Heroin High

The small amount of heroin that goes to the brain is probably what produces the heroin high. The high or euphoria can last for 30 seconds to 5 minutes. It seems that addicts become tolerant to this euphoria and eventually inject heroin only to prevent withdrawals (getting sick), with very little high or euphoria from the drug.

§ 9.5.10 Visible Effects of Acute Heroin Influence

Basic Physiologic Effect	Signs / Symptoms
Autonomic nervous system	Decrease in pulse, respiration, reflexes, blood pressure, body temperature
Neck Relaxation	"Nodding"
Eyelids Relaxation	Droopy
Face / mouth Relaxation	Licking of lips, Sleepy appearance, Drooling
Larynx Relaxation	Slurred or slow speech
Extremities Relaxation	Slow gait
Release of histamine	Itching
Stimulation of eye center in brain	Constricted pupils, Nonreactive pupils

The acute physiologic effects of heroin usually begin within 15 minutes after heroin is injected, and they usually last about 4 to 6 hours with a normal dosage. If dosages of 8 mg or more are used, effects may be slightly longer than 6 hours. Persons who are tolerant to heroin may show few, if any, physiologic effects, with the exception of the eye signs.

§ 9.5.11 Non-Visible Effects of Acute Heroin Influence

Heroin has many **acute or immediate** effects that are not visible to an observer.

—Euphoria
—Emotional stabilization
—Psychic stimulation
—Cough suppression
—Nausea
—Bowel and bladder suppression
—Pain relief

If heroin is taken chronically and the user becomes tolerant, most of the above effects disappear, although emotional stabilization may persist. Constipation may also develop and be persistent.

§ 9.5.12 Criteria for Physical Evidence of Acute Heroin Influence

Pupil Size:	Under 2.9 mm in. diameter (normal adult is 2.9 to 6.5)
Pulse:	Under 60 beats per minute(normal is 72/min.)
Blood Pressure:	Systolic under 100 mm Hg.(normal is 120 mm Hg.) Diastolic under 60 mm Hg.(normal is 80 mm Hg.)
Respiratory Rate:	Under 12 respirations per minute(normal is 20/minute.)
Temperature:	Under 97° F(normal is 98.6° F)

§ 9.6 BODY FLUIDS

A urine or blood test will detect the presence of narcotics. Heroin, codeine, methadone, Darvon and Demerol in the urine can be readily tested in most toxicologic laboratories. It takes two hours from the time of the injection for the morphine to be found in the urine. Ninety percent of the morphine is gone from the urine within 24 hours and 98 percent is gone within 48 hours. Be sure to obtain at least 10 cc of urine. The white powder in the urine bottle is boric acid, a preservative. The lab will tell you if the urine is positive or negative for morphine (heroin) but will not identify the percentage of the drug.

Heroin converts to morphine in the body. Most of the other opiates (morphine, opium, Percodan, Dilaudid and Demerol) can be specifically detected.

A person charged with being under the influence of a narcotic may request a urine test (which will be given at the jail). The reporting officer should offer the subject an opportunity to request the test and record his decision on the report form in the space provided (see sample below).

PART VI: CHEMICAL TEST

Statement to Defendant: You may take a chemical test to determine the presence or absence of a narcotic in your body. If you wish to take a chemical test, it will be provided at the Jail upon your request.

☐ request
I   to take a chemical test.
☒ refuse   *John Doe*
                                                    SIGNATURE OF DEFENDANT

REPORTING OFFICER	SERIAL NO.	NO. SECOND OFFICER	WITNESS
A. Smith	1001 P	1002 P	9001 T

TF-680

The officer should urge the person to sign the form whether he requests or refuses the test, because it is not unusual for the defendant to take the stand and deny having had the opportunity. Be sure to explain that the purpose of the test is intended to prove or disprove the presence of opiates. Also, point out that a refusal can be used against him and may show consciousness of guilt. Occasionally, a lab report will indicate negative urinalysis. There are several reasons for this. It is possible that the individual was under the influence of something else. A negative urine might mean that the suspect had taken only a small amount of heroin 24 hours prior to giving the sample. Be aware that the quality and accuracy of the lab is questionable.

Oftentimes, you will find a person who appears to be under the influence of something but you do not specifically know what. Many drug users are "poly drug users." It is not unusual for users to mix or combine different drugs.

If you have arrested a person for Section 647(f) Pen. Code who is in such a condition that he is unable to care for himself, but you suspect possible heroin and other drug use, you should request both urine and blood tests. The medical technician should draw at least two vials of blood. Have the suspect take an Intoxilyzer test to eliminate alcohol as the cause of the condition. There are also tests available to law enforcement to detect marijuana in the body.

§ 9.6.1 Body Fluids Required for Testing Narcotic and Drug Cases

Due to the confusion existing among police personnel over the type of body fluids (blood or urine) to be obtained from drug suspects, the laboratory has recommended the following samples be obtained from the suspect(s) as required for proper analysis.

If you have a clear Section 11550 H&S influence case, only a urine sample is necessary. However, if you are unsure, it is advisable to take both blood and urine samples from the suspect(s), as many drugs on the market are a combination of amphetamines, barbiturates or tranquilizers, or are taken in conjunction with one another by the user.

§ 9.6.2 Best Drug Test

The Best Test List reflects the substances that most labs are able to detect in a sample of either urine or blood. However, some labs can find LSD in both blood and urine, and marijuana in the urine. Also, some narcotics can be detected in the blood.

Drug	Blood Test	Urine Test
Amphetamines		Yes
Heroin		Yes
Cocaine		Yes
Codeine		Yes
Chlorpromazine (Thorazine)	Yes	
Meperidine (Demerol)		Yes
Phencyclidine (PCP)		Yes
Barbiturates	Yes	
Chlordiazepoxide (Librium)	Yes	
Diazepam (Valium)	Yes	
LSD	Yes	
Marijuana	Yes	

§ 9.6.3   Quantity for Sample

Blood—Volume is handled by the technician (usually 2 vials).

Urine—As much as possible. The minimum: 1 ounce.

a.   Drugs—Just take the first urine sample for evidence

b.   Alcohol—Take a sample of the latest bladder void for evidence, but wait at least 20 minutes and take a second sample. Keep both samples for your lab sample. (void = empty the urine bladder)

If the suspect requires a blood sample, it will take place in a hospital setting. At this time, have the nurse or lab technician write on the medical records their observations and the suspect's condition, arms, needle tracks, etc. Medical personnel have seen many addicts and know how difficult it is to find a vein to draw blood. Get a copy of the suspect's medical records at the time of the test and include it in the police report. The nurse or lab technician can be subpoenaed as a witness for the prosecution.

§ 9.6.4   Opioid Urinary Detection

The detection times of opioids in the urine vary, depending on the analytical method used, drug metabolism, tolerant, person's physical condition, fluid intake, and method and frequency of use. But there are general guidelines that can be used.

Using the Enzyme Multiplied Immuno-assay Technique (EMIT) test, the following generalizations can e made:

1)   Heroin - Changes to morphine shortly after use, so morphine will be found in urine, not heroin. It will show up in the urine in

a new user in about 1-2 hours and trace amounts can be found in urine for up to 3 days.

2) Methadone - Found in the urine as methadone 204 hours after use and can be found in the urine 15 days after use.

3) Codeine - About 95% of the codeine used will be found in the urine 1-2 hours after use. Can be detected in the urine 1-5 days after use.

§ 9.6.5   Negative Urine Tests and How to Avoid Them

Causes

—Urine specimen collected too soon. Most abusable drugs will not show in urine for about 1 to 2 hours after use.

—Urine specimen collected too late. About 90 percent is eliminated by 48 hours after last use.

—Too little drug in urine specimen to detect, i.e., below .20 micro-grams/milliliter. This commonly occurs when low dosages of drugs are used.

—Laboratory error.

How To Avoid Negative Urine Tests

—Take more than one urine sample. Wait about an hour between collections.

—Check with laboratory to see how they want samples processed and labeled.

—Wait until the pupil is reactive and has returned to normal size to insure that enough time has passed to allow the drug to reach the urine.

Urine Test Standards

There are several techniques which will measure the qualitative presence of abusable drugs in urine. Various techniques have different costs, sensitivities, methodologies, and tests for different drugs. Urine testing can be done through one of the following techniques:

—Thin Layer Chromatography (TLC)

—Radioimmunoassay (aka Abuscreen)

—Enzyme Multiplied Immuno-assay Technique (EMIT)

—Gas Layer Chromatography (GLC)

Chapter 9

—Gas Chromatography/Mass Spectroscopy (GC/MS)

—High Performance Gas Liquid Chromatography (HPLC)

§ 9.6.6   Field Test

There are a number of presumptive color tests which can assist in the identification of opiates, such as forehyde, nitric acid, ferric chloride, and marquis. The marquis reagent is the most common test and consists of formaldehyde in concentrated sulfuric acid. This reagent is available to law enforcement in commercially produced drug testing kits and is also sold in packets of small glass vials. The officer should carefully read all instructions before conducting the test. The procedure is basically placing the suspected opiate into the reagent or a few drops of the reagent into the suspected material. If the reagent turns a red to violet color, the results are positive for opiates. Amphetamine will turn the marquis reagent orangish-brown. The officer should handle the reagent with care since it is an acid. Remember that this test is only a preliminary indication of opiates. For positive identification, the substance must be analyzed by a qualified chemist.

§ 9.7 USE OF HEROIN AND COCAINE

It is quite common today for people to use heroin and cocaine or other central nervous system stimulants like amphetamines at the same time. To some this presents a confusing picture and a difficulty in an arrest situation. However, it is quite easy to make an arrest for Section 11550 H&S when you understand a few facts. First of all, the pupils may not be constricted below 2.9 mm because cocaine dilates the pupil. However, since the activity level of cocaine is shorter (2 to 3 hours) than heroin (4 to 6 hours), pupillary constriction may occur after the cocaine wears off. Cocaine and amphetamines usually will not affect the sedating and muscle relaxant properties of heroin.

In order to make an arrest for Section 11550 H&S, heroin and cocaine/amphetamines, you will need either the admission of use, fresh needle marks or the evidence of sedation or muscle relaxation, droopy eyelids, slurred or slowed speech, abnormal gait, or nodding. You will also need a positive blood and/or urine sample showing a heroin derivative.

§ 9.8 USE OF HEROIN AND METHADONE

Occasionally, you will be involved with a methadone addict who is also using heroin. The important facts to remember is that doses of methadone given in methadone maintenance programs in California are not enough to sedate or cause the droopy eyelids, slurred or slowed speech, or abnormal gait of a heroin addict. Methadone, like heroin, causes pupil constriction. However, methadone constriction may last up to 18 hours after a methadone dose. Methadone is not given by injection, and methadone tests as "methadone" in urine tests and not as morphine or codeine.

If the person you have stopped claims to be on a methadone maintenance program but appears to be sedated or has muscle relaxation indicated by droopy eyelids, slurred or slowed speech, or abnormal gait, you have probable cause to arrest. Check for pupillary constriction below 2.9 mm. Also, take a blood or urine test. If a heroin derivative and methadone are found, then the person is under the influence of a combination of heroin and methadone. In this case, look for fresh needle marks.

The following conditions are necessary for making a diagnosis of heroin influence in a methadone patient:

1. Fresh needle mark.

2. Sedation or muscle relaxation as indicated by droopy eyelids, slurred or slowed speech, or abnormal gait.

3. Heroin derivative in urine or blood.

§ 9.8.1   Heroin/Morphine Overdose

It is difficult to state the exact amount of morphine that is toxic or lethal to man. In general, a normal, pain-free adult is not likely to die after oral doses of less than 120 mg or to have serious toxicity with less than 30 mg parenterally.

Dreisbach lists the minimum lethal dose of morphine for a nontolerant adult as 200 mg (Dreisbach). However, the lethal dose may be up to 2,000 mg in a narcotic-tolerant individual and as little as 2 mg in an infant. Toxic and lethal dosage levels of morphine may be drastically reduced by the concomitant use of barbiturates, alcohol, phenothiazines, monoamine oxidase inhibitors and imipramine-like drugs.[2]

Constricted pupils, coma and respiratory depression strongly suggests an opiate poisoning (overdose). An individual who has taken an excessive (toxic) dose of morphine or heroin will be stuporous or comatose. He or she may be in a deep coma and unresponsive to painful stimuli. The respiratory rate is usually low and cyanosis may be present. As the respiratory exchange becomes poorer, blood pressure falls progressively. The pupils are symmetrical and pinpoint in size. Urine formation is depressed. Body temperature falls, the skin becomes cold and clammy, skeletal muscles are flaccid, and jaw relaxed. The tongue may roll back, causing obstruction of the airway. If death occurs, it is usually due to respiratory failure; this is usually not the case in users of street heroin, where death is often due to unknown causes.

The most common reason addicts die is overdose. The second most common cause is accidents, i.e., suicide, auto accidents, homicide. An intravenous injection of heroin and a sharing of "outfits" (injection paraphernalia) and a failure to use hygienic techniques causes a high incident of endocarditis, hepatitis, and other infections.

---

[2] Monoamine oxidase (MAO) is a complex enzyme system widely distributed throughout the body. There are drugs that inhibit MAO in the body such as Nardic, Eutonyl, Parnate, etc.

Chapter 9

The true opiate overdose is caused by severe respiratory depression. It generally does not occur immediately but over a period of time of lethargy, stupor, and coma. There are times when collapse and death are so rapid that the syringe is found in the vein and the tourniquet is still in place on the arm. In these cases there is a sudden and massive flooding of the lungs with fluid, called pulmonary edema. In some cases there is also cerebral edema or accumulation of fluid in the brain. This sudden collapse and death is also called an overdose, but it may not be a true overdose caused solely by the opiate. Since addicts are poly-drug users, it is thought that sudden overdoses are caused by mixing substances.

For example, a heroin addict long accustomed to injecting heroin got drunk one day, took his customary injection of heroin, then collapsed and died. Subsequent X-rays showed pulmonary edema. In another case reported by the Haight-Ashbury Medical Clinic, an addict shot some "reds" (barbiturate acid) and then "fixed" himself with heroin. The cause of death was declared an "overdose of heroin," although the drug combination exacerbated the effects of the heroin itself. Autopsies have even shown that some deaths were caused by injections of heroin that left little or no heroin (morphine) in the body. In these cases, death is most likely caused by the adulterants (such as quinine) in the heroin mixture or by an allergic reaction to the heroin. In any event, the end result of these drug combinations is the same—death.

It is possible that a police officer will receive a call that someone is sick or in need of assistance, or the officer may find someone on the sidewalk or alleyway, unconscious. The clinical signs of an overdose are the following:

—pinpointed pupils (unresponsive to light); however, due to other factors, pupils may not be constricted.
—nausea, vomiting
—dry mouth
—sweating
—hypothermia; cold, clammy skin (lowered temperature)
—muscle twitching
—flaccid muscles
—marked respiratory depression
—slow, weak, regular pulse
—convulsions in some cases (from codeine and Demerol)
—unconsciousness; coma

What to do first in cases of drug overdose depends chiefly on how well the person is breathing. If the person is conscious and there is no problem with breathing, either call an ambulance or take the individual as quickly as possible to the emergency room of the hospital. There should be at least 10 reasonable deep breaths a minute. If need be, administer artificial respiration. Any drugs, bottles, etc., found near the person should be taken with the person to the hospital. If there are witnesses, ask what happened, what drug was involved. Does the person have a medical history of problems? If no such evidence is found, look on the bedside table or in the medicine cabinet for a bottle or container carrying the name of the person's physician or pharmacy. Fast and accurate information about a person's medications and medical condition from either source could be lifesaving.

However, the preservation of life and vital functions is always more important than immediate specific drug identification. Remember, protect the person, cover them lightly, turn them on their stomach if they're vomiting (face down on floor with the head turned to one side). Keep mouth and airway open and clean, keep the person breathing, call an ambulance or take them to a hospital emergency room. When the person gets to the hospital or paramedics, the medic will administer 1 cc of Narcan (Naloxone). The drug is a narcotic antagonist and produces a withdrawal syndrome in less than one minute.

The problem of drug overdose is frequently complicated by the use of drugs in combination. The classical signs and symptoms of overdose with one drug may be altered or masked by the effect of the other drug or drugs present. An otherwise safe dose may prove lethal in combination with other drugs. Disease, exposure and serious cerebral or visceral injury may also further obscure the picture.

The San Francisco Department of Public Health reported that heroin overdose is the third leading cause of death in San Francisco. Also:

—98% of heroin overdose victims have taken another drug or alcohol

—25% of overdose deaths happen within 7 days of release from jail or a detox facility

—80% of users inject with a partner, but 80% of people found by emergency personnel are alone

—Heroin users on methadone are 20 times less likely to die from overdose ("San Francisco" 2000).

Andrew Moss, Professor of Epidemiology at UCSF and investigator on the U-Find-Out (UFO) study in San Francisco, reported that nearly half of the 124 injection drug users aged 14-29 he studied had overdosed. Two-thirds of those had overdosed more than once, and one-third within the past year. Only 35% received medical attention via 911 or a ride to the hospital, and the second most important reason given for that was fear of arrest, despite the fact that only 5% of the study participants reported being arrested during an overdose situation. The UFO Study began in September 1999 to measure heroin overdose, seroprevalence of hepatitis B and C, and HIV among heroin users in San Francisco.

§ 9.9 USE OF HEROIN AND CRACK

Mixing crack cocaine and smokable heroin is common practice by some heroin addicts. The mixture combines the physical addiction to heroin with the intense high of crack, and is called by a variety of names like "crack" and "speedball" though it bears little resemblance to street drugs that have similar names but are used differently. (Speedball usually refers to the intravenous injection of cocaine and heroin.) The new mixture of crack and heroin is smoked in a pipe.

The smokable heroin lengthens the crack high and reduces the intensity of the depression that follows it. "It is not at all surprising that heroin is making a comeback," said Dr. Mitchell S. Rosenthal, president of Phoenix House, which operates 10 drug-treatment centers in New York and California. "We've been expecting something like this for the past three years. Crack users need some way to come down from that racing high," he said, "and it was inevitable for a large number to eventually turn to heroin. But we didn't expect to see so much so quickly." The drug combination is sometimes sold premixed, users said, and generally costs about $10-20 a dose, roughly twice as much as a dose of crack.

Drug experts said a reason for the mixture's popularity is the nature of the high from crack, which is a stimulant. The high is brief, from 8 to 10 minutes, and extremely intense. Some crack users refer to the high as all the pleasurable feelings they have ever had, crammed into a few minutes. But once the high abates, users say, they become jittery and depressed. To escape the depression or "crash," crack addicts are turning to a range of sedatives including marijuana, alcohol, and heroin. Smoking heroin, which is how it is ingested in much of the world outside of the United States and Europe, has only recently become economically practical as heroin has become more abundant and pure.

According to DEA, in 2004, heroin purity in New York City was as high as 96% compared to the average purity of 46% (NDIC 2004).

Lisa, a 28-year-old former crack addict enrolled in a Harlem drug-treatment center, said it was not usual to see people "chasing the dragon," an old term newly applied to smoking heroin with crack. "Crack hypes you up." she said. "The heroin gives you a calm, drowsy high. A lot of people," Lisa said, "are chasing the dragon now."

§ 9.10 USE OF HEROIN WITH CODEINE PROPOXYPHENE (DARVON) OR PENTAZOCINE (TALWIN)

There is often confusion when a person states they have heroin influence signs due to pain medications, such as codeine (Empirin), propoxyphene (Darvon), or pentazocine (Talwin). The diagnosis of "under the influence" of heroin, however, is relatively simple when a few pertinent facts are known.

PERTINENT FACTS

1. The doses of codeine, propoxyphene, and pentazocine prescribed by doctors and dentists for pain are not high enough (by multiples of 2 to 5 times) to cause the pupil to constrict under 2.9 mm in diameter.

2. The prescribed dose of the oral analgesics mentioned above are not high enough to produce sedation and muscle relaxation, e.g., droopy eyelids and slowed speech.

3. Regardless of the presence of codeine, propoxyphene, or pentazocine in blood or urine, a heroin derivative will still be present as will fresh needle marks on the arm from the injection of heroin. If heroin and codeine have both been used, ask the laboratory to determine which drug predominates in the urine.

4. Physicians do not normally prescribe codeine, propoxyphene, or methadone by injection, and so a fresh needle mark is usually evidence of heroin use.

§ 9.11   ACUTE USE OF HEROIN WITH SEDATIVES

There is often confusion when a person states they have heroin signs due to alcohol, PCP, marijuana, diazepam (Valium) or other sedative-type drugs. The diagnosis of "under the influence" of heroin, however, is relatively simple when a few pertinent facts are known.

PERTINENT FACTS

1. The drugs listed above (including alcohol, but with the exception of PCP) rarely constrict an adult's pupils below 2.9 mm in diameter.

2. All the drugs listed above can produce the identical sedation and muscle-relaxing effects that heroin does.

3. The dosage of diazepam (Valium) prescribed by physicians rarely produce visible evidence of sedation or muscle relaxation if they are taken as prescribed and not mixed with alcohol or other drugs.

4. All the drugs listed here, including alcohol, can produce nystagmus and cause nonreaction of the pupil.

To make a diagnosis of heroin influence, if any of the above drugs or alcohol are taken, there needs to be constricted pupils and morphine in the urine. Sedation or muscle relaxation and nonreactive pupil cannot be used as evidence by themselves since the above-listed drugs and alcohol may produce these findings.

§ 9.12   HEROIN SLANG

Bag .... quantity of drugs packaged in various containers such as paper, balloons, plastic bags, etc.
Balloon .... quantity of drugs, usually heroin, packaged in toy balloons
Behind stuff .... using heroin
Bindle .... quantity of drugs packaged in various containers, same as bag
Brown stuff .... heroin from Mexico with brown coloration
Cap .... capsule
Chiva .... heroin
Cold turkey .... stop using heroin suddenly with no assistance from other medicine

Chapter 9

Cook, Cook up........... prepare heroin for injection by heating it in water to dissolve

Cotton....................... small pieces of cotton with drug residue from using the cotton as a filter when preparing the drug for injection

Cut .... adulterate drugs to obtain a larger quantity

Do up .... inject

Down .... "get down"—inject a drug

Dried out.................. detoxified, withdrawn from a drug

Fit.............................. injection paraphernalia

Fix.............................. to inject a drug

Gee .... gasket between needle and syringe

Geeze .... to inject a drug

H................................ heroin

Habit.......................... need for a drug; addiction

Hard stuff.................. heroin, cocaine, morphine

Hit up .... to inject a drug; to borrow or attempt to borrow

Hooked .... addicted

Joy Pop .... irregular use of narcotics

Junk............................ heroin

Junkie .... heroin addict

Kick............................ stop; to stop taking a particular drug, especially heroin

Kit .... injection paraphernalia

Mainline..................... to inject the drug directly into the vein

Marks.......................... supravenous scars caused by injection of drugs

Mexican Brown .... Mexican heroin

Needle freak.............. one who injects drugs into the vein or skin

Nod............................. dozing as a result of drugs, usually heroin

O.D. .... overdose of a drug, many times fatal

Outfit......................... injection paraphernalia

Piece .... one ounce of a narcotic, usually heroin

Quarter .... twenty-five dollars

Quarter piece............ ounce of a certain drug

Rig.............................. injection paraphernalia

Shit............................. heroin

Shoot (up).................. inject a drug

Shooting gallery....... place used by users to inject drugs

Skin pop..................... inject drugs into the skin rather than into the vein

Smack......................... heroin

Spike........................... needle

Spoon.......................... quantity of a drug, approximately one to two grams

Step on .... adulterate drugs to obtain a larger quantity

Strung out .... addicted

Stuff........................... heroin

Sugar (milk).............. addict's desire for sweets due to heavy habit; amount of sugar mixed with everyday heroin

Tar.............................. tar heroin

Tie off......................... prepare for injection by placing a tourniquet on the arm to be used

Heroin Influence

Tie rag .... homemade or makeshift tourniquet used during the injection of drugs
Tools .... injection paraphernalia
Tracks .... supravenous scars from injection of drugs
White stuff .... heroin, usually Chinese
Withdraw .... stop using narcotics
Works .... injection paraphernalia

§ 9.12.1 Terms Related to Black Tar Heroin

Aceite .... Spanish word for "oil"
Ball
Black gum
Black heroin
Black tar
Brown gummy balls
Brown heroin
Bugger
Candy
Carga .... Spanish word for "load"
Chapapote .... Spanish word for "tar"
Chiclosa .... Spanish word for "Chicklet" (gum)
Chocolate
Chiva .... Spanish word for "goat" (due to its smell)
Cocoa
Dog food
Goma .... Spanish word for "gum"
Gomero .... Spanish word for "rubbery"
Gum
Gumball
Gummy
Mexican mud
Mexican tar
Mud
Peanut butter
Pedazo .... Spanish word for "piece"
Poison
Raw heroin
Redrock
Tar
Tootsie roll

§ 9.13   SAMPLE JURY INSTRUCTIONS ON URINE TESTS AS EVIDENCE

PEOPLE'S PROPOSED JURY INSTRUCTION NO. _____
REFUSAL   TO   PROVIDE   URINE   SAMPLE   AND CONSCIOUSNESS OF GUILT

You are instructed that in a case where a defendant is accused of violating Section 11550 of the Health and Safety Code, it is permissible to prove that the defendant was offered a urine test after he or she had been made aware of the nature of the test and its effects. The fact that the test is refused under such circumstances is not sufficient standing alone and by itself to establish the guilt of a defendant; however, refusal to submit to the test is a fact which, if proven, may be considered by you in the light of all other proven facts in deciding the question of guilt or innocence. Whether or not such conduct shows a consciousness of guilt and the significance to be attached to such a circumstance are matters for your determination.

People v. Sudduth, 65 Cal. 2d 543, 55 Cal. Rptr. 393, 421 P.2d 401 (Cal. 1966), cert. denied, 389 U.S. 850, 88 S.Ct. 43, rehearing denied, 389 U.S. 996, 88 S.Ct. 460.
Whalen v. Municipal Court of City of Alhambra, 274 Cal. App. 2d 809, 79 Cal. Rptr. 523 (Cal. App. 2 Dist. 1969).

GIVEN _____
GIVEN AS MODIFIED _____
REFUSED _____
JUDGE _____

§ 9.14   SAMPLE EXAMINER'S ADMONITION OF URINE TEST

EXAMINER'S ADMONITION OF URINE TEST
Per PEOPLE V. SUDDUTH
(65 Cal. 2d 543, 55 Cal. Rptr. 393, 421 P.2d 401 (Cal. 1966)

DATE _____ TIME _____
NAME _____

You have been placed under arrest for a violation of Section 11550 of the Health and Safety Code, under the influence of a controlled substance. Incident to that arrest you are requested to submit to a urine test to determine the presence of heroin in your body. UNDER CALIFORNIA LAW AND THE UNITED STATES CONSTITUTION YOU DO NOT HAVE THE RIGHT TO REFUSE TO SUBMIT TO SUCH A TEST. When you submit to such a test the results will be made available to you and if the test indicates that there is no heroin in your body you can and will be able to use such evidence to demonstrate your innocence; but if the test indicates a presence of an opiate in your body such evidence can and will be used against you in court. If you refuse to submit to a urine test it constitutes a wrongful refusal to cooperate with law enforcement officers in their investigation and your refusal can and will be used against you in court as an indication of your consciousness of guilt in attempting to suppress evidence. You do not have the right to talk to an attorney or to have an attorney present before stating whether you will submit to a test or during the administration of the test.

I acknowledge that I have been advised by ______________ of my obligation to submit to a urine test. Having this obligation in mind I choose:

______________ to submit to a urine test.
______________ to refuse to submit to a urine test.
Examiner ______________
Signature of Arrestee ______________
Witness ______________

§ 9.15 EXAMPLES OF ARREST AND NARCOTICS INFLUENCE REPORTS

CONSOLIDATED ARREST REPORT 212-536-252 (4/75) **CA00109 Oakland Police Department**

1. DEFENDANT'S TRUE NAME (Leave Blank)
2. PFN
3. RD NUMBER
4. BKG AGENCY
5. DEFENDANT'S NAME: Doe, John M.
6. ARREST NUMBER
7. CODING
8. AKA or NICKNAME: Prune
9. OCCUPATION: None

10. DOB	POB	HEIGHT	WEIGHT	HAIR	EYES	RACE	SEX	AGE
06 Aug 46	Tx	6'	165	Blk	Bro	N	M	30

11. JAIL USE
12. SALIENT CHARACTERISTICS: Pockmarked face
13. CLOTHING: Blu/Whi long sleeve shirt, Blu levis, Bro cap
14. HOLD FOR
15. DEFENDANT'S RESIDENCE ADDRESS: 1210 Union Street
16. RES. PHONE: N/P
17. DEFENDANT'S BUSINESS ADDRESS — SCHOOL: – –
18. BUS PHONE
19. DRIVER'S LICENSE NO.: – –
20. SOCIAL SECURITY NO.: – –
21. DATE ARRESTED: 01 Jan 77
22. TIME ARRESTED: 1930

RIGHT INDEX FINGER

23 CODE SEC.	M/F	COURT	CC	WARRANT NO.	BAIL	CEN	FIN NUMBER
11550 H&S	M		1				

CII NUMBER
FBI NUMBER
CASH AT BOOKING
ID CONFIRMED BY
CHECK ☐ FIN ☐ NCIC
CITATION NUMBER
COURT
COURT DATE/TIME
SIGNATURE OF PERSON PRINTED X
SIGNATURE OF PERSON TAKING PRINTS

☐ NONE ☐ CONTINUATION ☐ OFFENSE REPORT ATTACHED:

24. LOCATION OF ARREST: IFO 1850 San Pablo Ave.
TOTAL
25. SUPERVISOR: 3/1
26. ARRESTING OFFICER: A. Smith — SERIAL NO.: 1001 P — ARRESTING OFFICER: 1002 P — SERIAL NO.
27. TRANSPORTING OFFICER: 1003 P — SERIAL NO. — TRANSPORTING OFFICER: 1004 P — SERIAL NO.
28. VEH. LIC. NO. — STATE — YEAR
29. YEAR — MAKE — MODEL — COLOR
30. TOWED TO — HOLD FOR — TOW TAG

I HEREBY ARREST THE ABOVE DEFENDANT ON THE CHARGE INDICATED AND REQUEST A PEACE OFFICER TAKE HIM INTO CUSTODY. I WILL APPEAR TO SIGN A COMPLAINT AGAINST THE PERSON I HAVE ARRESTED (SEE REVERSE SIDE FOR INSTRUCTIONS)

31. SIGNATURE OF ARRESTING CITIZEN
32. ARRESTING CITIZEN'S RES. ADDRESS
33. RES PHONE
34. ARRESTING CITIZEN'S NAME — SEX–RACE–AGE
35. ARRESTING CITIZEN'S BUS. ADDRESS
36. BUS. PHONE
37. COMPLAINANT'S NAME — SEX–RACE–AGE: A/O
38. COMPLAINANT'S ADDRESS — CITY
39. ABC PREM. INVOLVED
40. CO-DEFENDANT — SEX–RACE–AGE — CO-DEFENDANT — SEX–RACE–AGE — CO-DEFENDANT — SEX–RACE–AGE
41. ☐ ARMED WITH DEADLY WEAPON ☐ USED A WEAPON ☐ CAUSED GREAT BODILY HARM ☐ ACTED IN CONCERT
42. BURGLARY CLASSIFICATION
43. VALUE OF LOSS (Petty Theft Only)
44. INSTRUCTIONS: List charges by name and code section. Document your admonishment of the arrested person. Enter the names and charges of other arrested persons who are not co-defendants. Enter the reason for physical arrest (misdemeanors only). If you are completing an offense or continuation report, DO NOT start the narrative on this sheet.

11550 H&S Under the Influence of Narcotic
Quoted TF 361 -- Verbal statement taken.
Refused to submit to chemical test. Signed form.

EXTRA COPIES TO:

NARCOTICS INFLUENCE REPORT
Oakland Police Department

DATE 01 Jan 77	TIME 1930	LOCATION OF ARREST IFO 1850 San Pablo Ave	R.D. NUMBER
DEFENDANT'S NAME Doe, John M.		SEX-RACE-D.O.B. M N 06 Aug 46	DEFENDANT'S ADDRESS 1210 Union Street

PART I: PHYSICAL OBSERVATIONS (check as applicable)

EYES (PUPILS)
- X Constricted
- ___ Dilated
- ___ Watery
- ___ Sensitive to Light
- ___ Reaction Test
  - 1.0 mm to 1.5 mm
  - Comparison: 9001 T
  - 4.0 mm to 4.5 mm
- ___ No Reaction Observed
- X Eyelids Droop
- ___ Squints
- X Glassy Appearance
- ___ Other:

LIGHTING CONDITIONS
- ___ Daylight
- X Nighttime
- X Artificial Light
- ___ Other:

BALANCE COORDINATION
- ___ Normal
- X Sways
- X Staggers
- ___ Unable to Stand
- ___ Other:

SKIN
- ___ Normal
- X Scabs
- X Cold-Clammy
- ___ Sweating
- ___ Other:

OTHER
- ___ Nose – runny, sniffing
- ___ Yawning
- ___ Scratching
- X Dry Mouth
- X Drowsy ("On the Nod")
- ___ Drooling
- ___ Nauseated
- X No Odor Alcoholic beverage
- ___ Other:

MENTAL STATE
- ___ Cooperative
- ___ Depressed
- X Confused
- X Passive
- ___ Argumentative
- ___ Nervous
- ___ Other:

SPEECH
- ___ Normal
- X Slurred
- X Incoherent
- ___ Excited
- ___ Other:

MECHANICAL AIDS USED
- X Flashlight
- X Pupilometer
- X Photos taken by 2001T
- ___ Other:

PART II: LOCATION OF MARKS

RIGHT ARM — Old Puncture Marks

LEFT ARM — Punctures, Redish swollen; Old Puncture Marks

Heroin Influence

PART III: ADDITIONAL INFORMATION
(Note defendant's remarks; clothing condition; describe additional symptoms.)

1. Susp's shirt, BLU/Whi Long Sleeve, depicting Blood Stains
   at Left Arm, inner area. Suspected as being worn when
   Susp Fixed.

2. Susp voluntarily stated he couldn't be "loaded" because he only fixed
   half a T and normally he has to shoot more heroin to get loaded.

3. (Search of Susp's person revealed injection paraphernalia --
   if applicable)

(see reverse side)

PART IV: ADMONITION OF RIGHTS

1 YOU HAVE THE RIGHT TO REMAIN SILENT 2 ANYTHING YOU SAY CAN AND WILL BE USED AGAINST YOU IN A COURT OF LAW	3 YOU HAVE THE RIGHT TO TALK TO A LAWYER AND HAVE HIM PRESENT WITH YOU WHILE YOU ARE BEING QUESTIONED	4 IF YOU CANNOT AFFORD TO HIRE A LAWYER ONE WILL BE APPOINTED TO REPRESENT YOU BEFORE QUESTIONING, IF YOU WISH ONE

THE ABOVE STATEMENT WAS READ TO THE ARRESTEE BY ___Smith, A.___ SERIAL NO ___1001 P___ TIME ___1930___

DO YOU UNDERSTAND EACH OF THESE RIGHTS I HAVE EXPLAINED TO YOU? Yes, I know them. | HAVING THESE RIGHTS IN MIND, DO YOU WISH TO TALK TO US NOW? (WAIVER STATEMENT) Sure. You got me now.

PART V: INTERVIEW

Are you under a doctor's care? By Whom and Why? NO.

Are you taking medication? What? When? Yes. Valium, Methadone

When did you first use narcotics? What Kind? When I was 18, in the Marines.

What kind of narcotics, if any, are you using now? Stuff, H., Little coke when I can get it.

Have you ever used heroin? When did you start?

When did you last "fix" and with what? About 2 hours ago.

What part of your body do you inject? In my left arm.

How much do you use? How often? About 1/2 a T

PART VI: CHEMICAL TEST

Statement to Defendant: You may take a chemical test to determine the presence or absence of a narcotic in your body. If you wish to take a chemical test, it will be provided at the Jail upon your request.

I ☐ request ☒ refuse to take a chemical test. _____John Doe_____
SIGNATURE OF DEFENDANT

REPORTING OFFICER	SERIAL NO.	NO. SECOND OFFICER	WITNESS
A. Smith	1001 P	1002 P	9001 T

TF-680 (12/76)

Chapter 9

References

Dreisbach, R. H. <u>Handbook of Poisoning: Diagnosis & Treatment, 8th ed</u>. Los Altos: Lange Medical Publications, 1974.

National Drug Intelligence Center. "National Drug Threat Assessment 2004." Washington, D.C.: U.S. Department f Justice, 2004.

Oakland Police Department. "Training Bulletin." <u>1150 H.S. Enforcement Manual</u>. Oakland: 1977.

"San Francisco Board of Supervisors Hold Heroin Overdose Hearing." March 23, 2000.

Tennant, Forest S. <u>Identifying the Heroin User</u>. West Covina: Veract, Inc., 1985.

Yeh, S. Y., and McQuinn, R. L. "GLC Determinations of Heroin and Its Metabolites in Human Urine." <u>Journal of Pharmacology Science</u> 64 (1975): 1237-1239.

CHAPTER 10

DESIGNER DRUGS

§ 10.1   INTRODUCTION

It seems likely that early human beings wanted to escape reality and found some natural drug to satisfy this desire. The use of the coca leaf (cocaine) and the opium poppy (narcotic) dates back at least 3400 years ago and the use of peyote dates back to as early as 1000 BC.

Perhaps due to the long history of opiate products, one of the first derivatives of a natural drug to be used pharmaceutically was heroin. Accepting heroin as a pharmaceutical established the concept that certain structural modifications of physiologically active compounds can result in new compounds that cause biological responses that are not only similar, but are enhanced as compared to those of the parent compounds.

In the following years, much knowledge has been gained regarding biologically useful derivatives of naturally occurring drugs. This knowledge has allowed researchers to find many of the structural relationships associated with specific biological responses.

The sum of this hard-won knowledge allows one to produce pharmaceutically useful compounds, which have no counterpart in nature, from off-the-shelf chemicals. Unfortunately, there are those people who would take this body of knowledge and, rather than use it for the enhancement of medical science, use it for their own financial gain. Individuals such as these have created the so-called "designer drug" phenomenon.

Perhaps the easiest way to explain designer drugs is to take a look at the chemical structure of amphetamine and how slight modifications of its chemical structure produces a different drug.

Amphetamine

If a chemist were to make changes to the chemical structure of amphetamine, they could easily come up with ephedrine, pseudoephedrine, phenylalanine.

Ephedrine

Pseudoephedrine

Phenylalanine

Change the chemical structure of a known drug and some of these new drugs (analogs) will have the same or similar actions as the original parent drug.

That is basically what designer drugs are, new drugs based on another drug. No need to start from scratch, just take an existing drug and by 'design' make changes to its chemical structure so the resulting drug is not illegal.

The term "designer drugs" was coined in the laboratory of Dr. Gary Henderson at the University of California, Davis. Originally, the term referred to the increasing sophistication of illicit drug chemists who were developing the ability to produce drugs designed to fit the tastes of individual clients.

Therefore, "controlled substances analogs" refer to substances of abuse that are allegedly "designed" by clandestine chemists. The aim of these chemists is to manufacture compounds that produce the "high" or euphoria of controlled substances (such as narcotics, depressants, stimulants, or hallucinogens), but that are chemically different and

Designer Drugs

thus are not subject to the provisions of the Controlled Substances Act (CSA). By selling these chemical variants (analogs), the clandestine manufacturer can profit from the distribution of dangerous, abusable compounds while avoiding the penalties that would be levied against those illegally trafficking the controlled substances.

This concept of designing pharmacologically active, chemically related substances is neither new nor restricted to illicit clandestine laboratories. In fact, most controlled substance analogs were first developed by legitimate pharmaceutical chemists and publicized through articles in scientific journals. In the quest for better medicinal agents, pharmaceutical companies will synthesize and test numerous analogs of a parent compound. These analogs mimic the qualitative actions of the original compound but may vary in potency (the dose required to produce maximal effects) and in duration of action. For example, within the benzodiazepine family there are numerous variations on the "parent" drug, chlordiazepoxide (Librium). These Librium analogs (e.g., Valium, Dalmane, Serax, Ativan, Centrax, etc.) are now on the market and have similar psychoactive and therapeutic effects.

The use of chemical analogs for the purpose of avoiding the laws regulating controlled substances was first noticed in the 1960s with the synthesis and sale of the amphetamine analogs of mescaline (MDA, MMDA, DOM, TMA, PMA, DOB, and DMA). Within this group of hallucinogenic amphetamines, MDA, MMDA, DOM, and TMA were controlled under the Drug Abuse Control Amendments (a predecessor to the CSA). PMA, DOB, and DMA were subsequently controlled administratively under the Controlled Substance Act. In the 1970s three PCP analogs (TCPy, PCE, and PHP) and the methaqualone analog (mecloqualone) were all controlled administratively via the CSA. An amphetamine analog, N-ethylamphetamine, was controlled in 1982.

Today, designer drugs are universally understood to belong to a group of clandestinely produced drugs which are structurally and pharmacologically very similar to a controlled substance, but are not themselves controlled substances.

In October 2, 1987, the United States Government amended the Controlled Substance Act (CSA) in an effort to curtail the illicit introduction of new designer drugs.

This amendment states that any new drug that is substantially similar to a controlled substance currently listed under the Code of Federal Regulations (CFR), Schedule I or II, and has either pharmacological properties similar to a Schedule I or II substance or is represented as having those properties, shall also be considered a controlled substance and will be placed in Schedule I. The amendment further contains provisions which exempt the legitimate researcher as well as compounds that are already being legally marketed from the provisions of the amendment.

However, in spite of the law, illicit chemists will continue to manipulate the basic molecular structure of intoxicating compounds to create

265

new drug analogs. The main motivation for illicit chemists to custom-design a drug is money.

The most popular designer drugs currently used in the United States are: GHB, GBL, Rohypnol, MDMA, MDE, PMA, DXM, 2C-B, 5-MeO-DIPT, AMT, CAT, ICE, YABA, and China White. Some of these drugs will be discussed in this chapter. The rest of the drugs will be covered in other chapters. These drugs are created in clandestine labs by unlicensed and, for the most part, untrained amateur chemists with little quality control. Therefore, it is possible that there is great variation of quality from batch to batch.

§ 10.2   FOXY and AMT

The synthetic substances 5-MeO-DIPT, known by the street name "Foxy" or "Foxy Methoxy," and alpha-methyltryptamine (AMT) are being reported as new drugs of abuse in limited areas of the United States. These substances, which produce hallucinogenic effects, are part of a class of chemical compounds known as tryptamines. Since 2001, law enforcement authorities in Arizona, Delaware, Florida, Idaho, Illinois, New Jersey, Oregon, Virginia, Washington, and the District of Columbia have seized many samples of AMT and Foxy. Although Foxy and AMT are relatively new drugs of abuse, the abuse of tryptamines is not a new phenomenon in the United States. In fact, the appearance of Foxy and AMT are indicative  of a trend where many noncontrolled synthetic substances are sold to capitalize on the current popularity of club drugs, especially MDMA. Foxy and AMT are not currently listed as controlled substances in the Controlled Substances Act of 1970.

Many tryptamines can be obtained from chemical companies in the United States and overseas, usually via the Internet.

§ 10.2.1 Effects

Users of tryptamines typically experience a multitude of effects. These effects include hallucinations, euphoria, dilated pupils, empathy, visual and auditory disturbances/distortions, "feelings of love," and emotional distress. Some users may experience nausea, vomiting, and diarrhea. Tryptamines, like Foxy and AMT, are very dose-dependent, which means that the doubling of a moderate dose could result in effects similar to LSD. The duration of effects from 20 mg of AMT usually lasts between 12 and 24 hours, while the effects from 6 to 10 mg of Foxy reportedly last from 3 to 6 hours.

§ 10.2.2 Appearance

Foxy is found in tablet and capsule form. The capsules usually contain a powder that is blue, green tan, orange, pink, or gray. Tablets containing Foxy, analyzed by a private laboratory, have been purple in color and embossed with a spider or alien head logo. Foxy tablets analyzed by DEA laboratories have been red and purple. AMT is also found in tablet and capsule form and contains either an orange or off-white powder (DEA "BZP" 2001).

Although Foxy and AMT are relatively new drugs of abuse, their appearance is indicative of a trend whereby many noncontrolled substances are sold to capitalize on the current popularity of club drugs such as MDMA. Since 1996, formerly noncontrolled substances, such as 1-benzylpiperazine (BZP), 1-[3-trifluoromethylphenyl]-piperazine (TFMPP), and 2,5-dimethoxy-4-N-propylthiophenethylamine (2C-T-7), all of which produce effects similar to MDMA, have been distributed and abused throughout the United States. The chemicals used to produce the fake ecstasy tablets and capsules are sold legally for scientific use.

Many traffickers believe that by manufacturing and/or distributing noncontrolled substances, they are exempt from drug and chemical control laws. Consequently, in the future, more of these substances may appear among club drug users throughout the country. However, the DEA has determined that individuals and organizations currently trafficking these substances with the intent of human consumption can still be prosecuted under the existing federal drug-analog statute.

§ 10.3 BZP and TFMPP

Benzylpiperazine (BZP) and trifluoromethylphenylpiperazine (TFMPP) are increasingly trafficked as MDMA (ecstasy). These chemicals, which produce stimulant and hallucinatory effects similar to MDMA, are not currently listed under the Controlled Substances Act. In 2000, federal, state, and local authorities began seizing increasing amounts of tablets, capsules, and powder containing either BZP or TFMPP or more commonly, a mixture of both chemicals. Evidence indicates that some traffickers use these chemicals as substitutes for MDMA.

BZP and TFMPP are part of a class of chemical compounds known as piperazines, which are used as chemical intermediates in the production of certain detergents and pharmaceuticals. Piperazines are also used in medicine to treat parasitic infections, and are metabolites in some drugs used to treat depression, anxiety, and hypertension. Medical research continues on the use of piperazine derivatives as possible vasodilators and for tumor reduction. Current studies related to piperazines mainly concentrate on the effect these chemicals have on the serotonin in the brain.

Adolescents and young adults involved with the current rave culture are the primary abusers of these chemicals, sometimes referred to as "Legal E" or "Legal X." Dealers and abusers, however, may not know they are selling or ingesting BZP or TFMPP. In some seizures, tablets containing BZP and TFMPP were confiscated along with tablets containing MDMA.

BZP is reported to produce stimulant effects similar to amphetamine, while TFMPP has the reputation of having the psychoactive effects of MDMA. Increased heart rate, blood pressure, and body temperature also have been associated with the ingestion of some piperazine derivatives. In high doses, piperazines produce hallucinations, convulsions, and respiratory depression.

BZP, TFMPP, and other piperazine derivatives are legitimately manufactured in India and may be purchased in Europe, the United Kingdom, and the United States through several bulk chemical supply companies. BZP and TFMPP are relatively inexpensive, costing approximately $0.40 and $4.50 per gram, respectively. The clandestine manufacture of BZP and TFMPP has not been reported in the United States. However, BZP and TFMPP has been encapsulated or pressed into tablets by organizations operating in the United States.

The distribution of BZP and TFMPP is minor in comparison to MDMA. The primary illicit distributors of these chemicals are domestic organizations with connections to overseas sources of supply. Since BZP may also be obtained from both illicit and legitimate websites, some organizations and individuals may also use the Internet to facilitate purchases.

Illicit organizations are suspected of importing the chemicals either directly into the United States or through Mexico. Once the chemicals reach the United States, the BZP and TFMPP powder is processed into capsules and tablets, sometimes with logos so that they resemble MDMA.

BZP and TFMPP have been commonly marketed either as pink, tan, white, green, purple, or off-white pills. These tablets have been imprinted either with a fly, crown, heart, butterfly, or bull's head logo; however, some have no logo. In addition, these chemicals have also been seized in clear capsules containing an off-white powder.

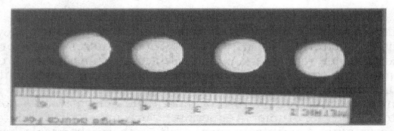

Combination BZP/TFMPP Tablets Seized by the Salem, VA PD

BZP Tablet Seized

by DEA, Sacramento

Combination BZP/TFMPP Tablets

Seized by DEA, Sioux City, IA

§ 10.3.1 Seizures

Since 2000, seizures of BZP and TFMPP tablets, capsules, and powder have increased in the United States. Seizures have occurred in California, Connecticut, Florida, Illinois, Iowa, Louisiana, Minnesota, Rhode Island, Texas, and Virginia at the dealer and user levels. In 2001, federal, state, and local authorities effected several large seizures of BZP, TFMPP, and other piperazine derivatives in tablet and powder forms. Approximately 5,000 tablets were seized in Norwich, Connecticut; 1,008 tablets in Sioux City, Iowa; and 1,000 pounds of powder in Austin, Texas.

§ 10.3.2 Conclusion

The Drug Enforcement Administration continues to investigate and gather intelligence on organizations involved with the importation, trafficking, and distribution of BZP, TFMPP, and other related substances. As previously stated, BZP TFMPP, and other piperazine derivatives are not currently controlled; however, efforts are underway to gather the necessary data to determine whether emergency or traditional scheduling is warranted. Individuals and organizations currently trafficking, distributing, or possessing these substances with the intent for human consumption can be prosecuted under federal and most state drug-analog statutes.

§ 10.4   PMA - PARAMETHOXYAMPHETAMINE

PMA, also known as 4-methoxyamphetamine, is an illicit, synthetic hallucinogen that has stimulant effects similar to other clandestinely manufactured amphetamine derivatives like MDMA.

In 1973, PMA was produced by clandestine laboratory facilities in Canada. PMA manufactured by these operations appeared in limited areas of Canada and the United States.

The first illicit use of the drug was encountered in the early 70s in the United States and Canada. Since 2000, PMA has reemerged in many states in the United States.

Currently, PMA is produced legally in the United States for limited commercial applications. A small quantity also is allocated for Schedule I scientific research.

Although PMA can be manufactured by several methods, the method used by laboratories to make the illicit form depends largely upon the availability of certain precursors. The exact synthesis procedure recently used to manufacture the PMA found in Florida, Illinois, Michigan, Virginia, and Canada is still unknown. Contrary to initial newspaper reports from Australia, the likelihood that PMA is inadvertently produced during the manufacture of MDMA is highly unlikely.

To date, four clandestine PMA laboratories have been seized worldwide: in Toronto, Canada, in 1973; in Worms, Germany, in 1991; and in 1999, two laboratories in northern Germany, one located in Brandenburg (DEA 2000).

A major trafficking network involving PMA has not been identified in the United States. Currently, illicit PMA distributors have targeted dealers primarily at rave clubs. Dealers may be unaware that they are buying or selling PMA rather than other club drugs like MDMA.

PMA is a potent and potentially lethal synthetic hallucinogen, which was placed in Schedule I of the Controlled Substances Act in 1973. The drug has been sold in tablet, capsule, and powder form, and its appearance and cost are comparable to MDMA. Common street names for PMA are "Death" and "Mitsubishi Double-Stack."

The effects associated with PMA vary, depending on the dose and whether other drugs are present. PMA typically is administered orally in pill or capsule form. PMA powder, although uncommon, may be inhaled or injected to accelerate the response. Ingesting a dose of less than 50 milligrams — usually one pill or capsule — without other drugs or alcohol, induces symptoms reminiscent of MDMA. Such effects include increased pulse rate and blood pressure, increased, labored respiration, elevated body temperature, erratic eye movements, muscle spasms, nausea, and heightened visual stimulation. Doses over 50 milligrams are considered potentially lethal, especially when taken with other drugs, such as amphetamine derivatives, cannabis, cocaine, prescription medications like fluoxetine (Prozac), and alcohol. Higher doses can produce cardiac arrhythmia and arrest, breathing problems, pulmonary congestion, renal failure, hyperthermia, vomiting, convulsions, coma, and death.

PMA Confiscated by McHenry IL PD. Photo courtesy of McHenry PD.

§ 10.5   DXM - DEXTROMETHORPHAN

DXM is a cough-suppressing ingredient found in a variety of over-the-counter cough medications such as Robitussin DM. Dextromethorphan is often sold as ecstasy at clubs or raves. DXM produces hallucinations and a heavy "stoned" feeling in users. DXM is used by mouth (swallowed).

The effects of DXM abuse vary with the amount taken. Common effects can include confusion, dizziness, double or blurred vision, slurred speech, impaired physical coordination, abdominal pain, nausea and vomiting, rapid heartbeat, drowsiness, numbness of fingers and toes, and disorientation. DXM abusers describe different plateaus of effects, ranging from mild distortions of color and sound to visual hallucinations and "out-of-body" dissociative sensations, and loss of motor control.

DXM is also sometimes abused with other drugs or alcohol, which can increase the dangerous physical effects.

The street names for DXM are: Dex, Robo, Skittles, Triple 6, and Tussin.

§ 10.6   2C-B, NEXUS
Distribution of the hallucinogen 2C-B (4-bromo-2,5-dimethoxyphenethylamine) has been sporadic since it became a Schedule I drug in 1995. Since 1999, however, seizures of this drug have increased. Law enforcement authorities in diverse locations across the country have recently reported seizures of 2C-B. Retail distributors of MDMA (3,4-methylenedioxymeth-
amphetamine), typically Caucasian males, market 2C-B as MDMA, and some dealers are unaware that the drug they are selling is 2C-B.

The drug 2C-B can be ingested orally in its pill and capsule forms or "snorted" in its powder form. Users report that 2C-B's effects are more intense when it is snorted. Some users consume 2C-B in combination with other illicit drugs including MDMA (called a "party pack") and LSD (referred to as a "banana split").

According to the DEA, 2C-B is a psychoactive substance that produces euphoria and increased visual, auditory, olfactory, and tactile sensations. Doses as low as 4 milligrams make users become passive and relaxed and the effects are similar to those of MDMA. Orally ingesting 8 to 10 milligrams increases 2C-B's stimulating effects and produces a completely intoxicated state. Mild hallucinations are also possible. Doses of 20 to 30 milligrams result in psychedelic hallucinations. Higher doses will produce extremely frightening LSD-type hallucinations and morbid delusions.

Proponents of its use describe the effects of orally ingesting 2C-B in different terms. They consider the drug to be both a psychedelic and an "entactogen" ("touching within"). At low doses, users report feeling "in touch with themselves and their emotions" and often report erotic sensations. At higher doses, users indicate that moving objects seem to leave "trails" behind them. Surfaces sometimes appear covered with geometric patterns and seem to move or "breathe." Listening to music in conjunction with taking 2C-B reportedly causes patterns, colors, and movements to be distorted.

The average duration of the euphoric effects from orally ingested 2C-B ranges between 4 and 8 hours. The table following represents estimates from various users of the inception and duration of the stages of the drug's effects.

Snorting 2C-B produces significantly more rapid and intense effects than orally ingesting it. Users typically snort one-third to one-half the oral dose.

§ 10.6.1 Effects of 2C-B

STAGE	TIME
Onset	20-90 mins.
Coming up	15-20 mins.
Plateau	2-3 hours
Coming down	2 hours
After effects	2-4 hours

Law enforcement agencies most often encounter 2C-B capsules and pills having the following characteristics:

• Off-white pills with brown specks

• Pink, red, or purple pills

• Small, off-white, thick pills with a bull's head logo stamp

• Clear, yellow, or gray and blue capsules

Because 2C-B is clandestinely produced, users are unaware of the dose they are ingesting and may be surprised by the drug's effects. Users who ingest relatively low doses of 2C-B and expect MDMA-like effects may actually experience frightening, LSD-like hallucinations. Individuals who snort 2C-B report extreme pain in their nasal passages and sinuses for up to 30 minutes after ingestion. Other side effects include nausea, muscle clenching, anxiety, and claustrophobia. Oral ingestion often results in gastrointestinal distress and increased mucus production that may result in coughing.

The Sioux Falls, South Dakota, Police Department recently discovered that the Marquis Reagent Field Test-902, a presumptive test for MDMA (ecstasy), amphetamine-type compounds (amphetamines and methamphetamine), and opium alkaloids (heroin and morphine) could be used to identify the presence of 2C-B. After receiving confirmation from the department's forensics laboratory that an exhibit submitted was 2C-B, investigators retested it using the field test described above. Detectives indicated that a bright green color resulted.

The manufacturer of the Marquis Reagent Field Test, ODV, Inc., confirmed this to be true. Although testing for 2C-B is not advertised on the packaging, it is the only drug known to produce a bright green color when using this test. The manufacturer originally designed the test to turn "orange to purple" for heroin or morphine, "black" for MDMA and "orange to brown" for amphetamine or methamphetamine (NDIC 2001).

Designer Drugs

Currently, NIDA-5—the most commonly used urinalysis test for cocaine, amphetamines, cannabinoids (THC), opiates, and phencyclidine (PCP) – is not capable of identifying 2C-B specifically. Normal urine screens for hallucinogens also do not detect 2C-B. Of the substances commonly tested for, 2C-B is most closely related to amphetamines. However, it is unknown what, if any, dose of 2C-B would trigger a positive amphetamine result in a standard drug test.

In the 1980s and early 1990s, several foreign companies legitimately manufactured 2C-B under the brand names Nexus, Erox, and Performax and advertised that it would alleviate impotence, frigidity, and diminished libido. It was sold at adult book and video stores, "head" shops, and some nightclubs. Although it has no formally recognized medical uses, some mental health clients took 2C-B in conjunction with traditional therapy.

The DEA first encountered 2C-B in 1979, before it was a scheduled substance. Law enforcement agencies concerned with club drug distribution and abuse should consider 2C-B a potential drug threat. Due to the broad range of dose-dependent effects, law enforcement personnel may encounter users exhibiting a variety of behaviors, from sedation to paranoia.

Encounters with 2C-B are likely to increase due to its marketing as MDMA and the rapidly increasing appetite for synthetic club drugs at raves and dance clubs. The recent reappearance of 2C-B in geographically diverse locations throughout the United States suggests that it is being sold through existing MDMA distribution networks.

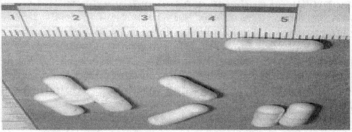

§ 10.7   Other names for 4-bromo-2,5 dimethoxyphenethylamine

–Nexus......................... 2C-B
–Bromo .... Toonies
–Performax................... 2's
–Spectrum .... Synergy
–Venus........................ Eve*
–Erox .... Zenith
–Cloud Nine................. Utopia
–Cee-Beetje.................. Afterburner Bromo
–BDMPEA .... MTF

–MDA is also referred to as "Eve."

§ 10.8 2C-T-7

2C-T-7 is a psychedelic phenethylamine developed by Alexander Shulgin around 1980. The effects of 2C-T-7 share some general similarities with LSD and 2CB, with its length of action more like that of LSD. The chemical has created an interest in the research community because of its recreational use, possible use in therapy, and recent interest for those searching for a religious experience. While most of the chemicals in its class are not known to cause acute physical dangers, it is not known today or currently researched to determine how safe 2C-T-7 is to consume. As with all new chemicals, it is difficult to be certain what the variety of reactions to the substance will be and the reports of use so far have many conflicting and confusing elements, including duration, physical stimulation, and dosage.

§ 10.8.1 Chemistry

2,5-dimethoxy-4-(n)- propylthiophenethylamine (2C-T-7) is a synthetic chemical in the phenethylamine class. It is related structurally to 2C-B and Mescaline.

§ 10.8.2 History

2C-T-7's chemistry was first published in Alexander Shulgin's book *PiHKAL* in 1991. This chemical was produced underground in college labs and by small commercial research labs until the late 1990s when it began being produced and sold commercially around the world.

§ 10.8.3 Effects

A standard oral dose of 2C-T-7 is between 10 - 50 mg. It is generally found in powder form although it is also produced and sold in pill format, most recently at 7 mg per tablet. Users should be extremely careful with dosages as 2C-T-7 can cause unexpected delirium and dissociation at high doses.

2C-T-7's primary effects can last as long as 10-12 hours, with aftereffects for another 4-6 hours.

2C-T-7's effects are unique but classically psychedelic, with some general similarities to LSD and 2C-B. 2C-T-7's effects can include psychedelic visuals (patterning, light sensitivity, color enhancement, etc.), mood lift, empathogenesis, anxiety or calmness, emotional volatility, increased sociability, associative/psychedelic ideation, etc. Some users have reported unexpected and disconcerting dissociation at high doses. Relatively prominent visuals are common with 2C-T-7, and at higher doses the visuals can overwhelm the visual field, creating a 'psychedelic soup.'

The most common problems reported by 2C-T-7 users appear to be nausea, vomiting, unpleasant dissociation, and overwhelming visuals at high doses. As with most psychedelics, there is also the possibility of anxiety or panic attacks. In a few higher dose cases, severe dissociation has been reported where the user experienced loss of memory, mental confusion, and extreme inability to deal with real-world situations while fully physically functional. This can lead to potentially dangerous situations if an individual is left unsupervised. Heavy dissociation and vomiting can be a life-threatening combination.

§ 10.8.4 Addiction Potential
2C-T-7 is neither physically addicting nor likely to cause psychological dependence. As with all substances, some people will use it more frequently than what they are comfortable with. There is a short period of tolerance after 2C-T-7 use. Using 2C-T-7 two days in a row is likely to lead to a diminished experience the second day, though when spaced 5 to 7 or more days apart, this effect is nearly nonexistent.

§ 10.8.5 Law
2C-T-7 is unscheduled and uncontrolled in the United States, making it technically legal to possess. Sales or possession could be prosecuted under the Analog Act, although no cases of prosecution have been brought to our attention. We are not aware of any country where it is specifically listed as illegal.

§ 10.9 KHAT
Although khat is illegal in the United States, it is legal throughout much of Europe, East Africa, and the Arabian Peninsula. Individuals of East African and Middle Eastern descent are most often responsible for the importation, distribution, possession, and use of khat in the United States.

§ 10.9.1 Background
Khat is a naturally occurring stimulant derived from the *Catha edulis* shrub. This shrub is cultivated in East Africa and the Arabian Peninsula. The use of khat is an established cultural tradition for many social situations in those regions. Khat is also known as Abyssinian tea, African salad, oat, kat, chat, and catha. Khat has two active ingredients, cathinone and cathine.

Cathinone is a Schedule I substance that produces a euphoric effect similar to amphetamine in that it stimulates the central nervous system. The cathinone in khat begins to degrade 48 hours after the plant has been cut. Khat that has been refrigerated or frozen will retain its cathionone potency for a longer period.

Cathine is a Schedule IV substance that produces a much less intense stimulant effect than cathinone; however, it does not lose its potency after harvesting (DEA "Khat" 2002).

Methcathinone, commonly called CAT, is occasionally confused with khat. Methcathinone is a synthetic Schedule I substance that has a similar chemical structure to the cathinone in the khat plant. Methcathinone is produced in clandestine laboratories and sold as a methamphetamine alternative. Ephedrine and/or pseudoephedrine are the main precursor chemicals used in methcathinone synthesis. The addictive properties and side effects of this synthetic are more intense than either of the naturally occurring khat substances. More information on CAT is found later in this chapter.

§ 10.9.2 Cultivation
Khat is an important part of the economy of many producer countries, particularly Somalia and Yemen. Press reports from Yemen state that more than US$2 billion are spent annually by Yemenis to purchase khat, which is often grown on land that is unsuitable for other crops.

Khat is grown in export quantities in countries such as Kenya and Ethiopia; it is Ethiopia's fourth-largest export according to United States embassy reporting, and the recreational use of khat is widely accepted there. Over 33 percent of Yemen's gross national product is associated with the cultivation, consumption, and exportation of khat. The World Health Organization reports that the cultivation and use of khat has profound socioeconomic consequences on countries and individuals. The cultivation of khat requires scarce land and water resources that could be put to other uses. Khat use is costly and potentially addictive. Widespread frequent use of khat impacts productivity because it tends to reduce worker motivation.

The only known case of khat cultivation in the United States occurred in September 1998, when 1,076 khat plants were seized in a raid in Salinas, California. Sophisticated irrigation techniques were used in this outdoor-grow operation. The individual involved was of Middle Eastern origin; he earned approximately US$10,000 per month in khat sales.

A close-up view of the khat crop in Salinas.

An investigator measures one of the khat leaves in Salinas.

§ 10.9.3 Use/Abuse of Khat

Khat has been used since antiquity as a recreational and religious drug by natives of Eastern Africa, the Arabian Peninsula, and the Middle East. Khat is legal in many countries, including Great Britain where khat can be legally imported, distributed, used, and/or exported. Khat has long been an acceptable substitute for alcohol among Muslims. During the period of Ramadan, the use of khat is popular to alleviate fatigue and reduce hunger. Although khat can be abused, it is often used in a social context similar to the manner in which coffee is consumed in other parts of the world. Reports from Yemen indicate that khat is consumed by 3 out of every 4 Yemenis, and accounts for more than 40 percent of the average family budget.

Khat is typically chewed like tobacco. The fresh leaves, twigs, and shoots of the khat shrub are chewed, and then retained in the cheek and chewed intermittently to release the active drug. Dried plant material can be made into tea or a chewable paste, but dried khat is not as potent as the fresh plant product. Khat can also be smoked and even sprinkled on food.

Chronic khat abuse can result in symptoms such as physical exhaustion, violence, and suicidal depression, which are similar to amphetamine addiction. Common side effects include anorexia, tachycardia, hypertension, insomnia, and gastric disorders (DEA 2002).

§ 10.9.4 Conclusion

The amount of khat seized in the United States has been steadily increasing; it appears to be related to the increasing number of immigrants from Somalia, Ethiopia, Yemen, Eritrea, and other countries where khat use is common. Although it is hard to predict future immigration trends, it seems likely that the importation of khat will continue to increase to meet the demand of those ethnic groups who are accustomed to using it.

It does not seem likely at this point that khat use will expand beyond the ethnic Somalian, Ethiopian, Yemeni, and Eritrean communities. There is no indication that khat is marketed outside these ethnic communities although it appears to be readily available.

Chapter 10

§ 10.10 ENTACTOGENIC DRUGS - MDA, MDMA, MDE

The widely used recreational drugs 3, 4- methylenedioxymethamphetamine (MDMA, ecstasy) and 3,4- methylenedioxyethamphetamine (MDE, Eve) occupy an intermediate position between stimulants and hallucinogens.

Besides stimulation similar to that caused by amphetamines, they usually induce a pleasant, easily controllable emotional state with relaxation, fearlessness, and feelings of happiness, but they sometimes also have stronger, hallucinogenic, effects. A number of pharmacological studies support the hypothesis that these drugs make up a distinct class of psychoactive substances, which have been designated "entactogens."

MDMA Tablets with Logos

§ 10.10.1 MDMA—Ecstasy

MDMA is 3,4-methylenedioxymethamphetamine. The following summarizes the current state of knowledge regarding MDMA and its manufacture, distribution, and abuse: 3,4-Methylenedioxymethamphetamine (MDMA) is a close structural analog of 3,4-methylenedioxyamphetamine (MDA) which is in Schedule I of the Federal Controlled Substances Act. MDMA is also structurally related to amphetamine and methamphetamine (Schedule II), mescaline, STP, PMA, and TMA (Schedule I), plus other Schedule I hallucinogens. MDMA was first patented by E. Merck in Germany in 1914 as a possible appetite suppressant. About the only other reference to it was as one of the eight psychedelics tested secretly by the Army in 1953.

Alexander Shulgin, a San Francisco Bay area chemist and drug designer, was working in the 1970s on synthetic derivatives of oil of sassafras and nutmeg that are structurally similar to mescaline and amphetamine. Other members of the family are MMDA and MDA. He came to believe that MDMA was something different. MDMA's active ingredient was the opposite isomer (an isomer is one-half of a molecule of any compound) from the one active in the hallucinogenic members of the family. The effect was much different than MDA. MDMA was not a hallucinogenic according to Shulgin. It seemed less toxic than MDA. When administered in small doses, there were few, if any, side effects; a slight tightening of the jaw, some nausea, and those would pass in the first half-hour. MDMA has amphetamine-like effects, such as increased blood pressure and pulse rate. Some people found it difficult to sleep after taking it and felt "hung over" the next day. The duration of action is about an hour in dosages of 100 to 150 mg orally. In most aspects, it is deceptively simple in action, leading to a sensory and verbal disinhibition, a state of mutual trust and confidence between subject and therapist, but without the distractions of visual distortion or compelling introspection reported by Shulgin.

MDA is one of a family of drugs whose members are amphetamine analogs of the psychedelic drug, mescaline (methoxylated phenylethylamine). This group contains more than a thousand different but related chemical substances. Only a few dozen have been tested on human beings—a few hundred on animals. Among those known to us are MDA, MMDA, DOM, DOET, TMA, DMA and DMMDA. All of these are similar in chemical structure and effect. They differ mostly in dosage and duration of effect. For example, MDA dosage is 100 to 150 milligrams and duration is 8 to 12 hours, while DOM (known on the street as STP) is potent at 5 milligrams and can last from 16 to more than 24 hours. With the latter, the effects of a high dose can last so long, ebbing and returning, the user may think that they will never end.

MDA and its analogs are synthetic but related to safrole, which is contained in oil of sassafras and oil of camphor and is the psychoactive agent in nutmeg and mace. They are produced by modifying the major psychoactive components of nutmeg and mace into their amines. MDA has been on the street since 1967, when it first appeared in the Haight-Ashbury drug culture.

Descriptions of MDA's effects tend to sound like the fulfillment of a psychedelic user's fantasy. Users have reported the onset as a warm glow spreading through their bodies, followed by a sense of physical and mental well being that gradually but steadily intensifies. Some have described a sense of increased coordination and an ability to do things they could not ordinarily do. Unlike most stimulants, however, MDA does not increase motor activity, but in fact, suppresses it. Thus, consumers can sometimes sit in meditation, or do yoga and related activities, for long periods of time. For clinical subjects in a 1974 research program, MDA served as an appetite depressant.

Researchers Grimspoon and Bakalor, in their book *Psychedelic Drugs Reconsidered*, concluded that MDA produces feelings of aesthetic delight, empathy, serenity, joy, insight and self-awareness, without perceptual changes, loss of control, or depersonalization; and it seems to eliminate anxiety and defensiveness. "The user actually feels himself to be a child, and relives childhood experiences in full immediacy, while simultaneously remaining aware of his present self and present reality."

MDA and MMDA showed some promise as an adjunct to psychotherapy in extensive research carried out in the late 1960s and early 1970s. In the mid 1970s, with MDA's inclusion as a Schedule I "narcotic," research on the methoxylated amphetamines came to a standstill.

As is true with all psychedelic drugs, effects vary with expectation and setting (the circumstances under which the drug is taken). MDA is not the sort of drug to be taken with alcohol and downers at wild parties. Its use can drain energy, leaving one tired and sluggish the next day. MDA may affect a woman's genitourinary tract and may even activate latent infections and other problems. Women should be aware of this danger. It is reported to cause tension in the face and jaw muscles to the point of "bruxism," involuntary teeth grinding. At least one researcher feels, however, that all these symptoms involve excessive dosage, poor setting, or counterfeit drugs. Anxiety, panic, and paranoid reactions occur but are rare.

It should be noted that, in the case of MDA, the synthetic is more benign than the natural. Nutmeg and mace do have some psychoactive properties, but the after effects are dire enough to make these poor drugs of choice.

MDA is toxic to certain individuals. Typical toxic symptoms are skin reactions, profuse sweating or confusion. Some of the more serious cases resulted in aphasia and, in one case, death. This serious neurological toxicity is a result of elevated blood pressure and effects on the brain associated with higher doses of MDA.

If such problems develop, medical care is required; antihypertensive medication and neurological care may be necessary. Anxiety, panic, or paranoid reactions can usually be handled by reassurance in a supportive environment. Occasionally, sedative medication such as Valium is recommended.

Antipsychotic medication is not needed unless a prolonged psychotic reaction occurs. This usually happens only in individuals who have major underlying psychological problems prior to taking MDA. In these rare cases, prolonged psychiatric care may be needed.

Slang terms for MDA include "the love drug" and "psychedelic speed."

From San Francisco to San Diego and in other areas of the United States, raves and warehouse parties are taking place. Hundreds of people are gathering to feel, listen, and dance to music. They are also taking Ecstasy. The recreational use of the drug began in the mid-1970s and by the mid-1980s was widespread on college campuses across the United States. Today it is still a popular drug at Raves.

§ 10.10.1(a)   The Drug and its Effects
3,4-Methylenedioxymethamphetamine (MDMA) is a Schedule I synthetic, psychoactive drug. Chemically, it is an analog of MDA, and is considered a designer drug. MDMA possesses variations of the stimulant amphetamine or methamphetamine and a hallucinogen, most often mescaline. MDMA is illicitly marketed as a "feel good" drug. Devotees say it produces profoundly positive feelings, empathy for others, elimination of anxiety, and extreme relaxation — hence the name the "hug drug." MDMA is also said to suppress the need to eat, drink, or sleep, enabling club scene users to endure all-night and sometimes two-to three-day parties.

MDMA is taken orally, usually in tablet or capsule form, and its effects last approximately four to six hours. Taken at raves, severe dehydration and, in some cases, death from heatstroke or heart failure may occur. An MDMA overdose is characterized by a rapid heartbeat or high blood pressure, faintness, muscle cramping, panic attacks and, in more severe cases, loss of consciousness or seizures. Other adverse effects include nausea, hallucinations, chills, sweating, tremors, and blurred vision. MDMA users also report aftereffects of anxiety, paranoia, and depression.

The effects of long-term MDMA use are just beginning to undergo scientific analysis. In 1998, the National Institute of Mental Health, Bethesda, Maryland, conducted a study of a small group of habitual MDMA users who were abstaining from use. The study revealed that the abstinent users suffered damage to the serotonin neurons in the brain. It further concluded that recreational MDMA users were putting themselves at risk of developing permanent brain damage, which may manifest itself in depression, anxiety, memory loss, and other neuropsychiatric disorders.

§ 10.10.1(b)   Medical Use

MDMA has no currently accepted medical use in the United States since the FDA has no investigational new drug (IND) or new drug applications (NDA) or approvals on file for MDMA. There is no manufacturer of MDMA registered with the FDA. Several psychiatrists and therapists are using MDMA in their practices as an adjunct to psychotherapy without FDA approval. These individuals are either making MDMA themselves or obtaining it from chemists.

Although chemically related, MDMA has never been proven to have the hallucinogenic properties that its parent drug, MDA, possesses nor the stimulating effect that is associated with methamphetamine usage. MDMA was first developed as an appetite suppressant by E. Merck and Company, but was never marketed. In the recent past, it had been used by therapists in psychotherapy and marriage counseling because it was said to have few negative side effects, it eased psychic trauma, and broke down barriers to communication between individuals. Normal therapeutic dosages range between 100 to 150 mg with the onset of effects occurring 25 to 30 minutes after intake and lasting up to one hour.

MDMA is available in most sections of the country as evidenced by its identification in submissions of drug evidence to DEA, state/local, and anonymous testing laboratories.

§ 10.10.1(c)   Manufacturing - Labs

Clandestine laboratories operating in Europe, primarily the Netherlands and to a lesser extent in Belgium and in Eastern European countries, manufacture significant quantities of the drug in tablet, capsule, or powder form. Although the vast majority of MDMA consumed domestically is produced in Europe, a limited number of MDMA laboratories operate in the United States. For instance, on May 8, 2004, DEA seized a fully operational lab in Nashville, TN. However, domestic production remains limited as evidenced by only a few MDMA lab seizures yearly (DEA 2004). As with many of the designer drugs, the clandestine production of MDMA is a relatively simple process and "recipes" can be found on the Internet. The synthesis of MDMA requires a few days to complete. It is generally produced from the immediate precursor, 3,4-MDP29, by reacting it with methylamine. 3,4-MDP2P is a List I Chemical under the Controlled Substance Act and is usually clandestinely produced from piperonal (also known as heliotropin), safrole, or isosafrole, which are also List I Chemicals. Several laboratories have used sassafras oil as a source of safrole, since the oil is usually greater than 80 percent safrole. Safrole is converted to isosafrole with potassium hydroxide in methyl alcohol. Isosafrole is then reacted with hydrogen peroxide and formic acid to produce 3,4-MDP2P.

The chemicals used in the production of MDMA are available primarily through specialty chemical supply houses in the United States for industrial and research purposes. Since these chemicals are controlled, they are not readily available to the general public.

§ 10.10.1(d) Trafficking

The synthetic drug market in the United States, particularly MDMA, traditionally has been supplied and controlled by Western European-based drug traffickers. In recent years, Israeli organized crime syndicates, some composed of Russian emigres associated with Russian organized crime syndicates, have forged relationships with the Western European traffickers and gained control over a significant share of the European market. Moreover, the Israeli syndicates remain the primary sources to United States distribution groups. The increasing involvement of organized crime syndicates signifies the "professionalization" of the MDMA market. These organizations have proven to be capable of producing and smuggling significant quantities of MDMA from source countries in Europe to the United States. DEA reporting indicates their distribution networks are expanding from coast to coast, enabling a relatively few organizations to dominate MDMA markets nationwide.

§ 10.10.1(e) MDMA Influence

MDMA can cause a wide variation in behavior. If you suspect a person is under the influence of MDMA, here are some of the symptoms to look for:

1. Pupils: normal to slight dilation with a slow reaction to light.

2. Increased blood pressure and pulse rate.

3. Horizontal nystagmus will **not** be present.

4. Vertical nystagmus will **not** be present.

5. The internal clock will be distorted.

6. Tightening of jaws and grinding of teeth.

7. Tensing of the neck muscles.

8. Occasional synesthesia (hearing colors, seeing sounds).

§ 10.10.1(f)   MDMA Identification

MDMA is found in tablet, capsule, powder form, or clear liquid. Ecstasy in the powder form is commonly packaged in clear gelatin capsules or pressed into tablets. The powder has a strong vitamin-type smell and taste and, unless it is cut with procaine or cocaine, it will not produce a numbing effect. The tablets weigh roughly one gram apiece. Each tablet contains approximately 100 mg of MDMA and the remainder is filler. Each tablet will be approximately 3/8 inch in diameter, 1/4 inch thick, various colors (white, green, red, pink), and sometimes with a design on the tablet.

§ 10.10.1(g)   MDMA Prices

Street prices currently range from $8 to $20 per dosage unit or $70 to $100 per gram. MDMA is sold as MDM, ecstasy, XTC, ADAM, Essence, cocaine, or MDA. A recent sample obtained in New York contained MDMA and PCP. Price quotations for MDMA are now included in *High Times* magazine, along with the prices of marijuana, LSD, cocaine, and hashish.

§ 10.10.1(h)   MDMA Law

MDMA is a Schedule I drug according to the Federal Controlled Substances Act (Section 812 of Title 21, U.S. Code), and the Uniform Controlled Substances Act of California (Section 11054 Health and Safety Code).

§ 10.10.1(i)   MDMA Advertisement

The street sale and use of MDMA is promoted through the distribution of pamphlets and circulars entitled "Ecstasy, Everything Looks Wonderful When You're Young and on Drugs," "Flight Instructions for a Friend Using XTC," "Ecstasy, 21st Century Entheogen," "How to Prepare for an Ecstasy Experience," and "Reflections on the Nature & Use of XTC."

§ 10.10.1(j)   Conclusion

MDMA abuse in the United States and the trafficking of MDMA to the United States are on the rise, posing serious social concerns. Once confined to major metropolitan areas on the East and West Coasts, MDMA trafficking is expanding to smaller communities throughout the country. Teenagers and young adults continue to be the primary targets of sophisticated crime syndicates who are supplying United States distribution groups with ever-increasing amounts of MDMA tablets. As the trend to consume MDMA in tandem with alcohol and other drugs continues, the harmful effects of the drug will be seen to increase exponentially.

§ 10.11   GHB AND ITS ANALOGS - GBL, BD, GHV, GVL

GHB (gamma-hydroxybutyrate) is a powerful central nervous system depressant that the human body produces in small amounts. A synthetic version of GHB was developed in the 1920s as an anesthetic; it was banned by the Food and Drug Administration in 1990. Originally sold in health food stores, GHB was marketed as a releasing agent for growth hormones that would stimulate muscle growth.

GHB is easily produced by combining gamma butyrolactone (GBL) with either sodium hydroxide or potassium hydroxide in a cooking pot or bucket. The final product does not have to be isolated or separated from the solution. The chemicals give off heat as they react, and the Internet recipes warn prospective chemists to monitor closely the pH level of the solution. Several companies advertise kits for sale over the Internet that provide the customer with GBL, sodium hydroxide, and litmus paper. Since the drug is easy to synthesize and manufacture, distribution usually is handled by local operators.

Individuals abuse synthetic GHB because of its euphoric and sedative effects. Because of its anesthetic properties, GHB also has been used by sexual predators to incapacitate their victims.

GHB analogs, which include GBL, BD, GHV, and GVL, are drugs that possess chemical structures that closely resemble GHB. These analogs produce effects similar to those associated with GHB, and they are often used in its place. GHB and its analogs typically are sold either as a white powder or as a clear liquid. The drugs often have a salty taste.

GHB and its analogs usually are taken orally. Because of the drugs' salty taste, they often are mixed with a flavored beverage. Sexual predators who administer GHB or an analog to their victims typically slip the drug into a drink, often at a bar or party (NDIC 2003).

Although information about the extent of GHB and analog use in the United States is limited, the data that is available indicates that these drugs primarily are used by young people.

§ 10.11.1   GHB: Use and Effects

The high associated with GHB can be described as a trance-like state similar to the sensation felt just before falling asleep and lasting between two and eight hours. According to the Food and Drug Administration, which banned GHB in 1990, GHB has poisonous effects. Drug effects occur 15 to 60 minutes after ingestion and may include one or more of the following: vomiting, drowsiness, drop in blood pressure, diminished activity, reduced heart rate, and vertigo. Tremors, irregular and depressed respiration, and unconsciousness may follow.

GHB generates feelings of euphoria and intoxication. Some users also report that it is an aphrodisiac. It is often used as a chemical method of counteracting the stimulant effect of MDMA. GHB is primarily available in liquid form, although it is sometimes encountered as a powder. It is highly soluble, and is often added to spring water or concealed in mouthwash bottles. Due to its salty taste, flavorings are often added, and it is sometimes passed off as a high-carbohydrate health drink. GHB is usually sold by the capful, and sells for $5 to $25 per cap. GHB is often added to alcohol, which enhances its effect and increases the potential for respiratory distress. Although it is not the primary reason for its abuse, GHB has been used in the commission of sexual assaults because it renders the victim incapable of resisting and may cause memory problems that could complicate case prosecution.

GHB has no legitimate medical use in the United States, though it has been sold to body builders as an alternative to anabolic steroids and as a sleep aid. The poisoning caused by GHB is not readily diagnosed, as its presence is not detected in urine and blood tests.

Sustained use of GHB or its analogs can lead to addiction, and chronic users experience withdrawal symptoms when they stop using the drugs. These symptoms include anxiety, insomnia, tremors, tachycardia (abnormally fast heart rate), delirium, and agitation. Users may experience these symptoms within 1 to 6 hours of their last dose, and the symptoms may persist for months.

The most common names for GHB are Georgia home boy, G, goop, grievous bodily harm, and liquid ecstasy. (See "Street Terms" below for additional names.)

§ 10.11.2   Street Terms for GHB and Its Analogs

—Cherry Meth	—Jib
—Salty Water	—Liquid-E
—Fantasy	—G-riffic
—Liquid-X	—Organic quaalude

§ 10.11.3   GHB and the Law

In the United States, the only legal use of GHB has been under specific FDA exemptions for investigational research protocols. In California, GHB is an unapproved drug product and is therefore illegal to sell, advertise for sale, or possess. Anyone advertising, selling, or possessing GHB is in violation of the Sherman Food, Drug and Cosmetic Law, Division 21 of the Health and Safety Code, Sections 109875 through 111915.

On February 18, 2000, the "Hillory J. Farias and Samantha Reid Date-Rape Prohibition Act of 1999" (Public Law 106-172) was signed into law, legislating GHB as a Schedule I controlled substance. GBL was also regulated under this law as a List I controlled chemical. Schedule I drugs, which include heroin and MDMA, have a high potential for abuse and serve no legitimate medical purpose. GHB analogs are treated as Schedule I drugs under 21 U.S. Code § 813 if they are intended for human consumption. Because the criminal penalties associated with GHB have been made more stringent and law enforcement pressure has rendered GHB more difficult to obtain, the distribution and abuse of GHB analogs have become an increasing concern.

§ 10.11.4   GHB Analogs

GHB analogs often are abused in place of GHB or are used to produce GHB. Common GHB analogs include GBL, BD, GHV, and GVL. Both GBL and BD metabolize into GHB upon ingestion. GBL is the most common precursor used in the production of GHB. GVL is abused in place of GHB because it metabolizes into GHV, which produces physiological effects similar to GHB.

The analog GBL is chemically known as gamma-butyrolactone, furonome di-hydro, and dihydrofuranone. They are precursors for the production of GHB and metabolize into GHB.

The analog BD is chemically known as 1,4-butanediol, tetramethylene glycol, sucol-B, and butylene glycol. They are precursors for the production of GBL and also metabolize into GHB.

The analog GHV is chemically known as gamma-hydroxyvalerate and methyl-GHB. They are not used as precursors and are not metabolized into another drug.

The analog GVL is chemically known as gamma-valerolactone and 4-pentanolide. They are precursors for the production of GHV and metabolize into GHV.

GBL is a chemical used in many industrial cleaners and is the precursor chemical for the manufacture of GHB. Several Internet businesses offer kits that contain GBL and the proper amount of sodium hydroxide or potassium hydroxide, along with litmus paper and directions for the manufacture of GHB. The process is quite simple, and does not require complex laboratory equipment. The kits sell for between $48 and $200. As with GHB, GBL can be added to water and is nearly undetectable. In addition to its industrial applications, GBL has been marketed as a health supplement. Products that contain GBL, such as Renewtrient, Longevity, Revivarant, GH, Revitalizer, Gamma G, Blue Nitro, Insom-X, Remforce, Firewater, and Invogorate were removed from the market. However, many of the products have been reintroduced under new names, utilizing 1,4 butanediol (BD) as a replacement for GBL. GBL is converted by dehydrogenase in the gastrointestinal tract to produce GHB. As a consequence, some partygoers drink small quantities of GBL straight. This often causes a severe physical reaction, usually through the violent regurgitation of the fluid. These chemicals increase the effects of alcohol, and can cause respiratory distress, seizures, coma, and death.

GBL became a List I chemical on February 18, 2000. BD is not scheduled under federal guidelines. Because GHB analogs either are metabolized into GHB by the human body or produce similar physiological effects when ingested, healthcare providers often are unable to distinguish between the abuse of GHB and GHB analogs.

§ 10.11.5   GHB Analogs: Use and Effects

GHB analogs are distributed as liquids and consumed orally. When ingested, these analogs produce effects such as relaxation, mild euphoria, and drowsiness. Such effects are similar to those associated with GHB abuse and may resemble the results of alcohol intoxication. GHB analogs also may increase libido, suggestibility, passivity, and cause amnesia — traits that make users vulnerable to sexual assault and other criminal acts. Users awakening or emerging from coma may exhibit extreme combativeness, a condition that is also observed among those in withdrawal from addiction to GHB and its analogs. GHB analogs are known to produce side effects such as topical irritation to the skin and eyes, nausea, vomiting, incontinence, a loss of consciousness, seizures, liver damage, kidney failure, respiratory depression, and even death. GHB analogs are physically addictive, causing addicts to experience severe withdrawal symptoms if they miss a dose or attempt to stop using the drug.

§ 10.11.6   GHB Analogs: Distribution

GHB analogs are readily available, and various methods are used to distribute these drugs. Because of legislation, GHB analogs are legally available only in products not intended for human consumption. Abusers and distributors may obtain commercial products such as chemical solvents legally and then illegally consume or distribute them. Illegal distribution of GHB analogs often occurs at raves, concerts, nightclubs, health clubs, gyms, and on college campuses. At these venues GHB analogs usually are sold for $10 to $20 per capful (approximately 1 teaspoonful). When distributors sell these drugs, they may fail to specify which analog they are selling, or they may misrepresent the analog as GHB.

GHB analogs often are sold with disclaimers that they are not for human consumption; however, many of the products have labels implying that the product may be ingested. One product marketed as an industrial solvent has a label that states "Warning! Accidental ingestion of [product] will produce GHB in your body. If you ingest some by mistake, don't take alcohol or any other drug!" Another product label states "Warning: Accidental ingestion may cause ... euphoria ... increases tactile sensitivity.". Many of the products are marketed as "Great Household Bargains" (GHB) in order to increase their exposure to individuals seeking GHB analogs.

In addition to the distribution methods discussed previously, supplies, kits, and recipes for producing GHB using GHB analog GBL are marketed and sold on the Internet.

§ 10.11.7   Test for GHB Analogs

Seized GHB analogs frequently are not identified because detection of such analogs requires specific field and laboratory testing. Three different color tests — cobalt nitrate, Marquis reagent, and Mandelin reagent — are useful for detecting the presence of GHB analogs. (Contact forensic laboratories to obtain specific instructions regarding utilizing these test kits.) Both the Marquis reagent and the Mandelin reagent tests are available commercially.

Routine toxicological screens do not detect GHB or GHB analogs; thus, law enforcement officers and medical personnel must order specific blood and urine tests when they suspect GHB analog abuse. The most common urine tests screen only for the "NIDA-5," five of the most commonly abused categories of drugs — amphetamines (amphetamines, methamphetamine), cocaine (powdered cocaine, crack), cannabinoids (marijuana, hash), opiates (heroin, opium, codeine, morphine), and phencyclidine (PCP). GHB in the blood or urine can result from the ingestion of GHB, GBL, or BD. To yield a reliable result, tests for GHB and GHB analogs must be performed not long after ingestion. Urine tests for GHB and GHB analogs must be performed within 12 hours after ingestion, and blood tests must be performed within 5 hours.

Federal, state, and local forensic laboratories may not routinely test for GHB in blood or urine. For example, the Florida Department of Law Enforcement (FDLE) began testing the GHB in urine on December 1, 2000, but tests are performed only if the suspect exhibits symptoms indicating the presence of GHB. FDLE does not have the resources to conduct blood tests; if blood tests are needed, the samples to be tested must be sent to outside laboratories — some of which are located in other states.

§ 10.11.8   GHB Factor in Auto Fatality

On November 21, 2000, a Florida woman under the influence of GHB crashed head-on into another car, killing a passenger in the other vehicle. Hours before the incident, the woman had been arrested after passing out at a red light. A Breathalyzer test failed to detect alcohol; however, the woman admitted to having drunk from a bottle that contained GHB. She posted bond and was released. Two weeks before the fatal collision, the driver had been ticketed for careless driving; police did not detain her because the officer at the scene did not smell alcohol and did not know to test for GHB. (Source: Florida Department of Law Enforcement; *St. Petersburg Times.*)

Because GHB analogs produce effects similar to GHB, driving under the influence of the analogs is just as dangerous as driving under the influence of GHB. As a result, some agencies have adopted aggressive strategies for identifying drivers who may have consumed GHB. The Pinellas-Pasco Medical Examiner's Office in Florida conducts GHB tests on drivers who are suspected of driving under the influence (DUI). In 2000, GHB was detected in approximately 8 percent of the suspected DUI cases that the office examined.

§ 10.11.9   Analogs and the Law

While federal law prohibits the sale of analogs for human consumption, GHB analogs are available legally as industrial solvents used to produce polyurethane, pesticides, elastic fibers, pharmaceuticals, coatings on metal or plastic, and other products. These analogs also are sold illicitly as supplements for bodybuilding, fat loss, reversal of baldness, improved eyesight, and to combat aging, depression, drug addiction, and insomnia. GBL and BD are sold as "fish tank cleaner," "ink stain remover," "ink cartridge cleaner," and "nail enamel remover" for approximately $100 per bottle – much more expensive than comparable products. Law enforcement's efforts to identify the abuse of GHB analogs are hampered by the fact that routine toxicological screens do not detect the presence of these analogs. In addition, distributors continually develop new analogs to avoid law enforcement detection.

GHB analogs are treated as controlled substances under federal law only if intended for human consumption. According to 21 U.S. Code § 813, "a controlled substance analogue shall, to the extent intended for human consumption, be treated, for the purposes of any federal law as a controlled substance in Schedule I." Thus, authorities can prosecute drug offenses involving GHB analogs in the same manner as offenses involving GHB. (NDIC 2002). (See also 21 U.S. Code § 802 (32) for the definition of a controlled substance analog).

§ 10.11.9   Conclusion

Deterring the distribution and abuse of GHB analogs poses unique challenges. Some analogs have legitimate purposes and are legally available. Distributors of illicit GHB analogs will continue to develop new products to disguise their activities, and illicit producers will continue to develop new GHB analogs for the same reasons. Web sites advertising these products will continue to be deceptive and everchanging. Distributors will develop new disguises for GHB analogs in addition to marketing them as cleaning fluids and dietary supplements. Sharing current information and associated trends relating to GHB analogs among medical personnel, law enforcement officers, and laboratory personnel is essential to stemming the distribution and abuse of these analogs.

§ 10.12 NARCOTIC ANALOGS

The novel aspect of the current wave of controlled substance analogs is the production of narcotic analogs. These substances consist of variations of the parent compounds fentanyl and meperidine (pethidine).

First synthesized in Belgium in the late 1950s, fentanyl, with an analgesic potency of about 80 times that of morphine, was introduced into medical practice in the 1960s as an intravenous anesthetic under the trade name of Sublimaze. Thereafter, two other fentanyl analogues were introduced; alfentanil (Alfenta), an ultra-short (5-10 minutes acting analgesic, and sufentanil (Sufenta), an exceptionally potent analgesic (5 to 10 times more potent than fentanyl) for use in heart surgery. Today, fentanyls are extensively used for anesthesia and analgesia. Duragesic, for example is a fentanyl transdermal patch used in chronic pain management, and Actiq is a solid formulation of fentanyl citrate on a stick that dissolves slowly in the mouth for transmucosal absorption. Actiq is intended for opiate-tolerant individuals and is effective in treating breakthrough pain in cancer patients. Carfentanil (Wildnil) is an analog of fentanyl with an analgesic potency 10,000 times that of morphine and is used in veterinary practice to immobilize certain large animals.

Illicit use of pharmaceutical fentanyls first appeared in the mid-1970s in the medical community and continues to be a problem in the United States. To date, over 12 different analogs of fentanyl have been produced clandestinely and identified in US. drug traffic. The biological effects of the fentanyls are indistinguishable from those of heroin, with the exception that the fentanyls may be hundreds of times more potent. Fentanyls are most commonly used by intravenous administration, bu, like heroin, they may also be smoked or snorted.

Fentanyl has been diverted by pharmacy theft, fraudulent prescriptions, and illicit distribution by patients, physicians, and pharmacists. Theft has also been identified at nursing homes and other long-term care facilities. Fentanyl oral transmucosal lozenges (Actiq) are typically sold at $20-25 per unit or $450 per carton (contains 24 units) while transdermal patches (Duragesic) are sold at prices ranging from $10-100 per patch, depending upong the dose of the unit and geographical area. There is evidence of large illegal distribution rings selling fentanyl products along with other opioid pharmaceuticals (DEA 2004).

Meperidine (Demerol) is another synthetic narcotic drug which has been mimicked by clandestine laboratory operators. A meperidine analog, termed MPPP, was first identified by a DEA laboratory in 1982. The MPPP compound is about 5 to 10 times more potent as an analgesic than meperidine and thus its dosage should be similar to morphine. Samples of the MPPP analog have also contained a neurotoxic by-product, MPTP. This by-product is formed during the synthesis of MPPP. A number of persons that used an MPPP/MPTP mixture developed a severe Parkinson's-disease-like state as a consequence. The neurological damage produced by exposure to MPTP is irreversible and appears to worsen with time. Another meperidine analog, termed PEPAP, has recently been detected in samples analyzed by the DEA laboratory system. The samples also contained a by-product that is chemically related to the neurotoxin, MPTP. Using emergency scheduling, DEA placed MPPP and PEPAP into Schedule I in August of 1985. More information on MPTP is available later in this chapter.

§ 10.13 SYNTHETIC NARCOTIC PHARMACOLOGY AND TOXICOLOGY

Synthetic narcotic substances such as meperidine and fentanyl derivatives are pharmacologically similar to opium-based narcotics such as morphine. Like morphine, the synthetic narcotics primarily act on the central nervous system (CNS) and the gastrointestinal (GI) tract. In addition to producing analgesia, drowsiness, and euphoria, these substances also produce varying degrees of respiratory depression, constipation, nausea and vomiting (except fentanyl), muscular rigidity, and changes in autonomic nervous system tone.

Natural and synthetic narcotic substances produce their effects on the body by way of biological molecules called opioid receptors. These opioid receptors are found on the surfaces of neurons and other types of cells. The narcotic substances bind to these opioid receptors and stimulate a cellular response. In general, the more tightly a narcotic substance binds to these receptors, the more potent it is (i.e., the lower the dose required to produce a response). The opioid receptors appear to consist of a number of different subtypes (delta, kappa, mu, sigma) and each subtype seems to affect different parts of the diverse actions of narcotics. At the present time, the mu subtype of opioid receptor is considered to be especially involved in the analgesic and addicting properties of narcotics.

Opioid receptors are found in high numbers in some areas of the brain and are also present in the GI tract. It is likely that narcotic analgesia is exerted through the opioid receptors located in CNS areas like the spinal cord and the thalamus (areas involved in pain transmission and perception). The euphoric actions, on the other hand, are more likely to involve stimulation of opioid receptors found in the limbic regions of the brain (areas that mediate mood and emotion).

The toxic actions of morphine-like narcotics involve depression of respiration and (except fentanyl) also release of histamine into the circulation.

Depression of respiration is caused by direct actions of narcotics on brain stem centers which sense carbon dioxide levels in the blood. Although this respiratory arrest is commonly responsible for overdose fatalities, the interaction of depressed respiration and histamine release also may be responsible for some deaths. The hypoxia (lack of oxygen) which follows severe respiratory depression may lead to a drop in blood pressure, and any release of histamine will produce further hypotension. Blood pressure may eventually become so low that cardiovascular collapse occurs and death results.

The chronic use of meperidine is associated with some additional toxic effects. These effects can include tremors, muscle twitches, hallucinations, seizures, and tissue fibrosis at injection sites.

Fentanyl and its derivatives depress respiration in a manner similar to morphine but these effects are much shorter in duration. Moreover, fentanyl seems to differ from morphine in that it does not provoke a release of histamine and thereby confers a greater measure of cardiovascular stability.

§ 10.13.1   Physical Description of Fentanyl: "China White"

The fentanyls are cut (diluted) with large amounts of lactose or sucrose (powdered sugar) before they are sold on the street so the amount of active drug present is exceedingly small, less than 1 percent. These amounts are so small they contribute nothing to the color, odor, or taste of the sample.

Color — The color of the samples obtained to date has ranged from pure white (sold as "Persian White") to light tan (sold as "China White," "Synthetic Heroin," or "fentanyl") to light brown (sold as "Mexican Brown"). The brown color comes from the lactose which has been heated and has caramelized slightly.

Texture — The texture of the samples observed in the laboratory has ranged from light and finely powdered to somewhat coarse, cake-like and crumbly, resembling powdered milk.

Odor — Occasional samples will have a medicinal or chemical odor, but this is not characteristic.

In summary, the fentanyls appear in all the various forms that heroin does and there is nothing characteristic about the appearance of any sample that will identify it as fentanyl.

§ 10.13.2   Routes of Administration
Intravenous injection is the most common route of administration for the fentanyls; however, they also may be smoked or snorted. In fact, because of their high lipid solubility, the fentanyls are used mostly by snorting and have become a popular drug among cocaine users. Fentanyl has been detected in the urine of individuals who used the drug only by smoking it.

§ 10.13.3   Pharmacological Effects of Fentanyl
It should be remembered that although the fentanyls are chemically quite distinct from other narcotics (morphine, heroin, methadone, etc.), they are pharmacologically equivalent; that is, they have all the effects and toxic effects of the classical narcotic. Therefore, all the actions of the fentanyls can be reversed by Naloxone (Narcan), although higher doses of the antagonist may be required.

Euphoria
The euphoria or "rush" from the fentanyls should be qualitatively similar to that of heroin, and the intensity of the effect would depend upon the dose and the particular derivative used.

Analgesia
Profound analgesia (absence of pain) is a characteristic effect of all the fentanyls. As little as 50 micrograms of fentanyl will produce analgesia while only 3 micrograms of the 3-methyl derivative would be required.

§ 10.13.4   SIDE EFFECTS AND TOXICITY
Respiratory depression — This is the most significant acute toxic effect of the fentanyls. The depth and duration of respiratory depression will depend on the dose and the derivative used. However, compared with other narcotics, this effect is relatively short-lived. For example, following 200 micrograms of fentanyl given intravenously, maximum depression occurs within 5 to 10 minutes, and normal respiration returns within 15 to 30 minutes.

Antidote —Naloxone (Narcan) is the antidote of choice for respiratory depression (or any other effect) produced by the fentanyls.

Bradycardia — Fentanyl produces a dose-dependent decrease in heart rate of up to 25 percent with a parallel drop in blood pressure of up to 20 percent. This effect is thought to be due to vagal stimulation (stimulation of vagus nerves) and can be blocked by atrophine. The role of this response in overdose deaths is not known.

Muscle rigidity — Sometimes called "wooden chest," muscle rigidity is the response common to high doses of all narcotics. Individuals using the fentanyls may describe this effect as a muscle tightness or tingling.

Addiction liability — The fentanyls produce both *tolerance* and *physiological dependence* following repeated administration. Controlled studies have shown that addicts perceive fentanyl derivatives as having heroin-like effects. In California, many individuals enrolling in methadone treatment programs have only fentanyl in their urine upon admission, yet are convinced they use only high-grade heroin. Therefore, when pharmacologically equivalent doses are used, most users probably cannot tell the difference between heroin and the fentanyls.

§ 10.13.5 Other Hazards of Fentanyl

Today fentanyl, norfentanyl, despropionyl-fentanyl, and other fentinyl-type drugs can be found in the serum (blood), urine, and hair. What is used is HPLC/MS/MS (tandem MS) test. The limit of detection for the various fentanyls is 10 pg/ml with a 1 ml sample. Fentanyl can also be found in the hair using the same test.

Why do they represent such a hazard and public health problem? There are several clear-cut reasons. First, these drugs do not require importation and all the costs and expenses thereby incurred. Secondly, they are much less expensive to make. Thirdly, of course, those making and selling synthetics may not be prosecuted because the substance may not be illegal. Fortunately, the DEA has been able to take action to control some of these substances. It is estimated that a single chemist working an eight-hour-day could, using the more potent fentanyl derivatives, supply the entire nation's heroin supply on an ongoing basis. A six-month supply for the United States could be stored in a closet. Hence, one can see the immense attractiveness of this approach in terms of cost and liability to those on the production side of the illicit drug market.

Fentanyl labs continue to be detected across the United States. What are the hazards? There are basically three. First, these chemists are obviously not required to carry safety trials with these new compounds as a legitimate drug company would be. Hence, the first subjects to receive them are not laboratory animals, but human beings using these compounds on the street. Secondly, there are no quality controls in the laboratories as there would be in a legitimate drug company. Therefore, contaminants or unwanted compounds are not removed and probably often not even detected. Thirdly, there is the issue of potency. The fentanyl variants, for instance, must be cut in microgram amounts. A dose of fentanyl as small as 40 to 80 micrograms will induce a heroin-like euphoria. To give an example of how small an amount this is, a postage stamp weighs about 60,000 micrograms. Hence, overdoses are common.

§ 10.14 MPTP AND MPPP

It was only a matter of time before a true poison "hit the streets." This is precisely what happened in Northern California in 1982, when a highly toxic compound known as MPTP was circulated. This compound is neurotoxic to a group of cells in the brain known as the substantia nigra. By pure coincidence, this happens to be the same area that is damaged in Parkinson's disease. A group of young adults came to the Santa Clara Valley Medical Center who resembled in every way elderly patients with end-stage Parkinson's disease. These young addicts had literally frozen up overnight and were totally unable to move or talk. Treatment with anti-Parkinsonia therapy was probably life-saving in three; however, these patients continue to be severely disabled and required medication every one to three hours just to be able to move and eat or drink. Two of them have undergone prolonged hospitalizations and the outlook for their futures is grim.

While there were only twenty severely involved young adults who were permanently crippled by this first "designer drug disaster," an additional 500 people were exposed to MPTP thinking it was a new "synthetic heroin." We now have evidence that damage to this area of brain, even if it is not enough to cause symptoms at first, acts like a time bomb with changes in the brain slowly ticking away. In other words, sooner or later, these young adults could come down with a Parkinson's-disease-like state. This concern was just theoretical, but then we started seeing a group of young people at Santa Clara Valley Medical Center who used MPTP two years previously and had just started to develop a myriad of symptoms suggestive of early Parkinson's disease.

MPPP is an analog of meperidine, a legal, federally controlled painkiller that goes by the trade name Demerol. MPPP has been blamed for causing the Parkinson's-like symptoms—including tremors of the hands, loss of motor control, and paralysis—discovered in drug abusers in California. The brain damage is done by a neurotoxin, MPTP, a contaminant unintentionally created in the MPPP manufacturing process. Unless clandestine chemists assay their batches, they cannot know if it is contaminated with MPTP.

§ 10.15 METHCATHINONE (CAT)

An analog of methamphetamine by the name of methcathinone or CAT has made an appearance in the illicit drug markets across the United States. It is known as ephedrine, 2-(methylamino)-1-phenylpropan-1-one, mono-methylpropion, UR 1432, CAT, goob, go-fast, crank, sniff, and wonder star.

The first CAT laboratories in the United States were seized in Ann Arbor, Michigan, in June 1991. To date, Federal, state, and local law enforcement continue to seize CAT laboratories across the United States. These CAT labs are usually small in size and utilize glass jugs, jars, and equipment usually associated more with kitchen glassware than typical lab equipment, making them more difficult to identify to the untrained eye.

The hazards and risks to health are serious and the utmost caution and training should be utilized when dealing with any clandestine laboratory situation. The immediate precursor used to manufacture CAT is ephedrine, which is also currently very popular with illicit lab operators in the United States. Ephedrine, the synthetic version of the active abstract from the ephedra plant and otherwise known as ma-huang, is a bronchial dilator used in over-the-counter cold medications. Ephedrine is usually obtained in pill form for its use in illicit metham-phetamine labs. The pills are either used in crushed fashion or the ephedrine hydrochloride powder is extracted by the use of solvents.

CAT hydrochloride (powder) is used in much the same way as methamphetamine: inhalation, injection, smoking, and oral ingestion. CAT can quickly deteriorate the sinus cavities causing chronic nose bleeding and sinusitis. An average dose is one line, or about to of a gram.

As with methamphetamine, the high obtained with CAT may last up to eight hours or more. With continued use tolerance to the drug will occur. Chronic users of CAT also use alcohol, sedatives, and/or mari-juana to reduce the side effects of the central nervous stimulation, such as nervousness, jerking behavior, paranoia, and insomnia. Like the "speedfreak" of the 1960s, CAT users may binge on the drug and stay up for days without eating or sleeping. They exhibit a gaunt and wasted appearance.

The market price for CAT is about the same as for cocaine and am-phetamines. CAT is packaged in plastic bags and less commonly in pa-per bindles.

Section 11550 H&S observations for stimulant influence are consis-tent with those of CAT, such as hyperactivity, increased heart rate, respiration rate and blood pressure, and dilated pupils. The typical user violence and the propensity to obtain weapons associated with the meth user are also consistent with CAT users. Therefore, the identification of a person under the influence of a stimulant such as methamphetamine would be the same for CAT.

It does not appear that CAT is included in Section 11550 H&S. How-ever, this should not stop you from making the appropriate detention and arrest for stimulant influence. The identity of the drug used cannot be made without the crime lab analysis of the blood or urine.

§ 10.16 CONCLUSION
In years to come, the development of highly selective, site-specific designer drugs may enhance our life and revolutionize mental health.

However, in the long run, irrespective of how clever our pharmacol-ogical interventions may one day be, we would arguably be better off taking no drugs at all. But then again, if there was nothing fundamen-tally wrong with our state of consciousness, why do we try so hard to change it? Tomorrow's bioscientists have a great challenge ahead.

§ 10.17 CONTROLLED SUBSTANCES ANALOGS ABBREVIATIONS

BDMPEA = 4-bromo-2,5-dimethoxyphenethylamine
DOB = 4-bromo-2,5-dimethoxyphenylisopropylamine

Chapter 10

DOM = 4-methyl-2,5-dimethoxyphenylisopropylamine; STP
MDA = 3,4-methylenedioxyamphetamine
MDE = 3,4-methylenedioxy-N-ethylamphetamine
MDMA = 3,4-methylenedioxymethamphetamine; ecstasy; XTC
MPPP = 1-methyl-4-phenyl-4-propionoxy-piperidine
MPTP = 1-methyl-4-phenyl-1,2,5,6-tetrahydropyridine
PEPAP = 1-phenethyl-4-phenyl-4-acetoxy-piperidine
DMA = 2.5 - Dimethoxyamphetamine
PMA = 4-Methoxyamphetamine
MMDA = 5-Methoxy-3, 4-Methylonedioxyamphetamine
TMA = 3,4,5-Trimethoxyamphetamine

References

Drug Enforcement Administration. Drug Intelligence Brief, BZP and TFMPP: Chemicals Used to Mimic MDMA's Effects. Washington, D.C: Domestic Strategic Unit of the Office of Domestic Intelligence, December 2001.

----------. Drug Intelligence Brief, The Hallucinogen PMA: Dancing with Death. Washington, D.C: Domestic Strategic Unit of the Office of Domestic Intelligence, October 2000.

----------. Drug Intelligence Brief, Khat. Washington, D.C: Domestic Strategic Unit of the Office of Domestic Intelligence, June 2002.

----------. Microgram Bulletin. Washington, D.C: Office of Forensic Sciences, 2004.

----------. Drug Intelligence Brief, Trippin' on Tryptamines: The Emergence of FOXY and AMT as Things of Abuse. Washington, D.C: Domestic Strategic Unit of the Office of Domestic Intelligence, October 2002.

National Drug Intelligence Center. GHB and Analogs Fast Facts, DEA, Product # 2003-L0559-009I. Johnstown, PA: NDIC, 2003.

----------. Information Bulletin, GHB Analogs-GBL, BD, GHV AND GVL Document # 2002-L0424-003. Johnstown, PA: NDIC, 2002.

----------. Information Bulletin, 2C-B (Nexus) Reappears on the Club Drug Scene. Johnstown, PA: NDIC, 2001.

Office of Forensic Sciences. Microgram Bulletin. Washington, D.C., U.S. Department of Justice, 2004.

Rocky Mountain Instrumental Labs, Inc. www.rockylab.com/Fentanyl.html. Fort Collins, CO, 2005.

CHAPTER 11

ANABOLIC STEROIDS

§ 11.1   INTRODUCTION

An estimated 3 million illicit users of anabolic steroids support a $100 million dollar a year market. This market incorporates the diversion of pharmaceutical drugs to illicit black market smuggling operations. Anabolic steroids are not generally thought of as drugs of abuse, and therein lies the problem. Adolescents, rushing to physically become adults, and athletes, willing to win at any cost, have discovered a short-cut to achieving their goals.

Recent research has determined that the nationwide abuse of anabolic steroids is a significant problem.

§ 11.2   HISTORY

Steroids are a synthetic version of the male hormone testosterone. Anabolic refers to a substance that promotes growth. When taken internally, steroids will, in conjunction with weight training, promote extraordinary weight gain and muscular development.

STEROID PRODUCTS AND THEIR TESTOSTERONE DERIVATIVES

This table represents only the most widely used steroid products; it is not all-inclusive.

PRODUCT	DERIVATIVE
Anadiol	Testosterone
Anadrol 50	Oxymetholone
Anavar	Oxandrolone
Cheque Drops	Mibolerone
Deca-Durabolin	Nandrolone
Depo-Testosterone	Testosterone
Dianabol	Methandrostenolone
Equipoise	Boldenone
Finaject	Trenobolone
Lyphomed	Nandrolone
Malogen	Testosterone
Nandrabolin	Nandrolone
Parabolan	Trenbolone
Primobolan	Methenolone
Primoteston Depot	Testosterone
Sostenon 250	Testosterone (Esters)
Sten	Testosterone
Stenox	Fluoxymesterone
Winstrol V	Stanozolol

Chapter 11

The idea of using male hormones to enhance performance originated in the 1890s when experiments linked testosterone with certain masculine traits like strength and muscular development. In 1935, researchers developed the first synthetic testosterone. The military experimented with steroids. Following World War II, Eastern European weightlifters began using steroids and as a result dominated international competitions. It did not take long for other competitors to realize why. Steroid use the spread from weightlifting to other athletic endeavors, and today steroids are used in any sport where athletes perceive a benefit.

Steroids were first introduced to athletes in the United States by a physician and weightlifter, Dr. John Ziegler. Dr. Ziegler was appointed as the team physician for U.S. weightlifters at the world championships of 1954 in Vienna, Austria. While on that trip, he discovered the use of testosterone among Soviet weightlifters. He and some close associates tried testosterone and found that it helped to improve their strength. Dr. Ziegler then worked with a pharmaceutical company to develop Dianabol (methandrostenolone) in the late 1950s. He administered Dianabol to some of the athletes training at the York Barbell Club and the rage began. Seeing the dangerous side effects of this new drug, Dr. Ziegler tried to stop its use, but it was too late.

A few of the more well-known anabolic agents are Dianabol, Winstrol, Durabolin 50, Decadurabolin, and Nilavar. Human growth hormone (HGH) or somatotropin could be added to the list today. The use of anabolic steroids has reached massive, worldwide proportions.

§ 11.3   STEROID SOURCES

At one time, American physicians readily prescribed anabolic steroids to their patients. However, when the U.S. Congress made steroids a Schedule III controlled substance effective in 1991, it limited the accepted medical uses of steroids to the "treatment of disease pursuant to the order of a physician." Clearly, enhancing athletic performance does not fit into this category. For this reason, many physicians are unwilling to prescribe steroids to athletes, but athletes, of course, use steroids extensively.

Probably the most notorious incident of anabolic steroid abuse by an athlete was the Canadian runner, Ben Johnson, who was disqualified from winning a gold medal in the 1988 Olympics in Seoul, South Korea, for the use of the steroid stanozolol. On May 18, 1992, former NFL all-pro Lyle Alzado died of a rare brain cancer he attributed to steroid abuse. Ben Johnson taught us that anabolic steroids work, but Lyle Alzado taught us another lesson. You might cheat and win on the playing field, but lose in the hospital bed. Before he died, Alzado spoke out against steroids, and he stimulated a nationwide assault on steroids just as Len Bias and Don Rogers did with cocaine.

More recently, a former Major League Baseball player said he used steroids during his career, including in 1996 when he was the American League MVP. Jose Canseco (who retired in May 2002) has said that

Anabolic Steroids

there is a drug problem in baseball and claims in his book <u>Juiced</u> that he shared steroids with some of the biggest names in baseball.

The major varieties of steroids sold are oil-based injectables, followed by tablets and water-based injectables. Syringes used tend to be 22-gauge needles. From where do athletes, and non-athletes, obtain these drugs?

Due to the use of steroids in veterinary medicine, veterinarians have become, both directly and indirectly, sources for individuals seeking anabolic steroids for their personal use. Veterinarians use anabolic steroids extensively, mostly in the treatment of horses. The steroids are administered for the treatment of injury and also to enhance the performance of the horse, causing considerable controversy in the horse racing industry. Some states like California have restricted the use of steroids in this area.

Although the Ben Johnson Olympic scandal and subsequent public hearings heightened public awareness in Canada of the consequences of using steroids, steroids were at one time more available in Canada than in the United States. To counteract this, Canada revised its statutes in 1991 to encompass all anabolic steroids, including those marked for veterinary use, which had previously been excluded. As a result, the supply of steroids arriving in the United States from Canada has decreased significantly.

The other major source of steroids for the U.S. market is Mexico. In Mexico, steroids, like many drugs that require a prescription in the United States, can be purchased over the counter. Individuals legally purchase steroids over the counter in Mexico, then illegally transport them across the border into the United States. Most of the steroids currently on the market in California are smuggled Mexican products.

Europe, including Eastern Europe and the former Soviet Union, also serves as a source for steroids. Some of the steroids coming from Canada originate in Europe. However, because of logistical problems and expense, the volume of steroids from Europe has not matched that from Mexico.

Most of the steroids currently on the market are smuggled Mexican products. Steroids diverted from medical uses have come from physicians, veterinarians, and pharmacists.

Anabolic steroids have generally been distributed either directly through or associated with popular workout locations. Dealers are contacted at the gyms and transactions occur at the gym, in the parking lot, or at the dealer's residence. The undercover buyer needs a good working knowledge of steroid products, prices, and abuse techniques, i.e., stacking, cycling, etc.

Mail-order distribution is also popular nationally and internationally. Most dealers utilize overnight express carriers and post office boxes.

Anabolic steroids that have been recently purchased and recovered by law enforcement officers include:

—Primobolon
—Nandrolone Decanoate*
—Methandrostenolone*
—Stanozolol
—Oxymetholone*
—Testosterone-Cypionate*
—Depo-Testosterone*
—Testosterone Enanthate
—Sten
—Primotestin Depot
—Winstrol-V
—Sostenone-250
—Methyltestosterone
—Halotestin-Fluoxymesterone*
—Testosterone Suspension

*Known counterfeits

Counterfeit steroid products are also commonly sold by gymnasium and tanning salon entrepreneurs who purchase bottles, stoppers, and labels from unsuspecting medical supply houses and private printers, and they then fill the bottles with only corn or cottonseed oil.

§ 11.4 COUNTERFEIT STEROIDS
Counterfeiters duplicate the carton and the container of legitimate steroids, but not the contents. Counterfeit steroids contain no or only trace amounts of testosterone. Generally, the counterfeiters mix vegetable oil with alcohol in about a 10 to 1 ratio. They add alcohol to destroy bacteria, which is a genuine problem because the counterfeiters usually take few precautions to sterilize the containers.

Stacking makes the marketing of fake steroids possible. When a distributor sells both fake and real steroids to a user who stacks, the user will experience gains from the real steroid and will assume all the steroids are real. This faith benefits the distributor, who acts as an consultant, advising the users which combination of steroids to take.

§ 11.5 CURRENT USE
Steroids have become prevalent in football, professional wrestling, track and field, swimming, and especially bodybuilding, where the abuse is the most widespread (Goldman et al). With regards to the use of steroids, individuals either inject steroids directly into the muscle tissue or take them orally in tablet form. They also usually cycle them, that is, they take them for a period of time, quit for a period of time, and then repeat the cycle. Dosages might gradually increase to a peak and then decrease, a process known as pyramiding. Users often time their cycles so that the steroid-free period coincides with bodybuilding competitions, which may be drug-tested. However, because some steroids remain in the body for long periods of time, users might take other substances to mask their steroid use.

Anabolic Steroids

The use of other drugs frequently accompanies steroid use. For example, steroid users often use Percodan and other prescription painkillers to diminish the various aches and pains associated with their strenuous workouts. Further, because the steroids and the physical activity make sleep difficult, many users take Valium or other depressants. Some also use cocaine to counteract the depression associated with steroid-free cycles. Cocaine also acts as an appetite suppressant, helping individuals decrease their body fat levels.

The different types of testosterone derivatives contained in the various steroid products yield different results, either real or perceived. Some build muscle, others increase definition. Bodybuilders call this definition being "cut" or "shredded." Because creating large but highly defined muscles is the object of bodybuilding, they often use more than one type of steroid at a time, a practice known as "stacking."

Bodybuilders, weight lifters, and power lifters are the easiest targets to condemn for steroid abuse, because they stand out from regular sports and are viewed as oddities that maintain a very extreme lifestyle. However, steroids are used and abused in every sport, without exception. Football, basketball, baseball, cycling, and swimming have all had athletes test positive for steroids.

ANABOLIC STEROID PERIODS OF ACTION

Steroid Type	Half Life	Preparation	Abuse Rate
Orals	few hours	Anavar Winstrol Dianabol Maxibolin Halotestin Adroyd	3-4 x/daily (20-100 mg/day)
Injectable Oils	1-3 days	Testosterone Propionate Testosterone Cypionate Durabolin Decadurabolin Primabolin	2-3 x/week (200 mg/week)
Injectable Waters	few hours	Testosterone Methandriol	4 x week (400 mg/week)

A major concern in steroid use and distribution is the involvement of public safety personnel. Fireman, policemen, correctional officers, and deputy sheriffs have all been investigative targets for possession and sales of anabolic steroids. Obviously, cases involving public safety personnel pose special concerns during covert operations and internal affairs follow-up. Public safety personnel who abuse anabolic steroids also present unique liability concerns for police chiefs.

§ 11.6   WHY USE STEROIDS

There are many reasons why people use steroids. The main reason is simple—steroids work. Ben Johnson proved it as he shattered the world record in the 100-meter dash and left American Carl Lewis far behind. Arnold Schwarzenegger proved it with seven Mr. Olympia titles. Brian Bosworth proved it by signing the highest rookie contract in NFL history. Ever-competitive athletes know that the potential of competing against a "chemical" athlete is very common in every sport.

Steroid use increases lean muscle mass. However, in order for steroids to be effective, the body must be subjected to intensive exercise. Steroids work by making the body's tissues more receptive to recuperation, nutrient absorption, intrinsic hormone release, and consequently, muscular tissue growth. In other words, steroids chemically manipulate the body's cellular receptor sites by first suppressing cortisol. Cortisol is one of many hormones called glucocorticoids. These hormones are catabolic; they break down muscle tissue. However, this catabolic response can only occur in the presence of corticosteroids, which lock into specialized receptor sites in muscle tissue. Steroids block these receptor sites, so catabolic action cannot occur. In response to this blocking action, the body tries to overcompensate by producing more cortisol and more receptor sites. When steroids are discontinued, the large quantities of hormones are then free to attach to their receptor sites and they literally eat the muscle away. The steroid user avoids this by gradually coming off the drugs or by staying on them continuously.

Steroids also suppress the enzyme monoamine oxydase, commonly referred to as "mayo." Mayo is the protein that breaks down the "happy" chemicals in the brain, which are the same chemicals that antidepressant drugs build up. Steroids are mood elevators in that they block mayo. As a result, mayo accumulates in the brain, and when steroid use is discontinued, depression sets in.

Euphoria and the feeling of invincibility are a direct result of the affect of steroids on the naturally occurring opioids and neurotransmitters, like dopamine, in the brain. These alterations also account for many of the withdrawal symptoms associated with steroid use. The invincibility or "Superman Syndrome" is a common manifestation of steroid-induced euphoria.

Steroids also increase sex drive and libido. Steroid use results in a massive quantity of synthetic testosterone in the body. This level of testosterone increases libido—the user becomes aggressive. This aggression manifests itself in intense workouts, but also is a factor in more instances of temper outbursts, arguments, and fights.

A clinical condition that is unique to steroid users causes them to keep using steroids, and this condition is called "reversed anorexia." This condition is characterized by the belief that the user's body is too small. No matter how great the gains, the steroid user is unsatisfied and wants to be even bigger, at any cost.

§ 11.7   MEDICAL USE

Today, different steroids are used for a variety of legitimate medical purposes. Steroid therapy is used to treat anemia, allergies, asthma, deep-tissue injury, gynecological abnormalities, dwarfism, and osteoporosis. There are many medical applications for steroids. However, the steroid use must be under the direction of a physician, and the dosages are significantly less.

§ 11.8   SIDE EFFECTS OF ANABOLIC STEROIDS

Side effects of steroids depends upon many factors, such as the type of steroid taken, the way the drug is taken (injection, oral, transdermal), the quantity of the dose, the number of different steroids taken at once, individual predisposition to the drug, the presence of other drugs in the body, the age and sex of the user, and the presence of any preexisting medical problems.

One of the biggest obstacles in dealing with anabolic steroids is a lack of understanding as to what they are, and to what they do to the human body. They are simply synthetic male hormones, or testosterone, and adult males are bigger, faster, stronger, and more aggressive that the average adult female because males have more testosterone in their blood. If anabolic steroids are taken, the man or woman becomes more "manly," and their strength, size, and aggression become more pronounced.

Therefore, women who take anabolic steroids may undergo profound physiological changes in that their breasts shrink, voice deepens, beard grows, and muscles bulge (Miller). Males normally have a shorter life span, partially due to their high testosterone levels. The taking of steroids, in effect, prematurely ages the man by increasing cholesterol levels and blood pressure. Heart disease and other cardiovascular problems are the most common serious effects of anabolic steroids (Kautor). Former professional football player Steve Courson believes his need for a heart transplant was caused by steroids.

Can steroids cause cancer? About 5 years ago, cancer of the liver was detected in steroid users, and there have been more documented cases since then. Did steroids cause Lyle Alzado's terminal illness of inoperable lymphoma of the brain? Alzado claimed that steroids and human growth hormones (HGB) caused his lymphoma. High, chronic doses of anabolic steroids alter the immune system by disturbing the metabolism of cortisone, endorphin, and testosterone, which in turn regulate the lymphocytes. When lymphocytes are disturbed, a lymphoma may result. Although they are generally uncommon cancers, lymphomas are relatively common in drug abusers.

It is suspected that in the future cancers of the testicle and prostate will be a common occurrence in former steroid users. Females who take high dosages of estrogen put themselves at excessive risk for cancers of the breast or uterus. Male athletes who take steroids usually take a daily dosage ranging from 10 to 200 times above the usual daily testicular production of testosterone.

Chapter 11

A newly established side effect from steroid use is addiction. Chronic steroid use fits the definition of addiction: loss of control, compulsive behavior, and continued involvement despite adverse consequences. Steroid use also involves denial, a tendency to relapse, and a predictable abstinence/withdrawal syndrome.

Research reports have shown that at least 70 percent of steroid users continue using the drug even when negative consequences occur. A group of Olympic athletes were asked the question, "If you could take a pill, in addition to your training, which would guarantee you a gold medal and a world record, would you take the drug under the following conditions?"

1.   Absolutely no side effects—98% said they would take it.

2.   Moderate side effects that might be debilitating in your later years— 95% said they would take it.

3.   You would be dead at age 40—80% said they would take it.

Loss of control with steroid use has two aspects: loss of control in social situations and loss of control in dosages. During steroid use, moods ranging from mania to major depression are a constant problem in addition to the changes in hormone levels, altered receptor sites, blocked neurotransmitters, and increased libido. Feelings of euphoria quickly turn to hostility and aggression while on steroids. Loss of control in dosages is another dangerous part of the addiction syndrome. It is not uncommon for athletes to use 100 times the recommended medical dosages and, in addition, to take up to twelve different drugs at the same time.

Denial is a state of mind that is created to protect the psyche from conflicting information. In the case of steroids, that conflict is increased performance versus the consequences and sacrifices that steroid use requires. In addition, steroids are expensive. It is hard to justify the expense without denial.

The physical addiction and especially the psychological addiction caused by steroids lead to frequent relapses and compulsive behavior. The athlete whose entire life is centered on his or her performance is driven to succeed at any cost.

The predictable withdrawal syndrome is now supported by the medical profession. The withdrawal syndrome is characterized by loss of muscle mass, increased body fat, slower recuperation, anorexia, suicidal tendencies, insomnia, poor self-image, joint pain, loss of strength, depression, decreased sex drive, fatigue, and a strong desire to resume steroid use.

By the nature of the way steroids work, they must be taken over time. This time frame is referred to as a cycle. These cycles can be as small as four weeks or over several years, but usually are from six to twelve weeks long. There are two primary formats for cycles: a broken cycle and a continuous cycle. A broken cycle begins with a minimal dosage of steroids. This dosage is gradually increased over the next several weeks until a high point is reached, about 5 to 10 times the original dosage. Then the amount of steroids is maintained at this peak level for several more weeks. As the cycle reaches about 75 percent completion, the dosages are gradually reduced to the initial starting point. A continuous cycle follows the same pattern as the broken cycle with a very important difference. At the point where peak steroid levels start to be decreased, an entire new series of similar steroids are gradually introduced. A continuous cycle is an overlapping of broken cycles and can last indefinitely. If steroids are cut out immediately, without the weaning process, the person crashes hard and suffers the most severe withdrawal symptoms. Most side effects that characterize steroid use occur at the end of the initial build-up component of the cycle and continue during the peak concentration phase. The withdrawal symptoms occur during the weaning phase of the cycle. These symptoms are less severe if the gradual downgrading is carefully administered over several weeks. The most severe symptoms occur during a crash.

§ 11.9   SIGNS AND SYMPTOMS OF USE
You should look for these warning signs of steroid use: sudden weight gain; male breast enlargement; acne; thinning hair; change in voice; facial hair; mood swings such as euphoria, giddiness, aggressiveness or depression.

§ 11.10   DESIGNER STEROIDS
THG, or tetrahydrogestrinone, thrust the world of designer steroids into the headlines when it was discovered in 2003. DMT is Desoxy-Methyl-Testosterone. The World Anti-Doping Agency in 2005 received an anonymous e-mail tip that led the agency to investigate a substance seized by Canadian customs. The substance is a clear, oily compound that is a modification of the steroid methyl-testosterone (Zinzei).

These designer steroids are not the first to appear on the shelves of athletes nor will they be the last. As long as anabolic steroids can improve the body's capacity to train and compete at the highest level, athletes will take them and will search for new analogs that cannot be detected in the body during a drug screen test.

§ 11.11   STEROID SUPPLEMENTS
Some steroidal supplements are banned by the new Anabolic Steroid Control Act of 2004 and other supplements are not.

In the United States, supplements such as dehydroepian-drosterone (DHEA) and androstenedione (street name Andro) can be purchased legally without a prescription through many commercial sources, including health food stores. They are often referred to as dietary supplements, although they are not food products. They are often taken because the user believes they have anabolic effects. Steroidal supplements can be converted into testosterone or a similar compound in the body. Whether such conversion produces sufficient quantities of testosterone to promote muscle growth or whether the supplements themselves promote muscle growth is unknown. Little is known about the side effects of steroidal supplements, but if large quantities of these compounds substantially increase testosterone levels in the body, they also are likely to produce the same side effects as anabolic steroids.

§ 11.12 HOW NEW DRUGS GET INTO SPORTS

The story of how EPO, erythropoietin, came into sports is an informative example. Erythropoietin is a naturally occurring hormone, produced by the kidneys, which stimulates the body to produce more red blood cells. An American pharmaceutical company, Amgen, was the first to manufacture a recombinant (synthetic) version of EPO, which they called Epogen. It began to be used widely — and effectively — in medicine in the late 1980s as part of the treatment of anaemia, a condition caused by a low number of red blood cells. Sportsmen soon realized that EPO would also boost the number of red blood cells in a healthy person's body — meaning their blood could carry more oxygen, so their bodies could work harder longer. It was picked up by athletes in endurance sports — cycling, distance running, swimming — and by the late 1990s had become the key battle in the anti-doping war.

§ 11.12.1   HGH in Sports

HGH, or Human Growth Hormone, occurs naturally in the body. HGH supplements are outlawed by the International Olympic Committee. However, its abuse is presently impossible to detect because it occurs naturally in the human body. So, athletes are able to use HGH with impunity because it does not show up in existing drug tests. There are currently many countries working on the detection of HGH. The chemists are dealing with a substance which is both endogenous (produced within the body) and exogenous (originating outside the body), and the exogenous HGH is absolutely similar to what is produced by the body. Therein lies the problem of developing a urine/blood test to detect exogenous HGH.

§ 11.13 FEDERAL LAW

The illegal sale of anabolic steroids has been a felony under federal law since 1988. Congress passed the Anabolic Steroids Control Act of 1990. This law placed 27 anabolic steroids and their derivatives into Schedule III of the Controlled Substance Act. Schedule III drugs by their definition have a potential for abuse but less than those drugs in Schedule II or I, which have a high potential for abuse. Abuse for a Schedule III drug may lead to moderate or low physical dependence or high psychological dependence.

Classifying steroids as controlled substances allows for the forfeiture of any property used to facilitate the distribution of steroids and any profit traceable to the sale of steroids.

The manufacture and distribution of fake steroids are prosecuted federally under two statutes. Because the counterfeit steroids are mislabeled as real, dealers can be prosecuted under the sale of misbranded drugs (Title 21, USC, Sections 331 (a) and 333 (a)(2). Part of the Food and Drug Act, this law is enforced by the FDA and the FBI. The seller of fake steroids using registered trademarks or any other counterfeit mark belonging to legitimate drug manufacturers can be prosecuted for trafficking in counterfeit goods (Title 18, USC, Section 2320).

§ 11.13.1   Anabolic Steroid Act of 2004

Steroid use has been in existence for a long time. It is, however, only recently that steroid abuse has become a national concern. It all started when the U.S. Anti-Doping Agency was contacted by an anonymous coach who claimed that several top athletes were using THG. Not much was known about the steroid analog. The U.S. Anti-Doping Agency identified BOLCO (Bay Area Laboratory Cooperative), a company which makes nutritional supplements, as the source of THG. Victor Conte, owner of BOLCO, denies he is the source of THG, and claims that his company analyzes blood and urine from athletes and then pre-scribes a series of supplements to compensate for vitamin and mineral deficiencies. Among its clients are top athletes Marion Jones and Tim Montgomery, as well as baseball star Barry Bonds and NFL's Bill Ro-manowski. Bonds has been a BALCO client since the winter of 2000 and has credited the company for a personalized program that includes nutritional supplements.

The furor over the THG steroid scandal prompted lawmakers to take action. The U.S. Congress passed the Anabolic Steroid Control Act (H.R. 3866) of 2004. The concern of the lawmakers in the passage of the Act extended far beyond professional sports.

Steroid use among young Americans has already passed a dangerous level. The 2003 Monitoring the Future Study conducted by the Univer-sity of Michigan indicates that approximately 3.5 percent of American high school students have used illegal anabolic steroids at least once by grade 12. In the same study, an incredible 45 percent of all 12th graders did not believe taking steroids posed a great risk.[1] This report came on the heels of earlier studies, including the National Institute of Drug Abuse (NIDA) report of 1999, which stated that more than a half mil-lion 8th and 10th grade students were using anabolic steroids. A Youth Risk Behavior Surveillance Survey conducted by the Centers for Dis-ease Control and Prevention (CDC) indicated that in 2001, five percent of all high school students reported use of steroids pills/injections with-out a physician's prescription during their lifetimes. Compounding the dangerous perception among young people that steroid use is harmless is the high-profile use of steroids among professional athletes. And be-cause sports figures are prominent role models for our younger citizens, the President has focused on preventing doping and cheating in sports.

"To help children make the right choices, they need good examples. Athlet-ics play such an important role in our society, but unfortunately, some in professional sports are not setting much of an example. The use of perform-ance-enhancing drugs like steroids in baseball, football, and other sports is

---

[1] These data are from the 2003 Monitoring the Future Survey, funded by the National Institute on Drug Abuse, National Institutes of Health, DHHS, and conducted by the University of Michigan's Institute for Social Research. The Survey has tracked 12th-graders' illicit drug use and related attitudes since 1975; in 1991, 8th- and 10th-graders' were added to the survey. The latest data are online at http://www.drugabuse.gov.

dangerous, and it sends the wrong message — that there are shortcuts to accomplishment, and that performance is more important than character. So tonight, I call on team owners, union representatives, coaches, and players to take the lead, to send the right signal, to get tough, and to get rid of steroids now." (President George W. Bush, 2004 State of the Union Address)

§ 11.13.2 CALIFORNIA LAW

In California law, steroids are in Schedule III, subsection (f) of Section 11056 H&S Code. Possession of steroids is found in Section 11377 (b) H&S Code. Possession for sale of steroids is found in Section 11378 H&S Code. Sale of steroids is found in Section 11379 H&S Code. The use of a minor or sales to a minor of steroids is found in Section 11380 H&S Code. Selling fake steroids is found in Section 11382 H&S Code. There is no section that covers being under the influence of steroids.

§ 11.14 CONCLUSION

Despite the efforts of law enforcement, the media, and others to educate the public on the problems of steroid use, there will always be individuals willing to risk long-term, potentially severe health problems for short-term athletic enhancement. Aspiring athletes should not have to use steroids to reach the pinnacle of their sport. Steroid use perverts the goals of sports and athletic competition. A victory achieved through steroid use is hollow, at best. At worst, the athlete may face prosecution or even death.

References

Alen, M. "Androgenic Steroid Effects on Liver and Red Cells." British Journal of Sports Medicine 5.6 (March, 1985).

Goldman and Klatz. Death in the Locker Room II. Chicago: Elite Medicine Pub., 1992.

Kautor, Mark A. "Androgens Reduce HDL2-Cholesterol and Increase Hepatic Triglyceride Lipase Activity." Medicine and Science in Sports and Exercise 17 (August, 1985).

Miller, Roger W. "Athletes and Steroids: Playing a Deadly Game." FDA Consumer, 1987.

Voy, Robert. "Illicit Drugs and the Athlete." American Pharmacy 26.11(November, 1986): 41-44.

Windsor, Robert E., and D. Dumitru. "Anabolic Steroid Use by Athletes. How Serious Are the Health Hazards?" Postgraduate Medicine 84.4 (September, 1988): 37-49.

Zinzei, Lynn. "Drugs: Scientists Find New Designer Steroid." New York Times, 3 February 2005.

CHAPTER 12

CENTRAL NERVOUS SYSTEM
STIMULANT DRUGS

§ 12.1   INTRODUCTION

Stimulants are sometimes referred to as uppers, and reverse the effects of fatigue on both mental and physical tasks. Two commonly used stimulants are nicotine, found in tobacco products, and caffeine, an active ingredient in coffee, tea, some soft drinks, and many non-prescription medicines. Used in moderation, these substances tend to relieve malaise, and to increase alertness. Although the use of these products has been an accepted part of U.S. culture, the recognition of their adverse effects has resulted in a proliferation of caffeine-free products and efforts to discourage cigarette smoking.

A number of stimulants, however, are under the regulatory control of the Controlled Substances Act (CSA). Some of these controlled substances are available by prescription for legitimate medical use in the treatment of obesity, narcolepsy, and attention deficit disorders. As drugs of abuse, stimulants are frequently taken to produce a sense of exhilaration, enhance self esteem, improve mental and physical performance, increase activity, reduce appetite, produce prolonged wakefulness, and "get high." They are recognized as among the most potent agents of reward and reinforcement that underlie the problem of dependence.

The stimulant drugs most frequently abused are cocaine and the amphetamines (this also includes drugs chemically related to amphetamines).

§ 12.2   COCAINE
§ 12.2.1 Introduction

Cocaine (benzoylmethyl ecognine—$C_{17}H_{21}NO_4$) is a white crystalline alkaloid found in the leaves of the coca bush (*Erythroxylon coca*) that acts as a stimulant on the central nervous system (CNS).

Cocaine is the principal active ingredient of the South American coca plant. The coca plant is an evergreen native to South America, particularly the countries of Peru, Bolivia, Brazil, Chili and Colombia. It has been successfully cultivated in Java, West Indies, India and Australia.

The use of chemical substances to prevent or treat local pain had its origin in South America. It was known that CNS stimulations occurred among the natives of Peru who chewed the leaves of the indigenous coca plant. Numbness in the mouth was believed to have occurred as a by-product of this custom.

§ 12.2.2 History of Coca Use

The coca leaf is commonly chewed by the natives of South America. The natives claim that the cocaine depresses their hunger and increases their strength.

The leaves are very bitter when chewed and are often flavored with another substance such as lime. It has been estimated that over 90 percent of the Native Americans chew the coca leaf. The natives chew, on an average, about two ounces of coca leaf daily and are often characterized by blackish red deposits on their teeth. The cocaine is sprinkled with alkaline ash that increases the absorption of oral cocaine. Besides being consumed by the natives of South America, the coca leaf is also exported to other countries for consumption.

Coca Flower

Chewing leaves of the coca plant gave the Native Americans energy to withstand the long hours needed to cultivate their rocky, mountainous terrain, as well as to reduce their hunger. Cocaine raised the body temperature, and by constricting surface blood vessels, held onto the increased body heat. Cocaine also thinned their blood, and this allowed them the ability to work at high altitudes without getting dizzy or sick. The Native Americans claimed cocaine was a gift from the gods, and necessary for their survival. However, as often happens, it had ill effects when transported from the culture that has safely assimilated it.

By 1840, most of the important medicinal alkaloids—morphine and codeine from opium, nicotine from tobacco, and atropine from belladonna—had been isolated and were being utilized. Cocaine was extracted, identified and named in 1860. But aside from the discovery that it numbed the tongue and that it could have potential as a local anesthetic, it was not assigned a practical use until 1878.

In 1878, a medical report advocated the use of cocaine for the treatment of morphine addiction. In 1883, another report was written by a German physician reporting beneficial effects of cocaine in combating fatigue when issued to Bavarian soldiers during war maneuvers (Inaba).

Coca Bean

Central Nervous System Stimulant Drugs

By 1880, cocaine was touted as a cure for fatigue, asthma, stomach ailments, "women's illnesses," and nose inflammations. Parke-Davis sold cocaine in cigarettes and tablets, and patent-medicine quacks peddled it from brightly painted wagons.

Cocaine was soon sold over-the-counter. Until 1916, one could buy it at Harrods: a kit labeled "A Welcome Present for Friends at the Front" contained cocaine, morphine, syringes and spare needles. Cocaine was widely used in tonics, toothache cures and patent medicines; in coca cigarettes "guaranteed to lift depression"; and in chocolate cocaine tablets. One fast-selling product, Ryno's Hay Fever and Catarrh Remedy ("for when the nose is stuffed up, red and sore") consisted of 99.9% of pure cocaine. Prospective buyers were advised—in the words of pharmaceutical firm Parke-Davis—that cocaine "could make the coward brave, the silent eloquent, and render the sufferer insensitive to pain" (www.cocaine.org).

When combined with alcohol, the cocaine alkaloid yields a further potently reinforcing compound, now known to be cocaethylene. Thus, cocaine was a popular ingredient in wines, notably Vin Mariani. But perhaps one of the most popular forms was a concoction of John Pemberton's, a Georgian pharmacist, containing kola nuts and cocaine: Coca-Cola.

Coca-Cola was introduced in 1886 as "a valuable brain-tonic and cure for all nervous afflictions." It was promoted as a temperance drink "offering the virtues of coca without the vices of alcohol." The new beverage was invigorating and popular. Until 1903, a typical serving contained around 60 mg. of cocaine. Though the Coca-Cola company had switched to decocanized coca leaves by 1906, even as late as 1920, the drink could be ordered by asking for a "shot in the arm." Sold today, it still contains an extract of coca leaves. The Coca-Cola Company imports eight tons of coca leaves from South America each year. Now, however, the leaves are used only for flavoring since the drug has been removed.

By 1914, the addictive and psychosis-producing nature of cocaine was apparent. For example, in New York State, illegal sale of opium or heroin was considered a misdemeanor, while sale of cocaine was a felony. On the federal level, the Harrison Narcotic Act of 1914 restricted cocaine to doctor's prescriptions and imposed fines and imprisonment for its illegal sale or distribution.

Cocaine use declined after the 1920s as a result of law enforcement and drug education and, in 1932, due to the appearance of the cheaper synthetic stimulant amphetamine. But suddenly in the 1970s, its use began again.

In 1970, the old federal narcotic laws were replaced with the Comprehensive Drug Abuse Prevention and Control Act. This placed cocaine in Schedule II, retaining it as a valid medical drug but with severe restrictions because of its high potential for abuse. Both the new law and the old Harrison Act classify cocaine as a narcotic, a misnomer.

Chapter 12

Cocaine and coca are stimulants, similar in effect to amphetamine, but unrelated to the depressive narcotic drugs.

§ 12.2.3 The Illicit Processing of Coca

When discussing the illicit processing of coca, it is important to consider the conditions under which the processing is performed. The illicit processor rarely has access to the wide range of quality chemicals available in the United States and Europe. The illegal process is carried out by "cooks" who know little about chemistry and routinely use substitute solvents and chemicals, depending on what is available. As a South American cook once said, "All you need to make cocaine is three buckets and two sheets." Many cooks actually use this method. The work is done in makeshift laboratories more reminiscent of kitchens, and the sheets (complete with multiple kilos) are often hung on a clothesline to dry in the sun. Time is of the essence. One never knows when a cocaine kitchen may have to be moved at a moment's notice, and, as a result, lengthy procedures are abbreviated to meet this criterion. Quality is often sacrificed in the process.

There are three kinds of laboratories that are utilized in the procedures. The pasta lab is usually located at or near the growing area and is used to extract all the alkaloids in the form of a water soluble paste. This crude cocaine sulfate, called pasta, is far less bulky than the leaves themselves, and the extraction procedure and laboratory requirements are simple enough to be performed by the coca growers. (It takes 100 to 150 kilos of dry leaves to produce one kilo of dry pasta.) All that is required is to soak the dried leaves in water, add a strong alkali like lime to release the alkaloids, and stir in a solvent like kerosene or gasoline, which will dissolve the alkaloids while remaining separate from the water. The water is then drained out the bottom of the container, and the solvent is poured off the top. Once the solvent has been separated, sulfuric acid is added to precipitate the alkaloids. The precipitate—the pasta—is separated from the solvent by filtration and put out in the sun to dry. (In Bolivia, where the predominant alkaloid is cocaine, hydrochloric acid is often substituted for sulfuric acid, and the resultant hydrochloride is the finished product.)

The dry pasta is usually tannish brown, which is the color coming from plant material, dirt, etc. Usually all its compounds will precipitate with lime, and will dissolve in gasoline. If a stronger alkali is used, then more compounds will be present.

The next step of the process is to convert the pasta to base. This is usually done in a base lab located in Colombia and is critical because it determines the amount and proportions of different alkaloids that will be present in the finished product. Parts of this conversion are routinely left out due to the time involved, weight losses, and potential risk to the cocaine. When properly performed, the conversion to base will eliminate cinnamylcocaine and the hygrine, as well as most organic impurities. The conversion is properly performed by dissolving the pasta in water and adding sulfuric acid to further acidify the solution. Potassium permanganate is added to the solution, which causes it to turn a violet color. This oxidation process does not appreciably affect the cocaine, but the oils and impurities are attacked almost immediately. The critical part of the process is deciding when to add an alkali in order to stop the action of the permanganate. If the decision is made too early, the resultant base will contain more impurities and other alkaloids; if the decision is made too late, some cocaine will be destroyed by the permanganate. Any experienced cook has over-oxidized the pasta at one time or another.

Note that the owners of the pasta are not involved for the fun of it—their purpose is to make money. Pasta converted to base without being oxidized with permanganate rarely results in cocaine hydrochloride, which is over 60 percent cocaine base, whereas cocaine hydrochloride made from properly oxidized base may equal as much as 82 percent cocaine base. Since the loss of a quantity of cocaine due to over-oxidation of the pasta is an ineffective means of increasing the profit, more often than not, this part of the process is eliminated. Why take the chance when the cocaine will sell anyway?

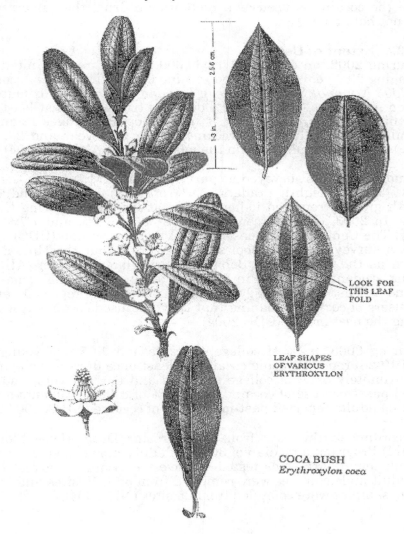

2.56 cm.

1-3 in.

LOOK FOR THIS LEAF FOLD

LEAF SHAPES OF VARIOUS ERYTHROXYLON

COCA BUSH
Erythroxylon coca

The last step of the process is to convert the base to "crystal," the South American term for cocaine hydrochloride. This is usually done in a crystal lab located in or near a major city in Colombia. The base is dissolved in ether, and hydrochloric acid is added to precipitate the cocaine hydrochloride crystals. These are collected by filtration and then are dried. While as many as 50 kilos may be done at one time, it is rare for this process to be performed with less than 3 kilos. The crystallization is performed as quickly as possible, taking as little as 15 minutes, whereas a more professional procedure might take hours.

Because most illicit cocaine is made the quick way—with the emphasis on quantity—it often contains an alkaloid proportion similar to that which existed in the leaves themselves. This is not necessarily bad, because most consumers of cocaine seem to prefer the mellower high of mixed-alkaloid cocaine to the speedy but clear high of the pharmaceutical product. In medicine, since cocaine is used as a local anesthetic, the presence of other alkaloids makes it less effective as such. However, when the cocaine is used as a recreational drug, the same reasoning may not hold true.

§ 12.2.4 Extent of Use

During 2002, an estimated 1,059,000 persons in the United States, averaging 20.3 years of age used cocaine for the first time. According to the *2003 National Survey on Drug Use and Health*, approximately 34.9 million Americans, ages 12 and older, had tried cocaine at least once in their lifetimes, representing 14.7% of the population ages 12 and older. 5.9 million (2.5%) has used cocaine in the past year and 2.3 million (1.0%) had used cocaine within the past month (SAMHSA 2004).

Among students surveyed as part of the 2004 Monitoring the Future study, 3.4% of eighth graders, 5.4% of tenth graders, and 8.1% of twelfth graders reported using cocaine at least once during their lifetimes. In 2003, these percentages were 3.6%, 5.1%, and 7.7%, respectively. The Centers for Disease Control and Prevention (CDC) also conducts a survey of high school students throughout the United States, known as the Youth Risk Behavior Surveillance System (AIRBASE). Among students surveyed in 2003, 8.7% reported using some form of cocaine at least once during their life. Around 4.1% reported being current users of cocaine, meaning that they had used cocaine at least once during the past month (CDC 2004).

During 2003, 9.2% of college students and 14.7% of young adults (ages 19-28) reported using cocaine at least once during their lifetimes. Approximately 5.4% of college students and 6.6% of young adults reported past-year use of cocaine, and 1.9% of college students and 2.4% of young adults reported past-month use of cocaine (NIDA 2004).

According to the data from the Arrestee Drug Abuse Monitoring (ADAM) Program, a median of 30.1% of adult male arrestees and 35.3% of adult female arrestees tested positive for cocaine at arrest in 2003. The adult male samples were compiled from 39 U.S. sites and the adult female samples were compiled from 25 sites (NIJ 2004).

§ 12.3   TYPES OF COCAINE

There are a few types of cocaine on the illicit market today. The first product made from the leaves of the coca plant is coca paste, which is used to produce cocaine base. Dried cocaine base is usually dissolved in ethyl, acetone, or a mixture of both, and is filtered to remove solid impurities. Acetone or ethanol, combined with concentrated hydrochloric acid, precipitates cocaine hydrochloride. The precipitate is filtered and dried carefully using bright light to produce the white, crystalline powder, cocaine hydrochloride, or otherwise known simply as cocaine.

Cocaine hydrochloride, available on the street at 30 to 40 percent purity, remains the most common coca product in the United States. The predominant methods of cocaine abuse continue to be through inhaling and, to some extent, injecting cocaine hydrochloride. Normally, only the intravenous use of cocaine could be expected to deliver the more potent and rapid hit, however, very strong cultural prejudices against injecting recreational drugs developed and users grew dissatisfied with the enhanced mood and euphoria derived from just snorting cocaine HCL. So, users were introduced to the smoke-able form known as "freebase" cocaine.

Since the hydrochloride salt decomposes at the temperature required to vaporize it, cocaine is instead converted to the liberated form. Initially, freebase cocaine was typically produced using volatile solvents, usually ether. Unfortunately, this technique is physically dangerous as the solvent tends to ignite. Hence, a more convenient method of producing smokeable freebase became popular. Its product is crack. To obtain crack-cocaine, an ordinary cocaine hydrochloride is concentrated by heating the drug in a solution of baking soda until the water evaporates. This type of base-cocaine makes a cracking sound when heated; hence the name "crack". Base-cocaine vaporizes at a low temperature, so it can be easily inhaled via a heated pipe.

§ 12.3.1 The Appearance of Crack

Crack is an off-white color resembling coagulated soap powder or pieces of soap. Crack made either with baking soda or ammonia is smoked in a water pipe or sprinkled over a tobacco or marijuana cigarette and smoked. The word "crack" may also have come from the crackling sound made when it is smoked before it dries, or from its occasional resemblance to cracked paint chips or plaster.

§ 12.3.2 The Appearance of Cocaine Hydrochloride

Cocaine sold on the street is in the form of a white powdery substance, which resembles snowflakes, crystal, or lactose. This accounts for two of its nicknames: "crystal" and "snow." It is "cut" for street sale, much like heroin. (This means the drug is diluted with some other substance.)

The major visual indicator of cocaine is the consistency of the crystal formation. It has been said that cocaine crystals are like snowflakes, each being similar, but no two looking exactly alike. Good cocaine will come apart in layers. When cut with a razor blade it should crumble and be rather brittle. Moistness may mean the product has been stepped on recently. If you drop one of the crystals (chips) on a mirror, you should hear a tile-like click and not a dull thud. When the cocaine is pushed along a mirror with the razor blade to make lines, the lines should be uniform and not clumpy with a filmy trace on the mirror (white cut with mannite). Generally, good street cocaine will have a uniform off-white color with a bit of pearl luster as opposed to a harsh, bleached out brightness.

Some cocaine has been reconstituted in a lab. Reconstitution is a process whereby a pure product is broken down, then adulterants are added to it, making it impossible to distinguish crystal variations.

A gram of street cocaine contains approximately 10 "doses." This gram of cocaine is not the pure drug smuggled from Colombia or Peru, but rather has been "stepped on," with sugar or other substances. Cocaine is cut with mannitol, lactose, insitol, B-2 vitamin, amphetamines, caffeine, pseudo-cocaine, (Toot, super cocaine) and synthetic cocaine or local anesthetics such as procaine, benzocaine, lidocaine. These external pain killers found in sunburn lotions and toothache preparations have properties similar to cocaine and are a common rip-off. While they numb or freeze the nose and are bitter to the taste like cocaine,, they lack any stimulant properties.

§ 12.3.3 The Appearance of Black Cocaine
In February 1998, law enforcement discovered a new cocaine. It was developed by Columbian traffickers to avoid detection.

Cocaine HCL is mixed into a red/black powder substance, leading officials to dub it "black cocaine." The unique quality of this substance is produced by a combination of elements that create a reddish-black color and render most drug detection test kits (the ones based on color) useless. The DEA's El Paso Intelligence Center reported in 1999 that drug-detection canines also are not alerting on the presence of cocaine. According to German forensic analysis, the presence of iron thiocyanate prevents or masks a positive reading for cocaine during color reaction-based tests (i.e., Becton Dickinson test kits). However, the "Secured Drugwipe-Test" is one field test that is still effective.

Europe, Africa, South America, and North America have all experienced the phenomenon of black cocaine. Columbia has been the only reported country of origin, and according to DEA reports, high-ranking officials within the Colombian National Police have remarked publicly about their concern over this "new substance." Traffickers ship black cocaine from Colombia to market through fictitious companies, as well as through legitimate companies that are unaware of their involvement in the drug's transport.

The first seizure of black cocaine was reported by German Customs officials in March 1998 in their weekly information bulletin (*RG - INFOR*). A 15-kilogram postal package was intercepted and found to contain a homogeneous black powder labeled as industrial dye. After a Drugwipe-Test indicated the presence of cocaine, HCL further testing revealed that iron and potassium thiocyanate were mixed into the cocaine. The cocaine HCL would not have been sold in "black" form but instead would have been extracted by using a commonly available solvent, such as acetone or ether.

§ 12.4 METHODS OF USE OF COCAINE
§ 12.4.1 Oral Use

The historical literature on cocaine is filled with people who preferred other methods of ingestion besides snorting it. Oral ingestion of cocaine by chewing coca leaves with lime, of course, has been used by the natives of Andean South America for thousands of years. Circa 3,000 B.C., the natives of Valdivia, Ecuador, discovered that alkalinizing the mouth greatly facilitated the release of cocaine from coca and improved its absorption through the oral membranes. They did this by chewing lime made from burnt shells or plant ashes with coca. Lime, however, is very caustic and can burn the lips and mouth severely. Chewing coca is probably the best way to absorb cocaine. The effects are pleasingly different: more moderate and less harmful to the body than sniffing coke. But coca leaves are hard to find outside the Andes.

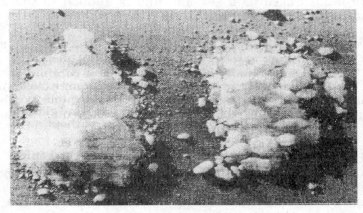

There is a much easier way to alkalinize the mouth for cocaine use. Dissolve one-fourth teaspoon of fresh baking soda in a cup of warm water and gargle several times with this solution, washing it around and spitting it out. Or simply put that amount of baking soda under the tongue and let it dissolve slowly. Alkalinizing the mouth in this way will facilitate the absorption of cocaine.

For many years, researchers thought that oral cocaine was inactive because it was changed chemically in the gastrointestinal tract. However, studies by Richard B. Resnick, M.D., and his co-workers have shown that oral coke gives a greater, though rather different, subjective high with much less cardiovascular effect than snorting the substance.

The disadvantage of oral ingestion, however, is that it is difficult to control the dosage, thus increasing the possibility of cocaine poisoning. Reactions to cocaine differ significantly, depending on the individual's tolerance and setting.

Another method of oral cocaine use is a hot-water infusion of coca sweetened with a little raw sugar, called Agua De Coca in the Andes, which is and used as a remedy for indigestion. Coca leaves also make an excellent tea. Angelo Mariani's Coca Tea sustained President Ulysses S. Grant in his later days, and gave him the strength to finish his memoirs.

The most famous alternative of all was concocted by Mariani in the 1860s—a comforting red wine made with coca-leaf extract added to a Bordeaux. In the 1880s, U.S. Surgeon General William Hammond, M.D., discovered that infinitesimally small doses of pure cocaine in wine—two grains of the hydrochloride to a pint of wine—was an excellent tonic for therapeutic purposes. Sigmund Freud noticed this and commented that Hammond himself "was for a long time in the habit of taking a wine glass full after the day's work and found himself refreshed each time, without any subsequent depression" (Byck). Freud's own favorite method of taking cocaine was to dissolve 0.05 grams of the hydrochloride in water (1 percent solution) and drink it.

Cocaine is also used as a sex aid, and is applied to the genital organs. A sprinkle of coke on the clitoris or just below the head of the penis will anesthetize the tissues and retard sexual climax. However, when cocaine was widely used as a surgical anesthetic early in the 20th century, doctors discovered that the urethra (the tube inside the penis or vulva through which urine is eliminated from the bladder) is very sensitive to cocaine; several patients died from constriction or collapse of the urethral canal. Also, cocaine severely dries delicate membranes, which explains why rubbing coke directly on the gums or membranes increases the likelihood of gum disease.

§ 12.4.2 Injecting of Cocaine

Some users inject the cocaine directly into the veins, a process similar to that of injecting heroin. They claim that when injecting cocaine, it is not advisable to heat the water solution because the heat and boiling tends to evaporate the cocaine. Also, cocaine is extremely soluble in water. By injecting cocaine, the person experiences an rush or euphoria within seconds. Users claim that the high from injecting cocaine will last from 45 to 90 minutes.

The intravenous route leads to paranoid states more often than when equivalent amounts are inhaled. Intravenous cocaine injections also carry with them the strong desire to repeat the event, much more so than the nasal route. The repetitious exposure of the cerebral neurones to high concentrations of cocaine produces alterations of brain metabolism that provoke distortions in thinking and perception in addition to the well-known emotional changes.

§ 12.4.3 Snorting Cocaine

A common method of using cocaine is by snorting, i.e., inhaling the cocaine into the nostrils. Snorting cocaine produces an immediate euphoric effect or rush that takes place within about 30 seconds and the user feels under the influence from 30 to 90 minutes. The rush from snorting cocaine allegedly is not quite as intensified as from injection or freebasing.

When snorting cocaine, the user will bring the powdered cocaine up to one nostril while holding the other nostril closed and sniff the cocaine into the nose. The user may vary from one nostril to another, but usually holds the other nostril closed for better suction. The immediate effect of snorting cocaine is a burning or freezing of the nostril area, depending on the purity of the cocaine and the substance with which the cocaine has been cut. If it has been cut with procaine, there will be more of a freezing. The user will normally snort anywhere from to gram at one time. Some users who want to maintain a constant high can snort cocaine all day long.

When the cocaine is snorted, a portion of the cocaine moves through the passages and bits are taken down through the throat. Other portions are taken in by the small capillaries in the mucous membrane and carried throughout the body to the brain. At times, however, some of the drug becomes lodged in the hairs of the nose and, if it remains for any length of time, tends to irritate the membrane, causing sores and bleeding. Cocaine constricts the blood vessels and anesthetizes the cilia that keep the mucous blanket moving over mucous membranes. Thus, the membranes dry out and stop functioning, leading very quickly to dryness, crusting, and ulceration in the nose. Small amounts of the drug can also become lodged in the sinus cavities resulting in congestion and related discomfort. In order to prevent such problems and maintain clear and unirritated nasal passages, many users will attempt to keep the cocaine very finely grained. This is achieved by chopping the cocaine with a razor blade or other sharp-edged instrument, or grinding the powder with a mortar and pestle. It is alleged that the finer the grain, the smaller the possibility of some of the cocaine being lodged in the nose or sinus. Some users will snort or drop water into the nose to help dislodge and dissolve any piece that may be held by the hairs.

§ 12.4.4 Smoking Cocaine Paste

Cocaine can be smoked either by freebasing it or by mixing the paste into a cigarette. In South America, a cocainized tobacco cigarette is called a pistola, or if mixed with marijuana, a "banana with cheese." Chemists in South American cocaine refineries often smoke paste, a crude and very impure form of cocaine sulfate, in this manner. But smoking paste, freebase or the hydrochloride can be very harmful to the lungs.

The first report of coca paste smoking came from Peru in 1974. Since then, the practice has spread to Colombia, Bolivia, Ecuador, Panama, and other countries. Sporadic instances of use are being seen in Los Angeles, San Francisco, and other cities. Coca paste is the first extraction product made during the manufacture of cocaine from the leaves of the coca bush. The leaves are mashed, then alkali, kerosene, and sulfuric acid are added. This procedure produces a white paste or semi-solid. It may contain up to 80 percent cocaine sulfate, other alkaloids that are found in coca leaves, benzoic acid, kerosene, sulfuric acid, and other impurities. It is usually sprinkled on tobacco or marijuana and smoked.

§ 12.4.5 Freebasing Cocaine

Resembling coca paste smoking in many ways is the smoking of alkaloidal cocaine in this country. Its popularity has been sufficient to generate a subindustry: the production of kits designed to convert the cocaine hydrochloride from street cocaine to freebase, or basic cocaine. These freebase kits are advertised and sold in paraphernalia shops. Freebase, then, is ordinarily made by the consumer.

Freebase is never sold as such. Rather, street coke—containing cocaine hydrochloride (a salt), various sugars (mannitol, glucose), and other cutting agents (xylocaine)—is treated, reducing the mixture to pure cocaine alkaloid; a white, slightly shiny powder. This process increases the potency of the drug.

Freebase is not soluble in water, not bitter to the taste, and is ineffective if snorted or eaten. What it does is vaporize more easily than cocaine hydrochloride, melting at body temperature and making it readily suitable for smoking. Because freebase doesn't burn, it must be either sprinkled on a cigarette or consumed in a pipe designed for this purpose. These freebase pipes consist of a bowl with multi-layered screens. A flame is applied to the bowl, volatizing the drug as it melts and drips from screen to screen.

Freebase enters the bloodstream through the lungs, and the high is felt before the smoke is exhaled. The euphoria lasts for only a few minutes and the primary kick is the instantaneous and intense rush. So strong is the brief high that repetitive and excessive usage is common. Compulsive consumption of this expensive drug is far greater among "baseballers" than among the cocaine snorting contingent.

Overdosing is a greater risk with freebase because of the increased purity, more efficient route of administration, and the compulsive desire to re-experience the ultra short rush.

§ 12.5 COMPARING CRACK AND FREEBASE

Crack was first detected in Southern California in 1981, and was documented in New York City during the summer of 1985.

§ 12.5.1 Processing

Freebasing is a process of converting cocaine hydrochloride (HCL) back to cocaine base for smoking. Traditional freebasing involves heating ether or other flammable solvents as the critical part of the extraction process.

Central Nervous System Stimulant Drugs

Crack is made by adding baking soda (or ammonia) and water to cocaine HCL. The mixture is heated and cooled, then filtered to collect the crystals. The result of the process is cocaine base (crack).

There are differences and similarities between crack and traditional cocaine freebasing. Freebase processing creates an extremely hazardous situation in which the risks of explosion and fire are quite high. Crack processing, on the other hand, eliminates the use of flammable solvents and the risks of explosion and fire.

FREEBASE PROCESS	CRACK PROCESS
Removes dilutents	Removes dilutents
Solvents used	Does not require solvents
Danger of explosion/fire	No danger of explosion/fire
Powdery material produced	Hard flaky material produced
End product is cocaine freebase	End product is cocaine freebase

§ 12.5.2 Use of Crack and Freebase

Traditionally, cocaine freebase is smoked through a water pipe in which the substance was originally produced or sprinkled on a marijuana or tobacco cigarette and smoked. Crack is sprinkled on a marijuana or tobacco cigarette, or mixed with either of these substances and smoked in a pipe.

Upon inhalation, both freebase and crack are rapidly absorbed by the lungs and carried to the brain within a matter of a few seconds. The user experiences a sudden and very intense "rush" with euphoria that suddenly subsides into a feeling of restlessness, irritability, and, in cases of sustained use, post-euphoric depression. This post-euphoric period may be so uncomfortable that freebase and crack smokers continue smoking, often in marathon binges, until they become exhausted or run out of cocaine.

Crack is sold on the streets, usually packaged in small vials, glassine envelopes, or film canisters, at purity levels between 60 and 90 percent. Although amounts vary, a small vial contains an average of $1/10$ to $1/2$ gram, priced as low as $3 to as high as $50; generally, prices range from $10-20. A vial of 100 milligrams can provide one, two, or three inhalations when smoked in a pipe, depending on how deeply the user breathes.

The low price per dose attracts buyers, while giving the dealer a substantial profit. Since crack users often crave more immediately after smoking, they purchase more cocaine in the crack form than they may have if they had used cocaine hydrochloride regularly.

Crack is sold on the street or in crack houses, also known as rock, base, freebase, or smoke houses. Crack houses generally are apartments or houses. The definition of what constitutes a crack house varies from city to city. In some cities, a user can both purchase and smoke the drug on the premises. In others, a user can only purchase the drug and is not allowed entry. Still in others, a user must bring his own crack, because the drug is not sold on the premises; the house simply provides a room and a pipe for smoking crack.

It is generally believed that the desire for a more intense "high" without the complications and dangers involved in freebasing with ether, or injecting cocaine with hypodermic needles that could spread AIDS, has been the reason for smoking crack as an alternative form of use.

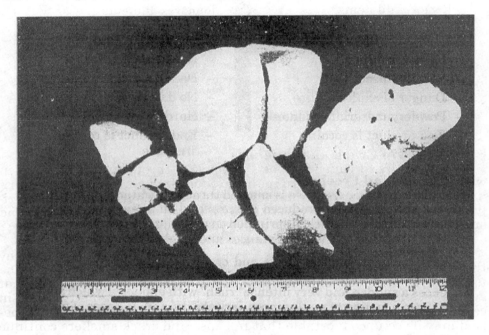

WHOLESALE QUANTITY OF CRACK COCAINE

§ 12.5.3 Popularity of Crack
In Los Angeles, crack accounts for 90 percent of street-level cocaine seizures.

The advent of crack can be held responsible for the recent broadening of the cocaine market into lower-income populations, as it appears to be the almost exclusively preferred form of use by low-income cocaine users.

Some confusion has arisen, both in law enforcement and among laypersons, as to what purpose rock cocaine serves the user. Freebasing was uncommon during the original cocaine vogue of the 1970s and early 1980s. Cocaine hydrochloride is also a perfectly usable form of the drug. So why does today's user go to the trouble of making rock cocaine?

Central Nervous System Stimulant Drugs

The main attraction of crack is that it renders cocaine smokeable. Cocaine in the bloodstream, regardless of its form before ingestion, is rapidly metabolized to its relatively inert components. The cocaine high is therefore dependent on how rapidly the drug can be absorbed. The serious cocaine user's goal is to get quantities of cocaine into the bloodstream as quickly as possible. In this respect, smoking is much more efficient than snorting as the lungs give much more surface area for absorption than the nasal passages and deliver absorbed substances to the bloodstream much more directly. The same difference also accounts for the swiftness of the freebase high. Smoking cocaine delivers the drug to the body all at once—where it is quickly eliminated. Snorting, by contrast, dribbles cocaine into the system a little at a time, giving a less intense, but longer-lasting, effect.

Cocaine must be freebased to be smokeable because normal cocaine hydrochloride vaporizes at a very high temperature. Freebase cocaine vaporizes at 187° C, a temperature within the reach of an ordinary butane lighter (and tolerable to the human lungs). Hydrochloride can be smoked, and occasionally is, but it will burn rather than vaporize, causing most of the drug to be wasted in the process. Conversely, freebase has to be smoked in order to be used efficiently, since it is not very soluble in water. Freebase cocaine works best when delivered through the lungs as a gas.

Another advantage of smoking over snorting is that, by smoking, the user protects himself from the famous "rat's nose" syndrome. By trying to absorb large quantities of cocaine through the small surface area of the nasal membranes, coke snorters often suffer severe corrosive damage to these tissues. Smoking freebase spreads the burden over the much larger surface area of the lungs. Of course, chronic smoking may turn out to be just as bad for the lungs as chronic snorting is for the nose.

§ 12.5.4 Los Angeles Crack

Newspaper reports crack cocaine in Los Angeles did not appear until late 1985, more than 5 years after smoking base cocaine had already become popular among specific groups in south central Los Angeles. The use of former drugs such as heroin and PCP began to decline in 1980, coinciding with the growing popularity of cocaine smoking at neighborhood parties and social clubs. In south central Los Angeles, simple conversion recipes that made use of baking soda for rocking up cocaine circulated at parties. The method was spread to adjacent areas by drug dealers who had observed the process.

By 1983, neighborhood drug dealers saw an opportunity to enhance their profits by marketing cocaine pre-prepared in a smokeable form. By 1984, competition led to new marketing strategies. Some dealers sold base or rock cocaine in small, more affordable amounts. They gave the substance catchy names like "crack." Between 1984 and 1985, base cocaine rose precipitously in popularity, overwhelming municipal and county agencies. Police developed new tactics to close down street and indoor market for crack or rock.

Chapter 12

§ 12.5.5 "Crack" Cocaine Cut with Procaine Base

The DEA Western Laboratory, San Francisco, California, received an exhibit of "crack" cocaine containing 2418.5 grams of 69 percent cocaine base with most of the balance of the material being procaine base. The sample consisted of large solid chunks of a uniform yellowish-white waxy material. The material was collected in Oakland, California, and was referred to on the street as "Mr. Coffee" because some of the larger chunks of the material appeared to conform to the shape of the inside of the glass coffee pot used with the "Mr. Coffee" coffee machine.

The Western Laboratory also received two additional samples of a similar material from the Seattle-Tacoma, Washington area. One sample consisted of 110 grams of 24 percent cocaine base with most of the balance being procaine base, and one contained 28.5 grams of 45 percent cocaine base also mixed with procaine base (USDOJ 1991).

Rock cocaine seems to be solidly entrenched as a major part of the narcotics industry.

§ 12.5.6 Effects of Freebasing Cocaine

Smoking freebase has a tremendously stimulating physical effect. The rush lasts only a short time, but it can be extremely exhilarating. The user gets a sensation of floating off on a wonderful cloud of euphoria, a feeling that rivals a hang-glider ride or a cruise in a sailplane.

The chronic cocaine user progresses through three phases with continuous drug use: euphoria, dysphoria, and paranoid psychosis.

Smoking freebase with its two-minute super-high evokes an enormous desire to keep on "basing." Again, the rapid shift from ecstasy to misery impels many users to keep smoking until they or their freebase are exhausted. This is understandable. After all, relief from their desolation is at hand from a single puff.

The results of smoking freebase, either in a special pipe or sprinkled on a cigarette, are identical to smoking coca paste or injecting cocaine hydrochloride intravenously. Mydriasis, tachycardia, increased blood pressure, and respiration rates are the autonomic effects. The rush is sudden and intense, producing feelings of energy, power and competence. After a few minutes, the euphoric high subsides into a restless irritability. The residual "wired up" state is so intolerable that a heroin habit may be started to relieve the tense and over-strung feeling. Sleep is impossible during a freebase binge, but exhaustion eventually supervenes. Enormous weight loss takes place in heavy users due to the anorectic action of cocaine. Manic, paranoid, or depressive psychoses have been seen. Overdose can cause death due to cardiorespiratory arrest.

Chronic users of freebase sometimes report bizarre skin phenomena like amber crystals and/or, more commonly, black specks that appear to come right out of the skin. These experiences are not commonplace, and the casual or part-time user of freebase may never encounter them; however, they deserve mention because they do occur and are therefore a possibility for anyone who freebases. These phenomena are so peculiar they are talked about very little.

In Siegel's book, *Freebasing: Hazards from Smoking Cocaine*, he estimates it takes about three months to lose control of use. Siegel writes: "Unlike LSD where you observe the hallucinations, with freebase the hallucinations become a direct part of your reality." Siegel does extensive counseling. He goes on to recite the already famous case of one of his patients who became convinced that worms were crawling out of his body and brought Siegel bits of skin he had tweezed from his arms. "The guy was totally convinced the worms were real," Siegel says. "All he wanted to know from me, in fact, was how they could have contaminated his cocaine supply to begin with."

§ 12.6   MEDICAL USE OF COCAINE
Cocaine is a local anesthetic used to control topical pain and in surgery on the nose, mouth, throat, as well as the eyes. Largely replaced in today's medical armamentarium by synthetic anesthetics such as lidocaine and procaine, it has some attractive abilities. It lasts longer and its vasoconstrictive properties prevent bleeding. But even with these advantages, the abuse potential severely curtailed medical application.

Recently, however, there has been a renaissance in the medical use of the drug, which is the result of a preparation whose value in terminal care is unsurpassed. Formulated in England and called Brompton's Mixture, its British recipe contained heroin and cocaine with gin or brandy. Transported to America, it is generally prepared as morphine and cocaine with gin or another alcoholic vehicle. Most observers working with the terminally ill report marked improvement. The stimulating effect of the cocaine apparently counteracts the dull, lethargic effect of the pain killer morphine. For with morphine and the other narcotics, the price paid for freedom from pain is often a listless patient who can barely distinguish between the dreams induced by the narcotics and the real world around him. The addition of cocaine in many cases gives bedridden and incoherent patients the ability to become ambulatory and lucid.

While relief for the painfully dying is welcomed, the increased use of medical cocaine means greater opportunity for diversion and the need for increased monitoring by law enforcement agencies.

§ 12.7   COCAINE COSTS AND PACKAGING
The pure cocaine that Merck Company sells to the pharmacists for $1.35 a gram (1 oz. costs $39) has little resemblance to the street cocaine. Pure cocaine is a light, extremely shiny, flaky white powder. Illicit cocaine is dulled by the cut. The amount of the remaining gleam is often in direct proportion to the percentage of cocaine.

The varied measurements of street cocaine can be as confusing as the amount of pure cocaine in the "buy." Generally sold by the gram, it is also retailed by "lines" (four lines, "two by two") or by the "spoon," approximately a teaspoonful. One author calculated the cost of heroin

Chapter 12

to cocaine, concluding that to stay high on cocaine costs 10 times as much.

§ 12.8   THE CHEMISTRY OF COCAINE

The alkaloid content of the coca leaf is about 0.5 percent to 2.0 percent, with cocaine representing about 50 percent to 75 percent of total alkaloid. The crude alkaloid may be extracted with dilute acid, made alkaline, and re-extracted into organic solvents. It is also quite possible to hydrolyze the alkaloid mixture to re-esterify and purify the cocaine through ethanolic recrystallization. Cocaine in its free form has molecular weight of 303 and a melting point of 98° C. Cocaine as hydrochloride salt has a molecular weight of 339 and a melting point of 197° C. The hydrochloride is soluble in water and ethanol, the freebase of cocaine, is soluble in organic solvents such as ether or chloroform.

Studies on the bodily distribution of cocaine in various animals clearly show penetration of the drug into all tissues examined, with the highest levels in liver, kidney, heart, and fat tissues (Dendow et al). Significant concentrations of cocaine were present in the brain and appeared to persist at low levels for several weeks after use. The drug was readily metabolized and primarily excreted in the urine and feces during the first 24 hours. In the animals studied, cocaine was metabolized to norecgonine, ecgonine, and a host of hyphoxylated derivatives. All these compounds are quite active pharmacologically, except for ecgonine, which does not appear to exhibit cocaine-like effects.

Studies in humans, although limited in scope, indicate that peak plasma levels of cocaine are reached at the first sampling (five minutes) after IV administration (Fischman et al). Eight hours after injection, the drug was no longer detectable. Benzoylecgonine, however, was detectable for a period of at least 24 hours after IV use. Interestingly, the biological half-life of cocaine following either IV or intranasal use was about 2.6 hours. Although both cocaine and benzoylecgonine were detected in urine for a full 8 hours, the cocaine levels were generally one-tenth that of the metabolite benzoylecgonine. Cocaine is generally excreted from humans in a form containing the following substances: the free drug itself, the metabolites benzoylecgonine, norcocaine, and ecgonine, as well as several hydroxylated derivatives of these metabolites.

§ 12.8.1   Physiological Effects

The primary medical use of cocaine today is as a local anesthetic in surgery because of the well-controlled vasoconstrictive action. In the central nervous system, cocaine alters neurotransmitters and can concomitantly alter electrical activity in the brain. Although some conflicting data appear to exist regarding the effect of cocaine on neurotransmitters, it most likely stimulates the release of dopamine, norepinephrine, and serotonin while blocking the reuptake of these same substances in the nerve terminal.

Concerning the electrical alterations that occur following cocaine administration, some studies showed that persistent low voltage fast waves occurred in the electroencephalogram (EEG) with subsequent increases in alertness as well as heart and respiratory rates, which lasted for periods of one to two hours (Dackis et al). Chronic administration of cocaine caused permanent changes in the EEG and in behavioral depression, along with the apparent development of tolerance to the convulsant and cardiorespiratory effects of the drug (Fischman et al).

The effect of cocaine on the cardiovascular system is direct. The heart rate increases and the blood pressure is raised through vasoconstriction. Respiration, however, is stimulated primarily through a direct effect on the medullary respiratory center. Through peripheral vasoconstriction as well as increased muscular activity, cocaine also causes an increase in body temperature (ASPET).

Generally 1 to 2 grams of cocaine are considered to be a lethal dose in humans; however, the route of administration plays an important role in overall toxicity. Death through cocaine overdose normally consists of convulsions coupled with cardiorespiratory failure. However, the data available on cocaine deaths frequently indicate the involvement of other drugs (opiates, amphetamines, barbiturates) ("Implications of Crack"). Therefore, the actual percentage of deaths due to cocaine alone is smaller than the total number of deaths involving cocaine.

§ 12.8.2 Psychological, Neurochemical, and Behavioral Correlates

As indicated previously, cocaine may be taken in a variety of ways: intravenous injection, oral ingestion, smoking, snorting (intranasal), or simply applied to a variety of mucous membranes—genital, oral, or rectal. Certainly the immediacy, the intensity, and the duration of the cocaine effect is related to the mode of administration. These methods produce euphoria, hyperstimulation, increased heart rate, increased respiration, hyperflexion, alertness, and feelings of grandiosity and power. These effects are accompanied by an increase in the level of 5-hydroxytryptophan and, to some extent, the levels of dopamine, norepinephrine, and epinephrine in the brain (Hammer et al).

The tremendous desire to repeat the experience and counter any depressive effects leads to compulsive chronic use of cocaine. Such activity usually causes a decrease or depletion in the neurotransmitters (DA=dopamine; E=norepinephrine; 5HT=5-hydroxtrytophan) and over time causes overt depression, dysphoria, paranoia, hallucinatory experiences, and sometimes destructive anti-social behavior.

In addition to the primary neurotransmitters mentioned, cocaine has effects on acetylcholine, and these effects may alter locomotor function and interfere with mental activity leading to confusion and poor coordination. In effect, cocaine can cause serious central neurochemical imbalances or changes that must be restored in order to achieve normal functioning after sustained chronic use of the drug. Unfortunately the myriad changes occurring in the CNS are not yet well understood nor in fact fully revealed. Full knowledge of the central and peripheral neurochemical changes may well lead to more effective means of treating the problem clinically.

§ 12.8.3 Tolerance

Most drug abusers show development of tolerance to the pharmacological effects after continued chronic use. However, in the case of cocaine there is a belief that chronic use leads to an increase in sensitivity or essentially no changes in the effect of the drug in man. In animals, however, a definite tolerance occurs to the convulsive dose and to the cardiovascular and respiratory action of cocaine when given repetitively. The issue of physical dependence is also raised following chronic use of cocaine. Certainly depression, insomnia, agitation, and lethargy (behavioral depression) were observed following cessation of chronic cocaine use and were indicative (along with the neurochemical changes) of some degree of physical dependence. The high-level drug-seeking behavior exhibited by cocaine users clearly demonstrates the existence of psychological dependence. It is, of course, the psychic drive to repeat the cocaine experience that encompasses compulsive obsessive behavior and is the core problem associated with illicit cocaine use. It is this pernicious drug-seeking, drug-reinforcing effect of cocaine that engenders continued abuse by the user with subsequent detrimental effects to both the individual and society.

§ 12.9 COCAINE ADDICTION

Many scientists are now revising their notions about cocaine addiction. People do seem to develop tolerance, which is part of the classical definition of addiction. They need larger quantities of the drug to get high, and may never again experience the ecstasy of their first episodes. Some believe that a person's brain chemistry makes the addict: "The brain and cocaine may be like a lock and a key." Or, "cocaine addiction—like alcoholism—isn't a sign of psychological weakness. It's a result of the drug's interaction with a person's brain chemistry." Some people say, "That's what's been missing from my life to make me feel wonderful," while others remain unaffected.

Scientists concede that there are those who can use small amounts of cocaine infrequently without showing any obvious physical damage or becoming obsessed with the drug (Erickson et al). The latest hypothesis, however, is that cocaine may damage the brain by slow steps. Charles Schuster, a professor of pharmacology at the University of Chicago, found that amphetamines lower the overall amounts of some neurotransmitters in the brains of rats, monkeys, and guinea pigs (Wagner et al). In Schuster's studies, the reduction persisted for as long as three years after the last time the animals were given the drugs, leading Schuster to believe that the neurons involved may be permanently incapacitated (Preston). Although more experiments are under way, the prognosis doesn't look good. Schuster concludes, "I suspect that cocaine will also damage the brains of these animals. When something happens across several species, you think more seriously about the pertinence to humans." At present, doctors don't know how to predict who will develop a physiological need for cocaine and who won't.

§ 12.9.1 Cocaine Toxicity

Cocaine toxicity occurs regardless of the route of administration. Frequently, the cocaine toxicity is what actually brings a person in for medical treatment, rather than any great desire to stop using the drug.

Central Nervous System Stimulant Drugs

Cocaine can have an adverse effect on the mucous lining of any part of the body. In addition, it can adversely affect the sinuses, the trachea, and the lungs. It is not uncommon for persons who are freebasers to complaint of severe respiratory problems. Freebasers may destroy the ability of their lung cells to process gases, leaving them with a constant cough and often shortness of breath. It is felt that the side effects experiences with freebasing are as much due to the propane torch used to heat the cocaine as from the drug itself. The iris and the conjunctivae are irritated at a result of persons snorting cocaine via the nasal route of administration, and there have been instances of cocaine crystals ending up in the retina, apparently as a result of retrograde circulation from the nasal cavity. Skin abscesses and cellulitis occur in individuals who are "skin poppers." After the veins are destroyed, these persons will begin injecting the drug directly into the skin and subcutaneous tissue.

X-rays of the sinuses are taken on individuals who have a 6-month or longer history of continuous cocaine snorting. Sinus X-rays of a 23-year-old referred for cocaine abuse demonstrated a large abscess of the right maxillary sinus (The Narc Officer 1990). This is not at all uncommon. Three days after admission, this young man sneezed and saved the material in a tissue, as it was unlike anything he had ever sneezed out before. This material was actually the remaining third of his nasal septum. Ear, nose, and throat surgeons generally do not surgically repair the nasal septums of cocaine abusers. Rather, they replace the nasal septum with a prosthetic device, the nasal septum button. This is placed in the nasal cavity and rides on either side of the remaining bone. The person wears this for the rest of his or her life.

Sudden death from cocaine use is usually a result of seizures of cardiac arrhythmia (Wetli et al). There is a misconception that persons who snort cocaine cannot die from these complications. There appears to be a lowering of the seizure threshold in many people who have a long history of cocaine abuse (Inaba et al). This phenomenon of subcortical stimulation by a particular drug that results in seizures and sometimes death is referred to as "kindling." This is not a new phenomenon and has been identified in the past with amphetamine abuse. This minimum lethal dose, taken orally, has been demonstrated to be 1.4 grams. Certainly, this is not a large amount of cocaine to be consumed on a one-time basis. Many cocaine abusers use several grams on a given day. The minimum dose that produces seizures of a nonfatal variety was in the case of a cocaine-addicted physician. He convulsed after orally consuming only one gram of cocaine. Acute fatalities are generally in people who have been abusing cocaine over an extended period of time. Sometimes cocaine crystals are found around the nose, or the syringe with which the cocaine was administered may be still lodged in the vein. When death is caused by cocaine-induced seizure, the person very often has such a violent tetanic reaction that the fingernails will be buried in the palms of the hand and the teeth will have bitten through the lower lip and the distal third of the tongue—in some cases, biting all the way through the tongue itself.

The route of cocaine administration will sometimes dictate compulsive use. It appears that as many as nine out of every ten individuals who abuse cocaine via the nasal route are able to continue to do so on a recreational basis. It also appears, however, that when users change from the nasal route to the system of freebasing, the brain is so enamored of the freebasing method that the person quickly develops a compulsive use habit. With this sort of change in the route of cocaine administration, a $300 per week habit may be quickly replaced by a $300 per day habit.

§ 12.9.2 Cocaine and Alcohol (Cocaethylene)
Cocaethylene is a psychoactive ethyl homologue of cocaine and is formed inclusively during the co-administration of cocaine and alcohol. The human liver combines cocaine and alcohol and manufacturers a third substance, cocaethylene.

Not a natural alkaloid of the coca leaf, cocaethylene can be identified in the urine, blood, hair, and neurological and liver tissue samples of individuals who have consumed both cocaine and alcohol. It is similar to cocaine. It increases dopomine (brain chemical) synaptic content, provoking enhanced stimulation resulting in euphoria, reinforcement, and continued use. Cocaethylene appears to be more euphoric and rewarding than cocaine. The combination of cocaine and alcohol appears to exert more cardiovascular toxicity than either drug alone in humans. Alcohol appears to potentiate cocaine toxicity in both humans and mice (Landry).

§ 12.9.3 Under the Influence
Being under the influence of cocaine means that there is physical evidence of cocaine present in the body, e.g., dilated pupils, hyperactive nervous system, muscle relaxation, and cocaine found in blood or urine. Since cocaine's activity level in the body is 3 to 6 hours following use, the term "under the influence" is restricted to users who show physical evidence of cocaine during its activity period of 3 to 6 hours.

Cocaine can be found in the blood for as long as 6 to 8 hours after a single dose. Since cocaine in blood correlates with the activity of cocaine and "influence," the presence of cocaine in the blood should be considered absolute evidence of "influence."

Because cocaine affects people differently, there are various situations in which you may encounter a user under the influence of cocaine. It is essential to find cocaine in the urine. In addition to this essential evidence of cocaine influence, it is necessary to have supporting evidence in the following types of arrest situations.:

—Observe dilated pupils above 6.5 mm and cocaine derivative in the urine.

—Find pupils between 5.0 and 6.5 mm with 1 or 2 control subjects who have smaller pupils in the same light (photographs of pupils of user and control subject should be taken for documentation) and the presence of fresh needle marks or cocaine residue in the nasal passage and cocaine derivative found in the urine.

—Observe evidence of muscle relaxation that would include droopy eyelids, slurred or slow speech, abnormal gait, and nodding. There must also be the presence of cocaine residue in the nasal passage or fresh needle marks and a negative alcohol breath, blood, or urine test, and, of course, cocaine derivative in the urine.

—Observe evidence of central nervous system hyperactivity, including increased speech rate, excessive sweating, pulse over 110 per minute, respiration over 25 per minute (requires two observers), and presence of cocaine in the nasal passage or fresh needle marks. Cocaine derivative must be found in the urine.

—Observe evidence of paranoia, hallucinations, or delusions and the presence of cocaine in the nasal passage or fresh needle marks and cocaine derivative found in the urine.

§ 12.9.4 Examination of a Cocaine Suspect

When you are examining a cocaine suspect for evidence of cocaine use, look for the following:

–Rapidity of speech (low dose)
–Slowing or slurred speech (high dose)
–Agitated or hyperstimulated appearance (low dose)
–Sedated or sleepy appearance (high dose)
–High pulse and respiration rate
–Pupil size (compare the control subject in the same light)
–Needle marks
–Presence of cocaine in nasal passages
–Hallucinations or delusions
–Cocaine in blood or urine

Remember that cocaine's acute physical effects may last only 1 or 2 hours after use. Some acute effects of cocaine are rapid speech, local anesthesia, pupil dilation, increase in heart rate and blood pressure, mood elevation, increase in respiration and reflexes, relaxation, and impaired motor functions. However, when the physical effects such as increase in speech rate, pulse, pupil dilation are observed, there is almost always evidence of the presence of cocaine in the nasal passage or a fresh needle mark. Also, cocaine has a short duration of activity that correlates with the influence on the human body. A single dose may last about 3 to 4 hours, and cocaine cannot be found in the blood past about 6 hours.

Nasal examination is indispensable for cocaine documentation. After snorting cocaine, residue remains in the septum, which makes excellent evidence. The residue is brown, black, white, or gray, often resembling plain dirt. To examine for residue, have the subject lean back the head, and look at septum of nose with a flashlight.

Although in very small and occasional doses, it is no more harmful than equally moderate doses of alcohol or marijuana, and infinitely less so than heroin, cocaine has a dark and destructive side. The euphoric lift is often followed by a letdown. Regular use can induce depression, edginess, and weight loss. As usage increases, so does the danger of paranoia, hallucinations, and a totally "strung out" physical collapse, not to mention a devastation of the nasal membrane. Says one initiate, "After one hit of cocaine I feel like a new man. The only problem is, the first thing the new man wants is another hit." This pattern can lead to a psychological dependence by which the effects are not all that different from addiction. Moreover, there is a growing clinical evidence that when coke is taken in the most potent and dangerous forms—injected in solution, or chemically converted and smoked—it is addictive.

§ 12.9.5 Miosis and Stimulants

The evaluation of a person under the influence of methamphetamine, a CNS stimulant, is the presence of pupil dilation called mydriasis. However, there have been many reports from California law enforcement where the chronic cocaine users did not always have dilated pupils, but, in fact, the pupils were slightly constricted. The eye is made up of the sclera, iris, and pupil. One possible answer to this phenomenon of constriction or miosis concerns the iris, which controls the opening and closing of the pupil in relationship to various light stimuli. The eye, in a person not affected by drug influence or some other medical or physical reason, should work like a camera. The pupil should dilate in minimal light and constrict in bright light.

A group of chemicals that regulate the opening and closing of the iris are the catecholamines. Catecholamines are important endogenous regulators of hormone secretions from a number of glands and major body organs and functions. In the human liver, the effects of catecholamines are mediated by beta receptors. One of the major catecholamines is epinephrine or adrenaline. Adrenaline activates beta receptors in certain vessels, leading, consequently, to total peripheral system failure. The iris function is a part of this peripheral system.

Central nervous system stimulants like cocaine are similar to adrenaline. However, they enter the central nervous system much more rapidly and have a marked effect on mood and alertness, and a depressant effect on the appetite. Peripheral actions are mediated primarily through the release of catecholamines. There is a condition called Horners' syndrome, a condition resulting from the interruption of the sympathetic nerves to the face, including the eyes, in which it causes pupillary constriction. The abnormally constricted pupil in such a case will not dilate in response to a drug like cocaine or amphetamines. It seems that this phenomenon, which has been reported throughout the law enforcement community and usually involves chronic drug users, should provide some explanation of eye miosis when the eyes should be dilated.

§ 12.9.6 Cocaine Overdose

The average quantity of cocaine necessary to produce death by overdose is 1.2 grams ingested within 30 minutes. This amount may vary considerably depending upon such factors as body weight, metabolic rate, or condition of health. One common symptom of overdose is a loss of control. Frequently the user will not be aware of his or her condition. The user may tremble, yet say, "Oh, it's nothing"; the person may tell you everything is fine, but not be able to stop moving. Observe the following overdose symptoms as well:

—Extremely nervous, irritable, and belligerent
—Excessively cold
—Dilated pupils
—Unnaturally pale
—Nauseated: feels queasy, throws up, or tries to throw up
—Seek medical aid immediately if the person
—Passes out (loses consciousness)
—Has a seizure or convulsion
—Is disoriented: Does person know who you are? Does person know who/where he/she is?
—Is hallucinating, jumping uncontrollably, hysterical, or babbling
—Has tachycardia (extremely rapid heartbeat). Cocaine stimulates the flow of adrenaline, which can increase the heart (pulse) rate to a dangerous level.

A person showing signs of overdose will continue to come on to the drug for at least another half an hour, so it is important to remove the drug at the first sign of overdose. If help is unavailable, get the person to lie down and be quiet in a peaceful atmosphere. Elevate the legs and slightly lower the head.

People fearing involvement, for whatever reason, and facing the alternative of totally abandoning the overdosed person have used the following option: They took the overdosed person to a hospital emergency room with a note pinned or put in a pocket briefly stating the problem (cocaine overdose) and left immediately refusing to answer questions, or just left the person outside near a main entrance to the emergency room.

Summary of signs indicating cocaine use:

1. Cocaine paraphernalia

2. Dilated pupils

3. Redness and sores around the nose

4. Rapid breathing and pulse rate

5. Hyperactive, bizarre and/or paranoid behavior

6. Skin itching

7. Perspiration on the forehead and neck

8. Extreme desire for liquid

9. Redness in the eyes due to lack of sleep

10. Dark brown deposits on the tongue and teeth

11. Needle marks and tracks

12. Sunglasses to shield the eyes

§ 12.9.7 When to Suspect Chronic Cocaine Use in Someone

Only a blood or urine test will definitely diagnose cocaine use. However, you should suspect chronic cocaine use if you observe a combination of any of the following:

—Dilated pupils
—Talks and walks too fast
—Nose may constantly run, appear red, or person may sniff frequently
—Sudden disappearances from work or school
—Work or school performance deteriorates
—Time distortion, including tardiness, unusual meal times, and missed appointments
—Chronic forgetfulness or broken promises
—Frequent auto accidents and/or traffic violations
—Falls asleep during the day
—Loss of interest and motivation at work or school
—Needle marks with intravenous use
—With freebasing, tips of fingers and nails may erode
—Weight loss
—Mental confusion or paranoia
—Chronic cocaine use may cause the following health complications:
—Rhinitis, sinusitis, bronchitis, and respiratory ailments
—Nasal ulcers and/or perforation of nasal septum
—Paranoia
—Severe depression and lack of energy
—Addiction or dependence
—Chronic insomnia
—Weight loss and malnutrition
—Skin eruptions due to excessive itching

Note: Available studies show that chronic cocaine use may deplete the brain of the chemicals norepinephrine and/or dopamine. Loss of brain chemicals provides a rational explanation for many of the behaviors and symptoms of the chronic cocaine user (Smith et al).

Some social problems associated with chronic cocaine use include the following:

—Loss of desire to work or attend school
—Disregard for time deadlines
—Marital discord
—Resorting to illegal activities to support habit
—Switching to heroin or alcohol abuse
—Accidents
—Violence and fights

§ 12.9.8 Cocaine Withdrawal Symptoms

Below is a table of the most common cocaine withdrawal symptoms. These symptoms and their frequency among cocaine users were determined in a study of 49 cocaine-dependent persons conducted by Dr. Forest Tennant.

Symptoms	# Who Experienced Symptoms*
Craving for cocaine	41 (83.7%)
Depression	39 (79.6 %t)
Irritable	35 (71.4 %)
Increased appetite	35 (71.4 %)
Sleep increase	33 (67.3 %)
Lethargy	32 (65.3 %)
Weakness	23 (46.9 %)
Confused thoughts	19 (38.8 %)
Loss memory	19 (38.8 %)
Abnormal taste and smell	19 (38.8 %)
Anxious	13 (26.5 %)

*It should be noted that subjects experienced and reported more than one symptom during withdrawal.

§ 12.9.9 How to Make a Diagnosis of Cocaine Addiction of Dependence

Addiction or dependence is to be assumed to be present if the following are evident:

—Person states he/she has used cocaine 4 to 5 times/day for 30 or more consecutive days.
—Person states he/she cannot stop without medical assistance.
—Person states that he/she experiences withdrawal symptoms or sickness when stopping for over 24 hours.
—Cocaine is present in urine or plasma.

§ 12.10 COCAINE METABOLISM

If taken intranasally, cocaine reaches its peak plasma level after about 30 to 60 minutes. If taken intravenously or by freebasing, it reaches peak plasma levels within 5 to 10 minutes.

Cocaine is converted in the blood to benzoylecgonine. This metabolite is what is usually detected in the urine. Cocaine metabolite appears in the urine about one hour after it is used, and it can be detected in urine for about 48 hours.

Cocaine can be found in the plasma for up to 4 to 6 hours after ingestion, although it is present in very low plasma concentrations after 1 to 1.5 hours. A plasma concentration of 10 mg/ml or greater should be considered to be evidence of cocaine "influence."

§ 12.10.1   Urine and Blood Testing for Cocaine Detection

Urine or blood testing is essential for diagnosing cocaine use. There are several techniques that will accurately detect the qualitative presence of cocaine metabolite in urine. The amount of cocaine in the urine is not very important—only the fact that it is present or absent.

Hindrances to accurate blood testing:
—Cost
—Lack of equipment
—No qualified blood drawers or technicians to operate equipment
—Test performed too seldom for technician to be competent
—Lack of adequate veins to draw blood from the user

If cocaine is present in plasma at a level above 10 ng/ml, cocaine activity can be assumed to be present.

§ 12.10.2   Negative Urine Tests: Causes & How to Avoid Them

Causes of negative urine tests:
1. Urine specimen collected too soon. Most abusable drugs will not show in urine for about 1 to 2 hours after use.

2. Urine specimen collected too late. About 90 percent is eliminated by 48 hours after last use.

3. Too little of the drug in urine specimen to detect, i.e., below 2.0 ng/ml to detect.

4. Laboratory error.

How to avoid negative urine tests:
1. Take more than one urine specimen. Wait about an hour between collections. Check with laboratory to see how they want samples processed and labeled.

2. Wait until the pupil is reactive and returned to normal size to ensure enough time has passed to allow the drug to reach the urine.

§ 12.11   TESTING AND STORAGE
§ 12.11.1   Street Tests for Cocaine

Often traffickers in cocaine check purity by using chemicals. Cobalt thiocyanate, hydrochloric acid, and chloroform are the ingredients for the classical test for cocaine. Clorox tablets (sodium hypochlorite) is sometimes used as a test. When cocaine powder is dropped into a Clorox solution, a white halo appears as the powder falls to the bottom of the glass. Any red coloring indicates a synthetic anesthetic. When heated on aluminum foil, pure cocaine produces a gray or red-brown stain. A black residue means sugar. Sounds upon heating can be significant; a popping sound means amphetamine and a sizzling one indicates procaine.

§ 12.11.2   Preliminary Field Tests for Law Enforcement

Until recently, investigative field testing for cocaine was a messy, many-stepped procedure. However, many simple test kits are now available to drug enforcement agents. B-D Company in Arlington Texas, makes a series of tests for controlled substances called "Nik." The cocaine tests consist of a thick clear plastic envelope containing three sealed glass tubes containing liquid. A small portion of the suspect powder is placed in the envelope, closed, and the glass tubes broken in sequence— a simple, convenient procedure. While a positive presumptively identifies cocaine and in most cases would warrant arrest, further assay is generally required for subsequent court proceedings. The preliminary field test is called a cobalt test.

§ 12.11.3   Cocaine Storage

Cocaine loses potency due to passage of time, light, heat, and moisture. Therefore, cocaine is stored in places to maximize the storage life.

§ 12.12   ARRESTS & SENTENCING

The Drug Enforcement Administration (DEA) made 10,518 cocaine-related arrests (includes crack) during FY 2003, representing 38.7% of the total arrests made by the DEA during the year.

During FY 2002, most of the drug arrests made by the Federal agencies were for cocaine. Cocaine was involved in 12,500 Federal drug arrests or 37% of all Federal drug arrests in FY 2002. The DEA made 7,261 arrests for powder cocaine and 4,400 arrests for crack cocaine during FY2002 (BJS 2004).

Of the 26,023 Federal drug offense cases during FY 2003, powder cocaine was involved in 5,867 (22.9%) and crack cocaine was involved in 5,166 (20.17%) (USSC 2004).

§ 12.13   PRODUCTION & TRAFFICKING

Cocaine is extracted from the leaves of the coca plant, which is indigenous to the Andean highlands of South America. During 2000, the majority (approximately 75%) of the Andean coca was grown in Colombia, with Peru and Bolivia ranking second and third, respectively (Department of State 2001).

The U.S./Mexico border is the primary point of entry for cocaine shipments being smuggled into the United States. Sources indicate that approximately 65% of the cocaine entering the U.S. crosses the Southwest border (DEA 2001).

Law enforcement, epidemiologic, and ethnographic *Pulse Check* sources indicate that price for powder cocaine range from $25-$35 per gram in New York to $75-$150 in Detroit. One gram of powder cocaine usually sells for $100 in most cities reporting to *Pulse Check*. Crack cocaine tends to be sold in 0.1 and 0.2 gram rocks that generally sell for

$10, but prices can range from $2-$40 depending on the size of the rock (ONDCP 2004).

Most of the *Pulse Check* sources indicate that powder and crack cocaine are both sold in central city areas. Suburban areas are also frequently mentioned as areas for powder cocaine sales. Settings for cocaine sales include cars, parties, schools, college campuses, raves, supermarkets, and shopping malls (ONDCP 2002).

Sources also indicate that adulterants are often found in powder cocaine. These adulterants include caffeine (in Miami), chalk, laundry detergent, and rat poison (in Memphis), meat tenderizer (in Boston), baby laxatives (in Baltimore and Memphis), and talcum or baby powder (in Billings, El Paso, and Washington, D.C.) (ONDCP 2002).

During FY 2003, Federal agencies seized 245,499 pounds of cocaine under the Federal-wide Drug Seizure System (FDSS). FDSS contains information about drug seizures made within the jurisdiction of the United States by the DEA, Federal Bureau of Investigation (FBI), U.S. Customs & Border Protection (CBP), and U.S. Coast Guard. For FY 2004, the CBP reports that its officers made 2,095 cocaine seizures totaling 44,560 lbs. while its Border Patrol agents made 510 cocaine seizures totaling 14,222 lbs (U.S. Customs 2005).

§ 12.14 COCAINE AND VIOLENCE

The association of cocaine with overt violence takes many forms. It begins in the growing fields and extends to assaults on concealed laboratories where coca paste and cocaine are made. It spreads to the transportation system protecting the material from hijackings by rival mobs. Its most visible and violent forms are seen in the capital cities. In Bogota, for example, the assassinations of police, judges, and newspaper editors who would try to oppose or deter the narcotraficantes is commonplace. The violence is random, and bystanders in the field of fire are murdered without compunction.

When cocaine arrives at the portal of entry of the consuming nation, violence begins again, and it continues until the ultimate consumer has delivered it to his brain. As one dealer said, "If you aren't paranoid in this business, you don't survive." Everyone carries a weapon and uses it without particular restraint. Some gangs specialize in "ripping off" cocaine dealers and transporters because "that's where the money is."

It should be recalled that the expression "dope fiend," coined during the first decades of this century, referred not to heroin addicts but to cocaine addicts. It was supposed to denote the crazed, demonic assaultiveness of the cocaine users.

The plight of the compulsive cocaine consumer is a difficult one. Cocaine hunger probably exceeds heroin hunger in intensity. If it is measured by what people will do for a fix, the drive to obtain cocaine is at least as great as that of a heroin-dependent person in withdrawal. When the craving is great, but money, liquid assets, or cocaine are not at hand, cocaine users may become desperate. Their dysphoria is great, and cocaine represents the only possible relief. They are compelled to obtain cocaine just like the starving rat might deliver a dose of cocaine rather than go to the food pellets in the cage.

Cocaine psychosis is common. It varies in degree from mild suspiciousness, to overwhelming delusions of death threats, to subsequent attempts to defend one's self by aggression against the threatener or threateners. With mild delusional disorders, some ability to evaluate reality may be retained. When paranoid thinking overwhelms the ability to sort out reality from delusion, however, insight into the false ideas is absent. Appropriate hallucinatory incidents accompany the deluded thought process.

The level of violence associated with the trafficking of cocaine, especially crack, exceeded that of all other drugs and is largely due to competitions between violent gangs over market shares. While in some cities, congestions among rival groups involved in retail cocaine distribution has led to a decrease in street level violence, other cities have experienced an increase. However, the level of violence today does not compare to that of the 1980s (NDIC 2001).

§ 12.15 SOME COCAINE TREATMENT PERSPECTIVES
From 1992 to 2002, the number of admissions to treatment in which cocaine was the primary substance of abuse decreased from 267,292 in 1992 to 241,699 in 2002. The cocaine admissions represented 17.5% of the total drug/alcohol treatment admissions during 1992 and12.8% of the admissions during 2002 (SAMHSA 2004).

Broken down by type of cocaine, the number of treatment admissions for non-smoked cocaine decreased from 84,010 in 1992 to 65,685 in 2002 and admissions for crack cocaine decreased from 183,282 in 1992 to 176,014 in 2002. The average age of those admitted to treatment for cocaine in 2002 was 37 years for smoked cocaine users and 34 years for non-smoked cocaine users (SAMHSA 2004).

There are aspects of cocaine abuse that are now being seen in treatment centers. For example, blackouts have been long recognized as a common amnesic episode for the alcoholic patient. This same phenomenon of blackouts in people who are cocaine abusers are observed by treatment personnel.

Craving is another common phenomenon during the abuse of cocaine and is especially intense during the first 6 months after stopping its use. It may be triggered by a favorite song heard while abusing cocaine. Many factors can immediately trigger intense craving, palpitations, and sweating.

Paranoia is quite common during cocaine abuse and during the initial period of abstinence. The person will suddenly develop an intense paranoid state without provocation. This will lessen with the passage of time and will not respond to the use of antidepressants.

Treatment personnel also commonly see patients who experience visual and auditory hallucinations. Peripheral blue lights, seen out of the lateral aspects of the field of vision, are frequently reported. Also frequently noted are the tactile hallucinations of "bug bites." The sensation that the skin is crawling with bugs is also seen in patients who abuse Talwin and pyribenzamine. It is thought that this is related to the adulterants added to the cocaine, rather than to the cocaine itself.

Weight loss is common for the cocaine abuser, and personal hygiene frequently deteriorates.

Treatment professionals believe that it is extremely important that patients who have completed their program of inpatient treatment and who are participating in NA and/or AA on a regular basis receive reassurance that the overwhelming cocaine craving they experience is not abnormal and that this will lessen with time, though probably never completely disappear. During their recovery, cocaine abusers also will develop "dry-highs" very much analogous to the alcoholic who has "dry drunks." The person may develop a sudden tachycardia, diaphoresis, an appearance of being "high"; some even believe they can taste the cocaine in their mouths and feel the numbness in their noses. This is very common during the recovery process and requires reassurance from the helping professionals that this will come and go frequently during the first six months of recovery, and will lessen with time. It is thought that the reasons for these phenomena are that dopamine and norepinephrine are depressed during the abstinent phase. However, the production is not steady and may occur in an erratic fashion, and may account for the distressing symptoms that occur during recovery. There are studies in progress that appear to indicate that persons who continue to abuse cocaine chronically develop permanent suppression of these chemicals. It is hoped that with the necessary support systems such as NA and AA and family education regarding the cocaine abstinence phenomena, the recovering cocaine abuser will become able to deal with and overcome the abstinence syndrome (Grabowski et al).

The widespread abuse of cocaine has stimulated extensive efforts to develop treatment programs for this type of drug abuse. NIDA's top research priority is to find a medication to block or greatly reduce the effects of cocaine, to be used as one part of a comprehensive treatment program. NIDA-funded researchers are also looking at medications that help alleviate the severe cravings that people in treatment for cocaine addiction often experience. Several medications are currently being investigated to test their safety and efficacy in treating cocaine addiction (NIDA 2005).

In addition to treatment medications, behavioral interventions, particularly cognitive behavioral therapy, can be effective in decreasing drug use by patients in treatment for cocaine abuse. Providing the optimal combination of treatment services for each individual is critical to a successful treatment outcome.

§ 12.16   LEGISLATION

Cocaine was first Federally-regulated in December 1914 with the passage of the Harrison Act. This Act banned non-medical use of cocaine, prohibited its importation, imposed the same criminal penalties for cocaine users as for opium, morphine, and heroine users, and required a strict accounting of medical prescriptions for cocaine. As a result of the Harrison Act and the emergence of cheaper, legal substances such as amphetamines, cocaine became scarce in the U.S. However, use began to rise again in the 1960s, prompting Congress to classify it as a Schedule II substance in 1970 (USDOJ App. C). Schedule II substances have a high potential for abuse, a currently accepted medical use in treatment in the United States with severe restrictions, and may lead to severe psychological or physical dependence (DEA 2003). Cocaine can currently be administered by a doctor for legitimate medical uses, such as a local anesthetic for some eye, ear, and throat surgeries (NIDA 1999).

The California State Legislature passed an amendment to the Controlled Substances Act changing cocaine from a Schedule II to a Schedule I drug, effective January 1, 1987. The law exempts cocaine hydrochloride, the accepted medicinal form of the drug, which remains on Schedule II (until recently, this was also the most commonly abused form). This change has the effect of stiffening the penalties for offenses involving rock cocaine, which is largely cocaine freebase.

§ 12.17   AMPHETAMINES
§ 12.17.1   Introduction

Most stimulant drugs are amphetamines, or drugs very closely related to amphetamines chemically. The most potent form of the drug is methamphetamine (commonly called methedrine). There are other amphetamines called dexedrine and benzedrine.

Amphetamines have an interesting history. They were discovered in 1927 by George Allas who was trying to find a way to more efficiently counteract depression in mental hospitals. He found that when patients started taking this drug that many lost their appetite. The loss of appetite proved to have a large market value. Amphetamines and their chemical analogues were once common ingredients in "diet pills."

§ 12.17.2   Definitions

A stimulant is defined as an agent that arouses organic activity, strengthens the action of the heart, increases vitality, and promotes a sense of well being. However, as per the medical definition, the effects produced by a stimulant drug may not be a very accurate term for the effects sought by those who *abuse* these compounds. For instance, at dose levels usually equated with heavy abuse, both amphetamine and methamphetamine are thought to be psychotogenic. Therefore, several of the amphetamines could be discussed as hallucinogens; however, it seems most likely that a substantial portion of the abuse of stimulant drugs is performed with the intention of inducing a state of euphoria.

§ 12.17.3   Medical Uses

Amphetamines are used to reduce appetite, overcome fatigue and sleepiness, improve mood, and increase attentiveness and motivation for work and learning. The usefulness of stimulants for reducing appetite, however, has been strongly challenged in many medical and research circles. Paradoxically, amphetamines also are used to reduce the overactivity and distractibility of hyperactive children.

CNS stimulants such as amphetamines and methylphenidate (Ritalin) are being used today to treat some medical conditions. Ritalin is a medication prescribed to individuals, usually children, who have an abnormally high level of activity or attention-deficit hyperactivity disorder (ADHD). According to the National Institute of Mental Health, about 3 to 5 percent of the general population has the disorder, which is characterized by agitated behavior and an inability to focus on tasks.[1]

Methylphenidate is a CNS stimulant. It has effects similar to, but more potent than, caffeine and less potent than amphetamines. It has a notably calming effect on hyperactive children and a "focusing" effect on those with ADHD.

Recent research at Brookhaven National Laboratory may begin to explain how methylphenidate helps people with ADHD (Volkow 2001). The researchers used positron emission tomography (PET - a noninvasive brain scan) to confirm that administering a normal therapeutic dose of methylphenidate to healthy, adult men increased their dopamine levels. The researchers speculate that methylphenidate amplifies the release of dopamine, a neurotransmitter, thereby improving attention and focus in individuals who have dopamine signals that are weak, such as individuals with ADHD.

When taken as prescribed, methylphenidate is a valuable medicine. Research shows that people with ADHD do not become addicted to stimulant medications when taken in the form prescribed and at treatment dosages (Volkow 1998). Another study found that ADHD boys treated with stimulants such as methylphenidate are significantly less likely to abuse drugs and alcohol when they are older than are non-treated ADHD boys (Biederman).

Although central nervous system stimulants are effective in treating ADHD, their use is controversial, especially in children. Because the stimulants may cause unwanted side effects, parents and doctors or children who need the drugs must carefully weigh the risks and benefits. There is also concern that these drugs are being prescribed for some children who do not need them. Other physical and mental conditions can have some of the same symptoms as ADHD, so it is important to rule out other causes before starting treatment with CNS stimulants.

---

[1] This fact sheet highlights information from the June 2000 meeting of NIDA's Community Epidemiology Work Group (CEWG). CEWG members meet twice yearly to share emerging trends in drug abuse for 21 major U.S. metropolitan areas. CEWG reports are on NIDA's Website at www.drugabuse.gov.

Methylphenidate also is occasionally prescribed for treating narcolepsy, an uncontrollable desire to sleep or the act of suddenly falling into a deep sleep. The medication is prescribed in an effort to reduce the frequency and severity of attacks of narcolepsy.

Ritalin (methylphenidate), a Schedule II substance, has a high potential for abuse and produces many of the same effects as cocaine or the amphetamines. The abuse of this substance has been documented among narcotic addicts who dissolve the tablets in water and inject the mixture. Complications arising from this practice are common due to the insoluble fillers used in the tablets. When injected, these materials block small blood vessels, causing serious damage to the lungs and retina of the eye. Binge use, psychotic episodes, cardiovascular complications, and severe psychological addiction have all been associated with methylphenidate abuse.

Historically, the abuse of stimulants (euphoriants) has been largely confined to amphetamine, derivatives thereof, and cocaine. Some of the amphetamine derivatives that have been controlled under U.S. law are dextroamphetamine (Dexedrine, DextroStat), methamphetamine (Desoxyn), pemoline (Cylert), and methylphenidate (Ritalin) and many others.

Central nervous system stimulants should not be used to increase alertness or to substitute for sleep. Although they can cause loss of appetite and weight loss, they should not be used as "diet pills."

A number of drugs have been developed and marketed to replace amphetamines as appetite suppressants. These anorectic drugs include benzphetamine (Didrex), diethylproprion (Tenuate, Tepanil), mazindol (Sanorex, Mazanor), phendimetrazine (Bontril, Prelu-27), and phentermine (Ionamin, Fastin, Adipex). These substances are in Schedule III or IV of the CSA and produce some amphetamine-like effects. Of these diet pills, phentermine is the most widely prescribed and most frequently encountered on the illicit market. Two Schedule IV anorectics often used in combination and phentermine (phen-fen combo), fenfluramine, and dexfenfluramine, were removed from the U.S. market due to heart valve problems.

§ 12.17.4   Appearance
Amphetamines are found as tablets, capsules, crystals, and liquids. The tablets are found in many colors, sizes, and shapes (round, heart, square, triangle, oval, etc.). The tablets may be scored once or twice, meaning that they have a line indented into one of the flat surfaces. This is done so the tablet can be easily broken into two or four sections to decrease the dosage. The shape and color give rise to many of the slang terms for the amphetamines: "hearts," "cartwheels," "greenies," "oranges," "peaches," "roses," "whites," and many others. The amphetamine capsules also come in a variety of sizes and colors, but they generally resemble time-release cold capsules.

The crystalline form and liquid solution are almost always "meth" methamphetamine. The crystals are white, and the liquid is clear and contained in glass ampules. Meth is also found in tablet form.

§ 12.17.5   Method of Use

The tablets and capsules are swallowed. Methedrine crystals are soluble in water, and like the liquid solution, are administered by injection. However, because the crystals are water soluble, the solution does not have to be "cooked" first, like heroin. The methamphetamine crystals are sometimes sniffed into the nostrils like cocaine.

§ 12.17.6   Effects of Amphetamine Abuse

All amphetamines tend to excite the user and induce talkativeness, restlessness, trembling, dilated (or enlarged) pupils, insomnia (sleeplessness), and heavy perspiration. There is a loss of appetite—which is the reason they are used for weight control—and hallucinations may occur. Much like the cocaine user, the amphetamine user may become violent, and you should exercise extreme caution when arresting the offender.

Methedrine (or methamphetamine) appears to be much stronger than amphetamines. It produces the following symptoms, which are easily observed: dry mouth, confusion, aggressiveness, nervousness, and the impression that time passes quickly (which gives rise to the slang term for the drug: "speed"). Other symptoms that are less obvious are insomnia, impotence, loss of appetite, abnormally rapid heartbeat, loss of weight, blurred and double vision, headache, nausea, and diarrhea with vomiting, and if used for a lengthy period of time, collapse and depression.

If the speed is taken orally or sniffed, it will produce similar symptoms as injection—but it takes longer for the rush to be felt. The method used to sniff it is exactly the same as the method used to sniff cocaine.

§ 12.17.7   In Summary

These drugs stimulate the central nervous system, which lead to increased wakefulness, alertness, arousal, activity, talkativeness, restlessness, pleasurable sensations, and reduced appetite. Larger doses may produce irritability, aggressiveness, anxiety, suspicion, excitement, auditory hallucinations, and paranoid fears (delusions, psychotic reactions). Stimulants also dilate the pupils, increase sweating, quicken breathing, raise blood pressure, and produce tremors (shaking) of the hands. These drugs have high potentials for psychological dependence. Tolerance develops to their use (sometimes to an astonishing degree), and there are some withdrawal effects after extremely high doses.

§ 12.17.8   Withdrawal Symptoms

Tolerance develops with the amphetamines, requiring larger and larger doses. There is also evidence that chronic users of large amounts of amphetamines can experience withdrawal symptoms—generally a deep depression and a general fatigue. For this reason, it is apparent that extremely high doses, taken over a long period of time, can be considered physically addicting.

§ 12.17.9   Main Dangers

The stimulants produce high levels of pleasurable feelings and, occasionally, the feeling of greatly increased power; also, there are sexually orgasmic experiences when the drug is taken intravenously. One is easily seduced into the repeated use of these agents. Overdosage can be rapidly achieved, with marked impairment of judgment, greatly increased suspicion (paranoia), aggressive behavior, and serious interruption of normal patterns of eating and sleeping (which produces physical deterioration). Constant heavy use often leads rapidly to psychotic-like behavior that can be indistinguishable from paranoid schizophrenia. Suicides have occasionally been triggered by the prolonged depressions of mood that often follow the intense stimulation produced by continued use of high doses of amphetamines. Intravenous amphetamine users learn, in time, that heroin produces a similar orgasmic feeling when injected with none of the deteriorative effects of speed on health and performance. Thus, there is some tendency to switch from amphetamines to heroin use.

Summary of Amphetamine Abuse Symptoms

1. Dilated pupils

2. Sweating (heavy perspiration)

3. Shaking — tremors of the hands

4. Talkativeness

5. Possible weight loss (due to reduced appetite)

6. Paranoia (increased suspicion)

7. Quickened breathing

8. Aggressiveness

9. Irritability

10. Potential for violence

§ 12.17.10   Handling People Under the Influence of Stimulants

People in the medical, psychiatric, and law enforcement fields talk about three major categories of dangerous drugs—cocaine and amphetamine, PCP, and alcohol—from the point of view of how dangerous the individual who uses them is. Particularly in the case of amphetamine or cocaine users, you are dealing with people who are extremely dangerous. This kind of individual will be very jumpy, extremely active, and unable to keep still, possibly wringing his or her hands, talking very fast, talking about a lot of different things, talking about being followed, and chain-smoking. If the person is a long-term user of amphetamines or cocaine, he or she may be very drawn and emaciated, appear extremely suspicious of everything that is going on, and may lick his or her lips frequently, since one of the side effects of amphetamine/cocaine use is extreme dryness of the mouth and lips.

This person is someone you should never let out of your sight, and never turn your back on. The primary intervention is to immobilize the individual as soon as possible. If you don't, it is quite likely that someone will get hurt. Immobilizing the individual should be undertaken with the recognition that he or she

1. Will be very quick.
2. Will be very strong.
3. Will defend him- or herself in every way conceivable.

Immobilizing the individual is probably going to take more officers than one would suspect it should. There is relatively little need for the kinds of reassurance and gentleness that you might want to exercise with the person on a bad trip.

Remember to control the person as soon as possible. The chance of the user trying to escape is great and the potential for violence is great.

§ 12.18   METHAMPHETAMINE HYDROCHLORIDE

Methamphetamine is a form of amphetamine, a CNS stimulant. Stimulants are either natural, such as epinephrine and norepinephrine, or synthetic, such as amphetamine and phenmetrazine. The first natural stimulant was epinephrine (adrenalin) and the effects were first described in 1899. The first synthetic stimulant of any significance was prepared in 1919 by a Japanese chemist and was later identified as methamphetamine.

Methamphetamine is available under the trade name "Desoxyn." It is a Schedule II drug. Commonly called "meth," or "crystal," methamphetamine has often been called the poorman's cocaine and has traditionally been the drug of choice of outlaw motorcycle gangs. In Honolulu, "crystal" or "ice" is referred to as the rock methamphetamine, while "crank" is the term used for the powder form.

Methamphetamine has been around illicitly for decades. It was made illegally in makeshift labs by motorcycle gangs in the 1960s. It got a bad name in the late 1960s and early 1970s when many users learned the truth behind the phrase "Speed kills."

§ 12.18.1   Forms of Methamphetamine

Commonly referred to on the street as *speed, meth, ice, crystal,* or *glass,* methamphetamine is a synthetically produced central nervous system stimulant that produces effects similar to cocaine. Because it metabolizes much slower than cocaine, methamphetamine has longer lasting effects. It produces a number of dose-related effects, including increased alertness and euphoria, as well as increases in heart rate, blood pressure, respiration, and body temperature. Agitation, tremors, hypertension, memory loss, hallucinations, psychotic episodes, paranoid delusions, and violent behavior can result from chronic abuse. Withdrawal from high doses of methamphetamine often produces severe depression. Methamphetamine may be either injected, ingested orally, snorted, or smoked.

Illicit methamphetamine, which is almost exclusively methamphetamine hydrochloride, is sold in powder, ice, and tablet forms. Powder methamphetamine, the most common form available in the United States, is produced domestically and is also smuggled into the country from Mexico. Traditionally, Asian-produced ice was almost exclusively found in Guan, Hawaii, and parts of California; however, increased domestic production of this form of methamphetamine has increased availability to several other areas of the country previously untouched by exposure to ice. Methamphetamine tablets, primarily manufactured in Burma, have been smuggled into the United States, especially to northern California and the Los Angeles area.

§ 12.18.2   Powder

Powder methamphetamine—also known as crystal methamphetamine—is the form most commonly encountered across the Untied States. It is a bitter-tasting, water-soluble powder, with colors ranging from dingy white to reddish brown, depending on the manufacturing process. The method of administration varies across geographic regions, but powder is usually injected or snorted; however, it can be orally ingested or smoked.

Powder methamphetamine was once primarily made and sold by outlaw motorcycle gangs such as the Hells Angels. However, since the mid-1990s, Mexican criminal groups have dominated the market. They manufacture methamphetamine in large clandestine laboratories, primarily located in Mexico and California, and distribute it across the United States. "Cooks" also produce powder methamphetamine in small independently operated makeshift laboratories, especially in the Midwest. Although the manufacturing process is relatively simple, fires and explosions often occur due to a combination of inexperience and careless handling of volatile chemicals. Dumped toxic waste and fumes emitted from these laboratories also create significant health hazards. Regardless of size, clandestine methamphetamine laboratories exact a great toll on local communities.

Although thousands of small laboratories operate in the United States, the majority of methamphetamine distributed across the country is manufactured in "super labs"—laboratories capable of producing 10 pounds or more of methamphetamine in a 24-hour period. The capability to produce 10-pound quantities of methamphetamine generally indicates a large organizational structure rather than a small independent operation. Super labs are almost exclusively located in California.

Once considered a West coast phenomenon, methamphetamine abuse and illicit manufacturing have spread across the nation to the Midwest, Northwest, and portions of the South. Some indicators currently show stabilization in the abuse of methamphetamine; nonetheless, the record amounts of powder methamphetamine trafficking and abuse in the United States during the 1990s resulted in a devastating impact on communities across the nation.

§ 12.18.3   Methamphetamine Use
Methamphetamine can be taken orally, by injection, or smoked in both a glass pipe (referred to as a "meth bowl" or "bong") and creased aluminum foil.

§ 12.18.4   Paraphernalia/Use
The meth or ice pipe, or bong, has one section where the ice or meth crystals are placed through a hole on the top of the bowl or the stem. The meth pipe or bong may have a vent hole on the stem between the chamber and mouthpiece. This pipe is available for "burning incense" through some Korean liquor stores to avoid paraphernalia laws.

§ 12.18.5   Packaging
Methamphetamine is sold in various forms. Purchase may include glass vials, paper bundles, or clear heat-sealed cellophane packets. Most recently it has been found in pieces of plastic straws that are heat-sealed at both ends.

§ 12.18.6   Description of Methamphetamine
Methamphetamine is normally a white powder. The formula used and the amount of washing determines the color and consistency of the final product, such as the difference in production methods using copper hydrocenenators that produce a green color methamphetamine.

Methamphetamine ice is a clear or translucent crystal in rock form that resembles shaved-ice, rock candy, pieces of glass, or Hawaiian rock salt, with a purity of 90 to 100 percent. This is a water-based product.

Yellow methamphetamine is an oil-based product.

§ 12.19   YABA
The tablet form of methamphetamine has been popular throughout much of Southeast and East Asia; however, Southeast Asian-produced methamphetamine tablets are recent phenomena in the United States. To date, most methamphetamine pills have been found in northern California and the Lost Angeles area. Frequently referred to by their Thai name, *yaba*, the tablets are a composite of methamphetamine and caffeine. In the United States, the tablets are commonly reddish-orange or green, and fit inside the end of a drinking straw. They have a variety of logos, with "WY" the most common. Methamphetamine pills are

normally ingested orally, although they can be crushed into powder and administered.

Southeast Asian methamphetamine tablets are produced by large drug trafficking organizations in Burma. The United Wa State Army, a former insurgent group and Burma's largest heroine trafficking organization, is the preeminent producer of methamphetamine tablets in Southeast Asia. Its primary market is the neighboring country of Thailand.

Southeast Asian traffickers, mainly Thai and Lao nationals, and U.S. citizens/resident aliens whose families have emigrated from those countries, dominate the trafficking of methamphetamine tablets in the United States. The tablets are primarily sent from Southeast Asia by mail, and, to a lesser extent, by either courier, air, or maritime cargo. Most of the tablets seized in the United States arrived through the international mail system and were destined for recipients in northern California and the Los Angeles area.

YABA Tablets

Although it is currently believed that Southeast Asian methamphetamine pills are brought to the United States primarily for sale to the Asian community, demand may expand to other communities. It is possible that methamphetamine tablets will become popular within the "rave" party scene, given the similar appearance to other tablet forms of "club drugs," such as 3, 4-methyl-enedioxymethamphetamine (MDMA), also known as ecstasy.

§ 12.20 CAPTAGON (Fenethylline)

Fenethylline, commonly known by the trademark name Captagon, is one of the most popular drugs of abuse among the young affluent populations of the Middle East. Since the cessation of legal production of Captagon, this synthetic amphetamine-type stimulant has been clandestinely produced in southern Europe and trafficked through Turkey to the consumer markets on the Arabian Peninsula.

Fenethylline has been a controlled substance on Schedule I of the Controlled Substance Act since 1981. Fenethylline does not have an accepted medical use in the United States, and is not approved for distribution.

Fenethylline is a central nervous system stimulant with effects similar to amphetamine. In small to moderate doses, amphetamine causes elevations in heart rate, body temperature, respiration, and blood pressure. In addition, a user initially experiences a dilation of bronchial vessels, extra energy, and appetite suppression. Over the long-term, however, amphetamine use can have a number of side effects, including, but not limited to, extreme depression, lethargy, sleep deprivation, heart and blood vessel toxicity, and malnutrition (Inaba et al).

The primary market for clandestinely manufactured Fenethylline has traditionally been the Arabian Peninsula. According to the United Nations (U.N.), it is the primary amphetamine-type stimulant consumed in the region. Authorities in Saudi Arabia, Kuwait, and Qatar, report that use is prevalent among their younger, affluent citizens.

In response to frequent diversions in the 1980s, Fenethylline was placed under international control midway through the decade. According to the International Narcotics Control Board (INCB), Captagon has not been legally produced since 1986. Despite the cessation of legal production, demand for Captagon has remained strong. The U.N. maintains that illegal stockpiling and clandestine Fenethylline production has continued unabated, primarily in southern Europe and Turkey, for consumption in the Middle East.

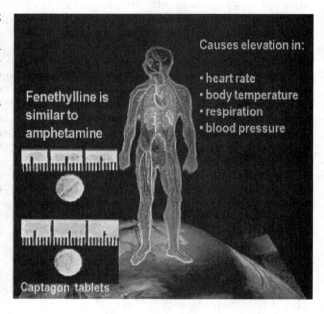

Fenethylline is similar to amphetamine

Causes elevation in:
• heart rate
• body temperature
• respiration
• blood pressure

Captagon tablets

Traditionally, clandestine production of Captagon has been reported in southeastern Europe. Over the past few years, the International Police Organization (INTERPOL) and the INCB have reported the seizure of clandestine laboratories in several countries including Bulgaria and Slovenia. Suspected Captagon laboratories were also seized in Serbia-Montenegro and Turkey. The laboratories vary in production capacity: some produce small quantities, while others are large, sophisticated operations with professional-grade equipment capable of producing large quantities.

Counterfeit synthetic drugs are commonly sold on the illicit market. Throughout Europe and the United States, tablets containing a variety of compounds are regularly sold as MDMA, or ecstasy (3,4-methylenedioxy-methamphetamine) at rave events, night clubs, and other venues. Though the physical appearance of these tablets, emblazoned with logos, etc., resembles ecstasy, the chemical composition may differ significantly. With dwindling stocks of diverted Fenethylline and fluctuations in the availability of precursor chemicals for clandestine production, counterfeit Captagon tablets are appearing in the primary consumption markets (DEA 2003).

§ 12.21 CRYSTAL METH OR ICE
The island of Oahu in Hawaii has been known as the place where the smoking of ice started. Although smoking crystal methampheta-

mine did not make the front pages of Oahu's newspapers until 1988, one form of ice known as "Batu" had emerged among certain of the island's ethnic groups, in particular communities before 1980. During the early 1980s, cocaine smoking became popular, although most resident drug users preferred or could only afford to use "pakkalo" (Hawaiian grown marijuana). At the same time, Batu smoking also increased, especially among industrious immigrants from the far east who used the substances to stay awake while working both day and night.

Enterprising drug dealers on Oahu, realizing that potentially large sums of money could be made by marketing prepared smokeable crystal methamphetamine, developed the name "ice." Although more costly per hit than base cocaine, smokeable methamphetamine was nonetheless touted as a relatively inexpensive, pure, hard-to-detect, reusable drug that produced better and longer highs than cocaine.

By 1986, the Honolulu police began to investigate the drug and its use. Within months, police, in cooperation with other criminal justice agencies, health professionals, and educators, spread the word that ice use was a harmful practice. During 1987 and 1988, many agencies made comprehensive, coordinated efforts to curtail methamphetamine smoking and sales. By 1989, organized ice dealing appeared to have been generally suppressed, and use was dropping rapidly on Oahu. In the early 1990s, ice supply and use increased. However, the sales and use of ice appear to have remained at a much lower level than before (NIJ 1993).

In the mid-1990s, traffickers from Mexico, operating out of Los Angeles, began supplying powder methamphetamine to ethnic Asian criminal organizations and gangs on the west coast and in Hawaii for conversion to ice. Mexican criminal groups also are producing ice and selling it for significantly less than rival Asian trafficking groups. The increased availability of Mexican-produced ice has increased abuse in areas of the country that were previously untouched. Ice use is still most prevalent in Guam, Hawaii, and parts of California, but has spread to new areas including Ohio, Florida, New York, and Virginia.

§ 12.21.1 How Is Ice Recognized?
In California, methamphetamine is normally found as a white powder. "Ice" is the street name for crystal methamphetamine ("crank") in solid form. The slang term "ice" was designated for the drug due to its appearance, generally a clear, crystal-shaped, solid form (of medium to large size) that looks like glass. It has also been designated "crystal" and "glass." Crystal methamphetamine has been described as almost transparent with a light yellowish cast, a translucent milky white, and an almost pure white, similar in appearance to "rock candy" or "Hawaiian salt". Ice found in Hawaii is 98 percent to 100 percent pure.

Ice, also known as glass, is similar in appearance to rock candy, crushed ice, or broken glass. Ice contains the same active chemical compound as powder methamphetamine, but undergoes a recrystallization process in which some impurities in the methamphetamine are removed. The finished product is allowed to dry into crystal chunks that are broken into rocks for sale.

Ice methamphetamine

Ice is a very pure, smokeable form of methamphetamine that is more addictive than other forms of the substance. When smoked, highly concentrated doses of the drug are delivered instantaneously into the user's system and may cause more compulsive use, severed paranoid delusions, and hallucinations. Usually smoked in a glass pipe, a hollowed aluminum can, or a light bulb, several "hits" can be obtained from a single gram of this substance. In a method of smoking sometimes referred to as "chasing the dragon," a term commonly associated with smoking opium or heroin, users heat ice on a piece of aluminum foil and inhale the released vapors — usually through a straw or similar device.

§ 12.21.2   How Ice Is Used

Methamphetamine can be injected, inhaled, smoked or taken orally. The ice form of the methamphetamine is ingested by smoking and is extremely addictive. This substance is not unknown to the methamphetamine world; just the name and utilization are new.

Because it's often odorless, ice allegedly can be smoked in public without detection. Smoking is usually done using a glass pipe called a bong, which is a circular bowl with a pipe stem (usually 5" in length). The pipe has only one section where the meth is placed and heated. There are no screens or coolants in the meth pipe.

The top of the bowl usually has a "hole leading to the main chamber and may have a vent on the stem that releases the meth vapor when the bottom of the bowl is heated. The openings in the chamber and vent hole are sealed, most often with a finger, while the crystal is being heated. Once the crystal has turned to gas, it is inhaled by the user. One telltale sign of a meth user is a burn mark on the finger(s) used to seal the hole in the main chamber. Approximately 10 to 15 hits can be obtained from a one gram dosage.

§ 12.21.3   Form of Crystal

Information gathered in the Honolulu area reports that several forms of "crystal meth" are being used. Most prevalent is the translucent or clear rock crystal. This form of meth is said to be water based and burns quickly leaving a milky white residue on the inside of the bowl. Reports also show that a yellowish crystal meth is also available. This form of meth is said to be oil-based. This form of yellow meth is also said to burn slower and last longer leaving behind a brownish or black residue in the pipe.

§ 12.21.4 How Ice Is Sold

Ice is most frequently sold in heat-sealed cellophane packets. Ice is typically sold on the underground market in small "rocks," hence the additional street designation "Crack Meth." Quite surprisingly, the street value of ice is significantly higher than an equal amount of the powder form. This fact may lead to a rapid switch-over to ice by clandestine methamphetamine cooks. Similar to "crack cocaine," the typical mode of ingestion is via smoking.

§ 12.21.5 Street Names

Street names for the drug primarily on the West coast and the Far East include "ice," "glass," "batu," "slabu" and "hiropong." It should be noted that in some areas of the Eastern United States ice is also the current street name for 4-methylaminorex (also known as "U4Euh").

§ 12.21.6 The High

The "high" gained from ice lasts from 2 to 14 hours (some reports indicate 12 to 24 hours), depending on the amount ingested. When heated in a glass pipe, the crystals turn to liquid and produce a potent vapor that enters the bloodstream rapidly. As this happens, large doses may be excreted into the urine, unchanged, up to 72 hours after ingestion. When allowed to cool or cooled by a wet rag, the ice reverts to its solid crystal state. It is then reusable and easy to transport.

The following factors are believed to have contributed to the growing popularity of ice:

* In quality, ice is similar to or better than meth when used for injection.

* Smoking ice eliminates the use of a needle.

* Methamphetamine enters the body faster when it is smoked.

* The drug's effects are long lasting when compared to other drugs (particularly in comparison to a cocaine "high" of about 20 minutes).

* Ice is often odorless, colorless, and tasteless.

* Ice is easy to transport.

* Ice sells for more than cocaine but is much cheaper to produce.

§ 12.21.7 Physical/Psychological Effects

It is too early to tell what the long-term physical effects of ice will be. However, due to the potency of smokeable ice, it most likely will be worse than injecting methamphetamine. Symptoms of abuse include absences from work or school, paranoia, schizophrenia, and behavior that is unpredictable, uncontrollable, delusional, irrational, illogical, and often violent. Continued use of ice for days at a time causes (1) insomnia; (2) depletion of the body's stored energy; and (3) vitamin and mineral deficiencies. When the drug wears off, the user will then crash for 24 to 36 hours. Often the effects of the drug do not go away. In other words, some users do not return to normal health. Overdoses can lead to convulsions, coma and eventually death. People use crank to lose weight quickly, to stay up all night working, studying, etc., and for a feeling of excess energy.

Prolonged use can produce a high degree of tolerance and users find they need heavier dosages. Heavy use can also result in psychological dependence, leading to a psychotic state, anxiety, depression and fatigue.

§ 12.21.8 Problems Associated with Use

Withdrawal from methamphetamine does not involve physical discomfort but can involve acute depression and fatigue. Depression can reach critical proportions, since life seems boring and unpleasant. Progressive toxic effects of amphetamine abuse may include restlessness, tremor, talkativeness, irritability, insomnia, anxiety, delirium, panic states, paranoid ideation, palpitation, cardiac arrhythmias, hypertension, circulatory collapse, dry mouth, nausea, vomiting, abdominal cramps, convulsions, comas, and death.

Other problems include rapid deterioration of physical and psychological health since methamphetamine erases feelings of periods of time and creates the same sort of stress to the body that any long period of exertion creates; however, the user does not let his body recuperate and permanent damage or death is the result.

As of August, 1989, a survey of all newborn infants in Hawaii showed 25 percent of them to have traces of crystal meth in their systems. Queens Hospital was averaging approximately a half dozen meth overdoses per day compared to 1 a day in 1988. Between January 1 and September 11, 1989, 23 percent of all narcotic arrests in Honolulu were related to crystal meth. Ice has surpassed cocaine as the drug of choice in Hawaii (Kouri).

§ 12.21.9 Manufacturing

Ice is simply d-methamphetamine hydrochloride in very large, crystal-clear "rocks." It is prepared by slow evaporation of a saturated solution of the salt in (possibly) water or isopropanol. The appearance of the resulting product is in dramatic contrast to the traditional crystalline white powder, prepared by "gassing" an etheric solution of the free base with anhydrous hydrochloric acid.

Preliminary information suggests that ice is currently prepared by the hydriodic acid/red phosphorus reduction of ephedrine. It should be noted, however, that several clandestine methamphetamine laboratories in the western United States, possibly attempting synthesis of this variant, have been recently seized.

§ 12.21.10 Clandestine Drug Labs

Clandestine drug labs have been a concern of law enforcement officials since the 1960s when outlaw motorcycle gangs produced their own methamphetamine in clandestine labs, and dominated distribution in the United States. Clandestine labs typically produce other types of illicit drugs such as PCP, MDMA, and LSD, but methamphetamine has always been the primary drug manufactured in the vast majority of drug labs seized by law enforcement officials throughout the nation. Since 1997, 97% or more of the clandestine lab seizures reported to DEA were methamphetamine and/or amphetamine labs.

Methamphetamine is, in fact, a very simple drug to produce. A user can go to retail stores and easily purchase the vast majority of the ingredients necessary to manufacture the drug. Items such as rock salt, battery acid, red phosphorous road flares, pool acid, and iodine crystals can be utilized to substitute for some of the necessary chemicals. Precursor chemicals such as pseudoephedrine can be extracted from common, over-the-counter cold medication. A clandestine lab operator can utilize relatively common items such as mason jars, coffee filters, hot plates, pressure cookers, pillowcases, plastic tubing, gas cans, etc., to substitute for sophisticated laboratory equipment. Unlike fentanyl, LSD, or other types of dangerous drugs, it does not take a college-educated chemist to produce methamphetamine. In fact, less than 10% of those suspects arrested for the manufacture of methamphetamine are trained chemists, which may be one reason we see so many fires, explosions, and injuries including clandestine labs.

The majority of these laboratories produce relatively small amounts of methamphetamine. In some respects, the methamphetamine problem is synonymous with the clandestine lab problem. Although the methamphetamine problem and the clandestine lab problem are both parts of the same drug abuse mosaic, in reality, they are somewhat different issues, which may require a different law enforcement response in order to successfully combat the spiraling increases in both arenas.

The threats posed by clandestine labs are not limited to fire, explosion, poison gas, drug abuse and booby traps; the chemical contamination of the hazardous waste contained in these labs also poses a serious danger to our nation's environment. Each pound of methamphetamine generated in a clandestine lab can result in as much as five pounds of toxic waste, which clandestine lab operators routinely dump into our nation's streams, rivers, and sewage systems to cover up the evidence of their illegal operations. In addition, clandestine lab operators routinely show a blatant disregard for the health and safety of others as evidenced by the number of children who have been present at clan lab sites.

Because of the possibility of explosions and direct contact with toxic fumes and hazardous chemicals, law enforcement officers who raid clandestine drug labs are now required to take special hazardous materials (HAZMAT) handling training. The highly toxic and flammable chemicals involved make these rudimentary laboratories ticking time bombs that require specialized training to dismantle and clean.

Chapter 12

The size of the lab does not matter when it comes to the danger level involved in a clandestine laboratory raid. The smaller labs are usually more dangerous than the larger operations where the cooks are generally less experienced chemists who often have little regard for the safety issues that arise when dealing with explosive and poisonous chemicals. However, the size of the clandestine laboratory can be a significant factor in the costs associated with the hazardous waste cleanup. Larger production laboratories usually have larger quantities of toxic chemicals and therefore more significant hazardous waste disposal charges.

The face of methamphetamine trafficking has changed. Around 1994, for the first time in law enforcement history, Mexican-based drug trafficking organizations operating out of Mexico and California began to take control of the production and distribution of the methamphetamine in the United States. What was once controlled by independent, regionalized outlaw motorcycle gangs had now been taken over by Mexican-based criminal organizations and independent operators in Mexico and California. Outlaw motorcycle gangs are still active in methamphetamine production, but do not produce anywhere near the quantities now being distributed by the Mexican-based groups. This shift is due, in no small part, to the fact that Mexican-based methamphetamine trafficking organizations had ready access to the necessary precursor chemicals on the international market. These chemicals have fewer controls in Mexico and overseas than in the United States, and as a result, the Mexican-based organizations capitalized on this advantage by producing huge quantities of high purity methamphetamine in clandestine laboratories in both Mexico and southern California.

The dynamics of this shift are grounded in the resilience of Mexican-based drug trafficking organizations. The Mexican-based organizations had well-established polydrug distribution networks, and were already transporting drug shipments to the United States on behalf of the Colombian cartels. Using existing proven trafficking routes, the Mexican traffickers began shipping methamphetamine along with the heroin and marijuana that was being produced in Mexico. Since they could make their own stimulants (methamphetamine), they would not have to share the profits and/or rely upon the Colombian-based traffickers, as they had done in the past when distributing cocaine. To further entrench themselves in the methamphetamine trade, these Mexican organizations developed international connections with chemical suppliers in Europe, Asia, and the Far East. With these connections, which were steadily nurtured and developed throughout the history of their drug trafficking and production, Mexican-based organizations were able to obtain tons of quantities of the necessary precursor chemicals, specifically ephedrine and pseudoephedrine, to manufacture massive amounts of methamphetamine and amphetamine.

A factor in the methamphetamine lab epidemic is the evolution of technology and the increased use of the Internet. While in the past, methamphetamine chemists closely guarded their recipes, today's age of modern computer technology had made chemists more willing to

356

share their recipes and has allowed them to disseminate this information to anyone with computer access. Aside from marijuana, methamphetamine is the only widely abused illegal drug that is capable of being readily manufactured by the abuser. A cocaine or heroin addict cannot make his own cocaine or heroin, but a methamphetamine addict only has to turn on his computer to find a recipe identifying the chemicals and the process required for production of the drug. Given the relative ease with which manufacturers are able to acquire precursor chemicals and the unsophisticated nature of the production process, it is not difficult to see why this addictive drug and potentially explosive clandestine laboratories continue to appear across America.

Methamphetamine prices vary considerably by region. Nationwide, prices range from $21,000 per pound at the distribution level. Retail prices range from $350 to $3,00 per oz. and $20 to $200 per gram.

According to law enforcement sources in California, the illicit market of the kilogram level distinguishes between methamphetamine that has been "cut" usually with Methylsulfonylmethane (MSN) and uncut methamphetamine. A kilo of cut methamphetamine sells for $4,000; an uncut pure kilo sells for $9,000.

The average purity of DEA methamphetamine exhibits has declined from 71.9% in 1994 to 35.3% in 2000. A corresponding rise in amphetamine purity between 1995 and 1997 may be the result of traffickers responding to regulatory pressure exerted on distributors of precursors as ephedrine and pseudoephedrine by substituting the amphetamine precursor phenylpropanolamine (PPA), which is less strictly regulated in international commerce. Subsequent control measures by the U.S. and other countries with respect to the distribution of PPA have reduced its availability, and may have contributed to the decreased purity of amphetamine since 1997. Consequently, the national average purity for amphetamine has drooped from 56.9% in 1997 to 20.1% in 2000.

§ 12.21.11 Current Emerging Trends: The Methamphetamine Situation Overview

Statistics indicate two distinct components to the overall methamphetamine problem. One involves the emergence of the Mexican-based traffickers, while the other involves the identification and clean up of the growing number of smaller producing laboratories.

The Mexican-based trafficking organizations have expanded their operations to numerous cities, from California to the heart of the Midwest and beyond, and have placed organizational members within existing, established, law-abiding Hispanic communities in these areas in an attempt to thwart local law enforcement efforts to identify and immobilize their organizations. Traditionally, local law enforcement efforts in these areas, while effective in the short run, have not attacked these investigations on a national scale as has been done with traditional cocaine investigations.

Chapter 12

California is ground zero for meth production. The State is home to 80% of the nation's meth labs, making the drug the leading export to other states. Ninety-seven percent of the U.S. "super labs", those that produce 20 lbs. of meth in a single batch, are located in California. The problem is growing. In 1999, law enforcement agencies in California seized more than 2,000 meth labs. In 1994, there were 559 labs seized.

§ 12.21.12   Lab Take Down

Many labs are found because of fire. About three years ago, the frequency of such disasters led state regulators to analyze the chemicals used to produce speed. That, in turn, led to drastic and expensive changes in the ways speed labs are handled. Vats of seized chemicals used to be carted into courts along with the accused. Now, they are destroyed and cases are tried using photographs and sample bottles.

Most police officers do not enter a lab. They cordon off the area and wait for a state-licensed chemist to arrive. The chemist, in a fire-retardant jumpsuit and gas mask, takes samples of the evidence. He turns the rest over to workers from a private waste disposal firm, who remove and destroy the chemicals.

Disposing of an operating lab can cost taxpayers from $4,000 to $20,000 although sites where labs and excess chemicals are dumped usually cost less, said a spokesman for American Environmental Management Corp., the company contracted to dispose of lab waste in California.

Usually, cleanup costs are paid by the county, which later is reimbursed by the state or federal government.

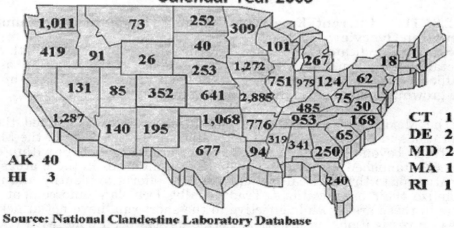

Total of All Meth Clandestine Laboratory Incidents
Including Labs, Dumpsites, Chem/Glass/Equipment
Calendar Year 2003

Source: National Clandestine Laboratory Database
Total: 17,356/ 47 States Reporting
Dates: 01/01/03 to 12/31/03

§ 12.22   PARAPHERNALIA

Common carriers for meth are opaque glass vials, paper bindles, or more commonly in Honolulu, clear heat-sealed cellophane packets. Common paraphernalia include syringes for the user who injects his drugs or glass smoking pipes (bongs).

There is a difference between a pipe used for cocaine and that used by the meth smoker. The basic difference is in the construction of the pipe. See illustration of the differences in the construction of these pipes.

METHAMPHETAMINE PIPE (GLASS)

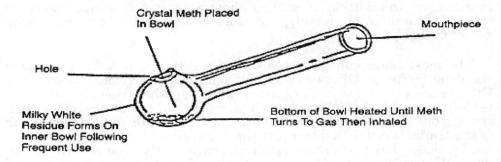

CRACK PIPE (GLASS)

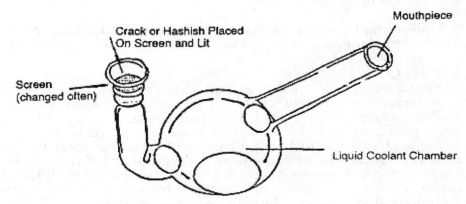

The cocaine pipe is made of two sections, one to hold the cocaine and the other section to hold a liquid coolant. The sections are separated by a screen or similar object. Cocaine smokers will ignite the cocaine in the top half of the glass pipe. The fumes are then inhaled, first through the coolant chamber and then into the mouth.

The meth or ice pipe has only one section where the methamphetamine is placed and heated. There are no screens and no coolants in the meth pipe. The pipes used for smoking meth usually have a hold on the top of the bowl leading to the main chamber and may have a vent hold on the stem between the chamber, where the crystal is placed, and the mouthpiece.

The ice is first placed into the chamber and heated with a lighter or other heat source until it turns to a gas. The opening in the chamber and vent hold are sealed, usually with a finger, while the crystal is being heated. Once the crystal has turned to gas, it is inhaled by the user. A telltale sign of a meth user are burn marks on the finger(s) used to seal the hold in the main chamber.

§ 12.23 TRUCKING INDUSTRY

Based on a year-long investigation of drug use in the trucking industry in California, it was found that the main drug being sold on the road is methamphetamine, which is frequently referred to as "go fast" by truckers. In addition to methamphetamine, which is also known as "speed," "crank" and "Lucille," cocaine, heroin and other drugs have been purchased.

The most remarkable aspect of this operation is how brazenly open the drug traffic is. Offers to buy and sell drugs fairly crackle over the CB airwaves from one end of California to the other. However, the center of the action is right around the truck stops. For the most part, truck stops themselves are not where these deals are going down. Much of the traffic is conducted by prostitutes and small-time dealers who are not truckers. The truck stops generally have pretty good security. They don't allow non-truckers inside. So the truckers looking for action, and the pushers and hookers looking to provide it, congregate in nearby parking lots or alongside roads.

Only a small fraction of truckers are involved in this kind of activity. The overwhelming majority of drivers are not on drugs of any kind.

§ 12.24 CONCLUSIONS

Stimulants are diverted from legitimate channels and clandestinely manufactured exclusively for the illicit market. They are taken orally, sniffed, smoked, and injected. Smoking, snorting, or injecting stimulants produces a sudden sensation known as a "rush" or a "flash." Abuse is often associated with a pattern of binge use, sporadically consuming large doses of stimulants over a short period of time. Heavy users may inject themselves every few hours, continuing until they have depleted their drug supply or reached a point of delirium, psychosis, and physical exhaustion. During this period of heavy use, all other interests become secondary to recreating the initial euphoric rush. Tolerance can develop rapidly; both physical and psychological dependence can occur. Abrupt cessation, even after a brief two or three-day binge, is commonly followed by depression, anxiety, drug craving, and extreme fatigue known as a "crash."

Therapeutic levels of stimulants can produce exhilaration, extended wakefulness, and loss of appetite. These effects are greatly intensified when large doses of stimulants are taken. Physical side effects, including dizziness, tremor, headache, flushed skin, chest pain with palpitations, excessive sweating, vomiting, and abdominal cramps, may occur as a result of taking too large a dose at one time or taking large doses over an extended period of time. Psychological effects include agitation, hostility, panic, aggression, and suicidal or homicidal tendencies. Paranoia, sometimes accompanied by both auditory and visual hallucinations, may also occur. In an overdose, unless there is medical intervention, high fever, convulsions, and cardiovascular collapse may precede death. Because accidental death is partially due to the effects of stimulants on the body's cardiovascular and temperature-regulating systems, physical exertion increases the hazards of stimulant use.

Methamphetamine production continues to pose significant risks to public health. Of the 6,835 methamphetamine laboratories seized in the United States in 1994, 204 were classified as Mexican-based Super Labs. The vast majority of methamphetamine produced within the United States is manufactured by numerous, independent, Mexican-based labs located primarily within California who distribute and transport the methamphetamine in the United States.

Unfortunately, it seems to be an axiom that any compound which has any possibility of altering man's perception of himself or his surroundings will at some time be abused.

§ 12.25 STIMULANT SLANG TERMS

Beans .... pills, referring to benzedrine tablets or capsules
Basing .... baseballing; freebasing cocaine
Batu .... methamphetamine, "Ice"
Bennies .... benzedrine tablets
Black Beauty .... bi-phetamine capsules (methedrine capsule)
Blow .... cocaine
Bottle .... 100 pills
Bug .... itching sensation due to cocaine poisoning
C .... cocaine
C & H .... cocaine and heroin
Cap .... capsule
Cartwheel .... benzedrine tablets
Cocaine Blues .... depression from discontinuing the use of cocaine
Coke .... cocaine
Coke Out .... excessive use of cocaine to point of incoherence
Coke Spoon .... specially made tiny spoons for inhaling cocaine
Crack .... smoking cocaine
Crack cooler .... rock cocaine with wine cooler
Co-pilot .... benzedrine
Crank .... methamphetamine
Crash .... to sleep or come down from being under the influence of a stimulant
Crate .... large quantity of pills, usually 50,000
Cross-tops .... benzedrine tablets
Crystal .... methamphetamine
Dexies .... amphetamine tablets (dexedrine)
Diamonds .... amphetamine tablets
Flake .... cocaine
Flash powder .... methamphetamine
Freak .... heavy user of a drug; scared

Freeze	the numbness caused by using cocaine
Girl	cocaine
Glass	crystal methamphetamine
Happy Dust	cocaine
Hearts	amphetamines (dexedrine)
Hiropong	methamphetamine, "Ice"
Horn	to inhale drugs through the nose
Hot Rock	rock cocaine and tar heroin
Ice	crystal methamphetamine
Jug	1,000 pills
Keg	50,000 pills
King's Habit	use of cocaine
Lady	cocaine
Leaf	cocaine
Line	cocaine poured out in a thin line on a table, book, album, etc., for inhaling into the nose with a straw.
Lucille	methamphetamine
Meth	methamphetamine
Merck	pharmaceutical cocaine
Mini Beans	small benzedrine tablets
Nose Candy	cocaine
Pep Pill	amphetamine
Peruvian	cocaine
Pill Freak	user of any type of pills
Pillow	25,000 amphetamines tablets usually packaged in black plastic bags.
Pop	to take a drug by injecting or by mouth
P-2-P	Phenyl-2-propanone (chemical used to manufacture meth)
Roll	ten pills sold in a roll (usually tinfoil)
Script	drug prescription
Sheet Rocks	liquid LSD with rock cocaine
Slabu	crystal methamphetamines
Snort	to sniff the drug through the nose
Snow	cocaine
Spacebasing	crack dipped in PCP and smoked
Speed	methamphetamine
Speedball	mixture of heroin and a stimulant drug
Super crank	cocaine crank
Tabs	tablets
Toot	cocaine
Upper	amphetamines
Whites	benzedrine
White Girl	cocaine
Wired	to be under the influence of a drug

§ 12.26 THE STIMULANT DRUG LAWS

The following is a brief overview of some pertinent drug laws from the California Health and Safety Code. (F- Felony; M - Misdemeanor)

(F)   11350 H&S (Possession of cocaine);

Central Nervous System Stimulant Drugs

(F) 11351 H&S (Possession of cocaine for sale);

(F) 11352 H&S (Sales, furnishing, transporting, offering);

(F) 11377 H&S (Possession of amphetamine);

(F) 11378 H&S (Possession of amphetamine for sale);

(F) 11379 H&S (Sales, furnishing, transporting, offering);

(F) 11380 H&S (Use of minor, sales to minor);

As you can see, cocaine and amphetamine are regulated under different sections of the code. As discussed previously, the difference between possession of either drug for sale is the amount of the drug in possession. As a general rule, if the possessor has more than is needed for his own personal use, he is violating either section 11351 H&S (for cocaine) or section 11378 H&S (for amphetamine).

(M) 11550 H&S (Under the influence of cocaine):

It is illegal to use or be under the influence of cocaine or methamphetamine except when authorized by a physician. If there is probable cause to believe the person is under the influence of cocaine or methamphetamine based on the symptoms you observe, transport him to a narcotic expert for a drug evaluation.

In addition to these sections, other Health and Safety Code sections which apply to the stimulant drugs are:

(F) 11353 H&S (Adult inducing a minor to violate any section relating to the stimulant drugs)

(F) 11354 H&S (Minor inducing another minor to violate any section relating to the stimulant drugs)

(F) 11355 H&S (Substituting another substance for a stimulant drug during sale, furnishing, etc.)

(M) 11364 H&S (Possession of paraphernalia such as crack pipe or ice pipe.

(M) 11365 H&S   (Unlawful presence in a place where a stimulant drug is being used)

(F) 11366 H&S (Maintaining any place for the unlawful sale, use, etc., of a stimulant drug)

(M) 109575 H&S (Possession of look-alike drugs with intent to sell).

Chapter 12

There are many more sections involving drug crimes that are found in the Health and Safety Code, Business and Professions Code, Penal Code, and the Vehicle Code. Become familiar with them.

References

American Society for Pharmacology and Experimental Therapeutics & The Committee on Problems of Drug Dependence. "Scientific Perspectives on Cocaine Abuse." The Pharmacologist 29 (1987): 20-27.

Biederman, Joseph et al. "Pharmacotherapy of Attention-deficit Hyperactivity Disorder Reduces Risk for Substance Use Disorder." Pediatrics 104 (1999): 20.

Byck, Robert, ed. Cocaine Papers by Sigmund Freud. New York: Stonehill, 1975.

Bureau of Justice Statistics. Compendium of Federal Justice Statistics, 2002. Washington, D.C., U.S. Department of Justice, 2004.

Centers for Disease Control and Prevention. Youth Risk Behavior Surveillance — United States, 2003. Atlanta: CDC, 2004.

"CIA-Contra-Crack Cocaine Controversy, Appendix C." Washington, D.C., U.S. Department of Justice, 2004.

"Cocaine: The Great Addicter and Deceiver." Drug Awareness Information Newsletter: A Report in The Narc Officer, June, 1990.

Dackis, C.A., and M.F. Gold. "New Concepts in Cocaine Addiction: The Dopamine Depletion Hypothesis." Neuroscience and Biobehavioral Review 9 (1985): 469-477.

Dendow, G.A., et al. "Self-Administration of Psychoactive Substances by the Monkey: A Measure of Psychological Dependence." Psychopharmacology 16 (1969): 30-48.

Department of State. Major Coca & Opium Producing Nations: Cultivation and Production Estimates, 1996-2000. Washington, D.C: U.S. Department of Justice, 2001.

Drug Enforcement Administration. Black Cocaine. Prepared by the Europe-Africa-Asia Unit of the International Section, 1991.

----------. "Defendant Statistical System." Sourcebook of Criminal Justice Statistics. Washington, D.C: U.S. Department of Justice, 2004.

----------. Drug Descriptions: Cocaine. Washington, D.C: U.S. Department of Justice, 2004.

----------. Drugs of Abuse. Washington, D.C: U.S. Department of Justice, 2003.

----------. Drug Trafficking in the United States Washington, D.C: U.S. Department of Justice, 2001.

----------. "Federal-wide Drug Seizure System." Sourcebook of Criminal Justice Statistics. Washington, D.C: U.S. Department of Justice, 2004.

----------. Fenethylline and the Middle East: A Brief Summary. Washington, D.C: U.S. Department of Justice, 2003.

Erickson, P., et al. The Steel Drug: Cocaine in Perspective. Toronto: Lexington Books, 1987.

Fischman, M.W., et al. "Acute Tolerance Development to the Cardiovascular and Subjective Effects of Cocaine." The Journal of Pharmacology and Experimental Therapeutics 235 (1985): 677-682.

Fischman, M.W., et al. "Cardiovascular and Subjective Effects of Intravenous Cocaine in Humans." Arch. Gen. Psychiatry 33 (1976): 989-989.

Grabowski, J., and S.E. Devorkin. "Cocaine: An Overview of Current Issues." Int. Journ. of Addictions 20 (1985): 1065-1088.

Hammer, S., and L. Hazleton. "Cocaine and the Chemical Brain." Addictive Behavior: Drug and Alcohol Abuse. Colorado: Mortion Publishing Co., 1985.

Central Nervous System Stimulant Drugs

"The Implications of Crack." Drug Abuse and Alcoholism Newsletter 15.6 (July, 1986).

Inaba, D., and W. Cohen. Uppers, Downers, All Arounders. San Francisco: Haight-Ashbury Detox Clinic, 1989.

"In Search of the Big Bang." The Good Drug Guide. http\\cocaine.org, February, 2005.

Johanson, C.E. Assesment of the Dependence Potential of Cocaine in Animals." Cocaine Pharmacology, Effects, and Treatment of Abuse. Washington DC: NIDA Research Monograph 50 (1984): 54-71.

Kouri, James. "Ice: New Drug of Choice in Hawaii." The Narc Officer (December, 1989): 43-45.

Miller, Marissa. "Trends and Patterns of Methamphetamine Smoking in Hawaii." NIDA Research Monograph 115 (1991): 72-83.

Landry, MJ. "An Overview of Cocaethylene, An Alcohol-Derived Psychoactive, Cocaine Metabolite." Journal of Psychoactive Drugs 24.3 (1992): 273-276.

National Drug Intelligence Center. "National Drug Threat Survey 2003." Washington, D.C.:U.S. Department of Justice, 2001.

National Institute on Drug Abuse. Crack and Cocaine. Rockville, MD: Department of Health and Human Services, 2005.

----------. Cocaine: Abuse and Addition, Rockville, MD: Department of Health and Human Services, 1999.

----------. Monitoring the Future National Survey Results on Drug Use, 1975-2003, Volume II: College Students & Adults Ages 19-45. 2004.

National Institute of Justice. Drug and Alcohol Use and Related Matters Among Arrestees, 2003. Washington, D.C: U.S. Department of Justice, 2004.

----------. "The Rise of Crack and Ice." Research in Brief, March, 1993.

Office of Forensic Sciences. Microgram 24.6 (June, 1991).

Office of National Drug Control Policy. Pulse Check: Trends in Drug Abuse, July-December 2001 Reporting Period. Washington, D.C., Executive Office of the President, 2002.

Office of National Drug Control Policy. Pulse Check: Trends in Drug Abuse, Drug Markets and Chronic Users in 25 of America's Largest Cities. Washington, D.C., Executive Office of the President, 2004.

Preston, K.L., et al. "Long-term effects of repeated methamphetamine administration on monoamine neurons in the rhesus monkey brain." Brain Res 338 (1985): 243-248.

Resnick, R.B., et al. "Acute Systemic Effects of Cocaine in Man." Science 195 (1977): 696-698.

Short, P.H., and L. Shuster. "Changes in brain norepinephrine associated with sensitization to d-amphetamine." Psychopharmacology 48 (1976): 59-67.

Siegel, R. "Cocaine Freebase." Journal of Psychedelic Drugs 13 (1982): 297-317.

Smith, D.E., and D.R. Wesson. Treating the Cocaine Abuser. Center City: Hazelden Education Materials, 1985.

Substance Abuse and Mental Health Services Administration. Results from the 2003 National Survey on Drug Use and Health: Rockville, MD: Department of Health and Human Services, 2004.

----------. Treatment Episode Data Set (TEDS) Highlights – 2002, Rockville, MD: Department of Health and Human Services, 2004.

U.S. Customs & Border Protection. "U.S. Customs and Border Protection Made Over 56,000 Illegal Drug Seizures, Nearly 2.2 Million Pounds, in FY2004." January 11, 2005.

U.S. Sentencing Commission. 2002 Sourcebook of Federal Sentencing Statistics Washington, D.C., U.S. Department of Justice, 2004.

Chapter 12

Volkow, Nora et al. "Dopamine Transporter Occupancies in the Human Brain Induced by Therapeutic Doses of Oral Methylphenidate." Am J Psychiatry 155 (October 1998): 1325-1331.

Volkow, Nora et al. :Therapeutic Doses of Oral Methylphenidate Significantly Increase Extracellular dopamine in the Human Brain." The Journal of Neuroscience 21 (2001):1-5.

Wagner G.C., C.R. Shuster, and L.S. Seiden. "Methamphetamine-induced changes in brain catecholomines in rats and guinea pigs." Drug and Alcohol Dependency 4 (1979): 435-438.

Wetli, C., and R. Wright. "Death Caused by Recreational Use of Cocaine." JAMA 241.3 (1979): 2519-2522.

CHAPTER 13

HALLUCINOGENIC/PSYCHEDELIC DRUGS

"If we could sniff or swallow something
that would, for five or six hours each
day, abolish our solitude as individuals,
atone us with our fellows in a glowing
exaltation of affection and make life in
all its aspects seem not only worth
living, but divinely beautiful and
significant, and if this heavenly, world-
transfiguring drug were of such a kind
that we could wake up next morning
with a clear head and an undamaged
constitution-then, it seems to me, all
our problems (and not merely the one
small problem of discovering a novel
pleasure) would be wholly solved and
earth would become paradise."

–Aldous Huxley (1894-1963)

§ 13.1   INTRODUCTION

Chemical substances in this group are referred to as hallucinogenic
drugs. Psychotomimetic refers to drugs that mimic a psychological or
psychotic state. Hallucinogenic refers to the hallucinations these drugs
may produce. Psychedelic means mind expanding.

The drugs in this category all have the ability to induce visual, auditory or other hallucinations and to separate the individual from reality.
They produce a wide range of behavioral alterations. Thus, their classification by chemical structure is difficult. However, these drugs are
thought to alter synaptic transmission processes in the human brain,
and it is possible to classify these compounds by the transmitter upon
which the drug is thought to act. Several chemical substances are commonly thought to serve as synaptic transmitters within the brain. Such
substances include acetylcholine, norepinephrine and serotonin.

Thus, we could classify psychedelic drugs as follows:

I.   ACETYLCHOLINE PSYCHEDELICS

Atropine, scopolamine, muscarine—from plants such as belladonna
or deadly nightshade, jimson weed, stick weed, thorn apple and henbane. This group also includes muscarine, which is derived from a
mushroom (amanita muscaria) found in Europe and Scandinavia.

II. NOREPINEPHRINE PSYCHEDELICS

Mescaline, DOM (STP), MDA, MMDA, TMA, myristicin—from plants such as peyote and mescaline derivatives (DOM, TMA and MMDA); myristicin is from nutmeg and mace.

III. SEROTONIN PSYCHEDELICS

Phencyclidine (PCP) and ketamine. The neurotransmitters upon which these compounds exert their activity are unknown. These are synthetically manufactured compounds.

§ 13.2 GENERAL EFFECTS OF HALLUCINOGENIC/ PSYCHEDELIC DRUGS

A user who is under the influence of a psychedelic drug may speak of "seeing" sounds, "tasting" colors, and "hearing" motion. His sense of direction, distance and time become disoriented. Restlessness and sleeplessness are common until the drug wears off.

The greatest hazard of the psychedelics is that their effects are unpredictable each time they are taken. Toxic (or poisonous) reactions that cause psychotic reactions can even result in death.

Persons in psychedelic states should be closely supervised, taking extra care not to upset them—to keep them from harming themselves and others. They should be approached slowly and calmly.

§ 13.2.1 The Question of Addiction and Other Hazards

Unlike narcotics, hallucinogens do not give rise to true addiction. However, hallucinogens are not less dangerous than drugs of addiction. They are dangerous in a different way. The great danger associated with the use of hallucinogens without medical supervision is the possible occurrence of a "bad trip," which is characterized by the development of severe confusion, panic and anxiety. This may lead to suicide, or in a psychologically unstable or youthful person, a permanent psychological trauma may develop. Hallucinogens completely transform perceptivity and the dangers inherent in such a process readily explains why primitive people imposed a taboo on these organic substances. For these people, hallucinogenic substances were sacred and were reserved for the use of medicine men in religious ceremonial situations. Since these taboos no longer exist in our society, and the general trend is to throw aside inhibitions, government has no alternative but to impose strict controls on the use of hallucinogens.

However, like many of the addictive drugs, LSD produces tolerance, so some users who take the drug repeatedly must take progressively higher doses to achieve the state of intoxication that they had previously achieved. Most users of LSD voluntarily decrease or stop their use over time. LSD is not considered an addictive drug since it does not produce compulsive drug-seeking behavior as do cocaine, amphetamine, heroin, alcohol, and nicotine. Clearly, though, this is an extremely dangerous practice, given the unpredictability of the drug. NIDA is funding studies that focus on the neurochemical and behavioral properties of LSD. This research will provide a greater understanding of the mechanisms of the drug.

§ 13.2.2 Withdrawal Syndrome

There is no documented withdrawal syndrome related to abuse of the hallucinogenic drugs. For this reason, the psychedelics have been shown to produce no physical dependence.

Some of the drugs like LSD, DMT, and PCP are made in a lab. Other drugs are found in various plants like mushrooms, cactus, vines, bushes, weeds, etc.

We will confine our discussion to the most popular psychedelic drugs used—LSD, PCP, peyote (mescaline), psilocybin mushroom and some miscellaneous substances.

§ 13.3   LYSERGIC ACID DIETHYLAMIDE
§ 13.3.1 Introduction

In 1938, Dr. Albert Hofmann co-developed from a fungal plant rust called ergot, a compound called lysergic acid diethylamide (LSD). Five years later, Dr. Hofmann decided to see if LSD could be developed into an analeptic compound to stimulate blood circulation and respiration in elderly people. While crystallizing the LSD compound in the form of a tartrate, he absorbed "an immeasurable trace" of it through his fingertips. Dr. Hofmann described his first unintentional use as "a not unpleasant intoxicated-like condition" occupying two hours of interesting imagery. From 1943 to 1970, Hofmann used LSD about 15 times and concluded that there was simply no way to guarantee either a good or bad "trip." "The experience is handled best," Hofmann cautiously counseled, "by a stabilized person with a meaningful reason for taking LSD."

Even though LSD is made from a fungus that grows on certain grains such as rye, it can be produced easily and synthetically in a laboratory.

In the 1940s, interest is LSD was revived when it was thought to be a possible treatment for schizophrenia. Because of LSD's structural relationship to a chemical that is present in the brain and its similarity in effect to certain aspects of psychosis, LSD was used as a research tool in studies of mental illness.

Sandoz Laboratories, the drug's sole producer, began marketing LSD in 1947 under the trade name "Delysid" and it was introduced into the United States a year later. Sandoz marketed LSD as a psychiatric cure-all and "hailed it as a cure for everything from schizophrenia to criminal behavior, sexual perversions, and alcoholism" (Henderson).

In psychiatry, the use of LSD by students was an accepted practice. It was viewed as a teaching tool in an attempt to understand schizophrenia. From the late 1940s through the mid 1970s, extensive research and testing were conducted on LSD. During the 15-year period beginning in 1950, research on LSD and other hallucinogens generated over 1,000 scientific papers, several dozen books, and 6 international conferences, and LSD was prescribed as treatment to over 40,000 patients (Zenter).

In the 1960s, LSD emerged as a casual drug of abuse. LSD has remained popular among certain segments of society. It is popular among teenagers, college students, and other young adults. LSD has been integral to the lifestyle of many individuals who follow certain rock music bands, most notably the Grateful Dead. Older individuals, introduced to the hallucinogen in the 1960s, still use LSD.

LSD is sold under more than 80 street names. More than 200 types of LSD tablets have been encountered by law enforcement officers since 1969 and more than 350 paper designs have been acquired by the DEA since 1975.

§ 13.3.2 Illegal LSD Production

LSD has been manufactured illegally since the 1960s. A limited number of chemists, probably less than 12, are believed to be manufacturing nearly all of the LSD in the United States. Some have been operating since the 1960s. It is believed that most of the LSD is manufactured in the San Francisco Bay area.

Drug enforcement agents believe that LSD cookers form a fraternity of sorts. They have successfully remained at large because there are so few of them. Their exclusivity is not surprising given that LSD synthesis is a difficult process to master. Although cooks need not be chemists, they must adhere to precise and complex production procedures. Further supporting the idea that most LSD manufacture is the work of a small fraternity of chemists, virtually all the LSD seized during the 1980s was of consistently high purity and sold in relatively uniform dosages of 20 to 80 micrograms.

LSD is produced from lysergic acid, which is made from ergotamine tartrate, a substance derived from an ergot fungus on rye, or from lysergic acid amide, a chemical found in morning glory seeds. Although theoretically possible, manufacture of LSD from morning glory seeds is not economically feasible. Ergotamine tartrate is not readily available in the United States. It is acquired from Europe, Mexico, Costa Rica, and Africa. The difficulty in acquiring ergotamine tartrate may limit the number of independent LSD manufacturers.

It takes 25 kilograms of ergotamine tartrate to produce 6 kilograms of pure LSD crystal that could be processed into 100 million dosage units, more than enough to meet what is believed to be the entire annual U.S. demand for LSD.

Cooking LSD is time consuming. It takes from 2 to 3 days to produce 1 to 4 ounces of crystal. LSD is not produced in large quantities, but rather in a series of small batches. Production of LSD in small batches also minimizes the loss of precursor chemicals should they become contaminated during the synthesis process.

Over the past 30 years, the traditional dilution factor for manufacturing LSD has been 10,000 dosage units per 1 gram of crystal. Therefore, dosage units yielded from high-purity (95 to 100 percent) LSD crystal would contain 100 micrograms. However, dosages currently seen contain closer to 50 micrograms.

Pure, high-potency LSD is a clear or white, odorless crystalline material that is soluble in water. It is mixed with binding agents, such as spray-dried skim milk, for producing better tablets or is dissolved and diluted in a solvent for application onto paper. Variations in the manufacturing process can cause LSD to range in color from clear or white, in its purest form, to tan or even black, indicating poor quality or degradation. To mask product deficiencies, distributors often apply LSD to off-white, tan, or yellow paper to disguise discoloration.

LSD crystal is converted into tablet form (microdots, that are inch or smaller in diameter), or thin squares of gelatin (window panes), or applied to sheets of prepared paper (blotter paper). LSD is most frequently found on blotter paper.

§ 13.3.3 Phases of LSD Use

The first phase of LSD use mainly involved pharmacological and psychotomimetic studies. This was followed by experiments on creativity, treatment of character disorders and religious mysticism. The next phase (1965 to 1970) involved widespread indiscriminate use by mostly young people. This phase involved a combination of magical expectations created by the sensationalism of the mass media, the extremism of reactions by society and the ready availability and ease of concealment of the drug. It was this phase that people attributed to Augustus Stanley Ocusley III's purple haze, white lightning and blue cheer, or the orange sunshine barrels made by the Brotherhood of Eternal Love.

From 1970 to 1978, LSD was not publicized in the media, law enforcement made few arrests and, overall, though LSD use never disappeared, not much attention was given to the use of the drug.

The next phase (1980s) involved more use of LSD than at any time since the early 1970s. Most of the "acid" used today is of the blotter variety. Wizards, political symbols, chemical equations, flying saucers, zodiac signs, flowers and a menagerie of animals and cartoon characters are found on blotter paper.

In the 1990s, LSD is the fastest growing drug of abuse among the under 20 age group. LSD, along with marijuana, are currently the only drugs with an upward trend among high school students.

Since 1978, there have been changes in the LSD market. LSD is more uniform at 50 micrograms. It is easier to get today, with the shift away from pills and powders to blotter hits. There are even sugar wafer blotters. There have been few reports of "bad acid."

The popularity of LSD decreased in the early 1970s because of problems with the purity of the LSD in the market. There were rumors that

LSD was cut with strychnine and amphetamines. PCP and crude speed were often represented as LSD. However, since 1973, according to PharmChem Lab in Menlo Park, California, LSD has been a consistent 87 to 95 percent purity with the remaining ingredients inert substances (PharmChem 1989).

Standardization of doses has gone a long way in increasing the popularity of LSD. The big seller in LSD in 1979 was blotter acid featuring a tiny green or red dragon. Some counterfeit "dragon acid" appeared in 1980. There was the popular "wizard" or Mickey Mouse acid. It featured a four-color still of Mickey Mouse, wand in hand, from the classic cartoon, "The Sorcerer's Apprentice." The printing is not easy to duplicate cheaply or quickly. A "package" of this acid is sold wholesale for $2,000+ in 40 sheets of absorbent blotter paper, each sheet divided by perforations into 100 individual hits. Each package of 40 blotter sheets is sealed in tin foil and put in a cardboard box which is sealed with wax. The package contains 4,000 hits equal to one gram. Most middle-level LSD dealers buy acid in bulk and produce their own brand of blotter LSD using a stamp or silk-screen to put their logo on the sheets. It was reported in High Times (August 1981) that one West coast LSD dealer includes a marketing kit when a buyer purchases 100,000 hits of LSD in liquid form. The kit illustrates the fine points of commercial LSD preparation, how to dilute LSD, if it is to be "windowpane," how to mold the gelatin and at what temperature, and the logistics of impregnating and stamping blotter LSD.

In 2003 LSD made a noticeable resurgence in many areas of the United States. This "new" LSD on blotter paper is high purity. Even with high purity, "bad trips" are infrequent. Current speculation is that the LSD is so expertly refined that impurities are not present. Impurities are partially reacted chemicals that may have caused bad trips. Packaging of LSD sheets or individual hits is in baggies or aluminum foil. Those handling it apparently know touching and absorbing it may cause a trip. LSD has once again become popular because it is inexpensive, can be used without obvious signs and is perceived as non-addictive. Interestingly, the new generation of LSD abusers thinks of LSD as the new drug on the street. They are almost completely unaware of the history of LSD in the 1960s.

It seems inevitable that LSD will become a social phenomenon again for better or worse.

§ 13.3.4 Forms of LSD

LSD in its pure form is an odorless, tasteless and colorless crystal. It dissolves in water and cannot be detected except by chemical analysis. The drug is combined with other ingredients to obtain bulk for packaging. These ingredients then contribute to the odor, taste and color of the LSD sold on the street.

LSD is mixed with or put on almost anything which can be swallowed: sugar cubes, candy (such as "Necco" wafers), animal crackers, chewing gum, paper, any liquid for drinking, etc. It has been placed on stamps and envelope flaps which are licked, and it has been mixed with gelatin and formed into thin squares (called "window panes") which are chewed. It also comes in tablet form—such as a distinctive orange tablet called Sunshine. It is also commonly sold on the street in clear capsules (smaller than the common time-release cold capsules) which contain LSD in a white or light blue powder.

Liquid LSD is primarily associated with mid-level distribution. LSD in liquid or crystal form generally is sold in plastic film canisters or, occasionally, in small, opaque plastic bottles to prevent oxidation. Liquid LSD is mixed with a binding agent and pressed into pills ("microdots" that are only 3/32 of an inch or smaller); distributed in thin squares of gelatin ("window panes"); distributed in breath mint vials and treated sugar cubes; or dissolved and diluted and applied to blotter paper. Since variations in the manufacturing of LSD may result in an off-white color, the finished product is often applied to off-white, tan, or yellow paper with colorful designs to mask the impurities. The most common method of distributing LSD is blotter paper, and there may be as many as 80 street names for the drug, based upon the designs on the papers.

In short, any substance which can be introduced into the body can contain LSD. Also, it is difficult to find it because almost all forms of the drug are so easy to conceal.

§ 13.3.5 Pharmacology of LSD

The dosage level that will produce a hallucinogenic effect in humans generally is considered to be 25 micrograms. Over the past several years, the potency of LSD obtained during drug law enforcement operations has ranged between 20 and 80 micrograms per dosage unit. DEA recognizes 50 micrograms as the standard dosage unit.

The effects of LSD vary according to the amount and how taken. The average period for LSD effects to come on in the use of 1 to 2 g/kg orally is 45 minutes (anywhere between 15 to 120 minutes). Almost all effects of LSD are gone after 8 to 12 hours, in some cases, 24 hours. Very large doses may produce intense and substantial symptoms for 48 hours. When the drug is swallowed, there is a gradual build-up of physiological symptoms. These consist of numbness, a tingling of the extremities, feeling of chilliness, anorexia, nausea, vomiting (rarely), flushing and dilation of the pupils. These symptoms usually subside by the time the psychic symptoms appear.

§ 13.3.6 Distribution of LSD in the Body

LSD readily crosses the blood-brain barrier but is not concentrated in the brain. Higher concentrations are found in the hypothalamus, limbic system and the visual and auditory reflect centers. The half-life of LSD in man is 175 minutes.

Excretion of LSD proceeds by way of 2-oxidation of LSD in the liver, an inactive metabolite and eliminated by the kidneys.

Tolerance to LSD is lost as quickly as it develops so that there is no tolerance when used twice weekly. Cross-tolerance between mescaline, psilocybin, and DMT has been established (Rosenberg et al). Physical addiction, in the sense of withdrawal effects following the prolonged use of the drug does not occur with LSD.

Stimulants tend to potentiate and increase the effects of LSD. Sedatives, tranquilizers, and narcotics counteract the LSD effect with some exceptions.

The lethal dose of LSD for man is unknown. If man metabolizes LSD like a rabbit, the calculated lethal dose would be 20 mg (or 20,000 g). When death results in the course of an LSD experience (LSD behavioral toxicity), it is due to accident or suicide rather than its intrinsic toxicity.

The effects of 100 g of LSD varies widely. Ten percent of the population will not observe any substantial subjective change; the great majority will report definite psychic effects. Women appear more sensitive than men. Schizophrenics and alcoholics are somewhat resistant to 100 g of the drug. Body weight is not a reliable index of LSD effects. Those who do not want loss of ego control can fight off small doses of LSD. There are, however, some drug variables that account for drug effects. One would have to consider personality of user, security of environment and the expectations of the user.

The question of human brain damage remains unresolved. The precise manner by which LSD exerts its psychic effects is unknown.

§ 13.3.7 The LSD State

Perhaps the first psychological indication that LSD has started to act is a loosening of emotional inhibitions: spontaneous laughter, tears and smiling without cause, relaxation of tensions. In general, the mood tends to be euphoric, and expressive.

The user may experience changes in visual perceptions and extreme changes of mood. He may lose his sense of time and depth perceptions. Size, movement, color, spatial arrangement, sound, touch and his own "body image" will be distorted. For example, he might lose the ability to tell the difference between his body and the rest of his environment. He might even believe he can fly or float in the air. He might feel two very strong but opposite sensations at once—for example, he might feel both heavy and light at the same time. Because this new world is so fascinating, abusers of LSD will lose their desire to eat or sleep until the trip is over. Nausea is a frequent side effect.

All of these psychological effects prevent the LSD user from making rational judgments about even the most common dangers—for example, he might walk in front of a moving car, or step out of a window several stories up. It is easy to see how accidental deaths can occur while a person is experiencing the effects of a "trip."

The same individual may experience different effects at different times. Responses to this drug cannot be predicted, and abusers talk about "good trips" and "bad trips" or "bummers." Abusers can usually remember what happened to them while they were under the influence, but they are often not able to describe it. This is because some of the experiences are not in the verbal dimension—there are no words available to adequately describe their sensations.

§ 13.3.8 Side Effects from LSD

One of the most frequent aspects of LSD, for the user, is that the effects can recur days, weeks, months, and even years after the drug is taken. This is called a "flashback." Intensive use of the drug seems to cause this situation more often than infrequent use. This recurrence of symptoms is frightening, and may cause the abuser to think he is losing his mind.

Another common side effect of LSD use is the fear or the panic that is experienced by a user when he is unable to cope with the effects often brought on by the drug. This panic is often experienced by novice LSD users as opposed to individuals who have taken LSD frequently and are familiar with the effects of the drug. Medical and law enforcement personnel often encounter an individual who is experiencing an LSD panic or "bummer."

The panic reaction that some individuals undergo during the LSD experience are feelings of deep depersonalization, distorted perceptions, and the content of the drug-induced illusions or hallucinations may be very alarming, leading to anxiety, panic or uncontrolled excitement at the peak of the drug effect. These reactions are most likely to occur in inexperienced users when in disturbing or threatening environments, in subjects who have ambivalent attitudes toward the drug experience, or in persons who are emotionally and mentally unstable.

LSD use can also cause an extended period of psychosis, which may occur after a single exposure, and usually involves a person who was pre-psychotic or had a history of psychosis.

LSD produces a suggestible state, making the user susceptible to influences in his environment which can induce a bad reaction. This bad reaction may then become reality to the individual under the influence of the drug, who is then off on a "bummer."

In regard to prolonged psychotic episodes, there are many reports of this type of activity after LSD use. However, all drug-using communities attract many disturbed people so it is difficult to separate direct drug effect from episodes precipitated or caused by the person's condition when a person already psychologically ill ingests LSD.

It has not yet been demonstrated conclusively that permanent organic defects result from prolonged LSD use. However, there are studies that show chromosome damage. There are a number of chemicals known to have an effect similar to LSD on the chromosomes. Such drugs as alcohol, caffeine and even commonly used pharmaceutical drugs will increase the incidence of chromosome damage at about the same rate as LSD.

Early laboratory studies suggested that LSD could cause malformation of a fetus if the mother took LSD. There is no hard and fast proof to substantiate this, as other drugs could cause the same effect during the first trimester of pregnancy. LSD is an ergot derivative capable of contracting the pregnant uterus. There is evidence which suggests this effect has caused fetal death and abortion and pregnant women should not use LSD.

§ 13.3.9(a)   Breakdown of the LSD "Trip"

The actual LSD experience or "trip" can be divided into four stages. The first stage begins when the drug is ingested and lasts until the full experience develops. If LSD is taken orally, symptoms usually appear in thirty to forty-five minutes. The first phase, or the initial development of symptoms, usually lasts about an hour if a normal amount is taken, but the time can vary from twenty minutes to two hours.

In the second phase, the full effects of the drug are manifested, and this period usually lasts about four to six hours. The length and intensity of the psychological experience depends upon several factors, which include:

1.   Amount taken

2.   Frequency of use (which may have led to tolerance)

3.   Prior experience with the drug

4.   Concurrent use of other drugs

5.   Physical and psychological makeup of the user

6.   "Setting" (environment in which the drug is taken)

7.   "Set" (mental condition of the user—happy, depressed, etc.). Setting and set are important in reducing the incidence of "bummers" and "flashbacks."

The third phase, or the recovery, starts when symptoms of the drug experience begin to diminish. During this phase, the person experiences altering waves of LSD symptoms and waves of normal feelings. This period usually occurs seven to nine hours after drug ingestion.

The fourth and final phase of the LSD "trip" is the aftermath. This final phase is usually demonstrated by feelings of tension, restlessness, and feelings of chilliness and nausea. This feeling generally lingers for several hours but is usually gone by the following day.

The impact of LSD on the senses is normally very striking. The function of perceiving, organizing, and interpreting sensory impressions that reach the brain can be severely altered by the drug. The user may become aware of the onset of LSD by noticing that objects have begun to waver and appear distorted. For example, a wall might begin to waver or grow larger, objects in a painting may begin to move, or ordinary objects may suddenly appear luminous as though surrounded by a halo.

The term "hallucinogenic" implies that the drug may cause hallucinations. A true hallucination, be it auditory and/or visual, has no basis in fact but is very real to the individual experiencing the hallucination. While this occasionally happens with LSD, pseudo-hallucinations are more common. Pseudo-hallucination means that the user knows that what he sees or hears does not have a basis in external reality. For example, the user may see geometric forms, figures or brilliant colors, but he realizes that they do not really exist and that his visions are drug induced.

In short, LSD can seriously affect the grasp that a person has on the world, and in some cases it can altogether shatter what was once a firm relationship with that world. This is especially true when the user forgets that what he is seeing, hearing or feeling is drug induced and will, in time, disappear.

Changes in emotion are characterized by rapid swings from one mood to another. For example, it is not uncommon for users to laugh hysterically and then suddenly become very sad, depressed, and even cry for no apparent reason. Some users report feeling happy and sad at the same time. Such changes in emotions are not necessarily directly caused by LSD, but may arise from the individual's own personality having been enhanced or altered by the drug.

The effect of LSD on other thought processes is just as pronounced as in the area of emotions. On many occasions, perception of time may be sharply altered. Time may appear to stand still, causing the user to feel cut off from the future. This feeling is often accompanied by a strong sense of living exclusively in the present. Foresight may become diminished or non-existent. This facet of LSD use is said by some to cause a lack of the competitive spirit, which is normally very pronounced in a human being.

A second way that LSD affects the thinking is through personal perception. Often the individual's body image becomes extremely distorted or he may see himself as being totally dismembered, limb from limb. This effect can become terrifying and can lead to severe anxiety and panic.

LSD characteristically causes a lack of ability to think in abstracts or in terms of ideas and concepts. One theory to explain this deficiency is that the user becomes so preoccupied with the LSD experience that he loses interest in other things.

It is common to hear the term "consciousness expanding" or "mind expanding" in discussions about LSD. Despite the claims of LSD advocates, a person under the influence of LSD has a restricted rather than expanded range of consciousness. This belief of increased awareness or acuteness is caused by the blurring of certain psychological boundaries, perhaps between reality and fantasy. This ultimately results in the user falsely believing there is an extension of his awareness, but actually rational judgment or critical reasoning is often greatly impaired.

§ 13.3.10   Treatment for "Bad Trips"

Users of LSD often realize that they may experience a bad trip or "bummer." For this reason users will often keep tranquilizers or barbiturates on hand. In the past, physicians administered these types of drugs to individuals experiencing "bad trips," but found these types of drugs were not antidotes. Illicit users may still keep a supply of these drugs to attempt to counter adverse psychological reactions. A very real danger of using this type of drug when under the influence of LSD is the possibility of an overdose. An LSD user attempting to stop adverse effects by using hypnotics or tranquilizers may actually intensify his "bad trip," causing him to ingest still more "downers," leading to an overdose. Most physicians now agree that the best method of dealing with the "bad trip" is by using the "talk down" method of treatment which is basically a reassuring conversation with the individual regarding his well-being.

§ 13.3.11   Law Enforcement and LSD

Most often, law enforcement will be called to handle an individual who is having a bad trip on LSD and other hallucinogens/psychedelic substances. A bad trip usually occurs in someone who has taken a substance which produces some unpleasant effects, or in the unstable individual who now has all kinds of strange things going on in his head as a result of the drug.

The user is in a state of panic of what is going on within him. He may be talking about strange things, about seeing things in a peculiar way, about perceiving people as changing shapes in front of his eyes or about faces melting and changing into something else. He may talk about strange sensations in relation to his environment, such as seeing the walls move or go in and out as if the room was breathing. He may talk about feeling the floor moving under him. All of these bizarre-sounding things should give you a clue that the person is probably psychotic or having a drug experience.

Intervening in this situation is similar to dealing with a psychotic person. Approach the person calmly, in a way that is non-threatening and is not going to contribute to his feeling of panic. Keep in mind that you may be dealing with someone who fears police officers. It is especially important to approach the user very calmly and reassure him that he is going to be all right and that you are there for his protection and to help him. If there is a lot of noise around, a lot of movement or a lot of people, try to reduce the level of stimulation as much as possible.

The individual who is using the psychedelic is someone who is very sensitive to changes and to any kind of stimulation in the environment. The principal danger in this kind of situation is not that the individual is going to attack another person, but rather because of the panic, the user will inadvertently hurt himself or someone else. He may try to get away from something that is terrifying him. He may jump out a window because he doesn't know it is a window or because it seems that jumping through it is more desirable than being attacked by monsters. If there is some indication that he is a danger to himself or to others around him, you should restrain the individual. It is important to control the user so he won't hurt himself and at the same time try to reduce his panic by being reassuring. After you have the individual under control, a referral to a drug crisis center would be appropriate. A less desirable alternative is the county hospital emergency room. Unless the hospital has considerable experience with such cases, it may make the situation worse. The atmosphere may increase the individual's panic and treatment with drugs may produce serious reactions.

§ 13.3.12   Current Trafficking and Distribution

LSD trafficking has mirrored the demand for the drug. The illicit market has never experienced a serious shortage or glut of LSD and the overall supply of the drug has remained constant since 1980. It has been established by the DEA that the sources of supply of LSD are located in the San Francisco Bay area.

DEA reports indicate that LSD is available in all 50 states. More than half of the DEA jurisdictions field offices have reported an increase in LSD in the 1990s. Northern California appears to be the source of supply for most of the LSD in the United States.

At the wholesale production and trafficking level, LSD is controlled tightly by California-based organizations that have operated with relative impunity for 20 or more years. DEA reports also indicate that an increasing number of people nationwide are manufacturing LSD.

LSD traffickers sometimes supply or front consignments of LSD to distributors who have established an acceptable level of reliability. The traffickers are reimbursed once the LSD has been sold. For the most part, however, payment for consignments of LSD is made in advance by wire through Western Union or by postal money orders. Upon receipt of payment, LSD is shipped to the distributor. At the retail level, LSD is sold strictly on a cash-and-carry basis. Money laundering is not conducted on a sophisticated level, except by LSD traffickers with international connections. DEA investigative intelligence reveals that major trafficking organizations are attempting to boost LSD sales through extension of credit, especially to mid-level distributors and occasionally to low-level sellers. This suggests that competition at the highest levels of the traffic is increasing, possibly due to an increase in the number of LSD crystal manufacturers.

LSD is usually transported from the San Francisco Bay area by overnight delivery services; Express Mail, Federal Express, and DHL are used extensively to transport large amounts of LSD throughout the United States. LSD is shipped to major distributors in cities that host rock concerts. The "Grateful Dead" band concerts were the most popular until the band stopped touring due to the death of leader Jerry Garcia. The concerts are used as forums for large-scale LSD distribution, as well as low-level or retail sales. In addition, intelligence reveals that major transactions take place at these events.

Chapter 13

Distribution of LSD usually occurs in one of three ways. First, an individual attends a rock concert, meets a source of supply, and exchanges telephone numbers. Typically, these purchases are for retail quantities of 1 up to 100 doses. Second, individuals who decide to continue distributing call the source for additional amounts. Usually, the source has either continued on the concert tour or has returned home, which frequently is in Northern California. After the initial purchase, almost all transactions are made via the public and private mail systems. Third, some distributors travel directly to California to meet sources of supply.

The mail system is the primary means used to ship wholesale quantities of LSD to distributors nationwide. DEA reports indicate that LSD is concealed in greeting cards, in cassette tapes, or in articles of clothing that are mailed to a post office box. The post office box is listed under a fictitious name or business. No return address is provided on the package or envelope.

§ 13.3.13   LSD Distribution Levels
Retail, or user-level quantities, range from 1 to 10 dosage units. Low-level distributors sell 50 to 100 dosage unit quantities. Mid-level distributors sell 1,000 dosage unit quantities, as well as multiples of 1,000 units. These distributors normally have more than one source of supply and sell to several lower level distributors. The sources of supply for gram-distributors typically are located in Northern California. These sources normally convert LSD from crystal or liquid form to paper form. Multigram distributors travel to California to obtain LSD personally and are associated with numerous lower level dealers.

§ 13.3.14   The Packaging of LSD
LSD is sold in several forms, including crystal, liquid, tablets, gelatin, or applied to sheets of paper or sugar cubes. At the upper levels of trafficking, LSD is sold in crystal form. LSD in liquid form is destined for transfer to a paper medium, commonly associated with mid-level dealing. At the retail level, LSD is sold in paper form and sometimes tablets.

LSD, when diluted and applied to paper, begins to degrade quickly, necessitating a high rate of product turnover. LSD in liquid and crystal are sold in plastic film canisters or in small opaque plastic bottles to prevent oxidation, which turns the LSD darker than the preferred white or off-white color.

LSD in crystal or liquid form is applied to sheets of paper by traffickers who operate clandestine conversion laboratories. These labs can be set up quickly almost anywhere. The sheets of paper are prepared with colorful designs or artwork of many different characters or images. The designs often are applied commercially by printing companies using off-set lithography, screen printing, or silk screening.

The sheets are perforated to create small squares which represent a single dosage unit. The sheets are then ready for the application of LSD. The printed sheets are dipped into shallow pans containing LSD crystal dissolved in methanol, ethanol, or other solvent (water can be used, however, its slower evaporation rate increases the likelihood of degradation), and then are dried. The printing inks are insoluble in the solvents to ensure that the image does not run. The potency of LSD can vary from sheet to sheet or from square to square.

Once the paper sheets are printed, perforated, and impregnated with LSD, they are ready for distribution.

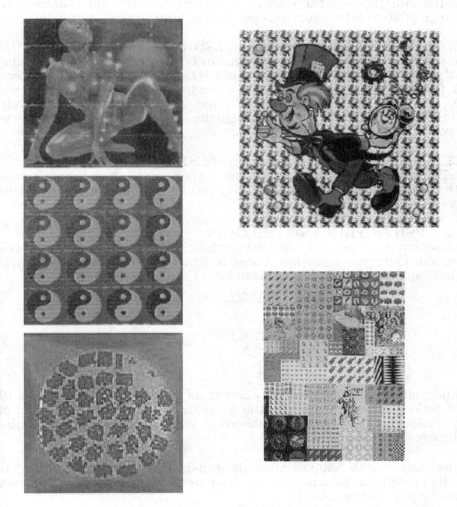

LSD Blotter Paper Designs

§ 13.3.15   Price of LSD
LSD is relatively inexpensive. The average price is $5 per retail dosage unit and less than $1 per unit in wholesale lots of 1,000 or more. Although LSD prices have fluctuated nationally during the past several years, overall prices remain relatively low (DEA 1995). The low cost of LSD has given rise to incidents where the drug is misrepresented as another illicit drug of abuse. For example, LSD can be applied to mush-

rooms to create "psilocybin" mushrooms that sell for $30 to $350 per ounce. It can be applied to tablets and sold as MDMA for $8 to $25 per dosage unit.

§ 13.3.16   Potency of LSD

LSD potency or strength is measured in micrograms. In the 1960s and early 1970s, LSD potency ranged from 100 to 200 micrograms per dose. In the later 1970s, LSD average potency was 30 to 50 micrograms. From the mid-1980s to the present time, LSD potency has remained in the range of 20 to 80 micrograms per dosage unit.

The distribution of lower potency LSD does two things. First, the same volume of LSD liquid or crystal can be diluted into a larger number of units, thus increasing the profits. Second, lower potency doses yield fewer adverse reactions on the scale of those seen during the 1960s and 1970s. Lower potency LSD has accounted for the relatively few LSD-related emergency room incidents noted during the past several years.

§ 13.3.17   Quantitative Analysis of LSD

LSD can be extracted from blotter paper and it has been demonstrated that gas-liquid chromatography can be used for the quantitative analysis of LSD (DEA 1993).

§ 13.4   PSILOCYBIN AND PSILOCIN

Psilocybin and psilocin are psychedelic agents obtained from the mushroom *Psilocybe Mexicana*. These mushrooms have a long history of religious and sacramental use throughout Central America.

Psilocybin is approximately 1 percent as potent as LSD—that is, 10 mg of psilocybin would produce the same degree of action as 0.1 mg of LSD. Psilocybin is effectively absorbed when taken orally and the mushrooms are eaten raw.

What appears to happen after the mushroom has been ingested is that the phosphoric acid is removed from psilocybin, producing psilocin, the active psychedelic agent.

Until the last 20 years, very little was known about the so-called "magic mushrooms" that grow in the southern portion of Mexico. Botanists have now identified at least 20 species of mushrooms from that area which contain psilocybin, which is the mind-altering drug in the mushroom. Also contained within the mushrooms is an unstable derivative of psilocybin, psilocin.

The ingestion of 32 dried specimens of *Psilocybe Mexicana*, weighing 2.4 grams, is considered a medium dose by Mexican Oaxaca Indian standards. It was possible to extract the active principals from the mushroom and to purify and crystallize them. The main active component was named psilocybin after the mushroom and the accompanying alkaloid was named psilocin. From this basic research conducted by Hofmann, other researchers identified other mushroom specimens which also contain psilocybin and psilocin (Heim et al).

§ 13.5   THE AMERICAN HALLUCINOGENIC MUSHROOM

The most common and the strongest hallucinogenic mushroom in the United States is known as *Psilocybe Cubensis*. The top of this mushroom, known as the cap, varies in color from a light tannish gold to a light gold which appears almost white. The edge of the cap will be either a darker gold if the center is white, or a whiter color if the center is gold-tan. The gold color is similar to that of broom straw. The cap of the mushroom will be covered with a sticky, slimy substance. Most of the caps have a slight knob in the very center, but this is not always the case. A slight rise or discoloration can be observed in the center of this knob on close examination. Because the size of the cap varies depending on the age of the mushroom, caps may vary from 1 to 2 inches in diameter, with some as large as 5 inches.

As the *Psilocybe Cubensis* mushroom first begins to grow, it may show small, whitish spots that disappear as it matures. As it grows, the stock becomes visible and the cap appears egg-shaped. The cap is curved inward and connects to the stem in order to protect the gills and spores that form on the underside of the cap. The gills are covered with millions of microscopic spores which later fall to the ground to produce more mushrooms. In a young mushroom, a white line appears where the cap joins the stem. After the cap opens up, this line, called the annulus or skirt, forms around the upper portion of the stem.

Once the mushroom starts to mature, it does so quite rapidly. The maturation period is from 24 to 72 hours depending on the weather and the temperature conditions. The cap first becomes conical, then bell-shaped and finally flatter. As the mushroom gets older, the color becomes somewhat darker but it will retain the golden color until it dies, turns black and falls to the ground.

One of the more definite identification characteristics of this mushroom is that the cap will turn blue with age where it has been scratched. The bluing of the cap will appear strongest around the edges. When the cap expands with growth, the gills underneath the cap become visible. The gills will be grayish-white in young specimens and violet-gray to nearly black in mature specimens. The gills are attached to the stem and may be slightly notched. The mushrooms are quite firm to the touch. The size of the stem depends on the size of the mushroom.

The skirt around the upper portion of the stem will be purplish-black from the dropping spore. The stem will be a little larger at the base and will be covered with a mass of white moss-like matting. The stem is usually the first part of the mushroom to turn blue, especially toward the base where it is torn or broken.

§ 13.5.1 Method of Ingestion

Once the mushrooms have been collected, there are several methods of ingestion.

The first method would be to eat the mushrooms fresh, including the cap and the stem.

Another popular method is to dry the mushrooms on a piece of window-type screen, which is placed to allow air to circulate underneath the screen. Drying is accomplished in about three days. Once they are completely dry, the mushrooms can be stored in a container and will reportedly keep for a period of years without losing potency. The weight of the mushroom is greatly decreased during drying as these mushrooms are 80 to 85 percent water. Some users freeze the mushrooms, but this is the least satisfactory method as the mushrooms spoil soon after they thaw.

Another method is to dry the mushrooms and grind them up in a blender or food grinder. The ground mushrooms are then placed in a shallow container, covered with methyl alcohol, and allowed to stand for 5 days. The alcohol is then strained off and the liquid placed in a dish until it evaporates. The remaining white crystalline substances is purportedly psilocybin.

§ 13.5.2 Psychological Effects

As one writer describes the effects of mushroom ingestion: "It permits you to travel backwards and forwards in time, to enter other places of existence, even to know God...our body lies in darkness, heavy as lead, but your spirit seems to soar and leave the hut and with the speed of thought to travel where it listeth, in time and space accompanied by the shamans singing...at least you know what the ineffable is, and what ecstasy means. Ecstasy! For the Greeks, ecstasies meant the flight of the soul from the body. Can you find a better word to describe this state?" (De Bald).

The hallucinations and distortions of time and space often produced by mushrooms are similar to LSD. Like LSD, side effects always precede development of the psychedelic action. Users feel symptoms associated with the fight/flight/fright response concomitantly with the psychological effect. With mushrooms, however, the duration of action is slightly shorter—2 to 4 hours.

The first clinical studies and analyses of the effects of psilocybin in humans were made at the University of Basle's Psychiatric Clinic in Basle, Switzerland. These studies were conducted on patients at the clinic by staff members of Sandoz Ltd. research laboratories (Steiner).

The effect of psilocybin may be described as follows: An oral dosage of 3 to 4 milligrams leads to changes in mental attitudes in 20 to 30 minutes. The psychological symptoms produced by doses up to 5 milligrams cause mood alteration and frequently pleasant environmental contacts. This feeling is usually accompanied by feelings of relaxation of both mind and body and by a seeming detachment from the environmental contacts. Commonly, the user experiences tiredness and weariness or a feeling of lightness and floating.

When higher doses of 6 to 20 milligrams are orally ingested, the psychological changes are much more pronounced. These higher dosage levels frequently cause severe changes in perceptions of time and space. The awareness the individual has of his or her self or "body image" changes markedly. As with LSD, psilocybin also causes the individual to experience illusions, perceptual alterations and hallucinations. Psilocybin has been used in psychotherapy because during the drug-induced dream-like state, the user will often recall events as far back as early childhood.

§ 13.6   THE PSILOCYBIN TRIP

The influence of expectation and mood seem to play an important part in any psychedelic experience including the use of psilocybin. Studies show that positive expectations before taking psilocybin usually lead to safe experiences during the drug "trip" (Fischer 1966). On the other hand, the reverse is also true. Anxiety or fear of the drug experience usually leads to an unpleasant "trip." Hence, the mood of an individual before the drug session is the best indicator of mood during the drug session. From this hypothesis, the following characteristics are said to be true of the psilocybin trip:

— Unpleasant, depressed, or anxious moods are intensified

— Pleasant moods provide a pleasant drug experience

— Religious expectations lead to a mystical or religious experience

— Ideas of gaining new insight reveal a drug experience that yields mind or consciousness expansion

From numerous studies conducted to date, it may be clearly seen that the type and depth of the drug experience depends to a decisive degree on the user's mental stability, expectations before the experience, and the environment in which the drug is used.

Another factor contributing to the success or failure of the drug experience is prior mental preparation. The drug will only release and activate that which is already present in the person taking it. An individual who does not realize a mental flaw in his or her character, yet has a positive expectation, may still experience the panic of a "bad trip."

§ 13.6.1 Psilocybin Investigation

In 1991, detectives of the Marin County major crimes task force and the Alameda County task force investigated a sophisticated large-scale psilocybin mushroom operation.

A subject was arrested in Alameda County who told detectives that his source for psilocybin lived in Berkeley and that his source was a man that lived in Bolinas, a small community in Marin County. Based on information obtained from surveillance and information provided by the informant, a search warrant was obtained for the suspect living in Bolinas.

During the course of the search, four structures were found on the property. One was designed to look like a workshop from the outside; however, the inside of the building concealed its true purpose. Inside was found a growing and drying room for the mushrooms. Thousands of mushrooms at all stages of their growing cycle were found. There were also three large drying closets and sophisticated electronic equipment used to monitor all the equipment used to grow the mushrooms. This included humidifiers, thermostats, an air circulating system and fluorescent lighting.

The interior walls were covered with Plexiglas to protect the walls from the humidity, and to maintain room temperature. Several pounds of wet mushrooms were pulled from the growing beds and several more from the shelves in the drying room closets.

Another building was found on the property which contained the lab portion of the operation. This room contained pressure cookers for sterilizing equipment, Petri dishes to begin the growing process of the spores, a Bunsen-type burner and refrigerator.

At the conclusion of the search, over 450 pounds of psilocybin mushrooms had been seized from the property. Three suspects were arrested in connection with this investigation (CA Narcotic Officer 1992).

In one of the more significant trafficking cases, on November 18, 1999, the DEA Medford, Oregon, Resident Office, in conjunction with the Federal Bureau of Investigation, the Internal Revenue Service, and state and local law enforcement authorities, reported the seizure of an indoor psilocybin mushroom growing operation. This operation resulted in the seizure of 66 pounds of dried mushrooms and 100 pounds of fresh mushrooms. The investigation revealed that the operator supplied psilocybin mushrooms to Oregon, California, Washington, New York, Nevada, Hawaii, Florida, Vermont, North Carolina, New Mexico, and Canada.

Mushrooms are not scheduled under the CSA, but both psilocybin and psilocyn are Schedule I drugs.

§ 13.7   PEYOTE AND MESCALINE
Peyote (*Lophophora Williamsii* or *Anhalonium Lewinii*), a plant common to the southwestern United States and Mexico, is a spineless cactus with a small crown or "button" and a long root. For psychedelic use, the crown is cut from the cactus and dried to form a hard brown disc, referred to as a mescal button. The dried button is softened in the mouth and swallowed. Because of its bitter taste, it is often ingested with tea, coffee or milk.

Hallucinogenic/Psychedelic Drugs

The "button" is eaten by some Indians in their traditional religious ceremonies. As a result of court action, the Native American Church, which is predominantly Indian in membership, may legally use peyote in its religious rites. For all other purposes, except legal research, peyote is illegal. Mescaline can be extracted from the peyote cactus, or produced synthetically in the laboratory. Its use is totally restricted.

§ 13.7.1 Appearance of Peyote

Peyote "buttons" are brown in color, approximately 1 to 2 inches in diameter, and resemble the underside of a dried mushroom. They are occasionally found on the black market for street sale. The "buttons" are more often found ground up into a brown powder and sold in clear capsules.

§ 13.7.2 Supreme Court Decision on Peyote

In 1990, the United State Supreme Court decided that the First Amendment's guarantee of the free exercise of religion does not bar a state from applying its general criminal prohibition of peyote consumption to those individuals whose religion prescribes sacramental use of the substance.

§ 13.7.3 Effect of Mescaline

Mescaline is the active ingredient in peyote. Mescaline dilates the pupils and increases pulse rate and blood pressure. The highest psychedelic effect is 2 hours after oral use of 12 to 20 mescal buttons (500 to 1500 mg). Twelve to 20 mescaline buttons is a common number for adults. Mescaline's half-life (activity of the drug in the body) is about 6 hours. Effects of a large dose may last up to 12 hours.

In about 24 hours after administration, approximately 87 percent of the mescaline is eliminated from the body by the kidneys. Repeated doses of mescaline have been shown to produce tolerance to the drug's psychological effects. For a high degree of tolerance to be established, a period of three to six days of use is required. Cross-tolerance between mescaline, LSD and psilocybin has been demonstrated, even though mescaline differs in molecular structure from the other two.

No known human deaths have been reported as a result of a mescaline overdose. However, when combined with certain other drugs such as insulin or barbiturates, there is a very pronounced additive effect which increases the mescaline's toxicity.

Mescaline produces effects similar to those observed during the fight/flight/fright syndrome: dilation of pupils, increase in blood pressure and heart rate, increase in body temperature, EEG and behavioral arousal and other excitatory symptoms similar to those produced by amphetamines. However, such actions are not the primary effects sought with mescaline. As one writer puts it:

"Interest in mescaline centers on the fact that it causes unusual psychic effects and visual hallucinations. The usual oral dose, 5 mg, causes anxiety, sympathomimetic effects, hyper-reflexia of the limbs, static tremors and vivid hallucinations that are usually visual and consist of brightly colored lights, geometric designs, animals and occasionally people; color and space perception is often concomitantly impaired, but otherwise the sensorium is normal and insight is retained" (Block).

In contrast to atropine and scopolamine, mescaline produces no delirium, amnesia or clouding of consciousness. Hallucinations are usually clear and vivid.

It has been known for a long time that "visions" are the most characteristic symptoms induced by mescaline. Like LSD, mescaline causes marked alterations in perception. Individual objects may take on new colors, shapes and may even seem to come alive while they move, wave and ripple. Many users experience synesthesia. This is where the senses become mixed, where the user will see sounds, hear colors, taste colors, etc. Objects normally seen in two dimensions may appear tridimensional. Tri-dimensional objects may seem more voluminous than usual. All objects, even the smallest and most unimportant ones, appear massive.

Usually subjects under the influence of mescaline are aware that the perceptual alterations have no basis in reality and are due to the effects of the drug.

In his book, Mescal and Mechanisms of Hallucinations, Heinrich Kluver states that euphoria is one of the typical mescal symptoms. In spite of marked nausea, many subjects "have a good time." Being in a state of mental exhaustion, they become talkative and jocular, they commit social errors and enjoy committing them; harmless remarks, even a potato salad or a catsup bottle are considered unusually funny. Sometimes the euphoric state may have no foundation whatever in objective happening.

"Suddenly I noticed that I lost control over myself through my laughing and was forced to continue laughing without any stimulus object." Some subjects refer to "cosmic emotions and to ecstatic states in which our exclamations of enjoyment become involuntary." A few records indicate that mescal may cause fear and "horrible depressions." One of the subjects of Prentiss and Morgan felt that his "life was leaving him." The drug apparently does not influence the sexual sphere in any specific way. The Indian peyote-eaters maintain that it inhibits sexual desires.

§ 13.7.4 Subjective Effects

There are multitudes of subjective reactions that may be experienced following the ingestion of mescaline. Emotional instability, significant mood changes and unprovoked emotional changes are common. As with subjects taking other psychedelic drugs and reporting an increased perception of truth, introspective and religious experiences are also common with mescaline use (Kluver 1966). Likewise, adverse or threatening reactions may also follow mescaline ingestion in both the naive and experienced user (Pelner). Bad trips on mescaline can usually be reversed or ended by a competent and supportive friend through the process of "talking down." This same technique is now employed in emergency hospitals for persons under the influence of LSD who experience a "bad trip." Although chemical intervention has been widely practiced by emergency wards in the past, it has been found unnecessary except as a last resort.

§ 13.7.5 The Street Packaging of Mescaline and Peyote

Peyote buttons are normally sold on the street as brown, dried discs approximately two to three inches in diameter and between one-half and one inch thick. Normally, a person will hold a button in his mouth until it becomes soft enough to swallow without chewing, because of the bitter taste. Four peyote buttons are usually adequate for one trip. Substances sold in the street as mescaline are almost always found to be entirely different drugs with contaminants. Usually, mescaline will be packaged in a clear, gelatin capsule containing a brown-colored powder and sell for $2 to $5 per capsule. Occasionally, peyote is seen in a ground-up form which is placed in large capsules to allow for ingestion without experiencing the bitter taste.

§ 13.7.6 The Synthesis and Extraction of Mescaline

A record of human studies with mescaline in it has been used in the form of the synthetic material and usually administered as the sulfate salt. In this form it has long glistening needles that are in a sense its signature and its mark of purity. It is also found in hydrochloride salt.

Mescaline has always been the central standard against which all other compounds are viewed. Even the United States Chemical Warfare group, in their human studies of a number of substituted phenethylamines, used mescaline as the reference material for both quantitative and qualitative comparisons. The Edgewood Arsenal code number for it was EA-1306. All psychedelics are given properties that are something like "twice the potency of mescaline" or "twice as long-lived as mescaline." This simple drug is truly the central prototype against which everything else is measured. The earliest studies with the "psychotomimetic amphetamines" had quantitative psychological numbers attached that read as "mescaline units." Mescaline was cast in concrete as being active at the 3.75 mg/kg level, meaning for an 80 kilogram (170 pound) person a dose of 300 milligrams. If a new compound proved to be active at 30 milligrams, there was an M.U. level of 10 put into the published literature.

So, mescaline can be extracted from peyote buttons or manufactured synthetically. The manufactured substance (mescaline sulfate) is chemically identical to the mescaline or 3, 4, 5 trimethoxyphenylethylamine extracted from peyote cactus and produces similar effects. The mescal button contains several alkaloids including mescaline, anhalamine, ankalamine and anhalidine.

§ 13.8 PCP—PHENCYCLIDINE
§ 13.8.1 Introduction

Since its emergence as a drug of abuse in the 1960s, phencyclidine (PCP) has been described as one of the most dangerous of all synthetic hallucinogens. Its niche in the drug world is usually one characterized by abusers exhibiting hostile behavior that manifests itself in extremely violent episodes.

§ 13.8.2 Current Market for PCP

Despite the negative effects associated with PCP, there remains an illicit market for the drug. Illicit organizations producing and distributing PCP are still active in the United States. These organizations, composed primarily of African-Americans operating mainly in Los Angeles, and, to a lesser extent, in Houston, supply most of the PCP available in the nation. The recent emergence of large PCP laboratories in other locations, such as Indiana and Maryland, are cause for concern because this may be an indication that the demand for PCP is on the rise. Lending support to this claim is a Drug Abuse Warning Network (DAWN) survey indicating that the number of PCP-related emergency room (ER) visits has increased 78 percent from 1998 to 2001. However, it is still too early to determine if PCP will return as a significant drug of abuse (DEA 2003).

PCP in tablet form is commonly sold under the guise of MDMA.

§ 13.8.3 Background

PCP is a synthetic drug. The initials PCP come from its full chemical name, phenylcyclohexyl piperidine, monohydrochloride. Although PCP was first synthesized in 1926, it was not until the mid-1950s that the pharmaceutical company Parke-Davis began to investigate PCP's use as a human anesthetic from a new family of chemicals.

The first chemical trial of the drug's effectiveness as an anaesthetic agent for humans was conducted in 1957.

In 1963, PCP was patented and marketed in the United States as a surgical analgesic and anesthetic under the trade name Sernyl. Medically, the PCP seemed to be more effective and safer than other anesthetics, but it did cause some other problems. When used as a surgical anesthetic, up to 30 percent of the patients manifested agitation, excitement and disorientation during the recovery period. People experienced body-image changes, feelings of loneliness, isolation and dependency. Their thinking was observed to become progressively disorganized.

However, due to adverse collateral symptoms (i.e., severe confusion, agitation, delusion, and irrational behavior), Sernyl was withdrawn from the market in 1965. PCP was subsequently marketed in 1967 as a veterinary anesthetic and tranquilizer under the trade name Sernylan. All legitimate manufacturing of PCP in the United States was discontinued in April, 1978.

§ 13.8.4 PCP Classification

The drug is sometimes referred to as an "upper or downer" with stimulant or depressant-like properties. Sometimes it is referred to as a "hallucinogen."

It is not related to any of the other chemical or known street drugs. It has also been stated that PCP is in a unique pharmacological classification of its own called the phencyclidine. Included in this new classification of drugs are 30 plus analogues. One of these analogues, ketamine, is currently used as a surgical anesthetic. The major difference between ketamine and phencyclidine is that ketamine has a shorter duration of action and produces convulsions less frequently.

§ 13.8.5 History of PCP Use

Phencyclidine was first discovered in illicit use in Los Angeles in 1965 (Educational Off-Print 1975). In 1967 it appeared in Haight-Ashbury in San Francisco under the name of "Peace Pill." It was not popular then because of some adverse reactions. Phencyclidine seemed to disappear from the drug scene in San Francisco, but in 1968 surfaced in the east coast under the name of "Hog." In the early 1970s, PCP was still a relatively unknown drug. However, in a review by PharmChem Research Foundation, from 1972 to 1979 phencyclidine spread throughout the United States.

The growing problem of PCP use was due to the simplicity of manufacture, large profits in manufacture, availability of drug and the effects on the users.

In California, PCP is a popular street drug and appears under a variety of names including crystal, crystal joints, KJ, angel dust, rocket fuel, Shermans, PCP, ozone, dust, elephant tranquilizers and many other names.

§ 13.8.6 Street PCP - Where Does It Come From?

The PCP sold in the United States is made in illegal laboratories, in bathrooms, garages and basements (Rainey et al). The person who makes it may or may not be a real chemist. It is not particularly difficult to make but it does take many complicated steps, and some of those steps are dangerous. A man died in San Jose, California from the inhalation of cyanide fumes caused by his preparations in making PCP.

The Los Angeles, California area is the primary source for the majority of PCP found in the United States. According to the El Paso Intelligence Center (EPIC) Clandestine Laboratory Database, 17 of the 24 PCP laboratories seized throughout the United States from 1998 to 2002 were located in California. As they have for decades, African-

American organizations and street gangs, operating primarily in Los Angeles and San Bernardino County, produce most of the PCP available nationwide. These groups typically produce PCP in liquid form and subsequently handle the wholesale distribution of the drug to mid-level distributors in Chicago, Houston, Los Angeles, Milwaukee, New Orleans, Newark, New York City, Philadelphia, and Washington, D.C. It has been determined that some of the individuals involved with these organizations were formerly part of PCP trafficking groups and street gangs that have operated in the Los Angeles area since the late 1980s and early 1990s. In July 2002, and more recently, in February 2003, the DEA and the Southern California High Intensity Drug Trafficking Area (HIDTA) seized two operational PCP laboratories in the Los Angeles area. These laboratories were operated by African-American members of a Los Angeles-based PCP trafficking organization (Rainey et al).

PCP is also produced by Mexican drug trafficking organizations operating in the United States. These organizations typically produce PCP in powder or crystal form versus the liquid form normally produced by African-American organizations. In addition, these organizations are suspected of distributing wholesale quantities of PCP powder to Hispanic street gangs and other distributors in San Jose, New York City, and various locations in Oklahoma. In 2001, a clandestine laboratory that produced PCP in powder and crystal form was seized in San Jose. A Mexican national serving as a laboratory operator in San Jose was recently released from prison, having served time for prior PCP-related offenses.

§ 13.8.7 Methodology
PCP is relatively easy to manufacture, and it is commonly produced in liquid form via the "bucket method." This method, in which chemicals are mixed in either a bucket or trash bin to produce liquid PCP, required approximately eight to ten hours to complete. Although easy to manufacture, it is extremely dangerous to produce PCP because most of the chemicals are toxic as well as highly flammable.

In California, independent operators have, for many years, been suspected of producing PCP. Because these operators normally produce small amounts of PCP for personal use and/or localized distribution, they are usually of little significance. However, in 2001, a large clandestine laboratory that produced crystal PCP was seized in California's Mariposa County. The Caucasian operators of this laboratory, described as "biker-types," appeared to be operating independently from other PCP trafficking organizations. As in the case of the San Jose laboratory, one of the operators of this laboratory was recently released from prison for prior drug-related offenses.

Despite California being the primary production area, significant PCP production operations recently have been found in Baltimore, Maryland, and Gary, Indiana. In November 2002, an operational PCP laboratory was seized at a residence in Baltimore. It was one of the largest PCP laboratories ever seized on the East Coast, as it contained an enormous amount of chemicals consistent with the manufacture of PCP and approximately 4 gallons of finished product. The African-

Hallucinogenic/Psychedelic Drugs

American operators of the laboratory apparently intended to lace marijuana with PCP to increase its marketability and profit margin. In December 2001, federal, state, and local law enforcement authorities disrupted an organization, responsible for the manufacture and wholesale distribution of PCP in Gary, and arrested many of its African-American members. This organization had been producing PCP for several years—primarily supplying a Chicago-based street gang.

§ 13.8.8 Why Do People Use PCP?

People use PCP for the same reasons they use other drugs: to get high, relieve boredom, escape or have fantasies, to feel powerful, to make some kind of spiritual connection, or simply, because it is there and everyone else is doing it.

§ 13.8.9 Physical Characteristics of PCP

PCP in its pure state is a clear liquid and as a powder is a white-colored substance. However, due to impurities in the manufacturing process it has a slight yellowish or brownish tint to it.

This does not preclude a dealer, however, from altering this standard appearance. In an attempt to make his product unique and thereby establish a reliable clientele, some dealers will add food coloring or other adulterants to the PCP. Purchases of "blue crystal" or "strawberry crystal" have been made by narcotics officers, and as a result the field officers should keep these possibilities in mind.

A substance suspected to be PCP can generally be detected by its distinctive chemical odor. The process of manufacturing PCP requires numerous chemicals, including ether, which is one of the strongest identifiable odors. The mere presence of this odor is a preliminary indication that the substance could be PCP. While the ether smell is a tell-tale sign, the police officer will find various physical forms of PCP on the street.

§ 13.8.9(a) Crystal PCP

The texture of the powder or "crystals" will range from a granular sugar to a loose powder to lumps. PCP crystals will be found packaged in zip-lock baggies, hermetically sealed in plastic, or wrapped in aluminum foil bindles. Crystals can be inhaled through the nose or, more rarely, sprinkled on a plant material and smoked. The terms crystals and powder are interchangeable.

§ 13.8.9(b) Liquid PCP

Phencyclidine liquid is generally clear or yellow colored, but can be disguised by any color. It may be found in eyedrop or vanilla extract bottles or similar containers. Phencyclidine may be sprayed, sprinkled or soaked into a leafy substance which, when dried, produces "angel dust." The substance can be:

1. Mint leaves

2. Parsley, oregano, or other vegetable spices or materials

Chapter 13

3.   Marijuana

Liquid phencyclidine may also be injected, although the practice is less common in most geographical areas than other methods of use.

Although PCP can be snorted and injected (rare), the most common vehicle for PCP usually encountered by the field officer is the hand-rolled cigarette or "joint." This PCP joint can be produced in two ways:

1.   The most common "joint" encountered by officers in the Northern California area is that produced using powdered PCP crystal. Approximately 35 to 50 milligrams of the drug is sprinkled onto a vegetable matter such as parsley, mint leaves or oregano, and then hand rolled into a cigarette. It is very rare to see a marijuana cigarette sprinkled with PCP as users generally do not like the combined effects of the two drugs. Breaking open a suspected PCP cigarette which has been manufactured in this manner, the field officer should be able to see the small PCP crystals.

2.   A second method of manufacturing the PCP joint is by making use of liquid PCP. The PCP is reduced to liquid form, sprayed on vegetable matter, and the vegetable matter is allowed to dry. This dried vegetable matter is then hand rolled into cigarettes for smoking. Generally a joint made in this manner will contain about half the quantity of PCP as that made with crystals and, as a result, will sell for about half as much on the street. Since it is difficult to detect the liquid PCP in a cigarette manufactured in this manner, the field officer should look for the obvious—a cigarette rolled with vegetable matter other than marijuana.

The police officer should also look for other containers holding vegetable matter which is not marijuana. Sprayed PCP has been found in plastic baggies, film canisters, tobacco pouches, spice jars, etc. While in and of itself there may not be probable cause for arrest, the officer should still seize the suspected material, write an offense report and submit the material to the crime lab for analysis.

Users of liquid PCP have devised ways to get around the obvious hand-rolled cigarette. One of the most common is by using a needle and absorbent string. The string is dipped into liquid PCP, allowed to dry and then threaded through a commercial cigarette. This method makes it very difficult to detect the PCP and has been used to enable friends and relatives to smuggle PCP into the jails.

§ 13.8.10   PCP Packaging & Storage
Phencyclidine is packaged in a number of ways. Those packaging methods which are most common include tinfoil, plastic, vials and paper bindles.

Phencyclidine is very popularly wrapped in tinfoil in both powder/crystal form, and when it is sprayed on vegetable matter. Generally it is found in small quantities such as grams or smaller when packaged in tinfoil. It is generally found in larger quantities when packaged in plastic zip-lock wrappers or baggies. Phencyclidine may be found in either glass or plastic vials. These glass or plastic vials come in all sizes, but most commonly contain a gram or less. These include containers such as eyedrop bottles. Many times paper bindles are avoided because they absorb moisture and the PCP will soak into the paper.

The most common quantity of PCP powder encountered on the street is the gram quantity. Generally packaged in the corners of plastic baggies which are then tied off and cut, PCP has also been seen compressed into small rocks and carried in any number of other containers. One gram of PCP is about the size of a dime and will enable the manufacture of approximately 20 to 25 cigarettes.

There are differences of opinion concerning the storage of PCP in a damp or cool environment. Many persons who have been arrested for possessing PCP, have the misconception the substance will lose its potency if subjected to heat for an extended period of time. PCP will remain moist and damp if refrigerated and this will increase the profit margin when sold in quantities by weight.

When searching locations for PCP, officers should pay particular attention to refrigerators, freezers, storage chests and other areas where the temperature would remain cool and constant.

§ 13.8.11   PCP Methods and Patterns of Use

PCP is a dry powder or granular, light-colored substance. In California, it is usually sprinkled on, or dissolved in liquid and sprayed on dried parsley leaves or marijuana. It is then rolled into a thin joint and smoked. Occasionally it is snorted (inhaled vigorously) or added to food or liquid and swallowed. Very rarely it is injected or smoked in a pipe.

There are probably a variety of other methods of using PCP. The users are limited only by their imaginations. One such method which is becoming somewhat popular in Los Angeles, California, is placing liquid PCP in the eye with an eyedropper. In this manner the many blood vessels, combined with the delicate tissues of the eyes and inner eyelids, are able to absorb the drug. PCP can be absorbed through the skin. There is at least one case where a U.S. Navy pilot was accidentally subjected to the influence of PCP when his suitcase and clothing were contaminated by a liquid spill. Following the wearing of his clothing from the suitcase, he exhibited bizarre behavior and had to be hospitalized for PCP toxicity. Also, PCP can be absorbed rectally.

There are three entirely different kinds of usage patterns. Each carries its own respective dangers.

One kind of user smokes PCP occasionally at parties, dances, concerts and other occasions. This person is least likely to know what he or she is getting, because a joint passed at a party contains an unknown dosage. Depending upon the amount used and the purity of the dose, the effect may be anything from a pleasant numbness to a violent freak out.

Another kind of user is considered a regular user. This person smokes PCP from twice a month up to three times a week. The regular user is likely to smoke on weekends and sometimes during the week.

Most of the regular users are hesitant about accepting the idea that they are "addicted," or having a problem with PCP. These individuals are "hidden users." Often, they maintain regular employment and appear to be functioning more or less normally. Their use of the drug can, however, result in tragedy. For example, in many cases single parents or housewives, whose husbands are at work, ingest the drug in front of their children. This has frequently led to accidental ingestion on the part of small children.

The third type of user is someone who uses PCP every day, or as often as it can be found. This person is much more likely to know what is being smoked because he or she is probably dealing PCP in order to support the expense of its use, or is buying it in quantity and rolling his or her own joints. So, problems do not arise out of not knowing what one is getting, but rather from the fact that when someone uses it regularly, memory, reasoning ability, judgment, and common sense disappear. Thus, the user thinks he can drive while stoned, or thinks nothing of selling joints on the corner in front of the school. Continued use, then, results in increasingly bizarre behavior and ultimately in severe memory loss.

Usually, it is the first type of user that is most likely to end up with a medical crisis. The second and third types are more likely to be arrested. All three are just as likely to be involved in violence.

§ 13.8.12 Pharmacology of PCP

PCP is distributed in the body's tissues, metabolized by the liver and excreted, unchanged, in the urine. The drug is highly soluble in lipid (fat) tissues. The cardiovascular effects include increases in blood pressure, heart rate, and cardiac output. PCP effects include hypersalivation and increased bronchial secretion. PCP also increases body temperature. After PCP use, respiratory rate is usually normal or slightly increased (Johnson).

§ 13.8.13 Signs and Symptoms of PCP Intoxication

PCP shares the properties of many commonly used street drugs. It may act like a depressant, a stimulant, a psychedelic, and a tranquilizer. It produces a unique combination of these effects in addition to removing physical pain.

§ 13.8.14 Physiological Effects

The physiological effects of PCP differ markedly with dose. At low doses, the most prominent effect is similar to that of alcohol intoxication—a generalized numbness. With increased doses, analgesia and then anesthesia can be observed. Large doses can produce convulsions, coma or even death. Most persons using PCP experience a confused state characterized by feelings of weightlessness, depression, anxiety, and hallucinations (Rainey et al). Users frequently report difficulty in reasoning and poor concentration (Reed et al). At least one study published in Clinical Toxicology has documented these physiological effects of PCP intoxication (Clinical Toxicology 1976). The study observed the effects of acute PCP intoxication in 18 individuals. Following is a summary of the study's results.

LOW to MEDIUM DOSE (Acute Confusional State)	HIGH DOSE (Stupor or Coma)
Clinical Features:	
A. *Responsiveness* Initially uncommunicative, may respond to simple; commands with nodding or eye movement; later incomplete verbal responses and then becomes talkative.	Appears awake; unresponsive to verbal stimuli, responds to deep pain with movement.
B. *Orientation* Disoriented for time and place, appears confused or fearful; amnesia for episode.	———————
C. *Behavior* Agitated, excited, combative; aggressive, self-destructive or bizarre behavior; insomnia, loss of appetite, incontinence, followed by depression, irritability.	———————
D. *Speech* Slurred, intermittently unable to articulate.	Moaning, groaning, inability to articulate.
E. *Eyes* Open "stare appearance" with drooping or eyelids, very little effect on pupil size.	———————
F. *Nystagmus* Bilateral, horizontal, and vertical.	Same; more jerky nystagmus.
Motor System A. *Gait* Unable to tandem walk; some muscle rigidity.	———————
B. *Muscle Tone* Rigidity.	———————
C. *Movements* Restlessness, repetitive movements.	Twitching movements, facial grimace.
Other A. *Increased Secretions* Drooling.	Same.

§ 13.8.15 Psychological Effects

The best subjective information on the psychological effects of PCP was published in a report by Doctors Baker and Amini in the Journal of Psychedelic Drugs in 1972. At one point Doctors Baker and Amini state:

The main effect on the psychological functioning of the subject was a progressive disintegration. This is meant quite literally in that the subject apparently became less and less able to combine and integrate all the information available to him. As a consequence, a progressive narrowing of his field of awareness was observed. Past and future disappeared, and the subject became unable to correctly integrate information from his own body with that from the environment.

Having feelings that the extremities did not belong to the body, did not belong to the subject himself, were typical. Although the subject knew intellectually it was he who was speaking, his voice seemed to come from a distance as if someone were talking to him. The changes in perception came somewhat later than the disturbances in body image. These perceptual disturbances manifested themselves quite suddenly.

In a study on the subjective effects of PCP it was found that in 1,008 of the cases, users experienced body image changes, estrangement, disorganization of thought (recent memory), drowsiness, and apathy; 78 percent of the users experienced feelings of inebriation; 67 percent of the users experienced negativism and hostility; 56 percent of the users experienced a hypnagogic state (a feeling of being far away); and 29 percent of the users experienced repetitive motor behavior or a parroting of questions (Tennant).

§ 13.8.16 Field Observation of PCP Intoxication

There are several obvious symptoms that a police officer will observe when coming into contact with a person under the influence of PCP. Some of these symptoms are also common to various stages of alcohol and barbiturate intoxication. These are the depressed abilities to walk and speak, redness of the eyes, flushing of the face, and sweating. With PCP intoxication, however, the officer should observe the "blank stare" appearance of the subject's eyes.

There are two field tests for PCP intoxication that can be performed by a police officer on the scene. When combined with the other physical symptoms of PCP intoxication already mentioned, these field tests provide enough probable cause for arrest for being under the influence.

Nystagmus: Have the subject keep his or eyes open with his head directed straight ahead. Hold an object in front of the subject's nose so that he can see it, then move the object to the subject's temporal area, directing him to follow it with his eyes only. Once the eyes are to the side, the police officer will be able to see that the eyeballs jerk uncontrollably from side to side. This test can also be performed for vertical nystagmus.

Pulse Rate: The police officer can take the subject's pulse manually. As noted previously, PCP generally increases the pulse rate, so the officer should not be surprised to find that the apparently "drowsy" subject has a pulse rate of over 100 beats per minute.

It should be noted that nystagmus is also present in some cases of alcohol and barbiturate intoxication. However, both of these drugs are depressants and subsequently would not be consistent with a high pulse rate. In addition, nystagmus in alcohol and barbiturate cases does not become evident until acute intoxication.

§ 13.8.17 Recognition of PCP Intoxication
The most common observable signs of PCP intoxication include:

—Horizontal and vertical nystagmus

—Gait ataxia—muscle rigidity

—Blank stare appearance

—Non-communicative appearance

PCP has three general effects: anesthetic, stimulant, and hallucinogenic. Chronic users become tolerant to many of these effects. Tolerance to the following effects is rapidly developed: increase in pulse, blood pressure, and body temperature, nystagmus, hallucinations, and anesthetic properties. Due to the development of tolerance, the regular user of PCP may have few if any physical signs of drug use.

The diagnosis of "under the influence" of PCP means that there is evidence of PCP activity present. Such evidence could be provided by nystagmus, muscle rigidity, hallucinations, delusions, and PCP in the blood or urine. The diagnosis of "under the influence" is made by finding more than one item of evidence. The most important evidence to find is the presence of PCP in the blood or urine (and the absence of other drugs in the blood or urine). As mentioned, two or more of the following physical symptoms must also be present to give an officer probable cause to arrest for PCP influence:

1. The presence of nystagmus.

2. Presence of muscle rigidity or muscle relaxation to include droopy eyelids, slurred or slow speech, abnormal gait and nodding.

3. Disorientation—subject does not know person, time or place, or shows presence of amnesia.

4. Hallucinations.

5. Delusions such as thinking one is Jesus Christ.

6. Non-reactive pupils.

Remember that these items of evidence may be considered subjective; therefore, at least two observers are required to avoid criticisms of bias. Although there are other symptoms of PCP use, the increases in blood pressure, pulse, body temperature and reflex are too nonspecific to use as medico-legal evidence.

In summary, the field officer's complete evaluation of the PCP suspect should include the following:

1. Examine the eyes for nystagmus (vertical and horizontal), pupil size, and pupil reaction.

2. Is the speech slowed or slurred? Is the subject unable to talk?

3. Smell the breath for the characteristic ether odor of PCP.

4. Observe gait for wide-stance.

5. Test arms for muscle rigidity.

6. Is the subject oriented as to person, time and place?

7. Is the subject seeing and hearing anything that may be a hallucination?

8. Is the subject having any obvious delusions?

9. Observe the subject for sedation by looking for droopy eyelids or general drowsiness.

10. Test the urine or blood for PCP and other drugs.

PCP can be easily detected in the blood or urine. It can be found in the blood 6 to 12 hours after last use. It can be found in the urine 24 to 48 hours after last use. If the suspect refuses a blood or urine test, this can be considered evidence of drug use. According to federal government regulations, refusal to give a urine sample in methadone programs is considered a positive or "dirty" urine.

Some other signs of PCP intoxication include:

—A fluctuating state of confusion or excitement

—Agitation or combativeness

—Aggressive or violent behavior

§ 13.8.18 Duration of PCP Effects

The effects of PCP will vary greatly depending on the purity and amount of PCP used, individual's metabolism, sex, age, mental state, psychological make-up, tolerance, etc.

The most popular method in California for use of phencyclidine is smoking the material on parsley, mint or other leaves. The onset of subjective effects after smoking is reported to occur within 1 to 5 minutes. The drug will peak or plateau in 15 to 30 minutes and the person will remain high for 4 to 6 hours. Generally 24 to 48 hours are required until the person again feels completely "normal."

With chronic use, the time required to return to normal may be increased to several weeks or years.

§ 13.8.19 Clinical Observation of Emergency Room Cases

A typical street dose of 5 mg produces a confusional state associated with a blank-stare appearance. Horizontal and vertical nystagmus and gait ataxia are almost always present. Muscle rigidity may be present. Most individuals are alert and oriented within 5 hours of admission to the emergency room. However, some users remain confused for periods of 24 to 72 hours.

Larger doses, 20 mg and greater, produce an unresponsive, immobile state where the eyes may remain open. Nystagmus, muscle rigidity and hypertension are common findings. With this dosage, it usually takes over 24 to 48 hours to recover.

Massive overdoses, exceeding 500 mg of PCP, result in periods of coma from several hours to days. Seizures are also common with such large overdoses.

PCP will remain in an individual's system for a prolonged time period. The drug is stored in both fat and brain tissue. Consequently, the frequency of ingestion is of paramount importance.

Studies have been conducted on persons who have chronically used PCP three or more times a week for a period of at least six months (Tennant). These studies have shown that, after use of the drug is discontinued, users experienced lingering problems with speech, memory, concentration, and abstraction for several years. They also continued to experience periods of bizarre, violent or amnesic behavior (flashbacks) (Showalter).

§ 13.8.20 Summary of Signs and Symptoms of PCP Intoxication

—The PCP intoxicated individual shows signs of recent memory loss.

—The PCP user is often uncommunicative and stares blankly. The communication difficulty is seen with users attempting to talk in words, or fragments of words, instead of sentences.

—The user is unpredictable. There are fluctuating levels of consciousness from mite to action involving agitation, pacing, aggression, impulsiveness, and loss of control.

—The PCP user may have hallucinations that change rapidly from auditory to visual and visual to auditory.

—The PCP user sometimes shows facial grimacing or jaw clenching. This symptom is an important warning sign of unpredictable or violent biting.

—The PCP user has difficulty estimating time.

—The PCP user experiences changes in body image. He or she has difficulty accurately perceiving bodily experiences and sensations; he or she may experience floating in and out of the body. Users are occasionally found nude. They often overestimate body size, shape, and height. Frequently they believe themselves to be powerful, very large, invulnerable and endowed with unique or super physical or mental abilities.

—It is difficult to make meaningful interpersonal contact with the PCP user. "Talking down" is not effective with the non-communicative PCP user and may, in fact, agitate the user and endanger the officer.

—The PCP user appears to have long-term neuropsychological impairment.

—Muscle rigidity.

—Gait ataxia—difficulty in coordination. When asked to stand on one leg, the PCP user will often fall down.

§ 13.8.21   Chemical Testing for PCP

There are some field test kits which allow the officer to perform a field examination on PCP using color reaction. The suspected substance is placed in the vial and a particular color will appear if the substance is positive. Remember that PCP can be absorbed through the skin so be careful when handling the evidence. Never touch, taste or smell PCP.

Phencyclidine can be identified in body tissues and fluids. Current techniques include thin-layer chromatography, gas chromatography, gas chromatography/mass spectrometry and radio-immunoassay. Since the drug rapidly disappears from the blood and is excreted in significant amounts in the urine, urine is the preferred body fluid for sampling. PCP can be detected in the blood and gastric content. PCP will usually be detected within 2 to 3 days after ingestion but can be detected for as long as 5 days. PCP will appear in urine about one hour after it is used.

The relative long life of PCP in the body is due to (1) its solubility in lipids and (2) its weak chemical base that allows it to readily ionize in the strong acid milieu of the stomach. A problem in detection is that PCP toxicity is sometimes mistaken for acute alcohol intoxication and that persons are mistakenly placed in a drunk tank or jail cell instead of being placed under treatment.

A urine sample will detect the presence of PCP. However, a blood sample will provide a quantitative analysis of the PCP in the body. There is no specific antidote for PCP intoxication.

§ 13.8.22 Negative Urine Tests

PCP will appear in the urine one hour after use. If you collect a urine sample before this hour, then the urine test for PCP may be negative.

About 90 percent of PCP is eliminated 48 hours after use. Collecting a urine specimen after 48 hours may result in a negative test.

When low dosage of PCP are used (below .25 □g/ml) there may be too little PCP in the urine to detect its presence.

A negative test may result from a laboratory error.

How to Avoid Negative Urine Tests: Take more then one urine sample. Wait about one hour between collections. It is a good idea to check with the laboratory to see how they want the urine samples processed and labeled.

§ 13.9 APPREHENSION AND CONTROL OF PHENCYCLIDINE USER

Department Policy: Because of the possibility of the person under the influence of phencyclidine to demonstrate psychotic behavior, departments should have established specific policies that set guidelines for contact with the phencyclidine abuser.

Detention vs. Booking: In all cases a person who is detained for being under the influence of phencyclidine should be examined by a competent medical authority prior to being placed in a detention setting. An alternative to booking would be commitment (under provisions of section 5150 WIC of California Codes).

Safety: Safety becomes an important factor for the officer, the public and the user himself when dealing with a person under the influence of phencyclidine.

The officer handling a person under the influence of phencyclidine must remember that because of the anesthetic effects of phencyclidine, the person's pain threshold will be increased, therefore rendering traditional police restraints ineffective. The officer should always request back-up, and when possible, wait for the user to become cooperative.

Chapter 13

A person under the influence of phencyclidine can occasionally be talked down and may become cooperative, eliminating the need for physical confrontation by the officer. "TALKING DOWN" SHOULD ONLY BE ATTEMPTED IF A USER IS COMMUNICATIVE.

However, if physical confrontation does become necessary, the most effective hold in dealing with a person under the influence of phencyclidine is the "carotid." However, it must be applied correctly to avoid serious injury to the suspect and the officer. With appropriate back-up (as many as eight officers) the best means of controlling the aggressive user is to hold him down by sheer body weight.

In all instances the "bar arm" must be avoided due to the possibility of the suspect suffering a broken neck. If the officer is unable to get backup, the "carotid" is the next best means of control. To reduce the possibility of respiratory failure, care must be used in applying weight to the chest.

If you have a PCP user who is communicative, ask the user questions that will help you determine what the problem is:

1.   What did you take?

2.   Do you have any amount of the drug left?

3.   Describe what you took (color, smell, taste).

4.   How did you take it?

5.   When did you take it?

6.   Have you ever taken it before?

7.   How do you feel?

Recently, several items have been developed to restrain a person under the influence of PCP. There is the PCP net. The use of the Taser (50,000 volts) has been found to be effective. The use of a heavy, nylon-braided cord around the ankles and attached to the handcuff chain is effective. Minimally, the user should be handcuffed with his hands behind his back and his legs restrained. Remember chemical mace does not work. The use of the baton is also ineffective. The use of arrest control techniques relying on pain compliance is ineffective. When transporting a PCP user, place him or her in the back seat of patrol vehicle face down on the floor. This will minimize any injury of the user falling off the back seat on to the floor. The PCP user is then transported to a medical facility (usually a county hospital emergency room) for a medical clearance.

If You Encounter a Non-communicative Person with a Blank Stare:

1.   Call for back-up

2. Wait it out

3. Use a show of force—sit on the person (5 officers)

4. Use methods of restraint

    a. PCP net

    b. Carotid

    c. 6 pt. restraint—both arms, both legs, stomach and upper chest

    d. Leg restraint hooked to handcuffs

    e. Leg restraint with end out of door

    f. Taser gun

Remember that sensory stimulation (sight, hearing, feeling) can induce violent reactions in PCP users. Loud or aggressive questioning, a body search for weapons, lights flashed in the eyes or an attempt to handcuff the user may set off explosive behavior. In summary, acts that tend to stimulate the senses (loud noises, flashing lights, etc.) may initiate violent reactions. On the other hand, conduct that produces calming, peaceful, and quieting effects have been successful methods of control. The officer should not, however, relax his or her guard or vigilance. Do not turn your back on a PCP user. Do not touch a PCP user unless it is absolutely necessary. There is no easy or dependable method of controlling the always unpredictable PCP user.

Custody personnel should be aware of the potential problem when detaining a person under the influence of PCP. Persons under the influence of PCP have demonstrated homicidal and suicidal tendencies. While under the influence, the person may suffer respiratory depression, seizures or coma.

§ 13.9.1 Arrest Report and Evidence Collection
The arrest report must include the specific objective symptoms of PCP intoxication which could be one or all or any combination of muscle rigidity, nystagmus, hypertension, blank stare, noncommunication, impaired coordination, etc. In addition to all of the elements of the crime, include the result of a comprehensive interview with the arrestee regarding the quantity of PCP taken, the method(s) used, the source of supply, and the location of any PCP not recovered during the initial arrest. Any uncovered PCP or chemicals for making PCP represent an extreme danger to other persons.

In the process of collecting evidence, certain hazardous situations should be avoided. A "contact high" could result during activities from exposure to PCP in any of its forms by touching, inhaling, etc. The same contact hazards exist during transportation. In addition, there is danger from exposure to the volatile chemicals used in manufacturing PCP.

The extreme danger of transporting chemicals used to manufacture PCP necessitates that a court order be obtained to destroy all chemical and containers except the quantity required for laboratory analysis and court presentation. Complete sets of sequential photographs are required to record the laboratory site, location of all chemicals and equipment in the laboratory, and a complete inventory prior to destruction. This is in addition to the quantity of chemicals retained for the prosecution. Limited amounts of all chemicals must be retained for use by the defense for their own analysis.

Limited amounts of all evidence must be preserved to satisfy the court requirements by both the defense and the prosecution. Consistent with the chain of evidence, chemicals should be stored in either airtight or well-ventilated areas where there can be limited or no contact or exposure to personnel.

In the process of booking, maintain the chain of evidence and book property in accordance with departmental regulations. However, due to the hazards, no more material should be retained as evidence than absolutely necessary for identification.

§ 13.9.2 Court Presentation
The qualifications, experience and expertise of all expert witnesses should be documented for submission to the court. Methods for the documentation and verification of evidence include witnesses, videotape, chemical analysis, cassette tape/audio, and urinalysis toxicology (blood and/or urine).

§ 13.9.3 Illicit Manufacture of Phencyclidine
Virtually the entire illicit supply of PCP is manufactured in clandestine laboratories. This synthesis process is not difficult and can be done by individuals who have only modest technical training. These laboratory operations vary in size and scope from a small quantity of chemical and a few pieces of glassware to a large facility with the production capabilities of a commercial scale which include barrels of chemicals, sophisticated industrial equipment and major distribution networks. Although there is considerable diversity among the clandestine labs, most that police encounter (1) have rudimentary equipment, facilities and are usually located in residential dwellings; (2) are small in size and usually produce a few pounds per batch, and (3) are dirty and usually contain byproducts and intermediaries from the reaction. Even though the size and production capability of the operations vary greatly, a small investment in a lab can yield enormous profit. An investment of $500 to $1,000 could yield the operator a $24,000 profit.

It is imperative that officers understand the inherent dangers surrounding any laboratory investigation. The chemicals used are often extremely toxic and may be highly volatile. For example, many laboratories contain the chemical cyanide and hydrochloric acid. These chemicals, when combined, produce a lethal gas. When a fire erupts, some of the burning chemicals can produce extremely toxic fumes. The inhalation of these fumes or prolonged exposure to some chemicals can cause poisoning or death.

An additional danger from fire exists when dealing with chemicals. A spark or inadvertent chemical mixture can cause an explosion of fire. Phenyl magnesium bromide may explode with the addition of one drop of water. Ether will ignite with a spark.

The presence of illicit laboratories has created a hazard to citizens, police officers and fire department personnel. It has become almost commonplace for these laboratories to explode and burn, causing personal injuries to bystanders and extensive property damage. When basic guidelines are followed, an investigation can be effectively conducted with minimal risk to officers and the public. Short of life-saving measures, there is no valid reason for an officer to enter an illicit laboratory, unless accompanied by a criminalist or other qualified personnel to render the laboratory safe.

The presence of an illicit laboratory may be discovered through a citizen's complaint or an officer's observation. The process of manufacturing or cooking PCP produces a strong and offensive odor, which in turn may generate complaints from neighbors. Thorough interviews of complaining persons or other neighbors will usually provide cause to believe an illicit laboratory is in operation. During the interview, personnel should determine if certain indicators of an illicit laboratory are present.

§ 13.9.4 PCP Defenses
Suspects involved in crimes such as homicide claim diminished capacity as a defense because they were under the influence of PCP at the time of the offense. This defense has proven satisfactory to the accused in several instances because it is not difficult to locate an "expert" who will testify that persons under the influence of PCP cannot be accountable for their actions while under the influence because they lose control of their minds. If a PCP user is encountered either in, or after, the commission of another crime, then certain questions should be asked to refute the possible defense of diminished capacity, primarily because the user's awareness of these facts supports his or her presence of mind at this time.

When investigating a crime, the officer should immediately document the orientation of the suspect as to person, place, and time to clearly show the ability or inability of the individual to respond. Additionally, a biological specimen (i.e., blood and/or urine) should be obtained for further documentation and evidence. This procedure also applies to the ability of the suspect to voluntarily waive his or her Miranda rights.

PCP has been increasingly linked to murders—at least by lawyers hoping to ease penalties against their clients. The most celebrated local case occurred in August 1976, when Barry Braeseke and David Barker shot Braeseke's parents and grandfather in hopes of inheriting the family's wealth. In his confession, Braeseke blamed crystal for the crimes. "The idea (of murder) seemed neat to me because I was under the influence," he told sheriff's detectives.

His lawyer, James Crew, used that defense in Barry's trial, but the jury was not impressed—Barry and his accomplice were convicted of first degree murder. Both Crew and psychologist Lerner, who testified at the trial, believe that Braeseke would not have killed but for PCP. Crew has the same opinion about another murder case he argued—the 1974 Hayward murder of 18-year old Steve McQuinn.

McQuinn was drowned by two friends, Dale Burdick and Michael Cortez, who decided during a session of PCP smoking that McQuinn was a police snitch. According to Cortez's court testimony, the pair took McQuinn to a flooded ditch in South Hayward and clumsily drowned him while McQuinn, apparently too stoned to resist, vainly called for help.

Crew, who defended Burdick, says this crime would never have happened but for PCP: "They would have beaten him up, to teach him a lesson, but they never intended to kill him." Both youths pleaded guilty to second degree murder before trial.

§ 13.9.5 What Is a Trip Really Like?
The following is a reprint of material presented by the PROJECT DARE PCP unit, which has dealt extensively with persons under the influence of PCP. For the occasional user, a normal trip goes through three stages:

Three to five minutes after smoking a PCP joint, the first effects are felt. The user will sit or lie down, because standing requires too much work. During this first "ozone" stage, which will last from 15 minutes to an hour and a half, depending on dosage and experience, the user will not feel like talking and speech will be slurred. He or she is "somewhere else" mentally. That somewhere else is different for each person. Some typical feelings a user has at this stage are of a deadening of body sensation, a disinterest in what is going on in the environment and sometimes feelings of being huge or tiny. But how the body feels is rarely the point for the user. The idea is to go off into the mental world where anything is possible.

The second, "intimate" stage usually lasts from one to two hours, and is very different from the first stage. Actually, the drug is now beginning to wear off, but the user does not perceive the situation this way. The smokers are feeling a real closeness to one another, a mental intimacy which sometimes seems to be telepathy. Each can tell the feelings of any of the others. Words and laughter come in waves of intensity. Now, too, it is easier to walk around and people may feel they are floating just above the floor. All powers of judgment are impaired. Users are as impulsive as puppies. If someone suggests they all do something, the whole group could just as easily jump in the ocean and swim towards Hawaii. If a trip is interrupted at this point by someone who is angry—a parent or policeman, for example, the easy, happy feelings can disappear suddenly and be replaced with hostile emotion, great strength and violence.

The third, "comedown" stage, which lasts from the end of the second stage until an hour or two later, but sometimes lasting until after the person has slept, is really an effect of the drug wearing off. Now users are generally more irritable and paranoid. They may become violent and/or demonstrate their ability to perform feats of strength and daring. The warm intimacy is gone, replaced by anger or resentment and a sense of isolation which is all the more devastating in contrast to their shared experience so short a time ago. Arguments or fights erupt. No one is happy anymore. Experienced users try to go home at this point and sleep it off, and so avoid trouble. The next day there is some leftover tiredness and fogginess of mind. The person may not feel "normal" for several days.

The daily or chronic user, as opposed to the occasional user, does not experience these three stages so sharply. He or she learns to maintain, or act as though the drug is not having a strong effect. The first stage may not be so incapacitating to this person. Gradually, over the weeks and months of using, it will take more and more PCP to create the high desired, and the joints will be smoked more frequently during the day so that the effects never really wear off.

This means that the power of judgment is constantly crippled. In addition, memory can become significantly impaired. For some reason that no one yet has explained, brain cells die and the mind is seriously affected. If regular use goes on long enough, serious mental handicaps develop, which do not go away when the user stops using. It may be several months or even years before the mind returns to normal and some people never seem to fully recover.

§ 13.9.6 PCP and Heroin

The availability and abuse of PCP has continued to increase in many major cities in the U.S., contrary to the downward pattern observed from 1979 to 1981. Concurrent with increasing PCP use has been the escalating abuse of PCP in combination with heroin.

Methods of administering PCP/heroin mixtures appear to vary by geographic region and ethnic background. Informal interviews conducted with treatment program staff and clients provided the following information:

—PCP/heroin combinations are known as "Sunshine" in the Washington, D.C., metropolitan area. Frequently, white users smoke PCP and inject heroin, while non-white users inject both PCP and heroin (either separately or in a pre-mixed powder).

—A new street drug known as "Black Dust" has appeared in certain minority sections of north Philadelphia. This combination, consisting of heroin, PCP, embalming fluid, and marijuana, is commonly smoked.

—A new street substance known as "the Boat" has surfaced in Washington, D.C., and minority sections of Prince George's County, Maryland. It resembles "Black Dust" and is now manufactured in the Washington, D.C. area, having first been discovered in Philadelphia.

—PCP/heroin injections are prevalent in Harlem, New York.

The motivations behind the abuse of this combination of substances allude to the complementary nature of PCP and heroin, and are summarized below:

—Due to the anesthetic and numbing effects of PCP, numerous heroin addicts have taken the drug as a method of self-detoxification to ease the pain of withdrawal.

—Informal discussions with ex-addicts indicated that heroin ameliorates the undesirable effects of PCP.

—PCP and heroin mixtures are often sold on the streets as high-quality heroin, since a small amount of heroin mixed with 2 to 5 milligrams of PCP will yield a larger profit and boost a low-purity heroin.

Because of the sophisticated techniques involved in detecting phencyclidine and the varying procedures employed by toxicologists in gathering information, heroin/PCP combinations are underestimated. Some counties conduct forensic analyses on a wider range of drugs than other counties. Coroners also have difficulty, when drugs are detected, deciding whether the death was by accident, suicide, homicide or natural causes, and to what degree, if any, a given drug contributed to that death.

Some facets of PCP's action within the body are not as yet fully understood. In most hospital emergency room admissions, patients are not routinely tested for PCP. Levels of PCP in the blood of patients may be so low that it may not be picked up by any but the most sensitive of analytical methods, and certainly will be missed by most screening tests. Levels in urine may be much higher, but PCP will be detected only if the urine is acidic.

§ 13.9.7 PCP Traces Found in Hair
A successful method of analyzing hair to detect previous phencyclidine (PCP) use has been reported from California (Baumgartner). Researchers from a number of Los Angeles centers used the radioimmunoassay technique with hair specimens of 10 to 20 strands in newly admitted psychiatric patients. To establish reliability, verified non-users of PCP and volunteers admitting to frequent PCP use during at least the last six months were treated. No false positive or negative results were obtained. Hair analysis, in addition to traditional methods of PCP detection from blood and urine samples, was then obtained from 31 consecutively admitted psychiatric patients and 16 patients selected by the admitting psychiatrist for PCP testing on the basis of either history or presenting symptoms. Of these 47 patients, hair analysis detected 11 who had used PCP, while blood and urine analysis did not

identify any positive samples. Although urine testing is more likely to identify PCP than blood testing, the researchers noted eight patients refused to provide a urine sample. Four of these were identified as PCP users by hair analysis. In three patients, the results of hair analysis helped establish a diagnosis of PCP intoxication. It is not known how the rate of appearance and accumulation of PCP in hair changes with time or is influenced by growth in amounts thought to correlate directly with the dose consumed (Sramek).

§ 13.9.8 Conclusion

At this point, it is still too early to determine if PCP is going to re-emerge as a significant drug of abuse. However, there are indications of a PCP resurgence. Recent large seizures of the drug, coupled with the discovery of clandestine laboratories operating outside of traditional source areas may be an indication that demand for PCP is increasing. Even though the trafficking and abuse of PCP is not as widespread as with other illicit drugs, the violent consequences of its abuse are always causes for concern.

§ 13.10   JIMSON WEED (DATURA STRAMONIUM)

Although jimson weed is not a controlled substance, instances of abuse are periodically brought to the attention of law enforcement. Jimson weed is a large annual plant which grows up to five feet tall.

The stems are green to purplish, leaves alternate and are up to 8 inches long, are irregularly toothed, and vary in size and shape. The flowers are white to violet and are funnel-shaped and usually form at the center of a forked branch. The wrinkled, black seeds are contained in an ovoid capsule with many sharp spines.

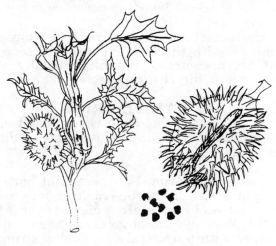

JIMSON WEED, *DATURA STRAMONIUM*

The plant is common to waste areas, pastures, and roadsides throughout North America. All parts of the datura plant are poisonous. Toxic effects have been reported after ingestion of teas brewed from plant parts, ingestion of leaves and flowers, and smoking stramonium cigarettes. Seed ingestion is now the most common route of toxicity.

§ 13.10.1   Why Jimson Weed Is Not Controlled

The two alkaloids found in this plant are so widely distributed that an analysis could not identify which plant they are derived unless accompanied by a botanical sample of the plant itself. Scopolamine and hyoscyamine are not exclusive to stramonium alone. Atropa (belladonna), hyoscyamus (henbane), solanum (nightshade), and duboisine myoporoides each contain one or both of these ingredients. By controlling scopolamine and hyoscyamine to control jimson weed, one would control these other plants and products made from them.

Over the counter (OTC) preparations such as "Compoz," "Sominex," and "Sleep-Eze" contain the active ingredient scopolamine. It would be difficult to control a substance when it is sold over the counter (Lewis).

§ 13.10.2   Pharmacological Effects
Except for the stimulant cocaine, all of the significant tropane alkaloids are found in the potato family (solanaceae). They include scopolamine (hyoscine) and hyoscyamine, the levo isomer of atropine. Datura stramonium is in the solanecea family and contains these alkaloids as its major pharmacologically active components.

The pharmacological action of the tropane alkaloids is well known. They are autonomic nervous system blocking. Because of this effect they commonly stimulate and then depress the medulla and high cerebral centers. They inhibit glandular secretions of the nose and bronchi, and relax smooth muscles there. They alter cardiac rate, dilate blood vessels, increase body temperature and pupil dilation.

Hallucinations usually involve simple images in natural colors in contrast with the brilliant displays seen with LSD. Seizures do occur but are uncommon. Fatalities usually result from associated trauma rather than direct toxic effects.

§ 13.11   SALVIA DIVINORUM
Even though this drug is not listed as a controlled substance, it is beginning to show-up in the streets of the U.S. and therefore worth reviewing.

Salvia divinorum is a perennial herb in the mint family native to certain areas of the Sierra Mazateca region of Oaxaca, Mexico. The plant grows in large groupings to over 3 feet in height. Characteristics of the plant include large green leaves, hollow square stems and white flowers with purple calyces. S. divinorum is one of several plants that have been employed by the Mazatec Indians for ritual divination and healing. In recent years the active ingredient of S. divinorum has been identified as Salvinorin A.

There has been interest among young adults and adolescents to discover ethnobotanical plants that can induce hallucinations, changes in perception, and other psychological effects. Since neither S. divinorum, or any of its constituents, are listed in the federal Controlled Substances Act (CSA), a variety of Internet sites have appeared advertising Salvia as a legal alternative to plant hallucinogens such as mescaline. Seeds, fresh and dried leaves, plant cuttings, whole plants, and various extracts are purported to be sold over the Internet.

Salvia divinorum has no approved medical uses in the U.S.

Hallucinogenic/Psychedelic Drugs

§ 13.11.1 Chemistry and Pharmacology

Salvinorin A, also called Divinorum A, is believed to be the ingredient responsible for the psychoactive effects of S. divinorum. Chemically, it is a neoclerodane diterpene found in the leaves, and to a lesser extent in the stems. Other substances have been isolated from the plant, but with the possible exception of Salvinorin C, none have been shown to be psychoactive.

In the U.S., plant material is either chewed or smoked. When chewed, leaf mass and juice are maintained within the cheek area with absorption occurring across the lining of the oral mucosa (buccal). Effects first appear within 5 to 10 minutes. Dried leaves, as well as extracts purported to be enriched with Salvinorin A, are smoked. Smoking pure Salvinorin A, at a dose of 200-500 micrograms, results in effects within 30 seconds and lasts about 30 minutes.

A limited number of studies have reported the effects of using either plant material or Salvinorin A. Psychic effects include perceptions of bright lights, vivid colors and shapes, as well as body movements and body or object distortions. Other effects include dysphoria, uncontrolled laughter, a sense of loss of body, overlapping realities and hallucinations (seeing objects that are not present). Adverse physical effects may include incoordination, dizziness and slurred speech.

Recent studies using tissue testing (in vitro) assays and functional assays show that Salvinorin A acts as a potent agonist on the Kappa opioid receptor. This may explain the psychoactive effects of Salvia divinorum and Salvinorin A since other drugs acting at Kappa opioid receptors have been found to cause dysphoria, illusions, and hallucinations (DEA 2004).

§ 13.11.2 Illicit Uses

Salvia divinorum is chewed or smoked to induce illusions and hallucinations, the diversity of which is described by users as similar to those induced by ketamine, mescaline, or psilocybin.

Anecdotal accounts of use of the herb, called Salvia divinorum, describe hallucinogenic trips that make the user feel like an inanimate object or worse. You've heard of watching paint dry, how about feeling like paint drying? "I don't know of anyone who has taken it and said, 'Gee, that was fun,' " said Dr. Ethan Russo, a Missoula, Mont., clinical neurologist and expert on psychotropic herbs.

The plant's effects can vary from mild to extreme, making even regular users wary.

Experts said interest in the plant, a member of the sage family, springs from its use as a ritual herb by an Indian tribe near Oaxaca, Mexico. Other hallucinogens, like the South American brew ayahuasca, have similar followings.

"People get captivated with the idea of using hallucinogens as a way of connecting with the spiritual world as used in indigenous cultures,"

413

said Jim Miller, curator and head of the applied research department at the Missouri Botanical Garden in St. Louis.

For now, the hallucinogenic plant is legal and is commercially grown in its native Mexico, as well as in Hawaii and California. However, the Drug Enforcement Administration is reviewing it.

How Saliva divinorum produces its hallucinogenic effects is unknown, since its active component, Salvinorin A, does not work on any neurotransmitter sites affected by other hallucinogens, including THC, the active component of marijuana. Nor does it contain nitrogen, which makes Salvinorin A unusual as a psychoactive molecule.

"We don't know much about its toxicity— we just don't know much about it, other than the experiences that many report, which don't sound very pleasant," said Dr. Alan Trachtenberg, who works for the substance abuse office within the U.S. Department of Health and Human Services (Register-Guard 2001).

Salvia Divinorum street names are Maria, Pastora or Salvia.

§ 13.12   KETAMINE HYDROCHLORIDE
Chemically ketamine is dl 2 (0-chlorophenyl)-2-(methylamino) cyclohexanone hydrochloride. It is a relative of PCP. It is made by Parke-Davis Company and sold under the trade names of Ketalar and Keta-set.

§ 13.12.1   Background
Ketamine hydrochloride, a Schedule III drug under the Controlled Substances Act, is a dissociative anesthetic that has a combination of stimulant, depressant, hallucinogenic, and analgesic properties. Legally used as a preoperative veterinary anesthetic, ketamine is abused for these properties and used to facilitate sexual assault. Common street names for ketamine are K, special K, ket, kit kat, vitamin K, purple, special la coke, cat valium, super acid, super C, lady K, super K, keta-ject, and cat tranquilizers.

Distribution of liquid and powdered ketamine typically occurs among friends and acquaintances, most often at raves, nightclubs, and at private parties; street sales of ketamine are rare. Caucasian males between the ages of 17 and 25 are the primary distributors of ketamine, but Mexican criminal groups are increasingly distributing the drug, particularly in the Rocky Mountain High Intensity Drug Trafficking Area (HIDTA). Retail quantities of powdered ketamine (100 mg to 200 mg) typically are packaged in small glass vials, small plastic bags, and capsules as well as paper, glassine, or aluminum foil folds. Law enforcement reporting indicates that liquid ketamine can be purchased for $20 to $140 per 10-milliliter vial, while powdered ketamine typically sells for $40 to $100 per gram.

Ketamine is produced commercially in a number of countries including Belgium, China, Colombia, Germany, Mexico, and the United States. Ketamine production is a complex and time-consuming process, making clandestine production impractical. For this reason most of the ketamine illegally distributed in the United States is diverted or stolen from legitimate sources, particularly veterinary clinics, or smuggled into the United States from Mexico.

Mexico is a significant source of ketamine available in the United States. The drug often is diverted from pharmaceutical manufacturers and veterinary clinics in Mexico and smuggled into the United States for distribution in markets throughout the country.

§ 13.12.2   Medical Use

Ketamine was first introduced to medicine in 1965 for pediatric and burn cases. In 1970, the FDA approved it as an anesthetic in veterinary medicine. It is a clear liquid injected intramuscularly in cats, dogs, horses, etc.

Ketamine is used medically today for short surgical procedures that do not require skeletal muscle relaxation. The IV injection of ketamine lasts 45 minutes with a half-life of 10 to 15 minutes (which corresponds to the anesthetic effect of the drug). It is a rapidly acting anesthetic. The IV dose at 2 g/kg (1 mg/lb) of body weight produces surgical anesthesia within 30 seconds lasting 5 to 10 minutes.

§ 13.12.3   Effects/Distribution

The anesthetic state produced by ketamine has been termed "dissociative anesthesia"; in other words, the patients feel detached from their environment. The drug elevates blood pressure, produces nystagmus and stimulates respiration (in large doses, respiration is depressed). Also, tonic and clonic movements resembling seizures, anorexia, nausea and vomiting occur. Animal studies indicate that ketamine is rapidly distributed into body tissues with high concentrations in body fat, liver, lungs and brain.

Psychological manifestations vary in severity between pleasant dream-like states, vivid imagery, hallucinations, and delirium. Some patients experience confusion, excitement, irrational behavior that can last a few hours up to 24 hours postoperatively. No residual psychological effects are known to have resulted from use of ketamine.

Ketamine produces physical effects similar to PCP, with the visual effects of LSD. Users report that it is better than PCP or LSD because the trip lasts an hour or less. Low doses of the drug produce an experience called "K-Land," a mellow, colorful "wonder world." Higher doses produce an effect referred to as "K-Hole," an "out of body," or "near-death" experience. Use of the drug can cause a delirium amnesia, depression, and long-term memory and cognitive difficulties. Due to its dissociative effect, it is reportedly used as a date-rape drug.

Ketamine may be used in drug-facilitated sexual assaults because of its sedative and dissociative properties. When used in the commission of this crime, offenders often mix ketamine into victims' drinks— usually without their knowledge—encourage victims to try it. Ketamine is included in the Drug-Induced Rape Prevention Act of 1996, and any offender convicted of using the drug to facilitate a rape or any other violent crime may face a prison term of up to 20 years (NDIC 2004).

Ketamine is rapidly metabolized by the body and therefore is difficult to detect through urine and blood toxicology testing beyond 48 hours after ingestion. Routine urine screening is often ineffective in detecting ketamine even within 48 hours. However, a number of advanced commercial toxicology tests will detect the drug and its metabolites.

§ 13.12.4 Recreational Use

Recreational use of ketamine was popular in the late 1970s and early 1980s, but fell out of favor. It is now making a comeback, especially on the East Coast. Ketamine is growing as a drug of choice among the "hip" crowd, whose members have begun to shy away from cocaine and heroin. Ketamine abuse has been reported at teen "rave" parties. Law enforcement agencies are encountering ketamine abuse when stopping drivers for what appears to be driving while intoxicated.

Ketamine is primarily used in a crystal form and is usually snorted like cocaine. Some users will inject it, either intravenously or intramuscularly (popular in Germany, where ketamine is taken by body builders to offset the effects of excessive dosages of steroids). Buyers prefer to purchase it in its original liquid state and crystallize it themselves, so that they know they are getting the real thing.

Ketamine is manufactured commercially as a powder or liquid. Users will evaporate liquid ketamine on hot plates, on warming trays, or in microwave ovens, a process that results in the formation of crystals, which are then ground into powder. Powdered ketamine is cut into lines known as bumps and snorted, or it is smoked --- typically in marijuana or tobacco cigarettes. Liquid ketamine is injected or ingested after being mixed into drinks.

§ 13.13 DMT—DIMETHYLTRYPTAMINE

A synthetic derivative of tryptamine, DMT provides central effects similar to LSD but of shorter duration, including behavioral excitability, visual distortions and hallucinations.

Dimethyltryptamin (DMT) has a long history of use and is found in a variety of plants and seeds. It can also be produced synthetically. It is ineffective when taken orally, unless combined with another drug that inhibits its metabolism. Generally, it is sniffed, smoked, or injected. The effective hallucinogenic dose in humans is about 50 to 100 mg and lasts for about 45 to 60 minutes. Because the effects last only about an hour, the experience has been referred to as a "businessman's trip."

§ 13.14 BUFOTENINE—COHOBA

Bufotenine has been isolated from secretion of the glands of toads and from the seeds of *Piptadenia peregrina*. South American Indians have long used the seeds to prepare a psychotropic snuff called "co-hoba." Bufotenine is chemically known as the N'N'-dimethyl derivative of 5-hydroxytryptamine and shares many of the same actions.

Intravenously, psychotic episodes and cardiovascular effects of short duration have occurred with the intensity being directly proportional to the dose of injection.

Some toads release hallucinogenic substances as well as toxins as part of their defense. The most commonly used toad for U.S. drug takers is the Colorado River Toad found in the southwestern United States and Mexico. It gives off a chemical called bufotenine. The toad is shaken about and agitated, which causes the toad to release the chemical through its skin. The user licks the chemical off the back of the toad. Bufotenine is in the same category of illegal drugs as LSD.

§ 13.15 DET—DIMETHYLTRYPTAMINE

DET is a synthetic derivative similar in action to chemically-related DMT (Siegel).

§ 13.16 STP—4-METHYL-2, 5-DIMETHOXY ALPHA METHYL PHENETHYLAMINE

STP is chemically related to mescaline and amphetamine. Studies indicate that STP will produce hallucinogenic effects in doses greater than 3 mg and mild euphoria in lower doses (Joffe). One report indicated a 2 mg dose would produce a mild reaction up to four hours, 3.2 mg would produce pronounced hallucinogenic effects lasting up to ten hours. Another study found that doses in excess of 5 mg always produced marked hallucinogenic effects whose intensity and duration were related to the dose. There have been reports that this drug could produce hallucinogenic reactions up to 72 hours and could be intensified with the use of chlorpromazine. STP was found to be 100 times more potent than LSD. Black market preparations of this drug are estimated to contain 10 mg in each dosage unit.

Pharmacological effects include pupillary dilation, increased pulse rate, increased systolic blood pressure, slight temperature increase, moderate euphoria and slight perceptual effects.

Toxic effects include nausea, sweating, paresthesia and tremors. Perceptual changes include blurred vision, multiple images, vibration of objects, visual hallucination, distorted shapes, enhancement of details, slowed passage of time and increased contrasts. Many persons who allegedly have used STP have suffered severe reactions according to reports from a number of hospitals.

Slang terms for STP are "serenity," "tranquility," "peace" and "DOM."

Chapter 13

§ 13.17 MORNING GLORY SEEDS

Evidence of morning glory seed use can be traced back in centuries. These seeds were used extensively by South American civilizations hundreds of years ago. Morning glory came into its own in this country in the early 1960s when a series of scientific articles were published demonstrating the connection between the morning glory and LSD. The popular and "beat" press provided complete coverage so that any individual who had not heard of the marvelous seeds was a rarity.

Morning glory seeds contain lysergic acid amide, an alkaloidal derivative about one-tenth as potent as LSD.

The seeds can be prepared as a tea or chewed to obtain the desired hallucinatory effect. Emesis, diarrhea and dizziness are frequent accompanying reactions and suicides have been reported.

§ 13.17.1   Morning Glory/Hawaiian Woodrose

Certain members of the common morning glory family, including "Heavenly Blue" and "Pearly Gates," and their close relatives, the Hawaiian baby woodroses, *Argyria nervosa* and *Ipomoea tuberosa*, were discovered in the 1960s to have psychedelic properties similar to those of LSD-25. The psychoactive principles of these plants comprise several forms of lysergic acid amide, chiefly ergine (d-lysergic acid amide) and iso-ergine, 5 to 10 percent as strong as LSD. These are called "ergot-alkaloids," because they're identical to the psychotropic LSD-type alkaloids found in ergot fungus. It is estimated that 100 morning glory seeds, or four to eight Hawaiian baby woodrose seeds, are equivalent to 100 micrograms of LSD.

Although ergot-alkaloid producing morning glories grow in many parts of the world, their ritual use as drugs was apparently confined to Mexico and Central America. The most notable ritual uses were the Aztec divine plant, ololiuqui (*Rivea corymbosa*) and the Mexican Indian drug tlitiltzin, or badoh negro, derived from *Ipomoea violacea*. These species of morning glory are cultivated in several ornamental varieties that include "Heavenly Blue," "Pearly Gates" and "Flying Saucer."

Modern use of these plants for their psychedelic properties began in the late 1950s and mid-1960s. In 1959, Dr. Albert Hoffman, the chemist who first synthesized LSD-25 from ergot fungus in 1942, isolated the lysergic acid amides in ololiuqui seeds. The psychoactive potential of Hawaiian baby woodrose was introduced to the public in 1965 in a scientific paper crediting these seeds with several times the potency of morning glory seeds.

Only the seeds of these plants are ingested. They are eaten whole, or ground and eaten, or leached with water and drunk. Despite wide interest in the seeds, use has never been widespread, and has declined in recent years. Woodrose seed use reached its zenith in the late 1960s and early 1970s; it was never extensive, but rather served as a substitute, albeit a poor one, for LSD when it was scarce and more desirable entheogens were unavailable.

The two primary liabilities of these hallucinogens are lack of potency coupled with a rapid onset of tolerance, and the abdominal cramping that seems to inevitably accompany a psychedelic dose. The cramping, nausea and frequent diarrhea that accompany use of these seeds gave rise to a street belief that they either contained strychnine naturally, or were coated with poison by seed companies to discourage ingestion. The general feeling among users is that the trip is not worth the side effects.

Given the low potency of the seeds, physical distress is much more probable than psychological disruption. There is a possibility of panic reactions and other psychedelic bad-trip symptoms, however, and especially in users who are unfamiliar with psychedelic effects. High doses can be dangerous and should be strictly avoided.

For adverse reactions, a talk-down similar to that used for LSD bad trips is effective. Be supportive and comforting. Remind the user that the drug's effects usually last less than six hours. Overdose victims should be taken to an emergency room or poison center.

Slang terms for morning glory: "Pearly Gates," "Flying Saucers," "Elephant Creeper."

§ 13.18   TRYPTAMINES - A REVIEW

Many analogs of a class of tryptamines are hallucinogenic substances that exist naturally in some plants, fungi, and animals, but also can be produced synthetically. These hallucinogens have been placed in Schedule I of the CSA. These substances include psilocybin, psilocin, bufotenine, alpha-ethyltryptamine, and dimethyltryptamine. There are numerous types of tryptamines available, including AMT and Foxy, that are not listed under the CSA. In addition to recent seizures of AMT and Foxy, law enforcement authorities have seized other non-controlled tryptamines, such as 5-MeO-DMT, over the past 2 years.

—Psilocybin (O-phosphoryl-4-hydroxy-N, N-ethyltryptamine)
—Psilocin (4-hydroxy-N, N-dimethyltryptamine)
—Bufotenine (5-hydroxy-N, N-dimethyltryptamine)
—Alpha-ethltryptamine (AET)
—Diethyltryptamine (DET)
—Dimethyltryptamine (DMT)
—Alpha-methyltryptamine (AMT)
—5-methoxy-N, N-dimethyltryptamine (5-MeO-DMT)
—5-metroxy-N, N-diisopropyltryptamine (5-MeO-DIPT)-Foxy

§ 13.18.1   Abuse and Availability

There have been limited reports of abuse of AMT and Foxy, sometimes at raves and clubs, in Arizona, California, Florida, and New York. According to the Florida Department of Law Enforcement (FDLE), reports of teens and young adults using these substances are emerging. The FDLE reports that AMT is now a popular designer drug in South Florida, although no seizures have occurred. In the August 2001 edition of DEA Microgram, the DEA Southwest Laboratory in San Diego reported that Foxy has been seen at clubs in Los Angeles and New York City.

References

Baumgartner, W. "Hair Analysis for Drugs of Abuse." Journ. of Forensic Sciences 34 (1989): 14-16.

Block, W. "Pharmacological Aspects of Mescaline." Chemical Concepts of Psychosis. Ed. Renkel and Denber. New York, NY: McDowell Obolensky, 1968.

The California Narcotic Officer. May, 1992.

Clinical Toxicology 9.4 (1976).

De Bald, R., and R.C. Leaf. LSD, Man and Society. Connecticut: Wesleyan University Press, 1968.

Drug Enforcement Administration. "LSD in the United States." Drug Intelligence Report. Washington, D.C.: U.S. Department of Justice, 1995.

----------.. Microgram, 23.6 (1993(.

----------. "PCP: The Threat Remains." Drug Intelligence Report. Washington, D.C.: U.S. Department of Justice, 2003.

----------. "Salvia Divinorum." DEA Diversion and Control Program. Washington, D.C.: U.S. Department of Justice, 2004.

Fischer, R., et al. "Personality Traits: Dependent Performance Under Psilocybin." Diseases of the Nervous System 31 (1970): 116-121.

----------. "Sympathetic Excitation of Biological Chronometry." Int. Journal of Neuropsychiatry 2 (1966): 91-101.

Gowdy. "Stramonium Intoxication, A Study of Symptomatology in 212 Cases." JAMA 22 (1972).

"Hallucinogen Legal, But Scary." The Register Guard, 4 September, 2001.

Henderson, Leigh. "About LSD." LSD Still With U.S. After All these Years. Lexington Books, 1994.

Heim, R., et al. "Botanical and Chemical Characteristics of a Forensic Mushroom Specimen of the Genus Psilocybe." Journ. of Forensic Science Society 6 (1966): 192-210.

Joffe, M. "Behavioral Effects of STP." Drug Dependence. Ed. Harris. Austin: University of Texas Press, 1970.

Johnson, K.M. "Neurochemical Pharmacology of Phencyclidine." Phencyclidine Abuse: An Appraisal. Rockville, MD: Department of Health and Human Services, 1978.

Kingsbury, J. Poisonous Plants of the United States and Canada. Englewood Cliffs, NJ: Prentice-Hall Inc., 1964.

Kluver, Heinrich. Mescal and Mechanisms of Hallucinations. Chicago, IL: University of Chicago Press, 1966.

Leonard, B.E., and S.R. Tonge. "Some Effects of an Hallucinogenic Drug (PCP) on Neurohumoral Substances." Life Sciences 9 (1970):1141-1152.

Lewis, J. Medical Botany Plants Affecting Men's Health. New York: John Wiley and Sons, 1977.

Lindgren, J.E., et al. "The Chemical Identity of 'Hog'—A New Hallucinogen." American Journal of Pharmacy 141 (1969): 86-90.

Metzner, R., et al. "The Relation of Expectation and Mood to Psilocybin Reactions." Psychedelic Review, 5 (1965): 3-39.

National Drug Intelligence Center. "Ketamine." Intelligence Bulletin. Washington, D.C.: U.S. Department of Justice, 2004.

Hallucinogenic/Psychedelic Drugs

National Institute on Drug Abuse. "Phencyclidine: An Up-Date." <u>Monograph</u> 64 (1986).

<u>The Narc Officer</u>. International Narcotics Enforcement Officers Association, 90.

"PCP (Phencyclidine): The New Delusionogen." <u>Educational Off-Print Series</u>. Madison: Stash Press, 1975.

Pelner, L. "Peyote Cult, Mescaline Hallucinations, and Model Psychosis." <u>New York Journal of Medicine,</u> 67 (1967): 2833-2843.

<u>PharmChem Newsletter</u>. PharmChem Laboratories. July, 1989.

Rainey, J.M., and M.K. Crowder. "Ketamine or Phencyclidine." <u>JAMA</u> 230 (1974): 466-467.

----------. "Prevalence of Phencyclidine: Street Drug Preparations." <u>New England Journal of Med</u> 290.8 (1974).

Reed, A., and A.W. Kene. "Phencyclidine (PCP): Another Illicit Drug." <u>Journ. of Psychedelic Drugs</u> 5 (1972): 8-12.

Rosenberg, D.E., et al. "Observations on Direct and Cross-Tolerance with LSD and D-Amphetamine in Man." <u>Psychopharmacology</u> 5.1 (1963).

Rush, J. "An Account of the Effects of the Stramonium or Thornapple." <u>Clinical Pediatrics</u> 2 (1973).

Showalter, C., and W. Thornton. "Clinical Pharmacology of Phencyclidine." <u>American Journal of Psychiatry</u> 134 (1977): 1234-1238.

Siegel, R.K., and M.E. Jarvik. "DMT Self-Administration." <u>Bulletin of the Psychonomic Society</u> 16 (1980): 117-120.

Sramek, J.J., et al. Hair Analysis for Detection of PCP in Newly Admitted Psychiatric Patients." <u>Aerican Journal of Psychiatry</u> 142 (1985): 950-953.

Steiner, J.E., and F.G. Sulman. "Simultaneous Studies of Blood Sugar, Behavioral Changes and EEG on the Wake Rabbit after Administration of Psilocybin." <u>Arch. Int. Pharm.</u> 145 (1963): 301-308.

Tennant, Forest S. <u>Medico-Legal Identification of the Phencyclidine (PCP) User</u>. West Covina CA: Community Health Projects, Inc., 1983.

Tennant, Forest Jr. <u>Research Studies in Phencyclidine (PCP)</u>. West Covina, CA: Veract, Inc., 1986.

Urich, Bowerman, and Levisky. "Datura Stramonium, A Fatal Poisoning," <u>Journal of Forensic Sciences</u> 4 (1982).

Zenter, Joseph. "The Recreational Use of LSD-25 and Drug Prohibition." <u>Journal of Psychedelic Drugs,</u> 8 (1976).

CHAPTER 14

CANNABIS (MARIJUANA)

§ 14.1   HISTORY

The first known textual reference to marijuana in India can be found in the *Atharva Veda,* which may date as far back as the second millennium B.C. Early references to cannabis also appear on certain cuneiform tablets unearthed in the Royal Library of Ashurbanipal, an Assyrian king. Ashurbanipal lived about 650 B.C.

In Asia, the use of cannabis can be traced to the Chinese text, *Herbal* (circa 1200 B.C.), in which the drug was described as a surgical anesthetic. Most likely, cannabis was used for other purposes as well. In 1090, Marco Polo returned from China with tales of a Persian religious cult that used hashish to induce visions of Paradise for cult members. The cult-leader, called the "Old Man of the Mountain," recruited men who were given the drug, subjected to ethereal pleasures and then sent on suicide missions of political murder. The promise of Paradise persuaded the recruits to commit the assigned crimes and assured them of their return. Although these recruited hit-men were called "hashishin" (etymological source of our word assassin), the legend has it that they were never permitted to use the drug during their acts of murder.

The ancient Greeks, on the other hand, used alcohol rather than marijuana as an intoxicant, but they traded with marijuana-eating and marijuana-inhaling peoples. Hence, some of the references to drugs in Homer may be to marijuana—including Homer's reference to the drug which Helen brought to Troy from Egyptian Thebes.

The date on which marijuana was introduced into western Europe is not known, but it must have been very early. An urn containing marijuana leaves and seeds, unearthed near Berlin, Germany, is believed to date from 500 B.C.

The first definite record of the marijuana plant in the New World dates from 1545 A.D., when the Spaniards introduced it into Chile. It has been suggested, however, that African slaves familiar with marijuana as an intoxicant and medicine brought the seeds with them to Brazil even earlier in the sixteenth century.

There is no record that the Pilgrims brought marijuana with them to Plymouth, but the Jamestown settlers did bring the plant to Virginia in 1611 and cultivated it for its fiber. Later, in 1629, marijuana was introduced into New England. From then until after the Civil War, the marijuana plant was a major crop in North America and played an important role in both colonial and national economic policy. In 1762, Virginia awarded bounties for hemp culture and manufacture; the state also imposed penalties upon those who did not produce it.

Three years later, in 1765, George Washington was growing hemp at Mount Vernon—presumably for its fiber, though it has been argued that Washington was also concerned with increasing the medicinal or intoxicating potency of his marijuana plants.

At various times in the nineteenth century, large hemp plantations flourished in such states as Mississippi, Georgia, California, South Carolina, and Nebraska. Hemp was also grown on Staten Island, New York. However, the center of nineteenth-century production was in Kentucky, where hemp was introduced in 1775.

The major factors contributing to the decline of hemp cultivation in the United States were the invention of the cotton gin, other cotton and wool machinery, and competition from cheap imported hemp.

The decline in commercial production did not, however, mean that marijuana became scarce. As late as 1937, the American commercial crop was still estimated at 10,000 acres, much of it located in Wisconsin, Illinois, and Kentucky. At this time, four million pounds of marijuana seed were being used each year in bird feed. During World War II, commercial cultivation was greatly expanded at the behest of the United States Department of Agriculture to meet the shortage of imported hemp for rope. Even decades after commercial cultivation had been discontinued, hemp could be found as a weed growing luxuriantly in abandoned fields and along roadsides. Indeed, the plant spreads readily to different territories. In 1969, the total area of Nebraska's land infested with "weed" marijuana was estimated at 156,000 acres (National Commission 1972).

§ 14.1.1 Early Recreational Use of Marijuana in the United States

Marijuana was readily available in the United States through much of the nineteenth and early twentieth centuries; its effects were known, and it was sometimes used for recreational purposes. But use was at best limited, local, and temporary. Not until after 1920 did marijuana come into general use, and not until the 1960s did it become a popular drug.

Rather than a change in the drug itself or a change in human nature, it was a change in the law that stimulated the large-scale marketing of marijuana for recreational use in the United States. When the Eighteenth Amendment and the Volstead Act of 1920 raised the price of alcoholic beverages, made alcohol less convenient to secure, and made it inferior in quality, there sprang up a substantial commercial trade in marijuana for recreational use.

Evidence for such a trade comes from New York City, where marijuana "tea pads" were established in 1920. These "pads" resembled opium dens or speakeasies, except that the price of marijuana was very low compared to the price of opium. A patron could get high on marijuana for a quarter in the marijuana pad, or for even less if the marijuana was purchased at the door and then taken away to smoke. It was said that most of the marijuana for these pads was harvested from supplies growing wild on Staten Island or in New Jersey and other nearby states. Domestic supplies were used because the marijuana and hashish imported from North Africa were more potent and were, therefore, more expensive. Much like the speakeasies of the time, these marijuana tea pads were tolerated by the city of New York. By the 1930s, there were said to be 500 of them in New York City alone.

§ 14.1.2 Marijuana Laws Since the 1930s

Due to the legalization of weak beer in 1933 and the return of hard liquor the following year, the modest, localized popularity of marijuana during the Prohibition years may have declined somewhat. The most important changes, however, resulted from legal intervention.

On January 1, 1932, the newly-established Federal Bureau of Narcotics, a unit in the Treasury Department, assumed responsibility for the enforcement of federal anti-opiate and anti-cocaine laws. As these responsibilities were taken over from the Alcohol Unit of the Treasury Department, former Assistant Prohibition Commissioner Harry J. Anslinger took over as commissioner of narcotics. Commissioner Anslinger had no legal jurisdiction over marijuana, but his interest in it was intense. The Bureau's first annual report under his aegis warned that marijuana, dismissed as a minor problem by the Treasury one year earlier, had now come into wide and increasing abuse in many states. As a result of increasing abuse, the report also stated that the Bureau of Narcotics had been endeavoring to impress on the various states the urgent need for vigorous enforcement of the local cannabis laws.

During his first year as commissioner of narcotics, Anslinger secured from the National Conference of Commissioners on Uniform Drug Laws the draft of a "Uniform Anti-Narcotics Act." This act was designed for adoption by state legislatures. The conference failed to include a ban on marijuana in the main text of this "model law," but it did supply to the states an "optional text" in addition to the basic act. Subsequently, state after state adapted the model legislation and began to enforce marijuana laws.

Later, Commissioner Anslinger continued to encourage states to adopt rigid marijuana laws. His 1935 report sent the following message to states:

> "In the absence of federal legislation on the subject, the States and cities should rightfully assume the responsibility for providing vigorous measures for the extinction of this lethal weed, and it is therefore hoped that all public-spirited citizens will earnestly enlist in the movement urged by the Treasury Department to adjure intensified enforcement of marijuana laws" (Smith).

By 1937, forty-six of the forty-eight states—as well as the District of Columbia—had laws against marijuana. Under most of these state laws, marijuana was subject to the same rigorous penalties applicable to morphine, heroin, and cocaine, although marijuana was often erroneously designated a narcotic.

Commissioner Anslinger's drive for federal as well as state anti-marijuana legislation shifted into high gear in 1937, when his superiors in the Treasury Department sent to Congress the draft of a bill that become the Marijuana Tax Act of 1937. Modeled on the Harrison Narcotic Act of 1914, the bill did not actually ban marijuana. It fully recognized the medicinal uses of the substance, specifying that physicians, dentists, veterinarians, and others could continue to prescribe cannabis if they paid a license fee of $1 per year; that druggists who dispensed the drug should pay a license fee of $15 a year; that growers of marijuana should pay $25 a year; and that importers, manufacturers, and compounders should pay $50 a year. At this time, only the nonmedicinal, untaxed possession or sale of marijuana was outlawed.

Since 1937, restrictive legislation on marijuana has increased in quantity and severity. Most state marijuana laws began to specify that marijuana penalties should be the same as heroin penalties. Thus, as heroin penalties were escalated through the decades, marijuana penalties were also increased. Moreover, the laws of nineteen states made no distinction between mere possession of one marijuana cigarette and the sale of large quantities of heroin. Under both federal and state laws, as noted earlier, marijuana was designated a narcotic; therefore, marijuana was included in legislation against the "sale" of narcotics such as heroin.

Along with federal heroin penalties, from time to time Congress escalated federal marijuana penalties. In 1951, mandatory minimum sentences were fixed for all marijuana offenses and all but first-time offenders were rendered ineligible for suspended sentence or probation. In 1956, the mandatory minimum for a first-offense possession was fixed at two years (with a potential ten-year term). The mandatory minimum for a second-possession offense was fixed at five years (with a potential twenty-year term); second-possession offenders were also denied parole, probation, and suspended sentence. For sale offenses, the mandatory minimum was set at five years for a first offense and ten years for a second, while terms of twenty years for a first offense and forty for a second were possible. Likewise, parole, probation, and suspended sentence were banned for all sales offenses.

On a national scale, anti-marijuana propaganda kept pace with the continuing anti-marijuana legislation after 1939. In its legislation, the United States was vigorously anti-marijuana. Then, in 1970, federal penalties for marijuana possession were reduced by the Comprehensive Drug Abuse Prevention and Control Act. When the federal penalties for marijuana possession were reduced, many states followed suit. Since 1970, marijuana laws have been reduced to reflect a more enlightened view of marijuana use in the United States. While the legal trend has been to reduce penalties for possession of marijuana in small amounts, most state laws have retained controls against traffickers and dealers. At present, federal and several state laws provide misdemeanor penalties for users or simple possessors. Some states are considering further reductions in penalties so that consumers will be charged with only a minor violation.

§ 14.1.3(a)   New Direction—Marijuana Laws

In 1996, California voters passed Proposition 215, also known as the Compassionate Use Act of 1996 (Health and Safety Code §11362.5). This act permits a patient to possess or cultivate marijuana for personal medical purposes upon the written or oral recommendation or approval of a physician. Stated specifically, the act will "ensure that patients and their primary caregivers who obtain and use marijuana for medical purposes upon the recommendation of a physician are not subject to criminal prosecution or sanction." Therefore, section 11357 of the Health and Safety Code regarding marijuana possession and section 11358 of the Health and Safety Code regarding marijuana cultivation do not apply if the requirements of section 11362.5(d) of the Health and Safety Code are met.

Federal law makes no provision for medical use of marijuana, and therefore the California law is subject to challenges in the federal courts. After Proposition 215 was passed, former U.S. drug czar Barry McCaffrey enunciated a policy under which doctors who recommended or prescribed marijuana could face federal criminal charges, lose their federal authority to prescribe medications and be denied Medicare and Medicaid payments. In late April 1997, a federal district court judge in California issued a preliminary injunction barring the federal government from taking any action against physicians who recommend personal use of marijuana for treatment of patients who have been diagnosed as HIV-Positive or with AIDS, glaucoma, cancer, seizures, or muscle spasms. Yet physicians who prescribe marijuana or attempt to help patients obtain marijuana are not protected from federal action. This is because possession and cultivation of marijuana are federal crimes (San Francisco Examiner).

Then, along came *Conant v. Walter*[1] in 2002. This case arises from the ongoing war between the federal government and the states that have authorized the use of marijuana for medicinal purposes. So far nine states have approved medical marijuana initiatives or laws—Alaska, Arizona, California, Colorado, Hawaii, Maine, Nevada, Oregon, and Washington—and others are considering measures. In early litigation, the Department of Justice (DOJ) established that federal controlled-substance laws preempt state laws permitting the use of marijuana. This was an extension of the litigation in the 1970s, which found that the Food and Drug Administration has authority to regulate and prohibit the drug Laetrile even if it was authorized by state law.

In *Conant v. Walters*, a group of patients suffering from serious medical conditions including HIV, and a group of physicians, sought an injunction against DOJ policy to revoke the DEA license of physicians who recommended the use of marijuana for medical reasons. The Ninth District Court granted a temporary injunction prohibiting the DOJ from investigating physicians for recommending medical marijuana

---

[1] *Conant v. Walters*, 309 F.3d 629 (9th Cir. 2002), *cert. refused*, Oct. 14, 2003.

and from revoking their licenses. In 2003, the U.S. Supreme Court declined to hear *Conant v. Walters*, letting stand the appellate court decision. It was found that the First Amendment protected physicians who merely recommended or discussed the medical use of marijuana with their patients. The case has an interesting discussion of the efforts by the federal government to control the medical use of marijuana.

The nine states that currently have medical marijuana laws basically involve the distribution of cannabis through "cooperatives" to people determined to have a medical necessity for marijuana such as cancer, AIDS, and patients with other illnesses.

On May 14, 2001, the United States Supreme Court, in the case of *U.S. vs. Oakland Cannabis Buyers' Cooperative No. 11-151*[2] ruled that the federal drug law allows no "medical necessity" exemption to the general population on selling or growing marijuana. They went on to say that Congress has made a determination that marijuana has no medical benefit worthy of an exemption. In the opinion written by Justice Clarence Thomas, "We hold that medical necessity is not a defense to manufacturing and distributing marijuana." Therefore, the Court upheld federal authority to obtain a court order shutting down the Oakland cooperative. The ruling does not directly invalidate the medical marijuana law in the nine states. Those states remain free to choose not to prosecute people who use marijuana for medical purposes, and the federal government does not often prosecute individuals for personal use of marijuana. As one California district attorney told me, "The Court decision says it is a violation of federal law for a club or cooperative to distribute marijuana, but I don't prosecute federal crime."

Based on this Supreme Court ruling, Congress would have to reclassify marijuana as a Schedule II controlled substance, allowing its use for medical purposes. Passing such a measure is unlikely.

There are certain to be more legal challenges to California's and other states' laws regarding medical use of marijuana in the future.

§ 14.2 MARIJUANA USE

Marijuana is one of the four most commonly used recreational drugs in the United States today; the other substances include ethyl alcohol (beer, wine, and liquor), nicotine (cigarettes, cigars, snuff, and other tobacco products), and caffeine (coffee, tea, and cola-based soft drinks).

Drug statistics vary from year to year and from one decade to another. An estimated 75 percent of current illicit drug users use marijuana. The National Drug Use and Health (formerly Household Survey) 2002 Survey found that marijuana is the most commonly used illicit drug, used by 14.6 million Americans. About one-third—4.8 million—used it on 20 or more days in the past month. There were 1.7 million youthful new users in 2001. The percentage of youth ages 12-17 who

---

[2] *United States v. Oakland Cannabis Buyers' Cooperative* (00-151), 532 U.S. 483 (2001), 190 F.3d 1109, reversed and remanded.

ever used marijuana declined slightly from 21.9 percent in 2001 to 20.6 percent in 2002 (SAMHSA 2003).

It is difficult to say what these statistics mean. It just might reflect society's and students' attitudes about marijuana, according to a University of Michigan study published in the June 1998 issue of the *American Journal of Public Health*. The analysis, conducted at the U-M Institute for Social Research by Jerald G. Bachman, Lloyd D. Johnston, and Patrick M. O'Malley, is based on data from the annual "Monitoring the Future" study of teen drug use and attitudes. The research is supported by the National Institute on Drug Abuse, one of the National Institutes of Health.

The new analysis by Bachman, a social psychologist, and his colleagues is based on surveys of 61,000 high school seniors from the classes of 1976 through 1996, and of 88,000 eighth-graders and 82,000 tenth-graders from 1991 through 1996. It examines how marijuana use is related to student attitudes about the drug itself and to a variety of general "lifestyle" factors, including school grades, truancy, hours spent working, average weekly income, religious commitment, political beliefs, and the number of evenings a week that teens hang out with friends. "Individual differences in some of the lifestyle factors we examined are important risk factors in determining which students are likely to use marijuana—or other drugs, for that matter," says Bachman. "But as important as they are, these lifestyle factors alone cannot account for the recent changes in marijuana use."

The data from the Monitoring the Future study show that seniors' use of the drug increased during most of the '70s and decreased throughout the '80s. Among all three age groups studied, use increased in the '90s.

Teen disapproval of the drug and perceptions of marijuana's hazards present a mirror-image of this usage pattern: in years when average levels of disapproval and perceived risk are high, average levels of use are low.

Earlier analyses from the Monitoring the Future study also have shown that marijuana use goes down when perceived risk and disapproval go up. What the new analyses show is that these changes cannot be explained by any shifts in the other lifestyle factors that were examined. "Young people did not become distinctly more conservative or conventional in the 1980s, nor did they become distinctly less so in the 1990s," says Bachman. "So if we want to know why marijuana use is on the rise again, there is little value in asking whether young people are somehow becoming more rebellious or delinquent in general, because the evidence indicates that this is not the case. "We need to ask why it is that young people have become less concerned in recent years about the risks of marijuana use, and why they do not disapprove of such use as strongly as students did just a few years earlier," says Bachman.

Another study by the University of Michigan assesses the extent to which trends in marijuana prices and perceptions of use risks predict cycles in youth marijuana use. Marijuana use among high school seniors declined to a recorded low between 1981 and 1992, when prices more than tripled. The trend reversed itself after 1992, when prices fell by 16 percent.

The study shows that perceived risk of harm from marijuana use had a substantial impact on the reduction of marijuana use between 1981 and 1992 (as perceived risk rose), and in the subsequent increase in use after 1992 (as perceived risk declined). These conclusions, now taking price into account, are consistent with ones reached earlier by the University of Michigan investigators, who for years have argued the importance of perceived risk in explaining trends in the use of various drugs.

Despite the increasing popularity of other drugs such as heroin, in the 1990s, marijuana was still the most popular illegal drug. The pervasive use of marijuana may have stemmed in part from the fact that it is a widely-known substance.[3] One study has documented the tendency of marijuana users to turn others on to the drug: 25 percent within two years of first use, and 29 percent within five or more years of first use (Voss 1984). 65 million Americans have tried it at least once, many of them during its heyday in the 1960s and 1970s (Gould's Penal Code).

§ 14.3   PHYSICAL CHARACTERISTICS OF MARIJUANA

The term "marijuana" commonly refers to the flowering tops and leaves of the plant *Cannabis sativa L.* The leaves make identification of the plant very easy. Domestic marijuana leaves are usually green in color, containing a number of serrated leaflets that are 2 to 6 inches in length and pointed at both ends. The flowers of domestic marijuana plants consist of light yellowish-green clusters of oblong seeds.

On the other hand, the leaves of marijuana plants grown in other parts of the world sometimes have a different appearance. They can be brown or slightly red in color, with a number of short, fat leaflets with smooth edges. In any case, the whole cannabis plant, including the leaves and the flowers, may attain a height of 20 feet.

The term "marijuana" legally refers to:

1.   All parts of the plant *Cannabis sativa L.*, whether growing or not;

2.   The seeds of the plant;

3.   The resin extracted from the plant (which is also legally referred to as "concentrated cannabis"—whether the resin is crude or purified); and

---

[3] The authors of "Marijuana and Youth" are Bridging the Gap researchers Rosalie Liccardo Pacula, RAND; Michael Grossman, National Bureau of Economic Research; Chaloupka, UIC; Patrick M. O'Malley and Lloyd D. Johnston, Institute for Social Research, University of Michigan; and Matthew C. Farrelly, Research Triangle Institute.

4.   Every compound, manufacture, salt, derivative, mixture, or preparation of the plant, its seeds, or its resin.

This definition from the California Controlled Substance Act (section 11018 of the Health and Safety Code) does not include the mature stalks of the plant, the oil or cake made from the seeds of the plant, the fiber produced from the stalks, or any other compound, manufacture, salt, derivative, mixture, or preparation of the mature stalks (except the resin extracted therefrom). The definition also excludes the fiber, oil, or cake of the sterilized seed of the plant which is incapable of germination.

FLOWERING TOP OF MARIJUANA PLANT

Dealers frequently include all parts of the cannabis plant (including the seeds, stems, and stalks) in the marijuana sold on the street. Not surprisingly, "street" marijuana has greatly increased in potency over the past years. Since THC is the active ingredient derived from the resin of cannabis, potency depends on the amount of THC concentrated in the marijuana. Confiscated cannabis in 1975 rarely exceeded 1 percent THC content. By 2000, samples as high as 5 to 15 percent THC content were common and sinsemilla averaged 15 percent THC with some samples as high as 25 percent. Furthermore, "hash oil," a marijuana extract distilled from the cannabis leaves, was found to have a THC content of 40-68 percent.

The THC content, or potency, is affected by how the cannabis is grown, the amount of sunlight, how the marijuana is prepared, and how it is stored. For example, sinsemilla is the cultivation of the female cannabis plant absent from the male cannabis plant. The Medical Cannabis Potency Testing Project analyzes samples of medical cannabis from various cooperatives and providers around the country. After many different tests they determined the average THC potency of sinsemilla samples was 15.4%—four or five times greater than NIDA's marijuana. They concluded that due to its higher THC content, patients need consume only a fraction of the harmful activators and gases in cannabis smoke to achieve the same effective dose (MAPS).

§ 14.4   CLASSIFICATIONS OF THC AND MARIJUANA
As mentioned above, the main psychoactive ingredient in the cannabis plant is trans delta-9 THC (tetrahydrocannabinol). THC is a diffi-

cult substance to classify. At low to moderate doses, it is a mild sedative and hypnotic agent; its pharmacological effects resemble alcohol and the antianxiety substances (such as Librium and Valium). Unlike the sedatives/hypnotics, however, higher doses of THC may (in addition to sedation) produce psychological effects similar to a mild psychedelic experience. Also unlike the sedatives/hypnotics, higher doses of THC do not produce anesthesia, coma, or death.

Marijuana has been classified as a narcotic, a psychedelic, and a sedative/hypnotic. Because of the difficulty in correctly classifying the substance, it is often thought that a separate classification entitled "Cannabis" would be most appropriate.

§ 14.5 VARIETIES OF CANNABIS

The several forms of the marijuana plant have been variously called "*Cannabis Indica*," "*Cannabis Africana*," "*Cannabis Americana*" and a variety of other names which represent the geographical regions in which the marijuana was grown. The hemp plant of India was once considered to be a distinct species, but the most observant botanists, upon comparing it with a plant cultivated in the United States, have been unable to discover any specific difference. Therefore, "*Cannabis Indica*" is now regarded merely as a geographic variety. Likewise, the many other forms of marijuana are simply geographical varieties of the true species, *Cannabis sativa L.*

The California Controlled Substance Act defines marijuana as all parts of the plant *Cannabis sativa L.* Thus, only *Cannabis sativa L.* is identified in the law. For this reason, many attempts are made to call each variety of the true species anything *but* the name *Cannabis sativa L.* because any other species, if known or determined, would logically be exempted from California statutes. This is one such contention of the growers, sellers, and users of many of the hybrid forms of marijuana such as sinsemilla.

However, a California Attorney General opinion stated that the true species of marijuana is *Cannabis sativa L.* and all the other forms of cannabis are varieties from *Cannabis sativa L.* They all contain THC and are all illegal under California law.

§ 14.5.1 Colombian

Colombian marijuana is considerably more expensive than the Mexican-grown variety, but its average THC percentage ranges from 3 to 1 percent. Colombian replaced Mexican marijuana in the early 1970s as the most common commercial marijuana because of its reputation for superior quality. With massive increases in production, quality declined, and now many users are interested in the more potent sinsemilla. Today, Colombia grows many species of marijuana as well as sinsemilla.

§ 14.5.2 Mexican

In the 1970s, there was much publicity about Mexican cannabis fields being sprayed with a herbicide called paraquat. Despite this bad press, Mexico is back in business, supplying large amounts of marijuana to U.S. customers. Mexico also grows sinsemilla.

§ 14.5.3 Thai or Thai Sticks

This variety of marijuana is grown in the country of Thailand or its neighboring countries, Burma and Laos. These three countries are commonly known by drug traffickers as the "Golden Triangle." These countries grow tremendous amounts of both marijuana and opium and are considered major contributors to the world market. Regardless of which country actually grows the marijuana, it is all referred to as Thai marijuana in this country. The Thai growers cultivate and harvest their marijuana in near-perfect growing conditions. The fertile soil, the weather, and the general geographic factors are highly favorable  to cultivation of marijuana. The THC content of Thai marijuana is comparatively high, ranging from 4 to 8 percent.

The Thai method of cultivation is to grow marijuana to maturity, allowing the plants to bud and flower. They then harvest these "flowering tops" and separate them from the stalks and leaves of the plant.

Even though the resin containing THC is found in all stalks and leaves of the marijuana plant, the highest concentration is always found in the flowering top. The Thai farmer then wraps these "tops" onto small bamboo shoots which are approximately 5 to 7 inches in length. The material which he or she uses to wrap the "tops" onto the shoots or sticks is the stringy material which can be peeled from the stalk of the plants. It is common for the growers or traffickers to wrap 15 to 20 individual Thai sticks into a bundle which weighs approximately one ounce. Again, these bundles are wrapped with the stringy material which is peeled from the stalk.

§ 14.5.4 Sinsemilla

Sinsemilla is a Spanish word meaning "without seeds." This variety of marijuana is cultivated to eliminate seeds from the final product. It is believed that this method of cultivation is the same that is employed in the cultivation of marijuana grown in Thailand or Hawaii. This process essentially involves isolating the female plants from the males to allow the female plants to mature without being pollinated. The theory, which has reportedly been tested successfully in many climates, is that the female plant puts at least 40 percent of her energy into the production of seeds once it has been pollinated by the male plant. If the female plant is isolated from the male, the energy of the female plant is channeled into the production of THC-laden resin, in an attempt to trap the pollen which has been denied as a result of the isolation process. The female marijuana plant attempts to reproduce so intensely that it will continue to produce resin until it is either pollinated or dead.

This is the practice of the sinsemilla growers throughout California. The mountainous regions of Northern California provide the ideal climate, elevation, fertile soil, and isolation necessary to the successful and prolific cultivation of marijuana. Specifically, the mountainous regions of Humboldt and Mendocino counties are popularly known as the birthplaces of sinsemilla cultivation in this state.

The most significant change in marijuana cultivation since the introduction of sinsemilla to California has been the importation of Cannabis Indica seeds. A good portion of California sinsemilla is of the Indica type; it is a more desirous crop than sativa because of the high THC and the resulting potency. However, due to a hybridization in California, many of the state's marijuana plants are now a mixture of Indica and sativa. The hybrid tends to produce large plants with several large buds. It might also be noted that Indica plants mature in September and October.

§ 14.5.5 Maui Wowie and Kona Gold

These popular varieties of marijuana are grown in the Hawaiian Islands. Maui Wowie and Kona Gold are similar to both Thai and California's home-grown sinsemilla; they contain approximately the same range of THC and are comparable in price. Some have said that the Hawaiian marijuana grown on the island of Maui (Maui Wowie) is especially popular and has become one of the island's chief resources.

§ 14.5.6 Other Varieties/Strains

There are numerous, popular, varieties of marijuana which are more costly than commercial, but generally less expensive than sinsemilla, Thai, or the Hawaiian varieties. Some examples of these are Guerrero (cultivated in the Mexican state of Guerrero), Oaxacan (pronounced Wa-hacon, and grown in the Mexican state of Oaxaca), Acapulco Gold (grown in the mountains surrounding the city of Acapulco, Mexico), and Panama (grown in the country of Panama). The name Panama Red refers to a reddish tint of the small hairs which grow around the flowering tops of certain plants. This phenomenon occurs in certain hybrid varieties as a result of cross-breeding. These kinds of plants have also been found growing in Southern California in the mountainous regions north of San Diego. The term "Red Hair" has also been applied to this variety of marijuana.

Marijuana Indica and sativa are the two basic marijuana families. There are crossbreeds that combine different sativa and Indica breeds to produce another strain. Some marijuana is developed for indoor growing versus outdoor growing; to control height, potency, and yields. There have been many strains of marijuana developed over the years, i.e., White Window, Northern Lights, Super Skunk, Big Bud, and Purple Haze. There are over 192 different kinds of marijuana strains on the market.

About five percent of marijuana in the United States comes from Canada. Canadian pot has a reputation for being especially potent. The featured brand is BC Bud, which is grown in British Columbia and has become synonymous with high-grade marijuana grown throughout Canada. Although the actual potency of BC Bud varies, depending on how it's grown, it is estimated to be 25% THC. The average potency of marijuana consumed in the United States today is about 7% THC.

§ 14.5.7 Kenaf

Kenaf is an annual plant, related to cotton and okra, that grows from one to four meters in height (about three to thirteen feet). Kenaf's thick stalk and palmate leaves have three, five, or seven lobes that are some-what serrated. From a distance, this plant looks very much like mari-juana. However, upon closer examination, kenaf has some major differ-ences. The most obvious of these are the large yellow flowers appearing at maturity.

Kenaf is grown in numerous states, but grows primarily in Louisi-ana. The plant is cultivated because its long stalks provide a fiber used to make burlap, rope, animal bedding, and packing material. It is also more profitable to grow than most farm crops. However, one of kenaf's two species may mislead some officers to believe that it is an illegal marijuana crop. The first species has leaves that look like a hibiscus plant, while the other, *Hibiscus Cannabinus L.*, has an appearance similar to that of marijuana.

When kenaf leaves are dried and examined microscopically, however, there are no similarities to marijuana. The only hairs are unicellular types, scattered on the veins in the leaves. The Duquenois-Levine test of this plant also proved to be negative, giving only a green color in both phases. Kenaf contains no THC.

The kenaf plant could cause confusion to law enforcement agencies due to its physical resemblance to marijuana when growing, especially prior to maturity (when it does not have large yellow flowers). Many people have mistaken it for marijuana. Awareness of the kenaf's exis-tence and characteristics will help prevent costly and embarrassing mistakes.

§ 14.5.8 Hashish

Hashish, or "concentrated cannabis" as it is legally and medically known, is simply the concentrated resin that has been extracted from marijuana. A general range of THC content in hashish is 10 to 20 per-cent.

The chief producers of hashish are reported to be India, Afghanistan, Pakistan, Morocco, Mexico and the Caribbean Islands. Hashish varies in color, but it is generally black, brown, or green; it may sometimes have a reddish tint. Hashish consists of the drug-rich resinous secre-tions of the cannabis plant, which are collected, dried, and then compressed into a variety of forms such as balls, cakes, or cookie-like sheets.

Many users prefer hashish because it produces a quicker and more intense effect. Hashish is occasionally mixed into food preparations or boiled into a tea, but the most common method of use is smoking.

One way of collecting the resin is to rub the buds gently between the palms of the hands until a uniform coat of green resin forms from the fingertips to the wrists. This is scraped off with a knife, rubbed into long finger-wads, pressed flat in the palms and wadded up again until the texture is smooth and uniform.

Hashish can be obtained from any marijuana plant. The resin can be collected by contacting the leaf with leather and scraping the resin from the leather. Hashish collected from the living plant by the use of leather is considered the finest form.

Another method used for gathering resin is threshing the cut plant. The hash falls from the dried plant in the form of dust and is collected on cloth. Likewise, a fourth method of collection is accomplished by pressing the cut (flowering) tops between coarse cloths to which the resins stick. Traders can tell whether hash has been obtained from the growing plant or from the cut, dried plant by the color of the substance.

The first quality hash is brown in color and becomes darker in aging. This quality of hash is generally sold in lumps or sticks and rarely exceeds one ounce per stick. The second quality (dried plant) has a brown-green or brown-gray color. It is sold in cloth bags and weighs one to three pounds.

§ 14.5.8(a)   Hash Oil

Sometimes called "marijuana oil" or "honey oil," hashish oil is legally considered "concentrated cannabis." This substance is an illicitly manufactured form of what was formerly known in the pharmaceutical and medical professions as "tincture" or "extract" of cannabis, a lawful product previously used for medicinal purposes. Although the medical preparations of *Cannabis sativa L.* were restricted in this country in 1937, marijuana and hashish continued to flourish. Interestingly enough, hash oil all but disappeared until the early 1970s when it cropped up in the Orange County area of Southern California. It soon spread throughout the state and is, today, a much used and desired drug. In general, hash oil is about 3 to 4 times stronger than hashish and 30 to 40 times stronger than "commercial-grade marijuana."

Hashish oil is produced by a process of repeated extraction of cannabis plant materials to yield a dark, viscous liquid. It varies in color, but can generally be found in amber, dark green, brown, or black. It has an average strength of between 20 to 60 percent THC, which makes it the closest thing to pure THC found on the street today. Although pure THC can be manufactured synthetically in a laboratory situation, the cost is prohibitive, the expertise is generally lacking, and pure THC has an extremely short "shelf-life" requiring storage under nitrogen. These complications prevent pure THC from being found on the street.

Most users smoke hash oil by adding it to a marijuana cigarette or a commercial cigarette. Some users have reported taking hash oil by mouth, or by adding it to food preparations or liquids such as hot teas. Due to its consistency and the presence of solvents or other chemicals used in its extraction process, hash oil must be preserved in an airtight container and should be kept away from light and heat. The air, heat, and light will cause the oil to harden.

There are many ways to produce hashish oil, but the basic principle used by most clandestine operations is similar to that of percolating coffee. A basket filled with ground or chopped-up marijuana is suspended inside a large container, at the bottom of which is contained a solvent, such as alcohol, hexane, chloroform, or petroleum ether. Copper tubing or similar material is arranged at the top through which cold water circulates. The solvent is heated and the vapors rise to the top where they condense, then fall into the basket of marijuana.

As the solvent seeps through the plant materials, the THC and other soluble chemicals are dissolved, and the solution drops back to the bottom of the container. Continued heating causes the process to occur over and over again. The solution becomes increasingly stronger until the plant material is exhausted of its THC. Sometimes new material is added and the same solvent reheated, yielding an even more potent solution.

The purity of the final product (i.e., the percentage content of THC) will depend on the degree of sophistication of the apparatus used, but it is presumed that with high vacuum distillation and further fractional distillation and use of chemical filters, the end product could approach 95 to 100 percent purity, as a clear liquid.

§ 14.6 MARIJUANA PACKAGING

Marijuana is packaged for street sale in a variety of different ways. The most common manner of packaging is to place the marijuana in a clear plastic sandwich bag which is then rolled up and taped, or simply tied at the open end. This is commonly referred to as a "bag" or "baggy" of marijuana. Pounds of marijuana are packaged in heavy plastic bags. Multi-pounds (kilos) are usually wrapped in heavy paper and shipped in large burlap bags.

Marijuana is frequently found in hand-rolled cigarettes. It might be sold in this form, but it is more often put into cigarettes by the user who has purchased a quantity of marijuana. The marijuana cigarette is shorter and thinner than a commercial cigarette, and the ends are crimped or twisted to prevent the contents from falling out.

There are several brands of rolling paper on the market. Some popular ones for marijuana smokers include "Zig-Zag" and "E-Z Widers." The paper may be yellow, white, or brown in color. Two papers are usually used to prevent any coarse material from piercing the paper.

§ 14.7 METHODS OF MARIJUANA USE

Marijuana may be brewed as a tea for drinking or baked in cookies or brownies for eating. The most common method of use, however, is by smoking it in hand-rolled cigarettes, pipes, or water jars. Marijuana pipes are sometimes specially made pipes with relatively small bowls, or they might be improvised from regular tobacco pipes which are lined with aluminum foil to decrease the size of the bowl. Sometimes a Middle Eastern style "hookah" is used. A "hookah" is a large jar with water inside and a long tube through which the smoke is drawn. It may also be called a "water pipe." Smaller water pipes, commonly called "bongs," are also used because they are less bulky.

Generally, the marijuana cigarette is smoked completely. When the user gets down to the butt (known as the "roach") he or she may use a device called a "crutch" or "roach clip" to smoke the remaining amounts of marijuana. This device can be made from almost anything: tweezers, paper clips, hairpins, alligator clips, etc. A "roach clip" may be very simple or very ornamental. Many are put on necklaces or other jewelry 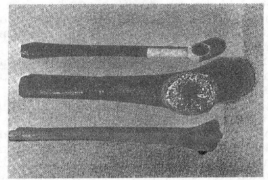 items. These "roach clips" are not illegal to possess, but possession of them could be used to support a case for drug use.

Many cannabis users will smoke in an enclosed area (such as a vehicle with the windows rolled up) to prevent the smoke from escaping. When smoking marijuana, the user holds the smoke in his or her lungs as long as possible to maximize the drug effects. A nonsmoking observer who is present in a location where there is a high concentration of marijuana smoke may also become affected but to a lesser degree than those actually smoking. This is referred to as a "contact high" and is sometimes used as a defense or excuse by abusers when they are apprehended for drug influence.

Burning marijuana has a very distinct odor, often described as sweet. It is easily recognized. It may be detected for a short time after smoking on the breath of the abuser, in the room or car where it was smoked, and on clothing.

A marijuana cigarette contains about 500 mg of plant material. If the marijuana contains approximately 1 percent delta-9 tetrahydrocannabinol (THC), then 5 mg of THC is available to the smoker. Half of the THC is destroyed by burning, 20 percent remains in the "roach," and 10 percent is lost in the sidestream smoke. This leaves about 20 percent or 1 mg of THC in the mainstream smoke that is inhaled by the user. Of that amount, the brain does not receive more than its share by weight, or about 0.015 mg. Within the brain, the distribution of THC reveals higher concentrations in the frontal and visual cortex, the cerebellum, and the limbic system.

§ 14.8   MARIJUANA, HEALTH, AND MEDICINE FACTS

One problem in sorting out fact from fiction about marijuana is that the "facts" keep changing into fiction. For example, in the 1930s, one "fact" was that marijuana was the dreaded "assassin of youth," a one-way ticket to a life of crime, madness, and despair. By the 1960s, that "fact" changed into the "munchies or harmless giggle," maybe not actually good for you, but at least it didn't do any real harm, like such legal drugs as alcohol and tobacco. In the early 1980s, a whole new set of "facts" was produced to justify a nationwide campaign against marijuana. Today the facts about marijuana are changing again. There are a lot of opinions masquerading as fact, but there is a growing body of scientific research that set down these facts as scientifically-proven truths.

Much more research on marijuana's effects on health in humans has been conducted outside of the United States. Even though some research in the U.S. has taken place, it is difficult to obtain marijuana from the government and time-consuming to obtain the necessary government research permits. SB295: California Marijuana Research Program was signed into law October 10, 2003, which allowed the continuation of marijuana research at the University of California. The purpose of the research program is to develop and conduct studies intended to ascertain the general medical safety and efficacy of marijuana, and if found valuable, to develop medical guidelines for the appropriate administration and use of marijuana. In 1995, the Multidisciplinary Association for Psychedelic Studies (MAPS) was created as a membership-based nonprofit research and educational organization. They assist scientists to design, fund, obtain government approval for, and report on studies into the risks and benefits of MDMA, psychedelic drugs, and marijuana.

Public opinion on the medical value of marijuana has been sharply divided. Some dismiss medical marijuana as a hoax that exploits our natural compassion for the sick; others claim it is a uniquely soothing medicine that has been withheld from patients through regulations based on false claims. Proponents of both views cite "scientific evidence" to support their views and have expressed those views at the ballot box in recent state elections.

Across the nation there is greater voter support for allowing the medical use of marijuana. California Proposition 215, the medical marijuana initiative, was passed in 1996 by 56% of state voters. Back in 1989, 16% of California residents agreed that the use of marijuana was no more dangerous than alcohol, while 75% disagreed. Now 50% believe that marijuana is no more dangerous than alcohol, while 46% disagree. We have seen some rather profound changes in the attitudes that Californians have about the drug (Field Poll 2004).

Californians' support for the medical use of marijuana has not eliminated some long-held reservations about the use of the drug in nonmedical situations. For example, in 1983, 65% of Californians agreed that the use of marijuana can make a person lose control of what he or she is doing. The current survey finds that a large majority of Californians (58%) still hold to this view.

The most contentious aspect of the medical marijuana debate is not whether marijuana can alleviate particular symptoms, but rather, what is the degree of harm associated with its use. It's a confusing and sometimes complex journey to uncover the facts about marijuana. So, as it turns out, the study of marijuana's health effects is at once more complex and less advanced than you might imagine. Interpretations of marijuana research may tell more about one's own biases than the data. For example, a prohibitionist might mention that THC often is found in the blood of people in auto accidents. Yet, they might omit the fact that most of these people also drank alcohol. Antiprohibitionists might cite a study that found no sign of memory problems in chronic marijuana smokers. Yet they might not mention that the tests were so easy anyone could perform them. The science of marijuana is young in the United States and contradictory, especially as to its potential medical uses.

In March 1999 the National Academy of Sciences' Institute of Medicine (IOM) completed a review of the medical use of marijuana and related issues. The report, "Marijuana and Medicine: Assessing the Science Base," was commissioned by the Office of National Drug Control Policy, in response to the successful ballot initiatives of 1996. The Institute of Medicine is the gold standard of American medicine and it was expected to broadly endorse the federal government's prohibition of marijuana for all persons. Instead, the IOM report recognized the therapeutic benefits of medical marijuana and urged that marijuana be made available to individual patients while research continued on the development of new drugs based on marijuana.

The Institute of Medicine's 1999 report on medical marijuana summarized the medical value of marijuana, saying:

"The accumulated data suggest a variety of indications, particularly for pain relief, antiemesis, and appetite stimulation. For patients, such as those with AIDS or undergoing chemotherapy, who suffer simultaneously from severe pain, nausea, and appetite loss, cannabinoid drugs might thus offer broad-spectrum relief not found in any other single medication. The data are weaker for muscle spasticity, but moderately promising. The least promising categories are movement disorders, epilepsy, and glaucoma. Animal data are moderately supportive of a potential for cannabinoids in the treatment of movement disorders and might eventually yield stronger encouragement."

Researchers do not know which cannabinoids are useful and how they act in concert with one another. What is known is that some people do not get relief from their conditions with the synthetic pill, but they do obtain relief from natural marijuana. As a result, the IOM recommended research and development of new drugs and new delivery systems; however, the IOM noted this could take many years and cautioned: "Patients who are currently suffering from debilitating conditions unrelieved by legally available drugs, and who might find relief with smoked marijuana, will find little comfort in a promise of a better drug ten years from now." The IOM concluded by recommending that smoked marijuana be medically available under limited circumstances, and the creation of clinical trials to continue studying the effects of smoked marijuana.

The IOM examined whether the medical use of marijuana would lead to an increase of marijuana use in the general population. This was a key concern of those opposed to medical marijuana. However, the IOM concluded that:

"At this point there are no convincing data to support this concern. The existing data are consistent with the idea that this would not be a problem if the medical use of marijuana were as closely regulated as other medications with abuse potential."

The report also stated that:

"this question is beyond the issues normally considered for medical uses of drugs, and should not be a factor in evaluating the therapeutic potential of marijuana or cannabinoids."

The IOM report also investigated the so-called gateway effect, which is the belief that using marijuana causes people to use other, more dangerous drugs like cocaine and heroin. IOM responded to this oft-made claim by stating:

"There is no conclusive evidence that the drug effects of marijuana are causally linked to the subsequent abuse of other illicit drugs."

The IOM also examined the physiological risks of using marijuana and cautioned that:

"Marijuana is not a completely benign substance. It is a powerful drug with a variety of effects. However, except for the harms associated with smoking, the adverse effects of marijuana use are within the range of effects tolerated for other medications."

The full IOM report can be viewed at or ordered from: www.nap.edu/readingroom/.

§ 14.8.1 History as Medicine
Marijuana has long been recognized as having medical properties. Indeed, its medical use predates recorded history. The earliest written reference is to be found in the fifteenth century B.C. Chinese Pharmacopeia, the Ry-Ya (NIDA 1975). Between 1840 and 1900, more than 100 articles on the therapeutic use of cannabis were published in medical journals (NIDA 1975). The federal government in its 1974 report "Marijuana and Health" states:

"The modern phase of therapeutic use of cannabis began about 140 years ago when O'Shaughnessy reported on its effectiveness as an analgesic and anticonvulsant. At about the same time, Moreau de Tours described its use in melancholia and other psychiatric illnesses. Those who saw favorable results observed that cannabis produced sleep, enhanced appetite and did not cause physical addiction."[4]

The 1975 report of the federal government began its discussion of medical marijuana by stating "Cannabis is one of the most ancient healing drugs." The report further noted: "One should not, however, summarily dismiss the possibility of therapeutic usefulness simply because the plant is the subject of current sociopolitical controversy" (NIDA 1975).

The list of medical uses of cannabis from historical references includes: Anorexia, asthma, nausea, pain, peptic ulcer, alcoholism, glaucoma, epilepsy, depression, migraine, anxiety, inflammation, hypertension, insomnia, and cancer (Mechoulam). Interestingly, relief of many of the symptoms marijuana was used for in these illnesses are many of the same symptoms that have been proven in modern research. This should not be surprising unless we want to assume that all of the experience of thousands of years did not have some factual basis.

§ 14.8.2 Chemistry and Metabolism of Cannabis

Marijuana is quite complex, containing at least 421 individual compounds. When smoked, some of the chemicals are further transformed by burning (pyrolysis) into other compounds. A great deal of research has been done on the principal psychoactive ingredient in cannabis, delta-9 tetraydrocannabinol (THC). However, THC is only one ingredient of the natural material.

The chemistry of marijuana smoke has commanded considerable attention in recent years. Some 150 compounds have been identified in the smoke itself. One of them, benzopyrene, a known carcinogen, is 70 percent more abundant in marijuana smoke than in tobacco smoke. There is also evidence that more "tar" is found in marijuana cigarettes than in high-tar tobacco cigarettes.

A confirmation of these earlier findings was published in 1982. It was found that when marijuana and tobacco cigarettes were consumed under similar conditions, marijuana produced 38 mg of tar, while 15 mg were produced from a popular brand of high-tar cigarette. When marijuana was smoked as it usually is (i.e., deeply inhaled and unfiltered) and compared with a cigarette of equal weight smoked as tobacco typically is, the marijuana cigarette yielded 3.8 times as much tar as the

---

[4] National Institute on Drug Abuse, Fourth Annual Report to the U.S. Congress, "Marijuana and Health," 1974, citing O'Shaughnessy, W.B., "On the Preparation of the Indian Hemp or Gunjah," *Translations of Medicine, Physiology and Sociology*, Bengal: 1838-1840; and Moreau de Tours, K., "Psychotic Depression with Stupor: Tendency toward Dementia: Treatment with an extract of Cannabis Indica," *Lancette Hospital Gazette*, 1857.

tobacco cigarette, suggesting that the health risk of one marijuana "joint" is much greater than that of smoking a modern high-tar tobacco cigarette.

These findings contribute to our current understanding of marijuana chemistry and metabolism. With respect to pregnancy, researchers have been able to demonstrate that marijuana constituents cross the placental barrier and, as a result, may affect fetal development. The presence of cannabinoids in the milk of the marijuana-using mother may also be transferred to the infant. Despite these possible dangers, research of marijuana's chemistry has also shown that one or more of the synthesized components of cannabis in its original or chemically-modified form may come to have therapeutic usefulness. Finally, our increased awareness of marijuana's chemical complexity and the ways in which components other than delta-9 THC modify the drug's effects may shed light on the common street belief that different types of marijuana have different effects not wholly related to their THC content.

The discovery of receptors in the central nervous system for cannabinoid compounds, and the presence of an endogenous ligand for these receptors, is of importance to the debate concerning the potential therapeutic uses of marijuana. This discovery supports a recommendation for more basic research to discover the functional roles of the cannabinoid receptors as a key underpinning for possible therapeutic applications. Such an approach allows the bridging of knowledge from molecular neurobiology to animal studies to human clinical trials.

§ 14.8.3 Risk Factors—Medical

Risks associated with marijuana, especially smoked marijuana, must be considered not only in terms of immediate adverse effects on the lungs, e.g., bronchi and alveoli, but also long-term effects in patients with chronic diseases. Additionally, age, immune status, the development of intercurrent illnesses, and concomitant diseases should be considered in the determination of the risk calculation. The possibility that frequent and prolonged marijuana use might lead to clinically significant impairments of immune system function is great enough that relevant studies should be part of any marijuana medication development research, particularly when marijuana will be used by patients with compromised immune systems. Of concern is marijuana's combustion byproducts, particularly when used for conditions requiring chronic therapy. It's likely that there will be developed insufflation/inhalation devices or dosage forms capable of delivering purer THC or cannabinoids to the lungs free of dangerous combustion byproducts.

§ 14.8.4 Cannabis and Dronabinol

There is growing evidence that there is no relevant difference in subjective effects between (Schedule III) dronabinol and cannabis. Thus, it can be expected that the abuse liability is similar for both agents.

In 1999, the Drug Enforcement Administration (DEA) reclassified Marinol from a Schedule II drug to the less-restrictive Schedule III category, according to the Controlled Substances Act. This essentially means that instead of being classified with drugs like morphine, Marinol is now classified with more widely used drugs like codeine.

According to the Associated Press of July 3, 1999, Barry McCaffrey, then the director of the White House Office of National Drug Control Policy, said the capsule form of Marinol is the "safe and proper way" to make components of marijuana available to the public. "This action will make Marinol, which is scientifically proven to be safe and effective for medical use, more widely available."

There are not many direct comparisons of the subjective and medicinal effects of cannabis and dronabinol (THC, Marinol). Recent experimental research has shown that the subjective effects of cannabis and THC are very similar. In a study by Wachtel and others, the authors write:

"There has been controversy about whether the subjective, behavioral or therapeutic effects of whole plant marijuana differ from the effects of its primary active ingredient, Delta(9)-tetrahydrocannabinol (THC). However, few studies have directly compared the effects of marijuana and THC using matched doses administered either by the smoked or the oral form."

Two studies were conducted to compare the subjective effects of pure THC to whole-plant marijuana containing an equivalent amount of THC in normal healthy volunteers. In one study the drugs were administered orally and in the other they were administered by smoking. In each study, marijuana users (oral study: n=12, smoking study: n=13) participated in a double-blind, crossover design with five experimental conditions: a low and a high dose of THC only, a low and a high dose of whole-plant marijuana, and [a] placebo. In the oral study, the drugs were administered in brownies, in the smoking study the drugs were smoked. Dependent measures included the Addiction Research Center Inventory, the Profile of Mood States, visual analog items, vital signs, and plasma levels of THC and 11-nor-9-carboxy-THC. In both the oral study and the smoking study, THC only and whole-plant marijuana produced similar subjective effects, with only minor differences. These results support the idea that the psychoactive effects of marijuana in healthy volunteers are due primarily to THC.

Since the abuse potential of a drug is mainly attributed to its subjective effects, it can be assumed that the abuse potential of THC and cannabis are quite similar.

Clinical research has also demonstrated similar properties of THC and cannabis with regard to therapeutic effects. This is shown in the data from marijuana research programs in six states on the anti-emetic effects of marijuana where patients who smoked marijuana experienced 70-100% relief from nausea and vomiting, and those who used the THC capsule experienced 76-88% relief (Musty et al). In the 2002 study by Abrams, et al., that investigated the interaction of smoked cannabis and Marinol (THC) with HIV medication, very similar effects were observed with regard to weight gain. The participants had been divided into three groups, with one set smoking marijuana (3.95% THC), another taking oral dronabinol capsules (three 2.5 mg doses daily), and a third taking oral placebo capsules. Researchers found that those using dronabinol (THC) or marijuana experienced significant increases in caloric intake and gained an average of 3.5 kg [7.7 lbs] (marijuana group) and 3.2 kg [7.1 lbs] (THC group) compared to 1.3 kg [2.9 lbs] in the placebo group. There was no significant difference between marijuana and THC with regard to side effects and benefits.

Marinol, or dronabinol[5] is available for treating nausea and vomiting associated with cancer chemotherapy and as an adjunct to weight loss in patients with wasting syndrome associated with AIDS. Although such approval currently applies only to orally administered THC, for practical purposes, smoked marijuana should also be expected to be equally effective.

Promising leads, also often fragile, suggest possible uses for treating chronic pain syndromes, neurological disease with spasticity, and other causes of weight loss. These indications require more study.

§ 14.8.5 Marijuana and Reproduction

It is now generally believed that the effects of cannabinoids on the hormones that modulate the reproductive process originate within the brain as a result of changes in neurotransmitters such as dopamine, norepinephrine, and serotonin. In monkeys, these amines alter the secretion of the gonadotropin releasing factor (Tyrey). A principal site of action of THC is in the hypothalamus, where production of the gonadotropin-releasing hormone is suppressed, which in turn inhibits secretion of the leutinizing hormone (LH), the follicle-stimulating hormone (FSH), and prolactin in the pituitary (Smith). These changes also induce decreases in the female sex hormones, estrogen and progesterone, interfering with ovulation and other hormone-related functions. When cannabis use is discontinued, however, these effects are reversible. After chronic administration of the drug, tolerance to the reproductive effects of THC is observed. Therefore, THC has its greatest effect upon the non-human primate's reproductive functioning when use is first initiated. The impact of marijuana or THC on human females requires further study.

Regular marijuana use during at least two developmental phases can be detrimental—during fetal development and during adolescence. The fetal risks will be discussed later. The endocrine events associated with puberty are strongly dependent upon a properly functioning hypothalamic-pituitary axis.

---

[5] Dronabinol is currently marketed in the United States for the stimulation of appetite in AIDS patients. The effects of smoked marijuana on cachexia associated with AIDS or cancer would need to be determined. Dronabinol is also marketed in the U.S. for the control of nausea and vomiting associated with cancer chemotherapy in patients who have failed to respond adequately to conventional antiemetic treatments. The effects of smoked marijuana for this indication merit consideration for further research.

As indicated, many of the endocrine effects caused by the chronic treatment of animals with THC are reversible as tolerance to the drug develops. Still, many questions remain regarding the long-term consequences of use, for example, on sperm formation, psychosexual maturation, and sex organ function. Until these and other issues are resolved, marijuana consumption by adolescents or males with marginal fertility poses uncertain reproductive hazards (Harclerode).

In laboratory animals, however, the administration of THC to male mice for five days has resulted in a reduction of sperm production and in an increase in abnormal sperm forms. In addition, testicular and seminal vesicle weights were decreased compared to the control group. These findings are consistent with a decrease in gonadotropin-releasing hormones in the hypothalamus and subsequent decreases in LH and FSH as well as a reduction of testosterone.

§ 14.8.5(a)   Effects Upon Fetal Development

In 1980, the Secretary of Health, Education, and Welfare's annual report released some important information on marijuana and health. This report was one of the first to address the effects of marijuana on fetal development Since then, additional information explaining the effects of marijuana on fetal development has been released.

Three studies have examined samples of sufficient size to adequately control for confounding effects. One of these studied 1,690 mother/child pairs (Hingston). Marijuana in varying amounts was used by 234 mothers during pregnancy. Use was found to be associated with lower infant birth weight and length compared to nonusers. Women who used marijuana less than three times a week delivered babies who were 139 grams lighter than those of the nonusing group. Marijuana use was the strongest independent predictor of whether the infant would have congenital features compatible with the fetal alcohol syndrome (FAS). In fact, marijuana use was a better predictor of FAS symptoms than alcohol use.

A larger study sampled 7,301 births for abnormal infant characteristics (Gibson). This research showed that women who used marijuana during pregnancy were significantly more likely than nonusers to deliver premature infants of low birth weight. The relationship of marijuana use to prenatal death did not achieve statistical significance, but was suggestive.

An even larger study sampled 17,316 women who gave birth at the Boston Hospital for Women (Linn). A total of 12,718 were interviewed to determine the impact of marijuana and other risk factors on their newborn offspring. Of the ten independent variables analyzed (which included tobacco and alcohol), marijuana use was most likely to predict congenital malformations. A 1984 report put out by Hingston et al. noted that tobacco and marijuana smoking, as well as alcohol and other drug abuse, frequently occur in the same women. Therefore, some of the adverse effects on fetal development attributed to maternal drinking or smoking may be due to an interaction with marijuana and other psychoactive substances. When a number of these toxic substances are consumed together, their toxic effects on the fetus may be cumulative.

Gross malformations in human infants due to prenatal exposure to cannabis have not yet been completely proven.

§ 14.8.6 Chromosome Abnormalities

While there were early reports of increases in chromosomal breaks and abnormalities in human cell cultures, more recent results have been inconclusive. Overall, there continues to be no convincing evidence that marijuana use causes clinically significant chromosome damage.

§ 14.8.7 Alterations in Cell Metabolism

The implications of laboratory findings on the inhibition of DNA, RNA, and protein synthesis (all of which are related to cellular reproduction and metabolism) are still unknown.

§ 14.8.8 Immune Status

Although additional information regarding possible reductions in immune responsivity has become available since 1980, the evidence that marijuana smoking in humans decreases resistance to infection remains inconclusive. The question is of particular importance because THC is sometimes used to reduce nausea resulting from cancer chemotherapy. Since cancer chemotherapeutic chemicals are themselves severely immunosuppressive, any additional THC-induced immunosuppression would be very undesirable. It has been determined that THC does decrease host resistance to herpes simplex virus, Type 2, in the guinea pig. This occurs in a dose-related fashion using amounts equivalent to human consumption levels (Cabral).

§ 14.8.9 Pulmonary Effects

Because marijuana is typically smoked, its possible adverse effects on the lung and pulmonary functions have long been of concern to researchers. It is noteworthy that one of the earliest attempts to assess the health and social implications of cannabis use, the "Report of the Indian Hemp Drugs Commission of 1893-94" includes observations about its pulmonary effects that are surprisingly similar to more contemporary observations. For example, this report mentions a possible value in the treatment of asthma because of the drug's pulmonary sedative qualities. However, it goes on to say that "long continued smoking...doubtless results in the deposition of finely divided carbonaceous matter in the lung tissues, and the presence of other irritating substances in the smoke ultimately causes local irritation of the bronchial mucous membrane, leading to increased secretion, and resulting in the condition which is described as chronic bronchitis in ganja smokers" (Indian Hemp Drugs 1894).

Thus far, there is no direct evidence that smoking marijuana is correlated with lung cancer. The American experience with marijuana has been too brief for this to be a likely outcome. Nevertheless, there is good reason for concern about the possibility of pulmonary cancer resulting from extended use over several decades. Like tobacco smoke residuals, or "tar," cannabis residuals, when applied to the skin of experimental animals, have been shown to be tumor-producing. Analysis of marijuana smoke has also found evidence that it contains larger amounts of cancer-producing hydrocarbons. For example, benzopyrene, a known cancer-producing chemical found in tobacco smoke, has been reported to be 70 percent more abundant in marijuana smoke. Therefore, the carcinogenic effects of marijuana smoking are a potential health concern for chronic smokers.

Extensive pulmonary macrophage infiltration of the lung has been documented in animals and by biopsy in humans. One report describes autopsies of 13 known marijuana smokers who died suddenly from trauma (Morris). This study indicates moderate to severe infiltration of the pulmonary alveolar spaces with pigmented macrophages leading to a fibrous tissue response and, finally, ulceration. The pigmentation was due to deeply inhaled marijuana smoke. Tobacco smokers of similar age (15 to 41) show little macrophage infiltration, and they do not develop the fibrosis and inflammatory changes until after many years of smoking. This suggests chronic obstructive pulmonary disease is a definite possibility in heavy users. One heavy marijuana smoker, 28 years old, had dyspnea on exertion due to alveoli being completely filled with macrophages.

From the total body of clinical and experimental evidence accumulated to date, it appears that daily use of marijuana leads to lung damage similar to that resulting from heavy cigarette smoking. Since marijuana users often smoke both tobacco and marijuana, the cumulative effects of the combination require additional study.

§ 14.8.10   Cardiovascular Effects
Marijuana significantly increases heart rate after smoking. There is evidence that in patients with already impaired heart function, use of marijuana may precipitate chest pain (angina pectoris) more rapidly and following less effort than tobacco cigarettes. Despite the limited evidence to date, heart patients and others who may have impaired cardiac function are at a higher risk of heart failure due to marijuana smoking.

§ 14.8.11   Brain Changes
Brain wave changes from cannabis generally consist of an increase and deceleration of waves. This is consistent with the state of drowsiness induced by the drug. Although scalp electroencephalogram (EEG) records show minimal alterations, electrodes implanted in deep brain structures like the septum, a center for emotionality, obtain marked changes in electrical activity (Heath).

The findings revealed by deep electrode recordings and by ultrastructural changes found in septal areas suggest that long-term, heavy use of marijuana or THC may produce microscopic changes. The possibility of macroscopic changes in the form of cerebral atrophy remains open, and additional imaging studies must be done.

§ 14.8.12   THC and Fat

THC and other cannabinoids dissolve readily in fat but not in water. This limits the possible formulations of cannabis and cannabinoid preparations, and slows down their absorption from the stomach. On the other hand, when cannabis is smoked (in a joint or "reefer" or in a pipe), THC is absorbed very quickly into the bloodstream, through the large surface area of the pharynx and the lungs. After smoking, the psychoactive effects of THC are perceptible within seconds, and peak effects are achieved within minutes. When cannabis or cannabinoids are taken by mouth, peak effects may not occur for several hours, but they last longer. After smoking or oral ingestion, the drug persists in the brain longer than in the blood, so the psychological effects persist for some time after the level of THC in the blood has begun to decline.

§ 14.8.13   Effects of Marijuana on Intellectual Functioning

A wide range of intellectual performance impairment due to marijuana intoxication is known. Cognitive tasks, such as digit symbol substitution, complex reaction time, recent memory, and serial subtractions are all performed more poorly when "high" as compared to performance during the sober state. Marijuana interferes with the transfer of information from immediate to long-term memory storage. Less demanding tasks, such as simple reaction time, do not appear to be affected by marijuana intoxication. A major unresolved question is whether long-term use produces irreversible effects.

§ 14.8.14   Marijuana Use and Sexuality

In a longitudinal study of white high school students, 61 percent of those who used marijuana and 41 percent of those who drank alcoholic beverages were sexually experienced compared to 4 percent among abstainers. It was also concluded that heavy marijuana users have higher rates of sexual experience than do light marijuana users (Jessor). These differences are as likely to be explained on the basis of congruent lifestyle behaviors as on any sexually induced drug activity. A fairly common finding was that marijuana use is associated with adolescent depression and poor self-esteem, with the drug serving as a form of self-medication.

Another study has determined that marijuana use is associated with increased sexual activity in many individuals, which, in turn, appears to relate to their sensation-seeking lifestyle (Abel). It might be said that many marijuana users take the drug to escape some unfavorable or unpleasant circumstance or as a social experience. It is common for adolescent marijuana users to openly provoke their parents with drug use or defy them in other ways. Defiance of school authorities is also common. Several users report that they "stone" themselves into unconsciousness or combine marijuana and alcohol to achieve this state. Adolescents repeatedly talk about using the drug to relax from tension and anger at home. Marijuana sometimes induces feelings of grandiosity that help adolescents deal with depression and poor self-esteem.

Combined with clinical studies, these patterns of use indicate that marijuana is often used as an escape, especially during adolescence, or is seen as a source of relief from coping with persistent difficulties

(Hendin). However, marijuana keeps adolescents in a condition of troubled adaptation and reinforces their unwillingness to master their problems. As an escape, the drug helps them dismiss serious problems as unimportant ones. Through marijuana use, adolescents avoid choices and challenges associated with becoming an adult and planning for the future.

§ 14.8.15   Psychopathological Effects
There have been few new developments in research on the psychopathological effects of marijuana use. An acute panic anxiety reaction is the most common adverse psychological reaction to use, especially when unexpectedly strong material is consumed. A number of clinicians have cautioned against use of marijuana by those with a history of serious psychological problems or who have previously had drug-precipitated emotional disturbances (so-called bad trips). While more serious psychiatric problems such as cannabis-related psychosis have been reported in countries with a long tradition of use, such reactions do not appear common in the United States. Nonetheless, concern has been expressed that availability of much stronger varieties of cannabis may result in more serious problems than in the past.

§ 14.8.16   Marijuana and Psychopathology
Cannabis may produce directly an acute panic reaction, an acute paranoid state or mania. Whether it can directly evoke depressive or schizophrenic states, or whether it can lead to sociopathy or even to amotivational syndrome is much less certain. The existence of specific cannabis psychosis postulated for many years is still not established. The fact that some users of cannabis may have higher levels of various types of psychopathology does not infer a casual relationship. The evidence suggests that virtually every diagnosable psychiatric illness among cannabis users began before the first use of the drug. It seems likely that psychopathology may predispose one to cannabis use rather than the other way around.

§ 14.8.17   Chronic Marijuana Use
In the current climate of debate about marijuana laws and interest in marijuana as medicine, one issue remains unresolved. Does heavy, frequent or prolonged use of cannabis lead to deterioration in cognitive function that persists well beyond any period of acute intoxication? Is the functioning of the brain altered in long-term use? Scientific evidence from past research clearly showed that gross impairment related to chronic cannabis use did not occur but was inconclusive with regard to the presence of more specific deficits. Recent studies with improved methods have demonstrated changes in cognition and brain function associated with long-term or frequent use of cannabis. Specific impairments of attention and memory have been found in cannabis users (Pop et al).

§ 14.8.18   Amotivational Syndrome
The occurrence of an "amotivational syndrome" in long-term heavy cannabis users, with loss of energy and the will to work, has been postulated. However, this is now generally discounted and thought to rep-

resent nothing more than ongoing intoxication in frequent users of the drug.

§ 14.8.19   Marijuana and Driving

There is ample evidence supporting the belief that marijuana use at typical social levels impairs driving ability and related skills. Studies indicating impairment of driving skills include laboratory assessment of driving-related skills, driver-simulator studies, test-course performance, and actual street-driver performance. Another important study, conducted for the National Highway Traffic Safety Administration, researched information on drivers involved in fatal accidents.

One example of these findings happened in California. In a study conducted by the California State Department of Justice, it was determined that of the 1,800 blood samples taken from drivers arrested for driving while intoxicated, 16 percent were positive for marijuana. Where no alcohol was present in the blood sample (about 10 percent of the samples), the incidence of marijuana detected rose to 24 percent (CNOA 1986).

In another study, in order to determine the role of alcohol and other drugs in fatal auto crashes, blood samples from deceased males between 15 and 34 years of age were obtained in four California counties. Driver responsibility for each fatal accident was determined. The blood was analyzed for 23 drugs or drug groups. The sample consisted of 440 drivers, slightly more than half killed in single vehicle accidents. In all, 88 percent of these drivers were considered responsible for the crash. Only 19 percent had no drugs present in their blood; 81 percent were found to have one or more drugs present. Alcohol was detected in 70 percent of the drivers, cannabinoids in 37 percent, cocaine in 11 percent, diazepam and phencyclidine in 4 percent, other drugs in 3 percent or less. Fifty-two percent of those who had alcohol present had blood alcohol concentrations (BACs) of 0.1 to 0.19 percent, and 30 percent had BACs of 0.2 percent or more. THC or its acid metabolite were present in 0.2 to 50 ng/mL (nanograms per milliliter) concentrations in blood. THC was found alone in 12 percent of those studied; it was found in combination with alcohol in 81 percent, and with other drugs in 7 percent (Williams et al).

Although alcohol is the prime cause of automotive accidents, marijuana and cocaine are currently being found frequently enough to suggest that they are potentially significant contributors. It has been well-established that marijuana and alcohol have additive effects upon driving skills. Since marijuana metabolites were found in more than a third of the drivers, impairment due to marijuana may be contributing to the problem. One study demonstrated that blood levels of THC correlate with impaired performance for several hours after smoking on tasks that are related to driving performance (Barnett et al). Using a more complex task, it has also been determined that pilots are impaired for 24 hours following the smoking of one marijuana cigarette containing 19 mg of THC. Ten experienced pilots familiar with marijuana smoking were tested 1, 4, 10, and 24 hours after smoking. At each point, the test resulted in significant impairment of the ability to perform a landing

maneuver. It might be noted, furthermore, that the 24-hour test occurred at a time that the pilots reported feeling alert and no longer under the influence of marijuana (Yesavage).

The parameter of impairment for the average driver under various
dosages of marijuana cannot yet be adequately specified. Nevertheless, it is important to develop reliable standards to discourage potentially dangerous driving. At present, it is clear that driving while "high"
presents a significant risk to highway safety and drivers should be
alerted to these dangers.

We know that once THC has entered the bloodstream, it is widely
distributed in the body, especially in fatty tissues. The slow release of
THC from these tissues produces low levels of drug in the blood for several days after a single dose, but there is little evidence that any significant pharmacological effects persist for more than 4-6 hours after
smoking or 6-8 hours after oral ingestion. The persistence of the drug in
the body, and the continuous excretion of degradation products in the
urine, however, can give rise to cannabis-positive forensic tests days or
even weeks after the most recent dose.

It is difficult to see how cannabis intoxication could be monitored.
There could be no equivalent of the breath test for alcohol to test for
marijuana intoxication—small amounts of cannabis continue to be released from fat into the blood long after any short-term drug impairment has worn off.

§ 14.8.20   Effects of Marijuana in Combination with Alcohol
Since marijuana is so commonly used in combination with alcohol
and other drugs, the combined effects of these drugs have potentially
important implications. Given the extremely wide range of possible
doses and interactions, it is not surprising that our present knowledge
is still quite limited. This is true even of the most commonly used combination: alcohol and marijuana.

Animal studies of the behavioral effects of the alcohol-cannabis (or
THC-alcohol) combination have generally found that the combined effect is greater than that of either alone. The limited human research to
date is generally consistent with the results of animal research. Experiments at alcohol levels within the range commonly used by social
drinkers showed that performance reductions from combined use are
greater than those from the use of either alone. Such detriments have
been detected in reasoning, manual dexterity, and standing steadiness.

§ 14.8.21   Cannabinoid Pharmacology
The term "cannabinoid" was originally used to describe the family of
naturally occurring chemicals found in cannabis, of which THC is the
principal member. It is now also taken to encompass all those substances capable of activating cannabinoid receptors. These include the
naturally occurring plant cannabinoids, some synthetic substances, and
recently discovered "endogenous cannabinoids." The most important of
these endogenous cannabinoids are the fat-like materials arichidon-
ylethanolamide ("anandamide") and 2-arichidonyl-glycerol (2-AG).

These discoveries have transformed the character of scientific research on cannabis from an attempt to understand the mode of action of a psychoactive drug to the investigation of a hitherto unrecognized physiological control system in the brain and other organs. Although the physiological significance of this system is still largely unknown, one of the principal actions of THC and the endogenous cannabinoids seems to be to regulate the amounts of chemical messenger substances released from nerves in the brain, thus modulating neural activity. The discovery of the endogenous cannabinoid system has significant implications for future pharmaceutical research in this area (Hirst et al).

It is now recognized that THC interacts with a naturally occurring system in the body, known as the "cannabinoid system." THC takes effect by acting upon cannabinoid receptors. When smoked or ingested, THC and other cannabinoids in marijuana attach to two types of receptors on cells in your body—like keys in a lock—affecting the cell once attached.

CB1 is one such receptor. CB1 receptors are found mainly in your brain, especially in areas that control body movement, memory, and vomiting. This helps explain why marijuana use affects balance and coordination and impairs short-term memory and learning, and why it can be useful in treating nausea, pain, and loss of appetite.

The other receptor, CB2, is found in small numbers elsewhere in your body, mainly in tissue of the immune system, such as your spleen and lymph nodes. The function of these receptors is not well understood. They may serve as brakes on immune-system function, which may help explain why marihuana suppresses your immune system.

The roles played by CB1 and CB2 receptors in determining the various effects of cannabis in the whole organism remain to be established.[6]

§ 14.8.22   At Risk

Clinical observations from many parts of the world have long suggested that regular heavy use of cannabis may produce lung damage, impair reproductive and endocrine functions, cause long-lasting disturbances of behavior and brain functions, and lower resistance to infection. What is not yet known is the frequency with which these health problems occur among cannabis users, the degree of use needed to produce them, and the percentage of users at risk.

It is believed that people especially at risk with even moderate doses include anxious, depressed or unrecognized psychotic individuals,

---

[6] In common with many other drugs, the effects of THC result from its ability to activate special proteins known as *receptors* found on the surface of certain cells. The drug binds specifically to these proteins and activates a series of processes within the cells, leading to alterations in the cell's activity. Drugs such as THC that are able to "switch on" a receptor are known as *agonists* at that receptor. Other substances, however, bind to the receptor and, rather than activating it, prevent its activation by agonists, such substances are known as recepter *antagonists*.

heavy users of other drugs, pregnant women, some epileptics, diabetics, individuals with marginal fertility, and patients with chronic diseases of the heart, lungs, or liver. In addition, as with any other psychoactive drug, adolescents who are undergoing rapid physiological and psychological development may be particularly susceptible to the development of a life-long pattern of use and to the health effects of long periods of cannabis intoxication.

The combination of the increasingly young age of current cannabis users, the greater frequency of use, and the greater potency of the smoked material completely changes the situation that existed only a few years ago. Therefore, what was believed then may no longer apply now.

A new educational effort is needed to bring potential or actual users up to date. Just as the scare campaign of the Anslinger era in the 1930s was not based on evidence, the benign reputation of cannabis during the more recent past also lacks a factual base. There are real areas of concern, some serious, that health professionals and the public should know about.

Most thoughtful members of all sides of the marijuana controversy would agree with the following statements:

1. Pregnant women should not use the drug.

2. Adolescents should be discouraged from use, especially heavy use.

3. People with heart problems may be further impaired by the heart-accelerating property of cannabis.

4. People with lung disease should not use the drug because of its irritant effects.

5. The infrequent use of marijuana (less than once a week) probably will not result in ill effects.

6. Continued work on the therapeutic potential of cannabis should proceed, especially in the control of nausea and vomiting and in open-angle glaucoma.

§ 14.8.23 Treatment of Cannabis Use Disorder

With more individuals seeking assistance in recent years because of higher potency marijuana and its more frequent use, it is becoming clear that the drug is capable of having adverse effects on physical and mental health (Jones). The typical heavy marijuana user is also an excessive user of alcohol and other abused substances. Marijuana-related cognitive or behavioral difficulties are not attributed to marijuana initially. Only later in treatment does the adolescent client become aware of the role marijuana plays in his/her dysfunction. Older marijuana users are more likely to recognize a connection between their drug use and impairment of their various relationships or their inability to curtail their use of marijuana. Persuading the user to remain abstinent for two to three months may be therapeutic in itself, because the individual often notices an emergence from mildly confused mentation, apathy, and loss of energy, whereas the entry into the state was imperceptible to him or her.

§ 14.8.24   How Does Marijuana Work in the Body?

The THC that is inhaled through marijuana smoking partially changes into two other compounds after it enters the human bloodstream. These two compounds are chemically known as C-THC and OH-THC.

THC is detectable in the human bloodstream (plasma) for only about two hours. It produces euphoria and may cause visual, mental, and muscle (motor) impairment during this time period. OH-THC stays in the plasma four to six hours and may cause a small amount of euphoria. Depending on the amount smoked, C-THC may remain in the plasma for as long as three to six days. It causes no euphoria but may produce visual, mental, and motor impairment. Consequently, users have no perception that they may be impaired.

SUMMARY OF MARIJUANA METABOLITES

Metabolite	Approx. Length of Time in Plasma	Causes Euphoria	Causes Visual, Mental and Motor Impairment
THC	2-3 hours	Yes	Yes
OH-THC	4-6 hours	Mild, if any	Yes
C-THC	3-6 days	No	Yes

C-THC stays in human plasma for so long because it is lipophilic, or fat-soluble. It goes into fatty tissue and "sticks" until it is released back into the plasma. Due to the fat-solubility of C-THC, it can be found in the urine for many days after one has stopped smoking marijuana. C-THC has been found in urine for up to about 45 days in chronic or addicted marijuana users.

§ 14.8.25   Marijuana Tolerance and Dependence

Tolerance to cannabis, i.e., a diminished response to a given repeated drug dose, is now well substantiated. Tolerance development was originally suspected because experienced overseas users were able to use large quantities of the drug that would have been toxic to United States users accustomed to smaller amounts of the drug. Carefully conducted studies with known doses of marijuana or THC leave little question that tolerance develops with prolonged use.

This is in some contrast with the original impression that users had a "reverse tolerance," i.e., a greater sensitivity to marijuana upon relatively low dose and infrequent use. Under those conditions, neophyte users may have become more aware of marijuana's subjective effects with repeated use partly as a result of social learning of what was to be expected from the experience and thus subjectively believed that its effects were enhanced.

Several more detailed reviews of tolerance development to the behavioral and physiological effects of marijuana in both animals and humans have been published.

The normal trend from tolerance to dependence does becomes complicated with respect to marijuana. The term "cannabis dependence" has often been used in an imprecise way with meanings ranging from a vague desire to continue use, if available, to the manifestation of physical withdrawal symptoms following its discontinuance. If "dependence" is defined as experiencing definite physical symptoms following withdrawal of the drug, there is now experimental evidence that such symptoms can occur, at least under conditions of extremely heavy cannabis use. However, this amount of cannabis use is not typical of the social marijuana user in the U.S.

Whether tolerance develops may depend on how much drug is consumed and how often. The repeated use of cannabis or cannabinoids does not result in severe physical withdrawal symptoms when the drug is withdrawn, so many have argued that these drugs are not capable of inducing dependence.

However, there is some indication that regular heavy cannabis users become dependent and they suffer withdrawal symptoms on terminating drug use. Fortunately, physical dependence is not common (Hall et al).

§ 14.9   IDENTIFICATION OF MARIJUANA INFLUENCE
§ 14.9.1 Introduction
Only a blood or urine test will definitively diagnose marijuana use. There are two major criteria to use to make a diagnosis of marijuana use when a person does not admit use. One is the presence of suggestive behaviors and signs and the other is marijuana derivatives in body fluids, i.e., blood or urine.

BASIC SIGNS AND BEHAVIOR ASSOCIATED WITH MARIJUANA USE ARE:
—Frequent absences from school or work
—Time distortion; unusual meal times
—Frequent missed appointments
—Constant use of eye drops (usually Visine)
—Wears marijuana-leaf jewelry, insignia, or has clips to hold cigarettes
—Wears sunglasses indoors
—Abnormal sleep pattern such as staying up late or daytime sleeping
—Repetitive forgetfulness or broken promises
—Frequent accidents, injuries, or traffic violations.
—Loss of interest or motivation in job, school, or relationships
—Deterioration of work or school performance
—Careless hygiene and grooming habits
—Recurrent respiratory infections
—Poor pain and stress tolerance
—Acne worsens
—Sudden personality changes; person is dull, bland, or humorless
—Binge eating of sweets and snacks between meals

Cannabis (Marijuana)

The effects of marijuana are subtler and less noticeable than the effects of many other drugs. A person under the influence may not be as easily recognized as such, compared with someone who is drunk on alcohol, tweaking on methamphetamine, or nodding on opiates. The effects of marijuana peak within twenty minutes and last two or three hours.

Marijuana affects the parts of the brain involved in attention, memory, learning, and the integration of sensory experiences with motivation and emotions. Marijuana intoxication impairs driving skills because it diminishes reaction time, motor coordination, and the ability to maintain and shift attention. An adverse reaction to marijuana resembles a panic or anxiety attack.

Chronic marijuana use, like cigarette use, results in respiratory problems such as nagging coughs, frequent chest colds, chronic bronchitis, and increased risk of pneumonia.

Be familiar with the smell of marijuana. Like cigarettes, the odor of the smoke is very noticeable and can be detected on the clothes, inside the car, in the air of a closed space, or on the breath.

Marijuana releases norepinephrine from neurons, which can reduce blood sugar and cause craving for sweets. It may impair a person's job or school performance. Marijuana may disrupt the endorphins and adrenaline producing chemicals in the brain which motivate a person to carry out normal day-to-day activities.

Cigarette smoking is the single, biggest indicator that a person may be using illegal drugs. Approximately one-third of the adult population over age 18 years smoke cigarettes, and of these, about 25 percent abuse drugs and/or alcohol. This figure is higher for youth. The percentage of youth between 13 and 19 years of age who smoke cigarettes is about 20 percent; of those, nearly 50 percent also use marijuana. One reason youth who smoke cigarettes are likely candidates to use illegal drugs is because they are already knowledgeable about inhaling and are tolerant to the heat irritation produced by ordinary cigarettes. Physically and psychologically, it is a short step from cigarette smoking to marijuana or cocaine inhalation. Over 99 percent of heroin users smoke cigarettes; likewise, 90 percent of PCP and amphetamine users smoke cigarettes.

§ 14.9.2 Changes in Vital Signs with Marijuana Influence

Since marijuana has stimulant properties caused by its effects on norepinephrine, vital signs of marijuana users may show stimulatory effects:

Pupil Size	Over 5.0 mm (0.20 in.) in diameter
Pulse	Over 100 beats per minute
	(Normal—72 per minute)
Blood Pressure	Systolic: over 140 mm Hg
	(Normal—120 mm Hg)

Respiratory Rate	Over 25 respirations per minute *(Normal—20 per minute)*
Temperature	Over 100°F *(Normal—98.6° F)*

Special Note: If two of the above are present and there is marijuana derivative in plasma, urine, or saliva, acute marijuana influence should be considered to be present.

§ 14.9.3 Vision Effects with Marijuana

There is growing evidence that some abnormalities and possibly other neuromuscular effects are present as long as marijuana's long-acting metabolite, C-THC, remains in the bloodstream (plasma). Essentially, this means that marijuana may produce impairment and meet the criteria for acute influence for as long as three to six days after the last dose of marijuana. Examples of marijuana's effects on vision include numerous drivers driving erratically, who are routinely arrested by the California Highway Patrol. Upon examination, they show eye findings of strabismus and slow or nonreactive pupils but claim to have not smoked marijuana for three to four days. Nonetheless, they show marijuana metabolite in their urine and no evidence of alcohol or other drug use. Chronic marijuana users have been studied to correlate eye and other physical abnormalities with the presence of C-THC in plasma (Tennant). Although strabismus (nonconvergence) and slow or nonreactive pupils were not present in every user, they were found in some marijuana users three to six days after they claimed to have ceased use. The importance of this finding is that drug influence and impairment may remain for several days after marijuana was last used, even though the user has no feeling of euphoria or perception of impairment. The presence of strabismus and nonreactive pupils can impair visual tracking ability, which may produce accidents and injuries.

SUMMARY OF MARIJUANA'S EFFECTS ON THE EYES

Finding	Presence	Approx. Time May Last After Smoking
Redness	Frequent	4 to 6 hours
Dilated Pupil	Sometimes	2 to 4 hours
Non- or slow-reacting pupil	Frequent	1 to 3 days
Failure to hold constriction (rebound dilation)	Sometimes	4 to 6 hours
Strabismus nonconvergence	Frequent	1 to 3 days
Droopy eyelid	Frequent	2 to 4 hours
Failure to estimate distance	Frequent	4 to 6 hours

§ 14.9.4 Physical Evaluation/Examination of a Person Suspected of Acute Marijuana Influence

Following is a list of physical evaluation procedures to be used when a person is suspected of acute marijuana influence. It is not necessary to do every procedure to make a correct medical and legal identification. Most of the following procedures can be performed by nonmedical personnel:

1. Listen for speech rate.

2. Observe gait and balance.

3. Look for sleepy appearance, droopy eyelids, mouth breathing, dry lips, and green tongue.

4. Smell for odor of marijuana.

5. Assess responses for attention span, concentration, and giddiness.

6. Assess depth perception by asking person to estimate a distance.

7. Examine eyes for droopy eyelid, pupil reaction, strabismus (non-convergence), and redness.

8. Determine muscle coordination and balance by finger-to-finger, finger-to-nose, step-test, and one leg balance count test (divided attention).

9. Take pulse, blood pressure, and respiratory rate.

10. Feel skin for sweating and tremor.

11. Note if hallucinations, delusions, or paranoia are present.

12. Instruct to give correct time, date, and place.

13. Observe for general physical and behavioral signs of acute drug influence.

§ 14.9.5 Background Evidence for Marijuana Addiction

Marijuana addiction was described in the United States over 60 years ago (National Commission 1972). In 1944, 35 "confirmed marijuana addicts" were admitted to a military hospital and developed withdrawal symptoms. Since this time, marijuana addiction has been reported in other countries. In addition, animals have demonstrated addiction to marijuana and there has been one carefully controlled trial where humans were given known quantities of THC; these humans developed withdrawal symptoms when marijuana was abruptly discontinued. Likewise, animals that are addicted to marijuana have demonstrated withdrawal symptoms when given naloxone. When naloxone precipitates withdrawal symptoms, it means that the addicting drug affects the body like an opioid (i.e., heroin, morphine, etc.). To complement these findings, another recent study in animals has demonstrated that THC will deplete endorphins in the nervous system. Furthermore, marijuana may also adversely affect the neurotransmitters norepinephrine and serotonin. Current evidence suggests that marijuana addiction exists, at least in part, as a result of depleted endorphin, nore-pinephrine, and possibly other neurotransmitters.

§ 14.9.6 Background and History of Marijuana Testing

Private industry has shown great interest in detecting the nonmedical use of drugs during the past. Since marijuana is the most frequently used illicit drug, it is of great interest to employers to detect its use in employees. In addition, the military services have pioneered mass urine screening for abused drugs because of their emphasis on alertness, the ability to make rapid decisions, and the need for unimpaired physical and mental functioning. More and more, large corporations are finding that accidents, breakage, absenteeism, theft, and poor productivity are associated with drug use—including marijuana use—in the workplace. Employers are testing urine (and, less frequently, blood) randomly, during pre-employment physical examinations, following accidents, and as a routine screening procedure for those who work in sensitive or public safety positions.

Acid metabolites of THC are found in the urine within an hour of smoking one joint. They fall below the 20 ng/mL (nanograms per milliliter) level after about three days. However, chronic smokers whose fatty tissues are saturated with THC may continue to excrete detectable amounts for a month after last use (Schwartz et al).

In addition to proper laboratory procedures and precise quality control, a supervised urine collection and a reliable chain of custody of the sample are necessary to provide accurate reports. A confirmatory test must also be performed after the positive screening test to assure that the positive result was definitely the acid metabolite of THC, 9-carboxy-THC. The possibility that a positive test was due to passive inhalation (second-hand smoke) is kept at 20 ng/mL or above. Due to the extended period of time during which urine tests for marijuana can remain positive, a positive result cannot prove use occurred at a specific time. A positive result simply indicates cannabis use at some point prior to testing which may have occurred hours or days earlier. While blood or sputum levels may eventually be correlated with intoxication, clearly defined criteria for impairment similar to those for alcohol do not yet exist.

Factors which can produce a false negative urine report for THC include drinking large amounts of fluids; adding water, bleach, vinegar, detergent, or blood to the urine specimen; or substituting the urine of another person. These efforts to invalidate the test can be counteracted by appropriate measures. For example, determining the specific gravity of the urine will reveal whether it has been diluted; likewise, careful supervision of the process for obtaining specimens will discourage substitutions (Schwartz et al).

§ 14.9.7 Retention of Marijuana in Plasma and Urine

A great deal of publicity has been generated as to how long marijuana metabolites may remain detectable in plasma and urine due to the fact that it is fat-soluble, so drug tests detect the drug as well as the

Cannabis (Marijuana)

drug metabolites. Metabolites are the byproducts of a substance after it has circulated through one's system.

When smoked, marijuana metabolites enter the fat, lodge there, and then leak out over a period of time. It is important to point out that it is only the regular, chronic user who keeps marijuana in urine for more than a few days. The length of time that marijuana metabolites can be detected in plasma is much shorter than in urine because the drug's concentration in the urine is 100 to 1000 times more than the concentration found in plasma or blood. Marijuana can be detected in urine much longer than in plasma due to the kidney's ability to concentrate drugs.

The half-life of the THC concentration in the body ranges between 0.8 to 9.8 days. Because of human variation, it is difficult to approximate how long THC will be detected in the urine of an individual. Infrequent users with a fast metabolism will have the shortest detection time. Frequent users with a slow metabolism will have long detection times. The only way to estimate a detection time is to consider the lower and upper bounds (3-45 days).

RETENTION OF MARIJUANA IN URINE

Frequency of Use	Approx. Length of Time in Urine
Once per week	2 - 20 days
Twice per week	5 - 30 days 15 - 45 days

*Varies as to amount used and whether use is chronic or occasional.

RETENTION OF MARIJUANA IN PLASMA (BLOOD)

Frequency of Use	Approx. Length of Time in Plasma
THC	2 - 3 hours
OH-THC	4 - 6 hours
C-THC	3 - 6 days

*Varies as to amount used and whether use is chronic or an occasional.

§ 14.9.8 Saliva Analysis

Saliva analysis for THC presence is possible because the marijuana smoke leaves THC residues in the mouth. If THC is found in saliva, then it usually means that marijuana has been smoked within the previous one to three hours. However, this test cannot be relied upon for confirmatory diagnosis of marijuana use because the smoker can easily spit or wash the residue out of the oral cavity.

§ 14.9.9 Marijuana Source

Despite 65 years of prohibition against marijuana, recent figures indicate that marijuana is ranked among corn, wheat, and soybeans as one of the four major cash crops grown in the United States in terms of dollar-volume of sales. Some researchers claim that marijuana is the leading cash crop, but the clandestine (often indoor) farming caused by strict marijuana laws makes specific figures impossible to obtain. It is certain, however, that a tremendous amount of marijuana is grown in the United States (<u>Register-Guard</u>).

An even larger quantity of marijuana is grown abroad, in Mexico, Colombia, Panama, and Jamaica. This huge quantity of marijuana is then smuggled into the United States on planes, boats, cars, mules, and individuals who sneak across the international borders on foot. Added to the multi-billion-dollar crop grown domestically, imported or smuggled, an enormous quantity of marijuana is trafficked throughout the United States.

Although Mexico is the primary foreign source country for marijuana sold in the United States, there is a growing indication that Canada is becoming the source country of hydroponically grown marijuana destined for the United States.

We have plenty of domestically grown marijuana. Indoor cultivation of marijuana provides a controlled environment conducive to the production of high-grade marijuana (sinsemilla). A healthy indoor-grown sinsemilla plant can produce about a pound of marijuana. According to 1998 Domestic Cannabis Eradication/Suppression Program (DCE/SP) statistics, the five leading states for indoor-growing activity are California, Florida, Oregon, Alaska, and Kentucky.

A review of marijuana eradication data from the DCE/SP for 1998 indicated that 11 percent of the cultivated plants eradicated last year were grown indoors, compared to 89 percent grown outdoors. These figures represent an increase from 1997, in which 6 percent of the cultivated plants eradicated were grown indoors. Major outdoor growing states for 1998 were California, Hawaii, Kentucky, and Tennessee, which accounted for approximately 75 percent of outdoor-cultivated plants. The largest DEA-reported eradication event for 1999 was the June seizure of over 51,000 outdoor plants near the Mississippi River in Arkansas (DEA 1999).

§ 14.9.10   Hemp Cultivation

In 2002, AB 388 was passed by the California legislature to allow California farmers to grow hemp. However, the governor at that time, Gray Davis, vetoed the bill so it did not become law. In 2005 another bill is being introduced by Assemblyman Mark Leno to legalize hemp production. To understand where we are with hemp production in the United States, a look at California House Resolution No. 32 will help.

House Resolution No. 32 Relative to industrial hemp.
WHEREAS, Industrial hemp was first domesticated 10,000 years ago; was required in 1619 to be grown by all farmers in Jamestown, Virginia; was legal tender in America and accepted as payment for taxes from 1631 to the early 1800s; was a cash crop grown on the plantations of George Washington and Thomas Jefferson; was grown in America and regulated by the Department of Agriculture until 1937; and was the domestic source of maritime rope during the 1942 to 1945 World War II "Hemp for Victory" campaign; and
WHEREAS, Industrial hemp provided the ropes and sails for Christopher Columbus' ships and the paper on which the Declaration of Independence was first drafted; and
WHEREAS, Industrial hemp has been used to produce more than 25,000 products; and

Cannabis (Marijuana)

WHEREAS, Industrial hemp is produced by thirty nations, including Canada, Britain, France, Germany, Romania, Australia, and China, none of which are classified by the Drug Enforcement Agency (DEA) as drug-producing countries; and

WHEREAS, The DEA permits industrial hemp to be grown under strict rules and regulations that are currently being revised; and

WHEREAS, The importation of industrial hemp is permitted by the General Agreement on Tariffs and Trade and the North American Free Trade Agreement; and

WHEREAS, North Dakota has legalized industrial hemp for commercial farming; Hawaii and Minnesota have legalized test crops of industrial hemp; the Legislatures of Colorado, Illinois, Iowa, Kansas, Kentucky, Maryland, Missouri, Montana, New Hampshire, New Mexico, Oregon, South Dakota, Tennessee, Vermont, Virginia, and Wisconsin are considering the legalization of industrial hemp; and the City and County of San Francisco is currently drafting an ordinance to permit its residents to grow industrial hemp; and

WHEREAS, Industrial hemp can be easily distinguished from marijuana by appearance, cultivation methods, and chemical analysis because industrial hemp is a nonintoxicating, benign form of the cannabis sativa plant that contains less than 1% tetrahydrocannabinol (THC), while marijuana contains 5 to 20 percent THC; and industrial hemp seeds are planted to yield more than 1,000 stalks per two square yards, while only one marijuana plant can be grown in the same size plot; and industrial hemp matures in 70 to 120 days and is harvested before it flowers, while marijuana is cultivated for its flowertops and takes 120-180 days to mature; and, when grown together, industrial hemp will pollinate marijuana, reducing its THC content to a nonintoxicating level; and

WHEREAS, Industrial hemp thrives without herbicides, reinvigorates the soil, requires less water than cotton, matures in three to four months, and can potentially yield four times as much paper per acre as trees, building materials that are twice as strong as wood and concrete, textile fiber that is up to eight times as strong as cotton, better oil and paint than petroleum, clean-burning diesel fuel, biodegradable plastics, and more digestible protein per acre than any other food source, and

WHEREAS, Industrial hemp can be planted and harvested in California several times per year, and gross $200 to $600 per acre per harvest at current market prices; and

WHEREAS, All industrial hemp raw materials currently must be imported to manufacture products that are distributed by, and sold in, more than 60 specialty shops and 250 general stores throughout California, with national sales and exports exceeding $100 million per year; now, therefore, be it

Resolved by the Assembly of the State of California, That the Assembly find and declares that industrial hemp is a vital, sustainable, renewable resource for building materials, cloth, cordage, fiber, food, fuel, industrial chemicals, oil, paint, paper, plastics, seed, yarn, and many other useful products; and be it further

Resolved, That the Assembly finds and declares that the domestic production of industrial hemp can help protect California's environment, contribute to the growth of the state economy, and be regulated in a manner that will not interfere with the enforcement of marijuana laws; and be it further

Resolved, That the Assembly finds and declares that the Legislature should consider action to revise the legal status of industrial hemp to allow for its growth in California as an agricultural and industrial crop; and be it further

Resolved, That the Assembly finds and declares that the Legislature should consider directing the University of California, the California State University, and other state agencies to prepare studies in conjunction with private industry on the cultivation, processing, and marketing of industrial hemp.

If the new hemp bill becomes law, farmers would be able to apply for state licenses to grow hemp. The law would be similar to regulations on industrial hemp in other countries such as Canada and the European Union.

§ 14.1.13(k)   DEA & Hemp

The DEA's war on hemp began in 2001 when it claimed jurisdiction over hemp products under the controlled substance statutes. Since hemp contained THC, the DEA said it had the right to regulate hemp products. The DEA's arbitrary interpretation of the CSA, however, was shot down in federal court, first in March 2002, when the court granted a temporary restraining order over DEA action on its ruling, and then when the Ninth Circuit granted a permanent injunction.

After three years and appeals, on July 2, 2004, the U.S. Court of Appeals for the Ninth Circuit denied the DEA's petition for a rehearing of the case. The DEA had the option of appealing the decision to the U.S. Supreme Court, but the allotted time for an appeal expired September 28, 2004.

Therefore, the court decision is now the law of the land. There is a federal industrial hemp bill that will probably be introduced in the 2005 congressional session.

§ 14.10 MARIJUANA AND CRIME

Several distinguished commissions have investigated evidence of the possible role of marijuana in criminal behavior. The different commissions reached strikingly similar conclusions: the behavioral effects of marijuana do not usually incite violent or sexual crimes; rather, the use of marijuana may reduce the possibility of aggression in most people. Laboratory and clinical studies support these conclusions and have demonstrated that while some individuals do commit crimes while under the influence of marijuana, most marijuana users tend to be underrepresented in studies of assaultive offenders. This is especially true when a comparison is made with users of alcohol, barbiturates, and amphetamines. Some sub-groups of marijuana users do commit crimes against property, but nonpharmacological variables are probably more important influences on such behavior than the effects of the drug itself (National Commission 1972). Thus, future research should analyze marijuana-crime interactions with the purpose of identifying and documenting these non-drug variables.

§ 14.10.1   California's Marijuana Laws

Possession of marijuana is a misdemeanor under California Health and Safety Code (HSC) Section 11357. Possession of *one ounces (28.5 grams) or less* is punishable by a maximum $100 fine. Jail time is possible for larger amounts or for hashish, which is an optional felony ("wobbler"). However, under Prop 36, effective July 1, 2001, first- and second-time possession-only offenders may demand a treatment program instead of jail. Upon successful completion of the program, their conviction is erased. Possession (and personal use cultivation) offenders can also avoid conviction by making a pre-guilty-plea under Penal Code 1000, in which case their charges are dismissed upon successful completion of a diversion program. Possession offenses are expunged from the record after two years under HSC Sections 11361.5 and 11361.7.

Possession of one ounce or less in a vehicle while driving may also be charged under Vehicle Code 23222, which is treated identically to Health and Safety Code 11357 B. No arrest or imprisonment is allowed for possession of less than one ounce of marijuana. However, police often get around this provision by charging minor offenders with intent to sell (see below).

Cannabis (Marijuana)

Possession with intent to sell any amount of marijuana is a felony under HSC 11359. Police often charge intent to sell if they see such indicia as: scales, cash, multiple packages, "commercial" packaging materials, "excessive" quantity, pay-owe sheets, address books, pagers, etc.

Cultivation of any amount of marijuana is a felony under Health and Safety Code 11358. People who grow for personal use are eligible for diversion under Penal Code 1000 so long as there is no evidence of intent to sell. There are no fixed plant number limits to personal use cultivation.

Medical marijuana: Medical patients and their designated primary caregivers may legally possess and cultivate, but not distribute or sell, marijuana under HSC 11362.5 (Prop 215) if they have a physician's recommendation or approval.

Sale, transportation, or distribution of marijuana is a felony under HSC Section 11360. Transporting or giving away *one ounce or less* is a misdemeanor punishable by a maximum $100 fine.

Sale or distribution to minors is a felony under HSC 11361.

Marijuana paraphernalia are illegal to sell or manufacture, but not possess, under Health and Safety Code 11364. All marijuana paraphernalia are subject to seizure by the police.

Driving suspension for minors: Any minor (age under 21) convicted of *any* marijuana, alcohol, or other drug offense faces a 12-month driver's license suspension, *regardless of whether the offense was driving-related*. The court may allow restricted license privileges if the minor demonstrates a "critical need to drive." Vehicle Code 13202.5. (Note: This penalty can be avoided by entering a diversion program.)

Driving under the influence: It is unlawful to drive while under the influence of marijuana (or alcohol or any other drug) by Vehicle Code 23152. "Under the influence" is not specifically defined in the statute, but is interpreted to imply some degree of impairment. Therefore, the mere fact of having taken a toke of marijuana does not necessarily mean one is DUI. For evidence of impairment, officers may administer a field sobriety test. Arrestees may also be required to submit to their choice of a urine or blood test under Vehicle Code 23612. Since marijuana is detectable for much longer periods in urine than in blood (several days versus several hours), a positive urine test constitutes much weaker proof of *recent* use and impairment than a positive blood test. Someone who smokes marijuana may realize that if he or she hasn't smoked marijuana recently and is not under the influence, it is better to choose a blood test, since he or she will probably pass it. However, if one is a chronic smoker or has smoked recently, that person is better off to choose a urine test; even though he or she can expect to test positive, the question will at least remain open as to whether that person was actually "under the influence" at the time of arrest.

Chapter 14

Marijuana in a vehicle: Drivers found in possession of less than one ounce of marijuana in their vehicle are liable for a maximum $100 misdemeanor fine under Vehicle Code 23222 (larger amounts are punishable under Health and Safety Code 11357(a) and 11359).

Forfeiture: Unlike federal law, California law requires a conviction for forfeiture of property involved in a drug crime. Also unlike federal law, state law does not permit forfeiture of personal real estate for marijuana cultivation. Vehicles may be forfeited only if 10 pounds or more of marijuana is involved. Health and Safety Code 11470.

California Law: search full text: www.leginfo.ca.gov/calaw.html.

Federal law: Marijuana is also illegal under the federal Controlled Substances Act. Federal charges are typically brought only in large cases where commercial distribution is suspected (e.g., cultivation of several hundred plants).

§ 14.11 CONCLUSION

It appears that cannabis use in this country is evolving in new directions that will increase its potential for damage. To prevent the mental and physical consequences, high priority should be given to deterring children from becoming involved and over-involved. Legalization of the drug is not indicated in view of the recent research findings. Decriminalization of the possession of small amounts remains a tenable position. The unsatisfactory attempts to arrest and prosecute the large number of marijuana smokers also supports decriminalization.

§ 14.12 GLOSSARY OF CANNABIS SLANG TERMS

Marijuana grass .... pot, weed, loco weed, tea, hay, Acapulco Gold, Mary Jane, J, 13, Colombian, Jamaican Red
Marijuana cigarette. joint, stick, reefer, number, roach
Sinsemilla .... sin
Hashish .... hash, soles
Hashish oil .... hash oil, honey oil

References

Abel, E.L. "Marijuana and sex: a critical survey." Drug and Alcohol Dependence 8 (1981): 1-22.

Barnett, G., et al. "Behavioral pharmacokinetics of marijuana." Psychopharmacology 85 (1985): 81-86.

Cabral, G.A., et al. "9-Tetrahydrocannabinol decreases host resistance to herpes simplex virus type 2 vaginal infection in the guinea pig." Marijuana 84: Proceedings of the Oxford Symposium on Cannabis. Ed. Harvey. Oxford: IRL Press, 1985.

California Narcotic Officers Association. The California Narcotic Officer. Winter, 1986.

Drug Enforcement Administration. "The Cannabis Situation in the United States." Drug Intelligence Brief. Washington, D.C.: U.S. Department of Justice, 1999.

----------. Drug Use in America: Problems in Perspective, Second Report. Washington, D.C.: U.S. Gov't. Printing Office, 1973.

The Field Poll. San Francisco: Field Research Corporation, 2004.

Cannabis (Marijuana)

Gibson, G.T., et al. "Maternal alcohol, tobacco and cannabis consumption on the outcome of pregnancy." Aust NZ Obstet Gynecol 23 (1983): 16-19.

Gould's Penal Code Handbook of California. Longwood, FL: Gould Publications, 1997.

Hall, W., Room, R., and Bondy, S. "A Comparison of the Health Effects of Alcohol, Cannabis, Tobacco and Opiates." The Health Effects of Cannabis. Ed. Kallant. Toronto: Addiction Research Foundation, 1998.

Harclerode, J. "Endocrine effects of marijuana in the male." Marijuana: Effects on the Endocrine and Reproductive Systems. Ed. Braude. Research Monograph Series 44. DHHS Pub. No. (ADM) 84-1278. Washington, D.C.: Supt. of Docs., U.S. Govt. Print. Off., 1984.

Heath, R.A., et al. "Chronic marijuana smoking: its effect on function and structure of the primate brain." Marijuana: Biological Effects. Ed. Nahas. Oxford: Pergamon Press, 1979.

Hendin, H., and A.P. Haas. "The adaptive significance of chronic marijuana for adolescents and adults." Advances in Alcohol and Substance Abuse 4 (1985) 99-115.

Hingston, R. et al. "Effects of maternal drinking and marijuana use on fetal growth and development." Pediatrics 70 (1982).

Hingston, R., et al. "Effects on fetal development of maternal marijuana use during pregnancy." Marijuana 84: Proceedings of the Oxford Symposium on Marijuana. Oxford: IRL Press, 1984.

Hirst, R.A., Lambert, D.G., and Notcutt, W.G. "Pharmacology and Potential Therapeutic Uses of Cannabis." British Journal of Anaesthesia, July 1998.

"Increasing U.S. Pot Crop." Register Guard, 8 January 1985, p. 1A.

Indian Hemp Drugs Commission Report, Simla, India: Government Printing Office, 1894.

Jessor, R., and S.L. Jessor. Problem Behavior and Psychological Development: A Longitudinal Study. New York: Academic Press, 1977.

Jones, R.T. "Marijuana: health and treatment issues." Psychiatric Clinics of North America 7 (1984): 703-712.

Linn, S., et al. "The association of marijuana use with outcome of pregnancy." Am J Public Health 73 (1983): 1161-1164.

Mechoulam, S.,et al. "On the Therapeutic Possibilities of Some Cannabinoids." Therapeutic Potential of Marihuana. New York: Penguin Press, 1976.

"Medical Cannabis Potency Testing Project." Multidisciplinary Association for Psychedelic Studies, MAPS 9.3 (Autumn 1999).

Morris, R.R. "Human pulmonary histopathological changes from marijuana smoking." J Forensic Sciences 30 (1985): 345-349.

Musty, R.E., Rossi, R. "Effects of Smoked Cannabis and Oral 9-Tetrahydrocannabinol on Nausea and Emesis after Cancer Chemotherapy: A Review of State Clinical Trials." J Cannabis Ther (2001).

National Commission on Marijuana and Drug Abuse. Marijuana—A Signal of Misunderstandings. New York: New American Library, 1972.

National Institute on Drug Abuse. "Fifth Annual Report to the U.S. Congress: Marijuana and Health, 1975." Rockville, M.D.: Department of Health and Human Services,1988 and 1995.

Pop, Gruber, Yurgelun-Todd. "The Residual Neuropsychological Effects of Cannabis: The Current Status of Research." Drug Alcohol Dependency. New York: McGraw Hill, 1995.

San Francisco Examiner, 30 April 1997.

Schwartz, R.H., and R.L. Hawks. "Laboratory detection of marijuana use." JAMA 254 (1985):788-792.

Chapter 14

Smith, C.G., and R.H. Ashe. "Acute, short term and chronic effects of marijuana on the female primate reproductive function." Marijuana: Effects on the Endocrine and Reproductive Systems. NIDA Research Monograph Series 44. DHHS Pub. No. (ADM) 84-1278. Washington, D.C.: Supt. of Docs., U.S. Govt. Print. Off., 1984.

Smith, Roger. "U.S. Marijuana Legislation and the Creation of a Social Problem." Journal of Psychedelic Drugs 2.1 (1968): 93-99.

Solomon, David, ed. The Marijuana Papers. New York: Signet Books, 1966.

Substance Abuse Mental Health Services Administration. "National Household Survey on Drug Abuse." Rockville, M.D.: Department of Health and Human Services,1988 and 1995.

Substance Abuse Mental Health Services Administration. "22 Million in U.S. Suffer from Substance Dependence & Abuse." Rockville, M.D.: Department of Health and Human Services, September 5, 2003.

Tennant, Forest. Identifying the Marijuana User. West Covina, California: Veract, Inc., 1986.

Tyrey, L. "Endocrine aspects of cannabinoid action in female subprimates: search for sites of action." Marijuana: Effects on the Endocrine and Reproductive Systems. Research Monograph Series 44. DHHS Pub. No. (ADM) 84-1278. Washington, D.C.: Supt. of Docs., U.S. Govt. Print. Off., 1984.

Voss, H.L. and R.R. Clayton. International Journal of Addictions 19 (1984): 633-652.

Wachtel, S.R., El Sohly, M.A., Ross, S.A., Ambre, J., De Wit, H. "Comparison of the Subjective Effects of Delta(9)-Tetrahydrocannabinol and Marijuana in Humans." Psychopharmacology (Berl), 2002.

Williams, A.F., et al. "Drugs in fatally injured young male drivers." Pharm Chem Newsletter. 14 (1985): 1-11.

Yesavage, J.A., et al. "Carry-over effects of marijuana intoxication on aircraft pilot performance: a preliminary report." Am J Psychiatry 42.11 (1985): 1325-1329.

CHAPTER 15

VOLATILE INHALANTS AND POISONOUS SUBSTANCES

§ 15.1 INTRODUCTION

There is much concern about illegal drugs such as marijuana, cocaine, and heroin, but little attention is given to inhalant abuse. Inhalants are breathable chemical vapors that produce psychoactive (mind-altering) effects. A variety of products common in the home and in the workplace contain substances that can be inhaled. Many people do not think of these products, such as spray paints, glues, and cleaning fluids, as drugs because they were never meant to be used to achieve an intoxicating effect. Yet young children and adolescents can easily obtain them and are among those most likely to abuse these extremely toxic substances.

§ 15.2 WHAT ARE INHALANTS?

Inhalants are volatile substances that produce chemical vapors that can be inhaled to induce a psychoactive, or mind-altering, effect. Although other abused substances can be inhaled, the term "inhalants" is used to describe a variety of substances whose main common characteristic is that they are rarely, if ever, taken by any route other than inhalation. This definition encompasses a broad range of chemicals found in hundreds of different products that may have different pharmacological effects. As a result, precise categorization of inhalants is difficult. One classification system lists four general categories of inhalants—volatile solvents, aerosol, gases, and nitrites—based on the form in which they are often found in household, industrial, and medical products.

§ 15.3 HISTORY OF INHALANT USE

The voluntary inhalation of toxic substances for the purpose of mood alteration is not a new phenomenon. In fact, the practice has endured for centuries. Its roots can be traced to the early Greek, Hebrew, and South American civilizations.

Abused volatile substances can be classified under three headings: anesthetics, solvents, and aerosols. Of these substances, anesthetics were the earliest to be abused. In the early 1800s, the anesthetics nitrous oxide, ether, and chloroform were used as intoxicants. Medical applications in the fields of surgery and dentistry followed. The use of anesthetics for recreational purposes continued throughout the 19th century in Europe and America. Recreational anesthetics re-emerged in the 1920s and 1940s. Among the solvents, petrochemicals—primarily gasoline—were the most commonly abused. One of the primary articles published on the origin of gasoline sniffing in the United States appeared in 1934. The first known report of glue sniffing appeared 25 years later on August 2, 1959, in the Denver Post.

Chapter 15

Although there were some isolated cases of inhalant use reported in the 1940s and 1950s, epidemiological interest in the use of inhalants did not become strong until the 1960s. Most cases from the 1940s through the 1960s were cases of "gasoline addiction." In the 1960s, many studies began to appear on the phenomenon of glue sniffing. During the 1980s, the use of aerosols as a means of intoxication also became widespread.

Since the early 1960s, the practice of solvent sniffing has spread across a wide spectrum of commercial products that contain volatile substances in their preparation. Paint and lacquer thinners, nail polish remover, shoe polish, lighter fluid, and aerosol products such as spray paints, non-stick coating substances, shoe-shine compounds, deodorants, hair sprays, and glass chillers are being sniffed for their intoxicating effects. The use of inhalants continued to increase dramatically during the 1970s and 1980s and continues to the present day. In fact, inhalant use has been reported not only in the United States, but worldwide.

§ 15.4 PREVALENCE OF INHALANT ABUSE

Initial use of inhalants often starts early. Some young people may use inhalants as an easily accessible substitute for alcohol. Research suggests that chronic or long-term inhalant abusers are among the most difficult drug abuse patients to treat. Many suffer from cognitive impairment and other neurological dysfunction and may experience multiple psychological and social problems.

§ 15.4.1 2004 Monitoring the Future Survey (MTF)[1]

According to the Monitoring the Future Survey, the nationwide annual survey of drug use among the nation's 8th-, 10th- and 12th-graders by the National Institute on Drug Abuse (NIDA), lifetime use by 8th-graders increased significantly in 2004 following a long and substantial decline in inhalant use through 2002 in all three grades. Between 1995 and 2002, 8th-graders' annual prevalence fell from 12.8 percent to 7.7 percent, as an increasing proportion of students came to see inhalant use as dangerous. However, annual prevalence rose significantly for 8th-graders, from 7.7 to 8.7 percent from 2002 to 2003. In 2004, 8th-graders' annual use was 9.6 percent.

---

[1] These data are from the 2004 Monitoring the Future Survey, funded by the National Institute on Drug Abuse, National Institutes of Health, Department of Health and Human Services (DHHS), and conducted by the University of Michigan's Institute for Social Research. The survey has tracked 12th-graders' illicit drug use and related attitudes since 1975; in 1991, 8th- and 10th-graders were added to the study. The latest data are on-line at www.drugabuse.gov.

Volatile Inhalants and Poisonous Substances

§ 15.4.2 2002 Drug Abuse Warning Network (DAWN)[2]

Emergency department/emergency room mentions of inhalants increased 187 percent, from 522 in 2001 to 1,496 in 2002, returning to the approximate level observed in 2000.

§ 15.4.3 2003 National Survey on Drug Use and Health (NSDUH)[3]

Among youths age 12 to 17, 11.2 percent were current illicit drug users in 2003, and 1.3 percent were current inhalant users. Among 12- or 13-year-olds, 1.4 percent used inhalants, the same percentage as 14- or 15-year-olds.

The number of new inhalant users was about 1 million in 2002. As in prior years, these new users were predominately under age 18 (78 percent), and just over half were male (53 percent).

The startling fact is that the actual number of abusers could be much larger. A complete count of the number of inhalant abusers in this country is particularly hard to obtain for the following reasons: (1) inhalant abusers are only identified when brought to the attention of the authorities or while presenting themselves for treatment; (2) inhalant abuse often goes undetected when it is part of multiple-drug abuse; (3) inhalant abuse will not be detected in standard urinalysis tests; and (4) most studies are completed on student populations, thus excluding the dropout, working, and adult populations. Due to these problems in data collection, several drug abuse experts believe that the incidence of inhalant abuse is severely underestimated.

Reports on inhalant abuse vary from about 1 percent in some populations to 60 percent in others. In most national surveys, the percentage ranges from the low to high teens. Among reported inhalant abusers, early adolescent Hispanic males represent a large percentage. Yet it is important to note that although the Hispanic population has been especially targeted by inhalant abuse research, the percentage of Anglo and African-American users has shown a steady increase (Media Projects 4).

People who abuse inhalants are found in both urban and rural settings. Research on factors contributing to inhalant abuse suggests that

---

[2] The latest data on drug-abuse-related hospital emergency department (ED) visits are from the 2002 DAWN report, from DHHS's Substance Abuse and Mental Health Services Administration (SAMHSA). These data are from a national probability survey of 437 hospital EDs in 21 metropolitan areas in the United States during the year. For detailed information from DAWN, visit DAWNinfo.samhsa.gov or call the National Clearinghouse for Alcohol and Drug Information at 1-800-729-6686.

[3] The 2003 NSDUH, produced by DHHS's Substance Abuse and Mental Health Services Administration, creates a new baseline for future national drug use trends. The survey is based on interviews with 67,784 respondents who were interviewed in their homes. Not included in the survey are persons in the active military, in prisons or in other institutionized populations, or who are homeless.
Findings from the 2003 National Survey on Drug Use and Health are available on-line at www.DrugAbuseStatistics.samhsa.gov.

adverse socioeconomic conditions, rather than racial or cultural factors per se, may account for most reported racial and ethnic differences in rates of inhalant abuse. Poverty, a history of childhood abuse, poor grades, and dropping out of school are all associated with inhalant abuse.

§ 15.5   TYPES OF INHALANTS
§ 15.5.1 Gases

Inhalants in the category of gases include medical anesthetics as well as gases used in household or commercial products. Medical anesthetic gases include ether, chloroform, halothane, and nitrous oxide. Nitrous oxide is the most abused of these gases and can be found in whipped cream dispensers and products that boost octane levels in racing cars. It is also used in hospitals and dental offices.

Nitrous oxide or "laughing gas"—a colorless, slightly sweet-smelling gas—was first synthesized in 1772 by Joseph Priestly. It was not until 1799, however, that a chemist named Sir Humphrey Davy first inhaled it and experienced its unusual effects. He and several others became enthusiastically involved in experimentation with this "gas of paradise" after discovering that, under its influence, they felt exhilarated and euphoric. After these initial experiments, several mid-nineteenth-century dentists became interested in the use of nitrous oxide as an anesthetic agent. By 1868, the gas was widely used as a painkiller. Nitrous oxide is still popular, not only as a dental anesthetic and analgesic, but sometimes as a social intoxicant as well.

Another anesthetic agent, ether, was introduced to the medical world in the eighteenth century by Friedrich Hoffmann. After its introduction, ether was frequently prescribed in liquid form as a "soothing tonic" for a variety of ills. The use of ether as a surgical anesthetic in 1846 by Thomas Morton, a Connecticut dentist, is often hailed as the birth of modern inhalation anesthesia. In addition to medical applications, ether drinking and sniffing for recreational purposes was quite popular in the nineteenth century; in fact, it was regarded as a harmless, cheap substitute for alcohol. Ether produced intoxicating effects similar to alcohol, was exempt from taxes, and did not cause hangovers. During Prohibition, when alcohol was unavailable, soft drinks were frequently "spiked" with ether. Numerous cases of ether habituation were reported during this time; users admitted inhaling as much as a pint a day over many years as a means to relieve anxiety, produce a sense of well-being, or induce sleep.

Like ether, chloroform is another highly volatile liquid that may be either ingested or inhaled. Chloroform was first produced in 1831, and in 1847 it was introduced as an anesthetic for women in childbirth. Recreational use began soon after its discovery; unfortunately, deaths from recreational overdose were not uncommon. Hence, chloroform never gained widespread popular acceptance as an intoxicant. Nonetheless, chloroform is an extremely versatile solvent; in addition to its many other uses, it appears as a common, though minor, ingredient in many cough and cold preparations.

§ 15.5.2 Nitrate Inhalants (Poppers)

In the era of Acquired Immune Deficiency Syndrome (AIDS), a discussion of nitrite inhalants is especially relevant. In the 1960s, clinicians began to note high rates of fatal infections and unusual tumors in homosexual men. A leading theory of this syndrome's origin was that the problems were caused by nitrite inhalants used by gay men in an attempt to enhance and prolong orgasm. While the deadly syndrome proved to be AIDS, there is some evidence that these substances may also contribute to immunologic problems, either exacerbating the syndromes associated with AIDS or causing additional problems on their own.

§ 15.5.2(a)   Amyl, Butyl, and Isobutyl Nitrite

These substances have had applications in medicine for years. One prominent action of nitrite inhalants is that they dilate blood vessels (they are vasodilators). Thus, these nitrite inhalants are often used in the treatment of angina (heart pain from exertion) and for diagnostic x-ray procedures where blood vessel size and flexibility are being evaluated. Some of these substances are also sold in adult sex stores under a variety of names including Rush, Kick, and Belt. The most potent form of the nitrite inhalants, amyl nitrite, is frequently prescribed for angina; however, it can be used "on the street" for the same reason as the other nitrites. These substances are generically called "poppers" because they are usually sold in small glass vials that are then broken or popped and sniffed when used.

§ 15.5.2(b)   Effects of Nitrite Inhalants

Inhalation of nitrite vapors in any form is usually associated with changes in psychological perceptions. First, these drugs produce a feeling of fullness in the head or a "rush," possibly caused by enlargement or dilation of cerebral blood vessels. Users also report a mild feeling of euphoria and a perception that time has slowed down; some users have mentioned an increase in sexual feelings or libido as well. These subjective effects usually last about a minute, but have been said to range in duration from five seconds or so to as long as fifteen minutes, depending upon the amount inhaled and the psychological state of the user.

Physical effects are also commonly observed with these inhalants. There is a general relaxation of both smooth muscles and the rectal sphincter. Increased heart rate is also a common effect. Research has not yet revealed whether the majority of homosexuals who use "poppers" take them in order to get the feelings of euphoria or if they are seeking some of the specific physiological effects. It may be a combination of the two.

§ 15.5.2(c)   Patterns of Nitrite Inhalant Abuse

Many individuals experimenting with drugs, not just homosexuals, try inhalants. A recent survey estimated that 17 percent of 18- to 25-year-olds have used these drugs. Those figures compare with 60 percent among homosexuals. The use pattern among gay men is estimated at approximately once per week, but as much as four times per week is not unusual. In another survey, 20 percent of the gay men surveyed had used some form of nitrite in the prior week.

The chances of a person having used a nitrite are determined through a number of variables. These drugs are more likely to be taken among urban individuals, men with a higher number of sexual partners, those who report having participated in group sex, and most likely among heavy drinkers. In one survey, the age of first use occurred at 22 years (range of 16 to 24 years), with the peak incidence at approximately 25 years. Apparently, individuals who take nitrites have a strong preference for the amyl form, with 78 percent in one study having used amyl nitrite only. Consistent with the information listed above, the use of these drugs is frequently associated with sexual activity, although almost 60 percent of the individuals sampled report that they inhale the drug mostly during masturbation. Only about a quarter of the surveyed users have ever taken these inhalants independent of sexual activity. Approximately half inhale nitrites in conjunction with other drugs, especially marijuana and alcohol (Lange).

§ 15.5.2(d)   Problems Associated with Nitrite Inhalants

The most disturbing data of nitrite inhalant abuse relates to the possibility (many would say the probability) that repeated heavy use of nitrites can impair immune functioning. There is evidence that many white cells, especially the T-lymphocytes, may not function normally in the presence of nitrites, and that there might be an additional suppression of natural killer cell activity. There is also some laboratory evidence that, in the presence of nitrites, certain normal body chemicals are converted into nitrosamines, a carcinogenic substance. It is felt that this combination of events might contribute to a high risk for Kaposi's sarcoma among homosexuals, even among those who do not have AIDS. It has also been hypothesized that the concomitant use of nitrites with "unsafe" sexual activity might facilitate the transmission of the AIDS virus.

A second medical difficulty associated with nitrite inhalants involves the respiratory system. When inhaled, these substances are irritating and can cause a bronchitis-like syndrome. In addition, in the presence of nitrites, the red blood cell component that is essential for carrying oxygen to the body cells, hemoglobin, can be converted to methemoglobin. This latter substance is not an efficient oxygen carrier; thus, repeated use of inhalants might contribute to a lack of oxygen in the body and associated respiratory difficulties.

Of course, as is true with most substances, it is also possible to overdose or have a toxic reaction with inhalants. While these are rarely (if ever) lethal, they can disturb the body's normal functioning. This is likely to include nausea, vomiting, headache, and dizziness. Through their vasodilation effects, these substances can also produce a significant drop in blood pressure. Moreover, some individuals develop allergies to nitrites that result in wheezing and itching. One final psychological syndrome is worth describing. The use of nitrites among individuals with little prior exposure to these drugs can cause a state of psychological panic. This panic usually centers on fears that the feelings will not go away and that the person might not come out of the "high." A similar syndrome can be seen with naive users of marijuana and hallucinogens. All such panic reactions can usually be treated with reassurance and education, as the symptoms are likely to pass within minutes.

In response to some of the problems described above, especially the fear of compromising the body's immune functioning, according to Newell et al, volatile nitrites had penetrated "every corner of gay life" by 1976. Surveys studying the use of nitrite inhalants found that in San Francisco, 58% of homosexual men were users in 1984 and 27% in 1991 (SFDPH 1991).

§ 15.5.3 Volatile Solvents

Volatile solvents are liquids that vaporize at room temperatures. They are found in a number of everyday products, including nail polish remover, lighter fluid, gasoline, paint and paint thinner, rubber glue, waxes, and varnishes. Chemicals found in these products include toluene, benzene, methanol, methylene, chloride, acetone, methyl ethyl ketone, methyl butyl ketone, trichloroethylene, and trichlorethane. When inhaled in sufficient quantity, all volatile hydrocarbons produce effects similar to alcohol intoxication. Almost all of these solvents have been misused by people seeking a cheap, easy high. Many factory workers who were continuously exposed to industrial solvents (prior to enactment of stringent health regulations) developed a strong attraction to the fumes and took to sniffing them deliberately. Gasoline, too, has its share of devotees, especially among children. Children were at the center of the highly publicized glue-sniffing craze of the 1960s, causing widespread alarm among concerned adults. The following chart shows some commonly abused commercial products and the solvents most often present:

Product	Main Solvents
model cement, airplane glue	toluene, acetone, naphtha
rubber cement	benzene
fingernail polish remover	acetone, ethyl acetate
lighter fluid	kerosene, naphtha
cleaning fluid	carbon tetrachloride
spot remover	trichloromethane, trichloroethylene
gasoline	benzene compounds, naphthenes, other aromatics
aerosols	dichlorodifluoromethane (propellant 12), trichlorofluormethane, isobutane

§ 15.5.4 Aerosols

These agents are liquid, solid, or gaseous products (or mixtures of the three), which are discharged by a propellant force of liquified and/or non-liquified compressed gas. Most aerosols contain three major components—propellants, solvents, and active ingredients—packaged under pressure in a disposable container. Commonly misused aerosol products include spray paints, insecticides, hair sprays, deodorants, glass chillers, and cooking oil sprays.

§ 15.6   PHARMACOLOGY AND CHEMISTRY OF INHALANTS

With the exception of the anesthetics, the commonly inhaled volatile substances are complex chemical compounds. Their contents generally belong to chemical groups variously consisting of aromatic hydrocarbons, aliphatic hydrocarbons, aliphatic nitrites, fluorinated hydrocarbons, dechlorinated and trichlorinated hydrocarbons, alcohols, ketones, and esters. Substance sniffing results in an immediate and effective reaction in the body. The inhalation of volatile substances through the lungs carries the chemicals via the bloodstream directly to the brain. Thus, the effects of sniffing are felt almost instantaneously. The "high" can last anywhere from one to fifteen minutes.

The inhaled chemicals are carried by and stored in fatty substances known as lipids, which are also found in high concentrations in the brain and throughout the central nervous system (CNS). Since volatile substances are stored by lipophilic substances until they are eliminated from the body, a cumulative buildup may occur if new chemicals are absorbed before any stored residue is expelled. With repeated "huffing" or sniffing of inhalants, the body may not be able to dispose of these chemicals quickly enough, and a cumulative concentration in the brain and CNS can occur. The body disposes of volatile substances through exhalation and metabolism by the liver, with excretion in the urine.

The effects of inhalants on an individual will vary in accordance with body size and weight, and the amount of chemicals inhaled. Also, since inhalants may contain more than one of a number of toxic chemicals, the effects of multiple toxins on the body must be considered especially dangerous.

§ 15.7   HOW DO INHALANTS PRODUCE THEIR EFFECTS?

Many brain systems may be involved in the anesthetic, intoxicating, and reinforcing effects of different inhalants. Nearly all abused inhalants (other than nitrites) produce a pleasurable effect by depressing the CNS. Evidence from animal studies suggests that a number of commonly abused volatile solvents and anesthetic gases have neurobehavioral effects and mechanisms of action similar to those produced by CNS depressants, which include alcohol and medications such as sedatives and anesthetics. Toluene, a solvent found in many commonly abused inhalants including airplane glue, paint sprays, and paint and nail polish removers, activates the brain's dopamine system. The dopamine system has been shown to play a role in the rewarding effects of many drugs of abuse. Nitrites, in contrast, dilate and relax blood vessels rather than acting as anesthetic agents.

§ 15.8   WHAT ARE THE EFFECTS OF INHALANT USE?

Although the chemical substances found in inhalants may produce various pharmacological effects, most inhalants produce a rapid high that resembles alcohol intoxication with initial excitation, then drowsiness, disinhibition, lightheadedness, and agitation. If sufficient amounts are inhaled, then nearly all solvents and gases produce anesthesia, a loss of sensation, and even unconsciousness.

Volatile Inhalants and Poisonous Substances

The chemicals found in solvents, aerosol sprays, and gases can produce a variety of additional effects during or shortly after use. These effects are related to inhalant intoxication and may include belligerence, apathy, impaired judgment, and impaired functioning in work or social situations. Dizziness, drowsiness, slurred speech, lethargy, depressed reflexes, general muscle weakness, and stupor are other possible effects. For example, research shows that toluene can produce headache, euphoria, giddy feelings, and inability to coordinate movements. Exposure to high doses can cause confusion and delirium. Nausea and vomiting are other common side effects.

Inhaled nitrites dilate blood vessels, increase heart rate, and produce a sensation of heat and excitement that can last for several minutes. Other effects can include flush, dizziness, and headache. Unlike other inhalants, which are abused mainly for their intoxicating effects, nitrites are abused primarily because they are believed to enhance sexual pleasure and performance.

A strong need to continue using inhalants has been reported among many individuals, particularly those who abuse inhalants for prolonged periods over many days. Compulsive use and a mild withdrawal syndrome can occur with long-term inhalant abuse. Additional symptoms exhibited by long-term inhalant abusers include weight loss, muscle weakness, disorientation, inattentiveness, lack of coordination, irritability, and depression (NIDA 2004).

§ 15.9 TOXICOLOGY OF INHALANTS

Although the toxic effects of sniffing most volatile substances are generally believed to be transient in nature, there are certain substances that present serious health hazards. Toxic effects of a transient nature include acute organic brain syndrome, which is characterized by dizziness, loss of memory, inability to concentrate, confusion, and unsteady gait. Beyond this fairly common reaction to inhalants, toxicity problems become specifically related to different chemicals and combinations of chemicals.

Volatile substances commonly found in commercial products that may represent dangerous, toxic effects when inhaled include the fluorocarbons (aerosols), benzene, tetraethyl lead, carbon tetrachloride, and n-hexane.

The most prominent threat to health associated with inhalant abuse is the Sudden Sniffing Death (SSD) syndrome related to sniffing the fluorocarbons contained in aerosols. The SSD syndrome is caused when the fluorocarbons (particularly trichlorofluoromethane) sensitize the heart to the adrenal hormone epinephrine, which is in itself a strong cardiac stimulant. By potentiating the effect of epinephrine on the heart, wildly erratic heartbeat and increased pulse occur, resulting in heart failure and death.

The prevalence of SSD syndrome has been confirmed by researchers at the U.S. Consumer Product Safety Commission; these researchers compiled accounts of over 300 deaths resulting from intentional inhalation of aerosol sprays. Their report states that "The hazard associated with aerosol containers that is most costly, in terms of loss of life, is intentional inhalation of aerosol spray vapors."

In addition to the aerosols, the substances benzene, carbon tetrachloride, and tetraethyl lead are among the most toxic. Benzene can cause death when inhaled in dense concentrations. The amount of benzene in gasoline is considered such a threat to health that the Occupational Safety and Health Administration (OSHA) gauges its standards for the amount of fumes gasoline workers may be exposed to on the percentage of benzene contained in the gasoline. The danger of benzene is that it deteriorates the blood-forming elements of the body and is believed to cause chromosomal abnormalities and leukemia in humans. Like benzene, carbon tetrachloride can also cause death in high concentrations. In lower concentrations with prolonged exposure, carbon tetrachloride may cause permanent kidney and liver damage. Another volatile substance used as an additive in gasoline is tetraethyl lead. This substance may cause permanent injury to the brain and the central nervous system if inhaled in sufficient quantities.

The most toxic propellant in aerosols is Trichlorofluoromethane (FC-11). The least toxic propellant is Difluoroethane (FC152a), which is rarely used in aerosols. Additional investigation is needed to determine which toxic effects are the important ones in deciding on the future use of these propellants.

Today, depending on end use, either liquified or compressed gases are used to dispense the product from the aerosol container. Liquified propellants, such as isobutane, butane, and propane are used. Compressed gas, such as carbon dioxide, nitrogen and nitrous oxide are also used as propellants today and are considered safer products.

Another widely used volatile solvent with adverse toxic effects is n-hexane. This solvent is frequently a component of model airplane cement. Excessive exposure to n-hexane through sniffing glue has been related to cases of nerve disorders resulting in either permanent damage and/or extended recovery periods.

The toxic effects of another common volatile solvent, toluene, are less clear than for n-hexane. Although it is generally believed that this widely abused substance is essentially harmless and any toxic effects are only transient in nature, there are documented cases which may indicate the contrary. These cases of chronic toluene sniffing presented bodily toxicities ranging from peripheral nerve damage to "permanent brain damage with diffuse cerebral atrophy."

According to Dr. Nancy Neff, an assistant professor of community medicine at the Baylor College of Medicine in Houston, individuals who regularly inhale the fumes of spray paint or similar chemical substances could also suffer permanent brain damage. "The primary physical effect of inhalant abuse is on the central nervous system (brain and spinal cord). It can cause organic brain syndrome, which is the diminished capacity to think, reason, remember, do calculations and abstract thinking," Dr. Neff says. Some spray paints and leather care products contain toluene which, when inhaled through the nose or mouth, is rapidly absorbed into the bloodstream and dissolves the fatty protective layer around nerves, thus causing them to wither and die. "Once a nerve is damaged, it is unable to regenerate and grow back. That's why I'm concerned that some of the neurological problems that we see may be permanent in these teen-age kids," says Dr. Neff.

In a four-year study of 97 teenage inhalant abusers at the Casa de Amigos Drug Treatment Program in Houston, Dr. Neff found that nearly half of them had evidence of long-term brain damage and physical deterioration. Simple neurologic tests, such as walking a straight line, touching the nose with a finger or maintaining balance while standing with eyes closed, were difficult for many of the inhalant abusers because of central nervous system damage.

In addition to brain damage, inhalant abusers may suffer nausea and vomiting, loss of appetite, ringing in the ears, a stuffy or runny nose, abdominal pain or cramps. More severe problems can include kidney damage, kidney stone formation, muscle weakness and paralysis. Female inhalant abusers who become pregnant face an increased risk of having a child with birth defects.

Moreover, serious personality problems may plague inhalant abusers. Previously stable teens can become violent and aggressive; feelings of anxiety, depression, and suicide are common. "Inhalant abuse, like many other forms of substance abuse, is probably a symptom rather than the problem itself," says Dr. Neff. "The kids get into it because they're unhappy, they're alienated from their families and other traditional support systems, they're bored, and they're subject to peer pressure" (DeBorona et al).

Treatment of the medical complications of inhalant abuse and individual and family counseling are the most common methods of preventing further physical damage and continued misuse of the chemical substance.

§ 15.10 METHODS OF VOLATILE SUBSTANCE ABUSE

The most common form of toluene abuse is by inhalation of the fumes. This may be done in various ways, but the most frequent method is to obtain a spray paint can that contains the substance. The paint is then sprayed onto a cloth material, usually a sock. The sock's toe area is generously coated with paint. The sock is then wrapped in a fashion so as not to have the paint come in contact with the skin. The sock is then placed to the nose and mouth area while the toluene fumes are inhaled into the body through a series of deep breaths. This is popularly referred to as "huffing." Silver and gold spray paints are rumored to contain higher contents of toluene.

"Bagging" is another popular method of inhaling volatile substances (like glue and cement), where one saturates the inside of a paper (or plastic) bag so the fumes can be contained at a concentrated level. The opened end of the bag is then placed over the mouth and the opening is sealed by holding the bag tightly to the cheeks. At this point the fumes are inhaled into the lungs, usually through one deep breath.

Other ways of abusing volatile substances include:

• "Sniffing" or "snorting" fumes from containers;
• Spraying aerosols directly into the nose or mouth;
• Inhaling from balloons filled with nitrous oxide.

Animal and human research shows that most inhalants are extremely toxic. Perhaps the most significant toxic effect of chronic exposure to inhalants is widespread and long-lasting damage to the brain and other parts of the nervous system. For example, both animal research and human pathological studies indicate that chronic abuse of volatile solvents such as toluene damages the protective sheath around certain nerve fibers in the brain and peripheral nervous system. This extensive destruction of nerve fibers is clinically similar to that seen with neurological diseases such as multiple sclerosis.

The neurotoxic effects of prolonged inhalant abuse include neurological syndromes that reflect damage to parts of the brain involved in controlling cognition, movement, vision, and hearing. Cognitive abnormalities can range from mild impairment to severe dementia. Other effects can include difficulty coordinating movement, spasticity, and loss of feeling, hearing, and vision.

Inhalants also are highly toxic to other organs. Chronic exposure can produce significant damage to the heart, lungs, liver, and kidneys. Although some inhalant-induced damage to the nervous and other organ systems may be at least partially reversible when inhalant abuse is stopped, many syndromes caused by repeated or prolonged abuse are irreversible.

Abuse of inhalants during pregnancy also may place infants and children at increased risk of developmental harm. Animal studies designed to simulate human patters of inhalant abuse suggest that prenatal exposure to toluene or trichloroethylene (TCE) can result in reduced birth weights, occasional skeletal abnormalities, and delayed neurobehavioral development. A number of case reports note abnormalities in newborns of mothers who chronically abuse solvents, and there is evidence of subsequent developmental impairment in some of these children. However, no well-controlled, prospective study of the effects of prenatal exposure to inhalants in humans has been conducted, and it is not possible to link prenatal exposure to a specific chemical to a specific birth defect or developmental problem.

§ 15.11 EARLY WARNING SIGNS OF INHALANT ABUSE
Many of the early signs and symptoms of inhalant abuse are similar to that of other forms of substance abuse:

—Sudden change in choice of friends
—Poor performance at school or work
—Sloppy dress, sudden lack of personal hygiene
—Lack of appetite, weight loss
—Sudden mood swings, defensiveness
—Withdrawal from family activities

The above signs by themselves do not indicate inhalant abuse, but parents, teachers, and health professionals should be aware of these signs when they are coupled with the following:

——Chemical odors on the breath or clothing
——Paint stains on clothing, fingertips, or around the nose or mouth
——Runny nose and other cold-like symptoms
——Red or glassy eyes
——Rashes around the nose and mouth

§ 15.11.1 Symptoms of Abuse
After inhalation, the toluene abuser will feel intoxicated and may appear to be drunk. The most visible objective symptoms are:

—Poor coordination
—Slurred speech
—Odor of the substance on the breath
—Excess nasal secretions
—Watering of the eyes
—Dilated (enlarged) pupils
—Sneezing and coughing
—Nausea and headache

While under the influence, the abuser will experience a feeling of euphoria, exaggerated well-being, vigor, and high spirits. This may be accompanied by or replaced with drowsiness and disordered perception. He or she may have hallucinations (seeing, hearing, and experiencing things that are not there), double vision, and may even become unconscious.

§ 15.12   INVESTIGATIONS OF VOLATILE SUBSTANCE ABUSE

The fumes of any inhaled substance may linger on for a long period of time after inhalation. In addition to recognizing the smell of volatile fumes, be sure to check the hands and facial area of suspected persons for tell-tale signs of paint. It is common for the paint to transfer onto the person's body when preparing and when ingesting the substance. If any skin areas have been exposed to the paint, they should be noted.

A check of the immediate area should also be made to attempt to locate the sock or other implements used in inhaling the substance. If this is found, a further check for the paint can or substance container should also be made.

A sobriety test of some sort should be administered to the subject when investigating the degree of intoxication. The symptoms noted previously should be documented, especially if the subject does have a strong odor of paint on his or her breath.

It is important to carefully secure any evidence obtained. If a sock or cloth material that is saturated with paint or some other substance is obtained, placement into a Mason-type jar with a screw-on-type lid is preferred. This will insure the freshness of the item for a later date in the event the matter goes to court. If no paint can is obtained, then this will further insure the quality of the evidence when it is sent to a crime lab for analysis. This last point is very important. The evidence, when obtained in the field, cannot be positively identified as containing toluene. A chemical test determining the chemical content is necessary. This is not possible in the field at this time, so analysis must be made at a lab. This is also the case when securing paint cans as evidence in the field. All paint cans or other substances that contain toluene are so noted on the label. As is most often the case, the subjects will remove the label in an attempt to conceal the fact that the substance does in fact contain toluene. If this does occur, a lab analysis is in order to definitely determine the chemical content of the substance.

§ 15.13   REPEAT OFFENDERS

There are habitual offenders of inhalant abuse. The most plausible explanation one can offer is that the individual, when low on money, will return to the abuse of toluene as the need arises for a cheap high. That is precisely what "sniffing" paint or glue is: a very inexpensive form of getting intoxicated.

Another motivation for repeated inhalation is social pressure. The general consensus, according to Lynn Miller of the Santa Cruz County Probation Department, is that although the inhaling of toluene is not physically addictive, it is socially addictive when those in the surrounding environment are continually in quest of activities to occupy their time. Referring to inhalant abuse and its socially addictive capacity, Miller said: "It is a destructive effort to find an alternate way to occupy free time when the individuals are left unsupervised for any great lengths of time, which is the case with a large percentage of the youth in the community."

§ 15.14 THE SOCIOLOGY OF INHALANT USE

Early studies suggest that the social backgrounds of inhalant users are fairly homogeneous (Cohen). Latinos (Puerto Rican or Chicano, depending on the region) have often been reported to be overrepresented among samples of inhalant users, while blacks have been underrepresented (Langrod). In addition, studies have generally shown that the majority of sniffers come from low-income backgrounds (Chapel). However, there are samples—such as Bass' of 110 youths who died "sudden sniffing deaths"—which are primarily from suburban white middle-class homes (Bass). Males have been reported to outnumber females as much as 10 to 1. Other samples of inhalant users suggest that they are well represented among all socioeconomic levels (Dorman). There is anecdotal evidence suggesting that, for many adolescent inhalant users, sniffing is primarily a group activity.

§ 15.14.1   The Causes of Inhalant Use

Implicit in most drug use research are assumptions about the causes of excessive drug use (even if "excessive" is seldom defined). Researchers have been remarkably consistent in assuming that the cause of excessive inhalant use lies in the disorganized existence of users, taking the form of either individual personality disruptions, massive familial disorganization, or both.

Here again, a distinction between kinds of inhalant use may distinguish between different causes, for the question of what causes a certain kind of drug use varies widely with the relationship between person and drug (the most obvious example being the occasional social drinker versus the severe alcoholic).

Cohen suggests that some kind of emotional disruption, from whatever source, stands out as the common factor pushing individuals into persistent use of inhalants. The most disturbed individuals are more likely to remain heavily involved because they obtain the most relief from their anxiety, depression, or other negative feelings. Cohen further suggests that some of the variables which influence the choice of intoxicant for adolescents are (1) what the microculture is using, (2) availability of the agent, and (3) the secondary gains, such as the "high" (Cohen).

The studies of drug use prevalence among young people in the United States all indicate that inhalants are only one of a number of substances used by youths; thus, several studies indicate that inhalants are used concurrently with other drugs or are associated with greater drug experimentation.

The inhalation of certain commercial substances is potentially more dangerous, both physically and psychologically, than the use of marijuana or other drugs popular among youths.

However, to generate hypotheses about what "causes" inhalant use without considering the larger circumstances influencing the lives of adolescents and young adults (including drug use and abuse) can lead to oversimplification and a narrow view of the problem. A broader picture of the contexts of drug use can also provide opportunities for the emergence of innovative treatment and other alternatives.

The fact that inhalant use by adolescents has been reported in many areas of the world—in many subcultures of the United States, in Canada, Mexico, England, Sweden, Japan, Australia—should indicate that such substance use is part of a process that extends beyond the cities and towns of the United States (Cohen). Many anthropologists would agree with the suggestion that it is a process tied to the universal problems of adolescents in finding their social and sexual identity.

Several reports offer suggestions about why inhalants might be the substance of choice among adolescents. The most obvious answer is the accessibility of the drugs. The range of commercial substances which will produce a high, including hallucinations, is vast. Many of them are household or workshop products. Particularly for children and adolescents, this factor must be an important influence. The most commonly mentioned factor in interviews with adolescents is the hallucinations, often described as vivid, mystical, and as a center for group rituals and communication. In addition, users often mention feelings of power and invulnerability as positive factors. However, there are acute negative side effects described such as headaches, nausea, etc., and undoubtedly not all young people who experiment with inhalants respond favorably to them.

Why, then, if inhalants are so accessible and have such desirable "highs," are they not used by higher percentages of young adults and adolescents? An initial approach to this question offers two possible answers. The first is the widespread fear of the permanent physical and psychological effects of inhalants. User anecdotes suggest that such a fear is pervasive. The second possible explanation is the association of drugs with certain groups—social class, ethnic, or age groups—an association which tends to make them less desirable for use by members of other groups, especially if the using group is lower status. Within some drug-using subcultures, inhalant use may be seen as lower status because of its identification with younger adolescents.

These suggestions indicate a need for more research on the use of substances in addition to inhalants by those who report current inhalant use and by those reporting past inhalant use. More information is needed on the factors which motivate drug use. This research might be initiated with user interviews to document their attitudes toward different drugs. The research might be augmented then by a study of those youths in drug- and inhalant-using communities who have not become involved with inhalants.

§ 15.15 POISONING INVESTIGATION
§ 15.15.1 Introduction

The preliminary investigation of a poisoning can be of critical importance in saving the victim's life. An experienced investigator can detect several poisons. In order to administer the appropriate treatment, doctors will depend on the officer's ability to quickly locate and possibly identify the poison. Also, any available physical evidence must be carefully collected and identified. The evidence can indicate whether the poisoning is suicidal, homicidal, or accidental.

CLASSIFICATION OF POISONS

Solvents:	Inorganic Poisons:
a. Ether	a. Arsenic
b. Acetone	b. Mercuric Chloride
c. Benzene	c. Antimony Compounds
d. Carbon Disulfide	d. Lead Salts
e. Carbon Tetrachloride	e. Phosphorous

Organic Poisons:	Gaseous Poisons:
a. Salicylate	a. Carbon Monoxide
b. Barbiturates	b . Illuminating Gas
c. Narcotics	c . Hydrogen Sulfide
d. Strychnine	d. Sulfur Dioxide
e. Nicotine	

§ 15.15.2   Investigating the Symptoms of Poisoning

Symptoms of poisoning may include vomiting, abdominal pains, convulsions, coma, and delirium. Documentation of symptoms should include all information concerning the victim's actions immediately prior to death or unconsciousness. Information from friends, family, or bystanders may be helpful in determining the substance used.

In determining whether or not death or illness is due to poisoning, one must remember that the symptoms preceding the illness or death, as well as the external appearance of the body, are of great importance. Many poisonings will produce some similar symptoms but when the outstanding symptom is one of those indicated below, there are definite poisons to look for first.

Symptoms Preceding Death

1. Convulsions — strychnine, nicotine

2. Delirium — atropine, hyoscyamine

3. Extreme drowsiness — opiates, hypnotics

4. Extreme rapidity of death — cyanide, strychnine, nicotine

5. Long, delayed death — metals

6. Abdominal pains — metals, food poisoning

7. Diarrhea — metals, food poisoning

8. Vomiting — metals, food poisoning

9. Burning of the mouth — corrosives, mercury, arsenic

Poisoning May Be Suspected If:
1. Nearby persons attempt to:

—Hurry embalming.

—Hurry funeral.

—Cremate body.

—Falsify death certificate.

2. There is sudden death of a healthy individual.

3. Death apparently due to unknown causes.

Preliminary Investigative Techniques upon Arrival at the Scene
1. Summon medical aid, if necessary (i.e., paramedics, ambulance, etc.).

2. Locate, separate, and interview the witnesses.

3. Identify, control, and separate the suspect(s), if present.

4. Follow the procedures for handling the source of poisoning, when located.

5. Try to ascertain the amount of poison ingested by the victim(s).

If and when this information is determined, notify involved medical personnel immediately.

6. Determine the actions taken by the victim prior to becoming comatose or dead.

7. If the poison is present in the atmosphere and is posing a danger to others, immediately evacuate the area.

Notify the fire department for a washdown and chemical neutralization, if necessary.

8. If the poison is criminally connected or there is suspicion of foul play:

Use the basic preliminary investigative techniques.

Do not overlook the possibility of latent prints. If the victim is in critical condition, accompany him or her to the medical facility in case a dying declaration is made.

§ 15.15.2(a)   Interviewing Victim/Witnesses

Questioning the Victim—If possible, question the victim. Prior permission should be obtained from the physician, and his or her recommendations as to length of questioning should be followed. During the questioning, develop as much essential information as possible. Keep informed of the recovery progress of the victim and continue questioning as necessary.

Questioning and Investigating the Witnesses—Witnesses should be questioned to develop information regarding the poisoning and should be investigated to determine if they participated in the poisoning. Witnesses may include:

—Persons who witnessed the act of poisoning, or persons who have knowledge of a suspect's utterances or actions that would tend to establish a motive for the crime.

—Persons who have knowledge of the victim's consumption of food or drink within the period of time he or she probably received the poison.

—Persons who sold the victim or suspects drugs or medicines.

—Persons who have knowledge of the victim's movements prior to the time he or she was stricken, or persons familiar with the victim's habits, particularly:

Eating and drinking habits.

Use of drugs and medicines.

Attempts at self-medication.

—Persons familiar with the victim's financial status, family background, and social life.

Essential Information—By questioning witnesses and the victim, the investigator should try to obtain answers to the following questions:

—Where was the victim when the symptoms first appeared?

—What were the symptoms?

—Did someone intentionally give the victim poison? If so, who? What was the person's motive?

—Did the victim administer the poison himself or herself? If so, was the poisoning accidental or intentional? What was his or her reason?

—Had the victim ever contemplated suicide or attempted it before?

—Who summoned assistance? When? By what means?

—Prior to the appearance of the symptoms, what did the victim do? With whom did he or she associate?

—What did the victim eat or drink prior to the appearance of the symptoms? Where did this consumption take place?

—Did the victim request food and beverages, or was it offered to urged upon him or her? Who prepared it? Who served it?

—Did the victim notice anything peculiar about the food or beverage? Did he or she regularly eat the food or beverage in question?

—Did the victim eat or drink anything after the symptoms first appeared? Was the victim in the habit of drinking any form of alcohol not intended for drinking purposes?

—Did the victim take any medicines prior to the appearance of the symptoms? Was this medicine prescribed by a doctor? Was the medicine given to the victim by someone other than a physician or a pharmacist? Where is the container in which the medicine was kept? Did the victim habitually take any kind of medicine? Was he or she addicted to any narcotic drug?

—Was the victim unhappy or depressed recently? Was he or she angry with, or jealous of, anyone? Did the victim have money on his or her person prior to the symptoms? Is that money still in the victim's possession? What was the condition of his or her estate? Did he or she owe large sums?

—Who would inherit the victim's estate? Has the person lost money recently? Does the victim handle money in his or her occupation?

—Did the victim have any recent difficulties with regard to his or her occupation or employment? Did anyone ever accuse the victim of misconduct or criminal actions?

—Was anyone jealous of the victim because of his or her position? Will anyone benefit, through promotion, from the victim's death? Did the victim recently receive any threatening letters or communications? How were they disposed of? Who sent them? If they were anonymous, who had a motive for sending them or who possessed the information on which they were based?

—Did the victim write any letters recently? To whom? What was the subject matter of the letters?

Investigating the Victim's Activities—Investigation should be made of the activities of the victim during the period prior to the poisoning.

Volatile Inhalants and Poisonous Substances

Ascertaining the Source of the Poison—Determining the source of the poison may furnish valuable investigative leads. Some possible sources that should not be overlooked are:

—Hospitals, dispensaries, laboratories, and pharmacies; offices, homes, and grocery stores. These may contain poisonous cleaning substances, rodent or insect poisons, and medicines that may be toxic if improperly used.

—Depots, warehouses, storage areas, farms, and similar places where rodent and insect poisons may be kept.

—Filling stations, garages, and other places where fuels with alcohol bases may be found.

—Establishments where cleaning and solvent compounds containing poisons are kept or used.

—Illicit narcotics channels

—Dealers in bad liquor.

The autopsy may disclose:

—The exact time of death.

—The affected organ that directly caused the death.

—The specific poison that caused the death.

—The identification and analysis of the poison (may be performed by a toxicologist subsequent to the autopsy).

—The approximate time the poison was taken.

—The food or beverage that contained the poison (this may not be possible if death is several days after the taking of the poison). The approximate time of death if the victim died before medical or public authorities could reach him or her.

—A disease or accident that may have caused death. Suicide victims may be surprised by the slowness of death and kill themselves by other means.

§ 15.15.2(b)   Collection of Physical Evidence

There are usually few witnesses to a poisoning; therefore, physical evidence is of vital importance. It is absolutely necessary that physical evidence be taken into custody in a legal manner, properly marked for identification, and safeguarded by a complete chain of custody covering every person who has such evidence in his possession from the time of the seizure until it is presented in court. In addition to the usual forms of physical evidence, the investigator or crime scene technician should obtain, when possible:

1. Remains of food and drink last taken.

2. Drugs, medicines, narcotics, or chemicals in the home of the suspect and victim.

3. Glasses, bottles, spoons, etc., from which the victim may have drunk.

4. Vomit, urine, feces, etc.

In every suspected poisoning case, the officer should make an immediate search for the following:

1. The possible source(s) of the poison agent.

2. The possible container(s) of the poison agent.

Once the source of the poison agent is located, it should be isolated.

1. If the source is identified, notify concerned medical personnel immediately.

2. If the source is not identified, immediately have the suspected substance transported as quickly as possible to one of the following:

   a. Police crime laboratory.

   b. Medical laboratory.

   c. Emergency facility where victim is treated.

Materials suspected as evidence should also be collected. These include:

1. All the contents of a medicine chest.

2. Freshly used drinking glasses.

3. Partially or fully emptied beverage bottles.

4. Used spoons.

5. Foods or beverages.

All evidence should be photographed before being collected and identified.

Volatile Inhalants and Poisonous Substances

All evidence to be analyzed at the laboratory should be:

1. Sealed in a clean glass container.

2. Labeled to identify the evidence.

3. Packaged in a suitable container to avoid breakage during transit to the laboratory.

If the evidence is not in a suitable container for shipment, it should be placed in a container provided by the investigator or evidence technician.

§ 15.16 WHERE CAN I GET FURTHER SCIENTIFIC INFORMATION ABOUT INHALANT ABUSE?

To learn more about inhalants and other drugs of abuse, contact the National Clearinghouse for Alcohol and Drug Information (NCADI) at 1-800-729-6686. Information specialists are available to help you locate information and resources.

Fact sheets on the health effects of inhalants and other abused drugs and other drug abuse topics can be ordered free of charge, in English and Spanish, from NIDA Infofax at 1-888-NIH-NIDA (1-888-644-6432); for deaf persons, 1-888-TTY-NIDA (1-888-889-6432).

Information is also available on the NIDA web site (www.drugabuse.gov) or the NCADI web site (www.health.org).

Chapter 15

References

Bass, M. "Sudden sniffing deaths." Journal of the American Medical Association 212 (1970): 2075-2079.

Chapel, J.C., and D.W. Taylor. "Glue sniffing." Missouri Medicine 65.4 (1968): 288-292.

Cohen, S. "The Volatile Solvents." Public Health Review 2.2 (1973): 185-214.

DeBorona, M., and D. Simpson. "Inhalant Users in Drug Abuse Prevention Programs." American Journal of Drug and Alcohol Abuse 10 (1984): 503-518.

Dorman, M. "Inhalant abuse: a psychological research model." National Institute on Drug Abuse: Third Technical Review on Inhalant Abuse. Rockville, MD, Department of Health and Human Services, 1976.

Lange, W.R., et al. "Nitrite Inhalants: Patterns of Abuse in Baltimore and Washington, D.C." American Journal of Drug and Alcohol Abuse 14 (1988): 29-39.

Langrod, J. "Secondary drug use among heroin addicts." International Journal of the Addictions 5 (1970): 611-735.

Media Projects, Inc. Inhalant Abuse: Kids in Danger/Adults in the Dark. Dallas, TX, 1990, p. 4.

National Institute for Drug Abuse. "Inhalant Abuse," NIH Publication No. 00-3818. Rockville, MD: Department of Health and Human Services, 2004.

Newell, G.R., Monsell, P.W., Spitz, M.R., Reuben, J.M., Hersh, E.M. "Volatile Nitrites: Use and Adverse Efforts Related to the Current Epedemic of the Acquired Immune Deficiency Syndrome." American Journal of Medicine 78 (1985): 811-816.

San Francisco Department of Public Health. "Lesbian and Gay Substance Abuse Planning Group, Gay Men, Lesbians and Their Alcohol and Other Drug Use: A Review of the Literature." San Francisco, California, 1991.

CHAPTER 16

THE EVOLUTION OF DRUG LAW

§ 16.1 INTRODUCTION

Throughout the history of chemical substance use, people have tried to regulate drugs by various laws or codes of conduct. Most laws have moral and sociological implications—for example, it is wrong to lose control of body and mind, to harm society, or to upset civilized codes of conduct. It is wrong to become unproductive, parasitic, or dependent on the community, or to be antisocial by stealing to obtain drugs, alcohol, etc. The enactment of laws depends on the prevalent moral and social codes and customs of the times. What may seem like a repressive law today may very well be changed over a period of time; strict laws may be replaced with light penalties or even be repealed. Again, these changes depend upon the desires of the people involved and the events that occur in any given historical era.

Over the years, the substances we call hallucinogens, depressants, narcotics, marijuana, coffee, tea, tobacco, and alcohol have all been subject to a wide range of controls, from none at all, to rigid. Laws were often changed: either so many people used a particular drug that it would have been impossible to enforce a ban, or because the government needed the tax revenue.

§ 16.2 HISTORY OF DRUG LEGISLATION UP TO 1989
§ 16.2.1 Early Drug Laws

The first significant piece of prohibitory legislation relating to drugs in the United States was an ordinance enacted in 1875 by the city of San Francisco prohibiting the operation of opium dens—commercial establishments in which the smoking of opium occurred. One Western state after another followed San Francisco's lead, and these states enacted legislation prohibiting opium smoking. In 1887, in response to U.S. obligations imposed by a Chinese-American treaty of commerce enacted in 1880, Congress prohibited the importation of smoke-able opium by Chinese subjects. Despite these first legislative efforts, the incidence of drug use and addiction increased, as did societal concern and illegal drug smuggling.

Some related substance control legislation was later put into effect in 1906. The 1906 Food and Drug Act required manufacturers to disclose the contents of patent medicines directly on the manufacturing label. Although this disclosure law had the beneficial effect of substantially decreasing the use of proprietary or patent medicines containing opiates, other forms of opium use continued at alarming rates.

Although estimates concerning the number of drug addicts during the 50 years prior to the passage of more specific drug legislation (the Harrison Act) in 1914 are inherently suspect, the available information suggests that drug abuse during that period was a "major medico-social problem." In fact, by 1909, the United States was confronted with a significant and growing drug abuse dilemma. The increased opiate use and addiction in the United States subsequent to the Civil War has been attributed to several factors, including the indiscriminate use of morphine to treat battlefield casualties during the war. The increase in morphine addiction was so extensive that the phrase "army disease" was used to describe the drug use among ex-soldiers. The widespread administration of morphine by hypodermic syringe also contributed to overall increases in opiate abuse. Other circumstances exacerbating the situation during the period of 1865 to 1914 included the spread of opium smoking from Chinese immigrants to American citizens. Opiate addicts tended to be middle-class and middle-aged women from rural areas or small towns. They took their morphine or opium orally and certainly were not regarded as criminals. Increases in opiate use were also caused by the manufacturing of opium and its derivatives in the American patent medicine industry. Beginning in 1898, this circumstance was particularly detrimental due to the marketing of heroin as a safe, powerful, and non-addictive substitute for the opium derivatives morphine and codeine.

It was said that "no remedy was heralded as enthusiastically as was heroin." Indeed, some physicians even recommended heroin as a treatment for "chronic intoxication" resulting from the use of morphine and codeine. It was not until 1910 that the medical profession began to recognize the dangers of substituting heroin for other opium derivatives.

In 1908, the American Opium Commission investigated domestic opium use. In response to the results of this investigation, Congress passed "An Act to Prohibit the Importation and Use of Opium for Other Than Medicinal Purposes" in 1909. Among other things, this act permitted the importation of opium for medicinal purposes, but only to 12 ports of entry. However, it did not regulate domestic opium production and manufacture or the interstate shipment of opium products. Opium products were still available without a physician's prescription and were being marketed throughout the country by retail outlets and a growing mail order trade.

§ 16.2.2 International Agreements

In 1909, the International Opium Commission met in Shanghai to discuss the possibilities of effecting international agreements aimed at restricting trade in narcotic drugs to the scientific and medical communities.

In Shanghai, the U.S. government took a position which has continued to be our hallmark in subsequent international discussions: pressing for more controls than other delegations were willing to support. At the 1909 Shanghai Convention, the U.S. delegation voted in favor of immediate opium prohibition as the ultimate goal in every country where opium is grown. Although the original purpose of the Shanghai Convention was to limit opium cultivation in the Orient, the Convention ended with a resolution advocating international opium control everywhere. Despite this resolution, the Shanghai Convention did not produce a treaty. A subsequent conference was necessary to make these resolutions binding.

The next significant international effort was held at The Hague in December 1911. When President Wilson signed the Harrison Narcotic Act on December 17, 1914, he said that this act was passed to fulfill our treaty obligations. The treaty obligations referred to by President Wilson were contained in the 25 articles set forth at The Hague Convention of 1912. In essence, the participants at The Hague Convention agreed that governments should control production, manufacture, and distribution of opium, certain opiates, and cocaine, both nationally and internationally.

It was further agreed that the control, manufacture, and distribution of opiate drugs would be limited to medical and legitimate uses only. The question of what constituted legitimate uses was a subject of debate and continues to be a subject of debate at all international conferences. Additionally, all nations which participated at The Hague Convention agreed to "examine the possibility of making possession of controlled drugs a crime." As a result, it was not surprising that President Wilson should characterize the Harrison Narcotic Act as a congressional statute passed in furtherance of an executive commitment.

Despite these agreements, The Hague Convention did not set up the proper machinery to enforce violations. Due to this inherent weakness, effective implementation of the treaty became impossible. Moreover, no mechanism was set up to monitor compliance with the treaty resolutions. In response to these weaknesses, the U.S. government quickly insisted upon the "limitation of production of opium," contending that unless production was limited, it would be virtually impossible to prevent smuggling.

In the early 1920s, the countries of Persia, Turkey, and Yugoslavia depended so heavily on opium as a commodity that abrupt cessation of production would have resulted in economic catastrophe. Because other nations failed to comply with the U.S. government's demands, we ultimately withdrew from the Convention.

At the Geneva Conference in 1924 and 1925, the U.S. government again strongly recommended all nations participating in The Hague Convention to fulfill their obligations under that Convention. It was clear that our position, in part, stemmed from our inability to control our narcotics problems at home. Although the Harrison Narcotic Act had been in effect for almost 10 years and law enforcement had been given the clear responsibility for handling the entire narcotics addiction problem, our failures, at that point, were glaringly obvious. However, the United States continued to pursue an unalterable course of action by thrusting upon law enforcement the responsibility for controlling conduct which seemed, even at that time, to be impossible to control. Although our government had committed itself to a research program in order to explore the course of drug addiction, we failed to implement that commitment and continued to rely totally upon the police to resolve our drug addiction problems. The Harrison Narcotic Act failed to curtail addiction; thus, crimes related to addiction continued to multiply. Since legitimate sources of drugs were completely unavailable to addicts, users turned instead to buying smuggled drugs or to smuggling drugs themselves. Here again, the U.S. government failed to control the flow of smuggled drugs across American borders. The total prohibition approach which we advocated and attempted to implement had only appeared to be a simple and certain way to solve our domestic addiction problem.

§ 16.2.3 Events of the 1930s

The events which effected drug legislation in the 1930s were varied and, to some degree, inconsistent. From the old Narcotic Unit within the Treasury Department's Bureau of Prohibition, a new and expanded federal enforcement agency was formed: the Bureau of Narcotics. Also situated within the Treasury Department, the Bureau was charged with the enforcement of the Harrison Act and other federal laws pertaining to narcotics.

With regard to the enactment of criminal laws, there were two other important developments in the 1930s. The National Conference of Commissioners on Uniform State Laws promulgated the Uniform Narcotic Drug Act, a recommended model for the states, which was eventually adopted by every state in one form or another. At the state level, the act criminalized the possession, use, and distribution of opiates and cocaine. These two classes of drugs were grouped together under the legal label of "narcotics." Although many states had enacted narcotic laws pre-dating even the Harrison Act, the element of uniformity among the states had been missing until the Uniform Act.

The United States Congress was also active in the creation of additional prohibitions. Acting upon the advice of the Bureau of Narcotics, Congress enacted the Marijuana Tax Act, placing cannabis under the same restrictions that were in effect for opiates and cocaine. Enforcement responsibilities were assigned to the Bureau.

The Bureau's articulated rationale for promoting the marijuana legislation was fear of the crime-inducing effects of the drug. Harry J. Anslinger, the renowned Commissioner of the Bureau, cited numerous anecdotal case studies relating ingestion of cannabis and commission of violent and bizarre criminal acts. Although critics cited the obvious inaccuracies of Anslinger's claims, the lawmakers were sufficiently convinced of the possible dangers of "reefer madness" and passed the act.

A number of theories abound in regard to the motives of Anslinger and Congress. Cynics charge that Anslinger merely wished to augment the size of his agency and chose re-definition of the Bureau's mission as the most convenient means. Others claim that passage of the Marijuana Tax Act was intended as an anti-Mexican measure aimed at discouraging immigration into the Southwest. Adherents of this theory also hold that the opiate and cocaine laws were racially motivated (against Chinese and Blacks, respectively). Finally, some observers link the Marijuana Tax Act with the repeal of Prohibition (in 1933), the marijuana law serving as a replacement for the loss of federal control over alcohol.

In response to the legacy of drug abuse that continued despite new laws, the U.S. government formally opened its first "narcotics farm" at Lexington, Kentucky in 1935. This facility provided a psychiatrically-oriented in-patient setting for the treatment of opiate addicts. The second "narcotics farm" was opened at Fort Worth, Texas in 1938. Established as a result of a 1929 Congressional enactment, the Lexington and Fort Worth facilities offered treatment to specially assigned federal prisoners and to voluntary admissions.

The primary impetus for creating these hospital facilities was to alleviate the overcrowding of addicts in federal prisons. Federal prisons were ill-equipped to handle narcotics addicts as the post-Harrison Act addict inmates presented significant medical problems beyond the resources of conventional prisons. Thus, addict prisoners were permitted to serve their sentences at the Lexington and Fort Worth facilities. Fortunately, these inmates—in addition to the numerous voluntary admissions—served as ideal research subjects. Most of the early medical and behavioral knowledge of the addictive process was gained from the research at these hospitals.

§ 16.2.4 The 1940s

During the 1940s, America was preoccupied with the serious problems of war and post-war recovery. Consequently, little activity occurred with respect to control of psychoactive drugs. One of the few noteworthy actions was an amendment of the Uniform Narcotic Drug Act placing cannabis under its purview. The states thus followed the lead of the federal government in criminalizing marijuana cultivation, possession, use, and distribution.

§ 16.2.5 Changes in the 1950s

Major changes in drug law penalties occurred in the 1950s. First, in 1951, at the urging of Commissioner Anslinger and the Bureau of Narcotics, Congress passed the Boggs Act which imposed stiff mandatory minimum sentences upon narcotics offenders. Many states emulated this punishment and deterrence model, enacting more local versions of the Boggs Act. Only four years later, federal narcotics penalties were again increased, fortifying its feature of a mandatory minimum sentence. Under the 1956 law, at the option of the jury, the death penalty could be imposed upon offenders convicted of sale of narcotics to a minor. The legislation also authorized the Bureau of Narcotics to conduct training programs for state and local enforcement personnel and to collect national statistics relating to narcotics patterns.

Analysts of the stiff penalty legislation in the 1950s are not in agreement with regard to their causes. Some of the often-cited causal factors include fear of widespread new narcotics usage, reaction to allegations of the Mafia's control over the narcotics trade, a general conservative drift in American politics, and effective law enforcement lobbying. One fact is clear, however: as a result of the statutes of this era, the United States had adopted one of the strictest narcotics control policies in the world. The lengthy and inflexible mandatory minimum sentence, later to be considered for more serious and violent crimes, had been specifically designed for the narcotics violator and exemplified the American commitment to a retributive-deterrent theory of addiction control.

§ 16.2.6 The 1960s

The decade of the 1960s was dominated by a spirit of experimentation. Lawmakers, executive officials, and the courts indicated a willingness to innovate and test new drug control policies. Much of the intellectual and political energy behind this movement stemmed from the joint American Bar Association/American Medical Association report on drug addiction released in 1961. The report, Drug Addiction: Crime or Disease? criticized the popular law enforcement approach to addiction control and recommended a more balanced prevention policy. The report and the spirited debate evoked by its conclusions signaled a renewed sociopolitical interest in the medical treatment of drug abuse. A year after its publication, President Kennedy convened a White House Conference on Narcotics and Drug Abuse. Rehabilitation, rather than punishment, of drug abusers emerged as the theme of that conference.

Taking the lead from the White House resolution on rehabilitation, the State of California enacted legislation in 1961 which authorized the involuntary civil commitment of narcotics addicts in need of treatment. New York passed a similar law in 1962, as did Congress in 1966. The civil commitment laws served both humanitarian and social control purposes. These statutes permitted long-term institutionalization of addicts, typically as an adjunct to the criminal process but sometimes as a diversionary substitution. Since then, however, poor treatment success, high operational costs, frequent civil libertarian criticism, and more attractive community alternatives led to de-emphasis of the civil commitment programs.

On the international scale, a major new multi-national agreement was formulated. In 1961, after nearly two decades of negotiation, the international community agreed on a new narcotics control compact. The Single Convention on Narcotic Drugs limited the production, manufacture, import, export, trade, distribution, use, and possession of opiate, coca leaf, and cannabis drugs to medical purposes only. The Single Convention replaced the earlier international agreements, and the United States quickly approved the pact.

In 1962, the United States Supreme Court then re-entered the narcotics control arena with a landmark decision. In Robinson v. California, 370 U.S. 660, 8 L.Ed.2d 758, 82 S.Ct. 1417 (1962), the Supreme Court ruled that a California misdemeanor provision prohibiting the condition or status of addiction was unconstitutional. The Court defined narcotics addiction as an involuntarily contracted disease not subject to the criminal law and urged states to adopt involuntary addict commitment laws based on the mental health model. The Court said it was cruel and unusual punishment, and therefore against the 8th Amendment of the Constitution, to arrest an addict for being an addict. Six years later, the Powell v. Texas decision (392 U.S. 514, 20 L.Ed.2d

1254, 88 S.Ct. 2145 (1968)) narrowed the scope of the Robinson rule in refusing to invalidate public intoxication laws and explicitly disavowing some of the involuntary disease rhetoric of the Robinson decision. Yet, to this day, Robinson v. California remains a potential precedent for expanded judicial intrusion into drug control policies.

As noted earlier, the White House Conference on Narcotics and Drug Abuse supported a more balanced approach to addiction control. In 1966, Congress implemented the Conference recommendations and passed the Narcotic Addict Rehabilitation Act. This act permitted federal judges and prison officials to send narcotics addict probationers and inmates to the Lexington and Fort Worth treatment facilities as a condition of sentence. Release from the hospitals was followed by mandatory after-care supervision. The Act also permitted voluntary self-commitments by motivated addicts. As with the California and New York civil commitment programs, the Narcotic Addict Rehabilitation Act (NARA) program has been significantly restructured and de-emphasized.

New criminal laws regarding drugs also appeared in the 1960s. Depressant, stimulant, and hallucinogenic drugs were brought under federal control for the first time with the passage of the Drug Abuse Control Amendments of 1965. Possession, use, manufacture, and distribution of these substances were subjected to criminal control mechanisms. Nonetheless, the penalties established for violations involving these classes of drugs were less stringent than the comparable laws pertaining to narcotics.

Enactment of the Drug Abuse Control Amendments was a Congressional reaction to abundant evidence of rapidly increasing "soft" drug usage by American youth. Reports indicated that use of the specified drugs was pervasive, touching all strata of American society. Considering the extensive and varied nature of the abusing population, Congress opted for fairly mild actions, limiting possession for personal use to the misdemeanor level. Deterrence was intended, but Congress hoped to avoid criminalization and incarceration of such a large segment of the youthful population.

At the suggestion of the federal government, and utilizing the model promulgated by the Food and Drug Administration, the states adopted uniform legislation regulating the possession, use, manufacture, and distribution of depressant, stimulant, and hallucinogenic drugs. Again, the penalties for violation of these laws were less stringent than the penalties for similar offenses involving narcotic drugs. Generically, these laws became known as "dangerous drug laws," while the earlier state legislation (covering opiates, cocaine, and marijuana) continued to be referred to as "narcotics laws."

The final event of the 1960s was an administrative action by the President. The two major federal drug law enforcement agencies, the Bureau of Narcotics (Treasury Department) and the Bureau of Drug Abuse Control (Food and Drug Administration) were consolidated into a single agency, the Bureau of Narcotics and Dangerous Drugs

(BNDD). Situated within the Justice Department, the new agency was assigned substantial responsibility for the enforcement of federal drug laws. The reorganization was intended to centralize drug enforcement decision-making and to avoid the crippling jurisdictional disputes which had plagued prior federal agencies.

The 1960s witnessed rapid and major changes in American drug control policies. Public attention was dramatically turned to the drug abuse phenomenon in the early part of the decade when public health and law enforcement officials announced the onset of a previously unparalleled epidemic of heroin use. The attendant rise in street crime and social decay aroused the American public to demand action. Reports of widespread drug use among the military in Vietnam then stimulated decisive Congressional action.

§ 16.2.7 The 1970s

In 1970, Congress passed the Comprehensive Drug Abuse Prevention and Control Act, popularly known as the Controlled Substances Act. The existing scattered federal drug laws were repealed in favor of this unified act. All drugs subject to federal regulation were entitled "controlled substances" and subjected to increasing levels of control on the basis of abuse potential and lack of therapeutic usefulness. The act furnished the Attorney General and Secretary of Health, Education, and Welfare the flexibility to add new drugs to the "controlled substances" list, to modify the degree of regulation of drugs already classified, and to delete drugs from the list on the basis of new evidence pertaining to abuse capacity or medical usefulness. The formerly stringent, mandatory minimum penalties were substantially reduced while education, research, and rehabilitation projects were encouraged as adjuncts to enforcement. Modeled upon this federal legislation, a state-level Uniform Controlled Substances Act was drafted later that year and has been adopted by over forty states.

Two other benchmark pieces of drug abuse legislation were enacted in 1972. As a direct response to the rising heroin epidemic and the impending return of the Vietnam veterans, Congress and the President created the Special Action Office for Drug Abuse Prevention. The office was mandated to coordinate and strengthen federal drug abuse prevention efforts. Although the Special Action Office registered significant gains in achieving coordination of existing resources and in stimulating new programs, it was discontinued in June of 1975. The major functions of the office were later resumed by the National Institute on Drug Abuse (NIDA) situated within the Department of Health, Education, and Welfare.

Simultaneous with the creation of the Special Action Office and its emphasis on improved treatment and rehabilitation, Congress created the Office of Drug Abuse Law Enforcement (ODALE) to develop a fortified approach to drug law enforcement. During its brief but spirited tenure, the office focused its efforts upon high level intra-city trafficking with national and international enforcement responsibilities remaining under the jurisdiction of BNDD. Later, in 1973, some executive re-organization dismantled ODALE.

The Evolution of Drug Law

In the same year, at the request of the President and Congress, the United States State Department undertook a planned campaign to diminish Turkish opium production. Supported by an agreement of $35.7 million of aid from the United States as compensation for losses resulting from crop substitution, the Turkish government banned the cultivation of the poppy plant. Two years later, however, a newly formed Turkish government repealed the ban and permitted replanting of the opium poppy. Hence, the creation of BNDD in 1968 did not achieve its intended goal of centralizing and coordinating federal drug law enforcement resources. Jurisdictional overlap and role confusion were not eliminated by that reorganization. As a result, the President ordered a new executive reorganization in 1973 to achieve the original objective of increased effectiveness.

By executive order, in 1973, the drug law enforcement resources of the Bureau of Narcotics and Dangerous Drugs, the Office of Drug Abuse Law Enforcement, the Bureau of Customs, and the Office of National Narcotics Intelligence were consolidated into a single federal enforcement agency: the Drug Enforcement Administration (DEA). All of the functions performed by the predecessor agencies were integrated into the new umbrella agency.

Once established, the DEA played an increasingly crucial role in the coordination of federal drug law enforcement. During the 1970s a number of inter-agency efforts were launched. Among the coordination efforts undertaken by the DEA was the development of mechanisms to provide timely and accurate narcotics intelligence to drug law enforcement personnel at the federal, state, and local levels.

One result of this DEA effort was an amendment to the 1970 Controlled Substances Act. Congress passed the Narcotic Addict Treatment Act of 1974 to require the annual registration of practitioners dispensing narcotic drugs, including methadone for maintenance or detoxification purposes. This legislation, which imposed standards for the legal dispensation of drugs, was deemed necessary because of the increased diversion of methadone for illegal sale and use.

That year also saw the passage of the Alcohol and Drug Abuse Education Act Amendments. The act placed greater emphasis on the need for prevention and early intervention programs, recognizing the crucial role of family, peer group, school, church, and other community institutions in influencing young people's behavior.

Enacting the 1974 Alcohol and Drug Abuse Education Act Amendments alerted Congress to the fact that most of the previously adopted federal programs to reduce demand had been directed primarily at the person who was already in serious trouble with alcohol and/or drugs. The focus of the Drug Abuse Education Act of 1970 was significantly different in that it was directed toward those who had not yet experimented with drugs or those who had just begun to do so.

Five years later, the Drug Abuse Prevention, Treatment, and Rehabilitation Amendments of 1979 were enacted. The 1979 legislation au-

501

thorized the NIDA's state formula grants, special grants, and contract programs for drug education and prevention to remain in effect through September 30, 1981. It did so because it found that the growing extent of drug abuse indicated an urgent need for prevention and intervention programs designed to reach the general population.

In the early 1970s, as amphetamines became increasingly difficult to obtain, street suppliers found it necessary to defraud their customers with phony products. In the mid-1970s, the traffic in "phony amphetamines" became big business when the marketing operation turned to the "truck stop market." Business cards, catalogs, and local suppliers for these products sprang up all over.

The marketing venture in phony amphetamines was so successful that these entrepreneurs began looking for other markets. At first, their venture into advertising seemed restricted to handing out business cards and small cards containing pictures of their products. The suppliers seemed to concentrate their efforts on shopping centers, campuses, rock concerts, or other areas where young people might be found. The success of this effort and the lack of any enforcement against it eventually lead to a nationwide phony amphetamine campaign with full-page color ads in magazines and newspapers.

Due to the success of phony amphetamines, reports of deaths and injuries to several young people increased. Finally, in the late seventies and early eighties, state and federal authorities became alarmed and took action. The efforts of the federal government were unusually strong, coordinated, and effective on the targeted distributors.

At about the same time, states reacted with a variety of legislative efforts. Most states enacted legislation to severely restrict trafficking in counterfeit controlled substances. In the majority of states, it became a criminal offense to possess, sell, manufacture, or advertise counterfeit controlled substances.

As a result of historical circumstances, the decade of the 1970s was an important one in the evolution of the federal drug abuse effort. It began with a comprehensive restructuring of federal laws relating to drugs and included a major reorganization of federal drug law enforcement agencies in an effort to reduce inter-agency rivalries and to promote efficiency and leadership in the fight against drug trafficking. Equally important was the recognition that strategies to reduce the demand for drugs must be an essential component of the overall drug abuse policy and that the nation's drug abuse problem could not be regarded as a crisis susceptible to quick resolution. In addition, new laws were passed to respond to particular aspects of the drug problem, and new enforcement approaches were attempted in an effort to disrupt drug trafficking more effectively.

Unfortunately, some disagreements over certain fundamental issues remained unresolved at the end of the 1970s. Among these were the role of the federal government in drug policy negotiations and the appropriate balance of strategies to reduce supply and demand. An even more disappointing fact of this decade was that, despite legislation, massive reorganizations, new enforcement techniques, and necessary attitudinal changes, the problems of drug abuse and trafficking continued on an increasingly widespread scale.

§ 16.2.8 The 1980s

On January 21, 1982, in a major policy shift, the FBI was given concurrent jurisdiction with the DEA for drug law enforcement and investigation. In addition, the Administrator of the DEA was required to report to the Director of the FBI, who was given the responsibility of supervising general drug law enforcement efforts and policies.

In giving the FBI concurrent jurisdiction for enforcement of U.S. drug laws, the Attorney General followed the recommendation of a committee that he had established to study the need for increased coordination of the DEA and the FBI in the drug field. Although FBI expertise in organized crime and financial investigations would be available in drug enforcement work as a result of concurrent jurisdiction, the DEA would continue to function as a "single-mission narcotics enforcement agency" that would give the drug problem the kind of focus it needs.

Several other important legislative initiatives were adopted in the 1980s. For example, the Department of Defense Authorization Act of 1982 contained a provision entitled, "Military Cooperation With Civilian Law Enforcement Officials," which was intended to codify the practices of cooperation that had developed between military and civilian law enforcement authorities. The act was also designed to improve the level of cooperation by delineating precisely that assistance which military commanders could provide and by permitting military personnel to operate military equipment that had been lent to civilian drug enforcement agencies. This legislation was deemed necessary for the following reasons:

The rising tide of drugs being smuggled into the United States by land, sea, and air presents a grave threat to all Americans. Only through the dedicated work of all of federal, state, and local law enforcement agencies can we begin to stem this tide. In fighting this battle, it is important to maximize the degree of cooperation between the military and civilian law enforcement. At the same time, we must recognize the need to maintain the traditional balance of authority between civilians and the military.

The most important and innovative part of this legislation was section 374, which permitted the Secretary of Defense to assign Department personnel to operate and maintain military equipment that had been made available to an agency with jurisdiction to enforce the Controlled Substances Act. This relatively simple change greatly increased the potential interdiction capability of federal drug law enforcement agencies.

The year 1984 was a prolific one for legislation dealing with discrete areas in drug law enforcement. The Controlled Substance Registrant

Protection Act of 1984 made it illegal, among other things, to steal any quantity of a controlled substance from a registrant. In addition, Congress passed the Aviation Drug-Trafficking Control Act, which among other things, requires the Administrator of the FAA to revoke the airman certificates and aircraft registrations of those convicted of violating any federal or state law relating to controlled substances, except where the violations involved minor possession offenses.

Although the Controlled Substance Registrant Protection Act of 1984 and the Aviation Drug-Trafficking Control Act were necessary laws, by far the most important drug law enforcement measures passed in 1984 were contained in several provisions of the Comprehensive Crime Control Act of 1984. The act included:

1. Bail Reform Act of 1984. This act comprises many sections, but the most important and most controversial stipulated that when a person charged with an offense appears before a judicial officer, the judicial officer must order that, pending trial, the accused be either released on personal recognizance or upon execution of an unsecured appearance bond; released upon certain listed conditions; temporarily detained to permit exclusion or deportation if not a U.S. citizen or lawful permanent resident; temporarily detained to permit revocation of a prior conditional release; or detained.

2. Comprehensive Forfeiture Act of 1984. This legislation made extensive revisions to federal, civil, and criminal forfeiture laws and procedures, which target the assets of racketeering and drug trafficking organizations. With respect to the Racketeer Influenced and Corrupt Organizations Act, the 1984 Comprehensive Forfeiture Act did several things, including confirming the Supreme Court's decision in Russello v. United States, 464 U.S. 16, 78 L.Ed.2d 17, 104 S.Ct. 296 (1983) that a defendant's ill-gotten profits from racketeering were forfeitable.

3. Controlled Substances Penalties Act of 1984. In essence, this legislation enhanced the penalties for violations of the Controlled Substances Act.

4. Dangerous Drug Diversion Control Act of 1984. This legislation represented the first major updating of the regulatory provisions of the Controlled Substances Act and the Controlled Substances Import and Export Act since their enactment in 1970.

5. Currency and Foreign Transactions Reporting Act Amendments. Without the means to launder money, thereby making cash generated by a criminal enterprise appear to come from a legitimate source, organized crime could not flourish as it now does. The 1984 amendments of the Currency and Foreign Transactions Reporting Act were designed to fine tune the active currency reporting laws in effect at that time.

The Evolution of Drug Law

As a whole, the Comprehensive Crime Control Act of 1984 was intended to, and did in fact, provide federal law enforcement agents with better tools for combating drug traffickers.

§ 16.2.8(a)   Controlled Substance Analog Enforcement Act of 1985

This act was intended to help law enforcement curb the fabrication of drugs that are chemically similar but not identical to controlled substances (also known as drug analogs and designer drugs. The act gives federal drug enforcement agents authority to arrest analog manufacturers and dealers before the new substances are federally controlled.

§ 16.2.8(b)   The Drug-Free American—October 1986

Some of the highlights of this act included the following:

—Grants to the states for prevention, treatment, and rehabilitation.

—Development of treatment evaluation programs.

—The Alcohol, Drug Abuse, and Mental Health Administration (ADAMHA) will consolidate the prevention activities of the Drug Abuse and Alcohol Institutes under an Office of Drug Abuse Prevention which will include the clearinghouses of both institutes to disseminate information on the health hazards of alcohol and drugs.

—The desirability of health warning labels on beverage containers is to be studied.

—The entertainment and media industries are requested to refrain from producing materials that in any way glamorize the use of illegal drugs and alcohol. In fact, they should develop materials that discourage drug and alcohol abuse.

—A survey to be conducted by the National Academy of Sciences to study and report on the best available treatment for alcoholism.

—A large-scale, school-based drug abuse education and prevention program will be funded. Curriculum development, teacher training, family participation and specially designed programs for high-risk youth and athletes are planned. Models to prevent youth and child drug use will be created with demonstration grants. The overall goal is drug-free schools.

—The severe problem of drug and alcohol abuse, especially among Native American adolescents and adults, is approached through additional education, prevention, and treatment initiatives.

—The Secretary of Labor will produce a study of the nature and effects of drugs in the workplace as well as a program to deal with them.

—Additional funds will be appropriated for research.

—Government employees and corporate supervisors will be educated and trained in identifying alcohol and drug abuse on the job. The Employee Assistance Program will be mandated. A study by the Institute of Medicine will examine the extent and adequacy of insurance coverage for substance abuse treatment.

—A media commission on alcohol and drug abuse prevention is designed to study the public information programs already in existence. It will also coordinate the voluntary donation of resources from the media, sports, and business sectors. The de-glamorization of alcohol and drugs in the audiovisual media is reemphasized.

§ 16.2.8(c) The Anti-Drug Abuse Act of 1988

Some of the provisions of the Anti-Drug Abuse Act of 1988 are as follows:

—Drug users can lose public housing and a vast array of other federal benefits.

—Government contractors may lose contracts unless they provide for a drug-free workplace.

—A high priority is placed on preventing AIDS by providing treatment for IV drug users. Whenever feasible, treatment on demand (within 7 days) is the goal.

—The act includes grants and contracts to establish employee assistance programs (EAPS).

—A program of assistance to state and local narcotics control agencies has been set up through the Bureau of Justice Assistance in the Department of Justice.

—There is a provision for developing a training program through the National Institute of Corrections that will assist in developing and improving rehabilitation programs for criminals convicted of drug-related crimes.

§ 16.2.8(d) Comprehensive Crime Control Act of 1989

Listed below are the four principles which provide the foundation of this anti-crime act:

1. A primary purpose of government is to protect citizens and their property. Americans deserve to live in a society in which they are safe and feel secure.

2. Those who commit violent criminal offenses should, and must, be held accountable for their actions.

3. Our criminal justice system must have as its objective the swift and certain apprehension, prosecution, and incarceration of those who break the law.

4. Success in accomplishing our criminal justice system goals require a sustained, cooperative effort by federal, state and local law enforcement authorities.

The Comprehensive Crime Control Act of 1989 is a four-part act designed to strengthen current laws, enhance enforcement and apprehension of criminals, facilitate prosecutions, and expand federal prison capacity. In 1989, it responded, in part, to the increasing need for restrictions against widespread drug trafficking.

Strengthening Current Laws

To ensure that those who commit violent criminal offenses are held fully accountable for their actions, it is essential to eliminate certain gaps in existing laws and to strengthen some current statutes.

Laws will be strengthened by enhancing penalties for firearms violations, restricting plea bargaining, enacting death penalty procedures, restricting imported weapons, preventing circumvention of imported laws, restricting gun clips and magazines, limiting access to weapons by criminals, and making drug testing a condition of parole/probation release.

Augmenting Enforcement

A primary purpose of government is to protect citizens and their property. This protection requires the sustained cooperative commitment of federal, state, and local law enforcement officials. Apprehending violent offenders requires increased enforcement personnel, improved cooperation among law enforcement authorities, and a cessation of evidence exclusion due to supposed legal technicalities.

This goal of increased protection is accomplished in the Comprehensive Crime Control Act of 1989 by providing additional ATF (Bureau of Alcohol, Tobacco and Firearms) agents, U.S. Marshals, and FBI agents as well as developing coordinated task forces. In addition, the act establishes a "good faith" exemption to the exclusionary rule regarding evidence.

Enhancing Prosecution

In order to assure that criminals are held accountable for their offenses, certainty of prosecution must accompany severity of punishment. Federal, state, and local authorities must expand and coordinate their prosecutorial efforts. This goal is accomplished in the act by additional assistant U.S. Attorneys, Criminal Division Attorneys, additional housing for unsentenced prisoners, additional money to the courts to process criminals, and the reform of habeas corpus.

Expanding Prison Capacity

Prison overcrowding remains a national problem. The most acute problem is at the federal level. At both the federal and state levels, prison overcrowding continues to affect sentencing. At the state and local levels, overcrowding is often responsible for the early release of convicted criminals.

The goal of reducing prison overcrowding is accomplished in the Comprehensive Crime Control Act by expanding federal prison facilities, converting unused federal properties, deporting criminal aliens, encouraging state prison construction, and reviewing court-ordered prison cops.

§ 16.2.8(e) Drug Paraphernalia Laws

Drug paraphernalia is any legitimate equipment, product, or material that is modified for making, using, or concealing illegal drugs such as cocaine, heroin, marijuana, and methamphetamine. Drug paraphernalia generally falls into two categories:

—User-specific products
—Dealer-specific products

User-specific products are marketed to drug users to assist them in taking or concealing illegal drugs. These products include certain pipes, smoking masks, bongs, cocaine freebase kits, marijuana grow kits, roach clips, and items such as hollowed-out cosmetic cases or fake pagers used to conceal illegal drugs.

Dealer-specific products are used by drug traffickers for preparing illegal drugs for distribution at the street level. Items such as scales, vials, and baggies fall into this category. Drug paraphernalia does not include any items traditionally used with tobacco, like pipes and rolling papers.

§ 16.2.8(f) Drug Paraphernalia Sales

With the rise of the drug culture in the United States in the 1960s and 1970s, the country began to see the appearance of "head shops," which were stores that sold a wide range of drug paraphernalia. While some of the paraphernalia was crude and homemade, much was being commercially manufactured to cater to a fast-growing market. Enterprising individuals even sold items openly in the street, until anti-paraphernalia laws in the 1980s eventually ended such blatant sales.

Today, law enforcement faces another challenge. With the advent of the Internet, criminals have greatly expanded their illicit sales to a worldwide market for drug paraphernalia. For example, in a recent law enforcement effort, Operation Pipedreams, the 18 companies targeted accounted for more than a quarter of a billion dollars in retail drug paraphernalia sales annually. Typically, such illicit businesses operate retail stores as well as websites, posing as retailers of legitimate tobacco accessories, when in reality the products are intended for the illegal drug trade.

The U.S. Supreme Court in *Posters 'N' Things, Ltd. v. U.S.*, 511 U.S. 513, 128 L.Ed.2d 539, 114 S.Ct. 1747 (1994) held that the Mail Order Drug Paraphernalia Act, 21 USC 863, was constitutional. This act makes it unlawful to sell or offer for sale listed drug paraphernalia, or to use the mails or any other facility in interstate commerce to transport listed drug paraphernalia. 21 USC 863, Posters 'N' Things, Ltd. v. U.S., supra.

Under the Federal Drug Paraphernalia Statute, which is part of the Controlled Substances Act (CSA), it is illegal to possess, sell, transport, import, or export drug paraphernalia as defined. The law gives specific guidance on determining what constitutes drug paraphernalia. Many states have also enacted their own laws prohibiting drug paraphernalia.

§ 16.2.9 Drug Legislation of the 1990s
§ 16.2.9(a)　The Crime Control Act of 1990
The Crime Control Act of 1990 contained the following provisions relating to drug laws:

Drugs: Added 12 new chemicals to the list of precursor chemicals; enhanced the penalties for offenses involving "ice" (methamphetamine) and strengthened the drug paraphernalia statute.

Asset forfeiture: Improved the government's ability to dispose of real estate and other assets seized from drug traffickers.

Anabolic steroids: Placed anabolic steroids on Schedule III of the Controlled Substances Act and provided criminal penalties for the possession and distribution of these dangerous drugs.

Money laundering: Made essential improvements in the federal money-laundering statutes; included a provision to improve cooperation with foreign governments when prosecuting money-laundering cases.

Firearms: Made needed changes in several firearms statutes which had been requested by the DEA.

"Rural drug initiative": Funded increased drug law enforcement efforts by local police and prosecutors in rural states.

Drug programs: Increased funding for DARE—Drug Abuse Resistance Education—and other successful drug education programs.

"Drug-free zones": Extended the area of drug-free zones around public playgrounds.

§ 16.2.9(b)　International Narcotics Control Act of 1992
The International Narcotics Act of 1992 provided for continuing funds for international narcotics control and provided for increased reporting on money laundering and precursor chemicals. Requirements of bilateral narcotics agreements between the United States and foreign countries were listed. Bilateral assistance and loans or other utilization of funds of multilateral development banks could be withheld if a country designated as a major illicit drug producing or drug transit country is determined not to be cooperating in achieving the objectives of the

bilateral agreement. The agreement specified that the foreign country agrees to show efforts to (A) reduce drug production, drug consumption, and drug trafficking within its territory, including activities to address illicit crop eradication and crop substitution; (B) increase drug interdiction and enforcement; (C) increase drug treatment; (D) increase the identification of and elimination of illicit drug laboratories; (E) increase the identification of, and elimination of trafficking in, essential precursor chemicals for use in the illicit production of narcotic and psychotropic drugs and other controlled substances; (F) increase cooperation with United States drug enforcement officials; and (G) where applicable, increase participation in extradition treaties, mutual legal assistance provisions directed at money laundering, sharing of evidence, and other initiatives for cooperative drug enforcement.

§ 16.2.9(c)   The Latin-American Drug Conference of 1992

On February 28, 1992, President Bush and six Latin-American leaders ended a two-day conference on the drug problem with promises to broaden the War on Drugs. The President hosted the conference in San Antonio, Texas; it was attended by the Presidents of Colombia, Bolivia, Peru, Ecuador, and Mexico, as well as a delegation from Venezuela.

At a press conference, President Bush stated that the seven leaders "established an aggressive agenda for the rest of the century" for battling drugs.

The top 9 priorities of the drug-fighting strategy included:

1.   Reducing the demand for drugs.

2.   Continuing economic reforms, economic assistance, trade and investment.

3.   Improving eradication, interdiction, arms control, chemical controls, and asset seizure.

4.   Concentrating on judicial system reforms.

5.   Coordinating strategies to understand the needs of other countries.

6.   Helping Mexico and Colombia stop heroin production.

7.   Educating the media and public about progress in the War on Drugs.

8.   Remembering that our efforts transcend borders.

9.   Ensuring that the anti-drug effort conforms to democratic principles.

This was the second drug summit in which the President of the United States met with Latin American leaders to discuss means of counteracting international drug trafficking. The first was held in 1990 in Colombia where Bush met with the leaders of the Andean nations of Colombia, Bolivia, and Peru. The recent San Antonio conference added Mexico, Ecuador and Venezuela, which have seen increasing involvement in illegal drug trafficking as the Andean nations crack down.

Initiatives now include new legal efforts to curb money laundering, international control on the sale of chemicals used to manufacture cocaine, and missions to Canada, Japan and Europe to involve the rest of the industrial world in the anti-drug battle. The leaders of Mexico, Colombia and Venezuela—the more industrialized Latin American nations at the meeting—generally called for new measures to increase their countries' (legal) exports to the United States, thereby creating jobs and bolstering their economies.

The leaders of two less-developed South American nations, Peru and Ecuador, pressed the conference participants for outright grants to create new industries and agricultural markets in their countries; these would replace those industries and markets now consumed by the drug trade. Similarly, the Bolivian leader urged Bush to spur United States business investment in the Bolivian economy to create new jobs. In essence, the aim of all six was to provide new employment for thousands of peasants who now grow coca leaf or opium poppies or otherwise earn their livelihood in the drug trade.

At the conclusion of the conference, President Bush announced that the U.S. had given 12 UH-IH Huey helicopters, a total value of $20 million, to Mexico for interdiction efforts.

§ 16.2.9(d)   Domestic Chemical Diversion Control Act of 1993

The Domestic Chemical Diversion Control Act of 1993 amended the Controlled Substances Act and the Controlled Substances Import and Export Act with respect to certain listed chemicals used in the illicit production of controlled substances such as methcathinone and methamphetamine. The Drug Enforcement Administration will require that manufacturers of products that contain these chemicals maintain transaction records. The regulation of ephedrine, an over-the-counter drug which is used in the manufacture of methamphetamine, was the primary concern in enacting this legislation.

§ 16.2.9(e)   Violent Crime Control and Law Enforcement Act of 1994.

The Violent Crime Control and Law Enforcement Act of 1994 included many drug-related provisions as follows:

—Developing alternative methods of punishment for young offenders, including innovative methods that address the problems of young offenders convicted of serious substance abuse, including alcohol abuse.

—Establishing a program of drug testing of federal offenders on post-conviction release.

Chapter 16

—Establishing residential substance abuse treatment and arrangements for aftercare upon release from custody for eligible prisoners in federal and state prisons.

—Establishing "drug courts" which provide programs that involve continuing judicial supervision over offenders with substance abuse problems who are not violent offenders.

—Specialized training in the investigation of drug trafficking and related crimes for officers from rural agencies.

—Makes unlawful any written advertisement (in newspapers, magazines, catalogs, etc.) with purpose of seeking or offering illegally to receive, buy, or distribute a Schedule I controlled substance.

—The "Drive-By Shooting Prevention Act," which provides that the death penalty may be imposed if a person, in furtherance or to escape detection of a major drug offense, fires a weapon into a group of 2 or more persons with intent to intimidate, harass, injure, or maim, and kills any person.

—The death penalty may be imposed for gun murders during federal crimes of violence and drug trafficking crimes.

—"Three strikes you're out"—Mandatory life imprisonment for a person convicted of a serious violent felony who also has two previous serious violent felony convictions or one or more serious violent felonies and one or more serious drug offenses. A "serious drug offense" means an offense that is punishable under sections 841(b)(1)(A), 848, or 960(b)(1)(A) of Title 21 of U.S. Code or an offense under State law that, had the offense been prosecuted in a federal court, would have been punishable under those sections.

—Increased penalties for drug trafficking in prisons, illegal drug use in prisons, and smuggling drugs into prisons.

—Increased penalties for drug dealing in "drug-free zones", including schools, public playgrounds and swimming pools, etc., and an area surrounding them (see Title 21, USC section 860).

—The Drunk Driving Child Protection Act, which provides for an additional term of imprisonment for an offense for which any term of imprisonment is provided when such offense is committed by a person operating a motor vehicle under the influence of a drug or alcohol if a minor was present in the vehicle when the offense was committed.

—Enhanced penalties for use of a semiautomatic firearm during a crime of violence or a drug trafficking crime.

—Enhanced penalties for smuggling firearms in aid of drug trafficking.

—Enhanced penalties for possession of firearms by violent felons and serious drug offenders.

—Increased penalties for employing children to distribute drugs near schools and playgrounds.

—Increased penalties for drug trafficking near public housing.

—The Drug Free Truck Stop Act, which provides increased penalties for distributing or possessing with intent to distribute a controlled substance in or on, or within 1,000 feet of, a truck stop or safety rest area.

§ 16.2.9(f)   Comprehensive Methamphetamine Control Act of 1996

The Comprehensive Methamphetamine Control Act of 1996 increased penalties for the manufacture, distribution, possession, or trafficking in methamphetamine and precursor chemicals. The act contains provisions for the following:

—Penalties for manufacture of listed chemicals outside the United States with intent to import them into the United States.

—Increased penalties for manufacture and possession of equipment used to make controlled substances.

—Enhanced penalties for offenses involving list I chemicals.

—Enhanced penalties for dangerous handling of controlled substances.

—Regulations for limiting retail and mail order sales of over-the-counter drugs which contain ephedrine, pseudoephedrine, and phenylpropanolamine by establishing threshold quantities for products in a single transaction. Pseudoephedrine and ephedrine are used to manufacture methamphetamine. Phenylpropanolamine is used to produce amphetamine.

§ 16.2.9(g)   Drug-Induced-Rape Prevention and Punishment Act of 1996

The Drug-Induced-Rape Prevention and Punishment Act of 1996 provides for increased penalties for the use of controlled substances to sedate people, usually women, for the purpose of committing a violent crime, usually rape. In particular, additional penalties are provided relating to flunitrazepam, brand name Rohypnol, often referred to as "roofies" or the "date rape drug." Penalties for distribution and for simple possession of flunitrazepam as well as import and export of the drug are provided. A study was directed to be made on rescheduling flunitrazepam as a Schedule I controlled substance.

§ 16.2.9(h)   The Higher Education Amendments of 1998

The Higher Education Amendments of 1998 include a new student eligibility provision. It provides that a student is ineligible for federal student aid if convicted, under federal or state law, or any offense involving the possession or sale of a controlled substance (generally meaning illegal drugs). The period of ineligibility begins on the date of conviction and lasts until the end of a statutorily specified period. The student may regain eligibility early by completing a drug rehabilitation program or if the conviction is overturned.

§ 16.2.10   Drug Legislation: 2000s
§ 16.2.10(a) USA PATRIOT Act

The Uniting and Strengthening America by Providing Appropriate Tools Required to Intercept and Obstruct Terrorism Act of 2001 (USA PATRIOT Act, H.R. 3162, S. 1510, Public Law 107-56) is a United States legislative law, enacted in response to the September 11, 2001, terrorist attacks. This law provides for indefinite imprisonment without trial of non-U.S. citizens whom the Attorney General has determined to be a threat to national security. The government is not required to provide detainees with counsel, nor is it required to make any announcement or statement regarding the arrest. The law allows a wiretap to be issued against an individual instead of a specific telephone number. It permits law enforcement agencies to obtain a warrant and search a residence without immediately informing the occupants, if the Attorney General has determined this to be an issue of national security. The act also allows intelligence gathering at religious events. With few exceptions, provisions of the act are due to expire on December 31, 2005.

The act is 342 pages long and amends over fifteen statutes. The following summarizes the new powers granted by the law:

Sec. 104: Allows the Department of Defense to share information with the Department of Justice during "emergency situations" that involve "weapons of mass destruction."

Sec. 106: Allows the President of the United States to seize property belonging to foreign nationals connected with terrorism. If the seizure is based on classified evidence, then the judge reviewing the case cannot share that evidence with the defense attorneys.

Sec. 203: Allows information collected by the police or presented to a federal grand jury to be shared with intelligence agencies. This information sharing is limited to evidence of terrorist activities. (Section 203(a) & (b) doesn't sunset/expire.)

Sec. 206: Allows a wiretap to be granted against an individual, instead of a particular phone. Previously, for example, if a person had a cell phone, a home phone, and an office phone, the government had to obtain separate warrants on each.

Sec. 207: Increases the duration of a wiretap "permitted for non-U.S. persons who are agents of a foreign power."

Sec. 208: Increases (from seven to eleven) the number of district court judges designated to hear applications for and grant orders approving electronic surveillance. (Section 208 doesn't sunset/expire.)

Sec. 209: Permits the seizure of voice-mail messages under a warrant.

Sec. 213: Allows FBI agents to conduct a search of a business or a place without notifying the owner that the search has been conducted until later. The agents still need a warrant, and only a federal district court judge can issue this type of warrant. Further, this type of warrant may only be issued if notifying the owner of the search would result in "adverse consequences." (Section 213 doesn't sunset/expire.)

Sec. 216: "PEN/Trap Authority." Allows law enforcement in ordinary criminal cases to get a warrant to track which websites a person visits and collect general information about the emails a person sends and receives. Law enforcement doesn't have to prove the need; the judge only has to determine that law enforcement has "certified" that this relates to an ongoing investigation. In other words, the judge cannot reject an application based on the merits. Furthermore, people not named in the warrant can be subject to the warrant if law enforcement "certifies" that the warrant was meant to apply to those unnamed people. (Section 216 doesn't sunset/expire.)

Sec. 217: Allows the government to intercept the electronic communication of a computer trespasser, i.e., a hacker, without a court order in certain circumstances if the owner of the hacked computer consents.

Sec. 402: Triples the number of Border Patrol, Customs Service, and INS personnel stationed along the U.S. borders.

Sec. 411: Expands the definition of a terrorist for the purpose of the act. Before passage, only members of the groups designated as terrorist organizations by the State Department could be denied entry to or deported from the United States. The law extends those actions to any foreigner who publicly endorses terrorist activity, belongs to a group that does, or provides support to a group that does. The definition of "terrorist activity" is extended to include any foreigner who uses "dangerous devices" or raises money for a terrorist group, if that person knows or reasonably should have known that the group is engaged in terrorism.

Sec. 412: Extends the power of the Attorney General to detain aliens. The Attorney General can order the detention of any aliens if he certifies that he has "reasonable grounds to believe" involvement in terrorism or activity that poses a danger to national security. He does not need to explain his reasoning or show evidence. Criminal or immigration violation charges have to be brought against such people within seven days, but they can be held indefinitely. However, they retain their right to petition the U.S. Supreme Court, the U.S. Court of Appeals for the District of Columbia, or any district court with jurisdiction to entertain a habeas corpus petition.

Chapter 16

Sec. 416: Directs the Attorney General to implement fully and expand the foreign student monitoring program to include other approved educational institutions like air flight, language training, or vocational schools.

Sec. 503: Requires DNA samples of convicted terrorists to be collected and added to a DNA database of violent convicts.

Sec. 814: Allows wiretaps for suspected violations of the Computer Fraud and Abuse Act, including anyone suspected of "exceeding the authority" of a computer used in interstate commerce, causing over $5000 worth of combined damage.

There has been strong criticism of the act on the grounds that parts of it violate the Constitution and endanger civil liberties. The American Civil Liberties Union (ACLU) alleges that its search and detention provisions violate the Fourth Amendment. Some say that the act's secret warrants resemble the general warrants which were one reason the colonists fought the American Revolutionary War.

Critics also say the law was passed without serious review in a climate of fear, and that it represents a reactionary agenda that has little to do with the 9/11 attacks. They note that there were unsuccessful attempts to pass similar laws, such as the Methamphetamine Anti-Proliferation Act of 2000, long before 9/11.

Supporters of the law argue that terrorist acts may result in the loss of thousands or millions of lives, so waiting until after the fact to hunt the perpetrators down would be a deadly mistake. They admit that the law may result in some rights abuses, but argue that the most basic civil right is the right to live without perpetual fear. They further argue that, unless the Supreme Court rules otherwise, the law is constitutional. However, since the Supreme Court does not seek out laws to countermand, the constitutionality of the Patriot Act must remain a question until someone brings the dispute before the court.

§ 16.3   CRIMINAL JURISDICTION

Federal expansion of criminal jurisdiction, while not specifically preempting state laws, diminishes the role of state legislatures by permitting federal and state prosecutors to circumvent state law. The choice to prosecute in federal court based upon federal penalties entails a choice to bypass state legislative responsibility. Federalizing state criminal offenses should be avoided because federalism is weakened and because the role of federal courts as court of limited jurisdiction is thereby undermined. Specific crimes may be appropriate for federal action if a systemic failure makes state action impossible or ineffective; such crimes may include those that have complex international or interstate implications, relate to the protection of civil rights, or where conflicts prevent effective state or local prosecution. Inadequacy of state resources is not sufficient reason for federal takeover of criminal jurisdiction (National Conference of State Legislatures).

§ 16.3.1 Police Powers of the Federal Government and State Government

An example of the police powers of the federal government is the federal and state regulation of the sale and possession of alcoholic beverages, tobacco products, and a wide range of other "controlled substances." The distinctive history of Prohibition, repealed by the Twenty-First Amendment to the U.S. Constitution, gives particular complexity to the mix of federal and state law governing alcohol.

Absent any specific regulation, these substances are treated like all other forms of personal property. However, the general rights of property are subject to so-called "police power" regulations of the state, local, and federal governments.

The regulation of alcohol is generally focused on "intoxicating beverages" with the exact definition of "intoxicating" varying from statute to statute. In many jurisdictions, it has been held that the list of liquors subject to regulatory or prohibitive enactments, particularly when such a list is followed by an expression akin to "or other intoxicating liquors" must be intoxicating in fact. Many statutes either refer to "intoxicating liquors" generally, or prescribe an alcoholic percentage cutoff. In Mississippi, it has been held that the prohibition of the sale of alcoholic liquor does not apply to a beverage containing less that 2/10ths of 1% of alcohol.

The police powers of the federal government are limited to regulating matters which are connected with one of the powers expressly granted to the government by the U.S. Constitution and which do not infringe on the police powers of the states. This means that the federal government lacks the power to regulate liquor sales by one citizen to another within the territorial limits of a given state or to prescribe liquor-related business within any state. Because of the commerce clause, however, the federal government can and does regulate the importation and interstate transportation of intoxicating liquors—see the Federal Alcohol Administration Act of 1935, 27 USC §§ 201 et seq. The federal government also has the power to regulate liquor sales in D.C. and where it has exclusive authority, such as on government-owned military installations, Indian reservations, and with Indian tribes. In all other situations, the states' police power controls alcoholic beverage law. The federal government has, however, used financial incentives built into its funding of highways to establish a national minimum drinking age. See 23 USC §158.

§ 16.4 THE PRINCIPLE OF THE NATIONAL DRUG-CONTROL STRATEGY

The fundamental principle of the national drug control strategy is to reduce drug use through a mix of supply and demand policies and programs. This strategy recognizes the key roles of federal, state and local governments, the private sector, as well as communities and individuals across the nation. The strategy calls for applying pressure across all fronts of the drug war simultaneously, recognizing that prevention is the only answer in the long run, but that in the short run increased interdiction, international cooperation, and law enforcement efforts are necessary. The strategy also acknowledges the need for adequate medical treatment of those currently abusing drugs.

The National Drug Control Strategy declares that, as a nation, we must:

—Establish meaningful and effective programs to prevent people from using drugs in the first place.

—Provide effective treatment for those who need to and can benefit from it.

—Hold users accountable for their actions and thereby deter others from using drugs.

—Target and dismantle drug trafficking organizations.

—Prosecute drug dealers and traffickers.

—Punish those convicted of drug crimes.

—Disrupt the flow of drugs, related chemicals, and drug money.

—Engage other nations in efforts to reduce the growth, production, and distribution of drugs.

—Support basic and applied research, medicine, and technology.

—Improve our intelligence capabilities in order to attack drug trafficking organizations.

§ 16.4.1 Limitations of Tactics Affecting Supply

Traditionally, efforts to reduce the trafficking and abuse of illicit drugs in this country have been based on the theory that significant reductions of drug supplies would lead to equal reductions in drug-related problems. While this seems plausible, a review of the 75-year history of these efforts reveals that they have not reduced social, economic, or criminal problems related to drugs. Despite continuing expressions of sincere determination, America's war on drugs seems nowhere near complete success. Now more than ever, drugs present problems of vast proportions.

This critique does not suggest that efforts to reduce supply—such as crop eradication, border interdiction, and prosecution—have failed. On the contrary, these efforts have achieved a measure of success. Crop eradication programs were significantly expanded in Colombia, where most of the world's cocaine is processed and nearly one-half of the marijuana consumed in the United States is grown. Moreover, indictments and convictions of some of the world's most notorious traffickers have been obtained in recent years.

The Evolution of Drug Law

Despite these efforts, however, American consumption of cocaine has continued. Cocaine, heroin, amphetamine, and methamphetamine-related deaths have increased. Likewise, cocaine, PCP, and methamphetamine-related emergency room visits have multiplied. In short, strategies to reduce supply are "working" by some standards, but only to a limited degree.

The effectiveness of these tactics is limited by several inherent factors. One is the fact that source country crop eradication or substitution efforts often fail in countries whose governments lack the resolve or power to effectuate these programs. The constantly changing patterns of drug trafficking compound the problem. Interdiction of drugs is extremely difficult because of the vastness of U.S. borders, the constantly changing nature of drug smuggling methods and routes, and the ease with which most drugs, particularly cocaine and heroin, are concealed. For example, five kilograms of heroin valued at more than one million dollars on the wholesale market, can fit into a shoe box. Furthermore, interdiction does not reach many of the most widely abused dangerous drugs, such as PCP and methamphetamine, which are produced in domestic clandestine laboratories. In view of these limited successes, it might be argued that the real problem lies in the overwhelming and continuing demand for illicit drugs among Americans. Millions of people want illicit drugs and are willing to violate the law, spend billions of dollars, and in many cases, risk their lives to obtain them.

§ 16.4.1(a)   Supply Versus Demand

Although the supply of drugs and the demand for drugs have often been considered separate issues, by both the public and private sectors, they are in fact inseparable parts of a single problem. The success of supply efforts are related to commitments made to reduce the demand for drugs through drug abuse education, treatment, research, vigorous enforcement of drug abuse laws, and effective sentencing. Drug supply and demand operate in an interrelated and dynamic manner. The strategies employed to limit each should be jointly undertaken.

The national fight against illicit drugs relies on two fundamental strategies: organized crime policy and drug abuse policy. Organized crime policy targets specific criminal groups and seeks to destroy those already in existence and prevent the emergence of new ones. This effort focuses on reducing supply. In contrast, drug abuse policy attempts to reduce drug use and its associated adverse effects. This effort is directed toward reducing the demand for drugs. Theoretically, organized crime policy and drug abuse policy can conflict. However, reducing the demand for drugs advances the goals of both organized crime policy and drug abuse policy. A significantly smaller drug market (which should result from a substantially reduced demand for drugs) would attack organized crime groups by limiting the huge profits currently available in drug trafficking. Simultaneously, this effort on the demand side of the equation should reduce the number of drug users, the goal of drug abuse policy.

§ 16.4.1(b)   Tactics to Reduce Demand

More successful tactics to reduce demand may in the long-run decrease the need for current high levels of funding for approaches to reduce supply. A significant reduction in the demand for drugs as a complement to aggressive enforcement efforts is likely to make drug trafficking less lucrative for organized crime and thus prompt many organized crime groups to drop out of the drug business.

Skeptics have argued that past tactics to reduce demand have not been successful. However, the history of drug abuse prevention and treatment programs has been relatively short. It was not until the upsurge of drug use in the 1960s that these programs developed. Some early prevention approaches were ill-conceived. For example, they often presented information about drugs without persuasive arguments to deter their use, and other programs used exaggerated information (Polich). Such programs have been criticized for unintentionally encouraging experimentation with drugs or squandering the credibility of anti-drug information.

The most effective drug abuse education and prevention programs focus on the psychological and sociological factors that contribute to the onset of drug use (Shore). Many of these programs are based on the anti-smoking campaigns of the 1970s and 1980s because it has been found that many of the same factors which lead to cigarette smoking also contribute to drug use. These efforts employ the "social pressures model" of drug prevention to teach adolescents how to resist peer and other social pressures to smoke cigarettes and to change attitudes about smoking. Today these efforts are considered a success. After reviewing several studies of anti-smoking campaigns, the Rand Corporation has concluded that these studies provide cumulative evidence that programs based on the social pressures model help reduce the smoking onset rate among adolescents.

Thus, drug education programs must be continually evaluated and improved to keep pace with changing drug abuse patterns. Prevention efforts targeted at adolescents and teenagers may significantly reduce the overall demand for drugs.

In a model program, the National Institute on Drug Abuse (NIDA) used the strategy of the anti-smoking campaigns of the late 1970s, which many feel were effective, to develop its "Just Say No" campaign against drug use. The "Just Say No" campaign recognizes and focuses on the impact of social pressure. NIDA seeks to show adolescents through a music video, television commercials, and other media that they can turn down drugs by simply saying "no" to those peers or dealers who attempt to coerce them into experimentation or frequent use.

While it is difficult to accurately measure the effectiveness of such anti-drug advertising, it is clear that the media can help shape attitudes. Just as beliefs about cigarette smoking have changed in recent years, so too can attitudes about drugs. In fact, many adolescents have endorsed the "Just Say No" campaign and organized youth groups of their own to help combat the prevalence of drugs in schools.

Furthermore, anti-drug advertising has an advantage over the anti-smoking campaigns: drug dealers cannot openly advertise their product. According to the New York advertising firm of Trout and Ries:

Unlike cigarette manufacturers, drug producers and sellers cannot use advertising to promote a fashionable image for their drugs. Quite the opposite, the government can use advertising to make drugs less and less fashionable to use. Thus, if America runs true to form, advertising will dramatically reduce demand. When it's "out" in America, it doesn't sell.

Any effort directed toward reducing the demand for drugs will require a long-term commitment; it takes time to change attitudes. This commitment must be made by federal, state, and local governments as well as the private sector. Each sector must unequivocally reassert that any and all illicit drug use is unacceptable in light of the effects of drugs on individuals, families, communities, and governments. Only in this context can a war against drugs be effective in reducing both the supply of drugs and the demand for them.

§ 16.4.2 Do Drug Laws Work?

Penalties against drug use in the United States have escalated dramatically since crack began infiltrating the nation's cities in the 1980s. During that time, Congress and nearly every legislature has overhauled drug laws to make them stronger, more consistent and, in a few cases, more creative.

Nonetheless, all signs suggest that the tougher laws have not been sufficient to prevent drug abuse from spreading; but there is little doubt that those who are caught are paying a higher price. While statistics on convictions and sentences for drug crimes are scarce, those in existence suggest that more people are going to prison for drug crimes than ever before.

In New York State, for instance, the number of people serving time for drug crimes rose more than 400 percent during the 1980s. Federal drug convictions jumped 161 percent, and the percentage of federal inmates serving time for drug crimes more than doubled. Approximately half the inmates in federal prisons in 1992 were convicted of drug crimes. That figure is in addition to the high percentage of convicts who were "under the influence" of drugs when they committed non-drug crimes such as murder.

In contrast to more recent drug-related legislation, drug laws in the 1970s appeared to be in remission. The recreational drug use that had become popular during the late 1960s had fostered a new sense of permissiveness in the following decade. In the 1970s, marijuana was decriminalized in some states, while laws against it went unenforced in other states. Strong laws against cocaine, heroin, and methamphetamines remained in place, but the judicial system was less eager than it once was to enforce them.

Chapter 16

The appearance of crack, the highly addictive form of cocaine, ended that permissive trend. Crack appeared on the scene just as public concern over cocaine use seemed to be reaching a peak, and pushed concern into panic. Lawmakers responded with much tougher laws.

Although the goal of drug legislation in the 1980s was a drug-free America, the only certain result so far has been overcrowded prisons and overburdened courts. Yet, even critics acknowledge that courts have become less hospitable places for drug users and dealers.

The federal government has been a leader in the crackdown, with Congress passing numerous anti-drug bills throughout the 1980s and 1990s. The laws established mandatory prison terms and fixed sentences for drug offenders, taking much of the sentencing discretion from judges.

Similar laws have been passed by most states, and some have adopted more severe measures. Virtually every state has raised the penalties for drug crimes that occur in or around schools. More than half have established stronger penalties for crack than for traditional powder cocaine. Furthermore, some states have extended the death penalty to include murders committed during drug transactions. About two-thirds of the states have enacted laws allowing the seizure of drug dealers' property.

Given that the drug problem continues to grow, it is difficult to prove the effectiveness of these laws. Some people believe the drug laws have not been effective. This ineffectiveness may be due, not to the strength of the laws, but to the application of them.

In addition to the need for increased enforcement, it might also strengthen drug laws to reconsider the rationale behind them. The common rationale for drug laws includes the following reasons: (1) drug use equals drug abuse, and drug laws that prohibit use automatically decrease abuse; (2) by controlling or eliminating people's access to psychoactive drugs, drug dependence can be curtailed. While this rationale has been effective to some degree, a slightly different approach may better address the problem of addictive behavior that is associated with drug abuse and creates such a high demand for drugs.

In their text, Drugs and Alcohol, Jones, Shainberg and Byer also review the so-called "epidemiological" approach to the drug problem. In one passage, the authors summarize this approach as follows:

Drug laws have been enacted to protect society. Legal controls such as quarantines, isolation, and penalties have always been necessary to stop the spread of various diseases and ailments. Since the best evidence supports the view that compulsive drug abuse is an indication of an emotional illness in an individual, society is justified in insisting on some type of regulation on the manufacture, distribution, and use of drugs. Such regulation can be viewed as part of preventive medicine.

Essentially, this approach holds that society must focus prevention efforts on target groups (such as young people) through education. Society must also isolate contagious people (i.e., drug users and drug sellers) through jail sentences. Society must vigorously treat chronic drug users as if they were deathly ill. The armament in this public health battle include the police, who quarantine abusers and sellers via arrest; courts, which sentence users to jail and/or remand them to compulsory treatment centers; drug educators (prevention experts) who strive for complete abstinence from drugs in their students (inoculation via education); and drug therapists who attempt to cure drug abusers by modifying the user's self-perceptions, coping skills, and behavior through a myriad of intervention techniques.

Despite various rationales behind anti-drug legislation, many social critics believe that drug laws do not help in the battle to prevent drug abuse. Their arguments often diverge wildly from each other, but enough similarities exist to delineate four positions: (1) drug laws simply do not work, as evidenced by drug use statistics; (2) crime increases as a function of prohibitions; (3) true drug abuse (i.e., where measurable harm to the individual or society stems from inappropriate use of drugs) is not reduced by prohibition, but is perhaps even increased; and (4) laws that attempt to dictate morality or styles of living threaten civil liberties.

In addition to reconsidering the rationales behind anti-drug legislation, it may also be productive to address the claim that drug laws are biased against certain ethnic groups and socioeconomic classes.

§ 16.4.3 Are Drug Laws Biased?

Although anti-drug legislation has had only limited success, the good news in the war against drugs is that the crack epidemic appears to have peaked and even appears to be subsiding. The bad news is that black defendants convicted of selling and using crack cocaine are over-represented in federal prisons.

The disproportionate number of blacks in prison may be due to the fact that crack cocaine users are treated differently than users of powder cocaine. Congress, responding to alarming reports about the highly addictive nature of crack and its association with gang violence, passed tough anti-crack laws in the 1980s. See 21 USC 841(b)(1)(A) as amended. The result of this legislation for sentencing purposes is that crack has 100 times the value of an equivalent amount of powder cocaine. In section 841 of 21 USC, for example, it stipulates that being convicted of a drug offense involving 50 grams of crack will fetch the same 10-year minimum sentence as a conviction involving five kilograms of powder cocaine. Generally speaking, most of those convicted of crack-related drug offenses are black, while those convicted of using the powder form of cocaine are white. This disparity has caused some controversy over the possible biases of legislators and law enforcement officers.[1]

---

[1] For a discussion of this controversy, see Heaney, G.W. "The Reality of Guidelines: No

Exploring the possibilities of biased legislation, defense lawyers have raised the issue of racial disparity in several federal circuits; however, they have had little success. Courts have consistently held that Congress could find a rational basis for treating the crack form of cocaine as a greater menace to society than other drugs.[2]

The Minnesota Supreme Court is perhaps the only state court to condemn the disparity in the treatment of crack and cocaine use in its state laws. In the case, *State of Minn. v. Russell* (1991) 477 NW2d 886, the court examined a year's worth of trial records and found that blacks comprised 96.6 percent of those charged with crack possession, while whites made up 76.6 percent of those charged with possessing the powder form of the drug. The court suggested that this disparity should be further investigated.

On the other side of the debate, prosecutors emphasize that crack is treated differently because of its different effect on society. "The crisis of crack led Congress to react to what it perceived as an immediate and serious threat to the whole social fabric," says Joseph Russonello, former U.S. attorney for the Northern District of California. He explains the disproportionate number of blacks convicted of crack-related crimes as follows: "The results you see are incidentally racially disparate. But as long as you have this perception that crack is a special and serious problem, law enforcement will continue to direct its focus and resources to those people who are most obviously in harm's way."

Others, however, have some slightly different opinions. In an article for American Criminal Law Review, Judge Gerald W. Heaney of the Eighth U.S. Circuit Court of Appeals wrote that African Americans, on average, are sentenced to federal prison terms that are 50 percent longer than terms given to whites and Latinos. Heaney said the harsher treatment of those convicted of crack use is one factor in the longer prison terms. Another factor, he said, is that local law enforcement officials divert "relatively minor offenses" into federal court to take advantage of the longer sentences. Pointing out that "blacks are vastly overrepresented in arrest records for street crimes," Heaney added that many of the affected defendants are drawing mandatory extended sentences under federal sentencing guidelines.

In the end, singling out crack as a greater social evil than other drugs may have little basis in fact. Dr. Darryl Inaba, director of the Haight-Ashbury Free Clinic drug program in San Francisco, says other drugs—such as methamphetamine and heroin—can be as lethal and as disruptive as crack. Methamphetamine use is increasing in white suburbia, Inaba says, and is also the drug preferred by runaway teens. Latinos tends to favor heroin and the animal tranquilizer PCP, he adds, while Asians tend to favor Quaaludes and crack. When talking about

---

End to Disparity." 28 Am Crim L Rev 160, 1991.
[2] For court decisions, see *U.S. v. Dumas*, 64 F.3d 1427 (9th Cir. 1995), cert. denied, 116 S.Ct. 1341, 134 L.Ed.2d 490; *U.S. v. Moore*, 54 F.3d 92 (2nd Cir. 1995), cert. denied, 116 S.Ct. 793, 133 L.Ed.2d 742.

the drug of choice for different groups, Inaba frequently refers to a 1989 study conducted in Rockville, Maryland by the National Institute on Drug Abuse. Whites were more likely to abuse drugs, the study concluded, followed by Latinos and Asians. In contrast, African Americans were least likely to abuse drugs among the various ethnic groups.

§ 16.5 SHOULD DRUGS BE LEGALIZED?
§ 16.5.1 Introduction
As discussed above, there are several arguments against the effectiveness of drug legislation. Some critics claim that the laws are ineffective because they are not adequately enforced; some argue that the rationale behind the laws themselves should be reconsidered; still others argue that some drug legislation is biased. Furthermore, there are those who argue for the medical usefulness of some drugs such as marijuana. If marijuana were legalized, several physicians say they would prescribe it as a treatment for glaucoma. All of these arguments for reconceiving anti-drug legislation raise the issue of legalizing drugs.

§ 16.5.2 The Case for Legalization
There are several good points in the case for legalization of drugs. For example, as a society, we pay a high price for keeping drugs illegal. Once these drugs were declared illegal, millions (or perhaps billions) of dollars had to be invested through the Customs Service, police agencies, and the armed services in an attempt to stop the drugs from coming into the United States. These costs are still incurred today. Unfortunately, the effectiveness of this program of interdiction is difficult to evaluate because, in part, it is virtually impossible to have a free society and to stop all drug importation. In addition, many of the drugs can be produced within our national boundaries, making it almost impossible to determine whether interdiction has been effective at all or whether the costs have been justified. From this standpoint alone, it is worthwhile considering whether a change in social policy might save a great deal of money and allow us to abandon a program whose effectiveness is difficult to establish.

Second, as a consequence of the continued high usage rate of illegal drugs in our country, the relative lack of competition has allowed the drug underworld to set street values that allow for the accumulation of immense profits. This has given resources to an underworld that is becoming increasingly vicious and physically destructive, and has created profits that are then used to produce and underwrite other forms of crime. Thus, if an effective step can be taken to undercut the price of street cocaine or other drugs, there is the possibility that the underworld and its crimes could be curtailed.

Third, reflecting the high cost of these drugs, the user frequently resorts to crime in order to support his or her habit. Again, any steps that decrease the cost and increase the availability of illicit drugs might help law enforcement agencies to minimize burglaries, theft, and robberies by drug users.

Fourth, the production of street drugs offers the user no guarantees of quality control. Thus, individuals are likely to inject substances that are dangerous, variable in quality, with resulting reactions to "fillers" as well as inadvertent overdoses. The latter occurs when individuals self-administer drugs of a quality that are higher than expected; thus, they inject greater concentrations of active ingredients than can be tolerated. The legalization of drugs would increase the probability that a user will get a more safe, standardized drug. Similarly, if along with legalization of drugs comes the supply of syringes and needles, it is possible that many severe medical complications such as HIV virus, hepatitis, abscesses, etc. can be minimized.

Finally, if drugs are legalized, they will be taxed. Especially if many people continue to use drugs (or the number of users increases), this step can be looked at as a potential revenue enhancer for the entire nation.

In summary, there are several logical arguments in favor of legalizing drugs. These include possible cost savings, a possible decrease in street crimes, and an increase in the assurance to users of avoiding inadvertent overdoses and unwanted infections, as well as the possibility of an additional revenue source. However, despite the logic of these arguments, it is important to look closely at the potential price that society would pay for legalization.

§ 16.5.3 The Case Against Legalization
If the United States is to make a major change in its policy on drugs, it is important that the best data possible are used in order to project accurate consequences. On the issue of legalization, these center on the probability of increased use, the consequences likely to be associated with a higher prevalence of drug intake, and the costs likely to accrue from the continued need for enforcement against use by minors.

§ 16.5.3(a) Increased Availability Is Likely to Result in Increased Use
There is data from several sources indicating a high likelihood that if a drug is more available, more people will use it. With alcohol, there appears to be an increased prevalence of use with an increasing number of alcohol outlets as well as with decreasing cost. Similarly, fairly consistent (although indirect) data demonstrate that "epidemics" of such drugs as heroin and crack, along with associated medical problems including fatal overdoses, are likely to be seen when more street drugs are available, especially if they are available at a lower cost.

The ideal cost for any drug would be a balance between making the drug inexpensive enough so as to undercut the drug dealer while keeping the price high enough to discourage "heavy" use. According to one recent expert reporting on cocaine, however, the drug is so cheap to produce that it would cost as low as $2.00 or $4.00 per gram on the street. In such an instance, the cost of a "hit" of cocaine would be 40 to 80 cents—a price highly unlikely to do anything but encourage heavy regular use.

§ 16.5.3(b)   Problems Associated with Increased Use

All drugs of abuse have dangers. However, the brain stimulants (such as cocaine and amphetamine) and opiates (such as heroin) are capable of producing a fairly rapid onset of tolerance and subsequent intense psychological and physical dependence. The intoxication associated with stimulants such as cocaine is very intense, likely to last less than one hour, and is usually followed by a period of sadness and lack of energy which is often subsequently relieved by another dose of the drug. Thus, the stimulants are highly reinforcing and are capable of producing an intense level of psychological dependence over a very short period of time. Similarly, tolerance and physical dependence develop very rapidly, with the latter resulting in physical and psychological symptoms likely to persist for months following heavy use.

Also, whether taken through an official "prescribed" dose or from the street, the acute effects of an intoxicating dose of cocaine can have severe physical consequences. At the very least these include an increase in heart rate and blood pressure, while at the other extreme it is capable of causing fatal heart-beating irregularities, life-threatening increases in body temperature, and severe convulsions.

Cocaine and other stimulants can produce severe states of emotional and psychiatric symptoms. With increasing doses, everyone is capable of developing a severely psychotic state (with hallucinations and paranoid delusions) that resemble schizophrenia. While this condition is likely to disappear within several days to several weeks, it is associated with chronic behavioral problems and can precipitate violence, including murder. Also, acute intoxication is likely to be associated with intense anxiety. Likewise, cessation of use (even after several days) is almost always accompanied by relatively intense levels of depression. Although the depression may continue at a decreasing level of intensity, it is likely to continue for many months.

In summary, while it is possible to project cost savings in interdiction and law enforcement, increased availability of these drugs is likely to result in increased use which will subsequently cause large costs in the treatment of physical and psychiatric difficulties.

§ 16.5.3(c)   Enforcement Costs Will Continue

Any "legalization" of drugs is likely to involve restrictions against the use of drugs by certain subgroups. Likely examples would be individuals under the age of 21 and, perhaps, men and women with psychiatric difficulties. Considering the fact that the age group with the greatest prevalence of experimentation with drugs includes individuals aged 20 and under, this would mean that a very large potential subgroup of users will still find that drugs are illegal for them. Therefore, an underworld of drug dealers will still exist and relatively high legal costs will remain due to the attempt to enforce the drug restrictions for this group.

§ 16.5.3(d)   Potential Problems with Legal Distribution

If drugs that are now illegal were to be legalized, who will distribute them? Will physician prescriptions be required? If so, many medical practitioners might be exceptionally reluctant to give out a drug with such dangers, raising the possibility that only the more unscrupulous individuals might choose to be involved in this "trade."

An alternative mode of distribution might be legal sales in government agencies. Perhaps, each state would develop a series of legal drug outlets with various ways of attempting to enforce the legal restrictions that remain. Once again, there will be costs of a bureaucracy, problems with enforcement, and legal difficulties if someone who buys a drug for "recreation" develops medical problems, or commits a crime while paranoid or otherwise impaired.

§ 16.5.4 Summary

As shown by the arguments briefly reviewed here, there are serious issues to be sorted out on both sides of the legalization controversy. When asking whether or not the war on drugs is succeeding, legalization may seem a feasible alternative. However, it is highly unlikely that all drugs will ever become legal for everyone. Some anti-drug legislation must remain in place. Thus, the issue of legalization might be best addressed through a careful review of the options for reconsidering the legislation and rationales that already exist.

References

Drug Enforcement Administration. "Drug Paraphernalia: Tools of the Illegal Drug Trade." www.DEA.gov.

Jones, Shainberg, and Byer. Drugs and Alcohol. New York: Harper and Row, 1979.

National Conference of State Legislatures. 2004-2005 Policies for the Jurisdiction of the; Law and Criminal Justice Committee.

National Institute on Drug Abuse. "Substance Abuse Among Blacks in the United States." CAP 34. Rockville, MD: Department of Health and Human Services, 1989.

Polich, J.M., et al. Strategies for Controlling Adolescent Drug Use. The Ad Corporation, February, 1984.

Shore, Million F. "Correlates and Concepts: Are We Chasing Our Tails?" Etiology of Drug Abuse 127, 128. Rockville: NIDA Research Monograph 56 (1985): 27-28.

Trout and Ries Advertising Agency. "A Way to Decrease the Demand for Drugs." Paper prepared for the President's Commission on Organized Crime, October, 1, 1985.

CHAPTER 17

DRUG LAW ENFORCEMENT AND INVESTIGATIONS

§ 17.1 INTRODUCTION

The responsibility for enforcement of narcotic and drug laws is entrusted to law enforcement agencies at three government levels: local (including municipal and county), state, and federal. Inevitably, the duties and responsibilities of these agencies will overlap to some degree.

Local Responsibility — Primary responsibility for enforcing narcotic law violations rests with local law enforcement agencies. The local agency is responsible for detection, arrest, and prosecution of persons who illegally use, sell, distribute, or manufacture dangerous drugs and narcotics within their community, regardless of the sophistication of the illicit operation.

Local agencies can be very effective in disrupting local illicit narcotic distribution patterns. They can diminish opportunities for dealers to develop new users. Moreover, local departments can furnish state and federal agencies with information so that these agencies are better able to pursue large-scale operations.

In numerous parts of the country, local and state police agencies have pooled their specialized narcotic enforcement personnel and resources to establish multi-agency narcotic units entrusted with either the partial or whole responsibility of narcotic enforcement in their respective areas. Combined units of this type fill a void created by the inability of local police departments to devote the necessary resources to narcotic enforcement or the inability of these departments to pursue the enforcement of narcotic law outside the boundaries of their respective jurisdictions.

State Role — State narcotic enforcement units are responsible for providing local agencies, upon request, with the resources necessary to identify, investigate, and arrest narcotic traffickers. State narcotic units are also available to communities that need assistance with investigations that cross local jurisdictional lines or that require an undercover operation when local agencies cannot provide one. State law enforcement agencies also assist by providing local agencies with laboratory facilities for handling and processing narcotic evidence.

In areas where local enforcement units or general resources are absent, the state agencies assume primary responsibility for investigating narcotic cases. These state agencies also assume partial or whole responsibility for training local patrol officers and specialized narcotic investigators.

Federal Role — Federal enforcement agencies assume the primary responsibility for preventing illegal entry of drugs into the country and for providing assistance to local and state agencies whenever possible. The responsibilities of federal agencies extend to the investigation of large-scale illegal operations involving more than one state. These federal agencies also assist local agencies in identifying and eliminating large organizations which manufacture and sell drugs illegally; they provide drug intelligence data to both state and local agencies. Furthermore, federal enforcement agencies are largely responsible for ensuring that drugs manufactured legally in this country do not appear on the illicit market. The federal agencies supplement state enforcement efforts and operations which are weak or nonexistent. In such areas, the federal government assumes some responsibility, consistent with federal jurisdictional limits, for providing training, intelligence, and investigative assistance.

FIELD PROCEDURES FOR THE STREET COP

§ 17.2 DRUG-RELATED CRIMES AND BEHAVIOR

Ninety percent of drug arrests in the United States are made by uniformed patrol officers. The arrests often result from observations made of suspicious or unlawful activities, or from radio calls and citizen requests. The largest source of unlawful conduct observations are traffic violations.

What does all this mean? It means that the police officer should always be alert for drug-related behavior—whether on routine patrol, answering a radio call, processing an arrestee, or making a citizen contact. All of these activities can result in uncovering drug violations.

Additionally, there are some specific things a police officer should know: where addicts hang out and how to recognize a drug addict.

Some crimes are very closely related to drug abuse and drug trafficking. Burglary, theft (such as shoplifting), some robberies, and forgery are the crimes most frequently committed by abusers who are supporting a heavy habit. Many female addicts resort to the crime of prostitution. You should keep these facts in mind while conducting preliminary investigations of these crimes. Also, when making arrests for these crimes, be alert for possible drug-related behavior by the arrestee. It is not uncommon for a shoplifting arrest to result in a drug-related booking.

One of the ways a police officer may come in contact with a drug abuser is when the officer finds drugs during a routine check or in the course of arrest for a totally unconnected offense. He or she may actually see a person taking drugs or find evidence of unusual behavior. The officer may also act in response to information from an informant.

Most investigations involving "buys" of drugs are made by an undercover officer or a reliable informant under immediate supervision. In most circumstances, the suspect is arrested and searched after the third or fourth sale, and the drugs found are seized as evidence. The charges lodged against the suspect will be for the illegal possession and sale of drugs.

The case will stand or fall on the testimony of the undercover officer and the officer who observed the transactions, as well as the lab analyst who examined the purchased drugs.

§ 17.3   PROBABLE CAUSE TO ARREST IN DRUG CASES

Probable cause to arrest has been judicially defined as "such a state of facts as would lead any man of ordinary care and prudence, given the training and experience of a police officer, to believe and consciously entertain an honest and strong suspicion that a person is guilty of a crime."

A variation of this definition states: "The facts establishing reasonable cause to arrest must be sufficient to allow any prudent officer with similar experience and training to believe that a crime has occurred and that the suspect is responsible."

§ 17.3.1 Probable Cause and/or Reasonable Cause

The terms "probable cause" and "reasonable cause" are nearly interchangeable. However, for the purposes of this chapter, probable cause will remain the standard term.

Knowledge of both what constitutes probable cause and the laws of arrest is an officer's best defense against possible criminal or civil action taken against him or her.

To have probable cause to arrest, a police officer need not be absolutely certain that someone is guilty of a crime. Typically, in situations that require action, you lack time for extensive investigation. You must act on the facts and circumstances as they appear to you at the time. Even if you have some doubt, you may still have probable cause to arrest.

§ 17.3.2 Probable Cause: A Dependent Variable

Probable cause does not conform to one fixed definition. It is a versatile standard. In each case, it depends on the facts and circumstances as they were found to exist at that time. It is dependent on the person viewing the facts and the circumstances at the time.

To a certain extent, probable cause is in the eye of the beholder. An officer of greater experience than another may look at the same set of facts as the less experienced officer and come to a different conclusion. Likewise, the man or woman "of ordinary care and prudence" may fail to see probable cause in a situation that is obvious to the trained police officer. This is why case law allows the man or woman "of ordinary care and prudence" to be assumed in possession of the training and experience of the officer actually making the arrest.

If the validity of an arrest is later challenged, the courts will decide whether the officer making the arrest had probable cause to arrest at the time he or she acted. This standard alone—that of reasonable or probable cause—determines whether or not an arrest is valid.

It must be remembered that the standard of reasonable or probable cause is applied at the time of arrest and not later. Reasonable or probable cause must exist prior to making an arrest. In making arrests, court interpretations of probable cause have become guidelines for officers to rely on, in addition to their own educated powers of observation and sound judgment.

§ 17.3.3 Probable Cause: Two Aspects
—A lawful arrest is based on probable cause.

—Probable cause is based on facts sufficient to establish the following:

1. The officer has reason to believe that a crime has occurred; and that,

2. The suspect is responsible.

In other words, the arresting officer must have probable cause to believe that a crime was committed, based on the establishment of the *corpus delicti*, or elements of the offense.

The arresting officer must have probable cause to believe that the person he or she is arresting is the perpetrator of the crime or is a principal to the crime committed. The officer may not arrest on a hunch, a guess, or on a mere suspicion that the person is guilty. If the officer cannot reasonably conclude on the basis of facts and circumstances that guilt exists, there is no valid reason for arrest.

Facts are the essence of probable cause. An arrest based on insufficient fact is an unreasonable arrest. An arrest can never be justified by the notion that the courts will later declare the suspect not guilty if he or she is really innocent.

The highest law in this country, the U.S. Constitution, assures protection of the individual's freedom from unreasonable arrest and search (Fourth Amendment).

§ 17.3.4 Factors Establishing Probable Cause to Arrest
What gives the officer probable cause to believe that a crime has occurred and that the suspect is responsible? It may be direct observation, coupled with his or her expertise, which is based on training and experience.

One day, officers driving down a residential street happened to look up at a first-floor apartment window, where they saw a marijuana plant. Their subsequent arrest of the tenant was based on the officers' observation of evidence in plain view. In this case, another factor also was present: the officers' knowledge of what a marijuana plant looks like.

Probable cause may also rest on *information supplied by others.*

Consider this case: you receive information from an apartment manager who suspects one of his tenants is dealing drugs. He states that people frequently visit the suspect's apartment, staying for only a short period of time. He has passed some of the people in the hallway and they seem high. He gives you several license numbers that he took down from cars of some of the people visiting the apartment. You run the numbers and they belong to people who are known drug users and dealers. You also find that the tenant has a past record for dealing narcotics. You go to the suspect's door and he attempts to run away. Do you have probable cause to believe the information supplied by the manager? When you locate the tenant, will you have probable cause to arrest him? The answer to both of these questions is yes.

It should be remembered that not every bit of information from an informant will establish probable cause. In every instance you need to evaluate the reliability of the source. You must consider the informer's motivation in supplying the information and his ability to observe, interpret, and report facts accurately.

Information you receive through official channels—i.e., your supervisor, a fellow officer, the police radio—can be assumed to be reliable. However, you should carefully consider the word of a witness or of a victim before accepting a statement as true. Under what circumstances might you doubt the statements of a witness? You doubt the statement when there is any possibility that the witness would have vindictive or other intentions which would raise a question in your mind as to the reliability of the information. Why might you doubt the story of a crime told by the victim? You might doubt it because the victim may be trying to protect his or her own interests, or the victim may have been injured emotionally and/or physically to an extent that his or her perceptions are unclear or his ability to relate is impaired.

How can you attempt to resolve any doubts about a witness' statement? Proceed with further questioning. As you do so, ask yourself: "Could the witness have observed what he is telling me from where he was when the crime occurred? Was the witness in a condition, mentally and emotionally, to make an accurate observation? Was he or she a victim, or was he in some way involved as a co-principal?"

Time and/or Place May Be Used to Establish Probable Cause—For example, you are in an area of the city where there have been frequent muggings, purse snatchings, and many complaints by merchants in the area that shoppers during the hours of 4 to 6 p.m. are particularly susceptible to these attacks. If you see a suspicious person loitering in this area between the hours of 4 to 6 p.m. with no apparent reason for being there, would you have probable cause to stop and talk to this individual and conduct a field interview? Yes.

Officer's senses (smell, hearing, observation)—The officer may also rely on senses, such as the sense of smell, for probable cause to arrest. For example: an officer stops a vehicle and asks the driver to roll down the window. The officer smells the odor of burning marijuana. In this case, the officer has probable cause to arrest for Section 23152 of the California Vehicle Code, driving under the influence of an alcoholic beverage or any drug.

Officer's training and experience—What appears to be innocent behavior by the average citizen may, in the eyes of a trained police officer warrant an investigation or even an arrest. For example: a suspect is negotiating a sale on a street corner; the officer, based on experience, suspects illegal activity and supports the conclusion when the suspect attempts to run from the officer and throw away the evidence.

§ 17.3.4(a) Emergencies

Emergencies may also be a contributing factor for probable cause. Generally, an officer needs fewer facts to establish probable cause in an emergency situation. For instance, circumstances in which you are endangered or in which a suspect is about to escape or destroy valuable evidence would be considered emergency situations. Factors such as flight are not ambiguous or neutral, but can be incriminating or guilt-laden facts and can be used to establish probable cause.

For example, while on patrol you notice two people standing on the sidewalk. When they see your police vehicle they throw some small items to the ground and take off running. Do you have probable cause to investigate why the suspects are running? Yes.

§ 17.3.4(b) Totality of Circumstances

In the final analysis, the court will decide that you had probable cause to arrest only if the "total circumstances" gave you an honest and strong suspicion of a law violation. There are no magic formulas for deciding whether the circumstances "add up" to probable cause. One overwhelming fact may be sufficient by itself while a dozen "maybes" could be insufficient. Also, one strong reason not to arrest may outweigh several weaker reasons for doing so. Finally, each case has its own set of circumstances; and while your past experience in similar cases may help you decide, you must still judge the present case on its own merits.

When establishing probable cause, the field officer might bear in mind the following court decision: "There is no mathematical formula to determine what specific facts constitute reasonable cause for an arrest; each case must be decided on the totality of facts and circumstances at the time an arrest is made" (*People v. Superior Court (Holquin)*, 72 Cal. App. 3d 591, 140 Cal. Rptr. 234 (Cal. App. 2 Dist. 1977)).

The police officer can rely on the following information for probable cause to arrest in drug cases. Remember: just one piece of information may not justify probable cause to arrest.

Drug Law Enforcement and Investigations

Physical description—When an officer receives information from a police bulletin as to the description of a known narcotics violator, if he sees the person, he has probable cause to arrest. The defendant's physical appearance or condition in terms of drug use may also give the officers probable cause to arrest.

Failure to explain—This in and of itself is not probable cause to arrest. However, misleading statements can lead to probable cause. Probable cause for arrest might be justified when the suspect is confronted by the officers and he provides an implausible explanation for his presence near the scene of a crime, or attempts to mislead the officers.

Admissions—These occur when an officer overhears that the suspect is in the possession of drugs, and when the officer asks the suspect if he is under the influence, the suspect states that he is.

Reputation of the premises—The mere fact of a person on the premises where officers have reason to believe there is criminal activity in progress will not alone justify probable cause for arrest. There must be other evidence.

The reputation of the residence or place alone is not enough for probable cause to arrest. However, the actions of occupants—such as staying short periods of time and suddenly departing—does warrant at least an investigation. Arrest is justified if the officer witnesses furtive conduct on his or her approach to the scene.

Furtive conduct—This is conduct with which a person attempts to hide contraband, evidence of the crime, attempts to secrete or destroy evidence, or exhibits abnormal behavior at the approach of the officers.

A narcotics violator will often attempt to swallow the evidence; thus, movement toward the mouth might establish probable cause. If the person cannot swallow evidence, he might attempt to throw it away. A drug violator may be arrested after his attempt to hide or conceal the contraband.

Flight and attempts to escape—Even though mere flight at the approach of an officer is not of itself grounds for an arrest, the officer can investigate the reason for the flight. Here are some examples of such flight:

A. While conducting a pat-down, the defendant hits the officer in the stomach and attempts to flee.

B. Officer observes the defendant looking in his direction, saying "cops," then walking away.

C. Upon hearing officers announce their presence at the front door, the occupants of a residence flee through the back door.

§ 17.4   PROBABLE CAUSE TO DETAIN

Prior to probable cause to arrest, the officer may obtain probable cause to detain. Furtive movements and unusual or suspicious conduct are examples of facts that may constitute probable cause to detain. The officer's right to detain is limited, but it increases in direct proportion to the number and severity of the facts unfolding before him or her. If the officer believes he may be dealing with a crime of violence, he is even less limited in his detention of a suspect. Generally speaking, a detention may continue as long as the investigation is in progress.

The test of sufficient probable cause to detain is outlined in *People v. Henze*, 253 Cal. App. 2d 986, 61 Cal. Rptr. 545 (Cal. App. 2 Dist. 1967). The requirements include:

A.   A rational suspicion by the peace officer that some activity out of the ordinary is or has taken place.

B.   Some evidence to connect the person under suspicion with the unusual activity.

C.   Some suggestion that the activity is related to the crime.

The facts the officer needs to justify detention are similar to those he needs to justify arrest. But the officer may detain on a basis of facts that are not, or not yet, adequate for arrest. The courts have ruled that there may be strong reason to investigate in the absence of a legal basis for arrest.

The officer who is genuinely pursuing suspicious or unusual facts has the right to stop a pedestrian or a motorist. He or she may then frisk for safety (if circumstances permit); the officer may then question and detain, even when the officer has insufficient facts to justify a formal arrest. He can, however, detain and frisk only when this is justified. The officer can also ask a person to remain at the scene while he investigates further.

Detentions can only be temporary. If, as a result of his investigation, an officer does not establish probable cause to arrest, the officer must release the suspect. In such a case, the proper method of ending the detention would be to explain the reason for the detention. If a problem arises, such as a likelihood of a personnel complaint, summon a field supervisor to the scene.

§ 17.4.1 Factors Establishing Probable Cause to Detain
§ 17.4.1(a)   Nighttime/High Crime Area

In recent years, California arrest and detention cases have placed less importance on some factors, such as "nighttime" or "high crime areas" (*People v. Madrid*, 208 Cal. App. 3d 822, 256 Cal. Rptr. 338 (Cal. App. 5 Dist. 1989)). It might be noted here that one frustrated judge said his entire city seemed like a high crime area these days. However, a police officer may still consider these factors, particularly if they are combined with additional specific facts. Furthermore, these factors are still given considerable weight by federal case law (*In re Frederick B.*,

192 Cal. App. 3d 79 237 Cal. Rptr. 338 (Cal. App. 1 Dist. 1987); *People v. Holloway*, 176 Cal. App. 3d 150, 221 Cal. Rptr. 394. (Cal. App. 2 Dist. 1985)).

California Supreme Court has stated: "An area's reputation for criminal activity is an appropriate consideration in assessing whether an investigative detention is reasonable under the Fourth Amendment," noting that "it would be the height of naivete not to recognize that the frequency and intensity [of criminal activities] are greater in certain quarters than in others." (*Souza* (1994) 9 Cal.4th 224, 241; see also *Wardlow* (2000) 120 S.Ct. 673, 676.)

Similarly, the Court also recognized that "The time of night is another pertinent factor in assessing the validity of a detention." (*Souza* (1994) 9 Cal.4th 224, 241; see also *Foranyic* (1998) 64 Cal.App.4th 186, 190.)

Fleeing from officers driving past in a high crime area at noon provided a sufficient basis to detain. (*Wardlow* (2000) 120 S.Ct. 673.)

An experienced narcotics officer observed a man participate in an apparent hand-to-hand exchange in a carport where the officer knew other drug deals had occurred, and which was in a known drug-ridden neighborhood. The officer had also seen the same man, just before and after the exchange, walk over and reach into an apparent hiding place, namely, the wheel-well of a pickup truck. HELD: There was reasonable suspicion to detain (and pat down) the suspect. Although a person may not be detained for merely being present in a drug-ridden neighborhood, "this setting is a factor that can lend meaning to the person's behavior." (*Limon* (1993) 17 Cal.App.4th 524, 531-534.)

If you spot someone you don't recognize who is standing alone on a street corner in the business district at 4 a.m., your suspicion would be more reasonable in a small town than in Los Angeles. Even so, by itself, this fact probably wouldn't justify anything more than a "consensual encounter." However, if you add another factor or two, such as that the person has bulging pockets, runs away when he sees you, gives you a phony answer, or is holding a "scanner" or a weapon, then you would have enough "reasonable suspicion" to detain him for further investigation. (*Brown* (1989) 213 Cal.App.3d 187.)

§ 17.4.1(b)   Race

Reasonable suspicion may not be based, in whole or in part, "on broad profiles which cast suspicion on entire categories of people without any individualized suspicion of the particular person to be stopped." (*Montero-Camargo* (9th Cir. 2000) 208 F.3d 1122, 1129-1130, quoting an earlier Ninth Circuit case.) In other words, generally speaking, race is simply not a factor which you may consider in calculating reasonable suspicion.

Indeed, racial profiling, that is, "the practice of detaining a suspect based on a broad set of criteria which casts suspicion upon an entire class of people without individualized suspicion of the particular person being stopped," is specifically outlawed. (Pen. Code, Section 13519.4.)

On the other hand, race or ethnicity *is* still a proper factor to consider if it is part of a description of a specific suspect you are looking for. "Hispanic appearance, or any other racial or ethnic appearance, including Caucasian, may be considered when the suspected perpetrator of a specific offense has been identified as having such an appearance." (*Montero-Camargo* (9th Cir. 2000) 208 F.3d 1122, 1134, fn. 22.) Even in such a situation, however, there would have to be additional factors, in addition to the suspect's race, which provide reasonable suspicion and thus justify the detention.

An officer observed one white male and several black males leaving a housing project populated by blacks. It was night, a high crime area, and in the past the officer had seen whites in that area at night only to buy drugs. The group dispersed as the officer approached. The Supreme Court said the detention of the white male was illegal. The reasons of race, the time of night and type of neighborhood were too flimsy to connect the individual with crime. (*Bower* (1979) 24 Cal.3d 638.) (But see *Wardlow* (2000) 120 S.Ct. 673, holding that "flight" in a high crime area is enough to detain (although race would remain irrelevant, of course.)

§ 17.4.1(c)   Flight

If you approach someone or a group and one or more of them walks or runs away, and you give chase, your act of chasing after the person does not constitute a detention. As the United States Supreme Court has made clear, there is no "seizure" until you have actually physically stopped the person, or he stops on his own and submits to your authority. (*Hodari D.* (1991) 499 U.S. 621, 626.)

When officers drove around the corner in their unmarked vehicle, a group of males who had been standing around a red car took off, and so did the car. One officer got out, ran around the block the other way, and approached within a few feet of the suspect, who was looking over his shoulder while running towards the officer, before the suspect looked up and saw him, whereupon he discarded a rock of cocaine before being tackled. The Supreme Court held that the suspect was not "seized" until he was tackled, because up to that moment, he had not submitted to the officer's assertion of authority. (*Hodari D.* (1991) 499 U.S. 621, 626; see also *Chesternut* (1998) 486 U.S. 567—driving along beside fleeing suspect did not constitute a detention; and *Arangure* (1991) 230 Cal.App.3d 1302, 1306.)

Even if you yell "stop" or "freeze," display a weapon, or assert your authority in some other manner, *Hodari D.* makes it clear that there still cannot be a detention until and unless the suspect stops fleeing in response.

The problem arises, therefore, when you *catch* the suspect, or when he stops in response to your actions or commands. For at that point, a detention has occurred, and it will be legal, as always, only if it is supported by reasonable suspicion.

The United States Supreme Court has declined to create a "bright line" rule regarding "flight." That is, the Court has refused to rule either (1) that "flight" alone will *always* justify a detention, or (2) that flight alone can *never* justify a detention.

Instead, both the U.S. Supreme Court and the California Supreme Court have held that "flight" is merely one factor in the "totality of the circumstances" which a court will look at in determining whether reasonable suspicion existed. However, it is an important factor, because fleeing from police officers, as opposed to simply refusing to cooperate, is inherently suspicious and therefore "can be a key factor in determining whether in a particular case the police have sufficient cause to detain." (*Souza* (1994) 9 Cal.4th 224, 235.) "Headlong flight—wherever it occurs—is the consummate act of evasion: it is not necessarily indicative of wrongdoing, but it is certainly suggestive of such." (*Marlow* (2000) 528 U.S. 119, 124; *Britton* (2001) 91 Cal.App.4th 1112, 1118-1119.)

Thus, when combined with other factors, such as a high crime area and/or time of night, you often *will* have a valid basis to detain. (*Fuentes* (9th Cir. 1997) 105 F.3d 487, 490; see *Garcia-Barron* (9th Cir. 1997) for a discussion of avoiding border checkpoints.)

Fleeing from officers driving past in a high crime area at noon provided a sufficient basis to detain. (*Wardlow* (2000) 528 U.S. 119.)

At 3:00 a.m. in a residential neighborhood known for burglaries and drug trafficking, an officer on routine patrol spotted two persons standing near a vehicle which was parked in a particularly dark location, apparently talking to someone inside the car. When he activated his spotlight and lit up the vehicle's interior, two persons inside ducked down out of sight, and one of the two persons outside (Souza) took off running. The officer chased him, stopped him, and patted him down, discovering cocaine in the process. HELD: The detention was lawful under the totality of the circumstances. The area's reputation, the time of night, and the suspects' efforts to avoid detection were all proper factors to consider, and together they provided reasonable suspicion of criminal activity. (*Souza* (1994) 9 Cal.4th 224, 240-242.)

§ 17.4.1(d)   Experience

Don't overlook your experience. "The specialized knowledge of a police officer experienced in police narcotics work may render suspicious what would appear innocent to a layman." (*Mims* (1992) 9 Cal.App.4th 1244, 1248; *Brown* (1985) 169 Cal.App.3d 159, 165; *Limon* (1993) 17 Cal.App.4th 524, 532.)

The suspect was in a park where marijuana sales often took place, doing nothing. An apparent stranger drove up, approached the suspect, gave him money for two small, thin, white, filterless cigarettes, and then drove away. Because of the officer's experience and the specifics of what he'd seen exchange hands, the court found probable cause to justify an arrest. (*Stanfill* (1985) 170 Cal.App.3d 420.)

Chapter 17

§ 17.4.1(e)   Officer Safety

Officer safety, as a justification for certain police action, exists in many areas of the law. It is perhaps best known as the basis for permitting a limited search for weapons, also known as a pat-down or frisk. (*Terry* (1968) 392 U.S. 1.)

However, there are also some cases, and helpful language in still more cases, which permit you to detain someone in the first place (but not necessarily to take the additional step of patting them down), on the basis of officer safety.

In *Terry* itself, the U.S. Supreme Court held that the lawfulness of the detention of a person based on something less than probable cause came down to "whether a reasonably prudent man in the circumstances would be warranted in the belief that his safety or that of others was in danger." (392 U.S. at p. 27.)

Later, in *Summers*, (1981) 452 U.S. 692, the Supreme Court repeated that courts must balance the extent of the intrusion upon the individual against the interests of the government, and that "the interest in minimizing the risk of harm to the officers" is a significant factor.

The clearest example, however, is the case of *Hannah*, (1996) 51 Cal.App.4th 1335, where police were told that a male juvenile, for whom they had an arrest warrant, was in a certain apartment. Three officers went to the apartment and entered after obtaining consent from the female who lived there to come in and look for the juvenile. Inside, they observed two males seated in the living room. While one officer "swept" the apartment looking for the juvenile, and while the second officer stood by the door, the third officer asked the two men "if they could just stay seated where they were at." He then asked them who they were, what their relationship was to the woman who answered the door, and why they were there. During this time, he noticed that one of the males (Hannah) had dilated pupils, and this soon led to Hannah's arrest.

In court, Hannah complained that he had been illegally detained. However, the Court of Appeal (5th District; Fresno) disagreed. It recognized that most of the other cases upholding the detention of persons who are on the premises involved narcotics *search* warrants, a situation which is very dangerous to officers, whereas this case involved only an *arrest* warrant. Nevertheless, the court applied the same test— balancing the extent of the intrusion against the needs of the government. Here, because the detention was so minimal (no force, no pat-down, brief duration, etc.), it was reasonable and therefore legal, since, viewed "from the perspective of the police officers who entered the apartment," the situation was still potentially dangerous for the officers (they were on unknown turf, did not know the floor plan, did not know the identity of the males or their relationship to the juvenile, etc.).

"Faced with these circumstances, any reasonable person would find an initial detention of the individuals encountered was necessary to ensure the safety of the police officers." (*Hannah* (1996) 51 Cal.App.4th 1335, 1346.)

In sum, there is now good, clear authority for the proposition that when it makes sense, from the standpoint of officer safety, to detain someone, the detention is lawful, even though the officer did not directly suspect the detainee of criminal activity. (In addition to the cases cited above, see also *Maleski*, (2000) 82 Cal.App.4th 837, 846-853.

§ 17.4.1(f)   Hearsay

In *People v. Hale*, 262 Cal. App. 2d 780, 69 Cal. Rptr. 28 (Cal. App. 2 Dist. 1968), an undercover agent answered the telephone at the residence of the defendant. The caller identified himself as Tony and asked if Bill had "scored the stuff." The agent said yes and told him to come up. The court held that: "Arrival at a given location of a person bearing the same name as that given by the caller in a telephone conversation indicates that the caller and the person at the door are one and the same person." The arrest and search of "Tony" was therefore proper.

§17.4.1(g)   Drug Courier Profile

The legality of detentions based on a "drug courier profile," meaning noncriminal factors about an individual, such as coming from Miami, looking nervous, using cash, not having luggage, etc., has traditionally caused difficulty for the courts. Courts have ruled, generally, that such a "profile" will not automatically justify a detention because, by itself, it does not rise to the level of "reasonable suspicion."

Therefore, it has traditionally been safer to use "profile" information simply as a basis for further observations and investigation, or for the initiation of a voluntary consensual encounter, unless you have some additional information indicating ongoing criminal activity, such as evasion or the use of an alias.

§ 17.4.1(g)   Information from Others

You can probably base a detention on information you receive from an eyewitness, victim, fellow police officer, dispatcher, or—if accurate—other "official channels," because the law generally considers such persons or sources to be automatically reliable (*Hensley*, 469 U.S. 221 (1985)).

Information from an identified "snitch" would also probably justify a detention if he had given you reliable information in the past (*McBride*, 122 Cal.App.3d 156 (1981)). As far as information from a totally anonymous source is concerned (like a telephone tape), there are two important United States Supreme Court cases: *White* and *J.L.* Together, they stand for the proposition that an anonymous tip, by itself, will normally *not* be sufficient to justify a detention or pat-down, although it *can* be *if* there is sufficient corroboration or other indications of reliability. (*White*, 496 U.S. 325, 327, 329 (1990); *J.L.*, 529 U.S. 266, 272 (2000).)

§ 17.4.2 *Miranda* Warnings

The general rule is that you do not have to give *Miranda* warnings to someone you have detained (1) on reasonable suspicion, (2) for a "site and release" offense (even though they may technically be under arrest), or (3) for investigative questioning at the scene of a crime (*Berkemer v. McCarty*, 468 U.S. 420, 104. S.Ct. 3138, 82 L.Ed. 2d 317 (1984)).

However, if your detention turns into an arrest because you use excessive force, extend the detention unreasonably long, or develop probable cause to arrest, then *Miranda* warnings would be required prior to questioning.

§ 17.5 CASES OF PROBABLE CAUSE THAT RESULTED IN ARREST

In *People v. Herrera*, 221 Cal. App. 2d 8, 10, 12, 34 Cal. Rptr. 305 (Cal. App. 2 Dist. 1963), after being qualified as a narcotics expert, the arresting officer testified that he observed what he considered to be hypodermic marks on the appellant's left wrist caused by the illegal use of narcotics. There were additional marks on the appellant's forearm. The officer then shone a light in the appellant's eyes and the pupils were pinpointed. This means that there was little or no reaction to light in the pupils and indicated, in the opinion of the officer, that the appellant was under the influence of narcotics at the time. The officer further testified that the appellant's speech was low and mumbled and at times..."he appeared almost to nod off or like he was about to go to sleep." The officer then said, "this would substantiate my earlier opinion that the defendant was under the influence of narcotics. The other two men had no marks on their arms and their eyes appeared normal. They were ultimately released from custody." Therefore, when the arresting officer, a Los Angeles policeman attached to the narcotics division and trained in that field, observed the marks on the appellant's arm, noted his pinpointed pupils, and saw his general somnolent condition, it was reasonable for him to conclude that the appellant was under the influence of narcotics and that an offense was being committed in his presence, for which an arrest could be made without a warrant. In summary, it should be noted that the officers detained all the suspects. As a result of the ensuing investigation, the officers established reasonable cause to arrest one suspect and released the other two. (See also, *People v. Di Blasi*, 198 Cal. App. 2d 215, 18 Cal Rptr. 223 (Cal. App. 2 Dist. 1961); *People v. Rogers*, 207 Cal. App. 2d 254, 259, 24 Cal. Rptr. 324 (Cal. App. 2 Dist. 1962); *People v. Newberry*, 204 Cal. App. 2d 4, 22 Cal. Rptr. 23 (Cal. App. 2 Dist. 1962)).

In *People v. Ferguson*, 214 Cal. App. 2d 772, 776, 29 Cal. Rptr. 691 (Cal. App. 2 Dist. 1963) the court held that the mere observation by officers of what they believe to be hypodermic marks, without more, is insufficient cause on which to base an arrest.

In another case in California, there was probable cause for the arrest of a person for violation of California Health and Safety Code Section 11550, which prohibits the use of narcotics and being under the influence of narcotics. The person had been observed by the arresting officers late at night, engaged in an apparent transaction of some kind in an area known for narcotics activity. In this area, the arresting officer, who had temporarily detained him for an interview, had observed that he was sniffling and that the pupils of his eyes were contracted. Furthermore, when the officers were about 40 to 50 feet from the corner, they saw the defendant and another individual "standing approximately six inches to a foot away from each other." Their hands were between them "like shuffling or exchanging merchandise or objects."

The officers left the vehicle to conduct an investigation which was to consist of talking to the defendant and his companion. First, however, the suspects were asked to take their hands out of their pockets. Something was said to indicate to them that the officers wanted to talk to them. A pat-down of defendant's companion produced a small automatic pistol from his front pocket. Apparently, it was when Officer Long was ready to pat-down the defendant that he observed him sniffle, as if he had a cold. On further observation he saw that his eyes were contracted. The officer then looked at the defendant's arms and noticed hypodermic needle marks on the inside of the elbow, above the vein. All these observations indicated that the defendant was under the influence of an "opiate type drug." He was then arrested.

The jury declared: "Even if we disregard the rather unsatisfactory proof concerning the visibility of the needle marks without an intrusion into the defendant's privacy by having him roll up his sleeves, we believe that the sniffle and the contracted condition of his pupils—particularly the latter, when viewed against the entire background—supports the assumption that the defendant was then under the influence of a narcotic" (*People v. Moore*, 69 Cal. 2d 674, 72 Cal. Rptr. 800, 446 P.2d 800 (Cal. 1968), overruled on other grounds in *People v. Thomas*, 19 Cal. 3d 630, 139 Cal. Rptr. 594, 566 P.2d 228 (Cal. 1977)).

§ 17.6 ARRESTS
§ 17.6.1 Definition
An arrest occurs when you take a person into custody. This means either that a police officer physically restrains the person or the person submits to the officer's authority (Pen. Code §835).

To be a valid arrest, the officer must take the person into custody "in a case and in the manner authorized by law" (Pen. Code §834).

§ 17.6.2 Who May Arrest
Under the proper circumstances, everyone has some authority to make an arrest. Furthermore, "citizen's" arrest is a poor label, since a person does not need to be a citizen to make a private arrest. Nonetheless, a peace officer has more authority to arrest than does a private person.

For a felony, a police officer may arrest a person (1) with a warrant (a private person may not) or (2) without a warrant if he has probable cause to believe the person committed a felony, regardless of whether or not it was committed in his presence.

For a misdemeanor, a police officer may arrest a person (1) with a warrant or (2) without a warrant if he has probable cause to believe the misdemeanor was committed in his presence (Pen. Code §836).

§ 17.6.3 How to Arrest

A police officer must either physically restrain the suspect or the suspect must submit to his authority. (Pen. Code §835.)

The police officer may use reasonable force to effect the arrest, overcome resistance, or prevent escape. (Pen. Code §§835, 835a, 843.)

Normally, a police officer must tell the arrestee (1) he or she is under arrest (2) the reason for the arrest, and (3) the officer's authority (i.e., that you are a peace officer) (Pen. Code §841).

§ 17.6.4 Must You Arrest?

An arrest initiates criminal proceedings against a person accused of a crime.

According to section 836 of the California Penal Code, an officer "may make an arrest in obedience to a warrant, or may...without a warrant arrest a person:"

1. Whenever he has reasonable cause to believe that the person to be arrested has committed a public offense in his presence.

2. When a person arrested has committed a felony, although not in his presence;

3. Whenever he has reasonable cause to believe that the person arrested has committed a felony, whether or not a felony has in fact been committed."

Note the wording of the Penal Code here: "the officer may arrest." The Penal Code does not dictate that the officer must arrest.

In a similar manner, a private person may arrest another person, but only when a crime in fact has been committed (Pen. Code §837). In other words, a peace officer, because of his or her professional training, is given greater discretion in determining probable cause than is a private citizen. With a few exceptions, the wording of the Penal Code is permissive. The laws of arrest are generally permissive. Even in the case of murder, the law is permissive. This gives the police latitude in their timing of an arrest, should there be good reason to postpone it. Especially in non-hazardous crimes such as petty theft, it is often wise to let a crime-in-progress continue to a point where criminal intent is easily proven, as long as the prolongation does not endanger life or property or allow a misdemeanor to become a felony.

However, departmental policies are usually less permissive than the Penal Code. A typical departmental policy would require that the officer take appropriate action promptly, especially in the case of a felony.

The officer is expected to enforce the law. If he felt that he might arrest, or might not arrest—more or less at will—he would undoubtedly be destined for a brief career as a police officer.

When an officer contacts a person who appears to be a drug abuser, the circumstances may not always supply probable cause to arrest. In such cases, the officer should take the opportunity to refer the subject to an agency which may be able to help him with his problem. The same referrals can be used when an officer is approached by a concerned third party (a parent, a spouse, or a friend).

By removing a person who abuses narcotics from the community, incarceration accomplishes two objectives: it places the individual in an environment where he must withdraw from drugs and gives him an opportunity to receive treatment; at the same time, it eliminates the possibility (at least while he is incarcerated) that he might commit crimes in order to obtain money for drugs. The reason to enforce narcotic influence laws in this manner is to reduce crimes against property.

Since some individuals take it upon themselves to seek aid in reducing or overcoming their own need for drugs, officers should be familiar with the drug treatment programs in their area. Most departments have a list of referral agencies.

§ 17.6.5 Recording Probable Cause
When making an arrest, it is important that the officer remembers, or in the case of complicated circumstances, records the probable cause of his or her actions. The officer should remember or record why he knows or believes that a crime has been committed and why he knows or believes that the person he is arresting is guilty of the crime.

Probable cause facts become a part of the arrest report prepared by the officer. If the arrest is later questioned, the officer may wish he had kept better records. Probable cause is often based on many bits of information and observations that, after a lapse of time, will be difficult to recall accurately and describe and relate before a court.

§ 17.7 SEARCHES DURING DETENTIONS (PAT-DOWNS OR FRISKS)
During a detention, a police officer has no power to conduct a general, full, exploratory search of the suspect. However, the officer may conduct a pat-down or limited weapons search of a person detained, but (1) only for weapons, (2) only of his outer clothing, and (3) only if the officer has specific facts which make him feel in danger.

"Standard procedure" isn't good enough (*Santos*, 154 Cal.App.3d 1178 (1984)). The officer must reasonably suspect that the person is armed or may be armed (*Pickerson*, 508 U.S. 366, 373 (1993); *Limon*, 17 Cal.App.4th 524, 532 (1993)), although he need not be positive.

The courts are quite supportive of officer safety (*Flippen*, 924 F.2d 163, 165 (9th Cir. 1991); *Frank V.*, 233 Cal.App.3d 1232, 1238 (1991); *Snyder*, 11 Cal.App.4th 389, 393 (1992); *Wilson*, 59 Cal.App.4th 1053,

1060-1061 (1997)). But at the very least an officer needs a potentially dangerous situation to justify a pat-down search. Dealing with a suspected dangerous felon is by definition enough cause.

However, he may conduct a search for contraband if the officer has probable cause to believe it is on the person—probably on the theory that his probable cause also provides a basis to arrest. In this case, the search is justified incident to that arrest, even though the search comes first (*People v. Valdez*, 196 Cal. App. 3d 799, 242 Cal. Rptr. 142 (Cal. App. 4 Dist. 1987)).

§ 17.7.1 Search and Seizure During Detention
The officer may seize any weapons or other hard objects usable as a weapon which are discovered during a pat-down. Contraband or other clear evidence of crime may also be seized, as long as objective safety factors exist to justify the pat-search in the first place.

If a valid pat-down leads to discovery of a closed container, you may open it if you have a basis for thinking that it contains a weapon; this is because of the inherent "exigencies" involved in a weapon situation. However, if you discover a closed container which you do not think contains a weapon, but rather some kind of contraband (e.g., a cigarette pack which you think contains marijuana), you will need a warrant in order to legally open the container, unless the contents are clearly obvious by plain view, smell, or touch.

§ 17.7.1(a)   Plain View
An officer may also seize any weapons, contraband, or crime-related evidence which is in plain view or plain sight during a detention. This type of seizure is lawful because observing something in plain view is not considered a "search."

Here is another case of plain view seizure: during a traffic stop, a "neatly folded squared piece of paper" fell from the driver's wallet to the ground. The experienced officer recognized it as a likely bindle of cocaine or heroin. Therefore, it was proper to seize the bindle.

§ 17.7.1(b)   Abandonment
Similarly, if the suspect discards an object during a detention, it is generally proper to seize and examine it. However, if you are going to detain the suspect longer or arrest him because of a discarded object (for example, a bindle containing white powder which you think is cocaine), be sure you have the training or expertise to justify your suspicion.

§ 17.7.1(c)   Plain View Is Not a Search
In one case, officers made a traffic stop and saw, from outside the vehicle, marijuana debris on the floorboards. The observation provided probable cause to enter the passenger compartment, seize the evidence, and search for more. In another case, an officer smelled marijuana during a traffic stop. He lawfully entered the passenger compartment (because he had probable cause) and saw a concealed weapon. In this case, it was proper for the officer to seize the weapon.

§ 17.7.1(d)   Plain Smell

Just like "plain view," "plain smell" is also not considered a "search;" therefore, it too can provide probable cause for searching parts of cars and containers within cars. Following are some cases of plain smell which would or would not lead to probable cause for a search.

An officer stopped Scott because the registration tag on his vehicle was not current. When Scott got out of this car, he was unsteady and had a blank stare. Scott told the officer that the officer could get the registration from the car. When the officer opened the door he smelled ether. As the officer's nose got closer to a box of Sherman cigarettes, his knowledge that Sherman cigarettes are often dipped in PCP gave the officer probable cause to open the box.

An officer, while making a traffic stop, smelled the odor of marijuana coming from the passenger compartment. He properly searched the passenger compartment. However, because he found only evidence of "casual use" (i.e., some debris, perhaps a few "roaches," etc.) his search had to end there. Small amounts of marijuana do not provide probable cause to search the trunk.

An officer made a traffic stop for speeding, then saw marijuana on the rear seat. While retrieving that marijuana, the officer smelled a further strong odor of unburned marijuana coming from the rear portion of the vehicle. That smell gave the officer probable cause to search behind the rear seat as well as in the trunk.

§ 17.7.1(e)   Undercover Entries

An officer may enter premises as part of an undercover operation if valid consent to enter is obtained from an occupant. The fact that you misrepresent your identity will not invalidate the consent (*Toubus v. Superior Court, Marin County*, 114 Cal. App. 3d 378, 170 Cal. Rptr. 697 (Cal. App. 1 Dist. 1981), cert. denied 454 U.S. 824)). Once inside, after the "buy" has taken place, you will then have probable cause to arrest and may do so without a warrant. Also consider the case below:

An operator poses as a friend of a friend and asks to enter to buy narcotics. The suspect lets the operator in and makes a sale. The warrantless arrest which follows is valid because the consent to enter is valid. The courts see no trick or misrepresentation of purpose because the officer's stated or implied purpose was to make a buy, and with that understanding the suspect agreed to let him enter. In other words, you can misrepresent your identity, just not your purpose. The suspect takes his chances about who you really are.

This type of entry has been upheld even where there was enough probable cause to arrest prior to entry (*People v. Evans*, 108 Cal. App. 3d 193, 166 Cal. Rptr. 315 (Cal. App. 4 Dist. 1980)). Nevertheless, be careful not to abuse this procedure. Get a warrant unless you intend in good faith to continue the investigation after you are inside (e.g., by making a buy) and not just to arrest the suspect.

§ 17.7.1(f)   Reentries

Be alert to another problem area with undercover operations. It is all right for the operator, while still inside, to signal for reinforcements who then also enter to actually make the arrest (*Toubus v. Superior Court, Marin County, supra*; *People v. Cornejo*, 92 Cal. App. 637, 155 Cal. Rptr. 238 (Cal. App. 2 Dist. 1979)).

However, if the operator physically leaves the premises to get assistance, his subsequent reentry could be invalid in some courts, making the arrest invalid also.

In one case, acting on a tip, an undercover officer went to the defendant's house to try to sell him some "stolen" guns. He got the suspect's consent to enter, made the sale, and then tried to signal for backup help. However, his transmitter was broken, so he stepped outside and was 15 feet from the residence when he signaled the others. The court said the warrantless (re)entry and arrest were unlawful. The original consent no longer applied and there were no exigent circumstances (*People v. Garcia*, 139 Cal. App. 3d Supp. 1, 188 Cal. Rptr. 868, (Cal. Super. 1982)). However, in *People v. Cespedes*, 191 Cal. App. 3d 768, 236 Cal. Rptr. 649 (Cal. App. 1 Dist. 1987), the defendant consented to the initial entry of the undercover officer. After the drug deal was complete, the officer signaled to the other officers over his transmitter that the transaction was complete, and then he left the building. The other officers entered the building and arrested the defendant,. The court held that the warrantless reentry into the defendant's house and the warrantless arrest were lawful even though they occurred after the undercover officer left the house.

§ 17.8   ARRESTS IN HOMES: THE WARRANT REQUIREMENT

As a general rule, you must have an arrest warrant in order to arrest someone inside his or her home (*People v. Ramey*, 16 Cal. 3d 263, 127 Cal. Rptr. 629, 545 P.2d 1333 (Cal. 1976)); *Payton v. New York*, 445 U.S. 573, 63 L.Ed. 2d 639, 100 S.Ct. 1371 (1980)). "Home" or "dwelling" can mean any place the suspect resides, such as his tent, motel room, boat, van, etc.

This same protection (the requirement of a warrant) also applies to those portions of a business or office which are not open to the general public.

The purpose behind this arrest warrant requirement (which also exists under federal law) is the same as the purpose behind a search warrant. "A man's home is his castle," and police simply are not permitted inside without judicial authorization (the warrant), an emergency (exigent circumstances), or valid permission from the occupant (consent).

§ 17.9   INVESTIGATION OF DRUG OFFENSES: CAR STOPS

A vehicle "stop" is an exertion of authority by an officer which is something less than a full arrest but more substantial than a simple "contact" or "consensual encounter." A detention occurs at the moment the officer turns on his red light or otherwise stops a vehicle to investigate a possible crime or to issue a traffic citation.

Note, however, that if an officer is dealing with a vehicle which is parked or already stopped for some other reason, it does not constitute a detention to walk up to the driver and ask (not demand) to see his or her driver's license or other identification (*People v. Gonzales*, 164 Cal. App. 3d 1194, 211 Cal. Rptr. 74 (Cal. App. 1 Dist. 1985)).

§ 17.9.1 Reasonable Suspicion

A detention following a car stop is valid only if you have a "reasonable suspicion" that:

—something relating to a crime has just happened, is happening, or is about to happen; and

—the vehicle or the person in the vehicle you are about to detain is connected with that activity.

The officer's "reasonable suspicion" must be based on specific facts which he or she can articulate to a court. The court will then decide if the facts were enough to make the officer's suspicion reasonable. The officer cannot make valid detention based on a hunch, rumor, intuition, instinct, or curiosity.

The officer may also make a legal detention, vehicle or person, based on a "wanted flyer" or similar bulletin issued by some other jurisdiction and relating to a completed crime, as long as the other jurisdiction had a reasonable basis for issuing it, and the detention is not impermissibly intrusive (*U.S. v. Hensley*, 469 U.S. 221, 83 L.Ed. 2d 604, 105 S.Ct. 675 (1985)).

§ 17.9.2 Traffic Stops

Observation of a Vehicle Code violation will always provide a valid basis to detain.

If the officer has a "hunch" a vehicle or its occupants are involved in a felony, but does not have enough specific information to make a valid detention for the felony, the officer may make a traffic stop to see what he can see (assuming, of course, that a valid basis for the traffic stop exists).

However, the officer's actions must be consistent with the legal basis for the traffic stop if he expects the detention to hold up. In other words, the officer should follow through on the traffic ticket and not undertake any unrelated investigation, or prolong the detention, unless he discovers something suspicious or incriminating in the course of issuing the ticket. In *Whren v. U.S.*, No. 95-5841 (1996), the U.S. Supreme Court held that the temporary detention of a motorist upon probable cause that he violated the traffic laws does not violate the 4th Amendment prohibition against unreasonable searches and seizures, even if a reasonable officer would not have stopped the motorist for such a violation. In *Whren*, while patrolling a high drug area, officers in an unmarked vehicle observed defendant's vehicle at a stop sign for more than 20 seconds. Then, the defendant's vehicle turned suddenly to the right without using a signal, and sped off at an unreasonable speed.

The officers followed and stopped the defendant's vehicle. On approaching the defendant's vehicle, the officers noted two bags of cocaine in the defendant's car. A reasonable officer would not have stopped the defendant for turning without using a signal, a traffic violation under Washington, D.C., law. The Supreme Court held that the officers could detain the defendant based on an observed traffic violation.

The officer should always concentrate on the specific facts which create the suspicion. Remembering each of them, or listing them in his report, may well "save" a case.

If the traffic stop turns out not to be "routine" because the officer sees contraband (marijuana "roaches") or discovers something suspicious, (non-matching names and vehicle identification numbers), the stop has become an "investigative detention."

It is impossible to give a specific rule on how long the officer may properly detain someone on reasonable suspicion for non-traffic offenses. The permissible length is determined by considering the officer's purpose, diligence, and choice of investigative means (*U.S. v. Sharpe*, 470 U.S. 675, 84 L.Ed. 2d 605, 105 S.Ct. 1568 (1985)). Twenty minutes might be perfectly reasonable under one set of circumstances but not under another.

Nevertheless, if the officer is not progressing in his attempt to obtain probable cause to arrest after a reasonable time of investigating, he should either:

—let the detainee go (possibly after filling out a field interrogation card or otherwise ensuring that he can be found later); or

—obtain the detainee's unequivocal consent to further detention.

§ 17.9.3 Ordering Occupants Out

Nevertheless, if the officer is not progressing in his attempt to obtain probable cause to arrest after a reasonable time of investigating, he should either:

—let the detainee go (possibly after filling out a field interrogation card or otherwise ensuring that he can be found later); or

—obtain the detainee's unequivocal consent to further detention.

The United States Supreme Court established many years ago that you have the right, during even a routine traffic stop, to order the *driver* to get out of the vehicle. You do not need any particular reason, such as danger, or suspicion of a crime. If the stop is lawfully underway, ordering the driver out during the detention is legal, period. This is because the courts believe that *all* traffic stops involve enough risk, inherently, to justify the minimal additional intrusion of ordering a validly detained driver to get out of the vehicle. (*Mimms*, 434 U.S. 106

(1977); *Maxwell*, 206 Cal.App.3d 1004 (1988); *Valencia*, 20 Cal.App.4th 906, 918 (1993); *Miranda*, 17 Cal.App.4th 917, 927 (1993).)

Twenty years after *Mimms*, the United States Supreme Court finally extended the same rule to *passengers*. "[T]he same weighty interest in officer safety is present regardless of whether the occupant of the stopped car is a driver or passenger." "[D]anger to an officer from a traffic stop is likely to be greater when there are passengers in addition to the driver in the stopped car. While there is not the same basis for ordering the passengers out of the car as there is for ordering the driver out, the additional intrusion on the passenger is minimal. We therefore hold that an officer making a traffic stop may order passengers to get out of the car pending completion of the stop." (*Wilson*, 117 S.Ct. 882, 886 (1997); see also *Ruvalcaba*, 64 F.3d 1323, 1327 (9th Cir. 1995).)

Remember, however, that your power to order passengers out of a vehicle is justified strictly by "officer safety."

§ 17.9.4 Consent
As long as you have some basis for asking, it will always be proper to search any part of a car or anything in it if you first obtain a valid consent. However, there are problem areas within the "consent" exception which you must fully understand. These areas include:

—"voluntariness" (was the suspect coerced or pressured into giving consent?);

—"authority" (did you get consent from someone empowered to give it?); and

—"scope" (were any limitations placed on the consent?).

ALWAYS SEEK CONSENT TO SEARCH NO MATTER WHAT OTHER AUTHORITY YOU MAY HAVE FOR YOUR SEARCH. Consent can never hurt and it may validate an otherwise bad search. In *Ohio v. Robinette,* No. 95-891, (1996), the U.S. Supreme Court held that the 4th Amendment does not require a lawfully seized defendant to be advised that he is "free to go" before his consent to search is recognized as voluntary. The officer lawfully stopped the defendant for speeding. After issuing a verbal warning and returning the defendant's license, the officer asked the defendant if the defendant had any drugs or weapons in the car. The defendant said "no". Then the officer asked the defendant if the car could be searched. The defendant consented. Methamphetamine was found in the car. The Court held that the consent to search was valid.

§ 17.9.5 Plain View
As mentioned earlier, "plain view" is not a "search." It is the observation of crime-related evidence from a place you have a lawful right to be (*Katz v. U.S.*, 389 U.S. 347, 88 S.Ct. 507 (1967)).

A.   Observation After Entry

If you are already lawfully within the vehicle, you may seize all crime-related evidence which you see. However, if you are not lawfully within the vehicle, it is illegal for you to seize any evidence. For instance:

1. An officer smells marijuana during a traffic stop. He lawfully enters the passenger compartment (because he has probable cause) and sees a concealed weapon. The officer may properly seize the weapon.

2. An officer stops a suspect on a traffic offense. The officer puts his head just inside the window and sees contraband. He may not legally seize the contraband because it was illegal for him to enter the vehicle before seeing the contraband.

§ 17.9.6 Plain Smell
Just like "plain view," "plain smell" is also not a "search," and it too can provide probable cause for searching parts of cars and containers within cars (*People v. Weaver*, 143 Cal. App. 3d 926, 192 Cal. Rptr, 436 (Cal. App. 2 Dist. 1983)).

§ 17.9.7 Observation Before Entry
In a vehicle context (as opposed to homes), it generally makes very little difference that you observe the contraband or crime-related evidence from outside the vehicle before you enter it. Typically, you may still enter for the purpose of seizing it, at least when the car is occupied. This is because the area you can observe from outside (i.e., the passenger compartment) carries such a low expectation of privacy (*Texas v. Brown*, 460 U.S. 730, 75 L.Ed. 2d 502, 103 S.Ct. 1535 (1983)).

§ 17.9.8 Using a Flashlight
The use of a flashlight, either from outside the car or after a lawful entry, changes nothing. You may use a flashlight to see anything which would have been visible during daylight hours (*People v. Rogers*, 21 Cal. 3d 542, 146 Cal. Rptr. 732, 579 P.2d 1048 (Cal. 1978)).

§ 17.10 SEARCHES BASED ON PROBABLE CAUSE: "AUTOMOBILE EXCEPTION"
§ 17.10.1 Parts of the Vehicle
Under both federal and California case law, a police officer may conduct a warrantless search of any part of a car which he has lawfully stopped on the road as long as he has probable cause to believe the object he is looking for may be located in that portion of the car.

The key to understanding this "automobile exception" is realizing that it is based on "probable cause," and that "probable cause" here means exactly the same thing that it does in a search warrant context; namely, enough facts, knowledge, training, etc., to make it reasonable to believe that the object a police officer is looking for may be located in the place (portion of the car) he wants to search.

Police officers' discovery of marijuana seeds in plain view on floor of automobile, in passenger area, gave the police probable cause to search the passenger area of vehicle. (*Wimberly v. Superior Court of San Ber-*

nardino County, 16 Cal. 3d 557, 128 Cal. Rptr. 641, 547 P.2d 417 (Cal 1976)). However, this did not provide probable cause for the police to search the trunk of the vehicle. There must be some specific facts to give the police reasonable cause to search the trunk of a vehicle.

Erratic driving, slurred speech, pinpointed pupils, and fresh puncture marks on the arm would provide probable cause to search the passenger compartment for narcotics (*People v. Low*, 148 Cal. App. 3d 89, 196 Cal. Rptr. 18 (Cal. App. 1 Dist. (1983)).

The key to understanding this "automobile exception" is to realize that it is based on "probable cause," and that "probable cause" here means *exactly the same thing that it does in a search warrant context*, namely, enough facts, knowledge, training, etc., to provide a "fair probability" that the object you are looking for will be found in the place (portion of the car) you want to search (*Pinela-Hernandez*, 262 F.3d 974, 978 (9th Cir. 2001); *Alien*, 78 Cal.App.4th 445, 450 (2000); *Nonnette*, 221 Cal.App.3d 659, 665-666 (1990)).

§ 17.10.2   Motor Homes

In 1985, the United States Supreme Court made it clear that the "automobile exception" applies to motor homes as well. It ruled that when a motor home (here a Dodge/Midas Mini Motor Home) is (1) being used on the highways, or (2) capable of such use and is found stationary in a place not regularly used for residential purposes, the two justifications for the vehicle exception come into play. First, the vehicle is readily mobile, and second, there is a reduced expectation of privacy stemming from the pervasive regulation of vehicles capable of traveling on highways (*California v. Carney*, 471 U.S. 386, 105 S.Ct. 2066 (1985); *People v. Black*, 173 Cal. App. 3d 506, 219 Cal. Rptr. 355, (Cal. App. 1 Dist. 1985)).

This ruling means that you do not need a warrant to search a motor home which you stop on the highway, or which you find parked on the street or in a parking lot.

The same is true for a "van," which also falls within the "automobile exception" since it is even more like a passenger car than a motor home (*People v. Chestnut*, 151 Cal. App. 721, 198 Cal. Rptr. 8, (Cal. App. 3 Dist. 1983)).

On the other hand, if the motor home is at a campground or other overnight facility, you should obtain a warrant, particularly if the vehicle is hooked up to outside facilities, especially plumbing.

§ 17.10.3   Federal Rule on Searching the Passenger Compartment

The federal "bright line" rule is relatively straightforward. When you make a custodial arrest of the occupant of a vehicle, you may search the passenger compartment of the vehicle, including the glove compartment, and including any containers you find, whether open or closed (*New York v. Belton*, 453 U.S. 454, 69 L.Ed. 2d 768, 101 S.Ct. 2860 (1981)).

In other words, no matter what the arrest is for, as long as you are taking the driver or occupant into custody, you may search the passenger compartment and everything and anything in it. It makes no difference that the arrestee is already out of the car and is, as a practical matter, not able to reach inside anymore (*U.S. v. Lorenzo*, 867 F.2d 561 (9th Cir. 1989)).

Note, however, that such a search is limited to the "passenger compartment" and may not include the vehicle's trunk.

§ 17.11 SEARCHES INCIDENT TO ARREST

As defined earlier, an "arrest" occurs when a police officer takes someone into custody, either by the use of physical restraints or by the arrestee's submission to the officer's authority. When the officer makes a custodial arrest of the driver or occupant of a vehicle, the law permits him to search the person and some portions of the vehicle incident to that arrest.

When a person is arrested in a home or other building, a limited right exists to conduct a warrantless search not of the premises but of his person, as well as the area within his "immediate control" ("arm's length," "lunging distance") (*Chimel v. California*, 395 U.S. 752, 23 L.Ed. 2d 685, 89 S.Ct. 2034 (1969)).

It is impossible to state exactly how much area is covered by this exception. However, it is supposed to include any place from which the suspect might otherwise grab a weapon or destroy evidence.

As you can imagine, the area a police officer may properly search can get quite limited as the chances of the suspect having quick access to the area diminishes. Such limiting circumstances would exit if:

—the arrestee has already been handcuffed (particularly if his hands are behind his back);

—an officer is standing between the suspect and the place being searched;

—there are numerous officers and only one arrestee;

—the area to be searched is locked, closed, or otherwise difficult to get at or into; or

—there are no particularly dangerous circumstances surrounding the arrest or the arrestee.

A search incident to an arrest is permissible only if it takes place at the same place and at essentially the same time as the arrest, i.e., just before, during, or immediately afterward (*Chimel v. California, supra*).

Normally, any evidence a police officer finds by searching beyond the suspect's "immediate control" will be suppressed unless he sees it in "plain view" while he is still within the "immediate control" area.

Furthermore, it is improper for a police officer to try to expand or enlarge the "plain view" or the "immediate control" area by moving the suspect from room to room (*Sanderson v. Superior Court of Stanislaus County*, 105 Cal. App. 3d 264, 164 Cal. Rptr. 290 (Cal. App. 5 Dist. 1980.)).

However, if the arrestee asks to go to another part of the premises (e.g., to get his billfold or shoes, to change clothes, to go the bathroom), it is perfectly legal for a police officer to accompany him for security reasons, and whatever you see in "plain view" while doing so may properly be seized (*Washington v. Chrisman*, 455 U.S. 1, 70 L.Ed. 2d 778, 102 S.Ct. 812 (1982)).

§ 17.11.1 Searching Persons

The federal rule for searching persons incident to a custodial arrest does not change just because the person is (or has just been) in a vehicle.

Briefly stated, the federal rule allows a full body search, including any containers, incident to any kind of custodial arrest, from murder to outstanding traffic warrants (*U.S. v. Robinson*, 414 U.S. 218, 94 S.Ct. 467, 38 L.Ed. 2d 427 (1973)).

§ 17.11.2 Stopping and Searching Vehicles

When making a car stop, the officer must keep the suspect under observation at all times. Watch the suspect's HANDS! All too often an officer will overlook a major law violation by being preoccupied with a "routine" car stop. While the officer is so engaged, the drug violator is busy throwing, or concealing contraband.

Once the decision has been made to arrest the suspect, search and handcuff the suspect IMMEDIATELY with his hands BEHIND HIM. Keep any recovered evidence out of the suspect's reach. How many times has this question been raised—"The suspect just ate the evidence. What do I do now?"

Request assistance as soon as conditions appear that additional help may be required. Whenever you can, make the car stop in an area where there is adequate light. Use the spotlight and headlights of the police vehicle to further illuminate the interior of the stopped vehicle. As you proceed with a routine stop, protect yourself. There has been an increasing number of attacks on police officers.

Conduct a thorough preliminary search. Check the obvious and not so obvious places of concealment such as trouser cuffs, inside of socks, inside of trouser waistband, items inside of other items such as a bindle of heroin inside a matchbook, fingernail clipper, or cigarette pack; and check inside the suspect's hand since drug users are very skilled at palming contraband until it can be thrown away or eaten. Keep in mind that weapons may be overlooked in a cursory pat search. Also, containers of narcotics are sometimes hidden in the body cavities such as the mouth, rectum, or vagina. For this reason, it is important to search the vehicle before the suspect is placed in custody and after the suspect is removed.

It might not be possible to conduct a thorough search of the body as you would like. Just remember that drug users will attempt to dispose of the evidence. When transporting the suspect, make sure to secure the suspect in the vehicle so no drugs can be disposed of.

Note: "Cite and release" traffic offenses are not included here because, even though the driver is technically under arrest, he is not in custody. The law treats such situations as a "detention."

§ 17.12   SEARCH AND SEIZURE ON PREMISES
§ 17.12.1   Abandonment
A person who voluntarily abandons his or her property no longer retains any reasonable expectation of privacy in that property. Although it seldom occurs that entry into a home can be justified on an abandonment theory, it is possible.

More frequently, it is rented apartments or motel units which might be considered "abandoned" either because the rental term has expired and/or because it appears from all the circumstances that the tenant has permanently departed (*People v. Ingram*, 122 Cal. App. 3d 721, 198 Cal. Rptr. 8, (Cal App. 3 Dist. 1983)).

§ 17.12.2   Personal Privacy
The United States Constitution guarantees everyone the right to be free from unreasonable governmental intrusion. This right is personal to every citizen. It can exist almost any time and any place as long as:

—the individual has indicated that he personally expects privacy;

—his expectation of privacy is objectively reasonable under the circumstances; and

—his expectation is one which society is prepared to recognize as legitimate (*California v. Greenwood*, 486 U.S. 100, 100 L.Ed. 2d 30, 108 S.Ct. 1625 (1988); *People v. Edelbacher*, 47 Cal. 3d 983, 254 Cal. Rptr. 586, 766 P.2d 1 (Cal. 1989)).

A person automatically has a reasonable expectation of privacy in his or her home. Of course, if he lives in a ground-floor apartment on a busy street and leaves his window shades wide open, he cannot reasonably expect his activities inside not to be observed. Likewise, the owner of undeveloped land exhibits a greater expectation of privacy the more he attempts to keep the public out (by fences, signs, gates, etc.)

§ 17.12.2(a)   General Rule for Searching Premises
It is illegal for a police officer to physically enter into an area where a person has a "reasonable expectation of privacy" in order to conduct a search or for the purpose of seizing something, unless:

—the officer has a warrant; or

—there are exigent circumstances (an emergency); or

—the officer obtained a valid consent.

§ 17.12.2(b) Garbage

Under the federal law (the Fourth Amendment), the United States Supreme Court has made it very clear that there is no reasonable expectation of privacy in trash or garbage, even if it has been bagged and placed at curbside or otherwise outside the "curtilage" of the residence for pickup (*California v. Greenwood,* 486 U.S. 100, 100 L.Ed. 2d 30, 108 S.Ct. 1625 (1988)). Therefore, it is lawful for an officer to conduct a search of garbage or trash for evidence.

§ 17.12.2(c) Other Items

If a person leaves an object behind, or disclaims any knowledge of it or interest in it, he is waiving any reasonable expectation of privacy he might have had in the object. Under such circumstances, it is legal for you to search the item. For instance, suspects were properly arrested inside a house where officers had reason to believe cocaine had just been delivered in a shoulder bag. The bag was discovered just inside the front door, but all the occupants/arrestees disclaimed ownership of, or any interest in, the shoulder bag. Therefore, it was legal for the officers to search it (*People v. Mendoza,* 176 Cal. App. 3d 1127, 224 Cal. Rptr. 145 (Cal. App. 4 Dist. 1986)).

§ 17.12.2(d) Specific Situations of Privacy

The following is a discussion of specific situations and how they relate to both a person's expectation of privacy and an officer's legal jurisdiction.

1. A Home

Everyone, of course, can reasonably expect privacy inside his own home, at least to the extent that no officer will enter unless the officer has a warrant, exigent circumstances exist, or consent has been obtained. On the other hand, a person can hardly claim he has a reasonable expectation of privacy in areas around his home where the general public (mailmen, salesmen, visitors, etc.) would reasonably be permitted to go. For example, the garage of a condominium apartment, which is available to all tenants and readily accessible by members of the general public, would not receive Fourth Amendment protection (*People v. Galan*, 163 Cal. App. 3d 786, 209 Cal. Rptr. 837 (Cal. App. 1 Dist 1985)). Almost anything, anywhere, can qualify as a "home," such as a boat, van, motel room, tent, etc.

2. A Driveway

It is normally proper for a police officer to view areas around the premises from someone's driveway (*People v. Bradley*, 1 Cal. 3d 80, 81 Cal. Rptr. 457, 460 P.2d 129 (Cal. 1969)).

In one case, footprints in a front yard, on the driveway and the front porch—visible to any visitor approaching the front door—were in plain view (*People v. Edelbacher*, 47 Cal. 3d 983, 254 Cal. Rptr. 586, 766 P.2d 1 (Cal. 1989)). In a similar case of "plain view" from the driveway, marijuana plants were visible 30-40 feet away (*People v. Johnson*, 105 Cal. App 3d 884, 164 Cal. Rptr. 746 (Cal. App. 3 Dist 1980)).

3.   The Front Yard

A person normally has no reasonable expectation of privacy in the areas around the front of his home "where members of the public having business with the occupants" would naturally go. Two examples of this "front yard" rule are recounted below:

An officer missed a turnoff and ended up driving on a circular "loop" road which provided access to seven houses. When he turned into a driveway to ask Gray (who was outside) for directions, he noticed that Gray was carrying a trash bag filled with marijuana which protruded from the top of the bag. The officer arrested Gray and seized the marijuana. His observations were legal. Even though the road had some "no trespassing" signs, the officer was not there searching for contraband in an area where the desire for privacy was obvious. The "loop" was open, accessible, and frequently used by the residents. Turning around in the driveway was an act which could have been done by any one of the residents or their guests who regularly used the roadway, and Gray could have been seen from the roadway as well as his own driveway (*People v. Gray*, 164 Cal. App. 3d 445, 210 Cal. Rptr. 553 (Cal. App. 2 Dist. 1985.))

An officer went through an unlocked gate in a chain-link fence to talk to the occupant/suspect who was standing in the front yard about 75 feet from the gate. Up close, the officer could see the suspect was under the influence of an opiate. The court held that the suspect had no reasonable expectation of privacy in his front yard, despite the fence, because the fence was more for "discouraging dogs, children, handbill deliverymen and others from walking across the front lawn and flower beds," than it was for "excluding the public." However, the result would probably have been different if there had been a locked gate, a high solid fence blocking the front yard from view, a written notice to keep out or "beware of dog," or perhaps a doorbell at the front gate, warning that the visitor was unwelcome (*People v. Mendoza*, 122 Cal. App. 3d Supp. 12, 176 Cal. Rptr. 293 (Cal. Super. 1981)).

4.   The Back Yard

Normally, a person has a higher reasonable expectation of privacy in his back yard than his front yard. This is because, by common sense and custom, members of the public are not normally invited into or expected to enter the back yard of an average residence. Therefore, a police officer may not normally enter the back yard to search or seize without a warrant, consent or exigent circumstances.

Officer went to a house to investigate a malicious mischief matter. Seeing no one inside the house, he walked into the fenced back yard through a closed, posted but unlocked gate and found marijuana. The warrantless entry was illegal. (*Winters*, 149 Cal.App.3d 705 (1983).)

5. Windows

If you look through a window from a place where the public (which includes police) has implicitly been invited, by means of a pathway, walkway, etc., then your observations will be legal. The fact you may have committed a "technical trespass" to stand there is irrelevant. And even from such a "public" place, your observations will probably be ruled illegal if you have to peek through a hole or small area, for example, a small gap in a blind, in order to make them. On the other hand, if you enter a back yard, side yard or other area where the public has not been implicitly invited, then your observations will definitely constitute an illegal invasion of privacy, even if the window, for example, is entirely uncovered (*Camacho*, 23 Cal.4th 824 (2000); *Lorenzana*, 9 Cal.3d 626 (1973)).

It was illegal for officers to look through a side yard window, located about 20' from the front of the house and 40' from the sidewalk, even though there was no window covering, and even though there was no "barrier" to the public, such as a fence or shrubbery, where there was also no implicit "invitation" to the public to go there, such as a pathway or entrance to the residence; where passers-by on the street or sidewalk could not see into the room; where the officers, who were responding to a "loud party" report, had not knocked on the front door first; where it was 11 p.m. and there was no exigency or any criminal offense discernable before they looked through the window (*Camacho*, 23 Cal.4th 824 (2000)).

6. Fences and Walls

The general rule is that if, while standing in a lawful place, you can see over or through the fence or wall (1) without extraordinary effort (e.g., without using a stepladder or standing on a car or cinderblock), or (2) without getting very close and "peeking," the viewing will normally not be considered a "search;" i.e, the person does not have a reasonable expectation of privacy in the area viewed.

An officer was told by an informant that Lovelace was growing marijuana. The officer went to the Lovelace residence and, while standing in the alley, looked through a small knothole in a six-foot-high wooden fence and saw marijuana growing. The officer then got a warrant and seized the marijuana (and other drugs in plain view). The evidence was suppressed because looking through the knothole was a warrantless "search." (*Lovelace*, 116 Cal.App.3d 541 (1981).)

7. Views from Neighboring Premises

A police officer may view the suspect's home or property from a neighbor's home or property if invited to do so, at least in situations where members of the public could also see the suspicious object. Below is one explanatory anecdotes.

Dillon's neighbor called the police and said that Dillon was growing marijuana in his back yard, which had a fence around it. An officer responded and viewed the marijuana from the neighbor's second-story window (40 feet away). The court ruled that this viewing was proper, but emphasized that "the view of the back yard was vulnerable to observation by any of the petitioner's neighbors, in essence, open to public view" (*Dillon v. Superior Court of Santa Barbara County*, 7 Cal. 3d 305, 102 Cal. Rptr. 161, 497 P.2d 505 (Cal. 1972)).

8. Open Fields

The "curtilage" of a home is the real property "so intimately tied to the home" that it is placed within "the home's 'umbrella' of Fourth Amendment protection." (*Dunn*, 480 U.S. 294, 301 (1987).) What falls within the curtilage is determined by (1) the proximity of the area to the home, (2) whether the area is included within an enclosure, (3) how the area is used, and (4) the steps taken by the resident to protect the area from observation by the public. (*Dunn*, 480 U.S. 294, 301 (1987).)

Areas beyond the curtilage are "open fields." Open fields don't have to be either "open" or real "fields" to qualify. (*Dunn*, 480 U.S. 294, 304 (1987); *Van Damme*, 48 F.3d 461, 464 (9th Cir. 1995).) Open fields are areas of land so open to public view that the owner or possessor is deemed to have "implicitly invited" the police to observe and seize his contraband.

Because of the lack of reasonable expectation of privacy in such areas, the Fourth Amendment has no applicability to them. Therefore, your warrantless entry into open fields is perfectly legal, as are any observations made from them. (*Lorenzana*, 9 Cal.3d 626 (1973); *Freeman*, 219 Cal.App.3d 894 (1990).)

Police, acting on an anonymous tip, went out to the suspect's property, walked past his house, went around a locked gate posted with "no trespassing" signs, and walked over a mile onto his private property to find a secluded parcel of marijuana that could not be seen from anywhere else around. The United States Supreme Court upheld all these actions as involving only open fields. The fact that the officers committed a technical trespass also made no difference. (*Oliver*, 466 U.S. 170 (1984).)

9. Surveillance

It is not a "search" for a police officer to conduct surveillance of private premises or to follow people who leave the premises, as long as the observations are made from a place the officer has a right to be (*Lorenzana v. Superior Court of Los Angeles County, supra; People v. Thomas*, 112 Cal. App. 3d 980, 169 Cal. Rptr. 570 (Cal. App. 2 Dist 1980); *U.S. v. Dunn, supra*).

10. Use of Binoculars

Binoculars may be used to look onto premises or into a building if what is being viewed could be seen with the naked eye from a lawful position (such as the driveway). In other words, you may properly use binoculars to get a "better look."

11. Federal Law on Overflights

Federal law is clear that persons on the ground have no privacy from warrantless aerial observations made from aircraft flying in a physically nonintrusive manner in publicly navigable airspace, typically 1,000 feet or more above the ground (*California v. Ciraolo*, 476 U.S. 207, 90 L.Ed. 2d 210, 106 S.Ct. 1809 (1986)).

Such aerial observations are legal regardless of whether the flight (1) is part of a random, routine surveillance program or (2) is carried out to look at specific property in response to a tip.

Likewise, in the case of marijuana, it makes no difference where the marijuana is growing. From a lawful altitude, you may look not only into "open fields," but also into the "curtilage" of the residence, i.e., the yard or private area immediately surrounding a home (*U.S. v. Dunn, supra*).

Although the observations in *California v. Ciraolo* were made with the naked eye, the United States Supreme Court ruled in a companion case (*Dow Chemical v. U.S.*, 476 U.S. 227, 90 L.Ed. 2d 226, 106 S.Ct. 1819 (1986)) that it is also legal to use aerial photography, including a camera which provides moderate enhancement. In both *Dow Chemical v. U.S.* and *California v. Ciraolo,* however, the court warned that its opinion might well be different if the police used sophisticated "hi tech" equipment, not generally available to the public, which would reveal "intimate associations" below, i.e., activities not otherwise visible.

The court also warned that overflights which are too "physically intrusive" (i.e., too low, loud, frequent, prolonged, etc.) could make aerial observations illegal. Concerning elevation, this means you should conform to FAA rules and stay a minimum of 1,000 feet above ground level in "congested" areas and 500 feet in other, sparsely populated areas, when flying a fixed-wing aircraft. Federal law permits helicopters to legally fly as low as 400 feet (*Florida v. Riley*, 488 U.S. 445, 102 L.Ed. 2d 835, 109 S.Ct. 693 (1989)).

12. Thermal Imaging

A thermal imager is a device that from outside a building can detect infrared radiation on a structure's surfaces and then produce images based on their relative warmth. This device is often used to discover or confirm that a suspect is using high-intensity lights in connection with an "indoor grow" of marijuana.

Federal and state court opinions have disagreed on whether the warrantless use of such a device is illegal, some ruling "yes" because it reveals, to some degree, what is going on inside the residence, and some ruling "no search" on the theory that the device only measures heat emanating from the exterior, or *outside*, of the structure, an area in which the occupant has no reasonable expectation of privacy.

In *Kvllo*, the United States Supreme Court has ruled, in a very close decision (5-4), that the warrantless use of a thermal imaging device upon a private residence *does indeed constitute an unreasonable, and therefore illegal, "search."* (*Kvllo*, 533 U.S. 27 (2001).)

13. Videotaping

Videotaping someone's activities is a form of surveillance and will be subject to the traditional Fourth Amendment analysis, that is, whether it constitutes an invasion of the suspect's reasonable expectation of privacy. Thus there can be civil, and possibly even criminal, ramifications. (Sacramento County, 51 Cal.App.4th 1468, 1477-1478 (1996); Civ. Code, § 1708.8; Labor Code, § 435.)

Furthermore, because a video recorder is a "recording device," the Privacy Act (Pen. Code, § 630 et seq.) may have to be considered, at least if the video is used to record a "private *communication*," which in turn would typically require an *audio* component. (See *Drennan*, 84 Cal.App.4th 1349 (2000).)

The owner of a condominium permitted DBA agents to install audio and video equipment inside his residence, which the owner's brother-in-law was planning to use for a few days to manufacture some methamphetamine. The recordings constituted a violation of the defendant's privacy. "Clandestine observations into a private residence from a vantage point inaccessible to the public or an uninvited guest is a search which, if conducted without a warrant, is the type of activity the Fourth Amendment proscribes." (*Henderson*, 220 Cal.App.3d 1632 (1990).)

Plain View

Under the general rule, when you see something in "plain view" (or "plain sight") from a place you have a right to be, no "search" has taken place in any constitutional sense, because the person has no reasonable expectation of privacy as to items which are in plain view. (*Horton*, 496 U.S. 128 (1990); *Edelbacher*, 47 Cal.3d 983 (1989); *Arango*, 12 Cal.App.4th 450, 455 (1993).) You may seize any object that is in plain view, as long as:

—you have a lawful right to be in the place from which you are viewing the object;

—the incriminating character of the object is immediately apparent, i.e., you have probable cause to believe it is crime related; and

—you have a lawful right of access to the location of the object. (*Dickerson*, 508 U.S. 366 (1993); *Hicks*, 480 U.S. 321 (1987); *Ortiz*, 32 Cal.App.4th 286, 291 (1995); *Calvert*, 18 Cal.App.4th 1820, 1829 (1993); *Horton*, 496 U.S. 128, 136 (1990); *LeBlanc*, 60 Cal.App.4th 157, 166 (1997).)

In other words, simply because you see an object in plain view—even contraband-does not *automatically* mean that you may legally enter without a warrant to seize it. You will need consent or exigent circumstances. (*LeBlanc*, 60 Cal.App.4th 157, 164, 167 (1997); *Hull*, 34 Cal.App.4th 1448, 1452 (1995).)

No amount of probable cause can justify a warrantless search or seizure absent consent or exigent circumstances (*LeBlanc*, 60 Cal.App.4th 157, 167 (1997)).

§17.13 WARRANTLESS ENTRY DUE TO EXIGENCY/ EMERGENCY

You may enter premises without a warrant or consent if there are exigent circumstances. An exigency is an emergency situation requiring swift action to prevent any of the following:

—imminent danger to life

—serious damage to property

—imminent escape of a suspect

—the destruction of evidence (*People v. Lucero*, 44 Cal. 3d 1006, 245 Cal. Rptr. 185, 750 P.2d 1342 (Cal. 1988); *People v. Duncan*, 42 Cal. 3d 91, 227 Cal. Rptr. 654, 720 P.2d 2 (Cal. 1986); *U.S. v. Wilson*, 865 F.2d 215 (9th Cir. 1989)).

Often, the above-mentioned justifications for a warrantless entry or further search will overlap.

§ 17.13.1 Protective Sweep

If a police officer is already lawfully inside or at a house and has some basis for believing there may be others inside who may pose a danger to him, he may undertake a "protective sweep"—a brief search (two or three minutes) to look for these other individuals (*Guidi v. Superior Court of Los Angeles County*, 10 Cal. 3d 1, 109 Cal. Rptr. 684, 513 P.2d 908 (Cal. 1973)). In such an instance, the officer can only search areas where a person could possibly be hiding (not drawers, small cabinets, etc.). f the officer sees crime-related evidence in plain view during such a search, he may seize it. It is normally better, however, to get a warrant for the evidence he saw and other similar evidence which may be on the premises.

§ 17.13.2 Victim, Injured or Ill Person Inside

If there is reason to believe someone (victim or other person) inside a house may be injured or ill and in immediate need of help, the officer may enter the house without a warrant (*People v. Roberts*, 47 Cal. 2d

374, 303 P.2d 721 (Cal. 1956))—officers heard moaning inside dwelling).

Remember, however, that once a police officer is lawfully inside, he still may only search or do whatever is necessary to resolve the emergency, nothing more. The case summarized below illustrates this principle:

Officers responded to a house where there had been reports of "screams." They knocked on the door and requested permission to enter and investigate. The man who answered the door appeared very nervous and ran back into the house toward a bedroom. Fearing for their own safety and that of a possible victim the officers followed the man and found weapons and contraband (narcotics) in the bedroom in plain view. After the defendant had been arrested and taken to the living room, one officer went back to the bedroom and looked around more closely. He found more narcotics in a cigar box. The court found the entry of the house proper. However, the search of the cigar box was invalid since it was not justified by either the emergency or by "plain view" (*People v. Frazier*, 71 Cal. App. 3d 690, 139 Cal. Rptr. 573 (Cal. App. 2 Dist. 1977)).

§ 17.3.3 Suspected Child Abuse
Courts will go fairly far in finding an exigency and permitting a warrantless entry into premises to prevent possible child-abuse offenses.

Late one evening, the brother of the victim personally reported hearsay information to the police that his father was right then having sexual intercourse forcibly with the cerebral-palsied and retarded daughter of the family. The officer had heard other information about prior acts of sexuality in the house from a probation officer who was working with the family. Accompanied by the brother, the officer entered the house and the father's closed bedroom, finding the sex offense in progress. The warrantless entries were upheld. (*Brown*, 12 Cal.App.3d 600 (1970).)

§ 17.13.4 Suspected Domestic Violence
It may be legal to enter a residence, without consent or a warrant, at the scene of possible domestic violence, on the basis of exigent circumstances, if the circumstances indicate that such entry is necessary to protect the victim by preventing ongoing or additional violence.

At 11:00 p.m., officers responded to report of "a man shoving a woman around." After knocking without success, they saw a man inside and heard a shout. Thirty seconds after knocking again, a woman answered. Although she claimed she was alright, she was extremely frightened, appeared (to the experienced officer) to have been the victim of felony battery, lied about being alone, and gave a suspicious story about having fallen down the stairs. Believing that she might be under the threat of continued violence and that there might be others in peril inside, the officers entered the residence where they encountered Higgins and observed signs of marijuana activity. After obtaining consent to search from Higgins, the officers discovered more contraband.

HELD: The warrantless entry was valid. The entry was motivated by the officers' legitimate safety concerns, and their belief was objectively reasonable here. The court warned, however, that officers must exercise discretion rather than "blindly following" a departmental policy to contact all the parties at the scene "without considering the facts at hand." (*Higgins*, 26 Cal. App.4th 247, 251-255 (1994).)

§ 17.13.5 Prevention of Serious Damage to Property
The warrantless entry of premises may be justified under the emergency exception to protect the property of the owner or occupant. If there is imminent likelihood of a fire, explosion, etc. (e.g., smell of gas or gasoline or PCP coming from a building), a warrantless entry is proper (*People v. Stegman*, 164 Cal. App. 3d 936, 210 Cal. App. 855 (Cal. App. 4 Dist. 1985)).

§ 17.13.6 Prevention of Suspect's Imminent Escape
It is proper to enter a residence without a warrant in order to prevent the escape of a suspect, especially if he is armed and dangerous or has just committed a violent felony (*People v. Parrison*, 137 Cal. App. 3d 529, 187 Cal. Rptr. 123 (Cal. App. 4 Dist. 1982)).

§ 17.13.7 Prevention of Evidence Destruction
A police officer may enter premises without a warrant or consent when there is immediate danger of destruction of crime-related evidence, at least where a serious crime is involved (*Welsh v. Wisconsin*, 466 U.S. 740, 104 S.Ct. 2091, 80 L.Ed. 2d 732 (1984)). For example, warrantless entry of the residence of a suspected cop-killer—seconds after the shooting—was proper to prevent destruction of the evidence (*People v. Parrison, supra*).

In addition to a serious offense, to prevail in court you must be able to prove that there was not enough time to get a warrant—possibly even a telephonic warrant (Pen. Code §1528(b)). For example:

An informant made a controlled buy of heroin from Ellers at Ellers' home and saw others doing the same thing. Afterwards, the officers met a mile away and spent 10 to 15 minutes planning the arrest. Then they returned, entered, and made a warrantless arrest. The evidence was suppressed. The court said the heavy traffic, without more evidence, did not justify immediate action, and that there was adequate time to get a warrant (*People v. Ellers*, 108 Cal. App. 3d 943, 166 Cal. Rptr. 888 (Cal. App. 4 Dist. 1980)).

Note: Once a police officer has a situation like this under control, it is normally better to secure the premises (from outside, when possible) and await the obtaining of a search warrant than it is to immediately seize the evidence you saw in plain view. (*People v. Daughhetee*, 165 Cal. App. 3d 574, 211 Cal. Rptr. 633 (Cal. App. 5 Dist. (1985); *People v. Larry A.*, 154 Cal. App. 3d 929, 201 Cal. Rptr. 696 (Cal. App. 1, Dist. 1984); compare *U.S. v. Segura*, 468 U.S. 796, 82 L.Ed. 2d 599, 104 S.Ct. 3380 (1984)).

§ 17.13.8 Warrantless Entry to Make an Arrest
A police officer may also enter a home without a warrant to arrest an armed or dangerous suspect he has been following in "hot pursuit."

§ 17.13.9   Creating an Exigency

A police officer may not use exigent circumstances as an excuse for a warrantless entry if he has "created" the emergency by his own conduct. For instance:

A reliable informant told officers that he had just seen contraband at Shuey's house, thereby giving probable cause to get a warrant. Instead, the officers went to Shuey's home, asked him about the contraband and requested consent to search. Shuey refused to talk or consent. The officers then secured the residence and got a search warrant. However, the evidence was suppressed because, although exigent circumstances existed to secure (Shuey would probably destroy the contraband), the officers had "created" the exigency themselves (*Shuey v. Superior Court for County of Los Angeles*, 30 Cal. App. 3d 535, 106 Cal. Rptr. 452 (Cal. App. 2 Dist. 1973)).

An anonymous tipster called officers and said that narcotics were being sold out of a certain apartment. An officer surveyed the apartment and saw many people come, stay a few minutes and then leave. One person left the apartment, drove erratically away and was stopped. Because the suspect had fresh marks on his arms, he was arrested. In a search incident to his arrest, the officers found a bag of "powdery substance." The officers then went to the door and knocked. When a person answered, the officers identified themselves and demanded entry. When the residents "began running," an officer "broke open the screen door." The officers then made arrests and seized evidence. The court ruled that, even assuming probable cause existed, the officers should have gotten a warrant. In suppressing the evidence, the court stated, "To the extent that their actions created an emergency it was of the "do-it-yourself" variety condemned in *Shuey v. Superior Court of Los Angeles County,* 30 Cal. App. 3d 535, 106 Cal. Rptr. 452 (Cal. App. 2 Dist. 1973) (*People v. Rodriguez*, 123 Cal. App. 3d 269, 176 Cal. Rptr. 798 (Cal. App. 2 Dist. 1981); *People v. Larry A.*, 154 Cal. App. 3d 929, 201 Cal. Rptr. 696 (Cal. App. 1 Dist. 1984)).

§ 17.13.10   Clandestine Drug Labs

Will the discovery of a PCP "lab" justify a warrantless entry? In one case, the court viewed the smell of ether, and even of PCP, as just contraband. The court held that the plain smell of contraband without evidence of the element of imminent danger did not provide a sufficient basis for entering the premises without a search warrant (*People v. Blackwell*, 147 Cal. App. 3d 646, 195 Cal. Rptr. 298 (Cal. App. 2 Dist. 1983)). In another case, the officers' actions, including a five-hour delay, belied their concern about an imminent explosion (*People v. Baird*, 168 Cal. App. 3d 237, 214 Cal. Rptr. 88 (Cal. App. 1 Dist. 1985)).

In a similar situation, however, other courts have reached the opposite conclusion, probably because the officers acted with genuine concern (e.g., called the fire department, or evacuated neighboring houses) and gave testimony stressing the danger involved, i.e., the risk of explosion if ether fumes were to contact flame or other heat source (*People v. Stegman*, 164 Cal. App. 3d 936, 210 Cal. Rptr. 855 (Cal. App. 4 Dist. 1985); *People v. Patterson*, 94 Cal. App. 3d 456, 156 Cal. Rptr. 518 (Cal.

App. 2 Dist. 1979); *People v. Messina*, 165 Cal. App. 3d 937, 212 Cal. Rptr. 75 (Cal. App. 2 Dist. 1985); *U.S. v. Wilson*, 865 F.2d 215, (9th Cir. 1989)).

The key is for the officer's actions to be consistent with his motive of preserving life or property (*People v. Duncan*, 42 Cal. 3d 91, 227 Cal. Rptr. 654, 720 P.2d 2 (Cal. 1986); *People v. Osuna*, 187 Cal. App. 3d 845, 232 Cal. Rptr. 220 (Cal. App. 2 Dist. 1986)).

Also, if you expect "exigent circumstances" to justify a warrantless entry, you will have to convince the court that it was reasonable to anticipate that an injury might have occurred before a search warrant, even a telephonic one, could have been obtained (*People v. Blackwell, supra*).

Once you have entered and controlled the situation, remember that if you leave, you will need a warrant to reenter and conduct a search (*People v. Blackwell, supra*) unless the emergency is still continuing (*People v. Duncan, supra*). For instance, if you were unable to turn off the furnace the first time, a subsequent warrantless reentry to do that task would still be justified (*People v. Stegman, supra*; *People v. Abes*, 174 Cal. App. 3d 796, 220 Cal. Rptr. 277 (Cal. App. 2 Dist. 1985)).

§ 17.14 KNOCK AND NOTICE

The general purpose behind the "knock and notice" requirements is to protect the privacy of a person in his home and to minimize the possibility of a violent confrontation between police and private citizens which might occur if the police made sudden, surprise, unannounced entries. In particular, before a police officer enters (not *while* he enters) he or she must:

—knock (or do something else which will alert the people inside to his presence);

—identify himself as a police officer;

—explain his purpose;

—demand entry and then wait a reasonable period before entering.

Knock loudly on the door and then say in a loud voice, "Police Officers. Open up. We have a search warrant (or an arrest warrant) for X."

The "knock and notice" requirements are excused when facts make it reasonable for an officer to believe, in good faith, that compliance would:

—result in increased danger to him;

—result in the destruction of evidence;

—frustrate the arrest by allowing a fleeing, dangerous suspect to escape.

However, a police officer cannot use generalizations or common knowledge in support of noncompliance. For example, it is not enough simply to believe that narcotics violators usually have guns and will use them on police, or that owners of guns will necessarily use them against approaching officers.

Instead, a police officer needs specific facts or reasons relating to the situation showing, for example, that a particular suspect on the premises is likely to shoot rather than submit peaceably to the entry. Below are two examples illustrating the "no knock" exception:

Officers serving a warrant had been told by a confidential, reliable informant that the informant had personally seen the suspect habitually answer the door with a gun in his hand. The court ruled that this was a sufficient reason for the officers to ignore the "knock and announce" requirements (*People v. Dumas*, 9 Cal. 3d 871, 109 Cal. Rptr. 304, 512 P.2d 1208 (Cal. 1973)).

The suspect's arrest record reflected a history of assaultive behavior, including a prior fight with a police officer because the suspect was carrying a gun. These facts were ruled enough to bring the officers within the "no knock" exception (*People v. Henderson*, 58 Cal. App. 3d 349, 129 Cal. Rptr. 844 (Cal. App. 2 Dist. 1976)).

Generally speaking, if exigent circumstances permit a police officer to enter the premises without a warrant, they will also excuse strict compliance with "knock and announce" requirements *People v. Kizzee*, 94 Cal. App. 3d 927, 156 Cal. Rptr. 784 (Cal. App. 2 Dist. 1979)). Nevertheless, it is good practice for a police officer to announce his or her identity and purpose whenever entering a residence.

§ 17.14.1 When Compliance Is Futile

A related exception excusing compliance with the "knock and announce" rule is when compliance would be "futile," i.e., when no purpose or reason to knock and announce exists because the occupant already knows your identity and purpose or has indicated that he is not going to cooperate (*Mann v. Mack*, 155 Cal. App. 3d 666, 202 Cal. Rptr. 296 (Cal. App. 2 Dist. 1984)). For example:

Officers went to a residence to investigate possible possession of marijuana in large quantities. As they approached, the occupant happened to come outside, yelling "Jesus, it's the cops." The occupant then ran into the garage, slamming the door behind him. In this case, it was proper for the officers to force entry into the garage without complying with "knock and notice" requirements (*People v. Bigham*, 49 Cal. App. 3d 73, 122 Cal. Rptr. 252 (Cal. App. 2 Dist. 1975); see also *People v. Mayer*, 188 Cal. App. 3d 1101, 233 Cal. Rptr. 832 (Cal. App. 2 Dist. 1987)).

§ 17.14.2   Ruse Entry

A police officer may use a false name or employ some other trick or ruse to obtain consent to enter if he already has a judicially authorized right to enter, e.g., a search warrant (*People v. McCarter*, 117 Cal. App. 3d 894, 173 Cal. Rptr. 188 (Cal. App. 3 Dist. 1981)).

§ 17.15   SEEKING CONSENT TO ENTER

A POLICE OFFICER SHOULD ALWAYS ASK FOR CONSENT TO SEARCH EVEN WHEN HE HAS OTHER AUTHORITY FOR THE SEARCH. It can never hurt, and it may help a great deal, if other grounds (e.g., exigency or warrant) are ruled insufficient.

Consider the following scenario: officers serve a search warrant and find lots of evidence. Later, the warrant is ruled defective and all of the evidence is suppressed. A simple question asked politely and prior to showing the warrant to the "consenter" might (assuming consent was obtained) have saved all of the evidence.

Never show the warrant before asking consent. If you do and the warrant is later ruled defective, the consent will also be invalid.

§ 17.15.1.   Do Not Seek Consent Instead of a Warrant

Never attempt a consent search instead of obtaining a warrant. If a police officer has probable cause to search a house but tries to obtain consent rather than a warrant to search, he takes the great risk that the resident will refuse to allow the search. If the resident does, the officer may be sure that the evidence will be destroyed while he or she is obtaining the warrant.

Furthermore, courts have ruled that in such circumstances the officer may not secure or "freeze" the premises because he "created" the exigency (*Shuey v. Superior Court for County of Los Angeles*, 30 Cal. App. 3d 535, 106 Cal. Rptr. 452 (Cal. App. 2 Dist. 1973)).

Therefore, if the officer has probable cause to search a residence (and no exigent circumstances exist), he should get a warrant first and then seek consent.

§ 17.15.2   Indications of Consent

To be valid, a person's consent must be clear, specific and unequivocal. This clear, specific and unequivocal consent may be indicated in many ways by the consenter, i.e., "Yeah," "Go ahead," "Do what you want." Silence, of course, is not good enough, because every person has the right to remain silent, thereby refusing consent.

Although physical conduct, such as pointing or waving, can also constitute a valid "implied" consent, the wise officer will always get verbal (or better yet, written) consent when at all possible.

§ 17.15.3   Misrepresenting Your Purpose

If a police office tells the consenter that he wants to enter for "X" purpose when his true purpose is to "search" (e.g., look for narcotics, stolen property, etc.), any consent he obtains will be ruled involuntary. Following are two examples of misrepresentation:

Undercover officers set up surveillance in an unoccupied apartment next door to a suspected dope dealer. One officer went to the suspect's door, knocked, and asked if he could come in to make a phone call. Once inside, the officer made the phone call, but also observed narcotics and elicited incriminating remarks from the suspect which were then used to obtain a search warrant. The court suppressed the evidence because the consent to enter was involuntary. The officer had misrepresented his purpose as being to use the phone, whereas his true purpose was to look for narcotics (*People v. Lathrop*, 99 Cal. App. 3d 967, 160 Cal. Rptr. 654 (Cal. App. 1 Dist. 1979)).

A refrigerator repairman observed marijuana in a home and phoned the police. An undercover officer went out to the house, knocked, and told the suspect that he wished to talk to the repairman. Inside, the officer confirmed the repairman's observations and then obtained a search warrant. The evidence was suppressed. The officer had misrepresented the real purpose behind his request to come inside (*People v. Mesaris*, 14 Cal. App. 3d 71, 91 Cal. Rptr. 837 (Cal. App. 2 Dist. 1970)).

§ 17.15.4 Misrepresenting Your Identity (Undercover Operators)

If a police officer's true purpose (stated or implied) for entry is to further an investigation or complete an undercover deal (i.e., buy narcotics or stolen property, sell illegal weapons, etc.) and the consenter lets the officer in, his consent is valid. The fact that the officer misrepresents his name, job, or identification makes no difference.

However, if the real reason of the officer's entry is to search for evidence, then he has misrepresented his purpose and the evidence will be suppressed. Thus, misrepresentation of an officer's identity is, for undercover operators, permissible; while misrepresentation of an officer's purpose is impermissible.

§ 17.16 KNOCK AND TALK

What do you do when you receive information that an individual is dealing drugs but you do not have probable cause to seek a search warrant, no informant to work the individual and surveillance is either impractical or fails to produce any useful information? The answer is the use of "knock and talk."

The method used is very simple. Under the circumstances described above go to the suspects' residence (or business or whatever place where the drug trafficking is occurring) and contact the suspect. Identify yourself as a police officer and tell him the purpose of your visit. Ask permission to enter the residence to talk about the problem. Once inside, provide the suspect with the information that you have and ask him if he would like to respond to the allegations that he is dealing drugs. After the suspect either affirms or denies the allegations, ask for permission to search the residence for controlled substances. Of course, if you find evidence to support an arrest, the suspect goes to jail.

Drug Law Enforcement and Investigations

Tom McCabe and Rich McGuffin of South Lake Tahoe Police Department first used this method in January, 1986, that resulted in the suspect voluntarily surrendering almost one pound of cocaine and $23,000 in cash. They utilized this procedure dozens of times thereafter. Officers in California have experienced a high rate of success in terms of consent to enter and search. With this method, officers have seized dope, money, and assets.

Keep in mind that the purpose of the contact is to determine if the suspect is, in fact, trafficking in controlled substances. Normally, the information in these cases comes from an anonymous source and most of the time the information is proven correct. However, in a few cases the informant gave false information as retribution for whatever reason. In those cases, the contact has served to remove suspicion from someone. Furthermore, in those cases where the informant gave false information, the "suspect" can usually tell who the informant is, giving us the opportunity to contact the informant and discourage future bogus calls to the police.

The element of surprise plays a significant role in the success of the "knock and talk" method. Suspects just don't expect the police to come to their house and confront them with the allegation that they are selling drugs. The contact should be low-keyed and polite. Always ask for the suspect's consent at every stage of the investigation.

Also bear in mind that there have been a percentage of cases where consent to search was denied. If you are asked to leave, then leave.

"Knock and talk" is a last resort procedure. If you have probable cause then get a search warrant. You cannot misrepresent your identity or purpose. You cannot coerce or trick. It is a straight up proposition and you must be prepared for that door to be slammed in your face. Nothing ventured, nothing gained. There is always tomorrow and at least the suspect will know you are there.

The suspect has the right to deny your request for consent to enter and search; he or she does not have to talk to you. Yet, each "knock and talk" will have its own set of circumstances and each will be judged on the facts of the individual case.

§ 17.17 SEARCH AND SEIZURE OF EVIDENCE ON A SUSPECT'S BODY

Occasionally an officer must obtain evidence from a suspect's body (e.g., hair samples). Evidence obtained from certain parts of a suspect's body may be seized without a warrant; evidence seized from other parts may be seized only with a warrant.

§ 17.17.1 When Evidence May Be Seized Without a Warrant

Normally, if there is no "bodily intrusion" (entry of the suspect's body) or only slight bodily intrusion to seize the evidence (blood sample taken in medically approved manner), the courts have ruled that no warrant is necessary. For example:

Officers searched Lara's jail cell and found a syringe. An officer then told Lara to strip and open his mouth. When Lara opened it a little, the officer saw a yellow balloon. The officer then put his left land on Lara's chest and his right hand behind his head, thereby forcing Lara's chin against his chest making it more difficult for Lara to swallow. Lara was told repeatedly to spit the balloon. Lara, however, tried to swallow the balloon. The officer then reached inside Lara's mouth and warned him, "If you bite my finger, I'm going to bust your head open." The court ruled that the balloon of heroin was admissible evidence because the method used to seize it was reasonable (*People v. Lara*, 108 Cal. App. 3d 237, 166 Cal. Rptr. 475 (Cal. App. 2 Dist. 1980)).

Choking a suspect to keep him from swallowing contraband may be excessive. If an officer must choke, he must be sure that:

—he has probable cause to believe the evidence to be swallowed is contraband and that it may be life-threatening if swallowed; and

—he must note in his report that the ingestion of the drug could have resulted in serious injury.

Can the officer have a physician pump the stomach of the suspect to recover narcotics? No, this is conduct that "shocks the conscience" of the court (*Rochin v. California*, 342 U.S. 165, 72 S.Ct. 205, 96 L.Ed. 183 (1951)). This procedure is possible only to save the life of the suspect.

Can the officer take photographs, fingerprints, palm prints and obtain handwriting from the suspect? Yes, and the officer need not advise per *Miranda*.

Can the officer request the suspect to speak for voice identification? Yes, the suspect has no constitutional right to refuse to speak for purposes of voice identification.

Can the officer force a urine sample? No, the suspect is obligated to provide a urine sample and has no legal right to refuse, but the officer cannot force a urine sample.

§ 17.17.2   When a Warrant Should Be Obtained
Normally a warrant is required to "enter" a person's body to seize evidence unless there are extreme exigent circumstances justifying the entry (*Rochin v. California, supra*—pumping Rochin's stomach to recover crime-related evidence was held unconstitutional).

The questions a court must answer in determining whether the warrant for an intrusion is permissible include the following:

—was there probable cause?
—would the method used normally work?
—how serious was the offense?
—how important was the evidence?
—was there an alternative to the intrusion?

Drug Law Enforcement and Investigations

—how unsafe, uncomfortable, and undignified was the intrusion?

(*People v. Scott*, 21 Cal. 3d 284, 145 Cal. Rptr. 876, 578 P.2d 123 (Cal. 1978))

Note: If possible, always contact a district attorney before attempting to obtain evidence from within a suspect's body.

§ 17.17.3 How to Conduct a Consensual Encounter

Narcotics officers are taught to investigate using a variety of techniques. Generally, those techniques include the use of informants, surveillance, electronic eavesdropping, PEN registers and undercover operations. The most potent weapon in an officer's investigatory arsenal, however, is his or her ability to communicate. At times, conducting a "knock and talk," a "walk and talk," or "consensual encounter," is the best or only method of proceeding. The results of these types of consensual ' encounters can be tremendous, if the officer operates within the law and with preparation.

§ 17.17.4 Five Stages of a Consensual Encounter

A five-step approach can be used when conducting a consensual encounter to ensure that you adhere to the legal requirements. Airport interdiction officers have been using this method of consensual encounters since Detroit and Los Angeles began transportation interdiction programs in 1975, and have been extremely successful in detecting and seizing drugs and arresting couriers based on consensual encounters and subsequent consent searches.

Step 1

First and foremost, you have to obtain consent to talk to the citizen. Displaying your badge or photo identification, you should state, "Hello, I'm a police officer. May I talk to you?" This request should be done in an unassuming, pleasant tone, and perhaps even with a smile. Citizens, whether committing a crime or not, are not likely to deny this request. Later in court, you can state, "I asked for permission to talk to the defendant and he/she agreed." Attention should be paid to the location of the encounter and every effort should be made to allow the citizen a clear path to walk away if he or she wishes to terminate the encounter. Although officers work in teams, only one officer should interview the citizen; any other team members should remain a distance away, providing back-up, making observations and taking notes if necessary. If possible, you should avoid conducting these encounters while in uniform, and weapons should not be visible.

Step 2

The next step is to ask questions, in a non-threatening manner, regarding the citizen's activity (whatever type of activity you are interested in, whether it is travel arrangements, home ownership, why they are in the hotel room, or why they are walking down the street). Generally speaking, you should have done some homework, and already have a reason to talk to the citizen. For instance, if an anonymous tipster tells you that marijuana is growing in a particular residence but you are unable to develop enough information through regular investigative methods to obtain a search warrant, do not let the information go unused. Instead, use the data (who owns the house, who else lives there, etc.) you've already obtained. Take the time to commit the information to memory, and question the occupants in a "knock and talk": "Hi, I'm a police officer I would like to talk to you. May I come in?" If you ask the questions to which you already know the answers, you can quickly assess whether the interviewee is lying about something or everything. Even seemingly innocuous questions such as, "Are you the owner of this house?" "When is the last time you slept here?" and "Who pays the electric bill?" often draw deceptive answers from the interviewee engaged in criminal activity. With each lie the interviewee tells you, you are developing reasonable suspicion, and perhaps probable cause.

This is easiest to describe in the interdiction scenario officers are able to do homework in with a traveler. The officer can easily determine the passenger's destination of travel, return itinerary, when the ticket was purchased, how it was purchased, where it was purchased, if the passenger is traveling with another person, and telephone numbers provided to reservation agents. Based on the information, in a matter of minutes officers can find additional information in available data bases.

At the time of the interview, interdiction officers already know the answers to the questions. If the passenger is a drug courier, he or she will lie about one or all of the questions. Even the least-experienced interdiction officer's expertise, combined with one or two lies, will often establish enough probable cause for a search warrant.

The officer already has the answers to the questions he is going to ask the passenger.

"Where are you traveling to today?" "Detroit." "What is your name?" "Bryan." "What is the purpose of your trip?" "To visit my sister." "Where did you stay?" "With my sister." "Where does she live?" "In Carlsbad." The officer then asks for and observes the passenger's ticket. It states the passenger's name is "Carl." The officer has now exposed two lies because he knows the driver picked the passenger up at the Motel 6 in Chula Vista, not Carlsbad, and "Bryan's" ticket is in the name of "Carl." Note that each time "Carl" responds to the name "Bryan" during the contact, he may be offering the officer another lie. As you can see, the officer is quickly establishing that the passenger may be engaging in criminal activity, and is moving toward establishing sufficient grounds to conduct an investigatory detention.

Step 3

The third step of the consensual encounter is to obtain a consent to search. Always ask permission to search the person as well as the property: "May I search you and your bag (house) (car)?" When requesting consent, ask if there are any illegal substances, weapons, or drugs present. As you may expect, the answer will generally be "no." Don't ask to "look" or "open," ask to "search," because that is what you are going to be doing - searching. Remember, a citizen has a right to refuse to consent, to limit the scope of your search, or to terminate the consent at any time. If the citizen consents to the search, have your partner begin searching immediately. Obviously, if you or your partner find contraband, you will arrest the subject. If you do not find anything, you should politely thank the person for his or her cooperation, and tell him to have a nice day.

If the subject has drugs or guns in the pr perty being searched, you can bet he is watching to see how close you get as you search. This is the dangerous point for the officer because of the fight-or-flight syndrome. Remember that you do not have to effect an arrest at that moment. Rather, you can pretend that you overlooked the contraband and let the subject's anxiety level decrease-

But what if the citizen refuses consent to search? If this occurs, you should consider moving to Step 4 in an effort to develop sufficient probable cause to apply for a search warrant.

Step 4

Your fourth step will be to use your K-9 and/or your own sense of smell. Do not be afraid to trust your own ability to smell drugs. If the K-9 alerts, or if you can articulate that you recognize the odor of the narcotics, use that information, combined with the other information you have gathered, to move to Step 5.

Step 5

The fifth step is to detain the property you want to search, and the subject, while you apply for a search warrant. An odor of narcotics detected by a K-9 or yourself can constitute probable cause. Remember that probable cause is completely fact-specific, and can rely heavily on your training and experience. Therefore, you must articulate everything in your affidavit, including the lies you are told and nervous behavior you have observed! Other subjects will tell you that they want to consent to the search once they have been detained or arrested. Do not accept consent to search in this situation because, in most instances, the consent to search will be viewed by the court as coerced. At this juncture, you are committed to obtaining a search warrant.

Conclusion

In law enforcement, we often think in adversarial terms, as part of our survival tactics on the streets. Being able to step back from that mindset and attitude can be difficult, but the rewards can be tremendous. To conduct an effective consensual encounter, you must work within the legal parameters and use the dynamics of everyday human interaction. Take a few moments to plan the encounter, be mindful of your demeanor and be aware of the setting you choose for the encounter. Above all, work with the information you receive, and build upon it. If you do that, and follow the steps suggested, you will conduct a legal and effective consensual encounter.

Chapter 17

§ 17.17.5   Wall Stops

A wall stop is (1) a traffic stop based upon probable cause to believe that a traffic violation has occurred, (2) but with the ulterior motive of seizing drugs, stolen property, illegal weapons, counterfeit or "dirty" money, and the like associated with an ongoing investigation, (3) while simultaneously attempting to ensure that the existence of the ongoing investigation is not prematurely revealed. A wall stop can involve either federal law enforcement officers, plainclothes local law enforcement officers, or a combination of federal and state task force officers working with uniformed, state and local law enforcement officers assigned to marked patrol units. Wall stops are often known by such other names as wall cases, hand-offs, and whisper stops.

The United States Supreme Court has granted police officers broad and various powers over motorists such that the uniformed officer responsible for conducting the wall stop is in a key position to initiate an investigation separate and distinct from the ongoing investigation.

In *Whren v. United States*, 517 U.S. 806 (1996), a unanimous Supreme Court held that "as a general matter, the decision to stop an automobile is reasonable where the police have probable cause to believe that a traffic violation has occurred." The Supreme Court also explained that the constitutional reasonableness of a traffic stop does not depend upon the "ulterior motives," "actual motivations," or "subjective intentions" of the officer conducting the stop. The temporary detention of a motorist based upon either reasonable suspicion or probable cause to believe a traffic law violation has occurred, therefore, does not violate the Fourth Amendment's prohibition ;against unreasonable seizures, even if a reasonable officer could not have stopped the motorist absent some additional aw enforcement objective. In other words, a uniformed officer can be called upon to observe and stop a motorist as soon as the officer observes the commission of a traffic violation, not for the sole purpose of issuing the offender a traffic citation, but as a means to stop the offending vehicle in an attempt to aid an unrelated investigation.

§ 17.18   POSSESSION OF A CONTROLLED SUBSTANCE

In short, a person cannot legally possess a controlled substance unless the substance was obtained upon the written prescription of a physician, dentist, podiatrist or veterinarian licensed to practice in the state.

When does a person have possession? How do you prove that a person has possession of a substance? To support a conviction of possession, it must be proven that the defendant had knowledge of the presence of the drug, that the drug was in his or her immediate possession and control, and that there was a usable quantity of the drug. However, actual physical possession is not required to be proven, so long as constructive possession is established. Because the element of knowledge is seldom susceptible of direct proof, knowledge is proven by evidence of acts, declarations, or conduct of the defendant from which it may be fairly inferred that he or she knew of the drug's existence in the place where it was found. Therefore, knowledge may be proven by the defendant's physical demeanor or appearance, drug debris on the person, drug paraphernalia, prior arrests, associates, literature, notes, and ledgers.

Where narcotics are found on the premises under the control of the defendant, this fact, in and of itself, gives rise to an inference of knowledge and possession by him which may be sufficient to sustain a conviction for unlawful possession, as long as there are no other facts and circumstances which might leave in the mind of the jury reasonable doubt as to his guilt. Whether there is possession and whether there is knowledge are both questions of fact to be determined by the jury or court.

Based on this rule of constructive possession, several court cases have discussed the fact of knowledge. For instance, in *People v. Traylor*, 23 Cal. App. 3rd 323, 333, 100 Cal. Rptr. 116 (Cal. App. 2 Dist. 1972), testimony was elicited from the officer, consisting of the officer's opinion that the defendant was a user of narcotics at the time of his arrest. With the addition of this opinion, the entire testimony became directly relevant to the culpability of the defendant as to one element of the crime charged. Thus, an essential element of the crime of narcotics possession is knowledge of the narcotic character of the article possessed (see *People v. Winston*, 46 Cal. 2d 151, 161, 293 P.2d 40 (Cal. 1956)). For establishing the fact of this knowledge, it is admissible to cite evidence of prior narcotics use—such as the presence of needle marks.

Remember that knowledge required for having possession is both knowledge that the substance is in one's presence and knowledge that the substance is a narcotic drug. Can one be inferred from the other? If the suspect knows the substance is in his possession, can it be presumed he knows what the substance is? Most courts accept the proposition that knowledge can be presumed where the defendant is in actual possession of the drug. Actual possession is when the drug is on your person, in your hand—when you have actual control over it.

Yet, when the drug is not in the actual possession of the defendant, possession can still be proven. The test for constructive possession (not actually in possession of the drug) is whether or not the defendant exercised dominion and control over the drug. In other words, the drug may not be in the actual possession of the defendant but within his reach, or in a place where he is storing it—in his car, lunch box, locker, desk, etc.—and where it is available to him for future use. According to *United States v. Salinas-Salinas*, 555 F.2d 470, 473 (5th Cir. 1979): "Constructive possession may be proved by ownership, dominion or control over the contraband itself, or dominion or control over the premises or vehicle in which the contraband was concealed." Thus, constructive possession can be established through the suspect's control over the drug, even if it is not directly on his or her person. "In essence, constructive possession is the ability to reduce an object to actual possession" (*United States v. Martinez*, 588 F.2d 495, 498 (5th Cir. 1979)).

However, a person's mere association with drug users who possess illegal drugs is not constructive possession. Nonetheless, if the individual is in close proximity to a location in which drugs may be found, this proximity could be considered constructive possession provided the circumstances clearly show that the defendant had dominion or control over the drugs. According to *United States v. Jones*, 764 F.2d 885 (D.C. Cir. 1985), "proximity may, under certain circumstances, amount to constructive possession." In this case, the court went on to say that "possession of a narcotic drug may be either actual or constructive...Constructive possession may be shown through direct or circumstantial evidence of dominion and control over the contraband..., and may be found to exist where the evidence supports a finding that the person charged with possession was knowingly in a position, or had the right to exercise dominion or control over the drug."

In yet another case, *United States v. Disla*, 805 F.2d 1340 (9th Cir. 1986), the court stated that constructive possession is a common sense notion that an individual "may possess a controlled substance even though the substance is not on his person at the time of arrest." The court further defined constructive possession as follows: "Constructive possession may be demonstrated by direct or circumstantial evidence that the defendant had the power to dispose of the drug or the ability to produce the drug, or that the defendant had the exclusive control or dominion over property on which contraband narcotics are found." The most important question is whether "the evidence establishes a sufficient connection between the defendant and the contraband to support the inference that the defendant exercised a dominion and control over the substance. Mere proximity to the drug, mere presence on the property where it is located, or mere association, without more, with the person who does control the drug or the property on which it is found, is insufficient to support a finding of possession." On the other hand, as the court points out, "It would be odd if a dealer could not be guilty of possession, merely because he had the resources to hire a flunky to have custody of the drugs."

Thus, constructive possession can be proved by dominion over the contraband. Evidence for dominion could even take the form of a key owned by the defendant. If it can be proven that the defendant possesses a key which opens the suitcase, locker, vehicle, or desk where drugs are found, then constructive possession may be established.

In addition, two or more defendants may possess a drug. This is called a "joint venture." Showing joint possession may be proved by constructive possession. In *Commonwealth of Pennsylvania v. Kitchener,* 351 Pa. Super. 631, 506 A.2d 941 (Pa. Super. 1986), the court stated that "possession of an illegal substance need not be exclusive; two or more can possess the same drug at the same time." (quoting *Commonwealth of Pennsylvania v. Macolino*, 503 Pa. 201, 469 A.2d 132 (Pa. 1983)). The court in *Kitchner* said, "The drugs were found in a dwelling where defendant and her boyfriend were the sole adult residents, (and in specific locations) which would be particularly within the access and knowledge of the residents," finding that, "it was reasonable for the fact finder to conclude that defendant knowingly or intentionally possessed the controlled substance."

§ 17.18.1   Usability

In addition to the fact of knowledge, analysis of the contraband is another essential element of any prosecution for violation of narcotics laws. Most of this analysis is straightforward, yet occasionally an issue of usability arises at the time of filing or trial. Of the many issues confronting the drug analyst, usable quantity is undoubtedly the thorniest. The issue of usability is really more legal than scientific. Over the years, courts have struggled with the idea that to sustain a conviction of possession of a controlled substance, the quantity of the substance must be "sufficient for use."

When is a given amount of cocaine a non-usable "trace," and insufficient for use? As a chemist, the analyst can rather easily extract microgram quantities of cocaine from an otherwise "empty" paper bindle. It is important to ask, "Is it reasonable to expect a drug user to manipulate quantities this small?"

With regard to usable quantity, different drugs will have different cutoffs. Marijuana would have to be present in quantities much greater than cocaine or heroin, for example. Another consideration is the method of packaging. Here again the analyst is asked to form an expert (although subjective) opinion. The method of packaging must be evident as an attempt to conserve the substance, as opposed to waste material. Of course, persons intent on recovering trace amounts of drugs could do so even from paper currency withdrawn from a bank. The operative question is, "What is reasonable?" A very large plastic bag which at one time held a kilogram of cocaine might now have only a thin film of cocaine dust clinging to it. A determined individual could perhaps recover a small bindle of cocaine from that same bag. But this "imaginary" bindle was not submitted for analysis, rather the bag was, and it is up to the analyst to decide if that amount is to be considered "usable." It may be suggested to the prosecutor that, "If the amount of residue had been collected and placed in a bindle, it would be usable."

Dosage form must also be considered. A tablet or capsule is by definition a usable quantity.

Fortunately, the issue of physiologic effect is not relevant to the question of usability, despite many attorney's attempts to make it so. Case law is generally in agreement that the state does ". . . not have to prove that the contraband possessed had a potential of producing a narcotic effect."

Another "red herring" frequently encountered is the "percent purity" argument. "Suppose," one is often asked, "that only a tiny speck of the drug was necessary to know what portion of the powder is a controlled substance." It is sufficient in most instances simply to show that there was sufficient powder to manipulate, that the tests for the drug were positive, and that the drug was packaged in an apparent attempt to conserve it.

Likewise, where a chemist found that the contents of some balloons contained heroin, the evidence was sufficient to show that the heroin was in a usable quantity even though the chemist did not perform a quantitative analysis and was unable to provide the percentage of heroin contained in the total volume of substance from the balloons (*People v. Piper,* 19 Cal. App. 3d 248, 96 Cal. Rptr. 643 (Cal. App. 4 Dist. 1971); *People v. Pohle,* 20 Cal. App. 3d 78, 97 Cal. Rptr. 364 (Cal. App. 4 Dist. 1971)).

§ 17.18.2   Possession of a Controlled Substance for Sale

In possession for sale and actual sales cases, knowledge of the narcotic nature of the substance is usually easier to prove. A defendant's heroin habit may be the motive to sell heroin or to possess heroin with the intent to sell. It is common knowledge that users often deal to support their own habit.

For example, in *People v. Perez,* 42 Cal. App. 3d 470, 117 Cal. Rptr. 195 (Cal. App. 4 Dist. 1974), a defendant sold heroin to an undercover officer. One week later, a search warrant was served on the defendant's house, where an outfit and a quantity of heroin were seized. The court allowed evidence of track marks on the defendant's arms to show MOTIVE to sell as well as KNOWLEDGE of heroin.

The elements of simple possession also apply to possession for sales cases—with two exemptions. Possession for sales involve an element of intent and a quantity and/or purity of the substance that would indicate more than personal use. In this respect, many courts have held that a conviction of possession for sales may be based upon evidence as to the quantity of the drug possessed.

One of the most important elements in possession for sale is quantity; large quantities (more than personal use) strongly suggest possession for sale. Thus, the following court cases have established the defendants' possession for sale (intent to distribute) based on the evidence of quantity: *United States v. Vergara,* 687 F.2d 57, 62 (5th Cir. 1982) (five ounces of heroin, valued at $8,500); *United States v. Edwards,* 602 F.2d 458, 470 (1st Cir. 1979) (165.49 grams of heroin); *United States v. DeLeon,* 641 F.2d 330, 335 (5th Cir. 1981) (294 grams of cocaine); *United States v. Mather,* 465 F.2d 1035, 1037-38 (5th Cir. 1972) (197.75 grams of cocaine); *United States v. Muckenthaler,* 584 F.2d 240, 247 (8th Cir. 1987) (147.09 grams of cocaine); *United States v. Love,* 599 F.2d 107, 109 (5th Cir. 1979), cert. denied 444 U.S. 944 (26 pounds of marijuana).

How do you prove the person intended to sell the drug? Intent may be indicated by observation of the suspect's movements, his associates, and the location of the two. Intent may also be shown by the way the drugs are packaged or by the possession of paraphernalia such as scales, cutting agents, paper bindles, penny balloons, or notebooks with names of customers. If at all possible to obtain, a statement by the defendant saying he intended to sell the drug is sure evidence.

In contrast to large quantities, possession of small quantities of a con-trolled substance usually indicates personal use rather than intent to distribute. For instance, *United States v. Washington,* 586 F.2d 1147,

1153 (7th Cir. 1978) (possession of 1.43 grams of cocaine) held that "proof of possession of a small amount of a controlled substance, standing alone, is an insufficient basis from which an intent to distribute may be inferred." However, possession of a small concentrated amount of a drug that can be adulterated, "cut," to make a larger amount to sell can be considered possession for sale. Purity levels are also important in considering whether or not possession is for sale.

In addition to quantity, however, there are other factors that would support possession for sale in most circumstances. For instance, *United States v. Staten*, 581 F.2d 878 (D.C. Cir. 1978) held that "intent to distribute may be inferred from possession of drug-packaging paraphernalia." Likewise, other courts have found that weighing scales, possession of significant quantities of glassine bags, foil packets, vials, etc. have supported possession for sale. In *United States v. Franklin*, 728 F.2d 994, 999 (8th Cir. 1984), the court found that possession of substances to cut or dilute a controlled substance would lead to an inference (circumstantial evidence) that the controlled substance is not for personal use.

Alongside paraphernalia, large amounts of money may also suggest possession for sale provided that a connection between the money and the drugs can be established. In other words, the money must have come from the sale of the drugs. (See e.g., *U.S. v. Tramunti*, 513 F.2d 1087, 1105 (2d Cir. 1975); likewise in *U.S. v. Marszalkowski*, 669 F.2d 655, 662 (5th Cir. 1982), possession of 38.2 grams of 84 percent pure cocaine along with cutting substance, a large amount of cash, and a weapon amounted to an intent to distribute.)

Furthermore, it is known that drug dealers protect themselves from "rip-offs." The possession of a firearm, along with the drug, can be considered evidence of intent to distribute. (See, *United States v. Moses*, 360 F.Supp. 301, 303 (W.D. Pa. 1973)—possession of a weapon and heroin sustained an inference of an intent to distribute; and *U.S. v. Marszalkowski, supra*, in which the weapon was evidence contributing to the inference of intent to distribute.)

In possession for sale cases, a slightly different form of evidence may be that of addiction to the drug. While *U.S. v. Ramirez-Rodriguez*, 552 F.2d 883 (9th Cir. 1977) stated that "a finding of addiction may support an inference that a larger quantity of the drug may be kept for personal use," the fact that the defendant is addicted to the drug may also support the inference that the defendant needed to sell the drug to support his or her addiction. This inference is especially true of the defendant who is in possession of a drug other than the drug to which he or she is addicted.

These different factors establishing constructive possession and possession for sale are easier to determine with experience. Once you become an expert witness (that is, qualified by the court as an expert in narcotics), you will be permitted to testify about controlled substances and drug activities that are not within the common knowledge of the average lay person. Many courts will allow you to testify about the processing, packaging, and characteristics of controlled substances, their street value, how they are used, the amount used, and what distinguishes a possession from possession for sale case.

§ 17.18.3 Transportation of a Controlled Substance

In the California Health and Safety Code, legislation on transportation of a drug can be found in the same section as sales of a drug. An essential element of the offense of transportation is the defendant's knowledge of both the presence of the drug and its narcotic character. The suspect must also have actual or constructive control over the substance.

Transportation is commonly proved by the circumstance of possession, even though possession is not an essential element of a transportation offense. Someone may transport drugs even though he or she is in the exclusive possession of another. For example, where the suspect was shown to have aided and abetted his passengers in carrying, conveying or concealing drugs in their possession, he can be charged with transportation. Thus, to prove transportation, it is not necessary to prove that the drugs were intended for sale or distribution.

In cases of the offense of being present where certain controlled substances are being used, there is a principle that in one's own residence or automobile one may have the responsibility to prevent the illicit use of the drug since the owner has some control over the premises or vehicle. An analogous principle should apply in cases of transportation. Regardless of purpose or intent, the driver or owner of an automobile has the responsibility to prevent the conveyance of contraband by himself or his passengers at least while the vehicle is under his dominion or control. Given this principle, proof of the knowledge of the character and presence of the drug combined with control over the vehicle is sufficient evidence to establish guilt without further proof of an actual purpose to transport the drug for sale or distribution.

§ 17.18.4 Selling a Controlled Substance

The legislation for selling drugs is similar to that for such acts as furnishing, administering, giving away, importing and transporting. Selling is defined as the act of exchanging drugs for money. The elements necessary to establish selling of a controlled substance include knowledge, dominion and control, usable quantity, and intent. Two of the most frequent ways to enforce this legislation are (1) for the police officer to purchase the drugs himself, or (2) for the police officer to use an informant—who is under his immediate and direct supervision—to purchase the drugs.

§ 17.18.5 Being Present Where Controlled Substances Are Unlawfully Being Used

Section 11365 H&S provides that it is unlawful to visit or to be in any room or place where narcotics, mescaline, peyote, THC, cocaine, etc., are being unlawfully smoked or used with knowledge that such activity is occurring. However, subsection (b) of section 11365 H&S provides that the section shall apply only where the defendant aids, assists, or abets the perpetration of the unlawful smoking or use of a controlled substance. Many suspects arrested for the offense will claim that they did not know about the drug activity. Knowledge is an important element to prove in this offense. The fact that the person was present and drugs were there would not constitute sufficient evidence to infer knowledge of its use on the premises.

If one purchases a ticket and enters a motion picture theater where one has every right to remain, and midway through the film one views a person in the theater using cocaine, must one leave immediately for fear of prosecution or force the person to stop using the drug? No. Yet in one's own residence or automobile, one has the responsibility to prevent the use of narcotics. The elements necessary to establish this crime are knowledge, the person's physical presence in the location where the substance is being used, and usable quantity.

§ 17.19 LOCATION, COLLECTION, AND PRESERVATION OF EVIDENCE
§ 17.19.1 Locating Evidence
A police officer will be faced with many situations requiring him to conduct a lawful search for drugs or evidence of drug abuse.

Where does an officer locate evidence? The answer is simple, but the method is very complicated. You may find drugs and evidence of drug abuse ANYWHERE. Therefore, you should never overlook any place when conducting a search. Look in any location that is capable of containing physical evidence, whether it is on a person, in cars, in houses, etc. Drug abusers will hide (or "stash") their contraband in places you wouldn't usually think about.

On a person, you might look:

—Under collars, lapels, cuffs and any folds of material in clothing.
—In the backs of watches, lockets or other jewelry.
—Behind belts or belt buckles.
—Inside any pockets.
—Inside packages of cigarettes, or inside the cigarettes themselves.
—Inside any body cavities.

BUT DON'T STOP THERE!

Inside a vehicle, you might look:

—In ashtrays or similar receptacles.
—Under the dashboard for secreted items or containers, like a hide-a-key box attached to some metal part.
—Behind sun visors, under seats, under floor mats, etc.

BUT DON'T STOP THERE!

Inside houses, you might look:

—In vents, electrical sockets, outlets, and similar receptacles.

—Under sinks and toilets, or inside toilet tanks or lids for items that might be taped down.
—For false bottoms in furniture or similar objects.
—Inside objects like cookie jars, sugar bowls, etc.

BUT DON'T STOP THERE!

Use a little common sense; it is always your best guide. The drug abuser has put some thought into hiding his or her "stash," and the officer will have to put some effort into finding it! Often the hiding places are so obscure, only a dope dog will find the evidence. If your department has a dog, it is well worth using the dog for searches.

§ 17.19.2   Collection and Preservation of Evidence

Successful evidence collection is the mark of the competent law enforcement officer. As every officer knows, evidence can be overwhelmingly persuasive to the police in charge of a case, but if it is inadmissible in court, the evidence is meaningless.

What is evidence? Evidence is anything which may be used in court as proof of a point in question. It may be found by the investigator at the crime scene or by one coming to or from the crime scene. It can include things understood and things not understood by the investigators. The important factor, from the officer's point of view, is that it be properly collected, properly preserved and, when necessary, subjected to evaluation and identification by an expert. Corroboration, preferably by another officer, is of paramount importance.

To ensure a systematic and thorough search, it is best to assign only one officer to direct the collection of evidence in a given case.

Areas of search should be exchanged to avoid overlooking facts. When evidence is discovered, the searcher should not attempt to move it. He should make sure that others see the evidence in sight, that photographs are taken, and that notes are made on its location. Frequently, drugs are stashed in several different hiding places, so it is important not to abandon the search after the first discovery. The officer should note any evidence that will prove that the suspected violator actually possessed the drug. Care should be taken to protect evidence so that it can be processed for latent fingerprints or foreign materials on the container that can identify the evidence with the suspect.

The investigating officer's responsibility does not end with the discovery of evidence. Evidence must be handled in such a way that its admissibility in court is not jeopardized.

Evidence is admissible in court only when a direct chain of custody can be established from the moment of discovery until the evidence is introduced in court. Every person handling the evidence is introduced in court. Every person handling the evidence is a link in the chain and must be known and available to the court in case the chain of custody is challenged.

Drug Law Enforcement and Investigations

Several steps must be taken to ensure the completeness and security of the chain of custody. The first is establishing the location of the evidence upon discovery. This can be done with photographs, sketches, and the observations of several officers.

When the evidence permits, permanent markings for future identification should be used. The name of the investigating officer, case number, date, time and location are normally sufficient. A complete inventory of the evidence should also be maintained. If evidence leaves the officer's possession, receipts should be obtained and preserved. (They form part of the chain of custody).

Even if it is not going to be shipped or mailed, evidence should always be kept in a tamper-proof container. If "lock-seal" envelopes are not available, sealing wax is an acceptable substitute. If the evidence must be mailed to a laboratory for analysis, it should be carefully wrapped and addressed correctly and completely (including return address). On the outside of the wrapper, print the instruction, "EVIDENCE—TO BE OPENED BY AUTHORIZED PERSONNEL ONLY." Evidence should be sent only by registered mail or Railway Express, and a return receipt should be requested.

Evidence should be stored only in a special evidence area or in a property safe until presented in court. If evidence is kept in a locker or file drawer, it may be lost or damaged and may prove inadmissible.

The officer's overall responsibility may be summed up with two points:

1. Make a legal, systematic, and thorough search for evidence.

2. Handle and preserve the evidence to maintain an accurate and direct chain of custody that can be established easily in court.

§ 17.19.3 Ten Points to Remember in the Collection and Preservation of Drug Evidence:

1. Before evidence is recovered by the finding officer, he should have the location witnessed by another officer.

2. All evidence should be marked with the initials of the finder and the date. These markings should be on the item of evidence itself whenever possible. If this is not practical for reasons of size, shape, contamination, etc., then the container in which the evidence is found or stored should be marked.

3. Evidence should be marked with a writing instrument that will not rub off. Most ball point or felt tip pens are not suitable. The purchase of a "permanent" type marking pen can save you needless hours of embarrassment on the witness stand trying to locate initials that have been rubbed off.

4. Evidence received from a citizen should be initialed and dated by the citizen prior to being received by the officer who in turn adds his initials prior to booking the evidence.

5. In cases where many items of evidence have been seized and must be marked for inventory, it is helpful to note the location of the find on the evidence tag. For example, glove compartment of vehicle, right front seat of vehicle, etc.

6. Collection of blood and/or urine samples should be taken from those who are suspected of being under the influence of a narcotic or dangerous drug, those who are being charged with "use," or specified cases where this type of evidence may be crucial to show knowledge on the part of the suspect.

7. Do not tie knots, staple, glue or otherwise make the evidence bags or containers semi-impregnable once you have placed the evidence in them. The follow up officer or perhaps you will have to untie or remove all of the encumbrances. All that is required is that the evidence be tagged for identification and placed in a secure locker.

8. Maintain the integrity of the evidence by not contaminating evidence obtained from one source with that of another. For example, marijuana found on the person of a suspect should not be mixed with marijuana found in another location.

9. Handle evidence carefully in order to preserve fingerprints.

10. Maintain the chain of custody.

§ 17.20 PROCESSING NARCOTIC/DRUG ARRESTEES

There are several different procedures for processing a narcotic/drug arrestee. We will consider each one separately.

Booking Approval - When a suspect (adult or juvenile) has been arrested for a drug violation which requires booking, you should transport him or her to the area of narcotic investigators for an interview and booking advice. Depending upon your department, procedures for booking could be different.

Preliminary Chemical Test - When contraband is involved in the drug arrest, the officer is sometimes required to complete a preliminary chemical test on the suspected drug. The type of testing equipment varies with the type of drug involved. Instructions for completing the test are usually listed on the testing equipment.

Remember - Never Taste Any Suspected Drug or Narcotic!

Obtaining Urine Samples - When an arrestee displays objective symptoms of being under the influence, a urine sample should be obtained and booked. The officer must include in the arrest report: the time the sample was obtained and the name and serial number of the officer who obtained the sample.

Photographing Hype Marks - When "hype marks" (the marks made by numerous injections—also called "tracks") are present on an adult arrestee, they should be photographed. For males and females this will generally be done at the booking location.

Booking the Arrestee - Generally, adult males being booked for a narcotic or drug felony are booked into the jail. Adult females being booked for a narcotic or drug felony are booked at a women's detention facility or other facility designated by your department. Information regarding detention for a juvenile arrestee may be obtained from your department.

Required Medical Treatment - The procedures for obtaining medical treatment for drug arrestees are the same as with any other arrestee, with one exception: a juvenile who is under the influence of drugs or narcotics and is to be detained MUST be examined by a doctor or county hospital to determine whether the juvenile should receive additional medical attention at a juvenile hall. If a juvenile is to be released to a parent or guardian, a chemical test should be administered before the release. However, if immediate treatment appears necessary, the juvenile shall be taken for medical treatment regardless of whether the juvenile is to be detained. The officer should also closely observe any narcotic arrestee for the possibility of an overdose. (See "Crisis Intervention for Drug Abusers" in the Appendix to this volume.) There are several reasons for this. Drug users are often unaware of the potency of drugs on the "black market." Also, users frequently try to destroy the evidence by swallowing the drugs, and you might not even realize that they have done so. The arrestee may appear to be O.K. when you first contact him or her, but after a little while, he or she may begin to show increasing signs of drug overdose. Be alert; if the arrestee is showing any signs of overdose, immediately transport him or her to a hospital.

Booking Evidence - As mentioned above, the "chain of custody" for drugs seized as evidence is very critical. It must remain unbroken. This means that the status of the evidence must be accounted for, from the time it was found, until it leaves the officer's custody. The officer must account for:

—Who found it.
—When and where it was found.
—Who marked it.
—Who transported it.
—Who booked it.
—Where it was booked.

It is very important to have only one officer involved in the collecting and processing of evidence. This will simplify the process required in court for establishing the "continuity" of the evidence. If "continuity" cannot be established, the evidence can be held inadmissible and the case may be lost.

Chapter 17

§ 17.20.1   Report Writing

The successful prosecution of a narcotics case depends upon the quality of the initial offense report. The police report must contain in chronological sequence who, when, where, what and why. For example:

On May 1, 1997, at 10:00 p.m., Officer Smith and Jones were east bound on Main Street approaching Almaden Avenue. Officer Smith was driving the marked police vehicle and Officer Jones was the passenger. At the intersection of Main and Almaden, a blue 1980 Chevrolet, 4-door, license #XYZ 123 was observed traveling north bound on Main Street at a high rate of speed. The vehicle was pursued and clocked at 60 mph (posted speed 35 mph), and subsequently stopped at First Street under a nearby street light.

As Officer Smith approached the vehicle from the driver's side, he observed the driver, later identified as Mr. John Brown, lean forward as if to be reaching under the front seat.

Officer Jones approaching the vehicle from the passenger side observed the passenger, later identified as Mr. Jim Black, throw an object, appearing to be a small colored object, out of the passenger's side window. The driver, Mr. Brown, and the passenger, Mr. Black, were asked for their identification by the respective officers. When the suspects were producing their identification, Officer Smith observed two rolled penny balloons in plain view on the floorboard of the vehicle.

Both suspects were removed from the vehicle, searched and handcuffed. Officer Jones retrieved the objects thrown by Mr. Black and identified the objects as two penny balloons, filled with some powder.

Both suspects were placed under arrest for violation of 11350 H&S, and were advised of their constitutional rights by Officer Smith. The interior of the vehicle was examined by Officer Smith and no further contraband was found. The vehicle was registered to Mr. Brown and was towed to Big M storage lot at 111 South, 10th Street. The suspects were transported to the detective bureau by Officers' Smith and Jones. The evidence seized remained in the custody of the receiving officers and was later booked into narcotic locker #33.

Both suspects were stripped and searched by Officer Smith prior to being photographed and interrogated by Detective Keith. Both suspects gave a recorded statement admitting to the offense charged—See supplementary report by Detective Keith. Both suspects were booked by Officers' Smith and Jones on 11350 H&S, possession of heroin—date May 1, 1997.

Report Officer:
J. Smith, Badge 101
S. Jones, Badge 329

While it is not possible to cover every eventuality, the example above serves to point out some basic rules about report writing:

1. Write your report as the event occurred in the case. Unless a continuity of thought can be established as to what happened and in what order, the report is of negligible value.

2. Whenever possible, keep specific events separated by using new paragraphs. This not only makes the report easier to read, but emphasizes specific action taken.

3. Careful attention to detail is a critical part of the report. Specific information as to the exact location of evidence, when it was found, who advised suspects of their rights, who searched the suspects, etc., are points that are sure to be brought up during a trial—a trial that may come too far in the future to depend on memory.

After your arrest, interview, and completed section 11550 H&S report, you must decide if you are going to book the suspect or release the suspect with a citation to appear in court after you have obtained a urine sample. Ask yourself the question, "Is the addict capable of caring for his safety or the safety of others?" If the addict cannot care for himself, then he must be booked on these charges, while the section 11550 is booked separately. In many jurisdictions, the only time an addict is booked into jail for an section 11550 charge is when he or she refuses to give a urine sample or when the addict is under the influence to such an extent that he cannot take care of himself or he is in need of medical attention.

§ 17.20.2   The Drug Abuser in Confinement
All drug suspects should be stripped searched prior to leaving them alone. Also it is important that the officer be sure of himself before taking a drug from a suspect. This is particularly true if the suspect is being jailed. In many instances, the drug could be vital to the suspect's health. Arrangements should always be made to continue essential medication while the suspect is in jail. Yet, special precautions are necessary for jailed drug abusers. To the drug abuser (particularly the narcotic addict), the most important thing in the world is his need for drugs, and he will go to tremendous lengths to satisfy his craving. Anything sent to him from "outside" must be inspected. Contact with visitors must be closely supervised. The drug abuser must not be given "trusty" status. Once the drug abuser establishes a source of supply, he may spread drugs throughout the confinement area.

Following the arrest of a person known to be or suspected of abusing drugs, a "skin search" is necessary. Drug abusers often place their supplies in body openings or swallow them via balloons for later recovery. The drug abuser is generally skillful at concealing his supplies, and it is important to prevent the smuggling of drugs into your confinement area.

§ 17.20.3   Testifying in Court
The arresting officer is often a non-expert witness. If you are not yet qualified as an expert witness in narcotics cases, the only way to obtain this qualification is for you to acquire knowledge through narcotics training and education and to develop your skills through experience (arrests).

Whether you are an expert or non-expert witness in narcotics cases, before going to court to testify, be sure to read your police report. If it is a heroin influence case, clearly state the defendant's symptoms and the reasons for arresting the defendant under 11550 H&S. While you are developing your expertise, it is a good idea to keep track of the narcotics schools or classes you have completed, your experience in narcotics arrests, drug books you have read, etc. In Appendix C, there is a form entitled Summary of Narcotics Expertise. Use this form to record your expertise.

Chapter 17

§ 17.21 INFORMANTS' BACKGROUND

Informants have gained a bad reputation. Most of the lay public has a stereotypical image of informants. The stereotype is usually of a "snitch," or criminal informant. However, that stereotypical image is in many cases a mistake, since informants range from undercover police officers to dope addicts, including "citizen informants," who act openly in aid of law enforcement, with no motive in informing except to rid the neighborhood of undesirables. This type of "citizen informant" often includes crime victims. Thus, an informant could be a fellow officer, a crime victim, a criminal suspect, or a police dispatcher. In essence, an informant is anyone who gives second-hand information to be used in court for obtaining a search warrant, or anything else. Information from an informant is regarded as hearsay when used in court.

§ 17.21.1   The Evolution of Reliability

In 1983, the U.S. Supreme Court changed the entire law regarding informants in the case of *Illinois v. Gates*, 462 U.S. 213, 103 S.Ct. 2317, 76 L.Ed. 2d 527 (1983).

To understand the *Gates* case, one must understand the law which preceded it. For years, the *Aguilar-Spinelli* rule stated the law on informants. There were two "prongs" to this rule, both of which had to be satisfied in order to obtain a search warrant, arrest warrant, etc., based on the informer's information.

After the *Gates* case, however, even though the same two factors are still considered by the courts under the totality of the circumstances, the two prongs are not strictly mandatory. In effect, the court said in the *Gates* case: "We're going to keep the *Aguilar-Spinelli* rule as a guide, but we're going to relax the rules to allow for common sense."

§ 17.21.2   The *Aguilar-Spinelli* 2-Prong Test

The two prongs of this test are as follows: an informant must be RELIABLE, and must speak from PERSONAL KNOWLEDGE.

PRONG ONE: RELIABILITY

The following people are considered inherently reliable:

—Law enforcement officers, by virtue of their profession. This kind of information is sometimes called "official channels."

—"Citizen" informants. There is a presumption that anyone who, with no ulterior motive, acts openly in aid of law enforcement is reliable and therefore needs no corroboration. The informant's name, address, etc. must be obtained, since, if it is not, the informer will be classified as an "anonymous" informant, and will require corroboration.

With citizen informants, make sure the citizen knows what he or she is reporting. For example, a person calls you and tells you that there is a narcotics party going on next door. Can you get a search warrant based on his information? Yes, but there will be questions from the defense, regarding the informer's knowledge of dope, and his experience to testify that what he saw was marijuana, cocaine, etc. If this was the first and only time he or she ever saw drugs being abused, chances are that the court will throw out the evidence.

The officer must make sure the informant is really a citizen informant before using him or her for probable cause on a search warrant. If the officer merely believes that the person with whom he is dealing is a citizen informer, and uses him on an affidavit without checking, the evidence obtained by such a search will be excluded, even if the informer turns out to be a legitimate citizen informant. It is assumed that citizen informants, since they have nothing to gain from lying, will tell the truth. It is just the opposite with criminals, who inform to stay out of jail, or to get better treatment by police.

In order to use a criminal suspect as an informant, you must make the criminal informant "reliable." There are three ways of doing this:

1. **Show the court that the informant has given accurate information in the past.** The mere fact that a criminal informant gave accurate information to police on even one occasion is enough. The information provided by such an unreliable informant need not result in a conviction, or even an arrest, so long as the informant gave information, and that information turned out to be correct.

2. **Use corroboration.** Any type of corroboration will do. Two or more untested informants may corroborate each other, so long as there was no collusion prior to such corroboration.

3. **Skelton affidavit.** For this reliability test, you bring an informant in front of a judge and have the judge examine him. If the judge determines that the informant is telling the truth, he may issue a search warrant based solely upon the informant's statement (*Skelton v. Superior Court of Orange County*, 1 Cal. 3d 144, 81 Cal. Rptr. 613, 406 P.2d 485 (Cal. 1969)).

PRONG TWO: PERSONAL KNOWLEDGE

Under the *Aguilar-Spinelli* rule, it is not sufficient to prove only that your informant is reliable. What if the information were third- or fourth-hand? The informant must also speak from personal knowledge. Think about the consequences of the officer's not being required to speak from personal knowledge.

Example: Officer X is testifying about information received from a C/I (confidential, reliable informant). He testifies that, "My C/I informed me that there was a narcotics party in progress at 312 Elm Street." This is good information, and will, assuming that the C/I is reliable, provide probable cause—but if and only if the officer knows how the C/I got the information. To verify the informant's personal knowledge, it is always best to say to the C/I, "And how do you know this information is correct?"

Example (from personal experience): I received word that one of my snitches wanted to see me. I was working in the Mission Beach area of San Diego. When we met, he was in a hurry, but told me that a large amount of narcotics was now being sold at an address he gave me. I recognized the address as one I suspected of selling dope. I thanked the C/I profusely, and called for a "telephonic" search warrant. After relaying my information to the D.A., I felt very good about the warrant I was about to get, and was already wondering how long it would be until I got my department commendation, when the D.A. asked me that giant mankiller of a question "How does your informant know the information you just gave me is correct?"

In essence, the D.A.'s question was: "Could this be second-hand information, or third-hand, or eighth-hand?" There was no way that the judge could tell from the conclusionary language used. In effect, the statement was double-hearsay; that is, hearsay on hearsay. Multiple-level hearsay is admissible only if you are able to find an exception for each level.

The lesson to be learned here is not to use conclusionary language. If, in the above example, I had asked the informer how he knew that dope was being sold from that address, and he told me that he himself was in the house an hour ago, and had seen sales himself, then the personal knowledge prong of the two-prong informant test would have been fulfilled.

However, in *Illinois v. Gates*, 462 U.S. 23, 103 S.Ct. 2317, 76 L.Ed. 2d 527 (1983), the Supreme Court abandoned the two-prong *Aguilar-Spinelli* test.

§ 17.21.3   *Illinois v. Gates*: Its Impact on the Subject of Informers

For years, and with good reason, prosecutors felt that the old *Aguilar-Spinelli* rules were cumbersome and overly technical. Finally, the U.S. Supreme Court granted *certiorari*, and subsequently ruled that the *Aguilar-Spinelli* test violated the due process clause.

In *Gates*, the Supreme Court adopted a less demanding standard for determining whether an informer's tip establishes a probable cause for the issuance of a warrant. The new test was received with mixed emotions in the law enforcement community. On the one hand, the new standard made a police officer's job much easier. On the other, however, the new guidelines were more vague and were subject to varying interpretations by lower courts.

The new ruling on informant reliability stipulates that a court must review the *totality of the circumstances*. Some facts of the *Gates* case may help to establish the rationale behind this ruling.

One day, the police department of Bloomington, Illinois received an anonymous letter. The letter explained that Brad and Susan Gates, who lived in the same area as the scrivener, made their living by selling narcotics. The letter went on to describe exactly how the Gateses obtained the narcotics. It detailed how Brad would drive and Susan would fly to Florida on a certain day of the week where they would meet with a distributor who sold them the dope. The letter even gave an exact description of the car in which they would drive back to Bloomington. Moreover, the letter explained that when the Gateses pulled their car in the garage on that one day of the week, it would always contain about $200,000 worth of narcotics.

Needless to say, this informant's letter was very incriminating for the Gateses. However, consider the legal implications of what happened (or didn't happen) at the end of the letter. There was no signature, no return address, nothing. The letter could not meet either prong of the *Aguilar-Spinelli* rule, since there was no indication that the writer was reliable; nor was there any indication of personal knowledge.

With the help of the DEA, Bloomington Police checked out the contents of the letter. They followed the Gateses as they went to Florida; the couple did everything that the letter said they would do. As they arrived back home, the police served a search warrant on their car and home, finding the narcotics described in the letter.

The Gateses appealed, arguing that neither prong of the two-prong test had been satisfied; whereas, case law under *Aguilar-Spinelli* held that both prongs must be satisfied.

The U.S. Supreme Court, in upholding the warrant, stated that the old *Aguilar-Spinelli* rule was too rigid and inflexible; the court then adopted a more reasonable "totality of the circumstances" test. This test holds that the relative weight of each prong (reliability and personal knowledge) should be measured only against the totality of the circumstances such that the "whole picture" would convince a reasonable and prudent person.

Although the *Aguilar-Spinelli* rule is no longer in effect as a rule of law, it must be kept in mind, since even under the more relaxed standards of *Illinois v. Gates,* both prongs are still relevant (*People v. Love,* 168 Cal. App. 3d 104, 214 Cal. Rptr. 483 (Cal. App. 5 Dist. 1985)).

§ 17.21.4   Other Proper Uses of Informants
§ 17.21.4(a)   Unknown, Untested Informants

Unknown, untested informants cannot be used to develop probable cause, at least not without further evidence. Nevertheless, any corroboration at all may supply probable cause, and the corroboration need not amount to probable cause itself (*People v. Lissauer,* 169 Cal. App. 3d 413, 215 Cal. Rptr. 335 (Cal. App. 1 Dist. 1985)).

§ 17.21.4(b)   Two Untested Informants May Corroborate

Probable cause for arrest, search warrant, etc., may be attained through two or more untested informants as long as each informant is a separate, unrelated source (*Clifton v. Superior Court, County of Humbolt,* 7 Cal. App. 3d 245, 86 Cal. Rptr. 612 (Cal. App. 1 Dist. 1970); *People v. Ballassey,* 30 Cal. App. 3d 614, 106 Cal. Rptr. 461 (Cal. App. 2 Dist. 1973)).

§ 17.21.4(c)   Statements Against Penal Interest

If an informant gives information against his or her own penal interest when implicating the suspect, then that statement alone may be used to develop probable cause even though the informant is not otherwise known to be reliable (*People v. Hall*, 42 Cal. App. 3d 817, 117 Cal. Rptr. 228 (Cal. App. 2 Dist. 1974)).

EXAMPLE: A and B commit a robbery/rape/murder. The next day, A calls B's girlfriend and tells her the story.

Note: This is not a situation where boyfriend tells girlfriend about a crime he has committed. If it were, then the second-hand confession would be admissible as a confession.

Here, however, the law presumes that when a person makes a statement against his own penal interest to a third party, it must be true, otherwise why would he make the statement? (*People v. Campa*, 36 Cal. 3d 870, 206 Cal. Rptr. 114, 686 P.2d 634 (Cal. 1984)).

§ 17.21.4(d)   Disclosure of Confidential Informants

The 6th Amendment to the United States Constitution guarantees every criminal defendant the right to "be confronted with the witnesses against him; [and] to have compulsory process for obtaining witnesses in his favor...."

The federal government and most states have enacted statutes, based on the common law we inherited from England, which gives law enforcement a privilege to refuse to disclose the identity of a person who has furnished information on criminal activity. One of the policies underlying this privilege is to encourage persons to communicate their knowledge of criminal acts to law enforcement without fear of reprisal (see *McCray v. Illinois*, 386 U.S. 300, 87 S.Ct. 1056, 18 L.Ed. 2d 62 (1967)).

The privilege is limited, however. When there is a conflict between the defendant's 6th Amendment rights and the government's privilege, the privilege must yield (see *Roviaro v. U.S.*, 353 U.S. 53, 77 S.Ct. 623, 1 L.Ed. 2d 639 (1957); *People v. Borunda*, 11 Cal. 3d 523, 113 Cal. Rptr. 825, 522 P.2d 1 (Cal. 1974)).

§ 17.21.4(e)   The Legal Test to Determine Disclosure

Almost all motions to discover the identity of an informant are in cases in which a search warrant was issued, based primarily on information from an informant. The test used to determine whether the informant's identity should be revealed is stated as follows: The informant is discoverable if the informant could give evidence material to the issue of guilt. If the informant only supplied probable cause, (i.e., simply points the finger of suspicion towards a person who has violated the law) the informant is not discoverable (see *People v. Borunda, supra*; *People v. McShann*, 50 Cal. 2d 802, 330 P.2d 33 (Cal. 1958)).

Since the rules of evidence require that witnesses, except experts, have personal knowledge of the matter they are asked to give testimony on, the legal test for disclosure can be correctly restated as follows: if the informant was percipient to an element of the crime or to a possible defense of the crime, and therefore potentially helpful to the defense, the informant is discoverable. If the informant was only percipient to those factors relied on for probable cause, then the informant is not discoverable.

§ 17.21.4(f) The Defense Evidence to Support the Motion to Disclose

The defense has the burden of demonstrating "a reasonable possibility that the informer could give evidence on the issue of guilt that might result in the defendant's exoneration. This rule of evidence is founded on the principle that nondisclosure in this situation would result in a denial of a fair trial to a defendant" (see *People v. Garcia,* 67 Cal. 2d 830, 839-840, 64 Cal. Rptr. 110, 434 P.2d 366 (Cal. 1967); *People v. Tolliver,* 53 Cal. App. 3d 1036, 125 Cal. Rptr. 905 (Cal. App. 2 Dist. 1975)). The defense may be able to demonstrate this possibility by calling an officer to the stand, by relying on statements in the affidavit, or most likely, by calling the defendant or someone closely associated with the defense to the stand (*People v. Garcia, supra,* at 839, fn.10; *People v. Tolliver, supra,* at 1044).

In this case, the witness will be asked questions concerning the person identified as the suspect in the affidavit. The witness will also be asked questions relevant to a defense such as entrapment, coercion, or planted evidence by the informant (see *People v. Fried,* 214 Cal. App. 3d 1309, 1312, 263 Cal. Rptr. 237 (Cal. App. 2 Dist. 1989)). The defense argument will be: "The informant will be able to testify that the person identified as the seller, or possessor of drugs in the affidavit, was not this defendant. The informant will testify that the defendant was not even at the place on the dates mentioned in the affidavit." Or, "the defendant did have the drugs on the date of the alleged offense, but only because the informant begged him to do it as a favor for the following reason: the informant...would be killed...lose face with his friends who were invited to a special party...tell the defendant's wife that the defendant was unfaithful..." (use your imagination here).

§ 17.21.4(g) The Government's Evidence for Non-Disclosure

The investigator must be aware of the elements to the crimes which may be charged against the defendant as well as the defenses to those charges. The best definitions can be found in the Jury Instruction books. The investigator has to develop evidence at the time of the investigation and execution of the warrant which will disprove any predictable defenses. At a minimum, the investigator should monitor, when possible, the informant's activities. The investigator, while searching for drugs (evidence of the crime), must also be looking for evidence which proves that the defendant didn't just happen to be in the wrong place at the wrong time. List evidence on the warrant, then try to find the evidence which proves that the defendant does occupy the place and is or was committing crimes there. Be prepared to prove that it was not possible for some other person to have been committing the crimes you are accusing the defendant of.

§ 17.21.4(h)   The In-Camera Hearing

If the prosecution is unable to convince the court that the informant is not material to an issue of guilt in the open court proceeding, and if you are claiming the privilege, then the prosecution is entitled to an in-camera hearing. This hearing is conducted outside the presence of the defendant and defendant's attorney. The record of this proceeding is sealed.

You must be prepared to offer "competent" evidence which refutes the defense claim as to why the informant is material to an issue of guilt. In many cases, the informant will be the only competent witness who can give testimony (see *People v. Lee*, 164 Cal. App. 3d 830, 836, 210 Cal. Rptr. 799 (Cal. App. 5 Dist. 1985)). Therefore, make sure the informant will be available to testify at the in-camera hearing, or be able to produce other witnesses, (even yourself) who could give evidence which proves the informant could not assist the defense (see *People v. Alderrou*, 191 Cal. App. 3d 1074, 1081, 236 Cal. Rptr. 740 (Cal. App. 2 Dist. 1987); *People v. Fried*, 214 Cal. App. 3d 1309, 1313-1314; 263 Cal. Rptr. 237 (Cal. App. 2 Dist. 1989)).

§ 17.21.4(i)   Sanction for Non-Disclosure

All the charges on which the "undisclosed" informant may be material to an issue of guilt must be DISMISSED! (*Eleazar v. Superior Court of Los Angeles County*, 1 Cal. 3d 847, 83 Cal. Rptr. 586, 464 P.2d 42 (Cal. 1970)).

§ 17.22   ENTRAPMENT
§ 17.22.1   Definition of the Entrapment Defense

Most legal defenses to criminal charges are what might be characterized as "true defenses." That is, they are circumstances which the law recognizes as *negating* guilt, rather than *excusing* it—for example, self-defense, defense of others, necessity, accident and misfortune, and insanity.   Other defense theories fall into a category of "technical defenses;" these are defenses which are created at law on public policy grounds which have nothing to do with the guilt or innocence of an accused, but simply represent the legislative or judicial view of procedural standards for criminal proceedings. This category includes, for example, the defenses based on double jeopardy, statutes of limitations, and lack of independent proof or corpus for a confessed crime. A defendant who asserts a "technical defense" is not necessarily claiming to be innocent of the charges—he or she is merely saying that some procedural irregularity prevents conviction on the charges, even though he or she may actually be guilty.

The entrapment defense falls into this latter category. A defendant who was improperly motivated by police to commit a crime is still morally guilty of the crime—he committed every element of the offense, and he has no "true defense" to negate his guilt. But the courts have decided that police conduct falling below a certain standard may be asserted—even by a guilty defendant—as a "technical defense" to his conviction.

§ 17.22.2 Rationale Behind the Entrapment Defense

In California, the reasoning for permitting a defense of entrapment is set out in a series of decisions:

California has recognized the defense of entrapment for reasons substantially similar to those which caused the courts to adopt the rule that evidence obtained in violation of constitutional guaranties is not admissible...the court refuses to enable officers of the law to consummate illegal or unjust schemes designed to foster rather than prevent and detect crime.

Although there is an instinctive sympathy for the originally well-intended defendant who is seduced into crime by persuasion and artifice, such a defendant is just as guilty where his seducer is a police officer as he would be if he were persuaded by a hardened criminal accomplice. Entrapment is a defense not because the defendant is innocent but because..."it is less evil that some criminals should escape than that the government should play an ignoble part" (*People v. Benford*, 53 Cal. 2d 1, 9; 345 P.2d 928 (Cal. 1959)). In essence, the courts have concluded that recognition of the defense of entrapment is crucial to the fair administration of justice. . . The function of enforcement officials is to investigate, not instigate, crime; to discover, not to promote, crime (*Patty v. BME*, 9 Cal. 3d 356, 364, 107 Cal. Rptr. 473, 508 P.2d 1121 (Cal. 1973)).

When the California State Supreme Court reexamined the entrapment doctrine in two 1979 decisions, it referred frequently to passages from other opinions indicating that the justification for permitting an entrapment defense was the necessity to "deter police misconduct":

"...courts must be closed to the trial of a crime instigated by the government's own agents"...because...deterrence of impermissible law enforcement activity [is] the proper rationale for the entrapment defense...."

The courts refuse to convict an entrapped defendant...because, even if his guilt be admitted, the methods employed on behalf of the Government to bring about conviction cannot be countenanced.

"...In People v. Benford, supra, this court unanimously embraced the public policy/deterrence rationale....(*People v. Barraza*, 23 Cal. 3d 675, 153 Cal. Rptr. 459, 591 P.2d 947 (Cal. 1979)).

...the test of entrapment we adopt herein is designed primarily to deter impermissible police conduct....(*People v. Barraza*, supra)."

We recently reviewed the entrapment doctrine in *People v. Barraza* and emphasized the deterrent purpose of the rule....Such an approach focuses on the methods used by the government to apprehend criminals and does not permit a defendant to be convicted when police conduct "falls below an acceptable standard for the fair and honorable administration of justice." (*People v. McIntyre*, 23 Cal. 3d 742, 745, 153 Cal. Rptr. 237, 591 P.2d 527 (Cal. 1979)).

Chapter 17

§ 17.22.3 Standards of Police Conduct

What standard did the court believe should apply to police participation in a criminal scheme? The California State Supreme Court decided the following:

> "...we hold that the proper test of entrapment is the following: was the conduct of the law enforcement agent likely to induce a normally law-abiding person to commit the offense?...it is impermissible for the police or their agents to pressure the suspect by overbearing conduct such as badgering, cajoling, importuning, or other affirmative acts likely to induce a normally law-abiding person to commit the crime (*People v. Barraza, supra,* at 689-690)."

As a guideline for measuring whether police conduct in any particular case violated this standard, the court announced two principles to be applied, and gave examples of each:

First, if the actions of the law enforcement agent would generate in a normally law-abiding person a *motive* for the crime *other than* ordinary criminal intent, entrapment will be established. An example of such conduct would be an appeal by the police that would induce such a person to commit the act because of *friendship* or *sympathy*, instead of a desire for personal gain or other typical criminal purpose.

Second, affirmative police conduct that would make commission of the crime *unusually attractive* to a normally law-abiding person will likewise constitute entrapment. Such conduct would include, for example, a guarantee that the act is *not illegal* or the offense will go *undetected*, an offer of *exorbitant consideration*, or any similar enticement (*People v. Barraza, supra,* at 690, emphasis added).

§ 17.22.4 Suspect's Predisposition

Under the federal law, the suspect's predisposition to commit the kind of offense in question is a proper subject of jury focus in deciding whether or not the suspect was entrapped. The argument for this doctrine is that a person who was ready and willing to commit the crime— as shown by his or her criminal record of similar offenses—needs little encouragement and has no cause to complain when his criminal inclinations lead him into a police trap (see *Sorrells v. U.S.,* 287 U.S. 435, 77 L.Ed. 413, 53 S.Ct. 210 (1932); *Hampton v. U.S.,* 425 U.S. 484, 48 L.Ed. 2d 113, 96 S.Ct. 1646 (1976)). In adopting a test which focuses on the inducement activities of the *police*, the California Supreme Court in *People v. Barraza* declared that the "character of the suspect, his predisposition to commit the offense, and his subjective intent are irrelevant." A defense of entrapment cannot be overcome, therefore, by offering to show that the defendant is a "known dealer," a "known fence," or a "known prostitute." Such evidence is *not admissible* on the entrapment issue (and is not affected by Proposition 8, which changed only the rules of admissibility of *relevant* evidence, but did not redefine what is relevant).

§ 17.22.5   Permissible Police Conduct

Even though the *Barraza* court was obviously concerned about criminal prosecutions involving police participation, the justices recognized that some kinds of crimes could never be detected or prosecuted without undercover police activity. The court approved police deception which does not violate its standard:

Official conduct that does no more than offer [an] opportunity to the suspect—for example, a decoy program—is therefore permissible (*People v. Barraza, supra,* at 690).

"There will be no entrapment...when the official conduct is found to have gone no further than necessary to assure the suspect that he is not being "set up." The police remain free to take reasonable, though restrained, steps to gain the confidence of suspects. A contrary rule would unduly hamper law enforcement; indeed, in the case of many of the so-called "victimless" crimes, it would tend to limit convictions to only the most gullible offenders" (*People v.* Barraza, supra, fn. 4).

Although the suspect's historical predisposition to criminality is irrelevant, the court said that in considering whether police conduct violated the entrapment standard, relevant circumstances could include the following:

"...the transaction preceding the offense, the suspect's response to the inducements of the officer, the gravity of the crime, and the difficulty of detecting instances of its commission" (*People v. Barraza, supra,* at 690).

§ 17.22.6   Origin of Intent

Before *Barraza*, a highly-relevant factor in the entrapment defense was the origin of the intent to consummate the subject crime: if the government "implanted the criminal design in the mind of the defendant," entrapment would come into play; if the defendant first suggested the crime, this would expose his criminal predisposition and negate any entrapment defense. (Police officers trained in the pre-*Barraza* era were routinely advised that if the police were the first to suggest to someone that he do something which would make him subject to arrest, the entrapment defense would prevent conviction.)

One consequence of California's rejection of the so-called "origin of intent" test of entrapment is that as long as the "normally law-abiding person" standard is observed, police *can* be the first to suggest a criminal enterprise without being guilty of entrapment. The *Barraza* test changes the emphasis from *whether* police conceived the idea of the crime to *how* police induced the suspect to go through with it:

"...*we are not concerned with who first* conceived or who willingly, or reluctantly, acquiesced in a criminal project. What we do care about is how much and what manner of persuasion, pressure, and cajoling are brought to bear by law enforcement officials to induce persons to commit crimes (*People v. Barraza, supra,* at 688, emphasis added)."

For example, where undercover agents originated the idea that defendants sell cocaine to an undercover officer, the defendants tried to base an entrapment defense on the fact that police made the first suggestion. However, the Appellate Court rejected this effort:

The defendant also urges that the jurors should have been instructed that a law-abiding person is any person who does not generate or originate the intent to commit the crime....Such a test, however, runs counter to the Supreme Court's explicit determination that *the sequence is not relevant* (*People v. Kelley*, 158 Cal. App. 3d 1085, 205 Cal. Rptr. 283 (Cal. App. 1 Dist. 1984), emphasis added). Likewise, where agents obtained prescriptions for controlled drugs from a medical doctor by simply requesting them, without any complaints of medical condition, the fact that the idea originated with the government did not mean the doctor had been entrapped:

Certainly, the agents lied to Douglass. But *Barraza* does not prevent government agents from lying....Here, the agents' conduct simply provided Douglass the opportunity to engage in unprofessional conduct for the ordinary criminal motive of pecuniary gain....Accordingly, there is no evidence the agents entrapped Douglass (*Douglass v. BMQA*, 141 Cal. App. 3d 645, 190 Cal. Rptr. 506 (Cal. App. 4 Dist. 1983)).

§ 17.22.7   Use of Civilian Agents

In those cases where an informant or other civilian agent is used against the suspect, the basic rules of agency apply: the agent is also forbidden to use improper or excessive means to induce the suspect to commit a crime, and if he or she does so under the direction of law enforcement officials, the defense of entrapment will arise. In fact, even if the agent is unaware that the person prompting him to influence another's actions is a police office, the defense still applies:

"...manipulation of third party by law enforcement officers to procure the commission of a criminal offense by another renders the third party a government agent for purposes of the entrapment defense, even though the third party remains unaware of the law enforcement object" (*People v. McIntyre*, 23 Cal. 3d 742, 748, 153 Cal. Rptr. 237, 591 P.2d 527 (Cal. 1979)).

Notice, however, that since entrapment is a "technical defense" and guilty defendants do not have any absolute right to assert it, the defense—like the exclusionary rules—is only to be invoked where its application may serve its purpose: to deter police misconduct. Logically, therefore, when police properly instruct an agent to observe the judicial rules on entrapment and the agent *independently* violates the standard by using improper motivations, there has been *no* police misconduct; there is nothing to deter; and so the entrapment defense should not apply.

To help prevent civilian agents from unwittingly laying the groundwork for an entrapment defense, *and* to aid the prosecutor in arguing to the court that no determinable police misconduct occurred (and therefore no entrapment instruction should be given to the jury), law enforcement agencies should require civilian agents to *read* and sign an advice form. (Undercover and uniformed officers should also be aware of this information, of course.)

Hopefully, agents will adhere to these guidelines and avoid entrapping a suspect. And if an overzealous agent violates the standards, the prosecutor can offer the information form as evidence that the agent was acting outside the scope of his or her agency, and that no determinable police misconduct was present (although the prosecution does not have the burden of proving the absence of entrapment—*In re Foss*, 10 Cal. 3d 910, 112 Cal. Rptr. 649, 519 P.2d 1073 (Cal. 1974)—it is still necessary to rebut defenses which might prevent a conviction).

§ 17.22.8   Entrapment vs. Solicitation

By coincidence, crimes of solicitation (such as prostitution, lewd conduct, subornation of perjury, soliciting murder, and offers to sell weapons or narcotics) are often the crimes where undercover or decoy operations are necessary for enforcement, and thus the defense of entrapment is most likely to be asserted. Unfortunately, this coincidence has created a tendency for some people to blur the distinction between entrapment and solicitation. The result is a confusion under which defendants often cry "Entrapment!" when what they really mean is that they did not commit the *solicitation* element of the crime.

For example, it is illegal to solicit anyone to engage in lewd conduct in public. If an undercover officer or agent approaches a suspect in a public toilet and asks the suspect to join him in a lewd act there and the suspect agrees, he has *not* been *entrapped*, because no undue influence was used. A normally law-abiding person would not have agreed to the act. However, it was not the *suspect* who did the soliciting in this example, but the *officer*. The suspect's proper defense is that *he* did not commit an essential element of the offense (solicitation). The distinction is simple, but it somehow frequently confounds police officers, attorneys and judges alike. *Entrapment* occurs when improper or excessive inducement is used; *solicitation* crimes require that the suspect do the soliciting. (But note that crimes committed by either soliciting, *agreeing to* or *engaging in* proscribed behavior can be committed by the suspect even if the officer is the first to suggest the act—e.g., Pen. Code §647(a), (b)—and as long as no undue pressures are used, no entrapment defense holds.)

§ 17.22.8(a)   Testing for Entrapment

The test for the defense of entrapment focuses entirely on the conduct of the officers. The central question can be formulated as follows: Was your conduct likely to cause a normally law-abiding citizen to commit the crime? (*People v. Barraza*, 23 Cal. 3d 675, 153 Cal. Rptr. 459, 591 P.2d 947 (Cal. 1979)). Other relevant questions would include: Did you appeal to friendship or sympathy? Did you offer extraordinary profit? The most common situations where the entrapment defense is asserted is, of course, where an officer or his agent buys contraband from the suspect (*People v. McIntyre*, 23 Cal. 3d 742, 748, 153 Cal. Rptr. 237, 591 P.2d 527 (Cal. 1979)). Entrapment can be asserted, however, in any situation where officers do substantially more than just provide an opportunity for the suspect to commit a crime.

Usually, suspects who assert the entrapment defense at trial are without other alternative defenses. If a suspect is questioned before he retains a lawyer, he will seldom assert the defense of entrapment. No matter how strong the evidence is against him, the suspect will almost always claim misidentification, or some other defense which can be easily rebutted at trial. Once the suspect has asserted a "bad" defense in his statement to police, he has committed himself to that defense at trial.

§ 17.23   DRUGS AND EVIDENCE IN COURT

Prosecution must prove two points:

1. The controlled substance is illegal—done by a chemist who analyzed the evidence.

2. Chain of custody—The prosecution must be able to prove that the same drugs in court are the drug seized at the time of arrest or purchased from the suspect at the time in question.

§ 17.23.1   Dope Lawyers

Lawyers who specialize in controlled substance cases are called "dope lawyers." According to attorneys and judges familiar with the craft, being a dope lawyer requires a different set of skills than those required of an attorney who represents defendants accused of other crimes. Even though many dope lawyers are skilled trial attorneys, the skill of presenting a case to a jury is not the most important. The reason for this is that very few cases go to trial, and when a case does go to trial, the police have overwhelming evidence and a solid case. The dope lawyer is most skilled in keeping evidence away from the jury. This involves skill in pre-trial motions aimed at getting evidence that has been seized thrown out of court on the grounds that the police misbehaved in obtaining it. Success in a "search and seizure motion" means that since there is no evidence, there is no crime. If the dope lawyer fails in pre-trial motions, then plea-negotiation is important. For example, the job is to get a charge of sales of cocaine reduced to simple possession.

§ 17.23.2   Qualification as a Narcotics Expert

To qualify an officer as an expert witness, the District Attorney will most often ask the officer the following questions:

1. Occupation, assignment, years of experience

2. Training

3. Courses, books, studies

4. Ever observed person under influence of narcotics? How many? Circumstances?

5. Ever observed injections of narcotics by hypodermic needle? Where? Where on the person? By whom?

6. Were the injections administered by physicians or persons acting under their direction? Have you noticed what traces, scars or scabs are left or form later, if any?

7. What have you observed about injections that are self-administered by narcotic users?

8. How long does it take a scab to form?

9. How long does it remain?

10. What size are those scabs? What is their appearance?

11. Did you interview the defendant? Where? When?

12. Did you examine the defendant's arms? What did you observe?

13. Please tell the court and jury what you recall of the details of defendant's arms.

14. Based upon your training and experience in hospitals and with physicians, together with your training and experience as a police officer, your observation of persons who use narcotics, their appearance, and the marks, scars and scabs upon such persons and further based upon your examination of the defendant's arms, and the appearance, number of location of the marks, scars and scabs on the defendant's arms, do you have an opinion as to the cause of those scars and scabs? Answer: Yes.

15. Based upon the nature of these marks, do you have an opinion as to whether they were administered by a physician or one under his direction or were they the result of a self-administered injection? Answer: self-administered.

16. Now, based upon the number, the location and the nature of those marks, do you have an opinion as to what was injected? Answer: Yes, a narcotic.

After answering the questions, the defense counsel has the right to take the investigating officer on *void dire*, the right to inquire in greater detail regarding the experience, schooling or any other endeavor claimed by the officer as establishing his knowledge of the subject. Remember, a witness is confined to testimony involving only those things coming in contact with one or more of his five senses. This is not the case with an expert witness who is expressing an opinion on a particular subject. Acceptance of his opinion is dependent upon his ability to express himself fully and understandably, particularly to a jury.

§ 17.23.3 Expert Testimony

A person is qualified to testify as an expert if he has special knowledge, skill, experience, training, or education sufficient to qualify him as an expert on the subject to which his testimony relates. Duly qualified experts may give their opinions on questions in controversy at a trial. To assist you in deciding such questions, you may consider the opinion with the reasons given for it, if any, by the expert who gives the opinion. You may also consider the qualifications and credibility of the expert. In resolving any conflict that may exist in the testimony of expert witnesses, you should weigh the opinion of one expert against that of another. In doing this, you should consider the relative qualifications and credibility of the expert witnesses, as well as the reasons for each opinion and the facts and other matters upon which it was based. You are not bound to accept any expert opinion as conclusive, but should give to it the weight to which you find it to be entitled. You may disregard any such problem if you find it to be unreasonable.

§ 17.23.4 CONTACT WITH NEWS REPORTERS

Many reporters for newspapers, radio, and television know little about amphetamines, barbiturates, tranquilizers, phencyclidine and narcotic drugs. Because of this, and because reporters often are under the pressure of deadlines, they frequently rely on the police for information. By giving news reporters accurate information about situations involving drugs, the officer can do assure that the public will receive accurate news reports. The officer will also want to make sure that he is conducting himself within the regulations, if any, set up by his own department. News reporters will usually appreciate anything the police can do to provide factual information about drugs. Performing a service of this kind enhances the reputation of law enforcement with the press and also serves to build public confidence in the police. Providing the press with accurate information is also important because inaccurate or exaggerated news reports can lead to embarrassment or other difficulties for law enforcement officers.

Here are some points an officer should remember when dealing with news reporters:

—You should confine your remarks to information about which you are positive. For example, you should never speculate about the identity of confiscated tablets or capsules.

—You should be careful in the use of slang expressions for amphetamines, barbiturates and other types of drugs. Although many people have heard about whites, downers, chiva, etc., few know the specific references for these terms.

Reference

Holtz, Larry E. <u>Contemporary Criminal Procedure</u>. Longwood, FL: Gould Publications, 1996.

CHAPTER 18

UNDERCOVER NARCOTICS AND CLANDESTINE LAB INVESTIGATIONS

§ 18.1 INTRODUCTION

Any careful approach to the overall drug problem must consider two main factors. First is the detection, arrest, prosecution, and incarceration of the drug traffickers, thus slowing the supply side of the pendulum. Second is the seizure of illicit drugs, supplies to make, process, and distribute the drugs, and any assets of the trafficker including vehicles, planes, boats, cash, bonds, and real estate. These seizures enormously inconvenience the traffickers and further weaken the supply side. Faced with possible incarceration for an extended period of time—and the loss of assets—the drug trafficker will become more cautious about those to whom he sells. Likewise, the clandestine meeting places will become much more hidden and difficult to locate or access by law enforcement or the drug buyer.

§ 18.2 ESTABLISHING AN UNDERCOVER INVESTIGATION

There are many steps involved in initiating a narcotics investigation. These include receipt and verification of information as well as planning the operation of the investigation. Since information is received from a multitude of sources, a determination must be made as to the value and validity of the information received and the credibility of the source supplying the information. Narcotics units routinely receive information regarding illegal drug activity from anonymous telephone callers. If the information is of any value or substance, then the unit may begin an investigation or write an Intelligence Information Report. Talking on the telephone to the anonymous caller helps the narcotics investigator to establish the validity of the information and to determine whether or not the caller has genuine first-hand knowledge of the information that he or she is giving. A large percentage of law enforcement agencies utilize a telephone recording device to receive these anonymous tips. This telephone number and recording device may be called secret witness, crime stoppers, TIP (turn in a pusher), or any other name to catch the attention of the public. With some agencies, a cash reward is offered for information; the caller is given an identification number to claim the cash reward. Regardless of whether a reward is offered, the anonymous caller is a valuable asset to any narcotics unit.

Another equally important source of information to a narcotics unit is the informant. The informant is often more reliable and the information the informant gives is generally easier to verify than that of the anonymous caller. The informant is generally a person who is actually involved in some facet of the particular crime being investigated. In the area of narcotics informants, the informant is almost always either a user or seller. Due to this fact, the informant can often introduce the undercover narcotics agent to a source of illicit drugs.

Once the determination has been made that the information received is of some merit and warrants an investigation, it is assigned to a narcotics agent for follow-up. Ideally, a narcotics agent would, through an introduction, infiltrate some level of an illicit drug distribution system. When an informant is available for assistance in a particular drug investigation, the infiltration is often easier and more successfully completed.

An overall objective must be established in each undercover narcotics investigation. Starting with an overview and synopsis of what is known about the current "target" operation, the narcotics agent can determine the most effective method of gaining access. There must be a well-defined plan to successfully complete a detailed undercover operation. Haphazard investigations could ultimately result in serious injury to or death of the narcotics agent, or the loss of a case in court.

Although undercover operations are crucial to the successful enforcement of drug laws, not all law enforcement officers are able to perform in an undercover capacity. Intricate and grueling mental work is involved. The requirements of the undercover officer vary with each investigation. Often the undercover agent is forced to assume the role of a drug dealer or drug user, and may be offered illicit drugs for personal consumption or use.

It should be noted that undercover operations may take place in virtually any facet of police investigations. However, undercover work is most generally associated with narcotics investigations. Narcotics agents must be fast on their feet and able to adapt to any situation. To preserve his undercover identity, the narcotics agent must be able to perform the roles of the drug dealer and buyer both physically (in appearance) and mentally. Most law enforcement officers find it unnatural to be involved in criminal activity. For the narcotics agent, this must become second nature. Due to the undercover officer's "participation" in criminal activity, it should be stressed that undercover narcotics agents must be dedicated, above all, to the enforcement of the law; they must maintain the highest integrity. The ultimate goals are the reduction of illicit drug trafficking, the apprehension of the perpetrators, and the conviction and incarceration of all parties involved in the manufacture, production, and distribution of illicit drugs.

§ 18.3   THE UNDERCOVER OPERATION

Before an undercover operation can be established, there must be some sort of objective and a "target." The term "target" refers to an individual or group targeted by a law enforcement officer/agency for apprehension. Once the target has been chosen, the investigators can decide the best way to accomplish the objective. The objectives are generally (1) an arrest with as large an amount of illicit drugs as possible; (2) the seizure of as many assets of the perpetrator as can be legally seized including cash, automobiles, planes, boats, homes, businesses, jewelry, stocks, and bonds; and 3) the incarceration of the perpetrator for as long as is legally possible. Even under ideal circumstances, all of these objectives are seldom obtained unless an extensive long-term operation is run on the target. Most municipal, county, and state narcotics bureaus do not have the manpower or budget to allow single-handedly for this type of operation. Therefore, when a long-term extensive operation can be run, two or more agencies frequently combine efforts. By combining efforts, the agencies can reduce the number of agents used, the cash outlay, and the man-hours invested. With a variety of officers and expertise, combined efforts may also lead to greater success in the undercover operation.

One requirement of multi-agency involvement is the distribution of assets seized during the investigation. Generally the distribution is determined by the each agency's level of involvement. The greater the involvement, the greater the amount of seized assets which go to that agency.

Another consideration of multi-agency involvement is that, depending on the particular target, the operation may require assistance from the Drug Enforcement Administration of the United States Department of Justice (DEA). If the only assistance rendered by the DEA is the furnishing of money or assets to purchase illegal drugs, then the amount of seized property disbursed to the DEA is generally minimal. If the DEA or the Federal Bureau of Investigation (FBI) is used as a means of asset condemnation, there is generally a percentage charge for administrative work performed to condemn the assets.

§ 18.3.1 Buy Operations

"Unlike most criminal offenses, the sale of narcotics usually occurs between two individuals neither of whom could realistically be classified as a victim" (DEA 99). Even though the above statement may be considered true, many administrators take it to heart in the most literal sense. The illegal sale of drugs is often called a victimless crime. True enough, the actual sale does not produce a victim as would an assault, robbery, or burglary. In reality, however, the sale may produce a multitude of victims. The drug addict will ultimately resort to other crimes to obtain the money necessary to finance his or her habit. Traffickers will combat one another for control of drug markets. Because of these facts, the illegal sale of drugs cannot truly be a victimless crime. In fact, the mere transaction of one sale has resulted from or results in a multitude of victims. Richard M. Smith, the Editor-In-Chief of Newsweek magazine, aptly summarized the chain reaction of drug trafficking when he wrote: "An epidemic is abroad in America, as pervasive and as dangerous in its way as the plagues of medieval times" (Smith).

Until very recently, the actual sale of illicit drugs took place in only the most private places. As a result, the law enforcement officer is often forced to go undercover to penetrate and hopefully make undercover buys which generally result in arrest. The private location for illicit drug sales is usually a location well-known to the dealer. Depending on the amount of a particular drug to be sold, the dealer may have counter-surveillance set up in an attempt to detect any law enforcement officers in the area of the sale. For this reason, the undercover buy becomes an even greater tool of law enforcement.

The ultimate goal of any undercover operation is the arrest of the drug dealer. As mentioned, this task will almost always be accomplished from an undercover buy. Accordingly, one of the most common ways for an undercover investigation to get initiated is through an informant. Informants are an invaluable asset to narcotics agents, and because of their knowledge of and involvement in the particular crowd of people being investigated, they become the safest means of leading an undercover officer to a target.

After initial introductions are made and the undercover officer has begun to gain the confidence of the target, then the buys are set up. In the safest method of undercover operation, the buy is made by undercover agents and arrest warrants are obtained and executed at a later time. Thus, a buy is made but no arrest is effected at the time of the buy. The number of buys made will be determined by several variables. The first, and administratively speaking, most important consideration is the amount of money allocated for drug buys. Depending on the size of the law enforcement agency, the money allocated for undercover narcotics operations could be dramatically limited. Since the illicit drug sale is viewed as a victimless crime by many police administrators, funds to support undercover operations are often very limited.

The next consideration is where the undercover buys will lead and how many buys will be made from a particular target. Depending upon the dealer who is being sought, there may be few or several buys made from one particular source. Assuming there are unlimited funds, if a source or target can be used to move up to a high-level dealer, several buys may be made.

After all the buys have been made on a particular operation, the arrest warrants will be obtained. The ensuing arrest—or round-up—is often a large operation with multiple suspects to be apprehended. Since drug dealers are generally transient in nature, undercover agents involved in the buy should always know where to locate and arrest the suspect.

§ 18.3.2 Buy/Bust Operations

Another form of undercover work is what is known as the "buy/bust" operation. As the term implies, the buy/bust operation utilizes an undercover officer to buy an illicit drug and, immediately thereafter, the seller is arrested for the drug sale.

With most agencies, the buy/bust is used for large buys where large amounts of money are needed to complete the transaction. Due to these large amounts of money, the investigating agency is often concerned about the possibility of a "rip-off" (rip-off referring to the actual robbery of the undercover agent by the drug dealer). Therefore, agencies prefer to utilize as many cover agents (support personnel or backup agents) as possible to assist in the bust part of the buy/bust operation.

Another major concern and reason for doing a buy/bust operation is the safety of the undercover agent. If there is a threat caused by the individual being targeted or if there is not enough information known about the target, a buy/bust is the best method to use for the safety of the undercover agent. After all, the safety of the undercover agent is tantamount to everything else and should be the first consideration. If the target is a major distributor for a particular region, the necessity for a buy/bust becomes imperative. Major drug dealers continue to mount serious and violent attacks on undercover drug agents, thus requiring the efficiency of the buy/bust.

The usual scenario for a typical police agency buy/bust operation is as follows:

1. The undercover agent either sets up the transaction personally or the deal is set up by a third party. This third party is generally an informant, but could be an associate of the target who is indirectly involved.

2. After the deal is set up and the quantity and price are negotiated, the location and time are set. This is the most critical consideration. The undercover agent must make the location of the deal a location that can be adequately covered by support and back-up personnel.

3. Prior to meeting the target, a predetermined bust signal is established to notify the cover team that the deal has taken place and the arrest should be effected. The cover team will know the deal has transpired, because either the undercover agent, the room, or both are equipped with audio surveillance equipment. This allows the cover team to monitor and record the conversation between the undercover agent and the target.

4. After the bust signal is given, the cover team will rapidly move in to make the arrests. For the safety of the undercover agent, and sometimes to protect his or her identity, the undercover agent is generally arrested at this point also. Since a greater number of drug dealers are armed with some type of weapon, the arrest must take place rapidly to minimize any risk to the agent.

§ 18.3.3 Reverse Sting Operations

Another type of undercover operation is the "reverse sting." This controversial operation, in which an undercover police officer sells narcotics to a suspected user, is technically illegal. Yet, a California state appeals court has ruled that this sort of operation is still a proper tactic in the war against drugs.

In *People v. Wesley*, 177 Cal. App. 3d 397, 223 Cal. Rptr. 9 (Cal. App. 2 Dist. 1986), three judges on a 2nd District Court of Appeals panel unanimously ruled that law enforcement's sale of drugs is valid and officers are immune from prosecution—even though the sales violate state health and safety codes. Prosecutors said Wesley is a case of first impression in the state. "It is a crime, but he [the undercover officer] is immune from prosecution if possession or sale occurs while investigat-

Chapter 18

ing narcotics violations in the performance of his official duties," the panel said.

The ruling also validated the use of contraband by police; it was deemed lawful for police officers to employ drugs confiscated in previous cases for the purpose of catching other criminals. The *Wesley* case involved a Pasadena policeman posing as a street corner drug dealer who was selling rock cocaine. One of his "customers" was Christopher Wesley, who allegedly approached the officer and said "I need a dime," street jargon for a ten-dollar rock of cocaine. Seconds after the exchange, two other undercover officers moved in to make an arrest (according to the panel's opinion). Wesley quickly threw down the rock, but police retrieved it.

At a preliminary hearing, public defenders moved to strike the charges, accusing the police of "outrageous conduct for selling illicit drugs." Superior Court Judge Gilbert C. Alston granted the motion. He ruled the sting operation was "fatally flawed," because the defendant did not have "uncontested possession" of the rock, and there was no competent testimony that the rock in question was actually cocaine.

However, the appeals court panel said the weight of evidence made it clear that Wesley had the rock in his possession, however briefly for his own use, and that he threw it down as he was about to be arrested. Likewise, even though it was not conclusively established that the rock was genuine cocaine, the appellate panel said it was sufficient that the undercover officer said, in his opinion, it was rock cocaine. "Evidence that will justify a prosecutor need not be sufficient to support a conviction," wrote Justice Mildred Lilly. Justices Earl Johnson Jr. and Norville Frederick Woods Jr. concurred.

The bulk of the appeals court opinion dealt with the legality of the "reverse sting." Deputy Public Defender Elizabeth Warner-Sterkenburg argued that the police were breaking at least two state laws by redistributing illegal narcotics on the street. Warner-Sterkenburg cited the State Supreme Court's ruling in *People v. Backus*, 23 Cal. 3d 360, 152 Cal. Rptr. 710, 590 P.2d 837 (Cal. 1979) which held that police officers who supply contraband drugs to informers are guilty of a crime.

"The police can lawfully arrest anyone for soliciting a purchase of narcotics. But that's only a misdemeanor," she argued. "So, in order to make a felony arrest (possession of cocaine), police are breaking the law by dispensing drugs on the streets." The appeals panel disagreed. It said that the "sting" appeared to stay within the rules. The undercover officer made no effort to solicit a sale, but merely nodded when Wesley solicited the sale.

As for the sale of contraband, the panel said police upheld the spirit of the law, which is to insure that confiscated drugs stay off the streets. "The cocaine was simply used as bait," the panel noted. "It was intended to be, and was retrieved by the officers after it served its purpose."

After winning the case, L.A. Deputy District Attorney Martha Bellinger said, "We're pleased because we now have a published decision that supports these kinds of operations." Bellinger argued the case on appeal for the county. "These sting operations are not the answer to our drug problem, but they are effective in cleaning out problem neighborhoods," added Bellinger (PORAC 1992).

§ 18.4   UNDERCOVER NEGOTIATING

An important variable in the success of any undercover operation is the negotiating skill of the undercover officer. Good undercover narcotics officers must possess a variety of interpersonal skills and talents. They must be able to put forward their own agenda, as contained in their operational plan, and maintain their position in spite of the stress and pressure placed on them by the very nature of their undercover role. They cannot allow themselves to be unduly influenced by the assertive and manipulative personalities of the suspects with whom they are interacting.

It is vital that their assertive personalities be supported by a well-developed understanding of the principles of effective negotiating. Very often, undercover narcotics officers approach their assignments with little more experience in negotiating than what they learned in the course of purchasing a major appliance. They often approach the negotiations of an undercover drug transaction as if they were a series of hurdles to be surmounted: the quicker the better. They tend to see each issue under negotiations as if it were a stumbling block to be avoided, rather than the vehicle that will eventually deliver them safely to their destination.

For the undercover narcotics officer, good negotiating skills are basic survival skills. For this reason, law enforcement agencies must not only develop training programs that will teach the elements of effective negotiating, but they must also tailor such training for the specific tasks required in undercover narcotics work.

In the case of the undercover narcotics officer, the innocent party is the agent himself, and while the threats may not be as direct, they are nonetheless real. The activities being negotiated are criminal in nature and generally involve relatively large amounts of money and highly valued contraband. The underlying premise, whether stated or implied, is that any failure on the part of the undercover officer to act in good (criminal) faith will be met with maximum retaliation on the part of the target. Furthermore, it can be presumed that any vulnerability or perceived weakness on the part of the undercover officer will also result in his victimization by the person with whom he is negotiating. This victimization will take the form of either some type of a "burn" (fraudulent deception during a transaction) or a straight "rip-off" or robbery. Because of the prevalence of weapons utilized in the drug trade, both of these forms of victimization can easily result in death or injury to the undercover officer. The officer is literally negotiating for his own life, and he is usually alone with his adversary at the time the undercover officer is really attempting to set his adversary up for eventual capture. While he endeavors to gain his opponent's trust and draw him into what seems to be a beneficial agreement, the officer is actually trying to lure his subject into a position that will eventually result in the neutralization of the adversary.

Undercover narcotics officers can benefit enormously from an analytical review of the negotiating process, and can do much to improve their skills by studying the methods employed by other successful police negotiators.

§ 18.4.1 The Elements of Negotiation

In his bestseller, You Can Negotiate Anything, Herb Cohen identified three variables that are critical to the successful outcome of any negotiation. These variables are information, time, and power. In a conventional narcotics transaction, the undercover officer begins with considerable information about his adversary. He knows that the drug trafficker is selling a contraband product that has no legal or legitimate market. The trafficker may have many potential customers for his product, but his market is limited to criminals, whom he can never totally trust. Furthermore, the undercover officer knows that the trafficker is driven by greed, tempered by concerns for self-preservation. In many instances, these two needs are compounded by substance abuse, resulting in both an extreme need for money and extreme paranoia.

Specific investigation of the target will add to the body of information available to the undercover officer prior to actually engaging in negotiations. The focus of this investigative research should center on the target's specific needs. What does he need from his negotiation? What are his short-term or immediate needs, and what might his long-term or ultimate needs be?

Undercover officers often presume that the suspect desires only financial benefit from any illicit transaction. However, this is never entirely the case. Even in those instances where the transaction being negotiated is a relatively small, street level purchase, the suspect couples his need for money with his need for security. He will generally conduct all such street-level transactions in a location of his own choosing— most likely a location over which he has a good degree of control.

The undercover officer may be able to get the dealer to compromise his security (i.e., control of location) if he can change the focus of the negotiation from a consideration of immediate needs to one of long-term needs. This might be accomplished by suggesting that the current transaction is nothing more than a "sample" in the eyes of the undercover officer. Therefore, the officer should direct his negotiations toward issues such as consistent quality, and ease and security of future transactions. The locations of future transactions are part of this consideration. By focusing on the future, the undercover officer can create a rationale for expressing concern over the location and circumstances of all transactions, including the current one. By appealing to what Cohen would call "the power of precedent," the undercover officer can insist that all major transactions such as this are conducted in a location of mutual agreement—typically a neutral location. Since this rather small transaction is really part of an ongoing series of larger transactions, then it is only right that it be conducted in a manner and location similar to those future transactions.

The second variable, which is time, is a major part of every undercover drug transaction. The traffickers consider themselves to be under severe time constraints by virtue of the fact that the longer they are in possession of contraband, the greater the chance of being discovered by either the authorities or criminal adversaries. In either case, the trafficker remains vulnerable, and will therefore choose to limit the time of his actual possession of drugs. He is likely to have his greatest quantity of illicit drugs at one time and, over time, he will reduce his inventory of drugs while increasing his capital. Because both of these commodities are of great value to the dealer, he will develop a strategy for protecting them. This strategy is his survival plan, and it will usually be directed against the undercover officer.

Cohen points out that, in any negotiation, there is a tendency for each party to perceive the other as being under fewer organizational pressures, time constraints, and restrictive deadlines. The effective undercover officer will attempt to emphasize and draw attention to those time constraints that favor his goals rather than those of the dealer. For instance, the undercover officer might carry with him an airline ticket envelope that is casually made apparent to the dealer while the officer explains that he is leaving town and thus has only a limited period of time in which to complete the transaction. By creating a time constraint, the officer is forcing the dealer into a schedule of the officer's choosing. Since this schedule is imaginary, the officer can change it or not, depending on what suits him, rather than becoming caught up in the dealer's schedule. The airline ticket envelope serves to reinforce the time constraint through the power of legitimacy; that is, printed words (in this case the envelope) carry an authenticity of their own.

In addition to these imagined time constraints, there is often real pressure on the undercover officer to rush or push the negotiations along. This pressure, arising from management or from fellow officers who are supporting the undercover officer by providing covering surveillance, may be articulated directly in terms of "time limits." The skilled negotiator will recognize that pushing for a deal before gaining his opponent's trust will only foster doubt and suspicion. Since the dealer really doesn't know the undercover officer well, his criminal survival instinct will cause him to suspect that the undercover officer might be out to hurt him—and might even be a police officer.

Nothing builds trust better than the passage of time. Experienced undercover officers are in almost unanimous agreement that nothing will instill greater trust in a trafficker than shutting a negotiation down and walking away. Therefore, it may be best to put off the transaction if it appears that the dealer is suspicious.

Negotiating an illegal drug transaction is similar to other high-stakes buyer/seller negotiations. The undercover officer will always improve his chances for success if he creates competition for his side of the equation. If he is conducting a conventional drug buy, he must let the dealer know that he has other possible sources of supply who are competing for his business. Obviously, it should not be represented as a "perfect" deal, since it would make no sense to negotiate with the target suspect in that case. On the other hand, the undercover officer must never express total satisfaction with the offer and the conditions being put forth by the suspect. By always maintaining a sufficient level of dissatisfaction, the undercover officer creates negotiating leverage, to be strategically applied under the conditions most conducive to his own safety and survival.

An example of the proper use of this negotiation ploy would have the undercover officer suggest to the target that there is another possible dealer from whom he can purchase a similar quantity and quality of drugs, and that the final price might even be slightly better. However, the competition has stipulated other conditions that are totally unacceptable. Naturally, the suspect will want to know what the conditions are, since his potential customer finds them so unacceptable that he might be willing to change suppliers, or even pay a slightly higher price.

When the suspect conducts this rudimentary market research (and he will), he will discover that the undercover officer is unwilling to take his money, by himself, into a location that favors the dealer. The officer might even describe a particular problem, such as a "rip-off" that grew out of an earlier episode in which he naively agreed to such conditions, only to regret it later. By informing the suspect indirectly about his needs in regard to the ultimate location and circumstances of the deal being considered, the officer has also suggested his limits in a non-threatening, non-confrontational manner. The dealer may then choose to make concessions in regard to these issues in an effort to finalize the deal. He certainly won't suggest the same set of conditions that have already been rejected.

The skilled undercover negotiator will use the suspect's failure to contest the location and conditions of the actual deal as an agreement to meet his own requirements. Naturally, the suspect will always pressure the officer to make last-minute changes in his favor. It is at this time that the officer will assertively exercise his leverage. He will insist that it is too late to make changes, emphatically reminding the suspect that they had already reached an agreement concerning these very points, and that any last-minute changes on the suspect's part are totally unacceptable. The undercover negotiator will then point out that if he is required to make these concessions, he would be better off doing business with his original source, where the price was better.

By making it clear that the suspect has created a problem that may cost him the sale, and by clearly demonstrating a willingness to walk away from the deal as it stands, the undercover officer will force the suspect to decide between his need for money and his need to control the location and conditions of the transaction. Most drug dealers will choose the money. If he does, the undercover officer will be able to manipulate the location and conditions of the actual transaction—whether it is a straight purchase or a "buy/bust"—using sound tactical planning to ensure his own safety and survival. If, on the other hand, the dealer refuses to comply with the conditions as negotiated, the negotiator must exercise his ultimate survival strategy by shutting the deal down and walking away.

It is not unusual for undercover officers who have not been properly trained in successful negotiation strategies to succumb to the pressure of completing a drug transaction under the conditions preferred by the suspect. However, any concessions to the last-minute changes demanded by the suspect, typically concerning the "flashing" of buy money, the locations and condition of the actual transaction, and the timing or sequence of the events of the transaction, will directly affect the tactical safety of the undercover officer. To be a successful undercover narcotics officer, confident negotiation skills are vital. No matter what the product, no matter what the price, the undercover negotiator is really dealing for his or her life.

§ 18.5 SURVEILLANCE
§ 18.5.1 Target and Objectives

In addition to undercover buy operations, surveillance may also play an important role in the eventual arrest of a drug trafficker or user. For instance, you may need to enact a process of surveillance in order to obtain information to warrant a legal search. In any case, the target of a surveillance is a person or group of people, a vehicle, or a place. The objectives of a surveillance are to obtain information concerning the activities and identities of individuals, to obtain evidence of a crime, and to protect undercover officers. A surveillance may also meet the following objectives:

—To locate persons by watching their hangouts and associates.

—To check the reliability of informants.

—To locate hidden property or contraband.

—To obtain probable cause for search warrants.

—To prevent an act or catch a suspect in the commission of an act or crime.

—To obtain information for later use in interrogating.

—To develop leads and information received from others.

—To know the whereabouts of an individual at all times.

—To obtain admissible legal evidence for court.

§ 18.5.2 Categories of Surveillance

To meet these objectives, there are several different categories of surveillance. These categories and their particular goals are listed below.

Chapter 18

Intelligence-Seeking Surveillance

—Learning everything you can about an activity or crime.

—Learning the suspect's source of supply (SOS).

—Identifying the suspect's couriers.

—Identifying the suspect's co-conspirators.

—Identifying the suspect's distributors.

Pre-Purchase Surveillance

—To gather intelligence to assist the U/C (undercover agent), who will attempt to purchase from the suspect.

—To identify associates of the suspect and their relationship or association.

—Attempt to determine the source of supply (SOS).

—Identify the suspect's couriers or distributors.

—Identify any counter-surveillance.

Cover Surveillance

—Primarily used for the protection of the U/C officer.

—To corroborate the U/C officer's testimony.

    a.   Corroborate times and locations.

    b.   Corroborate the transaction.

—Identify approaches to and escape routes from buy location.

—Determine the amount of force and manpower which will be necessary to assist the U/C officer.

Post-Purchase Surveillance

—To identify where the money goes after the sale.

—To identify other customers of the seller.

—To keep suspect under surveillance in case the U/C was sold "bunk."

—To identify suspect's residence, vehicles, associates, or source of supply (SOS).

—To obtain intelligence for future search warrants, buy-bust operation planning, and execution of search warrants.

—Planning of future meetings.

—Identify any counter-surveillance the suspect may have.

§ 18.5.3 Preparation and Equipment

Personnel

—Surveillance officers should be of ordinary appearance.

—Avoid anything which will attract attention.

—Make assignments based on factors such as race, appearance, ability to blend into the area or neighborhood.

—Must have the ability to act natural under any circumstances.

—Must have a high degree of alertness and resourcefulness.

—Must have good powers of observations and memory (events, description, contracts, or times of occurrences).

Pre-Surveillance Preparation

—Gather information and compile a file relating to the suspect's activities and criminal history.

—Get intelligence on the suspect's working and neighborhood environments as well as all vehicles involved or associated.

—Obtain detailed descriptions and photos of suspects, including, if possible, their habits and normal routines.

—Obtain identities and descriptions of known or suspected contracts or associates and the scope and extent of criminal activities of the suspect involved.

—Become familiar with the neighborhood or area where the operation will take place.

Equipment

—Props of certain dress or vehicles should blend into the area or neighborhood.

—Carry with you cameras, binoculars, telescopes, recording equipment, body wires, monitoring equipment.

—If assigned to fixed surveillance, think about personal needs and carry money and change.

—Carry clothes and personal hygiene items in the vehicle in cases of an extended long-term surveillance.

—Surveillance vehicles should fit the setting in which they are to be used.

—Vehicles should be occupied by two officers (one to drive, the other to handle the radio and take notes).

—Be prepared for emergencies:

    a.   Search kits.

    b.   Raid equipment.

    c.   Food/beverages.

Carry such items as jackets, caps or glasses to change your appearance, if necessary.

§ 18.5.4 Planning the Surveillance Assignments

When planning a surveillance, there are various assignments to make. Assign an officer in charge. If necessary, designate who will be involved in a stationary surveillance or foot surveillance. Coordinate a point car and assure rotation of the car if it is an extended surveillance. Assign arrest teams and an officer who will obtain search warrants; assign search teams and officers who will process in-custody suspects; and above all advise your supervisor and the watch commander of the surveillance's jurisdiction.

It is also very important to conduct a formal briefing to update the officers involved in a surveillance. Have a tactical plan, briefing sheets, and maps of the area. Distribute to all officers photos of the suspects, descriptions of the vehicles, license plate numbers, addresses of residence, and informants; most importantly, identify the undercover officer. Clearly explain the objectives of the surveillance, outline under what circumstances you want arrests to be made and under what circumstances you want the surveillance discontinued. Plan a debriefing after the surveillance is discontinued. Plan a debriefing after the surveillance to compare notes and put observations in chronological order and critique the operation for the success of future operations.

§ 18.5.5 Types of Surveillance
§ 18.5.5(a)   Foot Surveillance

One-man foot surveillance is extremely difficult and should be avoided. Two-man foot surveillance gives greater flexibility. Three-man foot surveillance, or the ABC method, is considered the best method. "A" is to the rear of the suspect, a reasonable distance behind the suspect. "B" is behind "A," at more distance than that between "A" and the suspect. "B's" responsibility is to keep "A" in sight. "C" is across the street from the suspect and slightly to the rear. "C's" responsibility is to keep both the suspect and "A" in sight.

Frequent changes between A, B, and C should be made. The most common mistake in foot surveillance by new agents/officers is too much distance between himself and the suspect. Also, make sure that you carry your handheld radio at all times during a foot surveillance.

§ 18.5.5(b)   Vehicle Surveillance

The appearance of your vehicle must fit into the environment of the area under surveillance. There should be two officers per vehicle: one can operate the radio and take notes, while the other is available for foot surveillance. For the officer operating the vehicle, driving skill and knowledge of the area are very important. Officers should also anticipate being stopped by the police, especially in other jurisdictions.

Use good judgment when violating any traffic laws (be sure the suspect does not see you). To protect yourself from discovery, have surveillance vehicles equipped with shut-off switches for the headlights, tail lights and brake lights. In addition, you should designate a point vehicle and rotate it frequently. Ensure that the point vehicle and its relief inform everyone when they are changing positions. The point vehicle must ensure that the relief vehicle is in position before pulling off or continuing straight.

Maintain strict radio procedures. The lead car should be the only one calling the surveillance (location/direction). Other units should only talk on the radio if absolutely necessary. While on the radio, the point vehicle should provide frequent locations, direction, approximate speed and number of the lane traveled. If the area is unfamiliar to the officers involved, provide landmarks such as businesses, schools, and service stations over the radio. While tracking the suspect, avoid giving directions such as "the suspect turned right" or "the suspect turned left." Use the directions east, west, north, and south to prevent confusion.

A two-vehicle surveillance should be avoided; you either lose the vehicle or the suspect will identify you. Only the lead vehicle should be in close proximity to the suspect. When following the suspect also keep in mind that, for surveillance, left turns are more difficult than right turns. A good rule of thumb is as follows: when the suspect turns, the lead vehicle should proceed straight; but make sure another vehicle is in position to take your place.

There are some situations during surveillance that require the lead vehicle to remain behind the suspect, in spite of the lead vehicle's best judgment that it needs to relinquish its position. In this situation, the lead vehicle should never become so anxious that they remove themselves before the number two vehicle can take the lead. Leading surveillance can also be used if the suspect's route of travel is known.

When following the suspect in a vehicle, care must be taken at intersections, especially if the suspect goes through a yellow or red light (in this case, a paralleled vehicle can assist). For this reason, an aircraft is very useful. Aircraft may also assist surveillance in sparsely populated areas, areas with very little traffic, or areas with congested traffic. Another aid is electronic surveillance; electronic devices may be used for different types of surveillance to prevent detection by the suspect.

In the event that the suspect on foot should board a bus, taxicab, or other form of transportation, a combination of foot and vehicle surveillance may be the most efficient.

§ 18.5.5(c)   Stationary Surveillance
Stationary surveillance frequently involves a great deal of manpower and long hours during the day and night. Therefore, a stationary surveillance van is frequently used.

The primary consideration in a stationary surveillance is whether the observation position affords the necessary vantage point to observe significant activity without being detected. Also, entry and exit points for stationary surveillance must be located so as to avoid attracting attention. Careless actions by the officers may end the surveillance and leave those involved with a feeling of being burned.

Technical Equipment:

—Binoculars.

—Radios/extra batteries.

—Infra-red scope.

—Electronically amplified night scope.

—Fluorescent markers and ultra-violet lights.

—Small flashlight/penlight.

—Cameras.

—TV and movie camera.

Personal Equipment (extended surveillance):

—Porta-Potty or some type of container.

—Changes of clothing.

—Food and beverage.

—Hygiene items.

Undercover Narcotics and Clandestine Lab Investigations

—Writing utensils.

—Safety equipment and raid gear.

Surveillance Log:

—Surveillance log should be constantly maintained.

—Notations should be made on events as they occur.

—Include all observations, even though they may appear insignificant at the time.

—Include descriptions of subjects, vehicles and activity; date, time, and place of occurrence.

—Include weather conditions, distance between observation point and the activity.

—Surveillance notes should be as accurate and complete as possible.

—Indicate who made the observations on the log.

§ 18.5.6 The Use of Surveillance Equipment

Before any surveillance operation always survey and preview the location prior to the surveillance operation. Drive a cold vehicle into the area and survey the location. Walk the area on foot and see what the area is like. Look at the surveillance location from different angles and see what pit-falls you observe from each angle. Determine the objectives for the operation, i.e., to identify vehicles or persons, etc.

When trying to identify vehicles, you can do this from a greater distance than when trying to identify faces. The overall distance should be determined by what type of equipment you are using. The best video camera for this type of operation is the Canon L-1 HI-8 mm.; the second best is the Sony EXC-10-PAC 8mm.

The period of surveillance should be determined by how hot the area is. Keep a keen look-out for how people react to your surveillance vehicle or location. In any given neighborhood location, do not do more than two days of surveillance in a row. Locals will very quickly identify your location and cause problems. The overall decision of surveillance duration may be further determined by how well you and your vehicle fit into the neighborhood. Thus, business or corporate environments are a lot easier since there is a lot more traffic in those locations and you should not to be too concerned with local neighbors identifying or dismantling your operation.

§ 18.5.7 Avoiding Detection by the Locals or the Suspect

Surveillance officers must fit into the location. If this requirement is not met, officers will stand out as not belonging there. In addition, watch out for little children. Children are very perceptive; they know

Chapter 18

what vehicles and people belong in a neighborhood and what vehicles and people do not. Be aware of the area in which you park. Children will stop and even ask what you are doing; so take precautions.

If using a van or fixed sight location, be very careful when you change shifts or when exiting or entering from the surveillance van. The best way to change shifts is to have a person drive the vehicle into the area and walk away from the van. Likewise, while you are in the surveillance van or away from it, do not leave the case file out in the open, on the seat of the car where people can walk up and read the information. Keep all case material and surveillance equipment hidden; you may simply keep these under a jacket or a towel.

Another way to blow the cover on your operation real fast is through radio transmissions. Use covert radio equipment whenever available. Furthermore, do not throw anything—even cigarette butts—outside the vehicle. Never leave anything behind. Never make yourself conspicuous.

§ 18.5.8 Narcotics Raid Planning

Once surveillance has confirmed preliminary information, it may be possible to enact a narcotics raid. Planning narcotics raids has proved to be one of the most challenging and dangerous responsibilities of law enforcement agencies. At the top of the priority list for law enforcement are concern for officer safety and the need to ensure that no innocent parties are injured. Furthermore, we live in an increasingly litigious society; no agency or its officers wish to suffer from a liability suit due to errors in planning for tactical raid operations.

Most raid planning will revolve around containment, locating personnel properly, eliminating confusion and maximizing observation of the suspect building. These principles are best applied by doing the following in a methodical manner:

When planning raids, always use a raid-planning checklist. This checklist will help to clarify the details of a dynamic entry; swift, confident, and complete room clearance; efficient apprehension of the suspects; and proper seizure of the evidence.

To facilitate and support planning strategies, surveillance should be conducted. The objective of surveillance is to evaluate procedures which will be used to initiate tactical raid operations. Surveillance is gathered so officers can become familiar with the suspects and can learn more about the type of crime committed, criminal patterns, etc.

In the planning process, tactical scouting reports can be authenticated, positions of cover evaluated, and access routes for convoying can be verified. Likewise, emergency medical personnel can be notified to the possibility of a medical rescue operation.

Planning will also necessitate a series of briefings conducted to explain all the phases of operation. This stage of planning will include the following members: Raid Operations Commander, Raid Team Personnel, representatives of appropriate divisions/units such as intelligence, patrol, and emergency services unit (SWAT), and legal representatives where necessary.

The briefing will encompass reviewing the planned approach to the location, personnel assignments (coordinated deployment), positioning of personnel for entry, entry technique, room clearance, suspect and bystander control, communications, and evidence management. In addition, an equipment check will be completed during one of the raid briefings to ensure proper and functional equipment is available. If an informant is being used, appropriate briefing information will be disseminated, as would be the case when using an undercover/covert police officer.

Often, narcotics raids uncover hazardous materials, as well as clandestine narcotics laboratory setups, which may vary from rudimentary to extremely sophisticated. Therefore, safety procedures for hazardous materials protocol will also be reviewed at a briefing. A representative of the fire service may be invited to attend a selected briefing with appropriate safety recommendations.

The following checklist provides information on the development of a raid management plan.

►	Records information (See I.)
►	Evidence management
►	Identify incident location and approach procedure. (See II.)
►	Minimize suspect control area (Kill zone)
►	Review approach to location (See III.)
►	Determine type and range of suspect's weapons.
►	Evaluate interior hazards (See IV.)
►	Select tactical frequency to be utilized; advise communications and responding units.
►	Establish perimeters, pedestrian evacuation control.
►	Check all equipment before initiating.
►	Cordon area and isolate from pedestrian and vehicular traffic. Identify those approved to enter area. Determine access routes and advise concerned units.
►	Evacuate citizens and interview them.
►	Be prepared to initiate Officer/Victim Rescue Plan
►	Provide officers stationed on perimeter with suspect photographs.
►	Designate Command Post Location and O.I.C. and Asst. O.I.C.
►	All personnel report to C.P. or police staging area prior to deploying.
►	All personnel are adequately briefed regarding problem, assignment and unit designation.
►	All personnel have communications capability.

►	Procedures for activating Emergency Services Team
►	Review "Hostage Negotiations" procedures.
►	Establish alternate routes for citizen traffic.
►	Acquire appropriate maps (Grid. Telephone)
►	Determine probable location of suspect
►	Personnel assignments
►	Maintain Incident Log for protracted operations
►	Physical layout of structures (See III and IV)

Notify:	
►	Watch Commander and Senior
►	Executive Personnel
►	Communications Division—Select tactical frequency
►	Area/Division Commanding Officer
►	Fire Department/Medical Services
►	Maintain incident log for Protracted operations.
►	Mutual Aid Agencies
►	Public Information Representative
►	Physical "layout" of structures. (See III and IV.)

I. RECORDS INFORMATION
Warrant #
Issuing Court:
Date Issued:
Address of Seizure:

II. DESCRIPTIVE INFORMATION ON LOCATION
a. Number of rooms, floors, attached and adjacent buildings, doors, cellar/attic, color, construction of building, i.e. brick, stucco.
b. Sketch of outside — location of abutting streets, driveways, outbuildings, doors, fences, shrubbery, etc. obscuring view from inside, exterior lighting on property/on street, etc.
c. Sketch of interior — indicating locations of rooms, doors, closets, stairways, large furniture.

III. EXTERIOR AND APPROACH INFORMATION
(Note answer: NONE, UNKNOWN, or describe details for items 1-8)
1. Gate locks (type: padlock/built-in)
2. Height of fences (type: wood, chain-link)
3. Alarms (type: motion, foil, trip wire, etc.)
4. Lookouts/dogs (location)
5. Motor vehicles likely to be on premises (reg. #s and description).

6. Exterior Doors (Type: wood, screen, metal, hollow-core).
   a. Location of doors
   b. Swing of doors (In-Right, In-Left, Out-Right, Out-Left, Sliding)
7. Door locks (Type: dead-bolt, chair, door-knob)
8. Presence of glass in door or one-way viewer.

IV. INTERIOR HAZARDS
1. If drug raid — type of operation (stash house, lab etc.)
2. Type of controlled substance(s) alleged to be on premises.
3. Location of contraband/evidence.
4. Chemicals, explosives, inflammables likely to be on premises.
5. Location of any structural defects/hazards.
6. Type and probable location of any weapons.
7. Dogs (describe: size, noisy and/or aggressive, etc.).
8. Persons likely to be on premises.
9. Note: Elderly, young children, and ill-disabled persons, hostages.
10. Alleged perpetrators (names, identifiable descriptions, reputations for violence, photographs).

§ 18.6   ENTRY
§ 18.6.1 Alternatives to a Forced Entry

Alternatives to a forced entry should always be considered. One of these alternatives is the "Soft Knocks" approach. Simply knock on the door courteously and state your purpose. Despite its calmness, sound safety principals must be used with this method. Another alternative is the "Ruse Entry." Using this method, the officer poses as a delivery man or salesman. Ruse entries must have immediate back-up available and the ruse man must be able to keep calm and play out the role effectively.

§ 18.6.2 Forced Entry: Use of the Ram

Often, however, a forced entry is unavoidable—especially when serving a search warrant at a fortified crack house. A forced entry consists of forcefully entering the premises and taking the suspect away from the location. Although it can be time-consuming, this method works well if you have both the time and the personnel.

Forced entry is often achieved through the use of a battering ram. As long as search warrants are served and dope dealers refuse entry, it will be important to know how to use a ram properly. Several narcotics agents have had bad experiences trying to enter a door that appears to have been welded shut. As long as the most serious setback from such a delayed entry is only some flushed dope, the matter is not so grave. Concern should lie with the possibility of an officer being injured because a dealer had the time to arm himself due to a delayed entry. To avoid such consequences, effective use of the ram can be broken down into five areas. These include: mental preparation, foot position, using your entire body, where to strike the door, and getting out of the way.

§ 18.6.2(a)   Mental Preparation/Focus

One of the most important members on the entry team is the person with the ram. If you can't open the door, your team's entry will be delayed. Anyone who has rammed a door knows that standing in front of a door with a holstered gun is an unpleasant thought. It's very natural to start backing for cover as your ram is halfway to its target. This, however, can cause the ram to fall short of making a solid, strong hit. A weak or glancing blow is often the result. This forces you to return to the same undesirable spot with a crook inside who has had 3 to 5 more seconds to destroy evidence or plan an assault. The proper technique is to focus not only on striking the door, but on striking through the door. You should envision the ram landing through the door. This mental preparation of the outcome will force you to stick around until after the mission is accomplished.

§ 18.6.2(b)   Foot Position/Balance

When preparing to strike the door, your feet should be positioned at shoulders width. Depending upon the length of your arms, your exact distance from the door will vary. Nevertheless, you don't want to be at a distance that causes the ram to land lazily on the door. If you find yourself lunging at the door just to make contact, you are too far away from it. At the same time, you don't want to be so close that you can't extend your arms completely. Take a few minutes, in a non-hostile environment, to find the right position.

§ 18.6.2(c)   Using Your Entire Body

Anyone involved in sports knows that the strongest person is not always the one who hits the ball farther or delivers the hardest serve. Likewise, brute strength alone will not knock down a door; yet, the speed generated by the ram will. If your ram hasn't reached top speed at the point it reaches the door, you're cheating yourself. If it reaches top speed before it strikes the door, you are also cheating yourself. The top speed of the ram is directly proportional to your body position, particularly your lower body. Velocity generated by a solid stance and a twisting torso is delivered right into your upper body and arms as they carry the ram into the strike zone. The importance of the lower body in generating velocity cannot be emphasized enough: imagine throwing an object from a kneeling position, thus eliminating the input from your lower body. Obviously, the velocity would be significantly decreased from such an inadequate position.

§ 18.6.2(d)   Where to Strike the Door

A battering ram can be lost through the middle of a door. Although everyone agrees that the deadbolt should be your target, it is still not uncommon to see such center-door or doorframe strikes. In most cases, the misplaced strike results from a lack of concentration at the moment of impact. After all, it's only a matter of inches between a successful strike and a lost ram through the middle of a door. Take care to ensure an accurate strike directly on the deadbolt.

§ 18.6.2(e)   Getting Out of the Way

By using the preceding tips, you will have better success in getting most doors to open. Yet, once the door is down, many officers will make the error of wanting to be the first through the door. While this may be noble, it is extremely dangerous. An armed suspect will have little difficulty in shooting at an unarmed cop who is trying to hide behind a ram as cover. You will also make it difficult for fellow officers to return fire if you are between them and the suspect. The proper move is a sidestep away from the threshold; discard your ram and take the wall as cover. As your team enters, you can safely unholster your gun and then enter the residence behind them.

§ 18.6.3 Forced Entry Considerations

If you do use a forced entry method, several considerations should be kept in mind. First, avoid parking in front of the location. If anyone has to be parked in front of the location it should be a marked patrol unit. Second, provide cover for both the containment team and the entry team while approaching the location. Allow sufficient time for the containment team to get into position prior to any entry. Third, all diversions, such as breaking windows, should be done away from the point of entry with the exception of gun-porting a window next to the door to cover the entry team. Finally, all precautions should be taken to avoid possible cross-fires between entry personnel and containment personnel.

Undercover Narcotics and Clandestine Lab Investigations

§ 18.6.3(a)   Door Breaching Techniques

When using a forced entry method, opening the doorway is the first and most important step. Team members should be provided with cover as they breach the door. Personnel with entry equipment should use the door jambs for cover as they work on the door. Furthermore, as the door is opened those personnel with the equipment should back away, secure their breaching gear, and then prepare to enter. Gloves and eye protection should be worn to avoid injury during the breach. If using a door pick on a metal door, try to pry the frame away using body weight and not arm strength.

§ 18.6.3(b)   Doorway Entry Techniques

At least two team members may use the cover of the door jamb to bracket the doorway. It might be noted that most residential doors open in. Strive to always have a team member at the hinge side of the door. This will facilitate a maximum view of the room when the door opens. When the door is finally opened, entry personnel should delay entering until the room is scanned for potential threats. Some further techniques of entry are detailed below:

1. "Quick Peek"

    a.   Look before you leap!

    b.   Allows you to gather intelligence before committing.

    c.   Works best when close to walls and when kneeling.

2." Roll Out"

    a.   Same principle as the quick peek but uses more room and allows more mobility.

    b.   Works best in hallways or while moving.

3. "Button-Hook"

    a.   Wrapping around the door frame after you have quick peeked, moving slightly into the room to avoid being backlit or to allow room for the next team member.

4. "Cross Method"

    a.   Simply crossing the doorway to the other side after quick peeking.

The above techniques should always be used with another team member covering while the one is moving. Proceeding at an even, controlled pace will allow you to move as a team while taking in as much as you can. During this process you should continually evaluate your movements. Keeping track of other members and yourself may prevent the "conga line" effect, which occurs when there is no organization or plan for movement. As a result of haphazard and inefficient entry, this effect endangers team members. Remember that stairways and hallways can be dangerous areas due to the lack of cover opportunities. You should maximize your efforts here by employing two team members on each side of the stairs or hall. This will facilitate two different viewing areas and provide immediate back-up and firepower. This rule of thumb also reduces the possibility of a one-on-one confrontation.

§ 18.6.3(c)   Post-Entry Considerations

After entering any room or hallway using the quick peek or roll out to gather intelligence, assess any major threat areas. Important considerations include darkened areas where you can be seen but you cannot see (such as closets) and partially closed doors to rooms. Once the danger areas have been assessed and the situation is under control, place the suspect out of view, walk through the entry and debrief. Prior to leaving the entry, draw a floor plan and diagram of the location and save it for future use. If the suspect is cooperative, ask him or her what happened during the entry and what their thoughts were.

§ 18.6.4 The Rock House or Crack House

One place that frequently requires forced entry is the "rock house." The "rock house," also known as a "crack house," is a specially fortified building used by drug traffickers as a headquarters, a distribution center, a warehouse, or a consumption area. The purpose of fortification is to delay entry time by police officers serving warrants, allowing enough time to dispose of the evidence down a drain or by some other disposal method. Fortified houses are not only used by crack dealers. They are in use by distributors of several other drugs, such as "meth."

Although drug dealers do not usually make special efforts to kill police officers (because they prefer to maintain low profiles), there have been enough instances of police officers killed in drug raids to justify strong precautions. A dealer trapped in his rock house may fight out of desperation; he may also use gunfire to delay entry by arresting officers.

Furthermore, a rock house is likely to have more than one occupant who is street-wise, tough, and unwilling to give up easily. Occupants are usually prepared for a raid by a competitor, and will have taken many defensive measures to slow down or stop anyone trying to get in. Some have well-rehearsed plans. For instance, one member will flush evidence down the drain whenever anyone gives the alarm, such as the shouted warning: "COPS!"

§ 18.6.4(a)   Rock House Defenses

Rock house occupants use a variety of defensive measures, including walls, fences, weapons, and combat tactics. Some are just obstacles and are not lethal. Others, however, are extremely dangerous, and many defenses are unseen from the street because occupants want to keep a low profile. Officers planning a warrant service on a rock house's external appearance may be easily deceived. In addition to "outer" defenses, rock house occupants frequently use weapons. Although drug dealers' arsenals may contain high-capacity semi-automatic and full-automatic weapons, most defensive measures use weapons which are perfectly legal and easily obtainable.

Barriers

At the edge of the rock house property is usually a fence. A major tactical reason for a fence instead of a wall is that it prevents entry while allowing a good view of anyone approaching. There may be barbed wire at the top of the fence. There may even be broken glass placed on a top of a slump block fence. Nearly always, the gate of the fence is locked—sometimes with a chain and padlock for extra security. The outer fence, with its dogs and booby-traps, keeps casual visitors off the property, thus avoiding inadvertent tripping of the alarms. It also helps provide early warning. The most important purpose, however, is to slow down an intruder. Therefore, even beyond the fence, doors and windows will be barred. Instead of wood hollow-core doors, there will be steel ones to resist both kicks and battering rams. Occupants may have gone to the trouble of installing steel bars set into wall brackets to further reinforce the door. There could be a wrought iron outer gate to protect the inner door. Glass windows may have been replaced with a polycarbonate material to prevent shattering. A panel of Lexan will stop a .38 Special bullet. More powerful bullets will penetrate this type of Lexan, but there won't be any danger from flying glass. Although Lexan is very expensive, drug wholesalers can afford it. Most importantly, Lexan panes are commonly available and perfectly legal to buy. In addition to these fortified windows, walls will probably be of block or cement construction. If not, there will most likely be reinforcements of sandbags or concrete inside the walls.

Alarms

Almost all commercially available alarm systems are suitable for a rock house. A special type of alarm system that is cheap and extremely reliable is the trip-wire connected to an alarm box. A fine, hair-thin wire follows the entire perimeter just inside the fence. Anyone breaking this wire will alert the occupants. There may be other wires to catch anyone who misses breaking the perimeter wire. This second type of alarm is battery-powered, a common model operating from four D-cells. It is a favorite among drug traffickers because it is portable, can be deployed anywhere, and is immune to power outages. Anyone encountering any sort of trip-wire has to be very careful, since it may set off a bomb instead of a mere alarm.

Dogs

Another type of rock house defense is a guard dog. A keen-eared and excitable family mutt who barks when anyone approaches is a simple and fairly reliable alarm. Some rock houses make use of specially bred and trained dogs, such as Shepherds and Rottweiler, to bark and to attack anyone who enters without authorization.

Chapter 18

Booby-Traps

Booby-traps are surprisingly cheap and easy to install. They can stop or delay an entry, and impede a search. They may be almost anywhere, depending on the intent and sophistication of the occupant. Literature and manuals on booby-trap designs are widely available in bookstores, on newsstands, and by mail-order. Most manuals have diagrams to help uneducated readers build very lethal weapons.

§ 18.6.4(b)   Indoor Defenses

The inside of a rock house will be as heavily protected as the grounds. To prevent an intruder's viewing the inside, windows are likely to have curtains or shutters. Interior walls may also be reinforced, for additional protection in case intruders breach the door. Steel plates and sandbags provide mini-bunkers for local defense. The layout of the house will be designed for defense. There is always more than one room, and often four or more. The "safe room" will be without any outside walls or windows. This will also have reinforced walls and a stout door, to delay anyone trying to enter. A toilet or sink will serve for flushing narcotics down the drain. A stove, fireplace, or paper shredder is usually present for destroying documentary evidence.

It should be noted that the safe room may have an escape tunnel. This might lead to a nearby garage where an escape vehicle is waiting, but in urban areas a better plan is to have the tunnel lead to a sewer, storm drain, or other underground conduit which already exists and which can take escapees miles away from the scene. The tunnel may also lead to a house in the next street, from which the escapees can emerge without attracting attention.

§ 18.6.4(c)   Defense Tactics

Hard-core drug wholesalers are not stupid, and many have had military experience. Others have studied military science at a training camp or trained themselves informally. They are likely to understand the basics of cover and concealment, and they understand S.W.A.T. operations through the media and reports from other lawbreakers. The media, showing explosive entries and officers repelling from helicopters, tend to exaggerate the facts. This alarms rock house occupants and probably results in more solid and thorough preparations than they would have taken otherwise. The occupants will most likely have gas masks, commonly available for only a few dollars on the surplus market. Since body armor is also commonly available, there is a good chance that the defenders will have some.

Because it is practically impossible to approach the premises undetected, defenders will be prepared. Unless they are tactically ignorant, they will have put the lights out, relying upon outside light to silhouette any intruders. Officers should remember that the interior of a building with obstructed windows can be very dark, even in daylight.

Defenders may also anticipate that police will cut the power. For nighttime, battery-powered external lights are commonly available in hardware outlets. Flashlights can provide the little interior lighting needed. Defenders will probably have enough tactical savvy to know that showing a light can draw fire.

Weapons used may include handguns, shotguns, and even full-automatic weapons in some cases. Because the suspects do not need to conceal these weapons on the person, they can easily chose shoulder weapons. Suspects are not likely to be concerned about stray shots injuring innocent parties, because they don't worry about lawsuits; thus, they will be more willing than police officers to open fire.

Since the interior will be set up for defense, not social calls, remember that furniture is likely to be just inside the doors and windows—to cause injury to anyone trying to dive into the room. Any entry team stopped by these obstacles provides stationary targets for the defenders. Trip-wires or marbles on the floor also slow up an advance. Additionally, spiked boards are quick and easy to deploy inside a doorway.

The occupant will probably know that an elementary precaution against tear gas, stun grenades, and gasoline bombs is to avoid defending a room from inside. This precaution also protects against cross-fire; thus, the defenders are unlikely to be in a room which has windows or doors leading to the outside. Officers who get inside are likely to find no targets in the same room. However, there may be loop-holes in the walls, or defenders may fire through a doorway. Another nasty prospect is the defender's use of tear gas or a gasoline bomb to cover his or her escape. Throwing a grenade or bomb into the outer room will delay officers long enough to allow escape down a tunnel. Officers must be aware that although "flak jackets" and ballistic vests will stop some fragments, they don't protect against gasoline bombs. Due to these significant risks, the best choice in coping with fortified premises is avoiding entry altogether.

§ 18.6.4(d)   Arrests

One alternative to entry is luring the occupants outside. Persuading them to emerge, using the "pizza man" and other subterfuges to bring the suspects away from their premises can avoid casualties. Isolating a suspect from his companions also reduces the chances of violent resistance.

§ 18.6.4(e)   Search Warrants

If you must enter a rock house to serve a search warrant be extremely careful. Because of booby-traps and the extensive precautions necessary when approaching rock houses, no search can be quick. Still, the best time for serving a search warrant is when the premises are unoccupied. With luck, it may be possible to find all occupants gone for a long enough time to send in a search team and set up a perimeter to detain any returning occupants. When caught outside their fortified premises, the occupants are unlikely to resist; but if they do, they won't have the defensive advantages of the rock house.

§ 18.6.4(f)   Assaults

If it becomes necessary to hold a full-scale assault, it is best to prepare carefully: try to nullify the defender's advantages. The basic preparation is to have accurate information about the defense. This information is often available only from an informant or undercover agent. If possible, officers should make themselves aware of all the rock houses within their jurisdiction, and collect as much information about them as possible. Technical surveillance techniques, exchanging information with other agencies, and probing suspects for additional information all help fill in the picture. Developing this preliminary information can save lives at the time of an entry.

§ 18.6.5 Preparing for Court

Once an arrest has been made on a target, through either a forced entry, a search warrant or through an undercover operation, the court preparation must begin. A detailed and often lengthy case file is assembled on the target for presentation to the prosecuting attorney. This enables the prosecutor to know what took place from the initial meeting until the arrest. It also gives the prosecuting attorney an idea of any offers or deals to be made with the defendant for the defendant's assistance—or the defendant's plea of guilty. Many times a defendant will plead guilty either as charged or to a lesser included offense after finding out the key witness in the case is an undercover agent.

§ 18.6.5(a)   Handwriting Evidence in Drug Cases

In a drug case, the question of who wrote the drug records is often important to answer when establishing the legal elements of control or knowledge. In the prosecution phase, these and other elements must be established, sometimes by no other means than documentary evidence. For example, drug prosecutors can satisfy the elements of control, knowledge and sale when the written documents are connected to an individual. The "resident" documents, such as rent receipts, leases, and drivers' licenses can establish the element of dominion and control by showing that a particular person resided at the drug location. There have also been cases whereby the drug records in one location were connected to another location by indented impressions, photocopier identification, and extraneous marks. Whatever role documents play in a drug case, certain methods of collecting handwritten evidence from the suspects will ensure greater success in connecting the suspect to the contraband.

With all document evidence, the best results come from cases where writing samples were collected early in the investigation and under the same conditions in which the questioned documents were written. For example, when the drug ledger consists of hand printed columns of dates, names and numbers on a 3 x 4 piece of lined paper—written in pencil—then the officer should obtain writing samples of hand printed columns of dates, names and numbers on a 3□ x 4□ piece of lined paper written in pencil, as well as some samples in ballpoint pen.

Of course, in the real world nothing is as easy as following simple rules and getting great results. Document evidence in drug cases is no exception. There are a few factors that can impede good results if the narcotics officer is caught unaware. First of all, drug busts are inherently dangerous. Therefore, a quick and efficient method of collecting documents and writing samples from the suspects must be created and followed.

Secondly, people involved with drug activity frequently do not have such written documentation ready at hand. Such documents might include bank accounts, job applications, and credit applications. However, these normal business records are crucially important in establishing the suspect's normal writing habits. Without them, it is difficult to establish whether or not the requested samples truly represent the normal writing habits of the suspect. Requested exemplars are far too often affected by nervousness or attempts to alter or change the writing. Therefore, all requested samples should be accompanied by some normal course of business record.

Third, many drug offenders learned to write under a different national system. A characteristic that appears to be unique or unusual to us is really quite common in a foreign system. This fact is important in evaluating handwriting for identification. A class characteristic which is common to many people is not as valuable for identification purposes as one which is unique to an individual.

Fourth, a drug bust may involve numerous suspects and only a couple of them will be associated with the record keeping. To make it even more complicated, there are numerous documents, and often more than one writer on a page. A narcotics officer in the heat of a seizure will not have time to study all the records to determine which are incriminating and who in the crowd is responsible. Therefore, samples must be obtained from all suspects and in a manner that is not too unwieldy.

Obtaining these writing samples brings us to the fifth and final factor: uncooperative suspects. Suspects may not want to give writing samples, claiming Fifth Amendment rights. However, there are no such rights in obtaining handwriting samples.

The best way to overcome these five obstacles is first to know about them. Different situations will dictate to the narcotics officer how to handle them. In addition, there are a few tips that have served officers in the past. These tips are explained below.

—Make up a generic exemplar form that contains the usual drug record information. This form will be much better than the traditional handwriting exemplar card that most police departments have on hand since that card was designed for check-forgery cases. Your generic exemplar form should be used in conjunction with the samples that duplicate the format of a particular drug record.

—Exhibit 1 is an example of a form that not only contains some letter and number combinations found in drug records but when folded in half, conceals the fact that the suspect is filling out a handwriting exemplar. The top portion of the form was designed to cause the suspect to concentrate on the content of the information, rather than the act of writing.

—Have pages of steno pads, notebooks, address books, accounting books, and note pads on hand. These are the usual source of paper used for most drug records; they will give you a ready supply for duplicating the paper size and format of the drug record that is found at the scene. When taking the samples, dictate the information in whole phrases in a normal speaking pace, pausing at the end for the writer to finish before continuing with the next phrase. This pace will cause the writer to think about the context of the message, rather than the act of writing, which only gives the writer time to think about the normal way he makes the forms and how he can alter them to avoid identification.

—Get enough samples that repeat the letters, words and figures at least four times. For example, if the drug record is one page of writing, get four pages of samples. If, on the other hand, the record is made up of numerous pages, chances are that the letters, words and figures are repeated throughout the pages, therefore one sample of each page should be sufficient.

—Have the suspect fill out the booking sheets. Again, the suspect has to think about the information rather than concentrate on the act of writing, and it is another writing sample usually taken at a different time and under different conditions. If the booking sheets are incomplete, illegible, or if your department has a policy that only the officer or booking personnel does this task, then a second set of booking sheets can be filled out simultaneously or afterward.

—Obtain a copy of the driver's license applications when requesting a soundex copy of the driver's license. There are samples of writing other than the signature on the driver's license application.

—When submitting the document evidence to the document laboratory, place the known documents in one package and the questioned documents in another. Avoid writing on documents that are placed on top of drug records, because the indented impressions you make may obscure indented impressions made by the suspect. If the drug records are going to be processed for fingerprints, always submit them to the document laboratory first and advise the examiner to take precautions.

—Only submit the "smoking gun" documents. Select the pages that make the best connection between the suspect and the contraband. Every scrap of paper and ledger is not necessary in most cases. It will only bog down or overwhelm the document laboratory.

These tips have made many successful identifications in drug cases. The main thing is to remember to duplicate the conditions of the questioned material. That's easy when you have the drug record and know what the test is and what kind of paper and writing implement was used. When you haven't had time to go through all the material before taking samples of writing, then use your generic form. This sample can be used as a gauge for subsequent samples which were taken after the suspect had time to think about how incriminating his writing may be.

Sometimes, the best efforts still fall short of full identification of a suspect. However, a probable or even possible conclusion from a document examiner can and has worked in the prosecution's favor when the supporting reason for the conclusion is that the known samples do not sufficiently represent all the normal writing habits of the suspect. This shows objectivity and care on the examiner's part, and uncooperativeness on the defendant's part, implying guilt.

Exhibit 1

NAME		PHONE NUMBER	DATE	
ADDRESS	CITY		STATE	ZIP CODE
DATE OF BIRTH	PLACE OF BIRTH		DRIVER LICENSE	
OCCUPATION	EMPLOYER		PHONE NUMBER	
IN CASE OF ILLNESS NOTIFY:		PHONE NUMBER	RELATIONSHIP	
ADDRESS	CITY		STATE	ZIP CODE

Signature _____ Date _____

☐ right

The above is a sample of my handwriting using my   hand.

☐ left

Witnessed by: _____

FOLD HERE		
JANUARY 28, 1976	JOSEPH S. FRANCK	$6,000.00
APRIL 30, 1988	MICKEY MOUSE AND DONALD DUCK PRODUCTIONS	$2,000.00
NOVEMBER 4, 1981	ROBERT S. THOMPSON	$50,000.00
DECEMBER 6, 1985	IGLESIA N. CRUZ CO.	$9,473.00
FEBRUARY 18, 1972	CATHERINE LINDA YUMA	$2,000.00
MARCH 11, 1986	GEORGE HOWARD WHITE, INC.	$937.45
SEPTEMBER 16, 1985	RINGO'S SALSA BAR	$7,456.00
JULY 22, 1983	MIGUEL ARTURO VALENTINO	$37.98
OCTOBER 16, 1987	E.B. PENNY, LTD.	$5,640.00
AUGUST 15, 1982	PAUL T. AND HARRY N. KANE	$12,450.00

§ 18.6.5(b)   The Legal Use of Dogs in Narcotics Cases

Another tool that officers may use to assist their arrest and prosecution of narcotics traffickers is the drug detection dog. Due to their highly developed olfactory sense, dogs have become common "equipment" used in narcotics investigations. However, since drug detection dogs are extremely effective, traffickers have attempted to thwart their efforts by packaging drugs with moth balls and garlic; traffickers have even gone so far as to put out contracts on the lives of certain detection dogs. Nonetheless, drug detection dogs have been successful; and the courts have recognized their value when they are well-trained and properly employed.

In any narcotics investigation, law enforcement officers must be careful to use detection dogs within the boundaries set by the courts. Those boundaries can be summarized as follows:

If the dog is used to sniff an area where the defendant has an extremely high expectation of privacy, then a warrant based on probable cause or an exception to the warrant requirement is a prerequisite;

If the sniff is to occur in an area of reduced expectation of privacy, then a mere showing of reasonable suspicion is all that is required; and

If the dog is used to sniff an item located in a public place or a place controlled by a third party, then no search will occur and Fourth Amendment proscriptions regarding searches need not be a concern.

Although other constitutional considerations may arise, such as the level of suspicion needed to seize luggage from a traveler or the amount of time an item may be detained prior to conducting a sniff test, law enforcement officers can help ensure the legality of the dog sniff itself by staying within these boundaries. For further information on the use of dogs in public places, see U.S. v. Place, 462 U.S. 696, 103 S.Ct. 2637, 77 L.Ed.2d 10 (1983).

§ 18.7   SEARCH WARRANTS AND TACTICS
§ 18.7.1 Why Warrants Are Preferable

Another legal consideration for law enforcement officers is the proper use of search warrants. The most important thing to realize is that a search made without a warrant is unlawful unless it falls within at least one recognized—and narrowly drawn—exception to the warrant requirement. This is the gist of the Fourth Amendment. In the courtroom, the burden of proof is on the prosecution to prove a warrantless search was lawful. The converse is also true—and herein lies a tremendous advantage accorded to warrant users: a search carried out pursuant to a search warrant is presumed lawful, and the burden of proof is on the defendant to prove it unlawful. The corollary to this rule will be explained later, but it basically adds up to the fact that a defendant has virtually no chance of successfully attacking even a marginally strong warrant as long as it was obtained and executed in good faith and is based upon a truthful affidavit. When there is no warrant, however, you may spend hours in court trying to explain that the defendant consented to the search of his home and that the consent was free, voluntary and knowing, notwithstanding the fact that he was surrounded by armed officers, was cuffed, speaks only marginal English, and signed the consent form only after the search was conducted because you didn't have a consent form handy at the scene.

If the defense does attack the warrant, it will be in a proceeding wherein the judge simply reads the warrant and determines its validity, and 99 percent of these warrants will be upheld, either because the warrant is supported by ample probable cause, or even if it isn't, the search will be saved under the holding of the "good faith" rule—*United States v. Leon*, 468 U.S. 897, 104 S.Ct. 3405, 82 L.Ed.2d 677 (1984). In essence, the Leon case ruled that even if the warrant is quashed for lack of probable cause, the remedy is not to suppress the evidence obtained during the search—as long as the officer conducted the search in good faith reliance on the validity of the warrant. The only exceptions are, (1) lies in the affidavit (or reckless mistakes or omissions), (2) a non-neutral signing judge who has wholly abandoned his or her judicial function, (3) a warrant so lacking in probable cause that no reasonable officer could have believed the warrant was good, or (4) the warrant is facially defective in that it totally fails to describe the places to be searched or items to be seized. As you can see by these exceptions, it is very difficult for a defendant to win a motion to quash.

§ 18.7.2 Obtaining a Search Warrant

To illustrate some of the circumstances under which a warrant may be obtained, let's assume that an informant with a very good history of reliability tells you that Josephine Smith is dealing ounces from her 1990 Honda, California license COKE4U. The informant also gives you Smith's home address on Main Street, and tells you that she has been in the house within the past week and has seen cash and about one pound of coke there. You run Smith and find that she has a five year old coke conviction, but is not currently on probation or parole and thus has no search conditions. You decide you'd like to search the car and house. A short surveillance of the house reveals little. You follow Smith away from the house, however, and see her make what you feel are deliveries from the car referred to by the informant. The informant is very valuable to you and has given information to you in the past which has allowed you to seize a lot of dope and prosecute several individuals, including some associates of Smith. What do you do at this point?

Well, you could catch Ms. Smith in her car and do an auto search under *U. S. v. Ross*, 456 U.S. 798, 72 L.Ed.2d 572, 102 S.Ct. 2157 (1982), which would be fully lawful. Then, you could obtain a consent for the house, depending upon what you did or didn't find in the car. Or, you could search the car under Ross and get a warrant for the house. Lastly, you could simply obtain a warrant for both the car and house. All are viable options.

Another very helpful tactic used by experienced officers and prosecutors is to structure the prosecution along the same lines as the facts set forth in your search warrant affidavit. For instance, there was a case against seven Colombian coke dealers caught with 1,000 pounds and $600,000. The search warrant involved weeks of detailed surveillance coupled with several expert opinions about such things as stash houses, mail drops, the lack of any visible employment by the suspects notwithstanding their rather upscale lifestyle, car switches, brief meetings in public places, beeper calls, cellular phones and the other things usually involved in such cases. The warrant was quite lengthy and was in effect, the blueprint for the jury trial.

Seventy-five percent of the trial in this case consisted of the narcotics agent explaining to the jury how a major narcotics organization operates, explaining beepers, cellular phones, car switches, etc., and then explaining how the defendant's conduct fit within that framework. The narcotics agent also offered the jury his expert opinions regarding various matters in controversy. Since the affidavit already existed well before the trial and, in fact, existed even before the defendants were arrested, the defense could in no way argue that the testimony had been tailored for the trial. Furthermore, since the cocaine, money, beepers and all other items sought by the warrant were in fact owned by the traffickers, the facts and opinions contained within the affidavit became self-fulfilling prophecies in a sense. The prediction of criminality in the warrant, coupled with its eventual and obvious uncovering at the time of arrest, became very compelling evidence at trial. The case basically tried itself from the plan laid out in the affidavit, and all that was needed on top was a correlation and presentation of the additional evidence found at various locations (bogus leases, phone records, pay-owes, etc.). In summary, the concept to be gleaned from this case involves the dual use of facts, both as probable cause for the arrests and searches, and as substantive evidence of guilt given to the jury.

§ 18.7.3 Warrants Will Save Time Later

It takes a couple of hours to write a warrant and two minutes to get a consent. It is true, on occasion you may spend more time in the field if you issue a warrant than if you don't. But if you have ever spent three days on the witness stand testifying about a series of warrantless arrests, searches and "securing" of residences, while six dope lawyers systematically seek to destroy you, I'll bet you would opt for the extra couple of hours in the field. Also, your increased chance of losing when you forego a warrant means that all of the time spent during your investigation and all of the prosecutor's time, as well as the judge's time are risked unnecessarily. The extra time you spend obtaining a warrant will pay off in better searches, more wins at trial, less court time for you, and less risk that the time you do spend is wasted by having your evidence suppressed. Also, the typical warrant does not take that much time to prepare. The affidavit accompanying most warrants is under 10 pages, with some as short as two or three pages. You can shorten matters substantially by having your expertise pre-printed and updated periodically for use as the first pages of your affidavit. Also, get a copy of the D.A. Search Warrant Manual if you don't already have one; keep it, some blank warrants, and some pre-printed expertise pages with you in your car. You should also learn to do telephonic and oral warrants.

§ 18.7.4 Most Judges Do Not Like to Suppress Evidence

Most judges, contrary to some popular wisdom, aren't really thrilled with setting an obviously guilty party free because the evidence must be suppressed. In fact, most judges frown upon this result. Believe it or not, the officer has much more control over this than does the judge. A judge simply cannot suppress evidence seized pursuant to a warrant without a darned good reason, or the appellate court will simply reverse. But a judge faced with a warrantless search or seizure that is weak can do you in, simply by making a credibility call against you. And no court of appeal can do a thing about it.

Furthermore, when an officer proceeds via warrant, he or she is reinforcing the image of police officers as professionals, concerned with making strong cases and conducting legal searches, and dispelling the image that some judges may hold of narcotics officers as cowboys who search first and come up with the bad taillight later. Obtaining a warrant from a judge also gives you the opportunity to interact with the judge on a one-on-one basis, usually outside of the courtroom. This is valuable to both the officer and the judge. Some bench officers, believe it or not, are not ex-prosecutors, and may have little empathy for or understanding of how the police operate. Some judges may have never socialized with police officers before becoming judges, and may even feel intimidated or threatened by them. Likewise, many officers who would never think of speaking to a judge unless absolutely necessary, perhaps viewing the judge as an enemy just looking for a way to free dangerous defendants. However, the cooperation of judge and police officer will only result in enhanced communication and a smoother trial.

Another reason for obtaining a search warrant is issue of civil liability. Let's assume you conduct a search of a suspect's home and come up dry; then this suspect decides to sue you. Would you rather go into the civil trial holding a document signed by a judge that ordered you to conduct the search in question (remember, a search warrant is an order in writing to conduct a particular search and seizure), or would you rather argue to the jury that the suspect consented to the search, although he and his eight family members claim you kicked the door and never mentioned consent?

§ 18.7.5 Serving the Narcotics Search Warrant

There are several kinds of search warrants. Their use may range from looking for evidence in cases of theft, narcotics, and explosives, or even murder. In this discussion, the focus is on the small-time dealer or dealer/user who is close to the bottom rung of the narcotics ladder. This person is extremely dangerous not only because he is usually a multi-time ex-con, but also because he cannot afford another arrest. In this case, and several others, serving a search warrant can be one of the most dangerous duties an officer encounters in his or her career.

To obtain a warrant, as discussed above, a "buy" is usually made by an undercover officer, special employee, or confidential and reliable informant. Right after the buy is made, an interview with the buyer may help to procure some necessary information which includes: description of suspect, layout of interior of house, weapons, where the narcotics are kept, and how many people live or stay in the house. It would also be helpful to get some details on such questions as how are the doors secured? With deadbolts? Are there booby traps? etc.

§ 18.7.5(a) Decisions

After the warrant is written and signed by a magistrate, you should decide when to serve the warrant. For legal reasons, it should be served as soon as possible after the magistrate signs it; but in most cases the warrant does not have to be served immediately. The more time between the "buy" and the serving of the warrant, the more likely the informant's identity can be concealed. You should also decide to serve the warrant in either the daytime or nighttime. There are many reasons to justify either time, but nighttime usually offers more concealment for the raiding party when approaching the house. On the other hand, early daylight offers the opportunity to catch the occupant of the house at home, hopefully, with his stash. The decision also depends on other factors, such as when the dealer gets resupplied and if you want to get more players and users in the house when you hit it.

§ 18.7.5(b) Warrant Serving Strategy—Seven People

5 front/2 rear. A game plan should be made up as to how many people are going to be used and how they will be assigned. There should be at least two uniformed officers utilized in serving the warrant; one positioned at the front door and one at the rear door. A good idea is to have a third person (detective) in the rear yard with the uniformed officer. They should each be placed diagonally away from the door, strategically out of the line of fire. Their main purpose is to prevent escape. Hopefully, if one of the dealer/users tries to escape, they can verbally stop him from exiting the rear door.

When serving the "average" search warrant, five persons should be used on the entry. The "knock and announce" should be made by the affiant, team leader or other person knowledgeable in the legalities of making a lawful entry. This person, along with all other non-uniformed personnel, should be dressed so that there could be no mistake that they are police officers. A good idea would be to wear an outer garment that is marked "POLICE" and to attach a badge to this outer garment. Have all participants wear bulletproof vests.

The person who knocks on the door should have the warrant in his hand and show it to the person opening the door. The entry in most narcotics cases should be done very quickly in order to prevent the destruction of evidence and to prevent officer injury; it must also be done legally. Therefore, the person who knocks on the door (known as the "knocker") has an extremely important position. If the "knocker" hears retreating footsteps or if the occupant refuses admittance, then forced entry should be made. The knocker must announce his purpose and authority and demand entry (in most cases) prior to forcing entry.

If forced entry is needed, the "door key" person will then, hopefully, open the door with one swing of the sledgehammer or ram. The first swing should hit the deadbolt lock mechanism and open the door. Upon entry, the first person through the house should be the uniformed officer. This officer should have his gun drawn in case firepower is needed. Before opening any other interior doors, this officer should also "knock and announce." When the interior situation is stabilized, he or she should be the one to open the rear door after loudly announcing "Police,

I am opening the rear door." The door key person should be the second one through the house. He or she should assist the uniformed officer in situations where a person needs to be controlled or arrested and fire-power is not needed. He or she is also responsible for forced entry if an interior door needs to be taken down.

The third and fourth persons through the house should be a team of shooters: the third person in case of a firefight situation and the fourth, a fighter, in case of a physical confrontation. This teamwork situation should help cut down on accidental discharges but should not preclude the "fighter" from pulling and using his or her weapon if necessary.

If a ruse is used to gain entry, such as an officer dressed as a deliv-eryman, letter carrier, etc., this person should take on the same re-sponsibilities as the "knocker." The "knocker's" responsibility is to allow no one to exit the front door and to prevent non-police personnel from entering the house.

This initial game plan should be set up without the need for radio transmissions. Many drug dealers monitor police channels, so it be-hooves the search warrant team to use hand signals, unless they are using scramblers or in the case of an emergency situation. If shots are fired within the house, the officers in the rear should maintain their position. They should not subject the other officers to a cross-fire situa-tion but instead maintain "cover" and listen for further communica-tions. If a firefight ensues, the Team Sergeant (who may be the 2nd, 3rd, or 4th team member) should radio via walkie-talkie for reinforce-ments. Depending on the situation, the Sergeant should generally call for setting up a double perimeter and command post. He or she should also determine if there is a need for a Special Response or S.W.A.T. Team.

§ 18.7.5(c)   The Search

The search should be made carefully and systematically. For best re-sults, every room and everything should be searched twice (by two dif-ferent people). There is no limit on where and how to search. Narcotics may be found anywhere from plain view to hidden in walls, toilets, wall sockets, safes, vacuum packed cans, furniture, body cavities, etc. If your courts allow it, the best scenario would be to have each individual offi-cer locate or spot the contraband and then have one officer be desig-nated as the finder. The finder systematically "finds" all the contraband and books it as evidence, which makes both accountability and court-room testifying easier.

§ 18.7.6 Searches for Narcotics Trafficking in the Workplace

Another situation in which an undercover officer may be required to do a search or a surveillance is in the corporate or industrial workplace. Increasingly, narcotics have been trafficked by workers at their place of employment. The prevalence of this phenomenon and the role of the undercover agent are discussed in the report below (INEOA 1990).

Chapter 18

UNDERCOVER INVESTIGATORS:
A NEW EMPLOYER DRUG WAR TOOL

Concerns about drug abuse in the workplace have led some employers to hire investigative services to place undercover agents in their work forces, according to representatives of private investigative agencies.

Ron Janick, vice president of investigative services for CPP/Pinkerton, headquartered in Van Nuys, Calif., said he has observed a 40 percent increase during the past six months in the number of employers requesting undercover investigations into suspected drug abuse.

Increasingly, employees are complaining to management—often anonymously —that other employees are working under the influence of drugs or selling drugs in the workplace, Janick said. Employees are concerned about their safety, he said, citing a recent example in which an employee who allegedly was using drugs had an accident while operating a forklift truck.

Spouses and relatives also sometimes tell employers about an employee's use of drugs on the job, according to Edward P. DeLise, a vice president with Investigations Corporation of America, based in Atlanta, Ga.

It is not always co-workers or family members who clue the employer that there is a drug problem. Employers sometimes observe behavior or other circumstances that leads them to believe there is a problem. Absenteeism, inventory shrinkage, increased workers' compensation claims, and diminished product or service quality are all potential signals of a drug problem, according to the investigators.

While absenteeism can be a signal of employee drug abuse, some employees involved in selling drugs have very good attendance records, according to DeLise. "Oddly enough, dealers are usually at work every day because that's where their connections are," he noted.

Theft in the workplace and drug abuse very often go hand in hand, according to Bobby Newman of Acta Investigations Inc., in Houston. Newman estimated that in some workplaces, employee involvement in the use or delivery of drugs runs from 10 to 30 percent of the workplace. He cited one instance where 100 employees out of a workforce of 150 were involved in narcotics use or transactions.

Corporate investigators say their clientele represents a broad range of U.S. workplaces, from banks to hospitals, schools to factories.

Surveillance: 'Preventive Medicine'

Although many employers request undercover investigations to target what they see as a specific problem, others use the investigations more as "preventive medicine." A Pinkerton advertisement suggests that undercover investigations can be "regularly used by sophisticated management as a precautionary measure—much like a surprise audit or annual physical checkup—to verify that operations are actually being conducted in accordance with the management's expectations and understanding."

Most operatives are placed in entry-level or secretarial positions, but they can be placed almost anywhere, the investigators said.

The fewer people who know about an undercover investigation, the better, investigators agree, noting that a human resource official is often one of the people appraised of the operation.

Pinkerton investigators usually suggest that a high-level human resource or personnel official be aware of the investigations, as these people often have to deal with the outcome, Janick said.

DeLise of ICA estimated that 80 to 85 percent of the time, a human resource official is aware of undercover operations conducted by his firm. A personnel official's cooperation often is needed to "get our operative in" to the work site, he said.

Secrecy Is Key to Investigation

DeLise said if more than three people from a company are aware of an undercover investigation into suspected drug abuse, he will not take the case "because it can be dangerous." He added that he doesn't use agents from the local area for this reason and because when the operation is over, he wants to get them out.

Most investigations range from one to four months, but some can take up to a year. Investigators agree that it can take time for the undercover operative to be accepted by co-workers.

The investigators said they bring the police in as soon as there is evidence of narcotics activity. It is particularly important to notify law enforcement officials in order to preserve the "chain of custody" of the evidence, DeLise said. In addition, since his investigators are often from out of town it is important that the police know of their presence so there is no confusion as to their role in the drug activity.

Worker discipline resulting from undercover operations usually sticks, according to the investigators. There is seldom a problem because the investigators often back up their observations with video or film, Newman said.

Although direct observation of workplace activity by management and supervisors is well accepted in employment law, new technology—especially electronic and video surveillance equipment—has raised fear among employees of privacy invasions, an employment attorney told a recent conference on employee surveillance.

The entry of new technology into the workplace sets up a clash between the employer's need to supervise its employees and the privacy rights of the employees, said Morton Orenstein of the San Francisco law firm of Schacter, Kristoff, Ross, Sprague & Curiale.

California and some other states have privacy guarantees in their state constitutions that could affect the ability of employers in those states to use various forms of workplace surveillance, he said.

§ 18.8   TARGETING SYNTHETIC DRUGS

Globally, the production and use of the synthetic drugs amphetamine, methamphetamine, and MDMA (Ecstasy) remain serious problems. There are numerous foreign sources for synthetic drugs and their precursors, including countries in Asia, Europe, and North America. Use patterns are strongly regional, with methamphetamine consumed in the United States and Asia. Amphetamines and Ecstasy are the drugs of choice in Europe. U.S. law enforcement continues to act in cooperation with law enforcement officials worldwide to disrupt foreign sources of the pseudoephedrine and ephedrine that are used to produce much of the methamphetamine used in the United States and Mexico.

Mexico is the largest foreign source of the methamphetamine distributed in the United States. Although flow estimates are elusive, production appears to be increasing in that the amount of methamphetamine seized within Mexico rose during 2003, as did seizures along the U.S.-Mexico border in 2003 and 2004. Moreover, Mexican criminal groups based in California and Mexico control most of the wholesale distribution of methamphetamine in the United States. In Asia, the largest source of amphetamine and methamphetamine in the world, the United States will continue to support efforts by law enforcement officials in the region to disrupt Asian synthetic drug traffickers. Although Asia provides only a minor amount of the methamphetamine used in the United States, it is the major source of the bulk precursor chemicals used by large, illicit methamphetamine production laboratories in Mexico and the United States. Europe supplies most of the Ecstasy distributed in the United States, but since the success of major enforcement efforts in the United States, Canada, and Europe, Ecstasy use continues to decline in the United States.

U.S. law enforcement officials are confronting and disrupting the synthetic drug markets through both organizational attack activities targeting major synthetic drug trafficking organizations and chemical control initiatives focused on keeping critical precursors out of traffickers' hands.

§ 18.9 THE INVESTIGATION OF CLANDESTINE LABORATORIES

There are several natural drugs (not illicitly manufactured) found on the street. The most popular ones are marijuana, psilocybin, and peyote. However, most of the drugs that police officers see on the street are clandestinely manufactured. Morphine is converted to heroin. PCP and LSD are synthetic and chemically manufactured. Based on the process required to manufacture any particular drug, there are different types of laboratories. Some basic manufacturing processes are described below.

1. Extraction: the raw plant material is changed into a finished product by the use of chemical solvents. The chemical structure of the drug is not altered. Examples include: cannabis to hashish, hashish to hashish oil, opium to morphine.

2. Conversion: a raw or unrefined drug product is changed into a finished or refined drug. Here the chemical structure is changed. Examples: morphine to heroin (diacetylmorphine), cocaine base to cocaine hydrocholride, cocaine hydrochloride to crack cocaine.

3. Synthesis: a combination of proper raw materials in required portions results in a finished drug product through chemical reaction. Examples: chemicals to phencyclidine, LSD, etc.

4. "Tableting": The machine processing of the final drug product into a dosage form (tablet).

§ 18.9.1 Where Are the Labs?

In the year 2000, approximately 6,700 clandestine methamphetamine laboratory sits were seized by DEA and state/local law enforcement, compared to 6,782 seized during 1999. The States of California and Washington reported the greatest number of laboratory seizures during 2000. The majority of the laboratories, approximately 95 percent, seized in the United States are considered "mom and pop" laboratories, capable of producing ounce quantities of methamphetamine. The remaining 5 percent are considered "superlabs," capable of producing 10 or more pounds of methamphetamine in a single cook. The majority of the superlabs are believed to be tied to Mexican criminal groups and are located primarily the California. Clandestine labs typically produce other illicit drugs such as PCP, MDMA, and LSD, but methamphetamine has always been the drug manufactured in the vast majority of labs seized by law enforcement.

LSD has been manufactured illegally since the 1960s. A limited number of chemists, probably fewer than a dozen, are believed to be manufacturing nearly all of the LSD available in the United States. Some of these manufacturers probably have been operating since the 1960s. LSD manufacturers and traffickers can be separated into two groups. The first, located in northern California, is composed of chemists (commonly referred to as "cooks") and traffickers who work together in close association; typically, they are major producers capable of distributing LSD nationwide. The second group is made up of independent producers who, operating on a comparatively limited scale, can be found throughout the country. As a group, independent producers pose much less of a threat than the northern California group inasmuch as their production is intended for local consumption only.

Drug law enforcement officials have surmised that LSD chemists and top echelon traffickers form an insider's fraternity of sorts. They successfully have remained at large because there are so few of them. Their exclusivity is not surprising given that LSD synthesis is a difficult process to master. Although cooks need not be formally trained chemists, they must adhere to precise and complex production procedures. In instances where the cook is not a chemist, the production recipe most likely was passed on by personal instruction from a formally trained chemist. Further supporting the premise that most LSD manufacture is the work of a small fraternity of chemists, virtually all the LSD seized during the 1980s was of consistently high purity and sold in relatively uniform dosages of 20 to 80 micrograms.

LSD commonly is produced from lysergic acid, which is made from ergotamine tartrate, a substance derived from an ergot fungus on rye, or from lysergic acid amide, a chemical found in morning glory seeds. Although theoretically possible, manufacture of LSD from morning glory seeds is not economically feasible and these seeds never have been found to be a successful starting material for LSD production. Lysergic acid and lysergic acid amide are both classified in Schedule III of the Controlled Substances Act. Ergotamine tartrate is regulated under the Chemical Diversion and Trafficking Act. Ergotamine tartrate is not readily available in the United States, and its purchase by other than established pharmaceutical firms is suspect. Therefore, ergotamine tartrate used in clandestine LSD laboratories is believed to be acquired from sources located abroad, most likely Europe, Mexico, Costa Rica, and Africa. The difficulty in acquiring ergotamine tartrate may limit the number of independent LSD manufacturers. By contrast, illicit manufacture of methamphetamine and phencyclidine is comparatively more prevalent in the United States because, in part, precursor chemicals can be procured easily.

Only a small amount of ergotamine tartrate is required to produce LSD in large batches. For example, 25 kilograms of ergotamine tartrate can produce 5 or 6 kilograms of pure LSD crystal that, under ideal circumstances, could be processed into 100 million dosage units, more than enough to meet what is believed to be the entire annual U.S. demand for the hallucinogen. LSD manufacturers need only import a small quantity of the substance and, thus, enjoy the advantages of ease of concealment and transport not available to traffickers of other illegal drugs, primarily marijuana and cocaine.

Cooking LSD is time consuming; it takes from two to three days to produce 1 to 4 ounces of crystal. Consequently, it is believed that LSD usually is not produced in large quantities, but rather in a series of small batches. Production of LSD in small batches also minimizes the loss of precursor chemicals should they become contaminated during the synthesis process.

LSD crystal produced clandestinely can be as much as 95 to 100 percent pure. At this purity—and assuming optimum conditions during dilution and application to paper—1 gram of crystal could produce 20,000 dosage units of LSD. However, analysis of LSD crystal seized in California over the past three years revealed an average purity of only 62 percent. Moreover, LSD degrades quickly when exposed to heat, light, and air and is most susceptible to degradation during the application process and once it is in paper form. As a result, under less than optimal, real-life conditions, actual yields are significantly below the theoretically possible yield: 1 gram of LSD crystal generally yields 10,000 dosage units of LSD, or approximately 10 million dosage units per kilogram.

Over the past 30 years, the traditional dilution factor for manufacturing LSD has been 10,000 doses per 1 gram of crystal. Therefore, dosage units yielded from high purity (95 to 100 percent pure) LSD crystal would contain 100 micrograms. However, dosages currently seen contain closer to 50 micrograms. This discrepancy stems in part from production impurities: during the synthesis process, manufacturers generally fail to perform a final "cleanup" step to remove by-products, thereby lowering the crystal's purity. Further, though average purity of tested LSD crystal samples is, as noted, 62 percent, the average potency of doses analyzed is approximately 50 micrograms rather than 62 micrograms, as would be expected. The diminished potency can be attributed to distributors who, when applying the crystal to paper, often "cheat" by diluting 1 gram of crystal to produce up to 15,000 or more dosage units.

Pure, high potency LSD is a clear or white, odorless crystalline material that is soluble in water. It is mixed with binding agents, such as spray-dried skim milk, for producing tablets or dissolved and diluted in a solvent for application onto paper or other materials. Variations in the manufacturing process or the presence of precursors or by-products can cause LSD to range in color from clear or white, in its purest form, to tan or even black, indicating poor quality or degradation. To mask product deficiencies, distributors often apply LSD to off-white, tan or yellow paper to disguise discoloration.

At the highest levels of the traffic, where LSD crystal is purchased in gram or multi-gram quantities from wholesale sources of supply, it rarely is diluted with adulterants, a common practice with cocaine, heroin, and other illicit drugs. However, to prepare the crystal for production in retail dosage units, it must be diluted with binding agents or dissolved and diluted in liquids. The dilution of LSD crystal typically follows a standard, predetermined recipe to ensure uniformity of the final product. Excessive dilution yields less potent dosage units that soon become unmarketable. LSD crystal usually is converted into tablet form (microdots" that are 3/32 inch or smaller in diameter), thin squares of gelatin ("window panes"), or applied to sheets of prepared paper (blotter paper—initially used as a medium—has been replaced by a variety of paper types). LSD most frequently is encountered in paper form, still commonly referred to as blotter paper or blotter acid. It consists of sheets of paper soaked in or otherwise impregnated with LSD.

Undercover Narcotics and Clandestine Lab Investigations

Often these sheets are covered with colorful designs or artwork and are usually perforated into one-quarter inch square, individual dosage units (DEA 1995).

Laboratories vary in sophistication. Some are expensively equipped and some consist of makeshift equipment such as plastic buckets, plastic barrels, and broom and mop handles. These laboratories can present a danger to the responding police officer in terms of the suspects therein and the inherent dangers posed by the improper manufacture of drugs. There are chemicals present that are highly toxic and highly explosive so the officer must exercise extreme caution. Since police officers are usually first on the scene, the officer must have a basic knowledge of how to go about handling a suspected clandestine laboratory.

§ 18.9.1(a)   Recognition of Clandestine Laboratories

Clandestine laboratories are not restricted to any particular geographical area. They may be found in a single family dwelling, an apartment complex, or in a remote area. The labs are usually detected by the strong odor of chemicals emanating from the site. When an informant calls the police or fire department, it is usually because of the odor of ether and other strong odors.

The following are the most common indicators of an illicit drug laboratory:

1. Usually, because of the danger of fire and the presence of toxic fumes, no one will actually live at the location. The laboratory operator will only periodically visit the location.

2. The doors and windows will be somewhat sealed in an attempt to conceal the strong odor.

3. The operator may, depending on the location, install large ventilation fans to disperse the fumes.

4. 55-gallon steel drums will be delivered to the location by a chemical company or common carrier.

5. Inordinate amounts of ice will be delivered to the location. (Ice is required for the cooling process during "cooking.")

6. A strong, distinctive odor of ether may be noticeable. If questioned, the operator will frequently indicate the odor is from a legal activity of plastic manufacturing or photograph developing.

7. The location will be sparsely furnished.

8. The neighbors notice that the operator appears to exit the location solely to get fresh air or to have a smoke.

9. The neighbor or a friend may have been inside and observed the laboratory in operation.

10. The operator may dump chemicals in the yard, causing destruction of plant life.

Upon responding to a suspected lab, a uniformed field officer should make contact with the informant and gain as much information as possible regarding the occupants of the building. The officer can then make a visual inspection of the location, looking for signs that a clandestine laboratory is in operation. One of the signs is chemical odors being ventilated from the building by fans, blowers, and other types of ventilating equipment. The officer should look for empty chemical containers around the building or in the trash.

Upon locating a suspected laboratory site, the field officer will generally back off and call for assistance while maintaining surveillance of the site. A narcotics unit should be called to the scene. If the officer feels there is an immediate danger to people in the surrounding area, he can call for the fire department and begin to evacuate persons from the area. He may also want to block off access roads to the area. The Uniform Fire Code allows fire departments to enter any structure if a hazard exists and authorizes police officers to assist fire departments in any function. The People v. Patterson decision, 94 Cal. App. 3d 456, 156 Cal. Rptr. 518 (Cal. App. 2 Dist. 1979), states that a residence, in its entirety, can be an extreme explosion hazard because petroleum ether creates a very volatile fume when improperly ventilated.

§ 18.9.1(b)   Search and Seizure
All investigative discoveries should be included in the affidavit. These might include persons ordering chemicals under false names; chemical odors around the suspected laboratory site; officer's observations from within the lab site; expert opinion; and the evasive movements of the suspect. When effecting entry without a warrant due to exigent circumstances, the fire department and a criminalist should always be notified immediately. As soon as the laboratory has been rendered safe, the search should be stopped and a warrant obtained.

§ 18.9.2 Safety Rules of the Clandestine Laboratory for Police, Firefighters and Public
Safety rules of the clandestine laboratory include the following:

1. Secure adjoining houses or apartments; evacuate surrounding area as necessary.

2. Have ambulance standing by, if necessary.

3. Have fire equipment standing by. After suspects are secure, move fire equipment into area.

4. Turn off gas and electricity at the outside source to the building.

5. Use gas probe to determine fire potential.

6. All personnel entering the lab should wear self-contained breathing apparatus.

7. A trained criminalist should always accompany investigators.

8. The criminalist should be responsible for shutting down the operations and the indication of possible dangerous chemicals.

9. Make sure the clandestine laboratory is well ventilated by opening doors and windows. Mechanical ventilation equipment should only be used outside the location.

10. Do not turn on lights to the location until it is well ventilated.

11. Do not smoke at the scene.

12. Do not allow acid and cyanide to be mixed or come together. This mixture is used in the gas chamber and is lethal.

13. Do not remove any flasks or containers from ice baths.

14. Photograph only with electronic flash.

15. Wash thoroughly after leaving the scene.

16. Curiosity seekers or unauthorized persons can only result in contamination of the scene and possible injury.

§ 18.9.2(a)   Safety

If you can, avoid entering a laboratory. If you have to enter a suspected laboratory site, the officer must remember that he is dealing with highly toxic and volatile chemicals. If there is a strong odor of ether, he must know that an explosion may result from a spark or flame. The officer should never turn on or off any electrical switch or appliance in the lab area. The fire department should stand by, and entry to the lab should be made with a qualified chemist. The building should be immediately ventilated to eliminate the danger of explosion. The officer must avoid accidentally mixing any chemicals present. Hydrochloric acid and sodium cyanide are commonly found at PCP lab sites and, when combined, they form cyanide gas. Cyanide gas is a very deadly substance.

§ 18.9.2(b)   Search Warrant

Usually, a search warrant will be obtained by the narcotics officers. The affidavit must allege facts sufficient to establish probable cause. For example, the odor of ether, alone, is not sufficiently distinctive to identify the manufacturing of PCP. If officers cannot establish an immediate danger to allow entry to the premises under fire code sections, they may have to set up a surveillance to establish further circumstances to obtain a search warrant.

§ 18.9.3   Chemicals Found at Clandestine Laboratories

There are certain chemicals that must be present to manufacture PCP or methamphetamine; these are called precursors. The necessary precursors for manufacturing methamphetamine are methylamine and phenyl-2-propanone. Other chemicals may be used in various combinations. Below is a list of the chemicals commonly used in PCP and Amphetamine labs.

PCP LABS	AMPHETAMINE LABS
1.Piperidine	1.Methylamine
2.Cyclohexanone	2.Phenyl-2-propanone
3.Bromobenzene	3.Petroleum ether
4.Petroleum ether	4.Aluminum foil
5.Anhydrous ether	5.Hydrochloric acid
6.Magnesium turnings	6.Acetone
7.Sodium bisulfite	7.Palladium
8.Sodium cyanide	8.Benzyl chloride
9.Iodine	9.Ephedrine
10.Hydrochloric acid	10.Phosphorus
11.Ammonium hydroxide	

§ 18.9.4   Alternative Method for Crank Synthesis

The recent seizure of a methamphetamine laboratory in Redding, California has revealed a synthesis method to produce phenyl-2-propanone (P-2-P) that has not been widely used in the past. This new method seems to be on its way to becoming more prevalent in clandestine lab activity.

The method is known as the "Nitrostyrene Route" and utilizes the uncontrolled precursors nitroethance and benzaldehyde. This reaction is quite simple and is analogous to the manufacture of phencyclidine in that it involves a two-stage reaction. The first stage is the synthesis of an intermediate called 1-phenyl-2-nitropropene. This is accomplished by way of refluxing the precursors listed above in a round-bottom flask with a solvent and catalyst. The reaction takes approximately 8 hours if using heat; or the chemicals can be simply set in a dark place at room temperature for 1 to 2 weeks. The trade off is time vs. heat. The resultant product (1-phenyl-2-nitropropene) is a yellowish crystal that has an indefinite shelf life.

The second stage involves the suspension of the intermediate in water in a reaction flask, adding again a catalyst and a reagent. The solution is heated and hydrochloric acid is added slowly over a period of hours, converting the intermediate to P-2-P. This process is known as hydrolysis (decomposition in which a compound is split into other compounds by taking up the elements of water).

Undercover Narcotics and Clandestine Lab Investigations

There are several dangers associated with this reaction: nitroethance can be explosive and is an irritant to the eyes and mucous membranes; the acid, of course, is corrosive; the solvents are flammable; and one of the catalysts is a mucous membrane irritant.

One the advantages of the "Nitrostyrene Route" is that this reaction does not have the nasty odor associated with the old phenylacetic acid route. The odor associated with this reaction is consistent with Maraschino cherries, which is quite pleasant comparatively. The down side to this process, for the user, is the fact that P-2-P crank is less reactant in the body due to the (dl) form of the methamphetamine rather that the (d) form, which is produced from ephedrine crank. Due to the availability of the precursors involved in this manufacturing method, the process may become more prevalent.

§ 18.9.5 Collecting Laboratory Evidence

Regardless of the type of lab you encounter, the process of collecting evidence is extremely important. All chemicals, apparatus, and the laboratory site should be photographed before collected as evidence; likewise, printable surfaces should be fingerprinted before collected as evidence. In addition, the criminalist should make a complete inventory of all chemicals at the location. The following evidence should be collected:

1. Samples of the precursor chemicals (liquid and solids).

2. Samples of intermediate compounds.

3. Samples of finished products.

4. Samples of all remaining chemicals.

5. Formulas and books, etc., to verify that illicit products were being manufactured.

6. Laboratory equipment.

§ 18.9.6 Disposal

When the investigation of a clandestine laboratory is concluded, the problem of disposing of the chemicals and equipment remains. After the chemist takes samples of the various chemicals found at the lab, a toxic waste disposal company, under contract with the city or county, will package the items in metal containers for disposal.

However, there are still other health and environmental concerns generated by illicit manufacturing at clandestine labs. For instance, the indiscriminate disposal of hazardous waste by outlaw laboratory operators may lead to contamination of surrounding water sources, soil, and air, as well as the building and its fixtures. Due to manifold health dangers, more comprehensive cleanup actions at laboratory sites—in addition to the immediate or planned removal of bulk chemicals and contaminated materials—are necessary to prevent harm to public health and to the environment. Factoring into this cleanup question are such pressures as a growing environmental awareness in the public and regulations forwarded by the U.S. Environmental Protections Agency (USEPA) and the Occupational Safety and Health Administration (OSHA). This complex rat's nest of issues has impacted law enforcement officers by requiring specialized medical training and the use of protective raid garments by any personnel involved in clandestine drug laboratory seizures. In addition, the federal government has mandated a more comprehensive cleanup program.

§ 18.9.7 Federal Cleanup Measures

On November 18, 1988, Congress enacted the Anti-Drug Abuse Act of 1988, Public Law 100-690. With respect to chemical cleanup issues, section 2405 of this act mandated the Drug Enforcement Administration (DEA) and the U.S. Environmental Protection Agency (USEPA) to form a joint Federal Task Force to formulate, establish, and implement a program for the cleanup and disposal of hazardous waste produced by illegal drug laboratories. The law also required the Task Force to develop and disseminate guidelines to law enforcement agencies that are responsible for the enforcement of drug laws. The law further stipulates that after the final guidelines are published and disseminated, the Attorney General shall make grants to and enter into contracts with state and local governments. These governments must agree to comply with the guidelines and the contracts will be made for demonstrations projects to clean up and safely dispose of substances associated with illegal drug laboratories—especially those substances which may present a danger to public health and the environment. The proposed guidelines are now available for review by state and local agencies and any other interested parties.

These proposed guidelines have integrated the experience of DEA Special Agents and Forensic Chemists and USEPA Emergency Response Technicians, including various guidance documents developed by USEPA for cleaning up hazardous waste sites and various health and safety programs established by the DEA, USEPA, and OSHA. The guidelines suggest that state and local law enforcement and environmental and health agencies implement a comprehensive approach to clandestine laboratory cleanup. The guidelines also outline measures which can be taken to reduce the hazards associated with clandestine drug laboratories and provide information on relevant and applicable hazardous waste statutes and regulations, such as the Resource Conservation and Recovery Act (RCRA), which may apply to cleanup activities at clandestine drug laboratories.

The guidelines contain information on chemicals commonly found at drug laboratory sites, DEA clandestine laboratory safety certification programs, and personnel medical requirements for participation in the clandestine drug laboratory program. The guidelines also include sample forms such as contamination reports, uniform hazardous waste manifests for transporting hazardous waste, and additional information that may be used to develop state or local clandestine drug laboratory cleanup programs. Requests for copies of the guidelines should be addressed to: Drug Enforcement Administration, Office of Forensic Sciences, Hazardous Waste Disposal Unit (AFSH), Washington, D.C. 20537.

§ 18.9.8 Summary

As a result of increasing clandestine manufacturing, the major illicit drug trafficker and manufacturer of the late 1980s and 1990s is far different from his counterparts of the 1960s and 1970s. Today's drug trafficker is much more clever, greedy, ruthless, violent, and dangerous. Drug trafficking and the illegal manufacturing of narcotics and dangerous drugs has become a multi-million dollar business. Stakes are high. A trafficker could invest 2 to 5 million dollars in a deal and make a profit of 25 million dollars.

When Congress passed the Racketeer Influence Corrupt Organization (RICO) and Continuing Criminal Enterprises (CCE) statutes, the stakes in the war on drugs rose even higher. Drug traffickers have taken severe steps to protect their assets from law enforcement and from each other. With asset forfeiture, traffickers have become acutely aware that if they get arrested by narcotics agents, then they stand to lose much of what they have. Many narcotics agents have been killed. Even juvenile drug dealers have become more violent nationwide. Thus, a well-educated and well-trained officer will be best prepared to deal with the changing drug world.

§ 18.10 POLICE WORK AND AIDS
§ 18.10.1   Introduction

The first cases of AIDS (Acquired Immunodeficiency Syndrome) were diagnosed in 1981. No one knows how many people are HIV (Human Immunodeficiency Virus) positive or how many have the full-blown AIDS disease. Nonetheless, one in twenty-five people in San Francisco, California is now infected with the HIV virus that causes AIDS. The international numbers are estimated to be in the millions. Much of the attention given to AIDS has assumed that it is a disease that primarily affects IV drug users and homosexuals. This is no longer true. AIDS is most commonly transmitted through heterosexual contact—sexual intercourse between man and woman—and this is its main method of transmission throughout the world.

§ 18.10.2   The Changing Face of AIDS

As the AIDS epidemic approaches its second decade, Americans are hearing less about it, so they may assume that the worst is over. However, both the number of new patients infected with HIV (the virus that causes the AIDS disease) and the number of full-blown cases of the disease are expected to continue rising sharply for at least the next few years in the U.S. and worldwide. This is true even though there is at least one drug, AZT, that may slow the progression of the HIV infection. It is even true considering the medications available to treat certain opportunistic diseases to which people with AIDS are susceptible. The Center for Disease Control (CDC) estimates that a million Americans are infected with HIV, most of them with no symptoms and no knowledge that they are carriers. Another 7 to 9 million people around the world are also infected, according to estimates by the World Health Organization (WHO). As of the end of 1990, more than 150,000 Americans have been diagnosed with AIDS, and two-thirds of them have died. The CDC estimates that by the end of 1993 there will have been between 390,000 and 480,000 Americans diagnosed with AIDS and between 285,000 and 340,000 deaths from the disease.

"The disease is becoming a generalized fact of American life, rather than the burden of well-defined risk groups," according to the National Research Council. In particular, heterosexual transmission (not via intravenous drug needles) is on the rise: though it still accounts for a relatively small percentage of cases in the U.S., such heterosexual transmission is the predominate mode of spread in most countries. Among American heterosexuals, sexual partners of IV drug users and people with multiple partners remain at greater risk. Here are some additional facts: By the year 2000, there will be 25 to 30 million people infected with HIV internationally, according to projections by WHO.

AIDS is rising sharply among American women, especially poor African Americans and Latinos. The death rate from AIDS among women aged 15 to 44 quadrupled between 1985 and 1988 and has undoubtedly continued to rise. By the year 2000, the number of new cases among women worldwide will begin to equal the number of newly diagnosed men, according to WHO estimates. As of 1990, about 700,000 infected infants had been born worldwide. Approximately 10 million infected infants will have been born by the year 2000, according to WHO. And there will be millions of uninfected orphans whose parents died from AIDS. About 6,000 infected American women gave birth in 1989 alone (and one-third of those babies born to HIV-positive mothers in the U.S. become infected).

AIDS is not just a disease of young people. Those over 50 account for about 10 percent of all cases in this country. AIDS-related symptoms are more likely to be misdiagnosed among these older people because doctors may assume that they are not at risk for the disease. Some people complain that too much money is being spent on AIDS research and care, pointing out that many more people die from heart disease and cancer. While more money should indeed by spent on research into heart disease and cancer, AIDS remains a priority because it is contagious and is one of the leading causes of death among young people. Moreover, the comparison between these diseases is not valid, since AIDS research is starting from scratch, whereas much of the basic research into heart disease and cancer has been continuing for decades. Furthermore, the information scientists are gaining from their studies into AIDS has important implications for research involving cancer and other diseases.

Researchers have discovered that it takes 12 to 15 weeks to develop the HIV antibody. During that time the only symptom might be a minor case of the flu which might go away. You will at that point be an infected carrier of the HIV virus, but may not be sick. People are highly infectious at this time. It may take several months or several years, but gradually you will have a reduced natural immunity and then you will start getting generalized symptoms which include swollen glands, night sweats, fevers, and weight loss. Then toward the end of the disease or when the disease is diagnosed, you will develop a progressive neurological disorder. Eventually, you will die; it is only a matter of how long your immune system can last, how much treatment you get, and how you are treated. This is true because the more illnesses you get, the less likely are your chances of longevity and survival.

The virus lives in very small amounts of saliva. If somebody was to bite you but not break the skin it is fairly clear that you would not get the disease; it would be very rare. But if the person had blood in their mouth mixed in with the saliva and broke the skin of the individual, there would be a distinct possibility of transmission. This scenario happened in New Jersey when a prisoner bit a corrections officer and the prisoner was sentenced for attempted murder. The case is now under appeal.

As for "safe" bodily fluids, tears may be considered among them. Also, urine is not of concern but if the person was kicked in the groin or received a seat belt injury in a motor vehicle accident there could be particles of blood in the urine, so infection control would be very prudent for this body fluid. For feces, the same holds true. Feces by itself does not harbor the virus as we know it today, but then again we do not know exactly what is going on in the individual's system, whether the person has hemorrhoids, bleeding somewhere in the body or has something causing blood in the feces. Furthermore, hepatitis lives in all these body fluids.

Hepatitis throughout the United States each year infects 12,000 hospital care workers of which 200 hundred die. Thus, there is a sustained risk in being unprotected and also getting involved with other people's bodily fluids. Whether it be AIDS, hepatitis or whatever, precaution is the key word. The virus is transmitted by these four other body fluids: blood, semen, vaginal secretions, and breast milk. A woman could deliver a baby HIV free, but later on during breast feeding, the baby could pick up the virus from breast milk. Any body fluid that is in the body, be it cerebral spinal fluid, synovial fluid, or the fluid around the heart, is also a highly contaminated fluid if the person is HIV positive. So again, the rule of thumb is anytime you are doing anything with any individual and there are any body fluids, take full precautions.

Among the common AIDS-related illnesses is a type of skin cancer which is mostly found in gay males. Keep your eyes open for any signs of this illness. Also, pneumonia is common in AIDS patients. This is usually the illness that takes the patient out; the patient may have several bouts or she might have one bout which becomes fatal. Furthermore, tuberculosis is coming back in the United States in epidemic proportions and is directly related to cases of AIDS—especially in New Jersey. Another possible illness is a yeast infection in the mouth, thrush, or trachea. This will not be life-threatening but it is very uncomfortable for the person with the disease and also a sign that they have cancer on the roof of the mouth and need extensive dental treatment.

The chronic symptoms of the AIDS disease are swollen glands in three places: under the neck, under the arm pits, and in the groin. The patient will also experience unexplained weight loss—called a "slim disease" in many parts of the world. There will be chronic and persistent fever and diarrhea for a month or more, resulting in the huge amount of body fluids lost. The most important symptoms for the field officer to remember are fatigue, night sweats, and yeast infections in the mouth and throat. If you were to arrest a person with dementia you may think that he or she is under the influence of alcohol or drugs. The person may not be able to understand you if you are giving commands such as "turn around and put your hands behind your head." The person may not understand why you are hand cuffing them; they might be agitated; they may experience memory loss. Remember that AIDS is a neurological impairment; therefore, it should be distinguished from intoxication or chemical impairment. Try to make this distinction when you are following arrest procedures. The disease is mainly a sexually transmitted disease whether it be between male and female, male and male, or female and female.

If, as a police officer, you are called to deliver a child or to assist in delivery, remember that the amniotic fluid and the fluid on the baby from the placenta may be infected with the HIV virus. You would not want to get this in your eyes, in your face—especially near your nose where there are a lot of surface blood vessels—in your mouth, or on unprotected skin that may have a small cut. Also exercise precautions with food—especially around prisoners. There was an incident in New Jersey where a prisoner bled into an officer's coffee while the officer left the room and the officer came back and drank the coffee; the prisoner then said he gave the officer AIDS. Of course, the heat of the coffee killed the AIDS virus because the AIDS virus is very fragile and it dies from heat immediately. But still the officer went through a so-called "health period" until he was to find out the individual did not have the disease. Thus, you should be wary of food stuff around prisoners and eat where you believe your food will be free from contamination. Despite these precautions, when dealing with prisoners or responding to calls, treat everybody the same regardless of their sex, race, social, or economic status. There should be no difference because you don't know who has the disease and who doesn't.

It might be noted here that one other concern among officers is for their K-9 dogs. It may be thought that K-9 dogs can get AIDS from biting someone with the disease. However, animals cannot get human AIDS and cannot transmit it to one another or to human beings.

§ 18.10.3 Infection Control Procedures
Given the many concerns of interpersonal activity and the spread of AIDS, the Center for Disease Control (CDC) has promulgated guidelines for the prevention of HIV transmission in the workplace. These guidelines are relevant to police officers and narcotic officers. Police officers should follow these control procedures.

—avoid needle sticks and other sharp instrument injuries;

—hypodermic needles should be placed in an impervious bag, tagged and marked for evidence;

—use a mask when administering rescue breathing or CPR;

—wear gloves when contact with blood or body fluids is likely;

—use disposable shoe coverings if considerable blood contamination is encountered;

—keep all cuts and open wounds covered with clean bandages;

—avoid smoking, eating, drinking, nail biting, and all hand-to-mouth, hand-to-nose, and hand-to-eye actions while working in areas contaminated with blood or bodily fluids;

—wash hands thoroughly with soap and water after removing gloves and after any contact with blood or bodily fluids;

—clean up any spills of blood or bodily fluids thoroughly and promptly, using a 1:10 household bleach dilution;

—clean all possible contaminated surfaces and areas with a 1:10 household bleach dilution; and

—place all possibly contaminated clothing and other items in clearly identified impervious plastic bags.

§ 18.10.4   Searches and Evidence Handling

Although the risk of HIV infection from being cut or punctured by contaminated needles or other sharp instruments appears to be very low, many criminal justice personnel are concerned about such incidents. Cuts, needlesticks, and puncture wounds might be sustained by officers while searching suspects, motor vehicles, or cells, or while handling evidence in a variety of settings. There is particular concern regarding searches of areas where sharp objects may be hidden from view—such as pockets and spaces beneath car seats. The following precautionary measures will help to minimize the risk of infection:

—whenever possible, ask suspects to empty their own pockets;

—whenever possible, use long-handled mirrors to search hidden areas;

—if it is necessary to search manually, always wear protective gloves and feel very slowly and carefully;

—use puncture-proof containers to store sharp instruments and clearly marked plastic bags to store other possibly contaminated items; and

—use tape—never metal staples—when packaging evidence.

Rubber gloves are currently the only type of gloves suitable for conducting searches. Although they can provide some protection against sharp instruments, rubber gloves are not, however, puncture-proof. Moreover, there is a direct tradeoff between levels of protection and manipulability. In other words, the thicker the gloves, the more protection they provide, but the less effective they are in locating objects. Agencies should select the thickness of glove which provides the best balance of protection and search efficiency.

§ 18.10.5   Orange County Program

With regard to the issue of puncture wounds and bodily fluids received by police officers, a program has been developed by Orange County, California that originally came from San Francisco and is also being used in New Jersey. In some cases of receiving wounds or fluids, it is known that the person has AIDS. Yet, in other cases—such as an abrupt physical confrontation—the person takes off and is unidentified. In these cases, because of confidentiality laws in some states, you cannot get the suspect tested for AIDS. In response to these cases, the Orange County program has been established; it offers the police officer the drug AZT or Retrovau for 40 days. In this 40 day period, the AIDS virus will not replicate and the person will be so-called "free" of the disease. This treatment is, essentially, chemotherapy. It should also be noted that the AZT is fully experimental even though it has been accepted by the FDA for treatment of people with AIDS. It causes a lot of side effects such as anemia, upset stomach, and nausea; but, luckily, officers who undertake this treatment will only experience these effects for 40 days.

Since a cure for AIDS is not likely to be developed for some time, police officers must take utmost precaution when they are in the field or on the street. It is important for an officer to understand the basics of infection control—putting barriers between your skin and someone else's as well as washing thoroughly. To protect ourselves, we have to go back to the basics and practice infection control at all times—especially since we are among the public on a regular basis. For more information about AIDS: The U.S. Public Health Service operates the National AIDS Hotline 24 hours a day, 7 days a week. Call 1-800-342-AIDS.

References

Drug Enforcement Administration. "LSD Manufacture: Illegal LSD Production." LSD in the United States. Washington, D.C.: U.S. Department of Justice, 1995.

----------. Narcotics Investigators Manual. Washington, D.C.: U.S. Department of Justice.

Peace Officers Research Association of California PORAC Law Enforcement News 24. 2 (February, 1992).

Smith, Richard M. "The Drug Crisis." Newsweek, 16 June 1986, p.15.

International Narcotic Enforcement Officers Association. International Drug Report. Albany, N.Y.: INECA, January, 1990.

CHAPTER 19

DRUG TRAFFICKING, TERRORISM AND ORGANIZED CRIME

§ 19.1 INTRODUCTION

The illegal drug market in the United States is one of the most profitable in the world. As such, it attracts the most ruthless, sophisticated, and aggressive drug traffickers. Drug law enforcement agencies face an enormous challenge in protecting the country's borders. Each year, according to the U.S. Customs and Border Protection, 60 million people enter the United States on more than 675,000 commercial and private flights. Another 6 million come by sea and 370 million by land. In addition, 116 million vehicles cross the land borders with Canada and Mexico. More than 90,000 merchant and passenger ships dock at U.S. ports. These ships carry more than 9 million shipping containers and 400 million tons of cargo. Another 157,000 smaller vessels visit our many coastal towns. Amid this voluminous trade, drug traffickers conceal cocaine, heroin, marijuana, MDMA, and methamphetamine shipments for distribution in U.S. neighborhoods.

§ 19.2 PATTERNS OF ORGANIZED CRIME

There is no single drug problem; rather, there are several separate drug problems, each interacting with and affecting the others. Similarly, there is no single pattern in the structure and operation of drug trafficking organizations. These organizations vary widely in size, sophistication, area of operation, clientele, and product. They have differing degrees of vertical and horizontal integration, differing propensities to violence, and differing patterns of interaction with other organizations.

On the other hand, drug trafficking organizations share the obvious characteristic that they are all engaged in some way in illicit activity; therefore, they do not have access to and are not subject to the normal channels of production, distribution, sales, finance, taxation, regulation, and contract enforcement that mold and shape both the playing field and the players in the legitimate world of commerce. However, these "businesses" are subject to the same economic laws of supply and demand, the same need for efficiency in operation, and the same need for a set of rules by which to operate as are other business operations.

Thus, drug traffickers must operate outside of the normal financial and legal structures of commerce while simultaneously remaining subject to all the market and social pressures which that structure normally accommodates and ameliorates. Understanding this dichotomy is one of the keys to understanding the nature of drug trafficking organizations. They must re-create the structures of the legitimate world of commerce—which they do with astonishing fidelity—yet they are skewed by the constraints and imperatives of the illicit nature of their activities.

Chapter 19

On the one hand, large, well-established drug trafficking organizations may have a board of directors, a CEO, and a bureaucracy that are disciplined and whose functions and benefits mirror those of executives and middle-level management in a modern corporation, complete with expense accounts, bonuses, and even "company" cars. On the other hand, the normal commercial concept of contracts, in which disputes are adjudicated by an impartial judiciary and restitution is almost always of a financial nature, is twisted into a system where the rule of law is replaced by the threat of violence and retribution. The very word "contract" is often used by drug trafficking organizations as a synonym for "death sentence."

Although there is no single type of organizational structure that serves to define major drug trafficking organizations, there are a few well-defined patterns. There are the major international, vertically integrated trafficking groups, which are best exemplified by the Colombian cartels. There are also groups such as the outlaw motorcycle gangs, which operate domestically and tend to have smaller, less sophisticated operations: lines of supply are shorter, bank accounts are fewer, and the quantities of drugs transported are not as great. Then there are city-based drug operations such as the California street gangs, which have even less sophisticated organizational structures at the management end, but which have extensive sales networks of low-level operatives, many of whom work directly on the street and who are primarily involved in local distribution and the retail sale aspect of trafficking.

A feature common to many of the largest organizations is an ability to tap alternative sources of supply and to adapt readily to changing conditions. Thus, the Colombian cartels can buy their coca leaf or paste in Peru, Bolivia, Ecuador, or in Colombia itself. When Turkish authorities clamped down on the illicit cultivation of opium-producing poppies, drug organizations shifted productions to the Golden Triangle region of Southeast Asia and to the mountainous regions on both sides of the Afghanistan-Pakistan border. This flexibility enables the major traffickers to regroup and to redirect a part of their operations without disrupting the whole.

In certain ways, the Colombian cartels are on the cutting edge of international technology. They are capable of operating easily across international borders, and the fluidity of their structures results in the ability to form joint ventures and transient limited partnership arrangements among themselves and with other groups for specific goals.

The broader organizations, like large legitimate businesses, have grown so large because they are good at what they do. They usually do not make careless errors; they do not take unnecessary risks. Moreover, their leaders are well aware of the advantages of insulating themselves and the upper echelons of their organizations from those who actually carry out the risk-taking activities involved in the enterprise.

The predilection for dealing in cash and for getting that cash into the legitimate economy so that it can be translated into legitimate goods and services is a characteristic that pervades the organized drug trafficking world—whatever the size, area of operation, or structure of the organization. This propensity creates problems for drug traffickers, problems that become increasingly hard to deal with as the organization grows. The need to "launder" large amounts of "dirty" money is the Achilles' heel of most large drug trafficking organizations.

There is so much cash involved in large, illicit drug trafficking operations that tracking the proceeds of such activities is often a more fruitful investigative endeavor than tracking the underlying criminal activities. Their ill-gotten wealth is the one part of their activity from which even the most cautious of drug kingpins will probably not isolate themselves. It is often through the tracking of their attempts to "launder" cash that the highest-level operatives in these organizations are identified and brought to final justice. In fact, monetary operations are such an overriding concern of drug trafficking organizations that an entire section of this chapter is devoted to exploring the mechanisms attendant to this aspect of the drug trafficking world.

Diverse groups traffic and distribute illegal drugs. Criminal groups operating from South America smuggle cocaine and heroin into the United States via a variety of routes, including land routes through Mexico, maritime routes along Mexico's east and west coasts, sea routs through the Caribbean, and international air corridors. Furthermore, criminal groups operating from neighboring Mexico smuggle cocaine, heroin, methamphetamine, amphetamine, and marijuana into the United States. These criminal groups have smuggled heroin and marijuana across the Southwest Border and distributed them throughout the United States since the 1970s. In addition to distributing cocaine and methamphetamine in the West and Midwest, these Mexico-based groups now are attempting to expand the distribution of those drugs into eastern U.S. Markets.

Likewise, the use of the drug 3, 4-methylenedioxymethamphetamine (MDMA), also known on the street as "Ecstasy," has increased at an alarming rate in the United States over the last several years. Israeli and Russian drug trafficking syndicates and Western Europe-based drug traffickers are the principal traffickers of MDMA worldwide, (which is primarily manufactured clandestinely in Western Europe), and this drug is smuggled into the United States by couriers via commercial airlines, as well as through the use of express package carriers. Finally, criminal groups based in Southeast and Southwest Asia smuggle heroin into the United States. Using New York City as a major distribution hub, these criminal groups move heroin up and down the eastern seaboard and into the Midwest.

Besides these criminal groups based abroad, domestic organizations cultivate, produce, manufacture, or distribute illegal drugs such as marijuana, methamphetamine, phencyclidine (PCP), and lysergic acid diethyamide (LSD). By growing high-potency sinsemilla, domestic cannabis growers provide marijuana that easily competes with other illegal drugs. With demand for methamphetamine remaining high, especially in the West and Midwest, so, too, does the number of illicit laboratories that supply methamphetamine to a growing number of addicts. Additionally, a small number of chemists manufacture LSD that is subsequently distributed primarily to high school and college students throughout the United States.

§ 19.3 PRINCIPAL DRUG TRAFFICKING ORGANIZATIONS
§ 19.3.1 Colombian Drug Cartels

The Colombian drug cartels are prime examples of the large, international, vertically-integrated trafficking groups. The major elements of this type of organization are present in the Colombian cartels. They are structured in what can be characterized as an onion-like layering of organizational power, with kingpins at the center, directing operations but insulated by layer upon layer of protective subordinate operatives, until one reaches the outside layer, the skin of the organization. Here are found the individuals who deal directly with the production, supply, and sale of the illicit product: the growers, the smugglers, the small-time distributors, and the street pushers. Nurturing and tending this structure are the providers of services: the accountants, the chemists, the lawyers, the paid politicians, and the corrupt customs officials who help to support the organization and who gain sustenance from it while never fully comprehending its entire scope or true nature. Here, the operatives' services are blindly given and easily replaced.

There are four principal cartels operating out of Colombia. The two largest, the Medellin and the Cali cartels, most closely approximate the model sketched above. These cartels are named after, respectively, Colombia's second and third largest cities, in which they are based. Between them they control approximately 70 percent of the cocaine processed in Colombia and supply 80 percent of the cocaine distributed in the United States. These cartels act as true cartels in the classic sense that they attempt, through collusion, to set prices and to eliminate any effective competition.

The Colombian cartels not only attempt to limit competition by making agreements to divide market segments, they also use wealth and force to corrupt and intimidate those government officials and law enforcement agencies charged with the tasks of shutting down their operations and bringing their members to justice. In Colombia, these coercive tactics have been widely used. When public officials cannot be bought, they are subjected to threats of violence. If this does not work, they are often assassinated. This intimidation is not restricted to government personnel. Business and community leaders, journalists, and anyone else who might pose a threat to their operations are subject to either the lure of corruption or the threat of violence.

Evidently, these tactics have been successful in Colombia, where the cartels are becoming more accepted and their employees, among the more well-paid in the society, are vesting themselves with the trappings of middle-class life. Cartel chiefs control most of the modern office buildings in the city of Medellin and many of the retail establishments in the El Poblado section, where most of them live.

Drug Trafficking, Terrorism and Organized Crime

The Medellin cartel is generally thought to be the strongest of the Colombian cartels. It was formed in the early 1980s by four major Colombian traffickers: Jorge Luis Ochoa-Vasquez, Pablo Emilio Escobar-Gaviria, Jose Gonzalo Rodriguez-Gacha, and Carlos Enrique Lehder-Rivas. Part of the impetus for the formation of this organization was the need to combat kidnapping gangs who had targeted the families of wealthy Colombian drug traffickers and businessmen.

Among the cartels, the Medellin cartel, directed by the late Pablo Escobar and others, has the most sophisticated organization. There are close ties to Colombian business interests and strong "home-office" control over overseas operations. Regular fax transmission links are maintained, and managers are sent, on a rotating basis, to supervise operations in the United States.

Jose Rodriquez, who operates out of the city of Pacho, about 80 miles from Medellin, has emerged as, perhaps, the most powerful of the Medellin cartel leaders. This development was, no doubt, facilitated by the apprehension and eventual conviction, in June 1988, of one of the cartels' other founders, Carlos Ledher. He was convicted of charges brought in the Middle District of Florida and sentenced to life imprisonment with no chance of parole.

Jose Rodriguez's organization differs slightly from those of his colleagues in the Medellin cartel. He maintains direct supervision of his transportation and distribution networks. He has representatives in South Florida and Southern California who are in charge of receiving, inventory control, accounts receivable, and general organizational support. Unlike the representatives of the Pablo Escobar group, who worked on commission, Rodriguez's U.S. representatives work on straight salary. They work regular business hours, wear suits and ties, and are instructed to keep a low profile.

Of the three other major Colombian organizations, the Cali cartel, begun in the late 1970s and early 1980s, comes closest to rivaling the Medellin cartel in wealth and influence. The Cali cartel works out of the Colombian cities of Cali and Buenaventura, and once worked closely with the Medellin cartel, dividing up trading areas and engaging in joint operations. This close working relationship has deteriorated to the point where, since 1988, the Medellin and Cali cartels have been engaged in a vicious trade war with one another, as well as with other cocaine trafficking organizations. For instance, a tacit agreement of 10 years standing, giving the bulk of the New York City cocaine trafficking distribution to the Cali cartel, was breached, as tons of cocaine were shipped directly into that market by the Medellin organization. In other areas, such as Miami, which has always been considered an open trading area, the two organizations have jockeyed violently for a more prominent position.

In 1995, the arrest of six of the seven top leaders of the Cali mafia represented a real blow to the most sophisticated organized crime syndicate in history. The Colombian National Police, in cooperation with the DEA and other U.S. agencies, tracked down the mafia leaders. The

Cali drug lords were indicted in the United States on drug charges. However, Colombia no longer allows extradition of its citizens due to the Cali cartel's influence in getting the extradition policy changed (DEA 1995). The U.S. government indicted dozens of operatives in the United States and Latin America along with six lawyers and the cartel's Colombian bosses. Thirty defendants, including four lawyers, pleaded guilty to lesser charges. In May, 1997, two American lawyers, who represented the drug leaders, faced trial in Miami on conspiracy and racketeering charges related to cocaine smuggling by the Cali cartel. Thirty-six defendants are fugitives outside of the United States (<u>Orlando Sentinel</u>).

The Bogota cartel has kept a much lower profile than the two major cartels described above. This organization seems to have been adept at buying police protection in Colombia. Originally a smuggling organization dealing in a wide variety of contraband, it entered the drug trafficking world through contacts with American criminal organizations—notably those connected with Miami—and Caribbean associates of the notorious Meyer Lansky group. By networking, leaders of the Bogota cartel have taken pains to become well-connected politically in Colombia. They have used their wealth to buy land and have set up processing plants near growing areas in eastern Colombia in an attempt to become more vertically integrated.

The North Atlantic Coast cartel is the smallest and least cohesive of the four major Colombian trafficking organizations. It is based mainly, as its name suggests, in Colombia's coastal cities—notably Cartagena, Barranquilla, Santa Marta, and Rio Hacha. Like the Bogota cartel, it was originally a smuggling organization. It graduated from marijuana to cocaine when it began providing fixed-fee shipping services to the Medellin and Bogota cartels. Operations were established in Miami, Jacksonville, Gainesville, Atlanta, New York, Boston, Los Angeles, and San Diego to support the cartels' efforts. Today, a major portion of the North Atlantic Coast cartel's activity is centered on providing smuggling and money laundering services for the other cartels.

All of these cartel operations working in the United States have been characterized by a propensity for violence that has not been seen in the American underworld since the bootleg days of Prohibition in the 1920s and early 1930s. Similar to the operations performed in their home bases in Colombia, the cartels have attempted to use their wealth and powers of intimidation as leverage to corrupt and intimidate American law enforcement personnel, public officials, and members of the financial and business community whose cooperation or complicity would expedite the illicit activities of the cartels. Likewise, the cartels have not been loath to back up their threats of violence with action. They have murdered informers and government witnesses, put out "contracts" on law enforcement personnel, and engaged in violent wars for "territory," which have produced record homicide rates in American cities from Washington, D.C. to San Diego, California.

By corrupting public officials in such places as the Bahamas, the Turks and Caicos Islands, and Panama, the cartels have been able, over the years, to develop a network of "safe haven" transshipment points. Using these points as stopover and staging areas, the Colombians found it relatively easy to transport drugs into the Southern District of Florida, sometimes using island hopping to disguise their activities and sometimes simply blending into the steady stream of legitimate traffic between the Florida coast and points south.

In the most notorious case of third country complicity in the Colombian drug traffic into the United States, Panamanian strongman Manuel Antonio Noriega was indicted for accepting payoffs from the Medellin cartel. It is alleged that Noriega provided services to the cartel that ranged from protecting a cocaine laboratory that the cartel was building in Panama, to arranging for the transshipment of intermediate chemicals needed to process cocaine, to permitting the laundering of millions of dollars through Panamanian banks.

Over the past decade, the cartels have found first the Southern District of Florida, and then the Central and Southern Districts of California, to be ideal areas in which to center their U.S. operations. These regions of the United States contain a combination of large metropolitan areas and close-by, relatively isolated rural areas with convenient landing strips. They also have long, hard-to-patrol coastlines or border areas, large transportation hubs, populations containing large numbers of transients and immigrants, a well-developed system of international banking and financial institutions, and access to sophisticated communications systems. This combination of elements has proven extremely advantageous to the cartels' operations.

In the early 1980s, for example, Florida became the point at which all cocaine trafficking roads converged. It became the cocaine capital of the United States. Miami, although a market for some of these drugs, was and is primarily a transshipment point to all areas of the United States. It also remains a banking center through which flow huge amounts of cash derived from illicit drug sales.

In the mid-1980s, as law enforcement pressure on drug traffic in South Florida grew, the cartels began to shift their transshipments through Mexico. From there, drugs could easily be transported across the border into California. Los Angeles and San Diego began to rival Miami as centers for distributing cocaine and for laundering the proceeds.

As this brief discussion indicates, the operations of the Colombian cartels, from the fields of coca cultivation in South America to the final sale of crack cocaine on a street corner in Des Moines or a schoolyard in Hartford, represent a massive production, distribution, and sales effort carried out over thousands of miles, using the nationals of various countries, the resources of several separate, coordinated organizations, and the expertise of hundreds of specialists in all aspects of drug trafficking.

This broad network allows trafficking activities to be widespread throughout the United States. The Colombian organizations operate in almost all sectors of the country, with many large urban areas serving as battlegrounds for drug wars between operatives of rival factions. Yet, even though their activities are concentrated in urban areas, they have spread to rural areas as well.

New York City has long been a central point of Colombian-dominated cocaine trafficking. This activity has been shown to extend to the Northern District of New York, to towns such as Minden, Flycreek, Fallsburgh, Coxsackie, Newburg, and Little Falls, where cocaine processing plants have been shut down by authorities. The processing plant in Minden was, purportedly, the largest in existence in North America. All of these factories had been run by a joint venture of the Medellin and Cali cartels. Furthermore, individuals tied directly to the Colombian cartels have been convicted in Minnesota in cases involving the transport of drugs through networks based in New York. Even in Massachusetts, a Colombian-controlled organization called the Triple X group was operated out of Framingham by a Colombian national. This organization had a client list of hundreds, and they kept meticulous accountings of its activities. It was run like a business, with workers in the organization receiving "company benefits" such as regular vacations (INEOA 1992).

As would be expected, the widespread success of Colombian cartels in the United States has led to massive needs for money laundering services. Thus, the Medellin cartel has affiliated itself with two groups in the State of Connecticut that provide them with money laundering services for their cocaine operations in New York City, Newark, Miami, Detroit, Chicago, Los Angeles, and San Francisco.

§ 19.3.2 La Cosa Nostra and the Sicilian Mafia

La Cosa Nostra (LCN), literally "Our Thing," was founded in the 1930s. It was an out-growth of the consolidation that occurred during a period of warfare among Italian immigrant ghetto gangs, which were created by a flood of over two million Italian immigrants in the early years of the century. The gangs were originally formed by the small number of immigrant criminals who belonged to the three major southern Italian secret societies—the Sicilian Mafia, the Neapolitan Camorra, and the Calabrian N'Drangheta. LCN soon emerged as the pre-eminent American criminal empire, distinct from its Italian antecedents.

Today, the organization has evolved from the original LCN, and consists of families which constitute formally recognized power structures within the organization. There are 25 known families, which among them have over 2,000 members and several times that many associates. The families are largely independent, local organizations joined together in a confederation that acknowledges the authority of a commission consisting of the heads of the most powerful LCN families.

Each family is led by a boss, who is supported by a principal underboss. Consiglieres or counselors, usually with significant contacts outside of the family, provide advice and mediate disputes but have no line of authority. Soldiers, the lowest-level family members, are organized into groups led by a caporegime (capo), or street boss. The structure of the various families is remarkably similar and has remained stable since LCN's early years.

Until the mid-1960s, LCN was run, on a day-to-day basis, by upper- and middle-level managers in the prime of life. Today, the seasoned upper- and middle-management level of this structure has been devastated by the government's continuous attack on LCN. The membership losses caused by this attack, and the resulting convictions, have presented LCN with a number of problems, including leadership vacancies and, as a result, operational difficulties. Within many families, a number of leaders at the caporegime level and above were simultaneously removed. This forced sudden promotions from lower, less experienced ranks, which, in turn, has led to a new breed of soldier who is greedier, who enjoys the high profile eschewed by the older capos, and who is less disciplined and more prone to violence. Because of their youth, the new middle-level leaders do not have the old, established lines of communication within the family or with other LCN families. Also, they are more willing to become involved in drug trafficking (President's Commission 1986).

From the outset, certain families have had prohibitions against drug trafficking. LCN has a tradition of not unnecessarily attracting the attention of law enforcement agencies, and older members were aware that drug trafficking would elicit a strong response from the law enforcement community. Older members also had a traditional distaste for drugs, which were considered a scourge and not a desirable LCN activity. A ban prohibiting involvement of LCN members in drug trafficking was allegedly ratified by the major LCN figures at a famous Apalachin, New York, conclave on November 14, 1957.

Despite this ban and the sentiment against involvement in drug trafficking among the older capos, individual LCN members have had a history of involvement with the importation and high-volume distribution of heroin from Southwest and Southeast Asia. Individuals found to be involved in drug violations have come from at least 19 of the 25 known families, despite official LCN opprobrium of drug trafficking.

A survey of LCN-related intelligence from the Boston FBI files indicated that, notwithstanding the family rule against involvement in drug activities, approximately 50 percent of New England LCN members have had some form of involvement in illegal drug trafficking or personal drug abuse. Observance of the prohibition is not widespread and is not enforced by the family hierarchy. Individual members and capos cannot resist the lucrative drug profits. The potential for tremendous wealth, when coupled with the changing LCN membership, has given rise to a new and potentially more violent role for the LCN in drug trafficking operations.

The most obvious drug trafficking partner for LCN is the Sicilian Mafia, which is independently active in the United States. Both groups associate and criminally interact in a number of areas of mutual interest. The Sicilian Mafia is primarily involved in international heroin trafficking and is associated with LCN in several locales, including Buffalo, Boston, New Jersey, Chicago, and Detroit.

In New York, the Sicilian Mafia conspired with LCN to import and distribute almost 4,000 pounds of heroin, and untold amounts of cocaine, over a 10-year period, realizing a 60-million-dollar profit. This famous case, popularly known as the "Pizza Connection" because many of the participants owned pizza parlors, resulted in the imprisonment of over 15 LCN/Sicilian Mafia kingpins for 20- to 45-year sentences.

Current estimates indicate that LCN and the Sicilian Mafia together are responsible for a significant portion of the total volume of heroin brought into the United States annually. Additionally, it has recently been reported that, with the assistance of LCN family members, the Sicilian Mafia is exchanging heroin for cocaine, as South American cocaine moves through the United States to Europe and heroin moves from the Middle East through Italy to the United States.

This middleman role in cocaine distribution has resulted in ties between individual LCN members and the Medellin cartel. These ad hoc relationships developed on the basis of a common desire to expand both their markets and their product lines. The relationships are generally initiated through introductions by mutual criminal associates. These relationships are rather tentative at first, but once trust has been established, extensive interaction results.

As LCN family members are involved in a broad array of criminal activities, it is realistic to expect them to further develop the avenues and methodologies to profit from the drug trade. They will not initiate direct confrontation with the Colombian or other major drug cartels. They are not in a position to, nor would they want to go head to head with the Colombians. They are, however, prepared to coexist and cooperate with the Colombian cartels and other drug-specific groups and organizations, as they have done for many years with the motorcycle gangs in the distribution of methamphetamine.

Although LCN maintains specific working relationships with certain other organized crime groups in order to fulfill its racketeering objectives, it is developing ties to South American drug trafficking cartels. The Gambino, Bufalino, and Bonanno families have strong ties to Colombian and Cuban drug cartels in the greater Miami area, providing these families with drugs for distribution in the United States. Individual LCN members work with Asian and Latin American organized crime groups and cartels that manufacture and smuggle narcotics. They also collaborate with ethnic street gangs and outlaw motorcycle gangs involved in high-risk, low-level distribution and street sales. Thus, the changing character of LCN membership and the potential profits to be realized continue to increase LCN's role in drug trafficking.

§ 19.3.3 Asian Organized Crime Groups

Within the past five years, Asian gangs have become a major force in the illicit drug market in the United States. Asian gangs, primarily of

Drug Trafficking, Terrorism and Organized Crime

Chinese origin, are operating on both coasts and have become significant players in the international drug trafficking scene. As with some other ethnic groups, Chinese Organized Crime (COC) leaders in this country have used their ties with overseas criminal organizations to assure a regular supply of whatever commodity they wish to distribute—whether the commodity is Chinese video cassettes, prostitutes, or heroin.

Since the mid-1960s, three events have had an impact on the growth of Asian organized crime in this country: the liberalization of quotas for Asian immigrants in 1965; the abatement of the Vietnam War; and the agreement between the United Kingdom and the People's Republic of China under which Hong Kong will revert to the latter in July of 1997, after more than 150 years of colonial rule.

These events wrought profound changes within Asian American society. The first two transformed conservative, insular communities, while the third may have led some of the most dangerous Hong Kong criminals to move their operations here. The Immigration and Naturalization Act of 1965 repealed restrictions on Asian immigration dating from the Chinese Exclusion Act of 1882. With the influx of immigrants from Southeast Asia, as the war in Vietnam drew to a close, the Asian American population increased dramatically. Between 1960 and 1980, the total number of Asian Americans grew from 878,000 to 3.5 million. By 1980, 91 percent of Vietnamese Americans, 66 percent of Filipino Americans, and 63 percent of Chinese Americans—but only 28 percent of Japanese Americans—had been born overseas. By then, Asian Americans had become the largest ethnic group among all immigrants in the United States (USDOJ 1989).

The increased immigration opened up the limited, rather circumscribed world of the older criminal groups. The new immigrants tended to be young; they knew little English and, like some immigrants before them, they were likely to see criminal organizations as the quickest road to advancement. In attempts to protect themselves from attacks by American-born Chinese, Chinese immigrant youth formed street gangs. Among the first were the Wah Ching in San Francisco and the Ghost Shadows in New York.

Including the street gangs, there are two primary classifications of Chinese Organized Crime groups operating in the United States today: American COC, and Triads. Hong Kong serves as the primary base of operations for the Triads. It is estimated that there are as many as 100,000 Triad members belonging to more than 50 Triads in Hong Kong. The major Triads are organized in five primary groups, the Wo Group and 14K being the largest. In Taiwan, the United Bamboo Gang boasts 1,200 members, and the Four Seasons Gang is 3,000 members strong.

The United Bamboo Gang has spread far beyond Taiwan in the 28 years since its founding. Today, the United Bamboo Gang has approximately 15,000 members worldwide. Charges filed in Houston and New York allege that Houston resident Chen Chih-Ye was the kingpin for

United Bamboo in the United States. In that role, he is alleged to have planned the murder of a California journalist, Henry Liu; conspired to import 660 pounds of heroin from Thailand to New York; and led Las Vegas gambling operations, protection schemes, and various gun and marijuana trafficking enterprises.

Traditionally, Triads have had rigid, hierarchical structures. At the apex of the organization is the Triad leader, the Shan Chu. Below the Shan Chu is the Deputy. Below the Deputy are two positions of comparable rank, the Heung Chu, the ceremonial officials, and the Sing Fung, who handles recruiting. They are joined by other senior Triad officials. Below this level are a number of "Red Poles," the enforcers and hit-men who have direct control of some operational Triad groups. At the same level as the Red Poles are a "White Paper Fan," the general administrative official, and a "Straw Sandal," who handles liaisons between and among the Triads and other groups. Ordinary members, or soldiers, comprise the remainder of the organization.

Currently, most Triads lack the traditional organizational structure. More are run by a chairman, who is usually a "Red Pole." There is also a governing central committee of six to nine members. A "White Paper Fan," as a member of the central committee, is usually the treasurer.

In its traditional origin, Chinese organized crime is similar to LCN. Like LCN, Chinese organized crime grew out of much older secret or fraternal societies which have evolved into criminal groups. The Triads originated in China during the 17th century to oppose the ruling Manchu dynasty. The organization then moved from political purposes into a variety of rackets. In the late 19th century, the Tongs (Chinese fraternal organizations) began as perfectly legitimate mutual aid societies for immigrants brought to the United States as contract railroad laborers. Today, while most American Tongs still serve legitimate business purposes, several are closely tied to organized crime.

Parallels between Chinese criminal organizations and the traditional LCN go even deeper than their historic connection to protective and fraternal societies. Both the Chinese groups and LCN place an unusually strong emphasis on family and group loyalty. They both practice retribution against those who reveal secrets to outsiders; their organizational structures are characterized by the same type of fragmentation into subgroups controlled by powerful leaders; and they have the same independence from their parent overseas organizations. Both the Chinese gangs and LCN practice the use of extortion and the corruption of public officials to promote their activities, and both gained their initial power and eminence through exploitation of large populations of non-English-speaking, innocent immigrants. Finally, both the Chinese groups and LCN have historically been involved in a broad range of criminal activities of which drug trafficking is but one part.

A much greater threat than that of the Triads is presented by the sophisticated criminal organizations that have evolved from the street gangs, for example, the Wah Ching, which is the most developed of such organizations on the West Coast. The Wah Ching's organization, with 600 to 700 members, 200 of whom are "hard-core," is extremely loose-knit and fluid. It has a central leader who is supported by four deputies under his normal control. Various deputies employ groups of Viet Ching (ethnic Chinese from Vietnam) to serve as enforcers under the direction of their lieutenants. It is believed that the Wah Ching are affiliated with the Sun Yee On Triad in Hong Kong.

In New York City, on the other hand, the street gangs are affiliated with the Tongs. The Tongs have a complex organizational structure. The organization includes co-presidents, executive officers, and a wide assortment of designated administrators and coordinators. This complex system allows for affiliations with various street gangs. For instance, the Flying Dragons Gang is affiliated with the Hip Sing Tong; the Ghost Shadows Gang is attached to the On Leong Tong; and the Tung On Gang and the Tung On Tong are both headed by the same person.

In Boston, the COC activity is dominated by the Ping On Gang, which is believed to have about 200 active members. However, the current internal functioning and degree of cohesiveness in this gang are matters of conjecture.

Since these gangs have grown, Chinese Organized Crime has expanded from Chinese gambling, extortion, pornography, and entertainment to include large-scale, international narcotics trafficking. While Chinese criminal organizations do not approach the scale of the Colombian cartels, the scope of their operations is impressive. Working with Asian nationals, Chinese American criminals are the largest importers of heroin from Southeast Asia, virtually all of it originating in the Golden Triangle at the juncture of Burma, Thailand, and Laos. The February 1989 seizure of more than 800 pounds of processed heroin in New York's Chinatown reveals the magnitude of this traffic.

Other reports from numerous areas on the East Coast underscore the growing prominence of Asian trafficking activities. Operation Bamboo Dragon in the District of Columbia (discussed later in this chapter) resulted in the arrest of 20 Asians in both the United States and Hong Kong for heroin trafficking. The Royal Hong Kong Police Narcotics Bureau described the operation as one of the most significant drug cases ever made there.

Likewise, in New York City, Chinese organizations are the dominant force in heroin trafficking, capable of smuggling loads of 10 to 50 kilograms into the city on a regular basis. In New Jersey, Chinese groups have become a major force in the importation and distribution of heroin at the highest levels. Chinese and other Southeast Asian trafficking organizations are also heavily involved in heroin trafficking in Massachusetts. In October 1988, Customs agents in Boston seized 180 pounds of heroin, the largest such seizure in New England history. The heroin had been carefully concealed in a piece of Chinese restaurant equipment—a bean sprout washer (USDOJ 1989).

Chapter 19

Like the heroin seized in Boston, most of the heroin that originates in the Golden Triangle is shipped to the West Coast of the United States via Hong Kong and such secondary transit as Singapore, Seoul, Tokyo, and Taipei. The destination is New York; from there, about half the heroin moves to other East Coast cities. Thus, Chinese criminal organizations operate mainly as shippers and wholesalers: they buy the raw product; process it; arrange for its transshipment; and, finally, turn it over to retailers. From what is known, Chinese traffickers also work through other groups, especially LCN, who distribute the product to the ultimate user.

Although the Hong Kong Triads are involved in drug trafficking, their role cannot be categorized easily. Some of the ethnic Chinese who smuggle heroin out of the Golden Triangle, and others who ship it to New York, are not affiliated with the Triads. Traffickers may be entrepreneurs who work with organizational crime groups on specific ventures, while in other cases drug trafficking is simply a means of transferring assets from Hong Kong to the United States.

To some extent, the magnitude of Chinese drug trafficking is reflected in the amount of money flowing out of Hong Kong to U.S. banks, especially those on the West Coast. However, much of this money simply represents assets that Chinese business people want to transfer to a safe haven before Hong Kong reverts to the People's Republic of China. By merely measuring the volume of foreign money entering the United States, we fail to distinguish between legitimate asset transfers and the laundering of drug money. The important point is that there is a huge and growing inflow of money from Hong Kong, primarily to banks in San Francisco, Los Angeles, and New York. This provides a wide stream in which laundered drug money inconspicuously flows. Some of these funds flow into large American commercial banks, with the rest going into some 100 Chinese-owned and operated banks. Most of these are small and cater exclusively to a Chinese American clientele; at some banks, tellers are assigned to service one or two accounts exclusively.

Traffickers in Hong Kong, Taipei, and Singapore can send funds by wire transfer or letters of credit to banks in Southern California, knowing that such transfers trigger no reporting requirements. Where such electronic transfers are impracticable, drug dealers can use Smurfs (see section on Money Laundering) to make several daily deposits under the $10,000 reporting limit. As with other regions, these transfers of drug money lead to huge surpluses at regional Federal Reserve banks. As of May 1989, the Los Angeles branch of the Federal Reserve had accumulated surpluses of approximately $4 billion (USDOJ 1989).

Compared to Colombian drug profits, more Asian-based drug money is invested in real estate than in personal property. An investigation centered in the Northern District of California positively identified one drug asset-related real estate empire. Numerous Hong Kong corporations, such as Dragonet, Ltd., and Tradewise Far East, Ltd., were found to be conducting no business in the United States other than holding title to real estate. In three instances, expensive properties held by these corporations had major drug dealers as residents. Subsequent grand jury investigations resulted in extensive seizures, numerous indictments, and, predictably, several fugitive warrants. Criminal organizations based in Asia are also investing heavily in shopping centers, apartment complexes, and office buildings. The result has been to drive up real estate prices, especially in those areas with large Asian American populations. Chinese American criminals, on the other hand, prefer investing in businesses where most transactions are based on cash: nightclubs, restaurants, travel agencies, and jewelry stores. The advantage of owning such businesses is that, besides serving as fronts for criminal activities, they are ideal for co-mingling legal and illegal funds in a way that avoids detection.

There is much that law enforcement organizations have to learn about Asian organized crime; only recently have they begun to give the problem the attention it deserves. The lack of agents with the background to infiltrate the Asian criminal organizations means that much about their operations remains unclear. It is clear, however, that the larger gangs—the Wah Ching on the West Coast, several New York gangs dominated by Tongs, and the Boston Ping On Gang—are powerful and sophisticated criminal organizations.

§ 19.3.4 Jamaican Posses

Approximately 40 Jamaican organized crime gangs, known as posses, operate in the United States, Canada, Great Britain, and the Caribbean. The combined membership of these gangs is conservatively estimated to number over 10,000, the majority of them convicted felons, illegal aliens, or both. Many of the mid- to high-level positions in the posse organizations are held by individuals who began their criminal careers in Jamaica and who are fugitives from justice there. The low-level positions in the posses are often filled by Americans, recruited primarily from black urban areas. Generally, these gangs grew out of specific geographic and political affiliations in Jamaica, but have long since become exclusively profit-oriented drug trafficking organizations.

The Jamaican posses, which began as marijuana traffickers, have been active in the United States since about 1984, and are now recognized as a major drug trafficking force. They are, perhaps, the ultimate example of stepping up to dealing lethal drugs, most notably crack cocaine. Almost all posses have connections in New York and Miami, which have large Jamaican populations.

The Jamaicans' operations are structured in a distinctive manner. For example, even more than the Colombians, the posses are vertically integrated in the United States. The operators are involved in the United States as importers, wholesalers, local distributors, retailers, and even money launderers. By excluding the middleman, the posses can substantially raise their profit margins, to the point where one posse controlling 50 crack houses can make $9 million a month.

The posses normally purchase cocaine from Colombians or Cubans in Jamaica, the Bahamas, Southern California, or South Florida—usually in small quantities of four or five kilos. Also, investigations show that

Chapter 19

Jamaican criminal groups are establishing new drug shipment routes distinct from Miami, the traditional entry point.

There are indications that Jamaicans have been entering the United States by wading across the Rio Grande into Texas and that these groups may be linked to Colombian drug suppliers arrested in the Houston area. In one instance, 15 Haitian and Jamaican aliens had arranged to be smuggled from Belize to Juarez, Mexico; from there, they would enter the United States with the help of a Jamaican involved in drug trafficking.

Distribution of the drugs is directed by key posse members at "controlling points." Drugs, drug paraphernalia, and weapons are stored at "stash houses," which supply the street-level distribution points known as "crack houses," "gate houses," or "dope houses." Those at the controlling points are responsible for re-supplying the street-level distribution points, usually located in apartments or rented houses.

Crack houses operated by Jamaican posses are often sophisticated distribution operations. They are shuttered from outside view, often with blackened windows. They have extensive defensive mechanisms in place, ranging from specially constructed entrance barricades composed of two-by-fours (known as "New York Stops") to lookouts using walkie-talkies to warn of police raids. Armed guards, or "managers," located at the crack houses, also keep intruders or law enforcement personnel from entering. Some Jamaican posses have reportedly told their guards to shoot any law enforcement officer who raids their crack house. The Northern District of Texas reports that, in many cases, a gun is held to a customer's head until the drug transaction is completed, in case the customer is found to be a troublemaker, an informant, or an undercover agent. In addition, the "houses" are usually equipped with secret hiding places for drugs and have ladders or other emergency exit routes. To frustrate police attempts at identifying trafficking locations, the crack house's site is often changed.

However, the posses do not restrict their operations to crack houses. In some cases, even more temporary quarters will do. Posse members in Columbus, Ohio, Frederick, Maryland, and Wilmington, North Carolina set up retail distribution networks in economy motels, usually located near interstate highways. It is believed that these operations were a form of market testing; where the market proved lucrative, the Jamaicans subsequently leased rental properties for use as crack houses.

Unlike most drug organizations, Jamaican posses often do their own money laundering. They have used Western Union for wire transfers of money, purchased legitimate businesses (restaurants, auto repairs, and record shops) as fronts, and bought real estate for quick resale. In one such case, investigators found that a doctor at the University of Mississippi Medical Center had conspired with a Jamaican dentist to launder money through a Panamanian front company that made false loans to the Jamaican (USDOJ 1989).

Drug Trafficking, Terrorism and Organized Crime

There are further indications that Jamaican organized crime is developing working relationships with West Coast street gangs, traditional organized crime, and Colombian narcotics cartels. The exact nature of the relationships among the posses and West Coast street gangs remains unclear. It is known that Jamaican drug dealers are operating in "the Jungle," a small area in Southwest Los Angeles known for drug activity and drug-related violence, and that the Los Angeles gangs known as the Crips are moving into crack distribution markets in Kansas City, Cleveland, and Dallas, where Jamaican criminal organizations are also operating. It is also known that Jamaican criminals have had long-standing relations with Colombians, as the former buys cocaine directly from the latter.

While informants have revealed the existence and operating locations of a few specific posses, the posses usually impose a code of silence on their members. A Jamaican criminal, when arrested, will rarely discuss his posse and will even deny that such bands exist. Of the posses identified thus far, the largest and most violent are the Shower and Spangler posses. Drug wars between the Spanglers and rival gangs led to between 350 and 525 murders during the late 1980s and early 1990s, and the posses as a whole have accounted for at least 1,000 murders in the United States since 1985. In general, these and other posses have demonstrated a willingness to turn to violence and torture at the slightest provocation, which is unusual even among drug traffickers. Victims in some homicides were apparently shot in the ankles, knees, and hips before being shot in the head. It also appears that other victims were subjected to scalding hot water before being murdered and dismembered (USDOJ 1989).

The posses' violence is directed at anyone who they feel is in their way: members of their group, rival groups, individuals who interfere with their drug territories, wives, girlfriends, and even children. Even witnesses who have been interviewed by the police—but gave no evidence—have been subsequently murdered. From the perspective of the posse, this has the advantage of intimidating a whole neighborhood and discouraging anyone from cooperating with the police.

The willingness of posse members to engage police in shootouts while resisting arrest makes them even more dangerous. They have not hesitated to issue contracts on the lives of police and federal agents who they feel are disrupting their business, even to the point of offering a $25,000 "award" in Virginia to anyone who killed a police officer. Jamaican criminals have attempted to entrap police by identifying their telephone and beeper numbers and luring them to staged shootouts.

From the time they enter the United States illegally to the point where they launder their drug profits, members of Jamaican organized crime are adept at throwing law enforcement officials off their track. This can involve anything from substituting photos or names on valid passports to forging Social Security cards, birth certificates and INS "green cards." In the course of breaking up a fraudulent document ring in Kingston, Jamaican police discovered electronic typewriters similar to those used by the Jamaican and U.S. Governments, as well as a variety of forged documents for each of the localities that Jamaican criminals wished to penetrate. In another case, an investigation in Pennsylvania exposed a veteran of the State Police who had been selling blank driver's license applications to members of the Shower posse, who then entered any name or date of birth that they wished (USDOJ 1989).

Equipped with multiple identities and adept at all types of identification and passport fraud, Jamaican posse members are extremely mobile; they are world travelers. In one case, the same passport was used by 15 different posse members, using the same name but with a different picture each time. Posse members are able to travel freely between the United States, Mexico, and Commonwealth countries such as Canada. This mobility is a distinct advantage when law enforcement personnel are often bound by the constraints of territorial and jurisdictional boundaries.

Although Jamaican organized crime is concentrated in metropolitan areas, it is starting to move outward. The experience of the Northern District of West Virginia is a case in point. After Jamaicans arrived in the Martinsburg area in the early 1980s as migrant workers to pick fruit at harvest time, many stayed on to peddle cocaine and crack. After a 1986 raid in which authorities closed down the Martinsburg operation, much of the street action moved to Charles Town, 16 miles away. In the spring of 1988, federal, state and local enforcement officers conducted a raid and made a series of arrests of suspected street-level crack dealers in Charles Town. What they found was a well-run operation, in which dealers were selling cocaine in gram quantities at the street level, with the crack running at a purity of 90 percent or better. These dealers received their supplies from couriers shuttling between Jamaican gangs in Miami, New York, and Washington, D.C.

Crack began appearing in Roanoke, Virginia (population 90,000), in the second half of 1988. The abundance of crack there was directly attributable to an influx of Jamaican nationals. The 25 to 40 Jamaican nationals residing in Roanoke were identified as being associated with the Jamaican Shower posse in New York City. They purchased guns in Virginia and exchanged them for crack from New York (USDOJ 1989).

The posses' mobility, their large networks of distributors and couriers, and their persistent use of aliases compel enforcement agents to use innovative techniques in investigating them. Among these techniques are the review of Western Union wire transfers, telephone toll analyses, and the tracing of firearms recovered from Jamaican criminals. An increasingly useful information source is the Federal Bureau of Prisons. The Bureau has computerized listings on the approximately 800 Jamaican criminals who have passed through the federal prison system, about a quarter of whom are still in custody. The violent nature of Jamaican posses and the threat they pose to security have led the Bureau of Prisons to attempt to set up a data base tracking links between Jamaican inmates and specific posses.

In December of 1987, the Jamaican Parliament ratified a treaty that broadened the category of offenders found in Jamaica who could be returned to the United States. Under the terms of the treaty, Jamaica must extradite fugitives wanted in the United States for any offense that would also be a crime in Jamaica. The treaty also covers fugitives wanted in the United States for conspiring to traffic in narcotics, a charge not extraditable before the treaty was ratified. The treaty and the legislation that implements it also permit the extradition of offenders wanted for offenses involving the unlawful possession or use of firearms, another crime not formerly covered.

§ 19.3.5 Outlaw Motorcycle Gangs

Outlaw motorcycle gangs were first thrust upon the American culture in the 1950s, when they were portrayed romantically in a number of Hollywood films. They again achieved notoriety in the early 1970s, when members of the Hell's Angels were hired to provide "security" for the Rolling Stones at an Altamont, California rock concert that degenerated into a deadly riot.

Like the films their activities inspired, the outlaw motorcycle gangs were originally created in California. Also like these movies, the gangs have achieved national "distribution." They no longer spend their days on the road terrorizing small California towns and their nights swilling beer and working on their "hogs." Today, they are highly structured, often national, drug trafficking organizations that control most of the amphetamine manufacture and distribution in the United States. These motorcycle gangs have also developed working relationships with a number of other drug trafficking organizations.

The Hell's Angels is the oldest, largest, and best known of the outlaw motorcycle gangs. It was founded in 1950 in Fontana, California. Throughout the 1950s and 1960s other gangs were formed. These gangs were generally structured into chapters, with a "mother" chapter and a number of subsidiary chapters. The formative years were ones of rapid growth in which gangs came and went, were absorbed and consolidated, and in which various forms of illegal activities were practiced. Even today, the gangs pursue a wide gamut of illegal activities: prostitution, burglary, rape, assault, murder, contract killings, and more sophisticated activities such as illegal banking, loan sharking, and financing of drug deals. It was not until the mid-1960s that the motorcycle gangs began to specialize in drug trafficking and to take on the highly disciplined structure that now characterizes them.

The organizational structure of the major outlaw motorcycle gangs has evolved from the "chapter" model described above to a structure resembling that of La Cosa Nostra (LCN). The national officers correspond to LCN commission members; chapter presidents perform the roles of LCN bosses; vice presidents act as underbosses; and road captains and sergeants-at-arms are the gang equivalents of caporegimes. Like LCN, these gangs operate legitimate businesses that function as fronts and/or as money laundering operations. In some parts of the United States the bikers actually work with LCN in arrangements in which the bikers control methamphetamine distribution through various LCN outlets.

Chapter 19

There are at least 500 outlaw motorcycle gangs currently operating in the United States. The four most important are the Hell's Angels, the Outlaws, the Pagans, and the Bandidos. These four gangs are national in scope and have a long record of drug trafficking.

The Hell's Angels got its start in drug trafficking in the mid-1960s, with local distribution of LSD in the San Francisco area. From this beginning, the Angels expanded into extensive trafficking in cocaine, PCP, marijuana, and methamphetamine. By the early 1970s, the Angels had moved into the clandestine manufacture of methamphetamine, an activity in which the gang is both highly skilled and highly influential. As a result of these activities, the Hell's Angels gang has grown to become the wealthiest and most powerful of the outlaw gangs. With between 500 and 600 members nationwide, the Angels' "Mother Chapter" is based in Oakland, California.

Another motorcycle gang, the Outlaws, was founded in Chicago in 1959 and later absorbed the Canadian "Satan's Choice" gang in 1977. This merger created the largest motorcycle gang in the United States and Canada, with approximately 1,200 to 1,500 members. It has 31 chapters, six of which are in Canada.

Yet another gang, the Pagans, was established in Prince George's County, Maryland, outside of Washington, D.C., in 1959. Located primarily in the Northeast, with their largest chapter in the Philadelphia area, the Pagans have structured their organization somewhat differently than the other national gangs. Instead of a geographically fixed mother chapter, a "Mother Club," composed of 13 to 18 chapter presidents, directs the Pagans' organization. There are 700 to 800 members in 44 chapters located between New York and Florida. In addition to developing a national network of drug dealers, firearms traffickers, and murderers, the Pagans appear to have ties to organized crime, particularly LCN.

Finally, the youngest of the four major criminal motorcycle gangs, the Bandidos, was established in Houston in 1966. In the 1970s, the gang expanded and eventually established chapters as far away as South Dakota and Washington State. Now, the Bandidos have approximately 500 members and a network of 2,000 associates.

Each of the major gangs specializes in some particular aspect of the drug trade. For example, the Bandidos are heavily involved in methamphetamine manufacturing, distribution, and sales. The Pagans dominate the PCP and methamphetamine trade in the Northeast, while the Outlaws, through their Florida chapters, which may be involved with Cuban and Colombian suppliers, are engaged in cocaine trafficking. The Outlaws also traffic in a bogus form of "Valium," manufactured in illegal Canadian laboratories and distributed from a base in Chicago.

As their structures have become more sophisticated, and their activities have become more widespread, the bikers have developed more sophisticated ways of defending themselves and their activities. The tire chain and the rumble have been replaced by more streamlined methods. The Bandidos and the Outlaws carry tape recorders to record conversations with any law enforcement officers who might confront them. They attempt to get the officers to make statements that will contaminate any case brought against them and record the conversations for later use by their lawyers. The major gangs have begun to exchange computerized information on law enforcement officers and their informants. They have also been known to place operatives in court houses, prisons, and police stations, to gather intelligence on law enforcement operations and planning.

As for their "home base," gang clubhouses vary in location and layout. They may be located on farms, in the center city, or in residential areas. While the clubhouses are used for business meetings, partying, and working on motorcycles, they must also be tightly secured against unexpected police raids or attacks by rival gangs. Some gangs place their houses under 24-hour guard, with steel-reinforced doors and standard chain-link fences topped with barbed wire as a perimeter defense. In many cases, the house itself is also protected by concrete cinderblock walls with built-in gun ports. Guard dogs often roam in the area between the fences.

Inside the clubhouses, other security measures are taken, including wooden or steel shutters that close from the inside, exterior walls fitted with sheets of armor plating, and electronic security equipment, including tracking devices, closed-circuit TV cameras, and telephone eavesdropping units. Even this is not enough to satisfy some gangs' security concerns; some have actually planted poisonous snakes in dresser drawers, kitchen cabinets, or boxes, ready to strike out at whoever rummages in their hiding place.

Therefore, the major outlaw motorcycle gangs are extremely difficult to infiltrate. Also, like Jamaican criminals, gang members go to considerable lengths to conceal their identities, using special "street names" in their everyday dealings. By forcing candidates to engage in bizarre rituals or commit major crimes, thus binding them to membership for life, and by playing on their fears of certain reprisal if they cooperate with the authorities, the gangs have largely succeeded both in screening out undercover agents and in tightening their grip on members' loyalty. Members are almost never allowed to leave a major biker gang alive.

However, law enforcement officials have had some success in "turning" members who fear that their days within the gang are numbered. They have also exploited intra- and inter-gang rivalries to gain information on gang activities. Law enforcement pressure on the West Coast has succeeded in causing the Hell's Angels to set up methamphetamine manufacturing businesses in other areas such as western Missouri. However, much more must be done before the goal of breaking up these gangs can be achieved.

It is not only the four major outlaw motorcycle gangs that are involved in drug trafficking operations. There are a number of local and regional motorcycle groups that are deeply involved in drug trafficking in their areas. These gangs often work closely with each other and with the major gangs to produce and distribute drugs. For example, members of the "Grim Reapers" motorcycle gang operated as a network of drug dealers in the Galesburg/Peoria, Illinois area. Reportedly, they were responsible for 80 percent of the cocaine trafficked in the Galesburg area and for a majority of the cocaine distributed around Peoria. One chapter of the gang also distributed methamphetamine in both areas. They received their cocaine from gang members located in California and Florida. The methamphetamine was manufactured by two members of the Bandido motorcycle gang in Texas and by members of the Satan Brothers gang in Oklahoma. In western Tennessee, outlaw motorcycle gangs involved in methamphetamine and other drug trafficking, besides the local chapter of the Hell's Angels, include the Outlaws, the Saints, the Iron Horsemen, and the Road Barons. Operating in the Middle District of Alabama are the Devil's Disciples, the Ghost Riders, the Peacemakers, the Rattlers, and the Iron Cross (USDOJ 1989).

§ 19.3.6 California Street Gangs

In addition to spawning the outlaw motorcycle gang phenomenon, California is home to one of the most dangerous and menacing developments in drug trafficking: the large-scale organized street gang. These gangs first appeared in Los Angeles in the late 1960s. Their activities have escalated from the instigation of neighborhood violence to large-scale drug trafficking throughout the United States.

Although there are many smaller independent gangs and minor organized gang groups in the Los Angeles area, the most successful and dangerous California street gangs are divided into two major organizations, the Crips and the Bloods. Each of these organizations is composed of numerous smaller gangs called "sets." It is estimated that there are approximately 190 Crips sets and 65 Bloods sets. Law enforcement officials believe that these approximately 250 sets have a combined membership of nearly 25,000.

The sets are generally geographically based. Some derive their names from local street names: "Five-Deuce Hoover Crips" (52nd and Hoover Streets) or "110 Main Street Gangster Crips" (110th and Main Streets), while others have descriptive names of arcane derivations— "Rollin 60 Crips," "Blood Stone Villains," and "Neighborhood Bloods."

The sets are structured along lines of seniority and function. They have caste-like subdivision within each set, notably (1) original gang members (O.G.); (2) gangsters, the hard-core members, whose ages range from 16 to 22; (3) baby gangsters, who are between nine and 12; and (4) in some gangs, tiny gangsters, who are even younger. While some age groups go to the late 1920s and early 1930s, the most violent and active members are those between 14 and 18, many of them "wannabes" who want to prove themselves in order to be accepted by other gang members and who are precisely the ones most useful as soldiers in gang activities.

Drug Trafficking, Terrorism and Organized Crime

The Crips and the Bloods organizations are primarily involved in PCP and crack cocaine trafficking. They have developed clandestine laboratories for drug manufacture in the Los Angeles area and have become adept at seeking out secluded areas where their manufacturing activities will be undetected. They have also developed supply sources for the constituent chemicals needed to fuel their production activities.

Since the advent of crack cocaine, the manufacture and distribution networks in the Los Angeles area have expanded tremendously. Crack is increasingly the drug of choice for the majority of users there. The usual arrangement is for an O.G. or former gang member to establish relations with Colombian or Mexican suppliers of powder cocaine HCL. The O.G. is at the head of the local distribution network and receives the cocaine either on consignment or with an up-front payment. First, he turns over multi-kilogram quantities of cocaine HCL for processing into crack, or rock cocaine. The newly produced crack is then given out in multi-ounce quantities by the supplier to street distributors, to be sold to the end user. The street distributors typically carry only small amounts, concealing the rest in convenient locations from which they can quickly replenish their stock.

California street gang sellers use a number of techniques for distributing crack. Sometimes they employ "spotters" to direct customers to where the street distributor is waiting, or they may sell to drivers of passing cars. Another approach is to make the sale from heavily fortified "rock houses," to which the customer has only limited access. The customer may have to wait outside until the transaction is completed—with the seller out of sight—or the customer may be admitted only as far as a caged area in the front end of the house. However, crack dealers are moving away from rock houses toward street sales and sales from motel rooms. In the latter case, dealers will usually pay in cash, rent multiple rooms, and use pagers and cellular phones to contact suppliers and purchasers of controlled substances.

The Los Angeles gangs are radiating out from the areas where they originated—up the West Coast as far as Seattle and Vancouver, into the heartland as far as Denver, Kansas City, and Chicago, and even to cities on the East Coast. Police in all these cities report that Los Angeles gangs are establishing branch operations to sell crack, sometimes in competition with other gangs who consider the cities their territory. This is the case, for instance, with the Samoan gangs in the San Francisco Bay area. In Baltimore, local law enforcement agencies identified a trend, as Los Angeles gangs sent cocaine HCL by way of their own gang members, "wannabes," or by way of local drug dealers looking for a purer or cheaper supply. Following the arrest of two Crips in Maryland and the Eastern District of Virginia, authorities began a special Organized Crime Drug Enforcement Task Force project to determine the extent of infiltration of the area by Los Angeles street gangs.

Kansas City, Missouri is another metropolitan area to which the Bloods and the Crips have migrated and established themselves. They were identified in Kansas City in the summer of 1987. They had sent representatives there to exploit the cocaine distribution market which, at the time, had a gap due to the successful neutralization of Jamaican drug factions. The gangs have generally taken up residence in the outlying areas of Kansas City but have targeted the inner city for cocaine distribution. Initially, the gangs were readily identifiable by their dress, language, and habits, but they now tend to avoid such dead giveaways to prevent unwanted attention from law enforcement.

After reviewing the situation in Kansas City, the Middle District of Tennessee feels it too is experiencing an expansion of Los Angeles drug gang activity. It is known for sure that a drug distribution network affiliated with street gangs has been operating in Nashville. The network stretches from Los Angeles to Nashville and involves at least 50 individuals. In response, the Metropolitan Nashville Police Department has increased its street gang unit from 6 to 50 fifty officers.

In Colorado, the Denver Police Department has documented 700 members of the Bloods and the Crips in the Denver area and reports that recruitment remains active there. Similarly, the migration of the Bloods and the Crips to the Seattle-Tacoma area was rated the "number one" news story of 1988 by readers of the Seattle Times. The Bloods even made it to Sioux Falls, South Dakota (population 100,000), where they were identified as the suppliers of a recently raided crack house.

One of the most frightening aspects of the California street gangs is their willingness to direct their violence at each other, at the police, at members of the public—at anyone who stands in the way of their operations. What makes this violence especially threatening is the amount of firepower at their disposal. Where the gangs once had to make do with zip guns, small-caliber revolvers, and sawed-off shotguns, they now have the wherewithal to acquire semi-automatic rifles and large-caliber handguns. In parts of Los Angeles, the weapon of choice is the AK-47 with a 30-round clip—a large-caliber (7.62 mm.) weapon that dramatically increases the chances of inflicting deadly injury. With so much firepower, gang-related homicides in the Los Angeles area have risen steadily.

Given the violent, elusive, and migratory habits of these street gangs, they are very difficult to investigate. The lack of audit trails, the high mobility of the principal drug dealers, and the relative absence of a formal organization have hindered attempts to infiltrate the gangs. However, as law enforcement agencies begin to understand the gangs better, they are learning to spot their weaknesses. For instance, many gang leaders outside the Los Angeles area will often return to Los Angeles for long periods, leaving their organizations more or less to fend for themselves. Additionally, when Los Angeles gangs try to move into new geographical areas, law enforcement officials can sometimes count on information from local dealers who resent being cut out of their own territories. Experience had led agencies to develop strategies for dealing with the gangs, such as using federal drug statutes (which tend to be more stringent than state statutes) to prosecute drug traffickers; to develop profiles of gang members dealing in drugs; and to build up case files of the gangs themselves.

§ 19.3.7 Other Domestic Trafficking Organizations

In addition to California street gangs, several traditional criminal organizations specializing in drug trafficking are known to be active in urban areas across the country. These organizations and their activities are well-documented in cities such as Detroit, Chicago, St. Louis, and East St. Louis, Illinois. The bosses, or kingpins of these operations supervise their highly structured and disciplined organizations which are composed, for the most part, of extremely violent career criminals. In some cases, the bosses retain control even if they have been convicted and are serving time.

The kingpin oversees the major distributors in his area as well as a body of "enforcers" who are often heavily armed with automatic weapons and explosives. These urban organizations seek to monopolize their segment of the drug trade in their area and routinely murder rival traffickers. They are also noted for using violence against witnesses; they have even been prone to attacking law enforcement officers and prosecutors.

The drug sources on which these urban trafficking organizations rely are often Mexican and South American nationals. The profit margins are unusually high in most of the cities where these urban trafficking organizations operate due to a combination of low supply and difficulty in transportation to the area. This high profitability becomes a great incentive to maintain control of trafficking territories and increases the propensity of these organizations for violent confrontation with rival groups.

Because of their relative stability and long-term involvement in their communities, many of these organizations have infiltrated the legitimate power structure of the jurisdiction and have formed close ties with city officials and local law enforcement personnel. These relationships often allow the urban trafficking organization to gather intelligence on law enforcement operations in their area, thus decreasing their vulnerability to prosecution.

An example of such an organization is the Alex Beverly group in Chicago. In operation for over 15 years, it was the city's largest black drug organization. The 100-member gang has been connected with a dozen drug-related homicides. Alex Beverly was convicted for conducting a continuing criminal enterprise (CCE) and was sentenced to 40 years, with no possibility of parole (USDOJ 1989).

On a smaller scale, there are some regional or even local, domestically based trafficking organizations which operate in areas throughout the United States. In some instances, these organizations are customers of the larger organizations. In other instances, the smaller organizations provide the larger ones with their local infrastructure and are hired by the large organizations to provide specific services or perform specific functions in the drug trafficking chain of operations. These local organizations are often drawn into overt conflict with larger organizations when their geographical or operational sphere of influence is invaded.

Chapter 19

Thus, Los Angeles is not alone among major cities in spawning drug trafficking street gangs. Although none are as active or as far-reaching in their activities as are the Bloods and the Crips, one other active drug trafficking street gang is the "Miami Boys," an organized crack trafficking gang from Florida whose activities have spread to the Atlanta area.

The "Miami Boys" handle the importation of crack into the Atlanta area, supervise young street dealers (most in their middle teens, but some as young as 10 to 12 years old), and handle crack trafficking revenues, which are wired daily to gang leaders in Florida. The "Miami Boys" are reported to be partial to the techniques of intimidating young welfare mothers into allowing the use of their apartments as rented "crack" distribution points. The welfare mothers are paid a going rate of $100 a day; in return they acquiesce to the use of their domiciles for the storing of drugs and as money collection points.

Farther north, Minneapolis-St. Paul is supplied with crack not only by the Crips and the Bloods from Los Angeles, but also by the Vice Lords and El-Rukins from Chicago. It has been estimated that 60 percent of the crack cocaine distributed in Cleveland, Toledo, and Akron is controlled by a combination of Los Angeles and Detroit based street gangs.

However, not all drug traffickers are members of large urban criminal organizations or motorcycle gangs. In the Western District of Washington, the prosecution of a cocaine distributor and several of his customers—business people and professionals—demonstrated the "yuppie" cocaine connection. The distributor was recorded as telling customers not to worry about being caught because "the police are after the black, inner-city dealers and not such people as us."

There are several high-level drug traffickers who do not fit the stereotypical profile of an inner city criminal. In Columbus, Ohio, the profile of the highest-level cocaine dealer is that of a middle-aged white residing in one of the city's more affluent suburbs. In Colorado, cocaine trafficking groups are composed primarily of upper middle-class individuals of Caucasian or Hispanic background. Moreover, a 1986 investigation in Lawrence, Kansas discovered that 19 prominent community citizens, including the executive Secretary to the Chancellor of the University of Kansas and a former Deputy Attorney General for the state of Kansas, were arrested and convicted on state and federal cocaine charges. Needless to say, the community was shocked that such respectable, high-level citizens were involved in drug trafficking.

Another "yuppie" connection was discovered in Pennsylvania. The Air America Organization in the Middle District of Pennsylvania was a consortium of airline pilots who brought 9 tons of cocaine into the United States, one of the largest quantities of cocaine ever smuggled by a single organization. In addition, tens of millions of dollars in cash were smuggled out of the country, directly to Colombia, by these pilots, who were paid $1 million per successful flight.

Drug Trafficking, Terrorism and Organized Crime

The individuals and informal organizations that fit these non-traditional patterns are differentiated by the circumstances of their origins and the surroundings in which they operate. Yet, both young urban professionals and rural or small-town locals may sometimes turn to selling drugs, either as a sideline or as a full-time occupation. In some instances, the operation of a drug trafficking enterprise is just a variation on criminal activities that predate any connection to drugs. In parts of the rural Southeast, some families who once produced moonshine or engaged in local criminal activities now cultivate marijuana or traffic in cocaine. The isolation of the rural areas in which these people operate creates ideal circumstances for drug-drops, as well as for marijuana cultivation. Many of these individuals start out trafficking in small quantities of cocaine and move on to working in clandestine rural drug laboratories.

A similar situation exists in the Northern District of West Virginia. In this state, drug trafficking is engaged in by several indigenous organizations whose members have been entrenched in the district for a number of years and who have extensive records of criminal activity.

Likewise, in the Northern District of Georgia a portion of the total drug traffic is attributed to a plethora of "southern style" career criminals, regionally referred to as the "Dixie Mafia." One of the district's most significant methamphetamine investigations targeted several "Dixie Mafia" defendants. The investigation determined that these established career criminals, who had well-documented records as marijuana and cocaine traffickers, were receiving monthly shipments of between 50 and 72 pounds of methamphetamine from a clandestine laboratory in Washington State.

On the other hand, the young professionals or "yuppies" who become involved in the drug trade bring a different background and perspective to their illicit activities. Many of those who went through college and graduate school experimenting with drugs either never gave them up or began using them again when the increased income and pressures of professional life made drugs both available and seemingly attractive. As stockbrokers, doctors, lawyers, and participants in other high-stress professions, some developed dependencies on an occasional snort of cocaine or on some other drug-related experience. Occasionally, these people are confronted with incentives and opportunities to become full time-traffickers, especially those professionals with access to essential chemicals or prescription drugs which can be diverted. In many instances, however, the yuppie drug dealer is driven by the same forces which motivate his professional life: greed and the desire to get rich quick.

The different perspectives and lifestyles of both the rural, blue-collar workers and young professionals engaged in selling drugs carry over into their trafficking operations. The rural traffickers usually live and operate in smaller, more stable communities and draw their partners in crime from family and friends. Young professionals form more collegial relationships, often engaging in short-term operations with old college friends or sympathetic office workers who are drawn together by an ini-

Chapter 19

tial common interest in obtaining illicit drugs. For example, a case in Montgomery County, Virginia, involved the arrest of 17 individuals for dealing in cocaine, marijuana, and other drugs. The group, whose customers included students at Virginia Tech, consisted of a number of the sons of prominent political figures in the area. These sons recruited people with whom they had gone to school and people whose other interests and backgrounds made them comfortable in forming a "business" relationship.

Rural organizations, on the other hand, tend to be structured more like traditional criminal organizations than are the yuppie groups, whose members usually do not consider themselves to be career criminals and whose idea of an acceptable relationship tends more toward the contractual and the communal rather than the hierarchical. Joint ventures are popular in yuppie trafficking organizations. Whereas the rural organizations seem to be more stable, with each person assuming a more or less permanent place in the trafficking hierarchy, yuppie groups are more ephemeral and more likely to be organized along the lines of the specific expertise that each member of the organization brings to an operation. Typically, yuppie organizations are established around short-term goals, while rural traffickers are more adaptable and more likely to be in for the long haul. It is not uncommon for these organizations to move their operations to a nearby town or urban center and proceed to transform into a full-fledged hierarchical trafficking organization.

§ 19.4 TRAFFICKING BY FOREIGN NATIONALS

The influx of immigrants, the changing immigration laws and patterns of the last few decades, and the increased mobility of residents in drug producing countries, have led to a great increase in the drug trafficking operations of foreign nationals in the United States. This new activity has in no way been restricted to the Colombian cartels, the Jamaican posses, and the Asian gangs cited above. Many less well-known trafficking organizations operate throughout the United States. The area of operation of any individual group of foreign nationals may be limited to a single locality or may encompass parts of several different states. In some instances, the traffickers operate through contacts with their fellow countrymen residing in drug import areas such as Miami and Los Angeles/San Diego, while also remaining in contact with nationals in their home countries. Distribution and/or importation is sometimes arranged through one of the larger trafficking organizations, such as the Colombians or the Jamaicans.

Mexican nationals represent one of the oldest groups of foreign nationals engaged in drug trafficking in the United States. They have been operating in the United States for years, especially in the Southwest and Far West. They traffic mainly in heroin and marijuana; however, trafficking in cocaine is also common, and over the past few years Mexico has become an increasingly important conduit for South American cocaine. A number of factors have combined to stimulate this activity: a long, hard-to-patrol border with the United States; an extensive rural Mexican countryside, with many mountainous areas, ideal for cultivating, processing, and manufacturing illicit drugs; a tradition of corruption in elements of the Mexican government and law enforcement agencies; and the growing drug market in the United States over the past decade.

Within the whole group of Mexican nationals, there are a number of different, often competing, Mexican organizations. These include the so-called "Mexican Mafia," with roots in Mexican "prison gangs;" loosely knit cartels, primarily specializing in one or more illicit substances; and smaller, less integrated trafficking groups of a less stable nature.

Reports indicate that the structures of Mexican drug trafficking organizations are much more family-oriented than those of other large-scale trafficking groups. A Mexican trafficking operation is often vertically integrated, using family members for each stage of the operation. For example, the Central District of California reports that the Sanchez-Carranza organization relies upon family relatives living in mountainous areas of Durango, Mexico, to cultivate its opium poppy fields. These family members send the crop to other family members in Mexico, who process it into heroin. The heroin is then smuggled into the United States by couriers, many of whom are family members, and delivered to yet another set of family members who live in the United States. The families in the United States oversee the heroin's distribution throughout California and the neighboring states of Washington, Idaho, Arizona, and Nevada. Some Mexican groups take the process a step further and employ family members in direct sales on the streets of U.S. cities. However, not all foreign nationals have penetrated the U.S. market to the extent that Mexicans have. In some cases, foreign nationals have found that they can engage in U.S. drug trafficking from "on the boat," without having to really "enter" the country. Pakistani nationals, members of the crews of boats docking at Baltimore harbor, have been reported to be engaging in heroin trafficking from their ships. They call at the Baltimore port every 4 to 6 weeks, usually in the middle or latter part of their itinerary. Their points of sale include most of Baltimore's inner-city heroin distribution organizations.

Other groups do get "off the boat" and spread to various parts of the country, blending in with legitimate refugees and immigrants and setting up their trafficking organizations in places where law enforcement may not expect to find them. For example, in Wichita, Kansas, two organizations of Dominican Republic nationals are engaged in separate but overlapping cocaine trafficking operations. Furthermore, the principal heroin distribution groups in Rhode Island are also composed of Dominican Republic nationals. Unlike many of the foreign nationals operating as traffickers in the United States, the Dominicans in Rhode Island, who form the country's third largest Dominican population after New York City's and Miami's, are reported to be interested in permanent residence. The more prevalent pattern is for nationals to be transitory residents, intent on returning to their country of origin and usually sending back home a large portion their illicit proceeds.

Another group of foreign nationals is operating out of Delaware. Haitian traffickers have become one of the primary sources of crack cocaine in southern Delaware. This network grew out of the influx of migratory

Haitian workers seeking employment in Delaware's agricultural and poultry industries. Members of the trafficking network in Delaware have connections with a Haitian community located in Ft. Pierce, Florida. This information was discovered because one of the traffickers prosecuted in Delaware was buying automobiles with the proceeds of his trafficking, sending them to Ft. Pierce, and having them shipped to Haiti, where he intended to open a taxi business.

As the Delaware case suggests, a foreign national may engage in drug trafficking operations independently, relying on connections with his fellow countrymen for supply and distribution. Yet, these traffickers can be just as dangerous as those with formal organizational ties. In the Southern District of Alabama, for example, a black Haitian male moved into an economically depressed housing project and began recruiting local street dealers. Considered unwanted competition by some local dealers, he showed his propensity for violence when confronted. In one instance, he shot a man in the back of the head in an attempt to execute him; miraculously, the victim survived.

Other groups of foreign nationals also exist. Nigerian heroin smugglers have utilized the London to New York commercial airline route as their main avenue of access. The couriers are recruited in Nigeria, usually from among those with legitimate reasons for travel to the United States. These "mules" bring the heroin into the United States for transport by automobile to its ultimate point of distribution. The Nigerian smugglers, even though not always professionals, have been uneager to cooperate with authorities against their source of supply, making it hard to develop a clear picture of the detailed structure of this heroin operation.

Moreover, organizations of Cuban nationals are reported to be involved in cocaine trafficking operations in the Western District of Wisconsin. Such organizations were first uncovered in the wake of their developments, in the early 1980s, and include many criminal refugees who arrived in this country during the Mariel boat-lift. These Cuban organizations are often traditional families in which the parents, brothers, and sisters operate different aspects of the narcotics trafficking business. In Wisconsin, as a result of their ties with other criminal refugees in Florida, these organizations developed a pipeline for bringing large quantities of cocaine into the state. Again, investigations of this operation have been hampered by its familial nature, as defendants have been reluctant to testify against family members. Other groups of foreign nationals are involved in drug trafficking in Cedar Rapids, Iowa. In the late 1980s, there were two major international heroin smuggling cases involving foreign nationals in this area. One case involved the arrest of a Lebanese individual who had smuggled several kilos of heroin and hashish from Lebanon on various occasions. Earlier, in 1985, over 20 individuals were prosecuted for involvement in a Nepalese smuggling operation (USDOJ 1989).

While most of these groups of foreign nationals do not represent a threat as great as that of the larger groups, they are cause for concern. They are highly mobile and difficult for law enforcement agencies to track and prosecute. They provide a local distribution network for the major importers and distributors in areas where these organizations have no local network in place. And, most disturbingly, they have the potential for developing organizations that could rival those of the Colombians and the Jamaicans, should the circumstances of supply, distribution, and organizational ability conspire to catapult one of them to prominence. For these reasons, it is necessary to maintain our constant attention to the activities of these trafficking organizations. It is also necessary to be vigilant in identifying any new or expanded areas of activity. This is an especially difficult task given the constantly shifting patterns of social, economic, and geographic status that characterize most populations of foreign nationals residing in the United States.

§ 19.5   1990s ILLICIT DRUG TRADE

During the 1990s, Mexico emerged as the most significant transshipment corridor for illicit drugs smuggled into the United States. Although cocaine continued to move through the Caribbean corridor, increased radar coverage from Aerostats along the Southeast coast deterred the use of aircraft flights directly to the United States. Traffickers thwarted the increased radar surveillance by combining drug airdrops with high-speed boats operating beyond the range of the new systems. The increased law enforcement and military presence in the Caribbean forced traffickers to explore more elaborate smuggling avenues, including the purchase of Soviet cargo aircraft, a surplus Soviet diesel submarine, and experimentation with semi-submersible vehicles.

Colombian traffickers increasingly relied upon Mexican and Dominican trafficking organizations to smuggle cocaine shipments to the United States. By the mid-1990s, Colombian organizations started paying Mexican transportation organizations with portions of the smuggled cocaine load, with up to half of the load provided to the transporters. This arrangement reduced the need for large financial transactions, and firmly established Mexico-based drug trafficking organizations as significant illicit drug wholesalers in the United States. The Central American corridor was increasingly used for air and overland cocaine shipments to Mexico. Aircraft were used to move cocaine from Colombia to Northern Mexico. Although smaller, twin-engine aircraft were most often used to smuggle cocaine, larger surplus jet aircraft were also used to transport multi-ton quantities of cocaine.

Drug-related violence continued to undermine government control in South America. Over 150 groups loosely organized in cartels operating out of Medellin and Bogota, dominated the cocaine trade. Colombian insurgent groups such as the Revolutionary Armed Forces of Colombia (FARC) and the Army of National Liberation (ELN) also benefited from the cocaine trade by taxing narcotics profits; protecting crops, laboratories, and storage facilities; and occasionally extracting payment in weapons. Insurgent groups also carried out kidnapping and terrorism in support of traffickers' alms.

By 1988, Southeast Asian (SEA) heroin dominated the East Coast heroin market, while Mexican heroin was supplied to users n the Western United States. New York was the primary importation and distribution center for SEA heroin, with San Francisco, Seattle, Los Angeles, and Washington also identified as points of entry. SEA heroin continued to dominate the market throughout the early 1990s, all but replacing Southwest Asian heroin. In 1994, however, a joint Royal Thai Government/DEA endeavor—Operation TIGER TRAP—led to the incarceration in Thailand and extradition to the United States of more than a dozen high-level violators who had played key roles in moving SEA heroin to the United States. These successful actions disrupted long-standing SEA heroin trafficking modus operandi, not only in Asia, but also in the United States.

Expanded opium poppy cultivation and heroin production in Colombia in the early 1990s allowed Colombian traffickers to fill the void created by the decreased flow of SEA heroin to east coast markets. During the mid- to late-1990s, Colombian heroin traffickers easily undermined the SEA heroin market with a readily available supply of high-quality, low-priced white heroin. They also undercut their competitors' price and used established, effective drug distribution networks to facilitate supply. Since Colombian heroin—often sold on the street with a purity of 90%—can be snorted like cocaine, it avoided the stigma of needle usage; thus, Colombian traffickers had a built-in marketing advantage over traffickers from Southeast or Southwest Asia. Throughout the 1990s, Mexico-supplied heroin continued to dominate user preferences in the Western United States.

By 1990, Mexico was the largest supplier of marijuana to the United States. The profit margin for marijuana not only fueled Mexican trafficking organizations, but led to an increase in domestic marijuana cultivation—particularly indoor-grow operations producing high-potency marijuana.

Synthetic drugs, especially methamphetamine, continued to be primarily produced domestically. In the early 1990s, high-purity "ice" methamphetamine (80 to 90% pure methamphetamine with a crystalline appearance) appeared on the West Coast. In addition to domestic production, primarily in California, ice was supplied from laboratories in South Korea and the Philippines.

Outlaw motorcycle gangs dominated the production of methamphetamine through the early 1990s. In the mid-1990s, however, Mexican drug trafficking organizations started large-scale production and trafficking of methamphetamine. The introduction of high-quality, low-priced methamphetamine undercut the monopoly once held by outlaw bikers. Some OMs, including the Hells Angels, reportedly relied upon Mexico-based sources of supply for their methamphetamine, preferring to avoid the risks associated with the manufacture of the drug. A sharp decrease in the purity of Mexican methamphetamine at the end of the 1990s reportedly pushed OMG back into drug production.

LSD and PCP remained available throughout the 1990s. In the late 1980s and early 1990s, methylenedioxymethamphetamine (MDMA), also called Ecstasy, gained popularity among young, middle-class college students in limited areas of the United States. Ecstasy use and availability greatly escalated in 1997 when clandestine laboratories, operating in Europe, began exporting significant quantities of MDMA tablets to distributors in the United States.

§ 19.6   2000s ILLICIT DRUG TRADE

The Southwest border remains the most vulnerable region of the United States for border security, followed by the Gulf Coast. DEA interagency assessments report over 60% of the cocaine entering the United States moves across the Southwest border. The U.S. Customs & Border Protection identified an increase in the movement of drugs between ports of entry over the last several years, as well as a trend toward smaller drug loads.

El Paso Intelligence Center (EPIC) reports that traffickers have not changed smuggling methods or routes following the September 11, 2001, terrorist attacks. Although the transportation centers are likely to be located near the border, the command and control centers could operate from nearly any location in the United States. Mobile communications and internet encryption allow Drug Trafficking Organizations (DTOs) to operate from remote locations.

The 9% decline in cocaine purity over the past four years illustrates a vulnerability of crop-based illicit drugs. One possible explanation for the increased use of cutting agents by Colombian DTOs is the expansion of the non-U.S. drug market beyond the traffickers' means to maintain world supplies. Cocaine and heroin production are limited not only by the same factors that affect any agricultural product, but also by the traffickers' abilities to either control production regions or to thwart government crop eradication efforts. Supplies of synthetic drugs, such as methamphetamine, MDMA (Ecstasy), PCP, and LSD are not limited by these same factors. The traffickers' capability to quickly move production sites of synthetic drugs presents a significant challenge to law enforcement authorities.

Colombian drug trafficking organizations increasingly rely upon the eastern Pacific Ocean as a trafficking route to move cocaine to the United States. Law enforcement and intelligence community sources estimate that 72% of the cocaine shipped to the United States moves through the Central America-Mexico corridor, primarily by maritime conveyance. Fishing vessels and go-fast boats are used to move multiton cocaine loads to Mexico's west coast and Yucatan Peninsula. The loads are subsequently broken down into smaller quantities for movement across the Southwest border. Despite the shift of smuggling operations to the eastern Pacific, the Caribbean corridor remains a crucial smuggling avenue for Colombian cocaine traffickers. Puerto Rico, the Dominica Republic, and Haiti are the predominant transshipment points for Colombian cocaine transiting the Caribbean (DEA "Evolution" 2002).

Traffickers operating from Colombia continue to control wholesale level cocaine distribution throughout the heavily populated northeastern United States and along the eastern seaboard in cities such as Boston, Miami, Newark, New York city, and Philadelphia. There are indications that other drug trafficking organizations, especially Mexican and Dominican groups, are playing a larger role in the distribution of cocaine in collaboration with Colombian organizations. Mexican drug trafficking organizations are increasingly responsible for the transportation of cocaine from the Southwest border to the New York market. Mexico-based trafficking groups in cities such as Chicago, Dallas, Denver, Houston, Los Angeles, Phoenix, San Diego, San Francisco, and Seattle now control the distribution of multi-ton quantities of cocaine.

New heroin users continue to be attracted to high-purity Colombian heroin because it can be snorted rather than injected. Reports of Mexico-produced white heroin continue to surface. Although heroin abuse indicators are stable, the increasing purity of Mexican heroin, as well as ready supplies of high-purity white heroin, may result in geographic "pockets" of overdoses as seen in Chimayo and Espanola, New Mexico, in the late 1990s. The high rate of overdose in these locations served as the initial impetus for Operation TAR PIT, which identified the operations of a Mexico-based heroin distribution organization that operated throughout the western United States and in sections of the Midwest.

Marijuana trafficking is prevalent across the nation, with both domestic and foreign sources of supply. Large-scale methamphetamine laboratories, located primarily in the western United States, and to a lesser extent in Mexico, provide the majority of the drug. However, even the smaller clandestine laboratories pose a significant public health and safety threat. The majority of the small toxic laboratories are not connected to large-scale drug trafficking organizations. "Super labs" (laboratories capable of producing in excess of 10 pounds of methamphetamine in one 24-hour production cycle), however, are generally funded and supplied by larger drug trafficking organizations. An increase in the number of super labs in the Midwest suggests an increased demand for methamphetamine. Although the majority of MDMA production takes place in the Netherlands, and to a lesser extent in Belgium, the transferability of the laboratories adds a dynamic to the drug trade that cannot be addressed at this time. Laboratories can be relocated to any nation in the European Union, Eastern Europe, or the former Soviet Union, as long as precursor chemicals can be obtained and transported.

§ 19.6.1 Post-September 11, 2001 Assessment
The September 11, 2001, terrorist attacks on the United States introduced a new set of variables to drug threat assessments: the reallocation of law enforcement, intelligence, and military assets from counternarcotics to counterterrorism reduces available enforcement assets, yet brings a concurrent strengthening of national borders. If history serves as a guide, DTOs will continue to identify and exploit vulnerabilities in order to maintain a steady supply of drugs to the illicit drug market in the United States.

§ 19.7   DRUGS AND TERRORISM: A NEW PERSPECTIVE
§ 19.7.1 Introduction
Prior to September 11, 2001, drug trafficking and terrorist activities were usually addressed by the law enforcement community as separate

Drug Trafficking, Terrorism and Organized Crime

issues. In the wake of the terrorist attacks in New York City, Washington, DC, and Pennsylvania, the public now perceives these two criminal activities as intertwined. For the Drug Enforcement Administration (DEA), investigating the link between drugs and terrorism has taken on renewed importance.

Throughout history, various aspects of the criminal world have been linked together, such as drug traffickers with connections to illegal gambling, prostitution, and arms dealing. Perhaps the most recognizable illustration of this linkage is the expansion of the Italian mafia in the United States during the early 20th Century. The links between various aspects of the criminal world are evident because those who use illicit activities to further or fund their lifestyle, cause, or well-being often interact with others involved in various illicit activities. For example, organizations that launder money for drug traffickers also launder money for arms traffickers, terrorists, etc. The link between drugs and terrorism is not a new phenomenon.

Globalization has made the world a smaller place, changing the face of both legitimate and illegitimate enterprise Criminals, by exploiting advances in technology, finance, communications, and transportation in pursuit of their illegal endeavors, have become criminal entrepreneurs. Perhaps the most alarming aspect of this "entrepreneurial" style of crime is the intricate manner in which drugs and terrorism may be intermingled. Since September 11, the public's image of terrorism is magnified. Not only is the proliferation of illegal drugs perceived as a danger, but also the proceeds from drugs are among the sources for funding for other criminal activities, including terrorism.

§ 19.7.2 Narco-Terrorism

The nexus between drugs and violence is not new; in fact, it is as old as drug abuse itself. The mind-altering strength of drugs has always had the power to create violence, but there is another kind of connection between drugs and violence: the use of drug trafficking to fund the violence perpetrated by terrorist groups.[1] Within the context of current world events, narco-terrorism is difficult to define. Historically, DEA has defined narco-terrorism in terms of Pablo Escobar, the classic cocaine trafficker who used terrorist tactics against noncombatants to further his political agenda and to protect his drug trade. Today, however, governments find themselves faced with classic terrorist groups that participate in, or otherwise receive funds from, drug trafficking to further their agenda. In this respect, are narco-terrorists actual drug traffickers who use terrorism against civilians to advance their agenda? Or are narco-terrorists first and foremost terrorists who happen to use drug money to further their cause? Perhaps, the correct answer is that narco-terrorism may apply in both situations.

---

[1] According to Chapter 22 of the U.S. Code (USC), terrorism is the premeditated, politically motivated violence perpetrated against noncombatant targets by subnational groups or clandestine agents. International terrorism involves citizens, or territory, of more than one country. A terrorist group is any group practicing, or that has significant subgroups that practice, international terrorism.

DEA defines a narco-terrorist organization as "an organized group that is complicit in the activities of drug trafficking in order to further, or fund, premeditated, politically motivated violence perpetrated against noncombatant targets with the intention to influence (that is, influence a government or group of people)."

§ 19.7.2(a)   The Pablo Escobar Example

One of the most infamous "narco-terrorists" was Pablo Escobar (DEA "Drugs and Terrorism" 2002). As leader of the Medellin cocaine cartel in Colombia, he became one of the wealthiest and most feared men in the world. At the height of his success, Escobar was listed in Forbes Magazine among the world's wealthiest men. While on the surface, he was nothing more than a street thug who became successful by trafficking in cocaine, Escobar had political aspirations and strove to project the appearance of legitimacy, claiming his wealth was the result of real estate investments. He eventually ran for Congress and campaigned for foreign policy changes that would prohibit the extradition of Colombian citizens to the United States.

Escobar had a penchant for violence. He wreaked havoc on Colombia while attempting to persuade the government to change its extradition policy. Due to the numerous assassinations of politicians, presidential candidates, Supreme Court justices, police officers, and civilians, as well as a number of bombings culminating in the bombing of an Avianca commercial airliner in 1989, Escobar enraged both Colombia and the world. These actions resulted in a massive manhunt and his death in 1993. Escobar was a drug trafficker who used drug-related violence and terrorism to further his own political, personal, and financial goals. Moreover, he funded his terrorist activities with the money obtained from his drug trafficking endeavors. He was the classic narco-terrorist; his cause was simply himself.

Terrorist organizations use a number of sources to garner funds for their activities, such as petty crimes, kidnap-for-ransom, charities, sympathizers, front companies, and drug trafficking. Most of the known terrorist organizations use several of these methods to collect funding, while preferring particular methods to others. Drug trafficking is among the most profitable sources. According to the Office of National Drug Control Policy (ONDCP), Americans alone spend an estimated $64 billion on illegal drugs annually.

Drug trafficking has always been a profitable means for criminal organizations to further or fund their activities. The complicity of terrorist groups in drug trafficking varies from group to group and region to region. In the broadest sense, some terrorist groups may be involved in all aspects of the drug trade, from cultivation, production, transportation, and wholesale distribution to money laundering. These groups may also provide security for drug traffickers transporting their product through territory controlled by terrorist organizations or their supporters. Finally, in some cases, terrorist groups or their supporters may require a "tax" to be paid on illicit products, or passage through controlled territory. No matter which form it takes, or the level of involvement in drug trafficking, many terrorist groups are using drug money to fund their activities and perpetrate violence against governments and people around the world.

§ 19.7.2(b) Afghanistan Under the Taliban

As in the case of formerly Taliban-controlled Afghanistan, narco-terrorism was not limited to terrorist organizations. Afghanistan is a major source country for the cultivation, processing, and trafficking of opiates, producing over 70 percent of the world's supply of illicit opium in 2000. Because of the country's decimation by decades of warfare, illicit drugs have become a major source of income. The Taliban's Afghanistan would be an example of a state primarily funded by illicit opium production. Through this drug income, the Taliban were able to support and protect Osama bin Laden and the al Qaeda organization. As in this case, drugs and terrorism frequently share a common ground of geography, money, and violence.

§ 19.7.2(c) Narco-Terrorism Versus Drug-Related Violence

When looking at the connection between drugs and violence, it is important to differentiate between drug-related violence and narco-terrorism. By definition, terrorism is premeditated, politically motivated violence perpetrated against noncombatant targets. With drug-related violence, we see financially motivated violence perpetrated against those who interfere with or cross the path of a drug trafficking organization. While we see drug-related violence on a daily basis on the streets of major cities, narco-terrorism is, in many cases, less visible. Drug-related violence permeates society at all levels and is visible at every stage of the drug trade, from domestic violence to turf warfare between rival drug trafficking gangs or groups. With narco-terrorism, the acts of terror are clearly evident, but the funding source is often well-disguised.

§ 19.7.2(d) Evolution of Narco-Terrorism

Any region, in which illegal drugs are cultivated, transported, distributed, or consumed, is susceptible to narco-terrorism. Throughout the world, insurgent groups, revolutionary groups, and ideological or spiritual groups, who use violence to promote their political mission may use drug proceeds to fund acts of terror in furtherance of their ideology. Leadership, cultural, political, and economic change may affect the ideology or mission of a group. Internal divisions and splinter groups may result, each seeking to pursue their goals via different avenues, be they legitimate political activity, perpetuation of violence, or criminal activity, such as drug trafficking.

History has shown that narco-terrorist organizations fall into different categories. One category includes politically motivated groups that use drug proceeds to support their terrorist activities; activities that will confer legitimacy upon them within the state. These groups usually call for a ceasefire with the government or take measures to establish a legal political party whereby their political goals are realized through nonviolent, legal means. Groups that fall into this category are generally viewed with skepticism by the state. An example of a group in this category is the Kurdistan Worker's Party (PKK).

Another category consists of groups that continually pursue their ideological goals while participating in aspects of the drug trade; for example, the Revolutionary Armed Forces of Colombia (Fuerzas Armadas Revolucionarias de Colombia or FARC).

There are notable examples of narco-terrorist groups in almost every corner of the world. Many insurgent and extremist groups are suspected of drug trafficking involvement, such as Hezbollah and the Islamic Resistance Movement (HAMAS) in the tri-border region of Paraguay, Argentina, and Brazil; Sendero Luminoso (the Shining Path) in Peru; and the Basque Fatherland and Liberty (ETA) in Spain. The level of involvement in drug trafficking by actual narco-terrorist groups and the evolution of the groups and their purposes are often very different.

§ 19.7.2(e)   Kurdistan Worker's Party
The PKK in Turkey was founded in 1974. Developed as a revolutionary socialist organization, the goal of the PKK is to establish an independent nation of Kurdistan. In 1984, the PKK began to use violence against Turkish security forces, gradually escalating the level of violence to include civilians. In the early 1990s, the group added urban terrorism to their repertoire of violent activities. The PKK, considered a terrorist organization by most Western Governments, is represented in Kurdish immigrant communities throughout the world and is particularly prevalent in Europe. The PKK is known to benefit from drug trafficking, but the extent of their involvement is often debated. The Government of Turkey consistently reports that the PKK, as an organization, is responsible for much of the illicit drug processing and trafficking in Turkey. Turkish press reports state that the PKK produces 60 tons of heroin per year and receives an estimated income of US $40 million each year from drug trafficking proceeds. According to historic DEA reporting, the PKK may receive funding from a number of illicit means, including kidnap-for-ransom and drugs.

Reporting from the early 1990s indicated that several large drug trafficking families were supporters or sympathizers of the PKK, and that direct funds from their trafficking organizations were provided to the PKK to buy supplies. However, recent changes in the structure of the organization, due in part to the group's founder declaring a peace initiative in 1999, have led elements of the PKK to strive for legitimacy and possible involvement in Turkey's political process.

§ 19.7.2(f)   Revolutionary Armed Forces of Colombia
The FARC is one of Colombia's major insurgent groups. The FARC is a pro-Communist group that wants to replace the current Colombian Government with a leftist, anti-U.S. regime. The FARC emerged in 1964 as the military wing of the Colombian Communist Party, with the goal of overthrowing the government and the ruling class of Colombia. The FARC is the largest, best-trained and equipped, and most effective insurgent group in Colombia. Over the past two decades, the FARC has controlled large areas of Colombia's eastern lowlands and rain forest, which are the primary coca cultivation and cocaine processing regions in the country. The FARC is an economically self-sufficient organization, supporting its mission through kidnapping, extortion, bank rob-

beries, and the drug trade. Some FARC fronts are promoting coca cultivation, managing cocaine processing, selling drugs for cash, and negotiating arms deals with international drug trafficking organizations to support their broad based weapons procurement program.

Recent DEA reporting indicates that some PARC units in southern Colombia are directly involved in drug trafficking activities, including controlling local cocaine base markets and selling cocaine to international smuggling organizations. At least one PARC front—the 16th Front—has served as a cocaine source of supply for one international drug trafficking organization. In March 2002, the United States announced its indictment of several PARC members. This case marks the first time that members of a known terrorist organization have been indicted in the United States for their drug trafficking activities, including selling cocaine in exchange for currency, weapons, and equipment.

Despite the differences between the PKK and the PARC, both were initially motivated to take action in furtherance of their ideological goals-the desire for independent homelands or political thought. The drug trade and terrorist activities were the means through which these groups furthered their missions. Changes in leadership, politics, and economics affected the varying outcomes; that is, movement toward political legitimacy for the PKK, and pursuit of an ideological mission through engagement in the drug trade by the PARC.

§ 19.7.2(g)   International Efforts Against Narco-Terrorism
There are three crucial elements to attacking narco-terrorism: law enforcement efforts, intelligence gathering, and international cooperation. Many terrorist groups rarely act within the borders of one state, but tend to have a more global view in regard to their activities and fundraising. This means that combating narco-terrorism requires a global network of law enforcement and intelligence officials tackling this issue wherever it appears. It is the cooperation at all levels of law enforcement and intelligence organizations that will prevent atrocities such as those financed by drug money in South America, Southwest Asia, and the rest of the world. Several international measures have been taken over the years to combat terrorism. According to the U.S. Department of State, there are 12 major multilateral conventions and protocols on combating terrorism. International efforts to combat narco-terrorism are focusing on asset seizure and control of all funding sources used by terrorist organizations. In 1999, the International Convention for the Suppression of the Financing of Terrorism was adopted. It required signatories "to take steps to prevent and counteract the financing of terrorists, whether directly or indirectly, through groups claiming to have charitable, social or cultural goals or which also engage in such illicit activities as drug trafficking or gun running." Under this convention, signatories also were required to hold those who finance terrorism to be criminally, civilly, or administratively responsible for their acts.

In response to the incidents of September 11, 2001, the international community is expanding their efforts to control and extinguish financing that supports terrorism. On September 28, 2001, the United Nations Security Council unanimously adopted an anti-terrorism resolution that called for the suppression of terrorist group financing, and improved international cooperation against terrorists. The resolution, identified as Resolution 1373 (2001), requires all states to prevent and abolish the financing of terrorism, and to criminalize the willful collection and distribution of funds for such acts. Furthermore, the resolution created a committee to monitor the implementation of the guidelines set forth in this resolution. The Security Council noted, "the close connection between international terrorism and transnational organized crime, illicit drugs, money-laundering, illegal arms-trafficking, and illegal movement of nuclear, chemical, biological and other potentially deadly materials, emphasizes the need to enhance coordination of efforts on national, sub-regional, regional and international levels to strengthen a global response to this serious challenge and threat to international security."

§ 19.7.3 CONCLUSION

The events of September 11th brought new focus to an old problem, narco-terrorism. In attempting to combat this threat, the link between drugs and terrorism came to the fore. Whether it is a state, such as formerly Taliban-controlled Afghanistan, or a narco-terrorist organization, such as the PARC, the nexus between drugs and terrorism is evident. Nations throughout the world are aligning to combat this scourge on international society. The War on Terror and the War on Drugs are linked, with agencies throughout the United States and internationally working together as a force-multiplier in an effort to dismantle narco-terrorist organizations. Efforts to stop the funding of these groups have focused on drugs and the drug money used to perpetuate violence throughout the world. International cooperative efforts between law enforcement authorities and intelligence organizations is crucial to eliminating terrorist funding, reducing the drug flow, and preventing another September 11th.

References

Drug Enforcement Administration. DEA Highlights. Washington, D.C: U.S. Department of Justice, 1995.

----------. "Drugs and Terrorism: A New Perspective." Drug Intelligence Brief. Washington, D.C: U.S. Department of Justice, 2002.

----------. "The Evolution of the Drug Threat: The 1980s Through 2002." Drug Intelligence Brief. Washington, D.C: U.S. Department of Justice, 2002.

International Narcotic Enforcement Officers Association. International Drug Report. Albany, N.Y.: Vol. 33.6 (June, 1992).

President's Commission on Organized Crime. "America's Habit: Drug Abuse, Drug Trafficking and Organized Crime." Report to the President and the Attorney General. Washington, D.C.: U.S. Government Printing Office. March, 1986.

"2 American lawyers helped Cali drug cartel, U.S. says." The Orlando Sentinel, 20 May 1997.

U.S. Department of Justice. "Drug Trafficking: A Report to the President of the United States." United States Attorneys and the Attorney General of the United States." Washington, D.C.: August 3, 1989.

CHAPTER 20

CHEMICAL CONTROL AND DRUG DIVERSION

§ 20.1   INTRODUCTION
With the exception of cannabis, every illicit drug requires chemicals to be refined to its final, consumable form (e.g. the coca plant to cocaine, the poppy plant to heroin), or is purely the result of chemical synthesis (e.g. methamphetamine, ecstasy, etc.). Chemical control offers a means of attacking illicit drug production and disrupting the process before the drugs have entered the market.

Law enforcement agencies are cognizant that chemical control is a critical element in the struggle against illegal narcotics and synthetic drugs. Because many legitimate industrial chemicals are also necessary in the processing and synthesis of most illicitly produced drugs, preventing the diversion of these chemicals from legitimate commerce to illicit drug manufacturing is a difficult job. Further, since so many chemicals listed as illicit drug precursors are manufactured all over the world, international cooperation combined with a comprehensive chemical control strategy is essential if long term positive impact is to be expected.

§ 20.2   THE LEADING SUPPLIERS
Chemicals critical to the production of cocaine, heroin, and synthetic drugs are produced in many countries throughout the world. Many manufacturers and suppliers exist in Europe, China, India, the United States, and a host of other countries. Historically, chemicals critical to the synthesis or manufacture of illicit drugs are introduced into various venues via legitimate purchases by companies that are registered and licensed to do business as chemical importers or handlers. Once in a country or state, the chemicals are diverted by rogue importers or chemical companies, by criminal organizations and individual violators, or, more typically seen in an overseas environment, acquired as a result of coercion on the part of drug traffickers. In response to stricter international controls, drug traffickers have increasingly been forced to divert chemicals by mislabeling the containers, forging documents, establishing front companies, using circuitous routing, hijacking shipments, bribing officials, or smuggling products across international borders.

§ 20.3   BRIEF HISTORY OF CHEMICAL CONTROL
The subject of the comprehensive need for chemical controls, as distinct from drug controls, was first examined in depth by an informal conference of U.S., Canadian and European drug control officials in Rome in May 1984. Thereafter, a series of special international conferences were organized on the subject: in Wiesbaden in 1986; Kuala Lumpur and Quito in 1987; and Washington, D.C. in 1989. These efforts resulted in the adoption of Article 12 of the 1988 Convention Against Illicit Traffic in Narcotic Drugs and Psychotropic Substances (known as the Vienna Convention), establishing the foundation for in-

ternational cooperation in chemical control. Also in 1988, the United States incorporated into its national controlled substances legislation the comprehensive Chemical Diversion and Trafficking Act (CDTA).

In 1990, the significance of chemical control was acknowledged at the Group of Seven (G-7) Houston Economic Summit in its mandate of a Chemical Action Task Force (CATF). The CATF's purpose was to develop effective procedures to ensure that precursor and essential chemicals are not diverted to manufacture illicit drugs. Results of the CATF's efforts included a recommendation that ten additional chemicals be added to the list of 12 in the Vienna Convention. Also, in December 1990, the European Community adopted a binding regulation on the commerce in listed chemicals, which was later modified and extended to include other chemicals as of January 1,1993. Additional chemical control action followed quickly in the 1990s. Thus, within a decade of the birth of the precursor and essential chemical diversion control concept, the legal framework for a concerted international control effort was firmly established.

§ 20.3.1 Chemical Control in the United States

The first major chemical control law in the United States was the Chemical Diversion and Trafficking Act (CDTA) of 1988, which instituted a control system for 20 chemicals, including those listed in the Vienna Convention. The regulatory and enforcement framework for precursor control was further enhanced through the Crime Control Act of 1990. The subsequent Domestic Chemical Diversion Control Act of 1993 specifically targeted the illicit production of methamphetamine and the related drug methcathinone (which has virtually disappeared as a clandestine product). The 1993 amendment began to close the "legal drug exemption" that had allowed traffickers to avoid regulatory requirements by buying thousands of legal FDA-approved tablets. The bill brought over-the-counter, single-entity ephedrine products under DEA regulatory control, and permitted DEA to add other products by regulation. It also required the registration of handlers of List I chemicals, similar to the requirements for controlled substances. In 1996, Congress enacted a major piece of methamphetamine-related legislation. The Comprehensive Methamphetamine Control Act (MCA) of 1996 broadened controls on listed chemicals used in the production of controlled substances and increased penalties for the trafficking and manufacture of methamphetamine and listed chemicals. This legislation removed the remaining CDTA-granted exemptions for combination ephedrine, pseudoephedrine (PSE) and phenylpropanolamine drug products. The Methamphetamine Penalty Enhancement Act of 1998, lowered certain quantity thresholds for mandatory minimum trafficking penalties. The recent Methamphetamine Anti-Proliferation Act of 2000 and Ecstasy Anti-Proliferation Act of 2000 enhanced the federal sentencing guidelines for these two substances.

§ 20.3.2 Chemical Situation

The world's leading chemical producers include the United States, the People's Republic of China, India, Germany and the Czech Republic. Ephedrine and PSE, precursors for methamphetamine, however, are not produced hi the United States or Canada. There are currently four countries that provide significant quantities of these chemicals to the international market: the Peoples' Republic of China, India, Germany, and the Czech Republic. Though Germany produces significant quantities of ephedrine and PSE, it maintains strict domestic controls of these substances, and has not been identified as a significant source country for these precursor chemicals in diversion investigations in the United States or Canada.

Four of the precursor chemicals potentially used for the production of Ecstasy (ethylamine, methylamine, nitroethane and piperonal) are produced in the United States, though not in significant quantities. These chemicals are regulated (List I) and domestic diversion is negligible. Imports and exports of these, and all List I chemicals, are monitored by the DEA Office of Diversion Control. The U.S. strategy toward international chemical diversion concentrates on chemicals destined for drug-producing regions.

§ 20.3.3 Domestic Movement of Chemicals

Sources of supply in the United States for methamphetamine precursor chemicals include convenience stores, liquor stores, gas stations, pharmacies, grocery stores, discount department stores, home improvement stores, tack and feed stores and other retailers. Decongestants and bronchodilators are purchased in drug and convenience stores, but there is no indication that they have been purchased in Canada and shipped to the United States. PSE tablets are also sent to individuals at their residences by mail order distributors, which often involves companies taking orders via the Internet. Increasingly, larger methamphetamine laboratories in the United States use PSE tablets manufactured in Canada and smuggled into the United States, often by traffickers who can no longer obtain large amounts from domestic U.S. companies. U.S.-based aromatherapy companies, using safrole, benzaldehyde, isosafrole, etc. as end products, are not required to be registered with DEA as List I chemical handlers.

§ 20.4   CHEMICALS
§ 20.4.1 Pseudoephedrine (PSE)

PSE is the most common precursor used in North American methamphetamine production. The diversion of PSE from legitimate Canadian suppliers to the illicit market is reaching a critical level. Massive quantities are being smuggled into the United States for use in methamphetamine "super-labs" (methamphetamine laboratories capable of producing 10 pounds or more per batch or "cook"), notably in the State of California. Since late 1999, DEA has documented more than 20 PSE and/or methamphetamine cases in the United States demonstrating a Canadian nexus.

Historically, the vast majority of the PSE diverted to clandestine laboratories in the United States was tablet product manufactured or distributed by U.S. companies. California has been the center of methamphetamine production and trafficking in the United States. As law enforcement attention increased and strong state precursor control laws were instituted in the State of California, making it difficult to obtain sufficient amounts of PSE locally, traffickers turned to suppliers nationwide. Traffickers purchased PSE at relatively low prices on the U.S. East Coast and moved the product to California, where the black market price reached between US$3,500 and US$4,000 per case. Nationwide networks of PSE suppliers, working together in loosely but not necessarily in identifiable hierarchies, provided ton quantities of PSE pill products to the market in California. These same operators also supplied distributors in other states who diverted product to local methamphetamine laboratories.

In response to the increasing diversion of PSE from U.S. sources, the MCA was enacted. When the provisions of the MCA went into effect in 1997, the ability of U.S.-based traffickers to acquire large amounts of PSE was curtailed, forcing the traffickers to find alternate sources of supply. During this time period, Canada began to emerge, on a small-scale, as a source of PSE for U.S.-based traffickers. The production, trafficking and abuse of synthetic drugs affects all Americans. DEA's strategy to combat the problem includes not only aggressive international, national and local law enforcement efforts, but also domestic and international precursor chemical controls and interdiction.

§ 20.4.2 Methamphetamine

Over the last decade, methamphetamine has become a significant drug threat facing the United States. The production, trafficking and abuse of the drug, coupled with the violence associated with all aspects of the trade, are concerns for U.S. policy-makers and law enforcement. The rise in production and trafficking of methamphetamine has resulted in expansion of abuse from the West and Southwest, to the Midwest and portions of the Eastern United States.

Prior to the 1990s, methamphetamine production and trafficking in the United States was primarily controlled by outlaw motorcycle gangs, including the Hells Angels. Mexican traffickers first became involved in methamphetamine production and distribution in the early 1990s, resulting in a significant increase in high-purity supplies of the drug. The growing popularity of the Internet also contributed to the accessibility of methamphetamine "recipes," resulting in a dramatic increase in the number of small-scale, or "mom-and-pop," laboratories throughout the United States.

According to the El Paso Intelligence Center's (EPIC) National Clandestine Laboratory Seizure System (NCLSS), during 2000, approximately 6,700 clandestine methamphetamine laboratory sites were seized by DEA and state/local law enforcement, compared to 6,782 seized during 1999. The States of California and Washington reported the greatest number of laboratory seizures during 2000. The majority of the laboratories, approximately 95 percent, seized in the United States are considered "mom and pop" laboratories, capable of producing ounce quantities of methamphetamine. The remaining five percent are considered "superlabs," capable of producing 10 or more pounds of methamphetamine in a single cook. The majority of the "superlabs" are believed to be tied to Mexican criminal groups and are located primarily in the State of California.

The supply of those chemicals needed to produce high-quality methamphetamine has been reduced through international chemical control efforts such as "Letters of No Objection" (LONO). DEA started issuing LONOs in 1995 to countries that require a letter stating that there is no objection to the export before allowing it to proceed. As a result of these efforts, the national purity level for methamphetamine, as well as amphetamine, has gone down dramatically. The average purity of methamphetamine exhibits seized by DEA dropped from 72 percent in 1994 to 31 percent in 1999. The average purity of amphetamine exhibits seized by DEA dropped from 41 percent in 1994 to only 21 percent in 1999. Emergency room mentions and overdose deaths involving methamphetamine show an analogous decrease. During 2000, however, there was a slight increase in the purity of methamphetamine to 35 percent and a slight decrease in the purity of amphetamine to 20 percent.

In addition, law enforcement efforts targeting both components of the methamphetamine trade, Mexican national organizations and "mom-and-pop" laboratory operators, have produced record arrests and seizures of methamphetamine, amphetamine and clandestine laboratories. In 2000, the Federal Drug Seizure System indicated seizures totaling 3 163 kilograms of methamphetamine, an increase from 2,774 kilograms in 1999.

§ 20.4.3 3,4-Methylenedioxymethamphetamine (MDMA/Ecstasy)
In the United States, the 1990s have been marked by unprecedented growth in the demand for MDMA/Ecstasy. The Rave phenomenon served as the primary vehicle for the perpetuation of the drug. Approximately 80 percent of the Ecstasy seized in the United States is produced in the Netherlands, and to a lesser extent, Belgium. Small-scale production is, however reported in the United States. International MDMA smuggling, according to DEA reporting, is largely controlled by ethnic Israeli drug trafficking organizations. The DEA Brussels Country Office (BCO), for example, reports clearly established links to Israeli groups in 12 of the 39 Ecstasy cases initiated by the BCO between 1998 and 2000. Ecstasy seizures in the United States have steadily increased over the course of the 1990s, from 11,913 tablets seized by DEA in 1996 to more than 3 million tablets in 2000.

Air couriers, mail parcels and air cargo shipments are the primary smuggling methods utilized by traffickers transporting Ecstasy shipments to the United States. New York, Miami and Los Angeles are the primary ports of entry for couriers arriving from both major and secondary European airports. Newark, Buffalo, Boston, Atlanta, Chicago, Detroit, Houston and San Diego are gaining popularity with Ecstasy traffickers as ports of entry into the United States. In Canada, Toronto and Montreal are increasingly utilized as transit points for MDMA entering the United States. As both trafficking organizations and law enforcement become increasingly sophisticated, routes are likely to diversify. INTERPOL reports for 1999 noted a movement away from the major European airports by international Ecstasy smugglers. Increasingly, couriers are utilizing secondary, or less heavily traveled, regional airports with direct connections to the United States, which include airports in Belgium, Germany, France, Spain, the Czech Republic and Iceland. During 2000, several Ecstasy seizures have been effected from couriers arriving at U.S. ports of entry from Iceland. These couriers obtained the Ecstasy and initiated travel in the Netherlands. The use of maritime containers and air cargo will likely increase as traffickers move larger quantities of Ecstasy from the source countries to destinations throughout the world. With Europe's sophisticated transportation networks and access to maritime commerce through the numerous container ports, these methods are likely to be frequently exploited in the future.

§ 20.4.4 Paramethoxyamphetamine (PMA)

PMA, also known as 4-methoxyamphetamine, is an illicit, synthetic hallucinogen that has stimulant effects similar to other clandestinely manufactured amphetamine derivatives like MDMA. Until recently, illicit abuse of PMA was briefly encountered during the early 1970s in the United States. However, since February 2000, PMA has reemerged in Florida, Illinois, Michigan, Virginia, and internationally. Like MDMA, PMA is currently distributed in the United States at Rave parties and clubs. Dealers may be unaware that they are buying or selling PMA rather than other club drugs such as MDMA.

§ 20.4.5 Gamma-hydroxybutyrate (GHB)

GHB has grown in popularity in the United States in recent years, especially among young adults active in the Rave and nightclub scene. According to the El Paso Intelligence Center (EPIC), during 2000, DBA seized seven clandestine GHB laboratories compared to five the previous year. GHB laboratory seizures by state/local agencies also demonstrated an increase during 2000, with 12 laboratory seizures reported, compared to eight during 1999. Access to recipes on the Internet has contributed to increased local production of GHB. The primary distributors of GHB are young adult Caucasian males, college students in particular.

§ 20.4.6 Ketamine

Ketamine, or "Special K", is an anesthetic in human and veterinary medicine. The Special K trip is touted as better than lysergic acid diethylamide (LSD) or phencyclidine (PCP) because it lasts only about 30 to 60 minutes as opposed to several hours. Ketamine is not manufactured in the United States, but is imported as a bulk powder. Once in the United States, it is converted into injectable dosage forms by U.S. firms. Illicit supplies are generally diverted from licit sources, with burglaries of veterinary clinics being the most frequently reported source. Increasingly, tablets containing amounts of ketamine have been seized in locations throughout the United States, including the states of Michigan, California and New York. These tablets are often sold as Ecstasy.

§ 20.4.7 Lysergic Acid Diethyimide (LSD)

The popularity of the Rave and nightclub scene has also given rise to a resurgence in the popularity of hallucinogens such as LSD. LSD is primarily produced in California, and more recently hi the Midwest. Manufacture remains arduous and time-consuming, and is limited by federal chemical controls on the primary precursor chemicals, ergo-tamine tartrate, lysergic acid and lysergic acid amide. Other limitations include the high price of the precursor chemicals and the high degree of skill required for the manufacture of the drug.

§ 20.5   ENVIRONMENTAL AND PUBLIC HEALTH HAZARDS

The threat to public safety from explosion, fire, poison gas, ground-water contamination, and hazardous by-products associated with clan-destine laboratories is likely to increase with the proliferation of syn-thetic drug production in the United States and Canada.

A growing number of children are present at clandestine laboratory sites in the United States. During 1999, approximately 974 children were present at laboratory sites—189 were exposed to toxic chemicals and 12 were injured. During 2000, the numbers increased, with 1,870 children present at laboratory sites—296 exposed to toxic chemicals, 12 injured, and three killed. As of June 2001, the number of children re-ported at laboratory sites was 738, with 271 exposed to toxic chemicals and 8 injured (DEA "Chemical Diversion" 2002). In response to this trend, a variety of policy and public safety approaches have emerged in the United States. The State of California, Office of Criminal Justice Planning, initiated the Drug Endangered Children (DEC) Response Teams in 1993. According to the Crime Prevention Coalition of Amer-ica, the primary goals of the inter-agency DEC Response Teams are to "improve the safety and health of children endangered by drug manu-facturing, distribution, and use environments by providing appropriate services; improve the community's response to drug endangered chil-dren by establishing a multidisciplinary team; and establish a consis-tent response from law enforcement and social services."

The risk of explosion and fire at clandestine laboratory sites is of great concern to the public and governmental agencies. The environ-mental degradation caused by the dumping of toxic by-products result-ing from methamphetamine production places heavy financial burdens on law enforcement agencies and all levels of government. On average, five to six pounds of toxic waste are produced for every pound of methamphetamine produced. In addition to the chemical and/or fire threat to the health and safety of the officers involved in the disman-tling of the clandestine laboratories, these sites often contain additional dangers such as blasting caps, dynamite, explosive booby-traps, explo-sives, grenades, pipe bombs and plastic explosives. Synthetic drugs continue to present a threat to North America. Domestic production of methamphetamine, MDMA and its analogues, and other synthetic drugs contribute to the overall drug threat in Canada and the United States. One of the primary strategies for combating the proliferation of synthetic drugs is the control and monitoring of precursor chemicals required for the production of these substances.

§ 20.6   WHAT IS BEING DONE INTERNATIONALLY?

The United States plays a vital role in coordinating chemical en-forcement operations in Latin American countries that produce cocaine or serve as transit points for cocaine chemicals. Operation Purple is a DEA driven international chemical control initiative designed to reduce the illicit manufacture of cocaine in the Andean Region by monitoring and tracking shipments of potassium permanganate (PP), the chemical oxidizer of choice for cocaine production. The cornerstone of the operation is an intensive PP tracking program aimed at identifying and intercepting diverted potassium permanganate; identifying rogue firms and suspect individuals; gathering intelligence on diversion methods, trafficking trends, and shipping routes; and taking administrative, civil, and/or criminal action as appropriate. Critical to the success of this operation is the communication network that gives notification of shipments and provides the government of the importer sufficient time to verify the legitimacy of the transaction and take appropriate action. The effects of this initiative have been dramatic and far-reaching. Operation Purple has exposed a significant vulnerability among traffickers, and has grown to include almost thirty nations.

Acetic anhydride (AA), the most commonly used chemical agent in heroin processing, is virtually irreplaceable. According to the DEA, Mexico remains the only heroin source country that has indigenous acetic anhydride production capability, producing 87,000 metric tons in 1999 alone. All other heroin producing countries must import large amounts of acetic anhydride. The diversion of this chemical to Colombian heroin laboratories is a continuing problem. However the largest markets for diverted acetic anhydride continue to be heroin laboratories in Afghanistan and Burma. Of particular note was a March 2000 seizure of 72.8 metric tons of AA in Turkmenistan, en route to heroin laboratories in Afghanistan. Authorities in Uzbekistan, Turkmenistan, Kyrgyzstan, and Kazakhstan routinely seize ton quantity shipments of diverted acetic anhydride.

The methamphetamine situation changed in the mid-1990's with the entrance of Mexican organized crime into production and distribution. According to the DEA, the seizure of 3.5 metric tons of pseudoephedrine (the primary precursor chemical used in the production of methamphetamine) in Texas revealed that Mexican trafficking groups were producing methamphetamine on an unprecedented scale, with potentially serious repercussions for drug abuse throughout the United States. DEA has developed several strategies to deal with the methamphetamine chemical diversion threat. First, the agency instituted a series of special enforcement operations directed against chemical traffickers. DEA instituted programs such as Operation Chemex and Operation Backtrack to track and seize chemicals destined for methamphetamine laboratories in Mexico. At the same time Congress has developed methamphetamine legislation, the Ecstasy Prevention Act of 2001 (S. 1208 and H.R. 2582). The legislation toughens sentences for methamphetamine production and trafficking and provide additional funds for cleaning up clandestine lab sites.

The thirty-five chemicals most commonly used in illicit drug production also have extensive industrial applications. For this reason, an important element in the U.S. drug-control policy is to ensure that all countries have a flexible monitoring system that regulates the flow of precursor chemicals without jeopardizing legitimate commerce. The Multilateral Chemical Reporting Initiative, formulated with international consensus encourages governments to exchange information on a voluntary basis in order to monitor international chemical shipments. Over the past decade, key international bodies like the Commission on Narcotic Drugs and the U.N. General Assembly's Special Session (UNGASS) have addressed the issue of chemical diversion in conjunction with U.S. efforts. These organizations raised specific concerns about potassium permanganate and acetic anhydride.

§ 20.7   DRUG DIVERSION/PRESCRIPTION DRUGS
§ 20.7.1 Introduction

Prescription drugs make complex surgery possible, relieve pain for millions of people, and enable many individuals with chronic medical conditions to control their symptoms and lead productive lives. Most people who take prescription medications use them responsibly. However, the non-medical use of prescription drugs is a serious public health concern. Nonmedical use of prescription drugs like opioids, central nervous system (CNS) depressants, and stimulants can lead to abuse and addiction, characterized by compulsive drug seeking and use.

Addiction rarely occurs among people who use a pain reliever, CNS depressant, or stimulant as prescribed; however, inappropriate use of prescription drugs can lead to addiction in some cases. Patients, healthcare professionals, and pharmacists all have roles in preventing misuse and addiction. For example, if a doctor prescribes a pain medication, CNS depressant, or stimulant, the patient should follow the directions for use carefully, and also learn what effects the drug could have and potential interactions with other drugs by reading all information provided by the pharmacist. Physicians and other health care providers should screen for any type of substance abuse during routine history-taking with questions about what prescriptions and over-the-counter medicines the patient is taking and why.

§ 20.7.2 Commonly Abused Prescription Drugs

While many prescription drugs can be abused or misused, these three classes are most commonly abused:

Opioids—prescribed to treat pain.
CNS Depressants—prescribed to treat anxiety and sleep disorders.
Stimulants—prescribed to treat narcolepsy and ADD disorders.

§ 20.7.2(a)   Opioids

Opioids are commonly prescribed because of their effective analgesic or pain relieving properties. Many studies have shown that properly managed medical use of opioid analgesic drugs is safe and rarely causes clinical addiction, which is defined as compulsive, often uncontrollable use. Taken exactly as prescribed, opioids can be used to manage pain effectively. Among the drugs that fall within this class - sometimes referred to as narcotics - are morphine, codeine, and related drugs. Morphine is often used before or after surgery to alleviate severe pain. Codeine is used for milder pain. Other examples of opioids that can be prescribed to alleviate pain include oxycodone (OxyContin-an oral, controlled release form of the drug); propoxyphene (Darvon); hydrocodone (Vicodin); hydromorphone (Dilaudid); and meperidine (Demerol), which is used less often because of its side effects. In addition to their effective pain relieving properties, some of these drugs can be used to relieve severe diarrhea (Lomotil, for example, which is diphenoxylate) or severe coughs (codeine) (NIDA 2000).

§ 20.7.2(b) CNS Depressants

CNS depressants slow down normal brain function. In higher doses, some CNS depressants can become general anesthetics. There are many CNS depressants, and most act on the brain similarly - they affect the neurotransmitter gamma-aminobutyric acid (GABA). Neurotransmitters are brain chemicals that facilitate communication between brain cells. GABA works by decreasing brain activity. Although different classes of CNS depressants work in unique ways, ultimately it is their ability to increase GABA activity that produces a drowsy or calming effect. Despite these beneficial effects for people suffering from anxiety or sleeping disorders, barbiturates and benzodiazepmes can be addictive and should be used only as prescribed.

§ 20.7.2(c) Stimulants

Stimulants are a class of drugs that enhance brain activity - they cause an increase in alertness, attention, and energy that is accompanied by increases in blood pressure, heart rate, and respiration. Historically, stimulants were used to treat asthma and other respiratory problems, obesity, neurological disorders, and a variety of other ailments. As their potential for abuse and addiction became apparent, the use of stimulants began to wane. Now, stimulants are prescribed for treating only a few health conditions, including narcolepsy, attention-deficit hyperactivity disorder (ADHD), and depression that has not responded to other treatments. Stimulants may also be used for short-term treatment of obesity, and for patients with asthma.

§ 20.7.3 Diversion and Distribution

Illegal acts by physicians and pharmacists are the primary sources of diverted pharmaceuticals available on the illicit market. In many cases, they create fraudulent prescriptions to obtain the drug for personal use or to provide associates with a supply of the drug for distribution purposes. To date, many physicians, pharmacists, and pharmacy technicians who have been illegally prescribing or diverting the narcotic OxyContin have been identified or arrested throughout the United States. One of the most popular ways to obtain prescription narcotics is through "doctor shopping." Individuals with real or fabricated ailments visit numerous doctors in an attempt to obtain prescription narcotics like OxyContin, Percocet, and Percodan. In many cases, certain physicians have earned reputations among abusers for easily dispensing prescriptions. An individual may obtain many prescriptions in a short period of time and get them filled at various pharmacies for personal use and/or distribution.

With the abuse of OxyContin on the rise, law enforcement authorities throughout the United States are reporting an increase in the number of burglaries, thefts, and robberies of pharmacies and residences. According to authorities, homes are being robbed and individuals are being targeted for their supplies of OxyContin. In some pharmacy thefts only OxyContin is stolen. Internet websites are potential sources for the diversion of prescription narcotics and other pharmaceutically controlled substances. Websites designed to facilitate the distribution of illicit drugs and diverted pharmaceuticals, including Oxy-Contin, are becoming increasingly popular with illicit drug dealers. These sites allow dealers or individual users to place orders for drugs and pharmaceuticals, and sometimes use encryption software to thwart law enforcement investigations.

Illicit prescription drug distribution is not limited to localized distributors as it also includes polydrug trafficking organizations. In the northeastern United States, a gang operating in southern Maine and New Hampshire obtained controlled substances, primarily OxyContin, using forged, stolen, and altered prescriptions. The drugs were illegally obtained from local pharmacies using cash and insurance cards. Gang members redistributed the drugs throughout areas in the Northeast. Pharmaceutical Drug Diversion is generally thought of as an offense that is perpetrated by humans visiting human practitioners—physicians, dentists, and others who treat people. The fact is pet owners who are interested in diverting pharmaceuticals have become part of the problem. Veterinarians can prescribe virtually any prescription drug. Veterinarians, especially those treating large animals or working at horse tracks, can be a source for those seeking anabolic steroids. Also, veterinarians themselves can be the source of the diversion because these drugs are readily available for self-abuse.

§ 20.7.3(a) Stopping Diversions

For the first time, the federal government is directing its fight against illegal drug use toward the abuse of legal drugs. "The nonmedical use of prescription drugs has become an increasingly widespread and serious problem in this country, one that calls for immediate action," said Drug Czar John Walters. "The federal government is embarking on a comprehensive effort to ensure that potentially addictive medications are dispensed and used safely and effectively" (Hawryluk). The 2005 National Drug Control Strategy will include greater scrutiny of labeling and marketing of opiate drug products, wider dissemination of educational materials for doctors regarding appropriate pain management, and a crackdown on Internet pharmacies that provide controlled substances illegally.

"This represents a somewhat new kind of threat," Walters said. "These drugs are legal, they have legitimate medical uses that need to be preserved, and they [sometimes leave] people to think they are safer and not subject to abuse. But they are." Nonmedical use of prescription drugs now ranks second only to marijuana use as the most common abuse of drugs in the United States. Steps are being taken to reduce "doctor shopping," in which patients get prescriptions from multiple physicians. Twenty states have implemented prescription monitoring programs that track the dispensing of drugs and can identify potential doctor shopping. In 2000, the five states with the lowest per capita number of prescriptions for OxyContin, a commonly abused prescription drug, all had monitoring programs, while the five states with the highest number of prescriptions per capita all lacked such safeguards.

The American Medical Association said more work is needed to prevent the illegal distribution of prescription drugs, particularly over the Internet. But the Association cautioned that controls must strike a balance between promoting pain relief and stopping drug misuse. "Preventing prescription drug abuse is a vital goal. However, it is just as crucial that those in chronic pain have continued access to pain relief medications," said AMA Trustee Rebecca J, Patchin, MD. "It is critical that in the rush to address drug abuse, we do not unintentionally discourage patients and physicians from appropriately treating chronic pain." The AMA launched a pain management education program in 2003 to provide primary care physicians with information about the assessment and management of pain. Prescription medications are now among the most commonly abused drugs in the United States (NIDA 2002).

—Marijuana: 14.6 million people
—Prescription drugs: 6.2 million people
—Cocaine: 2.0 million people
—Hallucinogens: 1.2 million people
—Heroin: 2.0 million people

§ 20.8   CONCLUSION

Although DEA statistics have consistently identified pharmaceuticals as almost 30% of the overall drug problem in the United States, many law enforcement agencies have spent little or no resources to combat the problem. Huge profits are made every year by a variety of prescription drug traffickers in this country, who go unnoticed and avoid prosecution in this lucrative market, A variety of regulatory agencies have recognized the problem for decades, pursuing health professionals through administrative processes. Law enforcement is a needed addition that could, and should, be working with the regulatory officers.

Health care professionals can become traffickers in enormous amounts of prescription drugs. Health professionals who are trafficking in prescription drugs can reap large monetary profits, exchange drugs for sex, and engage in health care fraud schemes that represent part of a $100 billion dollar business in the United States each year. False and forged prescriptions, "doctor shoppers," and other deception scams to obtain prescription drugs are commonplace in every community. These offenders feed addictions, become involved in trafficking offenses, and defraud government and private health care insurance agencies.

References

Drug Enforcement Administration. "Chemical Diversion and Synthetic Drug Manufacture." Intelligence Reports. Washington, D.C.: U.S. Department of Justice, 2002.

Hawryluk, Marian. "Focus on Stopping Diversion: Federal Officials Announce Crackdown on Illegal Use of Prescription Painkillers." AMNews Staff, March 15, 2004.

National Institute on Drug Abuse. "National Household Survey on Drug Abuse." Rockville, MD, Department of Health and Human Services, 2002.

----------. Pain Medications and Other Prescription Drugs. DHHS Pub #13553. Rockville, MD: Department of Health and Human Services, 2000.

CHAPTER 21

DRUG TREATMENT AND REHABILITATION

§ 21.1 INTRODUCTION

In the 1962 landmark case of *Robinson v. California*, 370 U.S. 660, 8 L.Ed.2d 758, 82 S.Ct. 1417 (1962), the United States Supreme Court established as a matter of law that drug addiction itself is an illness and not a crime; therefore, a person cannot be punished for the mere status of being a drug addict. Neither Robinson nor any federal or state Supreme Court ruling since that time has accepted the view that a criminal offender lacks the capacity to form the criminal intent (*mens rea*) to commit a crime because he or she, at the time of committing the illegal act, is under the influence of drugs. Hence, while the status of being a drug addict is not itself a crime, the sale of or knowing possession of illegal drugs by the addict, or the commission of drug-related crimes such as larceny to finance drug habits, continue to be punishable as crimes. Subsequent to Robinson, the federal government, with many of the states following suit, reorganized its drug laws in 1970 into a uniform Controlled Substances Act.

Furthermore, by holding that the states could not only require an addict to submit to treatment through a noncriminal avenue, but could also impose subsequent criminal penalties for failure to comply with this legal requirement, Robinson caused the drug treatment community and the criminal justice system to devise procedures for channeling drug-addicted criminal defendants into treatment.

Consequently, drug abuse treatment has become a significant industry in the United States. For example, the Federal Government's proposed budget for fiscal year 2005 proposed to spend 38.7 percent of the Drug Control budget ($4.81 billion) on drug treatment and drug prevention, and the remaining 61.3 percent ($7.61 billion) among Domestic Law Enforcement, Drug Interdiction, and International Drug Control.

For example, the Federal Government's proposed budget for fiscal year 2005 proposed to spend 38.7 percent of the drug control budget ($4.81 billion) on drug treatment and drug prevention, the remaining 61.3 percent ($7.61 billion) among domestic law enforcement, drug interdiction, and international drug control. Despite increased activity in the field of treatment, there is little consensus among practitioners about the best methods for treating drug abuse, or even the nature of the problem to be treated. Treatment programs vary widely, depending on whether the patient's drug abuse is ascribed to biological malfunctions, personality disorders, personal relationships, or other factors.

§ 21.2 WHAT IS TREATMENT?

Many intervention programs could be classified as either treatment or prevention. Whether an intervention is called drug abuse treatment or drug abuse prevention depends less on the actual mode of intervention than on the perceived degree of involvement in the drug by the person being treated. Less drug-involved people receive preventive measures while more drug-involved people receive treatment. Often the distinction between treatment and prevention is made from the frequency of use and/or the problems (dysfunctions) caused by excessive use. Generally, treatment is given to individuals who use drugs frequently, who take large amounts, and who experience significant dysfunctions or adverse effects as a result. Treatment is given to the addicted—to those who cannot say no, who have lost control, who are compulsive in behavior, and who continue to use drugs in spite of adverse consequences.

§ 21.2.1 Treatment in the United States

For all the ambiguity about what constitutes drug treatment, it is a major activity in the United States, involving government at all levels, private charitable organizations, private for-profit organizations, individual health care professionals, and concerned lay people. This multiplicity of service providers actually prevents knowledge of the extent of drug treatment. For example, if the child of a well-paid and well-insured lawyer obtains individual psychotherapy because cocaine use has caused a drop in high school grades, neither the treatment nor the money expended on it is likely to be incorporated into any statistical description of the extent of drug treatment.

Drug treatment in the United States was traditionally oriented toward opiates, while the popular image of drug treatment still focuses on heroin addiction. Indeed, the vast majority of treatment research and evaluation has dealt with heroin addiction and heroin treatment centers. However, this emphasis is changing as attention turns toward abusers of multiple substances (polydrug users), as other drugs such as cocaine and methamphetamine become more heavily abused, and as the relationship between alcohol and drug use is studied. Treatment for marijuana use has also become a more frequently researched topic, but efforts have concentrated on epidemiology and prevention.

§ 21.2.1(a) Modes of Treatment

There are four generally recognized modalities of treatment programs. These are detoxification (DT), methadone maintenance (MM), therapeutic communities (TC), and drug-free (almost always outpatient) treatment (DF). Each of these modalities has several variations within it.

§ 21.2.1(b) Detoxification (DT)

DT is a medical treatment intended to terminate current drug use via a safe withdrawal procedure. It largely involves supervised abstinence from the substance, with such medical and psychological support as necessary while the person goes through the trials of physical withdrawal. As such, DT is strictly physiological in orientation, and does not address the patient's psychosocial or economic well-being; these latter are deferred to post-DT treatment, if any. The early treatment programs at federal hospitals in Lexington, Kentucky and Fort Worth, Texas were stereotypical examples of detoxification institutions, spawning the popular detox image. However, these were institutionalized treatment programs enmeshed within the criminal justice system;

presently, over two-thirds of DT is done on an outpatient basis. Although many different drug programs have detoxification as the initial step in an overall treatment plan, a modality is classified as DT only if detoxification is the principal or only treatment provided.

§ 21.2.1(c)   Methadone Maintenance (MM)

MM is a treatment in which a synthetic opiate is administered to an addict as a substitute for the opiate of abuse, typically heroin. Although the client remains dependent on the substitute, there are several clear advantages to the change of opiate:

—The synthetic does not produce the intense "highs" or other sensations of the original drug of abuse.
—It blocks the effects of any other opiates taken during treatment, thus eliminating some motivations to continue those drugs.
—It is administered orally instead of by injection.
—It is longer-acting, therefore requiring fewer administrations than the typical opiate of abuse.

The underlying idea is that MM frees the client from the pressures of obtaining illegal heroin, from the dangers of injection, and from the emotional roller coaster that most opiates produce. Even though addicted to a substance, the addict can muster the effort required to gain social stability. Since its development in New York City by Dr. Vincent P. Dole and Dr. Marie Nyswander, it has become one of the most widely accepted of the treatment modalities for opiate addiction. It should be noted that MM is appropriate only for opiate addiction, and not for the treatment of abuse of other drugs such as cocaine, hallucinogens, or marijuana.

The synthetic originally used in MM treatment was methadone, hence the name now generically applied to substance substitution treatment. Methadone has since been supplemented by new substances that serve the same function but offer additional advantages. For example, LAAM (L-acetylmethadol) is quite similar to methadone in form and effects, but is longer-acting, thus requiring fewer administrations. Presently, any drug-substitution treatment of this form is known as MM. In a typical MM treatment, the addict comes to a clinic regularly (e.g., daily for methadone, or three times a week for LAAM) for administration of methadone and an inspection (typically urinalysis) to ensure that other drugs are not being used. Virtually all MM programs serve addicts on this type of outpatient basis. Many clinics provide long-term MM programs in keeping with a philosophical view of addiction as a long-term chronic condition. The original MM model offered chronic maintenance, with little or no psychosocial intervention. A second model, now more popular than the first, offers both psychosocial interventions and plans to taper off and withdraw all drug maintenance.

§ 21.2.1(d)   Therapeutic Communities (TC)

A TC is a residential treatment center in which the drug user lives, sheltered from the pressures of the outside world and from drugs, and in which he can learn to lead a new, drug-free life. The goal of TCs is to re-socialize the drug abuser by creating a structured, isolated mutual help environment in which the individual can develop and learn to function as a mature participant.

TCs developed during the 1960s in part as a reaction against the authoritarian treatment structure of the DT approach. The original TC was Synanon. Other communities, such as Daytop Village, Phoenix House, Pathways, CAPS (Combined Addicts and Professional Services), have achieved some reputation for success. Most TCs are largely staffed by ex-addicts. Some even view professional providers of drug abuse treatment with disdain, although professionals have had critical roles in the establishment of successful TCs. The original TC approach sharply restricted the personal freedom of people undergoing treatment and emphasized public self-criticism, criticism by others, and severe sanctions for violations of the community rules and norms. This practice has waned over time, with many present TCs replacing confrontational criticism with more supportive strategies.

Although originally used almost exclusively by heroin addicts, TCs have come to be a modality for pill takers, alcoholics, cocaine users, marijuana users, and even people who wish to change their food-taking habits. Many present-day TCs report large populations of polydrug users. Moreover, TCs have been founded to serve specialized communities such as blacks, women, youth, and born-again Christians who suffer from drug abuse.

§ 21.2.1(e)   Drug-Free (Outpatient) Programs (DF)

DF is a generic term for all of the remaining modalities of treatment, which are non-institutional, non-residential, and do not provide alternative drugs. Over 50 percent of all treatment is in this category, as is virtually all of the treatment of non-opiate drug abuse. Among the more commonly used techniques, especially with youthful drug abusers, are:

Crisis intervention centers. These are locations where users in distress can turn for help. They include walk-in centers, 24-hour telephone hot lines, "crash pads" for emergency living arrangements, and referral centers. They deal with overdoses, help during "bad trips," and other short-term services. As with TCs, crisis intervention centers are largely staffed by non-professionals with whom the addicts can identify.

Psychotherapy and counseling. Talking with abusers is the most common form of treatment, and occurs in every modality. As a primary mode of treatment, psychotherapy tries to help the individual behave in healthy ways. Additionally, many different types of therapeutic intervention have been attempted under DF. Among these are behavior therapies (both reinforcement and aversive), biofeedback, and hypnotherapy. In reinforcement behavior therapy, the addict is placed in a controlled environment where drug-related stimuli are presented to him, and is rewarded or punished depending on his response to the stimuli, so that the addict learns appropriate (drug-rejecting) responses. In aversive behavior therapy, the addict is presented with drug-related stimuli concomitantly with a noxious condition (such as being induced to be nauseous or receiving mild electric shocks), such that the drug-related stimuli become associated with the noxiousness and produce avoidance reactions (via conditioning). In biofeedback, addicts are presented with information based on electronic monitoring of biological processes (such as blood pressure, heart rate, or various brainwaves), and learn to maintain levels of these processes that are consistent with drug-avoiding behaviors. Hypnotherapy uses post-hypnotic suggestion in conjunction with behavior therapy techniques to reduce the psychological craving for drugs.

§ 21.2.1(f)   Summary

The four modalities of DT, MM, TC, and DF treatment are out-growths of different theoretical orientations towards drug abuse. DT and MM are largely based on theories of biological malfunctions and treat the abuser as having chemical dependencies in need of correction. TCs, on the other hand, are founded on theories of interpersonal problems and treat the abuser as needing re-socialization. DF treatment is based on theories of personality or interpersonal difficulties; if the problem is viewed as one of self, the treatment becomes individualized. In some cases, group psychotherapy may be used as opposed to family or other systems-based therapies.

§ 21.2.2 Narcotics Treatment in England

Serious considerations of the British approach to the treatment of heroin addiction have often been clouded by misinformation about the system, which ranges from the assertion that narcotics are legal in England to the belief that the British approach is identical to the American treatment policy. Neither statement is completely true. Although an addict in Great Britain can, through the proper channels, legally obtain heroin or morphine, narcotics are not legal. As in the United States, there has been increasing emphasis on switching the addicts to methadone maintenance and/or eventually encouraging them to undergo withdrawal. The history of British narcotics treatment policy may be divided into three major periods.

§ 21.2.2(a)   First Period: The Rolleston Committee (1924)

In 1924, the British Minister of Health appointed a group of distinguished physicians to consider the possibility that the practice of administering heroin to addicts might have been a violation of legal statutes. This committee, headed by Sir H. D. Rolleston, published a report in 1926 which concluded:

> "morphine or heroin may properly be administered to addicts in the following circumstances, namely (a) where patients are under treatment by the gradual withdrawal method with a view to cure, (b) where it has been demonstrated that after a prolonged attempt at cure that the use of the drug cannot be safely discontinued entirely, on account of the severity of the withdrawal symptoms produced, and (c) where it has been similarly demonstrated that the patient, while capable of leading a useful and relatively normal life when a certain minimum dose is regularly administered, becomes incapable of this when the drug is entirely discontinued" (May 351).

It should be noted here that this early decision of the Rolleston Committee has set the tone for subsequent British narcotics legislation.

Until the early 1960s, the number of known narcotics addicts in England remained insignificant; the total number of all known narcotic addicts averaged under 500 for any year between 1924 and 1960. In addition, almost all of these were not "street" addicts, but "therapeutic" addicts, i.e., initially addicted in the course of medical treatment (DHHS 1978).

In pre-World War II years, addicts were overrepresented among professional people, such as doctors and nurses; they were more often female than male and were usually middle-aged. The majority of these addictions were of therapeutic origin. Exemplifying the concept of the "stabilized addict," these British individuals were able to live useful and relatively normal lives with small, regular daily doses of narcotic drugs obtainable on prescription. The 1950s, however, marked a change in this pattern of narcotics use. The addicts during these later years tended to be younger and predominantly male. They congregated in groups in the music clubs of London. Throughout the 1950s, the medical profession in Great Britain jealously guarded its prerogative to prescribe heroin to addicts.

§ 21.2.2(b) Second Period: Convening of the First Brain Committee (1958)

In 1958, a committee was appointed under the chairmanship of Lord Brain to review the advice of the Rolleston Committee. The committee met to consider whether new methods of treating heroin addiction rendered the Rolleston recommendations obsolete and to decide if the increasing popularity of synthetic analgesics, such as pethidine and methadone, should come under stricter control or review. Their final report, published in 1960, recommended no major changes in British drug policy and reaffirmed the doctor's prerogative to prescribe narcotic drugs, including heroin. This decision was based on the belief that there had been no major increase in the number of new addicts per year.

§ 21.2.2(c) Third Period: Convening of the Second Brain Committee (1964)

In 1964, the Interdepartmental Committee reconvened to consider whether, in the light of recent experience, the advice they gave in 1961 in relation to the prescribing of addictive drugs by doctors needed revising; and if it did, the Committee was to make recommendations. Reports from the Home Office indicated that, although both organized trafficking in dangerous drugs and illicit importation of drugs remained at insignificant levels, there was now evidence of increasing heroin abuse, fed mainly by the activities of a few doctors whose over prescribing had created a surplus.

For example, in 1962, one million tablets of heroin (one-sixth grain each) were prescribed; 600,000 of these came from one doctor in London. In 1965, the Committee recommended a complete revision of the British approach to drug abuse treatment. The proposed controls more closely approximated the concept of a formal system than anything that had existed previously. Their conclusions were five-fold: (1) specific centers should be organized to treat addiction problems; (2) only licensed doctors should be authorized to prescribe heroin and cocaine to addicts for the purpose of treating their addictions—in practice, these licenses are issued on a selective basis to doctors working in the field of drug addiction; (3) a formal system for the notification of addicts should be established; (4) doctors at the centers should be given advice in cases where addiction was in question; (5) doctors at the centers should be given the power, in certain circumstances, to detain addicts in inpatient facilities without the addicts' consent. By the spring of 1968, all but the last recommendation were passed into law.

§ 21.2.2(d)   Operation of the British System After 1968

In the spring of 1968, seventeen clinics had been set up to provide both inpatient and outpatient facilities for the treatment of narcotics addiction. A patient who did not wish to undergo withdrawal treatment could be maintained on a minimum dosage of heroin with the understanding that the staff of the clinic would work to win his or her confidence and trust so that he or she might be eventually convinced to undergo withdrawal. The Advisory Committee on Drug Dependence, established approximately at the same time that the clinics were being set up, published a report emphasizing that outpatient clinics should not be "regarded as mere prescribing units without any positive objective. Outpatient clinics are also rehabilitation clinics. Their object should be to encourage the addict to accept hospital admission for withdrawal and to make use of the opportunity which prescribing gives to build a constructive relationship with the patient."

In 1969, the clinics were attended by approximately 1,300 patients a month. These patients attended the clinics every week and picked up daily prescriptions at local pharmacies. Efforts were made to spread prescriptions around town in order to avoid the problems that had existed earlier, when groups of addicts "hung around" specific pharmacies. Urine tests indicated that most patients used the drugs prescribed as well as other substances, primarily amphetamines and barbiturates. Many of the licensed physicians in the treatment clinics shifted from prescribing heroin to methadone, because the latter is a longer-acting drug and is available in sterile solution suitable for use in intravenous injections.

Beginning in 1960, the British began to see an increase in the number of new known addicts. In 1959, there were 454 known addicts; in 1960, 437; in 1961, 470; in 1962, 532; in 1963, 635; and in 1969, 2,881. By 1975, this figure had dropped to 1,954. By 1983, however, heroin addiction increased to 5,850 addicts. This was an increase of 1,750 addicts from 1982—a 42 percent increase. Many more of the new addicts were under 20 years old and seizures of heroin by police and customs officials doubled to more than six times the annual average of the 1970s. The addicts tended to be multiple drug users using cocaine as well as heroin.

§ 21.2.2(e)   Current Policies and Patterns of Drug Abuse in Britain

Patterns of drug abuse in Great Britain are changing. After 1968, there was a rapid increase in amphetamine and barbiturate misuse.

Chapter 21

When the prescription of heroin and cocaine was restricted, a few doctors irresponsibly switched their addicts to methamphetamine. Finally, a voluntary agreement was made between the pharmaceutical manufacturers and the Ministry of Health, whereby supplies of methamphetamine were restricted to hospital pharmacies; thus, a potential epidemic was averted. Currently, a number of methadone addicts who had no previous experience with heroin have been coming to the clinics as new patients. This suggests that a limited amount of the methadone prescribed by registered practitioners has been diverted to the black market. This may be due to the fact that the prescription of methadone has always been open to any registered physician.

Furthermore, methadone is replacing heroin as the drug of choice for maintenance therapy, even though the policy on prescribing drugs for the treatment of narcotics addiction has remained unchanged: it is still a clinical decision as to which drug to prescribe. Nonetheless, methadone—either orally or intravenously—is being prescribed much more frequently.

Since 1971, the British policy has been to treat the individual opiate addict as a medical patient rather than as a criminal. Furthermore, once the United States made treatment widely available in the 1970s and once the United States began to use methadone, the differences between the British and American approaches diminished greatly. As with the U.S. system, there has been considerable confusion over the success of the British system in curtailing the rising tide of individuals becoming addicted to heroin. In order for a narcotics addict in Britain to be accepted for treatment at one of the 35 narcotics addict treatment centers (15 in London and 20 in the Provinces), the physician in charge must be satisfied clinically that the addict is dependent on narcotic drugs and that he or she will be treated for his or her addiction. There is no regulation that there must be a 2-year history of addiction, as there is in the United States.

As noted earlier, the heroin legally produced in Britain is only available in one dosage form, a tablet of 10 mg (of a grain). The availability of this tablet dosage form led to a new trend in Britain from 1970 onwards: new addicts entering treatment were offered methadone instead of heroin, as methadone was available in sterile injectable dosage form.

By providing legally-produced heroin, it has been said that the British system has curtailed drug-related crime. However, arguments that the British system has been successful in undercutting the black market and destroying the incentive for organized crime seem to have been premature. The price of illegal heroin on the streets of London is about the same as the price on the streets of New York City. In light of this, it might be more accurate to say that the British pattern of narcotics control and licensed distribution served successfully to maintain pre- and post-war generations of therapeutic addicts. At that time, Great Britain did not have the street addict problem that has always characterized the American heroin experience. But, since the 1960s, addiction has been spreading to the streets and, as a result, stricter controls—like those in place in the United States—are necessary.

§ 21.2.2(f) Summary

The history of the British narcotics system is fraught with controversy. For years, debate has raged over whether or not the British drug program actually constitutes a system. Some say that a system can be just as much a loosely gathered set of regulations and customs as it can be a tightly structured organization of laws. Others insist that it has only been in recent years, when policies have been coordinated, that we can justifiably speak of a "British system." On the part of Americans, there has been much misunderstanding about what the British program intends to do and how it strives to reach its objectives.

§ 21.3 DRUG TREATMENT AND DENIAL

While it is difficult to draw precise inferences from the data available, the likelihood that an adult who uses drugs on at least a monthly basis (a so-called "current" user) will go on to need drug treatment is approximately one in four-high enough to constitute a substantial risk but low enough that many individuals are able to deny the obvious risks or convince themselves that they can "manage" their drug-using behavior. One drug treatment practitioner compares the problem to that of people who do not wear seatbelts. Although such people are risking self-destruction at every turn, every trip that ends safely actually reinforces the erroneous belief that seatbelts do not matter.

There is a word for this problem—"denial." Addicts deny the nature and severity of their problem even in the face of mounting evidence to the contrary. Denial explains why such a small percentage of the more than four million Americans who meet the clinical definition of dependence and are therefore in need of drug treatment actually seek it in a given year.

Not only does denial keep people from seeking help, it also maintains the destructive behavior long enough to allow the disease of addiction to gain an even firmer hold and be transmitted to peer groups and friends.

§ 21.3.1 What Type of Treatment?

One of the most perplexing issues in the treatment of drug users is determining which types of treatment are most beneficial to which types of drug users. Given the complex nature of drug dependency and the variable quality of treatment programs, only limited success in matching clients to treatments has been possible in the past. But classifying persons based on pretreatment characteristics may be useful in developing treatment programs for drug-involved offenders.

There is some evidence that young offenders with less serious drug abuse problems (no heroin use) and no prior treatment history can benefit from early intervention and treatment initiated by the criminal justice system. In another study, program offenders enter treatment in many communities through a program sponsored by the Bureau of Justice Assistance—the Treatment Alternatives to Street Crime (TASC) program—which refers these offenders to treatment in lieu of prosecution or probation revocation.

Criminal justice referral to treatment can be particularly effective because these persons tend to stay in treatment longer than those who enter treatment voluntarily. The length of time in treatment is a critical factor in post-treatment outcomes. Depending on the type of program, treatment usually must continue for several months and often 1 to 2 years to achieve substantial reductions in drug use and criminality.

§ 21.3.1(a)   In-Prison Treatment

Some in-prison treatment programs are designed to resemble the residential model that has been successful in community-based drug treatment programs such as Phoenix House in New York; other programs are less structured and more closely resemble a group counseling approach. In the former, prisoners usually spend some period immediately prior to parole eligibility in the treatment program, usually physically separated from the larger inmate population. Program directors draw staff from a wide range of professions.

Few in-prison treatment programs of this type operate in the United States, and evaluations of such programs are scarce. But available research suggests that intensive correctional drug treatment programs can have a substantial impact on drug-involved offenders if the offenders remain in the program.

An evaluation of a New York State prison program (Stay 'N Out) showed that participants who stayed in treatment for at least 9 months accumulated fewer parole violations than a comparable group that received only counseling or other less intensive in-prison drug treatment (Wexler). In another program for inmates in Oregon, 51 percent of program graduates had no subsequent convictions after 3 years, whereas only 11 percent of those who dropped out within 60 days had not been reconvicted (Field). Benefits increase when parolees are required to continue in community treatment as a condition of their parole.

It is not surprising that those who are motivated to stay in the program have better outcomes. However, most experts agree that if the in-prison programs were not available, the great majority of inmates with previous drug abuse problems would relapse once released from prison.

Successful implementation of in-prison drug treatment programs requires extensive planning and ongoing cooperation with correctional authorities, but there can be many positive outcomes of such programs, including reductions in recidivism, an improved working environment for staff, and positive publicity for the correctional system.

Drug abuse among correctional populations is a pervasive problem affecting between 60% and 80% of offenders under supervision. By requiring drug testing at the State and Federal levels, providing models of successful drug treatment programs, providing financial support for research and prevention, and looking to the future for a long-term commitment, the Federal Government will provide the basis for effective treatment programs for offenders to become productive, positive members of society.

Drug Treatment and Rehabilitation

§ 21.3.1(b) Alternatives to Incarceration

Created in the early 1970s, the Treatment Accountability for Safer Communication (TASC) program has demonstrated that the coercive authority of the criminal justice system can be used to get individuals into treatment and to manage drug-abusing offenders safely and effectively in the community. TASC's objective is to provide a bridge between the criminal justice system and the drug treatment community. Through TASC, some drug offenders are diverted from the criminal justice system and into community-based supervision, others receive treatment as part of probation, and still others are assigned to transitional services as they leave an institutional program. Community-based treatment and rehabilitation services are provided in concert with criminal justice sanctions and procedures that reinforce each other. TASC then monitors the client's progress and compliance, including expectations for abstinence from drugs, employment, and improved personal and social functioning. The progress of the individual in treatment is reported to the referring criminal justice agency (J. Drug Issues 1993).

Another promising alternative to incarceration is the drug court. Supervised by a sitting judge, a drug court is an intensive, community-based treatment, rehabilitation, and supervision program for drug defendants. The drug court movement, which began in Miami in 1989, has now expanded to all 50 States, the District of Columbia, Puerto Rico, Guam, and 2 Federal districts. There are more than 1,600 drug courts nationwide. The drug court movement continues to grow rapidly. The States with the most drug court programs include California, Florida, New York, Ohio, and Oklahoma (DCPO 2000).

Studies have shown that drug use by participants involved in a drug court program is very low. The percentage of clean drug tests for current drug court participants in a survey of 14 drug courts ranged between 84% and 98%. The percentage of drug court participants who are rearrested while they are in a drug court program is also very low (DCPO 1999). Drug court programs have a real effect on criminal recidivism. A National Institute of Justice study compared rearrest rates for drug court graduates with those of individuals who were imprisoned for drug offenses and found significant differences. The likelihood that a drug court graduate would be rearrested and charged for a serious offense in the first year after graduation was 16.4 percent, compared to 43.5 percent for non-drug court graduates. By the two-year mark, the recidivism rate had grown to 27.5 percent, compared to 58.6 percent for non-graduates (ONDCP 2005).

When compared with other offenders, drug court participants also have lower recidivism rates, even if they do not complete the program. A study of the Maricopa County Drug Court in Arizona found that after 36 months, 33.1% of drug court participants had been rearrested, compared with 43.7% of the control group. Findings were similar in a study of the Wilmington, Delaware, Drug Court. Drug court participants and a comparison group were followed for 12 months. One-third (33.3%) of the drug court participants were recidivists, compared with more than one-half (51.1%) of the control group (Belenko).

§ 21.3.1(c) Miami's Drug Court: "Saving Lives One Addict at a Time"

For Judge Jeffrey Rosinek, who runs the Miami Drug Court, drug court is so different from a traditional court that they might as well not be called by the same name. "In a traditional court, there is a prosecutor on one side, a defense attorney on the other side, and a judge in the middle," says Rosinek. "Here, the court is unified and non-adversarial. Everyone is here to get that person off drugs. These people have never seen a judge who does that. They have never had a team of people who are there to help them the way we are." Rosinek presides over the country's oldest drug court, founded in 1989. The court has roughly 1,600 clients at any given time—whom it keeps for a minimum of 12 months. Many stay for 18 months, and some for more than two years.

The drug court's mix of supportive cheerleading and persistent confrontation is what it takes to get many dependent individuals to start down the road to recovery, although the confrontation usually comes first.

"Our job is to use every way including coercion to get them off those drugs, because most people simply do not want help," says Rosinek. "The judge and their attorney might tell them, 'Try it and see how you feel when you have been clean for a few weeks,' at which point they are starting to feel that maybe it's working. And at the drug court, they have a whole team of people pulling for them." When clients come in for their monthly hearing, the judge receives a two-page report that spells out whether they are employed, what they are doing in treatment, and the results of the all-important drug tests. "If it's not a good report, I'll drug test them again right there," says Rosinek. "We try graduated sanctions. The final sanction is jail—but we always take them back." Clients can also earn special rewards, such as free bus passes, for good conduct.

The most recent drug court class graduated in February 2005, bringing the number of program graduates to well over 10,000. "We are saving lives one addict at a time," says Rosinek, "by convincing people that they have to give up their past life to have a life." Drug courts have demonstrated the potential to save funds. Jail and prosecutorial costs can be reduced and other costs can be avoided when a defendant is successfully diverted from the traditional system. For example, the drug court operating in Washington, D.C., has reported that a defendant processed through a drug court saves the District between $4,065 and $8,845 per client in jail costs; prosecution costs are also reduced by an estimated $102,000, annually (DCPO 1997).

§ 21.3.1(d) The Matrix Model

Established at the University of California at Los Angeles in 1984, the Matrix Institute on Addictions is a nonprofit organization well respected for its integrated approach to drug and alcohol treatment (The Voice 2005). Using the best established, empirically supported chemical dependency treatment principles, the Institute developed the "Matrix Model," a set of clinical outpatient protocols that have been documented for their success by the National Institute on Drug Abuse (NIDA), the

Drug Treatment and Rehabilitation

Center for Substance Abuse Treatment (CSAT), the National Institute on Alcoholism and Alcohol Abuse (NIAAA), and the Office of National Drug Control Policy (ONDCP) in its National Synthetic Drugs Action Plan. The Matrix Model: Intensive Outpatient Alcohol and Drug Treatment is a 16-week individualized program that has been continuously adapted and revised over the last two decades in order to give chemically dependent persons and their families the most thorough and up-to-date knowledge, structure, education and support possible so they might achieve long-term recovery from drug and alcohol dependence. It is the only specific comprehensive treatment program noted as a scientifically based approach in NIDA's Principles of Drug Addiction Treatment: A Research-Based Guide (1999), and the Matrix Adolescent Treatment Model is recognized as an exemplary treatment approach in Drug Strategies' Treating Teens (2003).

The curriculum addresses core clinical areas within five groups:

Weekly Individual/Conjoint sessions consist of eight one-hour meetings for the first two months and then once monthly for the next two months (although additional sessions may be necessary for some patients). Conjoint sessions are designed to orient the patient and, when possible, family members to the intensive outpatient (1OP) approach and to encourage treatment compliance.

The Early Recovery Skills Group meets twice weekly and consists of eight one-hour sessions during the first month of treatment. Here, patients are introduced to basic cognitive behavioral interventions and the value of Twelve Step participation. Because structure is so important, patients are taught to schedule and document each day of sobriety.

Patients and family members attend the Family Education Group weekly for 90-minute sessions over the first three months. Three videos and a facilitator's guide provide extensive information about addiction, treatment and recovery. Participants are taught how alcohol and drug abuse changes the way their brains function, and exercises take these neurobiological changes into account.

The Relapse Prevention Group meets twice weekly for 16 weeks to deliver information, support and camaraderie to patients as they proceed through the recovery process.

Patients who have attained a stable recovery and have completed 12 weeks or more of the Matrix IOP program meet weekly in the Social Support Group. For many patients, this group extends well beyond the initial 16 weeks of treatment. The Matrix Model also calls for weekly urine testing as part of its overall structure.

§ 21.3.1(c)   Buprenorphine Treatment

The Drug Addictions Treatment Act of 2000 allows physicians to treat opiate addictions. The FDA has approved two types of buprenorphine (Subutex and Suboxone) for opiate detox and maintenance, thus allowing doctors to treat opiate addictions in their office.

Chapter 21

Buprenorphine is an opiate that has been available since the 1980s for pain relief. It is made from thebaine, a derivative of opium poppies. Buprenorphine can be used for intoxication, but only produces a partial opiate high when compared to heroin or methadone. It can cause physical dependence, tolerance, and withdrawal. Some people will abuse it, but regulatory efforts and training of physicians should limit access and prevent wide scale abuse. Only properly trained physicians are allowed to prescribe it. Buprenorphine is available as a sublingual tablet in two different forms: Subutex, made of only buprenorphine, and Suboxone, a combination of buprenorphine and naloxone. Suboxone, rather than Subutex, will be used for maintenance therapy in an attempt to prevent the risk of injecting buprenorphine for its intoxicating effects. Both medications are intended to be used sublingually, not intravenously. Suboxone was developed in this combination so that if it is injected, the naloxone becomes effective and blocks opiate receptors. When this occurs the individual cannot become intoxicated. In fact, it's possible it could cause sudden, severe opiate withdrawal symptoms. This should prevent illicit intravenous use of Suboxone.

The law allows for office-based prescribing of buprenorphine in the privacy of the physician's office. This will improve the addict's ability to access this type of opiate addiction treatment and is much more private than methadone clinics. Addicts in buprenorphine maintenance treatment can obtain weekly prescriptions and only need to use the medication once every day or two. It is believed that more opiate addicts will seek maintenance treatment as a result (Seppala).

Physicians are being trained to select only stable patients for office-based buprenorphine treatment. This would exclude addicts who use other substances, those with little psychosocial support, and those with other significant medical or psychiatric problems. Safety and risk reduction are being emphasized in physician training. This screening process will limit the office-based use of buprenorphine in an appropriate manner. It will also help physicians who have little experience in addiction treatment as they enter into the unfamiliar territory of prescribing opiate medication (Seppala). The law requires physicians to have the capacity to refer patients for appropriate counseling and ancillary services. So the provision for at least some type of addiction treatment service beyond the isolated use of medication is in place. Addiction is a multi-faceted, biopsychosocial problem with physical, psychological, social, and spiritual consequences. Buprenorphine is not a cure. It should be as successful as methadone treatment in harm reduction, crime reduction, and in limiting some medical, social, and legal problems associated with opiate dependence. We know that drug maintenance alone is not the answer, but it will help.

§ 21.3.1(d)   Ibogaine
A botanical plant called ibogaine is a natural hallucinogen. It is illegal in the United States. Nevertheless, it is thought to alleviate or lessen withdrawal and drug dependency. It has been reported that addicts experience no withdrawal and new insights into their lives. Though it does not work for everybody, it is certainly worth any money spent on research to determine its effectiveness as a treatment tool.

§ 21.3.1(e) Substance Abuse and Mental Health Services Administration (SAMHSA)—Access to Recovery (ATR)

Through Access to Recovery (ATR), the government is providing individuals seeking alcohol and drug treatment with vouchers to a range of appropriate community-based services. By providing vouchers, ATR promotes client choice, expands access to a broad range of clinical treatment and recovery support services, and increases substance abuse treatment capacity. Vouchers may be used to access various services, including those provided by faith- and community-based programs.

§ 21.4 ADVANCES IN SPECIFIC TREATMENT MODALITIES

Since substance abusers suffer from such a complex of medical and social problems, it is not surprising that multiple treatments are often used in the same patient. Researchers usually try to isolate each element of treatment in order to study it scientifically. In practice, however, several treatment approaches are typically used simultaneously or sequentially. For purposes of discussion, various categories of treatments will be listed although there is a good deal of overlap. For example, specific types of behavior therapy or psychotherapy could be used either in patients on methadone maintenance or in drug-free therapeutic communities.

§ 21.4.1 Detoxification

Most treatment programs begin with detoxification. This simply means withdrawing the drug upon which the person is dependent. The withdrawal symptoms usually consist of the opposite effects from those produced by the drug. Cocaine, for example, produces euphoria and increased energy; however, cocaine-dependent persons usually become tired and depressed during withdrawal. Detoxification from sedatives can be life-threatening because of seizures and cardiac effects, but medical treatment with prescribed sedatives in decreasing amounts is usually successful. Detoxification from opioids—while less dangerous— is still quite uncomfortable without medical help. Detoxification from short-acting opioids takes seven to ten days, but subtle symptoms can continue for months. Protracted withdrawal symptoms can be a significant problem, especially for those trying to withdraw from such a long-acting opioid as methadone.

A significant development is the use of the anti-hypertensive drug clonidine to treat the symptoms of opioid withdrawal (Gold et al). Clonidine is not an opiate-like drug, but it relieves many of the symptoms of opioid withdrawal, particularly those which involve physical symptoms of autonomic nervous system hyperactivity. Since clonidine is not an addicting drug, it can be given in medical settings where amelioration of withdrawal symptoms by prescription opiate is not desirable. Interestingly, clonidine may relieve the symptoms of nicotine withdrawal in smokers attempting to quit (Glassman et al). This suggests that there may be a common neural pathway involved in the production of withdrawal symptoms among several classes of addicting drugs. Detoxification is also the first step in the treatment of cocaine-dependent persons. Often this step is quite difficult because the patient has a tremendous craving to resume the use of cocaine, and the presence of severe depressive symptoms makes participation in an overall rehabilitation program limited. However, the antidepressant drug desipramine has been reported to decrease cocaine craving on a long-term basis (Gawin et al).

It has also been theorized that cocaine-dependent patients suffer from a dopamine depletion syndrome and thus the dopamine receptor stimulant bromocriptine has been tried to relieve withdrawal symptoms. While detoxification has generally been viewed only as the first step in a long-term treatment program, there is some evidence that some addicts benefit from detoxification by itself (Newman et al). Detoxification programs provide a humane means of reducing drug dependency, an opportunity to break the cycle of addiction, and a chance to enter longer term treatment.

§ 21.4.2 Prevention of Relapse

After detoxification, patients are encouraged to enter a long-term treatment program to prevent their returning to drug dependence and to give them time to reconstruct their lives. A drug that aids in preventing relapse to opioid dependence is called naltrexone (Trexan), and it is one of a class of compounds known as opiate antagonists. It is not an opiate itself, and it is not addicting. The main effect of this antagonist is to occupy opiate receptors and prevent opiate drugs from exerting any effect.

Naltrexone is not a treatment by itself, but it has been shown to be effective within the context of a comprehensive rehabilitation program for prevention of relapse to opioid use. After detoxification, the patient can be given naltrexone as infrequently as two to three times per week. This medication will provide protection from re-addiction should the person impulsively take a dose of an opioid. The action of any opiate or opioid will be blocked resulting in no euphoria or reward. Unlike the alcoholic receiving disulfiram (Antabuse), there is no unpleasant reaction should the naltrexone-treated patient take an opioid. There is only a feeling that he has wasted his money because the effects of the heroin or other opiate have been neutralized.

Naltrexone is the product of many years of both NIDA-funded research and pharmaceutical industry investigations in pursuit of the "perfect antagonist." Naltrexone fits this description in many ways since it is effective against all opioids, is not itself addictive, is relatively long acting, and has few side effects. Unfortunately, such a drug appeals only to highly motivated patients who sincerely wish to give up experiencing opiate-induced euphoria. This describes only a minority of street addicts. Despite this limitation, naltrexone has become the treatment drug of choice in many centers for physicians, nurses, and white collar workers with opioid-dependence problems. In particular, physicians constantly exposed to the temptation of a return to opiate use seem to benefit from this new treatment aid.

§ 21.4.3 Behavioral Approaches

Several behaviorally based treatments have been studied. One of the most promising is known as "contingency contracting." This treatment involves setting up an explicit contract between the patient and therapist requiring specific behaviors from each (Crowley). Contingency contracting can be combined with other treatments such as detoxification, psychotherapy, therapeutic community, opiate antagonist, or methadone maintenance. It is then possible to analyze the relationship between treatments and determine what motivates a given patient. Contracts may include both rewards and punishments. Research has shown that external motivation imposed by a therapist or even a judge or probation officer can provide an important stimulus for the patient in early treatment. Eventually, the patient tends to incorporate the goals of treatment into his or her own value system and the new constructive behaviors become rewarding in themselves.

§ 21.4.4 Extinction of Conditioned Responses

Research dating back many years has shown that drugs of all types produce powerful conditioned responses. This means that the reliable pharmacological effects produced by drugs become associated with the environment or the situation in which the drugs were used. Even long after a person has stopped using drugs, the environmental stimuli may trigger a drug-like or a drug withdrawal-like response. Often these responses consist only of craving the drug, but sometimes strong physiological responses are evoked such as nausea, tearing, or sweating. These can occur when the former addict returns to his home or when he sees former friends using drugs. Of course, such reactions can lead to resumption of drug use and re-addiction. There is evidence that such conditioned reactions play a role in relapse to cocaine and opioid use and to the resumption of smoking.

Treatment research has been aimed at extinguishing these responses in the hopes that this will aid the patient to remain drug-free. The treatment consists of gradually exposing the patient to drug-related stimuli. These begin with mental images of the drug-using environment, progressing to images of the situations surrounding drug use. If the patient becomes anxious or develops withdrawal symptoms, he or she is taught to relax and deal with these feelings without resorting to drug use. Over several weeks, the program progresses to video tapes of drug-procuring and drug-using behaviors. Finally, the patient is given bags of heroin (or cocaine) to use for a mock drug-preparation ritual. The patient's responses are measured both by recording physiological responses using a polygraph and by obtaining the patient's subjective response to the procedure. This treatment is imbedded within a standard treatment program. The patients have first been detoxified and have received drug-free treatment in a therapeutic community. Results so far show that the extinction treatment procedures can reduce or even eliminate the conditioned responses to drug-related stimuli. The current research question is whether this extinction results in an improved ability to remain drug-free at long-term follow-up (Childress).

§ 21.4.5 Methadone Maintenance

For opioid (heroin) addicts, methadone has had a tremendously positive impact since its introduction in the 1960s. Patients who have been unable to completely stop heroin and detoxify or those who relapse shortly after detoxification can be easily transferred to a maintenance dose of oral methadone. Methadone prevents opiate withdrawal symptoms for 24 to 36 hours, and in proper doses it does not produce sedation or euphoria. Urine test results show that patients on methadone reduce or eliminate their use of street drugs. The best results have been achieved by those programs which utilize contingency management along with methadone.

Methadone is well accepted by most patients, and it enables them to turn their attention to social and occupational rehabilitation. Studies have shown that 65 to 85 percent of patients remain in methadone treatment for 12 months or more and during this time there is a dramatic reduction in crimes committed and an increase in gainful employment. Some patients remain on methadone for many years and it enables them to function well and in many cases make significant contributions to society. In response to possible negative effects, studies of long-term cases have failed to find evidence of toxic effects from long-term methadone ingestion (Kreek). Of course, most programs have as their stated goal achieving a drug-free state. But this is not practical for those patients who do not wish to stop methadone maintenance. Success rates for stopping methadone and remaining drug-free are reasonably good when both patient and therapist feel that the patient has made sufficient progress such that he or she is now ready to stop. Stimmel studied such a patient group and found that 57 percent were still drug-free at an average follow-up period of 31 months. Such patients, however, constitute a minority of those admitted to methadone programs (Stimmel).

§ 21.4.6 Residential Treatment
The primary residential treatment model is the therapeutic community (TC). As mentioned previously, TCs emphasize a self-help approach, frequently using former addicts as counselors, administrators, and role models. The atmosphere in the programs is highly structured, especially for newer members. Clients progress through the program in clearly delineated stages. Each successive stage usually carries more personal freedom and responsibility. Group counseling or therapy sessions, which are usually confrontational in nature—stressing openness and honesty—are a cornerstone of the TC approach to treatment.

TC treatment involves stays within the program usually measured in months; however, drop-out rates are fairly high. In seven programs surveyed by DeLeon and Schwartz, retention rates for a 12 month treatment stay ranged from 4 to 21 percent. In follow-up evaluations, improvements in drug use, employment, criminality, and psychological well-being were noted both for the program graduates and for the dropouts. In general, studies (not corrected for presence or severity of psychiatric disorders) indicate that those patients who remain in TCs longer, experience more successful and lasting treatment (DeLeon 1984).

§ 21.4.7 Outpatient Drug-Free Treatment
The outpatient drug-free modality subsumes a wide variety of approaches to treatment. In large surveys of treatment, this is the most popular modality, accounting for nearly half (48 percent) of all patients

in treatment. Programs vary widely from drop-in "rap" centers to highly structured programs mostly providing counseling or psychotherapy as the treatment mainstay. Simpson and Sells reported improvements in the opioid abusers who received treatment in outpatient drug-free programs. Daily opioid use declined from 100 percent pretreatment to 44 percent at the end of the first year and to 28 percent in the third year. Arrests also showed a significant decline, and employment increased after treatment. However, because individuals entering outpatient drug-free treatment have not been adequately described on a variety of severity variables, the significance of the above findings is not clear (Simpson et al).

§ 21.5 DOES TREATMENT WORK?

The effectiveness of current drug abuse treatment methods has been variously interpreted. Some people find that no general evaluation can be made; some find no evidence that treatment does any good at all; some do not discuss empirical evaluation; and some claim that treatment programs have been effective. It might be said that the field of drug treatment is in the stage that its cousin, psychotherapy, was in 30 years ago. Each of a variety of treatment approaches claims for itself at least some degree of success. Scientific evidence on the effectiveness of drug abuse treatment is limited. Most of the systematic evaluations contain design defects such as inadequate outcome measures, absence of appropriate control groups, or lack of randomized assignment to treatments. Nevertheless, the weight of the available evidence suggests that certain forms of treatment—methadone maintenance, drug-free therapy, and residential "therapeutic communities"—work better than no treatment at all. "Detoxification-only" treatment, which consists largely of custodial care during withdrawal, appears to have some benefits as well.

Research on drug treatment effectiveness also indicates that the longer an addict remains in treatment, the better the prognosis. "Graduates" have better outcomes than dropouts. Although it may be true that addicts benefit from greater amounts of treatment, we cannot rule out the alternate explanation of a "selection effect;" that is to say, more successful addicts may elect to remain in treatment. This election, rather than the treatment itself, may be the cause of better prognoses for addicts in long-term treatment. Much of the existing research on the effectiveness of drug treatment programs in reducing drug use and criminality is based on experience with heroin abusers in the 1960's and 1970's. Recent information on treatment effectiveness, especially for cocaine and methamphetamine users, is just beginning to emerge.

However, results from previous studies seem to be generalizable to many types of drug-involved offenders since most drug abusers share similar characteristics. Moreover, the basic elements of drug treatment (except for the use of specific drug therapies) are applicable to a variety of drug addictions, including illegal substances, prescriptions drugs, and alcohol (Speckart). All types of drug treatment have shown progress in reducing drug use and criminality. Drug-involved offenders in drug treatment commit fewer crimes and use drugs less often than such offenders not in treatment. In one large study, about two-thirds of persons who reported criminal activity before treatment, and who remained in treatment for at least 3 months, had ceased criminal activity in the year after treatment (Hubbard). However, recurrence of drug use and associated criminal activities is common after discharge, and several cycles of treatment are frequently necessary. Most experts believe that postrelease supervision or an aftercare program is an integral component of drug treatment and is essential for substantial behavioral change.

It is significant that despite some claims to the contrary, persons entering treatment under legal pressure do as well or better than other clients after discharge (Anglin). Drug-involved enrollees who committed crimes infrequently before their addiction either committed no crimes after release from treatment or committed crimes less frequently. Persons in treatment who had a history of serious criminal activity before their drug addiction continued to commit crimes at a moderate level after release from treatment. Moreover, treatment professionals are beginning to recognize that women may require different treatment strategies than men because of differences in reasons for drug use and responsiveness to treatment. Another critical issue related to effectiveness is the availability of treatment for adolescents. Many observers advocate "early intervention" with young people, before their drug abuse has become severe, but such intervention has not been empirically evaluated. A second approach, family therapy, treats the family as well as the patient, viewing the family relationships as the cause of the young person's drug abuse. Family therapy has received favorable evaluation as a treatment for other psychiatric disorders, and has proved effective in one well-designed randomized trial with adult heroin users. However, it has not been tested with adolescent non-opiate abusers, and its potentially high costs must be weighed against its benefits.

§ 21.6 FUTURE DIRECTIONS

Many studies are examining the effect of periodic urine testing on drug use and criminal activity during pretrial release, probation, and parole. Through the Focused Offender Disposition Project we will learn more about classifying drug-involved offenders for drug treatment and about whether traditional drug treatment programs are effective in treating all forms of drug abuse, from casual use to daily use of multiple drugs. A variety of studies are exploring whether the content of drug treatment programs should be tailored for specific groups: for example, for types of drugs, younger offenders, females, and extent of criminal activity. Both research and experience are reaching a consensus that criminal justice sanctions alone are not very effective in reducing drug use and criminality of drug-involved offenders on probation or parole. Similarly, numerous studies have found that a substantial proportion of substance abusers—possibly a majority—will not enter or remain in treatment unless some kind of formal pressure is applied.

The criminal justice system applies pressure, using the threat of incarceration or other sanctions to induce offenders who are under legal supervision to get into treatment programs. Typically, the longer legal supervision lasts, the more likely that offenders in drug testing or treatment will reduce their drug use and criminal behavior. Thus, joint efforts by the treatment and criminal justice systems are mo likely to be effective for reducing drug use and related criminality—a val crime control strategy for the foreseeable future. Incorporating di treat- ment programs in the sanctions imposed on drug-involved offu ers is an important step toward achieving this public safety objective.

§ 21.6.1 The Police Can Play an Important Role in Treatmen

To understand the underlying dynamics of drug-related crim police need to understand that not all addicts are the same. Ther e two kinds of drug addicts who commit crimes: the addict-criminal sorts to crime to pay for drugs; the criminal-addict uses drugs as par a broader pattern of criminal behavior.

The importance of the distinction is that the opportunities for la enforcement to make an impact differ dramatically, depending on the kind of addict that officers are dealing with. With the addict-criminal, if you treat the addiction, the person usually stops committing any crimes; without the drugs, the addict-criminal would not be involved with crime. With the criminal-addict, the original criminal activity usually persists even after drug treatment.

The police have a unique opportunity to use the threat of jail as a way to goad the addict-criminal into a recovery program. It makes sense for law enforcement officers to target these individuals for special attention, because once they are treated, the chances are good that they will not create problems for the police or the community in the future. Identifying the addict-criminal is difficult. But community policing, which puts officers in closer contact with members of a community, may assist in identifying those for whom treatment offers the best hope of living within the law. Dealing with the criminal-addict is much more difficult, since these individuals often continue to be problems in the community, even if their addiction is under control. Likewise, incarceration is less of a stigma, so the threat of jail may not induce them to seek treatment.

§ 21.6.2 Cost of Treatment

The goal of treatment for addicted offenders is twofold: to return a productive individual, free of addictions, to society and to reduce the expense of drug-related crime to society. The National Treatment Improvement Evaluation Study (NTIES) from the Center for Substance Abuse Treatment (CSAT) reports that the average cost per treatment episode was $2,941 between 1993 and 1995. The average treatment benefit to society was $9,177 per client. This resulted in an average savings of three to one: every $1 spent on treatment saved society $3. The savings resulted from reduced crime-related costs, increased earnings, and reduced health care costs that would otherwise be borne by society (SMAHSA 1999).

§ 21.6.3 Different Treatments for Different Types of Patients

As with other chronic diseases such as arthritis, it is best to speak of remissions and improvement rather than "cures" in treating substance abusers. Research has shown that substance abuse treatment is associ-

ated wit significant changes in drug use, employment, crime, and psy-
chosoc adjustment; but there was no indication that any particular
type treatment was any better or worse than any other form of
treat nt. Considering the major conceptual and practical differences
bet n such treatments as methadone maintenance and drug-free
th eutic communities, it was puzzling that there had been no dem-
o ation of outcome differences among these major forms of treat-
t.

Similarly, there had long been recognition of wide differences among
ubstance abuse patients in demographics, patterns of drug use, employment skills, crime backgrounds, etc. However, there was very little
evidence that this variability was associated with differences in treatment outcome across the different modalities, or even within a particular modality. There was, of course, general indication that those patients who entered treatment with more severe problems (particularly
crime problems) had poorer outcomes, but there was little evidence that
certain types of patients might be matched to specific kinds of treatments as a means of increasing the overall effectiveness and efficiency
of a treatment system.

The Addiction Severity Index (ASI) was designed on the premise
that addiction to either alcohol or street drugs must be considered in
the full context of those additional treatment problems that may have
contributed to and/or resulted from the chemical abuse. The objective of
the ASI was to produce a "problem severity profile" of every patient
through an analysis of seven areas commonly affected in alcohol- or
other drug-abusing patients. These areas include medical condition,
employment, alcohol and drug use, legal status, family relations, and
psychiatric condition. This ASI instrument was used in a four-year
study in 1982 of six programs treating alcohol/drug addicts, in an inpatient and outpatient program, and again in a series of studies in 1985.
Based on the findings of these studies, it was concluded that substance
abuse treatments do have specific and predictable effects on particular
patient subgroups; these subgroups can be easily and reliably identified
at the time of admission so that they may be assigned to the most appropriate and cost-effective treatments (McLellan 1982, 1983, 1985).

§ 21.7   SUMMARY

In the past, research on the treatment of substance abuse has been
concentrated on the management of narcotics addiction; however, the
rise in cocaine addiction in the United States has prompted a great deal
of activity in new areas. The increased awareness of drug abuse in the
workplace has also spurred the development of innovative programs for
early detection and treatment of workers before drugs have caused the
loss of their jobs. Moreover, the diversification of treatment approaches
has led to increased attention to the complex interactions of drug-use
behavior and social functioning, family problems, and occupational difficulties. Thus, effectiveness of any treatment may be influenced by
specific variables such as availability of family support for the patient
and more general factors such as the local economy and levels of unemployment. There is increasing recognition that substance abuse is a
multifaceted syndrome rather than a straightforward medical problem

requiring medical treatment. Substance abusers have been found to be a heterogeneous group who cannot be classified simply on the basis of their preferred drug. These issues are critical to research on treatment effectiveness because they call into question any simple measure of how severe the condition was before treatment and how much improvement there has been after treatment.

References

Advisory Committee on Drug Dependence. The Rehabilitation of Drug Addicts. London: Her Majesty's Stationery Office, 1968.

Anglin, M.D., M. Brecht, and E. Maddahian. "Pretreatment characteristics and treatment performance of legally coerced versus voluntary methadone maintenance admissions." Criminology 27 (1989): 1145-1149.

Anglin, M.D., and Y. Hser. "Treatment of drug abuse." Drugs and Crime Vol. 13. Chicago: The University of Chicago Press, 1990.

Belenko, S. "Research on Drug Courts: A Critical Review." National Drug Court Institute Review 1.1 (1998).

Childress, A.R., et al. "Behavioral therapies for substance abuse." Int J Addict. 20.687 (1985): 947-969.

----------. "Development of a procedure for assessing and extinguishing conditioned opiate withdrawal-like responses." Problems of Drug Dependence. Washington, D.C.: NIDA Research Monograph Series. 1987.

Collins, J., and M. Allison. "Legal coercion and retention in drug abuse treatment." Hospital and Community Psychiatry 34 (1983).

Crowley, T. "Contingency contracting treatment of drug-abusing physicians, nurses, and dentists." Behavioral Intervention Techniques in Drug Abuse Treatment. NIDA Research Monograph 46. DHHS Pub. No. (ADM) 84-1284. Washington, D.C.: Supt. of Docs., U.S. Govt. Print. Off., 1984.

DeLeon, G., and S. Schwartz. "Therapeutic communities: 'What are the retention rates?" Am J Drug and Alcohol Abuse 10.2 (1984): 267-284.

DeLeon, G., et al. "The therapeutic community: Success and improvement rates 5 years after treatment." Int J Addict 17.4 (1982): 703-747.

Dolan, M.P., et al. "Contracting for treatment termination to reduce illicit drug use among methadone maintenance treatment failures." J of Consult and Clin Psychol. 53 (1985): 549-551.

"Drug Abuse Treatment in Criminal Justice Settings." Journal of Drug Issues 23.1 (Winter 1993).

Drug Courts Program Office. Summary of All Drug Court Activities by State. Washington, D.C.: The American University, October 2000.

----------. 1997 Drug Court Survey Report: Executive Summary. Washington, D.C.: The American University, October 1997.

Field, G., "The effects of intensive treatment on reducing the criminal recidivism of addicted offenders." Federal Probation 53 (1989): 51-56.

Gawin, F.H., and H.D. Kleber. "Abstinence symptomatology and psychiatric diagnosis in cocaine abusers; Clinical observations." Arch Gen Psych. 43.2 (1986): 107-113.

Glassman, A., et al. "Cigarette craving, smoking withdrawal and clonidine." Science 226 (1984): 864-866.

Gold, M.S., et al. "Opiate withdrawal using clonidine." Journal of the American Medical Association 243 (1980): 343-356.

Chapter 21

Hubbard, R., M. Marsden, J.V. Rachal, H. Harwood, E. Cavanaugh and H. Ginzburg. Drug Abuse Treatment: A National Study of Effectiveness. Chapel Hill: University of North Carolina Press, 1989.

Kreek, M.J. "Health consequences associated with the use of methadone." Research on the Treatment of Narcotic Addiction: State of the Art. Ed. Cooper. NIDA Treatment Research Monograph Series. DHHS Pub. No. (ADM)83-1291. Washington, D.C.: Supt. of Docs., U.S. Govt. Print. Off., 1983.

May, Edgar. "Narcotics Addiction and Control in Great Britain." Dealing with Drug Abuse: A Report to the Ford Foundation. New York: Praeger Publisher, 1972.

McCarthy, J.J., and O.T. Borders. "Limit setting on drug abuse in methadone maintenance patients." Am J Psychia. 142.12 (1985).

McLellan, A.T., et al. "Increased effectiveness of substance abuse treatment: A prospective study of patient-treatment 'matching." J Nerv Ment Dis 171.10 (1983): 597-605.

-----------. "Is substance abuse treatment effective? Five different perspectives." Journal of the American Medical Association 247 (1982): 1423-1428.

-----------. "New data from the Addiction Severity Index: Reliability and validity in three centers." J Nerv Ment Dis. 173 (1985): 412-423.

Newman, R.G., and W.B. Whitehill. "Double-blind comparison of methadone and placebo maintenance treatments of narcotic addicts in Hong Kong." Lancet 8141 (1979): 485-488.

Nurco, D., T. Hanlon, T. Kinlock, and K. Duszynski. "Differential criminal patterns of narcotic addicts over an addiction career." Criminology 26 (1988): 407-423.

Office of National Drug Control Policy. Understanding Drug Treatment: An ONDCP White Paper. Washington, D.C.: U.S Government Printing Office: Washington, D.C., 1990.

----------. Healing America's Drug Users: Getting Tratment Resources Where They Are Needed. Washington, D.C.: U.S Government Printing Office: Washington, D.C., 2005.

Simpson, D.D., and S.B. Sells. "Effectiveness of treatment for drug abuse: An overview of the DARP Research Program." Advances in Alcohol and Substance Abuse 2.1 (1982): 7-29.

Speckart, G., M.D. Anglin, and E. Deschenes. "Modeling the longitudinal impact of legal sanctions on narcotics use and property crime." Journal of Quantitative Criminology 5 (1989): 33-56.

Stimmel, B., et al. "Ability to remain abstinent after methadone detoxification." Journal of the American Medical Association 237 (1979): 1216-1220.

Substance Abuse and Mental Health Services Administration, Center for Substance Abuse Treatment, National Evaluation Data Services. The Cost and Benefits of Substance Abuse Treatment: Findings From the National Treatment Improvement Evaluation Study. Rockville, MD: Department of Health and Human Services, 1999.

U.S. Department of Health and Human Services. "The British Narcotics System." April, 1978.

"The Voice: News and Opinion for Recovering People and Professionals." Hazelden 10.1, (Winter 2005).

Wexler, H., D. Lipton, and D. Johnson, A Criminal Justice System Strategy for Treating Cocaine-Heroin Abusing Offenders in Custody, Issues and Practices series. Washington, D.C.: National Institute of Justice 1988.

CHAPTER 22

DRUG PREVENTION AND EDUCATION

§ 22.1   INTRODUCTION

Concern about drug use and abuse is not new to our society and our time. For centuries, communities have addressed drug issues in a variety of ways, most commonly through legislation and education. The degree of interest in preventing drug use and related problems, however, has depended on the nature and level of the perceived problems, the political climate, agenda-setting by the media, and pressure from interested groups.

While the first half of the 20th century was marked by extensive efforts against drug use (the temperance movement of the first two decades and the campaigns against marijuana and heroin in the 1930s), concerted efforts to reduce youthful drug use did not arise until the late 1960s. By then it had become clear that drug use was widespread and growing among young people from all segments of society. In 1970, President Nixon called for preventive drug education at all levels of schooling from kindergarten through the 12th grade; subsequently, federal expenditures for drug prevention programs rose dramatically.

The reasons why people use illicit drugs, however, are complex; these reasons result not only from the legality or illegality of the drugs, but also from familial, societal, and cultural factors. It has become increasingly obvious that law enforcement can be but one part of any government's program to reduce drug use. Law enforcement must be supplemented by educational programs to inform people about the properties of various drugs and the risks associated with their use. These programs include public school drug education courses, mass media and other advertising campaigns, and grassroots programs (for example, the "Just Say No" movement).

Although the public may perceive that substantial resources have been allocated to drug use prevention through education and public information campaigns, the amounts spent on these efforts are small compared with those spent by agencies that enforce drug laws. This results from a historical emphasis on solving drug problems by reducing supply rather than demand. To measure the performance and effectiveness of substance abuse prevention programs, the office of National Drug Control Policy has developed a set of research-based principles upon which prevention programming can be established (ONDCP 2005).

The following 15 principles and guidelines were drawn from literature reviews and guidance supported by the federal departments of Education, Justice, and Health and Human Services as well as ONDCP, Some prevention interventions covered by these reviews have been tested in laboratory, clinical, and community settings using the most rigorous research methods. Additional interventions have been studied with techniques that meet other recognized standards. The principles and guidelines presented here are broadly supported by a growing body of research.

—Address Appropriate Risk and Protective Factors for Substance Abuse in a Defined Population

1. Define a population. A population can be defined by age, sex, race, geography (neighbor-hood, town, or region), and institution (school or workplace).

2. Assess levels of risk, protection, and substance abuse for that population. Risk factors increase the risk of substance abuse, and protective factors inhibit substance abuse in the presence of risk. Risk and protective factors can be grouped in domains for research purposes (genetic, biological, social, psychological, contextual, economic, and cultural) and characterized as to their relevance to individuals, the family, peer, school, workplace, and community. Substance abuse can involve marijuana, cocaine, heroin, inhalants, methamphetamine, alcohol, and tobacco (especially among youth) as well as sequences, substitutions, and combinations of those and other psychoactive substances.

3. Focus on all levels of risk, with special attention to those exposed to high risk and low protection. Prevention programs and policies should focus on all levels of risk, but special attention must be given to the most important risk factors, protective factors, psychoactive substances, individuals, and groups exposed to high risk and low protection in a defined population. Population assessment can help sharpen the focus of prevention.

—Use Approaches That Have Been Shown to be Effective

4. Reduce the availability of illicit drugs, and of alcohol and tobacco for the under-aged. Community-wide laws, policies, and programs can reduce the availability and marketing of illicit drugs. They can also reduce the availability and appeal of alcohol and tobacco to the under aged.

5. Strengthen anti-drug-use attitudes and norms. Strengthen environmental support for anti-drug-use attitudes by sharing accurate information about substance abuse, encouraging drug-free activities, and enforcing laws, and policies related to illicit substances.

6. Strengthen life skills and drug refusal techniques. Teach life skills and drug refusal skills, using interactive techniques that focus on critical thinking, communication, and social competency.

7. Reduce risk and enhance protection in families. Strengthen family skills by setting rules, clarifying expectations, monitoring be-

havior, communicating regularly, providing social support, and modeling positive behaviors.

8. Strengthen social bonding. Strengthen social bonding and caring relationships with people holding strong standards against substance abuse in families, schools, peer groups, mentoring programs, religious and spiritual contexts, and structured recreational activities.

9. Ensure that interventions are appropriate for the populations being addressed. Make sure that prevention interventions, including programs and policies, are acceptable to and appropriate for the needs and motivations of the populations and cultures being addressed.

—Intervene Early at Important Stages, Transitions, and In Appropriate Settings and Domains

10. Intervene early and at developmental stages and life transitions that predict later substance abuse. Such developmental stages and life transitions can involve biological, psychological, or social circumstances that can increase the risk of substance abuse. Whether the stages or transitions are expected (such as puberty, adolescence, or graduation from school) or unexpected (for example the sudden death of a loved one), they should be addressed by preventive interventions as soon as possible-even before each stage or transition, whenever feasible.

11. Reinforce interventions over time. Repeated exposure to scientifically accurate and age-appropriate anti-drug-use messages and other interventions-especially in later developmental stages and life transitions that may increase the risk of substance abuse-can ensure that skills, norms, expectations, and behaviors learned earlier are reinforced overtime.

12. Intervene in appropriate settings and domains. Intervene in settings and domains that most affect risk and protection for substance abuse, including homes, social services, schools, peer groups, workplaces, recreational settings, religious and spiritual settings, and communities.

—Manage Programs Effectively

13. Ensure consistency and coverage of programs and policies. Implementation of prevention programs, policies, and messages for different parts of the community should be consistent, compatible, and appropriate.

14. Train staff and volunteers. To ensure that prevention programs and messages are continually delivered as intended, training should be provided regularly to staff and volunteers.

15. Monitor and evaluate programs. To verify that goals and objectives are being achieved program monitoring and evaluation should be a regular part of program implementation. When goals are not reached, adjustments should be made to increase effectiveness.

§ 22.2   WHAT IS PREVENTION?

Prevention programs aim at the reduction, delay, or prevention of drug use before it has become habitual or clearly dysfunctional. On the other hand, treatment programs seek to reduce or eliminate drug use among people for whom it has become so dominant that it interferes with their lives. Thus, the major distinction among interventions aimed at potential or actual users is between prevention and treatment. The association between level of drug involvement and type of intervention provides a context for relating categories of prevention to the successive stages of drug use through which an adolescent might pass over time. Depicted below are four such stages based on frequency of use: (1) non-use, or never having tried the specific drug at issue; (2) experimental or episodic use; (3) social or recreational use; (4) regular or frequent use; and (5) heavy use.

Within these schemes, primary prevention is focused on the early stages—trying to keep young people from ever starting at all; or, if they have experimented already, trying to keep them from shifting into regular use. Secondary and tertiary prevention programs seek to prevent regular users from getting into serious trouble, e.g., from becoming habitual users who are psychologically or physically dependent on the drug or mired in other maladaptive behavior such as frequent school absenteeism or delinquent activities. Secondary prevention programs target youths who have not yet exhibited ill effects from drug use, but who are identified as "at risk" of becoming problem users. Tertiary prevention programs focus on groups that have already manifested some problems resulting from or associated with drug use (absenteeism, learning difficulties, delinquency, health problems, etc.), but have not yet become psychologically or physically dependent upon the drug. Both secondary and tertiary prevention programs serve specific target populations that have had prior drug experiences. The dividing line between tertiary prevention and treatment is indistinct, though treatment programs typically focus on people whose drug use is more habitual, extensive, or clearly dysfunctional.

§ 22.3   DRUG ABUSE ETIOLOGY AND PREVENTION/ EDUCATION RESEARCH

Understanding the factors associated with becoming a drug abuser and, ultimately, understanding the mechanisms of drug abuse etiology is fundamental to effective prevention. Our knowledge of the psychosocial and biological factors that play a role in smoking, use of alcohol, and other drug abuse continues to be limited, although it has grown significantly in the last decade. While experimentation with tobacco, alcohol, and other psychoactive substances is common in adolescence, certain risk factors are more common in children and adolescents who become heavily involved in smoking and substance abuse than in others who do not. These risk factors have been comprehensively studied in research funded by the NIDA (Hawkins). As with the risk factors for heart disease and other illnesses, these are characteristics that have been found to be associated with a greater-than-average chance of developing the problem. Individuals with one or more of these risk factors do not, of course, invariably become substance abusers. A brief review of the known risk factors, however, will provide a useful backdrop for discussing the basis of effective prevention strategies.

§ 22.3.1 Family Factors

1. A family history of alcoholism: Research has established a link between drinking problems in the family and adolescents or young adults abusing alcohol or other drugs. For example, the presence of an alcoholic family member approximately doubles the risk that a male child will later abuse alcohol or drugs.

2. A family history of criminality or antisocial behavior: Children from families in which other close family members have a criminal history are more likely to abuse alcohol and other drugs than children whose relatives have not been involved in such antisocial behavior.

3. Problems of parental direction or discipline: Unclear and/or inconsistent parental rules for behavior; inconsistent parental reactions to their children's behavior, unusual permissiveness, lax supervision of children's behavior or, conversely, excessively severe discipline, and constant criticism and an absence of parental praise or approval have all been found to be associated with higher rates of drug abuse among children.

4. Parental drug use or parental attitudes approving use are also associated with children later becoming drug abusers. Parents serve as models for their children's behavior in many ways. Children whose parents smoke, drink, or abuse drugs are more likely to do so than those children whose parents abstain from these activities. Parents who express favorable attitudes or approval of alcohol or other drug abuse also increase their children's likelihood of abusing these substances.

§ 22.3.2 Peer Factors

Children whose friends (or brothers and sisters) use drugs are much more likely to use them than those whose peers do not. Not only is having friends who are drug users a strong predictor of drug use, there is also sufficient evidence to estimate that most initiation into drug use occurs through friends rather than strangers.

§ 22.3.3 Achievement, School Commitment, and Social Alienation

1. Children who fail in school in their mid to late elementary school years are more likely to become adolescent drug abusers than those who do not. Children who fail in school for whatever reason—boredom, lack of ability, a mismatch with an unskilled teacher—are more likely to experiment with drugs earlier and to become regular users than those who do not.

2. Adolescents who are not interested in school and academic achievement are more likely to use drugs than those who are. Use of drugs, such as cocaine, other stimulants, or hallucinogens, is significantly less common among college-bound teenagers than among those who are not interested in their own education.

3. Children who feel alienated, strongly rebellious, and at odds with the dominant social values are at higher risk of abusing drugs than those with strong bonds to their family, their school, and to other conventional institutions.

4. Antisocial behavior during early adolescence, including school misbehavior, a low sense of social responsibility, fighting, and other types of aggression, have been found to be more common among drug abusers.

§ 22.3.4 Age of First Use

The earlier the child begins to drink or use other drugs the greater the likelihood of later developing drug problems. Using drugs before age 15 greatly increases the risk of later drug use. While the factors described are clearly associated with greater drug involvement, the reasons for this are often unclear. Vulnerability probably involves both psychosocial and biological elements. Having friends who are drug users or a parent who is an alcoholic may provide a "model" for use, but other neurophysiologic factors such as the drug being unusually reinforcing for the individual in relieving depression, anxiety, or producing euphoria may be decisive. For example, it is now well-established that children of alcoholics have a greater vulnerability to becoming alcoholics—even when raised by adoptive parents who are not alcoholic (Bohmen).

Furthermore, experimentation with one psychoactive substance has, on the average, a predictable relationship to the later use of other psychoactive drugs. Use typically begins with alcohol and tobacco; in contemporary American culture, use of these substances then "progresses" to marijuana use (Kandel). Some individuals may go on to use sedatives, stimulants, and psychedelics. Still fewer (in the general population) will go on to use opiates such as heroin. While alcohol and tobacco are often described as "gateway" drugs in the sense that their use usually (but not invariably) precedes the use of other drugs, the progression need not imply that some property of these substances "causes" later use of the other drugs. The more common—easily available—psychoactive substances may be used first simply because they are so readily obtainable. Thus, a shift in availability may alter this order of progression. Early use may also occur partly because those who are most tempted to use psychoactive substances are those who have an earlier sense of need in themselves that these substances can potentially satisfy.

§ 22.4 STRATEGIES

Prevention programs may vary widely, but generally are associated with information, education, alternative behaviors, and primary and early intervention activities. These services focus on reducing risk factors and building protective factors and may be directed at any segment of the population. Several prevention activities or strategies may be used effectively in combination.

§ 22.4.1 Control of Drug Abuse Through Education

Many attempts have been made to control the use and abuse of drugs (including alcohol and tobacco) through education. Society's readiness to seek educational solutions for social ills reflects the value it attaches to education per se, and its commitment to the notion of education based upon rational argument and experience. Educational strategies and programs to combat drug abuse differ in many regards, including the drugs and groups the programs target, their content and objectives, the media, settings, and processes they use, and their effectiveness. Drug abuse education is neither a simple nor a single concept; it refers, rather, to a collection of laws, policies, programs, and actions designed to influence the use of drugs. Today, there are thousands of drug prevention and education programs in schools and communities across the United States, but comparatively fewer federal dollars for financing them. Whether funded privately or publicly, however, most are based on one or more of four prevention models.

§ 22.4.1(a)   The Information Model

The information model constituted the dominant prevention mode for many years. It assumes that adolescents use drugs because they lack information about their negative effects and therefore have neutral or even positive attitudes toward trying them. This model sees providing information about drugs—their properties, their methods of use, and their consequences—as the solution. Such information is expected to produce less positive attitudes toward drugs. Those attitudes should, in turn, inhibit drug use.

Several states require drug education in the schools, but the specific content and amount of time devoted to the subject are usually left up to the school district, or even the individual school. Instruction therefore varies widely from one school to another, and examples of programs based on the information approach may vary from two pages in a school textbook to a highly structured, multiple-session health curriculum with audiovisual materials. Typically, these programs provide information about the physical and psychological effects of specific drugs, their pharmacology, and the legal implications of using illicit drugs. Most school-based information programs are presented by teachers using a didactic delivery style; some use outside experts such as a doctor, nurse, or narcotics officer, and some provide for class discussion. While the questionable "scare" tactics of early drug-education programs have largely been abandoned in favor of a more balanced presentation of the facts, the emphasis is usually on the harmful consequences of drugs, particularly the long-term effects of continued and heavy use. The content frequently goes beyond a "just the facts" approach to include an exhortation not to use drugs.

Chapter 22

§ 22.4.1(b) The Individual Deficiency Model

The individual deficiency model emerged as an important approach in the early 1970s. This model assumes that the problem lies within the child—that children use drugs to compensate for a lack of self-esteem, or because they lack adequate tools for making rational decisions. Programs based on this model seek to provide general skills that will enhance the youngster's self-esteem or decision-making skills. They also frequently seek to encourage a school or home climate that emphasizes each child's special qualities and individual value.

§ 22.4.1(c) The Social Pressures Model

The social pressures model is an approach to drug prevention which emphasizes the external influences that push adolescents toward drug use, particularly the subtle pressures of the media and the actual behavior and attitudes of key people in the adolescent's life; adults who drink, smoke, or use pills and, most importantly, friends and other peers who use drugs. The social pressures model also recognizes the special vulnerability of adolescents who are in a transitional status between childhood and adulthood: their general desire to appear grown up and to emulate what they perceive to be adult behavior. Accordingly, social pressures programs seek to provide adolescents with specific skills and support for saying "no."

§ 22.4.1(d) The Alternatives Model

Closely related to both the individual deficiency and the social pressures approaches, the alternatives model assumes that adolescents may start using drugs for a variety of reasons, including both internal and external pressures, but emphasizes providing alternative activities to keep them busy and productive as the solution.

§ 22.4.1(e) Current Trends

The current trend is to include a variety of components designed to influence knowledge, feeling, skills, and behavior. This multiplicity of program elements includes attempts to develop or enhance general interpersonal and coping skills, and specific skills related to drug use, such as assertiveness and refusal to use drugs

§ 22.4.2 Traditional Prevention Approaches

Considering the difficulty and cost of treating individuals with substance abuse problems, the prospect of developing effective substance abuse prevention programs has long held a great deal of appeal. Until recently, the standard prevention approach has involved either the presentation of factual information concerning the dangers of substance use or what is sometimes referred to as "affective" education. Informational tobacco, alcohol, and drug education programs are based largely on the assumption that increased knowledge about these substances and their hazards will effectively deter potential users (Goodstadt). In other words, this type of prevention strategy is based on the belief that if students are fully aware of the dangers of tobacco, alcohol, or drug use they will make rational decisions not to use them. Fear arousal messages are frequently used by such programs to frighten individuals into not smoking, drinking, or using other drugs. Such programs have been conducted by teachers and other school personnel as well as by outsiders such as physicians, the police, and ex-addicts.

A second type of substance abuse prevention involves "affective" or "humanistic" education. These programs are generally designed to enhance self-esteem, to encourage responsible decision-making and to enrich the personal and social development of students. Affective education approaches are based on the following assumptions: (1) substance abuse programs should aim to develop prevention-oriented decision-making concerning the use of legal or illicit drugs; (2) such decisions should result in fewer negative consequences for the individual; and (3) the most effective way of achieving these goals is by increasing self-esteem, interpersonal skills, and participation in alternatives to substance use. Consistent with these assumptions, prevention programs of this type attempt to increase self-understanding and acceptance through values clarification and decision-making; to improve interpersonal relations through communication training, peer counseling, assertiveness training, etc.; and to increase students' abilities to meet their needs through conventional social institutions. This material is generally taught through class discussion and a variety of experiential classroom activities (Swisher).

Although programs utilizing information dissemination/fear-arousal approaches as well as those emphasizing affective education have proliferated in past years, the available evidence suggests that neither approach is effective (Schaps). A great many programs have been able to show an increase in knowledge of the negative consequences of substance use; some have also shown an impact on students' attitudes. However, few programs have been successful in changing actual substance use. Due to this ineffectiveness, the challenge in prevention has been to demonstrate that there are approaches which can change substance use behavior—to show that substance abuse prevention can "work."§ 22.4.3Psychological Prevention Approaches

Substantial progress has been made during the past five years in new areas of prevention, and there is growing evidence supporting the effectiveness of some new approaches. Thus far, these techniques have been primarily used in preventing cigarette smoking, but the efficacy of this type of prevention beyond one or two years has not yet been proven. Researchers have focused on preventing adolescent cigarette smoking for several reasons. First, cigarette smoking is a major risk factor for such chronic diseases as coronary heart disease, cancer, and emphysema. It is widely recognized as the single-most important preventable cause of death and disability in the United States today.

Second, cigarette smoking is the most widespread drug dependence in our society. Moreover, cigarette smoking occurs toward the very beginning of the developmental progression of substance use (Kandel). There have been some reports that the prevention programs initially developed to deter adolescent cigarette smoking may also deter the use of other substances, notably alcohol and marijuana (Shaffer et al).

The substance prevention approaches which focus primary attention on the psychosocial factors involved in substance use and initiation show promise of increased effectiveness. Reviews of these programs not only highlight the evolution of the newer "psychosocial" approaches to substance abuse prevention over the past seven or eight years, but also describe the greater sophistication and increased methodological rigor of this research compared to earlier prevention research. These approaches fall into two general categories: (1) programs that focus on social influences believed to promote substance use and (2) broader life/coping skills and training approaches designed to enhance personal and social competence.

§ 22.4.2(a) Social Influence Approaches

The development of smoking prevention strategies focusing on social influences promoting use is based on the fact that peer and family influences have been consistently demonstrated to play important roles in beginning to smoke. Although not yet established empirically, media influences may also play an important role in influencing adolescents to begin smoking. In general, the social influence approach to smoking prevention involves (1) making students aware of those social pressures to smoke to which they are likely to be exposed, (2) teaching specific coping skills (e.g., refusal skills) with which to resist these pressures, and (3) correcting misperceptions of social norms regarding smoking (e.g., making students aware that, in fact, most adults and adolescents, do not smoke).

Most of the research that has been done with the social influence approach has been based on the pioneering work of Richard Evans and his colleagues at the University of Houston (Evans 1976). An underlying assumption of this approach is that students can be effectively "inoculated" against social influences to smoke by gradually exposing them to progressively more intense pro-smoking social influences. In addition, Evans' films provide students with specific tactics for resisting these pro-smoking influences. This approach, therefore, is based on the idea that students' resistance to group social pressures to smoke can be increased by making them (1) more aware of those pressures and (2) helping them develop effective counter-arguments.

Other investigators have elaborated on this model, placing more emphasis on actually training students to deal with both peer and media pressures to smoke. These intervention strategies go beyond the basic psychological inoculation model developed by Evans and place greater emphasis on social learning theory (Bandura). Two distinctive features of these expanded approaches are (1) the use of peer leaders (either older or the same age) to deliver some or all of the program and (2) the use of role playing and social reinforcement techniques to teach students specific skills for resisting group pressure to smoke. Some studies have also included a public commitment component in which students are encouraged to avow they will not smoke in the future.

Most research studies on the social influence approach have been targeted at junior high school students, with the intervention generally beginning in the seventh grade. Some studies have included students as young as fifth and sixth graders, while others have been aimed at high school students. All of the studies (over a dozen) have found reductions in smoking onset among students who have participated in the experimental programs when compared to those in the control group. As might be expected, these reductions are usually greatest shortly after the program is concluded (i.e., within a few weeks of completion) and tend to diminish over time.

Overall, the studies completed thus far have generally reported significant reductions in the proportion of individuals who begin to smoke following participation in the new programs compared to those who have not. Effects on individuals who are at an especially high risk of becoming smokers have not generally been studied using these techniques.

Although the social influence approach has been primarily evaluated in terms of its impact on cigarette smoking, there is limited evidence that it may sometimes reduce alcohol and marijuana use as well. Nonetheless, no firm conclusions can be drawn concerning the components that are most or least important, concerning who is most effective in conducting the programs, or concerning the age at which the programs should be presented to students.

§ 22.4.2(b)   Personal and Social Skills Training Approaches

Research has also been conducted on the efficacy of broader-based substance abuse prevention programs. In addition to including many of the components of social influence approaches, these programs emphasize acquiring more general personal and social skills. Their theoretical roots are largely based in social learning and problem behavior theories. From this perspective, substance abuse is a socially learned, purposive, and functional behavior that results from an interplay of social, environmental, and personal factors. Substance use behavior, like other behavior, is learned through modeling and reinforcement.

The modeling and reinforcement process occurs in several ways. Some individuals seek out others who smoke, drink, use drugs, or who are interested in doing so as an alternative means of achieving some desired goal. Adolescents who are doing poorly academically or socially and have no other basis for distinction, may begin to use drugs as a substitute means of enhancing their self-esteem or social status. Similarly, using tobacco, alcohol, and other drugs may be a way of coping with tension or anxiety, particularly social anxiety. Others may begin smoking, drinking, or using other drugs after repeatedly observing parents, siblings, or other esteemed role models doing so; they may also begin as a result of persuasive appeals by peers or advertisers. The extent to which individuals are susceptible to these influences may be related to their personal characteristics. For example, individuals with low self-esteem, low self-confidence, and those lacking a sense of personal autonomy appear most likely to succumb to social influences. Based on this principle, some researchers have hypothesized that susceptibility to substance abuse may be decreased by using broader-based intervention approaches that help develop personal characteristics associated with a low susceptibility to substance abuse (Botvin).

Researchers in such states as New York, Tennessee, and Washington have studied the effectiveness of personal and social skills training for substance abuse prevention. The research has shown that, as is true of the social influences approach, the content and structure of this training varies widely. While some programs contain material similar to that in social influences programs, others do not. Generally, the more broad-based programs emphasize two or more of the following:

1. Developing general problem-solving and decision-making skills (e.g., "brainstorming," systematic decision-making).

2. Developing cognitive skills for resisting a range of interpersonal and media influences (e.g., identifying persuasive advertising appeals and how they work, developing personal counter-arguments to these appeals).

3. Increasing self-control and self-esteem (e.g., self-instructional techniques, self-reinforcement, goal setting).

4. Learning non-drug coping strategies for anxiety and tension reduction (e.g., relaxation techniques, cognitive coping skills).

5. Enhancing interpersonal skills (e.g., the ability to initiate social interaction, conversational techniques).

6. Assertiveness training (improving the ability to make requests, how to say "no," expressing feelings and opinions more effectively).

These abilities are taught through instruction, demonstration, feedback, reinforcement, behavioral rehearsal (practice in class), and more extended practice is encouraged by the use of "homework" assignments. The underlying objective is to teach general life/coping skills with a broad range of applications rather than approaches that are situation- or problem-specific. However, these programs also emphasize applying these general skills in substance abuse-related situations (e.g., using assertion abilities to resist pressures to smoke or use other drugs). Virtually all of the studies published to date have reported significant behavioral effects in the form of sharply reduced numbers of initially non-smoking participants who became smokers in the experimental group compared to the control group on a short-term basis (under one year). Reductions range from less than half as many becoming smokers in the year following training to 75 percent fewer students in the experimental group becoming smokers at least over the short run (Dentz).

§ 22.4.2(c) Transferring Smoking Prevention Concepts to Drug Prevention

Can concepts used in cigarette smoking prevention be transferred to other drug prevention programs? While the prognosis appears favorable, there are reasonable arguments on both sides. On the positive side, we know that many of the factors that precipitate smoking also apply to marijuana, the most commonly used illicit drug among adolescents. The primary factors associated with smoking onset include the influence of friends and parents; attitudes and beliefs about smoking; rebelliousness and independence; low academic performance and motivation; and prior manifestation of problem behavior. Each of these factors plays a role in adolescent experimentation with other drugs.

On the other hand, it can be argued that anti-smoking programs are effective because the general social climate has changed so radically over the past twenty-years or thirty years. Today most people (both adults and adolescents) do not smoke; the great majority believe it is harmful to their health, and increasing numbers not only disapprove of smoking but feel much freer to ask others to refrain from smoking in their presence. One might argue that these are only preconditions for an effective anti-smoking program, and that these preconditions do not exist for other drugs. However, recent data provide evidence that beliefs about marijuana and cigarettes, at least, are converging.

§ 22.4.3 The Unanswered Questions

Although research on the newer prevention approaches is encouraging, particularly when contrasted with the evidence that earlier approaches were uniformly ineffective, fundamental questions remain unanswered. Perhaps the most basic is just why some individuals, by their biology or psychosocial development, are more predisposed to substance abuse than others. As the outline of risk factors indicates, there is evidence that both kinds of factors play a role, but neither is sufficiently well-understood to provide the foundation for more precisely focused prevention that exists in other areas of public health.

§ 22.4.4 More Questions to Address

Users or nonusers? For any program, there are several possible target audiences and corresponding objectives. The typical classroom, for example, is composed of a variety of subgroups representing a wide range of motivations and experiences with respect to drug use. The typical program may include any of these objectives, depending on the target groups:

—For committed users, to prevent or delay the onset of drug use.

—For former users, to reinforce the decision to quit drug use.

—For nonproblem drug users, to examine their drug use and, as a minimum, to keep their current use from escalating to problem levels.

—For problem users, to reduce drug use or effect a change in patterns of use.

It is important to realize that most young people and adults do not use drugs other than alcohol, most do not abuse drugs, and many drug users abandon drugs after a short period of experimentation.

Should a program direct its efforts toward youths or adults? It is reasonable to give special attention to educating young people about drugs; they are at higher risk and more accessible. Young people are more easily influenced than adults, and it is easy to reach them through schools and the media. Early patterns of thought and behavior will remain with them and guide their later behavior, and they are the principal resource for society's future.

There are, however, good reasons for giving attention to adults. Adults are more likely to abuse certain categories of drugs, especially the legal drugs, and some are particularly at risk—young adults who drink and the elderly who use medications, for example. Moreover, adults are important role models for younger members of society, in their positions as parents, teachers, youth leaders, public figures, and celebrities. Finally, adults are society's decision-makers; they set the norms and pass the laws.

Peers or parents? Recent emphasis on the influence of peers in stimulating adolescent drug use does a disservice to both adolescents and their parents. First, the portrayal of overwhelming, one-way peer pressure minimizes the active role of adolescents in selecting the peer groups to which they respond best. It also ignores the influence of individuals on other group members and fails to consider the importance of positive peer norms in regulating behavior.

Second, the attention given to peer pressure detracts from the importance of parental influence. Although responsiveness to peers increases during adolescence, parental influence still continues to be felt. Children's use of alcohol and tobacco is influenced more by parental use of these substances than by peer use. Parental attitudes toward illegal drugs also have an impact on children's illegal drug use, even though peers' attitudes drug are a powerful influence.

Knowledge, attitudes, or behavior? Since the onset of drug prevention programs, educators have faced a dilemma concerning the relationship between what people know, what they feel, and what they do. More significant questions explore the connections between the changes in knowledge and attitudes and changes in behavior. Research and program experience have demonstrated that changes in significant behavior, such as drug use, do not readily follow from modifications in knowledge and feeling. Educators now have greater appreciation for the complex nature of human behavior and for the need to take situational, social, and individual factors into account when attempting to change behavior. These new insights suggest that drug education programs should contain a variety of informational, affective, and behavioral objectives.

Informational objectives may include raising levels of awareness about the nature and effects of drugs, the role of drugs in society, appropriate ways of using drugs, alternatives to drug use, and sources of help for drug-related problems.

Affective objectives may be equally diverse, focusing on feelings, attitudes, and values regarding drugs, drug use, abuse, and addiction, as well as feelings about those people who use or abuse drugs. More ambitious objectives might include, among others, a concern for improving people's self-concepts.

Behavioral objectives may include a range of different aims.

—Abstaining totally from drugs.

—Retarding the onset of drug use.

—Reducing drug consumption.

—Promoting responsible use.

—Modifying the situations in which drugs are used (e.g., separating drinking from driving).

—Identifying problem drug use early.

—Helping those with drug problems.

—Improving social skills associated with communication and assertiveness; improving personal skills in decision-making, coping, stress management.

—Modifying lifestyles.

—Promoting alternatives to drug use.

—Supporting prevention efforts.

Abstinence or responsible use? One policy issue with which educators constantly struggle is whether to encourage complete abstinence from drug use or to encourage responsible use. Some people believe that responsible use of drugs is not an acceptable objective for education programs, especially for the young; but this position ignores some of the realities of drug use. First, use of alcohol and medications with parental supervision is usually neither harmful nor illegal. Second, it is unrealistic to talk to illegal drug users as if they do not, and would not, use drugs. Efforts to prevent drug abuse by reducing the most risky forms of drug use (for example, drinking and driving) need not condone illegal drug use. Third, it may be unrealistic to counsel immediate abstinence for chronic drug users; more responsible use of an illegal drug may be an appropriate intermediate objective for such a population.

§ 22.5 HOW CAN WE MAKE DRUG EDUCATION MORE EFFECTIVE?

Plan. Effective planning begins with an identification of needs, both those that are perceived to exist in a community and those that actually exist. Careful planning helps in specifying goals and objectives. Decisions regarding program content and processes should be based on a thorough understanding of the drug problems and an appreciation of the dynamics of individual and social change.

Take account of previous history. Too often, educators operate as if people had no previous history; yet from their earliest years, people are constantly exposed to drug-related messages and behavior. From these they acquire knowledge, form attitudes, and develop their own behavioral tendencies. Most important in this regard is the influence of parents, siblings, peers, and the public media.

Acknowledge the positive reinforcements of drug use. Drug use consequences are not all negative; if they were, nobody would continue to use drugs. Moderate use of some drugs offers physical, psychological, and social benefits for some people. Drug education programs that do not take into account this important aspect of the decision to start or continue using drugs diminish their credibility and effectiveness.

Establish links between the educational setting and the rest of the student's experience. Students will be exposed to powerful influences when they leave the classroom. By integrating drug education into other curriculum areas (for example, English, mathematics, science), and by implementing school-wide drug use policies for both students and teachers, educators can create a school environment that reinforces the positive efforts of the classroom and minimizes competing negative forces of students' social environments. The idea is for the desired behavior, skills, and attitudes to be rehearsed in the supportive environment of the school's educational program. And finally, the efforts of the school require reinforcement from students' homes and from their communities.

Implement programs. Educational programs lose effectiveness if information about them is not appropriately disseminated. The mere availability of programs does not ensure their use. Programs and supporting materials must reach the decision-makers and those who will implement the programs, and the latter must be adequately trained in all aspects of the program.

Allocate resources. Communities devote less attention and fewer resources to drug education than to law enforcement and drug abuse treatment programs. Within schools, drug education programs suffer from minimal allocations of curriculum time, poor staff training, and negligible teacher and student accountability.

Evaluate. It is clear that not all approaches are equally effective for all target audiences or for all drugs. Without evaluation, little progress can be made in identifying which forms of drug education are effective in preventing and reducing drug-related problems. In addition, careful research can clarify the reasons why some educational programs are effective and others are not.

§ 22.6   SIGNIFICANT TRENDS IN PREVENTION

It is important that other possible school- and community-based prevention alternatives be explored that may contribute to changed attitudes toward substance abuse by youth and the larger community. Programs in which youth themselves take the initiative to discourage substance abuse may be an important deterrent. Students Against Drunk

Driving (SADD) is an example. The family substance abuse prevention tactics, which have been advocated by the "parents' movement," is also an example of a community program organized by parents themselves to reduce the drug problem.

Another very visible effort by a parents' group has been carried out by MADD (Mothers Against Drunk Driving). Again, the impact on substance abuse is not easily measured, but may be important both directly by inhibiting irresponsible behavior and indirectly by making the community more aware of the hazards of substance abuse.

A number of professional associations in medicine, psychology, social work, education, and other areas concerned with young people have also begun to play greater leadership roles by developing their members' professional skills concerning substance abuse and encouraging them to be more active in prevention, early detection, and treatment of abusers. The burgeoning efforts of these groups will undoubtedly contribute to a "critical mass" that seems likely to substantially reduce the acceptability of smoking, alcohol, and other drug abuse throughout American society.

Finally, the more recent national interest in drug testing to prevent drug use and abuse in the workplace and in schools is assisting in the prevention of drug abuse.

§ 22.6.1 Screening and Intervening
§ 22.6.1(a)   Short-Circuiting the Path to Addiction
The first priority is to stop drug use before it starts. It should be obvious that robust efforts involving community action and public education are central to an effective drug control program - one that seeks to denormalize drug use by creating a climate of public intolerance toward the drug-using behavior that all too often leads to addiction.

Considerably less obvious is how to target drug users still on the pathway to addiction—those individuals whose drug use is on the verge of causing noticeable levels of difficulty with work and relationships. It is never easy to identify individuals with such an incipient problem. A new approach holds much promise, however, using the reach of physicians to identify problems as early as possible.

§ 22.6.1(b)   SBIRT
This new approach, known as Screening, Brief Intervention, Referral and Treatment (SBIRT)—and more informally as screen and intervene—is being fielded in medical facilities from major city hospital emergency rooms to a system of rural health clinics.

SBIRT has a special utility for addressing the under-reported problem of drugged driving on our Nation's highways. Almost eleven million drivers per year get behind the wheel of a car while under the influence of an illegal drug. Drugged drivers have a much higher than average likelihood of having a serious accident and thus coming into contact with medical professionals. In fact, it is estimated that illegal drugs are used by approximately 10 to 22 percent of drivers involved in fatal motor vehicle crashes.

The SBIRT approach capitalizes on this alarming fact by placing the drug screening resources where the users are likely to be. In an SBIRT setting, for instance, a motorist involved in an accident may be asked about his drug use history before discharge; this screening, in turn, may unearth a developing drug use problem.

§ 22.6.1(c) How Does SBIRT Work in Practice?
The answer to this question is coming from six state-level sites and one tribal council that are implementing the approach under a five-year federal grant.

Michael S. Cunningham oversees 21 SBIRT sites for the state of California. "The intent of SBIRT is to identify the nondependent drug users," says Cunningham. "These are people whose behavior is such that they are starting to show the strain of their drug use but who have yet to run afoul of those institutions that would result in a referral, such as the criminal justice system."

"We want to get to people before they become too entrenched in their bad habits," adds Theodora Binion Taylor, who oversees an SBIRT program for a large community hospital in Chicago. "We know from the research that the sooner we act, the greater the likelihood of sustained recovery."

§ 22.6.1(d) How Does an Individual End Up On the Receiving End of an SBIRT Screening?
"Let's say you have an automobile accident," says Cunningham, "and you present yourself as a patient in one of those hospitals where we have SBIRT services. Once you are stabilized, you are going to be interviewed by a health advisor. These people are very good at building rapport and guiding you through a list of questions. This in turn results in an assessment, which is provided to your doctor."

Doctors have always had the ability to refer patients to a treatment program, a traditional course but one that is appropriate only for individuals who are already dependent on illegal drugs or alcohol. Where SBIRT breaks new ground is by giving doctors a range of possible interventions, from a brief counseling session to a short treatment program of up to six sessions to a full-blown inpatient treatment admission complete with detoxification.

"Let's take the example of James," says Cunningham. "James just turned 21, and he and his buddies went through the ritual of '21 and 21'—having 21 drinks in a row. James ended up wrecking his car. This is the first time James drank that much, but we would still do an intervention with him. A doctor needs to sit down and say, 'Look where this behavior is leading you.' People are surprisingly receptive to being lectured when it's delivered by a doctor. They came for help, and this is part of their prescription."

"Tom, on the other hand, goes out with his buddies. They smoke some marijuana and use some cocaine," says Cunningham. "Tom is still gainfully employed and has not yet had any major family problems. But his drug use has been slowly increasing over time, he's starting to miss Mondays at work, and he's had some arguments with his wife." Problems are starting to show up, in other words. But Tom may not need detox or a full-blown course of treatment. "Tom might be a good candidate for brief treatments," says Cunningham.

In total, the pilot SBIRT sites have now interviewed some 113,000 patients. In 15 percent of cases the patient's drug use was deemed to warrant some form of brief intervention, while 2 percent of those interviewed were found to be in need of drug treatment.

§ 22.6.2 Student Drug Testing

There are a variety of prevention programs, including school- and community-based programs, student drug testing programs, and public service advertisements. These diverse approaches help parents keep kids away from drugs and alcohol. Yet none of these programs is enough to make a decisive difference without significant parental involvement. Student drug testing programs, for instance, reinforce parental admonitions against drug use but also provide parents with needed information, even when the information is the good news of a negative test result. A campaign of public service advertisements sponsored by a public-private partnership confronts parental misconceptions head-on by equipping parents with proven techniques for monitoring teen behavior. Community-level prevention strategies include programs that support parents' wishes when parents cannot be there to watch, multiplying the number of watchful eyes in the community to deter young people from using illegal drugs or alcohol.

But all roads lead back to parents—and for good reason. Available research is unambiguous about the importance of having parents discuss the dangers of illegal drugs and underage drinking with their children. Parents and other caregivers need to do more than simply talk about drugs and alcohol. They also need to act-by monitoring the behavior of teen children, knowing where their teenagers are at all times, particularly after school, and knowing whom they are with and what they are doing. Such techniques have proved remarkably effective in keeping teenagers away from drugs.

The greatest single barrier to increased parental monitoring seems to be self-inflicted—the view of some parents, particularly baby boomers, that monitoring their child is nagging or, worse, authoritarian behavior that could drive a wedge between them and their child. Such parents may be more comfortable reaching out to their child as a friend rather than in the more customary role of guardian, monitor, and guide. They may struggle to reconcile their own past drug use, wondering whether it is hypocritical to lay down an unambiguous line that drug use is wrong and will not be tolerated. Worse still, kids report that parents are not typically as vigilant as their parents believe themselves to be.

The good news is that parental monitoring has been shown to be remarkably effective in reducing a range of risky behaviors among young people. Studies indicate that kids who are monitored are one-fourth as likely to use illegal drugs and one-half as likely to smoke cigarettes as kids who are not monitored. Put another way, the research confirms what many parents of teenagers tend to doubt: kids really do listen to their parents, and they do respond to parental expectations. For example, surveys show that two-thirds of youth ages 13 to 17 say losing their parents' respect is one of the main reasons they do not smoke marijuana or use other drugs.

§ 22.6.2(a)   The Saint Patrick High School Experience

Founded in 1861, St. Patrick High School is Chicago's oldest Catholic high school for boys. Five years ago, St. Patrick formed a task force of parents, community leaders, administrators, and faculty to explore the idea of a student drug testing program. The upshot was a recommendation to drug test all students randomly at least once each year (ONDCP 2005).

"We have had amazing results from hair testing," says principal Joseph G. Schmidt. "We have 1,022 guys at St. Patrick. We have tested all of them, and only nine have tested positive. That's one percent." Each family with a child at St. Patrick pays $60 per year to administer the test, which can identify marijuana, cocaine, opiates, methamphetamine, phencyclidine (PCP), and MDMA (Ecstasy). A positive test triggers a notification of the student's family, at which point the student is typically referred to counseling. Consequences occur only if there is a second positive test anytime within a student's four-year high school career. "First, they have a confidential meeting with me," says Rudy Presslak, dean of students. "And if it was a one-time thing and they feel they can stop on their own, that's the end of it. We encourage them to meet with the counselors here at the school, however, and if the parents feel that it's a bigger problem, they can see an outside counselor."

"We pull 10 to 15 kids [at a time] for hair testing," adds principal Schmidt. "It takes maybe five minutes per kid, mostly for paperwork. We snip an inch and a half of hair, which tells us if they have used drugs in the past 90 days. The parents are very supportive. And they appreciate getting the letter saying, 'Your kid tested negative.'"

The students seem to appreciate the program as well. "For the kids who would be tempted to use, it's an incentive not to," Schmidt says. "And for the kids who wouldn't use anyway, it's an easy way to say no when someone pressures them." "The other day I heard a couple of our kids talking to a kid from another school," adds dean Presslak. "They were telling him, 'We don't have drugs here at St. Patrick.'" The purpose of testing, after all, is not to punish students who use drugs but to prevent use in the first place. Testing helps to ensure that users get the help they need through a student assistance program, to stop placing themselves and their friends at risk. Random drug testing is not a substitute for all our other efforts to reduce drug use by young people, but it does make those efforts work better. Years have passed since the U.S.

Supreme Court broadened the authority of public schools to drug test students, making this powerful tool available to any school battling a drug problem. Since that historic ruling, a number of schools across the country have seized this opportunity to implement drug testing programs of their own.

§ 22.7   RESEARCH

In the coming years, research advances in the following areas will significantly enhance prevention efforts:

—Understanding of the genetic and environmental risk and protective factors that can prevent or lead to drug abuse and addiction.

—Enhancement of the assessment of drug problems at a local level by providing communities with effective research-based tools.

—Translation of research-based prevention principles for the specific needs of local communities.

§ 22.7.1 Risk Factors

Understanding what determines vulnerability to substance abuse is crucial to the development of effective prevention programming. At this point, there is no evidence that a single, unique factor determines which individuals will abuse drugs; rather, drug abuse appears to develop as the result of a variety of genetic, biological, emotional, cognitive, and social risk factors that interact with features of the social context. Thus, both individual-level factors and social context-level factors appear to make an individual more or less at risk for drug abuse and influence the progression from drug use to drug abuse to drug addiction.

Studies supported by NIDA and SAMHSA have already identified many risk factors associated with the development of drug problems. These factors typically have been organized into categories that represent individual, familial, and social risks. For example, we now know that individual-level risks include shy, aggressive, and impulsive personality traits and poor academic achievement; and family-level risks include poor monitoring by parents and exposure to substance use by parents and siblings. School-level risk factors include a pro-drug-use norm and availability of drugs on or near the school campus; and community-level risks include lack of positive academic and recreational programming for children and adolescents after school hours and on weekends, as well as low levels of law enforcement with respect to minors' use of licit and illicit substances. This sampling of risk factors illustrates the breadth and complexity of the risks that can confront any one person.

§ 22.7.2 Protective Factors

For many years, our focus was on discovering the factors that put people, particularly children, at risk for drug use, abuse, and addiction. We now know that there are also protective or resiliency factors that protect individuals from developing drug-related problems. NIDA-supported research has already uncovered many such protective factors that operate at the individual and contextual levels through the family, peer group, school, community, workplace, and the media, among others. Examples of protective or resiliency factors include a stable temperament, a high degree of motivation, a strong parent-child bond, consistent parental supervision and discipline, bonding to pro-social institutions, association with peers who hold conventional attitudes, and consistent, community-wide anti-drug-use messages and norms. An accumulation of protective factors may counteract the negative influences of a few risk factors. The challenge for the future is to understand how risk and protective factors interact to make individuals more or less vulnerable to trying drugs, abusing drugs, and/or becoming addicted to drugs. Additionally, we must understand the unique risk and protective factors that contribute to drug abuse among minority populations. This knowledge will allow prevention researchers and providers to design programs that can be more effectively tailored to individual needs.

§ 22.7.3 Effective Research and Community Needs

To give communities the science-based tools to prevent drug abuse, we must have research in several emerging areas of prevention. Strategies that can help communities better determine their own local needs and their readiness for interventions are needed. For example, communities must be given the epidemiological tools to assess their needs. Research is needed also to aid understanding of the organization, management, financing, and delivery of prevention services. In the treatment arena there are established systems such as clinics, hospitals, outpatient centers, HMOs, and clinician training and certification systems. However, there are no defined systems for provision and financing of prevention services or training and credentialing of providers. Thus, it is difficult to determine how decisions are made about prevention implementation. A full understanding of these issues will help integrate prevention strategies and programs into existing community-level service delivery systems and sustain them (ONDCP 2005).

§ 22.8 SUMMARY

The most optimistic conclusions are related to prevention—not because past drug prevention programs have proven eminently successful (which they have not) but because we can see why past approaches have failed; they were grounded in outmoded assumptions of why adolescents begin using psychoactive substances. In contrast, there is encouraging evidence supporting the success of new smoking prevention programs, which are based on a more up-to-date model of adolescent behavior. Recent longitudinal studies have tracked the process by which adolescents start using drugs. It usually starts in a group setting, among their peers or relatives—social influences are the main influences on adolescent drug-taking. Secondly, young people have a strong desire to appear "grown up" and independent. If drug use is defined as an adult activity and adolescents see older youth or adults taking drugs, they are more likely to imitate that behavior in an attempt to claim a mature status. Third, young people are present-oriented. They are much more concerned with their life at school, their current social milieu, and their acceptance within the adolescent social group than with the long-term risks of their actions. Thus, warnings about future disease are likely to fall on deaf ears.

Drug Prevention and Education

Most drug use prevention programs do not focus on social factors. The majority of past "drug education" was based on an information-oriented approach. It provided facts about the pharmacology and effects of drugs, often as a lecture by a teacher, physician, police officer, or former drug user. Such programs assume that children use drugs because they are ignorant of the dangers. Unfortunately, there is a wealth of evidence suggesting that mere knowledge of the facts does not affect behavior directly, particularly if social influences contradict the facts. In addition, many previous education efforts were marred by exaggerations or "scare tactics," which today's sophisticated youth easily detect and discount.

Programs in "affective education" have been the other main approach in the past. These programs, including values clarification, skill development, and efforts to increase self-esteem, have been popular in the past decade but they have not been proven effective by any scientific evaluation. The model for such programs holds that adolescents start using drugs because they lack some essential trait or ability, such as self-esteem, interpersonal skill, or the capacity to translate values into rational decisions. Such traits are valuable, but there is no credible evidence that improving them reduces drug use. Indeed, the best-implemented example of such a program, which also contained a well-designed evaluation, showed virtually no effects on drug use.

In contrast, there are several successful programs based on a social influence model of adolescent behavior, all aimed at preventing cigarette smoking among junior high school students. These programs begin by identifying the messages and arguments in favor of smoking—messages that come explicitly or implicitly from peers, adults, and the media. They show adolescents how to counter those arguments, thus providing an "inoculation" against future pro-smoking influences. Then they teach students effective but socially acceptable methods of resisting pressure to smoke: how to "say no" gracefully. The reasons for wanting to "say no" are illustrated by the short-term effects of smoking, such as bad breath, discolored teeth, and increased carbon monoxide in the blood, rather than by long-term health effects that seem uncertain and far in the future to most young people. These themes are developed by group discussion in a 7th- or 8th-grade classroom, sometimes led by an older peer such as a high school student. Such programs have been successful in preventing adolescent cigarette smoking, reducing the number of smokers by one-third to two-thirds in a number of independent studies. Furthermore, in the NIDA Report on Drug Use Among American High School Seniors, 1975-1990, regarding attitudes and beliefs about drugs and their harmfulness, two-thirds (68 percent) of the seniors studied judged that regular use of cigarettes (one or more packs a day) entails a great risk of harm to the user. In addition, 78 percent of the seniors judged that regular use of marijuana involves a significant health risk (NIDA 1991). The 1993 high school seniors indicated they believed there is great risk in the regular use of marijuana (72.5%), cocaine (90%), heroin (88.3%), and LSD (79.4%) (BJS 1995). Thus, a healthy base of skepticism already exists among adolescents about the wisdom of using such harmful substances.

Chapter 22

References

Bandura, A. Social Learning Theory. Englewood Cliffs: Prentice Hall, 1977.

Bohmen, M. "Some genetic aspects of alcoholism and criminality." Arch Gen Psychiat 35 (1978): 269-276.

Botvin, B.J. "Broadening the focus of smoking prevention strategies." Promoting Adolescent Health: A Dialogue on Research and Practice. New York: Academic Press, 1982.

Bureau of Justice Statistics. Drug and Crime Facts, 1994. Washington, D.C.: U.S. Department of Justice, 1995.

Dentz, Mary Ann. "Prevention of Adolescent Substance Abuse Through Social Skill Development." Preventing Adolescent Drug Abuse: Intervention Strategies. NIDA Research Monograph Series. Rockville, MD: Department of Health and Human Services, 1985.

Evans, R.I., et al. "Deterring the onset of smoking in children; Knowledge of immediate physiological effects and coping with peer pressure, media pressure, and parent modeling." J of Applied Social Psychology 8 (1978): 126-135.

Evans, R.I. "Smoking in children: Developing a social psychological strategy of deterrence." Preventive Medicine 5 (1976): 122-127.

Goodstadt, M.S. "Alcohol and drug education." Health Education Monographs 6.3 (1978): 263-279.

Hawkins, J.D., et al. "Childhood Predictors and Prevention of Adolescent Substance Abuse." Etiology of Drug Abuse: Implications for Prevention. Ed. Jones. NIDA Research Monograph No. 56. Washington, D.C.: Supt. of Docs., U.S. Govt. Print. Office, 1985.

Hawkins, J.D., et al. "Childhood Predictors of Adolescent Substance Abuse: Towards an Empirically Grounded Theory." J of Children in Contemporary Society 18.1, 2 (1986): 1-65.

Kandel, D., ed. Longitudinal Research on Drug Use: Empirical Findings and Methodological Issues. Washington, D.C.: Hemisphere (Halsted-Wiley), 1978.

McAlister, Alfred. "Social-Psychological Approaches." Preventing Adolescent Drug Abuse: Intervention Strategies. NIDA Research Monograph Series. Rockville, MD: Department of Health and Human Services, 1985.

National Institute on Drug Abuse. "Drug Use Among American High School Seniors, College Students, and Young Adults, 1975-1990." Vol.I "High School Seniors. DHHS Pub. No. (ADM) 91-1813 Rockville, MD: Department of Health and Human Services, 1991.

Office of National Drug Control Policy. "Healing America's Drug Users: Getting Treatment Resources Where They Are Needed." The President's National Drug Control Strategy. Washington, D.C.: Executive Office of the President, 2005.

----------. "Stopping Use Before It Starts: Education and Community Action." The President's National Drug Control Strategy. Washington, D.C.: Executive Office of the President, 2005.

Swisher, J.D. "Prevention issues." Handbook on Drug Abuse. Washington, D.C.: National Institute on Drug Abuse, U.S. Govt. Print. Office, 1979.

Schaps, E., et al. "A review of 127 drug abuse prevention program evaluations." J of Drug Issues, Inc (Winter 1981):17-43.

Shaffer, H., et al. "The primary prevention of smoking onset: An inoculation approach." Journal of Psychoactive Drugs 15.3 (1983): 177-184.

CHAPTER 23

EFFECTIVENESS OF DRUG CONTROL ACTIVITIES AND CONCLUSIONS

§ 23.1   INTRODUCTION

It seems wrong—by some accounts, even evil—for drug traffickers to supply drugs to users, and it seems unjust that drug traffickers grow rich and powerful on their ill-gotten gains while regular users are often poor. These simple intuitions establish two quite different perspectives for looking at drug trafficking.

Drug trafficking as drug supply. From the perspective of drug control policy, the worst thing about drug traffickers is that they supply drugs. Too many drugs reach illicit users in the United States. The objective of drug trafficking policies should be to minimize the supply capacity of the distribution systems so that the smallest possible volume of drugs reaches users.

Drug trafficking as organized crime. Some criminal organizations engaged in drug trafficking grow rich and powerful. This situation, in turn, undermines citizens' confidence in their government. When drug trafficking is viewed as an organized crime problem, the objective of control efforts is to arrest and punish rich traffickers and to prevent new groups from arising.

To a degree, these perspectives and objectives are congruent. For instance, a principal means for minimizing the flow of drugs to the United States is to immobilize major trafficking organizations. In some circumstances, however, these objectives diverge. Aggressive law enforcement efforts directed at marginal trafficking organizations might well reduce the overall supply of drugs to illicit markets. But these efforts, by eliminating marginal traffickers, may increase the wealth and power of the drug trafficking organizations that remain by allowing them to gain effective control over the market.

§ 23.2   ALTERNATIVE APPROACHES

Choices between approaches for dealing with drug trafficking will depend on which aspects of the trafficking problem are deemed most important and on the costs and efficacy of particular policies.

§ 23.2.1 Legalization

The most radical approach to dealing with drug trafficking is to legalize drugs. Yet, legalization can mean many different things. At one extreme, it can mean complete elimination of any legal restrictions on the production, distribution, possession, or use of any drug. On the other hand, it can mean allowing limited uses of some particular drugs, producing the drugs only under government auspices, distributing them through tightly regulated distribution systems, and punishing with severe criminal penalties any production or use outside the authorized system.

The goal of legalizing drugs is to bring them under effective legal control. If it were legal to produce and distribute drugs, legitimate businessmen would enter the business. There would be less need for violence and corruption since the industry would have access to the courts. And, instead of absorbing tax dollars as targets of expensive enforcement efforts, the drug sellers might begin to pay taxes. So, legalization might well solve the organized crime aspects of the drug trafficking problem. Furthermore, drug use under legalization might not be as destructive to users and to society as it is under the current prohibition. Drugs would be less expensive, more pure, and more conveniently available. However, by relaxing opposition to drug use, and by making drugs more freely available, legalization might fuel a significant increase in the level of drug use. It is not unreasonable to assume that the number of people who become chronic, intensive users would increase substantially. It is this risk, as well as a widespread perception that drug use is simply wrong, that stops outright legalization.

An alternative is to choose a system more restrictive than outright legalization but one that still leaves room for legitimate uses of some drugs. Arguably, such a policy would produce some of the potential benefits of legalization without accelerating growth in the level of drug use. The difficulty is that wherever the boundary between the legitimate and illicit use of drugs is drawn, an illicit market will develop just outside the boundary. Indeed, if the boundary is more restrictive, the resulting black market will be larger and more controlled by "organized crime."

At present, the existing drug laws in the United States establish a regulatory rather than a prohibitionist regime. While most uses of heroin and marijuana are illegal, some research uses of these drugs are authorized under the current laws, and there is discussion of the possible use of these drugs for medical purposes such as the treatment of terminal cancer patients. So far, California and Arizona, and seven other states have passed laws making medical use of marijuana legal. Cocaine is legal for use as a medical drug, and barbiturates, amphetamines, and tranquilizers are legalized for a variety of medical purposes and distributed through licensed pharmacists and physicians. However, the fact that there are some legal uses of these drugs has not eliminated illicit trafficking. For marijuana, heroin, cocaine, and meth, the restrictions are so sharp relative to the current demand for the drugs that virtually the entire distribution system remains illicit and depends on drug trafficking. For amphetamines, barbiturates, and tranquilizers, the restrictions are fewer, so a larger portion of the demand is met from illicit distribution. Distribution of these drugs takes the form of diversion from legitimate channels rather than wholly illicit production and distribution.

§ 23.2.2 Source Country Crop Control
A second approach to dealing with drug trafficking is to try to eliminate the raw materials that are used to produce the drugs. For heroin,

cocaine, and marijuana, this means controlling opium, coca leaf, and marijuana crops in countries such as Turkey, Afghanistan, Thailand, Bolivia, Colombia, Peru, Mexico, and Jamaica. For marijuana, illicit domestic production is also important.

Efforts to control these foreign crops generally take one of two forms. Governments either try to induce farmers to stop producing the crops for illicit markets or attempts are made to destroy those crops that can be located. Sometimes the inducement takes the form of subsidies for growing other crops. Other times foreign crops are bought and burned before they reach illicit channels. Eradication may also be accomplished by airborne chemical spraying (which has the advantage of being controlled by a relatively small number of people, and the disadvantage of doing a great deal of collateral damage to legitimate crops), or by ground-level destruction of crops through cutting and digging (which has the disadvantage of relying on large numbers of people and of being quite visible well in advance of the operations).

In general, these efforts suffer from two major difficulties. First, there seems to be no shortage of locations in which the crops may be grown. If Turkey stops growing opium poppies, Mexico, Afghanistan, and Southeast Asia can eventually take up the slack. If Colombia stops growing coca, Peru can replace it. If Mexico eliminated marijuana production, the hills of California would be even more densely filled with marijuana plants than they are now. The second problem is that foreign governments cannot always be relied on to vigorously enforce crop control policies. Sometimes the difficulty is that the crops lie in parts of the country that are not under effective governmental control. Other times the problem is inefficiency or corruption in the agencies that are managing the programs. In the worst cases, the crops are sufficiently important to the domestic economy (or the personal well-being of high government officials) that the government prefers not to act at all.

When foreign governments are reluctant to cooperate, the United States government must balance its interest in advancing its drug policy objectives against other foreign policy objectives. One perplexing problem is posed by governments that acquiesce to drug trafficking but are important to the United States as regional bulwarks against terrorist expansion. In these countries, the U.S. government may feel required to overlook drug trafficking in order to maintain the other government's anti-terrorist activities. These observations do not imply that crop control policies can never be effective. In the early 1970s, more effective control of opium poppies in Turkey produced a 2- to 3-year reduction in the supply of heroin to the East Coast of the United States; it also produced an observable reduction in the rate at which new users were becoming addicted.

These observations do indicate, however, that crop control programs cannot be counted on as long-term solutions: they will take place sporadically and unpredictably. This suggests that an effective way to manage our crop control efforts is to position ourselves in foreign countries to notice and exploit opportunities when they arise, but not to rely on this approach as our major initiative for controlling drug trafficking.

§ 23.2.3 Interdiction

Interdiction efforts aimed at stopping illicit drugs at the border are compelling. If we cannot rely on foreign countries to help us with our drug problem, we will do it ourselves by establishing defenses at the border. The fact that government agencies have special powers to search at the border should also make it easier to find illicit drugs there. Forces of the U.S. Customs Agency and the U.S. Immigration and Naturalization Service inspect people and goods passing through official "ports of entry," and they patrol between "ports of entry" to ensure that no one can cross the border without facing inspection. The Coast Guard, the military, and civilian aviation authorities all have capabilities that allow the government to detect who is crossing the border and to prevent illegal crossings.

There are, however, two problems with interdiction. One is the sheer size of the inspection task. More than 12,000 miles of international boundary must be patrolled. Over 420 billion tons of goods and more than 270 million people cross these boundaries each year, yet the quantities of drugs are small—a few hundred tons of marijuana and less than 20 tons of heroin or cocaine. Moreover, the heroin and cocaine arrive in shipments of less than a hundred pounds.

That the volume of heroin and cocaine imported is much less than the volume of marijuana points to the second problem with interdiction. It is a strategy that is more successful with marijuana than with heroin or cocaine. Marijuana's bulkiness makes it more vulnerable to interdiction efforts. This situation is unfortunate because, in the eyes of many, marijuana presents fewer problems than heroin and cocaine. Moreover, marijuana can be grown easily in the United States. If foreign supplies are kept out, the supply system can adjust by growing more marijuana domestically.

That seems to be what has happened. Current estimates indicate that interdiction efforts are successful in seizing about a third of the marijuana destined for the United States. Yet, except for a few local areas, the impact on the price and availability of the drug has been minimal. To make matters worse, the current domestically-grown marijuana is more potent than the imported marijuana.

§ 23.2.4 High-Level Enforcement

A fourth attack on illicit trafficking is directed at the organizations responsible for producing, importing, and distributing drugs. The basic aim is to immobilize or destroy the trafficking networks. In the past, enforcement agencies have tended to view this problem as "getting to Mr. Big"—the individual kingpin who, it was assumed, controlled an organization's capacity to distribute drugs. If that person could be arrested, prosecuted, and imprisoned, the network would fall apart. More recently, the law enforcement community has become less certain that this strategy can succeed. Even when "Mr. Big" is in prison, he can continue to manage the distribution of drugs. Moreover, the organizations seem less dependent on single individuals than enforcement officials once assumed. Indeed, the whole drug distribution system is less centralized than was once assumed. Relatively small and impermanent organizations—freelance entrepreneurs—supply a large proportion of illicit drugs.

To deal with this decentralization, enforcement aims have shifted from stopping individual dealers to destroying whole networks. Federal investigators have been granted special powers to seize drug dealers' assets, including boats, cars, planes, houses, bank accounts, and cash.

The main problem with attacking illicit trafficking organizations is that it is enormously expensive. Convincing evidence can be produced only through sustained efforts to recruit informants, establish electronic surveillance, and insinuate undercover agents. It is difficult for prosecutions to succeed because of the complexity of conspiracy laws and the particularly intrusive investigative methods that must be used to gather evidence.

§ 23.2.5 Street-Level Enforcement

A fifth line of attack is to go after street-level dealers through the use of physical surveillance or "buy and bust" operations. In the recent past, this approach has been de-emphasized. It seemed to have no impact on the overall supply because dealers who were arrested were jailed only intermittently and when they were, they were easily replaced. At best, drug dealing was driven off the street temporarily, or to a different street. Many hours were spent to produce small, transient results, and these operations seemed to invite abuses of authority and corruption. As a result, many police were removed from street-level enforcement.

Police have renewed street-level enforcement efforts, but they have altered their objectives. To the extent that street-level enforcement increases the "hassle" associated with using drugs, it can make a contribution to the objective of reducing drug use. If drugs, already expensive, can be made inconvenient to purchase, some non-addicted users may be persuaded to abandon drugs. Street-level enforcement can also encourage criminally active drug users to reduce their consumption, or draw them into treatment programs. It can contribute to the objective of immobilizing major traffickers by identifying defendants who can provide information about major trafficking networks. Ultimately, it can contribute to the quality of life in neighborhoods by returning the streets to community control.

These rationales give street-level enforcement some plausibility. What gives it real force is that it seems to work. For example, Operation Pressure Point, carried out on the Lower East Side of Manhattan, reduced robberies by 40 percent and burglaries by 27 percent.

There have also been some important failures. An operation in Lawrence, Massachusetts failed to produce any important effect on levels of crime or drug use in that community. The reasons seem to be that the effort was too small relative to the size of the opposing trafficking networks, and that the effort was focused on cocaine rather than heroin. Similarly, an operation in Philadelphia failed to produce anything other than angry citizens and a stern rebuke by the courts because it was carried out without any consultation with the community and without any regard for evidentiary standards. Subsequent discussions of these results among academics and practitioners have produced several guidelines for successful street-level enforcement. First, the scale of the enforcement effort should be in some sense proportionate to the effective size of the trafficking network. Second, police should carry out the operation after obtaining widespread community support, and with scrupulous attention to the niceties of search and seizure. Otherwise, the operation will lack the legitimacy necessary to sustain continued support. Third, it is important to complement the street-level enforcement effort with other investments, not only in the criminal justice system, but also in the treatment system, otherwise the opportunities created by street-level enforcement will not be fully realized.

§ 23.3 LAW ENFORCEMENT

U.S. policy has always relied heavily on law enforcement to control the illicit drug market. When considering enforcement, the most fundamental point is that the supply of drugs can never be completely eliminated. Most of the illegal drug supply originates overseas, in regions where drug crops are the farmers' most profitable products. The central governments in these regions are often weak, and some are not sympathetic with U.S. concerns. Perhaps the most important consideration here is that most illicit drugs are exported by several source countries; when one source is shut down, other producers fill the vacuum. Accordingly, past efforts to reduce drug crops have had little lasting effect on the U.S. market, and we cannot expect more in the foreseeable future.

Nor is it likely that supply can be much reduced by stopping drugs "at the border." Although the federal government has greatly expanded its interdiction efforts, most drug shipments still get through and prices have not risen. Moreover, doubling interdiction would probably have little effect on retail prices. The key reason is that a drug's import cost is only a small fraction of its retail price. The price for a given quantity rises very steeply as it passes down the chain from producer to consumer. Hence, intervening at the top levels of the market can exert very limited effect on the final price. Other factors also work against interdiction, such as the smuggler's ability to adapt to enforcement pressure, and the capacity to recruit large numbers of foreign boat crewmembers at low wages.

Even within the U.S. borders, there are poor prospects for increasing pressure against retail drug dealers. Local police make many arrests, but retailers number probably over half a million. Therefore, only a small fraction are arrested, and an ever smaller proportion are imprisoned—probably less than 1 percent. With state prisons currently overcrowded and local courts backlogged, it is not feasible to raise those risks significantly. Even if it were feasible to arrest and incarcerate many more, the effect would be only a small price increase. The trade has simply become so vast that any reasonable increase in police pressure could deliver only a small impact on a very large market.

Undercover investigations of high-level dealers may offer better prospects, but even here the costs would be great and the results uncertain. Most of the innovative techniques that law enforcement agencies have developed can be evaded by dealer adaptations. Perhaps federal agencies could incarcerate more high-level dealers if their investigative budgets were greatly increased. However, such investigations are time-consuming and expensive. More intense law enforcement is not likely to substantially affect either the availability or the retail price of drugs in this country. This is not to imply that enforcement against drug traffickers should be abandoned. Past enforcement has certainly increased the price of drugs beyond what it otherwise would have been. In addition, enforcement may make it more difficult for novices to find dealers.

§ 23.4   TREATMENT

Another facet of the drug abuse problem involves treatment. Treatment of drug abuse is an extensive and multifaceted industry in the United States, accounting for over $500 million in annual expenditures. Originally, federal authorities conceived of treatment and law enforcement as complementary methods of containing the heroin problem; law enforcement would deter addicts and dry up drug supplies, so users would be forced into treatment centers. Treatment was, and still is, largely oriented toward heroin users.

A critical issue is the relative effectiveness of the various treatment approaches. For instance, many observers recommend "early intervention" with young people, before their drug abuse has become severe. Another promising approach, family therapy, is based on the premise that drug abuse often originates in family dysfunctions; accordingly, the therapy brings the family together into treatment in an attempt to resolve the underlying problem. However, even though family therapy has achieved demonstrated positive effects in a randomized experiment with young adult heroin users, it has not been systematically tested with adolescent drug abusers, and the costs could be quite high.

Some evidence suggests that it should be possible to develop effective treatment for drug abusers. First, evaluation studies indicate that certain forms of treatment—drug free-therapy, methadone maintenance, and residential "therapeutic communities"—work better than no treatment at all. Second, the longer a patient remains in treatment, the better are his or her chances of improvement; and patients who complete treatment have better outcomes than those who drop out. Although we cannot say with certainty whether this means that patients would benefit from longer treatment (because dropouts could differ from graduates in other ways), the relationship lends some credence to the belief that treatment, in general, produces positive effects.

§ 23.5   PREVENTION

It has become increasingly obvious that prevention programs offer brighter prospects for reducing adolescent drug use than any other method. There is now a considerable base of knowledge about how young people begin using drugs, plus some experimental evidence suggesting that prevention programs can keep adolescents from starting to smoke cigarettes. Preventing a phenomenon can best be done with a clear understanding of the processes that cause it. In the case of drug use, there is now abundant research supporting the hypothesis that the primary cause of initial drug use is social influence. Most people first begin using drugs because their friends do. This carries several implications for prevention programs. First, such programs should be designed to help individuals learn effective methods of resisting social pressure. Second, the programs should try to reinforce and solidify social norms against drug use. Third, the most effective appeals are likely to come from other adolescents, rather than from teachers, parents, or adult authorities.

Peer influence, of course, interacts with the individual's beliefs and orientations. Two aspects of adolescents' orientations are particularly important: (1) their desire to appear mature; and (2) their orientation toward the present rather than the future. Adolescents are vulnerable to pro-drug appeals because they wish to appear mature and free of the restrictions of childhood. Smoking, drinking, and using illicit drugs are all methods of demonstrating a new-found independence. Furthermore, young people are not likely to be deterred by warnings about adverse effects far in the future; most adolescents are much more concerned about their immediate circumstances, friendships, and activities than about future health problems. Therefore, prevention programs need to counteract the belief that drug use shows maturity, and to indict drugs for their short-term rather than long-term consequences.

The effectiveness of such an approach is illustrated by the contrast between older anti-drug programs and the newer anti-smoking programs. In the past, many prevention efforts assumed that drug use resulted directly from the user's lack of information or from their personal problems such as a lack of self-esteem. Early drug education programs based on these concepts produced disappointing results.

The more recent anti-smoking programs, based on a social influence model of initial use, have accumulated a more positive record. Such programs help children identify the pressures to smoke, particularly peer influences, and arm them with arguments against smoking. To tap into the adolescent's present orientation, these programs base their counterarguments on the immediate undesirable effects of smoking, especially those that harm one's appearance. And to counter the claim that smoking represents maturity, they often use nonsmoking older peers who can testify that smoking does not confer independence or adult status. These programs have been tested in several locations and evaluated by independent research teams, and they have generally shown significant effects in preventing cigarette smoking.

In this respect, national survey data suggest that for most drugs, prevention programs can be appropriately targeted at junior high school students. Even programs in elementary school on health, nutrition, drug use, abuse, and addiction may help promote a healthy lifestyle among students nearing adolescence. According to the National Household Survey on Drug Abuse, the average age of first use of cigarettes was 15.7 years (NIDA 1995). Furthermore, the study found that cigarettes were, on the average, used first before alcohol or illicit drugs.

It appears that a great majority of drug use can be prevented with strong, positive prevention programs aimed at elementary and especially junior high school students. These programs can take advantage of the anti-drug social norms that exist in a group of non-users.

Unfortunately, these arguments do not hold for alcohol. Alcohol is so common in American society that a substantial number of 7th grade students have already become regular users. Moreover, unlike cigarette smoking and illicit drug use, adults' use of alcohol is broadly accepted, and a "primary" prevention program suggesting that young people never start drinking is likely to be ineffective.

But there is a reasonable chance of adapting the anti-smoking model to other drugs. Marijuana is likely to be the best immediate target. Adolescent beliefs about marijuana and cigarettes have been converging; in 1991, about equal proportions of high school seniors believed that regular marijuana use and regular cigarette smoking posed great risks of harm (NIDA 1991). In 1993, 72.5 percent of high school seniors believed the regular use of marijuana posed great risks of harm (BJS 1995).

Longitudinal studies of adolescents have shown that drug use develops in a series of successive stages, beginning with use of alcohol or cigarettes; some of those users subsequently go on to marijuana, and some of the latter then proceed to other illicit drugs. This offers hope that a program starting early and targeting marijuana and cigarettes may not only prevent use of those substances, but may also "spill over" to prevent use of later-stage illicit drugs (Clausen).

Today, the scientific evidence is in favor of prevention approaches over the others. It seems, therefore, that prevention should receive greater credence in the future, and that a higher priority should be placed on developing and testing prevention methods that may ultimately reduce the demand for drugs. Thus, more appropriations for drug abuse should be directed toward prevention efforts.

§ 23.6 CONCLUSIONS

Drug abuse is fundamentally a social problem which cannot be solved by the government alone. Federal and state governments can support drug abuse prevention and treatment programs, conduct research, enforce drug laws, and provide leadership in the fight against drug abuse and drug trafficking. However, not until public and individual attitudes change will illicit drugs and the organized criminal groups that traffic in them be eliminated. Individuals need not accept drug use in their midst. There is no "right" to use drugs. Government efforts to combat drug trafficking and drug abuse are a vital effort, but they are ultimately only a holding action, while consensus continues to build among individuals concerning the utter unacceptability of drug use.

Despite this growing consensus, a profound disparity exists between principle and practice. Popular entertainment and advertising, sometimes subtle, sometimes not, regularly reflect and even promote the view that the use of illicit drugs is glamorous, exciting, and sophisticated, or at least harmless and amusing.

The illusion that drug use is glamorous is regularly, if somewhat indirectly, reinforced by revelations that drug use is commonplace among celebrities in the sports and entertainment worlds. In August 1985, for example, the New York Times reported cocaine's alleged use by players on virtually every baseball team in the major leagues, prompting the Commissioner of Baseball to declare drug use the "number one" problem facing the game. Drug-related controversy in major league baseball was then followed by a similar situation in professional football, reaching all the way to the National Football League's championship contest (Washington Post "It's a Crime").

There have been reports of purportedly responsible groups urging not only recognition but acceptance of drug use as a feature of daily life. An article in the January/February 1984 issue of Social Work, the journal of the National Association of Social Workers, prescribes the following for adolescent marijuana use: "Use should be moderate . . . no more than four to five joints per week seems advisable." Such acceptance of drug use may be shared by many who resign themselves to the fact that drug abuse is inevitable. However, such a view reflects a failure of will on the part of the American public. American society may view drug use in the abstract as wrong, and many people agree that heroin addicts who commit additional crimes to support their drug habits should be jailed. Yet, many people react with ambivalence to the drug use in their midst. Even while the U.S. government spends almost a billion and one-half dollars on drug law enforcement, threatens to cut off foreign aid to drug producing countries, and extradites and imprisons foreign nationals on drug trafficking charges, we appear to lack the same degree of resolve to hold this country's drug users, as well as those who directly or indirectly promote drug use, accountable for their actions and their consequences.

While attitudes are ultimately an individual matter, actions need not be. It is in combination with others that private citizens have been most effective in combating drug abuse. Private sector initiatives to combat drug use include the National Coalition for Prevention of Drug and Alcohol Abuse, comprised of private sector organizations representing millions of members, which seeks to expand drug abuse prevention activities. Member organizations include the American Medical Association, the International Association of Lions Clubs, the National Parent/Teacher Association, and others. Furthermore, the National Football League works with the International Association of Chiefs of Police, the Drug Enforcement Administration and the High School Athletic Coaches Association to carry anti-drug messages to student athletes across the country. The Newman Center, a private foundation in Los Angeles, California, offers technical assistance about drugs to the entertainment industry for its portrayals of drug use and provides awards to television writers, producers, and directors who present the best shows about drug use. McNeil Pharmaceutical company sponsors "Pharmacists Against Drug Abuse," a nationwide campaign in which local pharmacists are the focal points in the community for information about drugs. The National Broadcasting Company sponsored the "Don't Be A Dope" drug abuse awareness campaign, which was aired in 1983 and 1984. As discussed above, athletes, entertainers, manufacturers, advertisers, and the media can promote drug use by their individual examples or by favorable portrayals of drug use. However, these elements of society also have the power to shape different public attitudes about drug use by presenting the truth about drugs. The media and entertainment industries should carefully review their portrayals of drug use and its consequences to ensure their accuracy.

Efforts to combat drug abuse can also be successful in the workplace. Many businesses across the country have Employee Assistance Programs (EAP's), which seek to prevent drug abuse at the worksite, offering treatment and referrals. In addition, many businesses now test employees or prospective employees for drug use. According to a survey of 180 Fortune 500 companies in 1985, two-thirds refused to hire job applicants who failed such tests, 25 percent fired employees, and 41 percent required treatment for employees who failed (Dunivant). Drug testing protects businesses because they lose billions of dollars each year in reduced productivity as a result of drug use among employees and the public. Drug testing in certain "critical positions," such as in the transportation industry, law enforcement, and education is particularly important. Mandatory drug testing in the Navy reportedly reduced the drug abuse rate from 48 percent to three percent in two years (Washington Times). Also, the Federal Aviation Administration approved a plan requiring this country's air traffic controllers to submit to annual drug tests. The New York Times and Chicago Tribune have required drug testing of new employees for years. The Baltimore Orioles were the first professional baseball team to institute voluntary drug testing.

In addition to efforts in the workplace to combat drug abuse, health professionals—physicians, nurses, psychologists, and social workers—can help identify and treat drug users. Health professionals should be thoroughly trained before identifying and counseling drug abusers. However, formal training in the diagnosis and treatment of drug abuse is currently limited.

On a final note, it should be re-emphasized that decisions to use or not to use drugs are ultimately derived from values that are best inculcated and reinforced in families, churches, civic organizations, schools, and local communities. The efforts of organizations which seek to help families prevent drug use, such as the National Federation of Parents for Drug-Free Youth, are essential to the fight against drug use and drug trafficking. Relying on the task force approach which law enforcement officials have used successfully, parents, churches, schools, civic organizations, and business associations should form community task forces in every community across the country to provide a unified front against drugs.

Chapter 23

References

Bureau of Justice Statistics. <u>Drug and Crime Facts, 1994</u>. Washington, D.C.: U.S. Department of Justice, 1995.

Clausen, J. "Longitudinal Studies on Drug Use in the High School: Substantive and Theoretical Issues." <u>Longitudinal Research on Drug Use</u>. Washington, D.C.: Hemisphere Publishing Corp., 1978.

Dunivant, Noel and Associates. "Survey report in 'Firms Screen Workers.'" USA Today. 6 November 1985, p. 1B.

DuPont, R.L. <u>Getting Tough on Gateway Drugs: A Guide for the Family</u>. Washington, D.C.: American Psychiatric Press, Inc., 1984.

"It's a Crime." <u>Washington Post</u>, 30 January 1986, p. A24.

"Many Employers Test Workers for Drug Use." <u>Washington Post</u>, 2 February 1986, p. A14.

National Institute on Drug Abuse. "Drug Use Among American High School Seniors, College Students and Young Adults, 1975-1990." <u>Vol. I, High School Seniors</u>. DHHS Pub. No. (ADM) 91-1813. Washington, D.C.: U.S. Department of Justice, 1991.

<u>New York Times</u>, 19 August 1985, p. A1.

----------. <u>The National Household Survey on Drug Abuse</u>. Washington, D.C.: U.S. Department of Justice, 1995.

Smith, T.E. " Reviewing Adolescent Marijuana Abuse." <u>Social Work</u> (Jan./Feb. 1984): 17, 19.

<u>Washington Times</u>, 2 December 1985, p. 1D.

APPENDIX A

Federal Drug Scheduling

This document is a general reference and not a comprehensive list. This list describes the basic or parent chemical and does not describe the salts, isomers and salts of isomers, esters, ethers and derivatives which may also be controlled substances.

Schedule I			
Substance	DEA #	Non Narcotic	Other Names
1-(1-Phenylcyclohexyl)pyrrolidine	7458	N	PCPy, PHP, rolicyclidine
1-(2-Phenylethyl)-4-phenyl-4-acetoxypiperidine	9663		PEPAP, synthetic heroin
1-[1-(2-Thienyl)cyclohexyl]piperidine	7470	N	TCP, tenocyclidine
1-[1-(2-Thienyl)cyclohexyl]pyrrolidine	7473	N	TCPy
1-Methyl-4-phenyl-4-propionoxypiperidine	9661		MPPP, synthetic heroin
2,5-Dimethoxy-4-ethylamphetamine	7399	N	DOET
2,5-Dimethoxyamphetamine	7396	N	DMA, 2,5-DMA
3,4,5-Trimethoxyamphetamine	7390	N	TMA
3,4-Methylenedioxyamphetamine	7400	N	MDA, Love Drug
3,4-Methylenedioxymethamphetamine	7405	N	MDMA, Ecstasy, XTC
3,4-Methylenedioxy-N-ethylamphetamine	7404	N	N-ethyl MDA, MDE, MDEA
3-Methylfentanyl	9813		China White, fentanyl
3-Methylthiofentanyl	9833		Chine White, fentanyl
4-Bromo-2,5-dimethoxyamphetamine	7391	N	DOB, 4-bromo-DMA
4-Bromo-2,5-dimethoxyphenethylamine	7392	N	Nexus, 2-CB, has been sold as Ecstasy, i.e. MDMA
4-Methoxyamphetamine	7411	N	PMA
4-Methyl-2,5-dimethoxyamphetamine	7395	N	DOM, STP
4-Methylaminorex (cis isomer)	1590	N	U4Euh, McN-422
5-Methoxy-3,4-methylenedioxyamphetamine	7401	N	MMDA
Acetorphine	9319		
Acetyl-alpha-methylfentanyl	9815		
Acetyldihydrocodeine	9051		Acetylcodone

Appendix A

Acetylmethadol	9601		Methadyl acetate
Allylprodine	9602		
Alphacetylmethadol except levo-alphacetylmethadol	9603		
Alpha-Ethyltryptamine	7249	N	ET, Trip
Alphameprodine	9604		
Alphamethadol	9605		
Alpha-Methylfentanyl	9814		China White, fentanyl
Alpha-Methylthiofentanyl	9832		China White, fentanyl
Aminorex	1585	N	has been sold as methamphetamine
Benzethidine	9606		
Benzylmorphine	9052		
Betacetylmethadol	9607		
Beta-Hydroxy-3-methylfentanyl	9831		China White, fentanyl
Beta-Hydroxyfentanyl	9830		China White, fentanyl
Betameprodine	9608		
Betamethadol	9609		
Betaprodine	9611		
Bufotenine	7433	N	Mappine, N,N-dimethylserotonin
Cathinone	1235	N	Constituent of "Khat" plant
Clonitazene	9612		
Codeine methylbromide	9070		
Codeine-N-oxide	9053		
Cyprenorphine	9054		
Desomorphine	9055		
Dextromoramide	9613		Palfium, Jetrium, Narcolo
Diampromide	9615		
Diethylthiambutene	9616		
Diethyltryptamine	7434	N	DET
Difenoxin	9168		Lyspafen
Dihydromorphine	9145		
Dimenoxadol	9617		
Dimepheptanol	9618		
Dimethylthiambutene	9619		

Federal Drug Scheduling

Dimethyltryptamine	7435	N	DMT
Dioxaphetyl butyrate	9621		
Dipipanone	9622		Dipipan, phenylpiperone HCl, Diconal, Wellconal
Drotebanol	9335		Metebanyl, oxymethebanol
Ethylmethylthiambutene	9623		
Etonitazene	9624		
Etorphine (except HCl)	9056		
Etoxeridine	9625		
Fenethylline	1503	N	Captagon,amfetyline,ethyltheophylline amphetamine
Furethidine	9626		
Gama Hydroxybutyric Acid (GHB)	2010	N	GHB, gama hydroxybutyrate, sodium oxybate
Heroin	9200		Diacetylmorphine, diamorphine
Hydromorphinol	9301		
Hydroxypethidine	9627		
Ibogaine	7260	N	Constituent of "Tabernanthe iboga" plant
Ketobemidone	9628		Cliradon
Levomoramide	9629		
Levophenacylmorphan	9631		
Lysergic acid diethylamide	7315	N	LSD, lysergide
Marijuana	7360	N	Cannabis, marijuana
Mecloqualone	2572	N	Nubarene
Mescaline	7381	N	Constituent of "Peyote" cacti
Methaqualone	2565	N	Quaalude, Parest, Somnafac, Opitimil, Mandrax
Methcathinone	1237	N	N-Methylcathinone, "cat"
Methyldesorphine	9302		
Methyldihydromorphine	9304		
Morpheridine	9632		
Morphine methylbromide	9305		
Morphine methylsulfonate	9306		
Morphine-N-oxide	9307		
Myrophine	9308		
N,N-Dimethylamphetamine	1480	N	

N-Ethyl-1-phenylcyclohexylamine	7455	N	PCE
N-Ethyl-3-piperidyl benzilate	7482	N	JB 323
N-Ethylamphetamine	1475	N	NEA
N-Hydroxy-3,4-methylenedioxyamphetamine	7402	N	N-hydroxy MDA
Nicocodeine	9309		
Nicomorphine	9312		Vilan
N-Methyl-3-piperidyl benzilate	7484	N	JB 336
Noracymethadol	9633		
Norlevorphanol	9634		
Normethadone	9635		Phenyldimazone
Normorphine	9313		
Norpipanone	9636		
Para-Fluorofentanyl	9812		China White, fentanyl
Parahexyl	7374	N	Synhexyl,
Peyote	7415	N	Cactus which contains mescaline
Phenadoxone	9637		
Phenampromide	9638		
Phenomorphan	9647		
Phenoperidine	9641		Operidine, Lealgin
Pholcodine	9314		Copholco, Adaphol, Codisol, Lantuss, Pholcolin
Piritramide	9642		Piridolan
Proheptazine	9643		
Properidine	9644		
Propiram	9649		Algeril
Psilocybin	7437	N	Constituent of "Magic mushrooms"
Psilocyn	7438	N	Psilocin, constituent of "Magic mushrooms"
Racemoramide	9645		
Tetrahydrocannabinols	7370	N	THC, Delta-8 THC, Delta-9 THC and others
Thebacon	9315		Acetylhydrocodone, Acedicon, Thebacetyl
Thiofentanyl	9835		Chine white, fentanyl

Federal Drug Scheduling

Tilidine	9750		Tilidate, Valoron, Kitadol, Lak, Tilsa
Trimeperidine	9646		Promedolum
Schedule II			
1-Phenylcyclohexylamine	7460	N	Precusor of PCP
1-Piperidinocyclohexanecarbonitrile	8603	N	PCC, precusor of PCP
Alfentanil	9737		Alfenta
Alphaprodine	9010		Nisentil
Amobarbital	2125	N	Amytal, Tuinal
Amphetamine	1100	N	Dexedrine, Biphetamine
Anileridine	9020		Leritine
Benzoylecgonine	9180		Cocaine metabolite
Bezitramide	9800		Burgodin
Carfentanil	9743		Wildnil
Coca Leaves	9040		
Cocaine	9041		Methyl benzoylecgonine, Crack
Codeine	9050		Morphine methyl ester, methyl morphine
Dextropropoxyphene, bulk (non-dosage forms)	9273		Propoxyphene
Dihydrocodeine	9120		Didrate, Parzone
Diphenoxylate	9170		
Diprenorphine	9058		M50-50
Ecgonine	9180		Cocaine precursor, in Coca leaves
Ethylmorphine	9190		Dionin
Etorphine HCl	9059		M 99
Fentanyl	9801		Innovar, Sublimaze, Duragesic
Glutethimide	2550	N	Doriden, Dorimide
Hydrocodone	9193		dihydrocodeinone
Hydromorphone	9150		Dilaudid, dihydromorphinone
Isomethadone	9226		Isoamidone
Levo-alphacetylmethadol	9648		LAAM, long acting methadone, levomethadyl acetate
Levomethorphan	9210		
Levorphanol	9220		Levo-Dromoran
Meperidine	9230		Demerol, Mepergan, pethidine
Meperidine intermediate-A	9232		Meperidine precursor

Meperidine intermediate-B	9233		Meperidine precursor
Meperidine intermediate-C	9234		Meperidine precursor
Metazocine	9240		
Methadone	9250		Dolophine, Methadose, Amidone
Methadone intermediate	9254		Methadone precursor
Methamphetamine	1105	N	Desoxyn, D-desoxyephedrine, ICE, Crank, Speed
Methylphenidate	1724	N	Ritalin
Metopon	9260		
Moramide-intermediate	9802		
Morphine	9300		MS Contin, Roxanol, Duramorph, RMS, MSIR
Nabilone	7379	N	Cesamet
Opium extracts	9610		
Opium fluid extract	9620		
Opium poppy	9650		Papaver somniferum
Opium tincture	9630		Laudanum
Opium, granulated	9640		Granulated opium
Opium, powdered	9639		Powdered Opium
Opium, raw	9600		Raw opium, gum opium
Oxycodone	9143		OxyContin, Percocet, Tylox, Roxicodone, Roxicet,
Oxymorphone	9652		Numorphan
Pentobarbital	2270	N	Nembutal
Phenazocine	9715		Narphen, Prinadol
Phencyclidine	7471	N	PCP, Sernylan
Phenmetrazine	1631	N	Preludin
Phenylacetone	8501	N	P2P, phenyl-2-propanone, benzyl methyl ketone
Piminodine	9730		
Poppy Straw	9650		Opium poppy capsules, poppy heads
Poppy Straw Concentrate	9670		Concentrate of Poppy Straw, CPS
Racemethorphan	9732		
Racemorphan	9733		Dromoran
Remifentanil	9739		Ultiva

Secobarbital	2315	N	Seconal, Tuinal
Sufentanil	9740		Sufenta
Thebaine	9333		Precursor of many narcotics
Schedule III			
Amobarbital & noncontrolled active ingred.	2126	N	Amobarbital/ephedrine capsules
Amobarbital suppository dosage form	2126	N	
Anabolic steroids	4000	N	"Body Building" drugs
Aprobarbital	2100	N	Alurate
Barbituric acid derivative	2100	N	Barbiturates not specifically listed
Benzphetamine	1228	N	Didrex, Inapetyl
Boldenone	4000	N	Equipoise, Parenabol, Vebonol, dehydrotestosterone
Buprenorphine	9064		Buprenex, Temgesic
Butabarbital	2100	N	Butisol, Butibel
Butalbital	2100	N	Fiorinal, Butalbital with aspirin
Chlorhexadol	2510	N	Mechloral, Mecoral, Medodorm, Chloralodol
Chlorotestosterone (same as clostebol)	4000	N	if 4-chlorotestosterone then clostebol
Chlorphentermine	1645	N	Pre-Sate, Lucofen, Apsedon, Desopimon
Clortermine	1647	N	Voranil
Clostebol	4000	N	Alfa-Trofodermin, Clostene, 4-chlorotestosterone
Codeine & isoquinoline alkaloid 90 mg/du	9803		Codeine with papaverine or noscapine
Codeine combination product 90 mg/du	9804		Empirin, Fiorinal, Tylenol, ASA or APAP w/codeine
Dehydrochlormethyltestosterone	4000	N	Oral-Turinabol
Dihydrocodeine combination product 90 mg/du	9807		Synalgos-DC, Compal
Dihydrotestosterone (same as stanolone)	4000	N	see stanolone
Dronabinol in sesame oil in soft gelatin capsule	7369	N	Marinol, synthetic THC in sesame oil/soft gelatin
Drostanolone	4000	N	Drolban, Masterid, Permastril
Ethylestrenol	4000	N	Maxibolin, Orabolin, Durabolin-O, Duraboral
Ethylmorphine combination product 15 mg/du	9808		

Appendix A

Fluoxymesterone	4000	N	Anadroid-F, Halotestin, Ora-Testryl
Formebolone (incorrect spelling in law)	4000	N	Esiclene, Hubernol
Hydrocodone & isoquinoline alkaloid 15 mg/du	9805		Dihydrocodeinone+papaverine or noscapine
Hydrocodone combination product 15 mg/du	9806		Tussionex, Tussend, Lortab, Vicodin, Hycodan, Anexsia ++
Ketamine	7285	N	Ketaset, Ketalar, Special K, K
Lysergic acid	7300	N	LSD precursor
Lysergic acid amide	7310	N	LSD precursor
Mesterolone	4000	N	Proviron
Methandienone (see Methandrostenolone)	4000	N	
Methandranone	4000	N	?incorrect spelling of methandienone?
Methandriol	4000	N	Sinesex, Stenediol, Troformone
Methandrostenolone	4000	N	Dianabol, Metabolina, Nerobol, Perbolin
Methenolone	4000	N	Primobolan, Primobolan Depot, Primobolan S
Methyltestosterone	4000	N	Android, Oreton, Testred, Virilon
Methyprylon	2575	N	Noludar
Mibolerone	4000	N	Cheque
Morphine combination product/50 mg/100 ml or gm	9810		
Nalorphine	9400		Nalline
Nandrolone	4000	N	Deca-Durabolin, Durabolin, Durabolin-50
Norethandrolone	4000	N	Nilevar, Solevar
Opium combination product 25 mg/du	9809		Paregoric, other combination products
Oxandrolone	4000	N	Anavar, Lonavar, Provitar, Vasorome
Oxymesterone	4000	N	Anamidol, Balnimax, Oranabol, Oranabol 10
Oxymetholone	4000	N	Anadrol-50, Adroyd, Anapolon, Anasteron, Pardroyd
Pentobarbital & noncontrolled active ingred.	2271	N	FP-3
Pentobarbital suppository dosage form	2271	N	WANS
Phendimetrazine	1615	N	Plegine, Prelu-2, Bontril, Melfiat,

Federal Drug Scheduling

			Statobex
Secobarbital & noncontrolled active ingred	2316	N	various
Secobarbital suppository dosage form	2316	N	various
Stanolone	4000	N	Anabolex, Andractim, Pesomax, dihydrotestosterone
Stanozolol	4000	N	Winstrol, Winstrol-V
Stimulant compounds previously excepted	1405	N	Mediatric
Sulfondiethylmethane	2600	N	
Sulfonethylmethane	2605	N	
Sulfonmethane	2610	N	
Talbutal	2100	N	Lotusate
Testolactone	4000	N	Teslac
Testosterone	4000	N	Android-T, Androlan, Depotest, Delatestryl
Thiamylal	2100	N	Surital
Thiopental	2100	N	Pentothal
Tiletamine & Zolazepam Combination Product	7295	N	Telazol
Trenbolone	4000	N	Finaplix-S, Finajet, Parabolan
Vinbarbital	2100	N	Delvinal, vinbarbitone
Schedule IV			
Alprazolam	2882	N	Xanax
Barbital	2145	N	Veronal, Plexonal, barbitone
Bromazepam	2748	N	Lexotan, Lexatin, Lexotanil
Butorphanol	9720	N	Stadol, Stadol NS, Torbugesic, Torbutrol
Camazepam	2749	N	Albego, Limpidon, Paxor
Cathine	1230	N	Constituent of "Khat" plant
Chloral betaine	2460	N	Beta Chlor
Chloral hydrate	2465	N	Noctec
Chlordiazepoxide	2744	N	Librium, Libritabs, Limbitrol, SK-Lygen
Clobazam	2751	N	Urbadan, Urbanyl
Clonazepam	2737	N	Klonopin, Clonopin
Clorazepate	2768	N	Tranxene

Clotiazepam	2752	N	Trecalmo, Rize
Cloxazolam	2753	N	Enadel, Sepazon, Tolestan
Delorazepam	2754	N	
Dexfenfluramine	1670	N	Redux
Dextropropoxyphene dosage forms	9278		Darvon, propoxyphene, Darvocet, Dolene, Propacet
Diazepam	2765	N	Valium, Valrelease
Dichloralphenazone	2467	N	Midrin, dichloralantipyrine
Diethylpropion	1610	N	Tenuate, Tepanil
Difenoxin 1 mg/25 ug AtSO4/du	9167		Motofen
Estazolam	2756	N	ProSom, Domnamid, Eurodin, Nuctalon
Ethchlorvynol	2540	N	Placidyl
Ethinamate	2545	N	Valmid, Valamin
Ethyl loflazepate	2758	N	
Fencamfamin	1760	N	Reactivan
Fenfluramine	1670	N	Pondimin, Ponderal
Fenproporex	1575	N	Gacilin, Solvolip
Fludiazepam	2759	N	
Flunitrazepam	2763	N	Rohypnol, Narcozep, Darkene, Roipnol
Flurazepam	2767	N	Dalmane
Halazepam	2762	N	Paxipam
Haloxazolam	2771	N	
Ketazolam	2772	N	Anxon, Loftran, Solatran, Contamex
Loprazolam	2773	N	
Lorazepam	2885	N	Ativan
Lormetazepam	2774	N	Noctamid
Mazindol	1605	N	Sanorex, Mazanor
Mebutamate	2800	N	Capla
Medazepam	2836	N	Nobrium
Mefenorex	1580	N	Anorexic, Amexate, Doracil, Pondinil
Meprobamate	2820	N	Miltown, Equanil, Deprol, Equagesic, Meprospan
Methohexital	2264	N	Brevital
Methylphenobarbital (mephobarbital)	2250	N	Mebaral, mephobarbital

Midazolam	2884	N	Versed
Modafinil	1680	N	Provigil
Nimetazepam	2837	N	Erimin
Nitrazepam	2834	N	Mogadon
Nordiazepam	2838	N	Nordazepam, Demadar, Madar
Oxazepam	2835	N	Serax, Serenid-D
Oxazolam	2839	N	Serenal, Convertal
Paraldehyde	2585	N	Paral
Pemoline	1530	N	Cylert
Pentazocine	9709	N	Talwin, Talwin NX, Talacen, Talwin Compound
Petrichloral	2591	N	Pentaerythritol chloral, Periclor
Phenobarbital	2285	N	Luminal, Donnatal, Bellergal-S
Phentermine	1640	N	Ionamin, Fastin, Adipex-P, Obe-Nix, Zantryl
Pinazepam	2883	N	Domar
Pipradrol	1750	N	Detaril, Stimolag Fortis
Prazepam	2764	N	Centrax
Quazepam	2881	N	Doral, Dormalin
Sibutramine	1675	N	Meridia
SPA	1635	N	1-dimethylamino-1,2-diphenylethane, Lefetamine
Temazepam	2925	N	Restoril
Tetrazepam	2886	N	
Triazolam	2887	N	Halcion
Zaleplon	2781	N	Sonata
Zolpidem	2783	N	Ambien, Stilnoct,Ivadal
Schedule V			
Codeine preparations - 200 mg/100 ml or 100 gm			Cosanyl,Robitussin A-C,Cheracol,Cerose,Pediacof
Difenoxin preparations - 0.5 mg/25 ug AtSO4/du			Motofen
Dihydrocodeine preparations 10 mg/100 ml or 100 gm			Cophene-S, various others
Diphenoxylate preparations 2.5 mg/25 ug AtSO4			Lomotil, Logen
Ethylmorphine preparations 100 mg/100 ml or 100 gm			

Appendix A

Opium preparations - 100 mg/100 ml or gm			Parepectolin, Kapectolin PG, Kaolin Pectin P.G.
Pyrovalerone	1485	N	Centroton, Thymergix

APPENDIX B

UNIFORM CONTROLLED SUBSTANCES ACT OF CALIFORNIA

In 1973, California adopted the Uniform Controlled Substances Act, replacing the Narcotic Act. This act is Division 10 of the California Health and Safety Code. The act places narcotics and restricted dangerous drugs into five controlled substances schedules. The drugs are classified as to their potential for abuse, approved medical use, and dependency liability. The California Act corresponds with the Federal Controlled Substances Act adopted in 1970.

Schedule I substances are listed in section 11054 H&S and include heroin, LSD, marijuana, peyote, etc.

1. They have a high potential for abuse.

2. Except for marijuana, under the Compassionate Use Act of 1996 (section 11362.5 H&S), Schedule I substances have no currently accepted medical use for treatment in the State of California and cannot be prescribed or possessed except for legally approved research. (The Federal Controlled Substances Act does not provide for the use of marijuana for medical purposes; thus, the California law faces legal challenges from the federal government.)

3. Use of the substances can lead to severe physical or psychological dependence.

Schedule II substances are listed in section 11055 H&S and include opium, Percodan, Demerol, methadone, etc., along with cocaine, the amphetamines, methamphetamine, and phencyclidine (PCP).

1. They have a high potential for abuse.

2. They have a currently accepted medical use for treatment in the State of California with severe restrictions. The opiates and cocaine are prescribed on the triplicate prescription system. The amphetamines are prescribed on regular prescription blanks but must be written and cannot be refilled.

3. Abuse of these drugs may lead to severe physical and psychological dependence.

Schedule III substances are listed in section 11056 H&S and include barbiturates, anabolic steroids, and drugs which contain opiates in smaller amounts.

Appendix B

1. They have a lesser potential for abuse than Schedule I or II substances.

2. They have a currently accepted medical use for treatment in California. The prescribing regulations are more relaxed than Schedule II substances in that they can be called in and also refilled.

3. Abuse of these drugs may lead to moderate physical and psychological dependence.

Schedule IV substances are listed in section 11057 H&S and include chloral hydrate, phenobarbital, and other specific substances.

1. They have a lower potential for abuse than Schedule III substances.

2. They have a currently accepted medical use for treatment in California. The prescribing regulations are more relaxed than Schedule II substances in that they can be called in and also refilled. (Same as Schedule III)

3. They may lead to limited physical and psychological dependence relative to Schedule III substances.

Schedule V substances are listed in section 11058 H&S and include milder opiate compounds.

1. They have low potential for abuse relative to the other controlled substances in schedules I through IV.

2. They have a currently accepted medical use for treatment in California. The prescribing regulations are more relaxed than Schedule II substances in that they can be called in and also refilled. (Same as Schedule III)

3. They may lead to limited physical and psychological dependence relative to drugs in Schedule IV.

APPENDIX C

SUMMARY OF NARCOTICS EXPERTISE

Name

Rank

Department or Agency

Bureau/Division/Special Assignment Assigned to:

Years Employed as a Peace Officer

Years in Present Assignment

Education:

A.   Formal

High School Graduate: Yes   No

Number of College Units Completed

Degree   Major

Graduate Units _____ Degree _____ Major

Units in Police-related Field

B. Training

   1.   In-Service Training Schools —Narcotics
      List Hours and Dates Completed

  2.   Specific College Courses Completed in Narcotics

  3.   Specialized Out-Service Narcotics Training, i.e.

     a.   DOJ 80-Hour Narcotics Investigation School

     b.   80-Hour DEA Basic Drug Law Enforcement School

     c.   24-Hour Narcotics Enforcement and Case Development - Los Angeles State

     d.   40-Hour Narcotics Addiction and Drug Influence - OCSO List All Books

Appendix C

List all books read on Narcotics and Narcotics Investigations:

_____

_____

List all Technical Journals and Articles Read Relating Specifically to Narcotics:

_____

_____

Experience in Drug Investigation: (Update Monthly)

Hall	Heroin	Marij	Amphets	Barb	Coke

No. of Drug Purchases Made

No. of Posses. Cases Worked

No. of Drug Possess./Sale Cases Worked

No. of Times Affiant of Search Warrants

No. of Times Supervised Informant Purchases

No. of Times Testified as an Expert in the Following Categories:

Hall	Heroin	Marij	Amphets	Barb	Coke

Possession

Possession/Sale

Sale

Under the Influence

What Courts Have You Testified as an Expert in?

Municipal

Superior Court

County

APPENDIX D

SLANG TERMS FAVORED BY ILLICIT DRUG USERS AND DEALERS

There are many other slang terms related to drug abuse that may be heard on the street. The following is a partial list of drug-related slang terms:

Acid Head	One who uses LSD
Amped	High on stimulants, usually amphetamines
Bag	$10 to $25 worth of heroin
Baggy	A quantity of marijuana in a plastic bag
Balloon	A small amount of heroin, sold in a toy balloon or condom
Bindle	A small packet of narcotics
Blow a Stick (or Joint)	To smoke marijuana
Blow your Mind	To get high on a hallucinogenic drug
Bummer, Bum trip, Bad trip	Bad hallucinogenic drug experience
Burned	User has received phony or very weak drugs
Cap	A capsule of drugs
Carry, Carrying	To be in possession of drugs
Chip, chipping	An occasional narcotic user who takes small doses
Clean	Not in possession of drugs, or having withdrawn rom drug use
Crash	A stupor caused by an overdose of drugs
Cut	To dilute a drug with some other substance
Deal	To sell drugs
Dealer	Someone who sells drugs
Dime Bag	A $10 purchase of drugs (usually heroin)
Dirty	To be in possession of drugs
Drop	To swallow drugs
Dry up	To inject drugs
Dump, Flash	To vomit after taking drugs
Fix	To inject narcotics
Flipped out	Crazy
Guide	A babysitter for an abuser of hallucinogens during an experience
Head	An addict
Heat	The police or a narcotics officer
High	Being under the influence of drugs
Hit	Taking a drag of marijuana cigarette
Holding	Having drugs in possession
Hooked	Addicted to drugs
Hot Shot	A fatal dosage of narcotics
Keister Plant	Drugs which are hidden in the rectum
Kick (the habit)	Abandon a drug habit

Kilo	2.2 pounds, a common quantity of marijuana and narcotics for sale
Lid	1 oz. of marijuana
Light up	To smoke marijuana
Loaded	Being very high (under the influence) on drugs
Looking	Wishing to purchase drugs
Mainline	To inject drugs directly into the vein
Mainliner	A person who injects drugs directly into the vein
Make a Buy, Make a Meet	To purchase drugs
Matchbox	oz. of marijuana
Mule	A person who sells or transports for a regular peddler
Narc	A narcotics officer
Needle Man	An addict
Nickel Bag	$5 purchase of drugs
On the Nod	To get sleepy from heroin or depressants
O.D.	To overdose on drugs
Pad	A user's residence
Paper	A bindle of heroin
Plant	A location where drugs are concealed
Pop, Skin Popper	An injection just under the skin
Pothead	A marijuana user
Psychedelic	A mind-altering hallucinogenic experience
Push	To sell drugs
Pusher	A person who sells drugs
Rat	An informer
Rush, Flash	A strong, pleasurable feeling following a drug injection
Score	To purchase drugs
Shoot up	To inject drugs
Shooting Gallery	A place where narcotic addicts inject heroin
Snowbird	A cocaine user
Spaced Out	Out of touch with reality
Speed Freak	A chronic user of methamphetamine
Spike	A hypodermic needle (with syringe) used to inject drugs
Spoon	About 2 grams of heroin
Stash	A personal supply of drugs
Stepped on	A drug that has been diluted (same as "cut")
Stoned	Being under the influence of drugs
Stoolie	An informer
Strung Out	Being addicted; in bad physical shape due to drug habit
Swing Man	A drug supplier
Toke, Toke up	To smoke marijuana
Trip, Tripping	Being under the influence of a hallucinogenic drug
Turn on	To take a drug, or introduce someone else to drugs
User	Someone who takes drugs, or is an addict
Wasted	Being under the influence of drugs

Slang Terms

Weed Head................. A regular marijuana user
Wiped Out................. To have lost consciousness from abusing drugs
Works........................ Drug injecting equipment
Zonked, Zonked Out Really "loaded" or overdosed on drugs

Police officers: Study this list until you are very familiar with these terms. You will need to know what is really being said on the street when you hear terms like "I'm looking for my swing man," or "Let's go score a lid and start toking."

Slang Term Practice Exercises

Translate the slang terms into official terminology.

A narc is questioning Sam:

Narc: You dealing Sam?

Sam: I ain't even carrying. I'm clean, man!

Narc: Where's your stash?

Sam: Hey, I'm telling you, I've kicked it, man.

Narc: How come we caught you with a spike?

Sam: Some needle man gave it to me to hold for him. No law against that, is there?

Narc: That's the least of your worries, Sam. Freddie says he almost got a hot shot from you yesterday.

Sam: Freddie's stupid. If he O.D.'s, that's his problem.

Narc: Get off it, Sam. You're loaded right now! We'll see how smart you are when you crash.

———————

A pusher is talking to an addict named Harry:

Harry: I'm looking for a score.

Pusher: You don't need to look any farther, man.

Harry: Are you holding?

Pusher: I got it by the bag, and I got it by the bindle.

Harry: I only chip, man, so I'll score a bindle.

Appendix D

Pusher: You got the works?

Harry: Ya, I'm all ready to fix—just let me have the stuff.

Al is hooked. He's looking for his dealer, so he can buy a spoon of smack. The dealer has just received a kilo of the stuff, and has cut it and packaged it into dime bags and balloons. Al finds him and scores. He goes to his pad and gets his kit. Because Al is a mainliner, he cooks up his stuff, ties off, and fixes. Al feels the rush, and before long, he's on the nod. He starts thinking about how he got where he is. He remembers how he used to drop reds and blow a joint once in a while. Then, a user started him on shit, and he soon went from chipping to being totally strung out. Now, he wonders if he will ever be able to clean up.

APPENDIX E

CRISIS INTERVENTION FOR DRUG ABUSERS

HEROIN (NARCOTIC) OVERDOSE

Principal Manifestations

1. Coma.

2. Respiratory depression.

3. Flaccid muscles (tongue may fall back to occlude airway).

When you encounter someone who has overdosed on a narcotic, remember that a narcotic overdose causes severe respiratory depression. Emergency treatment should be sought immediately. With opiates, first aid is a must since you only have 3 to 5 minutes at most. Without oxygen exchange, the brain begins to deteriorate.

Principles of Emergency Treatment

Follow A, B, and C. Do not do B until A is working, and do not do C until A and B are working.

A. AIRWAY

—Place addict on his or her back with the head positioned so that the airway is not cut off. Tilt the head back.

—Check mouth for mucus, blood, broken teeth, etc.

—Maintain open airway.

B. BREATH

—Apply mouth to mouth resuscitation properly. Begin with 4 quick breaths, then 12 breaths per minute.

C. CARDIOVASCULAR

—Check pulse—carotid.

—If no pulse, start CPR.

BARBITURATE AND SEDATIVE/HYPNOTICS OVERDOSE

With sedative/hypnotics the emergency is the same as with a heroin overdose: establish a clear airway. You should never give a semiconscious person fluids; nor should you induce vomiting.

Principal Manifestation of Acute Barbiturate Withdrawal

Convulsions and preconvulsive symptoms.

Emergency Treatment

—Open airway.

—Support breathing.

—Assess cardiovascular system.

—In all cases, take the victim to a hospital. Barbiturate withdrawal is much longer and more physically dangerous than heroin withdrawal.

AMPHETAMINE OVERDOSE

Principal Manifestations

1. Irritability.

2. Hyperactivity.

3. Suspiciousness.

4. Possible violence.

5. Paranoia.

In suspected amphetamine overdoses, be careful. Try to come across to the person as non-threatening. Make no sudden moves, no threatening gestures. Do not touch the person. Toxic psychosis from amphetamines results from continuing use (3 to 5 days). It is characterized by vivid hallucinations, both visual and auditory, and paranoia. This happens 36 to 40 hours after taking large amounts of the drug. Toxic psychosis demands hospitalization. While fatal overdoses are rare, death by convulsions may occur. The signs are semiconsciousness, extremely high pulse, hyperventilation, and cold and clammy skin.

Emergency Treatment

—Reassurance, under constant observation, in quiet surroundings.

—Do not touch the person.

—Seek professional medical treatment.

ACUTE PHASES OF PCP INTOXICATION

Principle Manifestations

Crisis Intervention for Drug Abusers

1. Blank stare—very spaced out, may not respond to questions.

2. Ataxia—loss of limb coordination.

3. Catatonic appearance—rigid, fixed body posture.

4. Nystagmus—jerky eye movements.

5. Agitated and/or paranoid appearance—the presence of systematized delusions.

6. Unpredictability.

7. Violent behavior.

8. Combative aggression—fright or loss of control.

Emergency Treatment

—All approaches to the individual should be made slowly and calmly and only after clear identification is made.

—Request back-up—five officers minimum.

—Control user's actions—cumulative body weight—carotid restraint.

—Transport to emergency room.

—Reduce external stimulation.

—Remember that the user is unpredictable.

PSYCHEDELIC/HALLUCINOGENIC OVERDOSE

Principal Manifestations

1. Irritability.

2. Apprehension.

3. Suspiciousness.

4. Possible violence.

5. Panic.

Emergency Treatment

—Create a calm, reassuring environment.

—The "Talkdown."

Appendix E

a. The patient needs help to fully experience and complete his or her trip—this may take as many as eight hours.

b. Talk the patient down by reassuring him that he is in a safe place, is with sympathetic people, and can manage his own trip.

—Upon initial contact treat the person as you would an amphetamine user. Get help from the person-crisis intervention center; seek medical treatment, etc.

INDEX

M

MARIJUANA

INDEX

INDEX

INDEX

V

VALIUM (DIAZEPAM), §6.4.3
Driving under the influence,
§7.18.2

VIOLENCE AND CRIME, §2.1 to
2.10. *(See CRIME AND
VIOLENCE)*

W

WARRANTS
Arrests in homes, §17.8
Laboratories
Search warrant for clandes-
tine drug labs, §18.9.2(b)
Obtaining, §18.7.2
Preferability of warrants,
§18.7.1
Suppression of evidence,
§18.7.4
Time considerations, §18.7.3
Searches of suspect's person
Warrantless seizure of evi-
dence, §17.17.1
When to obtain a warrant,
§17.17.2
Serving, §18.7.5 to 18.7.5(c)
Decisions, §18.7.5(a)
Search, §18.7.5(c)
Strategy, §18.7.5(b)
Suppression of evidence, §18.7.4
Time considerations, §18.7.3
Warrantless entry due to exigent
circumstances, §17.13 to
17.13.10
Child abuse, suspicion of,
§17.13.3
Clandestine drug labs,
§17.13.10
Creation of exigent circum-
stances, §17.13.9
Domestic violence, suspicion
of, §17.13.4
Escape of suspect, prevention
of, §17.13.6
Evidence destruction, preven-
tion of, §17.13.7
Hot pursuit, §17.13.8
Person in need of assistance
inside, §17.13.2
Property damage, prevention
of, §17.13.5
Protective sweep, §17.13.1

X

XANAX, §6.4.2

Y

YABA, §12.19